THE PAPERS OF

Andrew Johnson

Sponsored by

The University of Tennessee

The National Historical Publications and Records Commission

The Tennessee Historical Commission

THE EDITORS

LeRoy P. Graf and Ralph W. Haskins are professors of history at The University of Tennessee, Knoxville.

An engraving of Andrew Johnson, Senator from Tennessee,
by A. B. Walter; J. Dainty, publisher.
Courtesy Library of Congress.

THE PAPERS OF

Andrew Johnson

Volume 4, 1860-1861

EDITORS
LEROY P. GRAF AND RALPH W. HASKINS
ASSOCIATE EDITOR, PATRICIA P. CLARK

1976
THE UNIVERSITY OF TENNESSEE PRESS
KNOXVILLE

Library of Congress Catalog Card Number: 67–25733
International Standard Book Number 0–87049–183–0
Manufactured in the United States of America

TO

J. Wesley Hoffmann

FRIEND AND COLLEAGUE

Contents

1860

1861

Illustrations

Introduction

It is a truism that an action may be assessed in a multitude of ways, depending upon the perspective of the observer. Andrew Johnson's stand for the Union, so dramatically displayed during the secession crisis, is a case in point. Should this self-proclaimed "sentinel on the watchtower" be praised as a man of courage, loyal to his principles and the Constitution, adhering to an indissoluble Union, or denounced as a traitor to state and section, deserting the South to gratify his lust for power and influence with the Lincoln administration? Was his position consistent with the attitudes he had taken in his earlier career? To what extent did he weigh the implications for himself, for his state, and for the nation?

Although the Johnson Papers provide no evidence for his assertion that his principles had become fixed as early as the nullification controversy, they leave little doubt that the rising politician of the forties and fifties was a staunch advocate of the Union. For some years prior to the election of 1860 he appears to have discounted the likelihood of secession while recognizing the grave danger that beset the American process. It may be that, like others of his generation, he had so often heard threats of disruption that he regarded them as mere buncombe and bombast. "You get up a great agitation, and settle it by a compromise; and then you keep up an agitation as to what the compromise means," he remarked in February, 1858; a year later he deprecated the propensity "to sing paeans and hosannas to the Union . . . done so often that it has got to be entirely a business transaction."[1] Yet if Johnson occasionally displayed some impatience with union-shrieking, it is also quite evident that he was deeply concerned about the impending crisis. In the wake of the settlement of 1850 he had expressed fears for the future, and by 1856, with the optimism born of compromise now clouded by the pessimism of renewed strife, he had warned that "The roaring can now be heard in the trees . . . the unerring indication of the approaching storm." Insisting that "our Southern institutions depend upon the continuance of the Union, and that the Union depends upon non-interference with our Southern institutions," he declared that the South must

---

1. Speech on Popular Sovereignty and the Right of Instruction, February 23, 1858, *Johnson Papers*, III, 64; Speech on Transcontinental Railroads, January 25, 1859, *ibid.*, 232.

stand united under the Constitution.[2] Consistent with this position, he had supported the Breckinridge "southern" ticket in 1860. On the day before Lincoln's election, we are told, he foresaw a Republican triumph, adding that the South would use it as a pretext to secede and predicting that the effort would fail. "When the crisis comes," said he, "I will be found standing by the Union."[3]

How did Johnson stand by the Union during the ensuing months? Believing that the border states might exert a moderating influence and thus hold the balance of power, he viewed Tennessee as pivotal to this middle area; hence she must be kept loyal at all costs. Partly because of his own considerable influence and partly because of optimistic reports from his correspondents, he was convinced that the state would not secede. The precise nature of his activities in behalf of border state solidarity remains unclear; nevertheless, the records demonstrate that the Tennessean was willing to try every possible expedient, however great or small, to hold the nation together. Well aware of the role of propaganda in influencing public opinion, he and others, during the weekend before the South Carolina secession convention met on December 17, aided the director of the census in compiling a list of southern voters to whom government clerks dispatched unionist speeches—just as Johnson himself would later respond to the landslide of requests which followed his own addresses.[4] In these months of denouement he introduced amendments and resolutions, offered his own compromise proposals while supporting those of others, and delivered speeches in the Senate and on the hustings—the latter directed toward confounding secessionist maneuvers in Tennessee.

During the early months of 1861 it became evident that Johnson's political status had undergone a veritable revolution. The partisan who had severely arraigned his Republican opponents now became Seward's "noble Senator" and Simon Cameron's "lion-hearted Johnson,"[5] while southern Democrats who had tolerated him in the past now excoriated his treason to the South. The Democrat who had spent nearly a quarter-century exorcising the demons of Whiggery now found Tennessee unionist Whigs standing with him shoulder to shoulder, while secessionists irrespective of party shot, stabbed, hung, and burned him in effigy from Memphis to Knoxville—one face of a profound political change subsequently labeled "the Revolu-

2. Speech at Nashville, July 15, 1856, *ibid.*, II, 431–32.

3. Robert W. Winston, *Andrew Johnson: Plebeian and Patriot* (New York, 1928), 150.

4. LeRoy P. Graf, "Andrew Johnson and the Coming of the War," *Tenn. Hist. Quar.*, XIX (1960), 219.

5. *Cong. Globe*, 36 Cong., 2 Sess., 341; Letter from J. Warren Bell, February 16, 1861.

tion in Tennessee."[6] The politician long deprived of his fair share of
the patronage now, ironically enough, saw himself chosen over John
Bell and other erstwhile Whigs as Lincoln's chief patronage dis-
penser for the Volunteer State.[7] The plebeian hitherto little known
outside Tennessee except as a leveler—the protagonist of the controversial homestead—now became a national figure, lionized by
northerners who fancied that his was the voice of a legion of unionists
in the South. For Andrew Johnson, the new year brought a dramatic
change which might well have turned the head of a man less convinced of his own rectitude.

So also was there a perceptible shift in his view of the conflict.
The fateful events of spring and summer—the burgeoning of the
Confederacy, the firing on Sumter and the battle of Bull Run, the
defection of the Harris regime and, in Johnson's word, its "over-
slaughing" of East Tennessee—produced a new note of intransi-
gence. The grim realities of secession and war brought in their wake
a heightening of passions on both sides; it would be surprising if he
had not mirrored the increasing bitterness of the time. That he became unforgiving, even vindictive, may be seen in his castigation of
the departing southern senators, men who had spoken earlier in
"sweet tones, euphonious utterances, mellifluous voice," but now become the victims of "Disappointed, impatient, unhallowed ambition"
which impelled them to break up the Union.[8]

An equally harsh temper was displayed in his "war guilt" resolution which declared "That the present deplorable civil war has been
forced upon the country by the disunionists of the southern States
now in revolt against the constitutional Government."[9] Of similar
tenor was his July speech in support of Lincoln's war policies. Epito-
mizing a realistic assessment of a situation "without much hope or
prospect of a speedy termination," it refuted the allegation of dictatorship in the North and charged that a tyranny was being created in
the South. Defending the President's call for volunteers, suspension
of habeas corpus, and additions to the armed forces, Johnson recalled
other occasions when customary privileges and immunities had been
suspended in the national interest. For palpable violations of human
rights, one must look to the Confederacy, that climax of a
long-maturing plot to dissolve the Union and to subvert the liberties

6. J. Milton Henry, "The Revolution in Tennessee, February, 1861, to
June, 1861," *Tenn. Hist. Quar.*, XVIII (1959), 109–14.

7. *Ibid.* Even an office seeker from "Yorkville N.Y. City" was advised to
"get a letter from Andy Johnson and it will car[r]y you through." Edwin Estes
to Johnson, August 21, 1861, Johnson Papers, LC.

8. Speech on the Seceding States, February 5–6, 1861; Speech in Support
of Presidential War Program, July 27, 1861.

9. Remarks on War Aims Resolution, July 25, 1861.

of the people. The secessionists, having "lost confidence in man's capacity for self-government" and contemplating a republic based exclusively upon slavery—one in which the great mass of the people were not to participate—had inaugurated a reign of terror. Under the circumstances "a violation of the Constitution for the preservation of the Government, is more tolerable than one for its destruction."[10] An unfriendly observer, contemplating this apologia, might well have maintained that Johnson had sold to the Republicans! Yet there is no evidence to suggest that his stand was in any way conditioned by hope for immediate political reward.

Actually, since Tennessee's June 8 plebiscite on secession, Johnson's attitude toward the conflict had been increasingly influenced by affairs in East Tennessee, where the situation of loyal men was daily becoming more precarious, and to a lesser degree by developments in Kentucky, officially "neutral" but wavering in sentiment between the opposing sides. By late July the line between unionist and secessionist had been drawn in East Tennessee, while rumor and fact mingled indiscriminately in both areas. Loyalists, begging for weapons, depicted in lurid detail their insecurity in the face of imminent invasion and argued the necessity for guerrilla warfare. Eastern Kentucky was obviously the funnel through which the beleaguered homeland was to be redeemed, but hundreds of enemy troops were alleged to be lying in wait at Cumberland Gap and elsewhere, not only to prevent the passage of "Johnson's arms," but to apprehend or even assassinate their purveyor. Meanwhile, badgered by the domineering and indefatigable Kentuckian William ("Bull") Nelson, the senator scurried around Washington, inaugurating an activity which would persist for the duration of the war—goading and prodding the bureaucracy, in particular the White House, the treasury, and the war department, to send aid to embattled East Tennessee. Enlisting legislative support for the cause of southern unionism, he introduced a bill appropriating two million dollars for arms to loyal citizens and for outfitting troops from among these citizens "for their own protection against domestic violence, insurrection, invasion, or rebellion."[11] Unlike most of Johnson's past legislative efforts, this measure, initiated on July 20, went through Congress virtually unchanged and became law only eleven days later.

But Johnson was not alone in his desire to save "the loyal mountaineers" of East Tennessee. In May Amos A. Lawrence, a Massachusetts industrialist turned philanthropist, had opened what he conceived to be an exchange with the senator, now at home rounding

10. Speech in Support of Presidential War Program, July 27, 1861.
11. Bill Appropriating Arms to Loyal Citizens, July 20, 1861.

up popular support prior to the election of June 8. That his correspondent was actually Knoxville Postmaster Charles W. Charlton, Johnson's onetime political ally now in cahoots with Governor Harris, came as a shock not only to the Bostonian but to Johnson himself when the Richmond *Enquirer*, acquiring one of Lawrence's letters, printed it with a denunciation of "so base a traitor" as Andrew Johnson. This comedy of errors—the hoary device of the interceptors intercepted and the revelation of a "caper" designed to mulct an idealist out of "5 or $10,000 in New England Currency, in *large bills*"[12]—was followed by an afterpiece in which the adventurer Parker H. French, alias "Carlyle Murray," led Johnson and Lawrence through a correspondence ostensibly designed to channel funds to Parson Brownlow, the doughty editor of the Knoxville *Whig*, but in reality intended to fatten his own purse or further the Confederate cause. Although these schemes to capitalize on the plight of East Tennessee were frustrated, so too were the earnest endeavors of Johnson and his new allies Brownlow, Maynard, and Bull Nelson to rescue the region. Effective aid was not to be forthcoming for months, and in the waning days of summer Andrew Johnson, now in exile, was on his way to being branded an "alien enemy" of the South.[13]

How had a southern senator become anathema to fellow southerners? Had there been an act, a conscious decision, a critical turning point at which he embarked upon the course which led to exile and rejection? Attractive as the "fateful decision" theory of historical change may be, the historian knows that change emerges from a series of choices—of actions taken or not taken, of positions embraced or rejected. So it was with the transformation of Andrew Johnson from southern spokesman to southern traitor. Yet one dramatic occasion, seen in retrospect, looms as a watershed toward which his previous decisions had been leading him, and from which his subsequent course logically grew. It was his Speech on Secession of December 18–19.

It came at a time when the nation stood on the brink of dissolution and the great American democratic experiment seemed doomed to failure. Southerners had threatened secession if a Black Republican became President; and in the wake of Lincoln's election northerners who had long scoffed at such threats eyed anxiously the assembling of the South Carolina secession convention. In these days of crisis Americans looked in vain to the President for leadership. Buchanan's message of December 4 displayed a studied ambiva-

12. Letter [from "Andrew Johnson"] to Amos A. Lawrence, June 6, 1861.
13. Writ of Sequestration, January 18, 1862; Michael L. Patterson to Johnson, January 31, 1862, Johnson Papers, LC.

lence, denying that a state had the right to secede but likewise denying that the federal government had the power to coerce a seceding
state. The "old public functionary" could offer only a few ineffectual
compromise proposals designed to pour oil on the troubled waters. It
was quite obvious that, for the future, he would leave the issue to his
Republican successor; for the time being he left matters to Congress.

It is difficult to say whether the legislators or their constituents
were the most excited; in any case, congressional deliberations during the secession winter were conducted in an atmosphere of high
tension. The galleries were generally crowded, often "packed" with
secessionists or unionists, who punctuated the proceedings with
cheers intermingled with hisses and the stamping of feet. "Order in the galleries" and "Clear the galleries" were phrases often
heard from presiding officers—phrases which frequently brought
protracted debate. That the senators now and then took liberties
with history is beyond question; that they often resorted to dema-
goguery is apparent; that they occasionally approached hysteria is
incontrovertible. Speculation was rife: according to one rumor, Ben
Wade of Ohio had a shotgun in his desk; according to gossip heard
some time later, Johnson had "shot Jeff Davis" and was about to
meet Wigfall of Texas on the field of honor.[14] Nevertheless the upper chamber maintained something of its traditional air of sobriety,
the senators restricting themselves to verbal salvos and adjectival
brickbats as they addressed themselves to the crisis.

During the fortnight which followed the presidential message, it
became apparent that Congress, reflecting the divided counsels of
the nation, had its polarities of viewpoint. Some regarded dissolution
as inevitable, a persuasion expressed by Alfred Iverson of Georgia,
who spoke of "an enmity . . . deep and enduring," never to be eradi-
cated. Let the separation be peaceful; otherwise "we will welcome
you with bloody hands to hospitable graves."[15] Others did not propose to let the erring sisters depart: "Without a little bloodletting,
this Union will not . . . be worth a rush," declared Zachariah Chandler of Michigan.[16] But amid these cries of disunion and threats of
coercion, there were other voices, largely from the border states
North and South, which spoke for compromise. Some, like William
Bigler of Pennsylvania and George Pugh of Ohio, are comparatively
unknown today; others, like Andrew Johnson and John J. Crittenden of Kentucky, were to achieve enduring niches in the national
pantheon. On December 10 Crittenden sponsored resolutions leading to the creation of a Senate Committee of Thirteen, and eight days

14. Letter from William M. Lowry, December 29, 1860.
15. *Cong. Globe*, 36 Cong., 2 Sess., 12.
16. Nevins, *Emergence of Lincoln*, II, 412.

later he offered the compromise proposals which came to bear his
name.

During these same days Johnson was also submitting proposals
designed to alleviate the crisis. On December 13 he introduced three
constitutional amendments. The first would place the selection of
President and Vice President in the hands of the people voting by
districts, with these posts to be alternated between North and South
so that at any given time one should be held by a northerner and the
other by a southerner. A second amendment stipulated that senators
were also to be chosen by direct vote. Similarly the Supreme Court
was to be made more responsible to the popular will, with appointments for twelve-year terms on a staggered basis and vacancies filled
one-half from the slave states and the remainder from the free.[17] In
a sense, none of these propositions were new, since Johnson had long
advocated direct election and had earlier introduced the court amendment into the House. What was novel for him were the provisions
calculated to assure the South an equal voice in the general government. Moreover, as with many such amendments, they were to be
unamendable. The idea of protecting a minority from the tyranny
of a majority and the proposition of alternating between North and
South are reminiscent of Calhoun's "concurrent voice." Yet the burden of these measures was clear: Johnson, the tribune of the people,
was concerned above all with the guarantee of southern rights *within the Union*.

The Tennessee senator's pivotal forensic on behalf of the Union
coincided with the deepening national crisis. Interrupted by other
business and by the heckling of southern antagonists, the speech
occupied several hours on December 18 and 19. It was timely: the
Senate was now considering the Crittenden amendments, the South
Carolina secession convention was deliberating, and five days earlier
thirty southern legislators had signed an open address to their constituents, in which they declared that the only hope lay in a separate
confederacy.

Identifying himself with southern interests but not with secession,
the speaker denied that Lincoln's election menaced the South. He
invoked the idea of a safety valve: let us keep the North to quarrel
with. That the South had just grievances he conceded, but he called
for joint action, insisting that the panacea for these ills lay inside the
Union—that the war for southern rights should be waged "upon the
battlements of the Constitution." He criticized northern states which
had violated the Constitution by passing personal liberty laws and
by impeding the execution of the Fugitive Slave Act. Where was the

17. Joint Resolution for Amendments on Presidential, Senatorial, and
Judicial Selection, *Johnson Papers*, III, 692–96.

logic in seceding and at the same time demanding that the North comply with the Constitution and the laws? Instead of mutual concessions—for "I am not a compromiser . . . in the usual acceptation" of the term—he preferred congressional legislation or constitutional amendments "upon the principle that they are right and upon no other ground." He emphasized his aversion to a "big" government; yet he demanded a government strong enough to preserve itself. If the right of secession were conceded, the Union was no stronger than "a rope of sand." Citing the opinions of Madison, Jefferson, Marshall, and Jackson, he rejected the heresy of secession and maintained that the compact was not temporary but perpetual, not voluntary but irrevocable. Although the federal government could not coerce a state, it could act upon the individuals within that state in order to enforce the law of the land.

The speech was fraught with grim forebodings. What would be the effects of secession? Assuredly the end of the Union would mean the end of slavery. And if the Palmetto republic made an alliance with a foreign power, the United States would be justified in using strong measures. What about the free navigation of the Mississippi? What significance would dissolution hold for the border states? Moreover, if one state seceded would not the nation ultimately be divided piecemeal

into thirty-three petty Governments, with a little prince in one, a potentate in another, a little aristocracy in a third, a little democracy in a fourth, and a republic somewhere else; a citizen not . . . able to pass from one State to another without a passport or a commission . . . with quarreling and warring amongst the little petty powers.

There were ringing phrases. If the government "was good enough for Washington, for Adams, and for Jackson," then "It is good enough for us. I intend to stand by it. . . . It is the last hope of human freedom." In a moving peroration Johnson besought the nation to "stand by the Constitution; and in saving the Union, we save this, the greatest Government on earth."[18]

How should this speech be assessed? The passage of a century provides historical hindsight and, in theory at least, a degree of detachment. If the southern point of view is apparent, it is equally obvious that the speaker valued the Union above all else. Although he minced no words, this speech, unlike his later ones, was basically conciliatory. In his allusions to the fate of slavery, the removal of a safety valve, and the evils of a consolidated government, there was what one biographer calls "prescience."[19] Many unionist speeches

18. Speech on Secession, December 18–19, 1860.
19. Lloyd P. Stryker, *Andrew Johnson: A Study in Courage* (New York, 1929), 60.

were heard in Congress during this time of troubles, but Andrew Johnson stood virtually alone as a southern unionist.

What was the judgment of contemporaries—men immersed in the crucible and lacking the Olympian detachment of a hundred years? The answer may depend upon the commentator's distance in point of time. While many people North and South, in Congress and among the public at large, sensed at once that the speech marked a significant milestone, evaluation of its impact appreciated enormously in the perspective of a successful war for the Union. Thus a panegyrist, contributing to the aura appropriate for a President newly sworn in, hailed it as "a great historical point not only in the career of the orator, but of his country at its most intense epoch."[20] An old East Tennessee Whig recalled that "Johnson at once became the most popular man in the North, excepting Lincoln"; while Alexander H. Stephens outshone all the rest, opining that it was "the most masterly effort ever delivered by man on earth."[21] In due time a modern biographer, himself a child of war and reconstruction, would say that "no sooner were the words spoken than they swept the country. North and South were alike astounded."[22] Allowing for a slight modicum of truth, it may be said that the historical evidence suggests more than a jot of creative imagination in such asseverations.

Indeed the historian's hindsight would suggest a strong caveat. Granted that this "masterly effort" marked a turning point in Johnson's career and enhanced his popularity North, it neither swept the country nor necessarily astounded the sections, though some senators on both sides of the aisle may have been taken aback. Whatever might have been said in the cloakrooms or corridors, in the boarding-houses or taverns, the *Congressional Globe* does not convey in any detail the reaction of the Senate. Only a few members, and certainly none from the South, praised it; only a few congressmen even alluded to it. Unquestionably northern legislators took a new interest in Johnson and some now discerned in him redeeming qualities once overlooked. But with southern extremists, it was another story. Joseph Lane of Oregon, occupying a most anomalous position— North Carolina native, ardent secessionist representing a state highly unlikely to secede, and a lame duck serving his last term—branded the Tennessean a coercionist, pontificating that neither "the gallant band of Democrats North" nor even the "honorable and bold people"

20. John Savage, *Life and Public Services of Andrew Johnson* (New York, 1866), 213.
21. Temple, *Notable Men*, 396; Stephens Interview with Victor Redfield in Cincinnati *Commercial*, February 1, 1875, quoted in George Fort Milton, *The Age of Hate: Andrew Johnson and the Radicals* (New York, 1930), 101.
22. Winston, *Andrew Johnson*, 167.

of Tennessee would "march with him under his bloody banner" in a crusade against South Carolina or any other southern state.[23] Johnson's old foil Jefferson Davis called him "an ally" of Ben Wade,[24] thus rendering a verdict of guilt by association. Johnson himself recalled subsequently that "a bevy of conspirators" came from the other chamber and he spoke bitterly of "the taunts, the jeers, the derisive remarks, the contemptuous expressions."[25]

The depth to which the speech stirred the nation "at its most intense epoch" remains a matter of conjecture. A brief sampling of press opinion suggests little more than a limited response, and the laudatory notice hailing Johnson as "the next Southern President of the United States"[26] almost certainly represents the exception. Few of the major journals gave the speech more than perfunctory attention, some ignored it entirely, others voiced strong disapproval. Perhaps this limited reaction was conditioned by the Tennessean's relative obscurity; several months would elapse before Americans became thoroughly familiar with the name of Andrew Johnson. Doubtless some editors, skeptical about the likelihood of permanent disunion, undervalued the significance of a strong unionist statement. Probably the fact that Johnson's unionism was at this time accompanied by vigorous arguments in defense of southern "rights" within the Union and stinging strictures on Republican extremists dampened the enthusiasm of many northern editors. But above all else, the high drama of a secession convention held far greater appeal than the declamations of a southern maverick. Unquestionably the reaction was strongly influenced by particular points of view. Thus the Washington *Constitution*, a persevering Breckinridge supporter, asked why such a speech had been heard from a southerner: "Was it genuine free-Soilism or the hope of reward?" On the other hand, its neighbor the *Evening Star*, politically neutral in 1860 but now a supporter of Lincoln and the Union, refuted the charge of treason: "Traitor to what, or whom?" and identified the speaker as "the representative of the laboring citizens of the South, and of the immense class there of quiet business men in all walks of life . . . deeply interested in the preservation of the many blessings of government now enjoyed by the people of every section of this country."[27] It may be argued with some plausibility that his criticism of the Republicans as a minority party delighted only the northern

23. *Cong. Globe*, 36 Cong., 2 Sess., 143.
24. *Ibid.*, 308.
25. *Ibid.*, 37 Cong., 2 Sess., 585.
26. Unidentified clipping in Charles Sinnickson to Johnson, December 24, 1860, Johnson Papers, LC.
27. Washington *Constitution* and Washington *Evening Star*, both December 20, 1860.

Democrats and that his sturdy defense of state prerogative rendered him something less than acceptable as a full-fledged unionist.

Secessionist editors generally gave him short shrift. The Knoxville *Register*, detecting no compassion for the South, judged that "The statesman was swallowed up in the politician," while an Arkansas scrivener suggested that "This scurrilous old puppy" be "rendered up into soap-greese, with which to make soap to wash the feet of Horace Greeley."[28] Probably the Cincinnati *Enquirer* came nearest to an accurate assessment when it observed that the speech "took both sections by surprise, the extremists at the North and South uniting in denunciation of it but the conservative men hail it as the dawning of a better day."[29]

The Johnson Papers afford still another opportunity for appraisal. Judging from the avalanche of correspondence which followed the speech, the rank and file was far ahead of the press and Congress. Between late December and April hundreds of letters poured in from all parts of the nation—far more from Tennessee and the North, far fewer from the deep South—and from all segments of society—the great and the small, the rich and the poor, the cultured and the illiterate. Communications came from prominent politicians and businessmen, from resident and transplanted Tennesseans, from old friends and utter strangers, from pacifists and laborites, from newspaper editors, and from members of all political parties. With but few exceptions they provide eloquent testimony of wide acclaim. His heart must have been gladdened, his conviction of rectitude strongly reinforced, and his dreams of higher office made more vivid—provided he found time to read these offerings and could cope with the vagaries of penmanship. As Lincoln would have said, they afforded a "public opinion bath."

Unfavorable reaction came principally, but not exclusively, from secessionists and their sympathizers. Now and then northerners, although endorsing his stand on the Union, took issue on particular questions. Several Republicans wrote at some length, defending the party as one of moderation rather than radicalism, and a Pennsylvanian, criticizing him as not strong enough on coercion, insisted that his assertion of state sovereignty was "fostering the ground work of Secession . . . encouraging the Bull frog to swell as big as the Cow."[30] Yet these letters from the North, taken as a whole, reflected strong approbation.

The severest arraignment came from below the Mason–Dixon

28. Knoxville *Register*, January 10, 1861; *Turner's Southern Star* (Camden, Ark.), quoted in Memphis *Appeal*, January 27, 1861.
29. Cincinnati *Enquirer*, December 20, 1860.
30. Letter from Walter S. Waldie, February 3, 1861.

line. Though his own state was not to secede until June, the tide of disunion was already running strong in its middle and western portions. There is no question that Johnson lost many friends among the Democracy; the ultras of all parties now considered him an enemy. In the legislature various moves were made to "instruct" or even to recall the senior senator, and in Knoxville he was denounced by Dr. J. G. M. Ramsey, John Crozier Ramsey, Charles W. Charlton, "and a few low down loafers."[31] There was an occasional response from the deep South, though the Johnson manuscripts contain very little material from that quarter for either the antebellum period as a whole or the secession crisis itself. It may be that the secessionists considered him a prodigal beyond redemption, but it is also possible that many letters were subsequently destroyed by accident or by design. A citizen of Mobile remarked that "no man having a drop of southern blood in his veins would openly proclaim such doctrines," while one Mississippian threatened to humiliate an impudent mulatto slave by dispatching him to Washington armed with a cowhide to give Johnson some *"marks* of *his attention."*[32]

But the bulk of letters from near and far eulogized him, and his correspondents, often touching in their homely patriotism, occasionally rose to the superlative. One reads such sentiments as "the man on the watch-tower," "the courage which dared to oppose the Catalines, Arnolds, and Burrs of 1861," "second Andrew Jackson," and "booked for the 'White House,'" with "a through ticket." The friend of the lowly must have had his spirits uplifted by the announcement that the people were with him: "the mountain boys— The wood choppers The rail splitters— Infact the bone and sinew of the country back you."[33] If he lost friends among Tennessee Democrats, he gained a host of new ones among former Whigs: a report that Parson Brownlow had declared that *"Johnson is right . . . a true Jackson Democrat . . .* and I will defend him to the last,"[34] attested that the age of miracles had not passed. Requests poured in for reprints of the speech, the *Globe* office receiving orders for more than thirty-six thousand copies. Johnson himself ordered ten thousand, and among other subscribers were such Republicans as Seward, Sumner, Hale, Chandler, Doolittle, and Trumbull.[35] From the backwoods of Tennessee came the assurance that "it would do

31. Letters from William R. Hurley, January 14, 1861, Roderick R. Butler and Robert Johnson, both January 15, 1861, Joseph C. S. McDannel, December 29, 1860.

32. Letters from Hiram S. Smith, December 26, 1860, and "Grand Junction," February 3, 1861.

33. Letter from William Crutchfield, January 14, 1861.

34. Letter from Joseph C. S. McDannel, December 29, 1860.

35. Order for Reprints of Speech [1861].

me and the old woman good to Read Enny thing that Andy Johnson send us."[36] Plainly the speaker had struck a responsive chord.

Yet his endeavors did nothing to slow the seemingly inexorable march of events. By late January South Carolina had been joined by other cotton states, and by February a Confederate provisional government was being organized. A peace conference, initiated by the Virginia legislature and presided over by former President John Tyler, had assembled at Washington; yet amid the deepening gloom of the hour, it evoked but little optimism. It was in this atmosphere that Johnson delivered a second major speech on February 5 and 6: a speech six weeks in preparation—"six weeks to study, and two days to disgorge," Lane said derisively; a speech which traversed much the same ground but was decidedly more militant; a speech which denounced secession as a political heresy and damned extremists, whether "run-mad Abolitionists" or "red-hot disunionists." Once again he conducted his listeners on an excursion into the past. If South Carolina were the historic southern culprit, Massachusetts was its northern counterpart; and the speaker pictured an idyll in which these marplots, "chained together as the Siamese twins," were convoyed to some sequestered part of the ocean, there to be purified before being returned to the nation.[37]

The rejoinders of the secessionists were predictable, but few reached the heights attained by Louis T. Wigfall, a South Carolinian long since gone to Texas, who indulged in an orgy of sarcasm, innuendo, and outright vilification. Johnson had lamented that Davis the warrior had deserted the rampart; Wigfall now impugned Johnson's patriotism, if not his courage, charging that he was not found "upon the battle-fields of Mexico," but instead "electioneering . . . trying to get place and office." His paramount object was to keep Tennessee in the Union—his "last and only hope of future promotion." Out of his arsenal of opprobrium, the Texan drew such phrases as "renegade," "Helperite," "Black Republican," "Red Republican," "sans culotte," "popinjay," and "jackal."[38] Nearly a month later, Lane remarked that Andrew Johnson, by this "unnatural speech," had abandoned the South, sold his birthright. Had it not been for the February diatribe, "we should have had a settlement of the difficulty before this"; for it "did more to strengthen the Black Republican party than all the speeches . . . on the other side of the Chamber during this session."[39] Lane's allegation was at once a severe indictment and a high compliment.

36. Letter from H. Warren Winfree, January 18, 1861.
37. Speech on the Seceding States, February 5–6, 1861.
38. *Cong. Globe*, 36 Cong., 2 Sess., 781–91.
39. *Ibid.*, 1347, 1349.

Unlike his February speech, Johnson's philippic of March 2 was largely extemporaneous, prompted by Lane's strictures of the same day. Like the earlier disquisition, it mirrored the increasing passions of the time: thus he now concerned himself with the theme of crime and punishment. Defining treason according to the Constitution, he sounded the notes of what would become a continuing cacophony: "Treason must be punished. . . . Were I the President of the United States . . . I would have them arrested; and, if convicted . . . by the Eternal God I would execute them." Speaking his lines before an audience now the more appreciative by the thinning out of secessionist senators and the predominance of Union partisans in the galleries, Johnson the actor combined word with gesture. Declaiming that "these two eyes never looked upon any being in the shape of mortal man that this heart of mine feared," he "rose to full height, pointing with two fingers at Lane, and smote his breast with a blow that reverberated through the Senate chamber."[40] Small wonder that Clingman of North Carolina, listening to the tumultuous reaction, could say caustically that the Senate "has been converted into a sort of theater for applause," and a reporter could write, "Such a scene never before occurred in the Senate. . . . For some minutes mob law ruled as completely over its galleries as ever in Tammany Hall, New York."[41]

Again there was a burst of enthusiasm from a multitude of correspondents—the same superlatives, the same comparisons with Jackson, the same rosy visions of the White House. Northerners were by this time fully awakened to his enduring virtues. The press, both newspaper and periodical, asked for photographs and sketches; collegiate literary societies besought him as an honorary member; city councils, civic organizations, and mechanics' institutes showered him with invitations to speak, with stipends running eventually as high as $125 per lecture.[42] The New York *Times* proclaimed him "the greatest man of the age."[43] While it would be a palpable exaggeration to say that he was on his way to apotheosis, it can be avowed with certainty that he had now won his "Union card."

Clearly "the greatest man of the age" had made his choice by the spring of 1861, and his subsequent activities would be devoted almost exclusively to the Union cause. Returning to Tennessee, Johnson labored until June alongside former Whig foes to rescue the

40. Speech in Reply to Senator Lane, March 2, 1861; Winston, *Andrew Johnson*, 180.

41. *Cong. Globe*, 36 Cong., 2 Sess., 1351; Washington *Evening Star*, March 4, 1861.

42. Boston Sons of Temperance to Johnson, January 31, 1862, Johnson Papers, LC.

43. Winston, *Andrew Johnson*, 180.

state from the grip of "King Harris." Thereafter he represented the state *in absentia*. Wandering around Kentucky and Ohio he boosted the morale of loyal men, harangued enthusiastic audiences, and exhorted refugees to organize for the salvation of East Tennessee. In Washington he busied himself in speaking, lobbying, and badgering, with indifferent success. Impatient with evasion, inertia, and procrastination, nonetheless he persisted doggedly in these endeavors throughout a frustrating fall.

What shall be said of the course pursued by the Tennessean during these months of turmoil? In one sense it represents a study in consistency, in another an adaptation to changing circumstances. His basic assumption, an article of faith demonstrated throughout his political career and one comporting with his essentially simplistic view of life, was the inviolability of the Union; from this premise it followed that the solutions attempted and the decisions reached must lie within the framework of the Constitution and the government erected thereon. For him, this choice was inescapable. As long as there remained hope of preserving the Union through persuasion, he bent his entire effort in that direction; the hope of reconciliation disappointed and the country dissevered, he turned his energies unstintingly to restoration by the sword. It was a shift in tactics but not in strategy, a change in posture but not in principle, a change reflecting the altered state of the nation yet retaining an inner core of idealism consistent with the realities of the situation and the nature of the man. His stance toward Tennessee is illustrative. As a spokesman for the state and her people on the eve of secession, he proclaimed her devotion to the Union while emphasizing her insistence on southern rights. Unsuccessful in keeping Tennessee from joining the Confederacy, he set about to reclaim by force of arms the homeland—seduced and torn from the Union, against the will of her people—for "this great, this good, this unparalleled Government."[44] Instructive, too, is his changing view as to the means for keeping the nation together. Against dissolution he was adamant; as to the mode of preservation, he became pragmatic. Thus in the early weeks of the crisis he was willing to entertain any stratagem short of actual dissolution. Inherently distrustful of compromise, he endorsed compromise; inherently distrusted by many southerners, he trumpeted for southern rights. With the coming of the war, he spoke in other tones—not in the "rounding, bounding, sounding periods" of the orator, but in the characteristic language of the stump speaker—demanding a vigorous, unrelenting prosecution in order that the nation might be restored. In a similar vein were his fluctuations toward the constitutional process—a literal interpretation when con-

44. Speech on the Seceding States, February 5–6, 1861.

fronted by secession, a liberal interpretation when war became an actuality.

Andrew Johnson would have understood the predicament of other Americans who have challenged the status quo: an outsider, a rugged individualist, and, indeed, a controversial figure, he was a nonconformist in a South which demanded conformity. It took courage to beard the secessionists in the impending crisis. But courage was one of his sterling qualities—a characteristic of the lowly tailor who had defied the Greeneville aristocracy, of the southern Democrat who had challenged the planter bloc, and of the President without a party who would resist the Republican radicals. And there were immediate rewards for courage. For the first time in his career, he enjoyed the approbation of national leaders, the recognition that accompanies political influence, and the satisfaction of popular acclaim. Although he suffered bitter disappointment—the nation disrupted and its defenders faltering, the state lost and efforts to succor East Tennessee thwarted, the righteous cause abandoned by longtime friends, the insecurity of family and neighbors a continuing source of anguish—the Tennessean had achieved undeniable success, steadfastly maintaining his principles, attaining a truly national reputation, enhancing measurably his prospects. For the defender of the Union, these momentous nine months were a time of travail and testing, of reversal and resurgence.

THIS VOLUME

The documents herein, covering approximately nine months of Johnson's term in the Senate, are primarily speeches and letters, with a scattering of miscellaneous items. Fundamentally they reveal the man's public posture rather than his private reactions. Taken in their entirety, his speeches afford new insight into his thinking on the issues of the day; they remind us of Johnson's inherent strengths and weaknesses as he struggled to accommodate his simple moral code to the complexities of public policy.

This volume shares with earlier ones a regrettable paucity of Johnson letters, totaling no more than twenty-two; moreover, unlike its predecessors, it provides no single instance in which he "unbosomed himself" to his son Robert or to an old crony like William Lowry, Blackston McDannel, or Sam Milligan. Absent also is the occasional political letter to a longtime friend and colleague, such as A. O. P. Nicholson, from whom he had become estranged. It may be that his intense preoccupation with the crisis and his feverish attempts to redeem East Tennessee precluded more than an occasional short letter or scribbled note; it is not unreasonable to believe that his activities "on the road" during the course of several months also kept him from writing. In these trying times Johnson seems to have relied heavily upon the spoken, rather than the written, word—unless, perchance, whatever letters he indited became victims of the hazards of war.

Equally difficult of explanation, though of less basic significance, is the sharp fluctuation in correspondence during these months. Voluminous for January, February, and March, 1861, it declines markedly thereafter. Unquestionably, the overwhelming mass of letters during the weeks between the December speech and the close of March reflects a spontaneous reaction to his emergence as southern spokesman for the Union. Perhaps his departure from Washington and the uncertainty of an address deterred his new northern "constituency"; again, these missives may have been lost during the mayhem of the war years in Greeneville.

Yet despite such manifest shortcomings, these documents not only record Johnson's reaction to the crisis—mainly in those speeches which illuminate his entry onto the national stage—but also dramatize the impact of disunion upon the rank and file, those Americans whose sentiments so often go unrecorded, lost to posterity. The great mass of correspondence emanates from the common man, almost invariably a protagonist of the Union, depicting his response to secession and war. In contrast to those in previous volumes, these letters, coming largely from writers either unknown to Johnson or at best peripheral acquaintances, take on a national complexion. Some are from transplanted Tennesseans who reveal their hopes and fears, their problems and speculations, but many, from natives of areas loyal to the Union, represent a much more extended clientele than he had enjoyed in the past. These outpourings offer vivid contrasts between the reasoned, literate, even pedantic unionism of a few and the emotional, homespun, often illiterate unionism of others. One gains insights into the dilemma of border states torn by divided loyalties and into the ordeal of local communities rent by dissension. Not least in human interest are those entries which reflect the vicissitudes of Johnson's family and friends.

Considerations of space have dictated a selection where sheer quantity has been prohibitive; thus certain routine and repetitious items are represented by samples. Following Johnson's major congressional appearances he was deluged with letters endorsing his stand and requesting copies of his speeches. Similarly, he received numerous letters concerning political appointments, speaking engagements, and honorary memberships, as well as patriotic effusions and maundering counsels on public policy—all testimonials to his growing prominence but not necessarily appropriate for inclusion here.

Despite the information that this volume conveys about Andrew Johnson in the secession crisis, it has certain inescapable limitations. As a correspondent Johnson leaves much to be desired: a "loner" with few intimate friends, a man not prone to wield the pen, one who resolved the problem of a reply by the terse endorsement "Attended to." The correspondence lost during the war remains an imponderable, as do the letters which may still be in private hands. Finally, there is the basic flaw inherent in the written word itself, or in the spoken word as recorded by others, which tends to screen out information to which we would be privy. Thus significant clues to Johnson's thought and his political decisions are lacking. With whom did he consort in Washington during these crucial times? What were his relationships with northern Democrats and prominent Republicans? What was his private assessment of Lincoln's leadership? Did he consider the long-term implications of the course he took? Was he ever troubled by doubts? To these and other tantalizing questions the following documents make no more than a modest contribution.

Yet the reader who seeks to understand the Tennessee plebeian will discover some tangible clues. Here may be observed the voyage of Andrew Johnson through the shoals of secession, out onto the seas of war; here is the written evidence on which his perception, both of the times and of his role therein, was based; here, once again, are revealed those virtues and defects which would define and limit his presidential capabilities.

ACKNOWLEDGMENTS

We owe much to numerous individuals and institutions without whose assistance an undertaking of this magnitude would be virtually impossible. Prominent among those who have contributed to this volume are the following: Oliver W. Holmes and E. Berkeley Tompkins, Emeritus and present Executive Secretary of the National Historical Publications and Records Commission, and their staff, particularly Sara Dunlap Jackson and Roger Bruns; Robert Bassett, Olive Branch, and John Dobson of the University of Tennessee Library; Cleo Hughes, Jean Waggener, and Naomi Hailey of the Tennessee State Library and Archives; William J. MacArthur of the McClung Collection, Lawson McGhee Library, Knoxville; James R. Bentley of the Filson Club, Louisville; John D. Cushing of the Massachusetts Historical Society; and John Ferguson, Arkansas State Historian.

An experienced and imaginative staff is a *sine qua non* of a project like ours. Working under the skilled leadership of Patricia Clark, a number of people have made significant contributions: William E. King and Richard A. Bland, National Historical Publications and Records Commission Fellows; Marjorie Yeomans, Edith Landis, and Edwin Hardison, research assistants; Patsy Graves, Wilma Nichols, Charlene Ashburn, secretaries; Barbara Bellows and Lynda Lasswell, graduate assistants; Denise R. Smith, Mike K. Smith, William H. Bass, Allen E. Stokes, work-study students. Mrs. Clark has assumed principal responsibility for the Index.

A list of repositories to which we are indebted may be found in Editorial Method, Symbols List A. We are under special obligation to Mrs. Margaret Johnson Patterson Bartlett of Greeneville, Philip Sang of Chicago, and the late Herman Blum of Philadelphia for their kindness in making available materials from their private holdings.

The three agencies most significantly involved in support of the Andrew Johnson Papers are the University of Tennessee, which provides housing for the Project, released time for the editors, and the services of its Press; the National Historical Publications and Records Commission, which makes available generous annual grants and a supplementary sum for printing costs; and the Tennessee Historical Commission, which contributes annual subsidies, as well as publication assistance.

Our families, with remarkable equanimity, continue to accept Andrew Johnson sight unseen as a denizen of the household.

LeRoy P. Graf
Ralph W. Haskins

Knoxville, Tennessee
July 1, 1975

Editorial Method

Like its predecessors, this volume is based chiefly on materials from Washington: the Library of Congress, the National Archives, and the *Congressional Globe*. Comparatively few documents come from scattered repositories and private collections. Especially noteworthy are the reports of speeches garnered from the daily press. While the volume contains all significant correspondence, speeches, and resolutions, it omits, except for representative samples, routine correspondence concerning recommendations, petitions, requests for speeches and public documents—especially voluminous in the weeks following his major congressional addresses—letters of introduction, honorary memberships, and speaking engagements.

In general, the sources of footnote information have been indicated. Absence of a citation may indicate that the subject is a matter of general knowledge, that the person has been previously identified (as reference to the Index will show), or that information is unavailable. Extended identifications provided in the first three volumes are referenced in the footnotes. Most city and business directories are to be found in the microform collection produced by New Haven Research Publications, Inc.

In transcribing documents the editors have sought to combine fidelity to the original text with consideration for the reader. Thus the writer's orthography is reproduced without change, except where confusion might occur; in such cases the bracketing of letters and words, or *sic* is employed to clarify the meaning. Where not otherwise cited, *Webster's Third International* has been used as the authority for spelling and definitions. Aside from the insertion of bracketed periods, the original punctuation has been retained. Repetitious words or phrases, when obviously slips of the pen, have been eliminated. Although information added by the editors is normally bracketed, exceptions are made when a correspondent's location or the date of a document are beyond doubt. Normally cities and towns without a state designation are in Tennessee.

SYMBOLS

A. Repositories

CSmH	Henry E. Huntington Library, San Marino, California
DLC	Library of Congress, Washington, D. C.

DNA	National Archives, Washington, D. C.

RECORD GROUPS USED

RG15	Records of the Veterans Administration
RG28	Records of the Post Office Department
RG46	Records of the United States Senate
RG59	General Records of the Department of State
RG60	General Records of the Department of Justice
RG94	Records of the Adjutant General's Office
RG107	Records of the Office of the Secretary of War
RG109	Compiled Service Records, War Department Collection of Confederate Records
RG156	Records of the Office of the Chief of Ordnance

ICHi	Chicago Historical Society, Chicago, Illinois
In	Indiana State Library, Indianapolis, Indiana
MH	Harvard University, Cambridge, Massachusetts
MHi	Massachusetts Historical Society, Boston, Massachusetts
PHi	Historical Society of Pennsylvania, Philadelphia, Pennsylvania
TKL	Knoxville Public (Lawson McGhee) Library, Knoxville, Tennessee

B. Manuscripts

AL	Autograph Letter
ALS	Autograph Letter Signed
ANS	Autograph Note Signed
Copy	Copy not by writer
D	Document
DS	Document Signed
L	Letter
LS	Letter Signed
Let. Bk. Copy	Letter Book Copy
Pet.	Petition
PC	Printed Copy
PI	Printed Invitation
PL	Printed Letter
RS	Receipt Signed
Tel	Telegram
Tel, draft	Telegram, draft

ABBREVIATIONS

GENERAL

A.; App.	Appendix
Adj. Gen.	Adjutant General
Appl. & Recomm.	Applications and Recommendations
Appt.	Appointment
c	About
Ch.	Chapter
Col.	Collection
Com.	Committee
Comp.	Compiler
Cong.	Congress, congressional
Corres.	Correspondence
fl	Flourishing
Gen. Let. Bk.	General Letter Book
H.R.	House of Representatives
LC	Library of Congress
Let.	Letter
Let. Recd.	Letter Received
Let. Sent	Letter Sent
M	Microcopy
Misc.	Miscellaneous
S.	Senate
Sec.	Secretary, section
Ser.	Series
Sess.	Session
Supp.	Supplement
Tr.	Transcriber

MILITARY

Adj. Gen.	Adjutant General
Brig. Gen.	Brigadier General
Bvt.	Brevet
Capt.	Captain
Cav.	Cavalry
Co.	Company
Col.	Colonel
Gen.	General
Inf.	Infantry
Maj.	Major
Rgt.	Regiment
Vols.	Volunteers

SHORT TITLES

Acklen, *Tenn. Records* — Jeannette T. Acklen, comp., *Tennessee Records* (2 vols., Nashville, 1933).

American Annual Cyclopaedia (1861) — *American Annual Cyclopaedia and Register of Important Events* (42 vols. in 3 series, New York, 1862–1903).

Appleton's Cyclopaedia — James G. Wilson and John Fiske, eds., *Appleton's Cyclopaedia of American Biography* (6 vols., New York, 1887–89).

Battles and Leaders — Robert N. Johnson and Clarence C. Buel, comps., *Battles and Leaders of the Civil War* (4 vols., New York, 1956 [1887]).

BDAC — *Biographical Directory of the American Congress, 1774–1961 ... (House Document* No. 442, 85 Congress, 2 Session, Washington, D. C., 1961).

Boatner, *Civil War Dictionary* — Mark M. Boatner, *The Civil War Dictionary* (New York, 1959).

Caldwell, *Bench and Bar* — Joshua W. Caldwell, *Sketches of the Bench and Bar of Tennessee* (Knoxville, 1898).

Campbell, *Tenn. Attitudes* — Mary R. Campbell, *The Attitude of Tennesseans toward the Union, 1847–1861* (Knoxville, 1961).

1860 Census, Tenn., Greene — U. S. Bureau of the Census, Eighth Census, 1860, Population, Tennessee, Greene County (original schedules on microfilm).

Clayton, *Davidson County* — W. Woodford Clayton, *History of Davidson County, Tennessee* (Philadelphia, 1880).

Collins, *Kentucky* — Lewis and Richard H. Collins, *History of Kentucky* (2 vols., Covington, Ky., 1874).

Confed. Mil. Hist. — Clement A. Evans, ed., *Confederate Military History* (12 vols., Atlanta, 1899).

Cong. Globe	U. S. Congress, *The Congressional Globe* . . . (23 Congress to the 42 Congress, Washington, D. C., 1834–73).
Coulter, *Civil War in Kentucky*	E. Merton Coulter, *The Civil War and Readjustment in Kentucky* (Chapel Hill, 1926).
DAB	Allen Johnson and Dumas Malone, eds., *Dictionary of American Biography* (20 vols., supp., and index, New York, 1928–).
ETHS *Publications*	East Tennessee Historical Society's *Publications*.
Filson Quarterly	*Filson Club History Quarterly*.
Folmsbee, *Tennessee*	Stanley J. Folmsbee, Robert E. Corlew, and Enoch L. Mitchell, *History of Tennessee* (4 vols., New York, 1960).
Goodspeed's East Tennessee *Goodspeed's Bedford* [and other counties]	Goodspeed Publishing Company, *History of Tennessee, from the Earliest Time to the Present* . . . (Chicago, 1886–87).
Gregory, *Union List of Newspapers*	Winifred Gregory, comp., *American Newspapers, 1821–1936: A Union List of Newspapers* (New York, 1936).
Heitman, *Register*	Francis B. Heitman, *Historical Register and Dictionary of the United States Army, from Its Organization, September 29, 1789, to March 2, 1903* (2 vols., Washington, D. C., 1903).
House Ex. Doc.	*House Executive Document*
House Misc. Doc.	*House Miscellaneous Document*
JP	Andrew Johnson Papers, Library of Congress. JP refers to the first series only; JP2, etc., to succeeding series.
Johnson Papers	LeRoy P. Graf and Ralph W. Haskins, eds., *The Papers of Andrew Johnson* (3 vols., Knoxville, 1967–).

Johnson-Bartlett Col. — Andrew Johnson materials in possession of Mrs. Margaret Johnson Patterson Bartlett, Greeneville, Tennessee.

Lanman, *Biographical Annals* — Charles Lanman, *Biographical Annals of the Civil Government of the United States during Its First Century* (Washington, D. C., 1876).

Mathews, *Americanisms* — Mitford M. Mathews, ed., *A Dictionary of Americanisms on Historical Principles* (2 vols., Chicago, 1951).

Moore, *Rebellion Record,* Doc. Diary Supp. } Frank Moore, ed., *The Rebellion Record: A Diary of American Events* (11 vols. and supp., New York, 1861–68).

Nashville Bus. Dir. (1855–56) — John P. Campbell, comp., *Nashville City and Business Directory, 1855–56* (Nashville, 1855).

—— (1860–61) — L. P. Williams & Co., *Nashville City and Business Directory, 1860–61* (Nashville, 1860).

Nashville City Cemetery Index — *Index to Interments in the Nashville City Cemetery, 1846–1962* (Nashville, 1964).

NCAB — *National Cyclopaedia of American Biography* . . . (54 vols., New York, 1967–73 [1893–   ]).

Nevins, *Emergence of Lincoln* — Allan Nevins, *The Emergence of Lincoln* (2 vols., New York, 1950).

——, *War for the Union* — Allan Nevins, *The War for the Union* (2 vols., New York, 1959–60).

Nichols, *Disruption of Democracy* — Roy F. Nichols, *The Disruption of American Democracy* (New York, 1948).

OED — James A. H. Murray and others, eds., *The Oxford English Dictionary* (13 vols., Oxford, 1933).

OR

War of the Rebellion: A Compilation of the Official Records of the Union and Confederate Armies (70 vols. in 128, Washington, D. C., 1880–1901).

Proc. E. Tenn. Conv. (Knoxville)

Proceedings of the East Tennessee Convention Held at Knoxville, May 30th and 31st, 1861 (First Session).

Proc. E. Tenn. Conv. (Greeneville)

Proceedings . . . at Greeneville, on the 17th Day of June, 1861, and Succeeding Days (Second Session).

Richardson, *Messages*

James D. Richardson, comp., *A Compilation of the Messages and Papers of the Presidents, 1789–1902* (10 vols., New York, 1903).

Robison Biog. Data

Dan M. Robison, Biographical Data concerning Tennessee Legislators (Tennessee State Library and Archives, Nashville, Tennessee).

Robison, *Preliminary Directory, Bedford* [and other counties]

Dan M. Robison and Robert M. McBride, comps., *Biographical Directory* (Preliminary) *of Tennessee General Assembly* (Nashville, 1967–).

Rothrock, *French Broad-Holston Country*

Mary U. Rothrock, ed., *The French Broad-Holston Country: A History of Knox County, Tennessee* (Knoxville, 1946).

Senate Doc.

Senate Document

Senate Ex. Doc.

Senate Executive Document

Senate Ex. Journal

Senate Executive Journal

Senate Misc. Doc.

Senate Miscellaneous Document

Speed, *Union Cause*

Thomas Speed, *The Union Cause in Kentucky, 1860–1865* (New York, 1907).

Speer, *Prominent Tennesseans*

William S. Speer, *Sketches of Prominent Tennesseans* (Nashville, 1888).

Stampp, *And the War Came*   Kenneth M. Stampp, *And the War Came: The North and the Secession Crisis, 1860–61* (Baton Rouge, 1950).

Stevenson, *Quotations*   Burton E. Stevenson, *Home Book of Quotations* (New York, 1964).

————, *Macmillan Book of Proverbs*   Burton E. Stevenson, *The Macmillan Book of Proverbs, Maxims and Famous Phrases* (New York, 1948).

Temple, *East Tennessee*   Oliver P. Temple, *East Tennessee and the Civil War* (Cincinnati, 1899).

————, *Notable Men*   Oliver P. Temple, *Notable Men of Tennessee from 1833 to 1875* (New York, 1912).

Tenn. Acts   *Acts of the State of Tennessee*

Tenn. Adj. Gen. Report (1866)   *Report of the Adjutant General of the State of Tennessee on the Military Forces of the State from 1861 to 1866* (Nashville, 1866).

Tenn. Hist. Quar.   *Tennessee Historical Quarterly*

Tenn. House Journal   *Tennessee House Journal*

Tenn. Official Manual (1890)   Charles A. Miller, comp., *The Official and Political Manual of the State of Tennessee* (Nashville, 1890).

Tenn. Senate Journal   *Tennessee Senate Journal*

Tennesseans in the Civil War   Civil War Centennial Commission, *Tennesseans in the Civil War: A Military History of Confederate and Union Units with Available Rosters of Personnel* (2 pts., Nashville, 1964).

U. S. Official Register   *Register of the Officers and Agents, Civil, Military and Naval in the Service of the United States . . .* (Washington, D. C., 1851–).

U. S. Statutes   *United States Statutes at Large*

Webster's Third International   *Webster's Third New International Dictionary of the English Language, Unabridged* (Springfield, Mass., 1968).

West Tenn. Hist. Soc. *Papers*   West Tennessee Historical Society *Papers*.

White, *Messages*   Robert H. White, *Messages of the Governors of Tennessee* (8 vols., Nashville, 1952–).

Wooldridge, *History of Nashville*   John Wooldridge, ed., *History of Nashville* (Nashville, 1890).

Wooster, *Secession Conventions*   Ralph A. Wooster, *The Secession Conventions of the South* (Princeton, 1962).

WPA   U. S. Works Project Administration, Historical Records Survey (Nashville, 1936–41).

Chronology

1808, December 29	Born at Raleigh, Wake County, North Carolina
1812, January 4	Death of father, Jacob Johnson
1822, February 18	Bound as tailor's apprentice to James J. Shelby, Raleigh
1826, September	Arrived in Greeneville, Tennessee
1827, May 17	Married Eliza McCardle, daughter of John and Sarah Phillips McCardle
1828, October 25	Birth of daughter Martha
1829–35	Served as alderman, then mayor, of Greeneville
1830, February 19	Birth of son Charles
1832, May 8	Birth of daughter Mary
1834, February 22	Birth of son Robert
1835–37; 1839–41	State representative
1841–43	State senator
1843–53	Congressman, first district
1852, August 5	Birth of son Andrew, Jr. (Frank)
1853, August 4	Elected governor of Tennessee, defeating Gustavus A. Henry, Whig
1855, August 2	Reelected governor, defeating Meredith P. Gentry, Know-Nothing
1857, October 8	Elected to U. S. Senate, defeating Neill S. Brown, Opposition
1860, May 1	Name placed before Democratic national convention, Charleston, S. C.
1860, December 18–19	Speech on Secession
1861, February 5–6	Speech on the Seceding States
1861, March 2	Speech in Reply to Senator Lane
1861, May–June	Canvassed East Tennessee for the Union
1861, June 12	Departed Greeneville to become an exile

THE PAPERS OF

Andrew Johnson

1860

Speech on Secession[1]

December 18–19, 1860

Mr. JOHNSON, of Tennessee. Mr. President,[2] by the joint resolution now before the Senate, three amendments to the Constitution
of the United States are proposed. One proposes to change the mode
of election of President and Vice President of the United States from
the electoral college to a vote substantially and directly by the people.
The second proposes that the Senators of the United States shall be
elected by the people, once in six years, instead of by the Legislatures of the respective States. The third provides that the Supreme
Court shall be divided into three classes: the term of the first class
is to expire in four years from the time that the classification is made;
of the second class in eight years; and of the third class in twelve
years; and as these vacancies occur they are to be filled by persons
chosen one half from the slave States, and the other half from the
non-slaveholding States, thereby taking the judges of the Supreme
Court, so far as their selection goes, from the respective divisions of
the country. This proposition, in substance, was offered many years
ago, in the House of Representatives;[3] it has been somewhat changed,
and is now offered again for the consideration of the Senate.

Mr. President, if these amendments had been made, or the Constitution had been in the shape now proposed, I think the difficulties
that are now upon the country would have been obviated. It would
have been required that either the President or the Vice President
should be taken from the South. That would have destroyed, to some
extent, the sectional character of our recent election. The next provision of the amendment would require the votes cast for President
and Vice President to be cast by districts; and if we are to take as
an indication the returns to the House of Representatives of a majority of twenty-seven against the incoming Administration,[4] it is
pretty conclusive that a President differing in politics and sentiments
from the one who has been recently elected would have been chosen.
Each district would have voted directly for the President and Vice
President of the United States. The individual having a majority of
the votes in that district would be considered as receiving one electoral vote, just as we count the votes for one member of Congress.

Hence, if all the votes in the respective districts had been cast on the same principle, we should now have a majority of twenty-seven in opposition to the incoming Administration; they would have given us a majority in the electoral colleges.[5] It seems to me, if these propositions were adopted and made a part of the Constitution, that, to a very great extent, the difficulty and complaint that is now manifested in different portions of the country would be obviated, and especially so with some improvement or modification of the law which provides for the restoration of fugitives from labor.

It is not my purpose, sir, to discuss these propositions to amend the Constitution in detail to-day, and I shall say but little more in reference to them and to their practical operation; but, as we are now, as it were, involved in revolution, (for there is a revolution, in fact, upon the country,) I think it behooves every man, and especially every one occupying a public place, to indicate, in some manner, his opinions and sentiments in reference to the questions that agitate and distract the public mind. I shall be frank on this occasion in giving my views and taking my positions, as I have always been upon questions that involve the public interest. I believe it is the imperative duty of Congress to make some effort to save the country from impending dissolution; and he that is unwilling to make an effort to preserve the Union, or, in other words, to preserve the Constitution, and the Union as an incident resulting from the preservation of the Constitution, I think is unworthy of public confidence, and the respect and gratitude of the American people. I say it devolves upon every one who can contribute in the slightest degree to this result to come forward and make some effort, reasonable in its character, to preserve the Union of these States by a preservation of the Constitution.

In most that I shall say on this occasion, I shall not differ very essentially from my southern friends. The difference will consist, as I think, from what I have heard and what I see published in the various periodicals of the day, in the mode and manner by which this great end is to be accomplished. Some of our southern friends think that secession is the mode by which these ends can be accomplished; that if the Union cannot be preserved in its spirit, by secession they will get those rights secured and perpetuated that they have failed to obtain within the Union. I am opposed to secession. I believe it is no remedy for the evils complained of. Instead of acting with that division of my southern friends who take ground for secession, I shall take other grounds while I try to accomplish the same end.

I think that this battle ought to be fought not outside, but inside of the Union, and upon the battlements of the Constitution itself.

I am unwilling, of my own volition, to walk outside of the Union which has been the result of a Constitution made by the patriots of the Revolution. They formed the Constitution; and this Union that is so much spoken of, and which all of us are so desirous to preserve, grows out of the Constitution; and I repeat, I am not willing to walk out of the Union growing out of the Constitution, that was formed by the patriots and, I may say, the soldiers of the Revolution. So far as I am concerned, and I believe I may speak with some degree of confidence for the people of my State, we intend to fight that battle inside and not outside of the Union; and if anybody must go out of the Union, it must be those who violate it. We do not intend to go out. It is our Constitution; it is our Union, growing out of the Constitution; and we do not intend to be driven from it or out of the Union. Those who have violated the Constitution either in the passage of what are denominated personal liberty bills, or by their refusal to execute the fugitive slave law—they having violated the instrument that binds us together—must go out and not we. I do not think we can go before the country with the same force of position demanding of the North a compliance with the Constitution and all its guarantees, if we violate the Constitution by going out ourselves, that we shall if we stand inside of the Constitution, and demand a compliance with its provisions and its guarantees; or if need be, as I think it is, to demand additional securities. We should make that demand inside of the Constitution, and in the manner and mode pointed out by the instrument itself. Then we keep ourselves in the right; we put our adversary in the wrong; and though it may take a little longer to accomplish the end, we take the right means to accomplish an end that is right in itself.

I know that sometimes we talk about compromises. I am not a compromiser, nor a conservative, in the usual acceptation of those terms. I have been generally considered radical, and I do not come forward to-day in anything that I shall say or propose, asking anything to be done upon the principle of compromise. If we ask for anything, it should be for that which is right and reasonable in itself. It being right, those of whom we ask it, upon the great principle of right, are bound to grant it. Compromise! I know in the common acceptance of the term it is to agree upon certain propositions in which some things are conceded on one side and others conceded on the other. I shall go for enactments by Congress or for amendments to the Constitution, upon the principle that they are right and upon no other ground. I am not for compromising right with wrong. If we have no right, we ought not to demand it. If we are in the wrong, they should not grant us what we ask. I approach this momentous subject on the great principles of right, asking nothing and demanding nothing but what is right in itself and which every right-minded man and a right-minded community and a right-minded people, who wish the preservation of this Government, will be disposed to grant.

In fighting this battle, I shall do it upon the basis laid down by a portion of the people of my own State, in a large and very intelligent meeting.[6] A committee of the most intelligent men in the country reported, in the shape of resolutions, to this meeting the basis upon which I intend to fight this great battle for our rights. They reported this resolution:

[Expressing sympathy for the southern states and affirming the "great and inherent right of revolution," the delegates nonetheless take a firm stand for secession and urge that the South, with the help of northern friends, resist "the aggression of Black Republicanism by remaining within the Union."]

This is the basis upon which a portion of the people of Tennessee, irrespective of party, propose to fight this battle. We believe that our true position is inside of the Union. We deny the doctrine of secession; we deny that a State has the power, of its own volition, to withdraw from the Confederacy. We are not willing to do an unconstitutional act, to induce or to coerce others to comply with the Constitution of the United States. We prefer complying with the Constitution and fighting our battle, and making our demand inside of the Union.

I know, Mr. President, that there are some who believe—and we see that some of the States are acting on that principle—that a State has the right to secede; that, of its own will, it has a right to withdraw from the Confederacy. I am inclined to think, and I know it is so in fact, that in many portions of the country this opinion has resulted from the resolutions of your own State, sir, [Mr. Mason in the chair,] of 1798 and 1799.[7] I propose to-day to examine that subject, for I know from the examination of it that there has been a false impression made upon my own mind in reference to those resolutions, and the power proposed to be exercised by a State in seceding upon its own will. When we come to examine those resolutions, we find that the third reads as follows:

That this Assembly doth explicitly and peremptorily declare that it views the powers of the Federal Government, as resulting from the compact, to which the States are parties, as limited by the plain sense and intention of the instrument constituting that compact, as no further valid than they are authorized by the grants enumerated in that compact; and that in case of a deliberate, palpable, and dangerous exercise of other powers, not granted by the said compact, the States who are parties thereto have the right, and are in duty bound, to interpose for arresting the progress of the evil, and for maintaining within their respective limits, the authorities, rights, and liberties appertaining to them.

The phraseology of the Kentucky resolutions is somewhat broader and more extensive than that a State, of its own will, has the right to secede or withdraw from the Union. The Kentucky resolution goes on to declare that a State has the right to judge of the infraction of the Constitution, as well as the mode and measure of redress. This is what is declared by that resolution which is repeated by so many in speeches and publications made through the country. Now, let Mr. Madison speak for himself as to what he meant by that resolution. Mr. Madison, in his report upon those resolutions, goes on and states expressly that in the resolution the word "States" is used, notwithstanding the word "respective" is used. Mr. Madison says: [8]

[Madison's salient arguments rested upon the right of the "States"— not a single state—to determine, "in their sovereign capacity . . . whether the compact made by them be violated" and to resort to interposition "solely" to arrest "the progress of the *evil* of usurpation" of the "rights, and liberties appertaining to the States, as parties to the Constitution."]

Now we find, by the examination of this subject, that Mr. Madison, in his report, explains it, and repudiates the idea that a State, as a member of the compact, has a right to judge of an infraction of the Constitution or any other grievance, and, upon its own volition, withdraw from the Confederacy. I will here read a letter of Mr. Madison to Nicholas P. Trist, in explanation of this very proposition: [9]

[Writing in December, 1832, in the midst of the nullification crisis, Madison declared that in a "free Government" the parties to the compact "are mutually and equally bound by it." No one party may withdraw "till released by consent or absolved by an intolerable abuse of the power created"; but the states, "having made the compact may do what they will with it." Asserting that the use of the plural "States" in the Virginia Resolutions was "intentional," Madison observed to Trist that the nullifiers cited Jefferson's authority in behalf of "their colossal heresy," while ignoring his remark that the right of coercion is "inherent in the nature of a compact."]

I have another letter of Mr. Madison, written in 1833, sustaining and carrying out the same interpretation of the resolutions of 1798 and 1799. I desire to read some extracts from that letter. Mr. Madison says: [10]

[Reiterating opinions expressed in the preceding letter, the Virginian warned "An inference from the doctrine that a single State has a right to secede at will from the rest, is that the rest would have an equal right to secede from it"—that is, expel it from the Union.]

When these letters are put together they are clear and conclusive. Take the resolutions; take the report; take Mr. Madison's expositions of them in 1832 and 1833; his letter to Mr. Trist; his letter to Mr. Webster;[11] his letter to Mr. Rives; and when all are summed up, this doctrine of a State, either assuming her highest political attitude or otherwise, having the right of her own will to dissolve all connection with this Confederacy, is an absurdity, and contrary to the plain intent and meaning of the Constitution of the United States. I hold that the Constitution of the United States makes no provision, as said by the President of the United States, for its own destruction.[12] It makes no provision for breaking up the Government, and no State has the constitutional right to secede and withdraw from the Union.

In July, 1788, when the Constitution of the United States was before the convention of New York for ratification, Mr. Madison was in the city of New York. Mr. Hamilton, who was in the convention, wrote a letter to Mr. Madison to know if New York could be admitted into the Union with certain reservations or conditions.[13] One of those reservations or conditions was, as Mr. Hamilton says in his letter, that they should have the privilege of seceding within five or seven years if certain alterations and amendments were not made to the Constitution of the United States. Mr. Madison, in reply to that letter, makes use of the following emphatic language, which still further corroborates and carries out the idea that the Constitution makes no provision for breaking up the Government, and that no State has a right to secede. Mr. Madison says:[14]

[Madison denied that "a *conditional* ratification" would make New York a member of "the new Union," for "The Constitution requires an adoption *in toto* and *forever*."]

I know it is claimed, and I see it stated in some of the newspapers, that Virginia and some of the other States made a reservation, upon the ratification of the Constitution, that certain conditions were annexed; that they came in upon certain conditions, and therefore they had a right, in consequence of those conditions, to do this or the other thing. When we examine the journal of the convention, we find that no mention is made of any reservation on the ratification of the Constitution by the State of Virginia. We find that Mr. Madison says, in his letter to Mr. Hamilton, that this idea was first mooted at Richmond, and was abandoned as worse than a rejection. His letter was written after the ratification of the Constitution of the United States by the State of Virginia. Hence he spoke with a knowledge of the fact that existed, that no reservation was made; and even if it had been made by one of the parties, and not sanctioned by the other parties to the compact, what would it have amounted to? Then we see that Mr. Madison repudiates the doctrine that a State has the right to secede. We see that his resolutions admit of no such construction. We see that Mr. Madison, in his letter to Mr. Hamilton, puts the interpretation that this Constitution was adopted *in toto* and forever, without reservation and without condition.

I know that the inquiry may be made, how is a State, then, to have redress? There is but one way, and that is expressed by the people of Tennessee. You have entered into this compact; it was mutual; it was reciprocal; and you of your own volition have no right to withdraw and break the compact, without the consent of the other parties. What remedy, then, has the State? It has a remedy that remains and abides with every people upon the face of the earth— when grievances are without a remedy, or without redress, when oppression becomes intolerable, they have the great inherent right of revolution, and that is all there is of it.

Sir, if the doctrine of secession is to be carried out upon the mere whim of a State, this Government is at an end. I am as much opposed to a strong, or what may be called by some a consolidated Government, as it is possible for a man to be; but while I am greatly opposed to that, I want a Government strong enough to preserve its own existence; that will not fall to pieces by its own weight or whenever a little dissatisfaction takes place in one of its members. If the States have the right to secede at will and pleasure, for real or imaginary evils or oppressions, I repeat again, this Government is at an end; it is not stronger than a rope of sand;[15] its own weight will tumble it to pieces, and it cannot exist. Notwithstanding this doctrine may suit some who are engaged in this perilous and impending crisis that is now upon us, duty to my country, duty to my State, and duty to my kind, require me to avow a doctrine that I believe will result in the preservation of the Government, and to repudiate one that I believe will result in its overthrow, and the consequent disasters to the people of the United States.

If a State can secede at will and pleasure, and this doctrine is maintained, why, I ask, on the other hand, and as Mr. Madison argues in one of his letters, cannot a majority of the States combine and reject a State out of the Confederacy? Have a majority of these States, under the compact that they have made with each other, the right to combine and reject any one of the States from the Confederacy? They have no such right; the compact is reciprocal. It was ratified without reservation or condition, and it was ratified "*in toto* and forever;" such is the language of James Madison; and there is but one way to get out of it without the consent of the parties, and that is, by revolution.

I know that some touch the subject with trembling and fear. They say, here is a State that, perhaps by this time, has seceded, or if not, she is on the road to secession, and we must touch this subject very delicately; and that if the State secedes, conceding the power of the Constitution to her to secede, you must talk very delicately upon the subject of coercion. I do not believe the Federal Government has the power to coerce a State; for by the eleventh amendment of the Constitution of the United States it is expressly provided that you cannot even put one of the States of this Confederacy before one of the courts of the country as a party. As a State, the Federal Government has no power to coerce it; but it is a member of the compact to which it agreed in common with the other States, and this Government has the right to pass laws, and to enforce those laws upon individuals within the limits of each State. While the one proposition is clear, the other is equally so. This Government can, by the Constitution of the country and by the laws enacted in conformity with the Constitution, operate upon individuals, and has the right and the power, not to coerce a State, but to enforce and execute the law upon individuals within the limits of a State.

I know that the term, "to coerce a State," is used in an *ad captandum* manner.[16] It is a sovereignty that is to be crushed! How is a State in the Union? What is her connection with it? All the connection she has with the other States is that which is agreed upon in the compact between the States. I do not now whether you may consider it in the Union or out of the Union, or whether you simply consider it a connection or a disconnection with the other States; but to the extent that a State nullifies or sets aside any law or any provision of the Constitution, to that extent it has dissolved its connection, and no more. I think the States that have passed their personal liberty bills, in violation of the Constitution of the United States, coming in conflict with the fugitive slave law, to that extent have dissolved their connection, and to that extent it is revolution. But because some of the free States have passed laws violative of the Constitution; because they have, to some extent, dissolved their connection with this Government, does that justify us of the South in following that bad example? Because they have passed personal liberty bills, and have, to that extent, violated the compact which is reciprocal, shall we turn around, on the other hand, and violate the Constitution by coercing them to a compliance with it? Will we do so?

Then I come back to the starting point: let us stand in the Union and upon the Constitution; and if anybody is to leave this Union, or violate its guarantees, it shall be those who have taken the initiative, and passed their personal liberty bills. I am in the Union, and intend to stay in it. I intend to hold on to the Union, and the guarantees under which this Union has grown; and I do not intend to be driven from it, nor out of it, by their unconstitutional enactments.

Then, Mr. President, suppose, for instance, that a fugitive is arrested in the State of Vermont tomorrow, and under the personal liberty bill of that State, or the law—I do not remember its precise title now—which prevents, or is intended to prevent, the faithful execution of that law, Vermont undertakes to rescue him, and prevent the enforcement of the law: what is it? It is nullification; it is resistance to the laws of the United States, made in conformity with the Constitution; it is rebellion; and it is the duty of the President of the United States to enforce the law, at all hazards and to the last extremity. And, to come back to the premises, if the Federal Government fails or refuses to execute the laws made in conformity with the Constitution, and those States persist in their violation and let those unconstitutional acts remain upon their statute-books and carry them into practice; if the Government, on the one hand, fails to execute those laws, and those States, by their enactments, violate them on the other, the Government is at an end, and the parties are all released from the compact.

[Jacob Collamer of Vermont, speaking briefly of his state's personal liberty laws, claims that the legislation reported in the press was passed in 1844, six years before the federal Fugitive Slave Law of 1850. Furthermore, the legislature has recently appointed a commissioner to review subsequent laws to determine their constitutionality. After an exchange involving Johnson, Collamer, and Judah P. Benjamin of Louisiana over the constitutionality of the Vermont laws and the interpretation of the Dred Scott decision, Johnson yields to a motion to adjourn until the following day.]

Mr. JOHNSON, of Tennessee. Mr. President,[17] yesterday, while I was pursuing a line of argument to prove that a State had no constitutional power to secede from the Union without the consent of other States, I was diverted from it to some extent by making use of an illustration in reference to the law of the State of Vermont upon the subject of fugitive slaves, which led to the Senator from Vermont [Mr. Collamer] making an explanation in reference to that law. I did not think his explanation was entirely satisfactory; and the answer that he made to the direct question that I propounded to him, I think is more unsatisfactory than the preceding portion of his remarks. That Senator being a gentleman of legal attainments, having presided in the courts of the country, and having been for a long time in the councils of the country, I asked him a plain question in regard to a law of his own State, about which there had been much controversy in the newspapers. I asked him whether he was of [the] opinion that it was a constitutional law, or whether it did not come in conflict with the fugitive slave law which was passed by the Congress of the United States in strict conformity with the Constitution of the country. I do not see him in his place; but if I remember his reply, it was an evasion. He said that it might or might not be unconstitutional.

I did not ask him what it might or might not be; I asked simply what was his opinion upon the subject, and there was no reply given to that explicit question.

I think it will be determined by the courts, and will be determined by the judgment of the country, that the acts passed in 1850 and 1858 by the Legislature of Vermont[18] are a violation, a gross, palpable violation of the Constitution of the United States. It is clear and conclusive to my mind, that a State passing an unconstitutional act intended to impede or to prevent the execution of a law passed by the Congress of the United States which is constitutional, is thereby placed, so far as the initiative is concerned, in a state of rebellion. It is an open act of nullification. It is true that, so far as my information goes, I am not aware that there has been any attempt in Vermont to wrest any persons out of the hands of the officers of the United States, or to imprison or to fine any person under the operation of this law; but the passage of such an act is to initiate rebellion. I think it comes in conflict directly with the spirit and letter of the Constitution of the United States, and to that extent is an act of nullification, and places the State in open rebellion to the United States.

I stated, yesterday, that there was no power conferred upon the Congress of the United States, by the Constitution, to coerce a State in its sovereign capacity; that there was no power on the part of the Congress of the United States even to bring a State into the supreme tribunal of the country. You cannot put a State at the bar of the Supreme Court of the United States. But, in this connection, I did say that the Congress of the United States had the power to pass laws to operate upon individuals within the limits of a State, by which all the functions of this Government could be executed and carried out. Then, in this case, if Vermont, either by an act of secession, which I take to be unconstitutional, or without first having seceded from the Union of the States by open force, in conformity with the laws of the State, should resist or attempt to resist the execution of the laws of the United States, it would be a practical rebellion, an overt act; and this Government has the power and the authority under the Constitution to enforce the laws of the United States, and it has the power and authority to call to its aid such means as are deemed necessary and proper for the execution of the laws, even if it was to lead to the calling out of the militia, or calling into service the Army and Navy of the United States to execute the laws. While I make this application to Vermont, I say the same principle applies to every other State placing herself in a like attitude in opposition to, and in contravention of, the execution of the laws of the United States.

I do not think it necessary, in order to preserve this Union, or to keep a State within its sphere, that the Congress of the United States should have the power to coerce a State. All that is necessary is for the Government to have the power to execute and to carry out all the powers conferred upon it by the Constitution, whether they apply to the State or otherwise. This, I think, the Government clearly has the power to do; and so long as the Government executes all the laws in good faith, denying the right of a State constitutionally to secede, so long the State is in the Union, and subject to all the provisions of the Constitution and the laws passed in conformity with it. For example: the power is conferred on the Federal Government to carry the mails through the several States; to establish post offices and post roads; the power is conferred on the Federal Government to establish courts in the respective States; the power is conferred on the General Government to lay and collect taxes in the several States, and so on. The various powers are enumerated, and each and every one of these powers the Federal Government has the constitutional authority to execute within the limits of the States. It is not an invasion of a State for the Federal Government to execute its laws, to take care of its public property, and to enforce the collection of its revenue; but if, in the execution of the laws; if, in the enforcement of the Constitution, it meets with resistance, it is the duty of the Government, and it has the authority, to put down resistance, and effectually to execute the laws as contemplated by the Constitution of the country.

But this was a diversion from the line of my argument. I was going on to show that, according to the opinions of the fathers, not only of the country but of the Constitution itself, no State, of its own volition, had the right to withdraw from the Confederacy after having entered into the compact. I referred yesterday to the last letter Mr. Madison wrote upon this subject—at least it is the last one that I have been able to find—in which he summed up this subject in a conclusive and masterly manner. In his letter to Mr. Webster of March 15, 1833, upon the receipt of Mr. Webster's speech, after the excitement had subsided to some extent and the country had taken its stand, Mr. Madison said:

[The passage set forth the broad role of the Constitution, "subject to the revolutionary rights of the people in extreme cases"—but, by inference, not subject to the right of secession.]

This is clear and conclusive, so far as Mr. Madison goes on the subject. I showed yesterday that in 1789, in making his report upon the Virginia resolutions, he gave the true interpretation to those resolutions, and explained what was meant by the word "respective" before "States." In his letter, in 1832, to Mr. Rives, and in his letter of 1832, to Mr. Trist, (to which I referred yesterday,) having had time to reflect on the operation of the various provisions of the Constitution upon the country, in the decline of life, when he had seen the experiment fairly made, when his mind was matured upon every single point and provision in the Constitution, he, at that late period, sums up the doctrine and comes to the conclusion that I am contending for on the present occasion.

In addition to this, Mr. Jefferson, who prior to the formation of the Constitution was in Paris, writing letters on the subject of the formation of a stable Government here, saw the great defect in the Federal head under the old Articles of Confederation, and he pointed with the unerring finger of philosophy and certainty to what is now in the Constitution, as what was wanting in the old Articles of Confederation. Mr. Jefferson, in his letter to Colonel Monroe, dated Paris, August 11, 1786, speaks thus:

> There never will be money in the Treasury till the Confederacy shows its teeth. The States must see the rod; perhaps it must be felt by some one of them. I am persuaded all of them would rejoice to see every one obliged to furnish its contributions. It is not the difficulty of furnishing them which beggars the Treasury, but the fear that others will not furnish as much. Every rational citizen must wish to see an effective instrument of coercion, and should fear to see it on any other element than the water.[19]

Here Mr. Jefferson, seeing the difficulty that, under the old Articles of Confederation, the Federal Government had not the power to execute its laws, that it could not collect revenue, points to what should be in the Constitution of the United States when formed. Mr. Jefferson, upon the same idea which was in his mind, and which was afterwards embodied in the Constitution, said, in a letter to E. Carrington, dated Paris, August 4, 1787:

> I confess I do not go as far in the reforms thought necessary, as some of my correspondents in America; but if the convention should adopt such propositions, I shall suppose them necessary. My general plan would be, to make the States one as to everything connected with foreign nations, and several as to everything purely domestic. But, with all the imperfections of our present Government, it is without comparison the best existing, or that ever did exist. Its greatest defect is the imperfect manner in which matters of commerce have been provided for. It has been so often said, as to be generally believed, that Congress have no power by the Confederation to enforce anything—for example, contributions of money. It was not necessary to give them that power expressly; they have it by the law of nature. When *two parties make a compact, there results to each a power of compelling the other to execute it.*[20]

"When two parties make a compact, there results to each a power of compelling the other to execute it." This is Jefferson's language. If it was not even expressed in the Constitution, the power to preserve itself and maintain its authority would be possessed by the Federal Government from the very existence of the Government itself, upon the great principle that it must have the power to preserve its own existence. But we find that, in plain and express terms, this authority is delegated. The very powers that Mr. Jefferson pointed out as being wanting in the old Government, under the Articles of Confederation, are granted by the Constitution of the United States to the present Government by express delegation. Congress has the power to lay and collect taxes; Congress has the power to pass laws to restore fugitives from labor escaping from one State into another; Congress has the power to establish post offices and post roads; Congress has the power to establish courts in the different States; and having these powers, it has the authority to do everything necessary to sustain the collection of the revenue, the enforcement of the judicial system, and the carrying of the mails. Because Congress, having the power, undertakes to execute its laws, it will not do to say that the Government is placed in the position of an aggressor. Not so. It is only acting within the scope of the Constitution, and in compliance with its delegated powers. But a State that resists the exercise of those powers becomes the aggressor, and places itself in a rebellious or nullifying attitude. It is the duty of this Government to execute its laws in good faith. When the Federal Government shall fail to execute all the laws that are made in strict conformity with the Constitution, if our sister States shall pass laws violative of that Constitution, and obstructing the laws of Congress passed in conformity with it, then, and not till then, will this Government have failed to accomplish the great objects of its creation. Then it will be at an end, and all the parties to the compact will be released.

But I wish to go a little further into the authorities as to the power of a State to secede from the Union, and to quote an opinion of Judge Marshall, given at a very early day. I know it is very common to denounce him as a Federalist; but I care not where the truth comes from, or where a sound argument may be found to sustain a proposition that is right in itself, I am willing to adopt it; and I have put myself to the trouble to hunt up these unquestionable authorities on this subject, knowing that they would have more influence before the country, and before my constituents, than anything that I could say. Though I am not a lawyer, though I have not made the legal profession my study and my pursuit, I claim to have some little common sense and understanding as to the application of general principles. I find that Judge Marshall, in speaking on the question of the right of a State upon its own volition to go out of the Confederacy, in the case of Cohans *vs.* Virginia, said:

It is very true, that whenever hostility to the existing system shall become universal—

That is, the system of our Government—

it will be also irresistible. The people made the Constitution, and the people can unmake it.[21]

I care not whether he speaks here of the people in the aggregate or not. The application of the principle is just as clear, whether you say the people, through the States, made the Constitution, or leave out the qualifying words "through the States."

It is the creature of their will, and lives only by their will. But this supreme and irresistible power to make and unmake resides only in the whole body of the people; not in any subdivision of them. The attempt of any of the parts to exercise it is usurpation, and ought to be repelled by those to whom the people have delegated their power of repelling it.—*Wheaton's Reports*, vol. 6, p. 389.

Now, whether you apply that, in a general sense, to the people in the aggregate, or to the States occupying the same relation to the Federal Government that the people do to the States, the principle is just the same; and when you speak of States ratifying and making the Constitution of the United States, one State, an ingredient—one of the community that made the Constitution—has no right, without the consent of the other States, to withdraw from the compact, and set the Constitution at naught. It is the principle that I seek; and the principle applies as well to a community of States as it does to a community of individuals. Admitting that this Federal Government was made by a community of States, can one of that community of States, of its own will, without the consent of the rest, where the compact is reciprocal, set it aside, and withdraw itself from the operation of the Government? I have given you the opinion of Judge Marshall, one of the most distinguished jurists that ever presided in this country, though he is called by some a Federalist. His mind was clear; he lived in that day when the Constitution should be understood, and when it was understood—in the days of Madison and Jefferson; and this is his opinion upon that subject, as far back as 1821.

In this connection, I would call the attention of the Senate to General Jackson's views upon this subject; and I would also call their attention to Mr. Webster's views, if it were necessary, for he is conceded, by some at least, to be one of the most able expounders of the Constitution of the United States. General Jackson, though not celebrated for his legal attainments, was celebrated for his sagacity, his strong common sense, his great intuitive power of reaching correct conclusions, and understanding correct principles. In 1833, General Jackson, in his proclamation, takes identically the same ground; and declares that, first, a State has no power of itself to nullify a law of Congress within its limits; and next, that notwithstanding a State may claim to have ceded, it has no constitutional power to withdraw itself from the Union of the States, and thereby set at naught the laws and the Constitution. He argues this question forcibly and clearly; and comes to the unerring conclusion, according to my judgment, that no State has the constitutional power to withdraw itself from this Confederacy without the consent of the other States; and it may do good to reproduce his views on the subject. He says, in his famous proclamation, speaking of the nullification ordinance of South Carolina: [22]

[Jackson, contending that the ordinance violated the citizens' responsibilities to the Constitution and the Union, rejected the argument that a state might at will impose its sovereignty over that of the United States. In his view the people, not the states, formed the Constitution through their legislatures and conventions, thereby surrendering some of their sovereign powers "to constitute, jointly with the other States, a single nation"; a state could not secede, since "such secession does not break a league but destroys the unity of a nation."]

Having traveled thus far, the question arises, in what sense are we to construe the Constitution of the United States? I assume what is assumed in one of Mr. Madison's letters, that the Constitution was formed for perpetuity; that it never was intended to be broken up.[23] It was commenced, it is true, as an experiment; but the founders of the Constitution intended that this experiment should go on and on and on; and by way of making it perpetual, they provided for its amendment. They provided that this instrument could be amended and improved, from time to time, as the changing circumstances, as the changing pursuits, as the changing notions of men might require; but they made no provision whatever for its destruction. The old Articles of Confederation were formed for the purpose of making "a perpetual union." In 1787, when the convention concluded their deliberations and adopted the Constitution, what do they say in the very preamble of that Constitution? Having in their mind the idea that was shadowed forth in the old Articles of Confederation, that the Union was to be perpetual, they say, at the commencement, that it is to make "a more perfect union" than the union under the old Articles of Confederation, which they called "perpetual."

What furthermore do we find? The Constitution of the United States contains a provision that it is to be submitted to the States respectively for their ratification; but on nine States ratifying it, it shall be the Constitution for them. In that way the Government was created; and in that way provision was made to perfect it. What more do we find? The Constitution, as I have just remarked, provides for its own amendment, its improvement, its perpetuation, its continuance, by pointing out and by prescribing the mode and manner in which improvements shall be made. That still preserves the idea that it is to be perpetual. We find, in addition, a provision that Congress shall have power to admit new States.

Hence, in traveling along through the instrument, we find how the Government is created, how it is to be perpetuated, and how it may be enlarged in reference to the number of States constituting the Confederacy; but do we find any provision for winding it up, except on that great inherent principle that it may be wound up by the States—not by a State, but by the States which spoke it into existence—and by no other means. That is a means of taking down the Government that the Constitution could not provide for. It is above the Constitution; it is beyond any provision that can be made by mortal man.

Now, to expose the absurdity of the pretension that there is a right to secede, let me press this argument a little further. The Constitution has been formed; it has been made perfect, or, in other words, means have been provided by which it can be made perfect. It was intended to be perpetual. In reference to the execution of the laws under it, what do we find? As early as 1795, Congress passed an excise law, taxing distilleries throughout the country, and, what were called the whisky boys of Pennsylvania, resisted the law.[24] The Government wanted means. It taxed distilleries. The people of Pennsylvania resisted it. What is the difference between a portion of the people resisting a constitutional law, and all of the people of a State doing so? But because you can apply the term coercion in one case to a State, and in the other call it simply the execution of the law against individuals, you say there is a great distinction! We do not assume the power to coerce a State, but we assume that Congress has power to lay and collect taxes, and Congress has the right to enforce that law when obstructions and impediments are opposed to its enforcement. The people of Pennsylvania did object; they did resist and oppose the legal authorities of the country. Was that law enforced? Was it called coercion at that day to enforce it? Suppose all the people of the State of Pennsylvania had resisted: would not the law have applied with just the same force, and would it not have been just as constitutional to execute it against all the people of the State, as it was to execute it upon a part of their citizens?

George Washington, in his next annual message to the Congress of the United States, referred to the subject;[25] and if my friend from California[26] will read two or three paragraphs for me, he will do me a favor, for I cannot see by this light. It will be seen from the reading of these paragraphs what George Washington considered to be his duty in the execution of the laws of the United States upon the citizens of the States.

[Justifying the calling out of the militia on the ground that the whiskey rebels were not merely resisting "a particular law," but were pos-

sessed with "a spirit inimical to all order," Washington averred that
the militia's response demonstrated that his fellow-citizens "feel their
inseparable union."]

Mr. JOHNSON, of Tennessee. We see that in that instance President Washington thought there was power in this Government to
execute its laws. We see, too, that George Washington considered
the militia the army of the Constitution. We see, too, that George
Washington refers to this Union as being inseparable. This is the
way that the laws were executed by the Father of his Country, the
man who sat as President of the convention that made the Constitution. Here was resistance interposed—opposition to the execution of
the laws; and George Washington, then President of the United
States, went in person at the head of the militia; and it showed his
sagacity, his correct comprehension of men, and the effect that an
immediate movement of that kind would have upon them. He ordered
fifteen thousand of his countrymen to the scene of action, and went
there in person, and stayed there till he was satisfied that the insub-
ordination was quelled. That is the manner in which George Washington put down rebellion. That is the manner in which he executed
the laws.[27]

Here, then, we find General Washington executing the law, in
1795, against a portion of the citizens of Pennsylvania who rebelled;
and, I repeat the question, where is the difference between executing
the law upon a part and upon the whole? Suppose the whole of Pennsylvania had rebelled and resisted the excise law; had refused to pay
taxes on distilleries: was it not as competent and as constitutional
for General Washington to have executed the law against the whole
as against a part? Is there any difference? Governmental affairs must
be practical as well as our own domestic affairs. You may make nice
metaphysical distinctions between the practical operations of Government and its theory; you may refine upon what is a State, and
point out a difference between a State and a portion of a State; but
what is it when you reduce it to practical operation, and square it by
common sense?

In 1832, resistance was interposed to laws of the United States in
another State. An ordinance was passed by South Carolina, assuming to act as a sovereign State, to nullify a law of the United States.
In 1833, the distinguished man who filled the executive chair,
who now lies in his silent grave, loved and respected for his virtue,
his honor, his integrity, his patriotism, his undoubted courage, and
his devotion to his kind, with an eye single to the promotion of his
country's best interests, issued the proclamation extracts from which
I have already presented. He was sworn to support the Constitution,

and to see that the laws were faithfully executed; and he fulfilled the obligation. He took all the steps necessary to secure the execution of the law, and he would have executed it by the power of the Government if the point of time had arrived when it was necessary to resort to power. We can see that he acted upon similar principles to those acted upon by General Washington. He took the precaution of ordering a force there sufficient for the purpose of enabling him to say effectually to the rebellious, and those who were interposing opposition to the execution of the laws: "The laws which we made according to the Constitution, the laws that provide for the collection of the revenue to sustain this Government, must be enforced, and the revenue must be collected. It is a part of the compact; it is a part of the engagement you have undertaken to perform, and you of your own will have no power or authority to set it aside."[28] The duties were collected; the law was enforced; and the Government went on. In his proclamation, he made a powerful appeal. He told them what would be done; and it would have been done, as certain as God rules on high, if the time had arrived which made it necessary.

Then we see where General Washington stood, and where General Jackson stood. Now, how does the present case stand? The time has come when men should speak out. Duties are mine; consequences are God's.[29] I intend to discharge my duty, and I intend to avow my understanding of the Constitution and the laws of the country. Have we no authority or power to execute the laws in the State of South Carolina as well as in Vermont and Pennsylvania? I think we have. As I before said, although a State may, by an ordinance, or by a resolve, or by an act of any other kind, declare that they absolve their citizens from all allegiance to this Government, it does not release them from the compact. The compact is reciprocal; and they, in coming into it, undertook to perform certain duties and abide by the laws made in conformity with the compact. Now, sir, what is the Government to do in South Carolina? If South Carolina undertake to drive the Federal courts out of that State, yet the Federal Government has the right to hold those courts there. She may attempt to exclude the mails, yet the Federal Government has the right to establish post offices and post roads and to carry the mails there. She may resist the collection of revenue at Charleston, or any other point that the Government has provided for its collection; but the Government has the right to collect it and to enforce the law. She may undertake to take possession of the property belonging to the Government which was originally ceded by the State, but the Federal Government has the right to provide the means for retaining possession of that property. If she makes an advance either to dispossess the Government of that which it has purchased, or to resist the execution of the revenue laws, or of our judicial system, or the carrying of the mails, or the exercise of any other power conferred on the Federal Government, she puts herself in the wrong, and it will be the duty of the Government to see that the laws are faithfully executed. By reference to the records, it will be seen that, on

December 19, 1805, South Carolina granted all the right, title, and claim of the State to all the lands reserved for Fort Moultrie, on Sullivan's Island, not exceeding five acres, with all the forts, fortifications, &c., thereon; canal, &c.; the high lands, and part of the marsh, belonging to Fort Johnson, not exceeding twenty acres; the land on which Fort Pinckney is built, and three acres around it; a portion of the sandbank on the southeasternmost point of Charleston, not exceeding two acres; not exceeding four acres for a battery, or fort, &c., on Blythe's Point, at the mouth of Sampit river; Mustard Island, in Beaufort river, opposite Parris's Island; not exceeding seven acres of land on St. Helena Island, for a principal fort; the whole on condition that the United States should, within three years, repair forts, &c.; the United States to compensate individuals for property; the lands, &c., to be free from taxes to the State.[30]

Here is a clear deed of cession. The Federal Government has complied with all the conditions, and has, in its own right, the land on which these forts are constructed. The conditions of the cession have been complied with; and the Government has had possession from that period to the present time. There are its forts; there is its arsenal; there are its dock-yards; there is the property of the Government; and now, under the Constitution, and under the laws made in pursuance thereof, has South Carolina the authority and the right to expel the Federal Government from its own property that has been given to it by her own act, and of which it is now in possession? By resisting the execution of the laws; by attempting to dispossess the Federal Government, does she not put herself in the wrong? Does she not violate the laws of the United States? Does she not violate the Constitution? Does she not put herself, within the meaning and purview of the Constitution, in the attitude of levying war against the United States? The Constitution defines and declares what is treason. Let us talk about things by their right names. I know that some hotspur or madcap may declare that these are not times for a government of law; that we are in a revolution. I know that Patrick Henry once said, "if this be treason, make the most of it."[31] If anything can be treason in the scope and purview of the Constitution, is not levying war upon the United States treason? Is not an attempt to take its property treason? Is not an attempt to expel its soldiers treason? Is not an attempt to resist the collection of the revenue, or to expel your mails, or to drive your courts from her borders, treason? Are not these powers clearly conferred in the Constitution on the Federal Government to be exercised? What is it, then, I ask in the name of the Constitution, in the meaning of the term as there defined? It is treason, and nothing but treason; and if one State, upon its own volition, can go out of this Confederacy without regard to the effect it is to have upon the remaining parties to the compact, what is your Government worth? what will it come to? and in what will it end? It is no Government at all upon such a construction.

But it is declared and assumed that, if a State secedes, she is no longer a member of the Union, and that, therefore, the laws and the Constitution of the United States are no longer operative within her limits, and she is not guilty if she violates them. This is a matter of opinion. I have tried to show, from the origin of the Government down to the present time, what this doctrine of secession is, and there is but one concurring and unerring conclusion reached by all the great and distinguished men of the country. Madison, who is called the Father of the Constitution, denies the doctrine. Washington, who was the Father of his Country, denies the doctrine. Jefferson, Jackson, Clay, and Webster, all deny the doctrine; and yet all at once it is discovered and ascertained that a State, of its own volition, can go out of this Confederacy, without regard to consequences, without regard to the injury and woe that may be inflicted on the remaining members from the act!

Suppose this doctrine to be true, Mr. President, that a State can withdraw from this Confederacy; and suppose South Carolina has seceded, and is now out of the Confederacy: in what an attitude does she place herself? There might be circumstances under which the States ratifying the compact might tolerate the secession of a State, she taking the consequences of the act. But there might be other circumstances under which the States could not allow one to secede. Why do I say so? Some suppose—and it is a well-founded supposition—that by the secession of a State all the remaining States might be involved in disastrous consequences; they might be involved in war; and by the secession of one State, the existence of the remaining States might be involved. Then, without regard to the Constitution, dare the other States permit one to secede when it endangers and involves all the remaining States? The question arises in this connection, whether the States are in a condition to tolerate or will tolerate the secession of South Carolina. That is a matter to be determined by the circumstances; that is a matter to be determined by the emergency; that is a matter to be determined when it comes up. It is a question which must be left open to be determined by the surrounding circumstances, when the occasion arises.

But conceding, for argument's sake, the doctrine of secession, and admitting that the State of South Carolina is now upon your coast, a foreign Power, absolved from all connection with the Federal Government, out of the Union: what then? There was a doctrine inculcated in 1823, by Mr. Monroe, that this Government, keeping in view the safety of the people and the existence of our institutions, would permit no European Power to plant any more colonies on this continent. Now, suppose that South Carolina is outside of the Confederacy, and this Government is in possession of the fact that she is forming an alliance with a foreign Power—with France, with England, with Russia, with Austria, or with all of the principal Powers of Europe; that there is to be a great naval station established there; an immense rendezvous for their army, with a view to ulterior objects, with a view of making advances upon the rest of these States: let me ask the Senate, let me ask the country, if they dare permit it? Under and in compliance with the great law of self-preservation, we dare not let her do it; and if she were a sovereign Power to-day, outside of the Confederacy, and was forming an alliance that we deemed inimical to our institutions, and the existence of our Government, we should have a right to conquer and hold her as a province—a term which is so much used with scorn.

Mr. President, I have referred to the manner in which this Government was formed. I have referred to the provision of the Constitution which provides for the admission of new States. Now, let me ask, can any one believe that, in the creation of this Government, its founders intended that it should have the power to acquire territory and form it into States, and then permit them to go out of the Union? Let us take a case. How long has it been since your armies were in Mexico? How long has it been since your brave men were exposed to the diseases, the privations, the sufferings, which are incident to a campaign of that kind? How long has it been since they were bearing your eagles in a foreign land, many of them falling at the point of the bayonet, consigned to their long, narrow home, with no winding-sheet but their blankets saturated with their blood? How many victories did they win? how many laurels did they acquire? how many trophies did they bring back? The country is full of them. What did it cost you? One hundred and twenty million dollars.[32] What did you pay for the country you acquired, besides? Fifteen million dollars. Peace was made; territory was acquired; and, in a few years, from that territory California erected herself into a free and independent State, and, under the provisions of the Constitution, we admitted her as a member of this Confederacy. After having expended $120,000,000 in the war; after having lost many of our bravest and most gallant men; after having paid $15,000,000 to Mexico for the territory, and admitted it into the Union as a State, now that the people of California have got into the Confederacy and can stand alone, according to this modern doctrine, your Government was just made to let them in, and then to let them step out. Is not the conclusion illogical? Is it not absurd to say that, now that California is in, she, on her own volition—without regard to the consideration paid for her; without regard to the policy which dictated her acquisition by the United States—can walk out and bid you defiance? Is it not an absurdity, if you take the reason and object of Government?

But we need not stop here; let us go to Texas. Texas was engaged in a revolution with Mexico. She succeeded in the assertion and establishment of her independence; and she became a sovereign and independent Power outside of this Union. She applied for admission, and she was admitted into this family of States. After she was in, she was oppressed by the debts of her war which resulted in her separation from Mexico; she was harassed by the Indians upon her border; and in 1850, by way of relief to Texas, what did we do? There was an extent of territory that lies north, if my memory serves me right, embracing what is now called the Territory of New Mexico. Texas had it not in her power to protect the citizens that were there. It was a dead limb, paralyzed, lifeless. The Federal Government came along as a kind physician, saying, "We will take this dead limb from your body, and vitalize it, by giving protection to the people, and incorporating it into a territorial government: and in addition to that, we will give you $10,000,000, and you may retain your own public lands;" and the other States were taxed in common to pay the $10,000,000. Now, after all this is done, Texas, forsooth, upon her own volition, is to say, "I will walk out of this Union!" Were there no other parties to that compact? We are told the compact is reciprocal. Did we take in California, did we take in Texas, just to benefit them? No; but to add to this great family of States; and it is apparent, from the fact of their coming in, that the compact is reciprocal; and having entered into the compact, they have no right to withdraw without the consent of the remaining States.

Again: take the case of Louisiana. What did we pay for her in 1803, and for what was she wanted? Just to get Louisiana into the Confederacy? Just for the benefit of that particular locality? Was not the mighty West looked to? Was it not to secure the free navigation of the Mississippi river, the mouth of which was then in possession of France, shortly before of Spain, passing about between those two Powers? Yes, the navigation of that river was wanted. Simply for Louisiana? No, but for all the States. The United States paid $15,000,000, and France passed the country to the United States. It remained in a territorial condition for a while, sustained and protected by the strong arm of the Federal Government. We acquired the territory and the navigation of the river; and the money was paid for the benefit of all the States, and not of Louisiana exclusively. And now that this great valley is filled up; now that the navigation of the Mississippi is one hundred times more important than it was then; now, after the United States have paid the money, have acquired the title to Louisiana, and have incorporated her into the Confederacy, it is proposed that she shall go out of the Union! In 1815, when her shores were invaded; when her city was about to be sacked; when her booty and her beauty were about to fall a prey to British aggression, the brave men of Tennessee, and of Kentucky, and of the surrounding States, rushed into her borders and upon her shores, and under the lead of their own gallant Jackson, drove the invading forces away. And now, after all this; after the money has been paid; after the free navigation of the river has been obtained—not for the benefit of Louisiana alone, but for her in common with all the States —Louisiana says to the other States, "We will go out of this Confederacy; we do not care if you did fight our battles; we do not care if you did acquire the free navigation of this river from France; we will go out if we think proper, and constitute ourselves an independent Power, and bid defiance to the other States." It is an absurdity; it is a contradiction; it is illogical; it is not deducible from the structure of the Government itself.

[John Slidell, Louisiana, remarks that he knows of no citizen living in the lower Mississippi region who would question the right of free navigation.]

Mr. JOHNSON, of Tennessee. That may all be very true; and I do not suppose that, at this moment, there is a citizen in the State of Louisiana who would think of obstructing the free navigation of the river; but are not nations controlled by their interests in varying circumstances? It strikes me so; and hereafter, when a conflict of interest arises; when difficulty may spring up between two separate Powers, Louisiana, having the control of the mouth of the river, might feel disposed to tax our citizens going down there. It is a power that I am not willing to concede to be exercised at the discretion of any authority outside of this Government. The Senator's assurance does not amount to anything. It depends entirely on the interest and condition of the surrounding country as to what power Louisiana would want to exercise in reference to that river. So sensitive have been the people of my State upon the free navigation of that river, that as far back as 1796, now sixty-four years ago, in their bill of rights, before they passed under the jurisdiction of the United States, they declared:

That an equal participation of the free navigation of the Mississippi is one of the inherent rights of the citizens of this State: it cannot, therefore, be conceded to any prince, potentate, Power, person, or persons whatever.[33]

This shows the estimate that the people fixed on this stream sixty-four years ago; and now we are told, if Louisiana does go out, it is not her intention at this time to tax the people above. Who can tell what may be the intention of Louisiana hereafter? Are we willing to place the rights of our citizens, are we willing to place the travel and commerce of our citizens, at the discretion of any Power outside of this Government? I will not; I do not care whether the other Powers be in Louisiana or the moon.

But, then, as we go on, let us follow the circle, and see where this doctrine will carry us. How long has it been since Florida lay out on our coast an annoyance to us? And now she has got entirely feverish about being an independent and separate Government, while she has not as many qualified voters as there are in one congressional district. What condition did Florida occupy in 1811? She stood in the possession of Spain. What did the United States think about having adjacent territory outside of their jurisdiction? Let us turn to the authorities, and see what proposition they were willing to act upon. I find, in the statutes of the United States, this joint resolution:

Taking into view the peculiar situation of Spain, and of her American provinces, and considering the influence which the destiny of the territory adjoining the southern border of the United States may have upon their security, tranquillity, and commerce: Therefore, *Resolved by the Senate and House of Representatives of the United States of America in Congress assembled*, That the United States, under the peculiar circumstances of the existing crisis, cannot, without serious inquietude, see any part of the said territory pass into the hands of any foreign Power; and that a due regard to their own safety compels them to provide, under certain contingencies, for the temporary occupation of the said territory. They, at the same time, declare that the said territory shall, in their hands, remain subject to future negotiations.[34]

What principle is set forth there? Florida was in the possession of Spain. English spies were harbored in her territory. Spain was inimical to the United States; and in view of the great principle of self-preservation, the Congress of the United States passed a resolution declaring that if Spain attempted to transfer Florida into the hands of any other Power, the United States would take possession of it. Yet Congress were gracious and condescending enough to say that it should remain open to future negotiation. That is to say, "Hereafter, if we can make a negotiation that will suit us, we will make it; if we do not, we will keep the territory;" that is all. There was the territory lying upon our border, outside of the jurisdiction of the United States; and we declared, by an act of Congress, that no foreign Power should possess it.

We went still further and appropriated $100,000, and authorized the President to enter and take possession of it with the means placed in his hands. Afterwards, we did negotiate with Spain, and gave $6,000,000 for the Territory;[35] and we established a territorial government for it. What next? We undertook to drive out the Seminole Indians, and we had a war in which this Government lost more than it lost in all the other wars it was engaged in;[36] and we paid the sum of $25,000,000 to get the Seminoles out of the swamps, so that the Territory could be inhabited by white men. We paid for it, we took possession of it; and I remember, when I was in the other House, and Florida was knocking at the door for admission, how extremely anxious her then able Delegate was to be admitted. He now sits before me, [Mr. Yulee.][37] I remember how important he thought it was then to come under the protecting wing of the United States as one of the stars of our Confederacy. But now the Territory is paid for, England is driven out, $25,000,000 have been expended; and they want no longer the protection of this Government, but will go out without consulting the other States, without reference to the effect upon the remaining parties to the compact. Where will she go? Will she attach herself to Spain again? Will she pass back under the jurisdiction of the Seminoles? After having been nurtured and protected and fostered by all these States, now, without regard to them, is she to be allowed, at her own volition, to withdraw from the Union? I say she has no constitutional right to do it; and when she does it, it is an act of aggression. If she succeeds, it will only be a successful revolution. If she does not succeed, she must take the penalties and terrors of the law.

But, sir, there is another question that suggests itself in this connection. Kansas, during the last Congress, applied for admission into this Union. She assumed to be a State, and the difficulty in the way was a provision in her constitution, and the manner of its adoption. We did not let Kansas in. We did not question her being a State; but on account of the manner of forming her constitution and its provisions, we kept Kansas out.[38] What is Kansas now? Is she a State, or is she a Territory? Does she revert back to her territorial condition of pupilage? Or, having been a State, and having applied for admission and been refused, is she standing out a State? You hold her as a territory; you hold her as a province. You prescribe the mode of electing the members of her Legislature, and pay them out of your own Treasury. Yes, she is a province controlled by Federal authority, and her laws are made in conformity with the acts of Congress. Is she not a Territory? I think she is.

Suppose the State of California withdraws from the Union. We admitted her. She was territory acquired by the United States, by our blood and our treasure. Now, suppose she withdraws from the

Confederacy: does she pass back into a territorial condition, remain
a dependency upon the Federal Government, or does she stand out
as a separate government? Let me take Louisiana, for which we
paid $15,000,000. That was a Territory for a number of years—
yes, a province. It is only another name for a province. It is a possession held under the jurisdiction of the United States. We admitted
Louisiana into the Union as a State. Suppose we had refused to
admit her: would she not still have remained a Territory? Would
she not have remained under the protection of the United States?
But now, if she has the power to withdraw from the Union, does
she not pass back into the condition in which she was before we
admitted her into the Union? In what condition does she place herself? When those States which were at first Territories cease their
connection with this Government, do they pass back into the territorial condition? When Florida is going out, when Louisiana is
going out, and these other States that were originally Territories go
out of the Union, in what condition do they place themselves? Are
they Territories or States? Are they merely on probation to become
members of this Confederacy, or are they States outside of the Confederacy?

Mr. YULEE. Will the Senator allow me to ask a single question
in this connection?

Mr. JOHNSON, of Tennessee. I hope the Senator will not interrupt me. I do not refuse out of any discourtesy.

Mr. WIGFALL. Let him alone.

Mr. JOHNSON, of Tennessee. Remarks of that kind never affect
me in the slightest degree; I never hear them. But, Mr. President, I
have referred to the acts of Congress for acquiring Florida as setting
forth a principle. Let me read another of those acts: [39]

[This measure authorized the President to take possession of the West
Florida country.]

What is the principle avowed here? That from the geographical
relations of this territory to the United States, from its importance
to the safety and security of the institutions of the United States,
we authorized the President to expend $100,000 to get a foothold
there, and especially to take possession of it if it were likely to pass
to any foreign Power. We see the doctrine and principle there established and acted upon by our Government. This principle was
again avowed by distinguished men at Ostend. A paper was drawn
up there by Mr. Buchanan, Mr. Soulé of Louisiana, and Mr. Mason
of Virginia, our ministers to the three principal Courts in Europe.
They met at Ostend and drew up a paper in which they laid down
certain doctrines in strict conformity with the act of Congress that

I have just read. They say in that paper, signed by James Buchanan, J. Y. Mason, and Pierre Soulé:

[Johnson reads that portion of the manifesto which contended that Cuba's geographic proximity, its strategic location, and its own internal instability made our possession and control of the Spanish-held island a justifiable response to "the great law of self-preservation." Should the American government decide that its own security was threatened by Spanish possession, it should offer Spain "a price for Cuba far beyond its present value" and, if the proposal were rejected, seize the island.]

We find in this document, signed by our three ministers, and approved by the American people, the doctrine laid down clearly that if the United States believed that Cuba was to be transferred by Spain to England or to France, or to some other Power inimical to the United States, the safety of the American people, the safety of our institutions, the existence of the Government, being imperiled, we should have a right, without regard to money or blood, to acquire it.[40]

Where does this carry us? We find that this doctrine was not only laid down, but practiced, in the case of Florida. Suppose Louisiana was now out of the Confederacy, holding the key to the Gulf, the outlet to the commerce of the great West: under the doctrine laid down by these ministers, and practiced by the Congress of the United States, would not this Government have the right, in obedience to the great principle of self-preservation, and for the safety of our institutions, to seize it and pass it under the jurisdiction of the United States, and hold it as a province subject to the laws of the United States? I say it would. The same principle applied to Florida. The same principle would apply to South Carolina. I regret that she occupies the position that she has assumed, but I am arguing a principle, and do not refer to her out of any disrespect. If South Carolina were outside of the Confederacy, an independent Power, having no connection with the United States, and our institutions were likely to be endangered, and the existence of the Government imperiled by her remaining a separate and independent Power, or by her forming associations and alliances with some foreign Power that would injure our free institutions, I say we should have a right, on the principle laid down by Mr. Mason, Mr. Buchanan, and Mr. Soulé, and upon the principle practiced by the Congress of the United States in the case of Florida, to seize her, pass her under the jurisdiction of the United States, and hold her as a province.

Mr. President, I have spoken of the possibility of a State standing in the position of South Carolina making alliances with a foreign Power. What do we see now? Ex-Governor Manning,[41] of that State, in a speech made not long since at Columbia, made these declarations:

Cotton is king, and would enable us in peace to rule the nations of the world, or successfully to encounter them in war. The millions in France and England engaged in its manufacture, are an effectual guarantee of the friendship of those nations. If necessary, their armies would stand to guard its uninterrupted and peaceful cultivation, and their men-of-war would line our coasts to guard it in its transit from our ports.

Ah! are we prepared, in the face of doctrines like these, to permit a State that has been a member of our Confederacy to go out, and erect herself into an independent Power, when she points to the time when she will become a dependent of Great Britain, or when she will want the protection of France? What is the doctrine laid down by Mr. Buchanan and Mr. Mason and Mr. Soulé? If Cuba is to pass into the hands of an unfriendly Power, or any Power inimical to the United States, we have a right to seize and to hold her. Where is the difference between the two cases?

If South Carolina is outside of the Confederacy as an independent Power, disconnected from this Government, and we find her forming alliances to protect her, I ask what becomes of that great principle, the law of self-preservation? Does it not apply with equal force? We are told, upon pretty high authority, that Great Britain is operating in the United States; that she is exerting a powerful influence. I find that, in a paper issued from the executive office, Little Rock, Arkansas, and addressed to the militia of the State of Arkansas,[42] the following language is used:

[Alleging the existence of a British plot to break up the United States and seeing in this discovery an end to "all discord between the free States and the slave States," Governor Conway abjured his people to "make *permanent and thorough preparations*" to repel the impending aggression.]

This is signed by "Elias N. Conway, Governor of the State of Arkansas, and commander-in-chief of the army of said State, and of the militia thereof." But ex-Governor Manning, of South Carolina, declares that cotton is king, and that the armies of Great Britain, and the fleets of France, and their men of war, would protect them; the one in the peaceful production of cotton, and the other in its exportation to the ports of the world. What sort of times are we falling on? Where are we going? Are these the threats that we are to be met with?

Is the United States to be told by one of the States attempting to absolve itself from its allegiance, without authority, and in fact in violation of the Constitution of the United States, that being disconnected with the Confederacy, it will place itself upon our coast to form an alliance with France and with England, which will protect her more securely than the protection which she now receives from the United States? The question recurs, have we not an existence, have we not institutions, to preserve; and in compliance with the great law of self-preservation, can we permit one of these States to take the protection of a foreign Power that is inimical and dangerous to the peaceful relations of this Government? Can we do it? I do not believe that we can. I repeat, for fear it may be misunderstood, that there are certain circumstances and conditions under which the remaining States, parties to the compact, might tolerate the secession of one State; and there are other circumstances and other conditions under which they dare not do it, in view of the great principle of self-preservation of which I have been speaking. When any State takes such an attitude what will be our course of policy? The case must be determined by the existing circumstances at the time.

But it is expected and said by some that South Carolina, in making this movement, intends to carry the other States along with her; that they will be drawn into it. Now, Mr. President, is that the way for one sister, for one rebellious State, to talk to others! Is that the language in which they should be addressed? I ask my friend from California to read an extract from the message of Governor Gist, of South Carolina.[43] He will do me a favor by so doing; and then we shall see the basis upon which we stand, and the attitude in which we are to be placed. Not only is South Carolina to go out of the Union in violation of the Constitution, impeding and resisting the execution of the laws, but the other States are to be dragged along with her, and we are all to be involved in one common ruin.

[Gist recommended to the legislature a prohibition on the introduction of slaves from states outside a southern confederacy, thereby preventing the nonaligned slave states from realizing "the money value for their slaves by selling them to us, and thus prepare them, without any loss of property, to accommodate themselves to the northern free-soil idea." He also asserted that the Constitution offers little protection from northern fanaticism.]

Mr. JOHNSON, of Tennessee. If my friend will read an extract from the speech of Mr. Keitt, of South Carolina,[44] it will show the determination and policy to be pursued. It is done with all respect to him; for he is a man upon whom I look as a perfect and entire gentleman, from all my acquaintance with him; but I merely want to quote from his speech to get at the policy they wish to pursue.

[In this Columbia speech Keitt urged, if need be, separate action by South Carolina to "shatter this accursed Union." If South Carolina could not do it alone, "she could at least throw her arms around the pillars of the Constitution, and involve all the States in a common ruin."]

Mr. JOHNSON, of Tennessee. Mr. President, I have referred to these extracts to show the policy intended to be pursued by our se-

ceding sister. What is the first threat thrown out? It is an intimidation to the border States, alluding especially, I suppose, to Virginia,
Maryland, Kentucky, and Missouri. They constitute the first tier of
the border slave States. The next tier would be North Carolina and
Tennessee and Arkansas. We in the South have complained of and
condemned the position assumed by the Abolitionists. We have complained that their intention was to hem slavery in, so that, like the
scorpion when surrounded by fire, if it did not die from the intense
heat of the scorching flames, it would perish in its own poisonous
skin.[45] Now, our sister, without consulting her sisters, without caring
for their interest or their consent, says that she will move forward;
that she will destroy the Government under which we have lived, and
that hereafter, when she forms a Government or a Constitution, unless the border States come in, she will pass laws prohibiting the
importation of slaves into her State from those States, and thereby
obstruct the slave trade among the States, and throw the institution
back upon the border States, so that they will be compelled to emancipate their slaves upon the principle laid down by the Abolition
party. That is the rod held over us!

I tell our sisters in the South that so far as Tennessee is concerned,
she will not be dragged into a southern or any other confederacy
until she has had time to consider; and then she will go when she
believes it to be her interest, and not before. I tell our northern
friends, who are resisting the execution of the laws made in conformity with the Constitution, that we will not be driven on the
other hand into their confederacy, and we will not go into it unless
it suits us, and they give us such guarantees as we deem right and
proper. We say to you of the South, we are not to be frightened and
coerced. Oh, when one talks about coercing a State, how maddening
and insulting to the State; but when you want to bring the other
States to terms, how easy to point out a means by which to coerce
them! But, sir, we do not intend to be coerced.

We are told that certain States will go out and tear this accursed
Constitution into fragments, and drag the pillars of this mighty
edifice down upon us, and involve us all in one common ruin.[46] Will
the border States submit to such a threat? No. If they do not come
into the movement, the pillars of this stupendous fabric of human
freedom and greatness and goodness are to be pulled down, and all
will be involved in one common ruin. Such is the threatening language used. "You shall come into our confederacy, or we will coerce
you to the emancipation of your slaves." That is the language which
is held toward us.

There are many ideas afloat about this threatened dissolution,
and it is time to speak out. The question arises in reference to the

protection and preservation of the institution of slavery, whether dissolution is a remedy or will give to it protection. I avow here, to-day, that if I were an Abolitionist, and wanted to accomplish the overthrow and abolition of the institution of slavery in the southern States, the first step that I would take would be to break the bonds of this Union, and dissolve this Government. I believe the continuance of slavery depends upon the preservation of this Union, and a compliance with all the guarantees of the Constitution. I believe an interference with it will break up the Union; and I believe a dissolution of the Union will, in the end, though it may be some time to come, overthrow the institution of slavery. Hence we find so many in the North who desire the dissolution of these States as the most certain and direct and effectual means of overthrowing the institution of slavery.

What protection would it be to us to dissolve this Union? What protection would it be to us to convert this nation into two hostile Powers, the one warring with the other? Whose property is at stake? Whose interest is endangered? Is it not the property of the border States? Suppose Canada were moved down upon our border, and the two separated sections, then different nations, were hostile: what would the institution of slavery be worth on the border? Every man who has common sense will see that the institution would take up its march and retreat, as certainly and as unerringly as general laws can operate. Yes; it would commence to retreat the very moment this Government was converted into hostile Powers, and you made the line between the slaveholding and non-slaveholding States the line of division.

Then, what remedy do we get for the institution of slavery? Must we keep up a standing army? Must we keep up forts bristling with arms along the whole border? This is a question to be considered, one that involves the future; and no step should be taken without mature reflection. Before this Union is dissolved and broken up, we in Tennessee, as one of the slave States, want to be consulted; we want to know what protection we are to have; whether we are simply to be made outposts and guards to protect the property of others, at the same time that we sacrifice and lose our own. We want to understand this question.

Again: if there is one division of the States, will there not be more than one? I heard a Senator say the other day that he would rather see this Government separated into thirty-three fractional parts than to see it consolidated;[47] but when you once begin to divide, when the first division is made, who can tell when the next will be made? When these States are all turned loose, and a different condition of things is presented, with complex and abstruse interests to be considered and weighed and understood, what combinations may take place no one can tell. I am opposed to the consolidation of Government, and I am as much for the reserved rights of States as any one; but, rather than see this Union divided into thirty-three petty Governments, with a little prince in one, a potentate in another, a little aristocracy in a third, a little democracy in a fourth, and a republic somewhere else; a citizen not being able to pass from one State to another without a passport or a commission from his Government; with quarreling and warring amongst the little petty Powers, which would result in anarchy; I would rather see this Government to-day—I proclaim it here in my place—converted into a consolidated Government. It would be better for the American people; it would be better for our kind; it would be better for humanity; better for Christianity; better for all that tends to elevate and ennoble man, than breaking up this splendid, this magnificent, this stupendous fabric of human government, the most perfect that the world ever saw, and which has succeeded thus far without a parallel in the history of the world.

When you come to break up and turn loose the different elements, there is no telling what combinations may take place in the future. It may occur, for instance, to the middle States that they will not get so good a Government by going a little further south as by remaining where we are. It may occur to North Carolina, to Tennessee, to Kentucky, to Virginia, to Maryland, to Missouri—and perhaps Illinois might fall in, too—that, by erecting themselves into a central, independent republic, disconnected either with the North or the South, they could stand as a peace-maker—could stand as a great breakwater, resisting the heated and surging waves of the South, and the fanatical abolitionism of the North. They might think that they could stand there and lift themselves up above the two extremes, with the sincere hope that the time would arrive when the extremes would come together, and reunite once more, and we could reconstruct this greatest and best Government the world has ever seen. Or it might so turn out, our institution of slavery being exposed upon the northern line, that by looking to Pennsylvania, to New York, and to some of the other States, instead of having them as hostile Powers upon our frontiers, they might come to this central republic, and give us such constitutional guarantees, and such assurances that they would be executed, that it might be to our interest to form an alliance with them, and have a protection on our frontier.

I throw these out as considerations. There will be various projects and various combinations made. Memphis is now connected with Norfolk, in the Old Dominion; Memphis is connected with Baltimore within two days. Here is a coast that lets us out to the commerce of the world. When we look around in the four States of Tennessee, Kentucky, Virginia, and Maryland, there are things about which our memories, our attachments, and our associations linger with pride and with pleasure. Go down into the Old Dominion; there is the place where, in 1781, Cornwallis surrendered his sword to the immortal Washington. In the bosom of her soil are deposited her greatest and best sons. Move along in that trail, and there we find Jefferson and Madison and Monroe, and a long list of worthies.

We come next to old North Carolina, my native State, God bless her! She is my mother. Though she was not my cherishing mother,[48] to use the language of the classics, she is the mother whom I love, and I cling to her with undying affection, as a son should cling to an affectionate mother. We find Mecklen,[49] who was associated with our early history, deposited in her soil. Go to King's Mountain, on her borders, and you there find the place on which the battle was fought that turned the tide of the Revolution. Yes, within her borders the signal battle was fought that turned the tide which resulted in the surrender of Cornwallis at Yorktown, in the Old Dominion.

Travel on a little further, and we get back to Tennessee. I shall be as modest as I can in reference to her, but she has some associations that make her dear to the people of the United States. In Tennessee we have our own illustrious Jackson. There he sleeps—that Jackson who issued his proclamation in 1833, and saved this Government. We have our Polk and our Grundy, and a long list of others who are worthy of remembrance.

And who lie in Kentucky? Your Hardings, your Boons, your Roanes, your Clays, are among the dead; your CRITTENDEN among the living. All are identified and associated with the history of the country.

Maryland has her Carroll of Carrollton, and a long list of worthies, who are embalmed in the hearts of the American people. And you are talking about breaking up this Republic, with this cluster of associations, these ties of affection, around you. May we not expect that some means may be devised by which they can be preserved together?

Here, too, in the center of the Republic, is the seat of Government, which was founded by Washington, and bears his immortal name. Who dare appropriate it exclusively? It is within the borders of the States I have enumerated, in whose limits are found the graves of Washington, of Jackson, of Polk, of Clay. From them is it supposed that we will be torn away? No, sir; we will cherish these endearing associations with the hope, if this Republic shall be broken, that we may speak words of peace and reconciliation to a distracted, a divided, I may add, a maddened people. Angry waves may be lashed into fury on the one hand; on the other blustering winds may rage; but we stand immovable upon our basis, as on our own native mountains—presenting their craggy brows, their unexplored caverns, their summits "rock-ribbed and as ancient as the sun"[50]—we stand speaking peace, association, and concert, to a distracted Republic.

But, Mr. President, will it not be well before we break up this great Government, to inquire what kind of a government this new government in the South is to be, with which we are threatened unless we involve our destinies with this rash and precipitate movement. What intimation is there in reference to its character? Before my State and those States of which I have been speaking, go into a southern or northern confederacy, ought they not to have some idea of the kind of government that is to be formed? What are the intimations in the South, in reference to the formation of a new government? The language of some speakers is that they want a southern government obliterating all State lines—a government of consolidation. It is alarming and distressing to entertain the proposition here. What ruin and disaster would follow, if we are to have a consolidated government here! But the idea is afloat and current in the South that a southern government is to be established, in the language of some of the speakers in the State of Georgia, "obliterating all State lines;"[51] and is that the kind of entertainment to which the people are to be invited? Is that the kind of government under which we are to pass; and are we to be forced to emancipate our slaves unless we go into it? Another suggestion in reference to a southern government is, that we shall have a southern confederacy of great strength and power, with a constitutional provision preventing any State from changing its domestic institutions without the consent of three fourths, or some great number to be fixed upon. Is that the kind of government under which we want to pass? I avow here, that so far as I am concerned, I will never enter, with my consent, any government, North or South, less republican, less democratic, than the one under which we now live.

Where are we drifting? What kind of breakers are ahead? Have we a glimpse through the fog that develops [sic] the rock on which the vessel of State is drifting? Should we not consider maturely, in giving up this old Government, what kind of government is to succeed it? Ought we not to have time to think? Are we not entitled to respect and consideration? In one of the leading Georgia papers we find some queer suggestions; and, as the miners would say, these may be considered as mere surface-indications, that develop what is below. We ought to know the kind of government that is to be established. When we read the allusions made in various papers, and by various speakers, we find that there is one party who are willing to give up this form of government; to change its character; and, in fact, to pass under a monarchical form of government. I hope that my friend will read the extracts which I will hand him.

[Latham reads first from the Augusta *Chronicle and Sentinel* of December 8, 1860, an editorial on the dangers of disunion: "If the Federal system is a failure . . . *is not the whole republican system a failure?*" Warning that the anarchy of disunion could bring a monarchy or, worse still, a military despotism, the writer raises the spectre of a vastly restricted suffrage and a chief executive, Senate, and judiciary all elected for life. The second extract, an undated letter in the Columbus (Ga.) *Times*, suggests a study of existing governments if the present system should fail and concludes, "I am one of a few who ever dared to think that republicanism was a failure from its inception"; if the Union were dissolved, he counsels a "return to a Constitutional Monarchy." The third article, from a correspondent in Columbia, South Carolina, printed in the Baltimore *American* on December 5, expresses concern for democracy and warns that the Charleston clique of the Rhetts and Thomas Y. Simmons inclines toward "dictatorship" or a "monarchical form of government."]

Mr. JOHNSON, of Tennessee. Mr. President, I have merely called attention to these surface indications for the purpose of sustaining the assumption that even the people in the southern States ought to consider what kind of government they are going to pass under, before they change the present one. We are told that the present Constitution would be adopted by the new confederacy, and in a short time everything would be organized under it. We find here other indications, and we are told from another quarter that another character of government is more preferable. We know that, North and South, there is a portion of our fellow-citizens who are opposed to a government based on the intelligence and will of the people. We know that power is always stealing from the many to the few. We know that it is always vigilant and on the alert; and now that we are in a revolution, and great changes are to be made, should we not, as faithful sentinels, as men who are made the guardians of the interests of the Government, look at these indications and call the attention of the country to them? Is it not better to

> Bear those ills we have,
> Than fly to others that we know not of? [52]

We see, by these indications, that it is contemplated to establish a monarchy. We see it announced that this Government has been a failure from the beginning. How has it been a failure? Now, in the midst of a revolution, while the people are confused, while chaos reigns, it is supposed by some that we can be induced to return to a constitutional or absolute monarchy. Who can tell that we may not have some Louis Napoleon among us, who may be ready to make a *coup d'etat*, and enthrone himself upon the rights and upon the liberties of the people? Who can tell what kind of government may grow up? Hence the importance, in advance, of considering maturely and deliberately before we give up the old one.

I repeat again that the people of Tennessee will never pass under another government that is less republican, less democratic in all its bearings, than the one under which we now live, I care not whether it is formed in the North or the South. We will occupy an isolated, a separate and distinct position, before we will do it. We will pass into that fractional condition to which I have alluded before we will pass under an absolute or a constitutional monarchy. I do not say that this is the design North or South, or perhaps of any but a very small portion; but it shows that there are some who, if they could find a favorable opportunity, would fix the description of government I have alluded to on the great mass of the people. Sir, I will stand by the Constitution of the country as it is, and by all its guarantees. I am not for breaking up this great Confederacy. I am for holding on to it as it is, with the mode and manner pointed out in the instrument for its own amendment. It was good enough for Washington, for Adams, for Jefferson, and for Jackson. It is good enough for us. I intend to stand by it, and to insist on a compliance with all its guarantees, North and South.

Notwithstanding we want to occupy the position of a breakwater between the northern and the southern extremes, and bring all together if we can, I tell our northern friends that the constitutional guarantees must be carried out; for the time may come when, after we have exhausted all honorable and fair means, if this Government still fails to execute the laws, and protect us in our rights, it will be at an end. Gentlemen of the North need not deceive themselves in that particular; but we intend to act in the Union and under the Constitution, and not out of it. We do not intend that you shall drive us out of this house that was reared by the hands of our fathers. It is our house. It is the constitutional house. We have a right here; and because you come forward and violate the ordinances of this house, I do not intend to go out; and if you persist in the violation of the ordinances of the house, we intend to eject you from the building and retain the possession ourselves. We want, if we can, to stay the heated, and I am compelled to say, according to my judgment, the rash and precipitate action of some of our southern friends, that indicates red hot madness. I want to say to those in the North, comply with the Constitution and preserve its guarantees, and in so doing save this glorious Union and all that pertains to it. I intend to stand by the Constitution as it is, insisting upon a compliance with all its guarantees. I intend to stand by it as the sheet anchor of the Government; and I trust and hope, though it seems to be now in the very vortex of ruin, though it seems to be running between Charybdis and Scylla,[53] the rock on the one hand and the whirlpool on the other, that it will be preserved, and will remain a beacon to guide, and an example to be imitated by all the nations of the earth. Yes, I intend to hold on to it as the chief ark of our safety, as the palladium[54] of our civil and our religious liberty. I intend to cling to it as the shipwrecked mariner clings to the last plank, when the night and the tempest close around him. It is the last hope of human freedom. Although denounced as an experiment by some who want to see a constitutional monarchy, it has been a successful experiment. I trust and I hope it will be continued; that this great work may go on.

Why should we go out of the Union? Have we anything to fear? What are we alarmed about? We say that you of the North have violated the Constitution; that you have trampled under foot its guarantees; but we intend to go to you in a proper way, and ask you to redress the wrong, and to comply with the Constitution. We believe the time will come when you will do it, and we do not intend to break up the Government until the fact is ascertained that you will not do it. Where is the grievance; where is the complaint that presses on our sister, South Carolina, now? Is it that she wants to carry slavery into the Territories; that she wants protection to slavery there? How long has it been since, upon this very floor, her own Senators voted that it was not necessary to make a statute now for the protection of slavery in the Territories? No longer ago than the last session. Is that a good reason? They declared, in the resolutions adopted by the Senate,[55] that when it was necessary they had the power to do it; but that it was not necessary then. Are you going out for a grievance that has not occurred, and which your own Senators then said had not occurred? Is it because you want to carry slaves to the Territories? You were told that you had all the protection needed; that the courts had decided in your behalf, under the Constitution; and that, under the decisions of the courts, the law must be executed.

Mr. Davis. I do not understand the Senator perhaps correctly, as asserting that any Senator from South Carolina said that.

Mr. Johnson, of Tennessee. I said they voted for the resolution.

Mr. Davis. They did not. They voted against both the resolution and the amendment, and voted for the resolution which declared the duty to protect.

Mr. Johnson, of Tennessee. The duty to protect now?

Mr. Davis. They did declare the duty to protect at all times and in every place, under all circumstances, wherever protection was needed.

Mr. Johnson, of Tennessee. When necessary.

Mr. Davis. And I suppose, if the Senator intends to make a plea on that word, that they intended to nail to the cross the miserable miscreants who would claim protection when it was not necessary, and shrink from it when it was.

Mr. JOHNSON, of Tennessee. The test was made before the Senate upon Senator Brown's proposition to give protection now.

Mr. WIGFALL. It was not. I corrected that the other day.[56]

Mr. JOHNSON, of Tennessee. Well, you just corrected it the way it was not—that is all. [Laughter.]

Mr. WIGFALL. Mr. President—

The PRESIDING OFFICER, (Mr. Fitzpatrick in the chair.) Does the Senator from Tennessee yield the floor to the Senator from Texas?

Mr. JOHNSON, of Tennessee. No. I will continue my remarks.

Mr. WIGFALL. Well, if the Senator chooses to pervert facts, and go on and publish them in his speech, I have nothing to say.

Mr. JOHNSON, of Tennessee. I will publish them as the records show them to be. I say that on Senator Brown's proposition to carry protection into the Territories now, it received but three votes.

Mr. WIGFALL. I say that never was proposed or voted on.

Mr. JOHNSON, of Tennessee. The record will settle it.

Mr. WIGFALL. Turn to it. I will read it for you.

Mr. JOHNSON, of Tennessee. I do not want to be interrupted now.

Mr. WIGFALL. I know you do not. You do not want the facts stated.

Mr. JOHNSON, of Tennessee. I know what the facts were, and in this Senate we voted for the passage of resolutions that Congress had the power to protect slavery, and that Congress ought to protect slavery when necessary and wherever protection was needed. Was there not a majority on this floor for it; and if it was necessary then, could we not have passed a bill for that purpose without passing a resolution saying that it should be protected wherever necessary? I was here; I know what the substance of the proposition was, and the whole of it was simply to declare the principle that we had the power, and that it was the duty of Congress, to protect slavery when necessary, in the Territories or wherever else protection was needed. Was it necessary then? If it was, we had the power, and why did we not pass the law?

Mr. GREEN. Will the Senator allow me to make one suggestion?

Mr. JOHNSON, of Tennessee. I hope the Senator will not interrupt me. I do not refuse out of any discourtesy. The Journal of the Senate records[57] that on the 25th of May last—

[Brown's motion calling upon Congress to extend "to slave property in the territories that protection . . . given to other kinds of property" had been supported by only three southern senators; the remainder had voted overwhelmingly against it.]

I was going on to say that the want of protection to slavery in the Territories cannot be considered a grievance now. That is not the reason why she is going out, and going to break up the Confederacy. What is it, then? Is there any issue between South Carolina and the Federal Government? Has the Federal Government failed to comply with, and to carry out, the obligations that it owes to South Carolina? In what has the Federal Government failed? In what has it neglected the interest of South Carolina? What law has it undertaken to enforce upon South Carolina that is unconstitutional and oppressive?

If there are grievances, why cannot we all go together, and write them down, and point them out to our northern friends after we have agreed on what those grievances were, and say, "here is what we demand; here our wrongs are enumerated; upon these terms we have agreed; and now, after we have given you a reasonable time to consider these additional guarantees in order to protect ourselves against these wrongs, if you refuse them, then, having made an honorable effort, having exhausted all other means, we may declare the association to be broken up, and we may go into an act of revolution." We can then say to them, "You have refused to give us guarantees that we think are needed for the protection of our institutions and for the protection of our other interests." When they do this, I will go as far as he who goes the furthest.

I tell them here to-day, if they do not do it, Tennessee will be found standing as firm and unyielding in her demands for those guarantees in the way a State should stand, as any other State in this Confederacy. She is not quite so belligerent now. She is not making quite so much noise. She is not as blustering as Sempronius was in the council in Addison's play of Cato, who declared that his "voice was still for war."[58] There was another character there, Lucius, who was called upon to know what his opinions were; and when he was called upon, he replied that he must confess his thoughts were turned on peace; but when the extremity came, Lucius, who was deliberative, who was calm, and whose thoughts were upon peace, was found true to the interests of his country. He proved himself to be a man and a soldier; while the other was a traitor and a coward. We will do our duty; we will stand upon principle, and defend it to the last extremity.

We do not think, though, that we have just cause for going out of the Union now. We have just cause of complaint; but we are for remaining in the Union, and fighting the battle like men. We do not intend to be cowardly, and turn our backs on our own camps. We intend to stay and fight the battle here upon this consecrated ground. Why should we retreat? Because Mr. Lincoln has been elected President of the United States? Is this any cause why we should retreat? Does not every man, Senator or otherwise, know that if Mr. Breckinridge had been elected, we should not be to-day for dissolving the Union? Then what is the issue? It is because we have not got our man. If we had got our man, we should not have been for breaking up the Union; but as Mr. Lincoln is elected, we are for breaking up the Union! I say no. Let us show ourselves men, and men of courage.

How has Mr. Lincoln been elected, and how have Mr. Breckinridge and Mr. Douglas been defeated? By the votes of the American people, cast according to the Constitution and the forms of law, though it has been upon a sectional issue. It is not the first time in our history that two candidates have been elected from the same section of country. General Jackson and Mr. Calhoun were elected on the same ticket; but nobody considered that cause of dissolution. They were from the South. While I oppose the sectional spirit that has produced the election of Lincoln and Hamlin, yet it has been done according to the Constitution and according to the forms of law. I believe we have the power in our own hands, and I am not willing to shrink from the responsibility of exercising that power.

How has Lincoln been elected, and upon what basis does he stand? A minority President by nearly a million votes; but had the election taken place upon the plan proposed in my amendment of the Constitution, by districts, he would have been this day defeated. But it has been done according to the Constitution and according to law. I am for abiding by the Constitution; and in abiding by it I want to maintain and retain my place here and put down Mr. Lincoln and drive back his advances upon southern institutions, if he designs to make any. Have we not got the brakes in our hands? Have we not got the power? We have. Let South Carolina send her Senators back; let all the Senators come; and on the 4th of March next we shall have a majority of six in this body against him.[59] This successful sectional candidate, who is in a minority of a million, or nearly so, on the popular vote, cannot make his Cabinet on the 4th of March next unless this Senate will permit him.

Am I to be so great a coward as to retreat from duty? I will stand here and meet the encroachments upon the institutions of my country at the threshold; and as a man, as one that loves my country and my constituents, I will stand here and resist all encroachments and advances. Here is the place to stand. Shall I desert the citadel, and let the enemy come in and take possession? No. Can Mr. Lincoln send a foreign minister, or even a consul, abroad, unless he receives the sanction of the Senate? Can he appoint a postmaster whose salary is over a thousand dollars a year without the consent of the Senate? Shall we desert our posts, shrink from our responsibilities, and permit Mr. Lincoln to come with his cohorts, as we consider them, from the North, to carry off everything? Are we so cowardly that now we are defeated, not conquered, we shall do this? Yes, we are defeated according to the forms of law and the Constitution; but the real victory is ours—the moral force is with us. Are we going to desert that noble and that patriotic band who have stood by us at the North? who have stood by us upon principle? who have stood by us upon the Constitution? They stood by us and fought the battle upon principle; and now that we have been defeated, not conquered, are we to turn our backs upon them and leave them to their fate? I, for one, will not. I intend to stand by them. How many votes did we get in the North? We got more votes in the North against Lincoln than the entire southern States cast.[60] Are they not able and faithful allies? They are; and now, on account of this temporary defeat, are we to turn our backs upon them and leave them to their fate, as they have fallen for us in former controversies?

We find, when all the North is summed up, that Mr. Lincoln's majority there is only about two hundred thousand on the popular vote; and when that is added to the other vote cast throughout the Union, he stands to-day in a minority of nearly a million votes. What, then, is necessary to be done? To stand to our posts like men, and act upon principle; stand for the country; and in four years from this day, Lincoln and his administration will be turned out, the worst-defeated and broken-down party that ever came into power. It is an inevitable result from the combination of elements that now exist. What cause, then, is there to break up the Union? What reason is there for deserting our posts and destroying this greatest and best Government that was ever spoken into existence?

I voted against him; I spoke against him; I spent my money to defeat him; but still I love my country; I love the Constitution; I intend to insist upon its guarantees. There, and there alone, I intend to plant myself, with the confident hope and belief that if the Union remains together, in less than four years the now triumphant party will be overthrown. In less time, I have the hope and belief that we shall unite and agree upon our grievances here and demand their redress not as suppliants at the footstool of power, but as parties to a great compact; we shall say that we want additional guarantees, and that they are necessary to the preservation of this Union; and then, when they are refused deliberately and calmly, if we cannot do better, let the South go together, and let the North go together, and let us have a division of this Government without the shedding of blood, if such a thing be possible; let us have a division of the property; let us have a division of the Navy; let us have a division of the Army, and of the public lands. Let it be done in peace, and in a spirit that should characterize and distinguish this people. I believe we can obtain all our guarantees. I believe there is too much good sense, too much intelligence, too much patriotism, too much capability, too much virtue, in the great mass of people to permit this Government to be overthrown.

I have an abiding faith, I have an unshaken confidence in man's capability to govern himself. I will not give up this Government that is now called an experiment, which some are prepared to abandon for a constitutional monarchy. No; I intend to stand by it, and I entreat every man throughout the nation who is a patriot, and who has seen, and is compelled to admit, the success of this great experiment, to come forward, not in heat, not in fanaticism, not in haste, not in precipitancy, but in deliberation, in full view of all that is before us, in the spirit of brotherly love and fraternal affection, and rally around the altar of our common country, and lay the Constitution upon it as our last libation, and swear by our God, and all that is sacred and holy, that the Constitution shall be saved, and the Union preserved. Yes, in the language of the departed Jackson, let us exclaim that the Union, "the Federal Union, it must be preserved."

Are we likely, when we get to ourselves; North and South, to sink into brotherly love? Are we likely to be so harmonious in that condition as some suppose? What did we find here the other day among our brother Senators, one of whom referred to a southern Governor?[61] I allude to it only to show the feeling that exists even among ourselves. I am sometimes impressed with the force of Mr. Jefferson's remark, that we may as well keep the North to quarrel with, for if we have no North to quarrel with, we shall quarrel among ourselves.[62] We are a sort of quarrelsome, pugnacious people; and if we cannot get a quarrel from one quarter, we shall have it from another; and I would rather quarrel a little now with the North than be quarreling with ourselves. Because the Governor of a southern State was refusing to convene the Legislature to hasten this movement that was going on throughout the South; and because he objected to that course of conduct, what did a Senator say here in the American Senate? The question was asked if there was not some Texan Brutus that would rise up and rid the country of the hoary-headed traitor! This is the language that a Senator used. This is the way we begin to speak of southern Governors. Yes; to remove an obstacle in our way, we must have a modern Brutus who will go to the capital of a State and assassinate a Governor to accelerate the

movement that is going on. If we are so unscrupulous in reference
to ourselves, and in reference to the means we are willing to employ
to consummate this dissolution, then it does not look very much like
harmony among ourselves after we get out of it.

Mr. President, I have said much more than I anticipated when I
commenced; and I have said more now (though external appearances
seem different) than I have strength or health to say; but if there is
any effort of mine that would preserve this Government till there is
time to think, till there is time to consider, even if it cannot be preserved any longer; if that end could be secured by making a sacrifice
of my existence and offering up my blood, I would be willing to
consent to it. Let us pause in this mad career; let us hesitate; let us
consider well what we are doing before we make a movement. I believe that, to a certain extent, dissolution is going to take place. I
say to the North, you ought to come up in the spirit which should
characterize and control the North on this question; and you ought
to give those indications in good faith that will approach what the
South demands. It will be no sacrifice on your part. It is no suppliancy
on ours, but simply a demand of right. What concession is there in
doing right? Then, come forward. We have it in our power—yes,
this Congress here to-day has it in its power to save this Union, even
after South Carolina has gone out. Will they not do it? You can do
it. Who is willing to take the dreadful alternative without making
an honorable effort to save this Government? This Congress has it in
its power to-day to arrest this thing, at least for a season, until there
is time to consider about it, until we can act discreetly and prudently,
and I believe arrest it altogether.

Shall we give all this up to the Vandals and the Goths? Shall we
shrink from our duty, and desert the Government as a sinking ship,
or shall we stand by it? I, for one, will stand here, until the high behest of my constituents demands me to desert my post; and instead
of laying hold of the columns of this fabric and pulling it down,
though I may not be much of a prop, I will stand with my shoulder
supporting the edifice as long as human effort can do it. Then, cannot we agree? We can, if we will, and come together and save the
country.

In saying what I have said on this occasion, Mr. President, I have
done it in view of a duty that I felt I owed to my constituents, that
I owed to my children, that I owed to myself. Without regard to
consequences, I have taken the position I have; and when the tug
comes, when Greek shall meet Greek,[63] and our rights are refused
after all honorable means have been exhausted, then it is that I will
perish in the last breach; yes, in the language of the patriot Emmet,
"I will dispute every inch of ground; I will burn every blade of

grass; and the last intrenchment of freedom shall be my grave."[64] Then, let us stand by the Constitution; and in preserving the Constitution we shall save the Union; and in saving the Union, we save this, the greatest Government on earth.

I thank the Senate for their kind attention.[65]

Cong. Globe, 36 Cong., 2 Sess., 117–19, 134–43; Pamphlet, *The Constitutionality and Rightfulness of Secession, Speech . . . in the Senate . . . on Tuesday and Wednesday, December 18 and 19, 1860* ([n.p., n.d.]).

1. This speech, characterized by an historian as "one of the memorable orations of the [secession] winter," was delivered during the discussion of Johnson's amendments (S. Res. 48) offered December 13 for consideration by the Committee of Thirteen. In essence these were the same proposals that Johnson had been sponsoring for ten years, but in face of the sectional crisis he added a provision for alternating the presidency and vice presidency between the North and South every four years. Nevins, *Emergence of Lincoln*, II, 390; see *Johnson Papers*, I, 604–7; III, 692–95.

2. Benjamin Fitzpatrick of Alabama was in the chair.

3. Johnson first submitted these proposals February 21, 1851. See *ibid.*, I, 604–7.

4. Although there was general agreement that legislators opposed to the Republican administration held a majority in both houses, estimates of actual numbers differed. The Washington *National Intelligencer* reported that the combined opposition had a majority of twenty-one in the House. Washington *National Intelligencer*, November 9, 1860.

5. It is doubtful that the speaker reached this conclusion through an independent study of the election returns; instead he seems to have extrapolated directly from his House of Representatives' figures, without considering the two electors-at-large in each state. Nor do his calculations take into account the reality of four candidates in the recent election.

6. The "State Rights" mass meeting held in Greeneville on November 24, in which he played a prominent role. Nashville *Union and American*, November 28, December 5, 1860. See also *Johnson Papers*, III, 673.

7. In alluding to "the resolutions of your own State," Johnson has in mind the Kentucky (1798, 1799) and Virginia (1798) Resolutions which sought to negate by joint state action the Alien and Sedition Acts. These "Principles of '98" contain, as he infers, the seeds of nullification and secession. See Henry S. Commager, ed., *Documents of American History* (New York, 1963), 178–85.

8. The following passages appeared in Madison's lengthy "Report on the Resolutions," drafted for the Virginia House of Delegates in early 1799. Gaillard Hunt, ed., *The Writings of James Madison* (9 vols., New York, 1900–1910), VI, 341–406.

9. *Ibid.*, IX, 489–92; also in *National Intelligencer*, December 10, 1860. Nicholas P. Trist (1800–1874), a distant relative of Thomas Jefferson and an intimate political friend of Andrew Jackson, had been appointed by President Polk to negotiate a peace settlement with Mexico in 1848. Although recalled, he completed the agreement, which was ratified by an embarrassed administration. Returning to his home at Alexandria, Trist unsuccessfully practiced law and, as his fortunes declined, accepted a job as a railroad paymaster in Philadelphia at $1200 a year. When the Civil War approached, he disavowed the doctrines of Calhoun, opposed secession, and voted for Lincoln; in 1870, Grant appointed him postmaster at Alexandria. *DAB*, XVIII, 645–46; Louis M. Sears, "Nicholas P. Trist, A Diplomat with Ideas," *Mississippi*

Valley Historical Review, XI (1924), 97; *McElroy's Philadelphia Directory* (1860), 1005.

10. The views of Alexander Rives appearing in the Charlottesville *Advocate* late in December, 1832, and signed "A Friend of Union and States Rights" prompted Madison's letter of January, 1833. Hunt, *Writings of Madison*, 496–98, 495n; Washington *National Intelligencer*, November 24, 1860.

11. Johnson later quotes from Madison's letter to Webster of March 15, 1833. Philip R. Fendall, ed., *Letters and Other Writings of James Madison* (4 vols., Philadelphia, 1865), IV, 293–94.

12. Buchanan's annual message of December 3 declared that the framers of the Constitution "never intended to implant in its bosom the seeds of its own destruction." Richardson, *Messages*, V, 633.

13. Hamilton to Madison, July 19, 1788, Harold C. Syrett and Jacob E. Cooke, eds., *The Papers of Alexander Hamilton* (15 vols., New York, 1961–   ), V, 177–78.

14. Madison to Hamilton, July 20, 1788, *ibid.*, 184–85.

15. That is, a government which has no bonding force. *OED*, VIII, 788.

16. An emotional, crowd-pleasing argument. *Webster's Third International*.

17. On the following day when Johnson resumed speaking, Solomon Foot of Vermont was in the chair.

18. To southerners these personal liberty laws seemed clearly designed to evade the Fugitive Slave Act. The Vermont law of 1850 required the state's attorneys "diligently and faithfully to use all lawful means to protect, defend, and procure to be discharged, every such person so arrested or claimed as a fugitive slave." Eventually all public officials were forbidden to arrest or to aid in the arrest of alleged fugitives. Slaves brought into Vermont by their owners were seemingly considered free by state law, since the antikidnapping statute of 1858 had declared, "No person within this State shall be considered as property, or subject as such to sale, purchase or delivery." A slaveholder attempting to assert his authority over an alleged fugitive slave was liable to a $2,000 fine and fifteen years in prison. Rowland E. Robinson, *Vermont: A Study of Independence* (Boston, 1899), 337; Stanley W. Campbell, *The Slave Catchers: Enforcement of the Fugitive Slave Law, 1850–1860* (Chapel Hill, 1968), 177–79.

19. Johnson uses the transcription found in earlier versions of Jefferson's writings; the modern edition exhibits minor variance in capitalization and renders "rational" as "national" and "than" for "but" in the last sentence. The reference to "water" is better understood in the light of Jefferson's next observation that "a naval force can never endanger our liberties" as might a land force. Julian P. Boyd, ed., *The Papers of Thomas Jefferson* (19 vols., Princeton, 1950–   ), X, 225.

20. *Ibid.*, XI, 678. The emphasis is Johnson's.

21. Selling tickets for a Washington lottery established in accord with a federal law, Cohens was arrested for violating Virginia's antilottery statute and appealed to the Supreme Court on the ground that his conviction had violated his rights under the federal lottery act. The case involved the questions of whether Congress had authorized the lottery in states where such sales were forbidden by law and whether Congress had any power to authorize such sales. Virginia argued that the Court had no jurisdiction, since the power to review decisions of state courts had not been "expressly" provided by the Constitution. Rejecting Virginia's position, Chief Justice Marshall held that the Court had jurisdiction in all criminal cases arising in state courts involving federal questions. However, having lost the case on the jurisdictional issue, Virginia won it on the merits: Cohens would go to jail because the Supreme Court decision stated that Congress did not intend its lottery law to authorize the sale of tickets in states where such lotteries were unlawful. Cohens v. Virginia was a signal triumph for Marshall's judicial federalism over the state sov-

ereignty arguments of the Jeffersonian Republicans. Charles Warren, *The Supreme Court in United States History* (3 vols., Boston, 1924), II, 5–12; Leo Pfeffer, *This Honorable Court: A History of the United States Supreme Court* (Boston, 1965), 102–3.

22. Richardson, *Messages*, II, 648.

23. Madison to Hamilton, July 20, 1788, Syrett and Cooke, *Hamilton Papers*, V, 184–85.

24. Johnson is in error. Hamilton's controversial excise tax on distilled spirits, which provoked the Whiskey Rebellion of 1794 in western Pennsylvania, became law on March 3, 1791. *U. S. Statutes*, I, 199.

25. In his sixth annual State of the Union address, November 19, 1794, Washington traced the development of the Whiskey Rebellion and the government's response. He observed, "to yield to the treasonable fury of so small a portion of the United States would be to violate the fundamental principle of our Constitution." Richardson, *Messages*, I, 164.

26. Milton S. Latham (1827–1882), a native of Ohio, began a law practice in Sacramento (1848) and was circuit court clerk (1848–50), moving to San Francisco in 1850. Elected to Congress as a Democrat (1853–55), he was collector of the Port of San Francisco (1855–57) and governor (1859–61), resigning to become senator (1861–63) upon the death of David Broderick. He was later manager of the San Francisco Bank, Ltd. (1865–78), removing to New York in 1878. *DAB*, XI, 13; *BDAC*, 1196.

27. Actually, although Washington accompanied the troops to their ultimate rendezvous at Bedford, Pennsylvania, he left Henry Lee in command and returned to Philadelphia to deliver his address to Congress, including a report on Lee's success in suppressing the rebellion. Douglas Southall Freeman, *George Washington* (7 vols., New York, 1948–57), VII, 198–220.

28. In all likelihood this passage is a rhetorical statement, not a verbatim quotation.

29. Possibly from "Do your duty and leave the rest to the gods." Pierre Corneille, *Horace*, Act II, last line. Stevenson, *Macmillan Book of Proverbs*, 648.

30. These deeds of cession are found in *Code of Laws of South Carolina, 1962, Annotated* (20 vols., Charlottesville, 1962), IX, 78–79.

31. A reference to the famous, though perhaps apocryphal, rhetoric indulged in during the debates on the Virginia Stamp Act Resolves, May 30, 1765. Samuel Eliot Morison, ed., *Sources and Documents Illustrating the American Revolution* (New York, 1923), 14–17.

32. This figure on Mexican War expenditures had been suggested by Congressman Alexander H. Stephens in July, 1848. In his December, 1848, report, Secretary of the Treasury Robert Walker had estimated $64 million for army and navy expenditures alone, a figure which did not take into account the $49 million added to the national debt, nor payments of bounty lands, pensions, and the assumption of American claims against the Mexican government. *Cong. Globe*, 30 Cong., 1 Sess., 912; Justin H. Smith, *The War with Mexico* (2 vols., New York, 1919), II, 266–67; Margaret G. Myers, *A Financial History of the United States* (New York, 1970), 137.

33. Tennessee Constitution of 1796, Art. XI, Sec. 29.

34. Approved January 15, 1811, and entitled "Resolution relative to the occupation of the Floridas by the United States of America." *U. S. Statutes*, II, 666.

35. Although the $100,000 figure is correct, the acquisition of Florida cost the federal government $5, rather than $6, million in American claims against the Spanish. *Ibid.*, III, 471; Commager, *Documents*, 224.

36. This seven-year conflict (1835–42), regarded as America's most expensive Indian war, cost from $20 to $40 million for the removal of 3,825 Indians; 1,500 soldiers were lost. Charlton W. Tebeau, *A History of Florida* (Coral Gables, 1971), 168; John K. Mahon, *A History of the Second Seminole War, 1835–42* (Gainesville, 1967), 321, 326.

37. Coming to Congress in 1841 as a delegate from the Territory of Florida, David Yulee worked to secure Florida's admission as a state; when his efforts culminated in success four years later, he was elected to the Senate. *DAB*, XX, 638; *BDAC*, 1862; *Cong. Globe*, 28 Cong., 2 Sess., 284–86; see *Johnson Papers*, III, 430n.

38. The Lecompton Constitution, drawn up in 1857 by a proslavery convention elected by a minority when the free-state majority refrained from voting, protected slavery as it existed, called for a large land donation from the federal government upon attaining statehood, set a referendum on the clause dealing with the future of slavery, but not on the Constitution itself, and included a section implying that the instrument could not be amended until 1864. After President Buchanan submitted the Constitution and his recommendations for admission, the Senate skirted the slavery issue and haggled over the other provisions, insisting that the land donation be reduced and the amending process altered. Although Congress ultimately passed a substitute bill hinging statehood upon the public land question, the people rejected the revised Lecompton Constitution in an August, 1858, referendum, and Kansas continued as a territory until 1861. Nichols, *Disruption of Democracy*, 125–38, 159–81; Nevins, *Emergence of Lincoln*, I, 229–45, 264–70, 301.

39. *U. S. Statutes*, III, 471.

40. The Ostend Manifesto of October 18, 1854, actually an embarrassment to the Pierce administration, was later repudiated. Perhaps Johnson regarded the Republican defeat in 1856 as an indication of popular approval of the declaration, inasmuch as the Republican platform had specifically attacked the "Ostend Circular" and its "highwayman's" threat of "might makes right," whereas the Democratic platform had urged the next administration to continue efforts "to insure our ascendancy in the Gulf of Mexico." Both Democratic platforms in 1860 contained specific wording favorable to the acquisition of Cuba. Kirk H. Porter and Donald B. Johnson, *National Party Platforms, 1840–1960* (Urbana, 1961), 26, 28; Roy F. Nichols, *Franklin Pierce* (Philadelphia, 1931), 367ff; Ivor D. Spencer, *The Victor and the Spoils: A Life of William L. Marcy* (Providence, 1959), 330–34.

41. Former Governor (1852–53) John L. Manning (1816–1889), although originally opposed to secession, became a member of Gen. Pierre G. T. Beauregard's staff. Elected to the Senate in 1865, he never served. One of the South's wealthiest planters, Manning on the eve of war owned 648 slaves and had $1,256,000 invested in real property. The quoted paragraph, from a speech "made not long since at Columbia," was taken from the *National Intelligencer*, November 24, 1860. *NCAB*, XII, 171; Wooster, *Secession Conventions*, 18, 261n.

42. Elias N. Conway (1812–1898), a native of Greene County, had ties to the Sevier family and political connections with the Andrew Jackson machine. Migrating to Arkansas in 1833, he developed, as auditor, a program of homestead legislation which formed the model for the bills before Congress during the forties. After two terms as governor (1852–60) he retired from public life. The extracts are from his address "To the militiamen of the state of Arkansas," August 27, 1860, printed in the Little Rock *True Democrat*, September 29, 1860, and in *Militia Laws of the State of Arkansas* (Little Rock, 1860). *DAB*, IV, 361–62; John L. Ferguson (Arkansas State Historian) to Andrew Johnson Project, September 15, 1971.

43. William H. Gist (1807–1874), Charleston-born planter, served in the state lower house (1840–44) and senate (1844–56) and was elected governor by the state rights faction in 1858. Calling the legislature into session on November 5, 1860, he signed the secession ordinance on December 20, completing his public career as a member of the executive council responsible for the defenses of South Carolina. His message, first appearing in the Charleston *Daily Courier* of November 27, was extracted in the *National Intelligencer*, December 13, 1860. *DAB*, VII, 325.

44. Lawrence M. Keitt (1824–1864), congressman (1853–60) and dele-

gate to the state secession convention, served briefly in the Confederate Congress (1861) before becoming colonel of the 20th S. C. Vol. Rgt. in January, 1862. Promoted to brigadier, he died on June 4, 1864, from wounds suffered at Cold Harbor. *BDAC*, 1149.

45. According to fable, scorpions committed suicide by stinging themselves if cornered by fire. *Encyclopedia Americana* (1972 ed.), XXIV, 426–27.

46. A reference to Samson's pulling down the temple, thereby destroying all within. Judg. 16: 29–30.

47. Speaking on December 10, Jefferson Davis had declared that he would prefer to have "this Union severed into thirty-three fragments" than have the government strengthened "to overawe the States, to coerce the people living under them as members of sovereign communities." *Cong. Globe*, 36 Cong., 2 Sess., 29.

48. A rendition of *Alma Mater*, a phrase normally associated with the school or college from which one has graduated. *Webster's Third International*.

49. In the pamphlet version of this speech, "Mecklen" has been corrected to "Macon." Nathaniel Macon, who fought in the Revolutionary War, had a long and distinguished career in the state legislature as well as in Congress, where he served as speaker of the House and as senator. *DAB*, XII, 158; see also *Johnson Papers*, I, 607n.

50. From William Cullen Bryant, "Thanatopsis," 1. 38.

51. The *National Intelligencer* on November 19, 1860, reported a speech by Francis S. Bartow of Savannah in which he proposed "that the Southern Confederacy should be a consolidated Republic" with "all State lines to be obliterated and all sovereignty to reside in the Federal power."

52. Shakespeare, *Hamlet*, Act III, sc. 1.

53. Scylla and Charybdis, the former a rock upon the Italian side of the Straits of Messina and the latter a dangerous whirlpool off the coast of Sicily, signified an undesirable choice between equals: if the mariner successfully evaded one, he was likely to be smashed against the other. In Homeric legend, Scylla was a sea monster who, perched on the rock to prey on mariners, destroyed a part of Ulysses' fleet. Edward Tripp, *Crowell's Handbook of Classical Mythology* (New York, 1970), 159–60, 523.

54. A statue of Pallas Athena whose preservation, according to legend, insured the safety of Troy. *Webster's Third International*.

55. These resolutions on congressional responsibility for protecting slavery, whether in the states or territories, were reintroduced by Jefferson Davis on March 1, 1860, and adopted in May. The debate here concerns the votes of James H. Hammond and James Chesnut, Jr., on amendments offered by Clingman of North Carolina and Brown of Mississippi: the one declared that it was not intended "*to assert, at this time*," the obligation of Congress "*to provide a system of laws for the maintenance of slavery*," and the other asserted that, inasmuch as territorial protection of slave property was inadequate, "*it has become the duty of Congress . . . to afford to slave property in the Territories that protection which is given to other kinds of property*." To Davis and his partisans, these resolutions posed questions of debatable fact rather than a statement of principle. Both South Carolinians voted against the Clingman proposal, while the Brown resolution was defeated with the votes of many southern senators—among them Chesnut and Johnson himself—though in this case Hammond appears to have abstained. *Cong. Globe*, 36 Cong., 1 Sess., 2310, 2322, 2344, 2347, 2349, 2350; *Senate Journal*, 36 Cong., 1 Sess., 203–4, 507, 512–15.

56. Wigfall refers to an exchange between himself and Stephen A. Douglas on December 11 concerning the justification for secession and disunion. When the Texan demanded federal protection for slavery in the territories, Douglas pointed out that Wigfall, by his votes against the Clingman and Brown amendments, had earlier denied the necessity for such protection. Retorting

that "I did not choose to be diverted from the direct path of duty which lay before me; and that was, to have a declaration of a great principle," Wigfall continued his explanation the following day, launching into an angry, gallery-pleasing tirade, defending his votes, declaring that "cotton is king," and denouncing northern transgressions against southern rights. *Cong. Globe*, 36 Cong., 2 Sess., 57, 58, 71, 73.

57. *Senate Journal*, 36 Cong., 1 Sess., 515.

58. Addison's *Cato*, Act II, sc. 1.

59. Had no resignations occurred, the 37th Congress would have contained 37 Democrats, 29 Republicans, 1 Whig, and 1 Unionist, making a majority of 6 Democrats. Of the latter, twenty-nine were from slave states. *BDAC*, 173–77.

60. Outside the South, 1,723,746 votes went to candidates other than Lincoln, whereas in the South the total number of votes cast was 1,109,597. Nevins observes, "it was a very curious, a very mixed, and except for its grand central result, a very inscrutable election." W. Dean Burnham, *Presidential Ballots, 1836–1892* (Baltimore, 1955), 246–56; Nevins, *Emergence of Lincoln*, II, 313.

61. On December 5 Georgia's Alfred Iverson inveighed against Governor Sam Houston of Texas, prophesying that, should "the hoary-headed incubus that stands between the people and their sovereign will" not yield and call for an ordinance of secession, some Brutus would arise to destroy him. Wigfall denied that fellow Texans would stoop to assassination but conceded that they might be forced into a revolution, circumventing a call to convene the legislature and meeting instead in a rump session which would later be recognized as a de facto, rather than a de jure, government. *Cong. Globe*, 36 Cong., 2 Sess., 11, 13.

62. Jefferson to John Taylor, June 1, 1798, Paul L. Ford, ed., *The Works of Thomas Jefferson* (12 vols., New York, 1904–5), VIII, 432.

63. Nathaniel Lee, *The Rival Queens*, Act IV, sc. 2: "When Greeks joyn'd Greeks, then was the tug of war." Stevenson, *Quotations*, 838.

64. Robert Emmet (1778–1803), Irish nationalist convicted of treason against England, reportedly uttered these words in an impassioned address before the court. Accounts actually differ on this wording, but all include the better-known injunction, "Let no man write my epitaph." *DNB*, VI, 780–81; Helen Landreth, *The Pursuit of Robert Emmet* (New York, 1948), 333.

65. Joseph Lane of Oregon spoke briefly in rebuttal, defending South Carolina and her senators, serving notice that neither the northern Democracy nor Tennesseans would ever join the Republicans in a "crusade" against the South, and appealing to that newly elected sectional party, the only one with the power to do so, to save the country and stop trampling on the Constitution.

From Charles W. Charlton[1]

Post Office Knoxville Tenn
Dec. 19, 1860

Private
Hon. Andrew Johnson
Washington D. C.
Dr Sir:

I have deemed it necessary & important to post you up with reference to some local matters at this place.

It is my purpose and determination to resign my office, as I am decidedly of the opinion that *no democrat* should accept office under Mr Lincoln.

There has been for sometime, in our midst, a gentleman by the name of Bell,[2] from California, and who was a *delegate* to the Chicago Convention. He was formerly a resident of this place, & has a number of relatives here. I understand he has the entire *programe* made out for the disposition of the federal offices among certain men of this town. The Post office he has promised to James C. Luttrell[3] —*the second edition of Brownlow.* Now, *"by the eternal,"* he shall *not have it if I can prevent it.* How shall I do it? In this way: I intend to tender my resignation in a few days, and designate my successor.[4] He voted, tobesure, for Bell, but he is honest, capable, and withal, poor, & is now laboring hard to support and take care of a widowed mother. If he is turned out, then a *fuss* is produced among themselves. When I present his name I want to secure your co-operation in the Senate for his confirmation. Meantime I will procure from Maj. Ramsey, Judge Swan,[5] & others of your friends, an endorsement of this young man.

The disunion sentiment is gaining ground every day in this State.

Respect &c.   C. W. Charlton

ALS, DLC-JP.

1. See *Johnson Papers*, III, 311n.

2. Edward Samuel Bell, son of Samuel Bell, a prominent Knoxville jeweler and former mayor, attended the Republican convention as a delegate from Mariposa County, and was later appointed by Lincoln as naval agent at San Francisco. Earlier he had represented his county as a Democrat in the California Assembly (1853), been elected controller of the state (1853–55), and passed, by way of Know-Nothingism, over into Republicanism, being one of nine names considered when the party selected its first gubernatorial candidate in 1857. William B. Hesseltine, *Three Against Lincoln: Murat Halstead Reports the Caucuses of 1860* (Baton Rouge, 1960), 293; Rothrock, *French Broad-Holston Country*, 379; New York *Herald*, March 9, 1861; Peyton Hurt, "The Rise and Fall of the 'Know Nothings' in California," *California Historical Society Quarterly*, IX, 42; Norman D. Brown, "Edward Stanly: First Republican Candidate for Governor of California," *ibid.*, XLVII, 255.

3. Luttrell, a former postmaster (1849–53), was again postmaster in 1863, serving until 1869. Rothrock, *French Broad-Holston Country*, 440; *U. S. Official Register* (1863), 629; *Johnson Papers*, III, 508n.

4. On March 30, 1861, in a telegram to Johnson, Charlton recommended Pryor L. Rogers (1830–1872), Knoxville clerk and later a bank cashier, for postmaster. Nevertheless, Charlton was still listed as postmaster in Sept., 1861. Johnson Papers, LC; WPA, Tennessee, Knox, Tombstone Records: Old Gray Cemetery ([Nashville], 1938), 1; *Williams' Knoxville Directory* (1859–60), 73; *Helms' Knoxville City Directory* (1869), 103; *U. S. Official Register* (1861), 266. See also Letter from John C. McGaughey, February 21, 1861, note 7.

5. For John Crozier Ramsey and William G. Swan, see *Johnson Papers*, III, 311n; II, 214n.

From "A Citizen of New York City"[1]

December 19, 1860

To the Hon Andrew Johnson
U. S. Senate.

I cannot refrain although a stranger, from expressing my admiration of your magnificent and patriotic speech before the Senate to day.

Your voice will ring through the nation from the Gulf of Mexico to Canada. It will meet with a response from the whole gushing heart of the north.—Thank God! the good old State of Tenessee stands, as from her antecedents we might well expect, with the Stars and Stripes wound around her, in this hour of national delirium. I would that I could have the honor of taking you by the hand.

The intimate financial relations that I have had for many years with your State Treasury officers, would warrant me in asking an introduction in person, were it not, that I leave in to morrow morning's train for New York.

As the descendant of one whose sword and fortune were devoted in the Revolution, to the erection of this noble fabric, which mad men & fanatics, are now shaking to its centre, I thank you.

Whatever is the result of the struggle, your name will go down to posterity, as that of a patriot, fearless, true, and devoted.

A citizen of New York City.

Washington   Wednesday eveni'g
Dec. 19th 1860.

ALS, DLC-JP.

1. It is perhaps symbolic that this, one of the earliest of the flood of letters which applauded Johnson's stand in behalf of preserving the Union on the eve of secession, should come from an anonymous northern correspondent. Johnson's clarion call for working out the sectional crisis under the benign aegis of the Constitution elicited a veritable avalanche of mail from men in all walks of life. Only a portion of this correspondence can be printed in this volume.

From Columbus W. Ford[1]

December 19, 1860

Hon Mr. Johnson

Sir—To be more explicit in my suggestion in the mode of electing P & V. P— Each representative and senatorial delegation to

nominate men from their own State and different names, that is no
nomination by the Rep, and Sen—delegation of the same person—
Also in reference to the election of Speaker by the house of Rep—
each delegation to nominate from their own delegation, and different
names— I would also suggest that the Senators be elected as they
are now— I deem it essential to maintain the rights of States— I
beleive it is an essential element in the preservation of our liberties
— The rights of States are our strongest guard against the absorp-
tion of all power by the general government— the people must have
something between them and the general government— Our forefathers in forming the government were afraid that the general government would overshadow the states and destroy the liberty of the
people— The rights of states were cautiously guarded—and the
Senate is the representatives of the states as states in contradistinc-
tion from the people, in mass as a state; The Sovereignty and
equality of the state is acknowledged in the representation and the
manner of representation or of election of the representative— If
the distinctive sovereignty and equality of the States is in the
slightest manner obliterated it will only add to the absorbing power
of the general government and be dangerous to the people— If the
mode of electing the Senate be removed from the legislature, the
Senate looses its particular necessity [and?] character [as] the representatives of sovereign powers or states—again it increases the
aspirants and lessens the quality of the Senate— It is a fact which
we cannot close our eyes to, that man is ambitious and that the most
undeserving, unworthy are the most ambitious, and too often get into
place— Again I would suggest, that the states be divided into Executive—Judicial, and diplomatic districts— That is the whole
number of states divided by the number of cabinet officers and one
be selected from each district— The whole number of states divided
by the number of judges of the supreme court, and one judge from
each, and the whole number of states by the number of foreign ministers and one from each— when the states or officers increase a new
division to be made— The consuls to be selected from the diplomatic
districts as equally as possible— [2]

Respy,   Columbus, W. Ford
North East Cecil Co. Md.

Dcr. 19. 1860

ALS, DLC-JP.

1. Columbus W. Ford (b. c1818) was a farmer with $4,000 in personal
estate. 1860 Census, Md., Cecil, 245.

2. As a congressman Johnson had urged, both in 1845 and in 1848, a
quota system based on congressional districts for federal appointments, including consular and diplomatic posts. See *Johnson Papers*, I, 192, 430.

From "A Southerner and a Lover of his Country"

Baltimore 19th December 1860

Hon Andrew Johnson
My dear Sir.—

My apology for this letter if it need one is that I am "an American citizen" & devotedly attached to this Great, this prosperous & happy Confederacy.—

But the Confederacy is in danger! This beloved country which we have all been taught aye by our *Mothers* to honor and love is in danger.

Fanatics & Politicians, must *now* give way to *Patriots* and *Statesmen.*

The mere politician rants & raves about his *constituents* and this is as far as his limited ideas & his patriotism (if he be possessed of any at all) extend.—

But the Statesman & Patriot while he honourably Serves his constituents feels also his responsibility alike & as Sacred to his country.

O My dear Sir in trying times like these when the noble, the true, & the patriotic heart of this Great Nation is throbing with fear & anxiety it is to such men as you, and Crittenden, Jeff Davis, Bigler,[1] John Cockrum,[2] Geo. S. Houston[3] & others of like acknowledged ability & sterling patriotism it is I say to such men this great Country looks under God's guidance and blessing to rescue us alike from Fanaticism & Political Trickery.—

O My dear Sir for God's sake for the sake of this great, this beloved Land—for the sake of Liberty, of Peace use all your good endeavours to this noble end.

All Abstract theories & opinions sink into utter insignificance when weighed in the balance with this Glorious Union.—

O Congress of 1860 immortalize yourselves in your countrys History as you surely will if you save this nation in this the darkest hour of her History.— Fear not! doubt not—God is with you.— He has pronounced His blessing on "The Peace-Makers"[.] Dont despair — Keep on in your Noble endeavours & all will yet be Well! Hurry on that day of Peace.

Yr friend in Sincerity
A Southerner & A Lover of his Country.

ALS, DLC-JP.

1. Senator William Bigler of Pennsylvania. See *Johnson Papers*, III, 194n.
2. John Cochrane (1813–1898), surveyor of the Port of New York (1853–57), was elected to Congress as a State Rights Democrat (1857–61)

and served as a delegate to both the Charleston and Baltimore Democratic conventions. An officer in the 65th N. Y. Inf., he later became a Republican and was nominated by the Independent Republican convention for vice president in 1864, an honor which he declined. Collector of internal revenue for the sixth district of New York in 1862, he was a delegate to the Liberal Republican convention in Cincinnati in 1872. *BDAC*, 714.

3. Congressman George S. Houston of Alabama. See *Johnson Papers*, II, 19*n*.

From Miles Benham[1]

Syracuse 20th Dec 1860

Hon. Mr. Jonson, Tenn
Dear Sir

I was interested reading your Speech in the Senate the 19th on the Union. I agree with you in part— You lay the Dificulty to the Republican party[.] in this I cannot agree with you— as I See it it has benn brought on by the Demicrat party, or the Learders, the Poletesions of that party has don the Deed for poletecal efect, the Northen Poletesions has falsely Represented the Republican party— I Contend they Are better friends to the South than the Dimecrat party or even the South is to them Selves— the Republicans party is for Stoping this agitation & have peace & not Keeping up this Slavery quetion but Stop it & let it rest Whare it now Stands, and that you Should be Satisfyed with, for the Dimecrat party has had the power for years in Congress, you have passed laws and Repealed them at your pleaser, and it would be nateral to Suppose that you would be Satisfyed with your own Doings— the Repeal of the Mesurea [Missouri] Line Was A Demecrat move which was the Foundation of all this trouble— the Republicans resisted the Repeal with thare full Streangth—but you Comited the Deed and I would ask you what has benn the result— You understand the result the loss of lives & property and the expence to the Goverment—and I ask for what onely to bring Slavery into the teritory that had been pledged to Free Labor— Did the South have any Idea the North would Submitt to Such anout rage when it was needed for Free Labor and not for Slave Labor— The South complains they have not Slaves Labor anough to work thare plantitations & here in the Free States we have thousands that needs that Soyl to Till and we think the Free Labor Should have the preference— The Telegraph has brought the news that South Carolina Had pass an ordinance in the convention to Leave the Union— I feel if the other States Should agree to stay content in the Union and Let South Carolina Leave in peace it would be a blesing to the Union, or if a few other States

Should assist [*sic*] on Leaving, the old States I would be in favor of leting them go in peace—but the States formed out of Teritory acquired Since the Constitution was framed I would not consent Should Leave— the Border Slave States would not Leave if they under Stand thare Intrest— They need the protection of the North & Western States which if they Leave they cannot have— I am for peace and I feel it better to let them withdraw peacebly if posibly— I think they would be glad to Come back— The excuse to Leave because Lincoln is Elected is Idle with out understanding what his polesy will be— I think it will be to Let the Slavery question alone & Bring this goverment back to its former Standing Stoping all fraud, extravegance and at peace with all Nations and at peace at home— Now Sir this would not Satisfy the Northan Dimecrat Politicens[.] this Strife between the North & South is thare onely Salvation— If the South wishes to Continue this State of things as we have had for the few years past and the Same plan of Administering the Goverment on this extravagant plan and continuing frauds in Goverment Oficers,[2] In this Case it would be better to Sepperate— The North is apposed to aney further Compromises to Have Broken — I think this has ben Brought on by reckless Poleticans North & South that had as Soon Distroy the Union as to preserve it— All I See thare is to do is to Stop all agitation— The Presidant does not intend to Stop it but Seemes to aid on this Sessesion Movements and places all power in to thare Hands, I think to get the coming administration in to Dificulty with the Southern States which I hope & pray can not be brought about— The Idea of War is Dredfull to me— I am Satisfyed if South Carolina Should Leave us we could then Live in peace[.]

                                        Yours Truley   Miles Benham

NB please excuse all Mistakes from an old Man 73 years old

ALS, DLC-JP.

    1. Miles Benham (b. *c*1797), a farmer, was currently living at 74 James Street, Syracuse, New York. *Syracuse City Directory* (1855–56), 39.

    2. Probably a reference to the recently exposed incompetence, if not outright fraud, on the part of Secretary of War John Floyd in selling military land to Virginia friends and New York politicians who then defaulted, and in purchasing at an over-inflated price Willett's Point, New York, for the government. Furthermore, Floyd's mismanagement of military contracts and those relating to construction on public buildings left President Buchanan no alternative but to request the secretary's resignation. In addition, the Covode Committee in the House, investigating the enormous profits garnered by the public printers, further embarrassed the Democratic administration. Philip S. Klein, *President James Buchanan: A Biography* (University Park, Pa., 1962), 377–78; Nevins, *Emergence of Lincoln*, II, 198–200; *Johnson Papers*, III, 29n.

From O. N. Chapin[1]

Nashville, 20th Dec. 1860

Hon. Andrew Johnson,
Dr Sir,

The telegraph reports your speech of a day or two ago in the Senate, and I am so much gratified in reading it that though always opposed to you in politics I cannot resist the impulse to thank you for the manly conservative stand you have taken for the Constitution and the Union. I am no submissionist but believe we can resist the agression of the northern fanatics and opponents of our institutions to far better advantage in the Union than out of it.

It seems to me that to go out of the Union to fight for our rights would be like the commander of a fortress going outside of his walls to fight mutineers who were left within, with all the advantage of arms, and works, while the commander exposed himself in the open field. We might possibly admire the bravery of the man, but what would we think of his judgment?

We have a million and a half good friends in the northern states, and it is not only suicide but ingratitude combined, to desert them when they would do us all the service in their power.

I hope you will go forward, and ignoring the mere ties of party by which you are *said* to be indissolubly bound, battle for our rights, in the only arena where battling can do much good.

Your Obedient Servant
O. N. Chapin

ALS, DLC-JP.
1. Chapin cannot be identified.

From William J. Cook

December 20, 1860, Chambersburg, Pa.; ALS, DLC-JP.

Requests copy of Johnson's speech; "had wise counsels prevailed and you have been the choice [for president], I sincerely beleive that the administration of the Government for the coming four years would have devolved upon you, and that the present National Crisis would have been avoided."

From Thomas N. Haskell[1]

E. Boston Mass. Dec. 20/1860.

Hon. And Dear Sir,

I have read extracts from your late Union Speech in the U. S. Senate with admiration and gratitude; and I write you to solicit the transmission of a copy of it if convenient for you, to my address.

In the language of a Carolina Statesman and Scholar[2] who addressed the Students of Miami University, my ALMA MATER, a quarter of Century Since, I "cling to the Union of these States with a patriots love, A Scholars devotion and a Christian's hope;" and though bound by the tenderest ties to Christian Ministers and men at the South as well as the North and myself a minister of the Gospel, I cannot approve the threats and coersing purposes of Southern Men to destroy the best historc government ever known and break into comparatively useless fragments the Federal Union planned by the wisdom and cemented with the blood of our pious and patriotic ancestors, nor can I be indifferent to the well being of either South or North in Such a time as this.

Having Spent the first four years of my ministry very pleasantly in the South[3] I am unwilling to judge her harshly; but I am compelled to infer that Secession now for the reasons urged would not only be Suicidal but the worst thing She could do. It was far better with the faith of Moses to "Stand and See the Salvation of the Lord"[4] (hemmed in on all Sides as She may be eventually by free states and the Sea) than like Pharoah and his hosts to rush into the Red Sea unbidden and be drowned. When living at the South I learned to regard her hope to be in the developement of her ample resources, the education of her citizens and the moral Culture of her Slaves, and I do not now believe her safety is in going out of the Union, even though it were possible to seceede in peace, nor is it in agitating any compromise which the Sentiment of the North will be Sure to resist or receive with a conscientious discontent[.] "Oh that we were as in times past!"[5] when the North and South could compare notes and *understand each other*! But the telegraph and R.R. are Symbols of haste & men do not stop to reason together as of old. The South misunderstands the North, the North misunderstands the South and in their haste the S. C. Convention will doubtless have repealed the ratifying act of May 1788 and thereby declared the Union dissolved, before this reaches Washington: perhaps the deed is now done; but it Seems as unsatisfying an Excommunication as that of a group of abolitionists who a few years since met and excommunicated the

Church and went from bad to worse till in the revival of /58 some of them were converted to Christ and again received into covenant with his people.[6] I beg that you will excuse my freedom in thus addressing you and believe me one who daily prays that "wisdom from above" may be given you and all our public men in this trying Emergency. I am pastor of a large church (orthodox) in this city[7] and my father Capt. Geo. Haskell and fatherinlaw Dr Justin Edwards[8] were national men[.] In their Spirit of patriotism I am very respectfully your fellow citizen[.]

T. N. Haskell.

ALS, DLC-JP.

1. Thomas N. Haskell (1826–1906), New York native, Miami University graduate (1851), and a founder of Colorado College (1873), served in various ministries, among them the Western Presbyterian Church of Washington, D. C. (1854–58) and the Maverick Church in East Boston (1858–62). Edgar S. Robinson, comp., *The Ministerial Directory*, I (1898), 299; Justin Winsor, *The Memorial History of Boston* (4 vols., Boston, 1881), III, 418; Caroline L. Goodenough, *Legends, Loves and Loyalties of Old New England* (Rochester, Mass., 1930), 73.

2. Thomas S. Grimké (1786–1834), South Carolina lawyer, orator, and reformer, spent a week at Miami University in 1834 at the invitation of the Erodelphian Society; contracting cholera, he died on his way to Columbus, Ohio. *DAB*, VII, 635–36; Walter Havighurst, *The Miami Years, 1809–1959* (New York, 1959), 78.

3. Presumably the Washington pastorate represented this pleasant interlude "in the South."

4. A variation of Moses' injunction to the Israelites as they fled from Egypt. Ex. 14:13.

5. The source of this quotation has not been found.

6. It is impossible to determine precisely which "group of abolitionists" Haskell had in mind. Since the 1830's throughout the North, zealous antislavery Christians, losing patience with the equivocations of organized religion, had, both individually and in groups, castigated the orthodox churches and divorced themselves from them. When the revivalism of 1857–58 brought these churches to a more assertive stand against slavery, these ardent abolitionists found it possible to return to fellowship with the now more congenial orthodox bodies. Timothy L. Smith, *Revivalism and Social Reform in Mid-Nineteenth-Century America* (New York, 1957), 180–224 *passim*.

7. Organized in 1836, the Maverick Church was Congregational. Winsor, *Memorial History*, III, 418.

8. Capt. George Haskell has not been further identified. Justin Edwards (1787–1853), a prominent Massachusetts Calvinist minister, was an organizer of the New England Tract Society (1814), corresponding secretary of the American Temperance Society (1829), president of Andover Theological Seminary (1836–42), secretary of the newly organized American and Foreign Sabbath Union (1842), and author of numerous tracts and sermons, many of which were widely circulated. *DAB*, VI, 39–40.

From Joseph C. G. Kennedy[1]

Census Office, Department of the Interior,
Washington, 20 Decr 1860

My dear Sir—

Your praise is in all lips and I hear none speak of your noble and patriotic effort in the Senate but in terms of the highest commendation— Permit me to congratulate you who seem destined to prove a benefactor to the Country & the Cause of Liberty.

Accept my humble thanks and believe gratefully & Respectfully

Your friend & Ob Servt

Jos. C G Kennedy

Hon Andrew Johnson Senator U. S.

ALS, DLC-JP.

1. Kennedy was superintendent of the census. See *Johnson Papers*, III, 615*n*.

From Amos A. Lawrence[1]

(Near) Boston.[2] Dec. 20. 60

Permit me, my dear Sir, to express to you the thanks of a private citizen who loves his whole country. In doing so, I am sure that I express the sentiments of thousands of yr fellow citizens in this part of the country—& of all parties, who admire the position wh. you have taken in yr patriotic speech in the Senate.

Respecty. & truly Yr Obt Svt

Amos A Lawrence

Hon. P. [*sic*] Johnson. U S. Sen.

ALS, DLC-JP.

1. Amos A. Lawrence (1814–1886), wealthy Massachusetts merchant-philanthropist, had joined Eli Thayer in his attempt to colonize Kansas, serving as treasurer and principal manager of the New England Emigrant Aid Company; a few years later, when Kansas became a state, the town of Wakarusa was renamed Lawrence in his honor. Thrice nominated for governor (1856, 1858, 1860) by former Whigs and Constitutional Unionists, he was treasurer (1857–62) and overseer (1879–85) of his alma mater, Harvard. *DAB*, XI, 47–48; William Lawrence, *Life of Amos A. Lawrence* (Boston, 1888); Lawrence, "Memoir of Amos Adams Lawrence," Massachusetts Historical Society *Proceedings*, XII (1898), 132; *Historical Register of Harvard College* (Cambridge, 1937), 294.

2. Presumably at Longwood, Lawrence's "winter" home some two and one-half miles west of the city. Lawrence, "Memoir," 136; William Lawrence, *Memories of a Happy Life* (Boston, 1926), 2.

From John Lellyett[1]

Nashville Dec 20, 1860

Hon Andrew Johnson
Washington D C

Dear Sir,— Judging by the telegraphic account I have seen of your recent speech in the Senate, I desire as an humble individual, to return you my sincere thanks. You may know that as an unimportant politician I have been decidedly opposed to you in politics for years past, though at no time, allow me to say, numbered with your revilers. But in this moment of our country's danger, I am on the side of those who "Keep step to the music of the Union,"[2]—and all the more so, if they are men of great influence with the masses of our people. My own conscience tells me that I have no reproaches for myself as to my own course in the late contest. *Very early* in that contest, I recognized the importance above all things of defeating Lincoln, at every hazard; and early I began to work in my humble way to bring about a result so desirable, even though Mr Breckinridge might thereby be made President. But our fathers made the term of the Presidential office only 4 years, and threw around the government various wisely devised checks and balances for the very purpose of cutting off the possibility of any necessity arising for the course now proposed to be pursued by the Cotton States. Let not the wisdom of the fathers be rebuked by their children's folly. I think we have one set of politicians South who want to save the Union *on the Sly*, and another who wish to destroy it in the same way. I sympathize with the former, but fear they will be caught in the meshes of their own net. The latter are among us. They have control of the Union and American of this place. They wish to pledge us all against coercion, and then how can the Union be preserved, if any body wishes to destroy it. I had already taken similar ground to that I understand you to occupy,—namely, that the government has no right to coerce a state in any matter at all; but has the power to coerce the people. In the sphere of the State sovereignty, the federal government has no power, and *vice versa*. Each has power to coerce the citizens—but each only in its own sphere of sovereignty. The federal government has just as much right to force a state out of the Union as a state has to go out. This cannot be done by either without violation of the sovereignty of the other.

Yours truly   John Lellyett[3]

ALS, DLC-JP.

1. John Lellyett (c1826–fl1887), native Ohioan, was part owner of

Lellyett and Smith, Nashville wholesale grocers. In 1859, as one of the editors of *The Opposition*, a weekly campaign newspaper, he had supported John Netherland for governor. Forced to leave Tennessee in July, 1861, he served for a time as a U. S. army intelligence agent in Kentucky and briefly as Nashville postmaster (March 20–early June, 1862); he later supported McClellan's bid for the presidency, and after the war practiced law in Nashville. 1860 Census, Tenn., Davidson, Nashville, 5th Ward, 180; *Nashville Bus. Dir.* (1860–61), 212; Clayton, *Davidson County*, 199, 236; *Tennessee State Gazetteer and Business Directory* (Nashville, 1887), 578; John Y. Simon, ed., *Ulysses S. Grant Papers* (5 vols., Carbondale, Ill., 1967–   ), IV, 35n.

2. A phrase used by Rufus Choate in his October 1, 1855, letter to the Worcester, Massachusetts, Whig convention. Stevenson, *Quotations*, 57.

3. In the margin of the second page of the letter is the note: "The indications are that the people of the rural districts will be with you. But your speech ought to be *circulated*[.]"

From James X. McLanahan

December 20, 1860, New York, N.Y.; ALS, DLC-JP.

A former House colleague applauds Johnson's sentiments—"*Your* trumpet utters 'No uncertain Sound'. . . . Your Speech has in it the right kind of metal—and possesses the ring of the old *Constitutional currency*."

From "A Northerner"

December 20, 1860, Brooklyn, N.Y.; ALS, DLC-JP.

Endorsing Johnson's Union sentiments, requests him to use his "influence to have a NATIONAL CONVENTION" to give "*People* [who] are honest at heart—even in Massachusetts" a chance to say, "The South *shall* have her Rights—her whole Rights, and nothing but her Rights—So help us God."

From Francis J. Parker

December 20, 1860, Boston, Mass.; ALS, DLC-JP.

Praises speech which "gives strength to every sinew of us who are contending upon the outer walls against 'rebublicanism,' and we will remember it four years hence"; would work to promote good feeling toward the South, even though "The greatest obstacle to our exertions is the craziness of So Carolina language."

From Thomas Shankland

December 20, 1860, New York, N. Y.; ALS, DLC-JP.

An old friend applauds Johnson's patriotic speech; "I always confidently looked forward to your occupying the White House, and I know that you would never leave it desolate and the country on the brink of dissolution."

From Herman Cox[1]

Nashville Decr. 21st, 1860

Honr. Andrew Johnson

Dear Sir. I have no doubt you will feel surprised at the receipt of this—but be that as it May—as stranger things are transpireing every day— I hope you will excuse Me for takeing this liberty, at a time when it seems that the destinies of our glorious Country for Weal or Woe, hangs upon the passing hour—. This is the emenation of an impulse free & volentary, yea Spontanious & irrepresable in its Character towards you, produced in My heart, & approved by my Judgment and attested by my Conceince, upon reading in our daily papers giving the proceeding of Congress, your proud, patriotice & Statesman-like position upon the presant alarming & Momentus issues of the day—. While I am pleased to say that I ever admired you as a Man, our political opinions have heretofore been antagonistic—but thank God, in Comon with many others in this Community—I am more then Willing to forget party—& Strike for my Country, her laws & institutions. Your position, & the true & patriotic Sentiments uttered by you in your recent remarks in the Senate, have struck the popular heart in Tennessee, and While there May be some, not so ready as Myself to award to you, that highest of all praise "Well done good & faithfull servant" still they feel as I feel—and their actions Will award what their hearts may reluctantly assent to— The first letter of your Collegue Mr Nicholson published,[2] produced alarm. Its tone seemed to Chime in with sentiments at War with the perpatuity of our union of States, but his recent letter[3] is not so regarded—& the opinion obtains somewhat —that you "Wrung it from him"[.][4] Our Legislature will soon Meet —then a Convention of the State upon Which Much depends. Govr. Harris it is believed will take [a] position (if not Straight-out) Strongly & closely bordering on *Cesession*—the lat[t]er in my opinion if he thinks he dare to venture.

No man in Tennessee in My opinion Can do More to form & Shape the action of her people, than yourself—and in this imergancy I feel & am assured, that you will exert yourself, & leave not a *line or a precept* unapplied, as far as May be in your power, to avert the threatened danger. This comes from, comparatively an obscure source, & May be worth but little— if so let that little enter into the great aggregate of patriotic sympathy which I know pervades the feelings & wishes of the people of Tennessee, & you Can not be insensible of it—should you need support from public approbation to Sustain you in your patriotic endeavor to save & perpetuate the Government.

Hopeing you will pardon the intrusion, and the liberty I have taken in writing to you—

I remain your Obt Servt.
Herman Cox

ALS, DLC-JP.

1. Herman Cox (c1815–c1866), a North Carolina native who became a Nashville lawyer and grocer, was an alderman (1854–58) and state legislator (1855–57). Appointed U. S. attorney for Middle Tennessee in 1861, he served for two years. Robison, *Preliminary Directory, Davidson*, 6; *U. S. Official Register* (1861), 192.

2. Probably a reference to A. O. P. Nicholson's letter of November, 1850, written after the second session of the Nashville convention and recently reprinted in the *Banner*. While actually an antisecession appeal and an endorsement of the Compromise of 1850, the letter nonetheless urged southern unity. Nashville *Republican Banner*, November 20, 1860; for Nicholson, see *Johnson Papers*, I, 73n.

3. Addressed to the editors of the *Union and American*, this letter of December 8 counseled a cautious course for the border states in view of the threat of secession by South Carolina and the Gulf states. Nashville *Union and American*, December 13, 1860; Nashville *Republican Banner*, December 14, 1860.

4. There is no evidence to support this statement; in fact, the presumption is against it, inasmuch as Johnson and Nicholson had for some time been quasi-estranged.

From Charles R. Cullen[1]

Richmond Va Dec 21st 1860

Mr. Johnson

Sir.   Though unacquainted with you yet I believe that your plans for the maintainance of the present Confederacy—to be on the right track. Union meetings are useless— I wrote to my old class mates in college—Hon S. S Cox[2] and Hon Eli Thayer[3] to push this plan and suggested an amendment that the Governors of the Several States give the vote for each candidate (for President & vice President) pro rata—according to the strength of each candidate in the field— Mr Thayer replied. "I think the proposition about electors (your plan) to be a fair one. Perhaps it would be better to vote directly for President and Vice President. I am ready for either. The present system is not a fair one." Under the plan I suggest—gerry mandering would be done away with and Black Republicanism killed practically and permanently— Mr. Cox—replied—that three months of actual suffering by the artisans at the North will bring about a change of opinion— That is true, but it does not come soon enough to prevent the Gulf States (it may now be too late for them) and the other Slave States from joining in the Secession movement. The States bordering on the Mississippi River and the border Slave States are most interested and should not be dragged into disunion— And yet (as I wrote Mr. Thayer) that the 'heel crushing bravado' of Senator Wilson[4] and Hale's coercion speech[5] were uniting Southern men in opposition to the present Union, and that coercion however constitutional could not be accomplished. Better let Secession take place peaceably—than attempt an impossibility. I beleive that the amendment to the Constition as suggested would bring about a change of feeling now going on in the South—among all parties in favor of secession— I believe Mr. Bell's views to be right[6]—and if Mr. Breckenridge and other leading conservative men would take up this tangible amendment to the Consitution—harmony may again be restored to our present Union. Speeches and Union meetings—and other exhibitions of popular feeling can do no good at the present crisis, and had I the position you occupy I would use all honorable means of stopping the present reign of sectional hate and distrust— which may lead to Civil war—in a month or so— May *God help you* and *govern* our country in His own way—

Respectfully   C. R. Cullen. MD.

ALS, DLC-JP.

1. Charles R. Cullen (1825–1899), Richmond physician, graduate of Brown University (1846) and Richmond Medical College (1848), began practice a year later in Los Angeles. Returning to Richmond in 1857, he served as an assistant surgeon, CSA (1862–64), and as a medical examiner for the state examining board (1884, 1889–99). *Historical Catalogue of Brown University, 1764–1904* (Providence, 1905), 205.

2. Samuel S. Cox (1824–1889), an Ohio lawyer and Democratic congressman (1857–65) and subsequently a New York congressman (1869–85, 1886–89), was also an 1846 Brown alumnus. Briefly secretary to the American legation in Lima (1855) and later an envoy to Turkey (1885–86), he is best known as the author of *Three Decades of Federal Legislation, 1855–1885* (Providence, 1885). *BDAC*, 745–46; David Lindsey, *"Sunset" Cox* (Detroit, 1959), 5, 6.

3. Eli Thayer (1819–1899), Massachusetts educator and Brown graduate (1845), served in the General Court as a Free-Soiler (1853–54), becoming deeply involved in attempts to colonize Kansas with free settlers. Obsessed with colonization as the panacea for various ills of society, Thayer, as Republican congressman (1857–61), alienated his fellow legislators and lost regular party support. Defeated as an independent in 1860, he spent the rest of his life trying to recoup his political fortunes. *DAB*, XVIII, 402–4.

4. Henry Wilson (1812–1875), Massachusetts schoolteacher, shoe manufacturer, and editor of the Boston *Republican* (1848–51), was a member of the state house (1841–42) and senate (1844–46, 1850–52). Elected to the U. S. Senate (1856–73) by a coalition of Free-Soilers, Americans, and Democrats, he served until he resigned to become Grant's vice president. In the tense months of 1860 Wilson responded unequivocally to the challenges of southern senators. When Clingman of North Carolina hinted at a "bloody struggle" and hoped that "the first-fruits of the collision may be reaped" in Congress, Wilson retorted that "the people of the free States have sent their

representatives here, not to fight, but to legislate; not to mingle in personal combats, but to deliberate for the good of the whole country; not to shed the blood of their fellow-members, but to maintain the supremacy of the Constitution, and uphold the Union." If in performing their duties they were assaulted, "those assaults will be repelled and retaliated by sons who will not dishonor fathers that fought at Bunker Hill and conquered at Saratoga." *BDAC*, 1830; *Cong. Globe*, 36 Cong., 1 Sess., 574. See also Ernest McKay, *Henry Wilson: Practical Radical* (Port Washington, N. Y., 1971); Richard H. Abbott, *Cobbler in Congress: The Life of Henry Wilson, 1812–1875* (Lexington, Mass., 1972).

5. When the Republican caucus met prior to the convening of the 36th Congress, it decided upon a policy of "masterly inactivity" until the party assumed power with the inauguration of Lincoln. For the most part they adhered to a policy of silence, but when Senator Wigfall of Texas boasted that, if war came, the next treaty would be signed "in Faneuil Hall, in the town of Boston, in the state of Massachusetts," a few Republicans perforce spoke out. John P. Hale of New Hampshire, condemning Buchanan for his indecisiveness, proclaimed that, if the voice of the majority in a constitutional election "will not be submitted to, then, sir, this is not a Union of equals; it is a Union of a dictatorial oligarchy on the one side, and a herd of slaves and cowards on the other." The issue was clear: "the majority must yield, or the minority; we cannot all prevail on every issue." The North had conceded and compromised too much; "if . . . war is the alternative, let it come in any form or in any shape." *Cong. Globe*, 36 Cong., 2 Sess., 9–10, 74; Stampp, *And the War Came*, 65–67; Richard H. Sewell, *John P. Hale and the Politics of Abolition* (Cambridge, 1965), 186; *Johnson Papers*, I, 508n.

6. In a letter recently appearing in the press, Bell cautioned southerners against hasty action, maintaining that their grievances could be redressed through constitutional means and that the new administration would be powerless should the South's congressmen and senators remain in their seats. He reiterated his earlier conviction that secession, merely another name for rebellion, was unjustified. Averring that Lincoln was no extremist, Bell declared his intention to "adhere to the Union." John Bell to A. Burwell, December 6, in *Republican Banner*, December 8, 1860; Joseph H. Parks, *John Bell of Tennessee* (Baton Rouge, 1950), 390–92.

From James F. Noble[1]

Cincinnati O. Dec 21/60

Hon Andrew Johnson
Washington
Dear Sir

Altho' a stranger to you, I cannot refrain from returning thanks for the pleasure afforded me in the perusal of your recent able and patriotic speech—And yet I have only read such portions as furnished by Telegraph.—

I am glad too, that you have made a move in the matter of changing the mode of electing President & Vice President[.][2] I have for years desired a change and Mr Bentons plan I have always thought would be popular with the people, and would if adopted prevent the election of Sectional candidates[3]—the source of a great deal of the present troubles—

I think though, his plan should be modified so as to have the electoral & congressional districts the Same and allow the two Senatorial votes to be given to the candidate having the greatest number of votes in the State— By this mode, objections may be obviated, that State Legislatures may Gerrymander in districting the State— If this mode of election had been in force at the recent Presidential election 8 if not 10 electoral votes could have been diverted from Mr Lincoln out of the 23 to which we are entitled—[4] By modifying in the way I have suggested, the first election for President could be held at the Same time Members of Congress are chosen & the law should be amended so as to require a Uniform day throughout the Union say in August— This would allow of the 2d election being held in Nov —in case no one has a majority of all the votes for President at the first trial[.] I never heard any one object to Bentons plan except on the ground it required too many elections in one year— By modifying in the way I have stated there would not be more than two elections in a year and perhaps but one, for I have no doubt if Congress would fix the day for holding elections for President & Congress the States would soon make laws making the elections for State officers conform to it.[5]

If this amendment can be put before the people, also one making an equitable division of the Territories between the free & slave states say by a restoration of the Mo compromise line and its extension to California and some modification of the Fugitive slave law, I think we should again see peace & harmony restored[.] I believe the measures I have suggested would be sanctioned by a large majority of the people of Ohio— All the Republicans of *the rank & file* I have conversed with, are willing for the restoration of the Mo Compromise line— If congress will do nothing I hope the members from the Border States—Slave & free will call a convention to be held at Louisville on 22d Feby—to agree on amendments to the Constitution— I believe it can be done and I believe whatever terms such a convention might agree on will be sanctioned by all the states except perhaps New England & Michigan & Wisconsin—& if our Union should be broken to pieces the Border & Middle States may form a Union—

From an old Clay Whig & supporter of Bell & Everett—

James F. Noble

ALS, DLC-JP.

1. James F. Noble, a bookkeeper "at N. Longworth's., h. 18 Barr," was a life member of the Cincinnati Independent Fire Engine and Hose Company. Longworth, whose occupation was unlisted in 1860, had been a wine dealer. *Williams' Cincinnati Directory* (1860), 234; Charles Cist, *Cincinnati in 1841* (Cincinnati, 1841), 294, 295.

2. See Joint Resolution for Amendments on Presidential, Senatorial, and Judicial Selection, December 13, 1860, *Johnson Papers*, III, 693–95.

3. Thomas Hart Benton, Missouri senator, advocated popular election of President and Vice President, thus eliminating caucuses, national conventions, and electors. If one candidate lacked a majority, another election would be held between the two with the largest number of votes. The only residence requirement was that the citizens of each state vote within their district for President and Vice President, "one of whom at least shall not be an inhabitant of the same state with themselves." Thomas Hart Benton, *Thirty Years' View* (2 vols., New York, 1854–59), II, 626–27, 629; *Johnson Papers*, III, 585n.

4. Although Lincoln carried the state and hence all its twenty-three electoral votes, the Ohio congressional delegation actually was composed of thirteen Republicans and eight Democrats. Perhaps Noble thought that his plan would have given the northern Democratic candidate, Douglas, an electoral vote equal to the congressional composition. Reinhard H. Luthin, *The First Lincoln Campaign* (Cambridge, 1944), 182.

5. In 1845 Congress had established a uniform day for presidential elections, designating the first Tuesday after the first Monday in November; the first national election occurred on November 4, 1848. The Constitution, which in Art. 1, Sec. 4, leaves to the states the decision as to time, place, and manner of choosing representatives, has never been amended to set a uniform day for congressional elections. In his third annual message, December 19, 1859, Buchanan recommended a law establishing a uniform day for congressional elections, but Congress failed to act. Gorton Carruth and Associates, eds., *The Encyclopedia of American Facts and Dates* (New York, 1970), 212; Bernard Schwartz, *A Commentary on the Constitution of the United States*, Part I: *The Powers of Government* (2 vols., New York, 1963), I, 99–102; H. Von Holst, *The Constitutional and Political History of the United States* (8 vols., Chicago, 1892), VII, 93–94.

From Ebenezer J. Penniman

December 21, 1860, Plymouth, Mich.; ALS, DLC-JP.

Approves Johnson's "appeal for a manly review by the northern States of their Legislation"; has long considered him "a representa[t]ive man of the great middle interests of the nation. . . . I should rejoice to see all the storms that surround us as a people, so quieted that it would be easy for me, a northern man, who honestly voted for Lincoln, to rejoice to see you succeed him[.]"

From Charles D. Smith[1]

Milwaukee Wis
December 21. 1860

Hon Andrew Johnson
Dear Sir

This letter may be a *bore* to you: if so attribute it to a desire to do something for my poor distracted country. I pray you read it through, it may afford you some aid and comfort in this dark period of our career.

During your gubernatorial term I was a citizen of the State of Tennessee residing at Memphis, and from the knowledge obtained of your character and public career while there, I have looked with no little degree of anxiety to see what stand you would take in this hour of peril to our common country.

I seize this early opportunity upon reading a telegraphic report of your remarks on the 19th instant, to thank you for the noble and patriotic opinions so boldly proclaimed. Go on Sir in the course so wisely adopted, and you will certainly obtain the attention of this *whole nation.*

It is useless perhaps for me to advise you to remain bold and firm, yet I cannot let this opportunity pass by without trying to *encourage at least.* I am no office holder or officer seeker, no brawling politician, having spent most of my life in commercial pursuits, but am always ready to give a reason for my democratic faith.

Our present difficulties arise in a great degree from the fact that the people of the North & South have received too much of their political faith, from mean, narrow minded selfish teachers. Our Members of Congress have taught their constituents to hate the constituents of others, merely for their own aggrandisement, this species of meaness has become of late years so prevalent, that patriotism and love of Country is almost discarded from the Councils of the nation, and now the fearful retribution is at hand. Treason walks forth boldly at midday without an effort to cover its deformities. Encounter it boldly and firmly, the *right must prevail.*

The administration of Lincoln is not to be feared, its disruption has already begun, and he will not occupy his office twelve months before his supporters will be as scarce as Tylers were.[2] There is a great change taking place among the people of the North. A member elect to our State Legislature from this City, a rabid Republican has already announced his determination to repeal the personal liberty laws upon our Statute.[3] Firmness, Coolness, & Determination on the part of the South, not *indecent haste* will procure for *all,* their rights, and this great nation may be still preserved, mans hope of liberty still strengthened, and that too under the guidance of democratic principles.

Go on as you have begun, do not swerve from the path you have taken, send your ideas broadcast over the land[.] yours will be the reward, and a nation will bless you[.]

If I can aid you in my humble way, command me[.]

Sincerely yours   Chas D. Smith

ALS, DLC-JP.

1. Charles D. Smith (b. c1821), New York native and a former cashier of the West Tennessee Bank, was secretary of the Milwaukee, Watertown and

Baraboo Valley Railroad. 1860 Census, Wis., Milwaukee, 4th Ward, 97; *Paschall and Riggs's Memphis Directory* (1856–57), 188; *Starr's Milwaukee Directory* (1860–61), 219.

2. John Tyler, elected to the vice presidency in 1840, was elevated to the presidency on Harrison's death. Declaring an independent course based on Jeffersonian principles, which meant a retreat from further enlargement of federal powers, Tyler managed to alienate his Whig supporters, who endorsed a program of internal improvements, a national bank, and a high tariff. By September, 1841, following his vetoes of the first and second bank bills, Tyler became virtually a President without a party. Smith evidently views Lincoln's relationship with the diverse elements within the Republican coalition as an omen of party disorder. Robert J. Morgan, *A Whig Embattled: The Presidency under John Tyler* (Lincoln, Nebr., 1954), 1–45; Oliver P. Chitwood, *John Tyler: Champion of the Old South* (New York, 1964 [1939]), 209–11; David M. Potter, *Lincoln and His Party in the Secession Crisis* (New Haven, 1942), 39–44, 127–28, 132–33.

3. It has not been possible to identify the legislator to whom Smith refers; in the forthcoming session of the Assembly, several efforts would be made to repeal these measures. See Milwaukee *Sentinel*, January 8, 15, 26, February 5, 9, 1861.

From Anthony Ten Eyck[1]

Detroit, Mich. Decr. 21/60

My dear Sir,

Permit me to Express to you my great gratification, at the perusal of the telegraphic Synopsis of your recent Speech in the Senate, on the present aspect of political affairs— You have demonstrated to the people (what I had learned before, from my short acquaintance with you) that you are not only an able Statesman, but an independent & unselfish Man & politician, & a genuine patriot[.]

If there were more just such men in Congress (especially from the Southern States) devoted to the Union, & determined to fight *in it*, for those rights which they feel have been invaded, rather than Seek them beyond—out Side of it, we of the North, who have battled long & faithfully to maintain them, might now have some encouragement to labour in effecting a change in the public Sentiment of the North, which would result in the Speedy overthrow of the Black republican organization[.]

If the Southern people will only remain true to the Union—if they will "bear the ills they have, rather than to fly to those they know not of,"[2] for only a little while longer,—until we of the North can get at the "Sober Second thought"[3] of the voters,—we can crush out the abolition Sentiment which has unfortunately misled a majority of our people, & a United Northern, Union loving, Constitutional democracy will again be in the ascendent, ready & willing, as they always have been, to sustain the Constitutional rights, & promote the best interests, of all Sections of the Country—

I do hope there is wisdom & patriotism enough in Congress, to devise Some plan for adjusting present embarrassments[.]

I like Senator Crittenden's resolutions,[4] & on them I believe we could rally a public Sentiment in the Northerm States, that Should Secure their adoption—

But I only designed congratulating you on your Speech, & expressing my gratification on its perusal—

You will oblige me by forwarding me a copy when published in EXTENSO—   Yours very respectfully
                                                              Anthony Ten Eyck

Hon. Andw. Johnson U. S. Senate

ALS, DLC-JP.

1. See *Johnson Papers*, III, 439n.
2. Johnson had used this quotation from *Hamlet* in his recent speech.
3. This phrase, recurring frequently in contemporary writings, seems to have appeared first in Matthew Henry's *Commentaries: Job*, VI, 29 (1708). Stevenson, *Quotations*, 1993.
4. On December 18, Kentucky Senator John J. Crittenden had presented a series of "unamendable amendments" which included the restoration of the Missouri Compromise line; a prohibition against Congress's abolishing slavery where it legally existed—especially in the District of Columbia—as long as Virginia or Maryland maintained the institution; federal compensation for runaway slaves; new fugitive slave legislation omitting the clauses obnoxious to northern citizens; and, finally, a strengthening of the laws prohibiting the African slave trade. *Cong. Globe*, 36 Cong., 2 Sess., 114; Albert D. Kirwan, *John J. Crittenden: The Struggle for the Union* (Lexington, Ky., 1962), 375.

From Edward H. East[1]

                                                       Nashville Decr 22' 1860

Hon Andrew Johnson
Dr Sir,—

I have watched with *much anxiety*, the proceedings, at Washington, and else where, relative to the present critical condition of the country[.] I felt some solicitude, to know what position our members of Congress, would take and have therefore been a close and critical reader, of every telagram, that would indicate anything. Our papers of this morning announced, in brief, your views on this subject, I belive you have struck the *popular heart* of Tennessee.

The people, had almost sickened under the *gruel and teas*,[2] of *policy* and *timidity*[.] I do not know, that it gives an emphasis or force to this letter, that you should know my political antecedents, they were not such at least, as would make me too partial in your favor, But justice to you as well as candor to my self and feelings has prompted this, much. It is some conselation to a public servant to know, that, in a great and trying emergency when the very *existence* of his country is put to the test, and the best government on the earth, destroyed, that sentiments uttered in times like these, by the man on the watch-tower, should find, a lodgment in the heart of his constituents, and extort a sustaining response. I do not know how many, that I am an index of but of the good, natural, patriotic sons of Tennessee, I feel that many will enthusiastically accord, in feelings kindred to mine[.]

I hope you intend to publish your speech in full, and send it home, it will do good I am confidant[.]

I trust that our other representatives will exhibit the same, bold, natural petriotic, sentiments as yourself[.]

I have the honor to be your Humble servant[.]

Edward H. East

ALS, DLC-JP.

1. East, a former Henry Clay Whig, remained loyal to the Union and served as Johnson's secretary of state during his military governorship. See *Johnson Papers*, III, 410*n*.

2. Probably a reference to the unappetizing diet of gruel and tea, the traditional lot of the poor and the sick. East is thus arraigning the "namby-pamby" leadership with which the citizens of Tennessee have been saddled during the current crisis.

From Joseph W. Merriam

December 22, 1860, Memphis; ALS, DLC-JP.

Requests copy of the December speech which "has called out a bitter article . . . from my old *confraree* of the Avalanche [Matthew C. Gallaway] in this mornings issue"; Johnson's speech "will be coolly received or denounced by most of the southern men, but still it will prove if properly circulated the best panacea yet administered for the pressing evils of the present."

From A. Waldo Putnam[1]

Nashville, December 22, 1860

Hon. Andrew Johnston
Senator in Congress
My dear Sir,

It is my *duty* and *pleasure* promptly to express to you,—and I rejoice in the opportunity to record,—my most hearty approbation of the sentiments uttered by you in the Senate on 18th inst.

I cannot but regard the course pursued by South Carolina as one of madness, demented folly, unparalleled in history only by that of the French Revolution—and that she has shown arrogance, dictation, disrespect and contempt of other States, which should make them scorn her advice and abhor her example. . . . It is absolutely a post of degradation to ask Tennessee. Ky. & Va. to follow the haughty lead of such a State as S.C.— *At last*—Jackson and his patriotic Tennesseans are to bow down at the nullification, yea *Disunion Despotism* of Calhoun and his successors, the aristocrats of the least oppressed, least democratic and most anti-republican State on this continent!

God grant to multiply the number of wise, prudent course & patriotic men, & may they soon peaceably adjust the fearful troubles of the times.

Very respectfully   A. W. Putnam
Nashville Dec. 22/60

ALS, DLC-JP.

1. Albigence Waldo Putnam (1799–1869), great-grandson of Gen. Israel Putnam, was born in Ohio and practiced law in Mississippi before moving to Nashville. An organizer of the Tennessee Historical Society, he served as its president from 1857 until 1869 and wrote the *History of Middle Tennessee* (Nashville, 1859). At the time of his death he was collector of internal revenue at Nashville. Harriet C. Owsley, "The Tennessee Historical Society: Its Origin, Progress and Present Condition," *Tenn. Hist. Quar.*, XXIX (1970), 231, 235; Stanley F. Horn, "Introduction," *History of Middle Tennessee* (Knoxville, 1971), xi; see also Cora B. Sevier and Nancy S. Madden, *Sevier Family History* (Washington, D. C., 1961), 321.

From William R. Hurley[1]

Nashville Dec 23d 1860

Hon A. Johnson.
Dear Sir:

You will doubtless be surprised to receive a letter from me. My apology is the present danger to which our country is exposed. From telegraphic reports of your speech I am of opinion that it will have a good effect upon the public. I am anxious to have a copy for publication in the Democrat.[2] I suppose that there will [be] a large number of your speeches circulated in pamphlet form. I am anxious that you shall send out large numbers to every point in Tennessee *especially*. All our papers or most of them in this state are *timid*. I shall fight a bold an[d] earnest fight, if I can sustain the Democrat. But as long as it can be sustained I will make an ea[r]nest contest in the union & for the union and our rights within the union. Secession is the short Cut to abolitionism especially in the border states and there is great danger of extermination of the African race from the continent. If our white people get the impression—that there is danger of establishing equality of the races, a war of extermination will set in at once. The Union & American and a few men of the *clique* are disposed to denounce you, but you will be sustained by a majority of men of all parties in this state, if you are reported correctly by telegraph. You and I differed very widely during the last can[v]ass, but when I see you stand up boldly for your cou[n]try, I say "well done good and faithful servant[.]" I am proud of a Representative who has the manliness to discharge his duty, and you will find the Democrat defending your position, boldly and earnestly, as long as it is sustained. Secession has been on the increase in this state but we calculate largely on the influence of your speech. My dear sir go on in the great work and save our bleeding country if possible.

I am yours in an effort to preserve the bonds of an everlasting Union.

W R Hurley

ALS, DLC-JP.

1. William R. Hurley (*c*1822–1865), Nashville physician and at this time co-owner and editor of the Nashville *Democrat* (1860–61), was a delegate to the state convention of 1860 and a member of the state Democratic committee. Breaking with the state central committee over "the secession tendency of the Breckinridge faction," Hurley established a separate Douglas organization and campaigned as the Little Giant's elector. In early December, 1860, he was chosen vice president of a bipartisan Nashville meeting which urged the governor to convene the legislature to consider calling a southern states convention on the state of the Union. With Douglas' political stock declining, the *Democrat*, "well known for its union sentiments" and suffering the consequences of having backed a loser, announced a temporary suspension pending the arrival of a new press. Beset with financial difficulties, the editor sought a government appointment in order to continue the paper; he received a clerkship in the sixth auditor's office and had resumed publication December 20. 1860 Census, Tenn., Davidson, Nashville, 3rd Ward, 83; Campbell, *Tenn. Attitudes*, 144; Milton, *Eve of Conflict*, 524n, 525n; Nashville *Union* and *American*, January 19, December 2, 1860; May 21, 1861; Nashville *Patriot*, March 8, 1860; *U. S. Official Register* (1861), 20; Hurley to Montgomery Blair, March 27, 1861, Johnson Papers, LC; Nashville *Banner*, December 21, 1860; Nashville *Press and Times*, September 21, 1865.

2. Hurley's laudatory comments on Johnson's speech appeared in the *Democrat* on December 25. See James Plunket to Johnson, December 25, 1860, Johnson Papers, LC.

From Levi P. Knerr[1]

Reading,   Penn. Decem. 23—1860

Honorable, Andrew Johnston,

Dear sir, Please send me in pamphlet form your speech made this last week in the senate on secession. I am of coarse an entire strainger to you but you must pardon me for this liberty that I take of addressing you at this time. I address you as a mechanic and therefore a

labouring man. I am a machinist employed at the Philada and Reading Rail Road Depot in this City and where their are employed some
five hundred men of every shade of polotics and nationality. And
amongst these men a man who is carefull observer can tell generaly
what public opinion is on all subjects. I sir got my first vote in the
fall of 1841 for Governer and I then voted for David R Porter the
Democratic nominee and sir I have continued to vote that ticket to
the present day. "The longer I vote the Democratic ticket the more I
think of Its Principles[.] Now sir, giving you these outlines I can say
to you that I cannot remember of having seen extracts of a speech or
heard of one that has left that universal charm and effect upon the
people that your speech has upon all classes hear. Sir It is lauded by
every man of all and every political complexion, It has been the universal talk this whole week hear in songs of praise. You sir have
made your mark in this crises of our countrys history never to be
obliterated, You sir have been designated the patriot of Tennessee.
And sir I and I know my fellow men delight to honour such men as
you. Would to god that all men in the senate and the house could
come forward as a band of brothers and save our beloved country
from ruin. I believe and always have that the South has just cause
of complaint and I want the North to conceed her her rights at the
same time I want to see South Carolina and all the other slave states
do what is right and demand and fight for their rights in the union,
And I for one will help them to get them. I for one can say what but
few men can say and that is this. My Grandfather was in the Revolutionary War. My father was in the war of 1812 and myself in the
Mexican war. Now sir hear are three generations of us in the three
wars of our beloved country. Can I look on and see this country distroyed without making an effort to stop It. Indeed I cannot, every
man should come forward and conceed something to save It. Your
speech and Crittendens and Pughs[2] have done a great [d]eal to heal
up bad feelings. Wades and Lanes[3] speeches are looked upon hear
with derision and perfect contempt. Their is no weight in them[.]
they are powerless whilst yours are talked about in praise by everybody as the moddle speech for any man to make. I fear that my country is in dainger, god forbid that one single star should be stricken
from her bright constellation. Was It for this that I went to Mexico
to fight for my native country to mantain her honour in a Just war to
be permitted to return to see her rent and torn in civil strife and In-
testine war. Better far that I to should have lost my life out their
where so many of my friends and companions lay. Better to that my
bones should lay bleeching beside theirs in the far off sunny plains
of Mexico than that I should ever returned to witness my countrys
degradation and ruin. What sir, distroy this Country on account of

the Negro[!] is It not preposterous that men will be so mad and lost to reason. I am satisfyed that public opinion has changed and that wonderfully at the north hear since the election of Mr Lincoln. one half of the men hear who voted for him had no Idea of this result or they would not have voted for him. I know plenty of men of this opinion. They are very sorry but It is now done. Yet he is powerless If the southern men did but know this and act accordingly. And my word for It the next Congressional elections in the north will be overwhelmingly against the Republican party. They hollowed before the election hear Vote for Lincoln and good times[.] they did so and now they have Lincoln and are thrown out of employment[4] and we now hollow and laugh at them. Touch a mans pocket and you make him sensable of his folly and he will vote afterwards accordingly. Senitor Bigler honored me with a commission as aid to him whilst Governer[.] he is a good man. Please do me this favour. And If you can send me the Presidents message for 1859, or any other books you can conveniently. I remain sir your friend

Levi P Knerr[5]

Late Lieut Compy A Second Penn Regiment in the war with Mexico

ALS, DLC-JP.

1. Levi P. Knerr (b. c1823), native Pennsylvanian and Mexican War veteran, was a machinist. 1860 Census, Pa., Berks, 1063; Boyd's Directory of Reading (1860), 56; Levi Knerr, Mexican War, Compiled Service Record, RG94, National Archives.

2. On December 18 Crittenden earnestly appealed to his fellow senators to lay aside petty differences, for with "The life, the existence of our country" at stake, "we must elevate ourselves to all those considerations which belong to this high subject." A week earlier George E. Pugh of Ohio, during a spirited exchange with Iverson of Georgia, had minimized the slavery issue, insisting that if "ninety-nine hundredths" of those voters supporting Lincoln gave any thought to the "subject of slavery in the States," a majority would be opposed to interfering with the institution in southern states. Cong. Globe, 36 Cong., 2 Sess., 51, 113.

3. Benjamin Wade of Ohio, in an inflammatory speech on December 17, attacked those southern senators who expressed fear of the incoming Republican administration. Asserting, "You have had the legislative power of the country" and own the executive, cabinet, and Senate "as much as you own the servant upon your own plantation," he denied any Republican culpability which would justify overthrow of the government. Lane of Oregon, following Johnson on December 19, defended southern rights and the course pursued by South Carolina. Claiming that Lincoln's statements constituted a threat to slavery, he contended that the North had determined to limit its extension, a policy inimical to the South. Ibid., 101, 144.

4. The predictions of Republican opponents that Lincoln's election would paralyze economic activity seemed to be borne out when a period of severe unemployment and precipitous drops on the stock market followed. It was claimed that over six thousand mechanics in Cincinnati alone were discharged, and it was sardonically suggested that "the same good times are experienced by thousands of mechanics and laboring men in every city of the Union." Laborers, inclined to blame politicians on both sides, adopted resolutions at meetings in late December and early January supporting compromise. Such

meetings occurred in a number of Pennsylvania towns, among them Reading. Philip S. Foner, *Business and Slavery: The New York Merchants and the Irrepressible Conflict* (New York, 1968), 196, 208–10, 215–23; New York *Herald*, January 6, 1861; Potter, *Lincoln and His Party*, 118–19; John R. Commons and Associates, *History of Labour in the United States* (4 vols., New York, 1935–46), II, 10, 11–13; Emerson D. Fite, *Social and Industrial Conditions in the North during the Civil War* (New York, 1910), 86, 105–8.

5. A marginal note reads: "I am the only mechanic in Berks County so far as I know that is the owner of a Library. I have about five hundred vollumes[.] I am always anxious to get books[.]"

From Return J. Meigs[1]

Nashville, December, 23, 1860.

My Dear Sir:

As yet I have only seen a telegraphic report of your late speech in the Senate; *but*, presuming that the report is correct, in the main, I beg to express to you my sincere thanks for this effort to maintain inviolable the laws and constitution of our country. That constitution and those laws were made by the *people*, to whom you appeal, to preserve their lives, liberty and property, and to maintain social equality, tranquility and peace. And what they were made and established for, has been obtained, through their instrumentality, to an extent and with a success, unexampled in the history of the human race. The men who are now attempting to overthrow them, despise the people and hate the political constitution which recognises the equality of man to man. I love this constitution, because it does maintain this very equality, and because it secures to every individual, however humble or obscure, the natural rights of man intact, and opens to the whole mass of men the same carreer and the same hopes. Have not the very oligarchs and aristocrats, who now would destroy this glorious order of government, been enabled, under its fosterig protection, to elevate themselves to the positions which they now occupy, and which they are trying to abuse and to turn to the ruin of their fellow citizens! Let them rave, let them utter their threats of assassination against the man who dare to resist their conspiracy. While they rave and swear, believe me, Sir, that the champions of the people will be sustained by the people, who will not be slow to discern their friends & their enemies.

R. J. Meigs.

Hon. A. Johnson.

ALS, DLC-JP.

1. Return J. Meigs (1801–1891), lawyer and Kentucky native who moved to Athens, Tennessee, in 1823 and to Nashville in 1834, was state

attorney general and reporter of the supreme court (1838–39), United States attorney for Middle Tennessee (1841), Whig state senator (1847–48), and publisher of a *Digest* (1848–50) of Tennessee superior and supreme court decisions; with William F. Cooper he compiled the *Code of Tennessee* (1858). Censured for his unionism by neighbors in Nashville, where he had been state librarian (1856–61) and active in civic affairs, Meigs moved to New York in 1861 and subsequently to Washington to serve as clerk of the District of Columbia supreme court (1863–91). *DAB*, XII, 510–11.

From James O. Shackelford

December 23, 1860, Clarksville; ALS, DLC-JP.

Wishes to bury their former political differences "and look only to the common welfare" as expressed in "your late speech"; asserts that men of violence are seeking to overthrow the government while "the qui[e]t citizens keep silent rather than encounter them, and the impression is made on the public mind the masses are with them[.]" Observes that "Cave Johnson of our place has spoken out on the questions as a patriot and statesman."

From Henry G. Smith[1]

Memphis   Dec 23/60

Hon. Andrew Johnson—Dear Sir,

I think you will be glad to know how we stand in this City & vicinity, upon the Union question.

Great efforts are made here to excite & sustain the disunion feeling, and the men of that stripe are very noisy & confident & exulting. Last night they had a grand jollification & torch light procession. Persons who counted & whose accuracy may be relied on, say there were just 246 in the procession. I hear you were burned in effigy[2]— which of course, is a low & small affair. A very prevalent feeling exists among our citisens, that the Union will be dissolved. Never theless, my opinion is, that there are not 500 men here who wish the Union to be dissolved—not over that number who do not hope & wish that the controversy may be honorably settled & the Union preserved. The feeling is general, that the South suffers grievances from the North which must be redressed, and that the South must be allowed to enjoy & expand her slave institutions peacefully & securely, otherwise the Union will be dissolved. Nearly every body hopes & wishes that the controversy may be settled, in the Union, honorably & safely.

Last night 30 or 40 of the solid men of Memphis—I mean of political & social & moral power—met at my office, to arrange for a

Meeting next Thursday "of those who desire to make an earnest & honest effort, to preserve the Union by an adjustment of the sectional Strife, in such manner as will be consistent with rights, honor & safety of the South."[3] The meeting I think will represent full 4500 of the voting population of Memphis. Two motives are operating, however, adversely—the fear of encouraging the North by Union demonstrations, to persist in the Anti-Slavery movement—and second, an apprehension of a hostile feeling from Miss. which will be injurious to our trade.

For myself—I am wedded to no plan. Any adjustment will suit me which withdraws the negro from Federal action totally (save the Fugitive Act) & as to territory, a line North of which [is] for the North & South of which [is] for the South & our institutions[.] I think the negro question may & ought to be settled now. If not, it will sooner or later overthrow our government. I am unwilling to live in a perpetual strife about the elementary & fundamental social & domestic & industrial institution of my section of country—and while I am by no means sure there is not more peril to them out than in the Union, I am ready to go out rather than endure the agitation within— I prefer to endure the extinction of slavery by the pressure of the outside world, if that must be risked, than go through the subjugation & extinction within the Federal Union by our Northern people.

So far as I gather the points of your speech from the brief newspaper abstract, I concur with you—that the Federal Government cannot coerce a State, if that proposition have any sense in it— But the Federal Law acts on individuals, and is executed on individuals, & coerces individuals who resist—whether they resist of their own will, or under pretext of authority of the State in which they live. A State or its people have no other right to divest individuals residing or citisen in it, of the obligation to submit to Federal Law, than the revolutionary right of superior might.

But this is getting long. I only write, that you may know how we stand here.

Shew this to my excellent friend Avery.[4] Tell him, not to allow himself to be thrown off balance by the violence or excitement about him—not to allow himself to be misled as to the strength of movements here. I greatly doubt whether Tennessee will go out *under any circumstances existing now*—and certainly will not until the last possible hope expires of living peacefully & safely within—& not until Kentucky & Virginia lead. I do not think the movement of the Cotton States will carry her at all.

Any document of interest from you or Mr. Nicholson will at all times [be] acceptable— & when you have leisure I would be glad to hear from [you], though that of course I scarcely expect in the multitude of your engagments—

Very respectfully & Truly
Henry G Smith

ALS, DLC-JP.

1. Henry G. Smith (1807–1878), Connecticut native and tutor at the University of North Carolina (1830–32), lived for a short time in Somerville before settling in Memphis (c1842), where he practiced law. Although a Unionist, he was commissioned county judge to buy arms and military equipment for Confederate Tennessee (1861); under Federal occupation he was a city councilman. Appointed by Governor Brownlow to the state supreme court (1867–70), he later served one term in the state senate (1877–79). Robison, *Preliminary Directory, Shelby*, 153–54; John W. Green, *Lives of the Judges of the Supreme Court of Tennessee* (Knoxville, 1947), 133–34.

2. Angered by Johnson's Union speech, a Memphis mob gathered on Saturday night, December 22, to hang and burn him in effigy. Nashville *Union and American*, December 25, 1860.

3. This rally, described as the largest and most enthusiastic assemblage ever held in the city, met on December 27 and approved a resolution condemning hasty, ill-advised separation of the slave states, despite the threatened aggression from the North. Nashville *Patriot*, December 31, 1860.

4. William T. Avery, Tennessee congressman. See *Johnson Papers*, III, 457n.

From Walter S. Waldie[1]

December 23, 1860

Hon Andrew Johnston.
Senator from Tennessee.
Dr Sir.   It becomes the duty of every Citizen who truly loves his Country, to aid if possible those who are struggling to produce harmony amidst this unholy excitement, and regarding you as one of truest men in the Senate from the Slave states I have by this letter ventured to intrude some impressions my mind has received—not in the vain expectation of your adopting them, but in the hope that they may supply some tint towards the Coloring of a National picture.

The errors North & South are tolerably well balanced, & even if they are not, to adjust past grievances, even in *private* life is almost a hopeless task, and in National affairs is an impossibility. Let us therefore, bury the past and start fresh.

A principle once accepted should ever advance in its application as increased Means are offered— An Indian paddling his Canoe is the simplest expression of propelling, but Mechanical & Chemical laws Combined enable the Steamship to be the expression, of the Same principle. The United States government was founded to Create *Human Happiness*. This is its great Vital principle. When we Compare the Congress of Washington, & the extent of its Means, with the present developed Condition of the people—We find the early Congress had the true spirit with limited knowledge and our present Congress, with Ample Means but failing in spirit. The paddling Indian happier than the Steamb[oat] Captain[.] Beginning afresh to develope human happiness it is wise to examine the materials Composing our Nation, and as the South is an element, the most Conspicuous of the *three* elements of our Republic, I have anxiously expected some of its representatives would enter a plea in its behalf, which it is entitled to, (and which Many of the great minds of private life in your section acknowledge & hold as true) I Mean the holy aim & immense responsibility of the true purpose of African Slavery.

When this Country was in course of settlement, almost every known civilized power had some Colonies here, and when the Declaration of Independence pronounced "So let it be" the Bible became a live book and its teachings What the Carpenter of Nazareth, failed to do in Jerusalem. Here for the first time Could Man Worship under his own Vine & fig tree. The divinity in man became his own, & not dependent upon Pope & Parliament. Civilized emigration poured in —but Was Our Father undmindful of the dark, benighted African— How was he to be advanced, how could his Canoe Carry him to the promised land. Happily Mans Cupidity could be brought into good service, and the Slave Ship, cursed as its Cruelties seemed to deserve, became the Messinger of God. To the Southern portion of our Country, settled as it was almost entirely by Nobility of Europe, this element of labor became actually Necessary, and high toned as the early Southerners were, the imported or stolen African became a happier being than at home. An immediate Necessity for these Negroes, created what would not have been done in a Convention. But be this as it May—Thousands of African Race are today developed into a humanity they never could have attained at home,— Now the question arises have we enough of this Race to do the work of emancipating the Race at home— I think we have. but that is for the Southerner to say—Would you, feeling your responsibility to the Great Creator, be willing to assume the task of enslaving the African to become a light unto his feet?[2] To do this free from mercenary motives becomes a Christian, and if the true men of the South, (and I know there are many such) would boldly proclaim to the World that Slavery was not a mercenary nor a power loving Measure but a true philanthropic principle, and show they respected & would give rights as soon as they earned them, there would be no need of a fugitive slave law, for the Negro would be a fool to run away, and true men North would be compelled from love to humanity to return such a runaway as we do absconding apprentices. If Southern gentlemen will by their voice repudiate Such Scum as Clingman, Yancy Rhett, &c, Who have no motive beyond political power,—a response from the *North* will soon settle Sumner, Phillips, Garrison &c. South Carolina by her threats made thousands of votes for Lincoln. Puritan stock is not a *threatenable* article. The *true republican* party must be of Southern growth, this Northern one so-called, is a Tariff party, aided by Southern hot heads. Seven eighths of those who voted for Gen Taylor, voted for Lincoln— they supported the Southern slave holder—& the Northern Mechanic, for the integrity &firmness of their Characters[.] Social economy is today a developed Sceince, and in its teachings are to be found the true means of our National prosperity. I hope to live to see the day when the Cotton States will be selling their Cotton at four dollars a pound in fine muslins instead of 10¢—and Geogia become the great silk producer of the world. You of the South have more means of Creating wealth, than we have but as long as you permit outsiders to make more money by selling your Cotton than you do by raising, we are bound to get rich faster. Northern gentlemen will never compromise with Such as Yancey, but to the Southern gentlemen they will do all that such men ask. In the Name of our beloved Country and with grateful remembrances to our early patriots, do stir up this element of which you appear to be imbued with—

Very truly   Walter, S. Waldie
Philada Dec 23/60   112b Chestnut St.

P S. I have written to Senator Cameron[3] of this State, urging him to meet you, with the olive branch.

ALS, DLC-JP.

    1. Walter S. Waldie was a clerk for the Philadelphia Bank. *McElroy's Philadelphia Directory* (1859), 735.
    2. A paraphrase of Ps. 119:105.
    3. Simon Cameron, soon to become Lincoln's secretary of war. See *Johnson Papers*, I, 508n.

From Oliver P. Baer

December 24, 1860, Richmond, Ind.; ALS, DLC-JP.

A doctor hails Johnson's speech as "good leaven, that will leaven the whole lump. . . . *all* agree that it hit the nail on the head"; Wayne, a Free-Soil county, has no more than "6000 Loid Garrettsen or Windel Philips *men* . . . 'ranting Abolitionists,' and these are as much hated

by the great body of the Republican party as they can be by the south";
hopes "this crisis will effectually crush out Garisonianism & secessionism
and leave us to b[r]eathe once more the free air of American freedom."

From Job J. Harvey[1]

Near Panola Ill's Dec 24th 1860.

Hon. Andrew Johnson—

My Dear Sir; Feeling the deepest possible interest in the preservation of our Glorious Constitution and Union, I take the liberty of
addressing you with a few lines.

Your position to "fight the Battles of the Union *within* the Union"
is the right one. Stand by the Union & do not let any State go out if
you can help it peaceably. But if the Abolitionists force division upon
us, I think division will not stop with a Southern & Northern Confederacy, but there will be a Western Division which I believe would
ultimately by sympathy & the natural laws of trade join the South
and leave Negro-worshiping N. England to her self when Mass
school of Politi[ci]ans would come to their senses.— But save the
Union, by all means save the Union.

I am very anxious to assure Our Southern Brethren that they have
thosands and tens of thousands of whole hearted friends at the North
who have done, & will do all they possibly can to secure them in
their Constitutional rights. I think it would be well to call a National Convention at once. Do you not think that could settle the
trouble for ever? I should like Chrittenden's amendment to the Constitution to prevail, with a further amendment added, *requiring* a
majority of all the votes cast North & South to elect Prest. & V.
President— Please suggest this. If this had been required from the
first it would have prevented the present sectional triumph— And
even now although it is admitted that the forms of the Constitution
and Laws have been generally complied with, at the late Election, I
think this is not true of Ohio, N. York, and Mass.—because in these
three states Negros were allowed to vote for President.[2] I contend
that this was not Constitutional, because the Supreme Court has decided that "Negros are not & cannot be citizens of the U. S."—[3]
Therefore Negroes cannot vote for U. States officers, Hence the
election of Nov 6,/60 in the three states named for Congressmen,
Prest. & vice Prest. is unconstitutional & should be overthrown &
Lincoln defeated. I suppose this should be looked into and finally
accomplished when Congress will count the votes in Feb next. For
God sake let the forms of the Constitution and Laws be more fully
observed in this particular than they have been in the case of negro
suffrage. There is no end of the frauds that the Abolition Republican

Nullifiers have committed at the late election, but we cannot get at any of them so well as in the cases named. And I believe those are sufficient to reach the point & defeat sectionalism at last. Oh how my soul would rejoice to see this effected according to the Constitution and laws. Grant it oh my God, for I believe it would be just in thy sight, to prevent those infamous hypocrits from exercising power in this Government, obtained by fraud[.] Mr Collamor is entirely wrong when he says that the Supreme Court decided that a "Negro had no rights a Whiteman was bound to respect."[4] The Court on that point simply states a Historical fact in relation to the "*Opinion*" of the civilised world touching the rights of the negro. Not saying *that* was the Opinion of the Court, but the opinion of Nations or the world, expressed for many years, (by their treatment of the negro, and otherwise)[.]

I am personally acquainted with Lincoln & regard him as a whole hearted Abolitionist & yet without moral honesty or courage to admit it. He is a great hypocrite, as his debates with Douglas show. In 58 he was forced to take all sides & assume all phases of the Negro, question just according to location. He has some cunning of a low vulgar order, is a fool wit Assuming that our Fathers included the Negro in the Declaration "that all men are created equal," and knowing at the same time that those Fathers made constitutional provision for the continuance of the Slave trade 32 yrs after July 4, 76: Knowing also that those Fathers made constitutional provision for the Fugitive slave law.[5] And yet this booby contends that the Negro slave was included in that[.] Oh my soul! how mortifying the result of the late election. Lincoln is a Tory, see his course on the Mex. War,—[6] I am sure you will accept my suggestions in the same spirit of kindness & patriotism I write them. I am a humble farmer & am anxious for my country. Please write me if there is any hope for Peace. Send me Speeches Documents &c &c and oblige   your friend

J. J. Harvey

ALS, DLC-JP.

1. Job J. Harvey (b. *c*1809), a native Pennsylvanian, was a farmer with $4,500 in real estate and $800 in personal property. 1860 Census, Ill., Woodford, 774.

2. Although the Ohio constitution specified that only "white male" citizens were franchised, during the 1850's there was considerable support in the legislature for Negro suffrage and the state courts had ruled that certain persons of mixed blood were to be considered citizens and allowed to vote; in practice such mulattos had been voting in strongly Free-Soil districts. In New York after 1821 strict property qualifications attached to Negro suffrage restricted, but did not prohibit, the franchise. These provisions were under constant attack during the prewar decade, but a referendum for equal suffrage was voted down in 1860. Although Massachusetts passed a literacy requirement in 1856, anyone previously registered to vote was excluded, and there

was no color bar in the elective process. Emil Olbrich, "The Development of Sentiment on Negro Suffrage to 1860," in *Bulletin of the University of Wisconsin, History Series*, III (Madison, 1912), 15–17, 22, 30, 36–39, 72–78, 103–5, 123–27; *The Constitutions of the Several States . . . in the Year 1859* (New York, [1879]), 113, 145–56, 401; Eric Foner, *Free Soil, Free Labor, Free Men: The Ideology of the Republican Party before the Civil War* (New York, 1970), 285, 286, 293.

3. The Supreme Court, in denying that Dred Scott was a citizen, opened the door to the interpretation that Negroes could not be citizens. Nevins, *Emergence of Lincoln*, I, 92.

4. A few days earlier, in an exchange with Johnson about Vermont's fugitive slave laws, Jacob Collamer had asserted, "our people understood the Supreme Court to say, that a colored man, a descendant of an African, is a man without any rights that any white person is bound to respect at all." *Cong. Globe*, 35 Cong., 2 Sess., 120. For Collamer, see *Johnson Papers*, I, 324n.

5. Art. IV, Sec. 2, declares that "no person held to service or labor in one State, under the laws thereof, escaping into another, shall . . . be discharged . . . but shall be delivered upon claim of the party to whom such service or labor may be due." This particular clause was superseded by the Thirteenth Amendment in 1865.

6. Lincoln, convinced that the soil upon which American blood had been shed was not American but Mexican and that Polk, in sending troops into the disputed territory, had provoked Mexico into an aggressive act, had opposed the Democratic administration's war; nevertheless, once the United States was formally at war, he supported the legislative measures necessary for its conduct. Roy P. Basler, ed., *The Collected Works of Abraham Lincoln* (8 vols., New Brunswick, N. J., 1953–55), I, 420–22, 451–52, 457–58; IV, 66.

From Sam Milligan[1]

Greeneville Ten
Dember 24. 1860

Confidential

Dear Governor,

I have not Seen your speech—not even a synopsis of your positions; but I have seen by the letter-writers that you took ground for coercing the south into submission.

I do not pretend to know what your position really is on this subject, and will not therefore attempt either to condemn or approve it.

But it seems to me without fully investigating the question, if Secession is revolution, there must be a power *inherent* in the Government to suppress it. The power is admitted, I suppose, to exist in the Federal Government, to suppress insurrection, and revolution in the citizens of a State or states, but as it is Contended, this power does not exist to suppress revolutionary action in a State. Why is this distinction? I have not seen any valid reason for it. The argument, I believe is, that the Federal Government can not declair war against a State. This is true, but I understand it to mean—A *Con-*

federated, and not a *revolted* State. One in the Union, and not one out of it.— Suppose some One State had refused to ratify the Constitution, and never come into the Union, would the Confederated States have had no power, for any offence, to have declaired war against it? I suppose that will not be Contended. What then is the difference, when one state, after she has ratified the Constitution, has disannuled it, and shaken off all her allegiance to it? Is she in any better condition than she would have been, if she had never ratified it? I do not see that she is; but in my opinion, she is in even a worse condition. She has broken her faith with the federal government, (if it be revolution to secede)—violated its laws; and cut off its revenues, and imperiled the peace and security of all the other states. Nor can this be done with impunity; or is it discretionary with the president whether he enforces submission or not? If any law is violated, any power usurped, any revenue cut off, or the security of any portion of the people imperiled, it is not the duty of the President to exercise any discretion about it, but he is bound to vindicate the law, protect the revenue and secure the rights of the people under the Constitution. The law is one thing; and the consequences another. The President should attend to the one, and God will look after the other.

This is the way the thing seems to be at present, without as I before stated having investigated it. And I suppose if the public mind was calm, and all our public men, perfectly disconnected with the excitement of the day, and as devoted to the Union and its constitution as our fathers were, there would be no diversity of opinion on the subject. Popular enthusiasm sometimes sways men's judgments, and they really see things in a light, which they have never seen before. In fact, they see them when they have never seen them before, and never will again, when the flare of popular enthusiasm has gone out. This I fear is too much the case with many of our public men now.

Your resolutions amendatory of the constitution, seems to cover the whole question; and if the slavey agitation was the cause of Secession, they ought to settle that question. But I fear it alone is not the cause. It is, I fear, only the pretext, and there are other objects undisclosed to be obtained by a disolution. But be it what it may, I feel well assured that there can be no secession or revolution without blood-shed. That would be an anomaly in the history of all revolutions. There never has been one without blood-shed, and I feel sure we will not be an exception to the general rule.

Send me out any thing you think would be of interest, and almost any thing will be—

I write hastily and without much consideration, hoping that by even a hasty effusion, I may get off some straggling idea which you can improve & make useful—

Your friend   Sam Milligan

ALS, DLC-JP.

1. See *Johnson Papers*, I, 114n.

From Stewart Pearce

December 24, 1860, Wilkes-Barre, Pa.; ALS, DLC-JP.

Favors a constitutional amendment providing "That no state or number of states shall ever secede from the Union without the Consenet of *three fourths* of all the states"; would also restore Missouri Compromise line and extend it to California, repeal the requirement of the Fugitive Slave Law that a citizen assist in arrest, forbid "anxation of any territory except by purchase and the consenet of three fourths or two thirds of both houses of Congress," and stipulate "that no negro should ever become Elegible as a voter juror or office holder in any of the states—."

From Alfred Williams

December 24, 1860, Circleville, Ohio; ALS, DLC-JP.

Johnson's speech "meets with the universal approbation of all men of all parties in Ohio[.]" Let the South "fight her battles in the Union. . . . no party can ever be successful in the North which desires in the least to interfere with the Constitutional rights of the South. Mr. Lincoln was elected by the conservative people of the North," and should he "infring upon the rights of the South . . . he would be at once almost unanomously repudiated by those who Supported him in November."

From Reuben F. Alexander

December 25, 1860, Memphis; ALS, DLC-JP.

A carpenter, describing Johnson's being burned in effigy in his city, assures him that the deed was done by a "contemptuable monority of our citizens," while the "masses are with you," as well as "the yeoman[r]y the Hardy sons of toile"; promises that the "conservativ[e] element," who plan a meeting, "will send the Secessionist[s] Howling from the field."

From John T. Blain

December 25, 1860, Columbus, Ohio; ALS, DLC-JP.

Ohio Democrat endorsing Johnson as "a true lover of our common country," avers, "if your counsels prevail, peace will again reign over our land, and in four years Lincoln & his coherts will be hurled from power, with the reigns of governmt in the hands of our noble Democracy."

From William Gammon[1]

Blountville Decr. 25 1860

Hon Andrew Johnson
Dear Sir

I saw on yesterday, a daily Globe containing the last part of your late Speech in the Senate but cannot get hold of the first part[.][2] I write to ask the favor of you to send me a full copy of it. I am well pleased with your positions so far as I have seen them and think you have taken the right position according to my judgment[.] Altho the sentiments of your Speech meet my approbation I am sorry to say, that from some remarks from some of our leading democrats which I have heard that they will oppose the views which you entertain[.] I mention this last opinion in confidence to you that you may have some Idea of what is going on here. I understand that the Editor of the Bristol News[3] intends to comment upon it, but I have for some months and do now look upon him as also the Editors of the Union and American[4] as being in favor of Secession. I think your Speech if generally circulated among the people would do much good in settling down public opinion on the right doctrine. Will you also send me Mr Pughs late Speech in the Senate,[5] and also one of Judge Douglas' when made. Where are we drifting! What are we to do! What is to be the result of this movement! and what is to become of us as a nation. Will you give me your views on these points[?] Yours Very Sincerely

Wm. Gammon

P S. I am a Subscriber to the States & Union[6] but have not rcd a paper in three weeks. Will you see them & know the reason[?]

WmG[7]

ALS, DLC-JP.

1. William Gammon (b. c1808) was a Blountville merchant with property worth $5,800. 1860 Census, Tenn., Sullivan, Blountville, 5th Dist., 74.

2. Johnson's Speech on Secession, delivered on December 18 and 19, had appeared in two issues of the *Daily Globe*, a publication of the congressional debates in newspaper form, edited by John C. Rives.

3. J. Austin Sperry, editor of the weekly Bristol *News* (1858–62) and a staunch secessionist, was later editor of the Knoxville *Register* until forced to suspend publication and flee for his life by the approach of Burnside in August, 1863. His Confederate sympathies earned him the unremitting enmity of Parson Brownlow, who fumed when Sperry was acquitted of treason charges late in 1865. Oliver Taylor, *Historic Sullivan* (Bristol, 1909), 299; Moses White, East Tennessee Journalism (Typescript, University of Tennessee Library), 8; E. Merton Coulter, *William G. Brownlow: Fighting Parson of the Southern Highlands* (Chapel Hill, 1937), 274.

4. In December, 1860, the Nashville *Union and American*, a former Breckinridge organ, bore the imprimature of John C. Burch, Leon Trousdale, Thomas S. Marr, and Francis C. Dunnington. Burch had been a prominent Democratic politician and legislator before embarking upon a career in journalism. Leonidas Trousdale (1823–*fl*1888), native of Robertson County and graduate of East Tennessee University (1841), migrated to Carroll County, Mississippi, and served under Jefferson Davis in the Mexican War. After several small publishing ventures in Mississippi, Arkansas, and Tennessee, he moved to Memphis, becoming part owner and coeditor of the Memphis *Appeal*. Following a dispute over editorial policy during the 1860 election, Trousdale left the *Appeal* for a similar situation with the *Union and American*. Aide-de-camp to Governor Isham G. Harris and a participant in the Chickamauga campaign, Trousdale edited the itinerant Chattanooga *Rebel*, publishing irregular editions at various locations just ahead of Federal troops marching south. After the war he published the Memphis *Commercial* briefly and for a time rejoined the *Appeal*. Later, he was appointed state superintendent of public instruction (1875–81) and surveyor of customs for the Port of Nashville in 1885. Marr (*fl*1880), Virginia-born, settled in Nashville in 1853, joining Trousdale in 1860 to purchase an interest in the *Union and American* which, together with other Confederate Nashville newspapers, ceased publication after the fall of Ft. Donelson in February, 1862. With the Federal occupation of Nashville and the passage of the National Banking Act of 1863, Marr became president of the federally–chartered Nashville Savings Company. Dunnington, a longtime political friend of Johnson, had been editor of the *Union and American* as early as 1856. Wooldridge, *History of Nashville*, 347; Wilbur F. Creighton, *Building of Nashville* (Nashville, 1969), 157; Clayton, *Davidson County*, 494; Speer, *Prominent Tennesseans*, 480–82. See also *Johnson Papers*, III, 204*n.*, 8*n.*

5. George E. Pugh of Ohio had spoken at some length on December 10. *Cong. Globe*, 36 Cong., 2 Sess., 33–35.

6. The Washington *States and Union* (April, 1857–April, 1861) was a Douglas organ until Lincoln's election, when it raised the standard of disunion "as a last hope of getting money out of some body," according to the Washington *Evening Star*. Wilhelmus B. Bryan, *A History of the National Capital* (2 vols., New York, 1916), II, 462.

7. A month later Gammon wrote asserting his unionism but declaring, "when all fails if we have to go let us go unitedly and peacably." Gammon to Johnson, January 22, 1861, Johnson Papers, LC.

From Samuel J. Pooley[1]

Liberty Corner somerset County
Dec the 25th 1860

Hon Andrew Johnson
Washington—
My dear sir,

I have seldom read a speech, of a public character, that gave me greater pleasure than yours, delivered in the United States Senate on the 19th Inst, on the subject of "Resolutions proposing amendments, to the Constitution,"

Of course we in the North, are surprised at the Opinion of the President on the great & vital question, touching the integrity of the union. If the President's reasoning is correct, then indeed "is the union, but a rope of sand,"[2] because each member at any moment, regardless of the circumstances which the nation might be placed in, could secede at pleasure. Can it be possible that the framers of the Instrument of union, could, have forgotten so important a requisite in their work, so essential to give its virtues permanency, & their posterity, the substantial fruits, of its blessings. I have always thought that our Fathers designed the instrument in question to be permanent & lasting, or else why have left, powers in Congress, to repeal an obnoxious law, & the United States Court, to hear & adjudicate causes touching their Constitutional powers &c.

An advocate as I have ever been of "State Rights," yet I have never forgotten that the United states had rights that should be upheld & supported with equal fidelity to those of the states. Indeed I have thought that the states could not long support, or preserve their independence, without upholding, in its fullest integrity, the strong & protecting arms, of the Federal union. By the bye, the great & I think in the end utopian view, of South Carolina (the leading state in the secession movement) is "That Cotton is King."[3] Those of us, that can remember, thirty to thirty-five years ago, recollect how Cooper[4] MacDuffie[5] &c advocated & upheld this idea. The result is, that this idea, has now permeated the whole state, hence her precipitate action, at Charleston, the other day. Of course this is to be supported by a policy of Free trade. Then South Carolina will become the El-dorado, all the Gold & silver, already coined, will be attracted by "King Cotton" to Charleston & her co-confederates[.] King Cotton, will then command "the Purse & the sword."[6] The great elements of peace & of war, will rest entirely in their hands. Well, well I think that some of our sothern Brethen, "have counted the chickens, before they are hatched."[7] I hope on seecession that our Brethen at the south will reflect deeply, on the subject & not blindly rush into "ills, they know not of."[8] The northern mind is ready to hear their complaints & will if a bill of grievances is presented to their several legislatures, in the form as suggested by Stephens, of Geo,[9] accept it favorably, & remove from their statutes all acts in conflict, with their obligations, letter & spirit of the general Constitution.

Yours very Respectfully
Samuel James Pooley

ALS, DLC-JP.

1. See *Johnson Papers*, III, 563n.

2. See Speech on Secession, December 18–19, 1860, note 15.

3. In speaking before the Senate in March, 1858, James H. Hammond of South Carolina had declared, "You dare not make war on cotton. Cotton is King." *Cong. Globe*, 35 Cong., 1 Sess., 961.

4. Thomas Cooper (1759–1839), president of South Carolina College

(1820–39), was a political economist and pamphleteer whose views strongly influenced the militant South Carolina leaders of the 1850's. An English-born reformer and political agitator, he migrated to Pennsylvania in 1794, embraced Jeffersonian principles, and, after teaching at Carlisle and the University of Pennsylvania, moved to South Carolina. Abandoning his earlier social philosophy, he viewed the Negro as naturally inferior and became an ardent defender of slavery and of the South's economic system, his published defense of the institution appearing in the November, 1835, issue of the *Southern Literary Journal*. Favoring nullification, he urged South Carolina to "calculate the value of the Union." *DAB*, IV, 414–16; Dumas Malone, *The Public Life of Thomas Cooper, 1783–1839* (Columbia, S. C., 1961), 387.

5. George McDuffie (1790–1851), South Carolina legislator (1818–20), Democratic congressman (1821–34), governor (1834–36), and senator (1842–46), was in early years a strong nationalist who subsequently became an ardent state rightist and one of the foremost advocates of nullification. *DAB*, XII, 34–36; *BDAC*, 1296.

6. During the debates in the New York convention to ratify the Constitution, Melancton Smith, a delegate from Dutchess County arguing against adoption, claimed the instrument gave to Congress too much power over "both the purse and the sword." The expression became a catch phrase during the discussions. Jonathan Elliot, comp., *Debates in the Several State Conventions on the Adoption of the Federal Constitution* (4 vols., Washington, D. C., 1836), II, 229, 233, 271.

7. An ancient and very popular proverb; one of the earliest versions occurs in Aesop's fable about the milkmaid and her pail: "Do not count your chickens before they are hatched."

8. Paraphrase of Shakespeare, *Hamlet*, Act III, sc. 1.

9. On November 14, Alexander H. Stephens, addressing the Georgia legislature, then considering a call for a secession convention, suggested that the South demand the repeal of northern personal liberty laws. For states refusing to rescind the offensive legislation, he urged, "Let your Committee on the State of the Republic make out a bill of grievances; let it be sent by the Governor to those faithless States, and if reason and argument shall be tried in vain . . . I would be for retaliatory measures." Moore, *Rebellion Record*, I, Doc., 225.

From Hiram S. Smith[1]

Mobile   26th Decr 1860

Hon. A Johnson
Dr Sir

I notice with much regret that you in a speech recently delivered in the U S Senate denied the right of Secession and urged coercion against any seceding state or states[.] Allow me to say that no man having a drop of southern blood in his veins would openly proclaim such doctrines. And allow me further to say that I consider you a *traitor to your country* And that you should receive your just deserts, which is the penalty that was given the tories in 1776. I must think that the state of Tennessee which you represent but disgrace has patriotism enough to mete out to you in due time the reward your conduct justly merits[.] This state will secede. and I would hail the hour with rejoicing to see you head an army to coerce her. You in the foremost ranks. I would like to meet you[.] I would consider that I had rid the country of an enemy, by spilling your hearts blood[.] I cannot I have not words to express my utter Contempt for any man occupying your position who would recommend coercion against his fellow man who was doing nothing more than Constitutionally defending their homes their wives their children & honor. I take the occasion to say that at a proper time your case shall receive due attention[.]

I remain Yours   H S Smith

ALS, DLC-JP.

1. Hiram S. Smith was a partner in Walsh, Smith and Company, cotton factors. Interestingly enough, this is one of the few adverse southern letters to be found in the Johnson Papers. *Farrow's and Dennett's Mobile Directory* (1859), unpaged.

From Richard K. Anderson

December 27, 1860, St. Louis, Mo.; ALS, DLC-JP.

Applauds "staunch Jackson union common sense speech" and declares that "the people of the North West . . . are beginning to regard Andrew Johnson as the 'Coming Man'" with a "through ticket" to the White House in 1864. Urges him "to stand fast and fight for the Union," since "the North will render justice . . . radicalism will be buried—the South appeased—and peace restored if these South Carolina Traitors can be prevented from dragging the Tobacco states with them this winter."

From N. F. Gad

December 27, 1860, Aberdeen County, Ohio; ALS, DLC-JP.

Charges that the northern clergy, having preached the "abolishon doctren for twenty-five years, has done more toward braking this greate republick then all the pestlance and fammons has ever done"; defends the slaveowner's right to recapture his servant.

From Daniel Keller[1]

Middletown Frederick County Md.
Dec 27th, 1860

To Hon Andrew Johnson (U. S. S.
Dear Sir.

Having Seen a few extracts from your Speech delivered during this Session on the State of the Country or rather opposed to disunion, for you deserve all the Honors due to mortals, in reading your views & determinations I came to the conclusion to write for the full speech if it can be had from you. we are for the Union and hope Rattlesnakes[2] will not succeed in their mad career in threats and Bullying. But the worst of this matter seems to be the old thing at the other end of the avenue has encouraged this Infernal bussines in his Message & in his actions Since, that silly paper was publised.[3] why did he not man the Forts, we think he stands a perjured villain before the whole World in not enforcing the Laws and in not supporting the Constution[.] we are almost sometimes led to believe that the matter has been understood between the traitors of our Country on all sides[.] Benedict Arnold could have done no worse. we are for the union at all hazards and if a separation should succeed, and old Maryland should be dragged over to the Cotton States she can never be held there[.] slavery is merely nominal in this state, only 5 or 6 strong slaveholding [counties] in the state out of 21.[4] all the Border counties are in a transition state for gradual emancipation though seem to be indifferent in the matter for the present[.] I saw in some of the papers that you was Burned in effigy by of course some of the tories of our Common country (S. C.) Rattlesnakes[.] you talk as a man who has a heart and that in the right place. you talk and reason as a man of good sense and not as a madman, or tory, who seem to be plenty at this time[.] we are rather inclined to think there will be a separation and as a natural result a war[.] we view the matter in this light[.] the Republicans have succeeded in electing their President by a heavy majority,[5] and as good Citizens always have done the majority get the advantage of the government patronage and one of the leading features or objections against the incoming Administration is that they are opposed to the extension of slavery into Free territory a principle we find by examining the Archives of our government has been carried out since Jeffersons ordinance of 1787 was adopted and passed over the great Northwestern territory and approved by all our great and good men up to the Administration of James K. Polk who signed the Oregon Bill with said proviso prohibiting slavery. enough for the present[.] we intend if spared in a few weeks of paying you a visit and any thing you may feel disposed to communicate shall be in strict Confidence. this the same to you[.] if you shall have any of your speeches for distribution Franked we will attend to the matter and will be thankfully received[.]

Yours most Respectfully
Daniel Keller (M. D.)

ALS, DLC-JP.

1. Daniel Keller (b. c1810), Maryland native, was a physician with $10,000 in real and $5,500 in personal property. 1860 Census, Md., Frederick, 279.

2. During the Revolution, South Carolinians had flown a naval flag of "red and blue stripes adorned with a rattlesnake"; now they were displaying a banner with a rattlesnake coiled around the traditional palmetto. *Encyclopaedia Britannica* (1971 ed.), IX, 402; Benson J. Lossing, *Pictorial History of the Civil War* . . . (3 vols., Philadelphia, 1874–77), I, 49, 106.

3. A reference to President Buchanan and his annual message of December 3, in which "the old thing" blamed the North for bringing on the crisis by threatening southern institutions. Denying the right of secession, he nonetheless disavowed the right of coercion, although he conceded the federal government had the responsibility to enforce the laws. Buchanan, hoping to avert war, and vacillating about manning the forts, had adopted a *status quo* position. At the time most of his countrymen agreed; there were others who felt his actions justified impeachment. His sanction of Interior Secretary Jacob Thompson's acting as commissioner from Mississippi to North Carolina, his refusal to adopt Gen. Winfield Scott's proposals for military measures, and persistent rumors that he would yield to South Carolina commissioners convinced many northerners that his actions bordered on treason. Klein, *James Buchanan*, 370–74; Richardson, *Messages*, V, 626–59; Stampp, *And the War Came*, 53–57; New York *Tribune*, December 5, 1860; Cincinnati *Enquirer*, December 5, 1860; Nashville *Union and American*, December 16, 1860.

4. According to the Census of 1860, Maryland had a population of 515,918 whites, 83,942 free Negroes, and 87,189 slaves, and only in Prince Georges and Charles were whites outnumbered by slaves; these counties, together with Anne Arundel, St. Marys, Montgomery, and Somerset, held over half the slaves. Joseph C. G. Kennedy, comp., *Population of the United States in 1860 . . . the Eighth Census* (4 vols., Washington, D. C., 1864–66), I, 211, 213.

5. Perhaps Lincoln's electoral vote of 180, as compared with 123 for his three opponents, might be considered a "heavy majority"; however, the popular vote of 1,866,452–2,815,617 reveals quite a different story. Nevins, *Emergence of Lincoln*, II, 313.

From John S. Craig

December 28, 1860, Maryville; ALS, DLC-JP.

Requests Johnson to send recent speech to forty-six residents of Maryville, Ellijay, Morganton, Unitia, and Louisville, some of whom have disunionist leanings. Secessionists have passed resolutions "denouncing your course, and charging you with going over to the Republicans, because you defend the right of coercion. . . . But a man who was at the meeting took down the names of the voters, and, *all-told*, they numbered a little over twenty, and not *twelve* of them for secession."

From Hu Douglas[1]

Nashville 28th Dec 1860

Hon And Johnson
My Dear Sir

I have just recivd yr speech. I thank you for it. I have not read it, but will to night. I have looked over it. I find nothing to Condemn, much to approve.

You have been much abused, slandered and, I think already some are ashamed of themselves. Some have threatened to throw you overboard, excommunicate you from the Democratic Party. You know the material of which that Party is composed here[.] You know them well, I am not of them. I am no Democrat, like yr Democratic president[.] if I had any Democratic blood in my veins I would let [it] out.

When I see you I will tell you much. I may write you again soon[.] I shall be glad to hear from you. I have a violent ultra Democrat readg yr Speech now to find fault with it. I refused to read until I had it either from you or the Intelligencer[.]

Yr frnd   Hu Douglas

ALS, DLC-JP.

1. See *Johnson Papers*, I, 21*n*; see also George H. Armistead, Jr., " 'He Is a Great Rascal': A Sketch of Byrd Douglas," *Tenn. Hist. Quar.*, XXVII (1968), 37–39.

From James W. Harold[1]

Greeneville Tenn December 28th 1860

Gov Johnson,
Dear Sir

I drop a line merely to give you some little information as regards the sayings and doings about this little town. the first of the week your friends were thunderstruck with articles that appeared in *Nashville* & *Memphis* papers & some here were complaining to wit Old Boyce Biggs[2] &c. we told them to hold still & wait for the wagon[3] untill they could see the entire speech. well sure Enough we read the speech the one you sent me is about wore out. I have not read it myself yet. only a portion of it, never had any thing to suit me better in my Life[.] tis the *verry* thing[.] tis the only grounds for an honest impartial statesman that loves his Country to take and the only grounds to take to attain any portion of what the south Contends for, I here of Burning in Effigee &c below here, *Great God* if it has come to this. that the Sentiments Endorsed or Contained in that speech, cant be Endorsed by Every Lover of his Country tis time that God almighty should visit some portion of it with his wrath. Tis not so here thank fortune, the most Ultra as far I have heard Express themselves say tis an able Effort.—and nothing that any could object to and others are delighted say tis thee, Great Effort of the age[.] we will have no Burnt Effigies here to give us light to walk by as in the case of John Tyler.[4]

for your friends are over, Joyd. & the opposition say tis the thing that is the Respectable position, G Jones[5] &c well pleased— Mc-Dowell[6] delighted with it— *Litle Bob McKorkle*,[7] may object[.] he has turned a summerset recently got verry southron all at once / McDannel[8] says tis the thing all *over*[.] if there is & I suppose there are some, that would like to pull down this government & go to Experimenting Prehaps such would not like your speech for tis a thousand brick upon their heads[.]

Tis the thing & no mistake[.]

I hope all may yet be well[.]

Your Friend   James, W. Harold

ALS, DLC-JP.

1. See *Johnson Papers*, I, 110n.
2. For William Boyce and Elbert Biggs, see *ibid.*, I, 422n; II, 391n.
3. "Wait for the wagon and we'll all take a ride" is the final line of the chorus in the traditional fiddle tune or square dance song "Wait for the Wagon." Ira W. Ford, *Traditional Music of America* (New York, 1940), 119, 422.
4. In August, 1841, a few nights after Tyler's veto of the national bank bill, a noisy mob gathered at the White House to protest. Although this group was frightened away, the President was burned in effigy "near the White House" the following night. Chitwood, *John Tyler*, 228–29; Oscar D. Lambert, *Presidential Politics in the United States 1841–1844* (Durham, N. C., 1936), 37.
5. For George Jones, Greeneville merchant, see *Johnson Papers*, I, 275n.
6. James P. McDowell (*c*1830–*fl*1870), a Virginia-born Greeneville merchant who served in the Tennessee house (1861–62), possessed in 1860 $6,550 in real and $18,500 in personal property. 1860 Census, Tenn., Greene, 10th Dist., 93; Robison Biographical Data.
7. Robert McCorkle (b. *c*1833) was a Greeneville merchant with $2,500 in real estate and $14,800 in personal property. *Ibid.*
8. For Blackston McDannel, see *Johnson Papers*, I, 184n.

From Samuel P. Tipton[1]

Summerfield, Illinoise
Dec the 28/60

Hon Andrew Johnson
Dear Sir

I write you this leter from the facte that I am a Tennessee my self was rased in Carter County & [k]now you from caracter[.] I moved to this state last October & I am a Invoalead pensoner from the Mexican ware from the state of N Carolina & refure you to T L Clingman fer my jenrel Caracter or Mr. Vance[.][2] my pensan Certificate was ishued on th 19 of January 1858[.] I was discharged as a Invalead which the papers in the pensan office will show in my case[.] Maj Stokes[3] certifies to that Efect[.]

now in justice to Invaleds that did not aply for a pensan as soon as dis charged which trid Ever means to be Curd of the diseas which they had contracte in Mexic & spent all they had & faild & nothing lefte But a broken Constitutio ther pay should comence from the date of ther Discharg from the army & as Congress pased a law fer Invoaleads before the Close of the Mexican war but did not so instructe the Comisenr of Pensans to date back it requers a bill to cover ther cases & beleaving thate frome you publick acts thate you will have a bill pased dating all Mexica Invalead Certifficts for Discharg from the army which I think is justice to them[.]

I am now living in this state bute if there is a disolution of this Union I goe south a gain[.]

The Democrats & Whigs her are all for the presavation of the Union, on homerabe principles but in cas of a disolution they ar all united with the south & I would note bee surprised if this state is Divided unless the Northren parte agrees to goe south[.] I live in the southern parte & the proment Democrats & Whigs whch United has largly the Majority will Certinly strike for the south[.]

Mr Lincon Vote was prinseple Fureners with a few desinig Amricans[4] & I asure you the Republicans has already regreted ther cours & if the Election was to take place here to day Lincon would bee fare behind all the candidats in the south parte of this state[.]

You cours meets the aprobation of Both Whigs & Demoats here with regard to the Unio[.] I have writen a much longer leter than I first contemplated but the love for this Glorious union has draw it out[.] let me hear from you[.]

your Truly & the Union S. P. Tipton

ALS, DLC-JP.

1. Samuel Tipton (b. c1806) was a Tennessee-born farmer who had served in the Mexican War as captain of a North Carolina infantry company; early in 1861 he would seek Johnson's aid for a mail agency on the Mississippi and Ohio Railroad. 1850 Census, Tenn., Carter, 389; Heitman, *Register*, II, 70; Tipton to Johnson, March 15, 1861, Johnson Papers, LC.

2. For Thomas L. Clingman, see *Johnson Papers*, I, 185n. Zebulon B. Vance (1830–1894) was a North Carolina lawyer, member of the house of commons (1854), Democratic congressman (1858–61), Confederate army officer (1861–62), governor (1862–66, 1876–78), and senator (1879–94). *DAB*, XIX, 158–61; *BDAC*, 1745; see also Glenn Tucker, *Zeb Vance: Champion of Personal Freedom* (New York, 1965) and Frontis W. Johnston, ed., *The Papers of Zebulon Baird Vance* (1 vol., Raleigh, N. C., 1963–   ).

3. Montford S. Stokes commanded a North Carolina infantry regiment in the Mexican War. Heitman, *Register*, II, 69.

4. Traditionally, historians have held that Lincoln could not have been elected in 1860 without the Midwest's foreign-born vote. Recent studies conclude that, while the effect of the German vote upon the outcome of the election is a matter of conjecture, the Republicans "oriented their appeals toward the Germans, mounted a special campaign to reach them, and adjusted the party platform in the immigrants' favor because they never considered them

'safe.' " Thus, because of their potential voting strength, the Germans were able to influence the campaign and the election. The other large ethnic group, the Irish, were principally Democratic. James M. Bergquist, "People and Politics in Transition: The Illinois Germans, 1850–60," in Frederick C. Luebke, ed., *Ethnic Voters and the Election of Lincoln* (Lincoln, Nebr., 1971), 225–26; Foner, *Free Soil, Free Labor, Free Men*, 259; Carl Wittke, *The Irish in America* (Baton Rouge, 1956), 106.

From N. M. Ellis

December 29, 1860, Phoenixville, Pa.; ALS, DLC-JP.

A Union Democrat insists that Lincoln has not been legally elected, inasmuch as black men voted in Ohio and Massachusetts despite the Supreme Court's Dred Scott dictum that the Negro is not a citizen under the Constitution.

From J[ames?] M. Jones[1]

Corinth Miss. Dec. 29th/60

Senator Andrew Johnson

Dear Sir: An apology might be due for this intrusion, being a stranger and a citizen of another state than the one you represent, if it was not that your recent speech in the senate and for which you have been so extensively denounced, demands of the friends of Constitutional Government a word of approbation. Even citizens of my State have felt called upon to *burn* the labeled figure of Andrew Johnson for Saying less than Andrew Jackson has been immortalized for saying.

But this is the Scum floating upon the mighty current of Mississippi sentiment under which clear and smoothe floats on an ever enduring flood of devotion to Constitutional Government. Your own State is little less attached to the Constitution than the northern counties of Mississippi, who are ready to coerce violators of law and the Constitution no matter whether in Maine or South Carolina. It seems to me that the question fairly stated is "Is this form of Government a failure"? If so then we ought to abolish it, if not we ought to maintain and correct abuses under it. But this is ground over which you have often trod. My purpose was merely to say to you, if you go to Memphis (which we learn your friends propose) that you call in our little city on your way and address your political sympathisers. If any thing can peril the rights of the South effectually and surely, hasty secession and consequent revolution by armed force will do it.

If you were disposed to engineer for the Conservative party in

Mississippi, you might give us considerable strength by influencing President Buchanan to appoint another U. S. Marshal in place of W. H H. Tison in the Northern District of Mississippi.[2]

Mr. Tison is now member elect to our State Convention upon the secession ticket and I suppose will soon resign (if the state secedes) and his place ought to be filled if the government aims to maintain itself[.] Rev. E. C. Gillenwaters,[3] a man of great personal popularity and withal a man of undoubted nerve and decision, and a Union Breckinridge man to the core will accept the position and enforce the law. At least 1,200 signatures might be obtained to such a petition in this Tishomingo County.

Our majority in this county for the Union ticket for the State Convention was the rise of 1,200 which has been gradually on the increase since the election, and should the Convention pass the ordinance of secession I verily believe the outside pressure will be so large as to force its submission to the people where it will be as signally rebuked as it was in 1851 in this state.[4]

I am not willing to give the Republicans this boon so much desired by them, if they really be anti slavey men for I cannot see how we can maintan our institutions bordered by a hostile foreign power. Already a strong patrol force must be kept to quiet the nerves of women and timid men of nights, and it only requires an outbreak to doom that race to almost extinction. Such a condition of affairs I cannot look upon with any degree of pleasure. In the Union our institutions are safe, with now and then an occasional abduction, for thirty years yet—out of it the irrepressible conflict is upon us.

Excuse these hasty and disconnected thoughts, and if worth an answer would be pleased to hear at what time you can address us and what you suggest as to the Marshalship &c.

I am &c.   J. M. Jones

ALS, DLC-JP.
    1. Possibly James Jones (b. c1830), English native and plasterer by trade, who declared $2,000 in property in 1860. 1860 Census, Miss., Tishomingo, 470.
    2. William H. H. Tison (1822–1882), Alabama native, was a member of the Mississippi legislature (c1855), U. S. marshal (1858–61), and a Confederate colonel. Irene S. and Norman E. Gillis, comps., *Genealogical Abstract of Goodspeed's Biographical and Historical Memoirs of Mississippi* ([Baton Rouge? 1962]), 617; *Senate Ex. Journal*, X (1858), 416; *U. S. Official Register* (1859), 17.
    3. Ed C. Gillenwaters (b. c1815) appears in the 1860 census as a Virginia-born minister with $10,000 in real and $6,000 in personal property. 1860 Census, Miss., Tishomingo, 410.
    4. In order to define Mississippi's position on the Compromise of 1850, a convention had met in November, 1851. Unionist candidates having been overwhelmingly elected over State Rights delegates, the convention voted to support the Compromise. Dunbar Rowland, *History of Mississippi* (4 vols., Chicago, 1925), I, 738–41.

From William M. Lowry[1]

Greeneville Ten Dec 29 1860

Gov Johnson

D Sir

I recd a copy of yr speech this morning[.] have not had time as yet to read, tho I regret to See our Democratic papers denouncing it in advance, admitting that you went farther in the Speech than you ought, charity ought at least to have estoped them until they could have read it and examined the points you made and a faithful Public Servant ought not to be Condemned without a fair hearing. I am under the impression from what I see that an attempt will be made to instruct you by the Legislature when called together. it would be well for you to forwd a copy of your speech to every member of the Legislature before they convene at Nashville so that they may examine it camly. We have been somewhat alarmed this morning by hearing a report passing on the wires that you had shot Jeff Davis.[2] I trust such is not the fact, but if so that you acted on the defensive[.] if however you are in a scrape let us know and we will stand at your back. our freinds differ Somewhat about the Secssion Question. Some Contend that it is peaceable others that is revolutionary. The objection to your speech so far as I can see is not beccause the Govt. has not right to coercion but against the principle in the present crisis. When I get home I will read yr speech carefully and as I told a freind the other day, that I did not know how you would come out with this controversy but as a general thing you were generally right and could Sustain your course before the country[.] do not neglect sending your speech to the members of the Legislature at once. let me hear from you. I wrote Vaughn[3] the other day that through you I had got his account allowd.

Yr freind   Wm M Lowry

Pps. Suppose the whole of the South like South Carolina desert the National Capitol abandon it to the Northern fanatics[.] I cannot for one moment tolerate the Idea[.] if we must have a dessolution I am for holding on to the National Capitol[.] it of right belongs to us and a Southern man deserting it at this important crisis. Shows the impolicy of the present Movement. My doctrine is to hold on to the Capitol and if any desert, let it be those Northern fanatics, and not the South, The South ought to meet in convention and in a respectful manner demand her rights and if not granted then let the whole South move together and take possession of the Capitol as belonging to us.

ALS, DLC-JP.

1. See *Johnson Papers*, I, 34n.

2. Under the caption "False Rumors," the St. Louis *Missouri Democrat* of December 27 denied the report which "flew from mouth to mouth yesterday that Senator Johnson . . . had shot and killed Jefferson Davis." Condemning idle gossip, the *Democrat* admitted that Davis' reference to Johnson as a "miscreant" after his recent speech "imparted a hue of probability to the story." Elsewhere in the paper, the story was credited to somone who kept Christmas "not wisely, but too well," and the spread of the news item to the exuberance of newsboys who sold out by crying, "*All about the murder of Jefferson Davis!*"

3. John C. Vaughn had been one of Lowry's assistants in taking the Census of 1860. See *Johnson Papers*, III, 469n.

From Joseph C. S. McDannel[1]

Knoxville, Tenn., Dec. 29, 1860

Hon. Andrew Johnson:

Dear Sir—

As there is a great anxiety here to see your *Union Speech*, you will do me a favor by sending me several of them as soon as possible.

You are being denounced here by a little clique calling themselves democrats. They have been trying for several days to get up a meeting to pass condemnatory resolutions in regard to your course, and to burn you in effigy, but as yet have not been able to raise a crowd. — If they do attempt it, I prophecy it will be a sore job for them.

Your worst political enemies, *Brownlow*, for instance, now speak of you in the highest terms. Brownlow said to me yesterday— "*Johnson is right— He is a true Jackson Democrat, and ocupies the same position now that he did in 1833, and I will defend him to the last.*" There is many others here of the same kind, but I mention this one because I know he has been your most bitter enemy. The people of Tenn. are with you, and no mistake.

You are being denounced by such men as General John Crozier Ramsey, U. S. District Attorney,[2] Old Parson Lewis, Pension Agent;[3] C. W. Charlton, P. M.; Wayne Wallace, Dr. J. G. M. Ramsey, John H. Crozier,[4] and *a few low down loafers*.

I am still a Johnson democrat, and for the Union all the time.

Be sure to send your speech.

Your friend,   Jos. C. S. McDannel

ALS, DLC-JP.

1. Joseph C. S. McDannel (1825–1901), Knoxville native and brother of Johnson's friend Blackston, was a printer for several local newspapers until the early fifties, when he opened the city's first confectionery shop, which became a casualty of the Civil War. Knoxville *Journal and Tribune*, February

11, 1901; St. George Sioussat Papers, Box 11, University of Tennessee Library.

2. See *Johnson Papers*, III, 311n.

3. Isaac Lewis (1801–1864), a native of Virginia, was pastor of the Methodist Episcopal Church at Knoxville (1827), trustee of East Tennessee College (1836), Knox County recorder (1838–54), and pension agent (1860). When the war began he supported the southern cause and after the battle of Knoxville was among those whom Brownlow's *Rebel Ventilator* admonished to leave town. Edward T. Sanford, "Biographical List of the Trustees . . . East Tennessee College, 1807–1840," University of Tennessee *Record*, I (1898), 229–67; Rothrock, *French Broad-Holston Country*, 141–42; *Senate Doc.* No. 1, 36 Cong., 2 Sess., 478.

4. For the remaining detractors mentioned here, see as follows: Charles W. Charlton, *Johnson Papers*, III, 311n; Wallace, *ibid.*, 402n; Ramsey, *ibid.*, II, 214n; Crozier, *ibid.*, I, 29n.

From David A. Wells

December 29, 1860, Troy, N. Y.; ALS, DLC-JP.

A Republican writes to clarify the position of northerners accused of hating the South; explains that he voted for Lincoln "not because I hated slavery, or thought it a sin, or wished in any way to do my neighbor a wrong—but because I was disgusted with the present administration, & wished for a change."

From Hu Douglas

Nashville 30th Dec 1860

Hon Andrew Johnson
My Dear Sir

I hoped to be able to send you the report of the Union Meeting on yesterday,[1] but cannot do it. I feel warranted however in saying that it almost resulted in a Secession Meeting. I am told that the Gazette[2] the organ of that party Claims it as Such. Some of ve[r]y best men were taken back v[er]y much, utterly surprised at the Course things took.

You will find herein the Comments of the U & A on your Speech.[3] I do not belive they would have published yr Speech at all but to publish the remarks of Gen Lane.[4] The fact is there are a great many old Sores to be cured that you have caused and we must begin to show our hand, the truth you must know is that you have been in the way of a good many of our would be great men for a long time. At heart many of us never wanted you to be Governor only none of the rest of us Could have been elected at the time and we only wanted you to use you. Then we did not want you to go to the Senate but the *people would send you.* Then Some of us wanted a *very distinguished man* to be Vice President and wanted to Commit our delegates in favor of him,[5] but instead of this (the people again interfered) they *expressed* a wish that you should have the nomination for President. Now we [are] afraid of the people and a little of you but notwithstanding this we must give vent to our feelings, we cant avoid it, the wounds are fresh & bleeding.

Now keep Cool, wait keep your powder dry,[6] dont write, but *when* you come home, Call us together and Call things by the right names, excuse me for making any suggestions, you know how to do it.

Just inform the people and they will [do] right. The people of this state of this Southern Country Cannot will not indorse S C if they can help it. They may be forced rather than see the *Genl* government coerse not otherwise.

read over old frind Cave Johnson's letters.[7]

I wish you would write to me. only what do you think? What will be the result? I am anxious for my Country, but if it is to be shattered, I would like to know how to set my own affairs in order. I assure you that I am at a loss to know what to do. I dislike to loose all I have after spen[din]g a life time to accumulate it[.]

Yr frind   Hu Douglas

ALS, DLC-JP.

1. A public meeting of the citizens of Davidson and surrounding counties had been called, ostensibly for the purpose of proclaiming a patriotic stand; however, two prosouthern resolutions, one attacking Johnson's speech of December 18–19 and the other praising Senator Joseph Lane's reply, were proposed and only with difficulty tabled. Nashville *Republican Banner*, December 30, 1860; Nashville *Union and American*, January 2, 1861.

2. During the fall and winter of 1860 the Nashville *Gazette* was blatantly secessionist and anti-Johnson, calling him "a bloody leader of bloody cohorts": "We hate him for his base treachery to the South." Founded in 1844, the *Gazette* continued until 1868, except for a period (1862–65) when its Confederate stance forced it to cease publication. Gregory, *Union List of Newspapers*, 660; Nashville *Gazette*, December 23, 1860.

3. On December 28, the Nashville *Union and American* announced that two days hence it would publish Johnson's speech and Lane's reply. This December 30 issue cannot be found.

4. In what his biographer considers one of Lane's most important speeches, the Oregonian, avowing his love for the Constitution, defended the right of secession, hinted that he would support a northwestern alliance with a southern confederacy, and savagely attacked Lincoln. *Cong. Globe*, 36 Cong., 2 Sess., 143–45; James E. Hendrickson, *Joe Lane of Oregon: Machine Politics and the Sectional Crisis, 1849–1861* (New Haven, 1967), 242–43. See also *Johnson Papers*, III, 372n.

5. Anti-Johnson Democrats in Tennessee had been hopeful that a national ticket would include Governor Isham G. Harris. *Ibid.*, 372n, 410–11.

6. An admonition attributed to Oliver Cromwell. Stevenson, *Quotations*, 1650.

7. Reference to a pro-Union letter of December 18, 1860, circulating in Tennessee, a copy of which appeared in the Nashville *Republican Banner*, December 30, 1860, and the Clarksville *Jeffersonian*, January 2, 1861.

From Adam Fergusson[1]

Carthage Tennessee
30th December 1860

Sir   You seem to be in the commencement of a Revolution at Washington as yet bloodless but tending fast to Anarchy and ruin affecting all the interests of the people of these United States throughout the length and breadth of their boundaries. North first and South next driving every wedge to split this glorious Union of States assunder. Well it is what some of us saw twenty years ago only we did not expect it so soon[.] We have seen the Democrasy of the South divided in 1835–6.[2] The vote of Tennessee transfered over to the Whigs in 1840 brought about by the money of the old United States Bank and Pensylvania US Bank used for printing Slanders against the only party that ever were worthy to hold the power of this Goverment and carry it on[.][3] They were printed and distributed to each family to read and to be learned by children who have since grown up and form the character who now rules this nation of White Men. And this has been done in a great measure by the cuning of these northern leaders. South Carolina has gone out as she believes, what madness! what a spectacle before the world! They forget that each and every Citizen of these United States owes allegiance and fidelity to these Same United States above all other laws. We have a common interest in every foot of land within all the States and Teritories. Also an eaqual right to the Navigation of the Seas with the most favoured Nastion. Permit me to ask you what can any of the southern or any other state or Teritory promise herself by separation[?] Is not the consequence Self destruction, too weak to protect herself and always inviting agression from stronger Goverments. Suppose a Southern Confederacy of States were formed could they protect themselves? They would undoubtedly as a matter Consequent loose our Democratic friends in the North, for they having stood up to us through every opposition would be compelled to join with their own people[.] Then the whole world is against slavery, and how long do you suppose will they last until they are called upon to defend themselves in oppen war? And such a war may Heaven forbid. Now the South is certainly right in demanding her rights under the Constitution; And the North has been wrong all the time and the cause of all this trouble, and long since ought their fanatical leaders to have been punished. I am a Southern Man and go with the South in her demands. I love the Union and the voice of the great mass of the people are for the Union[.] I do not think there are many disunion men in the fourth Congressional District. The old Democrasy of Smith County are as firm this day and their late vote show it as ever.[4] They are not willing to change their principles or prove ungrateful to long true faithful Publick officers[.] I make theese last remarks to counteract any impression that might be made by a recent disgracful occurrenc in our Town of Carthage to burn you in effigy on account of your late war speech as they would term it. It seems to have been gotten up by a Mr Brooks[5] a son of Doctor Brooks deceased who was Soninlaw to Col William Martin[6] of opposition Notoreity to General Jackson and Democrasy generally[.] He comes therefore out of a bad nest and has no right to be the exponent of Democratic principles. I am correctly informed that the most bitter Nonothings of our Town would not even countenance it nor open their doors to look at it consequently there was no one present but Some boys and Negroes headed by Mr Brooks. Personally I have no ambition against Mr Brooks[.] he came here as a young lawyer and settled about a year or two ago. These Demonstrations are not worthy of notice were it not for the impression that might be created abroad Towards you publickly and privately for your faithful Publick Services exists the Same esteem and regard. I could extend this letter further upon the views taken by others of sound Union Principles as well as myself; but I may be tresspasing upon your precious time and therefore leave the matter of further particulars to abler pens than mine. Be pleased to inform me by letter such views of the future as you think will show the final end of this mos[t] exciting State of Publick affairs[.]

Respectfully   A. Fergusson

Honble Andrew Johnson
United States Senate
Washington City

ALS, DLC-JP. Draft of letter in Fergusson Papers, Tennessee State Library and Archives.

1. Adam Fergusson (b. c1799), North Carolina-born Smith County farmer, in 1850 had real estate valued at $6,000. 1850 Census, Tenn., Smith, 423.

2. The division which produced the Whig party in the South was caused by differences on such issues as federal aid for internal improvements, a national bank, and a protective tariff, as well as by the presidential candidacies of Martin Van Buren, Jackson's designated heir, and Hugh Lawson White of Tennessee. John Bell, Ephraim Foster, Newton Cannon, and White were among former Tennessee Jacksonians who joined the Whig ranks. Folmsbee, *Tennessee*, I, 309–39.

3. In the "log cabin" campaign of 1840, disaffected Tennesseans rejected the Democratic party's standard bearer, giving William Henry Harrison the state by 11,572 votes. Unwilling, or unable, to explain the huge voter response in terms of an expanded electorate (Van Buren actually received more votes in defeat than in his 1836 victory), Democratic partisans quickly charged fraud, corruption, and chicanery. Although Democratic campaign practices

generally were similar to those of the Whigs, an unprecedented amount of money was available to subsidize Whig newspapers and other political operations. Robert G. Gunderson, *The Log-Cabin Campaign* (Lexington, Ky., 1957), 22–24, 158–59, 238, 254, 256; see also Thomas B. Alexander, "The Presidential Campaign of 1840 in Tennessee," *Tenn. Hist. Quar.*, I (1942), 21–43.

4. On the contrary, Smith County in recent years had been far from Democratic; after 1840 Whig majorities in both presidential and gubernatorial campaigns—including Johnson's—were substantial to overwhelming. In 1860 Bell had 1475 votes to 618 for Breckinridge and 60 for Douglas. In the fourth district congressional race, the Whig candidate, William B. Stokes, defeated his Democratic opponent, Savage, but only by the narrow margin of 6,633–6,160. Campbell, *Tenn. Attitudes*, 265–87; *Cong. Dir.* (1878), 645.

5. T. W. Brooks (b. c1837) was a young Carthage lawyer who attended the Nashville Democratic Convention of January 19, 1860. 1860 Census, Tenn., Smith, 8; Nashville *Union and American*, January 20, 1860.

6. Probably William Martin (1765–1846), Virginia-born Indian fighter and surveyor, who settled in Tennessee before 1800. A Jeffersonian Republican who early represented Sumner County in the Tennessee house (1803–5), Martin later moved to Smith County, became a Whig, and served as vice president of the Whig state convention in 1844. Robison, *Preliminary Directory, Sumner*, 55.

From William M. Bradford

December 31, 1860, Dandridge; ALS, DLC-JP.

State senator requests copy of recent speech "for my own reference" at forthcoming meeting of the legislature. Although Johnson's speech has met with some bitter reproof in Memphis and Knoxville, it is well received among the masses: "Even Brownlow, has recently taken occasion to give your views a complimentary notice in his journal."

From Mortimer F. Johnson[1]

Tellico Plains East Tenn Decr 31/60

Hon Andrew Johnson

I wrote you a few lines some days since and having mixed up with some of the One Horse Politicians and heard ma[n]y comments upon the positions taken by yourself from some of the Senators and representatives of our State who are about to assemble in Nashville, take the liberty of again addressing you[.] Your position interferes with the views of many of the hot brained politicians of our State and they are proposing to pass you out of the Senate by a Resolution asking you to resign[2] (There is many think you will do so at once) as they take great exceptions to your great scheme of Philanthropy the Home Stead Bill[.] Now all this is almost too absurd to repeat to you. But so many of our Citizens are under a state of excitement and talk about *Secession and revolution* as an ordinary matter and apparently without one thought of the ultimate Consequences— And as to the

Homestead Bill because you did not make it exclusively beneficial in its provisions to the South, you are to be denounced as not a true friend to the South. But I am happy to say to you, that the sober thinking men of the State, who have views that go beyond it, most unqualifiedly approve of your position and a large portion of those who have always been opposed to you Politically are most prompt in wishing you God Speed in your noble efforts for the Preservation of this glorious and powerful Nation[.] It is said "there is no excellency without great labour"[.][3] I sincerely trust you may be endowed with health and strength equal to the emergency[.]

I am a humble individual but have a large and abiding interest in the State of Tennessee and do trust that she may *Keep Cool*, and do that which alone Duty Honour and her best interests shall dictate[.] Without trespassing upon you any suggestions of mine be pleased to accept the assurances of my most unqualified approbation and esteem[.]

With assurances of great respect I am yours

M. F. Johnson

My father Hon Elisha Johnson[4] specially desires to be remembered to you, and he trusts you may never weary in well doing[.]

M. F. Johnson

ALS, DLC-JP.

1. Johnson was the Tellico Plains postmaster. See *Johnson Papers*, III, 430n.

2. See Letter from Michael Burns, January 13, 1861.

3. Possibly derived from Samuel Johnson's "Excellence in any department can be attained only by the labor of a lifetime." John P. Bradley, *et al.*, *The International Dictionary of Thought* (Chicago, 1969), 424.

4. See *Johnson Papers*, III, 430n.

1861

From E. B. Tuck[1]

Decaturvill Decatur county T 1861

Deir Sirr

afte[r] my respects to you after your manly proshin [position] that you tooke as ouer Sinertor in the Sinete of the united States I can Say to you that you have gained more frein than enny mane from the South for I can Say to you that all pairty is coming to your Rescue[.] now [no] mane Dair Say norte [naught] a gance Andrew Johnson proshin. and I can Say to you your proshin that you have taken is the Shalvation of ouer cuntry and if a complaing cane Bee maid a pon your ishu I tell you you nede note fear Eenny evel that may cum in the futher [future.] Soe andrew I wante you to Stand furme as a rock for I have alleewayes Bin your devotede frend for I [k]now I have hade a meny hard controversy for yo. for gode Sake preserv ouer union if you can[.] your motto is my moto[.] if I fite I wante to fite in the union note oute of it[.] I Rite to you Because I respect you[.] you and I Seirve ouer printes Shipe in the Same State and I respect you for your energe[.] I Sirve my printis Ship with D. A. Wilder[.][2] Soe I will clos By Saying wee have now [no] Secshion men in my county[.] all for the union and for your poshion you have taken[.] Soe I remane your persnel frend[.]

E B Tuck P. M   Decaturvill
Decatur couty Tennessee

ALS, DLC-JP.

1. E. B. Tuck (b. c1810), born in Virginia, was a Decaturville tailor and postmaster (1859). 1860 Census, Tenn., Decatur, 52; *U. S. Official Register* (1859), 354.*

2. Not found.

Order for Reprints of Speech[1]

[1861]

Speech of the Hon Andrew Johnson of Tennessee on the President's Message will be printed at the Globe Office @ $2.00 per hundred copies.

Names	Copies	Names	Copies
Andrew Johnson	10,000	Jno C [Frémont?]	100
William H. Seward	5,000	Z. Chandler, per J.	100
Charles Sumner per J.	500	J. R. Doolittle	100
K. S Bingham	50	L. Trumbull	100
J P Hale	100	Danl Clark	100
H B Anthony	100	L F S Foster	100
L M Morrill	100	Preston King	100

26,550

Commissions, $13.24

Mr Kennedy[2] of the census bureau wants 10,000 and the account sent to him[.]   A. Johnson

Copy, DLC-Gates W. McGarrah Col.

1. This order confirms the charge of his fellow Democrats, who asserted that Johnson's speech was being circulated all over the North by antislavery elements, particularly the Black Republicans. All the subscribers were congressmen or senators and by 1861 all were Republicans. *Cong. Globe*, 36 Cong., 2 Sess., 117–20, 134–42.

2. For Joseph C. G. Kennedy, see *Johnson Papers*, III, 615n. A Washington clerk writing to Howell Cobb complained: "Secession sentiments have become very offensive to the present powers and particularly with the Census Bureau. No sooner had Mr. Thompson retired than the *creature* of his misplaced confidence, Kennedy, by whose appointment he drew upon himself unmeasured abuse from divers quarters, commenced to exhibit his ingratitude by turning out every man in the Census Bureau who entertains the right of secession and has the boldness to express his sentiments." Kennedy, working with Johnson, Congressman John A. Gilmer, and others, assembled lists of voters, especially in the border and southern states, to whom Union speeches, addressed at night by "some twenty of Kennedy's clerks," were sent. Ulrich B. Phillips, ed., *The Correspondence of Robert Toombs, Alexander H. Stephens, and Howell Cobb*, American Historical Association *Annual Report, 1911* (2 vols., Washington, D. C., 1913), II, 540; Nichols, *Disruption of Democracy*, 400.

From Charles Johnson

Greeneville Jany 1st 1861

Dear Father

With this day commences another year and it will perhaps be a year that will stand out upon the record of time to be refered to by future generations as the year in which the closing scenes of the farce of mans self government was enacted. God forbid!— What will the future reader of history think when reading of the United States from its formation through its bloody revolution, through its years of prosperity and happiness down to its ignoble fall! And in what light will the south stand upon the pages of that history, they the rebellious party; tearing asunder the bonds of the union, in vindication of the right to enslave a portion of their fellow creatures; the north contending for universal liberty[.]

Your late speech seems to have excited some of our friends to a considerable extent, but in this county there is but one sentiment,— opposition men and in fact men of all parties heartily endorse it: — the Palmetto flag was hoisted on the streets one day by some irresponsible boys but it was soon forced to be hauled down and now the Stars and Stripes wave across the streets[.][1] I do not think there are twenty men in Greene County to day that would vote themselves out of the Union[.]

I have not seen a single man who does not endorse the doctrine of Coercion when they understand it, that is the right and the power of the government to enforce its law, if it can not do this it is no government. A German Philosopher I believe it was said "the soul of liberty is the love of law"[2] but as any thing I may say will have nothing to do with the saving the Country I shall close this part of my discourse[.]

On last saturday it rained all day, at night commenced snowing and snowed without intermission 36 hours— had the ground been dry it would now be three feet deep[.] As it is, the snow now is about 18 inches deep, with a fair prospect of more. I was up in Carter last week— We went to the mountains and killed seven Bear,— there has been killed up in those mountains this winter about 30.

I saw Mr. Henderson[3] a few days since; he did not know when he could pay that note; and at his own suggestion renewed the note[.]

John A. Brown marries Mrs Raby[4] next week; this I have pretty direct[.] We have nothing unusual going on here— All in our accustomed health.

Your Son Charles Johnson

ALS, DLC-JP.

1. This "battle of the flags" involved South Carolina's state ensign, whose designation arose from the emblem thereon, and the American flag, probably first identified as the "Stars and Stripes" in the 1795 edition of Philip Freneau's poem "A Prophecy."

2. Not found.

3. Joseph Henderson (b. c1800), a Kentucky-born farmer possessing, according to the Greene County tax list for 1853, 1,079 acres valued at $13,650, had by 1860 increased his wealth to $42,420 in real estate and $20,000 in personal property. His deeding of a 516-acre farm to Johnson on March 30, 1868, may possibly be connected with the note renewed at this time. 1860 Census, Tenn., Greene, 14th Dist., 94; Greene County Deed Book No. 35, p. 573.

4. John A. Brown, prosperous Greeneville merchant and farmer, married Rebecca L. Rabe (1827–1891) on January 3, 1861. Acklen, *Tenn. Records*, I, 133; II, 88; *Johnson Papers*, I, 36n.

From Robert Johnson

Greeneville Tenn   Jan'y 1st 1861

Dear Father,

I have not much news of interest to write you at this time— On Sunday last we had the heaviest fall of snow that has been for years and if the ground had been dry it would have been from twenty to thirty inches deep— as it was it laid to the depth of about fourteen inches— It turned very cold last night & to-day is the coldest day we have had this winter, although it is clear & bright—

Your speech is well received by all that have read it and have not heard of the first man that has read it, but endorses it— they are in great demand and ought to be circulated all over the State by thousands and at an early day— Such papers as the "Union & American" & "Avalanche" are condemning it very bitterly and are trying to create a prejudice against it, before it is read— circulate it as soon as possible— I am glad to see that the Nashville "Banner" endorses it out & out & says he will take you by the hand & bury the past—[1]

Milligan approves it & is very bitter on those that denounce it— If we can preserve the Union or keep Tennessee right, all will be well, & if Buchanan would sustain Anderson[2] & execute the laws, all would in my opinion turn out much better— but he seems afraid to do anything.

Send a copy of your speech to each member of the Legislature to Nashville— Send McDowell, McGaughey & Co a lot—also Lowry & Eason & Biggs—[3] Circulate them freely—

I presume you have heard of the burning of your effigy &c As John Tyler once said, they merely give light for a man to walk by—[4] let them burn, it will come home to roost—[5] I would like for you to write to me at Nashville & give me your views as to what the Legislature ought to do &c.

Excuse this writing, for my ink freezes almost as fast as I can write. We are all well— Charles all straight[.][6]

I will write tomorrow[.]

Your Son   Robt Johnson

ALS, DLC-JP.

1. Probably Hiram K. Walker (b. c1827), who was editor in chief. Originally of Vermont, he started with the Nashville *Whig* in 1850, becoming managing editor in 1856; the next year he bought an interest in the *Banner*. In a recent issue Walker, who had "heretofore opposed Mr. JOHNSON in all his political aspirations," now endorsed his stand, letting the "dead past bury its dead" and asserting, "We are ready to take by the hand every man, North or South, East or West, whatever may have been his past political associations,

who is to-day arrayed upon the side of *his country*, and lending his voice and his influence to a restoration of peace and a fair and honorable settlement of existing difficulties between the North and South." 1860 Census, Tenn., Davidson, Nashville, 5th Ward, 155; Clayton, *Davidson County*, 237, 238; Nashville *Republican Banner*, December 28, 1860.

2. Robert Anderson (1805–1871), commander at Ft. Sumter, was a native of Kentucky. A graduate of West Point (1825), he took part in the Black Hawk and Florida wars and served as a captain under Scott in Mexico. After the fall of Sumter he was promoted and given command of troops in Kentucky; however, his health failed and he was relieved in October, 1861. Throughout the remainder of the conflict he saw little duty, although he was privileged to raise the Union flag above Ft. Sumter exactly four years after his surrender of the post. *DAB*, I, 274–75.

3. Greenevillians Sam McGaughey (1816–1870), James P. McDowell, and T. J. Eason were merchants; William M. Lowry, a U. S. marshal; Elbert Biggs, postmaster. 1860 Census, Tenn., Greene, 10th Dist., 92, 93; Buford Reynolds, comp., *Greene County Cemeteries* ([Greeneville], 1971), 280; for Biggs, see *Johnson Papers*, II, 391n.

4. Tyler's August 16, 1841, veto of the bill to restore the United States Bank led to his being burned in effigy within sight of the White House on the following evening. Several months later he is said to have remarked that "the light of burning effigies has only helped me to make the path of duty more plain." Hugh R. Fraser, *Democracy in the Making: The Jackson and Tyler Era* (New York, 1931), 188–89.

5. From Edward Bulwer-Lytton, *The Lady of Lyons*, Act IV, sc. 2.

6. See Letter from Robert Johnson, May 8, 1860, *Johnson Papers*, III, 589.

From Washington C. Whitthorne[1]

Columbia Tennessee
January 1st 1861

Honl Andrew Johnson
Dear Sir,

I thank you for pamphlet copy of your speech delivered in the Senate 18 & 19th of last month— I have read it, and laid it by to read again. I am sure from your own nature, you will allow me credit for the frankness and candor, that has usually marked our intercourse, when in that spirit I say that I cannot wholly agree with you. I take issue more, with the "lodgement" that is made, in the mind, than with its wording, but I will not tresspass upon courtesy by arguing any question involved in it. I sincerely regret that differences of opinion have arisen and will arise amidst us in Tennessee. But to two or three have I expressed any view. I was satisfied that to my own peculiar one, I could give no strength, and all I could do was in a friendly social way express them. I could not run with the fastest, I could not stay with him, who rested— yet my conviction was that the times but hastened this issue, and that in all human probability, it would be the only one.

My own view in short has been to abide. Equality justice and right, peace and security upon this basis, with the whole 33 states. If not, then with an United South. If not, with an United South then with those who would stand with me upon it. I look to no name, however loved and hallowed, nor would I take counsel of any unmanly fear, but being a freeman, I would maintain the character, no matter who opposed. These are but general propositions, to which all would yield assent, who are in truth freemen, but their application is the mischief. Are the equal just rights of the Slave States now respected in this Confederacy? No! Will they be in the future? Does the past, does the attitude of parties, sects, and sections, authorize me to answer affirmatively? No[.] What then? Obviously I would answer endeavor first to secure it in the spirit of that *bond* which now unites you. Failing in that— Dissolve the compact, and stand upon your rights. This has been my programme, and hence I hailed with pleasure the introduction of those resolutions by Senator Crittenden, yourself and others in regard to the slavery question, trusting that their passage might eventuate in present harmony, and future peace. I desired no other means and never could contemplate the ideas of either prolonging the debatable issue, or of seeing a government of force. The present awful distress warns us that this question must no longer make the peace, happiness, prosperity, and ay, bread and meat of our people, its plaything. It should be settled, and if all avenues of hope in the Union are to be abandoned, and I confess that looking to the vote upon Crittendens resolutions I have well nigh despaired,[2] what must we do—the last fight in the Union has been had. Because a *blow of force* between the Sections destroys at once the character of the Goverment. It is the affection of the people, their confidence in each other's honesty & intelligence, that makes *our* Union, not the quantity of its armaments, or its capacity of force[.] Most assuredly, I would be unwilling, and I fain believe all of us, to see the 15 Slave States held in the Union in either an inferior or subject position and I am equally frank in saying that if we possessed the strength I would be unwilling to see the Northern States— I am utterly opposed to any form of goverment, which does not rely upon the honesty, affection and confidence of the great mass of its citizens, as well as their intelligence for its chief strength and support. If then the issue comes in this shape what should we do— Had we not better separate with popular goverments to each of the sections, trusting that the same habits, institutions & everything that makes each homogenous, will preserve such forms of goverments. I think so.

Our legislature will meet upon Monday next[.] Of course the subjects for our action will be determined by Govr. Harris message. I judge Tennessee will call for a convention of Southern States[3] for the purpose of Uniting in a demand upon the North unless events prior to that time shall destroy the hopes of the most sanguine (and tomorrow's election in Georgia[4] will have an important, if not conclusive bearing upon the whole question,) and if she *decides* for separate action, then the question of Tennessee's destiny may be put to the direct vote of her people, but how all these things may be God only knows for the judgement of to day may be reversed by the facts of tomorrow[.] I should be glad to hear from you at any time.

I am very truly yrs.
W. C. Whitthorne

ALS, DLC-JP.

1. See *Johnson Papers*, III, 384n.
2. Introduced on December 18, 1860, the ill-fated Crittenden amendments were currently in committee.
3. Tennessee legislators made several attempts to call a southern convention to meet on February 4, either in Nashville or in Richmond. After Virginia issued a summons for a peace convention representing all states to meet in Washington on the same date, a joint session of the General Assembly, held January 25, elected commissioners to that convention. A subsequent proposal to send three commissioners to a meeting in Montgomery was defeated. *Tenn. Senate Journal*, 1861, Extra Sess., 44–58 *passim*.
4. On January 2 Georgians voted for a convention to meet two weeks later to consider secession. Nevins, *Emergence of Lincoln*, II, 415–16.

From J. Warren Bell[1]

Springfield Illinois
January 2nd 1861

Friend Johnson

I cannot refrain from tendering to you my hearty congratulations for the noble stand you have taken in favor of "this union of states." I have not been able to obtain your speech entire, but only extracts. If not too much trouble send me a copy to my address at the "Saint Nicholas Hotel" in this place, as I shall remain here perhaps a few weeks. Johnson you remember in 1831 when quite a youth I predicted a portion of your then future political life. The prediction was more than fulfilled. In 1844 I again predicted that you would be Governor of Tennessee. I was right. In 1856 I predicted the "*White House*" would be your destination. *It will be.* I am not flattering nor am I prophesying. I have made myself a judge of human intellect, and the causes that effect the human judgment and sway the masses of the people, and from this "standpoint" I judge. But enough. I was aware, what your course on the question would be, and every where, have I told the people through the northwest when I have spoken in the late canvas, that, Andrew Johnson of Tennessee, the "Old Hickory" of this age would be always battling for the Union. I did this because I knew that Andrew Johnson is ever true to his country. I know "ambition like a mounting devil in the human heart, will play the Monarch and oerthrow reason",[2] but not often when love of country has the ascendency. I have often listened to Andrew Johnson when his soul was enlisted in the cause, as he proclaimed that "Man was not made for govement, but that govement was made for man"[3] and my mind would rush into the future and I could see the star of his fame ascending higher & still higher until it was lost in a blaze of unequaled eminence, in the history of man.

Andrew Johnson, you have no idea with what earnest and heart-felt joys I have ever watched your rising career, and how, I rejoiced at every success with which you have met in life. Your successful career is but another evidence of the truth that, he will *not* fail, who knowing the right, can summon the courage to bid difiance to all opposition and march boldly on. Such was Andrew Jacksons course[.] His courage always sustained him. And to Andrew Johnsons indominable will, is to be attributed his wonderful successes. Then permit me to bid you *God* speed. Stand firmly by the Union as it is. Uphold the Constitution. Demand submission from the north & the south, in their wild rage and all will be well[.]

The Administration of Abraham Lincoln will be all that can be asked or desired by all good citizens, north and south. He is no abolitionist[.] He is a firm Republican, and all the secession, and abolition elements in the states, cannot drive him from the principles to which he holds[.] He has more ability than one in ten thousand of our would be statesmen[.] Thus I tell you my friend he loves his country too well to peril any thing tending towards its destruction, and will ever guard with anxious care the prosperity and perpetuity of the Union, as our fathers made it. When Lincoln comes into power Andrew Johnson will sustain his administration, because it will be all that is right to the north and the south.

I am reliably informed that Genl Cameron of Pa Caleb B. Smith of Ind., Judge Bates of Mo. N. P. Banks of Mass. and I have no doubt Mr. Seward of N. Y. will all be in the Cabinet.[4] I wish Andrew Johnson were *there* too[.] But I am prolonging this beyond endurance. I intended when I commenced only to bid you *God* speed and ask a copy of your speech, and found myself drawn along by perhaps an overw[he]lm[in]g desire to assure you of the almost unbounded admiration with which your course meets in the minds of the masses of the Union loving people of all parties[.]

Pardon this intrusion and believe me now as heretofore

Your devoted friend
J. Warren Bell

I hope to see you 4th March—

ALS, DLC-JP.

1. Joseph Warren Bell (1814–1879), North Carolina-born unionist and Greeneville resident during the 1830's, had served with Johnson on a Greeneville mechanics' committee in 1843. Moving from Tennessee to Illinois, he became a Chicago lawyer who organized a cavalry regiment in 1861 and was discharged two years later. Designated a treasury agent (1867), he importuned Johnson for appointment as collector of customs in Galveston. Boatner, *Civil War Dictionary*, 57; *U. S. Official Register* (1867), 137; *Johnson Papers*, I, 251; Bell to Johnson, September 6, 1867, Johnson Papers, LC; Joseph W. Bell, Compiled Service Record, RG94, National Archives.

2. "How like a mounting devil in the heart / Rules the unreined ambition! Let it once / But play the monarch, and its haughty brow / Glows with a beauty that bewilders thought / And unthrones peace for ever." Nathaniel P. Willis, "Parrhasius," *The Complete Works of N. P. Willis* (New York, 1846), 834.

3. This is an idea consistently reiterated by Johnson. See *Johnson Papers*, II, 355; III, 51.

4. Of these, Simon Cameron became secretary of war; Edward Bates, attorney general; and William H. Seward, secretary of state.

From William H. Carroll[1]

Memphis Jany 2nd 1860 [1861]

(Confidential)

Dear Sir

You may rely upon the fact that a very large majority of our people will sustain your course and most cordially endorse the principles announciated by you in your late Speach in the Senate.

The Minute men[2] Secessionists and disunionists will not more than double the Breckeridge vote in this County— They are well organized and are trying to force *men* by bullying to join their organization— The outrageous attempt to insult you[3] meets the just condemnation of all good Citizens and has made for you hosts of friends who were your bitter opponents in the past.

We will proceed to organize this week and do it thoroughly.[4]

You will recollect what I stated to you at Washington after the adjournment of the Baltimore Convention—That Gov Harris was plotting to superseed you in the Senate— The attempt will be made — You can rely upon all the aid I can bring to bear in your behalf when the contest comes.

All you will have to do is let me know what you want done— Write to me and send me documents[.]

Very Respty   Wm H Carroll

Hon Andrew Johnson   Washington

P S You cannot rely upon the Appeal— Enclosed an article from the Bulletin.[5]

ALS, DLC-JP.

1. Carroll, a former Memphis postmaster, was later a brigadier general, CSA. See *Johnson Papers*, III, 392*n.*

2. Following Lincoln's election a revolutionary spirit swept the South, and it became fashionable for men to adorn their hats with blue cockades, the symbol of resistance since the old nullification days; a number of semimilitary marching groups formed, calling themselves variously "Minute Men," "Sons of the South," and similar appellations. The Memphis *Avalanche* reported that, after the news of South Carolina's secession, the oldest and most respectable citizens joined "the boys with the blue cockade" in demonstration. Companies of Minute Men soon appeared in the city. Bruce Catton, *The Coming Fury* (Garden City, N. Y., 1961), 111; Nashville *Union and American*, December 25, 1860; New York *Times*, January 26, 1861.

3. On the night of December 22 a Memphis mob had hanged and burned Johnson in effigy. Nashville *Union and American*, December 25, 1860; see also Letter from Henry G. Smith, December 23, 1860.

4. An attempt to marshal Union support in Memphis had begun with a rally on December 27; many of the movement's leaders later sided with the Confederate cause. Nashville *Patriot*, December 31, 1860.

5. The Memphis *Bulletin* for this period is not extant.

From Charles W. Charlton

Knoxville Tenn.   Jan 2d. 1861

Hon. A. Johnson
Washington D. C.
Dr Sir:

I thank you for a Copy of your speech. I was anxious to peruse it *for myself*, as many hard things had been said about you in consequence of it. And while I do not fully endorse all your views, yet, in the main, I think you are correct. Throughout the State you are very severely censured and how it will, finally, affect you, I am not prepared to say. Candor requires me to say that the democracy here, are disposed to dissent from you. I hope, however, that the "second sober thought," will incline them to your hearty support. Your former efficient services in the state—your war of utter extermination of Know-Nothingism, I hope, will rekindle their ardor in your behalf.

But enough of this. For myself, I can say I am still your friend, let the results be as they may. *You* favored me when I *needed* a friend, and now that I have no particular favors to ask at your hands, I should loathe myself to prove recreant to you.

In a few days I shall probably, send in my resignation. I would like to know of you if you will favor the confirmation of my successor, as I do not wish to resign, at present, if this cannot be done.

There is a gentleman by the name of C. A. Rice[1] who has been getting persons to sign a petition for the Office. This, of course, is in the absence of any information of my course. The gentleman I propose will be more acceptable to this community than he.

I see no prospect of any settlement of our difficulties. What is to be the result? The disunion feeling is gaining ground very rapidly in this State.

No news—   Respect, &c   C. W. Charlton

ALS, DLC-JP.

1. Charles A. Rice (1815–1881), a Connecticut native whose parents moved to East Tennessee about 1818, was Knoxville's first depot agent for the East Tennessee and Virginia Railroad. Engaged in the publishing business (1856–61), he was variously connected with such Knoxville publications as the *Presbyterian Witness*, *Register*, and *Whig*. During his later years, he was employed as a dead-letter agent in the Washington, D. C., Post Office. Rice did not get the appointment. Knoxville *Republican Chronicle*, June 30, 1881; WPA, Tenn., Knox: Old Gray Cemetery, 174.

From Richard M. Edwards[1]

Cleveland Tenn Jany 2nd 1861

Hon A. Johnson

Your late able speech in vindication of the constitution and the Union, has won back hundreds who have been temporarily estranged from you besides thousands who have never stood by you before. You have caused tremendous confusion among the seceders and disunionists; for there are disunionists even here. It afforded me great pleasure when I learned the position you had taken for there is no mistaking the fact that to the senators in Congress the great mass of the people are looking and upon the present senators most of the responsibility will attach for the events now transpiring and which will occur in the almost present portentous future. We are here taking the position that unless President Buchanan does his sworn duty by reinforcing fort Sumpter & retaking Fort Moultrie, that he should be impeached; and that should be done by some Southern senator, & a democrat. Believing that the Union can only be saved by decided prompt and energetic action of its friends; I believe that you ought to, at least enquire into the conduct of the president at once and show by your action that you intend to have the constitution of our country respected. The time is upon us for action. The controversy is already growing hot; and the issue is one involving the lives happiness and honor of us and our children; for already do secessionists talk glibly of the term "Tory" and it remains to be seen whether that term shall be applied to you and me & our children after us or shall that title with its attendant odium attach to those who from their position *of hostility to the present form of govern-*

ment, are more legitimately entitled to it. However the application of that or any other term of reproach depends upon the turn of affairs in the future. If the Revolutionists are successful we will bear all the odium; but if we are successful in maintaining the government then all the odium will attach to the other party. I have taken pains to sound the public mind here and at a large meeting here Union resolutions were passed notwithstanding Rowles Smith Harris Swan[2] & others moved Heaven & earth to defeat them. With all their ability and long speaking they only succeeded in getting 35 on their side and *they* are not real disunionists. The Union sentiment will win here. Send us if possible a large lot of your speeches & we can break the disunion movement down entirely.

Dreadful consequences are just ahead of us and they can not be averted by timid persuasive policy— such a policy is but the nursing the viper to life to sting you afterwards.

No reason is given for breaking up the government except that those who are leading in the movement *want to form a different one*. The love of a *different* government from this was the guiding star of the "Tories" of the Revolution. I have written thus much simply to encourage you to do your duty as you have heretofore.

Your friend   R. M. Edwards

ALS, DLC-JP.

1. Richard M. Edwards (1823–1907), a Bradley County lawyer who specialized in railroad and criminal cases, was a unionist who attended both the Knoxville and Greeneville conventions of 1861. The following year he organized the 4th Tenn. Cav., USA, serving as its colonel. After the war, he continued his law practice and was a candidate for governor on the Greenback ticket in 1880. John M. Wooten, *A History of Bradley County* (Cleveland, Tenn., 1949), 161; *Proc. E. Tenn. Conv.*, 5, 14.

2. Probably George W. Rowles, Cleveland attorney; Samuel A. Smith; Richard R. Harris, Cleveland attorney and state legislator; and either Robert M. Swan, Sam A. R. Swan, or Joseph L. Swan, all three prominent Bradley County rebels. Harris (b. *c*1832) served in the legislature (1859–61) and in the Confederate army; in 1884 he moved to Rome, Georgia, where he edited the *Tribune*. Robert M. Swan (b. *c*1797), Tennessee native, was a wealthy farmer ($8,000 in real and $12,000 in personal property) and the father of Sam A. R. (b. *c*1828), who fought in the Confederacy. Joseph L. (b. *c*1800), also a farmer, was a Pennsylvania native, with combined property valued at $20,000. Robison, *Preliminary Directory, Bradley*, 8; 1860 Census, Tenn., Bradley, Cleveland, 7th Dist., 21, 31; J. S. Hurlburt, *History of the Rebellion in Bradley County* (Indianapolis, 1866), 20; Wooten, *Bradley County*, 314. For Rowles, whom Hurlburt (135) characterized as "an unprincipled rebel leader" whose articles in the Cleveland *Banner* "tended to make it the bitter, relentless, dishonest and disgraceful sheet it proved itself to be," see *Johnson Papers*, I, 413*n*; for Smith, III, 447*n*.

From Hugh Graham

January 2, 1861, Tazewell; ALS, DLC-JP.

Requests copies of government documents and Johnson's latest Senate speech: "Some regards it in the light of coercion, others as giving a True picture of Disunion; which I fear many dislikes to read or Face." In Philadelphia, however, "my Soninlaw W. H. Patterson Says it has done more Good to open the Eyes of the People North & South, than any Speech made in Congress this Session."

From Cave Johnson

Clarksville   2 Jany 1861

Dear Sir,

I thank you for sending me your speech which I have hastily looked over and I can not see any reasonable grounds for the excitement produced in Memphis or Nashville. The principles advanced by you on secession & nullification and the power & duties of the Federal Government, cannot be successfully controverted and in my opinion your enemies instead of breaking you down will add to your strength in the State— the only danger to you individually arises from the division in our own ranks: it may be such as to elect an American—perhaps Mr. B.[1] Some of your democratic friends intend to supersede you by some secessionist but in that they will fail.[2] The publication of your speech has measurably quieted the Seceesh in this section & no objection is now made except as to the policy of doing so amidst the excitement now prevailing in the city— You will see from my letter,[3] I send you the paper to day that we do not materialy differ upon any one of the important questions discussed — There seems to be a madness prevailing in S. Carolina wholy unaccountable except upon the principles of selfishness & ambition among the agitators—

In this section of the State, we are, almost without an exception in favor of preserving the Union— Many think it however absolutely necessary that the north should *cease* their *attacks* upon the South and that *some means* should *be devised* to prevent it in future— if that be not done our State will very probably unite itself with the seceding States in despite of all that you or I can do— they say, the hostility between the two sections is so great that we cannot live together without some change and that we had better *now* have it setled than postpone it for our children. I think myself, if this thieving & robbery, slander & abuse and perpetual agitation can not be stopped, we shall soon be driven by the force of public opinion to seek security elsewhere— Surely the north would consent to an amendment of the constitution depriving Congress of the power to do any thing on the subject of slavery either in the States or territories and to enable it to punish attacks made by the citizens of one State on those of another or combinations in one state to injure another— The latter I suppose congress can over exercise but it had better be made definite— We are clearly entitled as good owners of the public lands to go with our slaves upon it upon the same terms allowed to citizens of the other states but the *right at present* is not worth a dime as we have no territory suited to slave labor— Why then should the north object to a declaration of such a right or why should the South insist upon it? We might very well postpone its settlement until a case arose requiring an adjustment. I think an amendment might also be made, allowing a State to secede upon such terms as might be agreed upon—say three fourths of the states consenting or to expel a state for misconduct such as refusing to abide by the Constitution or performing its Duties, three fourths consenting. The North should yield this much if for no other reason, than to protect the prudent & patriotic men of the South who are willing to stand by the Constitution and laws, against the fury & folly of the Fire-eaters of the South— the leaders of that class in my opinion do not care a dime for the action of *the North* upon the subject of Slavery & seize upon it & magnify the real evils we feel, to excite prejudices of the Southern people ag't the North, just as the abolitionists of the North have been doing for so many years— they seek a dissolution of the Union for other objects & other purposes wholy different from any thing connected with Slavery. Can it be possible that the prudent & sober minded men in both the great parties can suffer themselves to be controlled & their country ruined by these extreme factions composed of fanatics & mad men, who hope to profit by the Confusion among honest men, who have not sought or provided any organization to defeat their nefarious projects? I will not believe it— Sewards speech in N. Y[4] gave me some hope that he would finally take the control of his party & make some adjustment that we could all stand on— his humor brought to our minds, Nero fidling whilst Rome was burning, yet, before he closed, he said enough to give us some hope, that enough would be done to enable the patriots of the South to meet & overcome the enemies of the country.

As one of your constituents, I thank you for your manly and patriotic Speech, even if it shall turn out to have been ill-timed as some of your friends fear, yet I think it well timed for our protection at home— do excuse this long letter, I feel so much interest upon the subject that I never know when to quit, when I once enter upon it[.]

Yr. friend   C Johnson

Hon Andrew Johnson   Washington

ALS, DLC-JP.

1. John Bell.
2. That the legislators strongly disagreed over Johnson's course was reflected in house resolutions on the second and third days of the special session. On January 8 Jo J. Beaty of Giles declared, "We have read with profound regret, the late speech of the Hon. Andrew Johnson . . . in which he not only denies the right of a State peaceably to secede from the Union, but invokes the powers of the federal government to coerce the people of South Carolina [and] Believing as we do, that such sentiments will find no response among the majority of the people of Tennessee . . . we . . . respectfully request the Hon. Andrew Johnson to resign his seat in the United States Senate." The following day Daniel C. Trewhitt of Hamilton sponsored a resolution approving Johnson's stand on secession. Neither resolution was adopted. *Tenn. House Journal*, 1861, Extra Sess., 29, 35, 174.
3. Cave Johnson's letter of December 18, in response to one from "fellow citizens," was published in the Clarksville *Jeffersonian*, January 2, 1861.
4. Probably Seward's Palace Garden address in New York City on November 2, 1860—a conciliatory effort to demonstrate that the Republicans sought peace and union. Glyndon G. Van Deusen, *William Henry Seward* (New York, 1967), 235.

From Arthur S. Colyar[1]

Winchester Tenn
Jany 3d 1861

Hon Andrew Johnson
Dear Sir

You and I have been so wide apart in politics that we have had not even an acquaintance,[2] but I can not permit the occasion to pass without, in some way, tendering you my sincere thanks for what I conceive to be the strongest speech of the times.

I do this the more cheerfully because of the *excessive* bitterness from some quarters.

I hope you will not for a moment believe the Newspaper expression about your speech is any Criterion of the estimate put upon it by the people. This speech has undoubtedly given you more power with the people than any dozen speeches you ever made in your life. It has only been for a few days now that the people have been reading it but it is almost universally approved by the people while the politicians many of them denounce it.

I have never seen such a Conflict between politicians and people.

The Country people and in fact throughout the County towns in Tennessee, are almost entirely for standing by the Union and redressing our wrongs in the Union— They believe the madness of extreme men North & South is likely to bring ruin upon us—and they say almost to a man "stand by the Union" they say it with emphasis— If the question of *secession* comes before the people of Tennessee they wont leave a greasy spot of the secessionists.

The Turneys[3] have made strong efforts here for separate state action at once— But if we elect a delegate to the Convention the substance of your spirit will be made the basis of a platform and it will carry at least 1500 votes out of 1800 or 1900, against the strongest man they can start.

I am looking to you to do more than any man in the middle states in this terrible struggle and if we do succeed in saving the Country there is no telling what we will do for you.

All party lines are broken down here[.] And we feel after reading your speech like making one bold effort to save the Country. This Government is worth one *great* effort worth an appeal cost what it may directly to the whole people which will save the Country. In God's name let's not give it up because political wireworkers cant save the Country. We must not expect them to do it— it must be done in a different way.

I wish you could be among us to make a few speeches— No man ever had such crowds as you would have— our people are scared. Pardon this free letter in one whose position perhaps did not justify it but the crisis is my excuse.

Very Truly   A S Colyar

ALS, DLC-JP.

1. Arthur S. Colyar (1818–1907), a prominent Winchester Whig lawyer, had been a Bell-Everett elector in 1860 but, until elected to the Confederate Congress (1863–65), did not hold office. In 1858 he opened a law office in Nashville but did not move there until 1866. After the war he was a founder of the Tennessee Coal, Iron and Railroad Company and the author of a biography of Andrew Jackson. Clyde L. Ball, "The Public Career of Colonel A. S. Colyar, 1870–1877," *Tenn. Hist. Quar.*, XII (1953), 24–41.

2. Colyar disregards the fact that he and Johnson had shared the platform in Winchester during the presidential canvass of 1860, one speaking for Bell, the other for Breckinridge. On that occasion Colyar had provided the Nashville *Republican Banner* with what appears to be a reasonably objective report of Johnson's remarks. Nashville *Republican Banner*, October 2, 1860; Speech at Winchester, September 29, 1860, *Johnson Papers*, III, 661–64.

3. Probably Samuel Turney, former speaker of the state senate and his nephew, Peter Turney, the son of former U. S. Senator Hopkins L. Turney of Franklin County. The younger Turney, convinced that Lincoln's election doomed the South to an inferior position, was an early secessionist; in the February 9 vote for a state convention he was elected as a disunionist delegate. In April, without waiting for the state's withdrawal, he raised a volunteer

regiment, the 1st Tenn. Inf., assigned by the Confederate authorities to the Army of Northern Virginia. For Sam and Peter Turney, see *ibid.*, I, 112*n*; III, 427*n*; White, *Messages*, VII, 451–53.

From William H. Malone

January 3, 1861, Jacksboro; ALS, DLC-JP.

Campbell County lawyer, seeking appointment as district attorney for East Tennessee in the event John Crozier Ramsey resigns or is displaced by the Lincoln administration, comments on Tennessee's "insisting on our constitutional guarantees *within* the Union" rather than seceding and adds, "I heer of some complaint at your recent speech upon the *crisis* among the hot-heads in the larger towns & Cities, but I have no doubt the people will sustain your course when they properly understand the questions involved. . . . I can see no difference between secession and revolution."

From Harvey M. Watterson[1]

McMinville Ten Jan 4th 1861

Dear Governor

While the Madam is gone to Church to pray for the salvation of the Union, I will tell you what I think of your late speech in the Senate of the United States.

You have made out a clear case that the Federal Government has ample power to preserve its own existence. You have also shown beyond the shade of a doubt that the Constitution does not sanction the heresy of *secession*. Indeed, you have not laid down a principle that is not correct in itself and that has not been endorsed by all the great lights we have been following for three score years and ten. If you are wrong, so was Washington; so was Jefferson, so was Madison, so was Chief Justice Marshall, so was Jackson, so was Clay, so was Webster, and so was everybody else who sincerely desired the unity of these states. In a word, I consider your speech the ablest you have ever made in Congress. It is sound in doctrine and overwhelming to the enemies of the Union. Hence their bitter denunciations, their disreputable attempts to pervert, and their unpraiseworthy efforts to keep the truths you have set forth with such power from taking hold of the popular mind.

The *Nashville Union* and the *clique* who control it,[2] are delighted to have a pretext for assailing you. Fear them not. As sure as this Government lives, *they* will be lost. *It will live—it must live.* there are patriots enough in the country to save it, and the time has come when they should speak to the demagogues as the earthquake speaks of the coming eruption of Vesuvius.

What does Gen Lane mean?[3] Is he crazy? It seems so, or he would not have said so many silly things when attempting a reply to your speech. for example, that Washington was a seceder from the Old Confederation!!

I wish we had at least one hundred and fifty copies of your speech, in pamphlet form, for circulation in this county. They would not only do you but the country great good. The Nashville Union has a pretty large number of subscribers in Warren, and in addition to this fact, the McMinville New Era contained an editorial article on yesterday that I have no doubt was written by Tom Murray[4]—Col. Breckinridge-Elector in this district—and it wholly misrepresents your true position. Send a bundle to the address of each of the following gentlemen, and they will take pleasure in giving them the proper direction:

Col Wm Lowry 50 copies[5]
Col. Stokely D. Rowan[6] 50 copies   } McMinville
H. M. Watterson 50 copies   Ten

I have but little hope that Congress will do anything to settle our troubles. The people will have to rise in their majesty and take their destinies in their own hands, or certain madmen will shatter this Union to pieces.

Believing that such a measure at this time can not fail to operate favorably to the Union cause, I hope that the Pacific Railroad Bill will pass the Senate and become a law.[7]

I have not left the town of McMinville since Oct last, and [in] these Revolutionary times God only knows when I shall.

As I have plenty of time to read, I must beg you to send me the documents.

When Judge Douglas makes his speech, if it is published in pamphlet form, I would thank you for two or three copies. Compliments to him[.]

E. Pluribus Unum— Sine que non— God and Liberty!

Yours truly   H. M. Watterson

ALS, DLC-JP.

1. See *Johnson Papers*, I, 426n.

2. J. O. Griffith, owner and editor of the *Union*; Francis C. Dunnington, John C. Burch, Leon Trousdale, and Thomas S. Marr, editors.

3. Senator Lane had asserted that the northern Democracy would continue to defend the rights of other states and would never march with Lincoln against the South. In explaining the founding fathers' dissatisfaction with the Articles of Confederation government, Lane declared that, "They were seced-

ers then. George Washington headed the band." *Cong. Globe*, 36 Cong., 2 Sess., 143.

4.. Thomas B. Murray (b. *c*1817), a Virginia-born Warren County farmer with $8,000 in real and $7,000 in personal property, had been a Breckinridge elector, later becoming lieutenant colonel of the "Warren Guards," the first Confederate unit to be raised in that county. The McMinnville *New Era*, a weekly (1855–1906), is not extant for this period. 1860 Census, Tenn., Warren, 126; Walter Womack, *McMinnville at a Milestone* (McMinnville, 1960), 261; Will T. Hale, *Early History of Warren County* (McMinnville, 1930), 48; *Johnson Papers*, II, 235n.

5. William Lowery (1798–1877), a North Carolina native and Warren County farmer and saddler, had served in the legislature (1837–39). Robison, *Preliminary Directory, Warren*, 28.

6. Stokeley D. Rowan (1789–1870) was a pioneer Warren County lawyer with property valued in 1850 at $14,600, a figure which by 1860 had become $30,000 in real estate and $35,000 in personal property. *Population Schedule of the United States Census of 1850 (Seventh Census) for Warren County, Tennessee* (McMinnville, 1958), 8; 1860 Census, Tenn., Warren, 210; Hale, *Warren County*, 33; Acklen, *Tenn. Records*, I, 144.

7. Proposed during the Pierce administration as a military necessity for transportation of troops and delivery of the mails, the Pacific railroad question came to be entangled with the sectional crisis. In May, 1860, a bill reported from a select House committee proposed a road, to be built by private interests, which would start from two eastern points and merge into a single trunk line somewhere near the forty-first parallel. Defeated and returned to committee, the proposal was revived by the Republicans as a campaign issue and received considerable support when Congress met in December, 1860, but expired again "amid unhappy wrangling over routes." Nevins, *Emergence of Lincoln*, II, 195, 196, 301, 448.

From John Pat. Farrelly[1]

Memphis Tenn Jan 5th 1861

Hon Andrew Johnson
U. S. Senate Washington D. C—
My Dear Sir:

While the country is convulsed with political excitement, may I, by request, call your attention to a subject in which the people of Shelby and adjoining counties feel much interest—I mean the *Pacific Rail Road Bill*. I speak as the representative of Shelby, when I say, your support of this measure, would give Satisfaction to nine tenths of the people of this county—and as far as I have heard, a large majority of the people of this, the Tenth Congressional district.[2] I hope your views on this subject may meet the approval of our people hereabouts—

I have been from home some eight weeks, until Saturday last when I returned home, much talk is had about your recent speech in the Senate, on the subject of the crisis of the count[r]y— I have not had the pleasur of seeing your speech, but can say, notwithstanding you have been burnt and hung in effigy by *Some* of our people of Memphis, those who have read *the speech*, approve it— And I beleive I reflect the sentiments of the substantial men, with the majority of all classes, when I say you are right so far as your speech goes— Understand me, I am speaking from what I have heard,— I have not had the pleasure of seeing your speech— please send me a copy to Nashville, where I will be, by the time you receive this, to take my seat as one of the representatives from this county in the Legislature— I would say further, that I would be pleased to hear from you, in this the most trying period of our count[r]y—

Very Respectfully   John, Pat. Farrelly

ALS, DLC-JP.

1. See *Johnson Papers*, III, 427*n*.

2. West Tennesseans, particularly Memphians, were vitally interested in a transcontinental link to the Pacific with their city the prospective eastern terminus. Philip M. Hamer, *Tennessee: A History* (4 vols., New York, 1933), I, 445–46.

From Thomas M. Brennan[1]

Nashville Jany 7. [6] 1861

The Honble And Johnson
Dear Sir

Excuse the liberty I take in asking a favor that I hope you may not find troublesom to grant— I am desirous of obtaining a copy of report on 'Ordnance'[.][2] I do not Know the exact title but the object I have in view will suggest it and enable you to form an idea of the Report I desire,

It has occurred to me that the present very uncertain appearance of things in this State as indeed in the whole Union, may make it necessary for the Southern States to "Arm[.]" Ordnance, & Munitions of war, will be wanted, and as I do not expect much business in my line I thought I might turn attention to the casting of Cannon & balls & would be glad to have the advantage of any "Reports" or "orders" on the subject to assist me in carrying out my views[.]

This is a matter of business & I trust that the difficulties pending may be got over in time to preclude the necessity of any warlike preperation in our or any other State but it is well to prepare for the worst,

In connection with this subject you will excuse me if I compliment you on your recent success in Senate Speech[.] it suits many of your old friends and nearly all of your old enemies in this region, but the Phalanx of Democratic office holders who cling to the hope of demolishing a Southern Confederacy as they are trying to do with the Union are very much disgusted at your Coercion doctrine and call you an abolishnst[.]

I am glad there is one man from this State in the congress who has the boldness to take an independant stand & try and save this fabric that has been reared at the expense of so much blood and treasure but I cannot conceal from myself or you the fact that every effort is made here to make us Secessionists and complete the ruin that has been already commenced— I have been working over 100 hands in my foundry & Machine Shop all this year & in one month may have to stop altogeth altho I still provide for 75 to 80, & through them 250 mouthes, all commerce and manufacturs & enterprize are suspended or about to suspend, if this mad rush after dissolution is not stayed forthwith. Our legislatur meet tomorrow & I fear will adopt the popular or Secession principle, we are to have a meeting tomorrow night[3] that will I have no doubt be on the same side[.]

I am not an American born Citizen[.] I always thought I should have been one but if this Union is broken up, then will be cause for all true patriots North & South to weep galling tears, for God sake try to save this Union, and excuse the liberty I take in inflicting a letter on you[.]

Respectfully Yours   T. M. Brennan

ALS, DLC-JP.

1. Thomas M. Brennan (b. *c*1827), Irish-born and "himself a practical mechanic," had been a Nashville businessman for several years. Earlier the proprietor of the Nashville Foundry, he now owned the Claiborne Machine Works, described as "very extensive," with "facilities that are not . . . surpassed in the South for making steam engines and machinery of every species." 1860 Census, Tenn., Davidson, 10th Dist., 70; *Nashville Bus. Dir.* (1855–56), 22–23; (1860–61), 67.

2. While there had been many government publications relating to ordnance, the most recent, and probably the one to which the writer refers, was Col. H. K. Craig's Report of the Ordnance Department in the War Department (*Senate Ex. Doc.* No. 1, 35 Cong., 1 Sess., 1304ff.), issued in 1859. Donald A. MacDougall, The Federal Ordnance Bureau, 1861–1865 (Ph. D. dissertation, University of California, Berkeley, 1951).

3. At an "immense meeting" held in the courthouse on Monday night, January 7, resolutions were adopted condemning "coercion of a sovereign State," demanding that the federal Constitution be amended to guarantee and protect property in slaves, commending Lane for his defense of Tennesseans' honor, and announcing that "the first shot fired by the Federal forces" would be "the signal for Tennessee to withdraw from the Union and make common cause with the Southern States." Nashville *Union and American*, January 8, 1861; see also Nashville *Republican Banner*, January 8, 1861.

From Montgomery D. L. Boren

January 7, 1861, Carter's Depot; ALS, DLC-JP.

Thanks Johnson for his "patriotc Union Speech" which "Every boddy (except a few Disunionist)" approves; although there have been effigy-burning episodes in Memphis and Nashville, the attempt in Knoxville was "detered . . . by the Union Men of every party, who was armed Capapie"; assures Johnson, "You are a stronger man now in Tennessee, than you have ever been," to the extent that the "Whigs to a man, would support you for any office, against any Secessionists, dont think strange of this, for Brownlow is advocating your course."

From John Griffen[1]

Jan –7– 1861.

Hon Andrew Johnson
Washington D. C.
Sir

I was much pleased in reading your speech delivered some days since, to learn by it that you were in favor of the Union of these States, as it at present exists, A Government under which this country has prospered as no Country on which the Sun shines has prospered, it having risen in 84 years from 13 poor weak Colonies to 33 mighty States—one of the first powers of the earth.

I am an entire stranger to you, but as a citizen of the North, and one who voted for Mr Lincoln, I supposed it possible that the views of persons here, and particularly those of your political opponents, might be of use to you. I shall, therefore, without further preface proceed to say what I desire to say, merely premising that I am one of the constituents of Hon John Hickman,[2] by whom I am known personally, as I am also known by Col J W Forney, Clerk of the House of Representatives, Hon Thaddeus Stevens, and, I may add, by his Excellency James Buchanan[.]

There seems to be a very general mistake in the minds of Southern gentlemen, as to the aims and objects of the Republican party, I mean the rank and file—the voters. I am an old Henry Clay whig, one of those who beleived Henry Clay as near perfect as men generally come from the hands of their Maker. As long as the Whig party lasted I voted that ticket. In 1856, for want of a better man I voted for James Buchanan for the Presidency, and sustained him so long as he stood on the Cincinnatti platform. When he left that, on the Teritorial question, I left him, as did hundreds of thousands of others at the north, feeling that we had been betrayed by him. Mr Buchanan distincly enunciated the doctrine, that the people of a Teritory, like those of a State, should be allowed to manage their own domestic affairs in their own way. Upon that doctrine the battle, resulting in his election, was fought and the victory won. No one who voted for him then doubting that that doctrine met the approval of the people of the entire South, and would be adhered to, as we had listened to Speakers from the South, amongst the rest the Hon Howell Cobb of Ga, who boldly and unhesitatingly declared that to be the doctrine upon which the administration would stand. We, who voted for Mr Buchanan, beleived that if a man was fit to vote in a State he was none the less so when he had removed to a Teritory, and we were entirely willing that the majority of the bona fide inhabitants of a Teritory Should determine all questions relating to their domestic concerns for themselves. At that election there had been, here at the North, a pretty thorough reconstruction of the old parties. The repeal of the Missouri Compromise in 1854 and passage of the Kansas Nebraska bill created the Republican party, it being made up of about equal numbers from the Whig and Democratic parties, taking what were previously known as "Wooly heads"[3] from the Whig party, and the "free Soilers," or "Wilmot proviso men" from the Democrats, thus leaving three parties in the field. As the whigs for that Campaign made no nomination, the votes of the "Silver grey"[4] portion of them was cast generally for Mr Buchanan, and thus secured his election. Many of the whigs who voted for Mr Buchanan did so as the choice of two evils; not that they liked him, but that they thought he was honest and capable and would make by far a better President than Mr Fremont in whom they had no confidence. They were reminded by some of their brother whigs of Mr Buchanans treatment of Henry Clay in 1825,[5] and that such a man was not to be trusted, but other considerations prevailed, and although they regretted the repeal of the Missouri Compromise, and the consequent opening of the Slavery question, still they did not doubt but the fair carrying out of the doctrine on which Mr Buchanan was elected would prevent any disturbance in the Country on the exciting question of Slavery, and would prove satisfactory to the people. After Mr Buchanans inauguration, and his declared policy in relation to Kansas, and particularly, after Mr Walkers appointment as Governor, and his address made in Kansas[6] reached here, the Republican party, the men who had voted for Fremont said that if those doctrines were carried out it would use up their party, that they would have no ground to stand on. We, who supported Mr Buchanan, were jubilant, while the Republicans were dispondent. Their party was fast becoming disorganized, and would very soon have ceased to exist, but then came the Oxford and McGee frauds[7] as stated by Governor

Walker, the election of delegates to the Convention by but a part of the Counties of the Teritory, without the Census having been taken in more than half the Counties, although provided for by law, then the convention only providing for the submission of the Slavery Clause, instead of the whole Constitution to the people, for their ratification or rejection, as had been solemnly promised by Mr Walker, and which promise had been confirmed by many of the delegates to the Convention, the Submission being the more necessary, because so many had been deprived of any voice in the election of the delegates to frame the organic law, and, finally, the attempt to pass through Congress, on the recommendation of Mr Buchanan that Constitution, ignoring as it did the wishes of the people of Kansas, we saw, as we thought, that the people of Kansas were not allowed to express their opinion: that the whole thing was a fraud, and an infamous attempt to force upon the people of Kansas what they did not want, and what a majority of the people there protested against, we then saw, as we thought, an attempt of the administration, after the failure of Congress to pass the bill in its first shape, to get it passed as it was done by submitting the Constitution to the people for their ratification or rejection, when, if accepted by them, they were to be at once admitted as a State, but, if rejected by them, they were then to remain a Teritory until they should have population enough for one representative, instead of being allowed to elect new delegates to frame a new Constitution in accordance with their wishes. The north objected, and I think very properly objected, to the whole thing. They thought if Kansas had population enough for a Slave State, then she had enough population for a free state, and, although it was urged that no Teritory should be admitted as a state until there was sufficient population within its limits to entitle it to one representative under the apportionment law of Congress; while we admitted the force of that doctrine, as applied to the Teritories generally, still we insisted, and we thought with justice, that, as the people had been allowed to frame one constitution by their delegates, and upon a fair vote, even with a prospect of remaining a Teritory if it was not accepted by the people, it was voted down by them, they should have been promptly allowed to make another Constitution, more acceptable to them, which, upon being submitted fairly to the people, and ratified by them, should have been submitted to Congress, and, if found to be republican in form have been passed by Congress. In other words. If Kansas Contained population enough for a Slave State, then there was enough for a free state. It was not a question with us, however, whether the Constitution of Kansas allowed slavery to exist or not, that was regarded here so much as that the voice of her people was stifled; their wishes set at naught, and an attempt made to force a Constitution upon an unwilling people, and when they claimed the right to make one in accordance with their wishes, and which would have made Kansas a free state, the right of her citizens to do so was denied. We did not think it was just, then, nor do we think so now. Out of all these difficulties grew, very largely, the troubles in Kansas, distracting that unhappy country for years; troubles arising, I regret to say, in the effort to influence its chance as a future state, in which much property, and the lives of many persons were sacrifised, causing ill feeling in all parts of our land, such lawless acts as were perpetrated in Kansas were, I presume, condemned by all good citizens, whether they lived north or south, but, as the papers of the different sections gave but partial accounts from there, favoring in each case, their own views, each section, no doubt, considered itself the aggreived party and hence, no doubt, much ill blood was engendered. Probably when the impartial historian writes the accounts of the troubles there, each section will be found to have been about equally at fault. Such raids however, aside from the loss of life and property by the actors in them, must ever produce evil effects upon the whole Country, and produce an alienation of feeling very injurious to the true interests of the Country, and which it will require years of quiet to restore, if indeed, it ever can be fully restored. Be that as it may, the Republican party, which supported Fremont in 1856, and which had become disorganized and almost annihilated previous to the change of policy in relation to Kansas by the administration, after that change rapidly began to assume formidable proportions, many Democrats went over to them, and also many who had been Whigs, but had held aloof from either of the dominant parties, attached themselves to the Republican party. Every day, as the Kansas policy was more and more developed, new accessions were making to the Republican party, then came the meeting of the Democratic Convention in Charleston, with the determination, early evinced, to force what the north considered a Sectional Southern, certainly an ultra platform, on the Convention,[8] when failing in that, causing a disruption in the party, and the nomination of two tickets, both claiming to be Democratic and both to be regularly nominated. Mr Breckenridge occupying one, and Mr Douglass the other. It was then seen, at the north, that, if the nominee of Chicago was not objectionable he Could be easily elected, as he would have two men to run against, and that the opposition to him would necessarily be divided. Mr Douglass did not possess the confidence of the north, and therefore, there was no chance for him, and as Mr Breckenridge occupied the extreme Southern platform, there was no chance for him at the north. As to Mr Breckenridge, personally, he was every where highly spoken of, as a Union loving, talented, and unexceptionalle gentleman, and while it was conceded that, probably, no better man could have been nominated, the platform killed him. No man on that platform could ever take the northern vote, as the North is unwilling to believe that the Constitution, by its own force, carries slavery into all the Teritories, or that it does more than acknowledge slavery where it exists by law, and that it is a creature of Statute, and not of common law, and we are confirmed in this opinion from the fact that had it not been so considered the clause in the Constitution in relation to the re[n]dition of fugitives would not have been necessary. But, be that as it may, we felt that evil enough had been produced in the Country by the Civil war in Kansas on the subject, and that some means must be taken to prevent the recurrence of such troubles, or it might end in embroiling our whole land in Civil war, and, at best, it would be likely to still more alienate the two sections. That the north saw would not be done by the Breckenridge platform, nor yet again by the Douglass platform, as the doctrine of the Douglass platform had produced the present alienation. At the same time the Republican platform was liable to the objection that it denied the right of our Southern bretherin to take their property into any of the Teritories. The Breckenridge platform occupying extreme Southern ground, the Lincoln platform extreme northern ground [9] were therefore both Sectional, and therefore, both more or less objectionable; but, while the Breckenridge platform ignored the question affecting very many at the north, to wit, the tariff, the Lincoln platform declared that, while laying duties to raise revenue sufficient to carry on the Government, sound policy required that a discrimination should be made in favor of the manufactures of the Country. This, Coupled with the fact that the Republican members of congress genera[ll]y voted for what was known as the Morrill tariff bill last spring, induced hundreds of thousands at the north to vote for Mr Lincoln who cared but little about the Teritorial question, or, if they did care, subordinated that to an issue they thought much more important to them. All these causes combined rendered the election of Lincoln as easy matter, as the result shewed; not because he had the strength in his party to do it, but because upon the issue of protection he got the reserve whig vote, and because his opponents were divided. I have omitted to speak of John Bell who would have been the unanimous choice of the whigs, because for reasons now patent he could not combine that vote. They are as follows, first the whigs knew that without aid he stood no chance in the northern states, and that, therefore, his election by the people was impossible, second, they saw that, whoever was to be the President, it was very important that it should be determined by the people, as, in the first place John Bell could not possibly be elected by Congress, and thus their votes would be thrown away, and, secondly, seeing that the Country was convulsed last year from Maine to California, in the election by Congress of so unimportant an office as Speaker of the house,[10] they naturally argued that the election of a President would be likely to lead to very serious results, in view, therefore, of all these facts, they generally cast their votes for Lincoln, not, for a moment, doubting but that the Country would acquiesce in the election by the people of a president according to the forms of the Constitution, and, more particularly, as the President was without a party, both branches of Congress being in opposition to him, thus preventing any legislation that could be injurious to the South, and without the power to appoint even his Cabinet without the sanction of the opposition; his duty being to see that the laws in existence were enforced in accordance with the provisions of the Constitution. All the power he would possess would be of a negative character, and would, at most, consist in vetoing any bill he might think very objectionable. In view of all these facts it was not supposed by any person at the north that there would be any serious objection from any quarter to Mr Lincoln, certainly that it could not go to the extent of the destruction of the Union.

Much has been said, and very persistently said, to attempt to connect the Republican party with the John Brown raid in Virginia, and to hold them responsible for it, as being the result of the teachings of that party, if not, indeed, charging them with participation in it, at least charging them, generally, with sympathy for the hoary headed murderer and his gang of Villains, who went into the State of Virginia, making war upon her peaceful inhabitants, and attempting to create a servile insurrection. I need not say to you that the people of the north, without regard to party, viewed that act as a most cold blooded, feindish, and malignant attempt at one of the most brutal and hellish crimes of which any Sett of men could be guilty; that, while a few of the Abolitionists felt sympathy with the man, even they generally denounced the crime. They beleived, or affected to beleive, that he was not sane, or he would not have done what he did. All others think his crime of the most diabolical Charactre, and that he and his men suffered justly for their crimes. You will remember that Cook,[11] one of that band who escaped from Harpers Ferry, was taken up in Pennsylvania on suspicion of being one of the murderers, was held until evidence could be brought from Virginia to identify him, when he was surrendered by the Governor of this State to the authorities there, was convicted, and suffered the penalty of his crime. I do not wish to be understood as saying that no man who voted for Lincoln did not approve of the John Brown raid, as probably some of the abolitionists, and likely some of the most ultra of them, may have voted for him as the best they could do, but of this I know nothing, but I do know that, as a general thing, they are as much opposed to Lincoln as they would have been to Breckenridge, or Douglass, as they stigmatize our present Constitution as a "Compact with Hell, and, therefore, are in favor of a dissolution of the union. In that is proved the fact that "extremes meet": the Abolitionist of the north, and the secessionist of the South, are both aiming at the same thing, to wit, the destruction of the present Government, to be reconstructed in each case upon their own notions of right, regardless of Consequences.

But, to return again to the question of parties in the north, men may be considered as divided into three classes, some beleiving Slavery to be of divine institution, and, therefore meritorious, others who think that it is not of Divine institution, but, as it exists in our Country, it must be continued, as there is no possible way of getting rid of it, and who are entirely willing that the owners of Slaves shall enjoy their rights as fully as their nonslaveholding bretheren, the third class beleive slavery to be an evil, and, while they would make no change in the law where it exists, they would prevent its spread, and, hence, they deny the right of slave holders to take their property into the Teritories. Of these three classes the second one is by far the most numerous, the third next in number, the first the least numerous of the three. There is, of course, a fourth class here, the Abolitionists, but there are so few of them they are not worth taking into the account. They Certainly do not represent, taking the entire north, over five pr cent, if even so large a proportion as that. Our political parties are made up of the three first classes spoken of. The first named, as parties are now organized, are very nearly all Democrats, the third class are all in the Republican party, the most numerous, or second class, vote either one or the other ticket, as upon the examination of all the issues presented in a campaign, they find one or the other presenting those most Consonant with their views or feelings, and here let me say, that the course of the South on the tariff question, has tended to give the present sectional appearance to the vote north, not probably with the intention of doing so, but it has done it nevertheless. The Republican party, knowing that the north contained a very large number of Whigs, who cared very little about the Slavery issue, but were in earnest about protection, finding that the Breckenridge platform ignored that issue, and that the Republican platform declared protective doctrines, voted that ticket, and thus, incidentally, appeared to give prominence to what the South have seen proper to regard as the only issue, to wit; free Teritories[.]

Thus much seemed necessary to be said, in order to [have] a full

Comprehension of the position of the votes of the north, and to explain the seeming sectional position of the north, and to prepare your mind to beleive that there is, at this moment, a very large majority of the voters of the north who are entirely willing to grant their southern bretheren all the rights, under the Constitution, that they, in fairness, and a fratirnal spirit, will demand, provided that the demand can be made without being mixed up with other issues. For the reason stated above, the Representatives from the north, the Republican portion particularly, do not represent the veiws entertained by a majority in their district, on the slavery question, and although some of them boast they have in their pockets the endorsement of their Constituents, they would find that would not be true in very many of their cases. They would find that other issues tended to give them the majority by which they were elected. Therefore, in veiw of all these facts, it seems important that in some way the questions at issue between the north and south should be brought to the direct arbitrament of the people. If that can be done there is not a shadow of doubt but all that is desired will be yeilded; at any rate, all that a just man would think proper would be, beyond any doubt, but there is such a thing as pushing the north beyond endurance, and that would be the opening of all the teritories to slavery, and protecting it there by law, and for the following reason. While the north will not object to having a portion of our teritory set apart, and slavery protected therein, they will ask that another portion shall be devoted to freedom. They have seen the effects of that already in Kansas, and, therefore, know that it results in unmitigated evil, and that such a system cannot be satisfactory, either to the north or the south, and, aside from that, we have many persons in the north, both native and foreign born, who have but little Capital, but they have a stalwart frame, have children growing up around them, and wish to procure homes in the west. these men seek our frontiers, and are the pioneers in new settlements, they intend to till the ground with their own labor, and bring up their children to habits of industry, they wish to feel that they are the peer of their neighbour, and, as they know that in states where slaves are employed, labor is considered degrading, they earnestly desire that their future state shall be free, and they, therefore, desire that slavery shall not be permitted in that teritory, but they have no objections that other portions of the public domain shall have slavery in it, if it is desired by its inhabitants, for this reason it would seem desirable that the public domain should be equitably divided, and that irrevocably, except by the action of the future states to be carved out of such domain, either by an alteration of the Constitution; or in some way by the admission of such teritory into the Union as states, subject to subsequent division hereafter, on some equitable principle.

A very mistaken notion, I think, prevails at the south of the estimate put upon the negro at the north. While most of us beleive in the declaration of independence, that "mankind are created free and equal, and are endowed with certain inalienable rights, among which are, life, liberty, and the pursuit of happiness," and that, that includes the negro, as an abstract proposition; we are very far from considering the negros the equal of the white man, in any sense of the word, while living among the whites. Whatever may have been his status as God created him, we know that, here with the whites, he must ever occupy a very humble and I may very properly add, a very degraded position. This fact is well understood at the north, and it is very generally admitted that, physically and morally, the slave is, by far, better off where he is than he ever could be as a free man, and that his position as a slave is much more respectable than any he could attain in a condition of freedom in the north. The free negro is idle, improvident, vicious and degraded here, generally to the last degree, and occupies our Almshouses, our jails, and our prisons to such an extent as to be almost unendurable, and it is now a serious question whether we will not prevent any more negros coming into the state. Our Census shows that the number is diminishing yearly,[12] and it is hoped it may continue to be the case, as we should be relieved of a very serious burden, and a great amount of crime, by their absence. For these reasons, whatever may be our opinion in relation to Slavery, in the abstract proposition of its evil or good tendency, we are entirely unanimous as to wanting no more of the negros among us, and we are nearly as unanimous that they should remain in the condition they are at the south; none but the 4th class, or Abolitionists, wanting them freed. This may strike you as not being so, and it possibly is not entirely over the north, but it is so in this region, and yet, in this particular County Lincoln received a large majority of the vote. The question of the Condition of the Teritories, as discussed at the north, is not so much on any feeling they have against slavery, directly as such, as on account of the men who must settle the Teritories, and their known want of means, though many think, and probably very honestly think, that it should not be extended at this time, as they very often contrast the number of inhabitants in the slave states with their area, with the number of inhabitants in the free states, with the area of them, by which it appears that the population of the free states is very nearly twice as dense as the population of the slave states. By the Census of 1850 it was almost exactly twice as dense, there being a very little over 10 pr square mile in the slave, while there was nearly 21 pr square mile in the free states.[13]

Much has been said in the south, both in Congress and in the states, about the Personal Liberty bills, as they are called, and the

charge freely made that they are unconstitutional and interfere with
the operation of the Fugitive Slave law in the rendition of fugitives,
and, among the rest, I see that this good, conservative old Commonwealth is charged with having such a law upon her statute books. It
is true we have a law upon our statute books in relation to Kidnap-
ping, a crime that has first and last been practiced to a considerable
extent in this state, but it will be found that it in no way affects the
fugitive slave law, and was in existence when that law passed. The
only section that appeared to conflict with that law was repealed in
1852. I see, however, by the message of the Governor of this state,
that, while he states that our law is entirely Constitutional, still, as it
may be possibly misinterpreted, he advocates its repeal, wishing to
carry out the injunctions of St Paul to the Christians of his day,
"Avoid the appearance of evil,"[14] I have no reason to doubt it will be
done,[15] or so changed in its phrazeology that no doubt can arise in the
minds of any one as to its object. I think it will be found that the complaint against the laws of many of the northern states will turn out
to be not well founded, though it is possible there are three or four
exceptions. But suppose it had been true that all the northern states
had unconstitutional laws in relation to slaves on their statute books,
while it would have appeared unkind towards the southern states, I
apprehend that it could have done no harm, as a suit would have determined the question, when, if they had been pronounced unconstitutional, they would have fallen a dead letter. We claim to be a law
abiding people at the north, and, I think, with justice. We do not
like some of the provisions of the fugitive slave law, as under it any
of our Citizens may be turned into a negro catcher, but still that law
has been obeyed in this State. In every instance when a slave has been
arrested, and proved before a commission to be a slave, he has been
returned to the owner himself or to his agent, without a solitary exception. Indeed, in one case, that of a negro claimed as a slave belonging to a man living near Elkton in Maryland, the negro was sent to
Elkton to his supposed master, when it turned out that the man was
not his slave, but was a free negro, born in the State of New Jersey;[16]
but you will say, many negros escape through Pennsylvania, and get
into Canada without being arrested, true, and why? Every negro in
this state is Considered to be a free man, and, hence, he travels here
without any fear of arrest, and has no trouble in passing through on
his road to Canada, and that must ever be so, as, under the circumstances, it cannot well be otherwise.

We are also much misunderstood in relation to our entire freedom
of speech, and of the press, which is secured to us by the Constitution of the United States, and we consider them as sacred. We think
when they are abolished, or materially abridged, our liberties will

soon follow, besides, when the extreme licence is spoken of, we are reminded of the sedition law, passed under the elder Adams, and which was justly odious. We think that, though it may be sometimes abused, better that than in any way interfere with it, as we know that truth only shines with the more resplendent lustre by agitation;[17] and as all questions debatable have two sides, any proposition may be met by an opposing argument, besides, if we undertake to abridge, or prohibit, what shall be the subject, and who shall determine? For these reasons we accord the largest liberty of discussion, and writing, the party being always answerable to the law when libellous. Under our custom, then, a party having a room, may in that room discuss any subject with perfect impunity, without fear of disturbance from any quarter, without any regard to the sentiments of the people on the Subject, they being content not to go if they do not want to hear. Except in two instances lately, one in Boston and one in Philadelphia,[18] I do not know of any interruption. The one in Boston was prevented by the Citizens, the one in Philadelphia by the Mayor of the City. It may, under the circumstances, have been right in both cases, but all such interruptions are looked upon as not being right, without regard to the subject to be treated of by the speaker.

South Carolina, after twenty seven years quiet, or rather, Comparative quiet, again attempts Secession, this time it is an issue of Slavery, before it was duties. I apprihend one reason is just about as good as the other. When Jackson put down Nullification in 1833, he said the next outbreak of South Carolina would be on the Subject of Slavery.[19] His saying was prophetic. Why is South Carolina now in the front rank? It certainly is not because she loses so many slaves by the "underground rail road," or in any other way. The track cannot reach there, it would run through too many slave states to reach her. The border states, no doubt, have just cause of complaint on that subject, but she certainly has not. The question of the Teritories is at this time but an abstraction, there being no power in Congress for adverse legislation at this time, nor will there be, probably, at any time, but suppose the second reason a good and tangible cause of complaint, and that there was no remedy, while I can readily understand why she might be willing to cooperate with her sister states, many of which suffer much more severely, and might be willing to be governed by the wishes of a majority of them, in any ulterior movement, having for its objict a redress of the grievance, or failing in that a withdrawal from the Union. I cannot understand her precipitancy, except upon one hypothesis, and that is, that she desires to open the African Slave trade, which she knows cannot be done while she remains in the Union, and, hence, her overpowering desire to go out before any chance was given for cooperation for a ridress of greivances, or until her people had time for reflection. She has taken the fatal leap, has launched her frail bark on an unknown and stormy sea. God grant it be not wrecked! Her attitude is certainly not one of peace. She seems determined to leave the issue to the God of battles, and, probably, with the intention of drawing her sister states into the Conflict, and thus precipitate the revolution. If war must come we must meet it, and then "Dieu et Mon droit":[20] but who can Contemplate such a fratricidal strife without a shudder; and what for? Why shall brothers hand be raised against brother? No cause, certainly, exists at this time for such an arbiter. Will she not stay her already uplifted hand? Must the blow fall? Shall she, in her frenizy, lay her sacrilegious hands upon the pillars of this glorious temple, with the intention of prostrating it?[21] And shall she do it? Forbid it Heaven[.]

I see by the papers, that, recently, at a meeting held in Norfolk Va, one of the speakers said at the Conclusion of his speech, "let the Union go to H-ll".[22] Did he not know that, but a few years since, that place, and Portsmouth, were visited with Yellow Fever,[23] that it raged with great severity, that many of the inhabitants, nearly all who were able, left, and fled to a place of safety, that the exodus was so complete that not enough well persons remained to take care of the sick, that the voice of the Sufferers, imploring for aid, in that, their hour of distress, reached the ears of their northern brothers and sisters, that a noble body of our men and women left their homes here, and went down to that Charnl house, over which the Angel of Death was flapping his outstretched wings, and there attended the sick and the dying, that many of those who went were struck by the Destroying Angel, and they fell victims to the pestilence, leaving their bones to decay in Southern Soil. Such acts as that show that a brotherly and fraternal feeling existed between the two sections at that time, and why not now? The northern mind is the Same now as it was that time. I mean their settled Connections, their moral and religious feelings, and that, whatever they may be, I know that in their minds towards their brethern in the South they have none but feelings of kindness, that they would do any of them a favor if asked. I know, too, there is none of that feeling of hate in the northern mind that seems to have taken possession of the minds of many at the South.

However we may be divided here politically, we have but one opinion about the Union; we are all for that, come weal Come woe, under all circumstances, and for all time, we will stand by the Stars and Stripes, and, while we hope, for their own sakes, rebellion may not break out in the South, as we see no cause existing, sufficient to demand such a course, yet, if war must come, however we may abhor a fratricidal strife. War between brethren of the same Common Country, speaking the same language, mingled by blood, by marriage, by business, and in a thousand different ways, and, therefore, all the more to be deprecated. When the demand is made on us by the Constituted authorities, we will as one man, rally around that old, that honored flag, and will shed our best blood in its defense, and in the defence of our institutions as they were handed down to us by our fathers, the most precious legacy bequeathed to us by them, and, rallying under that flag, and our glorious institutions, under which we have been so prosperous, so happy, and so free, where, in deed and in truth, every man is sovereign, where, when he does not like his public servants, he by the ballot box can change them. I say, with that flag, and such institutions on the one side, and calling up the memories of the past, we cannot doubt upon whose banners, in the end, victory will perch; but then what? In place of mighty states what will we see? Desolation, destruction, Conquered provinces, and people; their Substance wasted, their hearth Stones desolate, the husband, father, son, the good Citizen, has been food for powder; the once mighty state, possibly, blotted from the map of nations; it may be to be settled by strangers. Who can contemplate all the evils, likely to result, without a shudder. Shall hope be allowed to settle into despair, will not the Southern States pause? Must they follow the lead of South Carolina, and by resolution declare themselves out of the Union, and then appeal to that last dread arbiter War! Do they not see that even if they are allowed to go without a struggle, that all they are contending for is lost. That, from the moment a separation is declared, even if it were possible mutually to declare it, that what was before a mighty nation is shorn of half its strength, that the expense of maintaining two Governments must be materially greater than one borne by the same people, that as two adjoining Governments, with a very extended border, without barriers, with institutions differing, with the alienation of feeling sure to result from separation, with the probable necessity of keeping troops on both sides of the line, with the possiblity, nay, almost certainty of colisions, under such circumstances, and with almost certainty that such colisions would lead to a general war. The consequences are too gloomy to contemplate with Composure, and thus when we come to contemplate what it is all for, and that by such Separation the South must be the losers by it, to by far the largest extent, as the north must also lose more or less. Then Slavery will, indeed, have been placed in the course of ultimate extinction, and that, inevitably. The protection from loss of slaves by the free states will be removed, Compelling the owners, however unwilling, to sell their slaves or remove farther from the border; the lands, thus left, will be purchased and occupied by persons using free labor, and this process would go on, until, in the end, the majority of the voters of the state would become in favor

THE CONSTITUTIONALITY AND RIGHTFULNESS OF SECESSION.

SPEECH

HON. ANDREW JOHNSON, OF TENNESSEE,

IN THE SENATE OF THE UNITED STATES,

ON TUESDAY AND WEDNESDAY, DECEMBER 18 AND 19, 1860.

The question pending being the Joint Resolution (S. No. 48) introduced by Mr. Johnson, on Thursday the 13th of December, 1860, proposing amendments to the Constitution of the United States.

Mr. JOHNSON, of Tennessee. Mr. President, by the joint resolution now before the Senate, three amendments to the Constitution of the United States are proposed. One proposes to change the mode of election of President and Vice President of the United States from the electoral college to a vote substantially and directly by the people. The second proposes that the Senators of the United States shall be elected by the people, once in six years, instead of by the Legislatures of the respective States. The third provides that the Supreme Court shall be divided into three classes: the term of the first class to expire in four years from the time that the classification is made; of the second class in eight years; and of the third class in twelve years; and as these vacancies occur they are to be filled by persons chosen, one half from the slave States and the other half from the non-slaveholding States, thereby taking the judges of the Supreme Court, from the respective divisions of the country.

Mr. President, if these amendments had been made, and the Constitution had been in the shape now proposed, I think the difficulties that are now upon the country would have been obviated. It would have been required that either the President or the Vice President should be taken from the South, and that would have destroyed, to some extent, the sectional character of our recent election.

The next provision of the amendment would require the votes cast for President and Vice President to be cast by districts; and if we are to take as an indication the returns to the House of Representatives of a majority of twenty-seven against the incoming Administration, it is pretty conclusive that a President differing in politics and sentiments from the one who has been recently elected would have been chosen. Each district would have voted directly for the President and Vice President of the United States. The individual having a majority of the votes in that district would be considered as receiving one electoral vote, just as we count the votes for one member of Congress. Hence, if all the votes in the respective districts had been cast on the same principle, we should in the next Congress have a majority of twenty-seven in opposition to the incoming Administration in the House of Representatives; for they would have given us a majority in the electoral colleges. It seems to me, if these propositions were adopted and made a part of the Constitution, that, to a very great extent, the difficulty and complaint that is now manifested in different portions of the country would be obviated, and especially so with some improvement or modification of the law which provides for the restoration of fugitives from labor.

It is not my purpose, sir, to discuss these propositions to amend the Constitution in detail to-day, and I shall say but little more in reference to them and to their practical operation; but, as we are now, as it were, involved in revolution, (for there is a revolution, in fact, upon the country,) I think it behooves every man, and especially every one occupying a public place, to indicate, in some manner, his opinions and sentiments in reference to the questions that agitate and distract the public mind. I shall be frank on this occasion in giving my views and taking my positions, as I have always been upon questions that involve the public interest. I believe it is the imperative duty of Congress to make some effort to save the country from impending dissolution; and he that is unwilling to make an effort to preserve the Union, or, in other words, to preserve the Constitution, and the Union as an incident resulting from the preservation of the Constitution, is unworthy of public confidence, and the respect and gratitude of the American people.

In most that I shall say on this occasion, I shall not differ very essentially from my southern friends. The difference will consist, as I think, from what I have heard and what I see published in the various periodicals of the day, in the mode and manner by which this great end is to be accomplished. Some of our southern friends think that secession is the mode by which these ends can be accomplished; that if the Union cannot be preserved in its spirit, by secession they will get those rights secured and perpetuated that they have failed to obtain within the Union. I am opposed to secession. I believe it is no remedy

---

Speech of December 18–19, 1860.
Courtesy Margaret Johnson Patterson Bartlett.

Balloon view of U. S. Capitol, from *Harper's Weekly*, July 27, 1861.

of its ultimate extinction in such state, such laws would be passed in relation to the institution as were passed at the north, and in this way, year after year, slavery would of necessity be driven back on itself from the borders; free states must surround it as with a cordon of fire, and, in the end, it must succumb to the pressure, not, to be sure, in this generation, or the next, but still it must come at some day, and that, too, with no guarantee from the north, and with none of the Teritories, as from [sic] the much larger population in the north would insist upon, and would keep the Teritories[.]

But peaceable secession will not be allowed by the North, as, when it begins we do not know where it will end, and, besides, our north-western States cannot allow the mouth of the Mississippi to be in the hands of a foreign state. Louisiana was purchased from France to give the Union the Control of that river when the west was almost a wilderness, now, that they are mighty states, and their existence al-most depends on the free navigation of that river, they will permit no power to take it from them, in which they would be prompted by self preservation, if from no higher motive, therefore, as I veiw it, peaceable secession is out of the question, even if secession were de-sirable to the South, and that it certainly cannot be. In veiw, then, of the fact that guarantees can be had in the Union; that it is the interest, both of the north and the south, that our present Union should be maintained in its integrity, those who favor the Union, both North and South, should come together, yielding all minor differences, and, as brothers, agree upon some plan, which, if not entirely satisfactory to one or the other, still is the best that can be done, and then say to those traitors, those rebelious Sons who would distroy this Union, stay your hands; touch not the sacred structure, cemented by the blood of our fathers, the patriots of the revolution, who, after the long and bloody struggle, through privation, through suffering, and almost despair, finally achieved our independence, and when Victory had perched upon their banners, and, when the Mother Country ac-knowledged our independence, they, the survivors of that struggle, headed by the immortal Washington, finding that the articles of Con-federation did not secure what was wanted, but that a more consoli-dated government was required, called a convention of the people to form "a more perfect Union", who, calling on the Almighty for aid, framed and prepared our present Constitution, full of concessions, but the freest, most liberal, and most perfect form of government ever vouchsafed to erring man, under which we have lived happily, and have flourished as no other Country has flourished, Capable of extension to an unlimited degree, because, only the general legisla-tion, that which is necessary for all of the States, is carried on by the general government, while local legislation is left to the individual states. Shall not the sons of such sires, the Unionmen of the United States, scattered though we may be through the different States, unite: and as one man say to the plotters of treason, "Go no farther with your fatal project; you shall not be allowed with your unhallowed hands to touch this sacred temple, reared by our fathers. It shall stand as it has stood faultless in proportion, the admiration of the world, sheltering under it[s] aegis the oppressed of all nations, and it shall be handed down to our children as the richest legacy which we bestow upon them, and to which they may add star after star, as we have added, until, if possible, the stars and stripes float over the entire Continent, constituting it one nation, a band of brothers, and so to continue through ages, that succeeding generations may bless the founders of so mighty an empire, so free and so glorious. That it may grow in the future, as it has in the past, growing larger and larger, and that the fires of liberty may grow brighter and brighter, that its beacon light may spread to the most remote parts of the habitable globe, and that other peoples, seeing our freedom and happiness, may rise in their might, and upon the ruins of Monarchies erict a form of Government like ours,"[24] is the sincere prayer of

Very Respectfully Your Obt Sert

John Griffen

Phoenixville Chester County Pa
Janry 7, 1861

ALS, DLC-JP.

1. John Griffen (b. c1812), a New York native, the possessor of $3,000 in real and $7,000 in personal property, husband of a well-to-do wife ($20,000 in personalty), and employer of two female Irish domestics and one Irish gardener, was superintendent of the Phoenixville Iron Company. 1860 Census, Pa., Chester, Phoenixville, 66.

2. John Hickman (1810–1875), West Chester lawyer and formerly a Democratic (1855–61), but now Republican (1861–63), congressman, had been district attorney of Chester County (1845–46) and later served in the Pennsylvania house (1869). *BDAC*, 1050.

3. The "Woolly Heads" were a Whig party faction which had espoused the cause of Negro liberation. Mathews, *Americanisms*, II, 1890.

4. "Silver-Grays" were conservative, and, by implication, elderly, Whigs who had supported the Compromise of 1850. *Ibid.*, 1546.

5. Griffen probably alludes to Buchanan's knight-errant venture on behalf of Clay in the aftermath of the disputed election of 1824, an imprudency that rebounded against Clay during the infighting that followed. When none of the candidates—Jackson, J. Q. Adams, Crawford, or Clay—obtained the necessary electoral majority, the choice was thrown into the House of Representatives, giving rise to stories of bargains on behalf of various candidates. On December 30, 1824, Buchanan, then a young Federalist congressman from Pennsylvania who, although supporting Jackson, hoped to see Clay made secretary of state, called upon Old Hickory and boldly asked whether the Old Hero had ever asserted that "in case he should be elected President he would appoint Mr. Adams Secretary of State?" Jackson replied that he had

kept, and would continue to keep, his own counsel about possible Cabinet appointments. Buchanan's inquiry was later used by Jackson and his partisans as evidence that Clay had first offered his support to Jackson and, when he received no assurances from Old Hickory about his future Cabinet role, had then turned to Adams. Buchanan was thus placed in the difficult position either of admitting complicity in a "corrupt bargain" attempt on Clay's behalf or of repudiating Jackson's contention and calling him a liar. Klein, *James Buchanan*, 50–59.

6. In his inaugural at Lecompton in late May, 1856, Robert J. Walker urged participation in the coming election for a constitutional convention and added that the resulting document would be submitted to public vote. Walker, former secretary of the treasury, hoped to build in Kansas a strong "Middle" party which would be Democratic. Nevins, *Emergence of Lincoln*, I, 151ff; *Johnson Papers*, I, 386n.

7. During the election of delegates to the Kansas territorial legislature, October 5–6, 1857, Oxford precinct in Johnson County cast over 1,500 pro-slavery votes and McGee County in excess of 1,200; neither had an adult white male population of more than a few hundred. Revealing the obvious fraud, Walker publicly exhibited the Oxford returns to prove that some 1,500 names, all in the same hand, had been copied from *Williams' Cincinnati Directory*. Nevins, *Emergence of Lincoln*, I, 173–74; Franklin G. Adams, ed., "Documentary History of Kansas: Governor Walker's Administration," Kansas Historical Society *Transactions*, V (1896), 316–18, 404–8.

8. Reflecting the Breckinridge faction's views, the majority platform committee report—endorsed by Oregon, California, and fifteen slave states—asserted that Congress had no power to abolish slavery in the territories, that a territorial legislature could not abolish, exclude, or even interfere with slavery, and that the national government must protect the rights of persons and property in the territories, on the high seas, or wherever federal authority was extended. When it became clear that such a plank could not be adopted, a majority of the southern delegates walked out. Nevins, *Emergence of Lincoln*, II, 214, 220–21.

9. Although Griffen is accurate in describing the Republican platform as extreme on the slavery issue, the framers of that document attempted to present their position in conciliatory language. Eschewing the perennial Wilmot Proviso, and asserting that the normal condition of the territories was freedom, they denied the authority of Congress or a territorial legislature to legalize slavery in a territory, at the same time opposing disunion, the reopening of the slave trade, the Lecompton Constitution, popular sovereignty, and interference with the domestic institutions of the states. Beyond the tariff position stressed by Griffen, the platform's attention to homestead legislation, internal improvements, and the Pacific railroad reflected the economic pragmatism of the Republicans. Porter and Johnson, *National Party Platforms*, 32–33; Nevins, *Emergence of Lincoln*, II, 253–54.

10. For the lengthy wrangle over selection of a speaker, see *Johnson Papers*, III, 366n.

11. John E. Cook (1830–1859), Yale-educated romantic and onetime legal clerk from Connecticut, emigrated to Kansas and joined the Brown guerrilla force just after the Pottawatomie massacre. In the summer of 1858, as advance scout for the Brown conspiracy, Cook worked at various jobs in the Harper's Ferry vicinity. When the raid failed he escaped to Pennsylvania, where he was captured and returned to Virginia. Convicted of murder and inciting slaves to rebellion, he was hanged with other conspirators on December 16, 1859, despite the vigorous legal efforts of his brother-in-law, Indiana Governor Ashbel P. Willard, to secure a lesser penalty. Stephen B. Oates, *To Purge This Land with Blood: A Biography of John Brown* (New York, 1970), 155, 218, 251–52, 275, 302, 328; Richard J. Hinton, *John Brown and His Men* (New York, 1968 [1894]), 466–90.

12. While Pennsylvania's free black population during the 1840's in-

creased 12.06 percent to 53,626, the Census of 1860 recorded a total of 56,849, a mere 6.01 percent increase. Geographically well situated to attract large numbers of Negroes, Pennsylvania from time to time considered restricting such immigration but never did so. Agitation for prohibitive measures came principally from the southern counties. Joseph C. G. Kennedy, *Preliminary Report on the Eighth Census* (Washington, D. C., 1862), 130–31; Leon F. Litwack, *North of Slavery: The Negro in the Free States, 1790–1860* (Chicago, 1961), 69; Edward R. Turner, *The Negro in Pennsylvania: Slavery-Servitude-Freedom, 1639–1861* (Washington, D. C., 1911), 153, 165–68.

13. The actual population density figures in 1850 show the free states with 21.91 persons per square mile and the slave states with 11.35. J. D. B. De Bow, *Statistical View of the United States . . . Compendium of the Seventh Census* (Washington, D. C., 1854), 42.

14. I Thess. 5:22.

15. In his inaugural address of January 15, 1861, Governor Andrew Curtin recommended the repeal of the personal liberty laws, but the legislature failed to act. Among northern states only Rhode Island repealed its 1854 statute, although Massachusetts modified its 1855 law to provide that persons held under due process in the custody of a U. S. marshal could not be seized under a writ of habeas corpus; however, the state reserved the right to question the validity of the arrest. William B. Hesseltine, *Lincoln and the War Governors* (New York, 1948), 122–23; New York *Herald*, January 16, 1861; Norman L. Rosenburg, "Personal Liberty Laws and Sectional Crisis: 1850–1861," *Civil War History*, XVII (1971), 41–42; Henry G. Pearson, *The Life of John A. Andrew: Governor of Massachusetts, 1861–1865* (2 vols., Boston, 1904), I, 167n.

16. This particular incident has not been authenticated.

17. Perhaps a paraphrasing of "Truth like a torch, the more 'tis shook it shines." Sir William Hamilton, *Discussions on Philosophy*, Stevenson, *Quotations*, 2050.

18. Probably the first reference is to the disruption of Wendell Phillips' address to an abolitionist meeting at Boston's Tremont Temple on December 2, 1860. When the mayor ordered the hall cleared, the antislavery group withdrew to Joy Street Church, where Phillips continued to address the gathering. In Philadelphia, when George W. Curtis, fiery abolitionist whose December, 1859, speech before the People's Literary Institute had been violently disrupted, was scheduled to speak to the same audience a year later, Mayor Alexander Henry, smarting under criticism for not having banned the earlier meeting, persuaded the owner of the hall to bar the assemblage. The Institute and its speaker were obliged to move to West Chester, outside Philadelphia. Oscar Sherwin, *Prophet of Liberty: The Life and Times of Wendell Phillips* (New York, 1958), 418; William Dusinberre, *Civil War Issues in Philadelphia, 1856–1865* (Philadelphia, 1965), 90, 103.

19. Writing to John Coffee in April, 1833, Jackson prophesied that "Nullification is dead, but the coalition between Calhoun, Clay, Poindexter, and the nullifiers in the South intend to blow up a storm on the subject of the slave question [and] try to arouse the southern people. . . . This ought to be met, for assuredly these men would do any act to destroy the Union." John Spencer Bassett, ed., *Correspondence of Andrew Jackson* (6 vols., Washington, D. C., 1927–33), V, 76.

20. "Dieu et mon droit," used by Richard I at the Battle of Gisors (1198), became a battle cry; displayed on the royal arms, it is the motto of the British army. Stevenson, *Quotations*, 546.

21. A reference to Samson's destruction of the temple. Judg. 16:29–30.

22. John Tyler (1819–1896), second son and private secretary of President Tyler, had thus concluded his remarks at the December 22 rally. Having succeeded his brother Robert in the land office, he subsequently served as

Confederate assistant secretary of war. Chitwood, *John Tyler*, 145, 226, 478; New York *Times*, December 25, 1860.

23. Yellow fever, first appearing in Norfolk on July 30, 1855, ravaged the city until the October frost killed the mosquitoes. As the mortality rate began to rise, volunteers had come from all over the Union; thirteen from Philadelphia died, and twenty-six of forty-five outside physicians succumbed to the disease. Thomas J. Wertenbaker, *Norfolk, Historic Southern Port* (Durham, N. C., 1931), 210–12, 215; George D. Armstrong, *The Summer of the Pestilence: A History of the Ravages of the Yellow Fever in Norfolk, Virginia, A. D. 1855* (Philadelphia, 1856), 51–52, 71.

24. These concluding sentiments, which reveal that they are not original with Griffen only by this solitary quotation mark, seem to reflect a passage in Henry Clay's "address" to Louis Kossuth on the occasion of the latter's audience with the mortally ill senator late in 1851. Calvin Colton, ed., *Works of Henry Clay* (10 vols., New York, 1904), III, 223–24.

From S. H. Stout

January 7, 1861, Midbridge, Giles County; ALS, DLC-JP.

Postmaster, convinced that "for near thirty years there has been on foot a conspiracy to destroy this government," expresses approbation of Johnson's recent speech; reports rumor that Giles County representative [Jo J. Beaty] intends to introduce a resolution instructing Johnson to leave Senate and urges him to be in Nashville during the legislative session so that "you may circumvent more effectually the machinations of your enemies, and advance the cause of truth."

From Sam Milligan

Greeneville Ten
January 8 1861

Dear Governor,

I know you are overwhelmed with cares and responsibilities, and for that reason I hate to trouble you about any thing. But the Circuit Court is Coming on, and we must prepare your Rail Road case[1] for trial. I will put in the pleas—any thing I can think of which will be availing; but then, if I understand it, you desire to have Cave Johnson's evidence. His deposition must be taken, and perhap some others.

I think we ought to prove that the negotiation for the bonds were made by you, and at the request of Cunningham. In other words that it was not a mere accommodation on your part; and that in the circumstances in which the road was then placed, your negotiation was worth to the Company $— — —[.]

If you have any thing else which you could prove, I would be glad to know it, at as early a day as convenient so I can get up the evidence[.]

Let me hear from you on this subject.

In certain quarters they are giving you thunder about your late speech. I am sorry to See it, but cant help it.

All you or any one else were ever effected by being burned in effigy,[2] amounts to nothing. It is the unerring evidence of a low vulgar mob, who are willing to become Condits of the Spleen of others who have neither the manliness, or courage to do so dirty a thing themselves. But after all, as I believe John Tylor once said, it is rather a good thing— *"It furnishes a man a good light to walk by."*

But that is nothing[.] the Speech itself is all sufficient to put at defiance evy passing effort that may be made by malace or revenge to destroy its author. It will, in my opinion, not only out live all its assailants but its author too; and when you and I ar both gone, and I fear, the glorious government and constitution under which we live, torn into piecs, the doctrines of that speech will remain unchanged, and its wholesome truths, I fear will then be seen, in a stronger light than the burning fires of its author's effigys.

Yesterday at a lage meeting here[3] we endosed it up to the hub; and if I am any judge, the indications of its acceptibility with the people is daily and rapidly growing. The only difficulty is, we have no copies to distribute. There is great demand for it, but no supply. The Whig papers are publishing it, but the county papers do not. They have all caught the slang of the Battle-arsed gentleman[4] of the Union & American, and denounce it as *"infamous,"* and withhold it from the democrats. This does you injustice with your own party.

I see Amos Kendal is writing a series of articles, in which he sustains you all over.[5] If they are published in pamphlet form, you ought to send out some of them.

The secession feeling gained ground here for a few weeks back, but now the Union feeling is evidently increasing in the State. Every body here are Union with an unimportant exception here & there.

What will be the result— I am calm, but uneasy? Where is it to end? I have full faith yet in preserving the union, and believe yet the great masses of the people out side the towns & villages are for the Union & th Constitution[.]

It is now—as it has been for a long time apparent—that all the Cotton states desire is disunion *per se*, and nothing short of it will satisfy them. In fact from the extract in Mr Benjamin's speech[6] which I have seen he virtually says so.

He says all compromises proposed now will be unavailing— They come too late. Too late how? If the seperation is to redress wrongs, and those wrongs are redressed, and guarantees given, why seperate? All he asks is a peaceable seperation. That is to say—we are going out no matter what you do, our mind is made up to rebellion, but because we have so determined, dont whip us. Such an appeal by a wayward child to a parent, would not be likely to satisfy him, even if the parent had injured him, and then made amends. The duty is reciprocal.

But I am wearying you, and will close—

Send me all the spee[ch]es you can on both sides.

How is old Geo W Hughs—[7] I am anxious to know?

Scott & Wool[8] are anxious to get into it.

All well but me— I am not ve[r]y well for a few days back. Write[.]

Your friend   Sam Milligan

ALS, DLC-JP.

1. In consequence of the loss of Greene County circuit court records, the nature of this case cannot be precisely determined. It may relate to bonds signed by Johnson as governor, or it may concern the senator's own railroad bonds. That there had been some litigation over the latter is revealed by a surviving document which shows that a suit of the East Tennessee and Virginia Railroad Company against Johnson was dismissed on October 10, 1865, with the costs assessed against the plaintiff. Fragment, dated January 13, 1870, Johnson-Bartlett Col., Greeneville.

2. Following his widely distributed Union speech, Johnson had been hung and burned in effigy in several Tennessee towns, including Memphis and Nashville. When disunionists conspired to do the same in Knoxville, Johnson's old political enemy, Parson Brownlow, came to his defense. According to the Parson, the chief culprits, John H. Crozier and one Dreyfous, labeled "a foreign jew," a "liquor dealer," and "a wife-beater," meeting in General Ramsey's office on the evening of January 1, made plans to burn Johnson's effigy on Gay Street. Although the deed was prevented by a large body of Knoxville citizens, "among them the best men in the place," equipped with "clubs, pistols, and other implements of husbandry," Crozier and Dreyfous apparently carried through their plans on another occasion, in the meantime having kept the effigy on display in the liquor dealer's establishment. With rumors current that the two were going to call upon Brownlow "for an explanation" of his biting attacks, the editor vowed that he would spend an entire day unaccompanied upon Gay Street to provide an opportunity for "these Godforsaken, Hell-deserving scoundrels" to mete out their punishment. Knoxville Whig, January 5, 19, 1861.

3. On Thursday evening, January 17, "the Mechanics of Greenville and vicinity" gathered at the courthouse to adopt a series of resolutions upholding the Constitution, denouncing secession, and counseling compromise. They expressed approval of the constitutional amendments proposed by Crittenden, Johnson, and T. A. R. Nelson and endorsed Johnson's recent Senate speech, expressing pride in "the position attained by one of our fellow mechanics." Milligan was appointed to canvass Greene County and "address the people on the questions now exciting the public mind and threatening the downfall of our Government." Ibid., February 2, 1861.

4. Presumably John C. Burch, editor. Milligan probably meant to say "bottle-arsed," a printer's term for type thicker at one end than the other, the result of wear; in short, the gentleman was broad in the beam. John S. Farmer, Slang and Its Analogues Past and Present (7 vols., London, 1890–1904), I, 302.

5. Amos Kendall (1789–1869), Massachusetts native become Kentucky newspaper editor and subsequently influential in Jacksonian circles, engaged

shortly before Lincoln's election in a public correspondence with James L. Orr, former speaker of the House (1857–59) and now a member of the South Carolina secession convention. Once opposed to secession, Orr had now become an ardent advocate, whereas Kendall vigorously denied the right to secede. These exchanges were followed by the series of twelve short articles mentioned here, which were published in the Washington *Evening Star* from November 16 into December, 1860. Addressed "To the People of the South," these letters denounced the abolitionists, arraigned the doctrine of secession, condemned South Carolina's action, and supported the right of the federal government to enforce the laws. Like Johnson, Kendall reviewed the development of the Constitution, quoted Madison on the nature of the Union and the sovereignty of the states, discussed the dim prospects of abolitionist success in view of Lincoln's election by a minority vote, and, sympathizing with the border states, appealed to moderates both North and South to maintain the Union. Like Johnson, Kendall asserted that the "avowed object of South Carolina is not a redress of Southern grievances, but the final irretrievable destruction of the Union." *DAB*, X, 325–27; William Stickney, ed., *Autobiography of Amos Kendall* (Boston, 1872), 471–80, 588–619.

6. On December 31 Judah P. Benjamin of Louisiana had cogently defended the right of a sovereign state to dissolve its compact with other sovereign states. His remarks included a jibe at Johnson's advocacy of force to retain South Carolina in the Union. *Cong. Globe*, 36 Cong., 2 Sess., 212–17.

7. Milligan's interest in George W. Hughes, a Democratic congressman (1859–61) from Maryland, dated back to the Mexican War; Hughes was military governor of Jalapa when Milligan and his Greeneville crony Blackston McDannel were soldiering in that area. During his one term in Congress, "old Geo" was one of the first to propose the establishment of a department of agriculture; he also staunchly defended the right of a state to secede. See *Johnson Papers*, I, 407, 410n.

8. Two other relics of Milligan's Mexican War experience, Gens. Winfield Scott and John E. Wool, were both advocating strong military measures to sustain Federal forts. Stampp, *And the War Came*, 58–59, 70.

Reply to Jefferson Davis[1]

January 10, 1861

Mr. JOHNSON, of Tennessee. When my speech is taken altogether, I think my meaning can be very easily understood. What I mean by fighting the battle in the Union, is, I think, very distinctly and clearly set forth in my speech; and if the Senator will take it from beginning to end, I apprehend that he will have no difficulty in ascertaining what I meant. But, for his gratification upon this particular point, I will repeat, in substance, what I then said as to fighting the battle in the Union. I meant that we should remain here under the Constitution of the United States, and contend for all its guarantees; and by preserving the Constitution and all its guarantees we would preserve the Union. Our true place to maintain these guarantees, and to preserve the Constitution, is in the Union, there to fight our battle. How? By argument; by appeals to the patriotism, to the good sense, and to the judgment of the whole country; by showing the people that the Constitution had been violated; that all its guarantees

were not complied with; and I have entertained the hope that when
they were possessed of that fact, there would be found patriotism
and honesty enough in the great mass of the people, north and south,
to come forward and do what was just and right between the contending sections of the country. I meant that the true way to fight
the battle was for us to remain here and occupy the places assigned
to us by the Constitution of the country. Why did I make that statement? It was because, on the 4th day of March next, we shall have
six majority in this body;[2] and if, as some apprehended, the incoming
Administration shall show any disposition to make encroachments
upon the institution of slavery, encroachments upon the rights of the
States, or any other violation of the Constitution, we, by remaining
in the Union, and standing at our places, will have the power to resist
all these encroachments. How? We have the power even to reject
the appointment of the Cabinet officers of the incoming President.
Then, should we not be fighting the battle in the Union, by resisting
even the organization of the Administration in a constitutional mode;
and thus, at the very start, disable an Administration which was
likely to encroach on our rights and to violate the Constitution of the
country? So far as appointing even a minister abroad is concerned,
the incoming Administration will have no power without our consent, if we remain here. It comes into office handcuffed, powerless to
do harm. We, standing here, hold the balance of power in our hands;
we can resist it at the very threshold effectually; and do it inside of
the Union, and in our house. The incoming Administration has not
even the power to appoint a postmaster whose salary exceeds $1,000
a year, without consultation with, and the acquiescence of, the Senate of the United States. The President has not even the power to
draw his salary—his $25,000 per annum—unless we appropriate
it. I contend, then, that the true place to fight the battle is in the
Union, and within the provisions of the Constitution. The Army and
Navy cannot be sustained without appropriations by Congress; and
if we were apprehensive that encroachments would be made on the
southern States and on their institutions, in violation of the Constitution, we could prevent him from having a dollar even to feed
his Army or his Navy.[3]

Cong. Globe, 36 Cong., 2 Sess., 309.

1. Speaking on Buchanan's state of the Union message, Davis took issue
with several senators. Quoting from Johnson's December address in which he
contended that the South had "just cause of complaint," but not enough for
withdrawal from the Union, Davis could not understand "how men remaining connected together in a bond as brethren, sworn to mutual aid and protection, still propose to fight each other," and he paused for Johnson to
explain.

2. See Speech on Secession, December 18–19, 1860, note 59.

3. Here Davis interrupted, declaring "I think I comprehend now that he is not going to use any force, but it is a sort of fighting that is to be done by votes and words," and consequently, "we are not in danger of much bloodshed in the mode proposed by the Senator from Tennessee." With this explanation, Davis resumed, continuing his critical analysis of Johnson's speech.

From Salmon P. Chase[1]

Columbus, Jany 11, 1861

My dear Sir,

Will you favor me with a copy of your speech, in pamphlet.

Andrew Johnson is Andrew Jackson differently spelled; and I am glad to see the identity is not in name only.

Yours truly   S: P: Chase

Hon. Andrew Johnson.

ALS, DLC-JP.

1. Salmon P. Chase (1808–1873), Cincinnati lawyer, early became involved in the antislavery movement. Originally a Whig, he was chosen senator (1849–55) by a Free Soil-Democratic coalition, served as governor (1855–59), first as an anti-Nebraska candidate and later as a Republican, and was mentioned prominently in 1856 and 1860 for the Republican presidential nomination. Returning to the Senate in 1860, he resigned to become secretary of the treasury—a post made extremely difficult both by his own presidential ambitions and by honest differences of opinion with Lincoln. By 1864, his position in the Cabinet having become untenable, he resigned, but shortly thereafter Lincoln appointed him chief justice, a position which he held until his death. *DAB*, II, 27–34; see also Jacob W. Schuckers, *The Life and Public Services of Salmon Portland Chase* (New York, 1894).

From John R. Howard[1]

Lindley, Grundy Co. Mo.
Jany. 12th 1861.[2]

Hon. Andrew Johnson: —

Senator in Congress from Tennessee: —

Dear Sir: —   Excuse this liberty in a personal stranger to you, in thus addressing you. Having been long a citizen of Tennessee, and having very near relations in that State, (one of whom, Mr. M. H. Howard,[3] a step-son-in-law of the late old Mr. Robt. Farquharson[4] (pronounced Ferguson or Farguson,) who lived nearly opposite the old U. S. bank building, on the So. West corner of the public square, (Nashville, with whom (M. H. Howard, who lived with him) you may have been acquainted, when you were Governor of Tennessee,) and that State containing the graves of a beloved wife and 4 children, a father, mother, and 3 sisters, of my own, I feel great interest in every thing pertaining to it; and having just read in the *Cincinnati Times*,[5] a glowing and eulogistic account of your speech delivered recently in Congress, in favor of the Union, I am anxious to get it, and wish you, on receipt of this, to do me the favor to send me a copy of it, addressed to *Dr. John R. Howard, Lindley, Grundy Co. Mo.* and I shall be under many obligations to you for the favor, as I am very anxious to read it.

Having always been an ardent friend of our great and glorious Federal Union, which has been the source to us of unnumbered, invaluable blessings, and under which we have grown, from a little handful of people, to be one of the greatest nations of earth; and being opposed to every thing like disunion and secession, I am rejoiced at the stand you have taken in favor of the Union, and its perpetuity.

It is the favorite and long-cherished notion of a "Southern Confederacy", that has, I have no doubt, caused South Carolina to secede, and take the lead in secession. If she had not believed, and have had no assurances of *other* Southern States following her example, I have no idea that she would have gone off. The election of Lincoln to the Presidency, afforded her, what she regarded as a justifiable pretext for a long cherished idea. It is to be hoped that but few *others* of the Southern States will imitate her example. She hopes, no doubt, that *all* the Slaveholding States will follow, and *believes* they will; but I think I know enough of the public sentiment to know that none of the border Slave States will secede—at least, will follow the secession of So. Carolina. Georgia, Florida, Alabama, Louisiana, and Mississippi will all pretty certainly go off—and no more at present, I think, unless N. Carolina does.

But before we can have any further Union of *all* the States, Slave & Free, an arrangement will have to be made—a provision will have to be incorporated into the Constitution of the U. S.—by which the Slave States shall have the choosing of *every other* President—alternately with the Free—making a *majority* of votes of the Slave States necessary to a choice. It is this Black Republican *domination*, that the South has long been foreseeing and been preparing for, and which has at last *driven* her into *secession*. She saw that they would get the *ascendency* finally (as they have gotten) in the General Government, and *inaugurate* a policy inimical to the South, and destructive to her most vital interests—a sort of "taxation without representation." Without such a Constitutional provision and such *assurance* as this, all other compromises will be in vain!—and the committee of 33 seemed strangely to have overlooked, or not given that importance to this that it deserves, as also Mr. Crittenden's compromises. — It is to be hoped (though almost "against hope!") that the present difficulties may be amicably settled, the seceding States "come back to their first love", and our glorious Union made firmer than ever, and peace, tranquillity, and prosperity restored to our distracted country!

I present the enclosed as my own individual suggestions to yourself and such other Congressmen or both Houses, to whom you may see fit to present them.[6] I think if incorporated (most of them) into the Constitution, they would restore peace and harmony and tranquillity to our distracted country— I believe that *amendments* to the Constitution, enough and of the right kind, would be better by far than any *reconstruction* of the Government, my reasons for which I will give you on another sheet, or half-sheet, of paper[.]

With sentiments of the highest esteem I am most respectfully,

Jno. R. Howard

Feb. 1st 1860 [1861].—Let me repeat it too, that no compromise as to the election of President, short of a constitutional arrangement, that will give the Slaveholding States the power to elect at least every other President—the next after Lincoln and then every other one after—will satisfy the South. I think also it would be well, in amending the Constitution, to place such guards around the powers and duties of the President, as to render it impossible for him to have any influence over any other sphere but that of executing or performing his duties—none, for instance for, or against slavery. And the power of turning men out of office, for changing their politics, or for difference of political sentiment, or using their political influence in any way they please while in office—in short, for any thing but misconduct in office, breach of duty, or proven incapacity —should be taken away from the President entirely. Jefferson's rule should be the one: "Is he *capable*?—is he *honest*?"[7]

I would have two bodies of Electors—one composed of those elected in the Congressional Districts, as I have suggested, who are to elect the President and Vice-President; and the other, to be composed of those for the State at large, a higher body, and to *decide* the election, when the former body cannot succeed, or no one candidate has a majority—all to be elected at the same time— But this by the way.

We have just had news from St. Louis, that there is a *majority* of at least *two thirds* of the people south of the Missouri river, in this State, who are for *secession* and you need not be surprised, to hear that she has *seceded* at the Convention to be held on the 18th. The secession sentiment is decidely on the increase here. The people are generally opposed to *coercion* and in favor of the Crittenden Resolutions.[8] I am for any compromises, that will give peace, harmony and union to the country.— I fear that the procedure of the Governor of Mississippi, in sending artillery to Vicksburg, to question all boats passing, will cause trouble.[9] I dont believe the States on the Ohio river and upper Mississippi will stand it.

I shall be pleased to receive any documents or communications from you.[10]

Jno R Howard, Lindley,
Grundy Co. Mo.

ALS, DLC-JP.

1. John R. Howard (1807–1870), North Carolina native, evangelist, editor, and physician, came to Henry County, Tennessee, in 1820. Converted to the Church of Christ in 1833, he was an organizer of congregations in West Tennessee and publisher-editor of two journals (the *Christian Reformer* in 1836 and the *Bible Advocate* in 1842), both at Paris. Following medical studies in Kentucky, he lived variously in West Tennessee and Missouri, preaching, teaching, writing, and practicing medicine. Herman Norton, *Tennessee Christians: A History of the Christian Church* (Nashville, 1971), 33–35.

2. Given the date of the postscript, this letter did not reach its destination until early February.

3. M. H. Howard (b. c1820), Virginia-born printer and member of the Nashville board of education (1856–63), later served in the 11th Tenn. Cav., CSA. 1850 Census, Tenn., Davidson, 74; *Tennesseans in the Civil War*, II, 213; Clayton, *Davidson County*, 253; Wooldridge, *History of Nashville*, 445, 447.

4. Robert Farquharson (c1777–1856), a Nashville merchant and businessman, held a number of civic offices, including those of alderman (1829) and bank director (1817, 1833–34). Randal W. McGavock, *Pen and Sword: The Life and Journals of Randal W. McGavock*, Herschel Gower and Jack Allen, eds. (Nashville, 1959), 609n; *Nashville City Cemetery Index*, 26.

5. This paper is not extant.

6. Howard's proposed amendments included direct election of the President by popular vote, with the stipulation that "a *majority* of at least *two-thirds* of the votes of the Slaveholding States be necessary to the choice (of at least *every other* President)"; or, failing that, a system in which electors would be chosen by congressional districts with two at-large for each state; a single five-year presidential term; the requirement that every presidential candidate should have served as governor, congressman, senator, and vice president; the reestablishment of the Missouri Compromise line and its extension to the Pacific Coast; the denial to Congress or a territorial legislature of the power to control or abolish slavery; the retention of the Fugitive Slave Law, with strengthening amendments; and the relocation of the capital at St. Louis or "some other more central point of the Union . . . not too far South to be unhealthy, nor too far North to be too cold."

7. A paraphrase of Thomas Jefferson to Elias Shipman and Others, July 12, 1801, Paul L. Ford, ed., *The Writings of Thomas Jefferson* (10 vols., New York, 1892–98), VIII, 70.

8. This assessment is essentially correct. Although Missouri was a slave state, the post-1850 migration, composed mainly of northerners and foreign-born—all nonslaveholders—had tended to neutralize the southern advantage. In the elections of 1860 Douglas won by a small plurality over Bell, and the new governor, Claiborne F. Jackson, while in reality prosouthern, won as a Douglas Democrat over his nearest competitor, the Constitutional Unionist candidate. In the new legislature the Breckinridge men were the largest group, but Douglas Democrats and Constitutional Unionists, representing a

more conservative view, could combine and make a majority. In his inaugural of January 3, Jackson had asked the legislature to call a convention to determine Missouri's future relations with the federal Union, to send delegates to any southern convention which might be called, and to provide for the reorganization of the militia. The legislature, spurning the last suggestion, granted the other two, providing an apparent victory for the South. Yet the unionists outpolled the secessionists in the election for delegates to the convention; the result was a basically conservative, conditionally Union, meeting whose final report, adopted on March 9, supported the Crittenden Compromise and, while denouncing federal coercion of any state, reaffirmed the conviction that no cause existed to sever relations with the federal government. Howard confirmed the majority of unionist votes for convention delegates in a later letter to Johnson. Arthur R. Kirkpatrick, "Missouri on the Eve of the Civil War," *Missouri Historical Review*, LV (1960–61), 99–108; Walter H. Ryle, *Missouri: Union or Secession* (Nashville, 1931), 193, 204, 210–11; Howard to Johnson, February 19, 1861, Johnson Papers, LC.

9. Governor John J. Pettus had just ordered a battery to Vicksburg to prevent any Union ships from passing that point on the Mississippi, an action which he reported to the legislature on January 15. John K. Bettersworth, *Confederate Mississippi: The People and Policies of a Cotton State in Wartime* (Baton Rouge, 1943), 11; New York *Times*, January 26, 1861.

10. In a postscript added to his proposed amendments, Howard asked for a copy of Jefferson Davis' recent speech and concluded, "Let me repeat it, that no compromises short of Mr. Crittenden's, will satisfy the South—at least this section of the slaveholding country."

From Michael Burns[1]

Nashville January 13 1861

Honl A Johnston
Dear Sir

I have been thinking for Some time of dropping you a line in order to give you My Idea of the Situation of our Political affairs[.] as you are aware there is a party in our Legislature and Some outside of It that would like to instruct you out of your Seat in the Senate[.][2] It is this that I want to particularly to warn you Not to be instructed out as I feel confident that they dont Reflect the will of the people[.] the people are with you and I think I have Some little Knowledge of the feeling in the state[.] I read your speech over attentively and can Say that any one Reading It over attentively who does not wish to wilfully missrepresent it, cannot find fault with It[.] I was very well pleased with your resolutions offered on the amendments of the Constitution and think they would be far more acceptable to the South than the Crittendens Resolutions[.] My principal object in writing to you was that you pay No attention to any instructions in refference to Resigning your Seat as this is a new question Sprung up and the people has had no chance be heard on It[.] when you come here you must if you can spare the time make a speech and I am certain that by you doing So you will Confound your Enemies[.] you will Excuse me in trespassing on your time but I thought I as one of your Supportes ought to give my opinion on your public course[.]

Your friend   M Burns

ALS, DLC-JP.

1. Burns was a Nashville businessman and friend of Johnson. See *Johnson Papers*, III, 376*n*.

2. On January 9 Representative Jo J. Beaty of Giles County offered house resolution No. 10 demanding southern rights within the Union, proposing a conference of southern states, and instructing Johnson to resign his Senate seat in order that someone more responsive to the wishes of the people might be selected. Referred to committee, the resolution was tabled on January 28. *Tenn. House Journal*, 1861, Extra Sess., 27–29, 36, 174; Nashville *Union and American*, January 13, 1861.

From Robert Johnson

Nashville Tenn   Jan'y 13th 1861

Dear Father,

Your letters of the 8th & 9th inst were both received yesterday, and I was glad to learn that you stand firm still in favor of holding on to the old Ship of State. I have mailed you every day our proceedings[1] which I presume you received. I telegraphed you last night that the House had passed the Bill calling a convention, and ordering the election of Delegates to take place on the 9th Feby & for the convention to assemble on the 18th Feby— The Bill provides for the people to endorse on their tickets, "Convention" or "no Convention" And if a majority vote no Convention, then the Convention not to assemble— Another provision of the Bill is, "That before any ordinance of the Convention changing the relation of Tennessee to the Federal government, shall have any effect or force, the same must be submitted to a vote of the qualified voters of the State on the basis of the last Gubernatorial election and ratified by a majority thereof[.] On this Amendment offered by Jones of Overton,[2] the fight was made in the House—the ultra men opposing it and the conservative supporting it— It was finally adopted by a vote of 44 yeas to 23 nays,[3] which was a most decided triumph for our side— the Bill then passed unanimously, & under the circumstance I voted for it—[4] The Same fight is being made in the Senate & our house has determined that the Bill shall not pass in any other shape[.]

Stokes[5] ruined Bob Payne[6] in the Senate yesterday on it— he made a most telling speech for the people & one that had great effect—[7] In our house Trewhitt of Hamilton made Some remarks on it, in which he endorsed your speech entire—[8] I find that almost all of the Opposition in both houses endorse it entire, while a great many Democrats denounce it, under the lead of the "Union & American.— Dr Beaty[9] member of the House from Giles introduced resolutions requesting you to resign &c— They met with but little favor & if they permit a vote to be taken on them will be defeated by a large majority. The opposition almost to a man will vote against them, and a large number of the Democrat[s]— The opposition were anxious for you to come out here, but I do not believe it would be policy now to do so— those that denounce you would get more bitter, impugne your motives &c. And since we know that we have a decided majority against them, It would be better in my judgment for you not to come at present— I have met more friends than I ever did here—who seem to be in earnest & sincere— The opposition here are almost unanimous for the union while a great many Democrats are— party lines seem to be entirely obliterated & the only question is Union or disunion &c[.] when the question is put to the people as it will be, in my judgment an overwhelming majority will be for the Union, unless things take a different turn from what I can now see. Various resolutions have been introduced & referred, but will be acted on this week— Conservatism will carry the day & that kind of resolutions will pass— Some of the ultra men are for making extensive military preparations, which would cost the people of the State from five hundred thousand to one million of Dollars, which cannot in my opinion be gotten through—and about all that will be done, will be a reorganization of the Militia on a more effective basis— I cannot vote for any extensive Military preparations now—[10]

I have seen but very little of Burch, Dunnington & Co[.] I do not trouble them & do not intend to do so— Whitthorne is pretty ultra[.]

If I deam it necessary for you to come out, I will consult friends & *telegraph you*. If I should do so & you come stop at the *Sewanee*[11]— As the proprietors tenders you the best room in the house and it is the best house in the City— I am staying at it, have a fine room, that Roberts the proprietor offered me after I came down here &c.

I wrote you last Tuesday & Thursday about matters & things generally & will write you now every day & give you in full all the goings on.

I would like to hear from you often as to the prospects of an adjustment &c.

My Bill to repeal the Conventional Interest Law will pass[.][12]

I do not think of any thing more at present & will defer writing more until tomorrow[.]

Your Son   Robt Johnson

ALS, DLC-JP.

1. Elected floterial representative (1859–61) from Greene, Hawkins, Hancock, and Jefferson counties, Robert was attending the called session which

convened January 7 to discuss Tennessee's relations with the federal government.

2. William E. B. Jones, Livingston lawyer and state representative (1859–61). *Johnson Papers*, II, 185n.

3. *Tenn. House Journal*, 1861, Extra Sess., 61.

4. On January 31, perhaps prompted by his father, Robert and his close political associate Daniel Trewhitt asked to record their votes in the negative, though the bill had become law nearly two weeks before. *Ibid.*, 208; *Tenn. Acts*, 1861, Extra Sess., Ch. I.

5. Jordan Stokes (1817–1886), Whig lawyer, represented Smith (1839–41) and Wilson (1851–53) counties in the Tennessee house, serving as speaker; elected to the state senate (1859–61), he was instrumental in defeating the bill to expel free Negroes. A unionist during the war, his conservatism forced him into the Democratic ranks following the conflict. Speer, *Prominent Tennesseans*, 467–69; Robison, *Preliminary Directory*, *Smith*, 104–5.

6. Robert G. Payne, senator from Shelby County and former commissioner of roads during Johnson's governorship. *Johnson Papers*, II, 232n.

7. On January 11, in an "eloquent and powerful" plea which "electrified all who heard it," Stokes proposed that the convention bill be so amended that the words "for Union" and "for Disunion" appear on the ballots; at the same time he defended himself against the insinuation that he was a "submissionist." In a sarcastic exchange, Payne demanded to know what "Union" meant in the context of the proposed amendment, to which Stokes replied that "the people [would] know what Union [meant]." Continuing their quarrel, Stokes finally asked Payne if he were for secession and suggested that the manly thing would be to "nail his colors to the mast." Nashville *Republican Banner*, January 12, 1861; Nashville *Patriot*, January 12, 1861.

8. As early as January 9, in resolutions aimed at reconciling northern and southern differences, Daniel C. Trewhitt had expressed approbation for Johnson's Union course. Trewhitt (1823–1891), born in Morgan County and raised in Cleveland, studied law under his father and began his practice in Harrison, Hamilton County, in 1852. Originally a Whig, he served in the lower house (1859–61) and was elected to the senate of the 34th General Assembly (Confederate), but did not attend. A member of the East Tennessee unionist convention at Knoxville in June, 1861, he served in the Union army during the following winter, resigning because of health and lack of aptitude for the military life. Appointed chancellor, second chancery division (1864–70), by Governor Andrew Johnson, Trewhitt was among the unionists meeting in Nashville (1865) to draw up a new constitution and nominate candidates for state office. In 1878 he was elected judge of the fourth circuit court, serving until his death. Robison, *Preliminary Directory*, *Hamilton*, 76–77; *Tenn. House Journal*, 1861, Extra Sess., 34–35.

9. Jo J. Beaty (b. c1820), a physician, was the Democratic representative from Giles County (1859–61). Enlisting in Confederate service, he was wounded at Ft. Donelson and retired. His resolution of January 8 asked Johnson to resign "in order that his place may be filled by one who knows our rights, and will dare to defend them." Robison, *Preliminary Directory*, *Giles*, 2; *Tenn. House Journal*, 1861, Extra Sess., 29.

10. On January 31 a bill was passed which repealed the act of 1857 abolishing military duty in Tennessee. The new measure, restoring the militia, called for the raising of three artillery companies, for frequent drills, and for arms to be provided by the governor. Although Robert first tried to alter the bill drastically, he supported it in its final form. *Tenn. Acts*, 1861, Extra Sess., Ch. XII; *Tenn. House Journal*, 1861, Extra Sess., 153, 156–58.

11. The Sewanee House, 26 North College Street, was operated in 1861 by William Roberts (b. c1800), a native of Connecticut, who owned personal property valued at $20,400 in 1860. One of his seven children, Thomas, worked as a clerk at the Sewanee House in 1860–61. *Nashville Bus. Dir.*

(1855–56), 104; (1860–61), 248; 1860 Census, Tenn., Davidson, 1st Dist., 31.

12. House bill No. 1, which Robert had introduced on January 8, repealed the act of February 21, 1860, entitled "An Act to amend the Usury Laws of the State, and to establish a Conventional Rate of Interest." The measure became law on January 31, after having been challenged in the senate and temporarily replaced by a substitute bill; the final senate vote was a close 12–10. *Tenn. Senate Journal*, 1861, Extra Sess., 137–38; *Tenn. House Journal*, 1861, Extra Sess., 31, 37, 91, 130, 216; *Tenn. Acts*, 1861, Extra Sess., Ch. IV.

To Sam Milligan, Greeneville

Washington City   Jany 13th [1861]

My dear frind

Your letter of the 9th inst has just come to hand and was more than gratified to find and know that my views met your approbation which I assure you has givn me much encouragemt—For there has been a great effort to get up a rign [of] terror here Similar to that in So Ca and have in fact intimidated some into silence who are in fact opposed to the Treasonabl move. As you say they have givn me "thunder" in some places, there one Comfort at least to be drawn from it, that is they feel the force of the blow and instead of answering the Speech and attacking the principles laid down in it, they rely upon misrepresenttion and personality in reference to me. The press of Tennessee and especially the democratic portion of it, has been subsidized and is now under the Control of a set of editors[1] who prefer mendacity to trueth, and treason to patriotism. I say to you that the country is rife with conspiracy and treason and full of Traitors who are ready and willing to destroy the Count[r]y. I hope that there is still intelligence enough and virtue in the country sufficient to save it. But it will require great effort to do it. If Tennessee Can be held firme for the present She Can hereafter be made to performe a Conspicuous part in Savi[n]g the Country from Civil and Servild [sic] war. Wee should all do what we Could in saving the Union from the hands of the spoilers. My dear f[r]iend, you now see that it is not guara[n]tees in reference to slavery they want: it is a go[vern]ment South so that they Can have the absolute Control of it in ther own hands—And would erect today a monarchy if they had in their power— I know what I say— It is not the free men of the north they are fearing most: but the free men South and now desire to have a goment so organized as to put the institution of Slavry beyond the reach or vote of the nonslave holder at the ballot box. The people of Tennessee in all matters of Legislation would differ as much with the

Gulf States as they do with northen states and would be more difficult to agree in regard to the organic law than they would with the north. The north in my opinion will give the middle States a[n]y reasonable guarantee they desire which would make us much more Secure in Slave property than if they were a separate hostile power. I did not sit down to write you a letter of any length and will not do it. For I am pressed to death both in body and mind. I would be much gratified if I were so situ[at]ed that I could see you occasionally & interchange and Compare thoughts. Nicholson as you will see from his Speech[2] is in a kind of betwee'nty and would like to pass through the Crisis without touching any body or b[e]ing touched by any body— I have taken my stand upon principle and the doctrin taught by the fathers of the republi[c] and intend to stand [by] them Come what will. The more I investigate the doctrin of Secession the more and more its fu[ti]lity and enormity becomes manifest— No Government now, or to be formd hereafter Can be preservd if this principle is recognized [or] Can Continue for any length of tim or hav ay Credit or Character— To admit that ay one mem[ber] of a Commu[n]ity either of stats or Inviduals Can withdraw at pleasure from the Community is a fundamental error and will result in its overthrow. In fine I look upon Secession when Carrid into a Social or political organization as beig the prolific mother of anarchy which is the next step to despotism— It is a political heresy and ought to be repudiated now as such. . . .[3]

On yesterday W. H. Seward of N. Y. made his speech[4] which was understood to reflect the sentiments of the incomig administration. The speech as a whole was rather Conciliatory in its character. He is willing to an amendment of the constitutn of the U.S.S. So as guard the states against ultimate interference with the institutin of Slavry in the states, the passage of laws to protect the states against "raids" or incursions from other states— The Territories after the admision of Kansas as a state— Then the remainder of the Territory to come in as two states and hereafter to be divide into States of Convenent Size &c to be admitted with or without Slavry as m[a]y be prescribed in ther Constitutns at the time of ther admission or some such plan. His speech was looked upon as a concession by some, yet it seemed not to Satisfy the extreme Southern men[.] I think upon the whole the speech conceded much and ought to [be] taken as a favorable indication— If the question could be once got before the people N & S I believe they would agree upon [it] and save the Country— Congress will not do it; but the people will.

Milligan the Country must be Saved and evry body must Come up to the work— So far as I am Concerned I do [not] Care one whit:

but let the Go[vern]m[en]t be saved— God Save Government is my pr[a]yer.

Give my respects to Mrs Milligan and accept for yourself the best wishes of a sincere heart[.]

Andrew Johnson

Genl Sam Milligan

Copy, Herman Blum, Letters of Our Presidents (Unpublished MS); ALS, Philip Sang, Chicago, Ill.

1. Tennessee's leading Democratic papers, all strongly secessionist, included the Nashville *Union and American*, the major voice of the "Southern Right Anti-Coercion" men under the leadership of J. O. Griffith and Company, including Leon Trousdale, Frank C. Dunnington, Thomas S. Marr, and John C. Burch; the Memphis *Avalanche*, edited by Matthew C. Gallaway, Memphis postmaster; and the Knoxville *Register*, with J. Austin Sperry at the helm. Campbell, *Tenn. Attitudes*, 172; White, *Messages*, V, 270; Rothrock, *French Broad-Holston Country*, 128; Folmsbee, *Tennessee*, II, 30.

2. A. O. P. Nicholson, Tennessee's other senator, speaking in defense of southern grievances on December 24, had asked for cooperation among Democrats and proposed a border, or middle, state convention. *Cong. Globe*, 36 Cong., 2 Sess., 185–89.

3. Blum "omitted here an irrelevant paragraph regarding a personal law suit."

4. In this speech Seward joined "the noble Senator from Tennessee" in declaring his "adherence to the Union in its integrity and with all its parts." *Ibid.*, 341–44.

To John Trimble,[1] Nashville

Washington City

Private   Jany 13th 1860 [1861]—

Hon John Trimble

My dear Sir

Your letter of the 27th ult was received a few days Since and was read with pleasure & interest and would have been answered sooner; but for the great press upon me at this time mentally and physically— And now write for the purpose of tendering to you my Sincere thanks for such a letter; for under the Circumstances I needed just Such a letter— While I was gratified to know that the views taken and the doctrins laid down in my Speech met the approbation of one esteemed So highly for talent and sterling integrity it was encouraging to press on the Cause of right and if possible thereby to Save the Gov[ernm]ent from Treason and disruption— I repeat I was more than gratified to recievee words of encourgment from Such a Source— There has been an attempt here[2] as in So'—Ca' to get up a reign of terror like that in charleston, for the purpose of Silencig the timid and to Carry the hesitatng along with them, and have here as well as there succeeded to some extent. I think the true policy for Tennessee to pursue is, not to be Committed to a[n]y moves that are now makig— There is no good reason why we Should act in Such haste— Tennessee had better stay where She is until She can See very clearly where She can do better— If there is a convention Called by the Legislature let it be put off to the latest period so that the people can have time to understand the whole question and the follies of So'—Ca' Can be made fully manifest— I do not see why there should be any Convention atall at present— The States which have seceeded would not wait to Consult the other States, and we should now have th full benefit of their future proceedings. My opinion is that if Tennessee will Stand firme that in the end she can and will act a very important part in bri[n]gi[n]g back the Seceding States into the confederacy; instead of being dragged out of the union or draw into a Southern Confederacy by them— I think and am satisfied that, if the middle States will remain in union that they can obtain any reasonable guarntee they m[a]y demand from the northern States which will protect and Secure Slave property in the border States, which would be much better than being Separated into two hostile powers and that hostility resulting from the instutution of Slavey— It would infact be movig Canada down to our northern border with the difference, of one being friendly and the other hostile— It will be as hard for the border states to agree with So'—Ca' (and the gulf States as they are Called) upon a forme of Govent as it would be with the northen States—[3] And if this doctrin of Secession is to become a fixed principle in any Govmt which my be organized including So' Ca'—It would hardly be six weeks before Sum of them would be for withdrawig again— I do not See what we are to gain by the operation except it is to be involved in the quarrels of So' Ca' and to incur the enormus expense of building anothr Govmt, Navy, Army &c[.] I Can See no good reason why the State Should be now involved in buying large amount of armes— The Genl Govmt is not goig to make war upon Tennessee nor no other state—unless we intend to join So'—Ca' in making war upon the Genl Govmt which I hope we are not prepared to do— How[ev]er, this [is a] matter which must be determind by future developemts— If Tennessee will stay where she is, that is in the Union there will be no necessity to run the state in debt as some of the States have been doing— South Carolina now begins to feel the wait of her folly with debt created in a few weeks of nearly a million and a half of dollars—[4] The federal Govmt does not intend to make war upon So'—Ca'; but she seems determind to make war upon the Govmt and infact has done So in Seizing the public property and in firing upon the "Star West" while Sailing undr the flag of the U. S.—[5] I hope that Tenn will keep out of the present move until she can see and understand what course she ought to take—

I must be candid and speake of the move as belie[v]ing it ought to be spoken of— The ostensible object is to obtain protection in regard to slave property— This is in my opinion a pretext and not the real design— The intention is to disrupt the Govmt and then to form one in the South as far removed from the people as they can get it— There is not merely a conspiracy on foot against the existing Govmt; but the liberty of the great mass of the people— Treason is rife in the land and the country full of Traitors— They are moving heaven and earth to cary the country before there is time for reflection by arousig theree apprehensions in refernce to Slave property— If we were in a Souther Confederacy now Tennessee would have her own slave property to protect[.] none of the States South of her would have it [to] do. So as to the protection of Slave property we have that to do our Selves either in a Northern or Southern Confederacy— Then what are we to gain by precipitating Tennessee out of the Union without knowig where we are going or what we are going to do— I do hope that Tennessee may be kept out of this treasonabl revolutiony move and when She does move let her Steps be guided by wisdom, discretion, and moderation— As to all the effigy burnig and rabble denunciations I care not, or the abuse of a subsedized and mendacious press, niether the one or the other will drive me from a discharge of my duty— I feel and believe that the best Govmt in the world is in the most iminent peril, that traitors are trying to overthrow it, and God being willing, to the utmost of my ability I intend to expose & rebuke the vile miscreants who are engaged in the nefarious work— I merly sit down to acknowledge the receipt of your vy welcome letter and hope you will pardon this incoherent Scroawl—

The Speeches you mentioned in your letter have been Sent. I thank you for your kind offer[.] all they will cost will be your trouble of distribution—

May God and the people Save the Country—for I fear Congress will not—

Your will please accept assurances of my high esteem and sincere regard

Andrew Johnson

ALS, PHi. Also printed in "Letters of Presidents of the United States and 'Ladies of the White House,' " *Pennsylvania Magazine of History and Biography*, XXVI (1902), 271–74.

1. Trimble was a Davidson County senator (1859–61) opposed to secession. See *Johnson Papers*, III, 409n.

2. In early January, 1861, wild rumors of a "southern conspiracy" to seize the seat of government circulated, as did stories that the incoming administration would impose a Black Republican "reign of terror," jeopardizing private

property and individual liberties. Respected Washington citizens formed a local unit of the "National Volunteers," a Democratic organization appearing in Baltimore and elsewhere, to oppose the Republican "Wide Awakes." Testifying before a House committee to investigate the "southern conspiracy," Gen. Winfield Scott read from letters which warned of a plot to seize by fifth-column tactics the principal government buildings in the early morning hours of March 3. Most other witnesses discounted the rumors, and the investigation ended without concrete evidence of a conspiracy. Constance Green, *Washington: Village and Capital, 1800–78* (2 vols., Princeton, 1962), I, 233–35.

3. Johnson's "middle States" and "border States" appear to include not only Delaware, Maryland, Kentucky, and Missouri, but also the second tier of Virginia, North Carolina, Tennessee, and Arkansas.

4. In picturing the seceded state as beginning to "feel the wait of her folly," the writer perhaps assumed that Governor Francis Pickens' estimate of about $1,450,000 for arms and troops actually had been implemented. Prior to January 13, the date of this letter, only some $550,000 had been appropriated; two days later, a bond issue of $150,000 was authorized. Charles E. Cauthen, *South Carolina Goes to War, 1860–1865* (Chapel Hill, 1950), 189–90.

5. In an effort to reprovision and reinforce Maj. Robert Anderson and his garrison at Ft. Sumter, Gen. Scott dispatched an unarmed light steamer, *Star of the West*. On January 9, warned by telegrams from Senator Louis T. Wigfall and Interior Secretary Jacob Thompson, the South Carolinians opened fire from batteries at Ft. Moultrie and Morris Island when the ship arrived offshore. Despite this "first overt act of the war," the Buchanan administration and most northerners received the news with a calm forbearance. Nevins, *Emergence of Lincoln*, II, 379–80, 432; Boatner, *Civil War Dictionary*, 793.

From William Crutchfield[1]

Chattanooga Jan 14th, 1861

Hon Andrew Johnson

Dear Sir— do not consider this letter as an intrusion on you for I take the bold ground of rendering unto you ample apology at the start— when I say to you that for twenty years I have spent time and money—and used every honorable means in my power to crush you politically—I speak only the truth— Let the past be forgotten —let the dead bury the dead— The old political *partys* are routed crushed—or obliterated— And Now it does most certainly become us as a free and independant people to guard well the palladium of our liberty—

Tennesse—the warrior state—the spartan band—The Key stone of the Arch of the confederacy, The land of heroes—The soil that has never yet produced a traitor—has found in you a worthy and true exponent of her position— Yes Gov—we are with you— The Stars & Stripes are yet near and dear to us— Yankey Doodle Hail columbia and The Star Spangled Banner—will never be surrendered by a Tennessean or given in exchange for hail to the *King*—or God save the *King*—[2]

I have most carefully read your speach— It is just the thing—and almost universally approved— The mountain boys—The wood choppers The rail splitters—In fact The bone and sinew of the country back you—entirely irrespective of party— this day I do most sincerely believe that 7-tenth of the people of Tennessee are with you— all of the fire eaters we have are men from *Ga—Ala—SC* or old renegade *whigs*—and other disappointed office seekers—anxious to create a storm so that they can ride.into power on top of the poli[ti]-cal wave— The cotton states now with the Gallant little State of South Carolina, that produced 9/10th of the Torys of the revolution are now using every means in their power to force on a rupture with this government for the purpose of keeping up the excitement and dragging the entire South into her den of *Treason*— oh yes they would like to have the Tennessee boys to do their fighting against the North, while they would rest securely at home— Then indeed we would be clever fellows certain— Gov—every thing looks dark and gloomy in the extreme— The North has done us Injustice— the south is running wild on secession and appears fully determined to go out whether it suits us or not—even admitting the possibility of a peacible dissolution of this union I do not believe that we could ever get along with South Carolina— her peculiar notions interests and views are so entirely antagonistic to those of the middle slave states that we never could agree— In fact the very first election in which she failed to get her choice—the fat would all be in the fire again— In case the cotton states secede and set up on their own hook—which it seems like our president is going to let them do—Then we the middle slave states—are forced to come to some understanding with the south—make some arrangement with the north—or set up on our own hook— really we are most certainly now entering upon the most trying crisis in the history of our beloved country— Excuse errors imperfections &&[.] I am the eldest son of Thos Crutchfield builder of the Greenville court house—[3] was introduced into this world, in a log hut 16 ft square belonging to the widow Harrington[4] in Greenville Tenn.

Respectfully yours &c
W. Crutchfield

ALS, DLC-JP.

1. William Crutchfield (1824–1890), Greeneville-born Chattanoogan, with his brother Thomas, operated the Crutchfield House (built in 1856 and forerunner of the Read House) and owned considerable property. Twice city alderman (1851, 1865), he was a Hamilton County delegate to the East Tennessee convention held at Knoxville May 30, and subsequently served in Congress as a Republican (1873–75). On January 22, only a few days after writing this letter, Crutchfield became involved in a personal altercation with Jefferson Davis, who, having stopped at the Crutchfield House, was persuaded

to make a secessionist speech which proved to be moderate in tone. When Davis finished, an excited Crutchfield denounced him in vehement language as a "future military despot," and violence was narrowly averted. Crutchfield was later forced to flee to the Union armies, with which he cooperated during the Chattanooga campaign and for the remainder of the war. Temple, *Notable Men*, 109–13; Zella Armstrong, *History of Hamilton County and Chattanooga, Tennessee* (2 vols., Chattanooga, 1940), I, 124–25; *BDAC*, 761; Gilbert E. Govan and James W. Livingood, *The Chattanooga Country, 1540–1951* (New York, 1952), 153, 174–75; *OR*, Ser. 1, LII, Pt. I, 150; XXX, Pt. III, 251–52.

2. Probably an allusion to the expressed preference of Robert Toombs and others for a return to British rule rather than a continuation in the Union, as evidenced in Toombs's speech before the Georgia legislature November 13, 1860. Moore, *Rebellion Record*, Supp., 368.

3. Thomas Crutchfield ([1808?]–1850), a native of Rockbridge County, Virginia, moved to Greeneville at an early age and became a prominent East Tennessee contractor, responsible for the "third" Greeneville courthouse, built during the 1820's, the Rhea County courthouse (1833), and "similar buildings" in seven other counties. *Goodspeed's Hamilton*, 929; *Goodspeed's East Tennessee*, 818.

4. Not identified.

From William R. Hurley

Nashville Jan 14th 1861

Hon Andrew Johnson
Dear Sir:

We are in the midst of a terrible excitement. The disunionists are exceedingly intolerant towards every union movement. The yeomanry of the land are with us, and you may rest assured that the voting massess are with us[.] There was a faint demonstration in the Legislature against you.[1] but it will fall still born before the people. I have letters from different parts of the State, saying that if their members, attempt to recall you meetings will be called immediately to *recall* the representatives. It is my opinion, that the people would be so indignant, that they would almost be ready to go to the capital and break up that body. We have a hard fight about towns and cities. The Democrat can not keep up the fight but a few days longer without money. Will you do us the favor, to call the attention of the friends of this union to the necessity of coming to our aid *immediately.* If we are compelled to stop, it will be a signal for general rejoicing among disunionists. Our circulation is very large but our advertising is small and the times require a great deal of matter to be set up, and hence it is the most expensive paper in the city.[2] We propose to take a loan and give a mortgage on our establishment[.]

It costs about $150 per week to publish the paper, and sometimes as much as $200[.]

Our circulation is increasing beyond any other paper in the city[.]

I am sorry to be compelled to call on our friends for a loan, and would not do so except for the extreme danger surrounding our beloved country[.]

Gov Harris, could not let the opportunity pass of roasting—you a little[.][3] He would be glad to cripple your influence. You may guess why. W. H. Polk endorses your speech entirely, and has so said in a speech.[4] Rest assured that if the people are kept posted you will be sustained. The Banner & Patriot have friends to serve and they, consequently enter into a lukewarm support[.][5]

Respectfully   W R Hurley

P. S. We have been looking for you here for several days. We will give you a handsome reception when you do come. H

ALS, DLC-JP.

1. The resolution requesting Johnson's resignation from the Senate had failed of passage and died on the table. *Tenn. House Journal*, 1861, Extra Sess., 29, 36, 174.

2. Lacking copies of the *Democrat*, one can do no more than offer some general observations concerning these problems. Obviously a new journal required time to build up an advertising clientele, a challenge rendered the more formidable by the *Democrat*'s unionist persuasion in an area strongly secessionist. Hurley's remark that "the times require a great deal of matter" attests to the changing size and sophistication of city newspapers, which carried an increasing burden of material designed for a larger and more diversified audience. Local and state news now shared the stage with the allurements of patent medicine, wondrous accounts of things exotic, serialized tales of derring-do, treatises on the art of husbandry, articles on homemaking and cookery, and detailed commentaries on fashion. Above all else, however, the press of that day was forced to devote a great deal of space to such great national issues as the reality of disunion and the imminence of war.

3. Probably a reference to Harris' January 7 message to the special session, in which he denied the right of the federal government to coerce a state and emphasized his belief that "there is no respectable portion of our people . . . who are so blind to reason . . . as to give countenance to a policy so fatal in its results, and so revolting to every sentiment of humanity." Johnson's December speech had been widely interpreted as endorsement of the policy of coercion. Nashville *Union and American*, January 8, 1861.

4. William H. Polk, brother of the President and an opponent of secession, ran against Harris for governor in August; this speech was not recorded by the contemporary press. For Polk, see *Johnson Papers*, II, 229n.

5. On the contrary, the *Patriot* and the *Republican Banner* did not follow the same editorial policy toward Johnson or the Union. Although both had adopted a conservative posture in 1860 and had supported Bell, the *Patriot* was certainly lukewarm, if not openly hostile, to Johnson and his position after South Carolina seceded, its editors terming his speech "impolitic and untimely" and accusing him of conveying the impression that he favored coercion. "If a dissolution is to be forced upon us by the action of the free States," the *Patriot* declared, "we desire a Union composed of all the slave States." The *Banner* came to the senator's defense, denying that he had advocated coercion and rejecting the contention that his speech was inopportune; although others might resort to shallow partisanship, "we unhesitatingly and heartily applaud him." Nashville *Patriot*, January 4, 16, 1861; Nashville *Republican Banner*, December 28, 1860, January 1, 1861.

From John C. Love

January 14, 1861, Louisville, Tenn.; ALS, DLC-JP.

A merchant, politically "opposed to you" in former years, approves "the bold open and manly stand you have done in defence of our Union"; mentions a disunionist meeting in Blount County designed "to give you a *Rub*," but adds that Union men plan a counter-meeting in Maryville which "wil be no little Humbug affair"; they expect to raise a company of "no hot headed minute men."

From Roderick R. Butler[1]

Nashville January 15th 1861

Hon A Johnson
Dear Sir

We have been looking for you, here for the last week[.] there Seems to be a General desire for you to come here[.][2] The instructing resolution was ignored in the committee this morning and there will sleep[.] your enemies are afraid to test it by a vote[.] they know well that they will receive the Severest rebuke that can be administered by a legislative body[.] I don't believe there would be more than half dozen votes cast for the [r]esolution. you have many warm frinds of both the old parties a sufficency to Sustain you. The disunion sentiment comes from the Democracy—and the leaders who want your place[.] The house passed a bill to call a Convention and Submit the action of the Same to the people taking the last Gubernatorial vote as the basis[.] Democracy fought hard to keep the action of the convention from the people and the Senate this day by a Strict party vote amended and Struck out that part of the bill fixing the Governors vote as the basis[.] the house will never in my opinion concur[.][3] The disunionist intend Some trick to take Tennessee out. The real people are for the union and all they want is a chance at it and they will give it fits[.]

yours respectfully   R R Butler

ALS, DLC-JP.

1. Roderick Random Butler (1827–1902), Virginia-born lawyer and sometime tailor, practiced law at Taylorsville (now Mountain City) and served as postmaster and justice of the peace before becoming state representative (1859–63, 1879–87), circuit judge (1865–67), congressman (1868–75, 1887–89), and state senator (April, 1865, 1895–1902). Butler was an outspoken unionist, serving as a lieutenant colonel of the 13th Tenn. Cav., USA (1863–64), and as chairman of the first Republican state executive committee. *BDAC*, 640; Robison, *Preliminary Directory, Johnson*, 41–42.

2. The expectation that Beaty's proposal requesting Johnson's resignation

would come before the General Assembly gave rise to rumors that he would come to Nashville: "Doubtless ANDY intends to be on the ground and see how the thing is done." Nashville *Republican Banner*, January 8, 1861.

3. Approved January 12, the house bill providing for the election of delegates to a convention to be held in Nashville February 25, for the purpose of examining the "existing relations between the government of the United States and the government and people of the State of Tennessee" passed the senate January 17 and became law two days later. The act stipulated that the voters were to cast a ballot either for, or against, a convention; if a majority demurred, there would be no convention. In any case, the action of the convention was to be submitted to the people before going into effect. *Tenn. House Journal*, 1861, Extra Sess., 62; *Tenn. Senate Journal*, 1861, Extra Sess., 59; *Tenn. Acts*, 1861, Extra Sess., Ch. I.

From Charles O. Faxon[1]

Jeffersonian Office Clarksvile Tenn
Jan 15 1861

Hon Andrew Johnson
U S. S.

I received your friendly letter several days ago but have deferred answering to this time on account of a pressure of business engagements.

As you are of course aware, many of your former friends are down upon your speech, but a large portion of the party sustain you and almost the entire body of the opposition sustain the speech and speak highly of your independence in making it. All conceed its great ability. The popular current here is against the designs of those who would overthrow this great goverment and establish upon its ruins a series of petty republi[c]s or a consolidated southern confederacy or Monarchy. The fire eaters called a meeting to be held here on last Monday.[2] Monday came and with it an immense crowd of the Sovereigns from every corner of the County, for the purpose of seeing personally that the position of Montgomery County was not mis represented. The court House was jammed with one of the most excited crowds I ever saw. The fire eaters soon found that they were under control but they had gone too far to evade the issue. They succeeded in getting a majority of their men on the committee and brought in a report about as hot as it could well be made. They tried to sugar coat a violent states right preamble with Crittendens proposition winding up with a flourish of trumpets of what we would do if that proposition was not accepted. No sooner was the report read than the resolutions recently adopted by the two conventions at Louisville[3] were presented (also embracing Crittenden's propositin) and passed by an overwhelmig majority, At least five to one. An effort was made to ring in a resolution about coercion which was intended as a slap at you, but it failed signally.

If the public mind is not further inflamed and exasparated by attempts to coerce the refractory States before our electin for the Convention. I think that we can beat the secessionists easy if they will only present the issue. The danger is that many secessionists will sneak into the Convention under the guise of cooperation and upon some pretext or other find occasion to vote secession. This the friends of the Union are endeavoring to guard against in the Legislature, by requiring that any action of the convention which proposes any change in our relations to the Federal goverment shall be submitted to a vote of the people[.]

The prospect is that we Shall have a severe fight on the election of delegates to the Convention and the friends of the Union will need all the help they can get. It has been suggested that you could do much good and greatly strengthen our cause by canvassing the State[.] Can you do it consistently with your public duties.

I am told that all of our old friends about Nashville are thoroughly infected with the disunion disease, and you have no idea of the irritation which has existed against me about here among the democrats on account of my effort to back you on the subject of your speech[.][4] Some of these are perfectly run mad.[5] There is Still, however, some who admire my Spunk while they damn my judgment. But the greater portion of the party I think stand firm[.]

But I have already spun this out too long

Respectfully Your friend

C O Faxon

ALS, DLC-JP.

1. Notwithstanding these unionist sentiments, Charles O. Faxon (1824–1870), native of Connecticut, Clarksville postmaster (1854–62), and editor of the *Jeffersonian* (1844–62), ultimately supported the South and ran unsuccessfully for the Confederate Congress. He subsequently wrote for the Chattanooga *Rebel*, the Louisville *Courier*, and the Clarksville *Tobacco Leaf*. 1860 Census, Tenn., Montgomery, 116; William P. Titus, *Picturesque Clarksville, Past and Present* (Clarksville, 1887), 270–73.

2. During an open meeting held on January 14, efforts to introduce extremist state rights resolutions were countered by resolutions endorsing the Crittenden Compromise. The latter were approved, with the significant addition of an amendment stating that, if the North should refuse to guarantee "the security of the South, Tennessee would then feel justified in withdrawing from the Union, or adopting such other measures for her own security as she might see proper." Clarksville *Jeffersonian*, January 16, 1861.

3. In a rousing joint session at Louisville (January 8–9), the Constitutional Union and Democratic Union conventions approved a series of resolutions upholding the Union and the Constitution, discounting the danger of Lincoln and the abolitionists, urging the repeal of personal liberty laws, and recommending the Crittenden propositions. In the event of disunion, however, one resolution advocated a confederacy of states under the Constitution

restructured according to the Crittenden proposals. Nashville *Republican Banner*, January 13, 1861; Cincinnati *Enquirer*, January 11, 1861.

4. Calling Johnson's December speech "undoubtedly the greatest speech of his life," Faxon, though protesting that he was not defending the doctrines advanced, praised "the ability with which he argues from his own premises, and defends and fortifies the positions he assumes." The editor insisted that the senator's meaning had been misinterpreted and that, "when fairly read and dispassionately considered," the speech would "in the main, receive the hearty and unqualified endorsement of the great majority" of Tennesseans. He pointed out that Johnson fell short of Jackson's stance on the federal government's coercive power—"yet he is denounced and execrated and burnt in effigy." Clarksville *Jeffersonian*, January 2, 1861.

5. In the context of the day, "To become wild with excitement."

From Jacob H. Holt

January 15, 1861, Monmouth, Ill.; ALS, DLC-JP.

Urges Johnson, if the Crittenden Compromise fails, to initiate amendments for popular election of President and Vice President and for replacement of the secretary of state with three regional ministers—one from each section of the country; takes exception to high interest rates on treasury notes and recommends that these notes be "issued in payment of debts due from the Government."

From Robert Johnson

House of Rep   Jany 15th [1861]

Dear Father

Nothing Interesting going on in the House to-day— The Senate is engaged on the Convention Bill— The disunionists are making strong efforts to Strike out the House Amendment requiring the convention to submit their action to a vote of the people[.] If the Senate strike out the Amendment, as the indications are that they will, the House in my Opinion will defeat the entire Bill, even if they have to resort to reducing the House below a quorum— The instructing resolutions cannot pass either House & are now in the tomb of the Capulets.—[1] I cannot say when we will adjourn, perhaps next week— A Strong effort will be made to pass a Mammoth Military Bill[2]—but will fail in the House in my judgment— I have not time to write more—but will write tonight—

Yours Son   R Johnson

ALS, DLC-JP.

1. Originating with Edmund Burke's *Reflections on the Revolution in France*, "the tomb of all the Capulets" implies a "repose in lasting oblivion." See William Rose Benét, *Reader's Encyclopedia* (New York, 1965), 177–78; Edmund Burke, *The Works of . . .* (12 vols., Boston, 1865–67), III, 349.

2. Robert refers to debate on house bill No. 17, which sought to restore the state militia, to all intents and purposes rendered ineffective four years earlier. Some of the ultra representatives sponsored various amendments to enlarge the militia, either by appropriating large sums of money or by authorizing a greatly expanded force of as many as 50,000 men. Others insisted that Tennessee—"Were Lincoln the Prince of Devils himself"—could repel any invasion with the forces already available. Amid ominous cannon salutes in the Capitol Hill area, Confederate speeches by itinerant fire-eaters, fateful preparations for the state convention, and the fashionable appearance of the blue cockade, the militia bill passed on January 31, thereby disproving Robert's judgment of its prospects. *Tenn. Acts,* 1857–58, Ch. XXXII; 1861, Extra Sess., Ch. XII; *Tenn. House Journal,* 1861, Extra Sess., 140–41, 147–50, 153, 222–23; *Tenn. Senate Journal,* 1861, Extra Sess., 122, 148; Nashville *Union and American,* January 25, 1861; Nashville *Republican Banner,* January 25, 26, February 2, 1861.

From Thomas M. Peters

January 15, 1861, Moulton, Ala.; ALS, DLC-JP.

Challenging Johnson to become a "Man for the times" and lead the loyal people in executing the laws and restoring peace at all costs, asserts that South Carolinians are "just about as free as Napoleon's french & Queen Victoria's Irish" and that, "in the end, unless we resort to a Military Government, there will be a revulsion, and as the Negro is the sole cause of our present troubles, the fury of the non-Slave holder will be turned on him & his Master"; asks, "Why do you not make the President, turn out the Post Master [Matthew C. Gallaway] at Memphis Ten. who abuses you so outrageously in the Avalanch."

From Milo M. Dimmick

January 16, 1861, Mauch Chunk, Pa.; ALS, DLC-JP.

Praises December speech, regrets that Johnson was not nominated at Charleston, and recalls their common service in the House (1849–53); "the day is not far distant . . . when your own constituents and posterity will accord to you that measure of justice 'of duty done' which will more than compensate for all the abuse [with] which prejudice & passion may now assail you."

From Charles Johnson

Greeneville Jan 16th [1861]

Dear Father

Your letter of the 13th inst came duly to hand;—and in reply I have nothing of moment to write;

The country is indeed in great perril and it seems there is no power to stay the sacriligious hand of a wild and madened rable; for such it is; I believe the sober and correct thinking men of the country, are opposed to this rebelious move, which can result in nothing but destruction; but I am fearful that even in Tennessee, contagion like it is spreading; it seizes upon men and in their wild and visionary schemes it seems that reason is dethroned; but if the masses can be checked and made to stare the monster in the face, they will put it down; and I further believe that the people, to day, if they had to meet the issue, and that issue was the exclusion of Slavery or the destruction of this Union; their verdict would be down with slavery but in the present excited condition of the public mind there is no foreteling what the result may be; yet I do not think Tennessee will vote herself out of the Union— this however depends upon the form in which the question is brought before them.

There is a great fuss and confusion attempted to be gotten up about Coercion, & submission, all to delude and divert the attention of the people[.] I usually reply to this; by saying that if the government has no power to execute its laws, it is no government; but that the government has the right and the power to enforce its laws and if this is coercion then I am for Coercion—that it is the duty of every good citizen to obey those laws, and if that is submission; then are all true friends of their country submissionists, and that is the whole of it.

Midshipman, Foute on his return home as I understand was for burning you in effigy; in consideration as I suppose, of the fact of your getting him a position in the Naval Academy,[1]— Capt Boyce also favored such a course, this I suppose is in return for the many favors shown him.[2] "such is life." The Democratic party of this state is in a nice fix;— it has been driven into this secession movement by the opposition; while they (the opposition) Press and leaders are left the champions of the rights of the people[.] I have heard nothing from Bob since he left; The Legislature I presume will adjourn in a few days[.]

There is nothing new here of a local character,—save the marriage of John Brown to Mrs. Rabe, to which I refered in a fo[r]mer letter. All well[.]

Your Son   Charles Johnson

ALS, DLC-JP.

1. Robert C. Foute, who had left Annapolis in December, 1860, subsequently joined the Confederate navy. *Johnson Papers*, III, 359*n*.

2. Johnson had been lenient with Boyce when the latter was unable, or unwilling, to pay his rent. *Ibid.*, 519.

ANDREW JOHNSON.

The following brief philippic from *Turner's Southern Star*, printed at Camden, Arkansas, is a fair specimen of Arkansas writing. Speaking of ANDREW JOHNSON's late speech, that paper says:

This scurrilous old puppy, who would not fight a yearling toad frog, if he could see a chance to run, has recently made a speech in the United States Senate, in which he advocated *coercion* in the very bitterest terms. Hanging is far too good for such a degraded old wretch. He should be made to eat Yankee nutmeg graters, until his life was grated out'; and then he should be taken to a "soap-factory" and rendered up into soap-greese, with which to make soap to wash the feet of Horace Greeley. Tennessee should hurl such a dispicable old traitor from her confidence immediately. We are satisfied that God had no hand in concocting such men.

Philippic from *Turner's Southern Star* (Camden, Arkansas), printed in Memphis *Daily Appeal*, January 27, 1861.

State of Mississippi, Feb. 3. 1861

Dear Sir

I have a mulatto slave remarkable for his impudence. This you know is often the case with africans having anglo saxon blood. Witness the case of Hannibal Hamlin. As a means of humiliating my slave it has been recommended to me, to send him to Washington City, with a Cowhide, and instruct him to give your back & shoulders some marks of his attention, with the instrument aforesaid. It is thought that ~~do~~ Coming in contact with you, will so effectually disgrace him, ~~that~~ that the effect on him will be so humiliating, that he will make a good obedient slave.

Thinking the suggestion a good one, I have concluded to try the experiment. If he shall happen to wound you badly in the encounter, employ Senator Sumner to send daily bulletins of your condition to your friends about

Grand Junction.

Letter from "Grand Junction," Mississippi, February 3, 1861.
Courtesy Library of Congress.

From Joseph W. Stokes[1]

Philadelphia 1 mo: 16th, 1861

Hon: And. G. Johnson
Washington D. C.
Esteemed friend

If not attended with too much inconvenience, I should be much obliged for a copy of thy speech, delivered in the Senate, on the state of the Union &c about amonth ago. As a republican I can say for myself and probably for the majority of the party in the middle & western states that we have no antagonism to slavery when it exists in the states, not considering ourselves responsible for its sins; fully acknowledging that it exists there by state law as allowed of in the Constitution, and therefore not wishing to interfere with it there. Neither is it the great love the majority of our people have for the negro, that induces our opposition to the introduction of slavery in the Territories but rather the love for ourselves and the interests of the country in the settlement of the great west; That is the section where many of our poorer but more enterprising people must & do look for their living, gotten as it must be by the sweat of their brow. But is it unreasonable or unnatural to suppose that the two institutions of free and black labor or rather slave labor, so diametrically opposite can flourish, or even exist together? I for one of the rapidly increasing population of the north think not. And it must be evident to the watchful statesman and the calm philosopher that as the radical changes in regard to the slave trade and slavery so ably alluded to by Seward in his recent speech in the Senate[2] have taken place in the nations of Europe; so those reformations are following their slow but steady course toward the west. It is not a question of abolitionism in our section but a question whether the working and industrious classes shall have the repelling institution of slavery to compete with in the territories[.]

I really had no idea of thus reasoning this subject with thee; but to appeal to thee, on the supposition of thy being probably more dispassionate and foresighted than most of thy colleagues, as a southern man to ask thy views, merely for my own satisfaction, as to the result of the reckless course of South Carolina and her sister cotton states, seeing the Crittenden compromise is not likely to be submitted to the people.

It has been truly gratifying to see one at least of our southern democratic senators stand up boldly for the maintainance of the

Union in opposition to the popular opinions of the south. Would there were others with the same self respect and independance. Is there not a probability of reaction? For certainly a continuance of such turmoil as exists at Charleston if continued much longer will prove the ruin of the whole place[.] Is it probable that Sewards speech will be allowed to circulate in the slave states?[3] For we are educated in the belief that we are not allowed a hearing with you. If not incompatable with thy position, atleast a recognition by the receipt of a copy of thy speech would much oblige thy very respectful friend[.]

Joseph W Stokes
of Williams & Stokes Philadelphia

ALS, DLC-JP.

1. Joseph W. Stokes (b. c1813) was a Philadelphia lumber dealer. 1860 Census, Pa., Philadelphia, 13th Ward, 134; *McElroy's Philadelphia Directory* (1860), 958.

2. In his speech of January 12 Seward had reflected on European opposition to slavery, noting that a hundred years earlier those same nations had been engaged in the slave trade. *Cong. Globe*, 36 Cong., 2 Sess., 342.

3. Evidence concerning the circulation of Seward's speech is lacking; but there is no question that many southerners knew about it, for the press both reported and commented unfavorably upon it. It is equally clear that despite laws forbidding interference with the mails, large numbers of southern postmasters intercepted objectionable political matter. Dwight L. Dumond, ed., *Southern Editorials on Secession* (New York, 1931), 395–96; Clement Eaton, "Censorship of the Southern Mails," *American Historical Review*, XLVIII (1943), 273–76; Nashville *Patriot*, January 18, 1861.

To Robert Johnson, Nashville

[Washington, D. C.]
January 16, 1861

Crittenden's proposition just defeated in the Senate by Benjamin, Slidell, and other Southerners not voting. Will come up to-morrow, and I think will pass.[1]

[Andrew Johnson]

Nashville *Republican Banner*, January 18, 1861.

1. William B. Stokes read this telegram to the state senate on January 17. The Crittenden proposals *per se* had not been defeated, but rather an amendment, submitted by Clark of New Hampshire, which proved to be the decisive action affecting the compromise, since subsequent efforts to reconsider the proposal as a whole were unsuccessful. Benjamin, Slidell, and the other southerners who abstained from voting were all from the deep South. Nashville *Republican Banner*, January 23, 1861; *Cong. Globe*, 36 Cong., 2 Sess., 409.

From William C. Jewett[1]

National Capitl
Washington Jany 17 1861

Senator

As representing the interests of your Country—permit me in the name of the great departed Statesman[2] to invoke you to oppose the present 100 000 000—Rail Road National debt measure[3]—& to offer to the Senate the grounds given in my petition—[4]

1st   The injustice of any measure but that of the Nation occupying the attention of Congress[.]

2d   Injustice of a National debt annd resolution—making questionable right of Congress to act—A Large debt curse of nations—

3d   Governmental aid not needed—The New Pikes Peak middle State[5]—with like means connecting all States—will give in due time a Middle—Southern & nothern road—thus preserving the great feature of the Constitution—State independent,—internal improvement —one of the Admirable points of our institutions—Calculated to sustain & perpetuate—

4th   The people will save the union through a new Constitution & change of representation[.] Truly—

W. C. Jewett of Pikes Peak

ALS, DLC-JP.

1. William C. Jewett (1823–1893), a New Yorker who migrated west, marrying in St. Louis (1848), stopping in San Francisco (1849), and subsequently settling in Colorado, was a delegate from Pike's Peak to the Washington Peace Conference in 1861. Convinced that he could mediate peace, he "harried European potentates and premiers with his personal, telegraphic, and epistolary communications," using personal funds amassed, according to detractors, "under false pretences," to write pamphlets and letters describing his activities. Regarded as "an irresponsible . . . adventurer," he spent most of the war years in Europe but in 1864 fell in with George N. Sanders and the so-called Confederate peace commissioners, who arranged a meeting for July 20 at Niagara Falls with Horace Greeley. Except for alienating some of Lincoln's conservative supporters, this venture came to naught. Jewett spent his last years mainly in Europe and died in Geneva. *DAB*, X, 73.

2. Possibly a reference to Andrew Jackson.

3. Under consideration by the Senate at this time, the Pacific Railroad bill (H. R. 701) provided trunk lines to the Pacific Coast at an approximate expenditure of $100,000,000; it was passed on January 30 and returned to the House with amendments. *Cong. Globe*, 36 Cong., 2 Sess., 609–18, 638–39.

4. Jewett's petition to postpone the Pacific Railroad question had been presented by Henry M. Rice of Minnesota on January 10. *Ibid.*, 304.

5. Colorado was then close to the territorial status it achieved February 28, 1861; hopes for early statehood were not realized until 1876. *U. S. Statutes*, XII, 172–77.

From Robert Johnson

House of Rep
Nashville Jany 17th [1861]

Dear Father

Your dispatch was received a few Minutes since and gave great Satisfaction to the Union Men— they are now in fine spirits— Disunionism not so rampant— If the Crittenden proposition will only pass, Tennessee will accept it by an overwhelming majority— Disunion will be burried so deep that it can never be resurrected— Payne is now speaking in the Senate— he is out and [out] disunionist— Trimble will reply and he will bring blood—[1] I was glad to find Andrew Ewing on the Side of the Union and against the treasonable Schemes of the disunionists—[2]

The Legislature is moving along very slowly and no telling when we will adjourn— I do not believe any appropriation will be made to arm the State— I am against it out and out— The Convention Bill has passed the Senate— they modified the House amendment so as to require only a Majority of the people voting to ratify any ordinance of Secession the Convention might pass—

I do not believe the House will agree to the modification—[3]

I will write to morrow[.] If anything extra occur I will Telegraph you[.]

Your Son   Robt Johnson

ALS, DLC-JP.

1. Robert G. Payne, declaring that the Union was dissolved, blamed the abolitionists for secession and observed that Lincoln was nominated not because of his great leadership, but because he espoused the "irrepressible conflict" doctrine and advocated "legal equality of the races." Trimble called for a dispassionate review of the crisis and appealed to all sections to "make their hearts the altar for the flame of that pure patriotism which lives for 'the Union, one and inseparable, now and forever.' " Nashville *Union and American*, January 26–27, 1861; Nashville *Patriot*, January 17, 19, 1861.

2. Long allied with the Middle Tennessee Democracy, Andrew Ewing had never been a close political associate of Johnson. On January 11 he had spoken of the "madness of pulling down this government" without considering alternatives and had urged maintenance of the Union and a review of "the alleged causes of grievance" before undertaking hasty action; three days later he embodied this moderate stance in a resolution condemning those who had "labored to prepare the public mind for a dissolution of the Union," deploring the thought of civil war, and endorsing the Crittenden resolutions. By the spring of 1862, however, Ewing had reassessed his position and "gone South." *Ibid.*, January 12, 1861; *Tenn. House Journal*, 1861, Extra Sess., 70–71; Clayton, *Davidson*, 120.

3. Robert was correct; the house did not concur in the senate's amendment, thereby forcing a conference committee. The final bill required that approval

of any convention action be by a majority of votes cast in the last election rather than by a majority of those voting at the time of a referendum. Nashville *Patriot*, January 19, 21, 1861.

From William P. Jones

January 17, 1861, Nashville; ALS, DLC-JP.

A Nashville physician, having "never liked you, never voted for you, and . . . never in fact had any special regard or use for you," now finds, after reading the December speech, that he honors Johnson for it; "though perhaps the tide is against" the senator in Tennessee, "& doubless largely in yr own party . . . . You have but to come home and do as did the leader of the Children of Israel 'Speak to the people that they go forward.' "

From William M. Lowry

Greene Ten Jany 18 1860 [1861]

Gov Johnson
Dear Sir
    for the first time in My life I have been Confined to my house for the last 2 or 3 weeks with an attack of Pneumonia[.] I am happy now to state that thro the kindness of Providence I am I think pretty near well tho I have not yet ventured out nor shall not do so for a few days[.]
I enclose you a letter I recd today from Col McCulley[1] of McMin[.] I do this merely to let you See that you have Still a few friends but the most people who have Condemned your Speech have went of half Cocked without ever reading it[.] I have not yet seen one who read the Speech but what was Satisfied with it and thought it all right. I feel Confident your enemys Cannot make any thing out of it but on the Other hand that it might make you and put them down[.] Stranger things than this has happened.
from What I can hear I fear We will have a Swarm of Candidates for the Convention and probably Some excitement[.] We must try and elect Some one who will cling to the Greenville resolutions[.][2] I have got behind with my buseness matters and it will take me Some weeks before I get up[.]
If you have leisure and are passing the U S Treas office I would thank you to Call and tell him I am in need of funds and that according to an adjustment of my account with the Comptroller their is Some 119 or 120 $ due me[.] if he Could transmit me a draft therefore I would be greatly obliged[.]
My friend J C G Kennedy of the Census office is also due me my

account for Superintending the taking of the Census[3] and some Other little items of which he is advised[.] Some 500 $[.] if you could do me the kindness to push up those payments I would feel greatly obliged[.] I presume it is pretty tight time with the Govermnt about money matters[.] probably Treas Notes might Suit me[.] I would however prefer drafts on New York[.] if Treas Notes would pass to Merchants in New York at par they would answer[.] I presume Mr Kennedy has paid most of the Marshals ere this[.] I was Some what Negligent in not Sending him forwd my account at an earlier date. I fear that you Can hardly make out this letter as it is so badly written[.] as my claim are So Small I hope upon a Suggestion of you that the Treas & Census office departmnt will forth with writ me the amts due by drafts on New York[.] We have had more rain in the last 10 days than I ever saw fall in Same lenght of time[.] health of the people pretty good[.] Your family all well[.]

Yr friend Wm M Lowry

ALS, DLC-JP.

1. Joseph McCulley [or McCully] (c1808–fl1866), McMinn County farmer (with real estate worth $7,000 and personal property valued at $8,000) and sheriff (1842–48), served as administrator of several estates; in 1855 he was commissioned to transport several freed slaves to Baltimore for passage to Liberia under the auspices of the American Colonization Society. After commenting on the unionist sentiment prevailing in his area, McCulley remarked that "Andrew Johnson can Lea[n] further into matters then any Southern Senator in congress." 1860 Census, Tenn., McMinn, 10th Dist., 58; McCulley to Lowry, January 15, 1861, Johnson Papers, LC; Reba B. Boyer, comp., *Wills and Estate Records of McMinn County, Tennessee, 1820–1870* ([Athens], 1966), 104, 127.

2. The unionist convention of November 24, 1860, had adopted resolutions opposing secession until all other means of redress had been exhausted, emphasizing that secession should await a direct attack upon southern rights—at which time all the states should withdraw as a unit—and demanding the repeal of northern personal liberty laws, the enforcement of the Fugitive Slave Act, and the protection of property in the territories. Although the Greeneville assemblage issued no call for a statewide convention, it urged that all counties hold preliminary meetings with a view to determining sentiment on secession. Nashville *Union and American*, November 28, 1860; see *Johnson Papers*, III, 673n.

3. As U. S. district marshal Lowry had been responsible for conducting the census in East Tennessee.

From H. Warren Winfree[1]

Marbell Hall hawkins County East Tennessee
January 18, 1861

Mr Johnson
Deare Sir

I hav allways Spread myself for you when I had a chance and I did the Same for Bob as we calld him[.][2] But I dont sopose you Recolect me[.] the Last time I was withe you was in walkers Hotell Rogersvill[3] a takeing a Littel oake Stave[.][4] But Enough of this[.] what I want to aske of you is if you please Send me your Speaches[.] I hav Nevere Seen Enny of them yet[.] I Liv in Sitch a out of the way place that we poore folks is Never thought of[.] I hav tolde my Neighbours (all of them for you) that I would write to you and aske you to think of me and that would do fore all[.] they is nothing talk of But your union Speach and it has made you more freinds than Enny thing you evere did[.] you Sent me 2 pattent office Reports 8 years ago and I hav them yet and Shall Keep them my Lifetim and Nevere forgit you[.] I Love to Reade But am two poore to furnish myself thease Long winter Nights[.] it would do me and the old woman good to Read Enny thing that Andy Johnson Send us[.] I Look over my Books mity often[.] they wear [were] for 1851[.] as old as they are I Still Look at them[.]

your friend forever   H. W. Winfree

Marbell Hall
Hawkins County E Tenn

ALS, DLC-JP.
    1. H. Warren Winfree [or Winfry] (b. c1820), was a North Carolina-born carpenter. 1860 Census, Tenn., Hawkins, 11th Dist., 3.
    2. Johnson's son Robert.
    3. Undoubtedly a reference to the tavern kept by Kentucky-born John Walker (b. c1800). 1850 Census, Tenn., Hawkins, 10th Dist., 771.
    4. Winfree's colloquialism reminds us that it was customary to store and age whiskey in charred-oak barrels. Esther Kellner, *Moonshine: Its History and Folklore* (New York, 1971), 229.

From John Olinger[1]

Pajaro valley Watsonvill, Cal.
Jan 20th, 1861

Col Johnson
    Dear sir; I read a speech that you delivered in the senate on the south Carolina secession movement. It was so consistent with my feelings on the subject that I could not help to exclaim huza for Johnson[.] I portrayed in my mind how you looked when you was charging S. Carolina with treason— notwithstanding we are now many miles apart I have all along been perfectly cognizant to all your course in congress since I left old Tennessee[.] I claim as having al-most grown up with you in the same political school (though we may have diffored in some topics)[.] But yet I still appreciate the views of those whome I have been so intimately acquainted. I helped to promote [you] from a Tailor (the canvass against Stephenson[2]) to

a representative in Congress or untill I left the state. I will now give you the political aspect in California. The State is decidedly democratic but inconsequence of a division of the party Lincoln got a small plurality vote. this State is represented by all kinds of people from every nation & from every State in the union & of all grades of color from the white man to the greasser (a kind of spaniard) cosequently there are too many foreign citizens here for Bell & Everett (know nothings) to get a very popular vote.[3] But the election is over and the Black Republican party has succeeded in electing their president & the great Secession crisis is exciting & agitating our glorious Confederacy. I very much deplore the consequences of a *Civil War*. it would create more calamity and distrees then ever was witnessed in America the Revilutionary war not excepted. I do hope (with your zeal & patriotism) that you will use your utmost influence & ability to quell the storm—restore the Missori compromise act, or any other compromise rather than a civil war. I dont think the South can gain any thing by a dissolution unless they conquer the whole *Union* & to do that would cause an internal war [and] our goverment would not be any better than Mexico—ruled by Military force. It is amusing to see hords of office seekers for the different Custom houses or ports in this Country under the New Administration[.] I live near two ports[.][4] there are some aspirents that turned Republican Just in time to get to vote for Lincoln. I would rather vote for a consistent Republican then such turn coats. though the offices doubtless will be filled by the party but still we have our choice in men. and knowing that you can have an influeng in the apointment of goverment officers or in other words that all the appointments are confirmed by the Senate. we therefore recommend the name of Alonzo R. Fall[5] (though a republican) for the position at Monterey[.] he is an intilligent man of good character—is worthy of the position and will do honor to his office & his Country[.] we pride in such *men* & *you would confer* a *favor* upon u s if you *could* succeed in PROCURING his appointment to that position. We are all well & in a tolerable prosperous condition— two of my sons are going to School at the great Paciffic Institute[6] the most renouned on th Paciffic coast. they will graduate in two or three sessions more; we live in a very fine Country[.] its climate & productions cannot be exceled by any country; society is not quite as good as it was in old Tennessee but it has improved very much since we came here[.] please write when the apointment is made for Monterey. give my respects to all my old friends in Tennessee and accept for yourself the best wishes of your sincere friend

                                                            John Olinger

To A Johnson

ALS, DLC-JP.

1. John Olinger (b. *c*1805), a farmer, was living in Pajaro in 1869. It has not been possible to determine which one of the two John Olingers listed in the 1830 Greene County census, both of whom were between twenty and thirty, removed to California. Monterey County Poll List for 1869 (Courtesy Valerie Rohrbaugh, Los Angeles Public Library); Byron Sistler, tr., *1830 Census, East Tennessee* (Evanston, Ill., 1969), 177, 206.

2. When Johnson first campaigned for the legislature in 1835, his opponent was Matthew Stephenson of Washington County, a man "of moral worth and high social standing," who had been prominent at the state constitutional convention of the preceding year. Temple, *Notable Men*, 363.

3. Out of a total vote of 119,876 for the four presidential tickets in California, Bell and Everett had finished a poor fourth with only 9,122 votes, nearly 25,000 behind Breckinridge and Lane, the third-running team. Burnham, *Presidential Ballots*, 256, 896.

4. Olinger probably refers to Santa Cruz on the north end of Monterey Bay and to Monterey, the former capital, on the south; the latter, an old whaling port, had but limited facilities and was losing its commercial advantage. Titus F. Cronise, *The Natural Wealth of California* (San Francisco, 1868), 83–85; Aubrey Drury, *California: An Intimate Guide* (New York, 1935), 200–203.

5. Fall cannot be identified.

6. The first chartered institution of higher learning in California, the College (now University) of the Pacific was founded by the Methodist Church in Santa Clara in 1851 and opened a year later. In 1871 the college moved to San Jose and in 1923 to Stockton. Only one of Olinger's sons, Thomas N., was listed in the Institute's 1859–60 catalog. A second son, John Harvey (b. *c*1839), may have been enrolled by 1861, inasmuch as he was pursuing a teaching career in Pajaro at the end of the decade. Sacramento *Union*, April 8, 1973; *Catalogue of the University of the Pacific, Santa Clara, California, 1859–60* (San Francisco, 1860), 5; Rockwell D. Hunt, *History of the College of the Pacific* (Stockton, 1951), 9 (Courtesy Martha S. O'Bryon, Curator, Stuart Library of Western America, University of the Pacific); Monterey County Poll List for 1869.

From John M. Seely

January 20, 1861, Maysville, Ky.; ALS, DLC-JP.

Agrees with Johnson's speech, but finds Seward's address of January 12 "full of Marked *deiseption*"; plans to look for work in Johnson's region, for, inasmuch as "northern mechanics have been compelled to leave the Lower country during the past 60 Days," the prospects of southerners are improved.

From William R. Sevier

January 22, 1861, Jonesboro; ALS, DLC-JP.

Applauds Johnson's stand, although "a few *fireside warriors* hereabouts indulge in abuse of you & your speech"; urges distribution of speeches in Washington County and, if possible, a visit to defeat editor William Graham's effort to nominate a disunion candidate [Landon C. Haynes] for the coming convention. "Your presence . . . would cast dismay into the ranks of the men who are laboring so assiduously for the destruction of the Union." Promises "a good crowd—*a regular old fashioned flag and . . . a more cordial reception* than you have Recd in 'these parts' for many years, *from all parties*[.]"

From John Lellyett

Knoxville   Jany 23, 1861

Hon Andrew Johnson
Washington City

Dear Sir.—About eight days ago I left Nashville, and have been traveling a little in Tennessee and Georgia. I have traveled with my eyes and ears open, and have made such observations as I was capable of making in regard to the progress of the prevailing rebellion. The reason why our friends in Georgia and Alabama were defeated[1] was simply this: They were *afraid*—overawed by the reign of intolerance and terror. They tried to compromise with treason. They tried to soothe a raging wolf by patting him gently and allowing him to taste a little of their blood by way of compromise. This thing of secession has become a most savagely raging lunacy;—and more, the people of the Cotton States are this day subjected to a most hateful and intolerable despotism. Once I thought strange that the first Napoleon should have become so universally popular in France by the successful use of strong and prompt coercive measures upon a raging mob.[2] Now I think I can appreciate it. We must meet the domineering career of this raging fanaticism in Tennessee by presenting a bolder, a more threatening and determined front, or we may be speedily overwhelmed, and bound hand and foot. No half way measures will do. For my part, I think we should denounce treason by its proper name; and let these men know that we will not consent to dissolving the Union at all for present grievances. None of those grievances can be any thing else than aggravated by secession, while tenfold greater evils will be brought upon us.

But you know enough about all that. My object is to urge you to come to Tennessee and make a number of speeches, *as soon as possible*—before the conventional canvass shall progress too far—in order to give proper tone and direction to the canvass. Our friends are still afraid—and they are still stupid and foolish. Look at the resolutions passed the other day in the House of Representatives of our State Legislature by a vote almost unanimous![3] Conditional disunion! Disunion unless impossible conditions can be obtained! Conditions involving amendments to the Constitution, by which we all swore only a hundred days ago! A man would hav been politically damned one hundred days ago, and repudiated by all parties, for the utterance of such sentiments. I believe you can do more than any man in the state to put down such sentiments. I am not willing to demand amendments to the constitution of our country at the point of the bayonet, nor with a threat of treason. I should vote for Crittenden's resolutions, to be sure; but how can we expect to obtain any concessions amid such an uproar of treasonable confusion? And then if I can obtain no amendment whatever, I have no right to *demand* any thing but the constitution as it is, and such amendments (if any) as *can* be obtained under its own provision made for the purpose. I would make no conditions with treason. The rebellion must be put down as you would *put* out a fire consuming your mansion. When the flames are subdued and the ruins have cooled off, we may reconstruct if we can. When this rebellion shall have been subdued, and the people have become willing to proceed about the business, peacefully, decently, lawfully, a National Convention may be called to amend the Constitution, if the people desire it. How can we know what the people desire now? Our convention must not be such a body as the Legislature—or we are ruined.

I thought to write you before, urging you to come home to your constituents, and set them right (as you could do to a great extent) on the issue now before the people. There was not a greater confusion of tongues at the tower of Babel, than of ideas now among our people—a chaos of ideas—an anarchy of ideas.

A manly declaration of the approaching Convention of Tennessee in favor of maintaining the Union and putting down rebellion would have a stunning effect on the rebel South. They are wild in anticipation that Tennessee will go with them. And the disunionists even here are sanguine of such a result. However, in East Tennessee the people are for the Union if they knew how. They absolutely don't know how to think speak or act, about it.

Yours Respectfully
John Lellyett

ALS, DLC-JP.

1. Following a convention vote of 166–130, Georgia's secession ordinance had been signed the day before this letter. Herschel V. Johnson, Benjamin H. Hill, and Alexander H. Stephens had led the losing battle for cooperation. In Alabama cooperationists nearly won a delay when a minority report calling for a Nashville convention of slaveholding states on February 22 to urge constitutional guarantees was defeated 54–45 on January 9, but a secession ordinance was adopted two days later. The fight for the cooperationists had been carried by former Congressman Jeremiah Clemens. Dwight L. Dumond, *The Secession Movement* (New York, 1931), 201–7; Allen D. Candler, ed., *Confederate Records of the State of Georgia* (6 vols., Atlanta, 1909–11), I, 15–17, 213ff.

2. During the revolt against the National Convention in Paris on October 5, 1795, Napoleon, directing the defense for the government, positioned the

artillery so that it could effectively shoot down the advancing rebels. *Encyclo-paedia Britannica* (1973 ed.), XVI, 2; André Maurois, *A History of France,* Henry L. Binsse and Gerard Hopkins, trans. (New York, 1968), 324–25.

3. Two days earlier, George Gantt of Maury County, speaking for the joint committee on federal relations, had offered a series of resolutions calling for a convention of slave states to clarify the basis on which they would remain in the Union, proposing constitutional amendments in support of slavery, and declaring that if such amendments were not adopted, the slave states should enact them and form a separate union. The resolutions passed by a vote of 56–7. *Tenn. House Journal,* 1861, Extra Sess., 125–28; Nashville *Union and American,* January 22, 1861.

From Horatio King

January 26, 1861, Washington, D. C.; ALS, DLC-JP.

In a *"Private & unofficial"* letter the acting postmaster general asks "to see and consult with you in reference to candidates and the propriety of making removals at several of the important offices in your State. . . . on account of the P. Ms. being active disunionists."

From McGill & Witherow[1]

Washington City Jan. 26, 1861.

Hon. A. Johnson,
Dear Sir,—

Inadvertently your a/c for speeches was placed among those given to the page. It was our intention to have seen you personally after having reduced the bill $15—which amount was agreed on after consultation with the Globe Office.

Enclosed please find $5, with bill and receipt for amount we intended to have charged.

Regretting the inadvertence alluded to, we are

Very respy. yours
McGill & Witherow

Whole Bill	$225.00	Received	$215.00
Reduction	15.00	Returned	5.00
	$210.00		$210.00

ALS, DLC-JP.

1. Thomas McGill and [James] Witherow were partners, trading as "Steam Press and Job Printers, 271 Penna. Av., between Tenth and Eleventh Streets." *Boyd's Washington and Georgetown Directory* (1858), 207, 329.

From Thomas J. Usrey[1]

Fayetteville Ark
Jany 26th 1861

Hon A Johnson
Dear Sir.

The recent [speech] of yours if correctly reported, is endorsed by a majority of the people in this section. While the majority are with you in sentiment they doubt the policy or expediency of using force. I published the abstract and endorsed it yesterday,[2] in debate, I defended your positions as I understood them, but frankly admitted that Coercive measures were at this stage of the revolution in[ex]pedient and dangerous to Republican liberty.

We elect delegates to a State Convention on the 18th of Feby. It is the purpose of Secession to rally under the cry of Democracy[.] This Co. elects four Delegates, and I am satisfied that if the election should come off tomorrow, Secession would be defeated 8 or 1000 votes. The Co. gave Breck[inridge] 300 majority. If the people are fairly dealt with Arkansas will stand by the Border States.

Please Send me a copy of your recent speech in full, with such facts and arguments as having a strong bearing on Secession.

Do you have any hope of an honorable adjustment. If so, let me know it for your influence is potent here among the great body of Tennesseans[.] Those who admire South Carolina'[s] Course, in Some instances endorse the Federalism in her state policy. What evidence or facts *can you* furnish me that intimate the purpose of Cotton States to organize a Con. Monarchy based on birth and property. I am with you to the end in resisting any government less democratic than the one in which we now live—

Pardon me for this trespass. Furnish me, as far as possible, with fac[ts] and arguments sought, for I am a volunteer [in] this Campaign against inconsiderate Secessio[n.] Written Compromise is t[he] ultimatum of the people here[.] Th[e]y are for it or Something Similar. The Speech of Judge Douglas, proves him a patriot—truly —.[3] I am Happy to [be] able to subscribe myself

Your Fellow citizen   T. J. Usrey

ALS, DLC-JP.

1. See *Johnson Papers*, III, 619n.
2. Usrey had gone from Tennessee to Arkansas to establish a Union paper, the Fayetteville *Democrat*; this defense undoubtedly appeared in that paper. *Ibid.*, 619; see Letter from Thomas J. Usrey, March 5, 1861; Gregory, *Union List of Newspapers*, 23.
3. Since his defeat for the presidency, Stephen A. Douglas had been ac-

tively engaged in efforts to save the Union. The reference here is probably
to his speech of January 3. *Cong. Globe*, 36 Cong., 2 Sess., App. 35–42;
George Fort Milton, *The Eve of Conflict* (Cambridge, Mass., 1934) 530–31.

From James W. Harold

Greeneville Tenn
Jany 27. 1861

Dear Sir

I concluded to drop you a line to inform you of some few things
going on. There was a pretty Considerable number of Powder Magazines in the Court House yesterday, & like to have been a row from
a verry small Circumstance. Yesterday was the day for a Convention for the purpose of Nominating Union Candidates for the Convention. There is an Immediate Secesion Element here though they
deny & say they are as good union men as any Body. Since there has
been such a strong Union demonstration from all parts of the County
the little Seccesion Crowd are as follows, Jacob Harris, Loyd Bullin
Old Boyce John Arnold, Joseph Galbreath Dr Foutte & Son he wants
to serve in a Southern Navy & Reuben Arnold, Gabriel F. Page and
Robert McKee James Rumbough, & Bill Williams[.][1] Now that is
about the Immediate Seccesion Crowd[.] Elbert Biggs though he
denies the above with Some boys are about the Crowd[.] Some of
the above are moved from the fact that the old Whig party Called
themselves the Union party in the last Election & they think Seccesion is a democratick move[.] Now if Immediate Seccesion is the
Democratick move the Lord deliver me from such, the bal[ance] of
my life[.] Tis not the means to obtain the End[.] the whole Country
is inflamed with Seccesion documints & Southern Speakers.

I forgot to mention Lowrys [a] firm f[i]re Eater through out[.]
Now the Convention met the day verry bad but a Large Crowd[.]
Every Secesion man nearly in the County here with a trick[.] still the
Union *Sentiment* 10 to 1—or nearly so & the Secesion Crowd by
Every hook or Crook trying slyly to Engender old party prejudices[.]
Bulen was the prime mover in this movement. I think he had &
[*sic*] object in view to wit to make a question Convention or no Con-
vention thinking that Milligan would be defeated as he favoured a
Convention & the Convention would nominate J P McDowell[2] &
then Bullen would pitch in as the democratick Candide. The Candi-
dates were taken through a fiery ordeal interogated on the stand[.]
Milligan Satisfied the most Ultra Union man in Every particular
Save one[.] When the question was asked whether he was for the
Convention he aswered Yes he thought it would be well Enough to
have one. then Come the row. the little secession crowd yelled for

Milligam, & that made Union men of all parties Cock their Ears. then a move was made to put Milligan through & he was Voted down Largely by Whigs & democrats the very men voting against him who had been doing all in their power to fix [the] publick mind united in his favour for Instance B McDannell standing Square toed & voting against him twice and myself along also & many others, the most perfect Excitement all the time. McDowell then was put in nomination & would have been Nominated if he had not Rose upon the Stand and protested & refusing to Come in Conflict with the Genl & Endorsing his Union Sentiments and requesting his freinds to support Milligan[.] the consqunce was that Milligan was put to the Crowd again & it was supposed he was nominated all the seccesionists shouting for him simply because they indorse him as they say which will injure Milligan by the straight out Union men of all partys[.] the Whigs are to a man nearly [all] against a Convention & all the straight out men of all partys[.] if the thing Could Come untrameled before the people of this County unbiased by whigEry or democracy th[e]y would give the Convention fits[.] But Bullen wants to mix it up with Whiskey & Democracy & with the aid of the inflamatory documents that the Country is filled with and the Treasonable Emisarys that are pasing through & Stoping along at Stations delivering their Lectures tis hard to tell what will be the result. it may be that the Convention proposition may Carry[.] tis pasing strange to me to see men but there are verry few here Condeming your position in your Speech, & shouting in the Convention, for Milligan[.] it shews there was a trick for he took the same ground[.] The fact is Milligan in private Conversation to me is the Strongest Coercion man about here[.] he is for Wools & Scotts origanal plan[3] says there would have been none of this. Bob Crawford[4] took the Bull By the horns Said he was opposed to the Call of a Convention, & they nominated him by acclination[.] But one single nay, for the Senate, & also Thornburgh[5] from Jefferson he followed Suit, Endorsing same views with Bobs made a verry strong Speech against Seccesion & was nominated for floater, & the Convention adjournd Simide [*sine die*]. I understand the Secessonists are going to have a Convention or meeting here Tuesdy next[.] they want pehaps to git up a Candidate for floater & Senate[.] thats the quistion the Secesionists are taking advatage of Convention or no Convention thus adopting the latter & Saying they are as good union men as any body when th[e]y utter a Lye when they say this Convention is a strange thing that ma[n]y Cant understand. Voting for a man for office & Voting against the office [at] the same time seems to be a contradiction that the people have not the time to understand. The seccesionists here Say that what the Convention does is final that it is a higher power

than the Legislature & Connot be Sent back to the people for ratification[.] now if in the Excitement of the moment if th[e]y were to pass
an ordinanc of Secesion & were to refuse to send it back in view of
the Act of Legislature to that Effect to ratify by the people there
would be a revolution & blood spilt right here in Tenn & no mistake[.]

Your Family are all well & nothing of interest that I know of Except what I have scratched down[.]

I dont know whether you can read it or not[.] if you can do so &
Burn[.] I thought you might like to hear what was going on[.] The
above is neare the history of Yesterday[.]

Your Freind Truly   James. W. Harold

ALS, DLC-JP.

1. Jacob Harris (b. c1816), Virginia-born farmer possessing real estate
worth $12,000; Lloyd Bullen, former state senator (1857–59); William
Boyce, Greeneville silversmith; John Q. Arnold (1842–1865), Thomas D.
Arnold's son and at eighteen captain of Co. F, 29th Inf., CSA; Joseph M.
Galbraith (b. c1807), a well-to-do farmer; Dr. George W. Foute and his son
Robert who joined the Confederate navy; Reuben Arnold, brother of John,
and a Greeneville lawyer who was lieutenant colonel of the 29th Inf., CSA;
Gabriel F. Page, Methodist minister; Robert M. McKee (b. c1834), railroad
postmaster and a Washington County delegate to the Greeneville convention;
James H. Rumbaugh and William D. Williams, both Greeneville merchants.
1860 Census, Tenn., Greene, 7th Dist., 227; 9th Dist., 18; 10th Dist., 82,
96; 13th Dist., 58; Johnson Papers, I, 333n, 393n, 497n, 534n, 538n; III,
359n, 473n; Reynolds, Greene County Cemeteries, 257; John Q. Arnold, Compiled Service Record, RG109, National Archives; Tennesseans in the Civil
War, I, 33, 235; Temple, East Tennessee, 573.
2. James P. McDowell, Greeneville merchant and a delegate to the Greeneville convention in May, 1861, was elected by that body, along with O. P.
Temple of Knox and John Netherland of Hawkins, as a commissioner from
East Tennessee to memorialize the legislature for a separate state. Temple,
East Tennessee, 569–71, 572.
3. Gen. Winfield Scott had recommended the immediate garrisoning of
nine southern ports and Gen. John E. Wool had proposed a "judicious application of army and navy." Stampp, And the War Came, 51, 70.
4. Robert Crawford (b. c1820), Greeneville attorney and unionist, was
a delegate to the Greeneville convention. 1850 Census, Tenn., Greene, 274;
Temple, East Tennessee, 572.
5. Probably Montgomery Thornburgh (1817–1862), a former Whig
state senator from Jefferson (1845–51) and state attorney general (1854–
62), who was an active participant in the Greeneville convention. Arrested in
1862 by Confederate authorities, he died in prison at Macon, Georgia. Temple,
Notable Men, 203–5; Tenn. Official Manual, 192.

From Sylvester Olinger

January 29, 1861, Birdville, Tex.; ALS, DLC-JP.

Requests Johnson's speeches and "other documents advocating the
Union"; "Secession is Rife in Texas & I Expect our present self Caled
Convention will pass an ordinance of Secession but if they submit it to
the people I think it doubtfull whether they will Ratify it or not[.]"

From William G. Leader

January 31, 1861, Philadelphia, Pa.; ALS, DLC-JP.

Renews invitation to address Union Club—this time for Washington's birthday; approves Johnson's constitutional amendments and hopes "the present difficulties may not be settled, without abolishing the Electorial Colledge, or else have the Electors elected by single districts, so this and another sectional candidate will never be elected President"; criticizes press for spreading abolitionist views; and favors constitutional amendment to silence and punish such traitors, as well as their counterparts, the southern fire-eaters. [Letter of January 23 had invited Johnson to speak March 15, Andrew Jackson's birthday.]

From William M. Lowry

Greeneville Jany 31 1861.

My Dear Sir

I wrote you Some days ago. Sins then I have got up to the Store this week having been confined to my house Some 4 Weeks, this probably is all well enough as I thereby escaped the turmoil and Strife of polatics, which is now getting pretty warm, a thing I regret to See[.] the people of Greene County, have had a good many Conventions, Milligan was nominated for the County, and has taken ground for Crittenden Compromise. I Can See from the few days I have been out that the Sentiment of the people are Some What divided about the propriety of a Convention. I am of the opinion from what I Can See that a pretty large Majority will vote against the Call of a Convention[.]

I See Some Controversy about where the Tennessee Commissioners should meet. My opinion is they ought to meet with the Virginia and No Car Comms at Washington[1] and I hope the Legislature may So instruct them. Milligan tells me he cannot go having, gone into the Canvass for the Convention[.][2]

I am beginning to think that no Compromise that Could be offered would Satisfy, Some of the extreeme Southern States. I have my Self, been for and willing to adopt the Crittenden Compromise and Settle the Question upon that basis.

I think our Southern States that have gone off have acted verry badly in retireing, from the Capitol and thereby throwing every thing, into the hands of the enemy, deserting the Capitol at the verry time when their services were needed. If the Crittenden compromise could only have been adopted and fixed upon the Country, now or at the time it was pressed it would have went far to have Settled the Controversy,

in all the border and Conservative States. I yet hope that it or Some
Kindred Measure may be adopted. I See from the papers of this
Morning, that the indications of Compromise are more flattering[.]
I hope that Ex Pres. Tryler may have done Some good in his visit
to Washington.[3] I Shall so far as I can throw oil upon the troubled
waters, and keep Our freinds from getting excited as it Seems that
Madness rules the hour. I have recd from the U S Treas a draft for
what they are due me[4] for which I presume I am in debt to you. I
have not yet had any thing from the Hon Mr Kennedy Census office
who owe me some 500$[.] I wrote to Mr Kennedy the other day
upon the Subject, that as my claim was Small and I had waited verry
patiently, that I hoped on recpt of my letter that he would forwd me
a draft for the amt[.] Not Much local news, one of James Johnstons
died the other day his Son James.[5] old Mrs Maloy[6] is also not expected to live— We have had a verry hard winter on all kinds of
Constitutions[.] Our traders to the South have generally done well,
the health of our town is pretty good. Your family all well.

with much regard Yr friend & obt. servt
Wm M Lowry

Hon A Johnson
Washington City D C

ALS, DLC-JP.

1. Tennessee sent twelve delegates to the Washington Peace Conference
of February 4, 1861. Of these, eleven stood staunchly for moderation. Folmsbee, *Tennessee*, II, 30.

2. Milligan, although in the midst of his successful candidacy as a "no-
convention" delegate to the proposed Tennessee convention, was convinced
by friends of the urgency of the mission and did attend the Washington Peace
Conference. Samuel Milligan, Memoir, 1863–1869 (Microfilm, Tennessee
State Library and Archives, original in possession of S. J. Milligan, Greeneville), 86–87.

3. Proposed by Virginia, the Washington Peace Conference represented
the last effort of border state conservatives to effect a reconciliation. Former
President Tyler presided over the meeting, which recommended constitutional
revision that included the reestablishment of the Missouri Compromise line.
Since no states of the deep South were represented and Republican radicals
scoffed at the "venerable" conclave, it was doomed to failure. Nevins, *Emergence of Lincoln*, II, 411; see also Robert G. Gunderson, *Old Gentlemen's
Convention: The Washington Peace Conference of 1861* (Madison, Wis.,
1961).

4. Probably the "119 or 120$" Lowry had mentioned in his recent letter
of January 18.

5. James A. Johnson [Johnston] (1839–1861), son of James Johnson
(1813–1889), a Greeneville farmer, died on January 29. Reynolds, *Greene
County Cemeteries*, 492; 1860 Census, Tenn., Greene, Greeneville, 9th Dist.,
11.

6. Possibly "old" Elizabeth Maloy (b. c1808), the wife of Thomas Maloy,
printer. *Ibid.*

From George W. Waite[1]

Hyde Park Cook Co. Ill
Jany 31. 1861

Hon. Johnsen U. S. S.
Washington D. C.
Dear Sir

I wish half a dozen or more of your late Speech on the State of the Union to distribute in this vicinity as they will do much good.

The people are very *Set* in their opinions, but can be approached by your border state men— They will hear most any thing from *you* and *your Class* in your State— But when a State has Seceeded, you Might about as well take [talk] to the fanatics of South Carolina as to talk to them. There is an uprising of the Masses here that is terrible to think of— God grant that wise Counsels may prevail and save the Country—

The Masses at the North have some how made themselves beleive, that the Slaveholders are trying to Crack their lash over them with a view to *dictate* terms, and would, had they the power, make Slaves of all the working Class— Till they can be disabused of this no person from the South that is not Conservative can gain their ears.

The North and South are in a bad fix. For Should a war break out the North would, with their present feelings, think that they *were* fi[gh]ting for *their* personal liberties, and would fight to desperation[.] Of course the South would do the same and God only knows the result. My own opinion is that both would get whipped and slavery exterminated and the Country ruined and we become food for foreign Mercinaries[.]

Please excuse this digression And believe Me your friend and well wisher

Geo. W. Waite   Post Master

ALS, DLC-JP.

1. George W. Waite, Hyde Park postmaster, organized a real estate and brokerage firm and served as president of the Mount Greenwood Cemetery Association No. 53. *U. S. Official Register* (1863), 341; *Lakeside Directory of Chicago* (1881), 1215.

From Spencer Henry[1]

Maryville Feb 1st 1861

Hon Andrew Johnson
Dear Sir

Our Court has been in Session this week, Baxter,[2] & Temple,[3] made Speeches on monday, to a very large crowd, as many as could be crowded into the Court house. The disunionists have not attempted during the week publickly, to defend their position[.] they are, nevertheless very *Zealous* and operate, where they can, in private circles, My Brother J. F. Henry[4] is the candidate to the convention for this County & will run perhaps without opposition. Robert Crawford of Greeneville I understand, is the candidate for the district. I do not think this County would give 300 votes to a disunion candidate. In Sevier County they grow *beautifully* less. In Cocke County they are more equally divided as I understand, your Speech in the Senate on the subject of Secession has been sought for during the week but unfortunately but few of them can be found. I happened by accident to get one of them in the lower end of the County last week, I have read it carefully. It contains the true doctrine I think, & I endorse every word of it. heartily, I read your Speech delivered in the Senate of Decr 12th 1860 [1859] on the invasion of Harpers Ferry. That Speech contained much matter of History in our Government to which I was a stranger, most of your old political friends of this County have discarded you entirely, they say you are Sympathising with the North and against Southeren interests. If those gentlemen will turn to your Speech in the U. S. Senate delivered 12th Decr 60 they will see from the manner in which you throttled Trumbull, Seward, & Doolittle, they *might* come to a different conclusion. But, Sir, you have lost nothing in the way of friends in old Blount ten to one, it has endeared some of your old friends to you, and made Hundreds of others. I fear Tennessee will Seceede with Gov Harris to urge it on. much depends on you, can you visit Tenn in this crisis. I hope you will employ every means in your power to save us from ruin. The Flag of our Country is now trailing in the dust. Is the genius of American liberty slumbering? Has the American Eagle let go her arrows of victory, folded her wings and perched uppon Some cragey Battlement of our Republic to look down with pitey uppon our ruins? God forbid! I have been urged by some of your old political friends to address you on this subject (Knowing that I am personally acquainted with you) "In the integrity of my heart I have done it"[5] Hoping that our Government may be perpetuated, and that she may Stand out as a beacon light to all the nations of Earth, and hoping also that you will pardon this intrusion uppon your patience I am as Ever yours

Respectfully   Spencer Henry

Feb 20th

The above was intended to reach you before our Election, owing to incessant rains & high waters &c I was prevented from doing So. I have concluded however to send it notwiths[t]anding. Tennessee is safe by at least 50.000[.] I can only utter my gratitude in the language of the Apocelypse "Halleluia for the Lord God omnipoten reigneth"[6]

I am no politician still, I have interests in common with other American citizens, in the future I want to keep better posted in the political affairs of our Country, but few of your Speeches can be found in this end of the County[.] Keep sending them, you have many fast friends here & throughout Tenn[.] I am certain your position will endear you to the conservative portio[n] of the American people[.]

S H.

ALS, DLC-JP.

1. Spencer Henry (b. c1806), a Blount County minister, served on a number of local committees, including the board of directors for the East Tennessee Masonic Female Institute. 1850 Census, Tenn., Blount, 76; Inez E. Burns, *History of Blount County, Tennessee* (Nashville, 1957), 41, 114, 115, 148.

2. John Baxter (1819–1886), a Knoxville Whig lawyer and former North Carolina legislator, opposed secession, though he was a slaveholder with strong southern sympathies. Following the war he tried unsuccessfully to organize a third political party to act as a moderating force between the Republicans and Democrats, chaired the influential judicial committee in the state constitutional convention of 1870, and served as United States circuit judge (1877–86). *DAB*, II, 63; Rothrock, *French Broad-Holston Country*, 376.

3. Oliver P. Temple (1820–1907), East Tennessee Whig lawyer, had unsuccessfully challenged Johnson for Congress in 1847. An elector for the Bell-Everett ticket (1860), he campaigned to keep Tennessee in the Union, helped organize the Knoxville and Greeneville conventions, and served as chairman of a committee to memorialize the legislature concerning the separation of East Tennessee. Remaining in Knoxville, he defended unionists arraigned before the Confederate courts, including the "Andrews Raiders," who were brought into the city in June, 1862. Chancellor of the 8th and 2nd Tennessee districts (1866–70, 1870–78), he was Knoxville postmaster (1881–84) and a member of the University of Tennessee Board of Trustees (1854–1907). After the age of seventy-five he wrote several historical works, among them *East Tennessee and the Civil War* (1899) and *Notable Men of Tennessee from 1833 to 1875* (1912). *DAB*, XVIII, 363–64; Fred A. Bailey, Oliver Perry Temple: New South Agrarian (M. A. thesis, University of Tennessee, 1972).

4. John F. Henry (1808–1884), Louisville merchant, had been a Whig state senator from Blount (1843–49) and after moving to Knox served as speaker of the senate (1849–51). He later returned to Blount County. Burns, *Blount County*, 99, 146, 267; Robison, *Preliminary Directory, Blount*, 25.

5. A slight variation of Gen. 20:5: "in the integrity of my heart and innocency of my hands have I done this."

6. Apocalypse: Revelation; a verbatim quotation from Rev. 19:6.

From "Grand Junction"[1]

State of Mississippi, Feb. 3. 1861

Dear Sir

I have a mulatto slave remarkable for his impudence. This you know is often the case with africans having anglo Saxon blood. Witness the Case of Hannibal Hamlin.[2] As a means of humiliating my slave it has been recommended to me, to Send him to Washington City, with a *Cowhide*, and instruct him to give your back & shoulders some *marks* of *his attention*, with the instrument aforesaid. It is thought that coming in contact with *you*, will so effectually *disgrace* him, that the effect on him will be so humiliating, that he will make a good obedient Slave.

Thinking the Suggestion a good one, I have concluded to try the experiment. If he shall happen to wound you badly in the encounter, employ Senator *Sumner* to Send daily *bulletins* of your condition to your friends about[.]

Grand Junction.

ALS, DLC-JP.

1. The envelope endorsement reads: "Signed 'Grand Junction.' THREATENED ASSAULT FROM MISSISSIPPI ATTENDED TO."

2. Because Hamlin, Lincoln's vice president, had an extremely swarthy complexion, it was rumored during the campaign, and believed by gullible southerners, that he was part Negro. *DAB*, VIII, 197; see also *Johnson Papers*, III, 112n; H. Draper Hunt, *Hannibal Hamlin of Maine* (Syracuse, 1969), 121–22.

From Walter S. Waldie

[Kensington Penn
February 3, 1861][1]

Hon Andrew Johnson "of Tennessee"
U. S. Senate.
Dr Sir

Accept my Thanks for a Copy of yr Speech and for your Manly support of righting all complaints *in the Union*. Because you wisely oppose the folly of Secession I feel it my duty to aid you with every power I possess, be it more or less, and to yeild much of any Cherished opinion to the calm and dignified request of a union loving neighbor, While to a secession traitor, I would make him buy the halter & then hang him. Agreeing with you in Sentiment I differ in your argument, and regret that you strengthen the argument of Toombs, Yancy & their Cohorts of Traitors.

The Colonies were settled by distinct Classes of persons, all owing allegiance to one Common government, that of Great Britain. In their vassalage they had no Government of their own— their local Councils were no more than County Commissioners of today. They did attempt to issue Bills of Credit & Coin Money and some other acts pertaining to Sovereignity, but under the articles or agreement of Common Defence, they found that a Union was already established by Necessity of their Wants. It was to satisfy this already Conceived & Created Union that the Confederation and after, our present Constitution were formed. Instinct of Safety made the Union, and so far perfect unanimity prevailed, but when the local peculiarities demanded also embodiment in the proposed expression of Government, then came the discussions followed by what are called the Compromises of the Constitution. The Puritan would have his severe Code of Morality or bigotry engrafted, while the Quaker was willing to eat with publicans & Sinners, keeping his own plate Clean. The most liberal ideas of the Constitution Came from Virginians, who at that time possessed the greatest political intelligence among our fathers, and their finest & best were most emphatic in opposing the idea of Slavery being in any degree Nationalised. Language was twisted in every direction to express the protection of fugitive Slaves without using the word Slave or implying property in Man. In all the discussions the Sovereign Superiority of the United States as *the* Government was never disputed. Every act of a Sovereign was embodied, but to no State was any power granted to do or Create a Citizen in its official Character. All Naturalization Certificates from any State require *Allegiance* to the U States, and obedience to local restrictions. The great idea of Citizenship, The protection of life & property is exclusively the Federal power, and it is only the Federal power that can execute for Treason, or demand his Services as a Soldier.

The Colonies Could not exist, therefore they had not the power to Create a new condition and bestow what they had not to give. But the combined, solidified unity of all the individual powers of a *Nation*, as the U. S. Could grant strength to local Communities to preserve their peculiar institutions inside of Such limits as were presented to the consideration of this power—this Unit of Strength in itself, and Creator or supporter of inferior satellites. Local peculiarities were never Sanctioned as Union. Blue Laws of Connecticut were allowed in that state, but does she Claim the right of Such laws in Territories? Once open the doors to Nationalising local peculiarities and Pandoras Box² would be a plaything to the Confusion of National affairs.

When you assert that the "Union sprung from the Constitution and that States have a Sovereign Capacity" you are fostering the ground work of Secession.

You are encouraging the Bull frog to swell as big as the Cow.³ Cotton may be King in the Gulf states, and Control the leading branches of industry therein but it has no claim beyond as Gov Hicks acknowledges.⁴ If Penna were to ordain Secession, and attempt to force my property to war against the U S, I Should at once apply to my *Sovereign*, to whom I owe Allegiance,— the Whole Nation, to my brothers in every State, and demand that their Chief Military Officer, the President, Should protect me. If I failed in obtaining protection, then I should have to decide whether to run away, be punished or submit.— In Austria, So Carolina or Penna, The U States is My only Country, and she owes me protection.

How can a man divide his love, & his duty without Weakening his powers? All the powers of a Man must be Subservient to our individual aim. and all Citizens must bow to one great purpose or power,— In republics Such a power is Created by intelligence, Such as it maybe,—in Monarchies the power of force. The More a Man has the More he Can give, and true also of Communities— New England as a Community works hard to develope each individual within its limits and hence the U. S. receives from Customs, P. O. &c the strength she does from a Community of *Individuals*— TheSe individuals are U S Citizens not *State*— The Corporate Capacity of the State is nothing to the U. S. nor the U States to it except as far the individuals ask intervention for protection. On page 7 of your Speech you quote from Judge Marshall—Claiming the *people* and not the states. There is a degree of inconsistency in some of quotations made by you. A nation of intelligence does not Combine into a Unity without having some high object. Common safety Created a Union of Strength, but after Securing protection, there must be a preserving idea, Something to keep alive the interest. Local ideas being kept within limits, what was to grow, to be cultivated? It must be something universal—for perpetuity Can only exist in universalism— & this was found in *labor*. Our Government was the first wherein labor ever discussed its provisions or had a voice in its Creation. Under the guise of "Pursuit of Happiness" was this idea Smothered, unfortunately, for stupid Counsels have ignored what they would never have dared to do, had a positive affirmation been expressed as the duty of the Union. That the interest of labor is distinctly a federal function, is apparent from the fact that all duties, imports & are all federal—as also the granting of Patents. *The right* of labor can never be disputed, but the Means best adapted to develop it, is a fair & noble subject of discussion, but is it ever done in Congress? Never and for want of some object beyond mere appropriation Bills (the Playthings of the Lobby)[5] there is not an idea presented but petty partisan debates, and the Once August Senate turned into a Cockpit for Presidential Candidates. Two lately and nearly a third in one term from the senate[6] looks very significant of Evil to the Country. Had Chicago been near to Washington—Seward would have recd the Nomination— When a convention—Called par excellence "the National Convention" Met & the idea of labor was presented—a Sneer went round and a drunken Irish Rowdy from N York publicly insulted My state.[7] The Candidate of that Convention, was claimed as *National* and the Convention that Claimed protection to labor as an object of Government Care is Called sectional —Black Republicans— Even you descend to this in your Speech.

What right have you or any one else to claim statesmanship when the great vital interest of 9/10 of the entire population of our Country is unworthy your Notice.? Do you think we are willing to forego the power we possess and permit such mis conduct? Do not judge from the Committee you have had lately in Washington,[8] they do not represent a tithe of the Working men, and was a dodge to bring Certain men prominent. We Who know our own power when properly prepared, will Come with a *Command* and not a treaty— We know that free discussion of labor is not permitted South of Tennessee—but we Sovereigns Can call a National Convention in any sou[t]hern town, we please, And Can go there strong enough to invite all the poor White men, and tell them Speak out. Protect them while they tell us the Cause of their unfortunate position. We will have Nothing to do, with the Negro. If these poor White Men want to Send one of their number to Congress to stand up for them, but dare not vote for fear of the Slaveholder—We will protect them at the election—use no force but permit No terrorism to be exercised. Working men never willingly elected such wretches as Yancy, Keitt,[9] &c. The Slave holder says that Slavery is the only National labor and we of the North have seen our Furnaces Mills & Shops all Closed at their Command.[10] Can you not see injustice in this? I know not nor care, if you are a Slave holder or not. You are a U S Senator and Charging Crime and Sectional Anmosity upon the most intelligent party that ever elected a President. Pledged to obey the Constitution—and asking the greatest good for all. No Congress man nor Senator from my state dare vote against labor. When your speech is read in the South, your Constituents are erroneously prejudiced against their fellow workman, in the North, and we who depend upon labor are both suffering. Northern papers being forbidden in the South, the only avenues of information are speeches of Southern Men, an[d] I have a right to Challenge any source that will tend to embitter feud between a Tennessee laborer & my self— A few years ago I was in your State, talked freely—frankly & kindly— our respective systems were canvassed and we did not differ much — those I talked with were *White* farmers near Pulaski.—

Could I do it now? No sir— Congressional partisan debates teeming with error have made them believe me their enemy. We of the North Read Southern papers as well as our own, and if a Congressman of ours makes an error, we know it— We read Wendell Phillips & Toombs—(would like to hang them both) but we do not get ang[r]y at Southern poor White men— We know they are not guilty— We pity them and will *protect* them. Our Hotels are filled with Southern (Many of them are not) gentlemen, but they are never disturbed unless they get drunk and insult some one. yet not a day passes but that Some Northern Mechanic or business man is maltreated.[11] And this even in Tennessee which is only nominally a Slave State—in Comparison with Mississippi &c.

In respect to your own honor, do not use the Words "Black Republican" and do not assert that "Lincoln a Million Minority Candidate"[12] when a vote *dare* not be polled for him in the South— Let Douglass & Lincoln go through the entire South as they went through Illinois, and I'll take your District system[13] and elect him in the South. Judas Yancy fears the republicanism of his own Constituents more than he does that of the North— Southern republicans would probably elect you—but never him nor Clingman. I with thousands other Lincoln men, worked and voted for Gen Taylor—a Slave owner — Were we sectional? You say no—but a Man born in a slave state, who freely of own accord moves into a free State, possessing all Gen Taylors integrity & views upon slavery Nationalizing—is elected, we are sectional— Partisan decision & not judgment from reason says this— Lincoln is not as emphatic against Slavey as Hy Clay— or Jefferson— I voted for Clay—You for Jackson I presume. We were both National— The Democratic Convention (I think the one that nominated Van Buren) gave the cold shoulder to Jno C Calhoun, who wished to embody his peculiar views upon the Democratic party.[14] Jackson men are now the most violent Republicans. If, in the proposed Southern Confederacy, power of plunder is not given to Yancy & Co—they will raise a Pirates flag in the Gulf or a negro insurrection—and Steal from the negroes what they filch from the whites. Do not let them pull wool over your Constituents eyes. I think your people are too intelligent to be long deceived by them for in Nashville there are book stores—but in the Gulf States they are like Angels Visits—[15] I am a working man capable of making $1000 a year in prosperous times but now squirming along on $5 p week. I regret my inability to convey in languge suitable for a Senators ears, my ideas, but asking your acceptance of my letter in the same kind spirit I entertain toward you & the Workmen of Ten. I remain

Very trul. Yr friend & U. S. Citizen—
Walter S Waldie

ALS, DLC-JP.

1. Date and address in a different hand.

2. In Greek mythology Jupiter gave Pandora a box containing all the world's ills which, when the box was opened, were let loose upon mankind. Stevenson, *Macmillan Book of Proverbs*, 1742.

3. An analogy suggested by Aesop's fable of the proud frog who, admiring "the size and majesty" of an ox and trying to expand itself to a comparable size, ultimately burst. *Select Fables from Aesop, and Others* (Philadelphia, n.d.), 251–52.

4. Although Thomas H. Hicks (1798–1865), Whig-American governor of Maryland (1857–61) and U. S. senator (1862–65), presided over a state of divided loyalties, ultimately he took a stand against secession. In a public letter to the "People of Maryland," dated January 3, 1861, Hicks declared that "the salvation of the Union depends upon the Border [States]. Without their aid, the Cotton States could never command the influence and credit and men essential to their existence as a nation." Speculating whether Maryland really wanted to fight the battles of the "*Cotton* States" without first attempting negotiation, or to be plunged into war simply because South Carolina decreed it, he asked, "Are we not equals? Or shall her opinions control our actions? . . . She refuses to wait for our counsels—are we bound to obey her commands?" *DAB*, IX, 8–9; *BDAC*, 1050; Frederick (Md.) *Examiner*, January 9, 1861.

5. Derived from the Latin "lobium," meaning a covered walk or cloister in a monastery, the word "lobby" first appeared in the English language around the middle of the sixteenth century, when it was used to describe the halls or corridors of the House of Commons. As early as 1808 the word appeared in the *Annals* of the 10th Congress; by 1829 it was in use at New York's state capitol as a designation for those who sought special privilege; and by 1832 the term "lobbyist" was used frequently in Washington. James Deakin, *The Lobbyists* (Washington, D. C., 1966), 54; Mathews, *Americanisms*, II, 985.

6. Two of the late candidates—Stephen A. Douglas and John C. Breckinridge—were senators at the time of the election, and Senator William H. Seward had been a leading contender for the Republican nomination.

7. It is impossible to determine the precise incident here alluded to; however, numerous fracases had occurred outside the Baltimore Democratic convention hall, two of them on June 21, the one a "severe personal altercation" between delegate William Montgomery and the son of delegate Robert Randall, both of Pennsylvania, and the other between John Clancy and William H. Ludlow, both of New York. New York *Herald*, June 22, 1860; see also Hesseltine, *Three Against Lincoln*, 220–21.

8. Claiming to represent fifty thousand Philadelphia workingmen, a thirty-three-man delegation presented to Congress resolutions supporting the Crittenden amendments. While hoping for a peaceful solution of the crisis they avowed their determination to "sustain the Federal Government in all legal means to enforce the laws of the land." Washington *Evening Star*, January 31, 1861.

9. Former Senator William L. Yancey of Alabama and Representative

Lawrence M. Keitt of South Carolina. For Yancey, see *Johnson Papers*, I, 185*n*.

10. Threatened by the possible loss of southern markets, northern commerce and industry experienced an acute economic recession in the winter of 1860–61. Stampp, *And the War Came*, 123–25.

11. Since John Brown's raid there had been occasional acts of violence against northern travelers and residents in the South. Recently the press had reported several such incidents: a northern resident working in Savannah was attacked by a "rough man" and then clapped into a "filthy dungeon" for seventeen days; a Philadelphia merchant, returning to Norfolk on business, was threatened with tar and feathers unless he departed the town. Ollinger Crenshaw, "The Psychological Background of the Election of 1860 in the South," *North Carolina Historical Review*, XIX (1942), 260–79 *passim*; Clement Eaton, "Mob Violence in the Old South," *Mississippi Valley Historical Review*, XXIX (1942–43), 366; New York *Tribune*, January 31, February 2, 1861.

12. See Speech on Secession, December 18–19, 1860.

13. Typical of the South, the recent Tennessee code divided the state into ten congressional districts which would also serve as districts for presidential and vice-presidential electors. Each voter cast a ballot for ten district, and two at-large, electors. Return J. Meigs and William F. Cooper, comps., *The Code of Tennessee* (Nashville, 1858), 89–90, 236.

14. Following his reconciliation with Martin Van Buren in December, 1839, Calhoun formally endorsed the President's reelection in 1840. Insisting that he did not wish to be President and that he hoped to retire from public life following the expiration of his Senate term, Calhoun nevertheless appeared to many to be the "logical man to suceed Van Buren in 1844." Confident that public opinion was "coming around" to his own state rights philosophy, Calhoun looked to his future political prospects with optimism and by 1842 was actively seeking the 1844 Democratic nomination. In December, 1843, at the opening of the 28th Congress, it was clear that Van Buren controlled most of the Democratic votes in the House, and Calhoun accordingly withdrew as a candidate. At the 1844 convention he "drew a scattering handful of votes but they were by courtesy only." Charles M. Wiltse, *John C. Calhoun: Nullifier, 1829–1839* (Indianapolis, 1949), 409; Wiltse, *John C. Calhoun: Sectionalist, 1840–1850* (New York, 1968), 146–47, 179; Gerald M. Capers, *John C. Calhoun—Opportunist: A Reappraisal* (Gainesville, Fla., 1960), 201–2, 204.

15. Contemporary directories give the lie to this piece of obvious flattery: Nashville had only four bookstores, whereas New Orleans listed sixteen and Mobile six. *Nashville Bus. Dir.* (1860–61), 126, 184, 223; *Hellier's New Orleans Business Directory* (1860–61), 5; *Farrow & Dennett's Mobile Directory* (1859), Index, v.

From Lindsey Sanders

February 5, 1861, Mt. Union; ALS, DLC-JP.

Staunch unionist of McNairy County in West Tennessee, concerned about the apparent effort "being made to chain Our noble Ten. to the Car of secession," regrets that "100,000 Copies of your celebrated Coersion speech (as it is termed)" were not distributed for "They would have saved Ten." Estimates "that ⅔ of the people of our Co. are loyal to the Union," but "that ⅔ of the Citizens of Purdy are secessionist," led by Martin Cross, who must be "in secret Correspondance" with Governor Harris, for "he is always a head of the news general[ly]." Cross's oldest son "is Capt. of the Minute Company" comprised of "13 all told."

From Harvey M. Watterson[1]

McMinville Ten
Feb. 5th 1861

Dear Gov.

I know that I express the sentiments of nine tenths of the people of this town when I say to you that our present Post Master, Smith Walling,[2] is shamefully unqualified to discharge the duties of the office he holds. He cant spell Sparta correctly and any thing like a big fat idea driven into his head, would tear it into one hundred pieces. This is not all: His heart is so inflamed with *disunion fire*, that he is totally incapable of being honest. He doubtless thinks it is right to suppress Union documents—such as your speech—and to give the widest circulation to everything that is intended for the manufactory of immediate secessionists. He ought to be removed, *forthwith*, and a good Union man put in his place. We have many such, but the gentleman I recommend is R. T. Martin;[3] and now a word in reference to Mr Martin. He is a merchant in McMinville— a sound national, Union-loving Democrat, and voted for Breckin- ridge at the late Presidential election. He is your friend, as well as the friend of his country; and withal he is popular and entirely com- petent. I believe that the removal of Walling and the appointment of Martin would please everybody in our town but the Disunionists, who number about 15! I therefore hope that you will loose no time in having this change made. I want you to file this letter in the Post Office department. You know me well enough to be satisfied that I would not deceive you. I have stated facts as they exist, and were it necessary, I could have them corroborated by a hundred townsmen.

Now, Governor, is the time for Union men to act; and most es- pecially is it the time for such ignorant *Disunionists* as Walling to be swept from office[.]

Yours truly
H. M. Watterson

Hon Andrew. Johnson
U. S. Senate

ALS, DLC-JP.

1. See *Johnson Papers*, I, 426*n*.

2. Smith J. Walling (b. *c*1814), Tennessee native and McMinnville mer- chant, became postmaster in December, 1854, serving until his removal in 1861 on charges of being a disunionist. Womack, *McMinnville at a Mile- stone*, 83; Horatio King to A. O. P. Nicholson, March 5, 1861, Letters Sent, RG28, National Archives; 1860 Census, Tenn., Warren, 200.

3. Raleigh T. Martin (b. *c*1830), McMinnville resident, was appointed on February 16 and reappointed in 1865, serving until 1868. Womack, *McMinnville at a Milestone*, 83–84; 1860 Census, Tenn., Warren, 216.

Speech on the Seceding States[1]

February 5–6, 1861

Mr. JOHNSON, of Tennessee. Mr. President,[2] on the 19th of December, I made a speech in the Senate, with reference to the present crisis, which I believed my duty to my State and to myself required. In making that speech, my intention—and I think I succeeded in it —was to place myself upon the principles of the Constitution and the doctrines inculcated by Washington, Jefferson, Madison, Monroe, and Jackson. Having examined the positions of those distinguished fathers of the Republic, and compared them with the Constitution, I came to the conclusion that they were right; and upon them I planted myself, and made the speech to which I have referred, in vindication of the Union and the Constitution, and against the doctrine of nullification or secession, which I look upon as a great political heresy. As far back as 1833, when I was a young man, before I made my advent into public life, when the controversy arose between the Federal Government and the State of South Carolina, and it became necessary for Andrew Jackson, then President of the United States, to issue his proclamation, exhorting that people to obey the law and comply with the requirements of the Constitution, I planted myself upon the principles then announced by him, which I advocated on the 19th of December last. I believed that the positions taken then by General Jackson, and those who came to his support, were the true doctrines of the Constitution, and the only doctrines upon which this Government could be preserved. I have been uniformly, from that period to the present time, opposed to the doctrine of secession, or of nullification, which is rather a hermaphrodite, but approximates to the doctrine of secession. I repeat, that I then viewed it as a heresy and as an element which, if maintained, would result in the destruction of this Government. I maintain the same position to-day. I then opposed the doctrine of secession as a political heresy, which, if sanctioned and sustained as a fundamental principle of this Government, will result in its overthrow and destruction; for, as we have seen already, a few of the States are crumbling and falling off.

I oppose this heresy for another reason; not only as being destructive of the existing Government, but as being destructive of all future confederacies that may be established in consequence of a disruption of the present one; and I availed myself of the former occasion on which I spoke, to enter my protest against it, and to do something to extinguish a political heresy that ought never to be incorporated upon this or any other Government which may be subsequently established. I look upon it as the prolific mother of political sin; as a fundamental error; as a heresy that is intolerable in contrast with the existence of the Government itself. I look upon it as being productive of anarchy; and anarchy is the next step to despotism. The developments that we have recently seen in carrying this doctrine into practice, I think, admonish us that this will be the result.

But, Mr. President, since I made that speech on the 19th of December, I have been the peculiar object of attack. I have been denounced, because I happened to be the first man south of Mason and Dixon's line who entered a protest or made an argument in the Senate against this political heresy. From what I saw here on the evening when I concluded my speech[3]—although some may have thought that it intimidated and discouraged me—I was inspired with confidence; I felt that I had struck treason a blow. I thought then, and I know now, that men who were engaged in treason felt the blows that I dealt out on that occasion. As I have been made the peculiar object of attack, not only in the Senate, but out of the Senate, my object on this occasion is to meet some of these attacks, and to say some things in addition to what I then said against this movement.

Yesterday the last of the Senators who represent what are called the seceding States, retired,[4] and a drama was enacted. The piece was well performed; the actors were perfect in their parts; it was got up to order; I will not say that the mourning auxiliaries had been selected in advance. One of the retiring Senators, in justifying the course that his State had taken, made a very specious and plausible argument in reference to the doctrine of secession. I allude to the Senator from Louisiana, [Mr. Benjamin.] He argued that the sovereignty of that State had never passed to the United States; that the Government held it in trust; that no conveyance was made; that sovereignty could not be transferred; that out of the gracious pleasure and good will which the First Consul of France entertained towards the American people, the transfer was made of the property without consideration, and the sovereignty was in abeyance or trust, and therefore his State had violated no faith, and had a right to do precisely what she has done. With elaborate preparation and seeming sincerity; with sweet tones, euphonious utterances, mellifluous voice, and great earnestness, he called our attention to the treaty to sustain his assumption. But when we examine the subject, Mr. President, how do the facts stand? I like fairness; I will not say that the Senator, in making quotations from the treaty and commenting upon them, was intentionally unfair; nor can I say that the Senator from Louisiana, with all his acumen, his habits of industry, and his great research, had not read and understood all the provisions of the treaty. In doing so, I should reflect upon his character; it might be construed as a reflection upon his want of research, for which he has such a distinguished reputation. The omission to read important portions of the treaty I will not attribute to any intention to mislead; I will simply call the attention of the Senate and the country to his remarks, and then to the treaty. The Senator, after premising, went on to say:

[Benjamin, citing Article III of the Louisiana Purchase Treaty, concluded that the United States "assumed to act as trustee or guardian of the people of the ceded province"; consequently ultimate sovereignty never rested in the federal government. In rebuttal, Johnson, citing Articles I and II, argues that both property and sovereignty were clearly conveyed to "the people of the United States"; Article III, on the other hand, provided only for subsequent admission of the area and its people on an equal footing in the Union.]

There is some order in that; one thing fits the other. There is the conveyance of sovereignty and property. There is a minute enumeration in the second article; and in the third article it is provided that as soon as possible, according to the principles of the Federal Constitution, they shall be incorporated into the Union, and protected in the enjoyment of the religion which they may profess. We see, then, how the thing stands. Have not all these things been complied with? But, by way of exonerating Louisiana from censure for her recent act of attempted secession, it is urged that, when this treaty was made, there was no consideration; but that, out of the good will that the First Consul had towards the American people, the sovereignty was given to us in trust; that we took the property in trust; that we took everything in trust. Sir, the Federal Government took the property, and the sovereignty with it, in trust for all the States. But how does the matter stand? The retiring Senator's speech— whether it was intended or not, I do not undertake to say—is calculated to make the false impression that some time afterwards, perhaps in some other treaty remote from that, some money was paid by the United States to France, out of the good will that this Government had towards them. And yet, sir, on the same day—the 30th of April, 1803—on which the other treaty was made and signed, the following convention between the United States of America and the French Republic was made:

[Quotes the preamble and Article I, in which the sum of 60 million francs was designated as payment for the ceded territory.]

What becomes of the specious plea, what becomes of the excuse tendered here, that we took it simply in trust, and that no consideration was paid? Turn over to the American State Papers; look at Mr. Livingston's letters, upon which these treaties were predicated; read his correspondence with Mr. Madison, who was Secretary of State, and you will find that France demanded the sum of 100,000,000f. independent of what they owed the citizens of the United States; but after long negotiations, the First Consul of the French concluded to take 60,000,000f.; and the first two articles of the treaty which I have read are based upon the 60,000,000f. paid by this Government in consideration of the sovereignty and territory, all of which was to be held in trust by the United States for all the States.

This was given to us out of the pure good will that Napoleon at that time had towards the United States. Sir, he had great hate for Great Britain; and by the promptings of that hate he was disposed to cede this territory to some other Power. He feared that Great Britain, whose Navy was superior to his own, would take it. He desired to obtain money to carry on his wars and sustain his Government. These considerations, and not love or partiality or friendship for the United States, led him to make the cession. Then what becomes of the Senator's special pleading? From the Senator's remarks, it may have been concluded that we got it as a gratuity. But after examining the State Papers and the correspondence, and looking at the tedious and labored negotiation previous to the making of the treaty, it is clear that at the time the first treaty was made, on the very same day, the consideration was fixed; and yet the Senators tell us that at some other time a treaty was made not referring to any amount of money agreed to be paid at this particular time, and that therefore they are excusable and justifiable in going out of the Confederacy of these States.

After all these things were enumerated, an appeal was made. It was a very affecting scene. Louisiana was gone; and what was the reason? Great oppression and great wrong. She could not get her rights in the Union, and consequently she has sought them out of it. What are the wrongs of Louisiana? What was the cause for all the sympathy expressed on the one hand, and the tears shed on the other? Louisiana was substantially presented to the country in a most pathetic and sympathetic attitude. Her wrongs were without number; their enormity was almost without estimate; they could scarcely be fathomed by human sympathy. It was not unlike the oration of Mark Antony over the dead body of Caesar. Weeping friends grouped picturesquely in the foreground; the bloody robe, the ghastly wounds, were conjured to the imagination; and who was there that did not expect to hear the exclamation: "If you have tears, prepare to shed them now?"[5] [Laughter.]

Sir, what are the great wrongs that have been inflicted upon

Louisiana? Prior to 1803, Louisiana was transferred from Spain to France, and from France back to Spain—both property and sovereignty—almost with the same facility as a chattel from one person to another. On the 30th of April, 1803, when this treaty was made, what was the condition of Louisiana? It was then a province of the First Consul of France, subject to be disposed of at his discretion. The United States did what? Came forward and paid to the First Consul of France 60,000,000f. for the territory. The treaty was made; the territory was transferred; and in 1806, in express compliance with the treaty, as soon as practicable, according to the terms of the Federal Constitution, Louisiana was admitted into the Union as a State.[6] We bought her; we paid for her; we admitted her into the Union upon terms of equality with the other States. Was there any oppression, any great wrong, any great grievance in that?

In 1815—war having been declared in 1812—Louisiana was attacked; the city of New Orleans was about to be sacked and laid prostrate in the dust; "beauty and booty" were the watchwords.[7] She was oppressed then, was she not? Kentucky, your own gallant State, sir, (and, thank God! she is standing erect now,) and Tennessee, (which, as I honestly believe, will ever stand by her side in this struggle for the Constitution and the Union,) in conjunction with the other States, met Packenham and his myrmidons upon the plains of New Orleans, and there dealt out death and desolation to her invading foe. What soil did we invade? What city did we propose to sack? Whose property did we propose to destroy? Was not Louisiana there gallantly, nobly, bravely, and patriotically defended, by the people of the United States, from the inroads and from the sacking of a British foe? Is that defense one of her oppressions? Is that one of the great wrongs that have been inflicted upon Louisiana?

What more has been done by this Government? How much protection has she received upon her sugar? In order to give that protection, the poorest man throughout the United States is taxed for every spoonful that he uses to sweeten his coffee.[8] How many millions, under the operation of a protection upon sugar, have been contributed to the wealth and prosperity of Louisiana since she has been in this Confederacy? Estimate them. Is this another of her wrongs? Is this another of her grievances? Is this another of the oppressions that the United States have inflicted upon Louisiana?

Sum them all up, and what are the wrongs, what the grievances which justify Louisiana in taking leave of the United States? We have defended her soil and her citizens; we have paid the price asked for her by the French Government; she has been protected in the production of her sugar, and in the enjoyment of every right that a sovereign State could ask at the hands of the Federal Government.

And how has she treated the United States? What is her position? Upon her own volition, without consultation with her sister States, without even consulting with Tennessee and Kentucky, who defended her when she was in peril, she proposes to secede from the Union. She does more: in violation of the Constitution of the United States, in despite of the plighted faith that exists between all the States, she takes our arsenals, our forts, our custom-house, our mint, with about a million dollars. Gracious God! to what are we coming? Is it thus that the Constitution of the United States is to be violated? Forts, arsenals, custom-houses, and property belonging to all the people of all the States, have been ruthlessly seized, and their undisturbed possession is the sum total of the great wrongs that have been inflicted upon Louisiana by the United States!

Mr. President, when I look at the conduct of some of the States, I am reminded of the fable of King Log and the frogs.[9] They got tired of the log that lay in their midst, upon which they could bask in the sun, or from which they could dive to the depth beneath, without interference. And these seceding States have got tired of the Federal Government, which has been so profitable to them, and loathe the blessings which they enjoy. Seemingly, its inability to take care of itself created their opposition to it. It seems, the inability of the United States to defend and take care of its own property has been an invitation to them to take possession of it; and, like the frogs, they seek a substitute for their log. They prayed to Jupiter, the supreme deity, to send them another king; and he answered their prayer by sending them a stork, who soon devoured his subject frogs. There are storks, too, in the seceding States. South Carolina has her stork king, and so has Louisiana. In the heavy appropriations they are making to maintain armies, and in all their preparations for war, for which there is no cause, they will find they have brought down storks upon them that will devour them.

What do we find, Mr. President, since this movement commenced? In about forty-six days, since the first State went out until the last one disappeared—the 26th of January—they have taken from the United States, this harmless old ruler, one thousand and ninety-two guns, without any resistance, amounting to $6,513,000. They are very much alarmed at the power of this Government. Thus the Government oppresses them; thus this Government oppresses Louisiana, pertinaciously persisting in allowing those States to take all the guns, all the forts, all the arsenals, all the dock-yards, all the custom-houses, and all the mints. Thus they are so cruelly oppressed. Is it not a farce? Is it not the greatest outrage and the greatest folly that was ever consummated since man was spoken into existence? But these are the grievances of Louisiana. I shall say nothing against Louisiana.

Tennessee and Kentucky have given demonstrations most noticeable that when she needed friends, when she needed aid, they were at her bidding.

But in the acquisition of Louisiana there was another very important acquisition. We acquired the exclusive and entire control of the navigation of the Mississippi river. We find that Louisiana, in her ordinance of secession, makes the negative declaration that she has the control of the navigation of that great stream, by stating that the navigation of the river shall be free to those States that remain on friendly terms with her, with the proviso that moderate contributions are to be levied to defray such expenses as they may deem expedient from time to time.[10] That is the substance of it. Sir, look at the facts. All the States, through their Federal Government, treated for Louisiana. The treaty was made. All the States, by the contribution of their money, paid for Louisiana and the navigation of the Mississippi river. Where, and from what source, does Louisiana now derive the power or the authority to secede from this Union and set up exclusive control of the navigation of that great stream which is owned by all the States, which was paid for by the money of all the States, and upon whose borders the blood of many citizens of the States has been shed?

This is one of the aggrieved, the oppressed States! Mr. President, is it not apparent that these grievances and oppressions are mere pretenses? A large portion of the South (and that portion of it I am willing to stand by to the very last extremity) believe that aggressions have been made upon them by the other States, in reference to the institution of slavery. A large portion of the South believe that something ought to be done in the shape of what has been offered by the distinguished Senator from Kentucky, or something very similar. They think and feel that that ought to be done. But, sir, there is another portion who do not care for those propositions to bring about reconciliation, but who, on the contrary, have been afraid and alarmed that something would be done to reconcile and satisfy the public mind, before this diabolical work of secession could be consummated. Yes, sir, they have been afraid, and the occasion has been used to justify and to carry out a doctrine into practice, which is not only the destruction of this Government, but which will be the destruction of all other governments that may be originated, embracing the same principle. Why not, then, meet it like men? We know there is a portion of the South who are for secession, who are for breaking up this Government, without regard to slavery or anything else, as I shall show before I have done.

The Senator from Louisiana, [Mr. Benjamin,] in a speech that he made some days since,[11] took occasion to allude to some authority that I had introduced from General Washington, the first President who executed the laws of the United States against armed resistance; and it occurred to him that, by way of giving his argument force, it was necessary to remark that I was not a lawyer, and that therefore I had not examined the subject with that minuteness and with that care and familiarity that I should have done; and hence that I had introduced authority which had no application to the question under consideration. The proof that he gave to show I had not examined the subject carefully, was contained in the very extract that I had quoted and which he said declared that General Washington had been informed by the marshal that he could not execute the laws; and from the fact of the marshal being incapable to execute them, General Washington was called upon to employ the means, under the Constitution and the laws, which were necessary to their enforcement. It may have been necessary for the distinguished Senator to inform the Senate and the country that I was not a lawyer; but it was not necessary to inform anybody that read his speech and that had the slightest information or sagacity, that he was a lawyer, and that he was making a lawyer's speech upon the case before him; not an argument upon the great principles of the Government. The speech was a complete lawyer's speech, and the authorities were summed up simply to make out the case on his side; and he left out all those that would disprove his position. It required no very great acumen or sagacity to discover that he was a lawyer; and, on that occasion, I think he showed himself to be a lawyer in the proper sense of the term, for he made a lawyer's argument, just suiting the case, leaving out and not noticing all authorities on the other side.

That Senator yesterday seemed to be very serious in regard to the practical operation of the doctrine of secession. I felt sorry myself, somewhat. I am always reluctant to part with a gentleman with whom I have been associated, and nothing had transpired to disturb between us those courteous relations which should always exist between persons associated on this floor. I thought the scene was pretty well got up, and was acted out admirably. The plot was executed to the very letter. You would have thought that his people in Louisiana were borne down and seriously oppressed by remaining in this Union of States. Now, I have an extract before me, from a speech delivered by that gentleman since the election of Abraham Lincoln, while the distinguished Senator was on the western slope of the Rocky Mountains, at the city of San Francisco. He was called upon to make an address;[12] and I will read an extract from it, which I find in the New York Times, the editors of which paper said they had the speech before them; and I have consulted a gentleman here who was in California at the time, and he tells me that the report is correct. In that speech—after the Senator had spoken some time with his accustomed eloquence—he uttered this language:

> Those who prate of, and strive to dissolve this glorious Confederacy of States, are like those silly savages who let fly their arrows at the sun in the vain hope of piercing it! And still the sun rolls on, unheeding, in its eternal pathway, shedding light and animation upon all the world.

Even after Lincoln was elected, the Senator from Louisiana is reported to have said, in the State of California, and in the city of San Francisco, that this great Union could not be destroyed. Those great and intolerable oppressions, of which we have since heard from him, did not seem to be flitting across his vision and playing upon his mind with that vividness and clearness which were displayed here yesterday. He said, in California, that this great Union would go on in its course, notwithstanding the puny efforts of the silly savages that were letting fly their arrows with the prospect of piercing it. What has changed the Senator's mind on coming from that side of the continent to this? What light has broken in upon him? Has he been struck on his way, like Paul, when he was journeying from Tarsus to Damascus? Has some supernatural power disclosed to him that his State and his people will be ruined if they remain in the Union? Where do we find the distinguished Senator only at the last session? On the 22d of May, last, when he made his celebrated reply to the Senator from Illinois, [Mr. Douglas,] the Senator from Louisiana, alluding to the contest for the Senate, between Mr. Lincoln and Mr. Douglas, said:

> In that contest, the two candidates for the Senate of the United States, in the State of Illinois, went before their people. They agreed to discuss the issues; they put questions to each other for answer; and I must say here—for I must be just to all—that I have been surprised in the examination that I made again, within the last few days, of this discussion between Mr. Lincoln and Mr. Douglas, to find that, on several points, Mr. Lincoln is a far more conservative man, unless he has since changed his opinion, than I had supposed him to be. There was no dodging on his part. Mr. Douglas started with his questions. Here they are, with Mr. Lincoln's answers.[13]

The impression evidently made on the public mind then, before the presidential election, was that Lincoln, the rank Abolitionist now, was more conservative than Mr. Douglas; and he said further, after reading the questions put by Mr. Lincoln, and his answers to them:

> It is impossible, Mr. President, however we may differ in opinion with the man, not to admire the perfect candor and frankness with which the answers were given; no equivocation; no evasion.

Since that speech was made, since the Senator has traversed from California to this point, the grievances, the oppressions of Louisiana, have become so great that she is justified in going out of the Union, taking into her possession the custom-house, the mint, the navigation of the Mississippi river, the forts, and arsenals. Where are we? "Oh, consistency, thou art a jewel, much to be admired, but rarely to be found."[14]

Mr. President, I never do things by halves. I am against this doctrine entirely. I commenced making war upon it—a war for the Constitution and the Union—and I intend to sink or swim upon it. [Applause in the galleries.] In the remarks that I made on the 19th of December, I discussed at some length the alleged right of secession. I repudiated the whole doctrine. I introduced authorities to show its unsoundness, and made deductions from those authorities which have not been answered to this day; but by innuendo and indirection, without reference to the person who used the authorities, attempts have been made to answer the speech. Let those who can answer the speech, answer the authorities; answer the conclusions which have been deduced from them. I was more than gratified, shortly afterwards, when one of the distinguished Senators from Virginia [Mr. Hunter] delivered a speech upon this floor, which it was apparent to all had been studied closely; which had been digested thoroughly; which, in the language of another, had been conned and set down in a note-book, and got by note [rote?][15]; not only the sentences constructed, but the language measured. In the plan which he proposed as one upon which the Government can be continued and administered, in his judgment, he brought his mind seemingly, irresistibly, to the conclusion that this doctrine of secession was a heresy. What does he say in that able, that methodical, that well-digested speech? He goes over the whole ground. He has been reasoning on it; he has been examining the principle of secession; he has gone to the conclusion to which it leads; and he is seemingly involuntarily, but irresistibly forced to admit that it will not do to acknowledge this doctrine of secession; for he says:[16]

[If the two sections representing two social systems could be made "mutually safe," then secession, which Hunter believed was not a constitutional right but one resulting "from the nature of the compact," could be regulated. His solution would require that a state with grievances could be voted out "in peace" by a convention of neighboring states sitting in review.]

Sir, I quoted the Old Dominion extensively before. I took the foundation of this doctrine and traced it along step by step, and showed that there was no such notion tolerated by the fathers of the Republic as the right of secession. Now, who comes up to my relief? When the States are seceding, when they are going off, the distinguished Senator from Virginia says, in so many words, that he admits the error, and the force of the principle that a State ought not to be permitted to go out of the Confederacy without the consent of the remaining members. He says, however, that the right to secede results from the nature of the compact. Sir, I have read Mr. Jefferson, and I am as much inclined to rely on the former distinguished men of the State of Virginia as I am on the latter. In the old Articles of Confederation, when the revenue required for the support of the Federal Government was apportioned among the States, and each State had to raise its portion, the great difficulty was, that there was no means by which the States could be compelled to contribute their amount; there was no means of forcing the State to compliance; and yet Mr. Jefferson, in view of that very difficulty, said, in 1786:

It has been often said that the decisions of Congress are impotent, because the Confederation provides no compulsory power. But when two or more nations enter into compact, it is not usual for them to say what shall be done to the party who infringes it. Decency forbids this, and it is as unnecessary as indecent; because the right of compulsion naturally results to the party injured by the breach. When any one State in the American Union refuses obedience to the Confederation by which they have bound themselves, the rest have a natural right to compel them to obedience.[17]

The Senator from Virginia says a State has the right to secede from the Union, and that it is a right resulting from the nature of the compact; but Mr. Jefferson said that even under the old Articles of Confederation, no State had a right to refuse obedience to the Confederacy, and that there was a right to enforce its compliance:

Congress would probably exercise long patience before they would recur to force; but if the case ultimately required it, they would use that recurrence. Should this case ever arise, they will probably coerce by a naval force, as being more easy, less dangerous to liberty, and less likely to produce much bloodshed.—*Jefferson's Works*, vol. 9, p. 291.

When was this? I have stated that it was under the old Articles of Confederation, when there was no power to compel a State even to contribute her proportion of the revenues; but in that view of the case, Mr. Jefferson said that the injured party had a right to enforce compliance with the compact from the offending State, and that this was a right deducible from the laws of nature. The present Constitution was afterwards formed; and to avoid this difficulty in raising revenue, the power was conferred upon the Congress of the United States "to lay and collect taxes, duties, imposts, and excises," and the Constitution created a direct relation between the citizen and the Federal Government in that matter, and to that extent that relation is just as direct and complete between the Federal Government and the citizen as is the relation between the State and the citizen in other matters. Hence we find that, by an amendment to the Constitution of the United States, the citizen cannot even make a State a party to a suit,

and bring her into the Federal courts.[18] They wanted to avoid the
difficulty of coercing a State, and the Constitution conferred on the
Federal Government the power to operate directly upon the citizen,
instead of operating on the States. It being the right of the Government to enforce obedience from the citizen in those matters of which
it has jurisdiction, the question comes up as to the exercise of this
right. It may not always be expedient. It must depend upon discretion, as was eloquently said by the Senator from Kentucky [Mr.
Crittenden] on one occasion.[19] It is a matter of discretion, even as Mr.
Jefferson laid it down before this provision existed in the Constitution, before the Government had power to collect its revenue as it now
has. I know that when, on a former occasion, I undertook to show, as
I thought I did show, clearly and distinctly, the difference between
the existence and the exercise of this power, words were put into my
mouth that I did not utter, and positions answered which I had never
assumed. It was said that I took the bold ground of coercing a State.
I expressly disclaimed it. I stated, in my speech, that, by the Constitution, we could not put a State into court; but I said there were
certain relations created by the Constitution between the Federal
Government and the citizen, and that we could enforce those laws
against the citizen. I took up the fugitive slave law; I took up the
revenue law; I took up the judicial system; I took up the post office
system; and I might have taken up the power to coin money and to
punish counterfeiters, or the power to pass laws to punish mail robbers. I showed that under these we had power, not to punish a State,
but to punish individuals as violators of the law. Who will deny it;
who can deny it, that acknowledges the existence of the Government?
This point, I think, was settled in the decision of the Supreme Court
in the case of Ableman vs. Booth.[20] When the decision of the Supreme Court is in our favor, we are very much for it; but sometimes
we are not so well reconciled to it when it is against us. In that case
the court decided:

[Johnson reads a passage supporting the reduction of the states' sovereignty in favor of the federal government, which "should be supreme,
and strong enough to execute its own laws by its own tribunals, without
interruption from a State or from State authorities." Without such central authority, "local passions or prejudices" on the part of one state
could lead to "acts of aggression" against the rights of other states.]

When the fugitive slave law was executed in the city of Boston, by
the aid of military force, was that understood to be coercing a State,
or was it simply understood to be an enforcement of the law upon
those who, it was assumed, had violated it?[21] In this same decision
the Supreme Court declare that the fugitive slave law, in all its details, is constitutional, and therefore should be enforced. Who is pre-

pared to say that the decision of the court shall not be carried out? Who is prepared to say that the fugitive slave law shall not be enforced? Do you coerce a State when you simply enforce the law? If one man robs the mail and you seek to arrest him, and he resists, and you employ force, do you call that coercion? If a man counterfeits your coin, and is arrested and convicted, and punishment is resisted, cannot you execute the law? It is true that sometimes so many may become infected with disobedience, outrages and violations of law may be participated in by so many, that they get beyond the control of the ordinary operations of law; the disaffection may swell to such proportions as to be too great for the Government to control; and then it becomes a matter of discretion, not a matter of constitutional right.

In this connection, I desire to introduce an authority from Virginia, for I do delight in authority from the Old Dominion; and from the indications that are now visible—although it is possible that before the setting of the sun I may receive news that will convert my present hopes and my present exhilarated feelings into despair—she is going to make a stand for the Union and the Constitution.[22] I delight in calling upon her for authority. In 1814 the doctrine that I am trying to inculcate here to-day was inculcated from Virginia; and I ask my friend from California[23] to read an extract which I have from the Richmond Enquirer of the 1st of November, 1814.

[The editors lambasted the Hartford Convention, demanding a cessation of its treasonous activities, for "no association of men, no State or set of States *has a right* to withdraw itself from this Union"; the power "to unknit" is reserved solely to the federal government. Calling upon "Countrymen of the East . . . to keep a vigilant eye" upon these traitors "who would plunge us into civil war and irretrievable disgrace," the *Enquirer* urged action "to SAVE THE UNION."]

Mr. JOHNSON, of Tennessee. Mr. President, I subscribe most heartily to the sentiment presented by the Richmond Enquirer of November 1, 1814. Then it was declared by that high authority that the Union was to be saved; that those persons who were putting themselves in opposition to the law were traitors, and that their treason should be punished as such. Now, sir, what is treason? The Constitution of the United States defines it, and narrows it down to a very small compass. The Constitution declares that "treason against the United States shall consist only in levying war against them, or in adhering to their enemies, giving them aid and comfort." Who are levying war upon the United States? Who are adhering to the enemies of the United States, giving them aid and comfort? Does it require a man to take the lantern of Diogenes,[24] and make a diligent search to find those who have been engaged in levying war against the United States? Will it require any very great research or observation to discover those who have been adhering to those who were making war against the United States, and giving them aid and comfort? If there are any such in the United States they ought to be punished according to law and the Constitution. [Applause in the galleries, which was suppressed by the Presiding Officer, Mr. Fitch[25] in the chair.] Mr. Ritchie,[26] speaking for the Old Dominion, used language that was unmistakable, that treason should be punished, springing out of the hotbed of the Hartford convention. It was all right to talk about treason then; it was all right to punish traitors in that direction. For myself, I care not whether treason be committed north or south; he that is guilty of treason is entitled to a traitor's fate.

But, Mr. President, when we come to examine the views of some of those who have been engaged in this work, we find that the foundation of their desire to break up this Government dates beyond, and goes very far back of, any recent agitation of the slavery question. There are some men who want to break up this Government anyhow; who want a separation of the Union. There are some who have got tired of a government of the people. They fear the people. Take the State of South Carolina. Although she has had Senators on this floor who have acted a portion of the time with the Democratic party, and sometimes with no party, there is, in that State, an ancient and a fixed opposition to a government by the people. They have an early prejudice against this thing called democracy—a government of the people. They entertained the idea of secession at a very early day; it is no new thing with them; it has not arisen out of the slavery question and its recent agitation. Even to this good day, the people, the freemen of South Carolina, have never been permitted to vote for President and Vice President of the United States.[27] They have never enjoyed that great luxury of freemen, of having a voice in the selection of their Chief Magistrate.

I have before me an old volume. In the frontispiece I find a picture of "William Moultrie, Esq., late Governor of South Carolina, and major general in the American revolutionary war." The book is entitled, "Memoirs of the American Revolution, so far as it related to the States of North and South Carolina and Georgia;" and the author is William Moultrie.[28] The Articles of Confederation, it will be remembered, were adopted July 9, 1778. South Carolina was one of the members of the Confederacy—a party to the compact. Charleston was besieged during the revolutionary war, in 1779, by the British. The defense of the town had been kept up for a considerable length of time, and at last General Moultrie sent a message to the British commander, desiring to know "on what terms he would be disposed to grant a capitulation." The answer of General Provost [sic][29] was submitted to the Governor, who summoned a council of war, and the result was the following message to the British commander:

[Moultrie refused to capitulate but later proposed to Prévost that South Carolina assume a position of neutrality with the undersanding that "the question whether the State shall belong to Great Britain, or remain one of the United States, be determined by the treaty of peace."]

The Governor, who was a major general, proposed a neutrality, and proposed to withdraw from the Confederacy, to desist from resistance to Great Britain, and leave it to the two Powers, in making a treaty, to say whether they should remain a colony of Great Britain or be one of the United States. At this early day, South Carolina was willing to go back and be subjected to the Crown of Great Britain under King George III.

Mr. Wigfall. I ask the Senator merely to permit me to correct him as to a fact.

Mr. Johnson, of Tennessee. I do not yield the floor.

Mr. Wigfall. I do not intend to interrupt you—

Mr. Johnson, of Tennessee. I do not yield the floor.

The Presiding Officer, (Mr. Fitch.) The Senator from Tennessee is entitled to the floor.

Mr. Wigfall. The Articles of Confederation were formed in 1781; that is all.

Mr. Johnson, of Tennessee. I have them before me: "Articles of Confederation and Perpetual Union;" and they end: "Done at Philadelphia, in the State of Pennsylvania, the 9th day of July, in the year of our Lord 1778."

Mr. Wigfall. They were ratified in 1781. If you will read history and inform yourself, you will not fall into so many errors: 1781 is the time; I know it.

Mr. Johnson, of Tennessee. I will just refer to the document.

Mr. Wigfall. While the Senator is looking over it, I will merely observe that I made the correction out of kindness to him.

Mr. Johnson, of Tennessee. I always prefer having correct ideas, and selecting my own sources of information. [Laughter.]

Mr. Wigfall. The year 1781 was the time the Articles of Confederation were ratified. You were simply mistaken; that is all.

Mr. Johnson, of Tennessee. I do not accept the correction, nor have I very much respect for the motive that prompted it. Let that be as it may, however, it does not change the great historical fact that at that day, instead of holding out with the other colonies who were members of the Confederacy and engaged in the war, South Carolina was willing to enter into an agreement of neutrality and go back under the protection of King George III. I have another document that I wish to read from; a book called "The Remembrancer, or Impartial Repository of Public Events for the year 1780."[30] In that year the people of Charleston, a large number of them, in view of the difficulties then upon the country, prepared an address, which I ask my friend from California, who reads so much better than I do, to read for me.

[In the letter, dated June 5, 1780, and addressed to General Henry Clinton and Admiral Marriot Arbuthnot, British commissioners, Charleston citizens indicated a desire to be "readmitted to the character and condition of British subjects." Claiming that the "doctrine of independency" originated in the North, the Carolinians declared that their "nature revolted at the idea"; they regretted the subversion of the English constitution "for which we always had, and ever shall retain, the most profound veneration," and the substitution of "a rank democracy, which . . . has exhibited a system of tyrannic domination only to be found among the uncivilized part of mankind or in the history of the dark and barbarous ages of antiquity."]

Mr. Johnson, of Tennessee. It will be seen, from these two documents, what the early notions of the people of South Carolina were. There never was, and I doubt very much whether, with a large portion of them, there ever will be, any ideas of the people governing themselves. They had a great aversion at that day to the idea of a government of the people. It was repudiated; and in the document which has just been read, signed by two hundred and ten citizens of Charleston, they proposed to pass back under the British Government. This carries out the previous proposition to remain with Great Britain by treaty stipulation, and not go through the revolutionary struggle with the colonies with whom they had formed a confederation.

Again: in 1833, under the pretense of resistance to the operation of our revenue system and to a protective tariff, they wanted to break up the Government. They were overruled then. Their pride was wounded by that failure; and their determination was increased, whenever it was in their power, to break up this Union, or go out of the Government. This feeling, I have no doubt, has existed there from that period to the present time. When we turn to the debates which recently took place in the South Carolina convention,[31] we find that Mr. Maxcy Gregg, Mr. Rhett, and others, said that their reason for going out of the Union now dates as far back as forty years; some of them said thirty years, and some twenty. Mr. Gregg said, in the South Carolina convention, on the 21st of December last:

If we undertake to set forth all the causes, do we not dishonor the memory of all the statesmen of South Carolina, now departed, who commenced forty years ago a war against the tariff and against internal improvements, saying nothing of the United States Bank, and other measures, which may now be regarded as obsolete.[32]

Mr. Rhett, on the 24th of December, said:

The secession of South Carolina is not an event of a day. It is not anything produced by Mr. Lincoln's election, or by the non-execution of the fugitive slave law. It has been a matter which has been gathering head for thirty years.[33]

Hence we see that there is a design with some to break up this Government without reference to the slavery question; and the slavery question is by them made a pretense for destroying this Union. They have at length passed their ordinance of secession; they assume to be out of the Union; they declare that they are no longer a member of the Confederacy. Now what are the other States called upon to do? Are the other States called upon to make South Carolina an exemplar? Are those slave States who believe that freemen should govern and that freemen can take care of slave property, to be "precipitated into a revolution" by following the example of South Carolina?[34] Will they do it? What protection, what security will Tennessee, will Kentucky, will Virginia, will Maryland, or any other State, receive from South Carolina by following her example? What protection can she give them? On the contrary, she indulges in a threat towards them—a threat that if they do not imitate her example and come into a new confederacy upon her terms, they are to be put under the ban, and their slave property to be subjected to restraint and restriction.[35] What protection can South Carolina give Tennessee? Any? None upon the face of the earth.

Some of the men who are engaged in the work of disruption and dissolution, want Tennessee and Kentucky and Virginia to furnish them with men and money in the event of their becoming engaged in a war for the conquest of Mexico. The Tennesseeans and Kentuckians and Virginians are very desirable when their men and their money are wanted; but what protection does South Carolina give Tennessee? If negro property is endangered in Tennessee, we have to defend it and pay for it—not South Carolina, that has been an apple of discord in this Confederacy from my earliest recollection down to the present time, complaining of everything, satisfied with nothing. I do not intend to be invidious, but I have sometimes thought that it would be a comfort if Massachusetts and South Carolina could be chained together as the Siamese twins,[36] separated from the continent, and taken out to some remote and secluded part of the ocean, and there fast anchored, to be washed by the waves, and to be cooled by the winds; and after they had been kept there a sufficient length of time, the people of the United States might entertain the proposition of taking them back. [Laughter.] They seem to have been the source of dissatisfaction pretty much ever since they were in the Confederacy; and some experiment of this sort, I think, would operate beneficially upon them; but as they are here, we must try to do the best we can with them.

So much, Mr. President, for South Carolina and Louisiana in this struggle. I do not think they are setting examples very worthy of imitation. But, sir, the speech that I made on the 19th of December seems to have produced some little stir; and among other distinguished Senators, the Senator from Oregon [Mr. Lane] felt it his duty, late in the evening, to make a reply to me.[37] I do not see why it was called for from the Senator from Oregon. I did not know that I had said anything that was offensive to him; it was not my intention to do so; it was an inadvertence, if I did. I felt that I had just come out of a campaign in which I had labored hard, and in which I had expended my money and my time in vindicating him and the present Vice President, who was a candidate for the Presidency, from the charge of favoring secession and disunion. Through the dust and heat, through the mud and rain, I traversed my State,[38] meeting the charge of the Opposition that secession was at the bottom of this movement; that there was a fixed design and plan to break up this Government; that it started at Charleston, and was consummated at Baltimore; and the charge was made that my worthy friend—if I may be permitted to call him such; I thought I was his friend then— was the embodiment of disunion and secession. I met the charge. I denied it. I repudiated it. I tried to convince the people—and I think I did succeed in convincing some of them—that the charge was untrue; and that he and Mr. Breckinridge were the two best Union men in the country. I did not see what there was in my speech that should extort reply from him, who resided away North. I had not come in conflict with anything that he had said or done. When he was striking these blows at me without cause, I thought it was, at least, unkind. I may not have defended him to his entire satisfaction. It so turned out that we were unfortunate; we were defeated; but I was willing to stand like a man; to stand upon the Constitution and the Union, and, if I must fall, fall decently. After I had gone through the canvass; after I had defended the Senator, and sustained him with my voice and my vote, I thought it was strange that he should attack me in the manner he did. I felt like replying to him, on the spur of the occasion; but it was late in the evening, and by the time he had concluded, the Senate was tired out, and I declined going on. I preferred to let it pass, and submit to all the wrong and injury inflicted upon me. In his speech upon that occasion,[39] the Senator from Oregon made use of the following language:

[Lane, addressing his remarks particularly to Johnson, had declared that the northern Democracy would never move to "strike down a gallant, chivalrous, and generous people contending for rights" denied them and would never march "under his bloody banner, or Mr. Lincoln's, to invade the soil of the gallant State of South Carolina" but would instead "meet him there, to repel him and his forces."]

I do not know that I used any argument that should have caused a reply like that. Did anybody hear me talk about a bloody battle? Did anybody hear me talk about going down upon South Carolina? Did anybody hear me speak about coercing a State? No.

Mr. LANE. Will the Senator allow me a word?

Mr. JOHNSON, of Tennessee. I would rather go on, sir. Why, then, answer positions I did not assume, or attribute to me language that I did not use? Was it in the speech? No. Why, then, use language and assign a position to me which, if not intended, was calculated to make a false impression? What called it forth? What reason was there for it? I saw the consternation which was created. I looked at some of their faces. I knew that I had stirred up animosity, and it was important that somebody from another quarter should make the attack. If the attack had been upon what I said or upon the position I had assumed, I should have no cause to complain; and I do not complain now. Sir, as young as I am, I have lived down some men.[40] I have survived many misrepresentations. I feel that I have a conscience and a heart that will lead me to do it again. But when I had said nothing, when I had done nothing, to be struck by him whom I have vindicated, I might well have exclaimed, "That was the unkindest cut of all."[41]

Again: the Senator said:

If it should come unfortunately upon this country, inaugurated by a tyrant, who would like to conquer and hold American citizens as vassals, then I will say to that coward who would do it, "You will walk over your humble servant's body first." I shall never coöperate with any portion of this country, North or South, that would strike down a people contending for their rights.[42]

I march down upon South Carolina! Did I propose any such thing? No. War is not the natural element in my mind; and, as I stated in that speech, my thoughts were turned on peace, and not on war. I want no strife. I want no war. In the language of a denomination that is numerous in the country,[43] I may say I hate war and love peace. I belong to the peace party. I thought, when I was making that speech, that I was holding out the olive branch of peace. I wanted to give quiet and reconciliation to a distracted and excited country. That was the object I had in view. War, I repeat, is not the natural element of my mind. I would rather wear upon my garments the tinge of the shop and the dust of the field, as badges of the pursuits of peace, than the gaudy epaulet upon my shoulder, or a sword dangling by my side, with its glittering scabbard, the insignia of strife, of war, of blood, of carnage; sometimes of honorable and glorious war. But, sir, I would rather see the people of the United States at war with every other Power upon the habitable globe, than to be at war with each other.

If blood must be shed, let it not be shed by the people of these States, the one contending against the other.

But the Senator went on still further in that discussion. Why it was necessary to follow up his attack upon me, I cannot tell. Alluding to the Senator from Tennessee, he said: [44]

[Reviewing Senate action upon the Davis resolutions, Lane contended that Johnson was unreasonable in his criticism of southern senators who supported Brown's amendment requiring protection of slavery in the territories, inasmuch as such a proviso could not possibly have passed the House. Instead, southerners should have "set forth the principles on which this Government reposed, and which must be maintained, or the Government cannot exist."]

Before I take up that proposition in connection with what I said before, I wish to say here that, had the Senator avowed the doctrine prior to the last presidential election that he avowed here in reply to me, expressing his secession and disunion sentiments, I give it as my opinion that he could not have obtained ten thousand votes in the State of Tennessee in the last election, and I think I know what I say. I give that, however, simply as my opinion.

But to come back to the point at which the Senator speaks of the resolutions introduced by the Senator from Mississippi, [Mr. Davis] [45] I had referred to those resolutions to show that there was no occasion for this immediate secession without giving the people time to think or understand what was to be done. I thought so then, and I think so now; and I want to show what the Senator's views were then, and see what has brought about such a change upon his mind since. We find that while those resolutions were under consideration, Mr. Clingman offered an amendment, to come in after the fourth resolution, to insert the following: [46]

[Quoting Clingman's amendment, "That the existing condition of the Territories . . . does not require the intervention of Congress for the protection of property in slaves," Johnson points out that only five southerners had voted affirmatively on Brown's proposal to strike out the word "not," the remainder sustaining Clingman's position.]

Thus, forty-three Senators recorded their vote during the last session of Congress that it was not necessary to pass a law to protect slavery in the Territories. The Senator from Oregon, in connection with other Senators, under the solemn sanction of an oath, declared that it was not necessary to pass laws for the protection of slavery in the Territories. What right has South Carolina lost since the last session? What right has any State lost since the last session of Congress? You declared that it was not necessary to pass a law to protect them in the enjoyment of their property in the Territories; and now, forsooth, in the short space of two or three moons, you turn around and tell the country that States are justified in going out of the Union because Congress will not pass a law to protect them in the enjoyment of their property in the Territories, when you said it was not necessary! That is what I call driving the nail in. [Laughter.] I will remark, as I go along, that the eloquent and distinguished Senator who made his valedictory here yesterday,[47] on retiring from the Senate, voted for that identical resolution. This protection was not necessary then. They said it was wholly unnecessary. But since that, they have waked up to a sense of its necessity, and resolved to secede if it should not be granted. To this same proposition Mr. Albert G. Brown offered an amendment. Mark you, this is the 25th day of May, 1860; and that is not long ago.

On motion by Mr. Brown, to amend the resolution by striking out all after the word "resolved," and in lieu thereof, inserting:

I wish I had the whole continent here to hear this paragraph.

That experience having already shown that the Constitution and the common law, unaided by statutory enactment, do not afford adequate and sufficient protection to slave property; some of the Territories having failed, others having refused to pass such enactments, it has become the duty of Congress to interpose and pass such laws as will afford to slave property in the Territories that protection which is given to other kinds of property.[48]

That is a pretty clear proposition. Upon that, Mr. Brown made an argument, showing the number of slaves in the Territories, and the action of the Legislatures, and concluded that if the time ever would arrive, it was then before Congress, and they should pass a law on the subject. What was the vote upon that? How does it stand? We find, after an argument being made by Mr. Brown, showing that the necessity did exist, according to his argument, the vote upon the proposition stood thus: The question being taken by yeas and nays, it was determined in the negative—yeas 3, nays 42.[49]

Forty-two Senators voted that you did not need protection; that slavery was not in danger.

The yeas and nays being desired by one fifth of the Senators present, Those who voted in the affirmative are: Messrs. Brown, Johnson of Arkansas, Mallory.

There were only three. Who said it was not necessary? Who declared, under the solemn sanction of an oath, that protection was not needed?

Those who voted in the negative, are: Messrs. Benjamin—

Ah! Yes; Benjamin!—

Bigler, Bragg, Bright, Chesnut, Clark, Clay, Clingman, Crittenden, Davis, Dixon, Doolittle, Fitzpatrick, Foot, Foster, Green, Grimes, Gwin, Hamlin, Harlan, Hemphill, Hunter—

Hunter, of Virginia, also!—

Iverson, Johnson of Tennessee, Lane.

Ah! [Laughter.] Yes, Lane, of Oregon, voted on the 25th day of last May, that slavery did not need protection in the Territories. Now he will get up and tell the American people and the Senate that he is for a State seceding, and for breaking up the Government, because they cannot get what he swore they did not need. [Laughter.] That is what I call putting the nail through. [Laughter in the galleries.]

The PRESIDING OFFICER (Mr. Fitch in the chair.) The galleries must preserve order.

Mr. JOHNSON, of Tennessee. Then, after voting that it was not necessary to have a proposition to protect slavery in the Territories, the original proposition, as amended, was adopted by a vote of 35 yeas to 2 nays; thus voting all the way through, even to the final action of the Senate, that no such protection was necessary.[50] You have not got protection, your rights, your equality; and then you tell me that I have done you injustice by defending you against the charge that you were in favor of a dissolution of the Union! Even if you approved it, it would only show that I was mistaken. You deceived me that time; that was your fault. The next time it will be mine. I assumed, on that occasion, in reference to the act of ratification of the Constitution by the State of Virginia, that so far as I was capable of examining it, Virginia had made no reservation, no condition, in her ratification of the Constitution of the United States. I had examined the question; I had looked at all the authorities that could be found upon the subject, and I could find no warrant for the assertion; but still the Senator from Oregon, in his reply to me, spoke with great familiarity of the proceedings of that convention ratifying the Constitution, as though he understood it; and with great confidence said it had made a reservation. I will read what he said:

That gallant old State of Virginia, that glorious Old Dominion, made a condition upon which she adopted the Constitution. It became a portion of the compact. And not only Virginia, but New York, made the same condition when she adopted the Constitution; and Rhode Island also.

He spoke with great confidence in this reply to me. He then said:

Now, I would ask the honorable Senator from Tennessee, if the time has not arrived when these States ought to resume the powers conferred on a Federal Government; or if it has not, I should like to know when the time can come.[51]

After declaring under the solemn sanction of an oath that no protection was needed, and nothing else has since transpired, he wants to know when the time will come, if it has not come, that they will be justified in breaking up this Confederacy? I saw a good deal of the confusion that was here that evening; the books were run around and figured about.[52] Sometimes a man had a great deal better read a thing and understand it before he pitches into it. I will not say that that is the case with the honorable Senator, for I should proceed upon the idea that he was laboring under the impression that he understood it exactly. It is not a very uncommon occurrence to be mistaken. Sometimes the mistake results from a want of examination; sometimes from an incapacity to understand the subject, and various other causes. So it is that it occurs very frequently we labor under false impressions. We find when we come to examine this subject of the ratification of the Constitution by Virginia, that a committee was appointed in the convention of Virginia, and that that committee reported a set of resolutions. They reported one resolution in lieu of the preamble. That resolution is as follows:

Resolved, That previous to the ratification of the new Constitution of Government recommended by the late Federal convention, a declaration of rights, asserting and securing from encroachment the great principles of civil and religious liberty, and the inalienable rights of the people, together with amendments to the most exceptionable parts of the said Constitution of Government, ought to be referred by this convention to the other States in the American Confederacy for their consideration.—*Elliot's Debates on the Federal Constitution*, vol. 3, p. 653.

Here was a proposition making conditions; and upon a vote to adopt this amendment it was voted down—ayes 80, noes 88. Then what follows? The committee reported an ordinance adopting the Constitution of the United States; but in their ordinance they go on and make a kind of preamble, or a whereas, a declaration as to their understanding—not conditions, not reservations—but a declaration of their understanding. What do they say:

We, the delegates of the people of Virginia, duly elected in pursuance of a recommendation from the General Assembly, and now met in convention, having fully and freely investigated and discussed the proceedings of the Federal convention, and being prepared as well as the most mature deliberations hath enabled us, to decide thereon—

Now, mark you—

do, in the name and in the behalf of the people of Virginia, declare and make known, that the powers granted under the Constitution, being derived from the people of the United States, be resumed by them whensoever the same shall be perverted to their injury or oppression.—*Elliot's Debates on the Federal Constitution*, vol. 3, p. 656.

They declare, in behalf of Virginia, that the powers of the Constitution are derived from the people of the United States, to "be resumed by them whenever they shall be converted to their injury or oppression." Who is to resume them? The people of the United States. That idea was always inculcated by James Madison.[53] What more do they say? This is not the ratifying clause. They say:

With these impressions—

Not these conditions, not these reservations—

With these impressions, with a solemn appeal to the Searcher of hearts, for the purity of our intentions, and under the conviction that whatsoever imperfections may exist in the Constitution, ought rather to be examined in the mode prescribed therein, than to bring the Union into danger by delay with a hope of obtaining amendments previous to the ratification.

Now comes the ordinance of adoption; and what is it:

We, the said delegates, in the name and behalf of the people of Virginia, do, by these presents, *assent to* and *ratify the Constitution,* recommended on the 17th day of September, 1787, by the Federal Convention, for the government of the United States; hereby announcing to all whom it may concern that the said constitution is binding upon the said people, according to an authentic copy hereunto annexed in the words following.—*Elliot's Debates on the Federal Constitution,* vol. 3, p. 656.

Is there any reservation or condition there? It seems to me that the sight of a man would be tolerably keen that could see a condition there. When was this? We find that Virginia adopted that on Tuesday, June 26, 1788. When did South Carolina come into the Union? Before Virginia did. If Virginia made a condition, South Carolina was already in. How many States were in? The covenant was formed and had been ratified by nine States before Virginia came into the Union. The idea of Virginia appending conditions after the Government was formed and the Constitution ratified by nine States!

But, to make this thing more clear, Mr. Madison, while in New York, received a letter from Mr. Hamilton,[54] stating that he had some doubts as to the ratification of the Constitution by New York; that they wanted some conditions, and one condition was, that they might have the privilege to recede within five or seven years in the event certain amendments were not adopted to the Constitution. I should have remarked, before passing to this, that they adopted it, not wanting delay, and then went in the same committee to report a long list of amendments to be submitted, and some of them were ratified afterwards by the different States. Mr. Madison writes, in reply to Mr. Hamilton, and tells him, if the Constitution is adopted, it must be adopted *in toto,* without reservation or condition. I am inclined to think Mr. Madison had some idea of this ordinance. I think he understood it. Here is his letter. That ordinance was adopted in Virginia, on June 26, 1778 [*sic*], and, in reply to Mr. Hamilton, in the following July, Mr. Madison said:

The idea of reserving a right to withdraw was started at Richmond, and considered as a conditional ratification, which was itself abandoned as worse than a rejection.[55]

Does not that show that I have put the correct interpretation upon it? James Madison understood it as being an abandonment. I would as soon rely upon his construction of the ordinance that brought Virginia into the Union as I would on that of the distinguished Senator from Oregon. I am inclined to think he was quite as familiar with the history of that transaction and with the whole subject as the Senator from Oregon, with all his familiarity and astuteness on the subject. So much in answer to that portion of the Senator's argument. We find upon an examination, as I before remarked, that nine States had ratified the Constitution before Virginia came in. New York, North Carolina, and Rhode Island came in afterwards. Mr. Madison so understood it. The fathers of the Republic so understood it. The country so understand it. Common sense so understands it. Practicability so understands it. Everything that pertains to the preservation and salvation of the Government so understands it, as contradistinguished from the admission of this doctrine of secession.

But let us see how this matter travels along a little. The Government was formed; the Constitution was ratified; and after the Constitution was ratified and the Government in existence, there is provision made, for what? New States may be admitted into this Union, not upon an equality, at all; but, new States may be admitted into this Union. It being an express grant to admit, the exercise of a power, I say the Federal Government can exercise incidents that are necessary and proper to carry the admission of States into existence upon such a basis as they believe the good of the Government demands. I am not so sure but the admission of a new State is placed upon a different ground to what was the admission of States coming in originally ratifying the Constitution. As the Senator seems to be so familiar with things of this sort, I will refer to the act admitting the State of Alabama:

[Quotes both the Alabama Enabling Act of 1819 and the state ordinance accepting its terms.]

This act was declared irrevocable.[56] They agreed to the conditions offered to them in the act of Congress with reference to the public lands and other subjects, and then the act of coming into the Union was declared irrevocable without the consent of the United States. Congress then passed an act accepting them upon the terms they imposed. That was the compact. What has been done to Alabama? What great complaint has she? Why should she leave the Union in such hot haste?

So much for that, sir. In the remarks that I made when I last addressed the Senate,[57] I referred to the constitution of the State of Tennessee, which was adopted in 1796, and their bill of rights, in which they declare that they would never surrender or give up the navigation of the Mississippi to any people. The Senator from Oregon, on that occasion, in reply to me, used the following language:

Then he is concerned about the navigation of the Mississippi river. He says that the great State of Tennessee and he, himself, are concerned about the navigation of that river. I believe it is recognized as the law of nations, as the law of all civilized nations, that a great inland sea running through several Governments shall be open equally to all of them; and besides, as the honorable Senator from Louisiana said, there is no man in Louisiana that would think for a moment of depriving Tennessee of the right of navigating that great river. No, sir, nor Kentucky either, nor Indiana, nor Illinois, nor any other State whose waters flow into that mighty stream. No such thing would ever be done.[58]

That was the Senator's declaration then, that nobody would question the right of those States to navigate that great inland sea. He seemed to show great familiarity with international law. I took it for granted that he had read Grotius and Wheaton upon international law,[59] and all the other authorities on the subject, for he spoke about it with great familiarity, as if he understood it well. How does the matter stand, sir? Before the printer's ink that impressed his speech upon the paper is dry, we find an ordinance passed, as I remarked before, to-day, by the State of Louisiana, declaring negatively that she has the right to control the navigation of that river under her act of secession. If the Senator had put himself to the trouble, as I presume he did, or ought to have done, to examine this subject, he would have found that the navigation of the Mississippi river has been a subject of negotiation for years upon years. He would have found that the navigation of various rivers throughout the world has been the subject of long, angry, and contested negotiation. While upon this point, I desire to present to the Senate an extract from a leading authority on this subject. I read from Wheaton's Elements of International Law: [60]

[Bodies of water entirely within a state's limits—those rivers "of which the use is inexhaustible, such as the sea and running water"— cannot be preempted so as to exclude others from using them. Wheaton expressly includes rivers flowing through a state under the term *innocent use* and states that the principle is derived from Roman law, "which considered navigable rivers as public or common property."]

Now, what are we told? That Louisiana, for which we paid $15,000,000, whose battles we fought, whose custom-houses, forts, arsenals, dock-yards, and hospitals we built,—in the exercise of the plenitude of her power, declares that she has control of the Mississippi, and such States may navigate that stream as are on friendly relations with her, she being the judge. Is not this what the dogma of secession leads us to? We see where it carries us; we see in what it will end—litigation, war, and bloodshed. As I remarked before, as we approach and advance in the investigation of the subject, we discover its enormities more and more. I repeat, it is the prolific mother of anarchy, which is the first step to despotism itself. The Senator from Oregon seems not to be apprehensive at all; and yet, before his voice has done reverberating in the Hall, we have the open declaration that they intend to exercise the control of the navigation of the Mississippi. Would it not have been better for Louisiana—

Mr. LANE. I think the Senator ought to allow me to say a word.

Mr. JOHNSON, of Tennessee. I do not want to be interrupted. I certainly mean no discourtesy at all to the Senator.

Mr. LANE. I only wish to say, in the way of explanation, that the people of New Orleans have had police regulations by which they have collected taxes to improve their wharves ever since New Orleans belonged to this country.

Mr. JOHNSON, of Tennessee. It is a very common thing in all cities where there are wharves, either on the river or ocean, to have what is commonly called a wharfage tax. We understand that. The navigation of the high seas and rivers is a different thing from paying wharfage and a little tax to defray the expense of keeping wharves and docks up. We understand all about that. That is a very different affair from placing batteries at this early day upon the banks of that great stream.

Mr. LANE. That was against the common enemy.

Mr. JOHNSON, of Tennessee. I did not know we had any enemies in these States. I thought we were brothers, and were entitled to free trade from one extremity of this Confederacy to the other. I did not know that the people of Indiana and Illinois and Kentucky and Tennessee, going along down that river, had got to be enemies. I suppose, however, when we look at these things our minds change and vary by varying circumstances. When we are candidates for the Presidency, we feel more like brothers; but when we have made the experiment, and signally failed, I suppose the enemy's line begins just at the line where our defeat was consummated. [Laughter and applause in the galleries.]

The PRESIDING OFFICER called to order.

Mr. JOHNSON, of Tennessee. How long has it been since we were prepared to go to war with the most formidable Power upon earth because she claimed the right of search? We would not concede to Great Britain the right of searching our ships on the high seas; and yet what do we now see? Batteries placed upon the banks of the

Mississippi to enforce the right of search.[61] Do we not see where it will lead? Do we not all know in what it will end?[62]

* * * * * * *

Mr. JOHNSON, of Tennessee. Mr. President,[63] yesterday I proceeded in the discussion, in answer to some of the attacks that had been made on me, to consider the question of the free navigation of the Mississippi river; and I shall leave my remarks on that subject at that point, and shall take up another sentence of the Senator from Oregon. I have no disposition to do the Senator from Oregon, or any other Senator, injustice. In this connection, I will say, as I have intimated before, that I thought his attack upon me unkind and uncalled for. Let that be as it may, it is not my disposition or my intention, on this occasion, to do him injustice. I intend to do him full justice. In the reply that he made to me—to which I yesterday referred—he gave the contradiction direct to what I stated in the presidential canvass, in answer to the charge that had been made that you, Mr. President, and the Senator from Oregon, were disunionists; were in favor of secession; and that you were used by what was called the seceding or disunion party for the purpose of disrupting and breaking up the Government. I met those charges—because I believed they were untrue, that they were not founded in fact—in various places, before large assemblies, and, I thought, successfully, at least to my own mind, exonerated you and the candidate for the Vice Presidency from the charge. I confess it was somewhat mortifying to me, after the reply which the Senator made, to have to say to the people, and the country generally, that I vindicated him against a charge which was true; for, when we take up his speech here in reply to the remarks that I made on that occasion, none of which had the slightest reference to him, involving neither his position before the country, nor his consistency as a legislator, we find that he took bold ground, advocating and justifying secession, arguing, in fact, that it was constitutional. I felt, after that speech, that I was involved in inconsistency before my people, an inconsistency in which I ought not to have been involved.

But in that same speech, in which the honorable Senator involved me in these contradictions, he goes on to state—and I will do him justice by reading his speech, for I do not want to misquote him:

> But, sir, understand me; I am not a disunionist. I am for the right, and I would have it in the Union; and if it cannot be obtained there, I would go out of the Union, and have that out of the Union that I could not obtain in it, though I was entitled to it.[64]

Mr. President, I have called the attention of the Senate to the paragraph of the Senator's speech which I have just read, in which he disavows disunion sentiments; but when you take the preceding part of his speech, you find that he advocates the doctrine of disunion and secession almost from the beginning up to the sentence that I have read. It seems to me it is paradoxical; but that may be my misfortune, not his. He may be capable of reconciling the conflict, the seeming inconsistency of first advocating the doctrine of dissolution, secession, and disunion, and then at the same time exclaiming that he is no disunionist. I do not know how a Senator can be for the Union, and at the same time concede the right that a State has the authority to secede under the Constitution; that it is justified in seceding, and ought to secede; that when it demands rights in the Union that it cannot get, it should go out of the Union to obtain that which could not be obtained in it. But let all that pass. I wish to do him no injustice; and therefore I desired to call attention, in the remarks that I am making, to his disclaimer of being a disunionist and a secessionist.

Mr. President, the Senator, in the sentence I have quoted, assumes that South Carolina, for instance, had the right to secede; and he assumes, also, that South Carolina can obtain that out of the Union which she has failed to obtain in it. Let us raise the inquiry here: what is it, since she entered into this Confederacy of States, that South Carolina has desired or asked at the hands of the Federal Government, or demanded upon constitutional ground, that she has not obtained? What great wrong, what great injury, has been inflicted upon South Carolina by her continuance in this Union of States? I know it is very easy, and even Senators have fallen into the habit of it, to repeat some phrases almost as a chorus to a song; such as "if we cannot get our rights in the Union, we will go out of the Union and obtain those rights; that we are for the equality of the States in the Union, and if we cannot get it we will go out of the Union," I suppose to bring about that equality. What is the point of controversy in the public mind at this time? Let us look at the question as it is. We know that the issue which has been before the country to a very great extent, and which, in fact, has recently occupied the consideration of the public, is the territorial question. It is said that South Carolina has been refused her rights in the Union, with reference to that territorial question, and therefore she is going out of the Union to obtain that which she cannot get in it.

Now, Mr. President, when we come to examine this subject, how does the matter stand? I showed yesterday, in reference to the protection of slave property in the Territories of this Confederacy, that South Carolina, in connection with the distinguished Senator from Oregon, had voted expressly that no slavery code was needed; that no further protection was needed, so far as Congress was concerned.

They decided it here in this body. South Carolina, by her own vote, on the 25th day of May last, decided that she needed no further protection in the Territories of the United States, so far as Congress was concerned. The Senator from Oregon voted with her. That vote seemed to be connected with and predicated upon the great fact that the Supreme Court of the United States had decided this question; that they had declared the Missouri compromise—in other words, the law excluding slavery north of 36°30′, and making it permissive south of 36°30′—unconstitutional and void;[65] and, according to our forms of Government, it was in fact stricken from the statute-book by the decision of the court. They thereby said to the country, the supreme arbiter of the land, so made by the Constitution of the United States, has decided that the people have a right, without regard to the character or description of their property, to carry it into all the Territories of the United States, and that under the Constitution of the United States it is protected there. It was said, the court having decided that they had a right to go there with this institution of slavery, and the Constitution finding it there, it was recognized and protected by the Constitution of the United States.

In this connection, permit me to go outside of the Senate Chamber, and state what occurred in my own State. There, those who were the best friends of the distinguished Senator from Oregon, and who are ultra upon this subject, before thousands of the people of that State took the bold ground that they wanted no further protection from Congress; that the Constitution of the United States and the opinion of the Supreme Court were all the slavery code they desired; that the question was settled; that the power was complete; and that protection was ample.[66]

In this connection, sir, we must recollect the decision made by the Senate upon the resolutions introduced by the Senator from Mississippi [Mr. Davis] on the 25th day of May last. On that day, under the solemn sanction of an oath, and all the formalities of legislation spread upon the Journals, the yeas and nays being taken, we declared, after an argument on the subject, that no further protection was needed at that time. The Senate went on and stated, in the fifth resolution—I give the substance, I do not pretend to repeat the words—that if hereafter it should become necessary to have protection of this kind, then Congress should give it; but they said it was unnecessary at that time. If South Carolina and the Senator from Oregon took this position then, what has transpired since that period of time that now justifies a State in withdrawing or seceding from this Union, on account of Congress not doing that which they declared was not necessary to be done?

But let us take the fact as it is. South Carolina, it is said, wanted protection in the Territories. I have shown that she said, herself, that further protection was not needed; but if it should be needed, then Congress should give it. But South Carolina—the Kingdom of South Carolina—in the plentitude of her power, and upon her own volition, without consultation with the other States of this Confederacy, has gone out of the Union, or assumed to go out. The next inquiry is: what does South Carolina now get, in the language of the distinguished Senator from Oregon, out of the Union that she did not get in the Union? Is there a man in South Carolina to-day that wants to carry a single slave into any Territory we have got in the United States that is now unoccupied by slave property? I am almost ready to hazard the assertion that there is not one. If he had not the power and the right to carry his slave property into a Territory while in the Union, has he obtained that right now by going out of the Union? Has anything been obtained by violating the Constitution of the United States, by withdrawing from the sisterhood of States, that could not have been obtained in it? Can South Carolina, now, any more conveniently and practically carry slavery into the Territories than she could before she went out of the Union? Then what has she obtained? What has she got, even upon the doctrine laid down by the distinguished Senator from Oregon?

But it is argued, striding over the Constitution and violating that comity and faith which should exist amongst the States composing this Confederacy, that she had a right to secede; she had a right to carry slaves into the Territories; and therefore, she will secede and go out of the Union. This reasoning on the part of South Carolina is about as sound as that of the madman, who assumed that he had dominion over the beasts of the forest, and therefore that he had a right to shear a wolf.[67] His friends remonstrated with him, and, admitting his right to do so, inquired of him if he had considered the danger and the difficulty of the attempt. "No," said the madman, "I have not considered that; that is no part of my consideration; man has the dominion over the beasts of the forest, and therefore he has a right to shear a wolf; and as I have a right to do so, I will exercise it." His friends still remonstrated and expostulated, and asked him, not only "Have you considered the danger, the difficulty, and the consequences resulting from such an attempt; but, what will the shearing be worth?" "But," he replied, "I have the right, and therefore I will shear a wolf." South Carolina has the right, according to the doctrine of the seceders and disunionists of this country, to go out of the Union, and therefore she will go out of the Union.

And what, Mr. President, has South Carolina gained by going out? It has been just about as profitable an operation as the shearing of the wolf by the madman. Can she now carry slaves into the Territories? Does she even get any division of the Territories? None; she has lost all that. Does she establish a right? No; but by the exercise of this abstract right, as contended for by secessionists, what has she got? Oppression, taxation, a reign of terror over her people, as the result of their rashness in the exercise of this assumed right. In what condition is her people now? They have gone out of the Union to obtain their rights, to maintain their liberty, to get that out of the Union which they could not get in it! While they were in the Union, they were not taxed a million and some six or seven or eight hundred thousand dollars in addition to their usual expenditures, to sustain standing armies and to meet other expenditures which are incurred by separation. But still she has the right to tax her people; she has the right to institute a reign of terror; she has the right to exclude her people from the ballot-box; and she has exercised the right, and these are the consequences. She has got her rights! She has gone out of the Union to be free, and has introduced a galling system of tyranny. She has gone out of the Union to be relieved from taxes, and has increased the burdens upon her people fourfold. All this is in the exercise of her right! [68]

Mr. President, when we examine this subject, and follow it step by step, to see what is gained by this movement, human reason deplores the folly which it exhibits. The public mind seems to have been inflamed to madness, and in its delirium it overbears all restraint. To some it appears that our admirable system of civil liberty is crumbling to pieces; that the temple of liberty is upheaved; that its columns are falling, and that nothing will remain but a general ruin; and in their consternation too many stand back appalled, and take no position for the relief of their country in the pending crisis. But, sir, the relations that we bear to the people of the United States, behoove every man, whether Senator or Representative, or even private citizen, to come forward as a patriot and lover of his country, and look at the condition of the country as it is. Without regard to the consequences upon myself, I have determined to meet this question, and to present my views to the country in such form as I believe to be right and proper.

Sir, let us look at the contest through which we are passing, and consider what South Carolina, and the other States who have undertaken to secede from the Confederacy, have gained. What is the great difficulty which has existed in the public mind? We know that, practically, the territorial question is settled. Then what is the cause for breaking up this great Union of States? Has the Union or the Constitution encroached upon the rights of South Carolina or any other State? Has this glorious Union, that was inaugurated by the adoption of the Constitution, which was framed by the patriots and sages of the Revolution, harmed South Carolina or any other State? No; it has offended none; it has protected all. What is the difficulty? We have some bad men in the South—the truth I will speak—and we have some bad men in the North, who want to dissolve this Union in order to gratify their unhallowed ambition. And what do we find here upon this floor and upon the floor of the other House of Congress? Words of crimination and recrimination are heard. Bad men North say provoking things in reference to the institutions of the South, and bad men and bad tempered men of the South say provoking and insulting things in return; and so goes on a war of crimination and recrimination in reference to the two sections of the country, and the institutions peculiar to each. They become enraged and insulted, and then they are denunciatory of each other; and what is the result? The Abolitionists, and those who entertain their sentiments, abuse men of the South, and men of the South abuse them in return. They do not fight each other; but they both become offended and enraged. One is dissatisfied with the other; one is insulted by the other; and then, to seek revenge, to gratify themselves, they both agree to make war upon the Union that never offended or injured either. Is this right? What has this Union done? Why should these contending parties make war upon it because they have insulted and aggrieved each other? This glorious Union, that was spoken into existence by the fathers of the country, must be made war upon to gratify these animosities. Shall we, because we have said bitter things of each other which have been offensive, turn upon the Government, and seek its destruction, and entail all the disastrous consequences upon commerce, upon agriculture, upon the industrial pursuits of the country, that must result from the breaking up of a great Government like this? What is to be gained out of the Union that we cannot get in it? Anything? I have been zealously contending for—and intend to continue to contend for—every right, even to the ninth part of a hair, that I feel the State which I have the honor in part to represent is entitled to. I do not intend to demand anything but that which is right; and I will remark, in this connection, that there is a spirit in the country which, if it does not exist to a very great extent in this Hall, does exist in the great mass of the people North and South, to do what is right; and if the question could be taken away from politicians; if it could be taken away from the Congress of the United States, and referred to the great mass of the intelligent voting population of the United States, they would settle it without the slightest difficulty, and bid defiance to secessionists and disunionists. [Applause in the galleries.]

The VICE PRESIDENT. There must be many persons in the galleries who have been warned again and again that order must be maintained. I hope not to have occasion to refer to the subject again.

Mr. JOHNSON, of Tennessee. Mr. President, I have an abiding confidence in the people; and if it were so arranged to-day that the great mass of the American people could be assembled in an amphitheater capacious enough to contain them all, and the propositions which have been presented here to preserve this Union, could be reduced to a tangible shape, and submitted to them, politicians being left out of view, the question being submitted to the great mass of the people, it being their interest to do right, they being lovers of their country, having to pay all, having to produce all, having to provide all, there would be but one single response, "Do that which will give satisfaction, ample and complete, to the various and conflicting sections of this glorious Republic."

But, sir, how are we situated? There are politicians here, and throughout the land, some of whom want to break up the Union, to promote their own personal aggrandizement; some, on the other hand, desire the Union destroyed that slavery may be extinguished. Then let me appeal to every patriot in the land, in view of this state of things, to come forward and take the Government out of the hands of the Goths and Vandals, wrest it from the Philistines, save the country, and hand it down to our children as it has been handed down to us.

I have already asked what is to be gained by the breaking up of this Confederacy. An appeal is made to the border slaveholding States to unite in what is commonly styled the Gulf confederacy. If there is to be a division of this Republic, I would rather see the line run anywhere than between the slaveholding and the non-slaveholding States, and the division made on account of a hostility, on the one hand, to the institution of slavery, and a preference for it, on the other; for whenever that line is drawn, it is the line of civil war; it is the line at which the overthrow of slavery begins; the line from which it commences to recede. Let me ask the border States, if that state of things should occur, who is to protect them in the enjoyment of their slave property? Will South Carolina, that has gone madly out, protect them? Will Mississippi and Alabama and Louisiana, still further down towards the Gulf? Will they come to our rescue, and protect us? Shall we partake of their phrenzy, adopt the mistaken policy into which they have fallen, and begin the work of the destruction of the institution in which we are equally interested with them? I have already said that I believe the dissolution of this Union will be the commencement of the overthrow and destruction of the institution of slavery. In a northern confederacy, or in a southern confederacy, or in a middle confederacy, the border slaveholding States will have to take care of that particular species of property by their own strength, and by whatever influence they may exert in the organization in which they may be placed. The Gulf States cannot, they will not, protect us. We shall have to protect ourselves, and perchance to protect them. As I remarked yesterday, my own opinion is, that the great desire to embrace the border States, as they are called, in this particular and exclusive southern confederacy, which it is proposed to get up, is not that they want us there out of pure good will, but they want us there as a matter of interest; so that if they are involved in war, in making acquisitions of territory still further south, or war growing out of any other cause, they may have a *corps de reserve*, they may have a power behind, that can furnish them men and money —men that have the hearts and the souls to fight and meet an enemy, come from what quarter he may.

What have we to gain by that? The fact that two taken from four leaves but two remaining, is not clearer to my mind that [*sic*] it is that the dissolution of the Union is the beginning of the destruction of slavery; and that if a division be accomplished, as some desire, directly between the slaveholding and the non-slaveholding States, the work will be commenced most effectually. Upon this point, I propose to read a short extract from South Carolina herself. Mr. Boyce, late a member of the other House, a distinguished man, a man of talent, and I believe a good man, and who, I have no doubt, in his heart this day regrets most deeply and sincerely the course which South Carolina has taken,[69] said, in 1851, when the same issue was presented:

Secession, separate nationality, with all its burdens, is no remedy. It is no redress for the past; it is no security for the future. It is only a magnificent sacrifice to the present, without in any wise gaining in the future. * * * * * For the various reasons I have stated, I object in as strong terms as I can, to the secession of South Carolina. Such is the intensity of my conviction on this subject, that if secession should take place—of which I have no idea, for I cannot believe in the existence of such a stupendous madness—I shall consider the institution of slavery as doomed, and that the great God, in our blindness, has made us the instruments of its destruction.[70]

He said then, that if South Carolina, in her madness, (but he did not believe she could,) should determine upon secession, he would look upon it that the great God had doomed the institution of slavery. This is the opinion of one of the most distinguished and, I conscientiously believe, best men of South Carolina.

But, sir, I pass on from the paragraph of the speech of the honorable Senator from Oregon to which I have referred; and as there seems to have been a sort of arrangement—at least it appears so to my mind—to make and keep up an attack on me, because I agreed with Mr. Boyce of South Carolina in this respect; because I agreed with many distinguished men; and because I advanced the doctrines of the fathers who formed the Republic, I shall take up these Senators in the order in which I was attacked. Without being egotistical, without being vain, when I feel that I have got truth on my side, when I feel that I am standing on principle, when I know that I have got facts and arguments that cannot be answered, I never inquire as to the difference of ability or experience between myself and those with whom I have to contend.

The next Senator in order that made an attack upon me on account of my previous speech was the distinguished Senator from Mississippi, [Mr. Davis,] who took occasion to do so in making his valedictory address to the Senate[71] after his State had passed her ordinance of secession. It has been the case not only with that Senator, but with others, that an attempt has been made by innuendo, by indirection, by some side remark, to convey the impression that a certain man has a tendency or bearing towards Black Republicanism or Abolitionism. Sometimes gentlemen who cannot establish such a charge, are yet willing to make it, not directly, but by innuendo; to create a false impression on the public mind—

Willing to wound, but yet afraid to strike.[72]

If the charge can be successfully made, why not make it directly, instead of conveying it by innuendo? The Senator from Mississippi did not attempt to reply to my speech, did not answer my arguments, did not meet my authorities, did not controvert my facts; but after reaching a certain point in his own argument, he disposes of all that I had said in these very few words:

I am here confronted with a question which I will not argue. The position which I have taken necessarily brings me to its consideration. Without arguing it, I will merely mention it. It is the right of a State to withdraw from the Union. The President says it is not a constitutional right. The Senator from Ohio, [Mr. Wade,] and his *ally*, the Senator from Tennessee, argued it as no right at all.[73]

Is that the way for a Senator, a distinguished Senator, an Ajax[74] of his peculiar sect—for when we come to examine this doctrine of secession, it is only broad enough to found a sect upon; it is not comprehensive enough, it has not scope enough, to found a great national party on—to notice the arguments of others? The Senator from Mississippi would not argue the right of secession. I say, that if any government be organized hereafter, in which this principle of secession is recognized, it will result in its destruction and overthrow. But the Senator says that the Senator from Ohio, [Mr. Wade,] and "his ally from Tennessee," regard secession as no right at all; and by that statement the whole argument is answered. What is the idea here?

Let us talk plainly, though courteously and respectfully. What was the idea which this remark was calculated, if not intended, to convey? I am free to say, that I think it was intended as well as calculated, to convey the impression that the Senator from Tennessee was an ally of Mr. Wade, of Ohio, who was a Republican, and the whole speech of the Senator from Tennessee, the authorities, the facts, and the arguments, are all upturned by that single allusion. Thank God, there is too much good sense and intelligence in this country, to put down any man by an innuendo or side remark like that. But, sir, so far as the people whom I have the honor in part to represent are concerned, I stand above innuendoes of that kind. They have known me from my boyhood up. They understand my doctrines and my principles, in private and in public life. They have tried me in every position in which it was in their power to place a public servant, and they, to-day, will not say that Andrew Johnson ever deceived or betrayed them. In a public life of twenty-five years, they have never deserted or betrayed me; and God willing, I will never desert or betray them. The great mass of the people of Tennessee know that I am for them; they know that I have advocated those great principles and doctrines upon which the perpetuity of this Government depends; they know that I have periled my all, pecuniarily and physically, in vindication of their rights and their interests. Little innuendoes, thrown off in snarling moods, fall harmless at my feet.

It was said that I was the ally of the Senator from Ohio. I turn to the doings of the committee of thirteen to show who were allies there.[75] I do not inquire what a man's antecedents have been when there is a great struggle to preserve the existence of the Government; but my first inquiry is, are you for preserving this Government; are you for maintaining the Constitution upon which it rests. If Senator Wade, or Senator anybody else, is willing to come up to this great work, either by amending the Constitution of the United States, or passing laws that will preserve and perpetuate this great Union, I am his ally and he is mine; and I say to every Senator; to every member of the House of Representatives; to every man that loves his country throughout the length and breadth of this great Confederacy, if you are for preserving this Union on its great and fundamental principles, I am your ally, without reference to your antecedents, or to what may take place hereafter. I say to all such men, come forward, and, like gallant knights, let us lock our shields and make common cause for this glorious people. If I were to indulge in a similar kind of innuendo, by way of repartee, where would the Senator from Mississippi find himself? In the committee of thirteen, a resolution was introduced by the distinguished Senator from New York, [Mr. Seward,] —who, I must say, since this question has sprung up, has given every indication of a desire for reconciliation and for compromise, and of a disposition to preserve the Government, that a man occupying his position could do—to this effect:

Resolved, That the following article be, and the same is hereby, proposed and submitted as an amendment to the Constitution of the United States, to be valid, to all intents and purposes, as a part of said Constitution, when ratified by the Legislatures of three fourths of the States:

1. No amendment shall be made to the Constitution which will authorize or give to Congress the power to abolish, or interfere, within any State, with the domestic institutions thereof, including that of persons held to labor or service by the laws of said State.[76]

That was a proposition which was calculated, to a very great extent, to allay the apprehensions and the fears that have been entertained in the South in reference to the institution of slavery. Why do I say so? We know what the argument has been before the southern mind. It has been: first, that the northern anti-slavery party wanted to abolish slavery in the District of Columbia, as an entering wedge; next, to exclude it from the Territories, following up the attack upon slavery; but these points were looked upon as of minor importance; they were looked upon as outposts, as the prelude to an interference with the institution within the States, which has been supposed to be the great end and the great consideration. Do you not know this to be the argument: that they were merely taking these positions as entering wedges to an interference with the institution of slavery in the States? Such is the real question, and such it will remain, the territorial question being substantially settled. What does Mr. Seward, who has acquired so much notoriety by his "irrepressible conflict," say? He comes here and proposes an amendment to the Constitution, which puts an estoppel upon his "irrepressible conflict" doctrine. He is willing to make it perpetual, so that the institution cannot be interfered with in the States by any future amendment of the Constitution. That is Mr. Seward's measure. Upon the adoption of that resolution, I believe every member of the committee voted for it, save two. The Senator from Mississippi [Mr. Davis] voted for it; Mr. Seward voted for it; and Mr. Wade, of Ohio, voted for it. Whose ally is he? Here we find Wade and Seward and Davis, and the whole committee, with the exception of two, in favor of amending the Constitution so that the institution of slavery cannot be interfered with in the States, making that provision irrepealable by any number of States that may come into the Confederacy. Who were "allies" then?

But, Mr. President, recurring to what I said yesterday, there are two parties in this country that want to break up the Government. Who are they? The nullifiers proper of the South, the secessionists, or disunionists—for I use them all as synonymous terms. There is a portion of them who, *per se*, desire the disruption of the Government for purposes of their own aggrandizement. I do not charge upon them that they want to break up the Government for the purpose of affecting slavery; yet I charge that the breaking up of the Government would have that effect; the result would be the same. Who else is for breaking up this Government? I refer to some bad men in the North. There is a set of men there who are called Abolitionists, and they want to break up the Government. They are disunionists; they are secessionists; they are nullifiers. Sir, the Abolitionists and the distinguished Senator from Mississippi and his party both stand in the same attitude, to attain the same end, a dissolution of this Union; the one party believing that it will result in their own aggrandizement South, and the other believing that it will result in the overthrow of the institution of slavery. Who are the disunionists of the North? Who are the "allies" of the distinguished Senator from Mississippi? We find that a resolution was adopted at the anniversary of the Massachusetts Anti-Slavery Society, convened in Boston, in these words:

Resolved, That the one great issue before the country is the dissolution of the Union, in comparison with which all other issues with the slave power are as dust in the balance; therefore we give ourselves to the work of annulling this convenant with death, as essential to our own innocency, and the speedy and everlasting overthrow of the slave system.[77]

This resolution was passed by the Abolition anti-slavery society of Massachusetts. They think a dissolution of the Union would result in the destruction of slavery, and absolve them from this "covenant with death," and attest their innocence, as far as the Government is concerned. On that, we find that Mr. Wendell Phillips made the following remarks:

I entirely accord with the sentiments of that last resolution. I think all we have to do is to prepare the public mind by the daily and hourly presentation of the doctrine of disunion. Events which, fortunately for us, the Government itself, and other parties, are producing with unexampled rapidity, are our best aid.[78]

Again: in reply to a remark made by Mr. Giddings, respecting the dissolution of the Union, the Boston Liberator says:

Mr. Giddings says truly, that the dissolution of the Union has long been held up as a scare-crow by the South; but when he adds that the friends of liberty never demanded it, his statement is untrue, unless he means to confine it to his political associates, who are but compromisers at last. We demand nothing short of a dissolution, absolute and immediate. The Union which was founded by our fathers, was cemented by the blood of the slave, and effected through his immolation.[79]

And still further: William Lloyd Garrison, at a Fourth of July celebration, at Framingham, Massachusetts, declared:

Let us, then, to-day, rejecting as wild and chimeral all suggestions, propositions, and contrivances for restraining slavery in its present limits, while extending constitutional protection to it in fifteen of the States, register our pledge anew before Heaven and the world, that we will do what in us lies to effect the eternal overthrow of this blood-stained Union; that thus our enslaved countrymen may find a sure deliverance, and we may no longer be answerable for their blood.[80]

The Union is to be overthrown by way of getting clear of the "great sin of slavery." Mr. J. B. Swassey [sic], on the same occasion, said:

In the olden times, I was what was called an anti-slavery Whig; but, Mr. President, it has come to my mind, like a conviction, that it is utterly in vain to hope that we can live under such a Government as this, with our professions, and with our pretended love of freedom and right. Why the thing is impossible. There cannot, in the nature of things, be any union between the principles of liberty and slavery. There never has been any union, except by the subjugation of the principles of liberty to those of despotism. For one, sir, I believe that the duty of every true man is to take the ground of secession.[81]

Again: Wendell Phillips, in a speech at Boston on the 20th of January, argued that disunion was desirable, because it would abolish slavery. He also argued that the North would gain by disunion, and used the following language:

Sacrifice everything for the Union? God forbid! Sacrifice everything to keep South Carolina in it? Rather build a bridge of gold, and pay her toll over it. Let her march off with banners and trumpets, and we will speed the parting guests. Let her not stand upon the order of her going, but go at once. Give her the forts and arsenals and sub-treasuries, and lend her jewels of silver and gold, and Egypt will rejoice that she has departed.[82]

He looks upon disunion as the beginning of the destruction and overthrow of the institution of slavery. Then, when we come to talk about "allies," whose allies are these gentlemen? Whose allies are the Abolitionists of the North, if they are not the allies of the secessionists and disunionists of the South? Are they not all laboring and toiling to accomplish the same great end, the overthrow of this great nation of ours? Their object is the same. They are both employing, to some extent, the same means. Here is Wendell Phillips; here is Garrison; here is the anti-slavery society of Massachusetts; and all, in the very same point of view, the allies of the distinguished Senator from Mississippi and his coadjutors; all in favor of disrupting and breaking down this Union, with the view of destroying the institution of slavery itself. "Allies laboring to destroy the Government!" Who else are laboring to destroy it but the disunionists and secessionists of the South, and Garrison and Phillips, and the long list that might be enumerated at the North? Here they stand, presenting an unbroken front, to destroy this glorious Union, which was made by our fathers.[83]

Mr. President, I have alluded to this subject of "allies" in order to show who is engaged in this unholy and nefarious work of breaking up this Union. We find first the run-mad Abolitionists of the North. They are secessionists; they are for disunion; they are for dissolution. When we turn to the South we see the red-hot disunionists and secessionists engaged in the same work. I think it comes with a very bad grace from them to talk about the "allies" of others who are trying to save the Union and preserve the Constitution.

I went back yesterday and showed that South Carolina had held this doctrine of secession at a very early day, a very short time after she entered into the Articles of Confederation, and after she had entered the Union by which and through which the independence of the country was achieved. What else do we find at a very early day? Go to Massachusetts during the war of 1812, and the Hartford convention, and there you will find men engaged in this treasonable and unhallowed work. Even in 1845, Massachusetts, in manifesting her great opposition to the annexation of Texas to the United States, passed a resolution resolving herself out of the Union.[84] She seceded; she went off by her own act, because Texas was admitted into the Union. Thus we find South Carolina and Massachusetts taking the lead in this secession movement. We find the Abolitionists proper of the North shaking the right hand of fellowship with the disunionists of the South in this work of breaking up the Union; and yet we hear intimations here that Senators who are not secessionists from the South are Black Republican allies! If I were compelled to choose either—I would not wish to be compelled to make a choice—but if I were compelled to be either, having the privilege of choosing, I would rather be a black Republican than a red one.[85] I think the one is much more tolerable than the other. If red republicanism is ever to make its way into this country, it is making its way in this disunion and secession movement that is now going on; for we see that right along with the sentiment of secession the reign of terror prevails. Everything is carried away by it, while the conservative men of the country are waiting for the excited tempest to pass. It is now sweeping over the country. Everything is carried by usurpation, and a reign of terror follows along in its wake.

I am charged with being "an ally" of the Senator from Ohio! I, who, from my earliest infancy, or from the time I first comprehended principle, down to the present time, have always stood battling for the same great principles that I contend for now! My people know me; they have tried me; and your little innuendoes and your little indirections will not scare them, even if your infuriated seceding southern men dare to intimate that I am an ally of Mr. Wade. The Senator charges me with being "an ally;" while he and the leaders of Abolitionism are uniting all their energies to break up this glorious Union. I an ally! Thank God, I am not in alliance with Giddings, with Phillips, with Garrison, and the long list of those who are engaged in the work of destruction, and in violating the Constitution of the United States.

So much, Mr. President, in regard to the argument about allies. I am every man's ally when he acts upon principle. I have laid down, as the cardinal point in my political creed, that, in all questions that involve principle, especially where there was doubt, I would pursue principle; and in the pursuit of a great principle I never could reach a wrong conclusion. If, in the pursuit of principle, in trying to reach a correct conclusion, I find myself by the side of another man who is pursuing the same principle, or acting upon the same line of policy, I extend to him my assistance, and I ask his in return.

But the Senator from Mississippi, in his reply to me, also said:

> I was reading, a short time ago, an extract which referred to the time when "we"—I suppose it means Tennessee—would take the position which it was said to be an absurdity for South Carolina to hold; and Tennessee still was put, in the same speech, in the attitude of a great objector against the exercise of the right of secession. Is there anything in her history which thus places her? Tennessee, born of secession, rocked in the cradle of revolution, taking her position before she was matured, and claiming to be a State because she had violently severed her connection with North Carolina, and through an act of secession and revolution claimed then to be a State.[86]

I suppose it was thought that this would be a poser; that it would be conclusive; and as Tennessee was "born of secession, rocked in the cradle of revolution," I was estopped; that my lips were hermetically sealed, so far as related to anything I could give utterance to in opposition to this heresy. When we come to examine the history of that subject, we find the Senator has fallen into just about as great a blunder and as great an error as he did in his allusion to allies. Tennessee had her birth not in secession—very far from it. The State of Frankland had its origin in that way. They attempted to separate themselves from the State of North Carolina. When was that? In 1784. Peace was made in 1783; but in 1784—I read from Wheeler's History of North Carolina:

> In 1784, the General Assembly, in April, at Hillsboro', among other acts for the relief of the General Government, ceded her western lands, and authorized her delegation in Congress to execute a deed, provided Congress would accept this offer within two years.

This act, patriotic and self-sacrificing, was worthy of the State; and although not then accepted by Congress, was the real source of the civil commotion which we are about to record.[87]

What was that civil commotion? The pioneers of that country had suffered great hardships, and they viewed with suspicion this act of 1784. On the 24th of August of that year, they held a convention at Jonesboro', and resolved to send a person to Congress to urge the acceptance of the offer of North Carolina. But I will read from this history:

[The passage presents an account of the state of Frankland: local residents, after repeal of the Cession Act, adopted a constitution, elected an assembly, chose John Sevier as governor, and established a system of courts. These acts brought immediate response from the mother state, whose governor, Richard Caswell, "was not of a temper to brook such high-handed measures." In the fall of 1785 the General Assembly, passing "an act to bury in oblivion the conduct of Frankland," held elections; thus two governments, one headed by Sevier, the other by John Tipton, were in operation. Frankland collapsed when both regimes tried to collect taxes from citizens who refused to pay either.]

All this shows, Mr. President, that the State of Frankland took its origin in 1784. A government was recognized, and it continued until September, 1787. The Legislature that year met at Greenville, the very town in which I live.

[The ensuing passage describes the final demise of the state of Frankland. After minor warfare between Tipton and Sevier, the latter was captured and charged with treason but escaped; pardoned by special act, he was elected to the North Carolina state senate.]

John Sevier was brave and patriotic, a man loved by the people; but he had fallen into this error of secession or separation from the State of North Carolina that I have called your attention to here in the history of North Carolina. We find that this doctrine of secession could not be borne by him, with his great popularity and with the attachment the people had for him. Instead of Tennessee having her origin or her birth in secession, the precise reverse is true. The State of Frankland had its birth in an attempt at disunion and was rocked to death in the cradle of secession; and its great defender and founder at that time, notwithstanding his great popularity and the attachment the people had for him, was lodged in irons. That is where secession carried him, with all his popularity, with all his patriotism, with all the attachment the people had for him. Yes, sir, this nefarious, this blighting, this withering doctrine of secession ended by placing that distinguished man in irons.

What next occurred? North Carolina passed a law for general pardon and oblivion for all those that had been engaged in this movement, with the exception of this great man, John Sevier. His name is even now venerated in the section of the country where I live; but, with all his talents and popularity, this infamous, this nefarious, this diabolical, this hell-born and hell-bound doctrine of secession carried him into chains. The State of Frankland had expired, rocked to death in the cradle of secession, and he went back to Greene county, and was elected a member of the Legislature of North Carolina. In passing this general oblivion and pardon, he was made an exception; and he was not permitted to take his seat in the Legislature until the exception was removed. It was removed, and he went back to the Legislature of North Carolina. Frankland had expired; it was no more; and yet we see the odious weight that was heaped upon him by this nefarious doctrine of secession.

Then what follows, Mr. President? When we turn to the act and follow it along, we find that North Carolina then made her cession act, completed it in 1790, and ceded the territory to the United States. A territorial government was established. General Washington himself appointed the first officers in the Territory, which was then styled "the Territory southwest of the river Ohio."[88] In 1794, the Council or Legislature of that Territory elected James White the first delegate to the Congress of the United States from the Territory southwest of the river Ohio—not Frankland or Franklin, for that is numbered with the things that were, but are not. Even with the popularity of the name of Dr. Franklin, it was consigned to oblivion, and now sleeps with the things that were. In 1794, the delegate to represent the Territory made his appearance here, and took his seat. In 1796, the constitution was formed; and then it was that Tennessee began her existence. The peace was made in 1783, and in 1796 Tennessee formed her constitution and applied for admission into this Union. Then it was that Tennessee was spoken into existence. She did not pass through this ordeal of secession; this probation of disunion. She germinated upon proper principles. The Territory was first organized by Congress after the death of the organization called Frankland; and in 1796, the people of Tennessee formed their constitution, and were admitted into the Union as a State. And, sir, who came into the Union with her when she was admitted as a State? Andrew Jackson. It may have been that his early knowledge of the country, it may have been that his early information upon the subject, made him understand and appreciate ever afterwards the value of the Union. When Tennessee was ushered into this family of States, as an equal member of the Confederacy, General Jackson took his seat as her Representative. The Senator from Mississippi said that Tennessee was "born in secession; rocked in the cradle of revolution." Sir, she has many fond recollections of the Revolution; but with all her revolutionary character, her people have never attempted secession. General Jackson first represented her in

Congress when she came into the Union; she brought him to the notice of the people of the United States as a public man. In 1833, when an attempt somewhat similar to the present was made, he was President of the United States; and it is unnecessary for me to relate what his views of secession were then. It is not necessary for me to refer to the acts of General Jackson in 1833. And now, sir, not intending to disparage others, but to give utterance to my conscientious belief, I must say that if such a man as Andrew Jackson were President of the United States at the present time, before this moment steps would have been taken which would have preserved us a united people without the shedding of blood, without making war. I believe that if Andrew Jackson were President of the United States, this glorious Union of ours would still be intact. Perhaps it might be jarred a little in some places, but not sufficiently to disturb the harmony and general concord of the whole. That is my opinion. I do not say it to disparage others; but I believe that this would have been the case, if he had been President, pursuing the policy which I feel certain he would have pursued in such an emergency.

Tennessee came into the Union in 1796. She was the third State that entered the Confederacy after the old thirteen ratified the Constitution. She was in this Union before Alabama, before Mississippi, before Louisiana, before Florida had an existence. There was a Union then, and she was in it. She has been in it ever since; and she has continued to contribute her money, her men, and her blood, to the defense of the flag of the Union; and though these other States may go out, I trust in God that she will still remain in the position she occupied before they were spoken into existence. We have been told that the Union is broken up—that it is already dissolved. Why, sir, according to the Constitution, nine States formed the Government; and provision was made for taking in new States. Taking in a State or taking out a State does not disturb the Union. It was a Union before the State came in; it is a Union after it goes out. We got along very well before these States came in; and where is the great injury now to result to Tennessee because they propose to go out?

I took occasion, in my former remarks,[89] to call the attention of the Senate, and of my constituents to the extent that I have the honor to represent them, to the kind of government that was likely to be formed by the seceding States, and the country they might acquire after they did secede. In relation to this, the Senator from Mississippi said:

But the Senator found somewhere, I believe in Georgia, a newspaper article which suggested the advantages of a constitutional monarchy. Does the Senator believe there is any considerable number of people in any of the States who favor the establishment of a constitutional monarchy?

The Senator from Georgia [Mr. Iverson] felt called upon to say something in the same connection. He said:

As allusion has been made by the Senator from Mississippi to an article which appeared in a paper in my own town, and about which a good deal of noise has been made, and which was referred to by the Senator from Tennessee, in his celebrated speech, the other day, as evidence that there was a party in the South in favor of a constitutional monarchy—[90]

He went on to state that that idea was suggested in some paper, he could not exactly tell how; but it was not by the editor, and it did not amount to much. I did not refer to a single paper; but I made various extracts from newspapers and speeches, simply as surface indications, as symptoms of what lay below, and what was intended to be the result. I referred to the Charleston Mercury; I referred to other papers; I referred to the speeches of distinguished men, some of them leaders in this movement. Is it not apparent, now, that unless the public mind is aroused, unless the people are put on the alert, there is a design to establish a government upon the principles of a close corporation? Can any one that has the least sagacity be so unobservant as not to see what is going on in the South? It is apparent to all. They seem to unite in setting out with the proposition that the new confederacy shall exclude every State which is not slaveholding, for the reason that those States which are interested in slaves should have the exclusive control and management of them. Here is a great family of States, some free and some slave, occupying, in one sense, the same relation to each other that individuals in the community do to one another. The proposition is started to form a government of States exclusively interested in slaves. That excludes all the free States? Is the argument good? Has not slavery been secure heretofore in the Union with non-slaveholding States; and will not our geographical and physical position be just the same after the present Union is dissolved? Where does the argument carry us? We must have a confederacy now composed of slave States exclusively. When we have excluded the free States, and we come to make a new government, does not the same argument apply that we must have a government to be controlled and administered by that description of persons among us who are exclusively interested in slaves? If you cannot trust a free State in the confederacy, can you trust a non-slaveholder in a slaveholding State to control the question of slavery? Where does your argument carry you? We see where they are drifting; and, as a faithful sentinel upon the watchtower,[91] I try to notify the people and sound the tocsin of alarm. If this idea be not carried out, it will be because the public feeling, the public opinion, is aroused against it.

I alluded yesterday to the fact that the freemen of the State of South Carolina have not been permitted to vote for a President since it was a State. There is a great terror and dread of the capacity of the people to govern themselves. In South Carolina, when the ordinance was passed to withdraw from the Union, did the convention trust the people to pass their judgment upon it? Were they consulted? Did they indorse it? Have they passed their judgment upon it to this day? Taking the language of Mr. Boyce as an index of their feeling, I have no more doubt than I have of my existence that if this reign of terror subsides, and the hearts of the people of South Carolina can be gotten at, it will be found that a majority of them disapprove and repudiate what has been done there. What do we find in the State of Georgia? There the proposition was moved to submit the ordinance to the people; and were the people consulted? The vote was 138 to 160, I think. It shows a great division. Did they submit it to the people? Oh, no.[92] I know something of the people of the State of Georgia; and I believe this day, if that seceding ordinance could be submitted to the voting population of Georgia, and the question be fully canvassed and fairly understood, they would repudiate and put it down. Go to Florida: were the people consulted there? Not at all. Look to Alabama; look to the arguments made there in the convention. It was said, "our power is ample; we must consummate this thing, and not let the people pass upon it." Louisiana refused to refer the matter to the people. The people have not been consulted. A reign of terror has been instituted. States have been called upon to make large appropriations of money to buy arms and munitions of war; for what end? The idea has been: "we can, almost with the speed of lightning, run States out of the Union without consulting the people; and then, if they dare resist, we have got an army, we have got the money to awe them into submission." These gentlemen are very fearful of coercion, exceedingly alarmed at the word "coerce"; but when you attempt to interpose and stop their career, they do not know of any other term but coerce. Look at the dispatch which Governor Pickens sent to Mississippi:

Charleston, *January* 19, 1861.
    Judge Magrath and myself have sent four telegraphs to you. Please urge Mississippi to send delegates to the Montgomery meeting of States, at as early a day as possible—say 4th of February—to *form immediately a strong provisional government*. It is the only thing to prevent war, and let that convention elect *immediately* a commander-in-chief for the seceding States. You may as well return, at least as far as Montgomery.
F. W. Pickens.[93]

To Hon. A. Burt Jackson.

South Carolina has a military establishment, with officers appointed, and the taxes necessary to support them now are grinding her people to the dust; but she expects in a very short time to transfer that military establishment, with her officers, to the southern confederacy that is to be established; and I suppose the great object in getting the leader appointed at once is that they may be able by military force to awe the people into submission. Have we not seen that nine regiments have been authorized to be raised in Mississippi, and a distinguished Senator, who occupied a seat on this floor a short time since, made the major general? [94] No doubt, when the scheme is consummated and carried out, when the military organization is complete, if the people offer to resist, they will be subdued and awed, or driven into submission at the point of the bayonet. Some of these gentry are very much afraid of the people.

Why, sir, a proposition was even started in my own State, to raise fifteen regiments; [95] for what? With whom are we at war? Is anybody attacking us? No. Do we want to coerce anybody? No. What do we want with fifteen regiments? And it was proposed to appropriate $250,000 to sustain them. There is a wonderful alarm at the idea of coercing the seceding States; great dread in reference to the power of this Federal Government to secure obedience to its laws, and especially in reference to making war upon one of the States; but the public property can be taken, your flag can be fired upon, your ships driven out of port, your gallant officer, with a few men, penned up in a little fort to subsist as best they may. [96] So far as the officer to whom I have just alluded is concerned, I will give utterance to the feelings of my heart when I express my profound approbation of his conduct. He was put there to defend the flag of his country. He was there not as an intruder. He was there in possession of the property owned by the United States, not to menace, not to insult, not to violate rights, but simply to defend the flag and honor of his country, and take care of the public property; and because he retired from a position where he could have been captured, where the American flag could have been struck and made to trail in the dust, and the Palmetto banner substituted, because he, obeying the impulses of a gallant and brave heart, took choice of another position; acting upon principles of humanity, not injuring others, but seeking to protect his own command from being sacrificed and destroyed, he is condemned and repudiated, and his action is sought to be converted into a menace of war. Has it come to this, that the Government of the United States cannot even take care of its own property, that your vessels must be fired upon, that your flag must be struck, and still you are alarmed at coercion: and because a gallant officer has taken possession of a fort where he cannot very well be coerced, a terrible cry is raised, and war is to be made?

I was speaking of the proposition to raise fifteen regiments in my own State, which has been brought forward. Sir, as far back as the battle of King's mountain, and in every war in which the rights of the people have been invaded, Tennessee, God bless her, has stood by that glorious flag, which was carried by Washington and followed by the gallant patriots and soldiers of the Revolution, even as the blood trickled from their feet as they passed over the ice and snow; and under that flag, not only at home, but abroad, her sons have acquired honor and distinction, in connection with citizens of the other States of the Union. She is not yet prepared to band with outlaws, and make war upon that flag under which she has won laurels. Whom are we going to fight? Who is invading Tennessee? Conventions are got up; a reign of terror is inaugurated; and if, by the influence of a subsidized and mendacious press, an ordinance taking the State out of the Confederacy can be extorted, those who make such propositions expect to have our army ready, to have their bands equipped, to have their pretorian divisions; then they will tell the people that they must carry the ordinance into effect, and join a southern confederacy, whether they will or not; they shall be lashed on to the car of South Carolina, who entertains no respect for them, but threatens their institution of slavery unless they comply with her terms. Will Tennessee take such a position as that? I cannot believe it; I never will believe it; and if an ordinance of secession should be passed by that State under these circumstances, and an attempt should be made to force the people out of the Union, as has been done in some other States, I tell the Senate and the American people that there are many in Tennessee whose dead bodies will have to be trampled over before it can be consummated. [Applause in the galleries.] The Senator from Mississippi referred to the flag of his country; and I will read what he said, so that I may not be accused of misrepresenting him:

It may be pardoned to me, sir, who, in my very boyhood, was given to the military service, and who have followed that flag under tropical suns, and over northern snows, if I here express the deep sorrow which always overwhelms me when I think of turning from the flag I have followed so long, for which I have suffered in ways it does not become me to speak of; feeling that henceforth it is not to be the banner I will hail with the rising sun, and greet as the sun goes down; the banner which, by day and by night, I am ready to follow. But God, who knows the hearts of men, will judge between you and us, at whose door lies the responsibility of this.[97]

There is no one in the United States who is more willing to do justice to the distinguished Senator from Mississippi than myself; and when I consider his early education; when I look at his gallant services, finding him first in the military school of the United States, educated by his Government, taught the science of war at the expense of his country—taught to love the principles of the Constitution; afterwards entering its service, fighting beneath the stars and stripes to which he has so handsomely alluded, winning laurels that are green and imperishable, and bearing upon his person scars that are honorable; some of which have been won at home; others of which have been won in a foreign clime, and upon other fields—I would be the last man to pluck a feather from his cap or a single gem from the chaplet that encircles his illustrious brow. But when I consider his early associations; when I remember that he was nurtured by this Government; that he fought for this Government; that he won honors under the flag of this Government, I cannot understand how he can be willing to hail another banner, and desert the one of his country, under which he has won laurels and received honors. This is a matter of taste, however; but it seems to me that, if I could not unsheath my sword in vindication of the flag of my country, its glorious stars and stripes, I would return the sword to its scabbard; I would never sheathe it in the bosom of my mother; never! never! Sir, my own feelings in reference to that flag are such as must have filled the heart of that noble son of South Carolina, Joel R. Poinsett, when, nearly thirty years ago, in an address to the people of Charleston,[98] he declared:

[Recounting his experience in Mexico City in 1828 when an uprising drove citizens to seek shelter in the house of the American minister, Poinsett described the effectiveness of the American flag in deterring attack by the mob and queried, "Should I have been here to tell you this tale if I had hung out the palmetto and single star? Be assured that, to be respected abroad, we must maintain our place in the Union."]

Sir, I intend to stand by that flag, and by the Union of which it is the emblem. I agree with Mr. A. H. Stephens, of Georgia, "that this Government of our fathers, with all its defects, comes nearer the objects of all good governments than any other on the face of the earth."[99]

I have made allusions to the various Senators who have attacked me, in vindication of myself. I have been attacked on all hands by some five or six, and may be attacked again. All I ask is, that, in making these attacks, they meet my positions, answer my arguments, refute my facts. I care not for the number that may have attacked me; I care not how many may come hereafter. Feeling that I am in the right, that argument, that fact, that truth are on my side, I place them all at defiance. Come one, come all; for I feel, in the words of the great dramatic poet:

Thrice is he armed that hath his quarrel just,
And he but naked, though locked up in steel,
Whose conscience with secession is corrupted.[100]

I have been told, and I have heard it repeated, that this Union is gone. It has been said in this Chamber that it is in the cold sweat of death; that, in fact, it is really dead, and merely lying in state waiting for the funeral obsequies to be performed. If this be so, and the war that has been made upon me in consequence of advocating the Constitution and the Union is to result in my overthrow and in my destruction; and that flag, that glorious flag, the emblem of the Union, which was borne by Washington through a seven years' struggle, shall be struck from the Capitol and trailed in the dust—when this Union is interred, I want no more honorable winding sheet than that brave old flag, and no more glorious grave than to be interred in the tomb of the Union. [Applause in the galleries.] For it I have stood; for it I will continue to stand; I care not whence the blows come; and some will find, before this thing is over, that while there are blows to be given, there will be blows to receive; and that, while others can thrust, there are some who can parry. They will find that it is a game that two can play at. God preserve my country from the desolation that is threatening her, from treason and traitors!

> Is there not some chosen curse,
> Some hidden thunder in the stores of heaven,
> Red with uncommon wrath, to blast the man
> Who owes his greatness to his country's ruin?[101]

[Applause in the galleries.]

In conclusion, Mr. President, I make an appeal to the conservative men of all parties. You see the posture of public affairs; you see the condition of the country; you see along the line of battle the various points of conflict; you see the struggle which the Union men have to maintain in many of the States. You ought to know and feel what is necessary to sustain those who, in their hearts, desire the preservation of this Union of States. Will you sit with stoic indifference, and see those who are willing to stand by the Constitution and uphold the pillars of the Government driven away by the raging surges that are now sweeping over some portions of the country? As conservative men, as patriots, as men who desire the preservation of this great, this good, this unparalleled Government, I ask you to save the country; or let the propositions be submitted to the people, that the heart of the nation may respond to them. I have an abiding confidence in the intelligence, the patriotism, and the integrity of the great mass of the people; and I feel in my own heart that, if this subject could be got before them, they would settle the question, and the Union of these States would be preserved. [Applause in the galleries.][102]

Cong. Globe, 36 Cong., 2 Sess., 744–50, 766–72; *Speech of Hon. Andrew Johnson, of Tennessee, on the State of the Union* (Washington, D. C., 1861).

1. By special order, Buchanan's message on resolutions from the Virginia legislature was called up for discussion; Johnson, under prior arrangement, had the floor.

2. Vice President Breckinridge was in the chair.

3. Lane of Oregon made an immediate, lengthy rebuttal, after which the Senate went into executive session. Johnson spoke subsequently of the "frowns" and "scowls," the "taunts, the jeers, the derisive remarks," from fellow senators, as well as that "bevy of conspirators gathered in from the other House." *Cong. Globe*, 36 Cong., 2 Sess., 143–45; *ibid.*, 37 Cong., 2 Sess., 585.

4. After reading into the record Louisiana's secession ordinance, John Slidell and Judah P. Benjamin withdrew. *Cong. Globe*, 36 Cong., 2 Sess., 720–22; for Slidell and Benjamin, see *Johnson Papers*, I, 367n, III, 245n.

5. Shakespeare, *Julius Caesar*, Act III, sc. 2.

6. Louisiana was admitted in 1812.

7. An expression of undetermined origin which appears to have enjoyed a revival during the Civil War.

8. The sugar industry had been granted protection in every tariff since 1789. The Act of 1846 placed a 30 percent ad valorem tax on "sugars of all kinds," and the principle was to be continued in 1861 legislation. Philip G. Wright, *Sugar in Relation to the Tariff* (New York, 1924), 95; William H. Michael and Pitman Pulsifer, comps., *Tariff Acts Passed by the Congress of the United States from 1789 to 1895* . . . (Washington, D. C., 1896), 124, 139.

9. One of Aesop's fables. See Benét, *Reader's Encyclopedia*, 646.

10. Resolution No. 3, passed January 26, the same day the convention adopted the secession ordinance, granted "egress and ingress" to "friendly states and powers." Three days later ordinances relating to the collection of revenues at the Port of New Orleans and providing that no duty be collected on imports from states "forming the late Federal Union" were adopted. "Ordinances Passed by the Convention of the State of Louisiana," *Louisiana History*, II (1961), 122–24.

11. A reference to Benjamin's speech of December 31. *Cong. Globe*, 36 Cong., 2 Sess., 216–17.

12. While in California defending a Mexican-American's mining claim (U. S. v. Castillero, October–November, 1860), Benjamin addressed a meeting of Episcopal ministers on the Wednesday following the presidential election. Contrary to Johnson's assertion, the *Times* carried no extract of this speech. Robert D. Meade, *Judah P. Benjamin: Confederate Statesman* (New York, 1943), 126–34, 141–42; Louisville *Journal*, February 4, 1861.

13. *Cong. Globe*, 36 Cong., 1 Sess., 2237.

14. A proverb of unknown origin. Stevenson, *Quotations*, 304.

15. Paraphrase of Shakespeare, *Julius Caesar*, Act IV, sc. 3.

16. Robert M. T. Hunter, in a speech of January 11. *Cong. Globe*, 36 Cong., 2 Sess., 330.

17. While minister to France Jefferson endeavored to assist Jean Nicolas Démeunier, who was compiling his *Encyclopédie Méthodique*, in understanding the political nature of the new American nation. The quotation is from Jefferson's letter to Démeunier of January 24, 1786. H. A. Washington, ed., *The Writings of Thomas Jefferson* (9 vols., Washington, D. C., 1853–54), IX, 291–92; Boyd, *Jefferson Papers*, X, 4, 19.

18. Eleventh Amendment.

19. Probably a reference to John J. Crittenden's January 7 speech in which he discussed the right to take slaves into the territories, stating that the Constitution did not grant Congress the power to legislate in matters of conscience. *Cong. Globe*, 36 Cong., 2 Sess., 265–66.

20. Ableman v. Booth, a decision supporting the Fugitive Slave Law, involved the rescue of a runaway slave in Wisconsin in 1854. Campbell, *Slave Catchers*, 157–60.

21. A reference to the case of Anthony Burns, a fugitive from Virginia whose return by federal authorities in 1854 was threatened by a Boston mob. Allan Nevins, *Ordeal of the Union* (2 vols., New York, 1947), II, 150–52. See also *Johnson Papers*, III, 374, 375n.

22. The outcome of a February 4 convention referendum in Virginia was not yet known. Of the 152 delegates elected, only 45 were "immediate secessionists," while 85 had supported Bell and 37 Douglas, an indication of a conservative trend. Henry T. Shanks, *The Secession Movement in Virginia, 1847–1861* (Richmond, 1934), 150–58; Wooster, *Secession Conventions*, 142–43.

23. Milton Latham, who had also read extended passages for Johnson's December speech.

24. Diogenes, a Greek philosopher of the fourth century B. C., carried a lantern at midday searching for an honest man. Benét, *Reader's Encyclopedia*, 298.

25. Graham N. Fitch of Indiana.

26. In 1814 Thomas Ritchie was editor of the Richmond *Enquirer* from which Johnson had just quoted. For Ritchie, see *Johnson Papers*, I, 386n.

27. South Carolina, still operating under its Constitution of 1790, was the only state which did not allow its citizens to vote directly for presidential electors, the selection of which rested in the hands of the legislature. Nichols, *Disruption of Democracy*, 351.

28. Moultrie (1730–1805), South Carolina planter and revolutionary general, saved Charleston in 1779 but was taken prisoner over a year later when the city fell; exchanged in 1782, he served as governor (1785–87) and was reelected in 1792. His two-volume *Memoirs of the American Revolution* was published in New York in 1802. *DAB*, XIII, 293–94.

29. Augustine Prévost (1723–1786), Geneva-born British general who had served in North America since the 1750's, was sent from East Florida in 1778 to command forces in the southern theater. Following his successful defense of Savannah in 1779, he returned to England. Mark M. Boatner, III, *Encyclopedia of the American Revolution* (New York, 1966), 889.

30. According to an undated, unidentified newspaper clipping (probably from the New York *Tribune*, December 28, 1860) found in Series 2 of the Johnson Papers, the speaker was reading from *The Remembrancer . . . 1775–1784* (17 vols., London, [1775–84]), X, Pt. 2 (1780), 83–84.

31. The South Carolina secession convention met first on December 17, 1860, and continued through four sessions, adjourning finally on September 17, 1862. Maxcy Gregg (1814–1862), a lawyer who became a Confederate general, and Robert B. Rhett, editor of the Charleston *Mercury*, were ardent secessionists. Wooster, *Secession Conventions*, 14–24; *DAB*, VII, 598–99; for Rhett, see *Johnson Papers*, I, 314n.

32. Washington *National Intelligencer*, December 27, 1860.

33. *Ibid.*, December 28, 1860.

34. In the secession convention Rhett had proposed on December 20 a resolution for a committee to draft an ordinance calling for "the assemblage of a Convention of the Slaveholding States . . . to form the Constitution of a Southern Confederacy." On January 1 the convention adopted resolutions providing for the selection of commissioners "to the various Southern States about to meet in Convention" and proposing that these commissioners set a date for an early conference of the states. The commissioners departed during the first days of January with instructions to urge immediate secession and the election of delegates to a southern convention in Montgomery in February. *Journal of the Convention of the People of South Carolina, Held in 1860, 1861 and 1862* (Columbia, S. C., 1862), 41–42, 150–62 *passim*; Cauthen, *South Carolina Goes to War*, 84–85.

35. In his December speech Johnson had quoted from Governor William H. Gist's message to the South Carolina legislature recommending that the introduction of slaves from states outside a southern confederacy be prohibited. See Speech on Secession, December 18–19, 1860.

36. Americans of that day were intrigued by the original Siamese twins, Chang and Eng (1811–1874), who had been born of Chinese parents in Siam and were joined at the waist by a cartilaginous structure. Brought to the United States in 1829 and placed on exhibit, they had accumulated a modest fortune, purchasing a farm in North Carolina, espousing two sisters, and raising large families. At this time they were once again in the public eye, on tour as a featured attraction with Barnum's museum. Their assets liquidated by the war, the brothers once more exhibited their peculiar deformity until Chang's intemperance led to the death of both men. *DAB*, IV, 2–3; New York *Times*, October 27–November 10, 1860.

37. *Cong. Globe*, 36 Cong., 2 Sess., 143–45.

38. It suits Johnson's purpose to exaggerate both the extent and vigor of his participation in the late presidential election—a canvass which he entered only in late September, even then campaigning less for his ticket than for the reunification of the Tennessee Democracy.

39. *Ibid.*, 143.

40. The senator had recently passed his fifty-second birthday.

41. Paraphrase of Shakespeare, *Julius Caesar*, Act III, sc. 2.

42. *Cong. Globe*, 36 Cong., 2 Sess., 144.

43. It would appear that this is not a reference to a specific religious denomination like the Quakers but rather to the general category of those seeking a peaceful solution for the current crisis.

44. *Ibid.*, 143.

45. On February 2, 1860, Davis had introduced resolutions, superseding those of his Mississippi colleague Albert G. Brown, which included a provision for the protection of slave property in the territories. *Ibid.*, 1 Sess., 494, 658. See also *Johnson Papers*, III, 467n.

46. *Senate Journal*, 36 Cong., 1 Sess., 513; *Cong. Globe*, 36 Cong., 1 Sess., 2343.

47. Slidell of Louisiana had delivered his farewell on February 4. *Ibid.*, 2 Sess., 720–21.

48. *Senate Journal*, 36 Cong., 1 Sess., 515; *Cong. Globe*, 36 Cong., 1 Sess., 2347.

49. *Ibid.*, 2349.

50. The evidence seems not to support Johnson's contention. The fifth resolution, to which this vote refers, clearly specifies that if territorial action does not adequately protect property in slaves, "it will be the duty of Congress to supply such deficiency within the limits of its constitutional powers." The final limiting phrases, beginning "within," are the portions of the amendment referred to. *Ibid.*, 2350.

51. *Ibid.*, 2 Sess., 143, 144.

52. Lane had quoted from several sources: two dealt with Virginia's and New York's ratification of the Constitution and three were passages from Lincoln's recent campaign speeches; however, two of these extracts came from the same address.

53. In Federalist No. 49 (February 2, 1788), Madison stated, "As the people are the only legitimate fountain of power . . . it seems strictly consonant to the republican theory, to recur to the same original authority . . . whenever any one of the departments may commit encroachments on the chartered authorities of the others." Jacob E. Cooke, ed., *The Federalist* (Middletown, Conn., 1961), 339.

54. Hamilton to Madison, July 19, 1788, Syrett and Cooke, *Hamilton Papers*, V, 177–78.

55. Madison to Hamilton, July 20, 1788, *ibid.*, 185. In this edition, the

final phrase of the quotation reads "which was itself considered as worse than a rejection."

56. Both the "Enabling Act for Alabama—1819" and the "Constitution of Alabama—1819" included an ordinance regarding public lands and waterways, the provisions of which were declared "irrevocable, without the consent of the United States." Francis N. Thorpe, ed., *The Federal and State Constitutions* . . . (7 vols., Washington, D. C., 1909), I, 94, 114.

57. Speech on Secession, December 18–19, 1860.

58. *Cong. Globe*, 36 Cong., 2 Sess., 144.

59. Hugo Grotius, *Freedom of the Seas* (1609), *The Rights of War and Peace* (1625); Henry Wheaton, *Elements of International Law* (Philadelphia, 1836).

60. *Ibid.*, Pt. II, 252, 253, 254.

61. On January 15 the governor of Mississippi had ordered volunteer companies in and around Vicksburg to erect batteries to prevent the descent of any hostile expeditions from the North. New York *Times*, January 26, 1861.

62. Upon motion of Hemphill of Texas and over the protests of Wigfall and Lane, the Senate adjourned. The deliberations of the following day were well along before Johnson resumed his speech.

63. Vice President Breckinridge was in the chair.

64. *Cong. Globe*, 36 Cong., 2 Sess., 144.

65. Four years earlier, in the Dred Scott decision, the majority had held that the federal government could not prohibit slavery in the territories. Nevins, *Emergence of Lincoln*, I, 95.

66. Although the Tennessee Democratic convention in January, 1860, had declared the views expressed in the Dred Scott decision "a true and clear exposition of the powers reposed in Congress upon the subject of the Territories . . . and the rights guaranteed to the residents in the Territories," Johnson is alluding directly to statements made during the presidential campaign, perhaps most notably at Brownsville, where his colleague Nicholson, speaking along with Governor Harris and Andrew Ewing, had endorsed the decision, while castigating "the hollow and infamous heresy of 'Squatter Sovereignty' . . . 'non-intervention' . . . and all that kind of clap-trap." Nashville *Union and American*, August 24, September 5, 1860.

67. Excessively fond of Edmund Burke's fable, Johnson had used it earlier in his speeches at Winchester, September 29, and Memphis, October 16, during the presidential canvass. *Johnson Papers*, III, 662–63, 670.

68. Faced with the immediate necessity of discharging the powers and responsibilities of an independent nation, the South Carolina legislature had passed an ordinance December 27 enlarging the powers of the governor, giving him responsibility for foreign affairs, and providing him with an official cabinet. The state assembly and the secession convention assumed powers formerly held by Congress, including the collection of customs duties. To meet her immediate needs South Carolina resorted to loans; however, tax rates were increased to provide a $200,000 increase in 1861 over the $600,000 total revenue in 1860. At the outset of secession various "unofficial military associations" sprang up in the state; committees of "Safety" or "Vigilance" established patrols for the purpose of apprehending those suspected of being traitors, and there were numerous arrests and acts of violence against "foreigners." Cauthen, *South Carolina Goes to War*, 79–81, 111–12, 188–91.

69. William W. Boyce (1818–1890), State Rights Democrat who served in Congress (1853–60) and in the Confederate Congress (1862–64), later moved to Washington, where he practiced law. Whatever views Boyce may have entertained "in his heart," he had earlier declared for secession in the event Lincoln was elected. *BDAC*, 582; Steven A. Channing, *Crisis of Fear: Secession in South Carolina* (New York, 1970), 235–36.

70. Extract from *Letter from W. W. Boyce to the Hon. John P. Richardson, President of the Convention of Southern Rights Association of South Carolina* (n. d., n. p., a five-page letter bound with *Resolutions and Addresses*

of the Southern Convention, in South Caroliniana Library, University of South Carolina, Columbia). Johnson had undoubtedly obtained this extract from the Nashville *Banner* where it had appeared on January 26. Although Boyce, as revealed by the passage quoted, was opposed to his state's secession in March, 1851, he was not categorically opposed to secession, as Johnson implies. Evidently the South Carolinian favored a southern confederacy if steps were needed to protect southern interests. Lillian A. Kibler, *Benjamin F. Perry: South Carolina Unionist* (Durham, N. C., 1946), 262–63.

71. Davis' farewell address had been delivered on January 21; the speech to which Johnson refers was given on January 10. *Cong. Globe*, 36 Cong., 2 Sess., 306–12, 487.

72. Alexander Pope, *Epistle to Dr. Arbuthnot*, l. 203; "but" is substituted for "and."

73. A passage from Davis' speech of January 10. *Cong. Globe*, 36 Cong., 2 Sess., 308.

74. Next to Achilles, the most famous hero of the Trojan War was Ajax, a giant in size and possessed of tremendous strength. Full of conceit, he went mad when Hector's armor was awarded Ulysses instead of himself. Benét, *Reader's Encyclopedia*, 17.

75. In order to consider the various compromise proposals, the Senate authorized on December 18 a Committee of Thirteen. Two days later Vice President Breckinridge appointed Davis (Mississippi) and Toombs (Georgia) from the deep South; Crittenden and Powell (Kentucky) and Hunter (Virginia) from the border states; northern Democrats Douglas (Illinois), Bigler (Pennsylvania), and Rice (Minnesota); and five Republicans—Seward (New York), Collamer (Vermont), Wade (Ohio), Doolittle (Wisconsin), and Grimes (Iowa). Nevins, *Emergence of Lincoln*, II, 390.

76. Report of the Committee of Thirteen, *Senate Report* No. 288, 36 Cong., 2 Sess., 10–11.

77. The sixteenth of eighteen resolutions adopted by the twenty-third annual meeting of the Massachusetts Anti-Slavery Society, January 24, 1856. *The Liberator* (Boston), February 1, 1856.

78. *Ibid.*

79. Editor Garrison's comment arose from Joshua Giddings' December 18, 1855, speech on the organization of the House. *Ibid.*, January 11, 1856.

80. *Ibid.*, July 11, 1856.

81. J. B. Swasey was a resident of Newburyport. *Ibid.*, July 18, 1856.

82. In his Music Hall address Phillips had also quoted somewhat inaccurately from Johnson's December speech: "If I were an abolitionist, and wanted to accomplish the abolition of slavery in the Southern States, the first step I would take would be to break the bonds of this Union. I believe the continuance of slavery depends on the preservation of this Union, and a compliance with all the guarantees of the Constitution." *Ibid.*, January 25, 1861; New York *Times*, January 22, 1861; Speech on Secession, December 18–19, 1860.

83. Johnson was not alone in believing that abolitionists of the Garrison and Phillips stamp were as eager to destroy the Union as were the secessionists; a northern editor would later observe, "They are the natural allies of the Secessionists of South Carolina." New York *Times*, January 17, 22, 1862.

84. For three consecutive years prior to the congressional joint resolution annexing Texas in March, 1845, the General Court of Massachusetts had formally opposed that step, and following annexation the legislature refused to acknowledge its legality, denouncing it as "an alarming encroachment upon the rights of the freemen of the Union . . . [and] a deliberate assault upon the compromises of the Constitution." Asserting that countermeasures were justified and that Massachusetts was ready to "cooperate with other states in any lawful plan for restoring the Constitution as an instrument for liberty," they declared that any future territory applying for statehood must exclude slavery.

It is interesting to note that the Andrew Johnson Papers, Series 18: Miscellaneous Papers, 1783–1862, contain a handwritten copy of the "Texas Resolves of the Legislature of Massachusetts 1843–4–5." Albert Bushnell Hart, ed., *Commonwealth History of Massachusetts* (5 vols., New York, 1966 [1927–30]), IV, 296; Martin B. Duberman, *Charles Francis Adams, 1807–1886* (Boston, 1961), 97–99; *Acts and Resolves Passed by the General Court of Massachusetts* (Boston, 1844), 319–29; (1845), 598–99, 651–53.

85. A "red" Republican was one who subscribed to radical ideas and advocated violent means to obtain political reform. Mathews, *Americanisms*, II, 1372.

86. *Cong. Globe*, 36 Cong., 2 Sess., 310.

87. John H. Wheeler, *Historical Sketches of North Carolina from 1584 to 1851* (2 vols., Baltimore, 1964 [1851]), I, 92.

88. Johnson's quotation is inaccurate; the 1790 act reads "the Territory . . . south of the river Ohio." *U. S. Statutes*, I, 123.

89. Speech on Secession, December 18–19, 1860.

90. For both extracts, see *Cong. Globe*, 36 Cong., 2 Sess., 311.

91. The phrase, rather universally used at this time, had appeared in Tennessee house resolution No. 18 introduced on January 9 by Unionist Daniel Trewhitt: "That the State of Tennessee be and remain as a sentinel upon the watchtower of our liberties." *Tenn. House Journal*, 1861, Extra Sess., 34; Knoxville *Register*, January 31, 1861.

92. William Martin of Lumpkin County, who had voted against the secession ordinance, was unsuccessful in his attempt to "secure the approval of the convention" for the submission of the ordinance to the people before that document was signed. Percy S. Flippin, *Herschel V. Johnson of Georgia: State Rights Unionist* (Richmond, 1931), 192–93; *Journal of the Public and Secret Proceedings of the Convention . . .* (Milledgeville, Ga., 1861), 46.

93. New York *Times*, February 5, 1861.

94. As part of the reorganization deemed necessary to establish the "Republic of Mississippi," Jefferson Davis one week earlier had been commissioned major general of the forces being mustered into service. Intimidation was real; following Lincoln's election secessionist newspapers in the state "poured out volleys of abuse" upon opponents in "almost every county"; unionists found themselves almost overwhelmed and driven from their course by the fury of secessionist pressure. Churches played a significant role in stifling opposition as ministers proclaimed the justice of the secession cause. "Such words as 'submissionist,' and even the unendurable epithet of 'coward,' were applied to those who hesitated to resist." Percy L. Rainwater, *Mississippi: Storm Center of Secession, 1856–1861* (Baton Rouge, 1938), 172–75; John Fulton, *Memoirs of Frederick A. P. Barnard* (1896), in James W. Silver, ed., *Mississippi in the Confederacy: As Seen in Retrospect* (Baton Rouge, 1961), 16–17; Richard A. McLemore, ed., *History of Mississippi* (2 vols., Hattiesburg, Miss., 1973), I, 446, 447.

95. Sitting in special session following the governor's January 8 message urging reorganization of the militia, the Tennessee legislature rescinded on January 31 an 1857 statute which had abolished the militia requirement. During discussion of two bills—senate bill No. 9 and house bill No. 17—suggestions were made to appropriate $500,000 for military expenses, but no appropriation appeared in the final act; however, the governor was authorized to raise three artillery companies as well as to reorganize the militia. Three other bills, which failed to pass, also related to the defense of the state. *Tenn. Acts*, 1861, Extra Sess., Ch. XII; *Tenn. House Journal*, 1861, Extra Sess., 141; *Tenn. Senate Journal*, 1861, Extra Sess., 69, 73, 87, 108, 114, 117, 135–36.

96. Concerned for the safety of his regiment on Moultrie, Maj. Robert Anderson moved to Ft. Sumter during the night of December 26; on January 9 the *Star of the West*, attempting to resupply that garrison, was fired upon and driven off. Nevins, *Emergence of Lincoln*, II, 367, 380.

97. *Cong. Globe*, 36 Cong., 2 Sess., 310.

98. A speech delivered "at a public meeting, held at Seyle's, in Charleston, S. C. October 5, 1832." *Niles' Register*, December 1, 1832, pp. 222–25; J. Fred Rippy, *Joel R. Poinsett, Versatile American* (Durham, N. C., 1935), 140–44.

99. From a speech to the Georgia legislature, November 14, 1860. Henry Cleveland, *Alexander H. Stephens, in Public and Private* (Philadelphia, 1866), 699.

100. Shakespeare, *King Henry VI*, Pt. II, Act III, sc. 2; "secession" is substituted for "injustice."

101. Addison's *Cato*, Act I, sc. 1.

102. Although Wigfall was to have replied immediately, the Senate postponed his speech until the following morning, when the Texan accused Johnson of being a spokesman for "Black Republicanism"—a man who professed love for the Union while his every utterance served to destroy it. *Cong. Globe*, 36 Cong., 2 Sess., 772–73, 781–91.

From Austin Packard[1]

No. 139 Maiden Lane
New York. Febry. 6. 1861

Dear Sir

Government to be useful to the People, must be progressive, it cannot stand still if it does it rusts out, if it does not cease in some other way.

Ours above all others, should be progressive and evry inducement should be held out to the young men of this land to settle and occupy the land and become tillers of the Soil.

We are now spending millions through the War department, on our frontier to keep hostile tribes from killing the white men & women. can not this money be spent for a better purpose than in keeping an army and have all the Officers thereof only drilling men & not teaching young men some good purpose?

I propose in short to create a School for young men, to learn them the art of farming on the Frontiers, and pay them say 8 $ per month some what on the Principle of the West Point School. Educate to fight as well as directing the Army[.]

Make Farm stations between the Missip. River and California on Each of which place say 1000 young men between 17 and 25 years of Age for say 3 years, and each year have an Examination and those that pass out with honor give them 160 acres of Land the title to be in them when they have occupied it and improved it for 5 years. These young men to be under a Farming & Military Education[.]

The young men who shall be competent for a scholarship shall have a certain degree of Education and each Member of Congress shall have the right of recommending from his District a certain number of young men and the senators a certain number from the state[.]

With a line of Schools, from the West, to California and branches north and South through our unsettled Wilderness we can dispense with an Army at the West as the *Natives* might be taught to culti-vate the soil by these Schools.

I will not try to picture the Effect it would have upon our Western wilderness to have it settled by Farme[r]s so Educated.

They would be a class of men generally known to one another and many young men who can find nothing to do would find this a way of life to their good[.]

Your Respectfully
Austin Packard

Mr Johnson U. S.

ALS, DLC-JP.

1. Austin Packard, who dealt in stoves, lived in Brooklyn. *Trow's New York City Directory* (1861–62), 660.

From Thomas Shankland[1]

New York Feby 6. 1861

My Dear Sir,

I rejoice, with thousands that your voice is again heard, rebuking Treason in Secession and I am only sorry that you should be reduced to the low necessity of noticing such a man as Joe Lane. The public mind, has been so long familiarized with the Cry of Secession and the venerable Chief Magistrate[2] so tender and tolerant of Traitors, that Treason ceases to be considered a Crime, and men rush into it for rank and respectability[.] Our valient old friend, the Great Shepherd of Texas,[3] writes me that he is for the Union, but he is in great tribu-lation surrounded by Traitors, and must be prostrated by clamours for Secession[.] In my correspondence for the Northern Newspa-pers,[4] I have endeavoured to do you justice, and hope, if you hold on your course corageously, that you may yet have the power to punish Traitors, and put down Treason & Secession[.] Geo Jones[5] & myself have been running you for the Presidency silently, for many years, and if Jehovah, who raises up one, and putteth down another[6] is only on our side, we shall yet see you in the White House. Would you not encourage the growth of Hemp?[7]

I think the Senate should elect a new Sergt. at Arms, and if you Hamlin & Preston King[8] would set about it quietly you could elect me. Why not? I am immensely poor, and in that position, I could do something for my country.[9] Excuse the liberty I have taken and believe me sincerely

                                    Your friend   Thos Shankland
Hon. Andrew Johnson Washington D C

ALS, DLC-JP.

1. Shankland (*fl*1869) was an attorney residing at 1405 Broadway. *Trow's New York City Directory* (1859–60), 772; Shankland to Johnson, June 28, 1869, Johnson Papers, LC.
2. President Buchanan.
3. Sam Houston, onetime president of the Republic of Texas and later U. S. senator.
4. Not found.
5. Former Congressman George W. Jones of Fayetteville. See *Johnson Papers*, I, 20*n*.
6. A paraphrase of Ps. 75:7.
7. A figurative reference to the hanging of traitors. Mathews, *Americanisms*, I, 795.
8. Senators Hannibal Hamlin of Maine and Preston King of New York. For Hamlin, see *Johnson Papers*, III, 112*n*; for King, I, 461*n*.
9. Shankland later served as U. S. consul to Port Louis, Mauritius (December, 1861–January, 1863). *Senate Ex. Journal*, XII (1861–62), 3, 25; XIII (1862–63), 32.

From Return J. Meigs

                                    Nashville, Feby. 7, 1861.

My Dear Sir

How shall I ever reward you as you deserve for the crushing blows you dealt upon the recreant heads of that arch-betrayer, Slidell, and that ChristKiller, Benjamin, as they slunk out of the Senate, ineffaceably marked with the brand of deceit and trason?[1] Of all the decepions, that of Louisiana is the most inexcusable; and then, for her representatives, in the Senat, to accompany the act by an ostentation of sorrow, aggravated the insult, and richly entitled them to the contemptuous Kick, with which you expelled them from the chamber, which has been too long polluted by their presence. They have sealed their fate politically, for ever & ever; and, in due time, will receive a dismissal from the regard of posterity, in the pages of history, as contemptuous as that with which you thrust them forth amidst the derision and scorn of every patriot in the nation.

The response that Tennessee will give day after tomorrow to the interrogatory: —"Union or disunion?"[2]—will give you a forecaste of the gratitude the people have in store for your fidelity to our beloved, but must abused and betrayed country. You have taught men to love you and to call you blessed, who have passed their lives in political hostility and opposition to you. You will be rewarded as a man who has shown himself capable, in the midst of treason and dissension, of sacrifing all party afiliations and ties on the altar of patriotism.

The disunionists here, who hoped for great results from the Legislature, have sustained a disastrous rout;[3] and the result of Saturday's vote will finish them, I trust, for good. We have been made happy here by the news, today, of the result in Virginia,[4] which was celebrated by a salute of 70 guns at 12 o'clock, as an offset to which, the destructionists are now, at sundown, firig one for the secession of Texas.

But I will not occupy your time; I began this to express the obligation of gratitude you have placed me under by your course this winter, and especially by your denunciation of Slidell and Benjamin, for whom I feel the bitterest scorn and contempt.

Truly   R. J. Meigs.

Hon Andrew Johnson:

ALS, DLC-JP.

1. A reference to Johnson's arraignment of the Louisiana senators in his speech of February 5–6.

2. On February 9 Tennesseans were to vote on calling a convention to consider the state's place in the Union.

3. In January, 1861, Governor Harris urged the legislature to strengthen the military by reorganizing the state militia and purchasing arms. Although a military bill passed the senate, it was postponed indefinitely by the house; unionists led by John Bell were credited with its defeat. *Tenn. Senate Journal,* 1861, Extra Sess., 17, 117; *Tenn. House Journal,* 1861, Extra Sess., 207, 217; Parks, *John Bell,* 393.

4. In January the Virginia legislature had passed a bill calling for a convention to consider the state's position on secession. Among the 152 delegates chosen on February 4, only 45 were clearly secessionist, while some 62 were unquestionably unionist. Wooster, *Secession Conventions,* 141–43.

From Fairfield (Iowa) Citizens

February 8, 1861, Fairfield, Iowa; L, DLC-JP.

Tendering their "unfeigned gratitude" for Johnson's patriotism and his "rebuke [of] the rampant treason now abroad in the Land," these "lovers of Our Glorious Union" assure him that "we of the North are not *your* Enemies—nor the Enemies of the South" but rather "stand by the Constitution as it is, and the faithful execution of the laws of the land."

From Henderson W. Johnson[1]

State of Iowa Jasper County
February 8 1861

Dear Cousin Andrew Johnson I take the present oppertunity of riteng to you a few Lines to let you [k]now that I am in the north and

I have six thousand dollars worth of land and I Can sell it and if you are serten that the union will be devieded[.] if so I am a goin to sell & leve the North and go to the South[.] If you please send me a few line and give me your sentiments Concerning the union and I will now whether to sell or not[.] my Father Moses Johnson Nicholas Johnson Washington Johnson my two Brothers[2] are all liven in Tennessee Carter County[.] I left Tennessee in 1849[3] but still I am infavor of my own native Country all the time[.] I am no secessionist[.] god frorbid I ever should be[.] ther are some hear was acquained with aunt Mary[4] and with you when you was a boy[.] there are several of your old Tennessee friends living close neighbor to me[.] so no more at present[.] only remain your friend[.] Direct your letter to Greencastle Jasper County Iowa

Henderson W. Johnson

Andrew Johnson

ALS, DLC-JP.

1. Henderson W. Johnson (b. c1819), a farmer living in Greencastle, Iowa, listed $2,000 in real estate and $375 in personal property in 1860. 1850 Census, Tenn., Carter, 340; 1860 Census, Iowa, Jasper, 886.

2. Moses (b. c1788), a mail carrier, and Nicholas (b. c1828), a carpenter, were natives of North Carolina. Probably "Washington" was the middle name of the North Carolina-born Moses Johnson (b. c1831), obviously the son of the elder Moses, found in the census. 1850 Census, Tenn., Carter, 340, 347; 1860 Census, Tenn., Carter, 120.

3. Henderson erred about the date of his departure, inasmuch as he, his wife, Jane C. Humphries of Carter, whom he had married in either 1841 or 1844, and their three children—Hester A., Nicholas, and John R.—along with Henderson's twenty-two-year-old brother Nicholas, were enumerated in the Carter County census of 1850. Hugh B. Johnston, Jr., Wilson, N. C., to Andrew Johnson Project, February 18, 28, 1973; 1850 Census, Tenn., Carter, 340.

4. Mary Johnson Daughtry, Andrew's mother. *Johnson Papers*, I, 3n.

From John W. Richardson[1]

Smyrna Tenn. Feby 8. 1861

Private
Dear Sir—

I take this opportunity, which I ought to have done sooner, to return you my sincere thanks for a copy of your speech, made 18, & 19th Dec. last.

Heretofore, on questions then of party character, I stood opposed to you in many particulars, which are doubtless known to you— All these things have passed away, or at any rate are overshadowed by the tremendous and vital issue now before the American People.

Union or Disunion is now the question. It cannot—it must not—it shall not be disguised. On this question I stand with you—doubting perhaps the policy of some expression & yet firmly persuaded that the time has come when the Sentinels whom the people have placed on the watch tower of the Citadel of Liberty[2] ought to speak out. Your speech has had a good effect. No speech has ever been more generally read, & none more severly & more unjustly criticized. The people—the real people—the men who labor—who stay at home and attend to their business are with you— The politicians—Street talkers—demagogues—Secessionists &C &C—are generally against you. I am sorry to say that much the greater portion of the Leaders, oracles; *talkers* of your old friends (party friends I mean) are opposed to you, and fight you with a vengeance even more desperate than they used to fight the Whig party. When they attack me, I reply to them, "He is not my Dog, *but you can't answer his speech* and whenever you can find a man who can & will agree to do it, *I'll be there to see*." They can't answer it— They misrepresent you & reply to that— They make a man of straw and have a glorious time in demolishing him. We had a hard time in the Legislature, but thank God, the Union men whipt the Seceders out of their boots, and Completely unhorsed his Excellency.[3]

Things were not done up just as we desired, but taking every thing into consideration we done nobly. The signs are that the people will not call a convention. This is a trick as I honestly believe to catch the unsuspecting, & altho' if a majority of the Delegates to the Convention (should one be ordered) be Union men, good may grow out of it— Yet I am afraid of it. I only voted to submit the call with the understanding that the action of the convention would be submitted the people. This requisition is not binding on the Convention, but I think they will not disregard it.

One suggestion I desire to make to you is this— If an adjustment is agreed upon, have it submitted directly to the people at their ballot box— Let the people vote directly for the adjustment or against it. On this view of the subject I tell our people there is no need for a Convention—at any rate, not until they themselves see the adjustment & endorse it. *All* the Secessionists & *some* union men are for a Convention— I fear these Conventions— they are the work of our enemies—and to my vision they are much like the Grecian Horse which destroyed Troy and robd. her of her liberties. In the language of the Roman, I am constrained to speak of these conventions, as he did of Grecian presents "Timeo Danaos, donas [*sic*] ferentes".[4] They may be gifts—peace councils—but they have not so appeared to me. Tennessee is passing through a fiery ordeal. All sorts of tricks and strategy are resorted to, to precipitate her into secession— If an adjustment is agreed upon by the border States at Washington,

North & South, we can save her from secession— If not, I fear all
is gone—

Vry Respectfully   Jno. W. Richardson

Hon. A. Johnson

ALS, DLC-JP.

  1. John W. Richardson (1809–1872), Virginia-born physician, was a
prominent Rutherford County Whig who served in the Tennessee house
(1843–47, 1851–53, 1857–59) and senate (1847–49, 1859–61). President
of both local and state medical societies and a crusader against "quacks and
nostrum venders," he also published numerous political and religious pamphlets. In 1860 his combined property was worth $54,000. Robison, *Prelimi-
nary Directory, Rutherford*, 46; 1860 Census, Tenn., Rutherford, 76; Philip
M. Hamer, *The Centennial History of the Tennessee State Medical Association*
(Nashville, 1930), 188–89.
  2. Johnson had used the same metaphor in his Speech on the Seceding
States, February 5–6, 1861, note 91.
  3. Governor Isham G. Harris.
  4. "I fear the Greeks, even when bringing gifts." The *Aeneid*, Bk. II, l. 49.
Stevenson, *Quotations*, 838.

From Benjamin Rush

February 8, 1861, Philadelphia, Pa.; ALS, DLC-JP.

Philadelphia lawyer and Democratic leader commends Johnson for his
patriotic course and suggests that Congress commemorate Washington's
birthday by a reading of the "Farewell Address" before a joint session,
by the printing of a million copies "in a handsome Pamphlet, on good
paper and with good type, *for distribution among the American People*,
as a rich gift from Congress . . . at this great crisis in the Nations
History," and by sponsoring local gatherings "of fifty or a hundred,"
at which the "Address" would be read. [Unsuccessful at this time, Rush
was instrumental a year later in getting Philadelphia support for a
resolution which Johnson introduced; see Resolution on Washington's
Birthday Celebration, February 11, 1862. *Cong. Globe*, 37 Cong., 2
Sess., 738.]

From C. H. Mills[1]

Hon Andrew Johnson   Cleveland East Ten
Washington D. C.   Feby 10th 61

Dear Sir

  You will have received no doubt before this reaches you, the gratifying intelligence: that Tennessee stands firm to her Constitutional
obligations: and means to resist Republican Encroachments within
the Union and in the Nations Capitol; It is now apparent that "No
Convention" will Carry in this state;[2] this action of Tennessee is
mainly attributable to the action of the Georgia and Alabama Conventions in refusing to refer their Secession Ordinance to the people;[3]

  The Southern border Counties of this state you will perceive have voted largely for "no Convention;" the sympathy and free interchange of sentiment between the people on the border has produced this result;[4]

they were fearfull that the same outrageouse disregard for the spoken will of the people in Georgia would characterise their Convention should they Elect One; In this I think they acted wisely; in veiw of the Commission sent by the Legislature to meet the Border states at Washington[.]

Bradly County Elects No Convention and Union Candidats by 1400 Maj. Hamilton McMinn. Polk and Rhea. votes *almost* unanimouse for the Union;[5]

A dispatch was received here last night from Mess Douglass and Crittenden with great Enthusiasm and joy, it was sent from Nashville— the people hail with unspeakable delight, anything promising settlement of the greviouse troubles that now surround Our Country;

The terrible blows you have dealt the Traitors, North & South have done much to restore Confidence and Courage to the true Men here and Elsewhere:— Boligny of La. has immortalised himself:[6] a reaction is dawning upon us that will hurl into merited oblivion: the Men who have forced this terrible crisis upon the Country— It is rumored here this Morning that a hostile Meeting is arranging between yourself and Wigfall:[7] in Gods name have no meeting with such a vagabond:—to Kill him would give you no credit: for him to Kill you would be a National Calamity, and to die at the hands of *such* a *Man* on the *field of honor* would be Esteemed by your Friends as a dishonorable death; The Nation has a better use for you, and need of your services;

Is there no hope of the Republicans *in Congress* yeilding to Compromise? Will we be Compelled to appeal to the people of the North? that Cannot be done by the 4th March: Is there no Argument potent Enough to bring Congressmen to their senses and yeild something for the honor and safety of their Country? The disunionist are taunting us Every day by quoting Expressions of Republican Members: There *must* be Something done very speedily to allay at least this bitter animosity, untill the people of the North can be reached through the ballot Box; I have no fears about the result if the people are allowed to Express their will: the great danger is that we may be precipitated before that Can be had; The disunionist are defeated, but they will work more unceasing to accomplish their design than Ever; They have Entered the wedge and they will continue to strike untill the Maul is wrested from their hands;[8]— Excuse this lengthy Epistle and tax upon your patience;

Yours Truly   C. H. Mills

ALS, DLC-JP.

1. C. H. Mills (b. *c*1824), a Maryland native, was at this time a Cleveland merchant and life insurance agent with real and personal property valued at $32,000. 1860 Census, Tenn., Bradley, Cleveland, 6th Dist., 7; *Mitchell's Tenn. State Gazetteer* (1860–61), 43.

2. The February 9 referendum for a state convention had failed, 69,387–57,798. Campbell, *Tenn. Attitudes*, 175.

3. There is no evidence to support this assertion. In both Georgia and Alabama the legislature had provided for conventions after the election of Lincoln. It is true, however, that in neither case was the secession ordinance submitted to a referendum. Walter L. Fleming, *Civil War and Reconstruction in Alabama* (New York, 1905), 27–37; Flippin, *Herschel V. Johnson*, 161–90 *passim*.

4. Once again Mills's explanation is debatable, but a more serious flaw is the inaccuracy of his facts. True, the four East Tennessee southern border counties had overwhelmingly opposed a convention, voting 4,028–1,140, yet only three other border counties (McNairy, Hardin, and Wayne) had voted anticonvention majorities, the remaining seven casting decisive votes for convention. Campbell, *Tenn. Attitudes*, 288–90.

5. This assessment is accurate, save for Polk County, where the contest was close.

County	For Convention	Against Convention
Bradley	242	1,443
Hamilton	455	1,445
McMinn	439	1,457
Polk	335	389
Rhea	79	573

The decisiveness of the Union victory is shown in figures which Mills himself reported to the Nashville *Banner*; according to his dispatch, two Bradley County unionist candidates led their disunionist opponents 1,109–163 and 1,103–162. *Ibid.*, 288; Nashville *Republican Banner*, February 12, 1861.

6. John E. Bouligny (1824–1864), a New Orleans lawyer elected to the 36th Congress (1859–61) on the American ticket, was strongly opposed to secession and became the only member of Louisiana's delegation to retain his seat after the state left the Union. *BDAC*, 576.

7. Following Louis Wigfall's February 7 castigation of Johnson for his speech in reply to Lane, the New York *Herald* circulated the rumor of an impending rencounter between the senators. Several of Johnson's correspondents expressed concern over the potential threat to his life. New York *Herald*, February 8, 1861.

8. A figure of speech stemming from log splitting. Mathews, *Americanisms*, II, 1036.

From Joseph H. Thompson[1]

Shelbyville Tennessee
Febry 10 1861—

Dear Sir

The election in Tennessee is now over and the returns thus far received, indicate that the state has gone overwhelmingly against the proposed Convention— If mistaken in this I am positive that but few (if any) secessionists have been elected[.]

This county (Bedford) has given a majority of one thousand

votes against the Convention[2]—but should other portions of the State successfully favour it we will be represented therein by M P Gentry Edmund Cooper & Jas S. Scudder everyone of whom are Union men[3] and will go there under the strongest anti-secession pledges[.] Gentry has laboured manfully for the Union but took strong for a convention urging that Tennessee could speak more effectively in that manner. The people thought differently however, and whilst the election of yesterday very forcibly demonstrated their attachment to the Union, it also disclosed their unwillingness to place it in the power of any Convention to vote them out of it by an ordinance of secession. Tennessee has indeed spoken in thunder tones and may we not hope that her voice will aid in hastening an adjustment of our difficulties? Her language of yesterday cannot be misunderstood. She has spoken and has spoken well. She has shown that she loves the Union and that the glorious memories which linger around its past achievements have not been forgotten. That the injunctions of Jackson are still cherished and that Treason & Rebellion can find no home or hiding place in Tennessee. Even more than this she has done. She has endorsed the course of her living patrot and statesman Andrew Johnson, and has said to him—well done thou good & faithful servant. Glorious Tennessee long may you remain a terror to Traitors and Rebels.

Much anxiety is felt here because of a probable difficulty between yourself & Wigfall of Texas. May it not [be] avoided. Your friends every where would deeply regret to see you placed in a position where the slightest harm might befall you. I can but indulge the hope that the difficulty if any exists may be adjusted in a peaceful mode.

Your dispatch to me on yesterday[4] giving assurances of a speedy compromise has inspired the union men with just hopes and in their behalf I thank you for it[.] A dispatch was seen here on yesterday purporting to be from Hon James H Thomas[5] declaring that all hopes were gone[.] I trust the despatch was *bogus* and that that gentleman would not be guilty of sending such dispatches to the Union loving state of Tennessee. With assurances of the highest regard I am &c &   Respectfully   Jos. H Thompson
Hon Andrew Johnson
Washington D C[6]

ALS, DLC-JP.

1. Joseph H. Thompson (b. c1831) was a Shelbyville attorney and county clerk. Deane Porch, tr., *1850 Census, Bedford County, Tennessee* (Nashville, 1968), 110; *Goodspeed's Bedford*, 868.

2. The vote was actually 828 for and 1,656 against. Campbell, *Tenn. Attitudes*, 288.

3. Ultimately, Gentry, Johnson's former gubernatorial rival, abandoned his unionism and served two terms in the Confederate Congress; Cooper

(1821–1911), a Shelbyville lawyer and legislator (1849–51, 1865), adhered to the Union, was later elected to Congress (1866–67) and appointed assistant secretary of the treasury (1867–69); Scudder (b. *c*1824) was a Shelbyville lawyer. *BDAC*, 735, 937; Robison, *Preliminary Directory, Bedford*, 14; Porch, *1850 Census, Bedford*, 109. For Gentry, see *Johnson Papers*, I, 366*n*.

4. Not found.

5. James H. Thomas (1808–1876), North Carolina-born Columbia lawyer and former law partner of James K. Polk, served as state attorney general (1836–42) and congressman (1847–51, 1859–61), resuming his law practice in Columbia during the war. *BDAC*, 1704.

6. Envelope endorsement: "Speech sent / 50 more to be sent—*Attended to*."

From Joseph R. Armstrong[1]

Rogersville Tenn Febry. 11th 1861.

Hon A Johnson,
Dear Sir.

Thinking you would [be] pleased to hear the election news of old Hawkins on the 9th I hasten to give it you. The Union ticket has carried every civil district in the county except one, and that is Mooresburg. The majority for no convention Netherland Kyle and Sevier[2] is between fifteen and sixteen hundred, a perfect Waterloo defeat for the secessionists.[3] Your late speech has made hundreds of votes for the union ticket not only in our county but all over the State. You have no political enemies with us now except in the secession ranks, such men as Riley Bynum the Powels[4] and other leaders in the defuncked Breckenridge party. the people are with you and will stand by you & Nelson Crittnden[5] and all other Conservative Statesman until the end of your earthly pilgrimage, and that is long enough[.] If you succeed in a proper settlment of our preasant difficulties—opposition to yourself and Nelson hereafter will be entirely useless. Your frinds without distinction of party were very anxious that you should have been with us during our late elections[.] the thing would still been worse for the secessionists.—

The people are anxious for Nelsons late speech.[6] he must frank a goodly number. to the people, Since writing the above I have hea[r]d from 4 districts in Hancock Co which gives the secession ticket but three votes out of about 300,[7] enought of this for the present in haste

Your friend   Jo R Armstrong

ALS, DLC-JP.

1. Joseph R. Armstrong (b. *c*1818), a Hawkins County justice of the peace with an estate valued at $2,000, later became clerk of the county court (1870–86). 1860 Census, Tenn., Hawkins, 10th Dist., 14; *Goodspeed's East Tennessee*, 880.

2. John Netherland, prominent Whig lawyer elected as a Union candidate in the February canvass, participated in the Knoxville and Greeneville conventions and was appointed one of the commissioners to present to the General Assembly East Tennessee's demand for separation. In 1864 he became a Democrat, remaining with that party until his death. William C. Kyle (b. 1813), Hawkins County farmer and slave trader of substantial means—$70,000 personal and real property in 1860—was elected as a Union candidate in February and later attended the Greeneville convention. "Sevier" is possibly James S. Sevier (1840–1909), proprietor of the Washington Hotel in Rogersville. Temple, *Notable Men*, 164–65; Temple, *East Tennessee*, 171, 353, 354; *Johnson Papers*, I, 617*n*; 1860 Census, Tenn., Hawkins, 10th Dist., 29; *Goodspeed's East Tennessee*, 1230; Acklen, *Tenn. Records*, I, 234.

3. Netherland, Kyle, and Sevier triumphed over their opponents 1,734–385, 1,742–384, and 1,770–38. Nashville *Republican Banner*, February 19, 1861.

4. Both John D. Riley and John G. Bynum (b. *c*1831) were Hawkins countians, the one a farmer and prominent Democrat, the other a young bachelor with real and personal property worth $140,000. It is difficult to ascertain the identity of "the Powels" to whom Armstrong refers. Samuel Powel, Hawkins County pioneer, judge, and congressman, was the progenitor of three sons, all of whom, by 1860, were prominent in the community; George R., a successful lawyer and former state legislator; Samuel, Jr., subsequently a Confederate colonel; and Robert D., editor of the Rogersville *Sentinel* and later a lieutenant in the 19th Tenn. Inf., CSA. *Johnson Papers*, I, 512*n*; II, 70*n*; III, 257*n*, 413*n*; 1860 Census, Tenn., Hawkins, 6th Dist., 152.

5. T. A. R. Nelson and John J. Crittenden.

6. On January 25 Nelson, in urging passage of the Crittenden resolutions, had expressed the sentiments of most Tennessee unionists. *Cong. Globe*, 36 Cong., 2 Sess., App. 106–11; Campbell, *Tenn. Attitudes*, 167–70.

7. Hancock County rejected the convention by a vote of 746–100. For convention delegates, unionists outpolled secessionists: Netherland (Union) 746; Kyle (Union) 744; Powel (Secession) 93; Arnold (Secession) 97. *Ibid.*, 288; Nashville *Republican Banner*, February 19, 1861.

From Richard M. Edwards

Cleveland Tenn Febry 11th 1861

Hon A. Johnston U. S. S.

Dear Sir:

I learn with regret that you are about to place yourself in a false position by meeting bully Wigfal on the field, of what fools call Honor— I emphatically say to you that the sentiment of all the Union loving men in Tennessee is that you should do no such thing. We have use for you in a higher capacity than that of Killing dogs. We need the services of all good men now, for God Knows they are getting scarce: and we can not consent for any of them to place themselves on an equality with ruffians in order that they may be ingloriously sacrificed to the gratification of bad men & their country's loss— No code of true Honor requires you to meet Wigfall. They might as well require you to meet a bull dog with teeth & claws because you had tramped on his toe, as to meet a regular duellist who has learned his trade in violation of all laws both human & divine.[1] No sir; the time for dog Killing has not yet arrived. When that time comes we will have hemp to do the work with; and it can be done without exposing the lives of good men.

Before this reaches you, you will have heard the glorious news from the land of Jackson Polk & Grundy.[2] I Know it will do you good & I wish I could be there [to] rejoice with the few good men who remain firm to duty.

Douglas & Crittenden dispatched to Wm H Polk that if we saved Tennessee the Union would be saved;[3] and we have responded to that dispatch with as I now believe 50,000 maj—

I Know the response will be a death Knell to Disunion while it also will carry gladness & joy to those noble men still true to duty it matters not where they may be.

The traitors in the seceding states were too smart to submit the ordinance of Secession to the people. We would have been treated the same way had we not Killed the thing at the start.

Gov Harris is buried so deep that no political resurrection horn can ever toot him up. You could be elected Gov now by 40.000 majority if you desired the place.

Your Speech has had a powerful effect on traitors here; we beat them about 1400 votes in this county.[4] Rowles & smith[5] have denounced your speech and have been overwhelmed; and although Smith has always been my friend yet *he deserved it*[.]

I have shown the foregoing to several who have always been your friends and they all endorse the Sentiment[.]

Send me a few of your late speeches in reply to Lane and others.

I may be in Washington in a few days; but can not yet say certainly how soon.

Your friend as in days of old
R. M. Edwards

ALS, DLC-JP.

1. Wigfall's "monomania" for dueling was well known. After the heated presidential campaign of 1840, he had engaged in two duels, as well as killing the nephew of one of his antagonists in self-defense. Firmly committed to the *code duello*, he fought no other duels, although he had faced several near engagements during college years and served as a second on at least one occasion. Alvey L. King, *Louis T. Wigfall: Southern Fire-eater* (Baton Rouge, 1970), 11–12, 21, 29–34.

2. A reference to Tennessee's unionist victory on the convention-no convention vote.

3. In an effort to bolster Union sentiment, Polk had solicited a telegram from John J. Crittenden and Stephen A. Douglas; this dispatch, dated February 5, appeared in the Nashville *Patriot* Extra the following day.

4. The Bradley County vote was 242–1,443. Campbell, *Tenn. Attitudes*, 288.

5. Both George W. Rowles and Samuel A. Smith, in whose office Edwards had studied law, cast their lot with the Confederacy. Although Rowles spoke against secession, when the state seceded he fled to Georgia and later to Alabama, returning to Chattanooga after the war. Smith, former congressman and briefly commissioner of the general land office (January–February, 1860), became a Confederate officer. Wooten, *Bradley County*, 160, 161; *Johnson Papers*, I, 413n; III, 588n, 447n.

From Charles O. Faxon

Jeffersonian Office
Clarksville Tenn Feb. 11 1861

Gov Johnson: —

The great news from Tennessee has of course reached you by telegraph before you read this[.] Tennessee has proved true to herself —to the Union and to you[.] The secessionists have been litterally overwhelmed[.]

Our returns from the State are yet meagre but enough is know[n] to show that the Union party have swept like an avalanche over the State. In this county our average majority is about 1800. The Convention Carries by about 1200.[1] The Union Men would have voted down the Convention but they were fearful that Gov Harris would call for another, and that it might happen that in a greater excitement than at present exists a Convention might be elected composed of men infected with the secession epidemic[.] For that reason they went for the Convention now and Gov Harris is Check mated. The Union maj[ority] in the State will almost defy computatin[.] So far as heard from the disunionists have carried but a single precinct. The Union and American Stands rebuked and damned before the people of the State[.] Threre is great anxiety here to see the official report of your last speech[.] Send me a lot for circulation.

Very Respectfully Your obt Servt
C. O. Faxon

ALS, DLC-JP.

1. Montgomery County voted 1,611–389. Campbell, *Tenn. Attitudes*, 289.

From B. M. McFarland[1]

Oakhall Weakeley Co Tenn Feb. 11, 61

Hon Andrew Johnson
Dear Sir—"There is a tide in every mans life if taken at the flood leades on to fortune"[2]

To you that *tide* is now—
Your generosity indused you to Send your Speach of the 13[*sic*]
Dec last to *blanke*
I got one and drank it as coolin *nectar*.
Was called on for a Speach at the poles for convention the 9th In—
I had all the news, with your able patrotick Speach for a data—
Began with the formation of thiss republick[.]
Showed Washingtons viewes and acts as to Pensyllveaney's resitance
of tax—
Showed Jeffison Madeson & Jacksons views as to the right of Ses-
sion—
Proved if Seporation took place Slavery was abolished— Adverted
to Garresons tratorous asertion that our constatution was a "covanat
with the grave and a leage with hell[.]"[3]
Showed that the mos effectual meanes to free negrows was to destroy
the constatution— Said the 4 Milions of Servile Slaves were now by
Southern fiereators reduced half— Showd a loss by that of 15 Milions at least to Slave owner— Thanked God that you whom I had
fought with had come out for your country[.]
Said you was imortal that I had written you to that effect—
Proved John A. Gardners[4] inconcistency[.]
He Said 5 monthes agoe he was for the union now against it & would
put his male negrows in front of battle, Showed he was recreant to
himself & the South[.]
Showed Lincons powerless condition & proved that no Sane man
wanted to Sweep from himself 15 States[.]
Shoed Yanceys subtra fuge—[5]
Adverted to Mexico for a Sampel of the Southeren confederacy [to]
prove the South could not be respected by other powers nor could
not bear the taxes of a Seperate Confederacy—
Told them 887 226 nothern men were for us.[6] Showed by a Separation they would become our enemames & then ower negrows would
not be worth a *read*[reed]—
Showed of all governments anarchy was most to be dreaded[.]
Proved that t[h]is was the best goverment on earth— Said the people
would do right if unexcited by demagogus and humbug clap-trap
office Seakeor[.] videcated Critendons resolution[.]
Asserted that the South had all to lose & nothing to gane[.]
She now rithed under opression reduction of property high taxes and
Stopage of trad[.] Showed the mutial conection betwen north and
South— Ast if they to pleas a fiew hotheaded Garresons & Yanceys
woul[d] ruin this great nation & drench it with fraternal *Blood*[.]
Adverted to the restrictions which Louisania migh[t] put on the
navegation the Missippi—

Ast [w]hat good would they accomplis by brakeing down the bes[t] govermet on earth—

Appealed to patrioticke fathers north & South— Showed but fiew negrows had excaped[.] Proved that Buckhanon had ordered and forsed mobes to give them up[.][7]

Showed that the negrow was Secure to his owner & they had lost thousands by the fuss[.]

Proved Southern Senators & representatives in congress had without cause agetated that vexed question and brought on the crices[.]

Will not det[a]in you longer but take backe all I have Said and written against you[.]

Adding Johnson is as noble a Tennessean as any[.] My talke came off with universal applase[.]

in hasete yours B. M McFarland

P. S. Will be in Nashville at the convention[.][8]

My home adress is Dresden Ten

The Union Ticket has carried in this the county of Weakley by about 1000 magority[.][9] Rogers & Somers elected by the above magority —[10]

Respectfully   B M McFarland

Isaac Williams[11] elected in Henry county union ticket carried by [illegible] majority[.]

Milton Brown beaten in the Carter district.[12]

B M M—

ALS, DLC-JP.

1. B. M. McFarland (c1803–fl1875), a delegate to the Whig state convention of 1840 and a successful farmer with real and personal property valued at $28,000, was a unionist. He later lived in Humboldt, Gibson County. 1860 Census, Tenn., Weakley, 161; B. M. McFarland to Johnson, October 10, 1873, January 26, 1875, Johnson Papers, LC.

2. An inexact quotation from Shakespeare, *Julius Caesar*, Act IV, sc. 3.

3. During his speech at a July 4, 1854, celebration in Framingham, Massachusetts, William Lloyd Garrison had dramatically burned a copy of the Constitution, which he termed a "covenant with death, and an agreement with hell." *The Liberator*, July 7, 1854.

4. John A. Gardner (1809–1892), lifelong Democrat and a leader of the Weakley County bar for over fifty years, had briefly edited two partisan papers, the Paris *West Tennessean* (1827) and the Dresden *Jacksonian* (1838), was state senator (1841–47), and supported secession in 1861. Following the war, he served as delegate to the constitutional convention of 1870 and as state representative (1879–81). Robison, *Preliminary Directory, Weakley*, 10–11; Nashville *Union and American*, February 17, 1861; Joshua W. Caldwell, *Sketches of Bench and Bar of Tennessee* (Knoxville, 1898), 331–34.

5. It is difficult to determine what aspect of Yancey's behavior prompted the allegation of "subtra fuge." To contemporaries of a unionist persuasion, he was a figure of intrigue and perfidy. Perhaps McFarland expatiated on Yancey's role in the disruption of the Democratic party, perhaps on his insistence—so insidious in the eyes of a unionist—that peaceful secession was possible, perhaps on the Alabamian's claim that he was a unionist, yet "only

under terms that he knew could never be met." Hesseltine, *Three against Lincoln*, 276; Nevins, *Emergence of Lincoln*, I, 415ff; II, 41, 334.

6. The source of this figure is a mystery. It bears no relationship to any part or combination of the 1860 northern popular vote which might be identified as "for us."

7. It would be interesting to see what evidence this earnest advocate presented for such a sweeping statement. That the Buchanan administration rigidly enforced the Fugitive Slave Act, despite increasing difficulties posed by northern personal liberty laws, is a well-documented fact; that the Old Public Functionary "ordered and forsed mobes" to surrender represents history which has apparently escaped students of the subject. For a discussion of Buchanan's policy, see Campbell, *Slave Catchers*, 107–9.

8. Since the state rejected a convention, no meeting was held. Campbell, *Tenn. Attitudes*, 290.

9. McFarland, in accord with Charles O. Faxon and contrary to most of Johnson's correspondents, saw a vote in favor of a convention as a unionist expression. Weakley County voted 1,472–483 for the convention. *Ibid.*

10. Job W. Rogers (1832–*fl*1887), a prominent physician, and John Somers (1827–*fl*1887), attorney and judge of the twelfth chancery division (1860), both of Dresden and both successful unionist candidates in this election, appear to have parted company during the war, Rogers serving for one year as assistant surgeon, 32nd Tenn. Vols., CSA, and Somers pursuing a course which led to his being commissioned by Governor Brownlow in 1866 as judge of the eleventh division. *Goodspeed's Weakley*, 1013, 1019; Worth S. Ray, *Tennessee Cousins* (Baltimore, 1966), 772; Nashville *Union and American*, February 17, 1861.

11. According to a Memphis paper, Isaac B. Williams (b. *c*1814), a Paris lawyer with property valued at $13,200, lost the February 9 election to secessionist candidate W. B. Travis by seven votes. 1860 Census, Tenn., Henry, 14; Memphis *Appeal*, February 14, 1861.

12. Brown, a former Whig congressman, was a Jackson lawyer. See *Johnson Papers*, I, 367*n*.

From A . Waldo Putnam

TENNESSEE HISTORICAL SOCIETY
Society Rooms, State Capitol,
Nashville, Tennessee, Feby 11th 1861

To Hon: Andw Johnston
Dear Sir

By advice of friends—(without going about to solicit names to a letter of commendation as some have been doing—) I make known to you and to Hon: A. O. P. Nicholson, that I wish my name presented to the President of the incoming Administration, for the situation of *Post Master* in this City.

I beg you to confer with Mr Nicholson,—who has known me intimately for many years.

I have resided here for more than twenty years,—and previously for about fourteen years in Mississippi[.]

My father was in the second immigrant party (from Connecticut and Massachusetts) to the North Western Territory, and I am a native of Ohio: But in Tennessee are all my worldly interests, and here were formed the most cherished ties of this life: My first and second wives were *grand-daughters* of *Govr. Sevier,*—the first Gov. of Tennessee: (And to his memory I have done what the State should have done—erected that beautiful Marble Cenotaph in the Nashville Cemetery.[1]) During the ten years past I have devoted much *time* and *money* to the acquisition and preservation of whatsoever appertains to the History of Tennessee[.] The original commission to my Great-grand Father, *Genl. Israel Putnam* is deposited among the many valuable and interesting articles in the Library of the Historical Society of Tennessee—and, besides my son,—I am the only person in all the Southern States, (by direct descent,) bearing the name of that Patriot of the Revolution[.]

You, my Dear Sir, know my character and standing in this community and in the State,—and that in these times of fearful commotion, of fear, of vacilation and of treason, I have contended for 'The Union and our Rights in the Union,' and have written and spoken freely and boldly—as you have nobly and truly done.

I take the liberty to furnish you two of the publications[2] made by me, under my own name, exposing the *absurdity* and *extravagance* of such a 'man of mark' as Gen Pillow: For these and some other publications, in defence of my country, I was *warned* that I should be "spotted," as a traitor to the South, and might get myself into trouble:

But thank God!— None of these things moved me from my integrity and duty to my country.

Thank God a thousand times! Tennessee has not been moved from her propriety; neither terrified, hoodwinked, corrupted or ensnared. . — Today this State stands higher before all enlightened patriots and before the civilized world, and will deserve to transmit her name with brighter glory to future ages—for what she has just endured and accomplished,—than by reason of her military achievements and civil services in the past. . . Glorious Tennessee! Calm, self-possessed independent, firm! The fanaticism of the North, and the despotism of the South, have met here a barrier high, stable and impassable: Here their proud waves are stayed.

The people of Tennessee have believed and *do believe*, that the great majority of people in the non-slave States, are conservative,— lovers of union lovers of concord, law-abiding, trust-worthy *fellow citizens*. The Wendel Phillips and the Yancey-Rhetts—God be praised,—are few indeed,—and *we trust and believe*, (that, like dogs,) "they have had their day."[3]

I can say, that at no time, have I despaired of a fair adjustment, and I have joined with a few christians here in daily prayer to the God of our fathers and our God, to bring order out of confusion, light out [of] darkness, and "restore unto us his Salvation: And 'though the vision tarry, we will wait for it': "Joy will come in the morning"[4] ... Yea the day begins to dawn, and all countenances in Tennessee are radiant with hope & joy.

You will have a jubilant reception on your return,—if the adjustment is made.

I presided at a Union meeting where Mr Wisener of Bedford,[5] your Son *Robert and Mr Bradford*[6] addressed the vast assembly: Party vanished before Patriotism.

My Dear Sir, I submit the manner and time of application in my behalf to the President elect for the P. O.[7]—into your hands in conjunction with your Hon: Colleague. . Be not wearied by letter—or to read my "comments upon *Genl. Pillow's* Letter"

Very Respectfully   A. W. Putnam
To Hon: Andw Johnston U. S. Senate.

ALS, DLC-JP.

1. This shaft, about fifteen feet high, was the first monument to John Sevier in Tennessee. The inscription reads: "Sevier, / Noble and Successful Defender / of the / Early Settlers of Tennessee. / The First and for Twelve Years Governor, / Representative in Congress, / Commissioner in Many Treaties with the Indians, / He Served His Country Forty Years Faithfully and Usefully, / And in That Service Died. / An Admirer of Patriotism and Merit, Unrequited, Erects This." Over this inscription a tomahawk encased in arrows holds up a wreath and crossed swords. As the anonymous author of the ten-page biography of Sevier in Wheeler's *History of North Carolina* (1851), Putnam had also paid homage to his wives' grandfather. Wooldridge, *History of Nashville*, 100–101; Stanley F. Horn, "Introduction to the New Edition," A. W. Putnam, *History of Middle Tennessee* (Knoxville, 1971), vii–viii, x.

2. Presiding at a meeting held Friday night, February 1, at Smith's Hall on Church Street, Putnam had delivered an address favoring preservation of the Union; this speech was probably one of the "publications" forwarded to Johnson. Nashville *Republican Banner*, February 3, 1861.

3. Found both in Homer, *Odyssey*, Bk. XXII, 1.35, and in Shakespeare, *Hamlet*, Act V, sc. 1. Stevenson, *Quotations*, 470.

4. Ps. 30:5: "weeping may endure for a night, but joy cometh in the morning."

5. William H. Wisener (b. *c*1812), lawyer and editor of the Shelbyville *People's Advocate*, was a Whig member of the Tennessee house (1847–49, 1851–55, 1859–61) and a Republican state senator (1864–65). A presidential elector for the Know-Nothings (1856) and the Republicans (1864, 1872), he ran unsuccessfully for governor in 1870 and for Congress four years later. Robison, *Preliminary Directory, Bedford*, 55.

6. William M. Bradford of Jefferson County. *Johnson Papers*, III, 615*n*.

7. Three days later, Putnam wrote again pressing his application for the postmastership. Reiterating his strong unionism and endorsing Johnson's course, he concludes, "You are the *first Democrat* I ever voted for." Subsequently he withdrew his name and supported William McNish. Putnam to Johnson, February 14, March 4, 1861, Johnson Papers, LC.

From John E. Helms

Knoxville, Tenn Feb. 12, 1861

Hon. A. Johnson;

Dear Governor:

You are acquainted by this time, with the result of our late election in Tennessee and have formed a pretty correct idea of the feeling at home. The thing is all right now—the object is to keep it so.

I have my heart still fixed upon the newspaper project that has been discussed by us so often. It seems to me that there is a better opening now, and really more use for an energetic new paper at this point than ever presented before. The Register office could be bought from Bradfield,[1] but at what price I do not know. It is an old fossil that I had much rather some one else would keep up than to attempt to keep up myself.

A new office can be brought out a new paper started upon less capital and much more favorable auspices than to trade for the Register. I do not contemplate any such thing. My idea is to buy new material and start a new neat Union sheet—not as the organ of Andrew Johnson par excellence; but as an honest reflection of Union sentiment in Tennessee and as such, I am sure it could not fail to be a better Johnson paper than is now published in the state.

I am disposed to try the enterprize at once, and energetically if I can meet with assistance sufficient to put the enterprise on a sure footing. Do you still favor such an undertaking? and to what extent can I rely upon you for pecuniary assistance.

Mr. Morrow[2] is the only one of our old friends here who is still true but there is a host of new ones who will aid somewhat, but not to the extent he will.

I send this through Mr. Maynard[3] and hope that your reply may be communicated in a prepaid envelope.[4] I haven't much confidence in the retiring officials.

Hoping to hear from you soon

I am Truly Yours   John E. Helms

P. S.—

Since writing the above I have met Mr. Morrow, and he encloses the following.[5] I hope with your assistance, we can put under way a newspaper institution, creditable to ourselves and of benefit to our state.

ALS, DLC-JP.

1. George W. Bradfield had purchased the Knoxville *Register* in 1859 and conducted it as an anti-Johnson organ. *Johnson Papers*, III, 315*n*.

2. Samuel Morrow (1816–1864), founder of the Exchange and Deposit Bank in Knoxville, and the father of Robert Morrow, later President Johnson's secretary, became sergeant of Co. H, 5th Tenn. Cav., USA. Laura E. Luttrell, tr., *United States Census 1850 for Knox County, Tennessee* (Knoxville, 1940), 51; *Goodspeed's Knox*, 846; WPA, Tenn., Knox: Old Gray Cemetery, 86; *Tenn. Adj. Gen. Report* (1866), 430.

3. Horace Maynard, congressman from Knox County. *Johnson Papers*, III, 286n.

4. Helms, justifiably suspicious of Postmaster Charles W. Charlton, urges Johnson, who normally would have franked his correspondence, to achieve anonymity through a postpaid letter.

5. Morrow wrote: "I have seen and approved of what Helms has written[.] Last September I urgd upon the party to buy out the Register and controll it: as I knew it was damaging the Democratic party by its disunion sentiments. Now to purchase it, with the odium that attaches to it, would be fatal. A new Paper is our only remedy. I will take *an interest in it* as a business man. will if proper means and associates are formed be a *paying* Stockholder. will if left to my controll see that every thing is done not only to make it an efficient organ of the Union Democrats of E Tennessee but a *paying concern* which I beleive can be done[.]" Morrow to Johnson, February 12, 1861, Johnson Papers, LC. See also Morrow to Johnson, February 16, 1861, *ibid*.

From William Lellyett[1]

Nashville, Feb 12, 1861.

Hon. Andrew Johnson:

Dear Sir,

I have just finished the perusal of your last speech in the Senate, and am determined, as a patriotic private citizen, to thank you for the service therein rendered to your country and mine, in an hour of trial and peril. These are not times for empty ceremony; I therefore make no apology for thus addressing you.

Having just been shown a letter from a Union member of the House, in which complaint is made, that *his* speeches have failed to reach their destination through the mails, I venture a suggestion to you, which, if acted upon, may render more efficient your efforts, and those who sympathize heartily with you, to save Tennessee from the hellish machinations of conspirators. I have noticed that Adams's Express[2] is very liberal of its services in forwarding papers and documents. As it is desirable your speech should be read by the masses of the people, could you not send considerable numbers, by that mode of conveyance, to trustworthy men in various portions of the State, for general distribution?

Too many of the Union men in Tennessee are fighting with weak, impotent weapons. If they dare speak the truth, it is muffled with such apologetic *ifs*, *peradventures*, and *contingencies*, as shame the lovers of truth. They fight with blank cartriges—and even these are made of soft material and damp powder. Whenever the piratical

forces of the conspirators shall attempt the capture of Fort Sumter
or Fort Pickens, my impression is, many of our so-called Union men
will be found to be wolves in sheep's clothing. Should the gallant
Anderson, or those in command at Pickens, knock out the brians of
a few traitors, they (the weak Union men) will cry "Murder!" and
throw down the stripes and stars. Others of them are so slenderly
fortified in their position, that should they prove true, all their work
must be done over. We need Stronger back-bone.

You have doubtless been advised by telegraph, and otherwise, of
the great Union victory in Tennessee. But I am persuaded it will only
make the traitors more desperate.

Very Respectfully   W. Lellyett.

ALS, DLC-JP.

1. William Lellyett (c1823–1872), a Pennsylvania native and brother
of John, was a Nashville wholesale grocer and commission merchant, as well
as a printer and editor of the Nashville *News*. 1860 Census, Tenn., Davidson,
Nashville, 1st Ward, 31; *Nashville Bus. Dir.* (1855–56), 70; (1860–61),
212; *Nashville City Cemetery Index*, 48.

2. Proclaiming itself the "Great Southern, Eastern, Northern and Western
Express Forwarders!," the Adams Express advertised the "safe and speedy
transportation of Freight, Money, Jewelry and valuable packages." Presumably Johnson's speeches might, under its aegis, be scattered over Tennessee,
thereby evading interception by "southern" postmasters. Nashville *Union and
American*, February 1, 1861.

From John McCook[1]

Steubenville Feb 12th 1861

Hon Andrew Johnson

Sir— I received your speech forwarded me—for which accept my
thanks—

I have given it a careful reading and as a whole it fully sustains the opinion I had formed of it, from the published newspaper
extracts—

I wish to God it could be read by the masses, for it must work
conviction in any honest heart and prove an antidote for the madness
that seems to threaten the destruction of our Government— In your
efforts to save the Union, Tennessee has lost none of the prestege
acquired in 1832 when her Great National Representative proclaimed "This Union must be preserved"— Your position is in the
Union, not out of it, and if the Border Slave States do not become
restive, and determined to heap burthens upon us too heavy to be
borne you will *obtain* all your *just rights* and every *guarentee* you
ask— The question of nigger once settled, the Republicans North
will have no *stick* to *whittle* and the second sober thoughts of the

people will dispose of them as they ever have done— It is only a question of time, for the Republican Party is already virtually disrupted, and nothing but the precipitate and unjustifiable action of the South can save them from total destruction— — The most respectable portion of the Republicans in this State are conservative and are denouncing Benjamin Wade & Co and if not compelled to stand together by the action of the Border States, their party must go by the board— But if, in the administration of the law the Border States shall unite, and defend the treason of the Gulf States this *Union* is gone—

All our hopes are in the Border States and if they desert us, "peaceble secession or the wager of battle" must settle the difficulty— I am very sor[r]y my old friend Vallandigham is so foolish as to talk about four Republics or of reconstruction,[2] it is a visionary project— there may be two (which I very much doubt) but not more— If Mr. V or any *other gentleman* is giving any comfort to any who would disrupt the Union, that the people of the North will not stand by the Stripes and Stars to the bitter end, *it is not so and they speak with out the record*— The Gulf States in their treasonable conduct, is bringing the people to have but one heart and one mind— —

I say to you Sir—in all frankness that it is the love and respect for the conservative position of the Border States, our love for the Union as our fathers gave it us and our unwillingness to precipitate civil war, has restrained the North from replying to the insults of Miss and Louisiana[.]

If the Government shall make a call upon the patriotism of the North and North West it will be responded to in a becoming man-[n]er— We may be neither "plucky" nor very chivalrous but we are a very stubborn and persistant people, perhaps to a fault— I am fearful the South have been lead into fearful error, by the misrepresentations of such traitors as Joe Lane & Co— the Democracy of the North will stand by the South in demanding their just rights within the Union, but sever the tie that binds as a confederacy and you change the whole aspect of the controversy—

The North will never recognize the right of a State to seeed, there can be no compromise on that question—

The right of revolution is inherent and the revolting States, in their efforts to throw off the yoke of oppression, real or immaginary might have received some sympathy, but the position they assume— and the line of conduct pursued forbids it— I know of but two *Breckinridge* democrats in our city who justify the conduct of the Gulf States and we are not more than a fair sample of the State— We all feel and know that the North has sins of omission and sins of Commission to atone to the South for and we, *will do it* and make the *amend honourable* if an opportunity be given us, but we will not be driven to the Mercy Seat—[3] conviction first converstion second and all the Christian virtues will follow in regular order—

In all this matter the South ought to deal with us in much charity, he that is without fault let him cast the first stone"—[4] If the South had not disrupted our party at Charleston Mr Douglass would have been triumphantly elected and all the evils that appear to be surrounding us averted—

In conclusion, I have no doubt, but that the Border State[5] or any other compromise that would be satisfactory to the *Southern B. States* would be *triumphantly endorsed* by the North— Little respect is due and less love is felt for the seceeding States in their rebellion and a feeling to apply the simple axiom, "withold not the rod where need requires and prudence directs",[6] increasing and will assume an imperative tone, unless the seceeding States stop short—

I hope you will excuse my taxing your time and patience, but aside from love of country, I feell all the better impulses of my nature revolt at the very idea of civil war— I have blood relations intermarried with Southreners from the "Manor born"[7] others equally near and dear who are in the service of their country and who I hope will stand by the Stripes and Stars as long as the[y] flutter in the breeze and other[s] await their countries call to the rescue— and shall I must I behold this fratricidal conflict— God forbid! and in mercy avert such a calmity—

If your late rebuke to Traitor Lane and his associates in treason, be published in pamplet form be so kind as to forward me one and you will much oblige

Yours truely   John McCook

ALS, DLC-JP.

1. John McCook (b. *c*1807), Pennsylvania-born physician who moved to Ohio from Connecticut, was an "old-line" Democrat. When the war came he and five sons joined the Union army; recalled home by "sad domestic afliction," he subsequently sought a collectorship of the seventeenth Ohio district. 1860 Census, Ohio, Jefferson, Steubenville, 3rd Ward, 76; McCook to Johnson, January 3, 1865, Johnson Papers, LC.

2. Borrowing from Calhoun's "concurrent minority" idea, Clement L. Vallandigham of Ohio proposed an amendment setting up four geographical sections: North, South, West, and Pacific. The election of President would be determined by a majority vote of the electors in each section, and on controversial questions before the Senate a majority vote of the senators in each section would be necessary for passage. In an additional amendment he suggested that a state might secede if the legislatures of all the other states in that section acquiesced. Vallandigham (1820–1871) was a Democratic congressman (1858–63) who opposed both abolitionism and disunionism. His obstruction of defense measures in 1863 brought about his arrest for treasonable utterances; sent into Canadian exile, he became a leader of the Peace

Democrats and campaigned unsuccessfully for governor in 1864. *Cong. Globe,* 36 Cong., 2 Sess., 794–98; Frank L. Klement, *The Limits of Dissent: Clement L. Vallandigham and the Civil War* (Lexington, Ky., 1970), 53–55; *BDAC,* 1743–44.

3. The gold covering of the Ark of the Covenant, considered as the resting place of God, and upon which was sprinkled the blood of the yearly atonement. *OED,* VI, 352.

4. A variation of John 8:7: "he who is without sin."

5. Perhaps the Crittenden Compromise or, more likely, the proposals of the Washington Peace Conference, then in session.

6. A variant on the hudibrastic "Spare the rod and spoil the child."

7. Corruption of "Though I am native here / And to the manner born." Shakespeare, *Hamlet,* Act I, sc. 4.

From Stokeley D. Rowan and William Lowery

McMinnville 12th Feby /61

Hon— Andrew Johnson:

Sir—

We have taken the liberty of writing to you on the Subject of the management of the Post Office at this place[.] the present incumbent S. J. Walling as we think is incompetent to the discharge of the duties devolving on him[.] There is considerable Complaint in regard to the distribution of letters & public-documents coming to this office[.] He is an unscrupulus partizan-*fire eater*—Secessionist pr se— We beg leave to give the name of Mr. Rolly Martin a merchant of this place a Brackenridge democrat Union loving man—who if appointed would accept and who would give general satisfaction to the Citizens[.] Will you be so good as to see to this matter— We assure you dear Sir—that we are not intermedling with a matter which does not concern ourselves & the public or through partizan feelings or malice but are actuated by a desire of promoting both private and public benefits & convenience[.]

Perhaps by the time this reaches you or even before—you will have seen the acct of the result of Our State Election for delegates to the Convention— It is a glorious triumph for gallant Tennessee[.] It is a rebuke—a most timely rebuke to Southern traitors— no convention—has carried by many thousands of votes[.]

We thank you Sir—for the Copies of your able Speech in the Senate recently—on the right of a State to Secede[.] We have made good use of them rest assured— they have had no small share in moulding public opinion in regard to the rights & the duties of the states. It imbodies the Cardinal doctrines of Our goverment from Washingtons time down to the present day—doctrines which must prevail or we must *fall*— go on Sir—final triumph awaits you[.] The people —the masses, who have no mot[i]ve to do wrong will flock to you[.]

Scores have already come that heretofore stood off— Let them Burn in effigy— the blood of the Saints is the seed of the church—[1]

Very respectfully Your friend and Obt Servt

S. D. Rowan

Wm Lowry[2]

ALS, DLC-JP.

1. Paraphrase of Tertullian, *Apologeticus*, Ch. L. Stevenson, *Quotations*, 1280.

2. Written by Rowan and signed by Lowery.

From Harvey M. Watterson

McMinville Te Feb 12th 1861

Dear Governor.

In my letter, of yesterday, I announced to you my election as a Delegate to the State Convention from the counties of Warren Cannon, Coffee, Grundy and Van Buren. I am indebted for the triumph to the popularity of *Uncle Sam*. I never considered myself anything more than *his* Elector, and thanks be to God and the intelligence of a patriotic people, the Star Spangled Banner still proudly flutters in this Senatorial district.

The Disunionists of Warren surrendered the county Delegate in order to insure my defeat. They met in McMinville and nominated, first, Col Josiah F. Morford,[1] a good Union loving man for the county, and *then* they put *forward* our quandom friend Hon H. L. W Hill as my competitor.[2] This was the pit they dug for H. M. W to fall in and be crushed beyond redemption; but they mistook the good sense and patriotism of the honest masses, who have risen in their majesty and consigned these traitorous demagogues to the grave they had prepared for me.

Hill professed to be a Union man, yet, his speeches were filled with *ifs* and *buts*. He would not vote for a secession ordinance *now*, *but if* War should break out he would. He denounced your speech publicly and in private denounced you as a renegade from the Democratic party. His friends scattered the Union and American by thousands, as well as Gov Harris' Message.[3]

I took the bull right by the horns[4]—defended any position you took and defied Hill to controvert a single principle you had enunciated. I told the people everywhere, and in all my addresses, that the Nashville Union had published falsehoods enough, within the last forty days, to sink forty thousand such establishments into the bottomless pit. I proclaimed on all occasions that an ordinance withdrawing Tennessee from the Union could never get my vote &c &c.

Hill and his disunion friends often asked me if I endorsed Gov Harris' Message. I replied, "No, Sir, I neither endorse Gov Harris nor his Message. One is a Disunionist—the other is a disunion document, and I am against both." I was determined, let the result be what it might, that nobody should misunderstand my opinions. I defied all enemies and looked alone to the Friends of the country for support. The *result* has given me an increased confidence in the capacity of man for self-government[.][5]

Col Lowry and Maj Rowan are two of the oldest, best-informed and most reliable Democrats in McMinville. Their letter explains itself.

I must repeat what I have said to you in a former letter that the removal of Walling as Post Master of McMinville and the appointment of Rolly Martin to fill his place would rejoice the heart of every Union loving man in and around this town[.] By all means, Governor, have this little job done by the present administration. The disunionists would make capital, if it were done by Lincoln. Now is the time—*certain*[.]

I have only room enough to add that I take it for granted that you will make speeches all over the state during the next summer. You will be gloriously sustained—and no mistake[.]

Yours truly   H. M. Watterson

ALS, DLC-JP.

1. For Morford, former state legislator, see *Johnson Papers*, II, 445n.

2. Hugh Lawson White Hill (1810–1892), son of J. A. Hill, one of the founders of Warren County, had served in the legislature (1837–43) and in Congress (1847–49); at this time he was a coal dealer and owner of a nursery and seed establishment. Robison, *Preliminary Directory, Warren*, 22–23; *BDAC*, 1053; *Mitchell's Tenn. State Gazetteer* (1860–61), 118.

3. Addressing the joint session of the Tennessee Assembly on January 7, Harris stressed the sovereign nature of each state, outlined the history of American Negro slavery, called for the election of a state convention to consider secession, proposed several proslavery amendments to the Constitution, and declared that, if these were not adopted, dissolution would be the only alternative. White, *Messages*, V, 255–69.

4. An old English proverb apparently first printed in this form in James Howell's *Proverbs* (1659). Stevenson, *Quotations*, 1442.

5. Although the five-county combined vote ran narrowly against convention (2,231–2,378), unionist Watterson was elected to represent these counties should the convention meet. Warren voted "for convention," 821–452. Campbell, *Tenn. Attitudes*, 289.

From William C. Kyle

February 13, 1861 [Rogersville]; ALS, DLC-JP.

Regales Johnson with news of the February 9 vote in Hawkins County— "the strangest election I have ever know[n] . . . the *leaders* on one side and the *people* on the other"—identifying leading Breckinridge men who supported secession, but speculating that the large union vote was indicative of sentiment among the rank and file; has seen "you hanging in Efigy at Tuscumbia Ala—to the telegraph post."

From John McGaughey[1]

Greeneville Feb 13th 1861—

Hon. A. Johnson—

Doubtless you have heard the result of the Ten. elections—giving a Strong rebuke to Harris Haynes[2] and others who have been advocating Secession— Tenessians are not willing for *Rebel* to be written upon her old glorious *flagg* that bares the *trophies* of the *Cross* upon it—[3]

I do hope and trust that the fate (politically) of Harris Haynes and others are forever sealed—and union men that have ben barred will *triumph*— the position taken by Ten will Stand as a monument between the two extremes—and your position will be better then— fighting fell and falling fought and being down he laid aboute—[4] you Can git up and I am going to take the liberty to tell you how[.] Just announce yourself (or let your friends do it) a candidate for *Governor*— you can beet the *field*[.] this is old *Johns prophecy* and in doing so you can mold the lagislature so as to have a majority that will place you back in the Senate of the united Stats—the Speaker of the Senate takeing your place as Governor of *Ten*— Standing as you do upon the constitutional plat form this can all be don against the first thursday in *August*[.] I hope you will upon the correct plea of Justification place yourself before the union men of Ten. as their candidate for Governor— this is no time for ceremony[.] the days of conventions are among the things of the past— the people want a man unpoluted with a party *convention*[.] do not delay[.] Som other union Candidate might Spring up and take from you a *victory* that is within your *grasp*—

the vote in Greene Cty no convention 2644 Convention 346— Arnolds[5] vote 333—

give my respects to Gnl. Milligan and tell him they must make a compromize[.][6] I would like to here from you in relation to the above—

Respectfully   John McGaughey—

ALS, DLC-JP.

1. John McGaughey, Greeneville farmer and unionist Democrat. *Johnson Papers*, I, 497*n*.

2. For Landon C. Haynes, see *ibid.*, 159*n*.

3. An obscure reference not to be taken literally. McGaughey may have regarded the bloodstains of the cross as "trophies," with the red field of the Tennessee flag conveying this symbolism.

4. "Till down he fell; yet falling fought, / And, being down, still laid about." Samuel Butler, *Hudibras*, Part I, Canto 3, ll. 93–94.

5. Official returns show 2,648 for no convention, 357 for convention. Reuben Arnold, the sole non-unionist candidate in Greene, polled only 339 votes to Milligan's 2,756, Crawford's 2,774, and Kyle's 2,626. Campbell, *Tenn. Attitudes*, 288; Nashville *Republican Banner*, February 19, 1861.

6. Sam Milligan was attending the Washington Peace Conference.

From Benjamin D. Nabers[1]

Memphis Tenn Feb 13, 1861

Private & Confidential

Dear Sir;

You have seen enough to know how Tennessee has gone—overwhelmingly for the Union. We had the fiercest contest I ever saw in Memphis. The Secessionist undertook to overawe the working men, but thank God they failed. The Union majority in this City is 722.[2] How much it is in the State I will not undertake to Say—

Now my dear Sir will the Republicans understand & appreciate our vote? We have Said that we wish to heal the breach between brethren & not submit to insult or injury. Tennessee comes in as Mediator— will She be heard? I trust She may. If the Peace Congress could now agree on the Crittenden or any Similar plan, Secession would be So dead in Tennessee that it would never raise its hedious form again[.] I beseech you & all our union men in Congress to increase, if possible, your efforts to accomplish a fair Settlement.

The Seceeders here altho writhing under a Waterloo defeat are calling their Scattered forces together for another effort. Tennessee they Say, Shall be redeemed from the foul blot Cast upon her, by the result of the election on the 9th inst. Altho, beaten by a majority unprecedented instead of yielding to a majority of our own people they Still insist, that whilst other States have a perfect right to go out of the Union Tennessee has no right to Stay in the union.

Why dont President Buchanan turn Galloway,[3] of the Avalanche, out of the Post office here? If I were President I would turn him out if I had but one hour to remain in office[.] See to this will you? His removal would have a good effect[.] We have good & true men here to fill the office & some of them ought to have it. The pay of the office is now used to break up the very government from which it is drawn. I would be willing to take the office myself or to See any union man in Memphis here rather than see it prostituted as it is now[.]

I will merely remark—that I served with you in Congress—the last Congress under P Fillmore—& that I had the Satisfaction of beating one Jacob Thompson[4]—late Secretary of the Interior under Mr Buchanan. This was in 1851. In 1857, I removed to Memphis—

and Served on the electoral ticket for President last year. These facts I mention merely to call your recollection to them. I am not anxious for the office, for my chances for office before the people are good but I will take it to get Galloway out, & my appointment I venture to Say, would be as Satisfactory as any other.

Galloway will hold the office until the last hour before the Enaugeration of Lincoln & then resign, with a flourish of trumpets & Say no man of the South can honorably hold office under Lincoln— Stop his wind in advance.

I would be very glad to hear from you as to the chances of an adjustment and all questions of interest[.]

Yours truly　　B. D. Nabers

Hon Andrew Johnston
Washington City D C

ALS, DLC-JP.

1. Benjamin D. Nabers (1812–1878), Franklin native, moved to Hickory Flat, Mississippi, where he was elected to Congress (1851–53) on the Unionist ticket. Moving to Memphis, he studied law, was admitted to the bar (1860), and stood as an elector for the Bell-Everett ticket. Returning to Mississippi during the war, he later served on the state penitentiary governing board. *BDAC*, 1378.

2. Although Union candidates received a majority of 722 votes over the secessionists, Memphis voters approved the convention by a majority of 4,511. Memphis *Appeal*, February 10, 1861.

3. Matthew C. Gallaway (1820–*fl*1888), born in Huntsville, Alabama, moved to Memphis from Aberdeen, Mississippi, in 1857. On January 1, 1858, he began publication of the Memphis *Avalanche*, a strongly prosouthern journal, and, with the exception of the years that the city was under Federal occupation, remained in the newspaper business until his retirement in 1887. Postmaster under both sides during the war (July, 1860–April, 1862), he later served as aide-de-camp to Nathan Bedford Forrest and bitterly opposed carpetbag government in Memphis during Reconstruction. John M. Keating, *History of the City of Memphis* (3 Pts., Syracuse, N. Y., 1888), II, 218–19; III, 131–35; Speer, *Prominent Tennesseans*, 346–50; 1860 Census, Tenn., Shelby, Memphis, 5th Ward, 65.

4. See *Johnson Papers*, I, 303n.

From John Rhea, Jr.

February 13, 1861, Bean Station; ALS, DLC-JP.

Believing Johnson "stronger in this county to day" than before, a Grainger countian reports on the February 9 Union vote and asserts that, if sufficient guarantees are forthcoming for the "Central Conservative States to justify them in remaing Loyal," the "secession stampede is ended with the act of Texas"; hopes "the designs of designing men" can be thwarted to preserve "the best government, the happiest homes ever enjoyed by man since his expulsion from the Garden of Eden."

From P. Henry Smyth

February 14, 1861, Burlington, Iowa; ALS, DLC-JP.

Former Tennessean, finding himself "in the midst of puritanical Yankeas, some of whom are as intolerant of the opinions of others as their ancestors were of Roger Williams," approves Johnson's patriotic stand and requests counsel for northern Democrats unwilling to accept southern secession or the alternate tactics of the "fanatical black republicans."

From J. Warren Bell

Springfeild Ill. Feb 16th 1861

Friend Johnson

The people in Illinois begin now to hav confidence in the continued existence of the Union. I am not flattering when I tell you that your name is a continual theme for praise and laudation from thousands of all parties save the poor advocates of Scession, who are in this state in a hopeless minority.

I am also in receipt of letters, memos, from Tennessee mostly from old friends all of whom (Sav, one) Speak in the highest terms of *Andrew Johnson*[.] Even those who have heretofore opposed you, now say you hav saved Tennessee from Secession[.] Yesterday I received one from a man who has always opposed *you* saying Andrew Johnson is now more than ever before popular, and beloved by Tennesseeans[.]

I also saw an influential man from Middle Tennessee here a few days ago who said the people were wild in worshiping Andrew Johnson. I see *my friend* General Cameron Senator in his speech in Phila Said among other things the "lion hearted Johnson[.]"[1] Such Sentiments fill me with pride for my native state and for the name and fame of him whom I have always admired and stood close to in all Conflicts[.] You may rest assured Johnson I dont set you back in this state[.]

A few days prior to Lincolns departure from this place Several visitors from Virginia pressed your name upon him for a Cabinet office[.] Mr Lincoln replied "Gentlemen I have no idea Mr Johnson would accept Such a position, His course is truly *noble* but just as is to be expected from a man possessing such a heart as his[.]"[2] This I had from one of the Gentlemen present at the time. My own opinion now is that the whole Country cannot dispense with your Services in the Senate[.] If this Union continu a few years longer as it is no man will be before *Andrew Johnson* in the hearts of Americans. I have heard more influential republicans declare a determination to use all efforts to obtain your nomination and election as Lincolns Successor[.]

Johnson I write this plainly to you because of the intimacy always existing between us and because of the kindly feelings I have for you[.]

Will you remain in Washington after the 21st? And will Lincoln be inaugurated in peace and quietness?

The Legislature will adjourn this day week or the Monday following[.] Then I shall return to Chicago[.] If not too much trouble just answer if you will the two questions above I asked & direct to me at the "Saint Nicholas Springfield" if you get this in time to answer by the 21st Inst[.] If not then to Chicago[.]

By-the-by—how is our friend *"Lizzie"*? Is she as *Smart* as ever?[3]

Your friend   J. W. Bell

ALS, DLC-JP.

1. Simon Cameron, senator from Pennsylvania and soon to be appointed secretary of war by Lincoln, spoke to the workingmen of Philadelphia on Saturday, January 26. He mentioned "the lion-hearted Andrew Johnson" among the "Union-loving men [who] . . . deserve and commend themselves to our kindliest sympathies." Washington *National Intelligencer*, January 30, 1861. See also *Johnson Papers*, I, 508n.

2. Neither the Springfield *State Register* nor the *Illinois State Journal* reported such a visit. The Washington *Star* twelve days later merely mentioned that Johnson was being considered for a Cabinet post. Washington *Evening Star*, February 28, 1861.

3. Inasmuch as Bell had known Johnson during the early thirties, it is possible that he refers to Eliza Johnson, whose reputed "booklearning" may have impressed both her husband and his associates.

From John M. Carmack[1]

Memphis Ten. Feb. 16th 1861

Hon. Andrew Johnson U. S. S.
Washington D. C.
Dear Sir—

You will see from the enclosed slip which I cut from the Avalanche of this morning that our Post Master has sent in his resignation to take effect on 5th of March.[2] This is I think intended to make his successor the appointee of Lincoln. If he is permitted to hold his office until the 5th & will not hold office under Lincoln's administration as he declares, then we are to have no Post Master from the 5th until one can be appointed & qualified under Lincoln after that time, or after the 4th. I do not suppose that Buchanan would have the right to make an appointment to take effect after the expiration of his term of office. Without discussing the motives that prompt the course of our present *mad* incumbent or the inconvenience that he would inflict upon a people who have repudiated him in his efforts to bully, dragoon & intimidate them into revolution I would suggest that it might be much to our interest to have a Post Master appointed & installed under the present administration, who can hold over without incurring the obnoxiousness of an appointment from Lincoln.[3] I admit that the same principle is involved in holding over & receiving an appointment under Lincoln, but as we live on or near the fretful edge of the *new conspiracy* it is important to our peace that we avoid as many causes of irritation as possible at this time. I would not compromise a principle nor propitiate fanaticism for the sake of peace, but where all the ends of the law will be answered, where our convenience & interests may be promoted & our peace preserved I deem it the very height of principle to consult policy. I suppose that Mr Lincoln will have to reappoint the incumbent even if one who will suit him be appointed by Buchanan, but that will be a private proceeding that will not excite so much objection as the induction of a new officer would. If you can do any thing for us in this matter you will greatly serve some of your (already) most grateful constituents. We apply to you because we regard you as the only representative we have in the National Council.[4] Our man Avery,[5] in the first place has not the ability to do any thing for us if he would & in the second place he no longer *represents* the people of his District in anything. Our plan is to have Gallaway removed at once & some good man put in his place, whom Lincoln will have the good sense to retain. He does not expect to appoint men of his party to office here. His policy as well as his duty in office would require a different course. Buchanan certainly owes Gallaway nothing.

In short if the thing is practicable & will not give you too much trouble you will much oblige many of your friends here, in whose behalf I write by doing what you can for us. This is prompted by no motive of personal interest on my part or of malice towards any one. If you can serve us I would suggest that Charles M. Carroll[6] or Wm A. Blythe[7] or any other good man would suit us.

Yours very truly   Jno M Carmack

ALS, DLC-JP.

1. John M. Carmack (*fl*1883), Memphis lawyer and former Whig, had assured Johnson two days earlier that while he was "engaged as you are now . . . on the side of the same issues you need not count me among your enemies." A personal and political friend of both Johnson and his son Robert —the governor having designated him a director of the Memphis and Charleston Railroad in 1857—Carmack had supported Douglas. Opposed to secession until Tennessee left the Union, he enlisted as a private in the Confederate army early in the war and was wounded during service in Virginia. Subsequently he served as judge of Memphis Common Law and Chancery Court (1869–70). Joseph B. Brady (Memphis Public Library) to Andrew Johnson

Project, September 4, 1974; Carmack to Johnson, February 14, 1861, and Carmack to Robert Johnson, July 10, 1865, Johnson Papers, LC; John M. Carmack, Compiled Service Record, RG109, National Archives.

2. Although Matthew C. Gallaway, *Avalanche* editor and current postmaster, announced his intention to resign March 5, he was subsequently reconfirmed by the Buchanan administration and did not step down until March 31, following the confirmation of Lincoln's nominee, Rolfe S. Saunders, March 27. Memphis *Avalanche*, February 16, 1861; *Senate Ex. Journal*, XI (1858–61), 346, 352.

3. During the month after Lincoln's inauguration and before Gallaway's departure from office, he reassured his readers that those who suspected "some collusion between the Black Republican Administration and the present postmaster to prolong his tenure," were mistaken and that he looked "with pleasure to the termination" of his duties. On March 21, commenting upon Saunders' nomination, the editor reiterated that he had been fully determined "to cease his official connection with the rotten power at Washington the very moment the obligations of his official bond relieved him." Memphis *Avalanche*, March 16, 21, 1861.

4. I.e., in Congress.

5. For William T. Avery, see *Johnson Papers*, III, 457n.

6. According to the *Avalanche*, Johnson was attempting to have Carroll named postmaster, while Etheridge was supporting Saunders. Charles M. Carroll (1821–fl1897), son of former Governor William Carroll and brother of former postmaster William H. Carroll, was assistant postmaster at Memphis and later a colonel of the 15th Tenn. Inf., CSA. Memphis *Avalanche*, March 9, 1861; Margaret L. Walker, The Life of William Carroll (M. A. Thesis, University of Tennessee, 1929), 157; J. Harvey Mathes, *The Old Guard in Gray* (Memphis, 1897), 292; *Williams' Memphis Directory* (1860), 115.

7. William A. Blythe (c1823–1864), Wilson County native, former Whig, and member of the Memphis bar since the early 1840's, was a partner of the well-known Edward M. Yerger. After building on the corner of Second and North Court streets a three-story lodging house, financed by his legal income and an inheritance, he reduced his practice. *Ibid.*, 81; John Hallum, *Diary of an Old Lawyer* (Nashville, 1895), 10, 67, 94; Carmack to Johnson, February 14, 1861, Johnson Papers, LC; Brady to Andrew Johnson Project, September 4, 1974.

From Blackston McDannel

Greeneville, Ten.
February 16, /61—

Friend Johnson

A few days ago Bob. told me he had written to you on the subject of a new Post Master at Knoxville, recommending J. C. S. McDannel[1] &c. Supposing that you might act on Bob's suggestion, and with a view of ascertaining whether or not Jo. would accept, I wrote him on the subject. To day I recvd a reply. He declines, on account of his present business arrangements, and if Charlton, the present disunion incumbent, is to be removed, he suggests the name of James C. Luttrell,[2] as the most acceptable man to the Union party. He says, "It is my candid opinion that Luttrell is the best man for that place that can be had. If any Democrat gets the appointment, the office will still be under the control of the little squad of infernal disunionists we have here." I suppose from this, that all the leading democrats about Knoxville, who are qualified, are disunionists.

Jo further says, that Luttrell is a good union man and your strong friend. In this connection, I will say, that the whole whig party appear to be, enthusiastically, for you, because you had the courage to throttle treason, disunion and secession, at the right time, and at a time too, when there was a probability of treason swallowing up Tennessee, and I believe they (the Whigs) are in good earnest, and mean what they say. How they may be in a year from now is a different matter—but I believe you have, by your late Union speeches, secured their good will, and that they would rather support you now than any other man in Tennessee. You have already the support of the Democratic party—save the secession part, which, thank god, is but a Corporals guard.

Gov. Harris, & Landon C Haynes, are nowhere. Haynes, openly avowed, secession here not long since. They are both as dead as hell, and buried, and upon their backs is written "No resurection—" However, if Tennessee, secedes hereafter, they may be resurected. But I think, the sentiment, to stand in the union, is deeply fixed in the minds of the people, and that if all the adjoining states secedes Tennessee will stand firm. I would rather stand with Massachusetts in the Union, than to stand with South Carolina out of the Union. I hope it will yet become necessary to whip this little upstart state, and hang a few of her leading traitors. All the forts, the Custom House and Arsenals and other public property now in the hands of the disunionists ought to be retaken at all hazards. This is due to the Federal government, for the outrage committed; and to maintain its character among the nations of the earth. So far, it has lost character, at home and abroad. Old Buck wont do for war. He is afraid somebody might get hurt. I differ with you on the subject of coercion. I think, if the government has no express power to *coerce a State*, or the authorities of a State, or the people of a state, it has implied powers necessary to punish treason and rebellion, wherever and in whatever shape it may be found, and to preserve the union. If it has not, the framers of the Constitution were a set of Jackasses.

Well, Johnson, if I ever was proud of my native state for any thing she has done, it is now, for the noble and firm stand she has taken against the disunion sentiment of the cotton states that seemed to be coming down upon her like a mighty avalanche. But she has withstood the shock, and hurled the avalanche back from whence it came, and stands now erect, proud and defiant, with no treason upon her bright escutcheon. Tennessee, the land of my birth and your adoption, has said to South Carolina and her confederates in crime and treason, thus far shalt thou come and no farther.

You remember the history of the Revolutionary war in the South, when the thunders of the British cannon, and the bristling of british bayonets, were sweeping every thing, as though victory was certain, until in the providence of God, terrorism was cut short at Kings Mountain, by the valor of Tennesseans and Virginians. By that great victory an impulse was given to the American arms, that saved the country. So now, in the providence of God, Tennessee, first in the list, and Virginia next, forms the barrier against Souther treason and fanaticism, checkmating the unholy crusade of Secession that will result in saving the union, at least, outside of the Cotton States. I place Tennessee first in the list, because she has i[n]dignantly placed her foot upon the Convention[.] Virginia has not done so, therefore I think, her position is equivocal, and deserves less credit.

But to return to Jo: McDannel, he says that if there is to be any change in the Custom House at Knoxville, he would like to have the appointment of Collector at that *Seaport*, as it would not materially interfere with his business— The Salary is about $300.

That damned fool *Crow* Ramsay, ought by all means, be turned out of office *now*,[3] Jo. Says as there is no union Democratic Lawyer about Knoxville, John M. Flemming,[4] "now a strong friend and defender of *Johnson and the Union*", would do to stop that hole with. I know nothing about this man. But I know Ramsay ought to be cut loose. And So ought *Billy be switched* the would be dictator of old Greene.[5] That House would not co-operate with the Union party here: That House belongs to the Harris *vein*. They would have underbid Judas Iscariot.

As usual   B. McD.

ALS, DLC-JP.

1. Joseph C. S. McDannel, a printer, was the writer's younger brother. Sioussat Papers, Box 11, University of Tennessee Library; Luttrell, *1850 Census, Knox County*, 54.

2. Luttrell, currently Knoxville mayor, received the appointment, holding it from 1861 to 1869. Robison, *Preliminary Directory, Knox*, 73. See also *Johnson Papers*, III, 508n.

3. John Crozier Ramsey, U. S. attorney general for East Tennessee, was on his way to becoming a Confederate. *Ibid.*, 311n.

4. John M. Fleming (1832–1900), sometime editor of the Whig Knoxville *Register* (1855–58), was prominent in the Knoxville-Greeneville conventions of May–June, 1861. Elected as a staunch unionist to the Tennessee legislature in 1861, he fled to Kentucky during the war. Although appointed by Lincoln U. S. district attorney for East Tennessee, he supported McClellan for President in 1864, opposed Republican Reconstruction policies in Tennessee, and became a loyal Democrat, editing several important news-

papers in Knoxville and Nashville, serving in the lower house of the legislature (1869–71) and as state superintendent of education (1873–75). Rothrock, *French Broad-Holston Country*, 417–18; Robison, *Preliminary Directory, Knox*, 39–40.

5. Probably a reference to their old friend William M. Lowry, who, as East Tennessee marshal, wielded considerable political influence and, like Ramsey, was moving toward secession. *Johnson Papers*, I, 34n.

From Joseph Powell[1]

U. S. of North America
One & Inseperable.
Bristol Ten Feb 16th, 1861,

Hon A Johnson
U-S-Senate   D. Sir

I have received your speech and read it with much satisfaction. And it is needless for me to say that I concur *fully* with every word of it. — — I regret my situation *just now*, as a Citizen of the U-S- For thirty years past I have resided in the State of South Carolina— But as She (with some other States) has assumed a position to the Goverment, that I do not recognize nor is it conceded by the supreme laws of the land— Yet, I am deprived of my immunities as a Citizen of the U-S- or forced to abandon, my home and my property or subject myself to outrage— I owe my first alleigance to the U-S- and I will never, (while I can have protection in it) acknowledge any other or higher power in the Country—

I believe that the Federal Constitution and the laws of Congress (Without any Amendment—of the Constitution) sufficent *for the present exigency* and every emergency that may arise in the future progress of the Government, *If faithfully administered.* and if Mr. Buckhanon has been too tardy or remiss in seeing the laws *promptly and* faithfully administered, I trust that Mr. Lincoln will see them *promptly executed*—and this comes from one who has his all of pecuniary interest in the Rebellious State of South Carolina, and who has resided upon her Soil for thirty years— I still hope that the power in the Government is ample to restore the Union and to protect its Citizens who still adhere to it—

I am Sincerely Your friend
J. Powell Bristol Ten

Hon A Johnson Senate U S.

ALS, DLC-JP.

1. Probably Joseph Powell (1801–1873) who is buried in Greeneville. Acklen, *Tenn. Record*, I, 133. See also Letter From Joseph Powell, May 24, 1860, *Johnson Papers*, III, 607.

From John P. White[1]

Nashville Tenn Feby 16th 1861

Gov Andrew Johnson
Washington D C
Dr Sir

My object in writing to you is to ask you if you have not made promises to others to assist them, to do me the favar of aiding Genl Clements[2] to retain his position as Marshall under the incoming Administration[.] it is true that he has had the office for a considerable time but it has allways taken all that he has made to support his family but for a considerable time to come at least till the country can raise two crops and relive the country of debt there will be a good deal of Suing and his office will be more profitable. I need not say to you that our family are under many obligations to you for past favors for I assure you that the family never had such a friend and we never will do anything else but stand by you when assailed by your enemies and you have many, who have pretended to be your frinds in days past but only wanted an excuse to abuse you and when you made your first Speech in the Senate they thought you had killed yourselfe so *dead* that you never could rise again but they now see that they have been disappointed and that you are sustained by the people by an overwhelming majority[.] the truth is they have been mistaken as the Know Nothings were in 1855[.] they know what was the sentiments of the people [in] the Towns & vileages but know nothing of the sentiments of the voters in the Hills & Hollows and the calm thinking portion of the State. I recd your speech that you sent me and all agree enimes & frinds that it is one of the best arguments that has ever been dileverd in the Snate but your enimes try to hold you to the doctrine of coersion yet, when your first speech is against it & your last also they still fight you on it[.]

I was pleased a few days ago to read your remarks in the Senate on Jo Lane—for I think he was made a tool of against you by ultra men south and think he will let you alone herafter for he must feel that he is smartly Blistered[.]

Peter Turney[3] was elected over Marks[4] in Franklin County to the Convention who you know is an unconditional disunion man but to day he could not be elected as I learn from my Brother Jim[5] who lives at Winchester. I learn from him that the causes that operated in Turney's favor are these and you will see at once that it was a powerful argument in his favor. They are building in that County what is called the university of the South which is to be built with money obtained from Ceceding States & they had Bishop Polk[6] going round tilling the people that if they did not vote for Turney & Cecession that the work would be stoped & the institution moved south & a great ma[n]y ignorent people were made to believe that the benefits to the County arising from this instituon would be worth more than the Union. I want no more cession[.] my hope is that the union will be saved but I think now is the time to settle it, not before the 4th of March for that is too soon for the people to act but let it be submited to the people the whole people not the Politicians & if they then decide to give us no gurantees & that they will not give us our rights under the Constitution then the Border States can act and go out peaceably but let this be the last last resort[.] this is the best govermet on the globe and I for one want to stick to it if there is any chance to live in it in peace and even then I dont know [but] what there would be as much peace in the present as there will be soon in the southern Confederacy for I think they will have great trouble in fixing up matters to suit South Carolina,

We would all be much pleased to see you in Nashville and to hear you talk about the tims, you was looke for during the late session of the Legislature and I assure you that if you had come you would have reced a welcome such as you never had from Nashville before. My Sisters Mary & Elizabeth arrived here a few days ago from Texas bringing with them the Corpse of my youngest Brother Jones who died in Austin Texas on the 17th of Decb last of Typhoid Fever[.]

I have not seen our frind G W Jones since he passed through here on return from his northern tour last spring. I know that it is the wish of the union men in his district that he should make the race for congress next summer against Thomas[7] and I hope you will urge him to do so, if he will run Thomas will not know what hurt him and then I think he will be better satisfied in political life. Make him run[.] I am satisfied that he will be governed to a great extent by your advice.

You will confer a lasting obligation from me by giving your influence to keeping Clements in his office one that I will allways be found trying to repay[.]

As ever your friend   John. P. White

I would be much pleased to recive a letter from [you.]

J P W

ALS, DLC-JP.

1. John P. White (b. c1825), Kentucky native, was a merchant in Franklin County (1850) before moving to Nashville as a member of the firm of Irby Morgan & Co., importers and jobbers in dry goods. V. K. Carpenter, tr., *Seventh Census of the United States, 1850, Franklin County, Tennessee* (Huntsville, Ark., 1970), 32; *Nashville Bus. Dir.* (1860–61), 275.

2. Jesse B. Clements (1799–1877), South Carolina native and White's father-in-law, had been a Polk appointment as marshal for Middle Tennessee, a position he retained until 1860, with some assistance from Johnson in 1853 and again in 1857. After serving as an assistant quartermaster general in the Provisional Army of Tennessee, he became Confederate marshal for the state. Nashville *American*, June 19, 1877; *Tennesseans in the Civil War*, I, 9; Johnson and Others to Pierce, March, 1853; Johnson to Buchanan, February 27, 1857, Appointments, Tennessee, RG60, National Archives.

3. See *Johnson Papers*, III, 427*n*.

4. Albert S. Marks (1836–1891), Kentucky-born, began law practice in Winchester in 1858. At first a Union supporter, he served as a colonel in the 17th Tenn. Inf., CSA, losing a leg in the battle of Murfreesboro. Later he was chancellor of the fourth chancery division (1870–78) and governor (1878–80). White, *Messages*, VI, 557–59; Caldwell, *Bench and Bar*, 349–50.

5. James White (b. *c*1830), a merchant, listed in the census as "General Trader" with $6,000 personal estate. 1860 Census, Tenn., Franklin, 1st Dist., 1.

6. As Protestant Episcopal bishop of Louisiana, Leonidas Polk (1806–1864) had urged the establishment of a southern university to educate young men and, at the insistence of Bishop Otey of Tennessee, founded his school at Sewanee, laying the cornerstone in October, 1860. Commissioned a lieutenant general by Jefferson Davis, Polk was killed at Pine Mountain in June, 1864. *DAB*, XV, 39–40; see also Joseph H. Parks, *General Leonidas Polk, CSA: The Fighting Bishop* (Baton Rouge, 1962).

7. Incumbent James H. Thomas of Columbia.

From Neill S. Brown[1]

Nashville Feb. 17th 1861

Dear Sir:

I have just read your last speech, and it gives me pleasure to be able to express to you my admiration for your heroic devotion to the Union— While it might have been more prudent in your first effort under all the circumstances, to have said less about force, yet I have not been able to except to your propositions, your logic or your authorities. You have done much good for your country as I believe, under the most trying & difficult circumstances— I am delighted with the scathing you have administered to the Southern conspirators, as well as to their northern allies & co-workers. It is the same mode which I have been attempting to pursue in our recent struggle— You have seen the result in Tennessee. Is it not most glorious? The happiest day of my whole life was the 9th inst. when I witnessed the stern verdict of the people of my native state in behalf of the Union. The mad waves of secession found an iron embankment around this proud commonwealth which dified all their fury— The large body of the Union Candidates favoured a convention as did also the candidates on the other ticket and yet the convention has failed by a large majority— It may be best in one event of things and prejudicial in another— If there should be no settlement of the strife in any reasonable time & if (what we most fear) there should be a collision at some of the southern points, it would create no small excitement among our people & give us much trouble & perhaps drive us to another convention under less favourable circumstances. The secession party per se, is small, but there is a large body of Union men who are such under the assurances of a fair settlement —many of whom would be carried off in a storm— Thus would be produced in our midst a formidable division animated by bitterness & violence— Whatever you & I may think of the causeless action of Secession & its diabolical tendencies & purposes, it becomes a matter of the highest importance to Tennessee as well as to the Union to have a final & fair settlement of the whole question— Crittenden's proposition or something equivalent would be amply satisfactory to Tennessee, & upon it all the *powers* could not seduce a respectable portion of her people. If the Republicans are wise they will close in at once & put an end to the struggle[.] They will sacrifice no practical advantage not even their construction of the constitution — They have all the territories that are valuable. We sacrifice nothing & gain nothing, except the peace of the country & the safety of the Union. It is then a mere peace offering, & not of fat lambs either, but of the mere hide & hoofs— Such a settlement would save the border states beyond doubt, & in the end bring back the Gulph states— the people of those states will at last gain the ascendancy, even at the point of the bayonet— But I need not say all this to you, for no doubt you are animated by similar views as a matter of sound statesmanship. The longer the exercise of force can be withheld in the south, the better for the great result of reunion—for the reign of terror is helping the cause. The heavy taxes will help powerfully, and if we can only hold up a fair settlement, it will be as magical in its effects upon the southern masses, as the rebuilding of the temple was upon the exiled Jews—[2] To such a settlement I pray you, use all your influence— & believe me, every step towards it, is an advance towards reunion[.] We all look with great anxiety to what Mr. Lincoln will say in his Inaugural— His speeches seem ambiguous, & strong fears are entertained that he will stand sternly on his platform, without making any advance[.] You have heard doubtless of your having been burnt in effigy in several points of the state — All this was the work of a few, & has the sympathy of no respectable class any where— It amounts simply to nothing & need not disturb your equinimity. It was done by those who never read your speech, & read but little of any thing[.]

                                    Yours truly   Neill S. Brown
Hon. Andrew Johnson

ALS, DLC-JP.

1. Neill S. Brown (1810–1886), Nashville lawyer, Giles County legislator (1837–39), Whig governor (1847–49), minister to Russia (1850–53), and speaker of the Tennessee house (1855–57), was a conservative unionist who acquiesced in secession and became a member of the military board which organized the Provisional Army of Tennessee. Arrested by Johnson in April, 1862, for treason, he was shortly after paroled and was a delegate to the state constitutional convention in 1870. Robison, *Preliminary Directory*, *Giles*, 7–8; Folmsbee, *Tennessee*, II, 78.

2. A reference to the rebuilding of the temple in Jerusalem after Nebuchadnezzar's sack of the city in 586 B. C. and the Babylonian Captivity. See Ezra 1–6.

From David S. Fraley[1]

Batesville Arkansas Feb 17th 61

To Hon A Johnson

Dear Sir   I am Still living, and in good health[.] hope this may find you well and at your post. I should not adress you this letter at this time only to endeavour to get you to Send me Several Copies of your last Speech. Your time is too valuable to the Country to Consume much of it in reading letters from Individuals like me. I carefully read your first Speech and endorse evey word of it even to the dotting of the i[']s and crossing of the t[']s[.] *Give it to them*. I have not been able to see your last speech[.] I would like to have some of them for distribution here. I am a strong union man and flatter myself that I have some influence too[.] On to morrow is our Election for Convention[.] this County will give ten to one for union Candidates[.][2] I am in the Northern portion of the State in Independance County[.] I think that the State will Secede as the Southern portion is that way. A Drunken Rabble has taken the Arsenal at the Seat of Government.[3] and I understand our Drunk Govenor distributed $60,000 amongst them under the Colour of pay for services.[4] I am a heavy, tax payer and do not feel reconciled to have my quota thus applied[.] my Taxes this year are over $300 and I am satisfied that 19 twentieths of the men that took the arsenal do not pay over a poll tax of one dollar each if even that. The fire Eaters in Tenn talked about Hanging you. I tell you now that they will hang you and I expect to live to see the day[.] It will not be now that they will do it but there is a time coming when they will do it and at that time I too as good a friend as you have on earth will help to do it[.] Yes the Boy you give the Shoes to and Stood his Bail in Greenville[5] many years ago will help to hang his *Old Crook*[.][6] Yes do not blame me for expressing myself thus for it is even so in these days traitors are brought almost by evey breeze and treachery and treason is the order of the day, but when these shall have passed away and our Country once more can get a breath of honest and pure air then I expect and hope that the hanging of Andy Johnson will commence. how[?] Just as the favourite Candidates for president in the last Contest were hung in beautiful Miniatures to the watch guards of their adherants. That is the way and then will be the time when you will be hung by the people of Tennessee and this portion of my State and I hope to see the day and I hope to be able to bring a good many in to the Hanging of Johnson. Look at the Map of S. Carolina[.] how often does the name of Marion or Washington occur in the naming of their towns or districts[.][7] It would not surprise me if the next act of that very Conservative Government under the rule of King Barnwell the first[8] would be to send a corporals guard and dig up the Bones of General Marion and throw him in Ashley or Cooper river[.] they always did both fear and hate him because he oftner saw how their "*coats fit in the back*" than in front that is when he could get near enough to them by making forced marches.[9]

Beautiful Stars for the erring Southron States to follow more like the Ignus Fatus[10] of their own rice swamps than Stars. Proud aristocrats one of them having twenty dollars in his possession will not speak to another that has orly nineteen dollars and Six Bits yet ready to fawn and truckle to one that may have twenty one dollars[.] degrees of aristocracy are measured by quarters of a dollar. I know them well[.] I *tramped* through the State once and it was truely laughable to hear a man that could stand in the middle of his ground and piss over the line anywhere talk about his possessions and plantation and crop in market &c[.] Though you must know them better than I do they are like old partee exactly the place where you told me you stayed all night six miles this side of Salisbury N. C when you were going west for the first time.[11] *Yancy*[12] I have not heard from him lately[.] I expect he is up in Rutherford County N. C. laying out in the woods living on cheese and crackers with some old tory sword girdled on waiting until the Siames Twins step out of their house to cut them apart[.][13] he no doubt thinks his mission is not fulfilled until he Seperates every thing living and then seperates his own head from his body. I wonder if he dont sometimes look at the quotations of the price of hemp in Ky[.] I do not want Kentucky to leave the union[.] her manufactures may be needed by the General Government and am opposed to buying much from foreign governments. This letter would look as though it ought to bear the Post Mark of some Massachusetts Town. not so[.] I own 8 slaves and live in the Southron States[.] neither does there a man live in the state of South Carolina or elsewhere who would Stand up for his Southern rights more readily than I would if I thought they were in danger of being lost. I do not belong to that class of Sailors who upon the first dark speck appearing in the heavens that would be eager to leave a good Staunch Ship and Jump overboard and strugling in the water to attempt to tear her to peices to build one smaller and less secure for fear a storm might come[.] I am for trying old Ironsides[14] a while longer and hope her pilot will steer her safe into port yet through all the piratical crafts that may attack her. I hope there may be no blood shed and reason may resume her sway in the minds of the fire eaters before it will have to be beat into their heads with Shot and Shell. The union the constitution and the enforcement of the laws is not a bad platform[15] for me either in peace or war. I own a Beautiful U. S. Flag[.] if to morrow is a sunshiny day I intend to sun it to take the mold off and if it is rainy I intend to hang it out to wash it and if it is cloudy Ill hang it out Just to see whether it will rain or shine[.] this county votes 3000[.] the large majority of the voters will be here in town on to morrow[.] the cupalo of our court house is about 75 ft high and god willing about the time our town clock strikes Six I shall nail it up there hoping it may assure some as the brazen serpent did in the wilderness that they may look upon it and be healed all Such as have been bitten by the Serpents of Secession.[16] Friend I have continued this beyond my expectations. But again *I Say give to them*[.] you can talk[.] you are posted. Send me such documents as will tell. Use well not waste[17] is my motto[.] I am with you and if ever I am in a country where there is an election held and your name is figuring and you should get but one vote at that precinct Just bet your bottom dollar that it was cast by

David. S. Fraley

I cant quit yet[.] Just to think of it[.] The day Andy Johnson was hung[.] now wouldnt that be a damned beautiful era to date from[.] no doubt some of the Fire-eating almanac makers are already in noting the memoriable days as they are generally given in almanacs say for instance Feb 1st 1861[.] Andy Johnson Hung by the people of Tennessee. That would look damned nice in print[.] I suppose they will put it in capitals (*Hung on a horse*)[.]

ALS, DLC-JP.

1. David S. Fraley (b. 1819–*fl*1884), a tailor from Salisbury, North Carolina, worked about a year in Johnson's shop around 1837. According to the *Carolina Watchman* (Salisbury), July 17, 1884, Fraley had served in the Texas navy (1836) and in the Mexican War. He probably moved to Arkansas in the mid-1840's, for by 1850 he was working in Batesville as a miller with real estate worth $3,500. In 1860 his declared property had increased to

$25,000 (his own estimate was $50,000) and he was again a tailor. Although a self-styled unionist, he joined Co. D, 7th Ark. Inf., CSA, in late November as a second lieutenant and quartermaster, resigning in May of the following year. James S. Brawley (Rowan County, N. C., Historian) to Andrew Johnson Project, January 28, 1973; John L. Ferguson (Arkansas State Historian) to Johnson Project, October 19, 1973; Fraley to Johnson, January 20, 1867, Johnson Papers, LC.

2. Although Independence was a poor county with few slaves, Fraley's estimate is not quite accurate. In the February 18 vote on convention, the county voted affirmatively, but elected three union candidates by a five to one majority (1500–300). Standing against secession at the convention, the delegates, when reconvened, voted for secession. John L. Ferguson, *Arkansas and the Civil War* (Little Rock, 1964), 237; Nola A. James, "The Civil War Years in Independence County," *Arkansas Historical Quarterly*, XXVIII (1969), 234, 236.

3. Fearing removal or destruction of the arms at the Little Rock arsenal, garrisoned by a small detachment of Federal artillery, "a mob—from Helena and Little Rock"—numbering around eight hundred voted to seize the installation. The mayor and city council opposed such action (the state had not yet seceded) and in panic requested Governor Rector to intervene. On February 6 the governor demanded surrender of the arsenal and, after the Federal unit marched out on the 8th, sent in state troops. John G. Fletcher, *Arkansas* (Chapel Hill, 1947), 141–42.

4. Henry M. Rector (1816–1899), a Kentucky native, moved to Arkansas in 1835 to manage the family's lands. After studying law, he was appointed U. S. marshal by President Tyler, served in the state senate (1848–51, 1855–57), and was surveyor general (1853–55) and associate justice of the state supreme court (1858–59). Elected governor (1860–62) as an independent Democrat in a three-way race, he alienated many Democrats. After his refusal in April, 1861, to supply troops to defend the Union, he ordered state troops to occupy Ft. Smith. There seems to be no evidence substantiating the "Drunk Govenor" allegation. Josiah H. Shinn, *Pioneers and Makers of Arkansas* (Baltimore, 1967), 401–4; Jack B. Scroggs, "Arkansas in the Secession Crisis," *Arkansas Historical Quarterly*, XII (1953), 194, 211, 219–20; Edwin C. Bearss and Arrell M. Gibson, *Fort Smith: Little Gibraltar on the Arkansas* (Norman, 1969), 241–43.

5. Apparently when Fraley, in a youthful "fishing frolic," was jailed "for breaking Old Dicksons oil [sic] mill dam," Johnson furnished his bond. See Fraley to Johnson, January 20, 1867, Johnson Papers, LC.

6. A slang expression derived from the verb "to crook" [the elbow], meaning to tipple or drink to excess. William A. Craigie and James R. Hulbert, *A Dictionary of American English on Historical Principles* (4 vols., Chicago, 1940), II, 682.

7. On the contrary, both Francis Marion and George Washington had been so honored. The name of South Carolina's revolutionary general is perpetuated in both a town and a district, the latter now a county; however, Washington District, created in 1791, ceased to exist nine years later. *Lippincott's Pronouncing Gazetteer* (1855), 1144; *Names in South Carolina*, X (1963), 118.

8. Robert Barnwell Rhett, former South Carolina senator who had earned the sobriquet "Father of Secession." See *Johnson Papers*, I, 314n.

9. Fraley may be implying cowardice, or again he may be suggesting that conservatives of any stripe—the British and their Tory allies in the Revolution or the "southrons" in 1861—regard the patriot Swamp Fox as inimical to their entrenched position.

10. *Ignis fatuus*, literally, in Latin, "foolish fire," was a phosphorescence hanging over marshy land, which receded as one approached it; thus the term referred to any elusive dream or hope. *OED*, V, 31.

11. Possibly Noah Partee (c1785–1841), a resident and the first post-master of China Grove, about fifteen miles from Salisbury. Unlike the im-pecunious but pretentious North Carolinian described in this passage, Partee was a man of considerable wealth who apparently welcomed sojourners—perhaps among them Andrew Johnson, traveling through from Salisbury to Charlotte. Brawley to Johnson Project, January 28, 1972; January 28, 1973.

12. Yancey had traveled extensively in September and October, speaking for the Breckinridge-Lane presidential ticket. His movements and speeches had been so widely reported as to give him the mark of ubiquity. John W. DuBose, *The Life and Times of William Lowndes Yancey* (2 vols., New York, 1942 [1892]), II, 489–535.

13. The Siamese twins, Chang and Eng, had their permanent residence in North Carolina.

14. Probably a play on words associating the *U. S. S. Constitution*—nick-named "Old Ironsides" during the War of 1812—and the national Constitution.

15. A reference to the 1860 platform of the Constitutional Union party. Porter and Johnson, *National Party Platforms*, 30.

16. See Num. 21:6–9. "And the Lord said unto Moses, Make thee a fiery serpent, and set it upon a pole: and it shall come to pass, that every one that is bitten, when he looketh upon it, shall live."

17. A variant of the familiar maxim "Waste not, want not."

From Levi P. Knerr

February 17, 1861, Reading, Pa.; ALS, DLC-JP.

Thanks Johnson for two copies of his December speech and requests copies of the February one, for which the "men in our shop at the Depot last tuesday dinnertime gave you nine harty cheers" when it appeared in the *Ledger*; feels the "tide in the north is turned in our favour" for the "republican party is split and devided Just where we [Democrats] want them" and "the conservatives are fighting the radicals and the radicals the conservatives."

From Isaac Anderson

February 18, 1861, New Haven, Conn.; ALS, DLC-JP.

A Republican, congratulating Johnson for "rolling back the tide of Treason & Rebellion," compares him to Andrew Jackson for his patrio-tism, yet warns that the " 'Oligarchy' are terribly down on you, and I fear some of them will be challenging you to a duel," which he hopes Johnson will not accept, for "The Country connot spare your valuable [life] at the demand of any duellist"; feels that "no name will create so much enthusiasm among the masses of the people of Connecticut, whether 'Democrat' or 'Republican', as the name of Senator 'Andrew Johnson' of 'Tennessee[.]' "

From Robert Anderson

Fort Sumter S C Feby. 18 1861

Hon Andrew Johnson
U. S. Senate Washington D C
Dear Sir:
Accept my thanks for the copy of your bold and manly speech on the State of the Union[1] and for the complimentary terms you were so kind as to use in it in my defense—

I am, Sir,   Very Respectfully,
Your obt. Sert.   Robert Anderson
Major U S A

ALS, DLC-JP.
1. See Speech on the Seceding States, February 5–6, 1861.

From William H. Carroll

Memphis Feby 18th 1861

Dear Sir
Mr. Gallaway[1] has resigned as Post Master of this city to take effect on the 5th of March next— The object, of his resigning in this manner, is that his paper can lampoon any one who may be appointed by Lincoln. If he was removed before that time your friends here would be better prepared to go into the fight next summer.
An appointment ought to be made by Pres Buchanan.
Gov Harris and other of your *particular friends* have recconed without their host—[2] They do not even die gentealy— By no means consult with Avery[3] upon any move conserning this District, he by no means represents the will of the people. I should be please to hear from you[.]

Very Respty   Wm H Carroll

Hon Andrew Johnson
U S Senator Washington City

ALS, DLC-JP.
1. Matthew C. Gallaway.
2. A proverb dating from the fifteenth century, of which a common version is "He that reckons without his Host must reckon twice." Stevenson, *Macmillan Book of Proverbs*, 1184.
3. William T. Avery, Democratic congressman from the Memphis district.

From Jesse B. Clements

Nashville Feby 18" 1861—

Honl. Andrew Johnson—

My friends in Middle Tennessee, will make application to have me reappointed to the Marshals office, for this District, I am informed that Several letters from Members of the Bar, have already been sent to Judge Catron,[1] others will be forwarded, and I have no doubt but that I will be pretty generally recommended for appointment— If from your knowledge of me as a public officer, you feel authorised to assist in having me reappointed, your Services will be fully appriciated and greatefully acknowledged,— I understand there will be Several applicants, but I know not who they are or will be— It is perhaps proper for me here to remarke that Some of my More *fire eating* friends, say that it will be disgracefull for any Democrat to hold office under Mr Lincoln's Black Republican administration and that they would not disgrace themselves in that way— I am of a differant opinion, Somebody has to and will hold the public offices, and if a Democrat can do so, why should he give way to a Know Nothing, I can see no good reason why he should—

I take it for granted that Mr Lincoln is under no particular obligations to either of the political parties in Tennessee—as he received no direct support—from Tennessee—and of course his object in filling the offices will be to get persen quallified, and whose integrity is undoubted— If I believed my appointment would injure the Democratic party in Tennessee, I would not hold the office for one hour—let my necessities be what they might—

Please give this letter such Consideration as in your judgment it deserves— in the meantime I would be pleased to hear from you— if Convenient—

Very respectfully   J B Clements

ALS, DLC-JP.

1. John Catron (c1786–1865), a native of Pennsylvania, moved to Nashville in 1812. A self-educated attorney, he served on the state supreme court (1824–35), becoming Tennessee's first chief justice in 1831. Appointed by Andrew Jackson to the U. S. Supreme Court in 1837, he was presiding over the circuit composed of Missouri, Kentucky, and Tennessee at the outbreak of the Civil War; because of his unionist sentiments, he was unable to return to Tennessee until late in the conflict. *DAB*, III, 576–77; *Tenn. Official Manual*, 178.

From Henry S. French[1]

Nashville 18 Feb 1861

Honorable Andrew Johnson
Washington City D C
Dear Sir

I have just finished reading your speaches and if ever Truth was powerful it is in you[r] late Speaches and iron Expreasn[.] thank god it just Come in the nick of time. how they did fall on the Right & Left[.]

Brags Batry at Vuena vista[2] was not half so destructive on the Disunion trators & bulshite plundlers and I want you to know you did not mistake the people of your place & state[.] Sir I for one and my Children will S[t]and by you in all Comeing time and by your son for his Manly and noble defence of his Countrys flag[.][3] I was opposd to you before but now and forever I am a Johnson man[.] your Speaches has done mor to quiet the Count[r]y than all [that] has bin done[.] Just go on in the good work may Almity god give you helth and strenth to Contend with all Trators Come from what quater it may[.]

Yours Truly   H. S. French

ALS, DLC-JP.

1. Henry S. French (1809–1883), Virginia native who moved to Nashville about 1850, was at this time a retired merchant and cotton broker with $90,100 in real estate and $10,000 in personal property. Subsequently he purchased the Felix K. Zollicoffer home at Sixth Avenue and Deaderick Street (later the site of the Andrew Jackson Hotel). 1860 Census, Davidson, Nashville, 4th Ward, 120; biographical data from Mrs. C. Somers (Alice Beeler) Miller, Knoxville.

2. A reference to Capt. Braxton Bragg (later a Confederate general) and his heavy artillery fire in the battle of Buena Vista during the Mexican War.

3. Robert Johnson, representing Greene, Hawkins, Hancock, and Jefferson counties in the extra session of the Tennessee house, spoke out both within that chamber and in Nashville public meetings against the convention and in support of the Union. Nashville *Republican Banner*, January 25, 26, 27, 31, 1861.

From John C. Love

February 18, 1861, Louisville, Tenn.; ALS, DLC-JP.

Applauds Johnson for "handling Treason with Gloves off" and requests that copies of his two speeches be sent to the Knoxville postoffice, since "the P. Ms. at this place and Maryville are Vile Disunionists and suppress such Docs. as those you sent to them to destribute." Avers, "In our election here on the 9th . . . we sustained your position by a vote of 158 to 31 and this too after you had been denounced in a Secession meeting."

From A. Waldo Putnam

TENNESSEE HISTORICAL SOCIETY.

Society Rooms, State Capitol,
Nashville, Tennessee, Feby 18th 1861

To Hon: Andw Johnson
Dear Sir

I sat down this, Monday morning, and enjoyed a rich treat—in the reading of your speech of 5th & 6th Feby. inst.—as reported in the Louisville Journal.[1] Your positions are right, your arguments sound, your facts incontrovertible your conclusions legitimate and your illustrations fair and happy—Good hits, well-given, timely and merited—and they were appreciated by your hearers, and will be by most of your readers.

I wish, as you said,—you could have "the people of all the continent to hear every word" of what you said: I wish that fifty thousand copies of that speech could be circulated in this State & in Ky. & Va. & N. C.

I cannot endure the thought that any one of these magnifi[c]ent States should leave the Govt. of our Fathers—the very Temple of Liberty with all its glories & guarantees—upon a freak, in passion —and with the object avowed to the civilized world and to posterity —to sustain Negro Slavery.

But, my dear Sir, it will not do to allow the impression to remain on the minds of Northern people that the Southern people or their leaders are engaged in the producing of this terrible disturbance of all the elements of Society, commerce and government, for mere political effect—that it is without any provocation or ground of reasonable apprehension of infringement of rights; that "it is only *artificial*," as the President elect has so often recently said,—and that it "will soon pass away,"—"and nobody be harmed."[2]

God, in mercy grant it may!

But, certainly,—however inadequate the cause; however hasty the measures; however pregnant of greater evils than all which have ever been known; however destitute of relief and of remedies for wrongs, —there is an *earnestness*, a fearful *earnestness* in the *leaders* and the mass of the people in the seceded States,—which must not be ignored or contemned:

And to encounter or assail it with *weapons of war*;—to attempt to crush it *now* or sudenly by any *invasion* of the territories of such States, to recapture the Forts &c.—will cause a commotion, will awaken a sympathy—in this State (and in Ky. Va. & other Slave States not yet inflamed,)—which would involve us in a war of desolation, the extent and duration of which no human Ken can limit. . . Had the firmness of Jackson been shown months ago,—the spread of the contagion might have been stayed—or the 'plague-spot,'— S. C. have been cut out and thrown into the sea to be cleansed,—or into the fire to be "purged so as by fire."

The imbecility of the Pub. Func.[3] has allowed of strong combinations in his very presence—and the Revolution has gained such headway, such volume and shape,—that,—if the Prest-Elect & his advisers can see and pursue the path of peace,—they must be endowed with 'wisdom from above.'[4]

I have relatives and connections in five of the Seceded States— nearly all of whom were opposed to the acts of Secession: But now they have lost confidence in the present and in the incoming administrations—have lost hope of healthy tone in Northern public sentiment—are disgusted with the double dealings of prominent politicians, are tired and impatient of delays of adjustment to come from or in concert with people of the free States,—and have yielded to the prevalent Southern spirit of action, decided action—precipitate action: They and thousands of others, recently conservative men—are now disposed to *accept the revolution*, help it—sustain it —make it as endurable as possible——Still hoping, that, like other violent fevers, it will not long endure,—whether it kill the patient, —or yielding to gentle purgatives, pass away, leaving its subject pale, depleted, a living skeleton.

They apprehend that the use of force at any point touching their inflamed borders, will aggravate the evils under which they now suffer—and that the flames may spread and kindle in the Middle Slave States, from whose *calmness* they now cherish their strongest hopes of *peace* and a *re-union*:

And will not the incoming administration be fully justified in pursuing the 'Hands' off' policy of this *Democratic?* administration, under whose sanction all of these mad eccentricities have occurred? If troops from Massachusetts or N. York or Ohio should be accepted & sent to fire a single gun into these infatuated States—whilst the people of the other Slave States not seceded, are in such a sensitive, nervous, emotional condition,—will not war kindle instantly and rage furiously?

Very Respectfully   A. W. Putnam

ALS, DLC-JP.

1. Louisville *Journal*, February 15, 16, 1861.
2. Speaking at Pittsburgh on February 15, 1861, enroute to Washington, Lincoln referred to the troubles confronting the Union: "In plain words, there is really no crisis except an *artificial* one! . . . My advice, then, under such circumstances, is to keep cool. If the great American people will only keep their temper, on both sides of the line, the troubles will come to an end . . . ." That same day at Cleveland, the President-elect observed that there was no occasion for excitement over the political difficulties of the day: "this crisis is all artificial." Minor variations appeared in the several press accounts. Basler, *Works of Lincoln*, IV, 211, 215, 216.
3. President Buchanan had originally called himself an "old public functionary" in his 1859 annual message. Richardson, *Messages*, V, 553.
4. James 3:17.

From Alexander B. Small

February 18, 1861, Knoxville; ALS, DLC-JP.

Reports that secessionists, "furious with rage at the result of the election on the 9th," are calling Union men "*submissionists*"; requests Knoxville postmastership or an appointment as railroad route agent. "The *people*, are speaking strongly of you as their leader in the gubernatorial race the coming summer."

From James Sullender

February 18, 1861, [Philadelphia, Pa.]; ALS, DLC-JP.

Hailing Johnson's "noble & fearless position," a hatter tenders a specimen of his handiwork, a token "for the unmerciful scathing you recently gave, In the U S Senate, to Nothen abolitionists & Southen Secessionists—."

From R. W. Whittington

February 18, 1861, Independence, Tenn.; ALS, DLC-JP.

Former political opponent who knows that Johnson has "love of the poor at hairt" writes that "the Rich nabob[s] of the South is agenst you" and have "said . . . that you had Runed yourself," but now that "Tennessee has endorsed you, the[y] say that the Country is Runend and that *Andy did it*."

From John W. Ford[1]

Chattanooga, Feby. 19th. 1861.

Hon Andrew Johnson.
Dear Sir:

I wrote you a letter on Saturday last,[2] asking your good offices in aiding me to procure a Route Agencey from this place to Nashville, informing you that Col Francis, the Special Mail Agent,[3] had promised to write both you and Judge Nicholson, asking your intersession in my behalf— On my return to Nashville on Monday, I inquired of him whether he had written to you? He informed me that he had not—that Genl Anderson[4] claimed the Agent for that end of the Route, and that he had acqu[ie]sced in the justice of the claim, and that he had joined Gen. Anderson in recommending a young man by the name of Haywood,[5] a clerk in the office for the appointment— that MCarty[6] one of the Agents on the East Tennessee and Georgia Road had resigned and that he would forthwith recommend me for that appointmet.

Now, there is no point whatever in the claim that the Agents shall live at any particular place on the Road— all that is required of them is that there shall always be one at each end of the Road in the regular course of running to receive the mails— The three Agents on the Memphis & Charleston R Road who run to Tuscumbia, all reside in Chattanooga—and the three who run from Tuscumbia to Memphis all reside at Tuscumbia— The whole thing arises out of opposition to me—and what has given cause to that opposition to me on the part of Genl Anderson I am totally unapprised—but it is as I tell you, and *I* should like to circumvent him, if possible, which I think can be done by your aid, and I think you will willingly afford it to an old friend, when you can do it, without doing injustice to any person else, but if I cannot get the Agencey to Nashville, I will take the other, if I can get it—and I certainly ought to have it, if there is any force in Gen Andersons claims, that at least one Agent should reside at each end of the Road—for all the Agents on the East Tennessee and Georgia Road reside in Knoxville— I leave this matter in your hands, feeling an abiding confidence that you will see that justice is done me— I think that I ought to have the Agencey, in view of the manner in which I lost my Agencey on the Road—[7]

Write me soon—

I beg leave to [subscribe?] myself truly your friend
John W. Ford

ALS, DLC-JP.

1. See *Johnson Papers*, III, 317*n.*

2. Ford to Johnson, February 17, 1861, Johnson Papers, LC.

3. Hu Francis (b. *c*1815) of Winchester possessed $7,000 in real and $1,700 in personal property. The agency on the Nashville and Chattanooga Railroad had been made vacant by the forced resignation of George I. Hooper. 1860 Census, Tenn., Franklin, Winchester, 1st Dist., 16; see Ford to Johnson, February 17, 1861, Johnson Papers, LC.

4. Samuel R. Anderson, Nashville postmaster. See *Johnson Papers*, II, 325*n.*

5. Willoughby Haywood (b. *c*1837), Nashvillian, an interim clerk after Hooper's removal. 1860 Census, Tenn., Davidson, Nashville, 3rd Ward, 84; St. John B. S. Skinner to Johnson, February 19, 1861, Johnson Papers, LC.

6. Route agent B. McCarty is otherwise unidentified. *U. S. Official Register* (1859), *429; *Nashville Bus. Dir.* (1860–61), 228.

7. Ford, who received the appointment, had served "the Department five years and a half in the same capacity." The reasons for his removal are not known. Ford to Johnson, February 17, 1861, Johnson Papers, LC.

From Homestead Club of Bergen, N. J.

Bergen N J Feb 19/61

Der Sir

Knowing you to be one of the oldest and firmest (if not the oldest) friend of the Homestead Bill in the Senate I am requested by the members of the Homestead club of this township to call your attention to this important and necessery measure and to ask you to do all that lies in your power to call it up and if possible to press it to a final passage before the close of the present Session of Congress[.][1] We think the passage of the Homestead Bill will do more to elevate the working men and to benefit all the people of this Country than aney measure that has ever come before Congress Since this Government was established[.] And we think it would have a benificial influance on the present diffculties that destract our Country by fixing the policy of our government in regard to the Public Lands and Teritories belongin to the United States[.]

The members of the Homestead club and the working men generally of this township and we believe a large majority of the people of the United States now fully indorse the doctrin anounced by that Illustrious Son of Tennasee who while filling the Executive Chair of this government Said in one of his messages to Congress that the time had arived when we Should no longer look to the Public Lands as a Source of revenue and that they ought to be administered and disposed of in Such a manner as would afford every industrious citizen an oppertunity to become a freeholder[.][2]

We fully agree with the above doctrin and believe the time has come when Congress Should put them into practice by passing the Homestead Bill which will aford every industrious Landless citizen an oppertunity to obtain a free and inaliena[ble] home upon the Public domain of the United States[.] In calling your attention to this Subject we feel confident that you will do all that lies in your power to promote the object we desire[.] Before closing this I desire in the name of the working men of this TownShip to thank you for the maney Services you rendered them by continually and Steadfastly defending their rights and advocating their interests while with Sincere regardes I remain your

Obediant Servant   Wm Rowe[3]
Ch of Homestead Club of Bergen Township N J

Hon Andrew Johnson

ALS, DLC-JP.

1. Upon Johnson's motion, a homestead measure (H. R. 24) had been referred to committee on December 10, 1860, and was not further considered during the session. This letter reflects the myopia of dedicated reformers who failed to recognize that any homestead legislation would receive short shrift in a Congress preoccupied with the secession crisis. *Cong. Globe*, 36 Cong., 2 Sess., 23; *Johnson Papers*, III, App. 714.

2. Andrew Jackson had made this recommendation in his fourth annual message. Richardson, *Messages*, II, 601.

3. Possibly William Row (b. c1818), a New York-born merchant, who had $5,000 of real and $3,000 of personal property. 1860 Census, N. J., Hudson, Bergen, 45.

From Francis W. W. Letournau[1]

Baltimore Feby 19th, 1861.

Dear Sir

Who are Patriots? who are Traitors? who are for War? Who for Peace? who are true to their Country? who are false to that trust, which was purchased so dearly, and handed down to us for safe keeping.

These are questions which can only be answered by United States Senators, in such a way as to bring about Peace, But we who have no power of Speach (in a Representative Hall) can answer, Could those United States Senators, feel the great responsibility now resting upon them, as they sit, in their Arm Chairs, and apparantly unconscerned about the things which make for the Peace of this once Happy, but now distracted nation, They feel not the sting of misery and want, they are provided with the comforts of this life. They, as they sit with their Feet upon the heated Furnace beneath their respective Desks,[2] They feel not the pinch of the extreem cold weather, They, retire to their finely furnished places of abode, They, feel not, hunger gnawing at their Heart strings, They sit at Tables bountifully spread with the luxuries of life, Their Ears, are strangers to sounds of *Bread, Bread*, Father I want Bread, and none to be had,

Could they, but penetrate the abodes, of many of those, who have by their influence (at the Ballot Box) elevateted them to the position[.] Yea! the exaulted position Oh! would they not wake up from their slumbers, and rush to the rescue of this once Happy People,

How oft have I repared to the Senate Chamber, to hear something said which had a tendency to bring matters to a Peaceful settlement, but as oft as I have gone, I have been disappointed[.] and What now? is there no one can save the Country? Let me say to you, I am willing to exculpate you from any sensure to ruin our Country, You have won a Name, which will live, after your Bones have crumbled to the dust, and when this Republic, (Gods, favoured Land,) has crumbled to dust,

Is it possible? that there is so few, who are able, and not willing to use an effort to save us,

Look sir a few months since, at the condition of our Happy Land, How sweetly could we worship our God according to the dictates of our conscence,

What enabled us to do so? because we as a people, confided in the *honour* of those, we have elected to such high *positions*, But to day? Oh look! The Minds of so many peoples destracted, Homes almost broken up, and soon to be entirely so, the hopes of many a Poor Mother, blasted forever,

Who knows how soon her only support must be torn from her Bosom? Young Man what are your prospects for the future? his Answer, is War, War, Civil War,

Your Lady, Sister? What are your prospects for the future? To be abandoned, and deserted, to be robbed, and neglected, and left without a protector,

Could Senators, take these thoughts home, and let them sink deep down in their Stoney Hearts, Oh! could their Hearts not be softened and made to feel,

But look at them as they sit, instead of being a blessing to their day and generation, they will be cursed, and marked by disgrace, and infamy to be handed down to future generation's, as Traitors to the People, and Country which gave them Birth,

Yes this great responsibility rests upon them, who have failed to put forth an effort to save this beloved country,

What success has the many appeals met with which have been presented? treated with indifferance,

What do we ask, as Mechanics? very little, only to be able to earn, something to eat, and feed those who are daly asking for food, We cannot expect the comforts which Senators enjoy, but mearly the necessary comforts of life,

What interest have we in the acqustion of Territory? When we cannot procure Bread, in that, in which we now live?

And are these Mechanics expected to be torn from their Families to carry on this Civil War? of which I have heard Senators speak? Or do those who inaugurate this Curse, intend to be first in the Field?

I feel it is upon us, and in a few months, we will not have it to look for, but will have it upon us, and wo be unto them who bring it about,

But the Voice of the Poor industrious Mechanic must be hushed up in his Bosom, and hushed up in Death, by the curse of a Civil War,

A Shaving from a Jack Plane[3]

Dear Sir

I have perused your last Speach, and I am convinced that you have not, been backward in expressing your true Union sentiments not only to those of your own State but to this entire Count[r]y,

And Gov.? would to high heaven, we had all such men as yourself, we should soon have Peace and plenty,

My object has not been to express my views, but I desire you to send me your first Union speach, that I may read it, and join it to the one delivered 5th 6th of Feby,

Will you oblige me by so doing, and I would have no objections to your sending your signature upon a slip of Paper, and other reading matter you might favour me with[.] I do appreciate your valuable services you have rendered your Count[r]y in the present Crisis,

I have expressed the opinion of a young mechanic and a devoted man, to those who make an effort to save our Count[r]y from Bloodshed[.]

I remain your Obt srvt
F W. W. Letournau

direct care of P L Perkins[4]
99 Bato St Bato Md

ALS, DLC-JP.

1. Francis W. W. Letournau, a carpenter, lived with his widowed mother on South Ann Street. *Woods' Baltimore Directory* (1858–59), 259.

2. Underneath his desk each member of Congress had a small forced-air register or duct constructed of perforated bronze and wire gauze. Fitted with diffusing boxes and valves, the registers allowed each congressman to regulate the airflow to his own satisfaction. Glenn Brown, *History of the United States Capitol* (2 vols., Washington, D. C., 1900–1902), II, 151; *House Ex. Doc.* No. 100, 39 Cong., 1 Sess., 3.

3. A medium-sized plane, somewhat over a foot long, used for general purposes. *Webster's Third International.*

4. A daguerreotypist, Palmer L. Perkins (c1825–1900), a New Jersey native, had been in business in Baltimore since 1850. Mrs. Susan Knight (Maryland Historical Society) to Andrew Johnson Project, March 12, 1974.

From John G. Winter[1]

Columbus Ga feby 19. 61

Hon A Johnston
U. S. Senate Washington—

D Sir—   Your courageous, Patriotic & States man like manner of discussing th diabolical heresy of Secession, has excited my warmest admiration & most profound gratitude— I think I am but one of Millions who entertain similar feelings & sentiments & one of your strong Common sense will not receive my humble endorsement otherwise than good naturedly— I have been so deeply interested for

months past in th movement of th proffessed Politicians, that is, the
hangers on of the public teat, that I have been scarcely able to attend
to business— the rascality of the movement has excited my most
intense disgust & the folly of the People in allowing themselves to be
so deluded by the base rebels, has creatd the most painful apprehensions for the results— The Terri *tory* has been the worst of all
Tories & now the hue & cry[2] of *no coercion*, caps the climax & I
think will demolish the Stars & Strips & bury the American Eagle
so deep that none shall live to see him resurected— I have always
believed in the adage that 'truth is mighty & will prevail',[3] but I
fear I have lived to see the Converse of the proposition realized— If
the People do really believe that the protection of ones property by
force of arms when the robber uses both force & fraud to deprive
the real owner of its possession, is *coercion* by the Party assailed,
then there is no limit whatever to the gullibility of the People & the
theory that man is smart enough to govern himself has culminated
as a most stupendous & magnificent humbug—A delusion & I fear
will prove in this country & in our day, a most disastrous one—

I am, (or shall be in a few weeks) 62 years old—served my country in a very small way in 1814— That is by working as a volunteer
in throwing up redoubts near New York, to defend the City against
British forces that were supposed to be en route from Washington—
At a time when every man (nearly) & every Boy entirely, *felt* that
the maxim of 'United we stand, divided we fall',[4] was a truism &
when not a soul could be found who would gainsay the verity of the
maxim[.] I have resided in Georgia 44 years & raised a large family
of Georgians[5] & for 30 years have combatted these nullifiers & secessionists in my humble way— I trust therefore you will excuse the
liberty I take in addressing you without th formality of an introduction[.] my excuse is a fervid love of the Institutions of Washington
& a painful anxiety for th welfare of a numerous progeny that are all
natives of th State & the adjoining one of Alabama— I wish to make
a suggestion & hope you will not think me presumptuous to do so—
The P. Off is terribly in th way of th rebels— To abolish them
directly by law, or by *authority* of law, may disaffect our friends,
who in truth are in the actual majority— I think they can be reached
by an indirection perfectly & without irritating our friends—
Get up a special oath of allegiance for P. Masters located in the infected districts— I would suggest whether it would not be well, to
make them give new securities residents of States not in a state of
rebellion— My opinion is that a suspension of mail facilities arising
from the P Masters refusing to take such an oath as is really requisite
for Governmental protection, will create a revulsion of popular
feeling which will overthrow the usurpers— I doubt whether any

thing more is necessary to accomplish the purpose named, than to require all P Masters in the seceded States, to be re-sworn, for I believe the oath prescribed places the State subordinate to the U. S. —an oath which would place th rattlesnake & the crescent[6] *beneath* the Stars & Stripes would be too humiliating for the compatriots of Quattlebaum & chesnut[7] & every mothers son of them would be compelled by 'vox populorum', to *shut up shop*— The men now in power, have not the capacity to Construct & carry on with any degree of regularity, a postal system— If they can only sail the Ship of State long enough to make a practical exhibition of the difference between talkers & actors, the Border States will be very far from joining & cerving under such a set of (business) asses—

I do not suppose that you can convert my letter to any useful purpose & hardly dare to hope that my suggestions will prove worthy of your acceptance— But do with it as you please, even to Committing it to the flames, but dont repeat my sentiments *as* mine, for this climate is dangerous & I might not be permitted to live to see the rascals brought to Justice[.] I am in the habit yet of speaking my mind, but to know that I had held counsel with a *'Black Republican'*, would bring down upon my head the vials of their wrath[8] & it is doubtful whether any thing but my blood could cool down their indignation— Every body is a Black Republica[n] now that is not in favor of the Confederate States & its usurpers & Dictators—

Hoping that you may achieve the most abundant success in your Defence of our Common Country & live to see its enemies, and especially her traitorous sons reap the proper reward of their treachery to the best Government that the world ever saw, is the honest & earnest wish of Yr M obdt hble Svt

John G. Winter

ALS, DLC-JP; also printed in LeRoy P. Graf and Ralph W. Haskins, eds., "The Letters of a Georgia Unionist: John G. Winter and Secession," *Georgia Historical Quarterly*, XLV (1961), 390–92.

1. John G. Winter (1799–1865), a native of New York City, migrated to Georgia during the second decade of the century and by 1841 had become a successful banker in Columbus. Beginning in 1844, he served two terms as mayor, followed by several years as a member of the county court; during this same period, he invested heavily in manufacturing and commerce. When the Civil War broke out, his outspoken unionism necessitated his exile, much of it spent in England. LeRoy P. Graf and Ralph W. Haskins, eds., "The Letters of a Georgia Unionist: John G. Winter and Secession," *Georgia Historical Quarterly*, XLV (1961), 385–88; biographical data supplied by Robert D. Thorington, Montgomery, Alabama.

2. Although "hue and cry" came to mean a written proclamation for the capture of a criminal or the recovery of stolen goods, the expression originally referred to a loud shout or cry by those pursuing a felon. All those within hearing were required to join the chase. *Webster's Third International*.

3. Popular paraphrase of "Great is truth, and it prevaileth." 2 Esd. 4:41 in the Vulgate Apocrypha.

4. "By uniting we stand, by dividing we fall!" is a line from John Dickinson's "Liberty Song," first published in the Boston *Gazette*, July 18, 1768. Stevenson, *Quotations*, 56.

5. Winter had seven children, all living in Georgia or Alabama, and "more grandchildren than it is convenient to count." Columbus (Ga.) *Sun*, April 16, 1861.

6. The "rattlesnake" and "crescent" devices appeared separately on two different South Carolina flags during the crisis of 1860. During the secession convention, a hand-painted cotton banner bearing the figure of a rattlesnake coiled about a palmetto tree hung behind the president's chair. On the same day that the secession ordinance passed, the convention adopted another flag, red silk with a blue cross and decorated with fifteen stars for the proposed Confederacy. In the upper left appeared the ubiquitous palmetto tree and in the right, the moon crescent, a device first introduced into the state flag in 1775. Lossing, *Pictorial Civil War*, I, 105–6, 111–12. See also Letter from Daniel Keller, December 27, 1860, note 2.

7. Paul Quattlebaum and James Chesnut, Jr., South Carolinians. Quattlebaum (1812–1890), a state legislator (1840–44) and senator (1848–52), had been an ardent nullificationist and was a delegate to the secession convention. A planter, he also operated a lumber industry, flour mill, and rifle works; Quattlebaum rifles were used by the Confederacy. Active in the militia, he had gained the rank of general by 1861, but age and a back injury prevented his serving in the Confederate army. Chesnut (1815–1885), U. S. senator (elected in 1858 and resigned November 10, 1860), was a lawyer, member of the lower house of the General Assembly (1840–46, 1850–52) and state senate (1852–58), and a delegate to the Nashville convention. He was also a delegate to the state's secession convention, helped draft the Confederate Constitution, served as an aide to Beauregard and on Davis' staff, was appointed brigadier general, and in 1864 commanded the reserve forces in South Carolina. Although disfranchised after the war, he played an active role in Reconstruction, serving as president of the convention of 1867 to protest against military rule, and attending, often as chairman, numerous state Democratic assemblies. His wife was the famous diarist Mary Boykin Chesnut. John A. May and Joan R. Faunt, *South Carolina Secedes* (Columbia, 1960), 196–97; *DAB*, IV, 57–58.

8. Rev. 16:1.

From Elias Beal[1]

Rogerville Hawkins County Febay 20 1861

Mr Andrew Johnson

dear Sir   My father is Very anxious to hear from you and har what chance thear is for pease[.] Mr Hughs your oald friend[2] waants hear from you in Regard to the deficency bill whitch imbracis his and my fathers[3] back pay as pensionors and you will con fer a graet favor on theas oald Soaldiers if you can give them some in couredgment a bout the union of theas oad States and allso if you think thear is any chanc for thear back pay you will if you can possable answer this Letter[.] thar is a great anxioty to hear from you here[.] any good union documents woud be vary hapely ricieved from you— ou[r] state Stands furm[.] oald Hawkins as She allways has for Johnson[.][4] you no I was vary glad to find Judg Paterson[5] So furm for the union[.] you have got friends in Hawkins now that you never had be fore and of the best Blud that Runs through the hewmon family[.] Mr hughs waunts to har from you if you ar not tou mutch presed[.] pleas answer as soon as possabl[.]

Elias Beal

To Andrew Johnson
the Savior of Tennessee

ALS, DLC-JP.

1. Elias Beal (b. c1819–1893) was sheriff of Hawkins County (1858–68). Enlisting in July, 1863, at Camp Dick Robinson as a private in Co. H, 8th Tenn. Inf., he was appointed captain by Johnson in January, 1864, and captured at Bull's Gap in April. After the war he successfully petitioned, through Senator David T. Patterson, for service as captain of the company from 1863 to 1865 in order to qualify for a pension, "having lost his health in service," and ultimately received twelve dollars a month beginning October, 1867, "for right hip injury." Johnson to Beal, January 27, 1864, Elias Beal, Civil War Pension Files, RG15, National Archives; Elias Beal, Compiled Service Record, RG94, National Archives; *Goodspeed's East Tennessee*, 880; *Senate Journal*, 39 Cong., 2 Sess., 229, 271, 457, 459; *Senate Ex. Doc.* No. 84, 47 Cong., 2 Sess., Pt. 5, p. 344.

2. Probably Cornelius Hughes of Hawkins, a veteran of the War of 1812, on whose behalf Johnson had worked diligently and whose pension was awarded in 1852. See *Johnson Papers*, III, 385n.

3. George Beal, an early Hawkins County taxpayer, served in the War of 1812 (November 11, 1814–June, 1815) as a private in Slaten's company, Booth's regiment of East Tennessee Militia. Pollyanna Creekmore, comp., "Early East Tennessee Taxpayers, Hawkins County," ETHS *Publications*, No. 32 (1960), 126; George Beal, War of 1812, Compiled Service Record, RG94, National Archives.

4. In the congressional races of 1847, 1849, and 1851, Johnson outpolled his opponents 1,309–1,148; 1,380–1,095; and 1,741–650. In gubernatorial races Johnson's vote in "oald Hawkins" was 1,180–805 (1853) and 1,158–887 (1855). Jonesborough *Whig*, August 18, 1847; August 18, 1849; Knoxville *Whig*, August 16, 1851; Campbell, *Tenn. Attitudes*, 268, 272.

5. David T. Patterson, Johnson's son-in-law, who had been judge of the first circuit court since 1854. *Tenn. Official Manual*, 182; see *Johnson Papers*, I, 110n.

From Jeremiah D. Mann[1]

Post office
Aberdeen Missi Febry 20 1861

Honl Andy Johnson

My Dear Sir Some years Since a Doctor Singleton[2] from your State Stayed in this city Some time[.] one day some person remarked that the car had run off the track in Georgia and that Andy Johnson was abord and was probbly Killed[.][3] Well Said Singleton I am a whig and don't like his pollitics much but Andey is mighty hard to be Killed. Some time Since I thought the Secssionist was about to Kill you in Tennessee. But your or somthing else has nearly Killed them in Tenn[.] A man like your Self could soon kill them in Missi. there are Some Good speakers in Missi but they are all Secessionist[.] all our Speakers Great & Small are Secessionist from the fact they exspect to be President or Somthing else[.] after all a bullet from a pistol in the hand of a Small Man might Kill andy. therefore dont you let any Wigfall Shoot at you tell you Kill all the Secessionist[.] Say nothing in connection with my name[.] if the Vote had been fai[r]ly put Missi would have Gone union 10,000[.][4] Verry Respectfully

J D Mann P.M.

P. S. Send me something like Seed Papers &C

J D M

(In Great hast)

ALS, DLC-JP.

1. Jeremiah D. Mann (c1798–c1863), North Carolina-born treasurer for Monroe County (1855–62) and postmaster of Aberdeen since January, 1859, possessed $2,000 in real and $8,000 in personal property. 1860 Census, Miss., Monroe, 517; Secretary of State, Register of Commissions, 1853–57, p. 493; 1858–64, pp. 519–20, RG28, Mississippi Department of Archives and History; Senate Ex. Journal, XI (1859–61), 33, 39.

2. Probably John Singleton (1826–1864), a physician of Louisville, who was practicing before 1850. WPA, Tenn., Blount County Tombstone Records: Mt. Moriah Cemetery, 257.

3. The accident, which occurred in February, 1857, resulted in a painful injury to his right arm, which had to be broken and reset after it had healed improperly. See Johnson Papers, II, xxix, 525–26.

4. The facts do not support this contention. Although the election of December 20, 1860, had been hotly contested in many counties, personalities, rather than fraud, seem to have played the larger role. Most candidates had not been nominated on specific platforms favoring union or secession, but had been men who the voters believed would follow the right course for Mississippi and the South. Moreover, apathy, rather than voting irregularities, appear to have ruled in certain instances. Only 60 percent of those who had voted in the presidential election just six weeks earlier returned to the polls to select delegates to the January 7 convention. Although the Mississippi contest was close in certain counties, the overall result was a significant victory for secession. The secessionists per se received 16,874 votes; those various Conservative-Unionist elements, called "cooperationists," polled 12,218, with the remainder going to coalition, and uncommitted, candidates. Rainwater, Mississippi, 177–201; Wooster, Secession Conventions, 28–29.

From Joseph S. Fowler[1]

Gallatin   Feb. 21st 1861

Hon. Andrew Johnson:
Dr. Sir,

I have read your late speech in the Senate with great interest. I congratulate you upon your patriotic effort and rejoice that one

Senator from the South still cherishes the love of his country and dare speak for freedom and equality. I mean for the equal rights of the uncorrupted peasantry of the land. The multiplied blessings of our matchless form of government, in which men may rise to the first official stations not by virtue of ancestry or still more debasing, wealth, but by courage moral & intellectual & by industry and merit, is still prised loved and defended. I must not say one alone—for the patriotic sage of Kentucky[2] stands with you. The memory of our illustrious ancesters, their fame and glory won by so much self denial and blood is not forgotten. The bones of our martyred patriots are still guarded as the consecrated relics of more virtuous days.

But what are we to do? The sesessionists hang their last hopes on the failure of the Peace Congress. They then think that Virginia will secede, and her course will determine the course of Tennessee. These results would tend powerfully to bring about that long and ardantly cherished effect.

For myself I can see no just cause for the disruption of our noble form of Government. We cannot hope to better it. Shall we have a higher object in destroying than our ancesters had in establishing? Will Virginia leave? If she does what shall we do? I speak for myself[.] never will I be found violating the convictions of my calmest deliberations and holiest impulses. This government is too importent too difficult to reconstruct to think for one moment of abandoning.

In the event that the Peace Congress fails shall we abandon the contest? If you think not—may I be permitted to suggest to you the propriety of canvassing the State. You would have a powerful effect if you could deliver your views to the people. The politicians have tried to misrepresent you[.] those too who never read it & some who could not comprehend it if they had. I am certain it is so here. But we carried old Sumner for the Union Candidate[.][3] If we are to go through another struggle you must try to be with us. It is time now that we were comeing to a definite stand. We should make the next fight for the government without any contingency or we will be compelled to undergo defeat— Your position in your fi[r]st speech was the one we should have boldly taken. The people would have sustained it. They will do it yet. But we must not suffer them to be corrupted by timid conditions and base contingencies. Send me a number of your speeches for distribution. Write me a line if possible on some of my enquiries soon. There is no time to loose.

Yours truly   Jos. S. Fowler

ALS, DLC-JP.

1. Joseph S. Fowler (1820–1902), Ohio native and graduate of Franklin College, New Athens, Ohio (1843), became a professor of mathematics at Franklin College, Davidson County (1845–49), and later served as president of Howard Female College, Gallatin (1856–61). Appointed by Johnson state

comptroller (1862–65), he was elected as a Union Republican to the U. S. Senate (1866–71) but did not seek reelection and subsequently became a Democrat. Enjoying a close friendship with Johnson during the presidential period, he spent his remaining years as a Washington attorney. *DAB*, VI, 564; *BDAC*, 910.

2. The elderly John J. Crittenden.

3. Probably Thomas R. Barry (1807–1891), Democratic state legislator (1839–42, 1851–53, 1869–71), who opposed secession in 1861, remained neutral during the war, and was appointed by Brownlow chancellor of the third division (1865–69); Barry defeated his opponent by a margin of fifty to one hundred votes. Robison, *Preliminary Directory, Sumner*, 19; Memphis *Appeal*, February 14, 1861.

From John C. McGaughey[1]

Knoxville Tenn Feby 21st 1861

Hon Andrew Johnson
Washington City
Dear Sir

Being personaly unacquainted with you I feel some delicacy in addressing you but the desire expressed in my letter must be my apology and allow me to say by way of introduction that I am a son of Jno McGaughey of McMinn County[2] hereto fore differing with you in politics but now standing firmly and squarely with you on the question of Union— The Post Master at this place[3] is an ardent secessionist and says he will resign and I have concluded thro you to make application for that Office— I have got no list of names to back me first because I thought it unnessesay and second I did not care about it being known that I had applied & failed, if fail I do. For responsibility and qualification for the Office I refer you to the citizens generally of McMinn Co—where I served as DPM under my Father—Col Brabson—& Judge Swan J C Ramsey Col. Baxter Temple[4]—Mabry[5]—M B McMahon[6] and others [in] Knoxville and Saml McGaughey[7] of Green & Dr R Birdwell[8] of Sevier— I dont ask any thing of Maynard because I do not want to be under any obligation to him and also because though I have been living here nearly four years I have no acquaintence with him— There are three other applicants that I know of Mr C. A Rice—P. L Rodgers[9] and Col Luttrell—[10] Rodgers is in the P O. now and I think it is Charlton's design to resign in his favor— He was for a convention & I think is an ultimatum man—[11] Col Luttrell is a very clever man but I should think the loose manner in which he acted when Comptroller[12] & his want of energy would be sufficient to prevent his appointment— As a test of my soundness on the Union—I have said & still say to my friends we had better live in this Union four years under Lincoln—bad as are his principles and much as I am opposed to them—with a fair prospect of routing them at the next race with a conservative man than to go with the Cotton States—

I make his request of you in all frankness and sincereity hoping you will aid me— if you can find it Consistent with your feelings and inclinations to aid me in this—to you and to no one else will I fell indebted for the office and to you will my gratitude will be due— & if you do not feel so inclined please burn and for get this letter[.] With many apologies

I remain Very Truly   Your Obt Svt
John C. McGaughey

ALS, DLC-JP.

1. John C. McGaughey (1838–1867) of Athens was at this time a Knoxville clerk. Acklen, *Tenn. Records*, I, 178; *Williams' Knoxville Directory* (1859–60), 64.

2. John McGaughey (b. *c*1797) was an Athens merchant and old-line Whig. A staunch unionist, he subsequently became provost marshal at Athens; in 1864, while engaged in raising a Federal regiment he was, according to O. P. Temple, arrested and murdered by "a lawless gang of Confederate guerrillas." Boyer, *1850 Census, McMinn County*, 63; Temple, *Notable Men*, 150–51.

3. Charles W. Charlton.

4. Reese B. Brabson, Tennessee congressman (1859–61); William G. Swan, Knoxville lawyer, soon to become a Confederate congressman; John Crozier Ramsey, Knoxville lawyer and district attorney; John Baxter, and Oliver P. Temple. For Brabson, see *Johnson Papers*, III, 452*n*; Swan, II, 214*n*; Ramsey, I, 317*n*.

5. Joseph A. Mabry (1826–1882), gentleman farmer and railroad promoter, supported the Confederacy and was instrumental in gathering supplies for Knox County volunteers. Later owner of a prosperous publishing firm, he was a member of the Tennessee Constitutional Convention of 1870. Ambushed in downtown Knoxville by Thomas O'Conner, an alienated business partner, Mabry, his son Joseph, and their assailant all died within five minutes. Rothrock, *French Broad-Holston Country*, 130, 134, 200, 228–29; *Goodspeed's Knox*, 1001; Jerome G. Taylor, Jr., The Public Career of Joseph Alexander Mabry (M. A. thesis, University of Tennessee, 1968).

6. M. B. McMahan (b. *c*1830), the owner of a mill and tannery (1853–60), in 1857 became cashier of the Knoxville branch of the state bank. *Goodspeed's Knox*, 846, 847; *Williams' Knoxville Directory*, 64; Luttrell, *1850 Census, Knox County*, 41.

7. Samuel McGaughey was a Greeneville merchant.

8. Reuel Birdwell, a physician. *Johnson Papers*, III, 448*n*.

9. Pryor L. Rogers. See Letter from Charles W. Charlton, December 19, 1860.

10. For James C. Luttrell, see *Johnson Papers*, III, 508*n*.

11. Probably a reference to those who espoused the stand taken by Governor Harris in his message of January 7 in which, after recommending constitutional amendments protective of southern interests, he declared that "If the non-slaveholding States refuse to comply with a demand, so just and reasonable . . . every consideration of self-preservation and self-respect require that we should assert and maintain our 'equality in the Union, or independence out of it.' " White, *Messages*, V, 263–64.

12. Although Luttrell's annual report of October 1, 1857, indicated that

disbursements had exceeded receipts by more than $51,000 the previous year, it should be noted that his predecessor had shown a deficit of $118,592. *Tenn. House Journal*, 1857–58, App. 133; Nashville *Patriot*, November 23, 1857; *Tenn. Senate Journal*, 1855–56, App. 5.

From William P. Johnson[1]

Columbia Texas Febuary the 22—1861

Dear Brother

I for the first time sit down to wright to you under imbaresments such as I wonce hoped never would come in my day of life I mean the state of the country and the affares of the Nation[.] our Country is in a desperate condition and as a concerritive I am allmost a lone but on tomorrow I shall vote for cecesion but I never will vote to be atached to a confedracy except it is a reunion of all the states as they ought have remained and as they would have don had not have bin so meney men that could git to Presedent or it would be so long before it would come to there turne they could not wait for there turne and by having two at a time ther [turn] would come sooner[.] I expect to see harder times than I ever saw in my life but if I had a home I would defend it to the last drop of my blood but as I have no home them that has Negrows must fight for them for I will not and I do most sincerly hope that nether of my two Sons will[.] if they have Negrows it is there duty to defend them[.] that I shear in common with my fellow men I am ready and wiling to defend[.] the people here are building up Goverments out of the fragmens of the Old union and a nice mes they will make of it and nasty dirty slinks[2] that is doing it calls them selves democrats and berades me for being a Nothing[3] one of the onley men that wanted to save the country or could have saved the country to the time they tried but there own country men would not help them and the foreners did want it saved and texas is made up of the damdest amegumation of humanity on the face of Gods earth[.] there is Mexicans Duch Irish Ingtish Scotch Indians Mulaters not a fue and quite a number of Negrows and some fue White People from N. States and scors of blue bellyed yankeys that are better Souther men than Georgians are or indeed eny Southern raised man and some men believe what they say but here is what dont [*sic*] you may depend narere [nary] a word of it but I feare there is going to be hell to pay but if I had no small children I would not care wat was to pay or what it was to be payed in but I have three small Children and two helpless Daughters that are Ladys to the letter with the exception Education and I have don all that my Sircumstances would allow me in that way[.] my oldest Daughter Elizebath is a stout well grown Woman of 19 years old the

17 of this month but our daughter Olive is in feble helth and has bin from her infincy[.] She is in her 16 year[.] She is small and delicate[.] my three Sons that I have with [me] are stout and harty[.] my Wifes helth is quite good[.] taking all in all my own helth is not as good as I could wish and my person is quite infebled but I am on the down hill of life but dont understan me as complaining of eny thing[.] I am s[t]ill sober and dos all the work that I am able to do[.] when I came to texas I came with the hope of geting a home but that is a lost ball I fear but never havin a home I have lost nothing that I ever had in the disapointment and there fore have nothing to complain of in being disapointed and takes nothing to hart seriously but I recon I have made my last move[.] I expect to live and die in Brazoria County Texas[.] my Brother I want you to receive in this letter the wormest Love of a Brother to his brother as long as mortal life shall last[.] answer my letter and let me here from you as I never Expect to see you in life[.] may God bless you and your family and I hope you may prosper in all your plausable undertakings[.]

I remain unalterabl your Brther

William P. Johnson

to Andrew Johnson U. S. S.

N. B. I have bin requested this eavning by my imployers J. H. Dance & Bros[4] and Mr A. R. Park[5] of this town to ask the favour of you to send them the last Patent Office report 1 to ea[c]h[.] they are both Patenttees of good and usefull machines one as a seed planter and other a grist Mill[.] they are both N. Carolinans one from Nash and other from Northhamton Countys[.] one is a joiner and other a Gunsmith and both Gentelmen of undouted Standing[.] your compliance will much oblige them and your Brother and if they are plenty you can send me one with rest but dont neglect them on my acount[.] I hope you will comply[.]

W. P. Johnson

ALS, DLC-JP.

1. See *Johnson Papers*, III, 683n.

2. A slinking, cowardly person. John S. Farmer and W. E. Henley, comps., *Slang and Its Analogues, Past and Present* (7 vols., [London], 1890–1904), VI, 250.

3. That is, a Know-Nothing.

4. J. H. Dance (b. c1825), a wheelwright with $8,000 in real and $9,000 in personal property, had living with him his brothers G. P. (b. c1832), D. E. (b. c1834), and J. C. [H?] (b. c1836), all millwrights, who had received in 1860 a patent for improvement in hanging millstones. 1860 Census, Tex., Brazoria, 11; *Senate Ex. Doc.* No. 7, 36 Cong., 2 Sess., 443.

5. A. R. Park (b. c1815) was a mechanic. 1860 Census, Tex., Brazoria, 51.

From William H. Morrow[1]

Nashville Tennessee
February 22d 1861

Hon Andrew Johnson
Dear Sir

Though I have once had the pleasure of an introduction to you I presume that you have long since forgotten even my name— I was introduced to you in July 1859 while passing through Greenville Tenn. on my way to N. Y in company with Mr A. J. McWherter[2] of this city, at about 9 oclock at night— I know you when I see you having had many opportunities of meeting you while Governor of the State— upon such a slight acquaintance as this I presume to address you. Though young in years I have for some time past had my political preferences and have acted with the party opposed to you—have never voted any other ticket Save that opposed to Democracy—have worked in my feeble way to do all in my power to defeat it and do not regret it— If the Breckinridge & Lane party in the last contest fought for the establishment of Democratic principles then am I truly glad at their defeat in this State[.]

While I have thus differed with you in the past I am with you *now* heart & Soul— I am glad that you had the boldness to beard the Lion in his den[3] & denounce as infamous the Spirit of Secession[.]

Your two great speeches lately delivered in the Senate have covered you all over with glory & Tennessee showed very plainly by her vote on 9th inst that she endorsed you fully and unhesitatingly — I bid you go on and crush the monster So deep that he will never again raise his hideous head.

A few days after you made your first speech you are aware that a figure representing you was burned in this City on the Corner of Union & College Streets immediately in front of the Planters Bank — I reached the spot in time to see the latter end of the farce & on going there early the next morning I picked up the veritable buckle that was on the vest & on getting up on the Gas Post to which the figure had been hung, I cut off a piece of the string which had been used for the purpose of swinging you up— I now Send them enclosed as I thought you would perhaps like to look at some relic of that most damnable act. I propose that when you next visit our City that you address our people from the identical Spot above named!

The Union loving men here have taken fresh courage from your recent Speech and they are determined not to be *dragged* out by the would be Southern Confederacy— *The Constitution as it is* Suit us much better than Yanceyism and as we have lived and prospered under it in days gone by we are not willing to yield it up to suit the wishes of a few men who had they lived in the days of Jackson would Long since have been hung as *Traitors—now* Some call them *"Patriots" "friends of the South"* &C &C.

As you are doubtless kept exceedingly busy I will not trespass further on your time— If you can find time I should be pleased to get a line from you— Do you yet hope for peace— if so upon what is that hope based?

Can you send me such documents of the present Congress as have a bearing on the question now agitating the Country— I shall be pleased to receive any that you may send. This day has been celebrated here by the appearance of the Military, firing of Cannon & a fine display of the Stars & Stripes suspended from many stores & dwelling houses.

Stand firm in your adhesion to the Union & Tennesseans will endorse you.

Very Respectfully You[rs]
Wm. H. Morrow

ALS, DLC-JP.

1. William H. Morrow (b. *c*1837) was part owner of John Morrow and Sons, saddlers. Deane Porch, tr., *Davidson County, Tennessee, 1850 Census* (Ft. Worth, 1969), 138; *Nashville Bus. Dir.* (1860–61), 224.

2. Andrew J. McWhirter (b. *c*1822), a wholesaler of dry goods, raised Co. G, 18th Tenn. Inf., CSA, saw service in the fall of Donelson, and was later assigned to the commissary department. Deane Porch, tr., *1850 Census of the City of Nashville* (Ft. Worth, 1969), 63; *Nashville Bus. Dir.* (1860–61), 232; Clayton, *Davidson County*, 173, 185, 430; *Tennesseans in the Civil War*, I, 212.

3. "And darst thou then / To beard the lion in his den, / The Douglas in his hall?" Sir Walter Scott, *Marmion*, Canto VI, st. 14. Stevenson, *Quotations*, 178.

From Jackson B. White[1]

Nashville Feb 22d 1861

Hon A Johnson
Dear Sir

I have been intending to write ever since the adjournment of our legislature to give you my thanks for the influence you exerted on the legislature as I believe for the best good of the state; others are praising you for your course in the senate, but in my opinion if it had not been for your influence with certain members of the legislature, Tennessee would to day have been out of the Union[.] Gov Harris was determined to have the state out, and he would have accomplished it, I believe if it had not been for your influence. Shortly after the legislature met at the call session a prominent democratic member approached me to know if the Bell men as he called us would help to kick you out of the senate, saying they had not the power to do it without assistance, I told him no we had no hand in putting you in the senate, and we would certainly have no hand in trying to turn you out, he said we might put any person in we pleased, and they would vote for him, I told him no I did not believe in the right of the legislature to instruct a senator, we seporated and he applied to others I have reasons to believe in the same way. And I have some reasons to believe Gov Harris was trying to encourage the idea. I do not know of course your own friends kept you posted all the time, of what was doing but I did not know that you had received any communication from our side, and I thought I would let you know how we acted and felt towards you in the present crisis[.] You know we have been denounced as Union shriekers John Bell subm[iss]ionists and Andy Johnson coertionist, traitors to the south, and black republican abolitionist and that any man will be damed that will except office under this administration[.] Now I wish you to say to Ole Abe or Gov Seward if they should ask your advice that I will accept a office if it is a good one a first class mission or something equal to it and I hereby tender to the administrat[ion] through you my se[r]vices, and that I am as clever a man as any in the state a big fat good natured lazy fellow with as much capacity as any man that was ever scent on a foreign mission from this state, and would represent the country as well as Jim Williams,[2] I have a plantation in Arkansas and my appointment would satisfy all the big negro holders, that a man was not to be proscribed because he held or owned negroes[.] But if Mr Lincoln & Gov Seward can get better men than I am to hold their offices, they ought to do so, the country is entitled to the best talent it possesses, No man can ever charge me with a want of fidelity to the south, but it is because I believe that my rights and property will be better protected in the union as it is than in the Southern confederacy that I shall go for the Union, and bid you God speed with all my heart in your efforts to preserve it[.] I should like to hear from you but I know you are very much oppressed about this time with correspondence and I do not wish to annoy you, I could have procured the reccommendation of every member I believe of the legislature but I will not do it[.] if I have any character, let me stand upon it, if not let the administration do better[.]

Yours respectfully J. B. White

ALS, DLC-JP.

1. Jackson B. White (1814–1893), a Nashville lawyer, was clerk of chancery court (1846–62) and an Opposition member of the legislature

(1859–61). He was more specific in a letter to Senator Nicholson, suggesting that his name be submitted for nomination as minister to Belgium. Failing to receive an appointment, he became politically inactive except for a term as mayor of Edgefield, now East Nashville (1870). Robison, *Preliminary Directory, Davidson*, 46; White to Nicholson, March 9, 1861, Letters of Application (1861–69), RG59, National Archives.

2. See *Johnson Papers*, II, 471n.

From Charles W. Charlton

Knoxville Tenn. Feb. 25, 1861

Dr Sir:

I thought, if you would not misconstrue my motives, I would venture to write to you. This I do in conveyance of some rumors which probably, reached your ears that I had detained your speech at my office. If this is so, I deem it my duty as a gentleman, to say to you that this is grossly & positvely *false*. Every document of every description, you sent to this office, has *been faithfully* & promptly sent off, & I challenge contradiction, let it come from what sourse it may.

And when you were burnt here in effigy, I raised my voice against it, as I can prove by men of all parties. And it is further due to say that the Democracy here *to a man* opposed it; and you were burnt by two *old line whigs*, one of them having voted for *Bell* & the other for Breckenridge.[1]

This much I have deemed it due to say to you, as a matter of justice to myself. That I am decided in my Southern feelings I do not deny, but that I am your *reviler* I *do* deny, & defy any living man to prove it. I simply wish to be put right *on the record*.

Respectfully   C. W. Charlton

ALS, DLC-JP.

1. Possibly John H. Crozier and William Swan; the former had converted to the Democracy in 1856. See A. A. Clingan to Johnson, February 17, 1861, Johnson Papers, LC; *Johnson Papers*, I, 29n; II, 214n. For Brownlow's description of the incident, in which he alleged that the culprits were Crozier and one Dreyfous, see Letter from Sam Milligan, January 8, 1861, note 2.

From F. A. Rice

February 25, 1861, Keysburg, Ky.; ALS, DLC-JP.

A physician urges Johnson to undertake a speaking tour of Kentucky and Tennessee, since "Every Secessionest to whom I gave your speeches turned promptly for the Union"; moreover, "Before you get over *Tennessee* there will be a majority in the State . . . of not less than *Eighty* thousand Warm Supporters."

From John C. Vaughn

Sweet water Tenn 25th Februry 1861

Hon Andrew Johnston
Dear Sir

Enclosed you will find my resignation as Post Master.[1] I understand Mr Brabson[2] is pressing my removal— I dont want to put them to any trouble.

I have been a grate sinner and a stumbling block in there way.[3] I have allways faught the oppisition hard & long with both my time & money both in Tennessee and in Mexico— they will rejoice over my removal in East Tennessee as much as any other mans—

I am as ever your friend[4]
John. C. Vaughn

ALS, DLC-JP.

1. The enclosure, dated February 24 and addressed to President Buchanan, indicated that Vaughn's resignation should be effective March 1. Denying the charges made by the "Bell and Lincoln party" men, he concluded, "I have allways been an unflinching Democrat—stood square at all times spent my money freely and time to defeat them." Johnson Papers, LC.

2. Reese Brabson was the congressman from Vaughn's district.

3. Rom. 14:13.

4. Ironically, Vaughn wrote Governor Harris a month later: "I do hope we may be able to Carry the legislator and elect you in the place of Andrew Johnson, U. S. Senator[.] nothing would do me more good . . . . Is it [not] humilliating for Tennessee to have *Johnston* in the Senate a worse enemy to the South today than Duglass or even a large no of Black republicans[.]" Vaughn to Isham G. Harris, March 28, 1861, Johnson Papers, LC.

From Samuel S. Cox

House Reps Washn
Feb. 26/61

Dear Gov/

Your paper for speech never went round our House.[1] Where can I get them?

Or can you today, send me ½ dozen.

Yours to the end: S. S. Cox

Gov. A. Johnson/

I send you a 'Dash' of mine! What do you say of my portrait of Giddings.[2] Can't you, by a slight change of feature, apply it to an Extreme Fire Eater in the South?

ALS, DLC-JP.

1. This "paper" was an order sheet for copies of Johnson's Speech on the Seceding States, February 5–6, 1861. For an example of a smiliar request, see Order for Reprints of Speech, 1861.

2. In a House speech of January 14, Ohio Democratic Congressman Cox had lashed out against his colleague Joshua Giddings for the latter's extreme antislavery position, which threatened to split not only the Republican party, which Giddings helped to found, but also the nation. Cox called upon Lincoln and other Republicans to moderate their views. *Cong. Globe*, 36 Cong., 2 Sess., 376.

From George I. Hooper[1]

Nashville Feby 26 1861

Hon Andrew Johnson
Dr. Sir.

Well I have gone through the ordeal of trial,[2] and stand acquitted, from any guilt or shame, a more persecuted, proscribed case, never came off in a Cou[r]t of Justice. Yes I demanded an investigation for I knew my innocence, And all I ask is for you to place me right on the Record, at Washington and restore to me back my position for I acted only as an honest man, would do in the matter, and I do think to be compelled to resign, without a cause is a hard matter for my labor, is my family dependence and that, has been wrung from me, without the slightest occasion for it.

Andy I have faced the storm, that has sprung up here against, you, and have "given blow for blow," in your behalf and to be breif I will refer you, to *Robert* who I know will do me justice for I was too deeply interested, in my Countrys good to be any thing else but a *Union Conservative Man* and I am proud to Say that I was the only Agent on the Route, that dared to assert my and your Rights, to stand by the Sheet Anchor, of all dear to us, the only hope, which can hold us as states together, a great many taunts and sneers, has been applied, to us, here, by this Southern Rights party, but dam them, they have had there day and like Know nothingism, "played out," completely and Tennessee to day stands proudly before the World that she is for the Union, and it must be *preserved*[.]

You Sir to day stand more endeared to her people then ever before, glad am I, to feel and Know it, for I see evidences of it every day, poor Bob your Son did look dejected, but myself, and my brother took him, consoled and cheered him, and in one day We satisfied him, that burning his "father in effigy" by craven, drunken, and hired scoundrels, was repudiated by the honest masses, here, and the vote just had in the State, is a Triumph and a glorious victory[.]

Now Governor, myself and Brotherinlaw Mr. Sands,[3] are both out of employment, if you can do any thing for us, do it, I know you will, and if there is not a man, in the State, that will not take office or position under Mr. Lincoln—here is two of us that will gladly accept, and will fill to the best of our judgement, and will thank you for any interest you may make in our behalf,   I am Sir
                              Truly Yours   George, I. Hooper
I Send you a Slip[.] read it[.] answer[.]
my respects to Bob, if there.

ALS, DLC-JP.

1. George I. Hooper (b. *c*1824), native of Pennsylvania and a mail agent for the Nashville and Chattanooga Railroad, possessed real estate valued at $1,000. 1860 Census, Tenn., Davidson, Nashville, 4th Ward, 130.

2. On February 17 the Nashville newspapers reported that Hooper had been arrested for robbing the mails and that the evidence strongly indicated his guilt. Examined before J. L. Bostick, U. S. commissioner, and actually charged only with removing a key from the post office, he was acquitted; however, he subsequently resigned and a successor was appointed. Nashville *Republican Banner*, February 17, 20, 1861; Nashville *Patriot*, February 18, 20, 1861; see also Letters from John W. Ford, February 19, 28, 1861; Ford to Johnson, February 17, 1861, Johnson Papers, LC.

3. Probably John E. Sands, in 1856 a Nashville and Chattanooga Railroad conductor and four years later a partner in "Hays & Sands, Wholesale Grocers and Commission Merchants." *Nashville Bus. Dir.* (1855–56), 102; (1860–61), 137.

From William H. Wetmore[1]

Wetmore Polk Co. Tenn.
February 26th, 1861

Gov. Johnson
Dear Sir

You have undoubtedly already received more information in relation to the varied effects produced upon the minds and feelings of the people of Tennessee by your late great Union Speech in the Senate than I can give you, for we of Polk receive but little intelligence of what is going on elsewhere[.] I desire to say to you however that so far as I have observed & do know, the patriotic & loyal Sentiments of that Speech have very largely increased your friends not in numbers only but in devotion & intensity. I hear you spoken of in such terms of confidence favor & admiration as are bestowed upon no one else except Mr Crittenden.

In our ardour for & deep devotion to this glorious Union of States our old political divisions and associations seem to be healed & forgotten[.] As to myself I have never been a partisan. I have never in my life joined in any parade or Shouted for any man or for any party. I have never till lately done more in reference to politics than to go quietly to the poles & deposit my vote as my own sense of my duty to my country dictated. Wishing to do what little good I might to the Cause of the Union, I did, at our late Election for delegates to a convention proposed to be held at Nashville, do myself or yourself the honor of reading to the assembled voters so much of your late Union Speech as my duties as Clerk of the election would allow, It was listened to with much attention & we gave our votes in accordance with its sentiments—Bating[2] the gross profanation, I was well pleased with the reply made to W H Ballew Esqr.[3] by your old friend Crawford Merchant of Athens[4] which I must give you.

On the morning of the day we lately elected delegates to Stay at home Crawford was assisting to raise a Union flag at his Store[.] Ballew rushes out in consternation & exclaims to Crawford Why you will ruin the party! Crawford an old veteran partisan replies "God Damn the party Sir!! My Country is in danger! I go for my Country! This I hold is the true sentiment which Should be fostered and encouraged by all everywhere—

The foregoing was written without other motive than the wish to give you a slight word of cheer in your labors when I received from my brother in Ohio the letter from him which is sent herewith.[5] I had written to him to get his influence in my favor for some appointment to a position that would enable me to support my little family. I had Known but little of my brother for 8 or 10 years. I knew him years ago to have position & influence with the New Hampshire Democracy—& supposing that he had got into the Republican party like most northern folks & had influence with that party I wrote to him asking him whether Mr Lincoln would refuse an applicant because he might be the owner of slaves as I am myself[.][6] The position I seek is quite an humble one but would be gladly accepted under all the present & pressing curcumstances[.] If nothing better can be had I would like to get the position of Mail Route Agent from Nashville to Chattanooga or if that cannot be had then from Knoxville to Chattanooga[.] Are your position and *dis*position such as that you can & will procure for me this position or appointment[?] If *not* will you indicate to me by writing how I should proceed to my efforts to procure it?

If your acquaintance with myself is too limited to justify you in procuring my appointment at once I would refer you to your very partial friends Col. William Biggs[7] or J H Alexander[8] Clerk and Master of the Chancey Court Benton Tenn—or will myself send you such a certificate or recommendation as you may require[.] It may not be improper for me to add in this connection as our acquaintance is somewhat imperfect that my wife is the daughter of the late Col.

S. H. Laughlin[9] with whom I suppose you were well acquainted when he was alive & taking his part in politics & in the practice of law in this State. As I am unsettled in business will you do me the favor of letting me hear from you at your earliest opportunity?— Direct as this is dated "Wetmore Polk Co Tennesse

I am & hope to be while I live upon earth your friend & fellow citizen in the Union of the old & new States & I was going to say of the north & the South States—

W. H. Wetmore

ALS, DLC-JP.

1. William H. Wetmore (c1816–1890), a Connecticut native and briefly postmaster at Wetmore, Polk County, was manager and part owner, with his brother Moses and cousin William S. Wetmore, a merchant rich from the East India-China trade, of the 6,000-acre Savannah Farm, said to be "the biggest thing in Polk County." Leaving his large holding worth $50,000, Wetmore fled North upon secession. Confiscated and sold by the Confederacy, the land was subsequently restored to the original owners, though they never returned there to live. 1860 Census, Tenn., Polk, Benton, 1st Dist., 15; Ben H. McClary, "Fun, Fact and Philosophy": The Diary of John Coffee Williamson, 1858–61 (M. A. thesis, University of Tennessee, 1957), lxxxiv–v; James C. Wetmore, *The Wetmore Family of America* (Albany, 1861), 382–83 (courtesy Dr. Watt P. Marchman, Hayes Memorial Library, Fremont, Ohio, to Andrew Johnson Project, September 9, 1974).

2. That is, "except for."

3. William H. Ballew (b. c1816), for several years secretary of Forest Hills Academy (1854–56), was an Athens merchant, selling general merchandise and groceries. Reba B. Boyer, tr., *Population Schedule of the United States Census of 1850 for McMinn County, Tennessee* (Athens, 1961), 66; see also his advertisements in the Athens *Post*, 1852–57.

4. John Crawford (1797–1862), the owner of Crawford and Sons, dealers in dry goods and groceries. Acklen, *Tenn. Records*, II, 176; *Mitchell's Tenn. Gazetteer* (1860–61), 9.

5. Nathaniel D. Wetmore (b. 1810), a Cleveland, Ohio, publisher and editor, who had lived in New Hampshire, where he was a member of the legislature (1846–48), had recently advised his brother "to get Andrew Johnsons letter in your favor, and such other men as may suggest themselves to you. Mr Lincoln will not decline any nomination offered to him in good faith, on account of the applicant being a holder of slaves[.] He has no bitterness toward the people South nor have his friends, nor the Republican party." *Loomis & Talbott's Cleveland Directory* (1861), 250; N. D. Wetmore to W. H. Wetmore, February 11, 1861, Johnson Papers, LC; Wetmore, *Wetmore Family*, 378–81.

6. In the 1860 slave census, Wetmore is listed as the owner of one male slave, aged thirty-eight. 1860 Census, Tenn., Slave Schedule, Tenn., Polk, 1.

7. William M. Biggs (1797–1878), Greene County native and an early settler in Polk County, had served as clerk of the circuit court (1840–44) and legislator (1849–51); at this time he was a farmer with property valued at $28,000. Robison, *Preliminary Directory, Polk*, 26; 1860 Census, Tenn., Polk, 2nd Dist., 44.

8. James H. Alexander (b. c1807), a Polk County farmer with property worth $36,000. *Ibid.*, 1st Dist., 47.

9. Samuel H. Laughlin, who died in 1850, had been one of Johnson's political associates in the state senate. When she married William Wetmore in 1849, Eleanor Laughlin was the widow of Timothy Keyser of Nashville. *Johnson Papers*, I, 60n; Wetmore, *Wetmore Family*, 383.

From Michael Burns

Nashville Feb 27 1861

Honb A Johnson
Dear Sir

I Received your speech by mail and I have read it attentively and have lent it to others and as Soon as a few friends Read it I am going to Send [it] to Mr Ellis[1] to Ark[.] there is only one opinion that It is the greatest speech that was made in the Senate for years and a credit to you and unanswerable[.] for Some cause or other a great many of the applicants for office beseiged me for letters to you[.] the letters given them were merely Saying that if they should get the offices they Sought I considered them qualified to fill. them and did not wish to Endorse them further[.] I write this as an appology for troubling you as I know your other dutys Engage all your time[.] I understand Mr Bell has started for Washington to day[.] Some think to take a Seat in Lincolns Cabinet[.] General Clemen[t]s is very anxious to be Marshal again[.] if you could help him I think It would be doing him Justice as when your first speech came out he was not one of the men that flew off but vindicated you[.] If he should not Succeed Either Glascock or Shaw[2] would make good officers[.] there is a good many applicants for the Post office. Buck. McNish[3] would be I belive very acceptable to the People as he has Experience and is a clever fellow[.] Nichol[4] is also an applicant and is Cave Johnson favourite[.] he is a very clever man and would act Honestly in the office[.] I write to you in Some hast to appologise for troubling you by adding another trouble to you in this letter[.] I Shall at all times be glad to hear of your prosperity as I never will forget Know Nothing times[.]

Yours Resp. M Burns

ALS, DLC-JP.

1. Not identified.
2. Edwin R. Glascock (b. c1819), a Virginia native, former Nashville constable, co-owner of the Nashville *Gazette* (1844–49), partner in the real estate firm of Glascock and Newsom, and a city alderman (1863), received the appointment, continuing in office until January, 1870. William C. Shaw (b. c1822), prosperous Davidson County farmer, had also been recommended by Burns a week earlier as a "gentleman and a man that would give Entire Satisfaction to the people at large." Wooldridge, *History of Nashville*, 124; Clayton, *Davidson*, 239; Porch, *1850 Census, Nashville*, 109; *Nashville Bus. Dir.* (1860–61), 176; *Senate Ex. Journal*, XVII (1867), 349; Burns to Johnson, February 21, 1861, Johnson Papers, LC.
3. William D. McNish (b. c1826), Virginia-born former post office chief clerk under Samuel R. Anderson, was named postmaster March 23 but resigned two and one-half months later. His secessionist tendencies were well

known and numerous complaints[were made about the appointment. According to a letter signed "Union Men" and addressed to the *Banner*, "The *Union and American* insinuates that our people are indebted to Senator Johnson for this appointment. If that is really so, the Senator owes it to his constituents to let them know how he has been so palpably deceived." However, Johnson was also advised that "nine tenths of the Citizens of Nashville" were pleasantly disposed toward the appointment with only a few "dissatisfied spirits," including William Lellyett, "co-assassin of Mr Poindexter—assisted by Mr French and some few others," who would probably send "a protest against appointment." McNish subsequently served as Confederate postmaster from June until the office was abandoned in February, 1862. 1860 Census, Tenn., Davidson, 18th Dist., 46; Wooldridge, *History of Nashville*, 129–30; Nashville *Patriot*, March 28, 1861; Knoxville *Whig*, March 30, April 6, 1861; Nashville *Republican Banner*, March 31, 1861; A. J. D. Thurston to Johnson, March 29, 1861, Johnson Papers, LC.

4. James Nichol (*c*1803–1878), a former Whig and one of Johnson's appointees as bank director, was a dry goods dealer. In applying for the postmastership, he noted, "I am fully aware of your position as to the incoming administration and of course I would not wish or desire you to do any act or recommend any thing in my favour . . . that would compromis you in the least," and referred Johnson to Cave Johnson, former state bank president. 1860 Census, Tenn., Davidson, Nashville, 3rd Ward, 66; *Nashville Bus. Dir.* (1855–56), 90; *Nashville City Cemetery Index*, 59; Nichol to Johnson, February 15, 1861, Johnson Papers, LC.

From Abraham M. Johnson[1]

Chattanooga Tenn Febry 27—61

Hon Andrew Johnson
Dear Sir

I enclose to you my resignation[2] as Route Agent on the Nashville & Chattanooga R R to be presented or not as you may think best to the P. O. Department[.]

You have doubtless noticed in papers the arrest and discharge of one of the Agents (Mr Hooper)[3] on this Road— before his arrest when everything was moveing on quietly—I determined to resign to take effect the 4th of March— Mr Hooper was acquitted but all that I have heard express themselves—believe him guilty— The investigation brought to light one fact *viz* that money has been lost on the Road. now should I resign could suspicion point to me— I do not wish to be *removed*[.] will it—or not—be Lincoln's policy to make a change with us— You know—I do not—can not—sympathize with him or his party— on the other hand my motto has been my rights in the union or independence out of it[.] I feel that I have done my duty in every respect and under all circumstances since I have been Agent—and have earned all that I received as a salary— The offices will have to be filled and after considering the matter I hardly think anyone would apply from Tennessee as a Lincoln man for office[.] I am sure nothing would induce me to do so— Under all the circumstances should you think it best I will continue as Rt Agt but should you think the policy of the incoming administration will be to change us—I would prefer mine to take effect the 4th of March—

Esqr Ford received his appointment yesterday[.] we all heartely endorse it and believe it will give general satisfaction. He ought not in my opinion to have been removed when he was[.][4] He expressed his sincere gratitude to you for his appointment.

Business of all sorts is at a stand still[.] dull times is the cry of every body. and all dread and fear the worst has not yet come[.]

An answer expressing your action or views in this matter—will add another to the many obligations I am under to you[.] I anxiously await it.—

Yours very Respectfully
A. M. Johnson

P.S. Will there be any seeds distributed this year from patent office
A. M. J—

ALS, DLC-JP.

1. Abraham M. Johnson (1830–1903), a Georgian who settled in Chattanooga in 1851, was postal agent on the Nashville and Chattanooga Railroad for eight years and later superintendent of the Wills' Valley Railway, continuing under the Confederacy. Resigning in 1869, he became superintendent of Chattanooga's new waterworks system and subsequently, while acting as general manager and part owner of the Lookout Rolling Mill, was largely responsible for the real estate development in the Lookout Mountain area. Charles D. McGuffey, *Standard History of Chattanooga* (Knoxville,1911), 439–44.

2. His resignation was attached. A. M. Johnson to Post Office Department, February 27, 1861, Johnson Papers, LC.

3. George I. Hooper, who was forced to resign.

4. The Nashville press announcement recalled John W. Ford's earlier service on the road, identifying him as probably the "first route agent . . . a position he filled for five or six years." Nashville *Union and American*, February 28, 1861.

From William M. Lowry

Greeneville Ten Feb 27 1861

Gov Johnson
Dear Sir

I have Just heard to day that two petitions for Post Master are being gotten up for the Post office at this place, one for Mr Jno Vance[1] a son of David G Vance the other for Lewis F Self.[2] I am of the opinion that it would be bad policy to remove Biggs. every one feels that Biggs is a Safe reliable man, and that the duties of the office will be faithfully and honestly attended too if he Continues in the office. I have no Idea the Course the incomeing administration will persue, presume they will Continue in office a faithful public Servant and not feel disposed to remove him unless obnoxious to the people who have business at his office[.][3] If you could say a word upon this Subject without embarrasment. it might have a good effect. I presume We will have the pleasure of Seeing you at home Soon[.] Mrs Johnson is improving[.][4] Nothing new[.]

in Haste   Yr freind
Wm M Lowry.

ALS, DLC-JP.

1. John Vance (b. c1837), probably because of his youth, has no occupation or trade listed in the 1850 census, but his father, David G. (b. c1812), and brother William (b. c1835) are listed as innkeepers. Inexplicably, John is not found in the 1860 Greene County census. 1850 Census, Tenn., Greene, 274.

2. See *Johnson Papers*, III, 647n.

3. Elbert Biggs was retained in office. *Ibid.*, II, 391n.

4. During these years Eliza Johnson was in poor health.

From Dunning R. McNair[1]

Senate Chamber, *February* 27, 1861.

Sir: In answer to your inquiry as to whether any one employed under my direction may not be dispensed with "without detriment to the public service," and also whether there are not abuses which require "reform and amendment,"[2] I have the honor to state that, in my opinion, the employment of three messengers now employed may be dispensed with *during the recess of Congress*, provided authority be given me, in case of any unforeseen emergency, to employ laborers. This, I respectfully trust, is an answer to the whole inquiry.

Very respectfully,   D. R. McNair,
Sergeant-at-Arms United States Senate.

Hon. Andrew Johnson, *Chairman*
Committee to Audit and Control Contingent Expenses of the Senate.[3]

Cong. Globe, 36 Cong., 2 Sess., 1521.

1. See *Johnson Papers*, III, 471n.

2. By resolution of June 18, 1860, the Senate had instructed the committee to audit and control contingent expenses to inquire into the number and salaries of Senate employees, whether the number employed could be decreased, and whether there were abuses in the system which needed reform. *Cong. Globe*, 36 Cong., 1 Sess., 3094.

3. On March 2 Johnson reported that the number of messengers had been reduced and that costs for laborers had been cut. *Senate Report* No. 309, 36 Cong., 2 Sess.

From Pitser Miller[1]

Bolivar Feby 27, 1861

Hon Andrew Johnson
U S Senate

D. Sir   I am not in the habit of writing on Politics but I feel
a good deal of Interest in the State of the Country[.]

I voted and done all I could for Union and no convention in our
late Election but if the Peace Congress breaks up without a settlement there will be a good deal of discontent and as Gov. Harris is
pretty well bent South he will call the Legislature again[.] I am fixed
and decided (altho it would be a sore thing) in my opinion that the
best thing that can be done for the Union is to withdraw the Mails
Troops officers from the Seceding States *in fact back down* give
them the Country without acknowledging the right of Secession[.]
do so with a conciliatory Proclamation then they will have no cause of
Irritation & no excuse for Drumming & fifing from morn till night
in every prominent place both in and out of the Seceded States[.] war
with the inexperienced is very popular[.] every man & Boy becomes
a Genl. Jackson[.] I think the war Cry gives them more than half
their Strength and the courage & Generalship of Jef Davis is divided
out to every man, this course would Satisfy every union Man that
I know the opinion of not that I think it right but the best the administration can do at the present[.] As to satisfying the Secessionists
I dont think it can be done[.] they will keep demanding until they
get a war[.] War is Jef Davis's Element & that he will have but by
acceding as above it will throw them in the wrong with thousands
& Rob them of a great deal of strength[.] much of their Strength
lies about the Towns and with Boys young men & agitators generally[.] Jno S Miller[2] writes me from Jackson that they are beating
up for volunteers there & Genl. Neely[3] who accompanied Jef Davis
to Montgomery has just returned has two Papers marching about
with Drum & fife for volunteers[.] one paper for our Rights the other
for Lincoln[.] this word our Rights I am willing to Stay in the union
if we can get our Rights is becoming much hackneyed and getting
into the mouth of a good many Union Men[.] a good deal of bluff is
used by the opposition Such as Licolnites Submessionists and putting
your Self down to vote with Free Negroes on an equality of New-
York and other northern States[.]

I have written Mr Seward & enclosed it to you[.] if you will hand it to him you will oblige me[.] of your Speech nothing can be Said against it except the truth should not always be told[.]

Your friend truly   Pitser Miller

ALS, DLC-JP.

1. Pitser [or Pitzer] Miller (b. c1801–fl1875), son of Jacob Miller (b. 1776) of Hawkins County and grandson of Peter Miller (1742–1810), inherited money and slaves from his father. He removed to Hardeman County, possibly in the 1820's, becoming a successful businessman and landowner; by 1860 he identified himself as a "retired merchant" with property valued at $287,000. During and after the war he was a Memphis merchant and served as a director of the Memphis and Charleston Railroad (1867), ultimately returning to Bolivar. 1860 Census, Tenn., Hardeman, Bolivar, 70; *Daughters of the American Revolution Magazine*, LXX (1936), 457; WPA, Hawkins County Wills, Bk. 1, 1797–1886, pp. 233–34; George C. Osborn, ed., "Writings of a Confederate Prisoner of War," *Tenn. Hist. Quar.*, X (1951), 174, 179; *Exhibit of the Condition of the Memphis and Charleston Railroad Company* (Memphis, 1867), 2.

2. See *Johnson Papers*, II, 323n.

3. Rufus P. Neely (1808–1901), Maury County native who moved to Hardeman County in 1832, became owner and publisher of the Bolivar *Democrat*. Register of deeds (1823–33), county court clerk (1833–[1861?]), member of the lower house (1839–41), and a soldier in both the Indian and Mexican wars, he became president (1856–61) and longtime officer of the Mississippi Central and Tennessee Railroad. Organizing the 4th Tenn. Inf., CSA, in 1861, he served as its colonel until his capture late the following year; after his exchange in 1863, he was commissioned to gather up Confederate troops trapped behind Federal lines. Robison, *Preliminary Directory, Hardeman*, 53–54; Speer, *Prominent Tennesseans*, 109–13; Mrs. Robert S. Owens and others, comps., *The Cemetery Records of Hardeman County, Tennessee* (6 vols., Huntsville, Ark., 1971–   ), II, 15–63.

From Hu Douglas

Nashville 28th Feby 1861

Hon. And Johnson
Washington City
My Dear Sir

I have been urged for Some days by different applicants for office to write to you urging their Claims. I have uniformly declined as I did not wish to either trespass upon your time or to embarrass you with my wishes. Knowing that you occupy a position that enables you to best judge, what Course to pursue, I have often thought of making some Suggestions, for your Consideration but I really have not been without fears that my letters would be mistaken. At the risk of this however I write you a few lines.

You should be extremely careful what you do[.] many of your old professed friends here are doing all they Can against you. While they assert that road to office from the President is through you then if you do any thing be sure to make as Major Downy[1] would say *a pint*[.]

Some of the old office holders have desired indirectly my influence with you. my reply has been that you certainly owed nothg to the Capitol P office Bk [bank] & Union office Cliqu or Junto.[2] Now you look out for Mockasin tracks[3] and be sure you are not Caught. Your Colleague in the Senate will represent their wishes.

Our Post Master will take Charge of the Bk on tomorrow.[4] I think he has had the P O & Bk for some time. May he not by some arrangement get the Bk and the P O?

I fear the Bk is gone—and I would have you to look out for the Same hard disclosures in regard to the Peniteniary[5] altho it was fortunate enough to have the endorsement of his excellency for its good ma[na]gement and this the Bk could not get while the Hon Cave Johnson man[a]ged it.

I sincerly trust that all will be fixed up and that we shall not be compelled to go with S. C and the balc[balance] of the mad states. If you can succeed in getting our rights in the Union, you may rely upon it that all with you will Commend and have the thanks and esteem of all good men.

You cannot however expect the approval of your professed friends who you long have known were your enemies.

But I tell you that you are Stronger to day in Ten than you ever were.

My letters are all Confidential to you and if you have any time I will be glad to hear from you[.] again I say as I often have said to you watch your friends[.] you know how to do the balc[.]

I am T[r]uly yrs,   Hu Douglas

ALS, DLC-JP.

1. Downing was a fictitious Yankee peddler, the creation of Seba Smith (1792–1868), political satirist and newspaper editor who established Maine's first daily, the Portland *Courier* (1829), in which the first "Major Jack Downing" letter appeared in 1830. These communications, featuring a humorous style widely copied during the Jackson era, were reprinted in various journals and published as separate volumes: *Life and Writings of Major Jack Downing* (1833), *Way Down East* (1855), and *My Thirty Years out of the Senate, by Major Jack Downing* (1859). Clarence L. Barnhart, ed., *The New Century Cyclopedia of Names* (3 vols., New York, 1954), III, 3636; Benét, *Readers' Encyclopedia*, 1043.

2. A reference to the Middle Tennessee Democratic faction associated with the late Aaron V. Brown, Gideon Pillow, and, more recently, Andrew Ewing. Johnson's fellow senator and former friend A. O. P. Nicholson was by now identified with this group. See *Johnson Papers*, III, 257n, 372n.

3. Douglas alludes to snakes rather than footwear.

4. Evidently Douglas had advance information, for Gen. Granville P. Smith, president of the bank, resigned from the board on March 7, his resignation to become effective April 5, and that body, by unanimous vote, elected Postmaster Samuel R. Anderson, who was also a bank director. Nashville *Union and American*, March 9, 1861.

5. Following Governor Harris' recommendation in 1859 that a convict-leasing system be established, a bill was presented in the senate and defeated on February 17, 1860; ten days earlier a similar bill introduced in the house had been withdrawn. Although the comptroller reported that the penitentiary was a drain on the state's resources, the report of the three inspectors, Dr. John D. Winston, William G. Harding, and James Overton, indicated that even with expansion and sanitation improvements the institution had produced a profit the previous year. The agent, William H. Johnson, elected by the board of inspectors in 1859, was commended by inspectors and governor for his good management. White, *Messages*, V, 121–22, 152–55; *Tenn. House Journal*, 1859–60, App. VI, 227–28.

From John W. Ford

Chattanooga Feby. 28 1861.

Hon A Johnson

Dear Sir: On the morning of the 26th inst. I received from the P. M. Genl.[1] the official notification of my appointment as Route Agent on the N. & C. R. R. in the place of Hooper "removed."— Knowing that I am indebted to your influence in my behalf in obtaining this appointment, you will please accept the tribute of a greatful heart. I was at Nashville yesterday— Genl Anderson expressed considerable surprise that Haywood did not get the appointment, when backed by the recommendation of himsef Francis and others; but said that as Haywood did not get it he preferred that I should have it.—

Hood[2] of the "Chattanooga Gazette," has gone on to Washington, for the purpose of trying to get Mr Phillips,[3] our present worthy and most efficient Post Master, removed and himself appoint instead— If he should be successful, it will be great outrage— Mr. Phillips is a modest, unassuming gentleman, and devotes his whole undivided attention to the duties of the office, and gives satisfaction to all— Hood has no qualifications and would not give satisfaction to anybody, and he certainly has no more claims upon the incoming Administration than Mr. Phillips has. If such a movemt should be made and you should think proper to interfere and prevent its consummation I know you will render a service to the people here that they will highly appreciate—

William McNish who has been Chief Clerk in the Nashville Post-office for the last ten years, has gone on to Washington for the purpose of trying to get the appointment of Post-Master at Nashville. If you have time to look through the immense list of names who have recommended him, you will see that it embraces the leading men of all parties in Nashville— John Bell has gone to Washington to press the claims of H Yeatman[4] who is also a candidate. If you can be of any aid to McNish I hope you will exert it— he was your warm friend, to my personal knowledge, in both your Canvasses for Governor.— so much on behalf of others—

Having obtained the appointment of Rout Agent, I have no wish to be removed in the advent of the incoming Administration. You understand me.

I should like very much that you would write me.—

I am as ever.   truly your friend
John W. Ford.

ALS, DLC-JP.

1. Horatio King (1811–1897) of Maine, assistant postmaster general (1854–61) and currently postmaster general (February 12–March 5), attempted to use his influence to avert the impending struggle. A loyal Democrat, he became one of Washington's outstanding lawyers. *DAB*, X, 391–92.

2. James R. Hood (*c*1838–1869), North Carolina native and editor of the Whig *Gazette*, was appointed Chattanooga postmaster in March, 1861, but because of his unionism was forced to leave the city during the war, returning in February, 1864, to reestablish his paper. Elected to the legislature in 1865, he was expelled from the house for having absented himself on too many occasions in order to prevent a quorum. Robison, *Preliminary Directory, Hamilton*, 39–40; see also Letters from James R. Hood, March 17, 31, 1861.

3. Harvey T. Phillips, see *Johnson Papers*, III, 292n.

4. Henry C. Yeatman (b. *c*1832), John Bell's stepson and ward, had inherited $58,000 from his father. Young Yeatman helped manage the family's considerable holdings, including the Cumberland Iron Works, and in 1860 had an estate worth $85,000. During the war he served as colonel and aide-de-camp to Gen. Leonidas Polk. 1860 Census, Tenn., Davidson, Nashville, 5th Ward, 148; Parks, *Leonidas Polk*, 307; Parks, *John Bell*, 115n, 208, 341.

From John G. Winter

Columbus feby 28. 1861

My dear Sir

I am very much obliged for your speech. It is a *crusher*— many facts, to me, were new & curious— Your replies to Davis & Lane precluded any other rejoinder than the one which Davis made— I feel desirious that the Pamphlet should be circulated in this part of the Country, among our friends for the purpose of furnishing them with the facts to fight the traitors with & to the moderates who went over from terror, but left their hearts behind them— In my list I will designate the Politics of the Parties—So that you can exercise your discretion as to the policy or propr[i]ety of the suggestions—

If I had my way, I would let the Cotton States go on the solitary condition that they should maintain a republican form of government— my reasons are manifold— If the Ballot Box is left open, we should vote ourselves back within two years— The experiment would terminate its miserable existence in a short period of time & Yancey & Co. would be buried tw thousand fathoms deep beneath its ignominious ruins— In the next place, the establishment of a despotism here, would create the necessity for one in the other States— The hydra headed Republic could not withstand the attacks of a talented Military despot, at an odds of half a dozen to one—I doubt wheth[er] Jeff Davis is a Louis Napoleon, but either of the Napoleons could take the Cotton States, as weak as we are & conquer the balance of the States by assaulting them in detail— If Clay & Adams had not made Peace in 1815, which they did most ingloriously by ignoring the cause of the war, under the Secession pressure of N England,[1] the republic would have lost first, all the Eastern States, then the middle States & then old England [could?] have done what she liked with the South—

Let the South go, even to the last Cotton State, protect the People of the South from falling into the hands of a military despost & I will guarantee that the indignation of the People would hurl the Freebooters into everlasting infamy, if they did not hurry them into another world— It is a bitter Pill to swallow, but if the friends of the Union could swallow the Pill, we should reconstruct the handi work of our Fathers & close up for many a long year, the cracks which have been made in our glorious Constitution by designing perfidious rascals— The poor deluded followers of the Traitors begin to wince under the operations of the new Tariff & the *tall saleries* which *short men* have voted themselves[.][2]

Pray forgive the inflection of my crude wr[i]ting & believe me

Yr devoted Svt
John G. Winter

P. S. I was told to day by a friend that you were the only Southern member of the Senate that recognized Mr Lincoln when he visted that honorable body—[3] Nobly and courageously done upon your part & the reverse is upon them[.]

John L. Mustian[4]	Columbus	A
W. L. Clark	"	A
W. R. Brown	"	A
Calvin Stratton	"	A
Justice Morton	"	B
Col. Jno Woolfolk	"	B
General Anderson Abercrombie		A
Wm. F. Luckie	"	B
Wareham Cromwell	. . . .	C
Col. Jos. B Hill	. . . .	B

Hon Jas Johnson   . . . .   B
Early Hurt Esqr   C
C. N. Terry   A
all the above reside in Columbus—
  G W Winter[5]   Augusta Ga.   C
  A—Staunch Union
  B—either half gone, or gone on the tongue, leaving the heart
    behind—
  C—rabbid secession—Secession being looked upon as salvation
  S. Woodfield—Manager Rail Road—Columbus Ga

ALS, DLC-JP; also printed in LeRoy P. Graf and Ralph W. Haskins, eds.,
"The Letters of a Georgia Unionist: John G. Winter and Secession," *Georgia
Historical Quarterly*, XLV (1961), 392–93.

1. New England's opposition to the War of 1812 had culminated in the
Hartford Convention of December, 1814, which called for a recognition of
state rights and a revision of the Constitution, with an implied threat of secession. When news arrived of the Treaty of Ghent, signed on Christmas Eve
by British and American commissioners, among them Henry Clay and John
Quincy Adams, tensions abated. Although the terms of the treaty virtually
ignored the original causes of the conflict—the impressment of American
seamen and the violation of other neutral rights—the war had been so widely
criticized that peace was welcomed. Nevertheless, Adams in private correspondence acknowledged that the actions of the New England Federalists had
had some detrimental effects on the peace negotiations. Samuel E. Morison
and Henry S. Commager, *The Growth of the American Republic* (2 vols.,
New York, 1962), I, 426–31; Worthington C. Ford, ed., *The Writings of
John Quincy Adams* (7 vols., New York, 1913–17), V, 219, 252–53.

2. The tariff measures of the Confederate Congress were used more to
regulate industry and commerce than to raise revenue; free trade was allowed
in war materials and food, but manufactured articles were restricted. The
Confederate President received $25,000 per annum, the vice president and
Cabinet members, $6,000, and congressmen at first received $8 per day, an
amount changed to $2,600 annually under the permanent government. Con-
temporary salaries for Union leaders were President, $25,000, vice president,
$8,000, and legislators, $6,000 with travel mileage. E. Merton Coulter, *The
Confederate States of America, 1861–1865* (Baton Rouge, 1950), 117, 173;
U. S. Official Register (1861), *passim*.

3. Lincoln, visiting the Capitol with William H. Seward three days earlier,
had spent about twenty minutes in the chamber, where a number of senators
were presented to him. The New York *Tribune* commented that the "Democratic side generally manifested much hesitation, but, Messrs. Douglas, Bigler,
Thomson, Andrew Johnson, and a few others, showed themselves superior to
any party feeling, and immediately asked to be presented." Washington *National Intelligencer*, February 26, 1861; New York *Tribune*, February 26,
1861.

4. For biographical information about Mustian and the others listed, see
Graf and Haskins, "Letters of a Georgia Unionist," 400–402.

5. George W. Winter (1824–1861), one of John's sons, was a banker
whose real estate holdings were valued at $87,000 by 1850. Four years later,
he with Randolph Mott and John L. Mustian, was among the purchasers of
his father's Palace Mills. Biographical data supplied by Robert D. Thorington, Montgomery, Ala.; 1850 Census, Ga., Muscogee, n. pag.; John H. Martin,
ed., *Columbus, Georgia* (2 pts., Columbus, 1874), II, 76, 147.

From Mathew B. Brady[1]

Bradys Gallery [March, 1861]
35 N. Pa. Ave. Washington

Dear Sir,

My stock of Imperial specimen Photographs having accumulated to such extent that I cannot exhibit one half of them, and believing it would be to my advantage to have yours exhibited in your district I propose to sell it to you for the merely nominal sum of ten dollars, much less than it cost to finish it.

If you can make it convenient to call and see it you will greatly oblige.

Very Resptly   M. B. Brady[2]

L, DLC-JP.

1. In 1842 or 1843 Mathew B. Brady (c1823–1896), the foremost American pioneer in photography, had established a New York studio which, because of the novelty and excellence of its work, attracted thousands of patrons. His *Gallery of Illustrious Americans* (1850) having added greatly to his prestige, he opened a branch office in Washington (1858). During the war he was commissioned by Lincoln to make a pictorial record, for which Brady and his assistants, under less than ideal circumstances, developed over 3,500 pictures, about two-thirds of which are still in existence. Nonetheless, he suffered heavy financial losses during the war, and the Panic of 1873 completed his ruin; he spent his remaining years in comparative poverty. *DAB*, II, 584–85; see also James D. Horan, *Mathew Brady, Historian with a Camera* (New York [1955]); Roy Meredith, *Mr. Lincoln's Camera Man* (New York, 1946).

2. A note in the hand of C. Percy Powell, Library of Congress, reads: "This is *not* the handwriting of Mathew B. Brady—"

From Jesse B. Clements

Nashville March 1st 1861—

Honl. Andrew Johnson
Dear Sir—

You have no doubt been annoyed untill you are tired of receiving letters from my self and friends upon the Subject of my re appointment to the Office of Marshal of this District— I have no idea of the number of letters you have received upon the subject—nor by whom written, except some few Gentlemen have told me that they had written to you— Letters have also been written to Genl. Quarles, Judge Catron, and Judge Nicholson, and perhaps some to Mr Wright —[1] I do not know how Genl. Quarles stands toward my re appointment, still I have the Confidence that he will do me no injustice[.]

Judge Catron I know is for my re appointment—and I presume the other Gentlemen mentioned will be for me, as I am the only Democrat in the field, that I know of—and I believe that I am the only one— If Mr Lincoln had a party in this state to Serve, it would be un necessary for my friends to present my name for re appointment, but he has no party here—and therefore it is an open field and a fair fight—and my friends have as much right to apply to Mr Lincoln for my reappointment as the friends of any Know Nothing have to apply— True many of my more fire eating friends almost denounce me for agreeing to hold office under a Black Republican Administration, this (I have written to you in a former letter)[2] but I must acknowledge, that I never have seen the good sense in my giving up the office to a political opponent if I could hold it myself— And as I have before stated to you that if my holding the office would injure the Democratic party I would not hold it one hour—

I am however entirely willing to leave this matter with you, if you believe I ought to hold and feel willing to lend your influance to that end, and the appointment is Confered upon me, I will most Certainty attend to the duties— I understand that Mr Shaw[3] carried with him to Washington a large petition directed to you, asking the appointment for himself— I have attempted to get up no petition, and to tell the trouth I have attempted to get no letters, except such as were offered— I further understand that I am represented at Washington, as being an *open*, *avowed*, *Sicessionest*, *this is false*. I am a Southern man in my feelings, and if a separation does take place, I want Tennessee to go with the South— but I have still hoped and trusted in God, that the difficulties would be fairly and honorably adjusted, and that there would exhist no necessity for a divission of the Government— I Still hope and trust there will not, but if Come it must, then I am with the South— I took no part in the late Conventional Election— I Split my ticket in voting, I voted for Andrew Ewing and Bu[r]ch, I neither voted for Foot, N. S. Brown, or Houston—having but little confidence in either of them—[4] The Object, of the Call of a Convention was perverted from the primary object of the call— it was not intended when the Election was ordered by the Legislature, that the Object was for the people to decide that they would Seceede, the Object of the Call of a Convention was to appoint Delegates to a Southern Conference, who were to agree upon an ultimattum which was to be presented to the whole people of the United States for a vote of the people, and if rejected then Tennessee would Consider what she would do— therefore the question of immidiate Secession raised by some of our more fire eating friend was untimely, premature, and simply, foolish— I never believed it mattered who we had in our convention, if we had good men, Tennessee must be united before any thing can be effective, towards staying in or going out—

I have not mentioned these things here for the purpose, of influancing any body in my favor[.] I mention them because, I have understood that I am misrepres[ent]ed at Washington, and because I wish at least to stand right before my friends— I am associated with what is Known here as the Post office Clique—[5] they are almost all open secessionist, but I have made it a rule to judge for my self and when I sease to do this, I shall be unfit to hold any office whatever—

Execuse this letter and do for me what you think is right— and I will be satisfied—

I am most respectfully
J. B. Clements

ALS, DLC-JP.

1. Congressmen James M. Quarles and John V. Wright, Supreme Court Judge John Catron, and Senator A. O. P. Nicholson. Quarles (1823–1901), Virginia-born lawyer from Clarksville, was attorney general for the tenth judicial circuit (1853–59) and a "National American" congressman (1859–61). During the war he served in the Confederate brigade led by his brother (William). Moving to Nashville in 1872, he was elected judge of criminal court (1872–82). *BDAC*, 1489.

2. See Letter from Jesse B. Clements, February 18, 1861.

3. William C. Shaw.

4. Clements seems to have voted on the basis of personal, rather than factional, considerations. Henry S. Foote, John J. McCann, John C. Burch, and William S. Flippin were the Davidson County secessionist candidates in the state convention election of February 9. Andrew Ewing, Neill S. Brown, Russell Houston, and John S. House were the unionist nominees who outpolled the former by more than 6–1. Nashville *Union and American*, February 9, 12, 1861.

5. The "Post office Clique" was composed mainly of remnants of the old Polk faction—Gideon Pillow, Nashville Postmaster Samuel R. Anderson, and William McNish, chief clerk soon to be named postmaster. Pillow and Anderson became Confederate generals; McNish served as Confederate postmaster.

From Samuel Tate

BURNET HOUSE,
JOHNSON, SAUNDERS, & CO., PROPRIETORS.
Cincinnati, Mch 1st 1861

Hon Andrew Johnson
U S. Washington
Dr Sir

I see a move is making to change the line of the Great Southern mail, from our line through east Tenn & Va, to the Baltimore & Ohio line via Louisville & thence to Memphis.[1] Is there any truth in this report, if so why is it done[?] is it to avoid Seceding states, as stated, and is the Tennessee Rail Roads to be ostracised by the Post office department, simply because they toutch a corner of Alabama & Miss. Will the Govt. recognize the right of Seceding states, by treating them as foreign nations and stopping the mails to their people. If so the sooner they make treaties with them for the regulation of inter-communication of mails & commerce the better, then for all[.] Such a policy might do very well if it was only to affect Seceding states & people, but I do not think Tennessee deserves such treatment after the late demonstration at the ballot Box, besides this the line over which it is proposed to be carried is much longer & if paid for per mile will cost much more. I as you know have always been an old line Whig and a Conservative man, and *now* seeing the disrupted state of our country am doing all I can to try & have it reconstructed if possible, but this ostracism looks like coercion and I am decidedly opposed to coercion, because I believe it will blast the last hope of those who desire a reconstruction & settlement of our difficulties. This move is gotten up by the new line of Rail Road from Louisville to Memphis, and you will confer a lasting benefit on the east Tenn Roads if you will put a stop to it at once. let me hear from you. I will be at home in a few days.

Yours Truly   Sam Tate Prest
Mem & Cha R R Co

ALS, DLC-JP.

1. Both Tate and Campbell Wallace, president of the East Tennessee and Georgia Railroad, were realistic in their appraisal of the situation; there patently was a movement afoot to redirect mail service to Memphis. [See Letter from Robert W. Humphreys, March 10, 1861, for more concrete evidence.] In 1861 the mails transported via the East Tennessee and Virginia, the East Tennessee and Georgia, the Nashville and Chattanooga, and the Memphis and Charleston network of roads touched, by means of the last named, a portion of Alabama and Mississippi. At the time of this letter, a House bill authorizing the postmaster general to suspend service which had to cross an insurrectionary state was pending in Congress. Amended by the Senate, the measure ultimately failed to pass; yet by April, the record of mail contracts reveals a shift to routes via Louisville for all Tennessee mail and a corresponding absence of movement through East Tennessee. Letters from Wallace and R. W. Humphreys to Johnson, March 5, 1861, Johnson Papers, LC; Folmsbee, *Tennessee*, I, 392–93; Stampp, *And the War Came*, 120–21; *Cong. Globe*, 36 Cong., 2 Sess., 498, 509–10, 1044–46, 1078–82, 1160–64; *House Ex. Doc.* No. 137, 37 Cong., 2 Sess., 552, 577.

From J[ames?] A. Cassidy

March 2, 1861, Morristown; ALS, DLC-JP.

Applicant for marshal of East Tennessee, "the only Democrat in this whole section of country who endeavored to defend your good name," sees a significant change in public sentiment: "those who were foremost in bitter denunciation are now not only silent; but begin to appreciate your great exertion in the cause of our whole Country." Denying that he is "acting the part of the sycophant," he assures Johnson that "the flames which curled around your effigy in Tenn. did more to consume the deamon, secession, than any thing else."

From James J. Wilson

March 2, 1861, Crossen's Store, Ark.; ALS, DLC-JP.

Native of Henry County, Tennessee, now living in Arkansas, seeks appointment as register of the Batesville land office: "I am 32 years old, a man of family . . . engaged in School teaching for the last 5, or 6 years. at 17 to 21 years of age kept the Post Office at Paris Tenn. have Farmed some[.]" Asks Johnson to "say to Father Abraham that I know how to split rails, and that I have split 2000 since christmas." If unsuccessful in his quest, "I can raise corn and Potatoes and teach the children Union Principles[.]"

Speech in Reply to Senator Lane[1]

March 2, 1861

Mr. JOHNSON, of Tennessee. Mr. President, it is painful for me to be compelled, at this late hour of the session, to occupy any of the time of the Senate upon the subject that has just been discussed by the Senator from Oregon. Had it not been for the extraordinary speech he has made, and the singular course he has taken, I should forbear from saying one word at this late hour of the day and of the session. But, sir, it must be apparent, not only to the Senate but to the whole country, that, either by accident or by design, there has been an arrangement that any one who appeared in this Senate to vindicate the Union of these States should be attacked. Why is it that no one, in the Senate or out of it, who is in favor of the Union of these States, has made an attack upon me? Why has it been left to those who have taken both open and secret ground in violation of the Constitution, for the disruption of the Government? Why has there been a concerted attack upon me from the beginning of this discussion to the present moment, not even confined to the ordinary courtesies of debate and of senatorial decorum? It is a question which lifts itself above personalities. I care not from what direction the Senator comes who indulges in personalities towards me; in that, I feel that I am above him, and that he is my inferior. [Applause in the galleries.]

[After the presiding officer, Trusten Polk, calls for order and threatens to clear the galleries should another demonstration occur, Johnson is allowed to continue.]

Mr. Johnson, of Tennessee. Mr. President, I was alluding to the use of personalities. They are not arguments; they are the resort of men whose minds are low and coarse. It is very easy to talk about "cowards;" to draw autobiographical sketches; to recount the remarkable, the wonderful events and circumstances and exploits that we have performed. I have presented facts and authorities; and upon them I have argued; from them I have drawn conclusions; and why have they not been met? Why have they not been answered? Why abandon the great issues before the country, and go into personal allusions and personal attacks? Cowper has well said:

A truly sensible, well-bred man
Will not insult me; no other can.[2]

But there are men who talk about cowards, courage, and all that description of thing; and in this connection, I want to say, not boastingly, with no anger in my bosom, that these two eyes of mine never looked upon anything in the shape of mortal man that this heart feared.

Sir, have we reached a point at which we cannot talk about treason? Our forefathers talked about it; they spoke of it in the Constitution of the country; they have defined what treason was; is it an offense, is it a crime, is it an insult to recite the Constitution that was made by Washington and his compatriots? What does the Constitution say:

Treason against the United States shall consist only in levying war against them, or in adhering to their enemies, giving them aid and comfort.

There it is defined clearly that treason shall consist only in levying war against the United States, and adhering to and giving aid and comfort to their enemies. Who is it that has been engaged in conspiracies? Who is it that has been engaged in making war upon the United States? Who is it that has fired upon our flag? Who is it that has given instructions to take our arsenals, to take our forts, to take our dock-yards, to take the public property? In the language of the Constitution of the United States, have not those who have been engaged in it been guilty of treason? We make a fair issue. Show me who has been engaged in these conspiracies, who has fired upon our flag, has given instructions to take our forts and our custom-houses, our arsenals and our dock-yards, and I will show you a traitor. [Applause in the galleries.]

[Polk directs the sergeant-at-arms to clear the galleries, but before the order can be enforced, a motion to suspend it is made and debated.]

Mr. Johnson, of Tennessee. I hope the execution of the order will be suspended, and I will go security for the gallery that they will not applaud any more. I should have been nearly through my remarks by this time but for this interruption.

[A lengthy discussion on the enforcement of the order ensues. When a consensus is finally reached that motions for tabling, adjourning, recessing, or moving into executive session are out of order and that Johnson has the floor, the chairman suspends his direction to the sergeant-at-arms and again warns the galleries before the speaker is allowed to continue.]

Mr. JOHNSON, of Tennessee. Mr. President, I was going on to remark, in reference to a general allusion to treason, that if individuals were pointed out to me who were engaged in nightly conspiracies, in secret conclaves, and issuing orders directing the capture of our forts and the taking of our custom-houses, I would show who were the traitors; and that being done, the persons pointed out coming within the purview and scope of the provision of the Constitution which I have read, were I the President of the United States, I would do as Thomas Jefferson did, in 1806, with Aaron Burr: I would have them arrested; and, if convicted, within the meaning and scope of the Constitution, by the Eternal God I would execute them. Sir, treason must be punished. Its enormity and the extent and depth of the offense must be made known. The time is not distant, if this Government is preserved, its Constitution obeyed, and its laws executed in every department, when something of this kind must be done.

The Senator from Oregon, in his remarks, said that a mind that it required six weeks to stuff could not know much of anything. He intimated that I had been stuffed.[3] I made my speech on the 19th of December. The gentleman replied. I made another speech, and now he has replied again; and how long has he been "stuffing?" How often has he been "stuffed?" [Laughter.] He has been stuffed twice; and if the stuffing operation was as severe and as laborious as the delivery has been, he has had a troublesome time of it, for his travail has been great, and the delivery remarkable. [Laughter.]

Again: he speaks of triumphant ignorance and exulting stupidity. In the West, where my friends Senator Douglas and Senator Bright are familiar, we sometimes do what we call "sawing a cross cut." It always requires two to perform the operation well. Repartee and satire, too, are not limited to one. I have no disposition to indulge in them; and, in fact, I think it is unsenatorial. Whatever may be the character of my mind, I have never obtrusively made it the subject of consideration. I may, nevertheless, have exhibited now and then the "exulting stupidity and triumphant ignorance" of which the Senator has spoken. Great and magnanimous minds pity ignorance. The Senator from Oregon, rich in intellectual culture, with a mind comprehensive enough to retain the wisdom of ages, and an eloquence to charm a listening Senate, deplores mine; but he should also be considerate enough to regard my humility. Unpretending in my ignorance, I am content to gaze at his lofty flights and glorious daring, without aspiring to accompany him to regions for which my wings have not been plumed, nor my eyes fitted. Gorgeously bright are those fair fields in which he revels. To me, alas! his heaven appears but as murky regions, dull, opaque, leaden. My pretension has been simply to do my duty to my State and to my country.

The Senator has thought proper to refer to the action of my State;[4] and I may be permitted to remark, that we in the South understand some things as well as they are understood in the North; and when we find one who calls himself a northern man, who boasts of his position there, making great professions of friendship, greater attachment to our institutions and our interests than we do ourselves, in some minds it may have a tendency to excite suspicion. The Senator from Oregon is more southern than the South itself. He has taken under his wing of protection the peculiar guardianship of the southern States, and his every utterance is upon the equality of the States, their rights in the Union, or their independence out of it. I think Dr. Johnson advised that when a man comes to your house, and makes great professions of his purity, his uprightness of purpose, his exalted character, of being far above suspicion and imputation, if you have any silverware, hide it.[5] When northern Senators and northern gentlemen make greater professions of devotion to our institutions than we do ourselves, our suspicions are somewhat excited.

The Senator has alluded to the action of my State; he has commented upon my devotion to the people; he has been reviewing my political history, and his penetrating mind has failed to discover anything extraordinary in it. That may be. My political history cannot be comparable with his. He has not discovered that I ever introduced or projected any great measure except the "homestead;" to that I had given great attention and labor. To the homestead policy I may infer that he was opposed. I believed it was a beneficent measure. I thought it was important that every honest and industrious head of a family in this Republic should have a home and an abiding place for his wife and children. I think so still. I can well remember the period of time at which I could exult in the assurance that I had a home for my family; and I know how to sympathize with those who are not so blest. Less gifted than the Senator from Oregon, I did not perceive that when, in the Senate, or House of Representatives, or before the people, I advocated a measure that I thought had a tendency to alleviate and ameliorate the condition of the great mass of mankind, I was incurring the censure that is due to a crime. Lamentably devoid of his wisdom, if I had succeeded in accomplishing the great object I contemplated, the measure of my ambition would have been full. I have labored for it long; I labor still. In 1846 it was introduced into the House of Representatives with but two friends.[6] In 1852 it received a two-thirds vote of that House. It came to the Senate of the United States, and during the last session of Congress thirty-eight Senators voted for it, and but eight against it. The Senator from Oregon himself, though he doubted and wavered, recorded his vote for it; but he is opposed to it now. I think it was one of the best acts of his life; and if it had succeeded, I think it would have been better for the country.

But he seems to intimate that I have been voting and acting with some that are not quite as southern as are some others. Sir, look at the Senator's course this morning. Who has tried to defeat the measures that are so well calculated to restore peace? Who is trying to eject the olive branch that has been brought into the Senate? Why does he not stand with his colleague from Oregon[7] when this measure of peace is held out to the country?

But he refers to what has been the action of my State. Well, sir, we all know that the issue was directly made; and what is the result? Tennessee has spoken in language not to be misunderstood. She has spoken in thunder tones that she is against violations of the Constitution and treasonable schemes, which have resulted in breaking up the Government. The Senator assumes a special guardianship over Tennessee. He had better try to take care of Oregon, and leave my colleague and myself, and the Representatives from Tennessee, to attend to Tennessee affairs. Where does he stand? His colleague is in favor of measures to restore peace and sustain the country, and he is against them; and did it occur to him that others might ask how he stood with the people of Oregon? Tennessee stands redeemed, regenerated, and disenthralled by the exercise of the elective franchise, that glorious lightning-rod that conducts the thunder of tyrants off the heads of the people. If the people of our sister States had enjoyed the same privilege of going to the ballot-box, and passing their judgment upon the ordinances of secession, I believe more of them would have stood with Tennessee to-day than now stand with her. But the people have been overslaughed, a system of usurpation has been adopted, and a reign of terror instituted.

The Senator is exceedingly solicitous about Tennessee. I am inclined to think—I do not intend to be censorious or personal, but entirely senatorial—that at twelve o'clock, on Monday next,[8] or a few minutes before, when the hand of the dial is moving round to mark that important point of time, instead of thinking about the action of my State, he may soliloquize with Cardinal Wolsey:

> Nay, then, farewell!
> I have touch'd the highest point of all my greatness;
> And, from that full meridian of my glory,
> I haste now to my setting: I shall fall
> Like a bright exhaltation in the evening,
> And no man see me more.[9]

If the Senator has received the news from Tennessee, if it has broken upon his mind, he may feel like Macbeth, when told by Macduff that he was not of woman born:

> Accursed be that tongue that tells me so,
> For it hath cow'd my better part of man:
> And be these juggling fiends no more believ'd,
> That palter with us in a double sense;
> That keep the word of promise to our ear,
> And break it to our hope.[10]

Yes, sir, I alluded to treason and traitors; and while I, her humble representative, was speaking, Tennessee sent an echo back, in tones of thunder, that has carried terror and dismay through the whole camp of traitors.

The Senator has alluded to my political course. What had that to do with the pending question? I did not attack the Senator from Oregon; he has attacked me. I had not even made an allusion to him in my speech, except in general terms; but he inquires into my consistency. How consistent has he been? We know how he stands upon popular or squatter sovereignty. On that subject, he spoke at Concord, New Hampshire,[11] where he maintained that the inhabitants of the Territories were the best judges; that they were the very people to settle all these questions; but when he came here, at the last Congress, he could make a speech in which he repeated, I cannot tell how many times, "the equality of the States, the rights of the States in the Union, and their rights out of the Union;" and he thus shifted his course. If the conflict between his speech made in Concord in 1856, and his speech made here on the 25th day of May last,[12] can be reconciled, according to all rules of construction, it is fair to reconcile the conflict. If the discrepancy is so great between his speech made then and his speech on the 25th of May last, of course the discrepancy is against him; but I am willing to let one speech set off the other, and to make honors easy,[13] so far as speech-making is concerned.

Then, how does the matter stand? There is one speech one way, and there is another speech the other way. Now, we will come to the sticking point. You have seen the equivocation to-day. You have seen the cuttle-fish attempt to becloud the water and elude the grasp of his pursuer. I intend to stick to you here to-day, as close and as tight as what I think I have heard called somewhere "Jew David's Adhesive Plaster."[14] How does your vote stand as compared with your speeches? Your speeches being easy, I shall throw in the scale against you the weight of what you swore. How does that matter stand? I intend to refer to the record. By referring to the record, it will be found that Mr. Clingman[15] offered the following as an amendment to the fourth resolution of the series introduced by Mr. Davis:

Resolved, That the existing condition of the Territories of the United States does not require the intervention of Congress for the protection of property in slaves.[16]

What was the vote on the amendment proposed to that resolution by Mr. Brown, to strike out the word "not."[17] I want the Senator's attention, for I am going to stick to him, and if he can get away from me he has got to obliterate the records of his country. How would it read, to strike out the word "not?"

That the existing condition of the Territories of the United States, does require the intervention of Congress for the protection of property in slaves.

Among those who voted against striking out the word "not," who declared that protection of slavery in the Territories by legislation of Congress was unnecessary, was the Senator from Oregon. When was that? On the 25th day of May last. The Senator, under the oath of his office, declared that legislation was not necessary. Now where do we find him? Here is a proposition to amend the Constitution, to protect the institution of slavery in the States, and here is the proposition brought forward by the peace conference, and we find the Senator standing against the one, and I believe he recorded his vote against the other.

But, let us travel along. We have only applied one side of this plaster. The Senator voted that it was not necessary to legislate by Congress for the protection of slave property. Mr. Brown then offered the amendment to the resolution submitted by Mr. Davis, to strike out all after the word "resolved" and to insert in lieu thereof:

That experience having already shown that the Constitution and the common law, unaided by statutory enactment, do not afford adequate and sufficient protection to slave property—some of the Territories having failed, others having refused, to pass such enactments—it has become the duty of Congress to interpose, and pass such laws as will afford to slave property in the Territories that protection which is given to other kinds of property.[18]

We have heard a great deal said here to-day of "other kinds," and every description of property. There is a naked, clear proposition. Mr. Brown says it is needed; that the court and the common law do not give ample protection; and then the Senator from Oregon is called upon; but what is his vote? We find, in the vote upon this amendment, that but three Senators voted for it; and the Senator from Oregon records his vote, and says "no;" it shall not be established; and every southern man, save three, voted against it also. When was that? On the 25th day of May last. Here is an amendment, now, to protect and secure the States against any encroachment upon the institution within the States; and there the Senator from Oregon swore that no further legislation was necessary to protect it in the Territories. Well, his speeches in honors being easy, and he having sworn to it in the last Congress, I am inclined to take his oath in preference to his speeches, and one is a fair set-off against the other. Then, all the amendments being voted down, the Senate came to the vote upon this resolution:

That if experience should at any time prove that the judicial and executive authority do not possess means to insure adequate protection to constitutional rights in a Territory, and if the territorial government should fail or refuse to provide the necessary remedies for that purpose, it will be the duty of Congress to supply such deficiency, within the limits of its constitutional powers.[19]

Does not the resolution proceed upon the idea that it was not necessary then; but if hereafter the Territories should refuse, and the courts and the common law could not give ample protection, then it would be the duty of Congress to do this thing? What has transpired since the 25th day of May last? Is not the decision of the court with us? Is there not the Constitution carrying it there? Why was not this resolution, declaring protection necessary, passed during the last Congress? The presidential election was on hand.

I have been held up, and indirectly censured, because I have stood by the people; because I have advocated those measures that are sometimes called demagogical. I would to God that we had a few more men here who were for the people in fact, and who would legislate in conformity with their will and wishes. If we had, the difficulties and dangers that surround us now, would be postponed and set aside; they would not be upon us. But in May last, we could not vote that it was necessary to pass a slave code for the Territories. On, no; the presidential election was on hand. We were very willing then to try to get northern votes; to secure their influence in the passage of resolutions; and to crowd some men down, and let others up. It was all very well then; but since the people have determined that somebody else should be President of the United States, all at once the grape has got to be very sour, and gentlemen do not have as good an opinion of the people as they had before; we have changed our views about it. They have not thought quite as well of us as we desired they should; and if I could not get to be President or Vice

President of all these United States, rather than miss it altogether, I would be perfectly willing to be President of a part; and therefore we will divide—yes, we will divide. I am in favor of secession; of breaking up the Union; of having the rights of the States out of the Union; and as I signally failed in being President of all, as the people have decided against me, we have reached that precise point of time at which the Government ought to be broken up. It looks a little that way.

I have no disposition, Mr. President, to press this controversy further. If the Senator from Oregon is satisfied with the reply he has made to my speech or my speeches, I am more than satisfied. I am willing that his speeches and mine shall go to the country; and, as to the application and understanding of the authorities that are recited by each, I am willing to leave an intelligent public to determine that question. I shall make no issue with him on that subject. I feel— and I say it in no spirit of egotism—to-day that, in the reply I made to his speech, I vanquished every position he assumed; I nailed many of his statements to the counter as spurious coin; and I felt that I had the arguments, that I had the authority; and so feeling, I know when I have my victim within my grip. I know an argument that cannot be explained away, and a fact that cannot be upturned. The Senator felt it; I know he felt it from the feeling he has manifested, from the manner in which he has nursed his feelings and his wrath until this occasion, to pour them out. Yes, sir, in that contest, figuratively speaking, I impaled him, and I left him quivering. He felt it. I saw it; and I have no disposition now, in concluding what little I am going to say, to mutilate the dead or add one single additional pang to the tortures of the already politically damned. I am a humane man; I will not add one pang to the intolerable sufferings of the distinguished Senator from Oregon.[20] [Laughter.] I sought no controversy with him; I have made no issue with him; it has been forced upon me. How many have attacked me; and is there a single man, north or south, who is in favor of this glorious Union, who has dared to make an assault on me? Is there one? No; not one. But it is all from secession; it is all from that usurpation where a reign of terror has been going on.

I repeat again, the Senator has made a set-to on me. I am satisfied, if he is. I am willing that his speech and mine shall go to the country, and let an intelligent people read and understand, and see who is right and who is wrong on this great issue.

But, sir, I alluded to the fact that secession has been brought about by usurpation. During the last forty days, six States of this Confederacy have been taken out of the Union; how? By the voice of the people? No; it is demagogism to talk of the people. By the voice of the freemen of the country? No. By whom has it been done? Have the people of South Carolina passed upon the ordinance adopted by their convention? No; but a system of usurpation was instituted, and a reign of terror inaugurated. How was it in Georgia? Have the people there passed upon the ordinance of secession? No. We know that there was a powerful party there, of passive, conservative men, who have been overslaughed, borne down; and tyranny and usurpation have triumphed. A convention passed an ordinance to take the State out of the Confederacy; and the very same convention appointed delegates to go to a congress to make a constitution, without consulting the people. So with Louisiana; so with Mississippi; so with all the six States which have undertaken to form a new confederacy. Have the people been consulted? Not in a single instance. We are in the habit of saying that man is capable of self-government; that he has the right, the unquestioned right, to govern himself; but here, a government has been assumed over him; it has been taken out of his hands, and at Montgomery a set of usurpers are enthroned, legislating, and making constitutions and adopting them, without consulting the freemen of the country. Do we not know it to be so? Have the people of Alabama, of Georgia, of any of those States, passed upon it? No; but a constitution is adopted by those men, with a provision that it may be changed by a vote of two thirds. Four votes, in a convention of six, can change the whole organic law of a people constituting six States. Is not this a *coup d'etat* equal to any of Napoleon? Is it not a usurpation of the people's rights? In some of those States, even our stars and our stripes have been changed. One State has a palmetto, another has a pelican, and the last that I can enumerate on this occasion, is one State that has the rattlesnake run up as an emblem.[21] On a former occasion, I spoke of the origin of secession; and I traced its early history to the garden of Eden, when the serpent's wile and the serpent's wickedness beguiled and betrayed our first mother. After that occurred, and they knew light and knowledge, when their Lord and Master turned to them, they seceded, and hid themselves from his presence. The serpent's wile and the serpent's wickedness first started secession; and now, secession brings about a return of the serpent. Yes, sir; the wily serpent, the rattlesnake, has been substituted as the emblem on the flag of one of the seceding States; and that old flag, the stars and the stripes, under which our fathers fought and bled and conquered, and achieved our rights and our liberties, is pulled down and trailed in the dust, and the rattlesnake substituted. Will the American people tolerate it? They will be indulgent; time, I think, is wanted; but they will not submit to it.

A word more in conclusion. Give the border States that security which they desire, and the time will come when the other States will come back; when they will be brought back—how? Not by the coercion of the border States, but by the coercion of the people; and those leaders who have taken them out will fall beneath the indignation and the accumulating force of that public opinion which will ultimately crush them. The gentlemen who have taken those States out are not the men to bring them back.

I have already suggested that the idea may have entered into some minds, "if we cannot get to be President and Vice President of the whole United States, we may divide the Government, set up a new establishment, have new offices, and monopolize them ourselves when we take our States out." Here we see a President made, a Vice President made, cabinet officers appointed, and yet the great mass of the people not consulted, nor their assent obtained in any manner whatever. The people of the country ought to be aroused to this condition of things; they ought to buckle on their armor; and, as Tennessee has done, (God bless her!) by the exercise of the elective franchise, by going to the ballot-box under a new set of leaders, they will repudiate and put down those men who have carried these States out and usurped a government over their heads. I trust in God that the old flag of the Union will never be struck. I hope it may long wave, and that we may long hear the national air sung:

> The star-spangled banner, long may it wave,
> O'er the land of the free and the home of the brave!

Long may we hear old Hail Columbia, that good old national air, played on all our martial instruments! long may we hear, and never repudiate, the old tune of Yankee Doodle! Long may wave that gallant old flag which went through the Revolution, and which was borne by Tennessee and Kentucky at the battle of New Orleans, upon that soil the right to navigate the Mississippi near which they are now denied. Upon that bloody field the stars and stripes waved in triumph; and, in the language of another, the Goddess of Liberty hovered around when "the rocket's red glare" went forth, indicating that the battle was raging, and watched the issue; and the conflict grew fierce, and the issue was doubtful; but when, at length, victory perched upon your stars and your stripes, it was then on the plains of New Orleans that the Goddess of Liberty made her loftiest flight, and proclaimed victory in strains of exultation. Will Tennessee ever desert the grave of him who bore it in triumph, or desert the flag that he waved with success? No; we were in the Union before some of these States were spoken into existence; and we intend to remain in, and insist upon—as we have the confident belief we shall get— all our constitutional rights and protection in the Union, and under the Constitution of the country. [Applause in the galleries.][22]

Cong. Globe, 36 Cong., 2 Sess., 1350–51, 1354–56; also published as a pamphlet, *Speech of Hon. Andrew Johnson, of Tennessee, in Reply to Senator Lane of Oregon* (Washington, D. C., 1861).

1. In the course of a speech opposing constitutional amendments suggested by the Washington Peace Conference and supporting the right of secession, Lane had defended himself against some earlier remarks made by Johnson. *Cong. Globe*, 36 Cong., 2 Sess., 1342–49.

2. Paraphrase of William Cowper, *Conversation*, l. 193.

3. Referring to Johnson's argument of December 18–19, Lane had opined: "Whenever it takes a man six weeks to study, and two days to disgorge, he never has a correct idea of what he has been cogitating." *Cong. Globe*, 36 Cong., 2 Sess., 1346.

4. The Oregon senator had recalled the 1860 presidential canvass in which Johnson took the stump for the Breckinridge and Lane ticket. Commenting that he was grateful for those services "so far as they were rendered to our party," Lane observed tartly: "if in his speeches in that contest he advanced such doctrines as he now proclaims, I am not so much surprised that we were defeated in that state." *Ibid.*, 1347.

5. Probably a reference to Samuel Johnson's rejoinder upon hearing that a certain man insisted there was no difference between virtue and vice: "if he does [think this], why, Sir, when he leaves our houses let us count our spoons." Humphrey Milford, ed., *Boswell's Life of Johnson* (2 vols., London, 1922), I, 289.

6. Johnson himself and Felix G. McConnell of Alabama. See *Johnson Papers*, III, 186.

7. Edward D. Baker (1811–1861), English-born lawyer, served as a Whig in the Illinois legislature (1837, 1840–44) and in the House of Representatives (1845–46, 1849–51) before moving to Oregon, where he was elected to the Senate as a Republican in 1860. A Mexican War veteran, he was a major general of volunteers when he was killed at Ball's Bluff in October, 1861. Baker, an ardent opponent of slavery, had concluded to support the Washington Peace Conference proposals which would have let the people decide on their adoption as amendments. *BDAC*, 505; *Cong. Globe*, 36 Cong., 2 Sess., 1314–16.

8. At noon on Monday, March 4, Lincoln's inauguration would launch the new Republican administration.

9. Shakespeare, *Henry VIII*, Act III, sc. 2.

10. Shakespeare, *Macbeth*, Act V, sc. 8.

11. In the pamphlet copy of his speech Johnson gives a verbatim quotation from Lane's Concord address of February 7, 1856, rather than the paraphrased version found in the *Globe*.

12. Here again, in the pamphlet Johnson quotes directly from Lane's speech and corrects the date to May 24, 1860.

13. An expression associated with whist and other card games, in which the four highest cards are referred to as "honors." *OED*, V, 368.

14. "Jew David or Hebrew plaster," a widely advertised popular remedy for rheumatism and "all seated pains" in "the back, side or breast," and likewise "efficacious in removing wens, tumors, corns, etc," was sold in a box "sufficient to spread 6 or 8 plasters" which, upon application, stuck tightly to the skin. Jonesboro *Whig*, July 1–November 18, 1846.

15. Thomas L. Clingman of North Carolina had submitted this amendment on May 24, 1860. *Cong. Globe*, 36 Cong., 1 Sess., 2322.

16. See Speech on Secession, December 18–19, 1860, note 55.

17. The amendment offered by Albert G. Brown of Mississippi was rejected, 43–5. *Ibid.*, 2343.

18. *Ibid.*, 2347.

19. *Ibid.*, 2349.

20. Lane's speech of March 2, in which he had castigated Johnson, represented his swan song. Defeated for vice president, he had been replaced as

senator and his Democratic machine in Oregon was in shambles. According
to his successor, James W. Nesmith, "Old Jo was regarded with universal
contempt." On his part "Old Jo" had been preparing to answer Johnson since
the latter's remarks early in February; writing to his son, he called the Tennessean "a low contemptible wretch that deserves the scorn and contempt of
all good men." Hendrickson, *Joe Lane*, 247.

21. Louisiana displayed the pelican, while "the wily serpent" was employed by both South Carolina and Alabama—one side of the latter's flag
depicting a rattlesnake coiled at the base of a cotton plant. Lossing, *Pictorial
Civil War*, I, 184; Clarence P. Denman, *The Secession Movement in Alabama* (Montgomery, 1933), 146.

22. On the order of the presiding officer, Graham Fitch, the galleries were
cleared after "three cheers more for Johnson." Other "expressions of feeling"
prompted Fitch to order arrests of any "guilty of this disorderly conduct." The
clearing process required more than ten minutes, during which time no business was transacted on the floor. *Cong. Globe*, 36 Cong., 2 Sess., 1356.

From Jesse L. Gross[1]

Sparta Tennessee March 3d 1861

Gov—Johnson sir:

I avail myself of the present opportunity of addressing you with
a few lines. You would confer a great favor on me by handing Mr.
Lincoln this letter. And tell him that my father and mother are
acquaintance of yours and Mother is a daughter Mordecai Lincoln[2]
who you were well acquainted with; and I think from the acquaintance you have with our family that you could recommend me to
Mr. Lincoln. I am as well qualified to fulfill a clerkship as any person
in Tennessee; and as Mr. Lincoln has offices to give to the people that
he would confer a great favor on me to give me an office.[3] I have
writting 2 letters to Mr. Lincoln and think the reason that I never
have received an answer that he receives so many that he has not any
time to read all letters that is sent him[.] I can bring good recommendation from any person in the neighborhood where I live he would
want if he so required it. I am a son of Milton Gross who formerly
lived in Greenville and Clara Gross[.][4]

Yours truly   Jesse Lincoln Gross

ALS, DLC-Lincoln Papers; also printed in David C. Mearns, *The Lincoln
Papers* (2 vols., Garden City, N. Y., 1948), II, 454.

1. Jesse Lincoln Gross (1839–*fl*1912), a native Tennessean and White
County farmer who later served as a second lieutenant in the 9th Tenn. Cav.,
USA (1863–64), received Johnson's endorsement for a Federal office. After
the war, Gross emigrated to Point Blank, San Jacinto County, Texas, where
he was a farmer and schoolteacher. 1860 Census, Tenn., White, 30; Johnson
to Lincoln, March 9, 1861, Lincoln Papers, LC; Jesse L. Gross, Volunteer
Service, RG94, National Archives.

2. Mordecai Lincoln, a first cousin of Abraham Lincoln's father, had been
a Greeneville tanner active in local politics. Jesse's mother was Paulina Emily

Lincoln Dinges Gross [variously spelled Grose or Groce], Mordecai's daughter by his first wife, Clara Paul of Hardy County, Virginia. First marrying William Dinges of Virginia and later Milton B. Gross of Sullivan County, Paulina, a widow by 1860, had evidently added her long-deceased mother's given name to her own, for she is listed in the census of that year as "C. P. E. Gross," hence the signature on the appeal quoted in note 4. For Mordecai Lincoln, see *Johnson Papers*, I, 5n; Samuel Cole Williams, *The Lincolns and Tennessee* (Harrogate, Tenn., 1942), 18–21.

3. There is no evidence that Gross, despite his tenuous relationship to the President, was successful in his application.

4. An appended message in the hand of Gross's mother reads: "Dear relation[:] I am a going to ask a favor that I never have ask the public. I have three sons that I have educated and spent most of my means in so doing. I am a widow and have no means to put my sons in to business with, and no relations to assist me in Tennessee[.] And you would confer a great favor on me if you would put than [*sic*] in to business[.]   Your niece   Clara P. Gross"

From William R. Hurley

Nashville March 4th 1861

Hon A Johnson
Dear Sir:

I propose to write to ask a favor. You are perhaps aware that I took charge of the Democrat[1] under the most unfavorable auspices. I have by persevering effort secured the largest daily circulation of any paper in Nashville. But we have no Press, and have to hire our printing—and while it takes all our profits, it is often inconvenient to have it printed at all[.] In view of these facts we propose to borrow some money from our friends, to place our paper on a permanent basis, and unless we can borrow some money we will be compelled to suspend the publication. We propose to give our notes & a mortgage on the establishment to secure the note holders against loss.

We are trying now to raise about $2000 from our friends, to purchase a Press &c. I have thought that there might be a Press (second hand) but good about Washington; that might be bought on good terms[.] would you do me the favor to make me a small loan and further inquire about a Press. Stokes is friendly to the Democrat & might also give us a small loan[.] What we do, must be done immediately: Or we will be compelled to suspend. If you can aid us we would be glad for you to Telegraph as soon as you receive this, and write also— We will decide what we will do in a very few days.

A number of my friends have asked me to take the Post office if I could get it.[2] In view of my necessity I agreed to do so but have not made it public. my friends, are anxious, on account of the aid it would afford me in sustaining the paper[.] I have not solicited the office nor will I, yet I would accept it. You are fully sustained in your own state, by the *people*[.] You have more friends to day than ever before in the state[.]

Respectfully Your &c   W R Hurley

ALS, DLC-JP.

1. The Nashville *Democrat* seems to have first appeared September 27, 1860, and was still being published in March, 1861. Guy H. Stewart, History and Bibliography of Middle Tennessee Newspapers, 1799–1876 (Ph. D. dissertation, University of Michigan, 1957), 129.

2. A telegram on March 4 from Thomas J. Kelly (Hurley's associate on the *Democrat*) and J. Richard McCann notified Johnson that "Dr Hurley would accept the Post Office at this Place— Is it possible that he could get it?" Kelly and McCann to Johnson, March 4, 1861, Johnson Papers, LC.

From Thomas J. Usrey[1]

Fayetteville Ark Mar 5th 1861

Hon. A. Johnson
Dear Sir

The telegraph has informed you of the results in this state[.] The Union Men have fine majority in favor of Co operation with Tennessee and the other Central States. This County voted nineteen hundred Union Two-hundred and seventy three secession.[2]

Most of the Indian Agents, the Land Registers and Receivers have resigned. Lincoln must either close the offices or send obnoxious individuals to fill them. Will you present my name to the President for an Indian Agency. I do not think there will be any impropriety in my Soliciting an office under the President (Lincoln) although I opposed his advent to power. I am of course a Southern man and am also consistently a Union *Man*. I hope you will act in regard to the foregoing request as you may deem best. Will you respond to this at your earliest Convenience that I may know what course to adopt in my private affairs.

Those in this state and the Indian Territory who have not resigned are the most determined secessionists. Yet they are equally, if not more intensely attached to spoils than Southern Rights. If you think I am privileaged to ask of you the favor and you do not consider it inconsistent with honor and self respect on my part, I hope you will present my name to the proper Department for an Indian Agency, Mail Agency or position in some one of the Land offices.[3]

The public interest requires the Continuation of the offices. Shall they then be retained by those who opposed to the existence of the government—or filled by men in the South, true to their native Section and also to the integrity of the Union.

In haste I close with request that you will favor me with an reply.

Your friend & fellow citizen

T. J. Usrey

ALS, DLC-JP.

1. See Letter from Thomas J. Usrey, January 26, 1861.

2. Usrey's interpretation of Arkansas' February 18 vote on matters related to the Union crisis is, at best, misleading. Although the Union delegates to a state convention to consider the issue of secession won, 23,626–17,927, over secession sympathizers, the unionists lost, 27,412–15,826 on the more basic question of holding such a convention. Only two counties—Washington and Crawford—returned a "no convention" majority. Again, Usrey overstated Union sentiment in his home county, Washington: the actual vote was against convention 1,541–569. The figures nearest to Usrey's were those for the most successful unionist delegates (1,921) and for the least successful secessionist candidate (353). Wooster, Secession Conventions, 157; John L. Ferguson (Arkansas State Historian) to Andrew Johnson Project, June 14, 1974.

3. Three days later he renewed his request, asking specifically for an Indian agency. See Usrey to Johnson, March 8, 1861, Johnson Papers, LC.

From H. M. Majors[1]

Shelbyville Ten March the 6 1861

Hon Andrew Johnson

Dear Sir haveing Some few weekes agoe wrote you a letter[2] informing you that I would be an applicant for the Post Office at Shelbyvill and Soliciting your aide and requesting you to answer it wich you have not done and the time is near at hand for the appointment to be maide and as there are Strong efforts makeing by other applicants I deem it Necessay to say Something more to you on the Subject[.] Sir I Some times think that it is folly for an individual in as humble circumstanes as my self to address a man in you Positon but when I turn to you biogrephy and Read thire that you was wonce a young man in humble circumstance like myself it Encourages me to write and this is sead [said] to be the working mans Administration[3] and you are a Taylor and So am I[.] there Should be a tendency of Feelling towards Each other and if there is I would Say to you Rememberest thou me in the Hour of need[.] When you made your first call upon the People of Tennessee & Sir nothing but a boy left the School Room took my Napsack upon my back my Riffle upon my Shoulder and march to the Feield of battle and bravely Set fourth your claim upon evy Stump through my own and surrounding Counties and in your Second Canvass I laid down my Needle and a gain march to the Field of batt[l]e and now Sir there is nothing that would induce me to belieav that you would hesitete to be [my] friend[.] I have sent up an able Petition to the PostMaster Geneal[4] and have Solicited the aid of many Friend, but there is no one that could do as much good as you from the Fact there is no man in Tennessee that would hav as much influence as you and as my request is neigher unkind nor unjust I cannot help but think that you will say Something to the Postmaster General in my Favor[.] it is true Sir that I differ with Mr Lincoln in reguard to Politic but that amount to nothing[.] Some Person is compelled to keep th PostOffice and if I Could get it would be of great help to me as I have aged Parent who are thrown on me by misfortune to take care of in thire declineing years and if I could get the appointment it [would] enable [me] to take care of them[.] now I will say Something in reguard to the other applicants[.] the First is Mr Richardson who is the Present Postmaster and is a very cleaver man but Mr Richardsen is wealthy and dosenet need the offic[.][5] the second is Mr Cleavelen who has sent his Petition to you and has ask you aide[.][6] Now Mr C is a Strong Opposition [man] and has for years been a Political emeny of you and Denounce your cours[.] Mr Cleavlend is ave[r]y clever man but I cannot [see] any justic in a man recomending his enemise in prefferane to his Friends[.] the next Applicant is Mr Brime who has no use for the office as he is extreamly whealthy[.][7] he has sent up a larg Pettion but I donot think a legal one for [he] got it up six or eight monts ago under Mr Buchanan Administration and Mr Richardson got the Apointment over him and he has transfered his Old Petition and sent it upa gain[.] the next Applicant is Mr Speer[8] who is now in Washington City[.] he has no Petition except one man John Edger[.][9] Mr Speer is a avolitionist and the auther of a letter recent Publish in the New York Tribune[10] and if he was to come back to Shelbyvll since the Publication of letter he would be kick out of town[.] now sir you have the History of the whol and I submit my case to your own good judgement and if you comply with my request you will be longe remembered[.]

vey Respectfully
H M Majors

To his Friend Andrew Johnson

ALS, DLC-JP.

1. H. M. Majors (b. c1839), a laborer in 1860, was mustered into Confederate service at Chattanooga in 1862, served as a private in Co. D, 23rd Tenn. Inf. and as brigade shoemaker until he was wounded at Petersburg in July, 1864, and medically discharged. 1860 Census, Tenn., Bedford, 6th Dist., 39; H. M. Majors, Compiled Service Record, RG109, National Archives.

2. Reporting that he had campaigned for Johnson, Majors contended that he took to the stump to defend the senator and his "Present Position in Congress and now in return I only ask you as a Friend to assist me in obtain[ing]

the Appointment of Postmaster." Majors to Johnson, February 17, 1861, Johnson Papers, LC.

3. When Lincoln and other Republicans spoke of "free labor," they were understood to espouse not merely absence of slavery but the cause of those who worked with their hands for a living—mechanics, laborers, farmers, even small businessmen—and the idea of social mobility, equal opportunity for all, was implied. The platform had justified the party's tariff policy as a program which would secure "to the workingmen liberal wages, to agriculture remunerative prices, to mechanics and manufacturers an adequate reward for their skill, labor, and enterprise." Arthur M. Schlesinger, Jr., ed., *History of American Political Parties* (4 vols., New York, 1973), II, App. 1241; Foner, *Free Soil, Free Labor, Free Men,* 11–18; Basler, *Works of Lincoln,* IV, 202.

4. Montgomery Blair of Missouri.

5. D. P. Richardson, printer and dealer in books, stationery, musical instruments, and wallpaper, sent his petition to Johnson March 14. Johnson Papers, LC; *Mitchell's Tenn. State Gazetteer* (1860–61), 285.

6. Hazzard P. Cleveland (b. *c*1817), who also solicited the appointment through Johnson, had in 1859 been postmaster at Wartrace Depot, Bedford County, achieved the Shelbyville postmastership during Reconstruction (1869–73), and in 1869 was named a commissioner to build the county courthouse. 1860 Census, Tenn., Bedford, Shelbyville, 15; *U. S. Official Register* (1859), 369*; *Goodspeed's Bedford,* 868; Cleveland to Johnson, March 14, 1861, Johnson Papers, LC; Record of Appointment of Postmasters, Vol. 28, p. 3, RG69, National Archives.

7. Perhaps William B. M. Brame (b. *c*1813), a Virginia-born merchant with $6,000 in real estate. Porch, *1850 Bedford Census,* 110; *Goodspeed's Bedford,* 874.

8. William S. Speer (b. *c*1823), with $14,500 in realty and $2,250 in personalty, later wrote Johnson in regard to a consulship. Subsequently he published *Sketches of Prominent Tennesseans* (Nashville, 1888). Speer to Johnson, March 15, September 29, 1861, Johnson Papers, LC; 1860 Census, Tenn., Bedford, Shelbyville, 22.

9. John T. Edgar (b. *c*1825), Kentucky native, son of the Reverend John T. Edgar, and ten years earlier a Nashville schoolteacher, possessed at this time $3,500 in personal property. On March 21 he was appointed U. S. consul to St. Thomas Island, where he served until recalled by President Johnson in 1865. *Ibid.,* 27; Porch, *1850 Census, Nashville,* 69; *U. S. Official Register* (1863), 6; *Senate Ex. Journal,* XI (1858–61), 321, 337; XIV (1864–66), Pt. 1, p. 308.

10. The New York *Tribune* of February 26 carried an unsigned communication "from Shelbyville," which declared that secession sentiment in Tennessee was diminishing and that four years hence "a Republican ticket in this State will make an excellent run" even under the slogan *"All men are created equal,"* inasmuch as many had indicated that they would *"willingly, cheerfully"* relinquish every slave they owned. For Speer's denial of authorship, see Letter from William S. Speer, March 12, 1861.

Response to Washington Serenade[1]

March 7, 1861

Mr. Johnson expressed his gratitude for such a manifestation of their appreciation of his efforts to save the Union. He did not believe that there was the least shadow of a reason justifying secession. The South had a majority in Congress and they could withhold money and cripple the administration, if they had been so disposed. But they had gone out of the Union simply because they had the right, without either consulting their own or the nation's interest. They had gained nothing, and lost all. The people had been hurried and dragged into secession by disappointed politicians, who were aspiring after office and the emoluments of place, and when these men found that they must go down they made this desperate struggle to elevate themselves at home. He pitied the people who had to submit to such rulers. He had met with them daily for many months; he had known them intimately for years, and was perfectly acquainted with their ideas of Government, and for himself he would rather be a subject to the autocrat of Russia than a citizen of the Southern Confederacy. He felt confident that Tennessee would remain firm and true to the Union. She had fought the battles of the South on many a field, and she felt that she had been wronged by them. He believed that the South could get more in the Union than they would ever obtain out of it, and he was willing to remain and battle with fanatics for the Union. He was confident that Tennessee could get all her rights secured to her by the North, and she would not yet sacrifice herself for a mere abstraction. If she could not get her just dues from the North, she would never join a southern oligarchy, but would unite with the other border States and set up a government of their own.[2]

Washington *Evening Star*, March 8, 1861.

1. A parade of well-wishers and office-seekers, after serenading Senators Crittenden and Douglas, and Gen. Winfield Scott, collected in front of the St. Charles Hotel and "called out" the Tennessee senator.

2. Tennessee Congressman Emerson Etheridge, stopping down the street from the National, was also cheered; "Yankee Doodle" was played and "the crowd quietly dispersed."

From Joseph C. Bradley[1]

Huntsville Alabama
March 8 1861

Hon Andrew Johnson
Washington City D. C.

I want to hear from you direct your opinion of the future of our Country— I cant see any thing warlike in Mr Lincoln Inaugeral"— but our papers are teeming with denunciations of it as being in every particular Coercive. The object—is plain— it is to run our people— politically mad if possible & prevent hereafter any reorganisation of the union. If Lincoln will only remain inactive—& make no attempts to repossess the forts—south—the Conservative feeling in the secedeng states will react. The precipitators greatly desire that Lincoln should make some demonstration on the Confederate States—so as to Create a warlike feeling among our people. Will not the people of the Free States take this matter in hand & save our Country, or are they determined to make every thing bend or yeild to Free soilism.

I will have much confidence in what you will say to me about the present & future of the country— I am deeply immersed in buisiness & have much at stake & of course feel verry uneasy in my present situation.

If Lincoln attempts to Blockade or Collect the duties at the Southern ports. a Collision will take place—as sure as you are a liveing man, & the whole Country will be involved in a civil war, as much as I have been opposed to the Precipitators in all of their moves. I cannot take part against my own State & Section, my fortune will be with the people of Ala—what a dilema,— may the God of Heaven evert the dire Calamity that is about to befall our once happy & beloved country.

a large Majority of the people of North Ala. would to day be in favor of a reunion of the States if we of the south could only get Constitutional safeguards for our Negro rights or property,—but if such are not granted our people will never be willing to reenter the Federal Union.

I was confident last Summer & fall—that it would not be many months before you would find out the great deception of some men with whom you acted. My political sentiments assimulate to yours— and I could never come to any satisfactory conclusion how you would allow yourself to be deceived by men who are at heart Monarchist & dispise you from the very bottom of their hearts,

If we have no immediate Collision with the U S—we the Co-operationist of Ala, will start a Candidate for Gov & try & get our state out of the hands of the Secessionist— but if difficulties should shortly occur, we will not be able to do so. It is my opinion that every thing now depends on the Course of Lincoln for weal or woe. If him & his friends are determined to Coerce, they will find a united people in the Confederate States to resist. all of us will go with our section[.] what will Va & North Carolina do— write me[.]

Yrs Truly   Joseph C Bradley

ALS, DLC-JP.

1. Joseph C. Bradley (c1813–fl1869), Virginia-born commission merchant with $20,000 in real estate and $230,000 in personal property, had been a delegate to the Baltimore Democratic Convention in 1860. Going "over to the enemy to save his property," he was gubernatorial candidate of the "peace party" in 1865 and a well-known "Scalawag" who interceded with Johnson on behalf of certain north Alabama unionists. 1860 Census, Ala., Madison, Huntsville, 50; Walter L. Fleming, *Civil War and Reconstruction*

in Alabama (New York, 1905), 146n; Edward C. Betts, *Early History of Huntsville, Alabama* (Montgomery, 1916), 102; Bradley to Johnson, September 8, 20, October 13, November 15, 27, 1865, May 22, 1866, Johnson Papers, LC.

From Genio C. Scott[1]

100 Waverly Place, & 156 Broadway New York
March 9th, 1861.—

Hon. Andrew Johnson
Dear Sir

On the occasion of talking with Mr. S. Prichett[2] of Nashville Tenn. yesterday, he suggested the wish that I could write to you, adding that you would know me, by reputation, at least. In complying with his request, I take more than ordinary pleasure in informing you that your conservative and patriotic political course meets with commendation from nearly every citizen of New York, including all the intellectual and virtuous among them.

I was a democrat, of that branch denominated the Hunkers;[3] but now, I am willing to be anything or nothing for the Union. I also think that the Union may be preserved without war. Do you think so? If Mr. Lincoln will but send an able letter, glowing with patriotism, to the Governors of the seceded states, couched also in the greatest frankness and ability, inviting them to state their grievances and whether they will be willing to unite with the other states in a national Convention to adjust them—placing great emphasis on their states never having stated their grievances constitutionally, and upon the patriotism of the masses, the known conservatism of Stevens[4] and other able men.—If, I say, he will postpone answer to the representatives from the states which have seceded declaratively, and man[a]ge the matter gingerly and at the same time diplomatically, I think he may heal the differences between the North and South. I was greatly pleased with your intention to so amend the Constitution as to allow every man to vote direct for President, and have advocated it in the N. Y. Courier, wherein I have suggested your nomination to the Presidency in 1864.[5] I belong to a family of Scotts who have scarcely ever held a civil office. Grandfather Scott[6] was the heir to the farm settled by Samuel Scott A. D. 1665, and Grandfather was the Col. Scott of our Revolutionary War. James Scott, father's brother, was wounded at Lundy's Lane, while an officer under Winfield Scott, now Lieut. Gen. & Commandant of the American army. Father was Capt. in the war of 1812, and was also with Peter B. Porter—surveyor of the state.[7] Martin Scott[8]—sec. cousin —was shot at the taking of the City of Mexico. It was to him that the [illegible] offered to come down and [give?] in if he would not shoot. Uncle James taught the military school[9] in N. Carolina after his health became infirm from his wound at Lundy's Lane, and he died in N. Carolina. My father died at Ft. Osage Missouri. I learned tailoring, then became a railroad and canal contractor, then published the N. Y. Transcript a daily paper and the Report of Tailor's Fashions.[10] I have resided in the city 26 years and published the fashions during all that time; and while soliciting subscriptions for the work, travelled to every town and village in the Union. I have several times travelled over Kentucky, Tennessee, Alabama, Ga. South and North Carolina on horseback, crossing over the Cumberland range of mountains from Huntsville Ala. to Egleton,[11] and from Huntsville to Knoxville, then by the Valley road to Winchester Va. I have also resided 18 months in Europe since I commenced my fashion publication, and was elected in Paris, a member of the *Commission des Modes*,[12] a membership of which body I still am. Mr. James G. Wilson—recent owner of the patent by Woodworth, for planing, tonguing and grooving boards and plank—was my partner in the fashion business for eight years. He also employed Hon. W. H. Seward three years, to assist with legal advise in sustaining the Patent.[13] It was on a tour of this kind to the South, that Mr. Seward visited many of the distinguished statesmen of that section of the Union.[14] I am a widower, with only one son—Winfield—who resides on my plantation near Geneva N. Y. I am no politician, but have some taste for literary pursuits, and have worked for years for Graham's Magazine, Arthur's Magazine, the Home Journal, and Wilkes Spirit of the Times[.][15] But, if I can be even a spoke in the wheel for getting you nominated for the Presidency, I will at once take the stump and ask for the great cause of bringing about the time prophesied by Carlyle, when the Tailors shall become the Hierarchs of the Earth, without an English King to confiscate their estates again in dread of their power, nor a Will. Shakespeare to pander to the Crown in the effort to write them down.[16]

In the present disaffection between the North and South, I think the North the first aggressors; but having inflamed and maddened the people of the Cotton States, they there have committed overt acts which cannot be justified by any views of clemency or charity. They have out Heroded Herod; and though too wrongs can never make a right, yet—'twere well, could they be made to realize the advantages of the Union.

The instinctive desire of the Napoleon family will be to favor the South.— At least I judge so from their talk during my residence in Paris, for having come from here to Paris with Prince Murat—as bearer of dispatches in the Spring of 1848,[17] and then at the fight in

June,[18] I became tolerably familiar with the family, and they prefer the people of the South, to those of the North. Excuse the above random letter, and accept the assurance of my highest and most friendly consideration for yourself and your interests.

Yours Very Sincerely
Genio C. Scott

ALS, DLC-JP.

1. Genio C. Scott (c1805–1879), born in Livonia, New York, taught school and was briefly connected with the Delaware and Hudson Canal before establishing himself in New York City (c1835); over the years from 1844 until 1879 he was identified in New York City directories as a reporter or publisher of fashions. An avid fisherman, he contributed articles to various sports journals and published *Fishing in American Waters* (New York, 1869). New York *Times*, December 20, 1879; Gunther Pohl (New York Public Library) to Andrew Johnson Project, January 10, 1975.

2. Samuel Pritchett (b. c1817), New Jersey native, was a prosperous merchant-tailor doing business at 54 North College Street and living in West Nashville. 1860 Census, Tenn., Davidson, Nashville, 13th Dist., 121; 1850 Census, Tenn., Davidson, 233; *Nashville Bus. Dir.* (1855–56), 97.

3. Hunker, a corruption of the Dutch word *hunkerer* ("a self-seeking politician"), came to be applied to a New York political faction which emerged about 1843 in opposition to the Locofocos and Barnburners, the radical and reform wings of the state Democracy. The Hunkers favored internal improvements at federal expense, state banks, and compromise on the slavery issue. Richard B. Morris, ed., *Encyclopedia of American History* (New York, 1953), 176, 192.

4. Alexander H. Stephens of Georgia.

5. The *Morning Courier and New York Enquirer* (1827–61) eventually gave way through subsequent mergers to the New York *World-Telegram* of modern times. Scott's communiqué has not been found. Gregory, *Union List of Newspapers*, 464, 482.

6. Neither the genealogical nor the military records available disclose information on Samuel, "Grandfather," James, or "Father" Scott.

7. Peter B. Porter (1773–1844), a Connecticut native, major general of N. Y. Volunteers (1812–15), and secretary of war (1828–29), was a lawyer and pioneer on the western New York frontier. A member of the legislature (1801), he served in Congress (1809–13, 1815–16) where he became a prominent "War Hawk." Also a surveyor, he was appointed one of the commissioners to determine the Canadian-U. S. boundary after the Treaty of Ghent. *DAB*, XV, 99–100; *BDAC*, 1471.

8. Martin Scott (d. 1847) of Vermont served as a lieutenant in the 26th Inf. (April 21, 1814–June 15, 1815) until honorably discharged. Reenlisting two years later he rose to lieutenant colonel; cited for gallantry in the Mexican War, he was killed at the battle of Molino del Rey. Heitman, *Register*, I, 869.

9. A vague reference which could allude to several North Carolina military schools; no record of Scott's teaching has been found.

10. Both a rival and an imitator of the New York *Sun*, the *Transcript* (1834–39) was "important in the history of sensational journalism." Despite its existence of more than thirty-five years, Scott's "Report of Tailor's Fashions" has not been specifically identified. Frank L. Mott, *American Journalism* (New York, 1947), 228.

11. Possibly Eagleville in Williamson County, south of Nashville.

12. Not identified.

13. Wilson, a New York businessman, held the patents on a planing machine designed by William Woodworth of Hyde Park, New York. Granted

originally in 1828, the patent was extended for seven more years in 1842; meanwhile it became so valuable that numerous infringements occurred. In January, 1846, Seward won an important case before the Supreme Court in James G. Wilson v. Lewis Rousseau and Charles Easton; he subsequently prosecuted a number of similar litigations. 4 Howard 646 (1846); Van Deusen, *William H. Seward*, 98.

14. While in Washington on the patent case, Seward encountered many of the leading politicians of the day, including President Polk and ex-President Adams. The Washington visit, side trips to Richmond and Norfolk, and a later tour of Maysville and Lexington, Kentucky, Memphis, and New Orleans early in 1846, brought the New Yorker in contact with Calhoun, Benton, Clay, Crittenden, Cassius Clay, and others. At the same time, he gained an awareness of the plantation regime, an experience which heightened his growing distaste for slavery. Frederick W. Seward, ed., *Autobiography of William H. Seward from 1801 to 1834* (New York, 1877), 767–806; Frederick Bancroft, *The Life of William H. Seward* (2 vols., New York, 1899), I, 152–55.

15. Under the shrewd business eye of George R. Graham, then part owner of the *Saturday Evening Post, Graham's Magazine* (1841–58) developed into a successful journal containing romantic fiction, poetry, occasional travel pieces, high quality illustrations, and colored fashion plates. Poe, Lowell, Bryant, Cooper, Longfellow, and Simms were among its distinguished contributors. *Arthur's Magazine or Ladies' Magazine of Literature, Fashion and the Fine Arts* (1844–46), edited by Timothy Shay Arthur of *Ten Nights in a Barroom* fame, published several famous pieces, including Longfellow's "Village Blacksmith," before merging with *Godey's Lady's Book* in 1846. Poet and essayist Nathaniel Parker Willis and Gen. George Pope Morris, author of "Woodman, Spare That Tree," edited the New York *Home Journal* (1846–1901), a newspaper which mirrored the city's fashions and fashionable people. Thriving on the clippings of sister journals, pirated fiction and essays from the Continent, and sprightly gossip and amusements aimed at the society-conscious, it had on its editorial staff at various times both Poe and Thomas Bailey Aldrich. *Wilkes' Spirit of the Times*, one of the most popular general sports periodicals of this period, was founded in 1859 by George Wilkes, who also launched the *National Police Gazette*. The *Spirit* covered a variety of special-interest topics including racing, field sports, and the stage. Frank L. Mott, *A History of American Magazines* (5 vols., New York, 1930, 1938), I, 544–55, 733–34; II, 203–4, 348–55.

16. The exact quotation in *Sartor Resartus* reads: "With astonishment the world will recognize that the Tailor is its Hierophant and Hierarch, or even its God." In the same work Carlyle satirizes the low opinion of the tailor held by Shakespeare and Queen Elizabeth, reminding that a nameless tailor appears in *The Taming of the Shrew* and one called "Starveling" in *A Midsummer Night's Dream*, and that Elizabeth, alluding to the proverb "Nine tailors make a man," reputedly addressed a group of eighteen tailors with "Good-Morning, Gentlemen both!" Thomas Carlyle, *Sartor Resartus*, Frederick W. Roe, ed. (New York, 1927), 235, 236.

17. In 1825 Napoleon Lucien Charles Murat (1803–1878), the second son of Napoleon I's brother-in-law, Prince Joachim Murat, came to the United States, where he constantly schemed to recover his father's Neapolitan throne. Returning to France in 1848, he became a senator and during the Second Empire was accorded formal recognition as a prince of the imperial family. *Webster's Biographical Dictionary* (Springfield, Mass., 1966), 1073; A. J. Hanna, *A Prince in Their Midst: The Adventurous Life of Achille Murat on the American Frontier* (Norman, Okla., 1946), 97–100, 232, 239–46.

18. A reference to the disorders of the "June Days" of 1848, which followed the Assembly's dissolution of the controversial national workshops. Donald C. McKay, *The National Workshops: A Study in the French Revolution of 1848* (Cambridge, 1933), *passim*.

From William Shanks[1]

March 9, 1861

To Mr Govnir A. Johnson

mi famley is in toleble health all but mi Self[.] I am a bad Criple
with Rheumtism[.] I Cante Shute nare [nary] hand[.] i can get mi
finger & thumbe to geather[.] i can walke alittle with mi sticker[.] i
caint gete up of mi Chear[.] mi gearles lifte me a baute fron place
to place[.] they Set me on mi horse & I Can ride[.] I have a large
femley all girls but one boy[.] mi famley be long to the flower
famley[2] of the world & it is likley you doant know the famley by the
name[.] I give the nam So you will know mi gearls is farmers[.] mr
gov A Johnson I thinke you have forgoten your frendes in Chop-
tack[.][3] I aint Saw you in a longe time[.] i aint for goten you[.] i all
ways go to the Poales with Johnson at the head of mi ticket[.] you
& I youst to to ake [take] on a little Buck hie juse [Buckeye juice][4]
to geaher[.] I read gin Laen [Gen. Lane's] Speech[.] I thoughte he
had give you fittes but whean I read your Speech i saw he haddent
made nare mark on you[.] I Juste Say your Speech that you deliverde
in the sennet of the united Steats is the best thing that eave [ever] fell
from the Lipes of any Gentleman[.]

I aint for forcen South Carolina back tho the Stronge pints in you
argument is if South Carolin was a re Publick to her Self & she
was gooing to form a alilen [alliance] with sone oathe [some other]
govermente you Said Snatch her in & I Say Snatch her in lete it
cost whate it may[.] some foles [fools] or crazy men ar burning &
hanging you in Effregy[.] hit all anounte to nothe [nothing.] your
ar Stronger in Tennssee tho you eavre was[.] I will bete the Shirt
of[f] mi back thate you Can beate are [ary] man in the State for
govnor[.] yes your ar like the Lady the loser of one is the gaine of
two[.] Mr O. Rice[5] Saide iddene [I didn't] get all of your Speech in
the weekly union & american[.] if ther was any more & as good as
what he had publich I think if he hade publich it all hit would have
kill the Editor[.] I juste Say the [that] know [no] State hase arite
to Seecede[.] if theay hav we Caint hoald Choptock Districk &
Rogersvll Districk to geather[.] the gentle men at Rogersvll a few
days before the laste presideter [presidential] in [inaugural?] sent
mee docamemt to Distribete a nough to Wait a pore mane horse
down[.] they knowed I was trubled[.] I put mi gearl on a horse &
she tuck [took] the districk & Distribete them[.] I expec[t]ed one of
yr Speeches in pam[p]h[l]et form frome thos gentle men but they
nay Come nare Speech to mi dick [district?] yet[.]

I undestande you have mad the second speech[.] if I get are wome [one] I will have to bie hit[.] I will gave mi Poaste office: Easten- nessee Hawkins County marble Hall. Post office[.] you will please Sende mee some those Speeches & whean you & I meate in Rogersvll we will take a dram of buck hie juse to geather & I will pay all damage[.] I want you to hoalde tennessee virginia & Kentucky to geather if you Can & we aint in any danger or i think we must have our juste rites[.] I am for your plane [plan] on the teritory question[.] if we Cainte gete our rites lete these Slave State that aint gone lete them all Come out to geathe & invite oathe States to join[.] I doante think ther is a nough of fooles in the uniteade States to Destroy this grate Repblickan governmente in the worlde[.] lete our Stares & Stripes floate any wheare & the People in places ar as fraide of our banner as me & you would be of a big lion that we woud meate in the Road[.] if the north doant give the South her rites & we have to fite I am for pease all the time[.] I say if we have to fite mi Plane is to man the army the eagle [equal] army of them[.] Coll for vlunteers & have the army largenough one third virginia one third Tennessee & one thi[rd] Kentucky[.] the worlde Cainte whipe sutch armies[.] they may kill all of our men but Cainte whip them[.]

Our most in truste [interest] is withe the South[.] I doante Ceare mutch whearthe South Caroninie is in the union or oute[.] she is all wais Cicken [kicking] up[.] we muste hav our just rites[.] if we Cane get a compemise to Suite the border states mi Plane [is] to whipe South Carolinia back[.] lete oald virginia Tennessee Kentucky In- diania Illinois & Ohio[.] lte [let] thoase States hoalde the meete Corne & flour back twelve moanths & the govne of South Carolina would Com troten back like a Pore Swampe Possom & agange of yonger ones folering him[.] I have alarge famley 10 in number 7 Daughtere 1 sone alive[.] I naim mi Sone Martean Van Burian Shanks after the Ex Preasideante[.] I voated for Van Burian fo preasidente[.] whean he was alected he got 3 voates at mi presink oute of a boute 160 voate[.] I am toal [told] tho we differ in politcks know [now] whean I was married I Coudeante read a plain noate of hande[.] I dideant k[n]ow the meaning of figers know [no] mor thean a hoge did of Sunday[.]

March 9 the 1861

William Shanks

ALS, DLC-JP.
    1. William Shanks (b. *c*1812) was a Hawkins County farmer with com- bined property worth $5,686. 1860 Census, Tenn., Hawkins, 11th Dist., 1.
    2. Not identified; although the census records show no such name, it is possible that the writer may be referring to a maternal kinship with the Flora family of Hawkins County.
    3. A Hawkins County village, five miles west of Rogersville.

4. One designation for home brew. A contemporary magazine, discussing smuggled liquor, observed, "It is nearly all *very bad*, owing to the quantity of the buckeye bean used in its preparation, to give it what is called a *head*." *Harper's Weekly*, December 7, 1867; Mathews, *Americanisms*, I, 202.

5. Orville Rice (1793–1879) of "Marble Hall" was a wealthy Hawkins County farmer with real and personal property valued at $168,550 at mid-century. Coming to Rogersville from Virginia in 1824, he became a successful merchant and tavern keeper, and amassed a fortune in the marble industry. 1850 Census, Tenn., Hawkins, 22; Prentiss Price, "Samuel Shaver: Portrait Painter," ETHS *Publications*, No. 24 (1952), 104; David L. Eubanks, ed., "J. G. M. Ramsey as a Bond Agent," *ibid.*, No. 36 (1964), 94n.

From Alexander A. Clingan

March 10, 1861, Cleveland; ALS, DLC-JP.

Former Bradley County sheriff praises Johnson's speech of February 5-6, urging that hundreds of copies be distributed in Tennessee. "I have Let one or two of my nabours Read your Speach[.] Theay say it is a bible Docament and if they Had one of them they would Sleep every night with it under their Head[.]"

From Jeptha Fowlkes

Richmond Va. March 10. 1861.

Private
Hon. A. Johnson
My dear Sir:

I regret I could not see you again but requested Genl. Richardson[1] to see you & Col Etheridge; stating my views "afresh," to avoid possible misapprehensions of my position, wishes & judgment! 1st. I hold that the disposition of the Federal patronage in Ten. shold be made in reference to *"the future"* rather than *the past*— 2nd. I hold *your* support as indispensible, to public interest, in the attitude you have & now stand! 3rd. I regard Col. Etheridge & yourself, co-operating for *future* good, to the State & Nation, vastly important; & hence, I sought as I did to effect that result. I had no object, & no wish for either, or my self or friends, but the great End of saving the Union & advancing public interests; & best done as above indicated, in my opinion.

Finding so far as Memphis be concerned *the past* & not the future governing the distribution of its offices; & that Col. E. occupied a position unchangeable as he declared I could not see, how, I could enforce my views on you without its Separating you & Col. E. rather than tending to unite yr. action, I felt it due to you, to him & my own views, to withdraw all suggestions & all interference & lest *mischief*, & not good be the fruit of my efforts. The patronage of Federal Gov. should be dispensed most to promote its own well-being in this Crisis—& not for personal benefits & past services—to your friends or kin but confer it on common friends, who will use discreetly, justly & wisely its influences for *public*, & not private advantage of friends! The patronage at Memphis could be dispensed so as to have effected a powerful control over the public mind by correctly & fully dispensing facts to the people.

I do not wish to be understood as entering objections to what is proposed, to be done, but I have this, to say, the patronage of our end of State ought to have gone, where & with whom, it would dispense light, most brightly; & produced most influences; & I believe, it is not proposed, so to dispense it—resulting from *past* considerations rather than looking to those of a *future* character!

I repeat you & Col. E., should understand & act *unitedly*[.] I labored for this & not "the spoils of office." & no consideration could induce me, to thwart this object—sincerely so desiring, *then* & *now*— no opinion, wish or object of mine can or shall interfere therewith— fearing evil results I withdraw all suggestions & commit matters solely to you & himself—acquiesing in whatever you shall do, heartily—acknowledging *no* responsibility nor obligations, for the results of a policy or acts, founded upon a rule of dispensation drawn from *the past*, rather than the *future* & which, are, not the offspring, of a compromise judgment!

Va. will not secede *now*— efforts making, & I think they will be successful, to carry out yr. views of a border State Convention![2] No war, is, the conviction! Avoid all that can excite or inflame— The fever is gradually subsiding—& soon our sick patients will be convalescent. you may regard Va. I think, in no danger from hasty, unwise action & I am more & more encouraged to hope for a happy termination of our national troubles.

I left Washington with Hon. J. Bell— he told me he made advances to you;[3] & expressed a gratification, that, you had recd. his approach properly. He goes home well assured of peace—while Senator Green[4] visiting Va. was strong in his conviction of war. Hon Mr. Cockrane[5] said to me, as we separated he for N.Y & I for this City—he had fearful apprehensions of the administration! All considered, I think we shall have peace—& with it, the Union will yet "be preserved." Hostilities once begun we have two Confederacies—Civil war long protracted & great loss to slavry if not its over throw on this Continent! When I can serve command me *freely*. You can let Col. Etheridge see this letter if you choose— he has been kind & useful to me—which I appreciate & shall not forget.

Very truly Your friend
J. Fowlkes.

ALS, DLC-JP.

1. Probably William A. Richardson (1811–1875), Kentucky-born Democratic lawyer, who served in the Illinois house (1836–38, 1844–46) and senate (1838–42) and was a Mexican War veteran. Illinois congressman (1847–56, 1861–63) and governor of Nebraska Territory (1857–58), he was chosen to complete the senate term of Stephen A. Douglas (1863–65). *BDAC*, 1518; Ben: Perley Poore, comp., *The Political Register and Congressional Directory. . . 1776–1878* (Boston, 1878), 596.

2. In response to the call, originating in Virginia, for "A Convention of the Border Slave States and such other slave States as have not passed ordinances of secession," a small group of delegates representing only Missouri and Kentucky met at Frankfort on May 27 to consider "the critical condition of the country, and agree upon some plan of adjustment." A lone Tennessean, John Caldwell, representing McMinn and Sevier counties, participated by invitation in the discussions but lacked the proper credentials to vote. Certainly Johnson would have approved the convention's appeal for a peaceful solution to the crisis and the suggestion for constitutional guarantees of slaveholders' rights. It is unlikely that he would have endorsed the neutral course recommended: "take no part in this war." Yet Governor Isham G. Harris, writing in early January to Johnson's friend Mrs. Lizinka Brown, made an intriguing observation concerning the senator's views: Tennessee's future, declared Harris, lay with "a Southern or Northern Confederacy, unless we should adopt the project of Johnson and Nicholson, who (in the event of dissolution) favor a middle confederacy." By the time the border state convention gathered in May, Johnson and Harris had little common ground. Moore, *Rebellion Record*, I, Doc., 350–56; Coulter, *Civil War in Kentucky*, 81–82; Harris to Brown, January 8, 1861, paraphrase and transcription in St. George L. Sioussat Papers, Box 11.

3. While there is no record of a Johnson-Bell interview, the former Constitutional Union candidate had gone to Washington for Lincoln's inauguration and was granted an extended conversation with the President-elect on the afternoon of February 26. Urging conciliation, Bell assured Lincoln that coercion by armed force would fail. Although receiving no definite commitments, he left with the impression that the new President would follow a peaceful course. In view of Johnson's growing influence with the new administration, particularly with regard to patronage, Bell may well have sought out the senator in the hope of furthering a conciliatory policy toward the South. Parks, *John Bell*, 395–96; David Rankin Barbee, "The Line of Blood: Lincoln and the Coming of the War," *Tenn. Hist. Quar.*, XVI (1957), 13–15; LeRoy P. Graf, "Andrew Johnson and the Coming of the War," *ibid.*, XIX (1960), 220.

4. James S. Green, Missouri Democrat. See *Johnson Papers*, III, 511n.

5. John Cochrane, Democratic congressman from New York.

From Robert W. Humphreys[1]

[Clarksville, March 10, 1861]

Hon A. Johnson

Sir—When I was in Washington City last week I laid before the Post Office Department a bid for the great South western Mail—from Washington to Memphis[.][2]

This bid was signed by all the RailRoads from Washington to Memphis—and as we were to carry the longest and most important Mail in the U States we put in the bid the Maximum compensation

$300—dollars per mile— We expect the Contract for the following reasons—

We will carry the mail the entire line from Washington to Memphis in 54 hours[.]

We will carry it with promptness and certainty far greater than on any other route—

We will cary it all the way over law abiding Territory—and the mail will not be liable to be overhauled at every cross Road or Station by a lawless mob— The Memphis and Charleston Road goes 250 miles or more through the territory that is now in Rebellion and the President and Directors of that Road have tendered it to the Gov of Miss for the transportation of troops and munitions of war *"free" of all charges.*[3]

Are the bounties and benefits and the public service of the U states to be placed in the hands of those who intend to destroy the Goverment—or in the hands of the law abiding Citizens—
Will the Goverment foster force and rebellion or Order and obedience.

We will carry the Mail for West Tennessee Mississippi, Arkansas Louisiana and Texas and we should have the highest compensation. We wish a Contract[.]

We now pay for Southern letters 25 cents each to Adams Express Co—and will the Goverment employ those Roads to cary the mail through the ceded territory to points beyond[.] in the face of this fact I beg of you to urge these matters before the Department and if they decline it then I wish the proposition filed by Mr Guthrie[4] and myself at 200 per mile accepted— By this you will greatly oblige your obt Servant

R W. Humphrys *Pres*

Hon Andrew Johnson

PS—I find there is considerable feeling among the soap locks[5] about town—and they claim that the secession feeling is on the increase— I see no evidence for it whatever[.] There are Some hypocrites who pretended to be for the Union but were Traitors at heart— They say that they are for the Union but not for Andrew Johnson[.] But they cannot make this distinction for we intend to make the point on your position as the Union platform[.] I think everything depends on your position for you are the head and front of our party—
Your Speeches will start to day in safe hands for Stewart Benton and Henry Counties along the line of the Rail Road—
Please call me at any time— I will freely give my labours for the good cause[.]

R W Humphrys

ALS, DLC-JP.

1. Robert W. Humphreys (1824–1878), a University of Nashville and Harvard graduate and a Mexican War veteran, was a prosperous Clarksville lawyer with $23,880 in real and $31,580 in personal property. In 1860 he became president of the Louisville, Clarksville, and Memphis Railroad, a branch of the L & N. Titus, *Picturesque Clarksville*, 30–34; Clarksville *Jeffersonian*, March 20, 1861; 1860 Census, Tenn., Montgomery, Clarksville, 18.

2. Seeking the lucrative mail contract for his railroad, scheduled to be opened to traffic the next month, Humphreys had gone to Washington for a February 26 meeting to discuss revising southern mail routes in order to avoid passage through seceding states. Humphreys to Johnson, March 5, 1861, Johnson Papers, LC; Ursula S. Beach, *Along the Warioto: A History of Montgomery County* (Nashville, 1964), 138, 176; Clarksville *Jeffersonian*, March 6, 1861.

3. It had been reported that Samuel Tate, president of the Memphis and Charleston, had offered free troop transportation over his line, one of eight railroads operating on Mississippi soil at the outbreak of the war. These railroads tendered their services either free of charge or on favorable terms until about May, 1861, when the Confederate government began paying fifty percent of the regular rates. Memphis *Avalanche*, February 28, 1861; Bettersworth, *Confederate Mississippi*, 132, 136–37.

4. James Guthrie, former secretary of the treasury, was president of the Louisville and Nashville Railroad. *Johnson Papers*, III, 461n; Robert S. Cotterill, "The Louisville and Nashville Railroad, 1861–1865," *American Historical Review*, XXIX (1924), 701–15.

5. Slang for a fellow who plasters his hair down with soap; a loafer or member of a "low set of fellows who lounge about the market." *Webster's Third International*; John R. Bartlett, *Dictionary of Americanisms* (Boston, 1877), 622.

From J. T. Thompson

March 10, 1861, Chattanooga; ALS, DLC-JP.

"*An Andy Johnson* . . . and a *Union democrat*" warns against the appointment of James R. Hood, "your old *traducer* & Slander," as postmaster and "in the name of the *Simon pure democracy*" recommends James S. Edwards.

From Henry S. French

Nashville 11 March 1861

Hon A Johnson
Washington C. D. C
Dear Sir

On my arrival here ifind [*sic*] two letters from my Son J C French[1] and there is Severl heer from our thur [other?] Union men and I find the Removel of Anderson would do more then Scott with 200 000 men in the feild[.][2] Remove evry Cause of irritation and you will beat them at their own game[.] do this at once and the C[o]unt[r]y is Safe[.] tell Hon Lincoln this[.] Cant you See it if this is done all their Woorke is lost[.] their plans and predictions falls to the ground harmless at the feet of the administration[.]

may God give you helth and Strength to go on with the good Woorke for the union[.]

your friend & Servant   H S French

ALS, DLC-JP.

1. Jefferson C. French (b. c1834) was a partner with his father in H. S. French, grocers and commission merchants. In 1860 he had $17,000 in real estate and $15,000 in personal property. 1860 Census, Tenn., Davidson, Edgefield, 39; *Nashville Bus. Dir.* (1855–56), 46.

2. A reference to Maj. Robert Anderson, commanding the Federal garrison at Fort Sumter, and to Winfield Scott, army general-in-chief (1841–61) until replaced by George B. McClellan in November. Scott had suggested to William H. Seward four possible alternatives in dealing with the rebellion, including an invasion of the South with an army of 300,000 "disciplined men." Boatner, *Civil War Dictionary*, 15, 728; Scott to Seward, March 3, 1861, Winfield Scott, *Memoirs . . .* (2 vols., New York, 1864), II, 627; Charles W. Elliott, *Winfield Scott: The Soldier and the Man* (New York, 1937), 698.

From James P. McDowell

March 11, 1861, Greeneville; ALS, DLC-JP.

Without wishing "to throw any thing in the way of Mr Lowry," solicits appointment as marshal for East Tennessee should the office become vacant. "I understand from my wife that Mrs. Johnson is considered on the mend and hope that She will now improve pretty fast until She is intirely recovered again."

From Alexander J. D. Thurston[1]

Nashville 11 March 1861

Hon A Johnson
Washington
Dr Sir

I am more than obliged to you for an official copy of your Speech in the Senate of last Month— it breathes the true doctrine— The dissatisfaction at your course in the Senate is fast dying out in our City, and where you have lost one friend you have gained two in the place of the one lost—

There is much fear and anxiety among the people, and I think we should have had a convention, but the course the Nashville Union & American and some of our public men took in relation to the action of the legislature in regard to submitting the action of the Conven-

tion to the people,[2] frightened them from voting for a convention—
they feared being drummed out of the Union without their consent to
so important a Measure—

There are many dissatisfied spirits among us, and I am afraid
their patriotism does not proceed from love of country, but more
from a thirst after the loves and fishes—

Our difficulties together with a short crop last year,[3] render all
business and financial matters gloomy indeed in middle Tennessee
and if the present troubles could be amicably settled it would indeed
be a Godsend to the people of this State—

Please accept my best wishes for your good health and prayers
that you may be instrumental in settling the present difficulties[.]

I am Sir Very Respectfully Yours &c
A. J. D. Thurston

ALS, DLC-JP.

1. Alexander J. D. Thurston (b. c1821), a Nashville post office clerk and
a member of the dry goods firm of Thurston and Bernard, 9 Union St., was
named lieutenant colonel of the 1st Tenn. Zouave Rgt., CSA, which seems
to have been authorized but not organized. 1860 Census, Tenn., Davidson,
Nashville, 13th Dist., 157; *Tennesseans in the Civil War*, I, 169; *Nashville
Bus. Dir.* (1855–56), 117.

2. The act authorizing an election for a convention which would consider
the "existing relations" between Tennessee and the United States stipulated
that no ordinance or resolution changing the state's position would be binding
until "adopted by a majority of the qualified voters." *The Union and American*, while endorsing the idea of giving the people an opportunity to register
their views, strongly implied that expediency might require the convention
to assume the initiative. That the paper had become a leading secessionist organ is evidenced by its frequent printing and endorsement of the views of ultra
groups like the "State Central Southern Rights, Anti-Coercion Committee,"
which asserted that "the only hope of peace and safety, consists in decided
action before the inauguration of Mr. Lincoln," and of such avowed secessionists as editor John C. Burch, ex-Mississippi governor Henry S. Foote, and
Shelby County senator Robert G. Payne. During the debates in the legislature Payne and others had opposed referring the convention's resolutions to
popular vote; indeed, "why call a convention at all?" asked a Sumner County
representative. Unionists in general, fearing that a convention, if it met, might
ignore "*that part of the resolution that refers its action to the people*," cast
their votes against the convention. *Tenn. Acts*, 1861, Ch. 1; Nashville *Union
and American*, January 12, 26, 27, 29, February 6, 7, 1861; Nashville *Republican Banner*, January 31, February 3, 5, 8, 1861.

3. In the summer of 1860 Middle Tennessee experienced a severe drought
which ruined crops, reduced yields of grains, produce, and livestock, and
contributed to a general scarcity of money, meat, and foodstuffs in certain
sections. Some agricultural societies curtailed or, in one case, cancelled, the
annual fair, perhaps reasoning like those in Wilson County that the money
would be "better and more wisely appropriated to the relief of the poor." The
farm depression preceded a more general economic dislocation in Tennessee
in the wake of Lincoln's election, characterized by lethargic trade, financial
panic, and discounted or suspended currency. Nashville *Republican Banner*,
October 10, November 21, 1860; Fayetteville *Observer*, August 30, September 13, October 25, November 15, 22, 29, 1860.

From Henry S. French

March 12, 1861, Nashville; ALS, DLC-JP.

Calling Johnson "the Secon Mosas" destined "to preserve the C[o]unt[r]y and lead and Conduct the peop[l]e to the promised Land," French berates "the moast bitter durty Hell for Saken artickel I ever red" which appeared [March 11] in the Memphis *Avalanche*. ["The bare mention of the name of Andy Johnson causes every true Southerner to hold his nose with the same instincts that would prompt them, on kicking the moulding carcass of a dead dog."]

From William S. Speer

Shelbyville Tenn 12 March '61

Gov. Johnson—
Dear Sir:

Rely upon my discreetness in what I may say or do in connection with your name and the Federal Appointments in this State. Rely also upon my judment *as it regards one point* in reference to the Marshalship of Middle Tennessee. Pardon me now when I say to you the best thing you can do towards *Johnsonising* Middle Tennessee will be to have Lewis Tillman[1] of this place appointed Marshal in place of Genl Clemens. It will secure ten thousand votes for the Union & for Gov. Johnson that will be lost with any other man for Marshal, That is my opinion. Tillman is a life time Whig—but he is a Johnson man on principle. He will turn more Whigs to you than any other man can—& he is dead out against secession.— He has the energy of a steam engine, and is very prudent.

My papers are all filed in the State Department for a foreign appointment. But I will be glad to accept a position at Washington or elsewhere. May I ask you to ascertain at some of the Departments a place to be filled and solicit it for me? My vouchers I think will satisfy the Administration and yourself.

I have sowed it from Bristol to Shelbyville that Gov. Johnson is to be returned to the United States Senate over all opposition—Bell & Neill Brown included. Our boys here are for it & that is saying much. I shall continue to operate in this direction.

An infernal letter from this place has just been published in the *Tribune*.[2] It is a lie out of whole cloth. It is an evident forgery, got up by the Secessionists to damage the union cause in this State & county. We *think* Sam. Whitthorne wrote it.[3]

If you were not crowded with letters & company I would write more.

With many thanks for your great kindness to me in Washington, and with unfeigned admiration for you as a man and a Statesman
I am, sir,

Yours very truly
Wm. S. Speer.

I recd a large batch of your speeches this morning—& shall distribute them to day.—

ALS, DLC-JP.

1. Lewis Tillman (1816–1886), a Shelbyville attorney, served as circuit court clerk (1852–60), clerk and master of chancery court (1865–69), and as a Republican congressman (1869–71). *BDAC*, 1717–18.

2. A week earlier another Shelbyville correspondent had categorically announced that Speer himself was the author of the objectionable anonymous letter in the *Tribune*. See Letter from H. M. Majors, March 6, 1861.

3. Samuel H. Whitthorne (b. *c*1828) was a Bedford County lawyer. Porch, *1850 Census, Bedford*, 117.

From Salmon P. Chase

Treasury Department
13 March 1861

My dear Sir

To no one more than yourself can I give an affirmative answer with greater pleasure and therefore I have directed your letter with others acompanying it in relation to Mr McNeil[1] of the 3d Auditors office to be placed on file with the endorsement "to be retained" which will insure him undisturbed in his position.

I am Very truly Yours
S P Chase

Hon And Johnson
U S Senate.

LS, DLC-JP.

1. Archibald McNeill (d. *c*1868), born in New York but appointed from Tennessee, was a clerk in the third auditor's office (1850–69). In addition to his recent letter on McNeill's behalf, Johnson had signed a petition for his retention in 1853, and in 1862 would attest to his loyalty. Johnson and others to James Guthrie, February 25, 1853; Johnson to Chase, March 9, 1861, January 31, 1862; Archibald McNeil [McNeill], Application File, RG56, National Archives; *Boyd's Washington and Georgetown Directory* (1868), 334.

From William Dawes[1]

Baltimore March 13th/61

Hon Andrew Johnson,

Dr. Sir   Not having time to call on my return home, I wish to present to your view a few facts, as Regards the appointment of Post Master at Jonesboro *Tenn* for which you are aware I am an aplcant. As you said on yesterdy that as Soon as you had the time you Would Examine the papers left by Mr Graham as to Mr *Williams*.[2] Now Mr Johnson if you look to the Wishes & Will of the citzens I Refer you to my Pettion[3] Signed by (107) names of the citzens & vincenity and indeed there was not (20) men in the place that did not sign my Pettion. Again if you look to our former position *politically* We Both ocupy the same position[.] *But* as to his (Mr W's) presant Position as I told you, I am unable to say. But as for Mr. W. H. Crouch[4] I know & presum you do *also* that he is a *disunionist* of the deepest *dye*[.] for two days before the Election *last* he quit his postoffice & went to fall Branch & made a disunionist Speach, for Mr S. T. Logan[5] & my self ware theaire & he Mr Logan Spoke Against Mr. *Crouch* & Harris & defended your Speach made in the Senate about which there was so much fuss. again if you look to location & have the Best in the place for access &c, and Sir, a Pecunarly *View*, I have a family & he (Mr Williams) has *none*, & he has *Means* & I have *none*[.] Besides all this if he (Mr W) had made his application *first*, I should not have opposed *him*, and if you Refer to my Pettion you will see that he Mr W signed it himself. But after that Mr Crouch Resigned in his Mr W.'s favour, after he Mr. C. having said he Would, not Resign in favour of any one. But Remember also, that Mr Crouches, Reckmendation Was made to the former administration & whether or not he would Still Give it to the Presant one to which he is so much *oposed* I leave for you to judge. But before you deside I would Beg your Refer to my Pettion & letters from Mr. Nelson & Mr. Bocock of Va.[6] all which are filed. I well know if you should deside in my favour, I will Get it & if against me you have the Right to so, do. But should you as said the other day, not deside betwen friends & prefer to leave the appoint ment with the Department I am perfectly Willing that you shall file the paper correspondence &C, and let them deside it. Hoping you may Give this your Ear[l]iest posible *attention* I Respectfully Submit the whole matter.

Yours Truly   Wm. Dawes

Hon A. Johnson U. S. Senate
Washington D C

ALS, DLC-JP.

1. William Dawes (b. c1823), native of Washington County and a Jonesboro merchant with personal property valued at $500, received the postmastership. 1860 Census, Tenn., Washington, 147; *U. S. Official Register* (1863), 629.

2. Albert G. Graham, Jonesboro lawyer and newspaper editor, recommended John E. Williams (b. c1837), a merchant, who was also endorsed by James M. Deadrick. Although not a family man, he was not as affluent as Dawes suggests, having only $150 worth of personal property. 1860 Census, Tenn., Sullivan, Brush Creek Dist., 9; Deadrick to Johnson, February 25, 1861, Johnson Papers, LC.

3. "Signed by (62) names [of] citzens of this place," this petition was forwarded to Congressman T. A. R. Nelson. Dawes to Johnson, February 14, 1861, Johnson Papers, LC.

4. William H. Crouch, to be replaced as postmaster at the end of this month, was a Jonesboro merchant with combined property valved at $23,000. 1860 Census, Tenn., Washington, 148; *Johnson Papers*, I, 418n.

5. Samuel T. Logan (1832–1901), Abingdon, Virginia, native, practiced law at Jonesboro (1855–64) and Knoxville, where he was a partner of T. A. R. Nelson until the latter's death in 1873. Elected to the state senate (1884–85), he subsequently served as circuit and criminal judge of Knox County (1886–94). John W. Green, *Bench and Bar of Knox County, Tennessee* (Knoxville, 1947), 83.

6. Thomas S. Bocock (1815–1891), Buckingham (now Appomattox) County Democratic lawyer, was a member of the Virginia house (1842–44) and congressman (1847–61), resigning to become a member, and later speaker (1862), of the Confederate Congress. After the war he remained active in state Democratic politics, serving several terms in the legislature. *BDAC*, 568.

From Jeptha Fowlkes

Nashville March 13—1861.

Hon. A. Johnson
my dear sir:

We reached here this mor[n]ing. I find some of yr. old Democratic friends very harsh & bitter towards you & Etheridge! Amongst them Genl. Anderson—[1] A. Ewing very well satisfied. The Whig & No-Nothing opponents Speak well & kindly—but how far you can rely on them after the chief battle is over, becomes a grave question. Gov. Harris is at Memphis— Col. Stevenson, (Douglass Democrat,) is Said, to be a *rabid* secessionist![2] He goes with me, to Louisville [I have not had] a talk with him politically yet— As soon as *you* can visit Nashville, Memphis & such leading points the better—to see, to hear & to judge & determine for yourself. Galloway[3] has bought out Enquirer & merges it, with Avalanche! Work must be done—before beginning a general survey of field of battle; & then forces pro & con must be reviewed by you!

Yr. friend   J. Fowlkes

ALS, DLC-JP.

1. Samuel R. Anderson, Nashville postmaster.

2. Vernon K. Stevenson, a railroad executive who had been chairman of the Douglas executive committee in Nashville, became quartermaster general of the Provisional Army of Tennessee. Nashville *Patriot*, July 23, 30, 1860; John T. Moore and Austin P. Foster, *Tennessee: The Volunteer State, 1769–1923* (4 vols., Nashville, 1923), I, 473; *Johnson Papers*, II, 251*n*.

3. Matthew C. Gallaway, Memphis editor.

From Robert W. Humphreys

March 13, 1861, Clarksville; ALS, DLC-JP.

Reports conversation in which Cave Johnson advocated that Union men concentrate their support on Johnson: "He says that Govr N S Brown cannot be used against you but thinks that Govr Campbell or A Ewing esqr will be put forward by the Secession influence." Adds that "Persons here without distinction of party will urge Cave Johnson for Governor."

From William M. Lowry

Greeneville   Ten Mar 13 1861.

Gov Johnson
D Sir

I have been requested by a young freind of mine to write you in his behalf. I herewith enclose you his letter that will better explain what he is wanting than I Could State it.[1] If you feel disposed to interfere in behalf of any one I could cheerfully recommend young Lowry as Competant and in fact a business man[.] he has belonged and for aught I know belongs to the Opposition Now[.] let that be as it may. I am of the Opinion he would make a good offi[c]er. he is a young Man and wishes to go to some new Country, is the reason I presume he wants the office in Question[.] If you Could say a good word for him, it would be duly appreciated by him and his freinds.

Not much local news, Some of the old Men are dieing towit Alexd Susong & Isaac Dearstone[.][2] Mrs Johnson is doing pretty well on the mend, tonight pretty good[.] the people are beginning to want to see you at home. Weather for the last few days verry fine[.] people are beginning to garden and clean up for spring work[.]

in Haste Yr freind
Wm M. Lowry

ALS, DLC-JP.

1. Willie Lowry, an Athens kinsman, "knowing that the relations existing between you and Senator Johnson have always been of the most friendly character," had requested Lowry to intercede on behalf of an appointment as agent for the Cherokee Indians. Willie Lowry to William M. Lowry, March 12, 1861; Willie Lowry to Johnson, March 13, 1861, Johnson Papers, LC.

2. Alexander Susong (b. *c*1798), a Greene County farmer with $3,200 in real and personal property; Isaac Dearston (1795–1861), Virginia-born farmer with $7,500 in real estate. 1850 Census, Tenn., Greene, 603; 1860 Census, Tenn., Greene, 3, 119; Reynolds, *Greene County Cemeteries*, 66.

From Felix A. Reeve[1]

Knoxville, Tenn., March, 13th, '61.

Hon. Andrew Johnson—
Dear Sir: —

I Should feel great delicacy in writing to you again, if I were *Sure* that the two former communications[2] which I addressed you several weeks ago, were received. But as I do not believe that you recieved either, I trust you will excuse the present one.

During the last few months, I have addressed several letters to Washington, but as yet, have no intimation that any of them were received!— But this may be irrelevant.

Last November, early after the election of *Mr. Lincoln*, I applied through the Representative of my former District (—Mr. Nelson) — for the office of Federal Att'y for this Division of the State.

Then, I had no rivals. *Then*, the whole political firmament was begloomed and ominous: but *now* as the soft rays of Peace dissipate the lowering clouds, there are numerous "Richmonds"[3] out for the various *Federal offices*. I have but one formidable opponent—John M. Fleming, Esq., who, as I learn, has *recently* become an applicant.[4] I suppose he has the advantage of Maynard's influence. I respectfully solicit yours, and feel assured that you can obtain the desired office. As regards my character, past and present, I need only refer you to Mr. Fletcher of Greeneville,[5] and to your sons, Charles and Robert, both of whom know me *socially* and *masonically*.

Hitherto, we have differed in political faith, but now we occupy the same platform—"The Union, the Constitution, and the Enforcement of the Laws."

Being *poor* and *destitute*, I apply to you particularly because I know that no one can more freely and fully sympathize with the poor young man struggling for knowledge and position. And to you, sir, I appeal with a Confidence above all political prejudices; and feel assured that I apply to one whose heart pulsates with nobler emotions than mere *party feeling* can ever inspire.— Like myself, Mr. Fleming is a *true Union man*. But he is a partner in the strongest law firm in East Tenn.—that of *Baxter, Haynes, & Co.*, and of course, does not need the office.

I have obtained license to practice law in the various Courts of the State, and the salary of the office, though Small, would enable me to purchase a library of legal works, and to thoroughly prosecute the study of a science which I find both noble and pleasing.

Any thing that you may effect for my interest, shall not be forgotten.

I have written twice to *Mr. Seward*,[6] but suppose he did not receive either letter.

As my handwriting is well known at the Knoxville P. O., I will have the superscription in an unknown hand.[7]

In both of my former letters, I requested a few copies of your late *Union speech.* Please Send me *half a dozen.*

Respectfully,   F. A. Reeve.

ALS, DLC-JP.

1. Felix A. Reeve (1836–1920), a Knoxville attorney, was colonel of the 8th Tenn. Inf., USA (1862–64). After the war he settled in Knoxville, where he practiced law and attempted to set up a political base. Unsuccessfully running for chancellor in 1870, he moved to Washington, D. C., obtaining first a temporary position in the treasury department and eventually becoming assistant solicitor. Felix A. Reeve, Compiled Service Record, RG94, National Archives; Reeve to O. P. Temple, May 5, 13, August 9, 1870, March 3, 4, 14, 1879, O. P. Temple Papers, University of Tennessee Library.

2. In earlier letters Reeve expressed his desire, as a young and needy lawyer, to be appointed district attorney for the eastern division of Tennessee and urged that John M. Fleming, Knoxville lawyer and also a candidate, be rejected, inasmuch as he already has a successful practice and "does not need an office that pays no more than five or six hundred dollars *per annum.*" Reeve to Johnson, February 22, March 2, 1861, Johnson Papers, LC.

3. A reference to Shakespeare, *Richard III*, Act IV, sc. 4: "I think there be six Richmonds in the field."

4. Fleming, who remained loyal to the Union, later received the appointment and served during the war. Rothrock, *French Broad-Holston Country*, 417.

5. Andrew J. Fletcher was a prominent Greeneville political figure who sided with the Union. *Johnson Papers*, II, 473n.

6. In these letters Reeve, as "an uncompromising union-man of the 'Old Line Whig' school," had sought Seward's assistance. He would do so again in April, displaying a partisan discontent entirely absent in this rather fawning communication to the Tennessee senator. Arraigning bitterly Johnson's employment of the state patronage "for his own *selfish motives*," Reeve would contend that he was using it as "a kind of cement to unite the two divisions of his party—the patriots and traitors," when, in reality, "THREE-FOURTHS *of the Union Party of Tennessee are Whigs!*" Reeve to Seward, January 16, March 2, April 6, 1861, in Tennessee, 1861–65, Appointments, RG60, National Archives.

7. O. P. Temple, under whom Reeve had studied law, chided him about his penmanship, remarking that his "time were better employed in attending a *writing school* than in addressing *hieroglyphic* letters." Reeve to Temple, March 15, 1860, Temple Papers.

From Charles Arnold[1]

Cleveland. O. March 14. 1861

Sir: I am informed that you, and several other patriotic men, are now engaged to settle and arrange the groundwork & basis of a

Union Party[2] which is to be composed of, and embrace all true
national men, irrespective of their antecedents; that such a movement
is indespensable to the reconstruction of our Union is clear to every
one who has witnessed the utter prosteration of the once invincible
Democracy of the North—and that either faction—alone, is incapable
of recovering the past supremacy—needs no demonstration—. The
MAN worship of the northern and nigger adulation of the southern
politicians has caused our ruin! Now therefore, the masses; the honest rank and file are prepared, ready and eager to Sustain and carry
out a movement of the kind suggested—:

How OUR leading Douglass politicians. i.e. Payne, Gray,[3] etc will
receive the proposition, I do not know for unless their Idol nods
assent they would not participate in a *feast* prepared by the immortal Gods themselves— but I am satisfied that their self-interest will
"EVENTUALLY force them to join the Army"—or else new Capitanos
might convince the people that in this great movement *cross-road*
politicians[4] and spoil-hunters can be dispensed with. But we will
take such measures as will arouse and concentrate the Democratic
& Union masses—depend on that. Now if We receive your "Union
Programme" in time preliminary to our charter election which takes
place early in April[5]—we will be enabled aided by the impetus—
given from such distinguished source, to arrange a Union ticket,
and then it might be possible that Cleveland not inaptly termed the
hot bed of abolitionism,[6] could again be redeemed— that such a
Union Victory—would lend a moral prestige to the "new orginiza-
tion" and strenghten the Union sentiment "all over this broad Land"[7]
there can be no doubt.

It will however be a hard job to restore harmony, and procure concert of action among our politicians. I hardly think that patriotism
or persuasion will accomplish that result—unless aided and seconded
by the "thunder of the masses[.]" We would respectfully solicit your
advice. how can we *compell* these "fellows" to forgit their past differences, and repress their egotism even if only temporarily—until
the storm-clouds of treason have passed away.

Now let me conclude— whether you will or not—we are determined
that you shall be—if possible—our canditate for President in 1864
—and we are determined to do everything from now until that time
to accomplish that purpose. In 1860 the Douglas epedemic ran to
high, and you were *comparatively* unknown among the masses, but
times have changed—. I assure you that among the PEOPLE of *all*
parties; in Northern Ohio—at least, you are to day the most popular
man in the U. S. Senate—this is owing to your firmness—versus—
treason and secession at a TIME when "the *mighty* were *silent* and
trembled with fear";[8] and your advocacy of the homestead bill—!

Now whatever myself and friends can do towards securing you the Democratic Union—nomination in 1864—*will be done*, and by that time many of our old fogy leaders will be *extinguished*, and others convinced that there are other "Giants" than the "Little one"—[9] In order to effectuate our purpose please send a quantity of your speeches, on secession etc, etc, and as "Old Joe,"[10] (: for which old rascle I worked and voted—, but that was before he avowed himself a traitor:) & I will circulate them among the most influential men —of the Democracy of Northern Ohio—and thus prepare in time— for the contest to come!

   Excuse this Long epistle[.]   Respectfully Yours
                                              Charles Arnold
            Attorney at Law   P.O. Box 3824.Cleveland.O.
One of the Executive Committee of the "National Democratic Club"
To Hon Andrew Johnson.
Sen. Elect. of Tenn.

ALS, DLC-JP.

1. Charles Arnold (b. *c*1836), a native of Germany, had an office at 90 Superior Street and resided at 265 Pittsburgh. 1860 Census, Ohio, Cuyahoga, Cleveland, 3rd Ward, 385; *Williston's Cleveland Directory* (1859–60), 46.

2. Ten days earlier the Washington correspondent of the Cincinnati *Enquirer* had reported: "I hear to-night that several Democrats, Andy Johnson, John Cochrane, and others, have drawn up a manifesto, to be signed by as many leaders of all parties as will sign it, setting forth the basis of the formation of a Union party. From what I can learn, it is very moderate in its tone, and is designed to include in the proposed party all who approve the policy of compromise." Louisville *Journal*, March 6, 1861. No copy of this "manifesto" has come to hand, and the precise reaction of contemporary political leaders remains unknown.

3. Henry B. Payne (1810–1896), New York-born lawyer and Democratic politician, was a member of the Ohio senate (1849–51) and delegate to the nominating conventions of 1856, 1860, and 1872. Eschewing involvement with the Vallandigham movement during the war, he subsequently served in the House (1875–77) and the Senate (1885–91). Joseph W. Gray (1814–1862), a Vermonter at one time employed in Payne's law office, spent most of his life in newspaper editing and politics. Purchasing the Cleveland *Advertiser* in 1841, he renamed it the *Plain Dealer*—a paper which, according to a contemporary, became "the Democratic voice in the wilderness of Whiggery." Appointed postmaster in 1853, he was removed five years later for his support of Douglas. *BDAC*, 1435; Milton, *Eve of Conflict*, 300–479 *passim*; Eugene H. Roseboom, *The Civil War Era, 1850–1873* (Columbus, 1944), 409, 432; William G. Rose, *Cleveland: The Making of a City* (Cleveland, 1950), 132, 184–85, 226, 259, 288.

4. A derogatory expression implying "smallness, cheapness, etc." Mathews, *Americanisms*, I, 440.

5. The Cleveland mayoral race ended with the victory of the "Democratic and Union" candidate over the Republican nominee by a majority of 718 votes. Cincinnati *Enquirer*, April 5, 1861.

6. Although abolition sentiment in northern Ohio was strong, Cleveland proper was considered conservative on the issue of slavery. Perhaps the appellation "hot bed of abolitionism" came as a result of the famous trials held in Cleveland during the first half of 1859. Thirty-seven prominent Oberlin

citizens, including a professor at the college, a former missionary, and a number of theological students, were charged with violating the Fugitive Slave Law in an attempted rescue of a slave held in custody by government officials in Wellington, some nine miles distant from Oberlin. Two defendants tested, unsuccessfully, the law itself, an action which carried the trials into June. Campbell, *The Slave Catchers*, 53–54, 164–67; Elbert J. Benton, *Cultural Story of an American City: Cleveland* (3 vols., Cleveland, 1943–46), III, 50–53.

7. From Lincoln's first inaugural. Basler, *Works of Lincoln*, IV, 271.

8. Not found.

9. The "Little Giant," Stephen A. Douglas.

10. Joseph Lane, vice-presidential candidate on the Breckinridge ticket.

From Herman Cox

March 14, 1861, Nashville; ALS, DLC-JP.

Applicant for U. S. district attorney, in renewing his request for "your aid & influance," mentions the death of Henry M. McEwing, who was also seeking the post; reports that the "rumor of the withdrawal of the troops from Forts Sumter & Pickens has taken all the Starch out the Secessionist here." [Cox received the appointment.]

From William R. Hurley

Nashville March 14th 61

Hon A. Johnson
Dr Sir:

I have no doubt but that you will be consulted in regard to the Tennessee appointments, and I write to day, to suggest, that no appointment will be satisfactory—where a secessionist shall be appointed. It is my opinion and the opinion of the people generally that no man who has favored the disunionists *in the least*, ought hold any, even the most trifling office, in the state[.]

This was suggested to me yesterday, by the remark, that there were several secessionists from this vicinity applying for office. I understood that Clemons was applying for the marshallship. a secessionist applying for District attorney, & McNish for the Post office.[1] If either of these officies should be filled by a secessionist, we would hold an *indignation* meeting immediately and protest against it. The secessionists in the Post office has done all in their power to injure my paper in its circulation—and I am sending most of the papers by Express (on that account.) whenever they can be sent in that way.

If the appointment for Post master at this place is not made, will you do me the favor, simply, to inform the proper department that I would like to have the appointment[.] As to character, I think it would be sufficient for them to know that I was endorsed by the Democracy of the state by being a member of the Central Committee *before* the disruption of the party, and afterwards chairman of the Douglas Central Committee and now Editor of an independent union paper[2] and would claim the right *and would exercise it*, of condemning any thing in Mr Lincoln's administration, and would commend what was wright. with these facts before Mr Lincoln, if he would give me the appoint[ment] of Post master I would like to have it— I need it. As you are aware, I have given up my profession[3] and unless the Democrat is sustained by the friends of the paper, or I have some income from other quarters, it will be impossible for me to sustain it. We are trying to get a patron to take an interest in it but have thus far failed. Our friends have not fulfilled their, promise and we may have to give it up[.] In that event I would take almost any office, and go any where that the duties of such office should lead me. I hope you will not consider me too importunate. I have no specil claim upon you, though I have always sustained you but would have sustained any other man of the Democratic faith who might have occupied your position. You have made a national reputation during the recent stormy Congress, which in my opinion—almost insures you the candidacy for Presidency four years hence[.]

I have stopped publishing the Democrat for a short time with the view of arranging for permanency— I only need a few hundred dollars now. My part[n]er[4] has gone to Cincinnatti to purchase a Press.

Very Respectfully Yours &c
W R Hurley

ALS, DLC-JP.

1. Jesse B. Clements, the incumbent marshal; probably Thomas B. Childress, the current attorney general; and William D. McNish.

2. The Nashville *Democrat*.

3. Hurley had been a physician. *Nashville Bus. Dir.* (1860–61), 198.

4. T. J. Kelly, associate editor of the *Democrat*, who became orderly sergeant, Co. C, 10th Ohio and was wounded in 1861 in Virginia. Stewart, *Middle Tennessee Newspapers*, 129; Cincinnati *Gazette*, September 18, 1861.

From Richard M. Edwards

Cleveland Tenn March 15th 61

Hon Andrew Johnson,
Dear Sir;

I yesterday was forced to do a thing which I did not sanction; but did so to keep down *family difficulties.* I *endorsed for.* Wm H. Grant[1] for the position he now holds. Wm. H. Craigmiles[2] had already signed it who is a brother-in-law of mine; and Grant is a cousin of my wifes, and taking all the circumstances in comunion I was forced to sign for Billy although he has been lately the most busy, impudent, annoying disunionist in our town—abusing all men of any note who are true to the Government.

Under these circumstances of course I disliked to endorse him, and did not do so till he promised to not let it be known publicly. The foregoing are the facts and now if you condescend to act in the matter at all you will know the character of the endorsement he has on his paper.

I am really sorry after reflecting the thing all over that I touched his paper; but he came to me in presence of my wife who would have thought hard of me if I had not endorsed for her cousin.

There are a few here who consider that you have gone over to the Black Republicans and Billy is one of that number with his father who holds the same doctrine.[3]

The Union men here desire you to come here at the earliest practicable period to show the fools the difference between a true friend of the Government and a Black Republican.

Truly Your friend & obt Servt
R. M. Edwards

ALS, DLC-JP.

1. William H. Grant (b. c1825), listed in the 1850 census as a "collector" with $1,400 worth of real estate, was in 1860 a "route agent" with $3,000 in real property. 1850 Census, Tenn., Bradley, 276; 1860 Census, Tenn., Bradley, Cleveland, 6th Dist., 8.

2. William H. Craigmiles (b. c1812) was a merchant with $11,000 in real estate and personal property. 1860 Census, Bradley, Cleveland, 6th Dist., 2.

3. William Grant had long been active in lower East Tennessee railroad enterprise as contractor and director for the East Tennessee & Georgia, the Hiwassee, and other lines; together with his son, he appears on Hurlburt's proscriptive list of "Leading Rebels in the Sixth District." James W. Holland, A History of Railroad Enterprise in East Tennessee, 1836–1860 (M. A. thesis, University of Tennessee, 1930), 153, 401; Wooten, *Bradley County*, 78; J. S. Hurlburt, *History of the Rebellion in Bradley County, Tennessee* (Indianapolis, 1866), 20.

From Blackston McDannel

Greenville Tennessee
March 15, 1861

Hon. Andrew Johnson
U. S. Senate Washington D. C.
D. Sir

I have concluded to apply for the Office of United States Marshall for the District of East Tennessee, through you, provided you do not stand pledged to the Support of any other person. You will there-fore confer a favor by calling on the President and communicate to him my wishes in such manner as may best suit you.

For thirty years, you have known me intimately, and I leave it with you to give me Such a reccommendation as you think I deserve. I had thought of getting up a petition to the President. Nearly every body here would sign it; but as petitions can be so easily gotten up by any person, with any number of Signatures, and as they are not regarded as of much consequence, I am advised to make application in the manner above indicated. You will receive letters from Some of my friends whom you know, on this subject;[1] all of which I hope you will make use of as you may think best.— Gen'l Lowry, as you know, is the present incumbent, and as I understand, his term ex-pires shortly. He has held the Office about eight years, and my in-formation is, that he will not be an applicant[.]

If there should arise any contest for this office between any applicant from Knoxville and myself, upon the grounds that I do not reside at that place where the U. S. Courts are held, I wish it to be under-stood, that even as a Knox*villian*, I have Some claims on that score, from the fact that I was born there in 1811—was raised there—my father's family now live there, and that I live only three hours ride, by rail, from Knoxville.

As the mail will arrive in a few minutes, I am necessarily com-pelled to make this letter Short, and will only add, that I desire you to See the President at your earliest convenience on this subject[.][2]

As usual   Your friend
B. McDannel

ALS, DLC-JP.

1. Sam Milligan wrote that McDannel "is as firmly identified with the Union party as any man in Tennessee." Milligan to Johnson, March 15, 1861, Johnson Papers, LC.

2. Twelve days later Robert reported that McDannel's nomination had been confirmed by the Senate. Robert Johnson to McDannel, March 27, 1861, Typescript copy, George Fort Milton Papers, LC.

From John McGaughey[1]

Athens Tennessee 15 March/61

Honl. Andrew Johnson

Sir—I have a friend at Cleveland Tennessee[2] that is desires of Reciving the appointment of Post Master at that place. I am well acquainted with him and beleive him to be a corect business Man, he is a no one [known] Union Man or I Should not of Said one word in his behalf[.] I am a union Man unconditionaly & expect to take a course next election regardless of former assosiations for the entire union ticket[.] I have diferd with you in times upon Politics[.] ther now is a differat and more dangerous Question befour us, one that I have great fears as to what the final Result will be, but we are hard at work and will work untill we remove every man out of office, that is not a good union Loving Man—. I expect to be with you next Summer in centiment and action—. aney thing that you may do for any of my friends or Relation Shall be corectly appreciated by your friend—

Yours with Respect   John McGaughy

NB you have my thanks for your Speach[.] J M

ALS, DLC-JP.
    1. John McGaughey (b. c1797), father of the John C. McGaughey who had recently applied for the Knoxville postmastership.
    2. Possibly Stephen Hempstead (b. c1787), a schoolteacher in 1860, who had served briefly as postmaster (January 20–April 4, 1853) and as county register (1852–56), or his son Stephen (b. c1839), or James Pearce (b. c1826), a farmer and former deputy postmaster who was the son-in-law of former Greene countian William Grant. 1860 Census, Tenn., Bradley, 1st Dist., 191; Cleveland, 6th Dist., 8; Wooten, *Bradley County*, 28, 178; see also John H. Payne to Johnson, February 19, 1861, Johnson Papers, LC.

From John C. McGaughey

Knoxville March 15/61

Hon Andrew Johnson
Dear Sir
    I wrote you some time since making application through you for the Office of Post Master at this place and have recd your Speech with notice that you had read my letter— Mr Charlton the Presant P M has been Canvassing the town to day for names to a petition for Mr Rogers—[1] Mr R—as I told you in my letter is now in the Post Office and has been for two months and let him have as many endorsements by Union men and as much as he claims to be a Union man his appointment would be regarded by the masses as a Secession triumph inasmuch as he is seconded by Charlton—One of the leading disunionist—and other disunionists[.] You will likely receive a letter from Col Brabson[2] and others urging my appointment— I hope you will find it consistent with your feelings to assist me in this—
    I learned that Mr Maynard had Said he would endorse Rogers— I Called on him & he told me he had Said no such thing—that he had

only Said he would see that it was put before the proper authorities
and Should have a fair Showing— I told him that all I wanted of
him was "hands" Off— this he promised—

I have nothing to Say about Rogers but will Say that Some of
his backers—and the most prominent ones:—are neither friends of
yours or the Union[.]

I am very Respectfully

Your Obt Svt   John C. McGaughey

ALS, DLC-JP.
  1. Pryor L. Rogers.
  2. Reese B. Brabson, Tennessee congressman.

From Sylvester Olinger

March 15, 1861, Birdville, Tex.; ALS, DLC-JP.

Acknowledges receipt of Johnson's speeches which "we prise highly &
they are doing a good Work here[.] I loned them out to secesionists,
& have kept them going and Evry Man that has Red them has publickly
declaired that hencefourth they are for the union if there is a Compromise of the presant difficulties"; claims that secessionists hold a majority
in the county because of election fraud, but that unionists are strong
in northern counties. "We have, Washington Greene, & Suliven County
men here & Evry Tennesseean is a gainst this secesion Moovement."

From John H. Steck

March 15, 1861, Philadelphia, Pa.; ALS, DLC-JP.

Concerning Johnson's prospective visit, remarks that "I have never
known so much desire expressed to hear any public man, as is manifested
in our community to hear you on the absorbing topic of the *Union*." The
Academy of Music, the city's largest building, probably will be engaged,
and financial success is assured; suggests that Johnson make the six-hour
trip within the next two weeks.

From George W. Mindil[1]

Philadelphia, March 16 1861

Hon: Andrew Johnson:
Dear Sir:

Through your kindness I have at length obtained a complete and
correct copy of your masterly address of December 18th, and allow
me to say, that, in my humble opinion it is the crowning address of

the last sessions of Congress—an address—devoid of the flimsy arguments of the politician and abounding with the sentiments of the patriot—and the spirit of the MAN. Although representing a Southern State, you have gallantly thrown yourself into the breach—and then—with your mind—arguing by the constitution,—then, with your noble heart, filled with love for the Union—you "will dispute every inch of ground, burn every blade of grass" and when everything else should fail, when treason and intrigue would overpower —loyalty and reason—you "will find your grave in the last entrenchment of freedom."[2] And depend upon it, if this awful doom should happen—if this country should be torn in pieces by fanaticism, the day will come, when the PEOPLE, rising in their might, clothed with the most exalted powers, will demand of their miscreant and usurping rulers—a return to their old and beloved Union; and then—the grave of Andrew Johnson—would recieve a monument, bequethed by millions of freemen proud of the martyr to Union principles. But, may Heaven prevent this doom, may God Allmighty give wisdom to our people and forethought and foresight to our rulers—and may Andrew Johnson long live to be the recipient of his people's blessings— And when, in after years, posterity shall write the history of the nation, and congratulate themselves upon the unity of their government, they will not fail to remember, that it was Andrew Johnson, who stemmed the currents of fanaticism, who drove back the forms of treason, and who kept this "Union" whole. I hope, you will pardon me, a stranger, for this outburst of the feelings of my heart—feelings for the good of the Union—feelings for the man, who dares to brave the assaults of enemies, and the mockeries of "would-be friends—," and if the country had more such minds and hearts as yours—this Union would not be threatened with destruction—nor this glorious people suffering from a stagnation of trade. Hoping you will answer and inform me that you can at least appreciate my sentiments

I remain Yours   G. W. Mindil—Box 1377

ALS, DLC-JP.

1. George W. Mindil was a Philadelphia bookkeeper living at 120 Arch Street. The letter is typical of patriotic effusions which Johnson's speeches elicited from his fellow citizens. *McElroy's Philadelphia Directory* (1861), 695.

2. These quotations, also used by Johnson in his Speech on Secession, December 18–19, 1860, are reportedly from the last words of the Irish patriot Robert Emmet before his execution for treason. Landreth, *Robert Emmet*, 333.

From Jeptha Fowlkes

Memphis Ten. March 17. 1861

Private

Hon. A. Johnson.

My dear Sir:

I reached home last night—passing by Nashville & Louisville—the exacerbation of Secession, is, coming down!— the excitement of the hour is passing away & "The sober second thought of the people", will I feel great confidence "Save this Union".

I find some old Democrats bitter towards you but generally I think the people will as a whole sustain you. From the individuals I have met with while travelling, I should conclude judging from them, much *less* disaffection, in the Seceded States, than I supposed to exist! Most, say, they are fixed & immovably *out.* none express to me dissatisfaction or a desire to return back! Arkansas will not go out, now: Bob. Johnson,[1] Hindman,[2] Rusk[3] & others from here & other states, are, using every effort, for the Secession of Ark at Little Rock. but I think, all these efforts will, probably fail, from all, I can gather![4] YOU have much, very much, to do, in Tennessee!

If no act of violence & no new cause of irritation be furnished the Secession feeling will rapidly lessen— the evacuation of fort Sumpter & promises of Peace by Admn. is doing vast deal to bring men to reason & to a commonsense view, of the issues before the country! I have said Seward, Weed & Cameron, are, all laboring intensely for Peace & the Union; & that all, will be yet rightly Settled— I have so far, & shall continue, to place you before the public—*rightly*! My feeble efforts I find not without benefits. People befogged by false impressions— You must soon visit the cheif places in Tene It is of great significance that you do so! I am outright defending not only yourself but insisting on a fair & just Consideration for Lincoln's Administration. Seward & Cameron are not distasteful to our sensible men whom I have presented the issues & the facts to in Tene [&] Ky.

Yr friend.   J. Fowlkes.

ALS, DLC-JP.

1. Senator Robert W. Johnson of Arkansas. *Johnson Papers*, II, 82*n*.

2. Thomas C. Hindman (1828–1868), Arkansas Democratic congressman (1859–61), was born in Knoxville, Tennessee, served in the Mississippi legislature (1852), and established a law practice at Helena, Arkansas, in 1853. Reelected to Congress in 1860, he declined to serve and soon afterward

raised "Hindman's Legion," becoming a Confederate major general in 1862. Following the war he spent three years in Mexico, returning to Helena, where he was murdered. *BDAC*, 1057.

3. Probably Albert Rust (*c*1818–1870), Virginia-born lawyer who was a member of the Arkansas house (1842–48, 1852–54), Democratic congressman (1855–57, 1859–61), member of the Confederate Provisional Congress, and brigadier general. It is not clear why Rust is mentioned here; though eventually a Confederate, he was at this writing a conservative unionist delegate to the Little Rock convention. *Ibid.*, 1552; Robert B. Walz, "Arkansas Slaveholdings and Slaveholders in 1850," *Arkansas Historical Quarterly*, XII (1953), 69; Marcus J. Wright, *Arkansas in the War, 1861–1865* (Batesville, Ark., 1963), 94.

4. In the wake of Lincoln's election, Johnson, Hindman, and others associated with the extreme southern faction of the Arkansas Democratic party, had inaugurated a campaign to take the state out of the Union. Successful in getting a convention called to consider secession, they found the assemblage, convened on March 4 and still in session at this time, controlled by unionists. Defeating a resolution providing for an ordinance of secession to take effect when ratified by popular vote, the convention adjourned March 21. After the fall of Sumter and Lincoln's appeal for troops, it reconvened on May 6 and, by a vote of 65–5, passed a secession ordinance. Ralph Wooster, "The Arkansas Secession Convention," *Arkansas Historical Quarterly*, XIII (1954), 172–84; Scroggs, "Arkansas in the Secession Crisis," 179–224.

From James R. Hood

Cincinnati, Ohio, March 17. 1861

Gov. Johnson—

Dea[r] Sir: Having to remain here for several hours, I have concluded to drop you a few lines.

I shall esteem it, a great honor if you will have my appointment[1] attended to before the Senate adjourns[.] No one need know but that I am indebted to Brabson[2] for the appointment. However, I shall know the facts; and be grateful accordingly. It is a matter of great importance to me.

I shall send you a copy of my paper regulaly, in order to show you that all former political differences are forgotten now, and will be for years hence.

I should be pleased, if possible, to get for my paper the publication of the laws passed by Congress,[3] and a[n]y governmental advertising that may be at the disposal of the administration.

I find from enquiry here that the Republicans are getting pretty sore of Abe, Seward, and even Chase; and I have heard the word "Tylerized"[4] more than once, as applied to the Republican party.

The Republican party is dead, and a great *national* triumph awaits the Union men. So be it. In haste,

Yours, very respectfully,   Jas. R Hood

Please send copy of your last Speech to Chattanooga.

ALS, DLC-JP.

1. Hood was in process of being appointed Chattanooga postmaster by the Lincoln administration. Brownlow's *Whig*, April 6, 1861, accused "little Hood" of being a party to a patronage conspiracy involving Johnson and Etheridge.

2. Reese Brabson.

3. Founded in 1838 as the *Hamilton County Gazette*, the Chattanooga *Gazette* was a Whig journal until 1859, when it was suspended following a fire. Although Hood revived the paper in 1861 and conducted a vigorous campaign against secession, he apparently did not receive the commission he sought. Armstrong, *Hamilton County*, I, 153–54; see also Hood to Johnson, January 1, 1860 [1861], Johnson Papers, LC.

4. An allusion to a party's being taken over by a leadership which betrays its principles—as John Tyler had been accused of doing with the Whigs in the 1840's.

From John C. Ferriss, Jr.[1]

Nashville, March 18th 1861

Hon And. Johnson
Washington City, D. C.

I do not know whether it will be propper or not to write to you again[2] in regard to the office of Attorney General; I will refer you to your son Robert Johnson for refference to me. it is true, that like yourself I have been an humble mechanic all my life up to within the last two years; since then I have been reading and practicing law.— I hope you will do all you can for me, for it is through you that we all act.— When I was a Democrat I always took you for an example, now you are for preserving the union and I go with you there; It is said by some here that Lincoln is president but Johnson is ruler.—that you have a great deal of influence, then I may have a chance of being appointed yet. I do hope that you will do all you can for me.

Respectfully   J. C. Ferriss jr

ALS, DLC-JP.

1. John C. Ferriss [variously spelled Farriss, Farris] (1837–*fl*1902), the son of John C. Ferriss of Rutherford County, came to Nashville in 1855 to learn the printing trade and had been on the staff of the *Tennessee Baptist*. Briefly publishing the Rutherford *Telegraph*, in 1859 he went to Pine Bluff, Arkansas, where he published the *Jefferson Independent*. Late in that year he returned to Tennessee, entered Cumberland Law School, graduated in 1860, and commenced his practice in Nashville. With the onset of the war he enlisted in Co. C, 2nd Tenn. Inf. serving under Gen. William B. Bate. He was for many years Davidson County court judge. Speer, *Prominent Tennesseans*, 289–90; Deane Porch, *1850 Census, Rutherford County, Tennessee* (Nashville, 1967), 29; William Waller, *Nashville, 1900–1910* (Nashville, 1972), 75, 79–80.

2. In February he had written Johnson asking him to "do all you can for me, I have never appealed to you in vain." Ferriss to Johnson, February 25, 1861, Tennessee, 1861–65, Appointments, RG60, National Archives.

From Blackston McDannel

Greenville Ten March 18/61

Friend Johnson

There is a damned secession traitor at Cedar Creek, a Post master, by the name Girdner.[1] He ought by all means be turned out. Old man Rumbough and his son Tom, are good union men,[2] and fought like hell through the late election. They have a store at Cedar creek and in the right place for a post office— Would it not be well to turn out that damnd impudent, rich man, Girdner, and put in Tom. Rumbough, or the old man.

I expect they are both whigs. I know of no Democrat *there*, that would suit.

I hope it will be so managed, that all damnd, traitors will have to walk the plank.

I understand that a petition has been started from the House of Lowry & Eason,[3] to retain Biggs[4] in the Post office— It was presented to me for my signature, by an anti-coercionist, but I declined upon the grounds that I am opposed to any man for any office, who refused to co-operate cordially with the union men during our late election. It makes some folks mad about here, if any person speaks disrespectfully of the damnd traitors of the South.

Perhaps Lowry thinks, that the same compliment may be returned by Biggs or somebody else by getting up a petition to retain him in office. He (Lowry) says he will not apply for the position of Marshall, but that the great Judge Humphreys will apply to have all, Judge, Marshalls, Attorney Generals &c retained— I understand, Humphreys is a Secessionist also.[5]

I mustered up courage the other day sufficient to send my application to you for the office of Marshall of East Tennessee. If I make a failure, why just let it go as a matter of Moonshine.[6] But still I would like to have it. and to hear from you on the subject. I told Lowry I intended to make application. He said, without my asking, that if he was not situated as he was then (in expectation of being retained through Humphreys, is what he meant) he would take great pleasure in reccommending me. I thought of the petitions I signed for him in times gone by for post master, and Marshall, and particularly of a special letter he would have me to write for his advancement for the Office of Marshall, in which I stated that he was *perfectly honest* &c, but still I didn't say what I thought.

Well in conclusion I will just Say, if there is any chance for McDannel, put him through. Patterson, Milligan, McDowell & Mc-

Gaughey[7] promised to write you— Geo. Jones wrote to Tom. Nelson to drop you a line on the subject. I hope they will convince you and the president that I would make a good *Sheriff* for the U. S. Court[.][8]

As usual   B. McDannel

ALS, DLC-JP.

1. William Girdner (b. *c*1818), the local physician, sawmill owner, and postmaster at Cedar Creek (1851–66), ten years earlier possessed real estate valued at $2,100. 1850 Census, Tenn., Greene, 410; *U. S. Official Register* (1851), 384*; (1865), 342*.

2. Jacob Rumbough (1791–1875) and his son Thomas S. (1837–1864) were Cedar Creek merchants. McDannel may have been blinded by class consciousness in his assessment of the Rumboughs. Young Rumbough was far from the dedicated unionist here depicted; not only did he become a captain in the 16th Tenn. Cav., CSA, which served in East Tennessee, but he was described in 1864 as leading a company of "about 100 men . . . calling themselves 'freebooters,' " who were "continually scouring the country, robbing loyal citizens of their horses, cattle, grain, clothing, bedding, and every other species of household furniture." Allegedly, they once seized a Methodist minister, cut off his ears, and "beat him to death with their guns." 1860 Census, Tenn., Greene, 3rd Dist., 52; Reynolds, *Greene County Cemeteries*, 281; *Tennesseans in the Civil War*, II, 351; *OR*, Ser. 1, XXXII, Pt. II, 29.

3. William M. Lowry and T. J. Eason were general merchants at Greeneville. Lowry, Johnson's longtime personal friend who had been Federal marshal for the eastern district of Tennessee since 1853, later sided with the Confederacy; Eason (b. *c*1828) a man of some wealth, possessed real and personal property worth $28,000. 1860 Census, Tenn., Greene, 10th Dist., 92; *Johnson Papers*, I, 34*n*; II, 134; *U. S. Official Register* (1853), 258.

4. For Elbert Biggs, see *Johnson Papers*, II, 391*n*.

5. West H. Humphreys, the Federal district judge for Tennessee, later accepted a commission as a Confederate judge. *Ibid.*, 387*n*.

6. "Ridiculous chatter or nonsense." *Webster's Third International*.

7. David T. Patterson, Sam Milligan, James P. McDowell, and John McGaughey.

8. McDannel received the appointment. *U. S. Official Register* (1861), 192.

From Harvey M. Watterson

McMinville, Te. March 18th 1861

Dear Governor.

I trust that this letter will reach you in Washington.

Our friend Raleigh Martin,[1] in conformity with instructions from the Post Office Department, (under the Buchanan Administration) sent on the bond he was required to give, but has not yet received his *commission*. Walling has refused, and still refuses to *abdicate* until Martin obtains this *commission*.[2] Thanking you for what you have already done in the case, I must ask the additional favor that you go to the Department and have, if possible, the *commission* forwarded. In a little matter like this I take it for granted that the new Post

Master General will be willing to accommodate you. By the by, I do not think Lincoln's inaugural is very alarming.

Our approaching political canvass will be different from any we have ever had in the state. I think the time has come when the *people* should select the candidates—and all the indications are that they intend to do it. The Union men of Warren, Coffee and Cannon, without a dissenting voice, so far as I know, are for Andrew Ewing as our candidate for Governor. I believe myself that, under all the circumstances, he is the very man. I am for him with a will.

I have not seen Stokes,[3] and know nothing definite of his views in regard to another race for Congress. I shall neither encourage nor discourage him. I think, however, that Hickerson[4] would be a much stronger candidate.

You will, of course, make us a speech in McMinville. Do not put it off too long. In this mountain country you can do great good. Your old friends are not all dead yet[.] What a H-ll of a fool old Joe Lane has made of himself. Cant you send me your last speeches?

Yours truly   H. M. Watterson[5]

ALS, DLC-JP.

1. Writing on the same date, Martin reported that he had not received his commission and also observed that Johnson's speeches were "mutch misrepresented by the disunionists and but little read." Martin to Johnson, March 18, 1861, Johnson Papers, LC. See also Letter from Harvey Watterson, February 5, 1861.

2. Smith J. Walling continued in the office, which he had held since 1854, until June; Martin served the remaining six months. *U. S. Official Register* (1861), 266.

3. William B. Stokes (1814–1897), a North Carolina native, was a DeKalb County farmer who served as a Whig in the state house of representatives (1849–52) and senate (1855–56). Elected to Congress (1859–61), he remained loyal to the Union, becoming colonel of the 5th Tenn. Cav. Rgt., USA. After the war he studied law, was admitted to the bar (1867), and served two more terms in the House (1866–71); for a short time supervisor of internal revenue for Tennessee, he returned to Alexandria to practice until his death. *BDAC*, 1661–62; *Tennesseans in the Civil War*, I, 329.

4. Probably William P. Hickerson (1816–1882), Coffee County merchant and lawyer, who was born in North Carolina and came to Tennessee as a child. Judge of the sixth circuit court (1865–67, 1869–77), Hickerson was a delegate to the Washington Peace Conference (1861). *Goodspeed's Coffee*, 933; Leighton Ewell, *History of Coffee County* (Manchester, 1936), 19; Coffee County Conservation Board [Corinne Martinez], *Coffee County: From Arrowheads to Rocketheads* (Tullahoma, 1969), 113, 162.

5. An endorsement written by Dr. Robert A. Lacey, a clerk in the postmaster general's office, urges Johnson to call on the postmaster general to dispel the latter's uneasiness about Martin, who had been appointed under the Buchanan administration. *U. S. Official Register* (1861), 1*.

From John G. Winter

Columbus Mch 18. 61

Dr Sir— The evacuation of Fort Sumter is doubtless a necessity &
a most deplorable one at that— The Devils will send up a shout of
exultation at the degradation of the Stars & Stripes, which will reach
the lowermost depths of the infernal regions— *But* if th administration will reestablish th Flag in th Bay of Pennsa. [Pensacola][1] It will
give *us* a hurrah which will *acend* to th third *heaven*—[2] It will be
policy to give our side the *conclusion* & that *right quickly*— If we
can take & hold Pennsa., we will effectually check the *big Steal* on
the Ocean—[3] They cannot use Steamers without *Coal Depots*—
Pennsa. will be as it has been, just th place for that, & our Steamers
can catch their boasted Yankee Pirateers as fast as they can put them
afloat— The lawful hanging of a dozen of those enterprising Gentlemen, will estop the operation— Let Government secure itself *well*
at Pennsa., firmly collect the revenues & the Traitors will exhaust
their naval Power at Pennsa. & I see not how Civil war can become
general— Pennsa. will not only be with them a point of honor, but
a stern necessity— The independence of the Cotton States Can never
be any thing but nominal, whilst Key West, Tortugas & Pennsa. are
in the hands of a Foreign Power— Secure them & secure the mouth
of th Chessapeake & the American Eagle is safe— But men who are
placed there should be thoroughly opposed to secession—men of my
views & I believe yours, who look upon secession as damnation to
human liberty here & elsewhere—as the culmination of every evil
now complained of, or by the Secessionists really or feignedly *apprehended*, & yet ten thousand others not now dreamed of— The Anglo
saxon machine is a powerful one & when the restraints of law &
order shall have been removed, he will be found as energetic in robbery & murder as he has been in the arts of peace & in treading its
virtuous paths—

Please accept my reflections as the offerings of a heart thoroughly
devoted to the Welfare of my Country & *not* the offsp[r]ing of vanity
— If I should be fortunate enough to offer any (even th smallest)
idea of value, I shall be agreeably disappointed & you will only be
acting your natural part in adopting it in spite of its humble origin[.]
I will excuse you from any ceremonial acknowledgement of my letter,
as your time must be fully occupied with the *substance* of things—
should you have *occasion* to write me, please let it be without your
frank— The infernal ruffle shirt mob[4] in this country have got the

hue & cry upon you & it is about as much as a mans life is worth to be identified as your supporter— I trust the time *will* come when you will be looked upon as one who saved the good old Ship of State by standing firmly to your post in the hour of her extremity—when honors justly your due will be showered upon you, instead of the obloquy which is now your portion throughout the Cotton States—
Let Pennsacola be the field of blood, if nothing but blood will satisfy & they will have neither blood nor money to expend elsewhere—
My opinion is that they are making large calculations on robbing the California Steamers—

To catch them at it & to hang the ring leaders as Pirates, will be a terrible blow upon their prestige— Let *them make* the fights & let uncle Sam *whip* them & the cry of *Coercion* will not Save them from ruin & degradation. Pennsa is a far better point for a fight than Charleston— The title to *that* property is beyond the *reach* of *sophistry*—as it was *never* in the State of Florida, they cannot alledge that it was ceded by Florida for certain purposes & the bargain being violated it *reverts* to the *grantor*—[5] It is a surer fight & success is *vitally* important—To us a *cheaper* fight—To them a dearer one & more remote from reinforcements— The expenses of an army large enough to tempt them to make th attack, would rapidly exhaust the finances of the Confederate States— If they *cannot* collect their revenues & persevere energetically in their efforts to take Pickens, the Fall elections will hurl them from power— The *outs* have Commenced *gr[o]wling*[6] & by the time th next elections come around they will *cry aloud*.

The weakness of Buchannon & the wickedness of Floyd & his compeers have placed the Country in a horrid dilemma,[7] but I hope there is enough of wisdom & virtue left on th side of th land of Washington to stay the tide of rapine & murder which is threatening to engulf in everlasting ruin the happiest People upon the face of Gods Earth—

Respectfully & Truly Yr devoted Sert.
John G. Winter

It is my candid opinion that if there were a fair vote taken in this part of the Country, untrammeled by *terror*, there would be found a large majority against the Seceders & in favour of reconstruction — All the gains are *for* us & there have been some recent converts who object to the tariff & the lavish expenditure of money—[8] Every time they lose a *fight*, they will lose ten thousand *votes*[.] Success makes the man, the want of it the fellow—[9] The adage will fit Yancy, Davis, Toombs & Co as well as oth[er] folks—

P.S. Just rumoured that the Cabinet has determined not to evacuate Fort Sumpter— To be repulsed there will I fear ruin every thing— will encourag th disorganizers in the Border States & enable them to carry their point— But if given up & the Traitors immediately Castigated at Fort Pickens, would have counteracted the damage to our prestige at the evacuation— But I suppose they know best— If they win the fight, all right & I trust in God they will— If they do, it will be a crusher & no mistake—

ALS, DLC-JP; also printed in LeRoy P. Graf and Ralph W. Haskins, eds., "The Letters of a Georgia Unionist: John G. Winter and Secession," *Georgia Historical Quarterly*, XLV (1961), 394–96.

1. Although the Federal government retained Ft. Pickens in Pensacola Harbor throughout the war, the Pensacola navy yard and adjacent Ft. Barrancas had been occupied early in January, 1861, by the seceding states of Florida and Alabama. Winter makes clear his opinion that recovery of the navy yard is essential to weakening the Confederacy and avoiding a general war, thereby paving the way for the collapse of secession. In reality, Federal control of Pickens kept the South from making effective use of the navy yard. Kathryn Abbey [Hanna], *Florida, Land of Change* (Chapel Hill, 1941), 271–73; William Watson Davis, *The Civil War and Reconstruction in Florida* (New York, 1913), 74–85 *passim*; Edwin C. Bearss, "Civil War Operations in and around Pensacola," *Florida Historical Quarterly*, XXXVI (1957), 125–65; Pt. II, XXXIX (1961), 231–55.

2. The third heaven, a concept which has its origins in early Christian mysticism and perhaps reflects the ideas of gnosticism. According to the Apostle Paul, "I knew a man in Christ above fourteen years ago . . . such a one caught up to the third heaven." 2 Cor. 12 : 2.

3. Winter feared that the Confederates planned to seize cargoes, including specie from California, carried by steamships plying between Panama and New York.

4. An expression used in contempt and referring to a person of some means—an aristocrat. Mathews, *Americanisms*, 1427.

5. The Federal government's title to East and West Florida, including the offshore islands, was clearly established in the Adams-Onís Treaty of 1819, which preceded by a quarter century the admission of the "sovereign state" of Florida. Hubert B. Fuller, *The Purchase of Florida: Its History and Diplomacy* (Gainesville, 1964 [1906]), 372.

6. Leadership in the Confederacy early fell into the hands of comparatively moderate secessionists, leaving the extremist fire-eaters disgruntled and restive, fearful that plans were afoot to restore ties with the Union. Indeed, insisted Rhett's Charleston *Mercury*, such a plan lay behind the deliberations of the Montgomery convention. To such ultras, the impasse would have to be resolved, either by the seizure of Sumter or by some other sharp blow struck in behalf of the Confederacy. Catton, *The Coming Fury*, 255–57.

7. The "wickedness of Floyd & his compeers" may imply more than Winter's acceptance of the allegation that John B. Floyd, Buchanan's secretary of war, had transferred "huge quantities" of materiel—100,000 stands of arms and 125 cannon, according to Allan Nevins—to southern arsenals. Floyd had also exhibited "negligence, blundering, and general misfeasance" in office. Although apparently not benefiting personally from the attempted sale of Ft. Snelling, a federal military reservation in the new state of Minnesota, and the purchase of Willett's Point, Long Island, for army use, he had allowed friends to use him and his office for fraudulent purposes. These actions led to

his resignation. The allusion to "compeers" reflects the domination of Buchanan by Floyd, Howell Cobb, Jefferson Davis, and others, known to contemporaries as "the Directory." Clement Eaton, *A History of the Southern Confederacy* (New York, 1954), 131; Nevins, *Emergence of Lincoln*, II, 199, 375.

8. As a temporary expedient, the Provisional Congress had adopted the Tariff of 1857, modifying it on February 18 to put food and some provisions of a free list. As this letter was being written, "the first distinct Confederate tariff," placing graduated ad valorem taxes on numerous articles, had just been passed (March 15). Although these taxes were all lower than corresponding Federal rates, further modification would follow to place the South nearer its free-trade philosophy. However, interestingly enough, Winter's state of Georgia, with some budding manufacturing interests, and Louisiana, with its sugar industry, had opposed the clause in the permanent Confederate Constitution which prohibited a protective tariff. Robert R. Russel, *The Economic Aspects of Southern Sectionalism, 1849–1861* (New York, 1960 [1924]), 261–66; John C. Schwab, *The Confederate States of America, 1861–1865: A Financial and Industrial History* (New York, 1901), 240–41; Augusta *Chronicle*, March 10, 16, 17, 1861.

9. Paraphrase of "Worth makes the man, and the want of it the fellow." Alexander Pope, *Essay on Man*, Epistle IV, l. 203.

From William S. Speer

Shelbyville Tenn 19 March 1861

Gov. Johnson—
My Dear Sir—

When I pledged you my poor efforts to Johnsonise the Whigs of Middle Tennessee *I meant something*—and when I reached home *I did something*. I openly told the boys I left Washington a Johnson man—and that the Whig Congressmen were Johnson men. My report has *driven the nail through* that your own speeches had "*driven in*".[1] Whereupon a petition was gotten up and signed numerously for the brief time and sent on to you requesting you to visit Shelbyville.[2] This is at least a straw in the breeze & I give it to show you I knew what I was talking about.

I think I can amuse you a little by an anecdote or two that I picked up in Washington. I fell in with poor *Maynard* in an Omnibus, and improving the opportunity I sounded him as to his position. Your name came up and Maynard said—

"Had one of us Whig Congressmen made the speech that Gov. Johnson delivered on the 19th Decr. he would not have been hung in effigy but in person in Tennessee— he would never have left Tennessee alive again. But Tennessee has indorsed that speech of Senator Johnson because it was right & truth in itself and came from the Democratic side."

Thus Maynard slily showed me his own position.[3] I smile a little broad every time I think of that singular disclosure. Maynard is my friend and I like him, but he lacks a little directness & boldness in these times. I am glad to find him courting good company—

I have spent six or eight hours with Col. Gentry[4] since my return. Without venturing to repeat a conversation with you in which you had spoken kindly of him, I did tell him the Washington programme which includes returning you to the U. S. Senate;—[5] he observed, half freely—half drily—

"That is a good programme if it can be carried out."

I have heard him approve your course—& he is with you on the pending questions. *He is sound.* When I endorse the soundness of a Union man you may take it for granted he *is* sound.[6]

Thus, Governor, as patriots we meet the greet and coöperate. God save our native land!

I thought it would please you to read this tit bit and hence I write it.— I am committed, and shall remain constant.

I have not heard a word from Washington since I left. Hoping this may reach you in the Federal City I will take advantage of the kind offer you made me to do what you can to further my object to obtain an office. Mr. Lincoln promised my brother in law Dr. Black[7] in Illinois to give me an appointment if I should be properly endorsed by Tennessee Congressmen—which I am.

By a five minutes interview with him or Mr. Seward or one of the heads of Departments I think you can obtain me a place. My papers are in the State Department. Send me as Charge to South America Europe or Asia— send me as Consul to Madeira, Valparaiso or Yeddo— Make me an Auditor, Clerk, Commissioner, *or what you can.* I will be satisfied. I want a place, I need it.—[8] Col. Gentry has again written to Mr. Seward on my behalf. I think *you* have only to ask and I shall be put in. As so many are pressing for places, I must ask my friends to act for me. You have kindly promised to aid me. Please do so. *I am ready for service* at a day's warning.

> With the highest regard I remain
> Your Constant Personal & Political Friend
> Wm. S. Speer.

ALS, DLC-JP.

1. This figure of speech had appeared in several of Johnson's recent public statements, most notably in his Senate address of early February. See Speech on the Seceding States, February 5–6, 1861.

2. Dated March 15, the petition with 300 signatures was enclosed in a letter from Joseph H. Thompson of Shelbyville. Thompson to Johnson, March 16, 1861, Johnson Papers, LC.

3. One can do no more than speculate about this observation. It may well have reflected Horace Maynard's inherent caution, evidenced generally during his term in the prewar Congress and demonstrated particularly in his reaction to the secession crisis. A unionist, he could readily endorse Johnson's position in private but would avoid taking such a decided stand in public. In his remark

about Tennessee's endorsing an address which "came from the Democratic side" but which a Whig could not safely have delivered, there was also a bit of irony which recalled the old party rivalry. For evidence of Maynard's position in the crisis, see Maynard to George T. Hillard, November 16, 1860, Horace Maynard Papers, University of Tennessee Library; *Cong. Globe*, 36 Cong., 2 Sess., 316, 1260; Gladys I. Williams, The Life of Horace Maynard (M. A. Thesis, University of Tennessee, 1931), 22–27.

4. Meredith P. Gentry, former Tennessee Whig congressman and Johnson's gubernatorial opponent in 1855. See *Johnson Papers*, I, 366–67n.

5. In the absence of specific evidence, we can but speculate that loyal Tennessee unionists of both parties, in an effort to counter strong secessionist currents at home, had met in Washington to devise a strategy for keeping the Volunteer State in the Union. Obviously, the keystone of any such "Washington programme" would be the retention of Johnson as the legitimate spokesman for the state, in the face of threats to remove him.

6. Contrary to Speer's asseverations, Gentry proved not to be a "sound" Union man, for he subsequently served in the Confederate Congress (1862–63). *BDAC*, 937.

7. Thomas G. Black (b. *c*1825), a physician, in 1860 had $10,000 worth of real estate. 1860 Census, Ill., Adams, Clayton, 907. See Black to Lincoln, February 23, 1861, Lincoln Papers, LC, for his recommendation of Speer.

8. Appointed consul to Zanzibar in November, 1861, Speer was recalled in early 1863; in 1865 he was still seeking a government place. Roger Bruns (National Historical Publications Commission) to Andrew Johnson Project, September 20, 1973; William Speer, Applications and Recommendations during Lincoln, Johnson Administrations, RG59, National Archives; Speer to Johnson, April 18, 1865, Johnson Papers, LC.

From William H. Tilford

March 19, 1861, Walter Hill [Rutherford County]; ALS, DLC-JP.

Asserting that Murfreesboro Postmaster Reuben Butler is "a rabid secessionist" whose supporters denounce Johnson daily as "a Republican and a Traitor to the South," asks Johnson to use his "influence with the department and have this man removed and all other avowed Secessionists in our good union state[.]"

From J. Knox Walker and E. W. M. King[1]

Memphis Tenn. March 19. 1861.

Confidential
Hon Andrew Johnson.
Dr Sir.

The Avalanche of yesterday morning intimates & the Appeal of this morning states positively that *McCallister*[2] *has been appointed Custom House Officer for this place.* The papers named are as you know out & out Secession papers & no doubt the wish is father to the thought—[3].for it would indeed be a hard blow upon the Union party here to remove Hulbert[4] who voted the entire Union ticket & appoint McCallister an unknown man, of doubtful reputation simply because he is kin to Montgomery Blair—or Mrs. Lincoln—.[5] It would be a sweet morsel for the Secession papers to roll under their tongues[6] each alternate morning for which we could find & give no justification.

It is the universal desire of your friends[7] that this thing be not done; let Henry Hulbert be either reappointed or at least let alone (for he has over a year yet to run) & it will give universal satisfaction to our friends[.]

Very Respectfully Yours.

J Knox Walker

E. W. M. King

ALS, DLC-JP. Letter in Walker's autograph.

1. For Joseph Knox Walker and E. W. M. King, see *Johnson Papers*, III, 295n, 427n.

2. John C. McAlister (b. c1820), Kentucky native, merchant, and operator of a Memphis boardinghouse at the "corner of Main and Beal streets," possessed $300 in real and $1,000 in personal property. 1860 Census, Tenn., Shelby, Memphis, 5th Ward, 71; Memphis *Appeal*, March 19, 1861.

3. Shakespeare, *King Henry IV*, Pt. II, Act IV, sc. 5.

4. Henry T. Hulbert (b. c1826), native Pennsylvanian, was surveyor at Memphis at a salary of $2,841.54 per annum; listed in the census as a lawyer, he had $40,000 in real and $5,000 in personal property. In 1864 he served on the council by appointment of the Union army. 1860 Census, Tenn., Shelby, Memphis, 8th Ward, 133; *U. S. Official Register* (1859), 75; Keating, *Memphis*, II, 30.

5. McAlister's wife, Almira J., was said to be related to the Blairs of Missouri. Memphis *Appeal*, March 19, 1861.

6. Adapted from Mathew Henry, *Commentaries: Psalms*: Ps. 36. John Bartlett, *Familiar Quotations* (Boston, 1968), 386.

7. A letter of March 18, signed by Walker, King, and five other Memphians, requested that Hulbert not be removed, for "this will be Exceedingly obnoxious to the Union Party— Secessionists will rejoice—." In the same vein former Mayor Edwin M. Yerger alleged, "Evry appointment in this State, so far meets our approbation," and vigorously asserted that the appointment of an unknown man like McAlister "would be destructive of our hopes, and might be a *death blow* to the cause of the Union in Tennessee." Yerger to Johnson, March 19, 1861, Johnson Papers, LC.

From Charles O. Faxon[1]

Clarksville Tenn March 20 1861

Hon Andrew Johnson:

Dear Sir:

In conjunction with Hon Cave Johnson I have by the mail which takes this, forwarded to the P M General an application for the appointment of two young gentlemen of this city as route agents upon the Rail Road just completed from Memphis to Louisville through this City[.]

Their names are R B Hickman and C B Wilcox.[2] They are worthy and would fill the positions well[.] By the addition of your influence to our recommendation I think their appointment can be secured. By doing so you will confer a favor which I shall appreciate most highly[.]

There is still much uneasiness in political circles in Tennessee[.] The secessionists are not yet dead and only wait an opportunity— Unless the nomination for Governor by the Union party is exactly what it should be we shall have difficulty[.][3] I would like very much to hear your views on this subject. The danger I think is, that some leading politician of the old whig school may be put up by the Union party and that the cry will be raised by the democratic secessionists that it is a trick to strengthen the opposition to the democracy and that many of our old democratic friends may thus be deceived into voting the secessionist ticket and the Union Strength be in that way divided and the secessionists strengthened[.]

Respectfully   C. O. Faxon

ALS, DLC-JP.

1. Faxon, Clarksville postmaster and editor of the *Jeffersonian*, had written Johnson a week earlier about the rumor that Congressman James M. Quarles was seeking the local post office for a brother-in-law. Faxon to Johnson, March 13, 1861, Johnson Papers, LC.

2. Robert B. Hickman and C. B. Wilcox. Hickman, described as "Faxon's man," was a clerk in the Clarksville post office, recommended by both Cave Johnson and Robert W. Humphreys. C. B. Wilcox (b. *c*1837), born in Kentucky, was the son of Dr. C. L. Wilcox, native of Tennessee and a Clarksville physician. Cave Johnson to Andrew Johnson, March 19, 1861, Johnson Papers, LC; see also Letter from Robert W. Humphreys, March 13, 1861; Ann E. Alley and Ursula S. Beach, trs., *1850 Federal Census of Montgomery County, Tennessee* (Clarksville, 1971), 3; *Johnson Papers*, III, 445n.

3. Subsequently, a unionist convention held in Nashville on May 2 failed to nominate a candidate but recommended ex-Governor William B. Campbell, a Whig, as a suitable choice. Meanwhile the *Republican Banner*, a former Whig paper, mounted a campaign for William H. Polk, Douglas Democrat and younger brother of President Polk, who ultimately ran and was defeated by the incumbent, Isham G. Harris. White, *Messages*, V, 321–32.

From J. K. Ingalls

March 20, 1861, New York, N. Y.; ALS, DLC-JP.

A land reformer, writing on New York Kansas Relief Committee stationery, requests that Johnson use his influence with the party in power to obtain some situation for Dr. William J. Young, "who has spent some sixteen years, in circulating Tracts, Petitions, reporting for papers, writing, speaking &C. for these principles."

From Jesse H. McMahon[1]

Memphis, March 20, 1861

Private

My dear Sir

If "misery makes strange bed fellows,"[2] *patriotism* brings about equally unexpected associations. Who would have expected that you and I should be politically, brothers?— how could I have dreamed that, avowed "liberalist"[3] as I have been, for twenty-five years, not harshly or unkindly but from patriotic cautiousness, distrustful of the competency of the unlettered masses of the people to decide complex political questions, should have been *converted* into placing the firmest reliance upon these same "mud-sills" of our social organization?[4] Yet so it is. Experience and observation have taught me, and teaches me every day, that in time of real peril to our free institutions, the "higher classes" (!) of intelligence are not to be depended on while the people—the real people—are firm and solid as granite. I owe *you* some atonement for misjudging your philosophy heretofore, and I offer it in the enrollment of my name, hence to my life's end, among the "rosin-heeled,"[5] "mud-sill," *honest*-hearted though possibly ignorant, *people*. By whatever *name* it may be called—democrat or radical—aye, even an "Andy Johnson democrat"—I shall not flinch, but claim, sympathy and membership.

I have to thank you for the kind appreciation which I learn through a friend you were willing to extend to me in the matter of the Post Office here. From the first suggestion I repelled it, believing, as I did, that its acceptance would cripple any power and influence in *our* summer canvass, and detract from the efficiency of the *Bulletin* in aiding in that coming revolution of the *people* in Mississippi, Alabama and Arkansas, which I believe is sure in the future, by which the upstart usurpers will be hurled from their ill-gotten and transitory power. The office was not attractive enough, either in distinction or emolument, to tempt me into imperiling *that* cherished object.

There is, however, an appointment under the Government, which if *offered* to me, I would willingly accept—the mission to *Belgium*, Sardinia, or Switzerland[6]—if the last named has attached to it a salary that would enable a plain man to *decently* represent his country and "lay up something" for his return. The first, however,— Belgium—would be peculiarly acceptable to me for the reason that I speak and write French—have a creole wife who has near relatives there in honorable employment under the Government (the male fellows in the military line, and some cousins married to Judges or something of that kind) —know "French ways" enough to live well there, and at the same time save something of the salary—and, above all, could carry on the education of my two girl children, practically and, sensibly, among the practical and sensible Flemish people of that country. The *distinction* is something not altogether valueless to one who has toiled many years to make others great in active political life, without any taste for or ambition of the doubtful honor of going to Congress or being Governor of a State, but who at the same time is not indifferent to an honorable recognition that he had not lived in vain.

I suppose there is an immense pressure for all those places, and I certainly shall not *scramble* for it. If *your* suggestion, and that of a few other friends to whom I have mentioned it, does not suffice, I shall not expose myself, or the Union cause, to the injury which an unsuccessful *effort* to obtain office from this administration might entail.

If I do not over-estimate my position, I think I do not err in supposing that the tender of such an appointment would give *strength* to the Government in the Southwest, and aid rather than retard those in the seceded States who, in good time, will lead the reversal of the apparently popular judgment; for it would argue, not only that the President was willing to be *national* in his distribution of preferments, but that he had an eye to the sustenance of the true friends of the Union, without regard to party. I have, by the folly of large numbers of my contemporaries, *here* and elsewhere in this region, who went down like bulrushes before the storms raised by the conspirators of disunionism, become a kind of *representative man* of a large though latent class, to whom my appointment would appear as, in a degree, a personal testemonial.

I am under the impression that both Mr. Seward and the President, could *see* all this, if pointed out to them, and that, most probably, *your* suggestion of it would be potential. Do about it, precisely as you think fit, and expedient. If nothing comes of it, let it remain confidential between us. If necessary, I could, at very short notice, get our Union Congressmen, and other decent, *live* people, to file such documents as would afford the Administration justification in "pre-termitting"[7]—(as the know nothings said, to which I never belonged or sympathized with).—the pretensions of others.

Pray write me, and send me a lot for distribution of both your much misrepresented speeches. In the bonds of the Union

Your friend   J. H. McMahon[8]

ALS, DLC-JP.

1. Jesse H. McMahon (b. c1812), native of Tennessee possessing $15,000 in real estate and $10,000 in personal property and earlier associated with the Whig Memphis *Enquirer*, was currently editor of the *Bulletin* which he had founded in 1855 and conducted until its merger with the *Avalanche* in 1861. According to a contemporary, McMahon "went south after the [Union] occupation of Memphis," but in late 1865 he helped reestablish the Memphis *Appeal*. 1860 Census, Tenn., Shelby, Memphis, 4th Ward, 50; Hallum, *Diary*, 157; Keating, *Memphis*, I, 257; II, 212, 218; *Goodspeed's Shelby*, 904–5.

2. Paraphrase of Shakespeare, *The Tempest*, Act II, sc. 2.

3. McMahon was apparently using "liberalist" in a Burkean sense: a person of "superior social standing" as distinguished from one engaged in *"servile* or *mechanical* pursuits." *OED*, VI, 237.

4. "Mudsill": a person in the lowest stratum of society. Used by Senator James H. Hammond of South Carolina in his famous Senate speech of March, 1858, to describe poor whites of the North, the derogatory term had been picked up immediately by Johnson and used in a flattering way in his Speech on Homestead Bill, May 20, 1858: to him, the mudsill constituted the foundation of the country.

5. "Rosin heel" was a term applied to the poor white. Craigie and Hulbert, *Dictionary of American English*, IV, 1975.

6. He apparently did not receive a foreign appointment.

7. "Pretermit": to let pass without notice.

8. On this same date, McMahon recommended for marshal of West Tennessee J. B. Moseley, a former sheriff of Shelby County, who was not appointed. McMahon to Johnson, March 20, 1861, Johnson Papers, LC.

From Elkenah D. Rader[1]

Bristol March 20th 1861

Private

To the Hon Andrew Johnson.

Dr Sir   I have just returned from the Blountville Court where I had Several interviews with Judge Patterson[.] I gave him a history of the doings of the Cecession party in Bristol, he requested Me to inform you of them[.] there is not an office holder Scarsely but what is a Cecessionist and you have bin written to by some of them claiming to be good Brackenridge men and wish to be retained in office[.] Now Sir they denounce you for every thing they can think of[.] Call you and Nelson Black Republicaning, Sutch men Should be turned out[.] it is the wish of all your frends of both parties, One of them runs as rout agent on the Ten & Va Rail Road.[2] Caywood[3] is a Union man and a strong friend of yours and So far as I have Knowledge is acceptable to the Party and wish him Retained[.] the one who denounced you is not from Greenville So you May Know who I mean. the Union Party in Sullivan is gaining Strngth[.] Nelson made a speech at court that done good[.] he Sustains you like a brother[.] I have never Seen Sutch a revolution[.] the Union Whigs applaud you in the highest degree and swear they would rather Support you for President than any man in the united States[.] but in Bristol we have a Strong Cecession Party[.] Not more than twenty union men[.] Joseph Anderson[4] and My Self are the only ones that give them battle[.] they Say you Shall not make a Speech in Bristol and if you make the attempt they will Egg you[.] we tell them that they Shall have a chance for it and if the attempt is made the first blood will be spilt on the line of Tenn. We have it in Contemplation to in vite you Nelson and others to make Speeches here after you return[.] Nelson is anxious for it[.] Jonesboro and the union men in Sullivan will be in attendance[.] I have just recd two Copy of your Speech of Feby the 5 & 6th[.] I have Sent them out in the hands of Union Whigs[.] I never heard Such a cry for a Speech in my life[.] it ought to be freely Circulated[.] I hope to receve your last reply to Lane and others[.] the battle in Tenn this Summer will be *feirce*[5] but the victory will be great, in a Conversation with Nelson Deadrick Arnold and Netherland[6] they Say the old Issues are gone and they will Support a[n]y Union Democrat for any office and will not Support a Cecession Whig and So it goes. you have Seen I Suppose Sperrys Comments in the Bristol News[7] on your corse in the Senate[.] You Should never Speak to him[.] he is the worst liar I have ever seen. I must close[.] I am trespassing on your tim[.] I hope to See you the hero of the union party Shortly and hea[r] from you[.] please Send me all good documents and I will Send them out[.]

Your frind   E D Rader

ALS, DLC-JP.

1. Elkenah D. Rader (b. c1817) was a Sullivan County house painter. 1860 Census, Tenn., Sullivan, 53; 1870 Census, Tenn., Sullivan, 17th Dist., 1.

2. Probably Andrew J. Blair, incumbent agent, who wrote Johnson earlier in the month that, while "not an applicant under [the new] Administration," he would like to continue in the office. Blair to Johnson, March 1, 1861, Johnson Papers, LC.

3. James J. Cawood [Caywood?] (b. c1813) was mail agent on the East Tennessee and Virginia Railroad. James M. Crockett, another applicant for route agent, however, claimed Cawood was disloyal to Johnson, had been "doun one[on] you . . . [and] s[a]id you arte [ought] to Bee Hung For that Speech you Maid[.]" Marion K. Burgner, tr., *Population Schedule of the United States Census of 1850 for Sullivan County, Tennessee* (Knoxville, 1963), 63; E. P. Cawood to Johnson, March 22, and James M. Crockett to Johnson, February 27, 1861, Johnson Papers, LC.

4. See *Johnson Papers*, III, 362n.

5. A reference to the impending race for governor.

6. T. A. R. Nelson, James W. Deadrick, Thomas D. Arnold, and John Netherland, all leading East Tennessee Whigs.

7. J. Austin Sperry, a founder of the Bristol *News*, who later took over the Knoxville *Register*.

From Sullivan County Citizens

March 20th 1861

Hon. A. Johnson
Greenville
Dear Sir

I suppose you will be surprised when you see the author[1] of this epistle. As I have always been opposed to your promotion since I came to Tennessee many wonder that I have taken the position I now occupy. I am where I have always been as regards the Union and I am glad to say that you have been consistent and loyal to our country, and therefore we naturally are allies and friends in this dreadful crisis. Neither of us have sacrificed to come together, but it is by devotion to our beloved country. This is therefore a strange crisis, one that has split the old parties asunder and has formed new associations and combinations, of the old fragments. When you come among us again you will find some of your old enemies still arrayed against you and some who were your strongest friends are now your bitterest enemies, and again many of your old enemies are your new recognised friends. I for one watched with anxiety your course and was rejoiced to see you found at your post and battling for the Union against the hordes of Northern and southern *Disunionists*—and thus I have been occupied until I have lost sight of all the old issues and have determined to go with that party that will be willing to compromise and settle on any safe ground that is right and fair to all sections. My object in writing to you sir is to request you to come to Blountville on the 1st Monday in April next County Court day to make us a speech[.][2] Many are on the fence wavering, many of whom you could forever make safe union men of. You can do more than any one else or I may say that [*sic*] all else put together just at this juncture[.] Desperate exertions are now making by the leaders to forestall your influence in this county. When you come you will have a storm to contend with and I am confident that you are the man for the Crisis. Threats were made before the election to mob you if you ever attempted to speak in Sullivan. You then had friends who would not have hesitated to stand against any odds in your defence and now you have any number. My reason for saying that you can do more than any one else is—that any one of note on the old Democratic side is a Secessionist whilst the Union men who were Whigs cannot have the effect desired as the Seceders are using every means to prejudice the minds of the democrats, and draw the old party lines when it is

to their advantage, and when they can succeed in making disunionists of old Whigs, it is by another kind of a game altogether. Tomorrow we will agree as to the time when we will make a demonstration
in Old Sullivan and I hope that when she speaks again she will confirm what she did last election.[3] If you cannot come on the said day
we wish you to make an appointment and notify us thereof and
oblige your friends for whom I write who also subscribe[.]

R. P. Fickle

E. P. Cawood
Thos B Rhea   J Hamilton
Gideon Cate   A Boy
Saml Snapp   E D Rader
John Spurgin   Saml Evans
        &c &c

P. S. I was not able to get this letter of invitation up as soon as I
expected and in the manner that I wished, owing to my duties at the
Court,[4] but I will refer to Judge Patterson who is familiar with all
the points—and I am urged again and again to press you to come, on
the day that I have suggested. If you cannot—then appoint one at
some public time, as every exertion will be made to keep the masses
from hearing you. Your speeches have been kept from circulation as
much as possible but many carry them along and read them by the
wayside to the common people. I have thus written you a few un-
connected paragraphs in haste which you will excuse[.]

R. P F

ALS, DLC-JP. In R. P. Fickle's autograph.

1. Although a unionist at this writing, Robert P. Fickle (1822–1895), a
Virginia-born farmer with $21,500 in real estate and $8,000 in personal prop-
erty, later served in the Sullivan County Reserves, a Confederate unit. 1860
Census, Tenn., Sullivan, 8th Dist., 23; *Tennesseans in the Civil War*, II, 152;
Ray, *Tennessee Cousins*, 174.

2. Johnson did not return to Tennessee at this time. Although he scheduled
a speech at Blountville for May 7, he was asked to cancel the engagement
because "of the excited state of the public mind." Knoxville *Whig*, May 4, 18,
1861; Thomas B. Alexander, *Thomas A. R. Nelson of East Tennessee* (Nashville, 1956), 84.

3. "Old Sullivan's" voice in the February 9 election was unclear; while the
vote for convention was 1180 to 734, the unionist candidates outpolled the
secessionist. Contrary to the hopes of Fickle and his associates, the June 8
vote went 1586 to 627 in favor of secession. Campbell, *Tenn. Attitudes*, 288,
291.

4. In 1860 Fickle had begun a six-year term as justice of the peace for
district 8, Sullivan County. Mrs. Cleo A. Hughes (Tennessee State Library
and Archives) to Andrew Johnson Project, October 30, 1974.

From Joseph L. Williams[1]

[Washington, D. C.]
Wednesday 20th March—1861

Dr Sir,

A personal friend, the Assistant Secy of the Treasury, Mr. Harrington,[2] suggested to me yesterday, that if you would see Mr Chase, in person, to enforce y'r own recommendation, it would settle the matter at once; as to the Office of Solicitor of the Treasury, at least; a more legal & technical office, than that of 1st Comptroller—& of the same pay—

Mr. H. also suggests, that this Office of Solicitor is the more readily attainable, by a man hailing from a Union Slavery State, now, than the others, because the late Solicitor,[3] was of Georgia & an avowed Disunionist[.]

That Mr. Chase & the President, cherishing really, views of equal consideration, yet, for the Loyal States, Slave & Free—are disposed to apportion incumbencies, as far as possible, as they have before existed; and, to place a man from the North, for example, in the 1st Comptrollership, because, a man from that section, is now the incumbent.[4]

That this idea, which would exclude me, from the latter place, would include me, as to the now vacant place of Solicitor of the Treasury; "provided always", I am deemed, otherwise eligible & appropriate for it; on which latter point, Mr. Harrington, thinks, your presence with Mr. Chase, to enforce y'r own recommendation, to-night, or, to-morrow morning, before 10, O'clock, would be instantly conclusive. Mr. Harrington has, in his possession, your letter for me, together with one from Senator Simmons[5] & another from Mr. Etheredge; for the final consideration of the Secretary of the Treasury, &, the President.

I am thus free & unreserved, in communicating with you, touching a matter so personal to myself—simply, because, with equal frankness & kindness, you challenged me to invoke your aid.

Soliciting an office, is a new thing to me. By the thousands, in times past, I have seen Offices distributed, without a temptation to compete for one.— Old Hickory, in personal good will, offered me, two. Old Tip[6] offered me, two— The Pierce Administration offered me, one. I declined all, for the mere pleasure of Welch independence.[7] Thro' the long series of these years, however, I must add, that I had, without "treasure in Heaven", far more 'treasure' of earth, than I now have—& far fewer demands on it, than I now have— If I can perfect my plan, to complete the proper education of my boys— it will enhance their chances of prospering in some honest trade or profession, hereafter; &, thus, become, only the more independent of other patrimony.

I mark this, as Confidential, altho' I have already named to our friend, Mr Browning,[8] Mr Harrington's suggestion as to y'r seeing Mr. Chase—

Yrs Faithfully,   J. L. W.

ALS, DLC-JP.

1. Williams, former Tennessee Whig congressman and practicing attorney in Washington, did not receive the treasury post but was appointed judge of the U. S. district court, Dakota Territory. Johnson had earlier recommended him for assistant attorney general. *BDAC*, 1823; see also *Johnson Papers*, III, 564n; Johnson to Edward Bates, March 7, 1861, Records *re* Appointment Assistant Attorney General, RG60, National Archives.

2. George Harrington (1815–1892), a native of Massachusetts and long-time clerk in the treasury department, became chief clerk in 1861; that same year he replaced Philip Clayton of Georgia as assistant secretary of the treasury. Minister to Switzerland (1865–69) under Johnson, Harrington subsequently served as president of the Telegraph Company of New York. Lanman, *Biographical Annals*, 188; *NCAB*, XII, 337.

3. Junius Hillyer (1807–1886), Georgia lawyer, circuit court judge (1841–45), and congressman (1851–55), had been appointed treasury solicitor by Buchanan (1857–61). *BDAC*, 1057.

4. William Medill (1802–1865), a Delaware native, was a Lancaster, Ohio, lawyer who served in the legislature (1835–38), in Congress (1839–43), as commissioner of Indian Affairs (1845–50), and as lieutenant, acting, and governor (1852–55). *Ibid.*, 1319.

5. James F. Simmons, senator from Rhode Island. See *Johnson Papers*, III, 245n.

6. President William Henry Harrison.

7. Probably a whimsical allusion to the storied individuality of the Welshman—a traditional foil for the anecdote, the conundrum, and even the canard.

8. Probably William A. Browning (1835–1866), who had just been appointed a clerk in the general land office. The son of a Washington tailor, Peregrine W. Browning, whose business was located on Pennsylvania Avenue near the St. Charles Hotel, young Browning became Johnson's secretary in the summer of 1861 and served until nominated secretary of the U. S. legation in Mexico in December, 1865. He died before his confirmation. New York *Times*, March 5, 1866; Washington *Evening Star*, April 5, 1861, March 2, 1866; *Senate Ex. Journal*, XIV (1864–66), Pt. I, 305, II, 717.

From Jeptha Fowlkes

Memphis Ten. March 21. 1861.

Private

Hon. A Johnson U.S.S.

My dear Sir:

I apprehend from private advices to-day that Ark. may pass Secession ordinance to be submitted to the people. Sebastian, Johnson

Hindman[1] & various parties from Seceding states have been sent to Little Rock to effect this object![2] I think, "the unknown policy" of the Administration, is, daily weakening the Union men! The seceders are "up &c doing—"

Our frinds Sewerd, Cameron, & Bates in the Cabinet should be made to realize the effect of delayed actin, want of sanity, on a "declared policy"![3] It is a mistake—& may prove fatal to us, & to this policy! So far as I can judge from persons & parties I have seen from Seceding states, that, the people are acquiescing & settling down to remain out of the Union— I go to Miss & to N. Orleans in 2 or 3 days— I will, then, write you again—giving, you *things*, as I may find them! Our people are excited—& will speedily Settle down for or against our Governt—for or again[s]t Southern Confederacy! It is but to elect. Our f[r]i[e]nds are too tardy. Douglass has made frinds & is much stronger than ever before South— All Union-men seem to do him justice & wish him well! The same feeling exists with them towards you—but while no bitterness be expressed towards D. old Democrats are pouring forth invectives on you. Yo should early visit chief places in Ten: in person— Will not the Democratic opposition attempt to "ensconce," themselves in power; & from our Division, if they can, throw you & all prominent Democrats over board? I urge you early to make a trip over the State. I am doing you all the good I can—& I am held to be a Sewardite & Cameronean— but I find both Seward & Cameron the hope of this Administration —possessing, much strength & embodying much to give them, free admittance, to the toleration respect & confidence of our people!

I percieve some tottering & some will fall towards Southern Republic—action with open, direct & bold line of policy is essential by Pres. Lincoln & his Cabinet.

Yr frind.   J. Fowlkes.

The doubts & distrusts have *alone* inclined far, & made Ark. yield to seceders! You can't *lead* without boldness & decision!— you & Douglass Seem to be, only public men, that the masses see clearly & fully understand!— offer Sen: Douglass my regards—[4]

ALS, DLC-JP.

1. Senators William K. Sebastian and Robert W. Johnson; Congressman Thomas C. Hindman.

2. The convention for deciding Arkansas' course convened at Little Rock March 4.

3. Evidently an allusion to Lincoln's First Inaugural, in which he spoke of a "declared purpose." Basler, *Works of Lincoln*, IV, 266.

4. A postscript is appended on a separate sheet: "Send me Copy of Congressional Globe 1860—last Session."

From Cave Johnson

Clarksville 21st March 1861.

Private

Dear Sir—

The appointment of P M at Nashville excites a good deal of feeling and I have thought I ought perhaps to have Said more in behalf of Nichol than I did in my former letter—[1] in the last few months parties have spawned a new aspect— the Union party is composed of the great body of the Democratic & American parties— it is Difficult to say which is the stronger— the leaders controlling the Union & American are the active politicians in our villages under their control, constitute the head & front of Secession from which neither you or I have any thing to hope in future and I suppose no one connected with the disunion movement can have any chance of getting the appointment or your Support—

The selection of Mr. Nichol would do more to strengthen and consolidate that portion of the Union party favorable to us than any other—. the selection of W Lelyette[2] would have a directly opposite influence & would strengthen those of the Union men who would likely be opposed to us— Lelyette is said to be a clever man and personally unknown to me— Nichol I have long known to be an honest, upright & reliable man & would make as good a P M as any body— both Union men—the former more intimatly connected & would be more under the influence of our former opponents— These are selfish considerations but I suppose legitimate where the qualifications are equal[.]

It is generally believed that the contest is between those two—and Mr. Quarles[3] has made every body believe here that the patronage of this State is in your hands & whoever gets it the credit or discredit will be given to you[.][4]

I hope there will be no collision with the Southern States— if a civil war should commence & any blame could be justly attributed to the Govr. we will be greatly troubled in our August elections— Any thing in preference to a civil war is the general feeling in this country— The late Tariff bill[5] strengthens the Southern movement & will embarrass the Admn. at every step—in the minds of many excited partizans a sufficient excuse for secession— If the Admn could stand still, the Southern leaders would soon kill themselves given more rope— the honor of the Country cannot be compromised by forbearance[.]

Your friend   C Johnson

Hon A Johnson

ALS, DLC-JP.

1. If Cave Johnson wrote a letter on James Nichol's behalf, it has not been preserved. There is, however, a brief telegram in support of his candidacy. See Cave Johnson to Andrew Johnson, March 19, 1861, Johnson Papers, LC.

2. William Lellyett.

3. James M. Quarles, Tennessee Whig congressman (1859–61). See Letter from Jesse B. Clements, March 1, 1861, note 1.

4. For a sampling of contemporary assessments of Johnson's patronage power, see letters from John A. Kasson, March 11, 1861, asking approval of a John Bell recommendation and from Mrs. Anna S. Plunket, of the same date, in which she, "hearing yesterday that you controlled the appointments in Tennessee," seeks post for her husband. Johnson Papers, LC.

5. The first truly protective tariff since 1832 had been introduced in the previous session by Congressman Justin Morrill of Vermont and passed by the House; taken up by the Senate during the first week of the new Congress, it had been adopted February 20, 1861. Designed particularly to attract Republican presidential votes in Pennsylvania and the Midwest, the Morrill Act not only increased duties on iron and wool but also provided for higher rates on other individual items. Western Democrats, including Douglas, recognized this legislation as discriminatory, and southern representatives, reflecting the section's longtime opposition to protectionism, struggled vainly against its passage. Their failure was due in no small degree to the departure of seceding senators: the final vote, 25–14, showed only senators from the upper South, together with a sprinkling of western Democrats, in opposition. F. W. Taussig, *The Tariff History of the United States* (New York, 1931), 158–59; Stampp, *And the War Came*, 162–64; *Cong. Globe*, 36 Cong., 2 Sess., 1065.

From Jeptha Fowlkes

Memphis Ten. March 23. 1861.

Private

Hon. A. Johnson.

My dear sir:

Great efforts are & will be made to adopt the Secession Ordinance in Ark—in August.[1] The seceded States, will send in orators & worthies—and, I have serious fears will adopt the ordinance!

First—The uncertainty of policy by Administration is weakening Union men— They, are, yielding daily!

Second—The Constitution of Confederate States,[2] is, now before people; & they can see & discuss it—& *it* is generally recd. well by all Union men! while applauded by seceders— vehemently—& is taking here! My opinion, is, soon, a large number of Union-Conservative men in Tene. will become reconciled to separation—and indeed, go over to the Seceders. This seems to me the tendency;—& rendered, so because they find, a something fixed—& definite South: while, all, is, doubt, hesitation & uncertainty, with our Northern friends! Fatal policy! Southern Seceders, are, active & intolerant & bend by *will* & *force*, all opposition to their views! "Milk & gruel,"[3] will not do!

Finally, unless you rouse the Administration, to realize the exigency & cause it to [adopt] some *avowed, direct* & *fixed* measures for adjustment, the whole, South, will early go over to Confederate States. Rely on it! Act accordingly! Soon "The Rubicon"[4] will be passed, & when passed, the fanaticism of southern disunionist will forever sever the union!

our people (many) are mad.

Yr. friend.   J. Fowlkes

[marginal note]

I am outright for you & all Union-men & I find Douglass, is, very strong—gaining— Seward, Weed, & Cameron our union men respect & appreciate— I loose no occasion for them & Lincoln's administration— The deep rooted in prejudice you can scarcely realize vs. north!

ALS, DLC-JP.

1. Meeting in mid-March, the Arkansas convention had set August 5 as the date for a referendum on "cooperation" or "secession," but because of events in April that body reconvened on May 6 and passed a secession ordinance. Scroggs, "Arkansas in the Secession Crisis," 215, 222–23.

2. The Confederate Provisional Congress, sitting as a constitutional convention, had basically utilized the old Federal Constitution, making only those modifications which reflected the southern viewpoint concerning state rights, internal improvements, and the tariff. Commencing its work on February 9, the committee presented its recommendations seventeen days later; Congress adopted the instrument on March 11. Edward McPherson, *Political History of the United States . . . during the Great Rebellion* (Washington, D. C., 1865), 98–100; Nichols, *Disruption of Democracy*, 462–65.

3. Possibly a variation of the expression "milk and water," meaning weak or insipid. Richard H. Thornton, *An American Glossary* (2 vols., Philadelphia, 1912), II, 580; *OED*, VI, 442.

4. This expression, derived from Caesar's crossing the river Rubicon, and implying that the die is cast, was first used in Plutarch's *Lives: Caesar*, Ch. XXXII, sec. 6. Stevenson, *Quotations*, 422.

From Frederick (Md.) Committee[1]

Frederick Mar 25, 1861

To Senator Andrew Johnson of Tenn

You are published throughout the county universally expected[.] we cannot dispense with having you here[.] you can take the first train in the morning & be with us in time. disappointment will leave us without resource[.] excuse our importunity[.][2]

James Cooper[3]
on behalf of Committee

Tel, DLC-JP.

1. Invited to address a Union meeting in Frederick on March 26, Johnson travelled on the B & O from Washington, using a ticket forwarded by the committee. James Cooper to Johnson, March 23, and W. P. Smith to Johnson, March 23, 1861, Johnson Papers, LC.

2. Although no detailed report of Johnson's March 26 speech seems to be available, the Frederick *Examiner* declared that the senator "made a most eloquent and able address in favor of the Union. . . . he touched on the cord of patriotic sympathy with a master hand, and the effect of his thrilling appeal was manifested in the repeated outbursts of applause, that interrupted him at the utterance of every national Sentiment and approved the force of every argument." According to the New York *Tribune*'s Maryland correspondent, Johnson found "the hearts of the Old Democratic and ancient Whig masses of Frederick City . . . in the right place. The meeting listened to him uninterruptedly for two hours and more, and when he had done the farmers crowded round him and gave him their hardfisted hands in token of their approbation of his old Jackson doctrines." A local correspondent—"Somewhat instrumental in Seducing" Johnson into visiting Frederick—assured the senator that his visit had given the Union men "an Encouragement, which has made them doubly brave." Frederick *Examiner*, March 27, 1861; New York *Tribune*, April 2, 1861; Ulysses Hobbs to Johnson, March 26, 1861, Johnson Papers, LC.

3. James Cooper (1810–1863), a Frederick native who had been a Philadelphia attorney since 1848, was a Whig congressman (1839–43), member of the Maryland lower house (1844–48), and a U. S. senator from Pennsylvania (1849–55). In May, 1861, he was commissioned by Lincoln to raise a brigade of loyal Marylanders. *BDAC*, 736; Boatner, *Civil War Dictionary*, 174; see also Cooper to Johnson, March 25, 1861, Johnson Papers, LC.

From William R. Hurley

Nashville Tenn March 25th 1861

Hon A Johnson,
Dear Sir:

I was suprised to learn, that McNish had received the appointment of Post-Master.[1] I did not calculate on getting the office myself. But I did not expect to have a disunionist, again forced upon us. For months past I have employed the Express Company to cary the Democrat. I am now still compelled to employ the Express[.] this same man has back this office and had done the Democrate great injustice[.] The same clerks, that have done so much to ruin the Democrat will be continued. The same set of the worst enemies you & I have had in this city. It is understood here that McNish went by & got your son to go to Washington to aid him in getting the position[.][2] *any* other appointment would have been more satisfactory[.]

This & such appointments will completely disarm the union men of Tennessee[.] Clemens[3] is a candidate for marshall and you are understood to favor his appointment. It would be an outrage upon a Union Community to have another Secessionist appointed over us. If you have any influence with the Administration, do not advise any man, who is a Secessionist[.] such appointments will ruin the Union men of the state[.] so far as I know all the applicants for Marshall-ship are union men except Clemens. *Personally* I have no choice so we have Union appointments.

Respectfully   W. R. Hurley

ALS, DLC-JP.

1. William D. McNish, who had been principal clerk.
2. Robert Johnson was in Washington at this time, apparently aiding his father with patronage and other problems. See Robert Johnson to Blackston McDannel, March 27, 1861, Johnson Papers, LC.
3. Jesse B. Clements.

From Harvey T. Phillips[1]

P. O. Chattanooga Ten
Mar. 25th 1861

Hon And Johnson
Dr Sir.

I have hitherto refrained from having anything to say or do in reference to my position in this office, or as to who shall succeed me —& I now depart from this reserve only for the purpose of making a single suggestion which may or may not be, pertinent or acceptable.

It is reported & believed here that the appointments in E Ten, are at your disposal. It is furthermore reported that J. R. Hood has the promise of this office, with *your approval*—
This latter report may be true, but your old friends here—myself among the number—are reluctant to believe it. If it is so, it must be from a misapprehension on your part, of the character of the man.
Besides being a new comer among us, he has been notorious for his wanton & vulgar attacks upon your public & private character, both in street conversation & through the columns of the "Gazette". True, during the last few months he has evinced a newborn love for your political course, but this is so superficial & selfish as scarce to deceive a[n]y one; & upon any other issue than the present, he may be relied upon as one of your most malignant political foes.

If the designation of my successor rests with you, I am confident that you can find one, in the ranks of those who have for years been your unwavering Supporters, & who still expect—even if differing somewhat at present—to continue good Johnson men, that would fill the position with far more acceptance to the commuity than Mr. Hood.

If no change is made for the present, I shall expect to give my

personal attention to the duties of the office with the same fidelity
that I have served for the past seven years.

I remain   Very Respt Yr obt svt

H. T. Phillips,

ALS, DLC-JP.

1. See *Johnson Papers*, III, 292n.

From James A. Rogers[1]

Brownsville Tenn. 25th. Mch. 1861

Hon. Andrew Johnson.

My Dear Sir,

I write to you to ask a personal favor, to use your influence with
the Administration to get for me the appointment of U. S. Mail Agt.
for Tennessee & North Carolina— You know me by character &
personally, and being a *modest* man, *I do not go* to Washington City
to *annoy my friends* or the President— I am the owner of upwards
of 50 slaves, I plant 300 acres in cotton, hence my appointment
would give satisfaction to this *ultra* end of the State— Your efforts
& influence for me will be duly and properly appreciated— I served
2 Sessions in the House and two Sessions in the Senate of the Tenn
Legislature— You remember me well, as the "Senator from Haywood", whilst you were Governor. The speeches you sent me I carefully distributed and wish you would send me more as they are in
great demand by our Union friends. Send me as many as you can
for distribution— If there are any copies of your last speech, please
send some of them as your three speeches have given more *joy* to
union men than any that have been made during the present session
of Congress.

The time will soon be upon us to nominate a Union Candidate for
Governor[.] I should be pleased to hear your views as to the proper
candidate, what you write will be kept in the strictest confidence—

Your Sincere Friend

James A. Rogers.

If the appointment I desire cannot be obtained for me, some one of
equal profit & trust, that would not take me too much from my family
would be acceptable[.]   J. A. R.

I have written to Etheridge Stokes & Nelson[2] about the same matter
but hear from neither of them— I *know you never neglect a friend*,
hence I trouble you also—

ALS, DLC-JP.

1. James A. Rogers (1817–1890), North Carolina native and Whig
member of the Tennessee house (1847–51) and senate (1851–54), was at

this time a successful Haywood County planter with real property worth $35,000 and a personal estate of $55,000. Although he subsequently avowed himself "an unflinching union man," his actions would seem to belie his claim. Responsible during the early days of the conflict for the construction of Fort Pillow on the Mississippi, he subsequently remained in Brownsville, converting most of his wealth into Confederate bonds and emerging "land poor" at the end of the war. 1860 Census, Tenn., Haywood, 8th Dist., 184; Rogers to Clinton B. Fisk, February 22, 1866, Johnson Papers, LC; Robison, *Preliminary Directory, Haywood*, 17; John H. Halliburton (Coral Gables, Fla.) to Andrew Johnson Project, December 27, 1974.

2. Emerson Etheridge, William B. Stokes, and Thomas A. R. Nelson, unionist congressmen.

From Samuel Williams[1]

Trenton March 25th 1861

Hon Andrew Johnson

Dear sir   I with pleasure Acknowledge the Re[ce]ipt of Pattent off Agricutural Reports Presids Message Documents &C and if it were entirely convenient should like to have the late Sensus of 1860 and then I am Rather inclined to complain that I have Recd no coppy of your January speeches[.][2] verry few of them have found there way into this Country[.] Post Masters may be at fault as our Union Papers all arive verry Tardily & irregularly[.] while I have not been able to see a coppy of your janary speech I have heard it much inquired after[.] there are other places where it ought to have been in greater demand as we are nearly all for the constitution & union[.] this County gave the Union Candidates over 2000 majority & will give a better majority in the August election & that majority is verry much attributable to your Decr. Speech which was fully endorsed by a large meeting of our Citizens the 1st Monday in January[.][3] in these North western County [*sic*] our Union men have only one thing to regret in the election for deligates to Convntion that is that they did not vote there whole strength against a Convention which they might have done just simply by preparing it for they unanimously rejoice over the Defeat of the Convention[.] our people will not consent to go into a southern Confederacy[.] we are preparing to husband all the strength of the union party during the Canvass of the coming summer[.] under all the circumstances we feel that you ought to give the County the full Benifit of your advice & experience in the approaching Canvas to maintain the ascendency which your Labours more than any other mans has brought about and to thoroughly defeat those who would involve the Country in hopeless Ruin for selfish purposes. shall be gratifyed at any time when other engagements permits to hear from you or to Receive any Documents that you may think would be Interesting[.]

I remain verry Truley yours &c

Saml Williams

ALS, DLC-JP.

1. For Williams, see *Johnson Papers*, III, 686n.
2. Johnson made no speeches in January; probably Williams is referring to the address of February 5–6.
3. Although the February vote for convention carried, 2,277–533, Union candidates outpolled secessionists by approximately 2,100 votes. A reading of the newspaper account suggests that the January 7 meeting in Trenton was not nearly as unionist as Williams would have Johnson believe; no mention of Johnson's speech was reported, and the committee on resolutions recommended the calling of a convention. At the same time, however, an anti-coercion motion was tabled. Trenton *Southern Standard*, January 12, February 16, 1861.

To Edward Bates, Washington, D. C.

Washington City March 25th 1861

Hon Edward Bates
Attorney General
Dear Sir,

I would recommend for the appointment of Marshal, for the Eastern Division of Tennessee Blackston McDannel of Greeneville — For Attorney General John L. Hopkins[1] of Chattanooga—

For the Middle Division of Tennessee, for Marshal, E. R. Glasscock[2] of Nashville— For Attorney General Herman Cox of Nashville—

For the Western Division of Tennessee, for Marshal Thos. J. Gardner[3] of Trenton[.]

For Attorney General John M. Carmack[4] of Memphis[.]

I have the honor to be &c.

Andrew Johnson

L, DNA-RG60, Appts., Tenn., 1861–65, "General."

1. John L. Hopkins (c1825–fl1911), lawyer and Chattanooga civic figure, was city attorney (1853) and alderman (1854, 1857–58). As an early supporter of secession, he had prevailed upon Jefferson Davis to address a Chattanooga audience on January 22, 1861. Later he became the adjutant of the 36th Tenn. Inf., CSA. Actually, Hopkins was offered the position of district attorney for East Tennessee but declined. After the war he moved to Atlanta, becoming a distinguished jurist and a compiler of the *Georgia Code* of 1895. Armstrong, *Hamilton County*, I, 124, 143; II, 293, 309; McGuffey, *Chattanooga*, 341; Allen D. Candler and Clement A. Evans, *Cyclopedia of Georgia* (4 vols., Spartanburg, S. C., 1972 [1906]), I, 414; Nashville *Republican Banner*, April 4, 1861; Memphis *Avalanche*, April 20, 1861.

2. Glascock and Cox were appointed. *U. S. Official Register* (1861), 192.
3. Thomas J. Gardner (b. *c*1820), a Trenton saddler, received the appointment. *Ibid.*; 1860 Census, Tenn., Gibson, 143.
4. John M. Carmack was appointed.

From Samuel R. Anderson

Nashville P. O March. 26. 1861.

Honl. Andrew Johnson
Senator
Dr Sir

Since the announcement of the appointment of W.D McNish, as PM. of this city John Lellyett, a late applicant, for the same office, has been trying to raise, a disturbance in regard to the appointment of McNish. Lellyett is very Sore headed, and is very bitter in his denunciations of you— the fact is he has allways been your *devoted enemy*. He has allways been your bitter enemy, and any profesion of friendship for you now, emanates from no real love but fro[m] the desire to receive the benifit of the Spoils—

I tell you what I know to be true, that the appointment of McNish, receves the unqualified approval of a very large majority of the business men & cittizens of Nashville[.] Mr. Andrew. Ewing requests me to say this you, and further to say to you that you ought not to Suffer, the appointment to be interfeared with— Lellyett & his parasytes are the only ones who are troubled— McNish will make a capital officer, and if the vote of the city was taken to day, between him & Lellyett, he would beat Lellyett two to one.

I deem it due to make this statement to you—So that you may not be imposed on in changing off a true and tried friend for One who has been your bitter enemy.

Yours Very Respty   S. R Anderson.

ALS, DLC-JP.

From Alexander B. Small[1]

Knoxville, March 26th, 1861.

Gov. Johnson,
Dear Sir,

I am asked often if you will visit us on the adjournment of the Senate and address our citizens upon the issues now distracting the country. Your speeches are highly satisfactory but they desire to see and hear for themselves. I have almost daily inquiries for copies of your speech. I should be glad if you could fix upon a time so as to give us some days notice.

If you have it in your power and it will not be inconsistent with your duty to your friends I desire light upon who will be the probable appointees for the several Federal office in East Tenn. Is Col. Lowry an applicant for reappointment? A freind of mine desires to know and if he is not will apply. He is the present Sheriff of Knox County[2] & would be entirely acceptable to people of this County— he is honest, honorable, capable & faithful & withal a "master workman." & union to the core. Will there be a change in the Pension agency here, if so can you tell who? Also I should like to know who will be District Attorney. Mr. F. Reeve desired me to mention his name to you in connection with the appointment.

There is more anxiety felt in our town as to who will be P.M. here than any other appointment. Can you enlighten me as to that? It is currently reported all over our place that I am an applicant for the place through you. How many applicants there are I do not know but I hold that no appointment should be declined from any false notion that one's honor was being compromised from holding a commission signed by a Republican President.

Who will be appointed secret [special?] Mail Agent in place of Hugh Francis? I have frequently been requested by my friends to apply for that or the Post office. Tell me what steps would be necessary for a man to take to secure an appointment as I have been asked to obtain this information. If you can consistently answer the above queries I can promise you they will be lodged in the "repository of a faithful breast."[3] I do not make the above inquiries from idle curiosity but that having the light I may govern my actions accordingly.

If your time is not too greatly taxed I should be pleased to have an early answer. Hoping you will excuse the liberty I have taken

I am Respectfully &C.   A. B. Small.

ALS, DLC-JP.

1. For Small, see *Johnson Papers*, II, 382n.
2. William P. Crippen (b. c1811), a Knox County farmer, was at this time sheriff (1856–62). Luttrell, *1850 Census, Knox County*, 67; *Goodspeed's Knox*, 814.
3. Not found.

From Eleanor F. Strong[1]

[March 26, 1861]

My dear Mr Johnson—

I received through Mr Anthony[2] yesterday the Photograph you so kindly sent me— I find it an admirable likeness, and cannot tell you how much gratified I was by your prompt attention to my request. I know that I was making an unwarrantable demand upon you now that your time is so engrossed by more important matters.[3] My great admiration for you, and my strong desire to possess some portrait of you, must plead my excuse—

We are here awaiting with the greatest anxiety some exposition of the policy of the administration feeling that any decision would be preferable to this uncertainty, but all look forward to an ultimate reconstruction.

We all hope for an Extra Session that this iniquitous tariff may be repealed,[4] for if there must be two separate Confederacies, We of the Loyal States wish to enter the lists upon equal terms at least[.] In case you are ever in New York, I need not tell you how proud and gratified I should be if you would allow me to see you—

With renewed thanks for your kindness and apologies for having trespassed so long upon your time I am

Most sincerely & gratefully yours
Eleanor F. Strong.

March 26th
38 East 22d Street.

ALS, DLC-JP.

1. Eleanor Burrill Fearing in 1850 married Charles E. Strong, cousin and law partner of George Templeton Strong of New York City. Impulsive, impressionable, and vain, a young woman of charm coupled with "a strange compound of cleverness and foolishness," she was friendly with a number of senators, among them Charles Sumner of Massachusetts and Henry B. Anthony of Rhode Island. In the summer of 1866, after an unhappy marriage touched by a hint of scandal involving the journalist W. H. Hurlbut, Eleanor, with her daughter Kate, left the United States to reside permanently in Europe. Allan Nevins and Milton H. Thomas, eds., *The Diary of George Templeton Strong* (4 vols., New York, 1952), II, xiii, 2, 7, 236, 495; III, 88, 107; IV, xiii, 70, 183n, 233, 437.

2. Henry B. Anthony (1815–1884), Rhode Island senator (1859–84), editor (1838) and publisher (1840–84) of the Providence *Journal*, had been a Whig governor of Rhode Island (1849–51). A Republican, he was several times elected president pro tempore of the Senate. *NCAB*, IX, 398–99; *BDAC*, 484–85.

3. Earlier, Mrs. Strong had requested a "carte de visite." Reminding Johnson of his promise, she had written, "I regret extremely, that I was unable to see you once more, to thank you, for your last most eloquent speech, & to urge upon you the fulfillment of your promise." Strong to Johnson [March 7, 1861], Johnson Papers, LC.

4. Enacted March 2, 1861, the Morrill Tariff levied specific duties and raised rates overall from 5 to 10 percent. Morris, *Encyclopedia of American History*, 519.

From William R. Hurley

Nashville Tenn   March 27th 1861

Hon A Johnson.

Dear Sir:

I dislike to trouble you so often, but my necessities are such that I am constrained to appeal to my friends for some sort of assistance. I have bought a Press & fixtures but have no means to [sic] left to run it. It is on that account that I have asked for an appointment. I had thought that I might be able to fill the Post Office[1] or some other position, and still edit the Democrat. I have tried to borrow money, —have tried to sell an interest in the Democrat but have thus far failed in every effort[.]

We have some government printing,[2] but our *present* necessities is what annoys me.

I should not write to *you* at all but for the fact that I know you are aware of the necssity of your having, a paper friendly to you during this year. I have stated fairly the condition of the Democrat hoping you may feel some interest in its success & that you may be able to aid in *Some* way[.]

Respectfully Yours &c
W. R. Hurley

ALS, DLC-JP.

1. On this same day Hurley wrote Postmaster Blair of the strong protest in Nashville against McNish's appointment and requested that he be considered "as an aspirant to the position," should a change be made. Hurley to F. P. Blair, March 27 [1861], Johnson Papers, LC.

2. During the second session of the 36th Congress, the Nashville *Democrat* received $187 for publishing the laws of the United States. *U. S. Official Register* (1861), 198.

From Michael L. Patterson[1]

Greeneville Tennessee
March 27th 1861.

Gov. A. Johnson

Dear Sir

You will please Do me the kindness to Speak to Judge Douglas, to give me a Reference to a good *Lawyer* that resides in *Chicago Illinois*.[1] I own Some three Lots in that City, and I want to write to Some good reliable Lawyer—to See about having my deed Recorded,

And to see whether the title is incumbered or not— In attending to this you will Do me a great kindness— I hate to trouble you— But it is the most reliable Source that I can reach at this time—

Yours Respectfully.
M. L. Patterson

ALS, DLC-JP.

1. For Patterson, see *Johnson Papers*, III, 388*n*.

2. In response to this request, Johnson wrote Stephen A. Douglas at once, asking for the name of a *"reliable Lawyer."* Johnson to Douglas, March 30, 1861, Princeton University Library.

From John G. Winter

Charleston Mch 27. 61

My dear Sir

I have been here one day & it makes me heart sick to listen to exulting tone in which the fire eaters speak of their success & of th seeming imbecility of our Government— They are boasting now that they will throw out Anderson & also Slemmer—[1] the apparent faltering of the Governmet is adding strength to their cause & weakness to ours— Human nature does not like to tie to a conce[r]n that exhibits signs of weakness—. This *is* a *strong* governmnt & will overcome a weak one of ten times its size in number, money & oth[er] warlike appliances. If they degrade us at Pickens, our cause is *lost past all hope*— The Borde[r] States will be lost if Government dont prove that it has strength enough to protect its adherents— 'Moral suasion' is not the treatment for Lunatics & robbers— Stripes until they *see* the Stars, is the only medicine which will answer—

Hastil[y] Yrs tly
J G W

I dare not write my name in full— I *wish to live for my Country*, & see the Rascals out to the bitter end—

ALS, DLC-JP; also printed in LeRoy P. Graf and Ralph W. Haskins, eds., "The Letters of a Georgia Unionist: John G. Winter and Secession," *Georgia Historical Quarterly*, XLV (1961), 396.

1. Maj. Robert Anderson at Ft. Sumter, and Lieut. Adam J. Slemmer, commanding officer at Ft. Pickens, Florida. Slemmer (1828–1868), a native of Pennsylvania and a graduate of West Point (1850), was promoted in May to major and served with the Army of the Ohio, rising to the rank of brigadier general. Boatner, *Civil War Dictionary*, 764.

From Jesse B. Clements

Nashville March 28/61—

Honl. Andrew Johnson—
Dear Sir
If you cannot effect my reappointment of Marshal, have the thing
stove off untill after the April term of our court— The Court of this
District meets on the third Monday in April—And will adjourn in
about forty days—Say by the first of June— The business of the next
term of the Court will be worth more to the Marshal than the Office
has been worth in the last three years— I have done all the business
of the next term of the Court, at an expense of four months labor
and at a Cost of five hundred dollars to me—

I do not know whether you are for my reappointment or not. I believe you are for me— At any rate, I am Satisfied with whatever you
do—and will abide your action, without one murmur—

If I have to be Superceeded do not have the appointment given to
this fool—Glasscock—[1] Give it to some man who has *Brains* enough
to discharge the duties of the Office—

Very respectfuly   J B Clements

ALS, DLC-JP.
1. Johnson had already recommended "this fool—Glasscock" on March 25.

From John C. McGaughey

Knoxville Mch 28th 1861.

Hon Andrew Johnson
Dear Sir
Having recently written you two letters[1] and aware that you are
overrun with Correspondence it is with reluctance I address you but
as I want to make a few suggestions which I hope you will receive
kindly I write you this— I understand from a reliable source that
Mr Alex Small is or will likely be appointed Post Master at this
place— As it is known that Mr S. is no better Union Man and no
better qualified than other applicants and understood that you have
a considerable if not a ruling influence in the Appointments in this
section the only apparent grounds for your favoring his appointment
is that he was of the same political faith as you before the recent
overthrow of all parties— Mr S. as one of the Union men of the
Breckinridge party in Knox Co represents certainly not more than

600 voters while in the Union party of Knox Co there is not less than 2500, Twenty five hundred, voters who were Bell men— It is not unnatural to suppose that when this 2500 find themselves set aside and the 600 favored merely because they voted for Breckinridge— it will not be very satisfactory to them— If Mr Small is appointed, it will appear that it was done not because he is a Union man now So much as that he was a Breckinridge Democrat before— I speak of course as regards Knox Co and this would not apply to democratic Cos[.] And this dissatisfaction whether right or wrong will be turned towards you—and if this course is to be followed it is not unreasonable that the Bell party through out the State will think as the Breckinridge men are to have the small offices that it [is] nothing but fair and just that Union Whigs should have the larger ones such as Govenor United States Senator &c— It will also give opportunity to Whigs who have not forgotten former blows and are anxious for a change in these Offices to press their schemes to success and this too without being charged with renewing old party divissions or if so they could reply that they did not begin it but the other side did and it would strike every one as fair that one party should not monopolise the Offices—

It is natural that the Bell men in Knox Co will expect one of their number to be Post Master and also fair that it should be one that would not be obnoxious to the Breckinridge Union men— Col Luttrell,[2] as he has been a very decided Whig and partisan would probably be as unsatisfactory to the Breckinridge men as a Breckinridge men [sic] would be to the Bell men— The proper Course would be I should think to harmonize these two parties— Of Mr Rodgers[3] I shall say nothing more than I did in my last letter— Of myself if you will not consider it egotistical I will Say that altho always a Whig I have generally let my party feelings give away—as in my support of Judge Swann[4] for Judge in his last race—when I found the best qualifications for an efficient officer on the other side— To make a faithful Officer, and character as a prompt efficient and accomodating business man is my ambition[.]

                                  I am very Respectfully Your Obt Svt
                                                      John C. McGaughey

ALS, DLC-JP.

1. See Letters from John C. McGaughey, February 21, March 15, 1861.
2. James C. Luttrell received the appointment. See *Johnson Papers*, III, 508n.
3. Pryor L. Rogers.
4. For William G. Swan, see *ibid.*, II, 214n.

From "Stability"[1]

New-York March 28, 1861

To the Hon. ANDREW JOHNSON, *of Tennessee.*

SIR:

The question which now engrosses the attention of the people of this country, is of such importance that I am sure you will permit me to address to you, and through you to the people of your section as well as of mine, some statements and suggestions which I trust are not unworthy of serious consideration.

A few months ago we believed that we were one people, a NATION with power, pride, and purpose equal to any. We had had different theories of the exact powers of our Government, and we had never, from the first day of our Union, been entirely free from the anomalous and disturbing element of Slavery. Our political experiment had always been affected by it, and our National progress has not been natural and healthy as otherwise it would have been. But we had carried on our political contests so far without violence. Within this last half year, however, the control of the machinery and power of our Government has passed in strict harmony with the Constitution from the slave sentiment to the free sentiment, and a change has been effected, second only to that of our Revolution. We cannot wonder that the deposed party should have struggled against this, but we are surprised that it should have been able to induce so large a majority of the people of seven States to disrupt the Union with precipitation and violence; and whatever our views may be as to what Mr. Buchanan should have done, or whatever our theories about the "Right of Secession," as it is called, we may now, I think, drop them and approach this as a practical question.

The present position of our Government, all will admit, is full of difficulty. To know what is best to do, is one thing, and to do it is another, both of which call for the highest wisdom, talent, and energy. It is clear that this complication and suspense should be terminated as speedily as possible, for enterprises of every kind are prostrated, and will continue to be, so long as any contest lasts, while the bitterness of private condemnation will ripen too fast into public hate, and will ensure further mischief.

There seem but three ways to resolve this miserable confusion, so suddenly precipitated upon a wonderfully prosperous country.

First. To maintain the integrity of the Union and the Constitution and the Union of the States at any cost and every sacrifice.

Second. To yield to the demands of the SLAVE POWER whatever they are now, or may be hereafter—in other words—to Compromise again.

Third. To not only allow the Cotton States to go out of the Union; but to request all the Slave States to leave us, and as speedily as possible.

Upon these three propositions allow me to offer a few suggestions. As to the first: "To maintain the integrity of the Constitution and the Union of the States at any cost and at every sacrifice."

This position is clear, logical, and constitutional. It involves, of course, the denial of any *right* of secession, which is simply insurrection or revolution. It demands prompt action to hold, defend and repossess the national property, to collect the revenues and to enforce the laws. It is direct and manly—we have the power to maintain it; and it will be pressed as the only proper one by a large portion of our people, and particularly of the party to which I belong. As a practical question, I am satisfied it means War—bitter and destructive; complicated with slave insurrections, and ending with the wiping out of Slavery; but carrying with it the destruction of the Slave States, and the temporary ruin of the Free. It will destroy in the Cotton States not the traitors only who have done this mischief, but will carry down also what loyal and honest men are there. "Secession" is foolish, illogical, anarchical, expensive and impracticable, and will by and by be contemptible. *War will dignify it.* Is it wise to sacrifice one honest life on so poor a thing, or to spend one charge of powder upon the political traitors, whom a betrayed people will yet hang?

The second proposition is—"To yield to the demands of the slave power—to Compromise again."

The mildest demand, of even the Union men of Virginia, and perhaps of your own yet loyal State, is that negro slaves shall be recognized by us of the Free States as property, the same as horses and hogs—that this fact shall be somehow asserted by the laws and the Constitution, and that we shall cease to think, or at least to say that we think, Slavery an evil and a wrong. This is demanded of us while you in the Slave States do not admit such positions. You do not kill or eat your slaves with quite the same ease as you do hogs and oxen; and you demand that they shall be represented in Congress as you do not for hogs and horses. Now, I beg leave to assert in the strongest manner to the people of your States who are demanding compromise and concession, my opinion that we shall certainly not do more than you do. We shall make no such concessions or compromises. We shall under our Constitution, *tolerate* Slavery in those States where it exists, but we shall not love it, nor cease to speak ill of it; and no hocus-pocus can persuade us to consent that our Government shall buy or steal more new lands in which to spread it. The public opinion of the whole civilized world is against such doctrines and practices, and it will grow stronger not weaker with us in the *Free States*.

But suppose some sort of a "Compromise" could be hit upon, I appeal to you, what would it be worth? Neither side would like it, and it would only serve to continue through another quarter of a century this miserable wrangle with all its degrading political consequences, and with certain and recurring financial and commercial disasters. I repeat it, if the people, the capitalists of the Slave States are bent solely upon Slavery extension and political domination, if they will neglect and sacrifice their agricultural, mining, and manufacturing advantages for these, if they will "rule or ruin,"[2] they must go on their way alone. If they will conquer Mexico and the West India Islands, they must do it without our help or protection, and they must suffer the consequences. We are sick of the whole business.

I can travel in foreign and despotic countries and in some barbarous ones and not have my *opinions* put upon trial. Actions and not opinions are liable to penalties in decently civilized countries—only this is an exception. If I violate a *law* I demand a calm trial of my peers, and not the tender mercies of a crazy mob; and whatever my opinion of slavery may be, I respectfully ask in my own *free country* that my body may be free from all tar, feathers, rails, pistols, bowie knives, gallows ropes and other like productions of the "Sunny South." I do not propose to meddle with the "institution" of Slavery; and I desire to be let alone. Whenever the Slave States are a foreign country I *think* I shall be unmolested—that then I shall be safe.

We, too, have rights, and I insist upon equality with the slaveholder, be he for Union or Secession. I am satisfied with the Constitution, and I ask that it shall be free henceforth from these fierce assaults of the slave interest; that it shall not be juggled with and interpreted to suit the caprices of a faction whose property happens to be negro slaves. I ask that legislation shall be decided upon the merits of the question, and not as to how it suits a faction. I wish the privilege of voting without either sword, or whip, or threat being suspended over my head. I must send my portion of the President to Washington on his feet, and not on his belly. I demand, too, for our politicians of the Democratic persuasion one chance before they die, and some of them are old now, to think, speak, and act as becomes freemen.

The Slave States are demanding guaranties that we will let them alone; are they willing to give guaranties that they will henceforth let us alone? I demand such guaranties.

Now does not "compromise" mean that we shall give whatever is demanded of us, and ask for nothing? What remains?

The third proposition, as follows: "To not only allow, but insist upon a separation of the Slave States from the Free."

Some of the Border States talk of a Convention to discover and declare their "ultimatum," which being granted, they will stay in the Union. Shall not the Free States save them the trouble by calling a CONVENTION, and requesting them to go at once? Six months ago this would have seemed hasty, if not preposterous; but now that the Union is so unsettled, is it not well to consider its propriety? It is a practical question. The difficulties in carrying out this separation will be great, of course; but are they not less than in either of the other plans? Let us see what some of the difficulties are—remembering that we have a satisfactory Constitution and all the machinery for government, ships, army, post-offices, &c., in working order:

1. The possible relinquishment of Washington by the Free States.
2. The almost certainty of a marauding border wrangle.
3. The necessity of interior custom-houses.
4. The impeded navigation of the Mississippi River.

These objections once seemed imperative—now they do not. Great as they are, let me briefly say: Maryland might prefer to remain with us with some fair compensation for her slaves. But if not, for myself there are no hallowed memories connected with the *City* of Washington which endear it to me, but rather the reverse. I should be glad to dispose of my share of it at a very large deduction from the cost, and remove the Government to some safer and more suitable place.

Border collisions would soon come to an end, because in a single year the slaves would disappear from the border, part going North and part South. Those inviting and genial States would then be enriched with the labors of white men, and would take the rank in the nation to which they are naturally entitled, from which they have been receding for a half century, and which they never will take until Slavery leaves them.

A line of interior Custom-Houses is not a great evil, and is found practicable in other countries. Some smuggling would grow up, but why more than on the Canadian border, or upon any frontier of a European country? Our manufacturers, too, will soon learn how much more enlarged and productive free-trade will be to them, and they will demand it.

The navigation of the Mississippi River was once a necessity of the great and productive Northwest, but the recent movements of trade have shown that it is now of secondary importance. Out of any interference by the Southern Confederacy with its free passage, would grow war, and thus in all probability there would be no interference. We of the manufacturing and commercial districts are charged by some people who live at a distance from us with disliking the smell of powder. I admit that I do prefer to inspect the breeches rather than muzzles of guns. But there exist in this State some 400,000 men who can fight in a good cause, and still leave enough for a "Home Guard" to keep our domestics and women in order; and in the great and growing Northwest are some men who have been raised with rifles, and have sucked powder; and I think Louisiana folks will not invite that kind down there with rifles loaded. Thus I suppose the Mississippi will not be interrupted. But should it be, it would be soon settled, and would be infinitely preferable to a war now, for then it would be war with a foreign country, not as now, with ourselves.

It seems that the political theorists of South Carolina have not only convinced themselves, but a certain number of other people, that "Secession" is a natural right, and is not Revolution. They seem to shut their eyes to the fact that it means no government—anarchy. They seem to have satisfied themselves and others, perhaps, that they can become rich and grow great if they can only try their plan of a slave-owning nation. Let us see for a moment how it looks. They have a region thinly settled without manufactories or the thrifty and industrious habits of more Northern States. They intend to make the negroes do the work and leave them the leisure and profit. They must have free-trade and free negroes from Africa, or from some quarter. They must support a government with armies, navies, light-houses, revenue service, post-offices, departments at home and ministers abroad. These are not cheap luxuries; and must not their taxation be ten times what it is now? and must it not be paid almost entirely by the wealthy class? But it seems they wish to try the experiment, and will it not be well to let them? for some follies can be brayed out in mortars only, while some cannot. And how can it hurt us, except that any change is expensive? So soon as they arrange their affairs, our trade with them will be the same as now; they will buy where they can buy the cheapest, for they are human, I believe; and we can undersell any other producers of our own articles. Again, is it not clear that this doctrine of "peaceable secession," as it is called, has been invented to meet an emergency; and is it not quite clear that no stability or certainty is possible, if it is once admitted as a fundamental principle of government? Revolution, of course, may always change a government if there is no provision made in the Constitution itself for such inevitable changes; but revolution means violence, and hanging if it does not succeed. Now, if any man, or any combination of men, are at liberty, without risk or cost, simply to defy all laws and overthrow the government of the whole, what stability or good government is possible? And must not the Cotton Confederacy look forward to speedy anarchy, to be succeeded by military despotism, or any other changes? Now, I ask of you as a practical and sensible man, do you or your people wish to join such a Confederacy? A SETTLEMENT and STABILITY only are needed to insure all just as prosperous a trade as ever—provided the Cotton Confederacy can pay for what they require.

Now one other point it may be well to touch upon—namely, Expansion. Is it likely that the Cotton Confederacy will be allowed to take possession of Cuba, the West Indies and Mexico? Is it not more than likely that England, Spain, France and Mexico will be very ready to protect their interests in those countries, and shall we not help rather than hinder them in checking the fillibustering tendencies of the Confederacy? Is not this clearly our policy? for under the auspices of a liberal Government in Mexico we look for a large and productive reciprocal trade, which will give work to our mechanics and business to our ships and sailors.

It is not necessary to press the importance of these considerations; you will see their value; and, I ask, is it not wise for the Free States at once to take some such steps as I have indicated, so as to bring about a speedy settlement of this imbroglio. What we all want is certainty; and can we not get that certainty by organizing ourselves under our present Constitution, which is perfectly satisfactory to us, free from the anomalous and disturbing element of Slavery. If the interests of the Border States are with the Cotton Confederacy, let them go there; if with us, let them remain. We see a large, generous and loyal party of men in the Border States, of which, permit me to say, we think you the bravest, trying to make head against the disorganizing doctrines and purposes of the Secessionists. If you can make head against them, then join us; if you cannot, we shall regret this separation from us much more than you can.

But I ask of you as a brave and candid man, to consider the effect of this separation—this non-dependence upon the slave sentiment with your own people. Should they continue with us and unite in a Government for white men, would they not begin to prosper just in proportion as they devoted themselves to free labor? Is it not certain, too, that the manners and customs of the people in the Cotton States, would sooner conform to the laws and usages of civilized society? And is it not certain that our public credit at home and abroad would be better than now? Is it not certain, too, that our people, having no hostile and encroaching element to contend against, would devote their undivided thoughts and energies to the development of our magnificent resources, and produce results which at present we cannot estimate.

Pardon the liberty I have taken in addressing you, and believe me, with great respect,

Your obedient servant,

For a Union with   STABILITY.

New-York, March 28, 1861.

New York *Tribune*, March 30, 1861; PL, DLC-JP.

1. The precise identity of "Stability" cannot be established, though the point of view is similar to that of Horace Greeley, *Tribune* editor. Shortly after this letter was printed an editorial appeared urging a "clearly defined programme" and declaring that no true ground existed for compromise—either let the seceding states go in peace, or fight! One historian, analyzing Greeley's position, suggests that he "used disunion to defend the Union, offered secession to defeat the secessionists, agreed to an abstract proposition to forestall its practical application," and that he "had no more idea of dividing the Union than Solomon had of dividing the infant; he depended on patriotism to refuse his offer, just as the wise king depended on maternal love to save the child." New York *Tribune*, April 3, 1861; David M. Potter, "Horace Greeley and Peaceable Secession," *Journal of Southern History*, VII (1941), 155, 158.

2. Paraphrase of John Dryden, *Absalom and Achitophel*, Pt. I, l. 174.

Remarks on Contingent Expenses[1]

March 28, 1861.

Mr. JOHNSON. The resolution upon which this report was made was introduced on the 18th of June last, but a short time before the adjournment of Congress. From the 18th to the 25th of June, the day on which Congress adjourned, the committee had not time to act on it, and hence it went over to the session which has just closed. It will thus be seen that there has been no great loss of time or delay, so far as the committee's action on this resolution is concerned; and when the report of the committee is read, it will be seen that every single inquiry contained in the resolution has been fully answered.

As to the abuses referred to by the Senator from New Hampshire,[2] the committee was not cognizant of them. The Senator does not say that the services required to be performed by those individuals who it is now assumed are absent upon other business and whose duties are said to be performed by others, are not necessary; but the committee was not cognizant of any such facts, and does not know of any case of the kind referred to by the Senator.

As I have said, every requirement of the resolution has been complied with; but the Senator has put the stress of his argument upon this clause of the report:

And by authority of the committee, a laborer at $1 20 per day; and, *during the session only*, a page to assist the account clerk, at the same pay as those in the Senate Chamber, namely: $2 50 per day.

This is an enormous discovery that the Senator has made! The only thing he finds fault with, or seeks to throw a doubt over, is the exercise of the power of employing a laborer, at $1 20 a day, and a page while Congress is in session, to wait upon members, to run backwards and forwards with drafts from the account-clerk's room to this Chamber, at $2 50 a day. It seems to me that the Senator has omitted to look at the large expenditures of the Government, where there may be just cause for complaints of extravagance, and he has got down to the wafers—the little details.[3] The committee felt, as they believed they had the authority, that it would be for the convenience of the Senate to have a page to attend during the sitting of Congress; and they have ventured, besides, to incur the enormous expense of employing a laborer, at $1 20 per day! That is a tremendous complaint! I think it is a pretty serious charge against the committee!

Now, Mr. President,[4] a word as to those abuses which are alleged to exist. The committee has had a good deal more trouble in some quarters, on other questions, than it has had as to the employment of a laborer that was needed about this building at $1 20 a day, and the employment of a little page at $2 50, to wait on the Senate and facilitate its business. If Senators themselves were as strict, and as exact, and as economizing, where they have privileges in reference to these little matters, we should not be complaining so much about pages and laborers. I will not say, I will not even insinuate, that this committee has incurred the displeasure of any Senator on this floor, because it would not authorize the purchase of some articles that the committee thought rather extravagant. I will make no allusion of that sort. It may be perfectly right for Senators to come forward and ask the Committee on Contingent Expenses to make heavy and extravagant orders for costly articles; but it is a very great offense to employ a little page at $2 50 a day, to wait on Senators, and a laborer at $1 20 a day; and there are grave doubts as to the authority of the committee to exercise so extraordinary a power! I think the Senator has certainly run out of material, for he is usually very prolific, both in wit and argument, in regard to anything which he sets his hand to; but I think he is pretty near run out in this case. The report was made in good faith, I know. I can speak for the other two members of the committee.[5]

This committee has really very little power. All these offices are created by law; the pay of the officers is fixed by law; their accounts are made out and sent to the committee. It is a mere mechanical, automatic operation to pass upon the accounts and direct the payment.

In reference to the three messengers that the Sergeant-at-Arms says in his letter may be dispensed with, that is based on the consideration that laborers may be employed to do what they do. If you dismiss them, laborers must be employed in their places; if you retain them, you will not have to employ the laborers; and that is all there is in this question. The report complies literally with everything that the Senator required in his resolution. If he knew of those things that he has referred to to-day, it would have been proper for him to call the attention of the committee to them. The committee was not cognizant of them, and simply reported the facts as they were understood to be.

[Reiterating his desire to prune unnecessary expenditures in the form of surplus employees, Hale reassures Johnson that he does not wish "to impeach his integrity. . . . I never met a man . . . who impressed me with the idea of more perfect integrity in every position . . . than the Senator from Tennessee." He continues: "I look upon him as the Aristides of Athens in this community and in this country; and if his constituents ever get tired of him they will get tired of him for the same reason that the Athenians got tired of Aristides—because they were tired of hearing him called 'the just.' "]

Mr. JOHNSON. I did not intend to indulge in anything personal at all. If the Senator will remember, there was a resolution passed by the Senate, on the recommendation of the committee, which dispensed with a certain number of messengers, whose places were not to be filled until the Senate so directed. Laborers, at a smaller salary, are employed in their places. Before employing them, the committee have always inquired of the Sergeant-at-Arms if their labor was needed or not; and if it was needed, they were employed; and then, when their accounts were made out, the committee audited them.[6]

Cong. Globe, 36 Cong., 2 Sess., 1524–25.

1. Just before the adjournment of the second session, Johnson, as chairman of the committee to audit and control contingent expenses, had reported on the investigation into Senate employee abuses which John P. Hale of New Hampshire had requested the previous June. [See Letter from Dunning R. McNair, February 27, 1861.] Preceding Johnson's remarks, Lyman Trumbull had moved that Sergeant-at-Arms McNair be authorized to make the removals suggested in his letter. Hale, while refraining from criticizing the committee, called for correction of the alleged abuses. At one point James Dixon, then chairman of the committee, assured Hale that Johnson, the former chairman, had "a character for economy quite equal to the Senator from New Hampshire." After some further discussion, Bright called upon Johnson to speak. *Cong. Globe*, 36 Cong., 1 Sess., 3094; 2 Sess., 1413; Special Sess., 1519, 1521–24.

2. Hale had charged that several Senate employees were absent from Washington touring Europe, that one was studying medicine, and that Johnson's committee not only had ignored McNair's request to eliminate three messengers but also had authorized the hiring of pages and clerks without specific fiat, either by law or by order of the Senate. *Ibid.*, 1523.

3. In the sacrificial ritual of the ancient Israelites, the wafer of unleavened bread was the last, and smallest, part of the peace offering. See Num. 6:19.

4. Solomon Foot of Vermont.

5. Lazarus W. Powell of Kentucky and James Dixon of Connecticut.

6. During the ensuing discussion it was revealed that a Senate clerk named Jameson had traveled in Europe for two years and was now studying law in Maryland. After further debate, with the inference that the sergeant-at-arms would dismiss the unnecessary employees, the Senate adjourned *sine die* without taking a vote on Trumbull's resolution. *Ibid.*, 1525–26.

From Clisbe Austin[1]

Tunnel Hill Whitfield County Georgia 29 March 1861

Hon Andrew Johnston

Dear Sir

Excuse me in troubleing with a broken scrawle fome one who do not recollect that I ever saw you not withstanding I was Born and raised in Jefferson County Tennessee & lived in Jeferson Hawkins & Grainger countys untill 11 years ago I mooved and settled at this place[.] am now 59 years oald[.] was a Clay Whig all my life and all though you have allways been a Democrat, yet Sir my verry heart is *now* so attached to your course that I ask you to indulge me in the expression of some of my feelings[.] I am as you will see from my letter butt a poore Schollar[.] I am an humble Farmer and also but a verry humble Minister of the Methodist Church with talents scarcely sufficient to fill the stand as a Local Minister[.] yet Sir I feel a great intrust in the salvation of our country[.] I have children and grand children that I wish well as well as the country at large[.] As above remarked I once lived at Austins Ferry Grainger county was apointed & served as Postmaster at that office through the kindness of Col McClelen[2] who was Member of Congress from that District at the time[.] after I mooved to this place I served as P. M here under Fillmoore administration[.] Hon A. G. Watkins[3] was my neighbor in Tennessee and *allways my special friend*[.] my personal acquaintance with other Polititians have been only limeted yet I read enough to make me feel a great intrust in what is now going on in the world[.] I have read your Speeches in the last Congress for which our Southern Traitors have denounced and annathimitised you so furiously for untill my verry hearts blood have broiled with in me in your behalf[.] Yes Sir all the Whigery & Dimocracy that devided us in former days is as entirely sunk in to obblovion as if they never had existed on earth & my daily prayre to Almighty God is to give you and all other good men of piece success—

I need only to say to you that all though we union men of Georgia was coaxed Flattered and Bullyed out of the union yet my self and

many others Lothe & detest the Draggooning principal that fills the
brest of our opponants yet we have to endure it there being no relief
for us. I tell you as an honest man this day that if they had the power
(many of them) would hang us as soon for defending Andrew
Johnson & W. G. Brownlow as any crime we could be gilty of[.] I
am apprised that if you read the Southern Fiereating papers that
they will tell you we are a satisfied & happy people but so far as
North Georgia is concerned[4] I contradict it most positively and I
dare them to give us a chance to vote our selves into the union[.] but
we are here and cant help our selves. We do not want ware by no
means & here permit me to express my cincere thanks and best wishes
to President Lincoln & Seward for there Patriotic corse in not bringing on a collesion with our Rebelious Fiereaters. *Please tell them
from me* & that I speak the voice of many of my country men that all-
though I am a Slave holder & know there viewes inregard to Slavery
yet I am one that is willing to think & let think and my daily Prayre
at a throne of Grace is that God may bless Lincoln and all his conservitive cabinett[.] Tell them they are makeing many *warm* friends
in my country and did the people only dare to do so they would
Huzaw for Lincolns *conservitive Peacefull* administration[.]
Do if you please tell him & Seward both what one humble Southern
Slave holder thinks of them and accept a full portion of the humble
respects also to your Self. Tell the President and Seward both any
document they think would interest me would be thankfully received
from there hands through the Post office and if you can send me any
it will be truely acceptible to your humble servant[.]

C. Austin

P. S Can you take time to write me a word. If you could send me one
of the Books containing the latest list of all the Post offices in the
U. S it would be a grea presant to me[.]
I do not know where I will get my letter mailed but will send it to
some other office on account of the Antipithy of the P M here against
you[.][5] I am a fraid he would not Mail it as he says you are a Abolitionist & ought to be hung &c &c but you will Mail to me Tunnel
Hill, Ga as this is my home[.]   C Austin

ALS, DLC-JP.

    1. Clisbe Austin (b. *c*1802), who had real estate of $14,000 and $11,000
in personal property, was postmaster at Austin's Ferry, Grainger County,
Tennessee (1840–42) and at Tunnel Hill (1851–53). 1860 Census, Ga.,
Whitfield, 544; Joseph B. Howerton (Civil Archives Division, National
Archives) to Andrew Johnson Project, July 11, 1974.
    2. For Abraham McClellan, see *Johnson Papers*, I, 112*n.*
    3. For Albert G. Watkins, see *ibid.*, 538*n.*
    4. Principally white and with few slaves, the hill counties of North Geor-
gia, were seats of strong unionist sentiment. A citizen of Walker County, ad-

jacent to Whitfield, wrote "If Surtern [*sic*] Georgia want to leave the union let her go but we the people of Cheroke [*sic*] want to Stay in the union So I hope you will let us go in peace." T. Conn Bryan, *Confederate Georgia* (Athens, 1953), 139.

5. T. R. Cherry was the postmaster at Tunnel Hill. *U. S. Official Register* (1859), *51; (1861), 202*.

From J. J. Bryan

March 29, 1861, Chattanooga; ALS, DLC-JP.

Doubts that there would be serious complaint if Harvey T. Phillips were retained as Chattanooga postmaster, but if change is to be made recommends James S. Edwards, "an Oald Seteler and will qualifed to fill the office." Observes in postscript: "I for one have not much love for Lincolns administration and I do not know whether in future a Tenn[essean] that is so very anxious for office under him will be looked on with the Same respect that he other wise would be[.]"

From Robert H. Hodsden[1]

Sevierville, Tenne. March 29th, 1861

Hon. Andrew Johnson
Dear Sir

I have just received a letter from my Brother (Col John G. Hodsden,[2] of Portsmouth, Virginia, who desires to get the appointment of Superintendant of the workmen in the Navy Yard at Gosport, or some other appointment there, of equel pay—

My Brother has been unfortunate in life, having lost several negroes who escaped to Boston, and on his pursueing them there, escaped to Cannada— He has also been burnt out with a good stock of furnature (having kept a furniture establishment in Portsmouth) which placed him in reduced circumstances, with a large family to support— He voted for the Hon. John Bell at the last Presidential election, and is now most decided for the preservation of the Union—

The Hon. Mr. Milson[3] of his Congressional District, refuses to recommend any person for Office under the present administration—

He therefore wishes me to precure a recommendation for him from some person who would likly have influence in the proper direction— And I believe, (and so dos my Brother) that the Hon. T. A. R. Nelson and yourself have the confidence of the President and his Cabinet, as much a[s] any Southern gentlemen could reasonably have; and that a recommendation from both or either of you would secure him the appointment—

I therefore ask you, if you can do so through my representation, to write to the proper department in his behalf— I know it is asking

something unusual, as you are not acquainted with my brother—
But you may rest assured I would not desire a recommendation
from you even for a brother, did I not know he was both honest and
capable—

My Brother will not go on to Washington City, because he thinks
it unnecessary—

If my request can be consistantly granted, I shall take it as a
favor long to be remembered—

I am Very Truly Your Obediant Sevant
R H. Hodsden

N B. Will you be so kind as to send me a copy of your Speach, in
which, (as my friend H. Manard informed me) you skined old Jo
Lane a live—or any other documents, interesting, in favor of the
Union—

R. H. H—

ALS, DLC-JP.

1. Robert H. Hodsden (b. c1807), Virginia native and Sevier County
physician, had $28,700 in real and $23,390 in personal property. Pollyanna
Creekmore and Blanche C. McMahon, trs., *Sevier County, Tennessee: Census
of 1850* (Knoxville, 1953), No. 806; 1860 Census, Tenn., Sevier, 4th Dist.,
73.

2. John G. Hodsden (b. c1811), identified as a farmer, had but recently
arrived in Sevier County from Virginia at the time of the Census of 1850.
Creekmore and McMahon, *1850 Census, Sevier*, No. 756.

3. John S. Millson (1808–1874), Norfolk lawyer, was a Democratic
congressman (1849–61). *BDAC*, 1336.

From William Henry Maxwell

Jonesboro, E. Ten March 29 1861

Private

Dear Governor

Wm. K. Blair[1] as you know has been pension agent here for a
long time and as I understand some one wants his place[.]

S. T. Shiply[2] is the applicant and I do not know whether you intend to interfere or not. I see in the Herald *that you have transfered
to Etheridge* the *bestowment of the Federal patronage in Tennessee*.[3]
I do not wish to be thought to be interfering But would say that as I
am informed Blair, claims that for 11 years he has recd no Compensation & thinks that by holding to the office until his claim can be
adjusted he will be more certain to get his *rights*.

I know that you are as well aware of the political Status of Mr Blair
as I am—As I do not really know where he stands in the present upon
the great question of Union or Disunion[.]

I know however that as a general fact—All the old opposition to you were jubilant at the prospect of your down fall and *mourning* over the *mistake* you had made.

I would not write except it had been by request and can only say that as between Mr. Blair & Shiply, under the circumstances it might be right to let Blair keep the place—

The secession party or *par Excellence* the States Rights party intend to make a fight in Tennessee[.] I am for the Union—As long as a white man Can hold to it, or live under our present Constution. Milligan myself Nelson & Deaderick spoke at Blountville—Haynes, McLin[4] & Reuben Arnold, also as States Right men— Nelson & I speak here Monday—

I am pressed with business today or wd write more.

Yours truly   Wm Henry Maxwell

ALS, DLC-JP.

1. For Blair, see *Johnson Papers*, I, 317n; II, 3–4n.

2. Shelby T. Shipley (b. c1817), a Jonesboro saddler, served as trustee (1856–62), sheriff (1865–68), and register (1878–86) of Washington County. 1860 Census, Tenn., Washington, Jonesboro, 146; *Goodspeed's East Tennessee*, 904.

3. Although the New York *Herald's* observation that "Messrs. Johnson and Etheridge control the Tennessee appointments" does not seem to warrant Maxwell's sweeping assertion, a paper nearer home, under the heading "Rumor," one week earlier had declared that the senator had "turned over to Mr. Etheridge the Federal patronage for Tennessee." New York *Herald*, March 13, 1861; Nashville *Union and American*, March 22, 1861.

4. Probably John B. McLin, who later organized a Confederate cavalry company from Greene and Washington counties and became colonel of the 1st Tenn. Cav. when it was reorganized in May, 1862; less than three months later he was relieved of command and his regiment reduced to a battalion. *Tennesseans in the Civil War*, I, 48–49.

From John Smith[1]

Osage Mill Arks. 29th Mar'/61

Hon A Johnson
Washington
Dr Sir

I am sure you cannot look on, with indiference, to the fight the people of Arks. are making in defence of their rights the Constitution and the Union, abandoned by every publick leading men of the State of both parties, (for we have had two parties here in relation to our local concerns) a majority of our Legislature, Gov. &C[.] The election forced on us on a few days notice, the issue unfairly presented, our speakers almost all on one side, the most popular men of the Counties selected to represent the Secession Movement, almost all the federal officers of Govt. throwing their immense weight and influence in the scale of disunion, add to this, the Country flooded with secession speeches and pamphlets, the press with a few noble exceptions prostituted our people embarrassed in their pecuniary affairs, with a fair prospect if they would consent to secession their foreign debts would not have to be paid[2] and I am sorry to add, the influence of some of our churches were and is being thrown in the scale against us. These and many other things, all brot to bear against us. on the other side, we had nothing to present against such immense influence, but simply our love of Country, its Constitution, Union and institutions. We appealed to the people, we appealed to each other, we appealed to the memory of the illustrious dead, to the memory of Washington Jefferson Jackson Clay and others. we did not appeal in vain. We ourselves were astonished at the result. We beat down secession all over the State.[3] We elected a majority of Union delegates. We had a majority of the popular vote, and here the fight should have ended, not so, true to their principles, the Secession party will not submit, their leading men are taking the field, the 1st Aug. We have again to submit the dispute to the arbitrament of the ballot box. We need help, public documents. All we can get is through our several friends. if not asking too much we Should like to have some of your speeches— many Tennesseeans in Arks. and Tenn. you know— I make no excuse for addressing you. We are working in the same cause, you in your place, I in mine.

Yours Truly   Jno. Smith

ALS, DLC-JP.

1. John Smith (b. c1813), a Tennessee-born merchant with $10,000 in real and $30,000 in personal property, became postmaster in November, 1854, serving until 1865. 1860 Census, Ark., Benton, Osage Mills, 199; *U. S. Official Register* (1855ff).

2. These "foreign debts" (probably those owed to northern merchants) amounted to more than $125,000,000; it was reported that southerners "seemed to delight in the fancied release from their obligations secession gives them." Quoted in Foner, *Business and Slavery*, 302.

3. On February 18 a statewide referendum on the convention bill which had been passed by the Arkansas legislature in January resulted in victory for convention, 27,412–15,826; however, an analysis of the votes cast for candidates reveals unionists leading secessionists by a smaller margin—23,626–17,927. In the March convention, despite pressure from secession delegates, from Governor Henry Rector, and from commissioners representing South Carolina, Georgia, and the Confederate government, unionists, by a vote of 40–24, were successful in postponing the issue of separation until an August 5 statewide referendum on the subject and in carrying a resolution to the effect that "Arkansas citizenry preferred to settle national problems by means of conventions and constitutional amendments rather than by changing or overthrowing the present form of government." Scroggs, "Arkansas in the Secession Crisis," 206, 208–15.

From Benjamin F. Smith[1]

Lindley Missouri March 30th 1861

Hon. A. Johnson,
Respected Sir,

Will you please send me a copy of each of your speeches in the U.S. Senate, on the political issues that have so direfully destracted our Country, for the last few months.= Many of your old Greene County (Tenn) friends are in this vicinity, and are generally unconditional Union Constitutional men. Occasionally a rebid secessionist though lifts his head among them and tries to live on top of the world by the light of political fires, that only consume his hopes as fast as fancied.

Indeed there has been great & intense excitement here for some time. A few wandering bewildered and rarely an ungodly Black Republican tries his hand and creates some extraordinary sensations, but soon goes down under the enraged thunders of popular indignation. =Abolition is=Disunion[.] Secession is=Disunion. Therefore secession is Abolition.

Disunion is in a pitiful minority here and presents but a noisy and contemptible disturbance as disgusting as a nigger weding and disregarded as Ned Buntlines[2] novels among professed Christians. Send me some of your speeches And oblige yours Truly

B. F. Smith

Address Lindley, Missouri
Grundy County
Dr. B. F. Smith.

Your old political friends Joseph Bowman George Smith, (my Father) Henry Dell & Tip Cooper,[3] would be highly gratified to receive a like favor from you.= each of them except Bowman wandered awhile after Disunion[.] But I think we have them on the square again. all same post office as above.   Yours   B. F. S.

ALS, DLC-JP.

1. Probably Benjamin Smith (b. c1827), former Tennessean, presumably a doctor, but listed as a farmer with $1,100 in real and $200 in personal property. 1860 Census, Mo., Grundy, 350.

2. "Ned Buntline" was the pseudonym of Edward Zane Carroll Judson, a former supporter of nativist causes and author of numerous dime novels deplored by the conventionally moral element of society. *Johnson Papers*, II, 320n; *DAB*, X, 238.

3. Joseph Bowman (b. c1828) was a farmer with $2,000 in real estate and $729 in personal property; George Smith (b. c1808), a farmer living in

Lindley, had only $350 in personal property in 1860; Henry Dell (b. c1802), a farmer, lived in Scottsville with $3,840 in real and $5,876 in personal property; and probably Christopher Cooper (b. c1799) who possessed $4,500 in real estate and $2,000 in personal property. With the exception of Cooper, a Virginian who lived for some time in Tennessee, all were natives of the Volunteer State. 1860 Census, Mo., Sullivan, 634, 654, 678, 621.

From Edward R. Chase

March 31, 1861, Ann Arbor, Mich.; ALS, DLC-JP.

Former patent office clerk, thanking Johnson for past kindnesses, assures him that "here your name is honored and your praises sung in such a manner as would turn the head of most men to hear it." Convinced that border states would have already left the Union except for the Tennessean's efforts, he observes that if those states go "I must go South. hundreds here will do the same."

From James R. Hood

Gazette office,
Chattanooga. Tenn. March 31, '61.

Gov. Johnson: —

Dear Sir: —   I note the Senate adjourned on the 28th; and that no action was taken relative to the Chattanooga Post office. I should not have addressed this letter to you, but for the fact that there is rumors in the city said to be "by authority" that there will be no change made in the office here. I would like very much to know the truth of these rumors. I see that many other appointments were attended to. If I fail in this application, it were an unfortunate day, indeed, when I went to Washington City. I came to Chattanooga in '59, without means, and with a family to support—a family of orphan sisters-in-law and have thus far succeeded very well; but the extraordinary "tightness of the times" induced me to apply for the Post Office, so as to enable me to get along easily, and meet all my obligations. Absence from home, and the expense of the trip, will seriously press me. Whatever the actions of those in power may be, I am anxious to know what to depend on. On the day that I left Washington I saw, in the Assistant P. M. General's office, the papers already made out removing Mr. Phillips and appointing me: hence my surprise and disappointment at hearing nothing further from it. Had I not seen these papers, I should not have spoken so freely to you as to my feelings in favor of your re-election. I took it for granted that the appointment was substantially made, and that I was indebted to your friendly aid for it. I sent you a copy of my last paper.[1] I have

waked up "ye animals" (the politicians) several of whom have come
"down on" me heavily. In my next issue I fight back. I tell them that
I know the people will be for you; and that they must and shall "knock
under."[2] I will send you my paper regularly.

I have already extended this letter to a greater length than I intended. I would be much obliged to receive an early reply.

Yours truly,   Jas. R Hood

P. S.—A petition was forwarded to the Post Office Department recommending my appointed, signed by most of the business men of
the city: all of them signed it, I believe, who were applied to.

ALS, DLC-JP.
    1. Hood's Chattanooga *Gazette* was reported in the Nashville *Patriot* of
March 28 as endorsing Johnson's reelection to the Senate; it is very likely
that this was the issue which the editor sent.
    2. Short for "knock under board," meaning to give in, acknowledging that
one is beaten; a variation of "knuckle under." *OED*, V, 739.

From John L. Hopkins

April 3, 1861, Chattanooga; ALS, DLC-JP.

Appreciates his appointment as district attorney for East Tennessee—
a position he cannot accept, though he does not wish to appear ungrateful
nor to seem to decline "because *Lincoln* tenders the office"; expects a
bitter state canvass this year with "unpleasant dissensions in our own
ranks."

From William C. Kyle

at home   Apl 3d 1861—

Hon A Johnson—

Your friend J Blevins[1] is a little mortified at not getting his son
in Law, a position with Lyons[2]—in the shape of a Deputy-Martial—

Could you get Pace[3] the appointment of *Post Master* at Rogersville— your old friend Edmonds,[4] has gone off with Powel Miller
&C[5]—on *sesesion* and I think dont expect to continue as Post Master.
— It was said at the start, that he wouldnt hold office under Lincoln
—but it is said now that he will not resign—& I have no doubt would
be glad to keep the place—

I saw your old friend A Gommon[6]—on the Cars yesterday on his
way to the Grand Junction[.][7] he was giving you fits & said you
Nelson & co were *all Black Republicans.*— the fight in Ten. this
summer will be Union or Disunion— the disunion men will call
themselves *states Right*[.]

I want you to come to Rogersville & make a speech as soon as you get home— I dont expect to take any part in politics this summer but will support my friends.—

Respectfully   W. C. Kyle

ALS, DLC-JP.

1. John L. Blevins (1817–1887), a farmer with real estate valued at $47,000 and personal property at $127,000, was a delegate to the Knoxville and Greeneville unionist conventions. His son-in-law has not been identified. 1860 Census, Tenn., Hawkins, 11th Dist., 22; WPA, Records of Hawkins County: Miscellaneous (Prentice Price Collection), 34; *Proc. E. Tenn. Conv.*, 7, 14.

2. Clinton G. Lyons (1829–*fl*1887), prominent Hawkins County farmer and merchant with $3,000 in personal property, was later a captain in the 12th Tenn. Cav., CSA. 1860 Census, Tenn., Hawkins, 8th Dist., 74; *Tennesseans in the Civil War*, II, 256; *Goodspeed's East Tennessee*, 1231–32.

3. James R. Pace (b. *c*1832), Virginia native and clerk of the Hawkins County court, received the appointment and remained postmaster during both the Confederate and Union occupation. *Ibid.*, 880; 1860 Census, Tenn., Hawkins, 10th Dist., 7; Frances Y. Schumacher, Confederate History of Hawkins County, Tennessee (Typescript, University of Tennessee Library), 7; *U. S. Official Register* (1863), 632.

4. Anderson R. Edmonds (b. *c*1797), a hotel keeper in 1860, served as postmaster from August, 1853, to June, 1861. 1860 Census, Tenn., Hawkins, 13; Records of Postmaster Appointments, 1857–1873, RG28, National Archives.

5. Either Robert D. or Samuel Powel, Jr., both of whom became Confederate officers, and Jacob Miller, president of the Rogersville branch of the Bank of Tennessee; in June, 1863, the latter organized the "Beech Creek Jerkers," a company of local Confederate defense troops. *Johnson Papers*, I, 512n; III, 257n; *Tennesseans in the Civil War*, I, 312.

6. Abraham L. Gammon, a Sullivan County merchant-farmer, who later raised a company for the 19th Tenn. Inf., CSA. *Ibid.*, 215; *Johnson Papers*, III, 653n.

7. Probably the Rogersville Junction, where the spur from that town joined the main line of the East Tennessee & Virginia Railroad.

From Eliakim Littell[1]

April 3, 1861

To THE HON. ANDREW JOHNSON, SENATOR FROM TENNESSEE.

THE spirit in which most of the speakers in Virginia address the United States, is not unfairly exhibited in the epigrammatic verses, copied above from *The New York Commercial Advertiser*.[2]

How different is the attitude of the States which refused to call conventions! It is said that "the woman who deliberates is lost;"[3] and every State which takes into consideration whether it will revolt or no, stains its own character in some degree. "Touch not, taste not, handle not the unclean thing."[4]

The people of the United States wait the progress of events with burning vexation, though willing to "let patience have her perfect work,"[5] and confidently trusting to the administration. But we are anxious to be *doing something* ourselves, and can hardly bear entire inaction while the "confederates" are sending their emissaries to propagate treason in the Border States and Territories. To sit still is to allow them to take us at disadvantage. "When bad men conspire, good men should unite."[6] Can we not organize a patriot band of brothers all over the country, whose fundamental principle shall be that our national government is one and indestructible, and that secession is only a new name for treason?

How is it that the loyal men of Virginia and some other of the Southern States, speak with bated breath of the revolutionists; and when they would defeat Secession, feel obliged to set up some middle ground instead of the Constitution? All the while they speak in this tone they are drifting away from their duty, and making their hearers familiar with disloyalty. We are mortified at such *contingent* patriotism.

How are we to know how far the virus of Calhounism has penetrated, unless we take some action against it? Let such a band of loyal men as I have suggested be formed in every State, and when they have ascertained their own strength let them call upon the Legislatures thereof, to "put the foot down firmly," proclaiming their adherence to "The Union and the Constitution." When we have thus ascertained what is sound, we can let the unsound go,— and proceed anew with the blessing of God, on our way to peace and renewed strength.

It seems a small thing, and yet it may be that a very great part of the success of the doctrine of "State Sovereignty"—and its descendant, Secession—has been, owing to our not having, *in one word*, a name for the nation like England, France, Spain.

I would propose as a name for the political brotherhood of private men—the title of *Washington Republicans*. Under this banner let us gather loyal men of every former denomination. Republicans, Democrats, Whigs, Union-men; holding no man obliged to give up his opinions upon the points which have formerly divided us; and pledged only to support our country, "however bounded," as "one perfect chrysolite" against the men who are endeavoring to break and destroy it.

Your voice in the Senate sounded like a trumpet of defiance to Treason, and it was paralyzed before you! Let us hear it again, brave and faithful Senator! Marshal the patriot hosts, and lead us to the rescue of our insulted nationality!

E. LITTELL.

Living Age Office, Boston, 3 April, 1861.[7]

Littell's Living Age, LXIX (1861), 130; clipping in DLC-JP.

1. Despite a limited education, Eliakim Littell (1797–1870), New Jersey-born editor and publisher, became one of the foremost journalistic figures of his time. Having achieved modest success with several Philadelphia-based reprint journals, he moved to Boston to found *Littell's Living Age* in 1844. Consisting initially of reprints from the British press, *Living Age* was the most successful of his publishing ventures. A shrewd businessman, a well-read editor, and a staunch unionist, Littell contributed greatly to America's knowledge of foreign affairs and culture through his magazine, which became one of the nation's most prestigious journals. Early in February Littell had sent Johnson a "plan for changing the Presidential Term"; a month later he observed that "*you* hav saved the Border States from joining the *Traitors*" and that northerners "would have rejoiced if you had taken a seat in Mr L's Cabinet!" *DAB*, XI, 295; Littell to Johnson, February 5, March 8, 1861, Johnson Papers, LC.

2. Entitled "Virginia to the North," the attached poem read: THUS speaks the sovereign Old Dominion / To Northern States her frank opinion. / FIRST. / MOVE NOT A FINGER: 'tis coercion, / The signal for our prompt dispersion. / SECOND. / WAIT, till I make my full decision, / Be it for union or division. / THIRD. / If I declare my ultimatum, / ACCEPT MY TERMS, as I shall state 'em. / FOURTH. / THEN, I'll remain, while I'm inclined to, / Seceeding when I have a mind to."

3. Addison's *Cato*, Act IV, sc. 1.

4. Col. 2:21.

5. "Best let patience have her perfect work, that ye may be perfect and entire, wanting nothing." James 1:4.

6. A variant of "When bad men combine, the good must associate; else they will fall, one by one, an unpitied sacrifice in a contemptible struggle." Edmund Burke, *Thoughts on the Cause of the Present Discontent* (1770), in Henry L. Mencken, *A New Dictionary of Quotations on Historical Principles* (New York, 1942), 476.

7. On the envelope Littell had written: "If Mr. Johnson be not in Washington—then Postmaster there will oblige the writer by forwarding this letter to him."

From Robert M. Barton[1]

Russelville April 4th 1861.

Hon. A. Johnson
Dear Sir

No one feels more reluctant than I do, to annoy public men with applications for office—and I only address you now because I believe I may be of some small service to you— Some time ago, I addressed a note to you in relation to the post master at Knoxville— I wrote for Charles Rice Esq—[2] I did not press his claim—nor do I now— He is a clever fellow—Competent for that position—No account as an architect of his own fortune—and as for who has the office at Knoxville, I have no right to interfere—

But, I was there on Monday & Tuesday,—and I find those great Union loving men, who only one short month ago, were much in advance of ME in their laudations of you, and their unequivocal endorsement of your course—now denouncing you—or rather saying that they were going to do so, in the event one Small was appointed post master—[3]

I know very well, that you are not to be driven from your purpose by fear of denunciation— But, it has occured to me, that it was due to that community that a descent regard should be had to their feelings— Small in past time has made himself very offensive to the great boddy of the Whigs—and I am by him, as I am by Brownlow— I think it wrong in principle for one section, or boddy of the Union party to present one, so odious to the other—

Whilst I have not a particle of respect (as I told those fellows at Knoxville,) for the patriotism that rises only to the grade of party— Puts party above country—Yet I do desire that you shall exercise some care in trying to cement the fusion so hapily begun— Let there be no Whig or Democrat—Never, never,

I have for years been a silent, pained & disgusted looker on in political warfare— I have believed that we were approaching some crisis— But, I little expected such a state of things as now exists—

I would like to know privately if you have had any hand in the appointment of the post master in Nashville—and what, if any in the appointment of Small at Knoxvill if he is to be appointed— My reason for wanting to know is, that I may be prepaired as your friend to act—

This is rather a singular letter Govenor, and one that I would not venture to write, but that I believe you *know me*— I hear my friend Milligon has a Judgeship— I am glad of that—Tho I hate to give him up as floater—[4] I would like to hear from you if not asking too much— Would you feel willing to give us a speach in this end of our vally?

Yours   R. M. Barton

P. S. I am not for Lutrel— His friends are getting up quite a muss—say you prevented his appointment by charging that he was a defaulter— I dont know any thing about that. But, assuming that Gov. Campbell swore the truth he is not fit for office—[5] Rice, they say then, would give satisfaction—

ALS, DLC-JP.

1. Robert M. Barton, a Greeneville Whig attorney and Johnson-appointed circuit court judge. *Johnson Papers*, II, 448n.

2. Charles A. Rice, Knoxville publisher. In recommending Rice, Barton wrote that he had been "an uncompromising political opponent of yours" but "one of the many thousand of *my* former political associates, that can now see how I could be true to my faith and vote for you!" Barton to Johnson, February 23, 1861, Johnson Papers, LC.

3. Alexander B. Small was not appointed. See also *Johnson Papers*, II, 382*n*.

4. A legislator representing more than one county where population is not sufficient for a separate, or direct, representative.

5. There appears to be no evidence which would clarify this rather obscure reference to William B. Campbell's swearing "the truth" about James C. Luttrell. Although John C. McGaughey, writing earlier in 1861, declared that Luttrell had been incompetent as comptroller during Johnson's governorship, no charges were ever placed against him. Neither the Nashville newspapers for 1857 nor such manuscript collections as the Sioussat Papers (University of Tennessee Library), which contain transcripts of Campbell correspondence, and the Thomas A. R. Nelson Papers (Lawson McGhee Library), disclose any information on the subject. See Letter from John C. McGaughey, February 21, 1861.

From John Lellyett

Nashville April 4, 1861

Hon Andrew Johnson
Washington City

Sir,—   I understand that Faxon of the Clarkesville Jeffersonian had the meanness to represent to you to my injury, that I was "rather too fond of carrying Shot guns" &C—alluding to the Hall-Poindexter affair.[1] I had just three things to do with that affair, viz.,

1st To advise Mr Hall not to fight, on account of his age and family,

2d. To approach a friend of Poindexter with the view of having the parties bound over to keep the peace,—in which I was repulsed,

3dly, To advise my brother (who did carry the gun) not to have any thing to do with the affair.[2]

This was all I had to do with that fight. I suppose it is of no importance to state this to you now. But I would rather you should know how damnably the fellow lied, who came sneaking to you to injure me with these representations.

Yours Respectfully   John Lellyett

ALS, DLC-JP.

1. During an editorial exchange in 1859, G. G. Poindexter of the Nashville *Union and American* imprudently accused Allen A. Hall of the Nashville *Daily News* of holding Black Republican sentiments. On November 18 Hall effectively ended the controversy, killing Poindexter with a blast of buckshot. A prominent Whig and native of North Carolina, Hall (*c*1803–1867) had served as chargé d'affaires to Venezuela (1841–45), assistant secretary of the treasury (1849–50), and editor of several newspapers, including the Nashville *Republican Banner* (1839–41), the Washington *Republic* (1850), and the Nashville *Daily News* (1857–59). After the Poindexter affair he fled the city, later becoming minister to Bolivia (1863–67), where he died. Lanman, *Biographical Annals*, 179; New York *Times*, July 14, 1867; Nashville *Republican Banner*, November 19, 1859, July 14, 1867; 1860 Census, Tenn., Davidson, Nashville, 3rd Ward, 89.

2. William Lellyett, city and commercial editor of the Nashville *Daily News*, testified that at Allen A. Hall's request he had asked a bookkeeper, James A. Fisher, to procure a gun. On the evening before the shooting, Lellyett deposited the gun in Hall's office. The morning of the affair, Lellyett testified, he advised Hall to meet Poindexter in the street, and at Hall's request wrapped the gun (which Fisher had earlier testified was his own) in a newspaper and carried it to the porch. A short time later Hall, armed with the loaded shotgun and standing in the main entrance to the *Daily News* offices, attempted to halt Poindexter as the latter advanced toward him with a pistol concealed by an umbrella. When Poindexter refused to stop after a third command to do so, Hall fired the fatal shot. Clayton, *Davidson County*, 235; Nashville *Union and American*, December 2, 1859.

From Lucy A. Glascock[1]

McMinnville, April 5th, 1861.

Hon: Andrew Johnson,
Sir:

Among the many letters soliciting *favors* with which you are doubtless overwhelmed, let *mine* too come in for a moment's consideration, and if it lies in your power to grant my request, I beg of you not to fail to exert your influence to that effect. And by way of introduction I will mention to you that I am a sister of Charlie Faxon's of Clarksville Tennessee, and I trust that your friendship for him will induce you to give my letter a reading. It is in behalf of my *husband* (James Glascock) that I now write, though he knows nothing of my intention to write, nor do I wish him *ever* to know that I have done so.

My mother[2] wrote to me some time ago, that there was to be a Route Agent appointed on the Memphis & Louisville Rail Road, and she as well as my brothers[3] are exceedingly anxious for my husband to receive the appointment. Before my brother Charlie knew that Mr Glascock desired a situation, he had already signed a recommendation for another person and had written to you to endorse it;[4] but he said he would write to you not to sign it but to use your influence toward having Mr. Glascock receive the appointment. The President and Superintendent of the Road[5] both wish him to receive the situation and said they would write to Washington to that effect. Whether or not they have done so now I do not know but I feel so much for my husband that I could not forbear writing to you *myself* to ask you if you could not secure that position for him, to use your influence to get him into some profitable business. And now, you will perhaps wonder what claims *I* presume to have upon *you*, that *I* should ask such a favor at your hands! Only the claim of humanity. The right that *every* devoted wife has to ask assistance for a husband who has never injured any one but has lost his all through the selfishness of an extravagant *father*.[6] Will you bear with me while I give you an outline of his business difficulties. His Father was unfortunate enough to have been born to wealth and luxury. The consequence was that although a man of talent and education, he had neither taste nor inclination for business of any kind, and in the past twenty years has gone through with three large fortunes which had been left him by different individuals. At the time of his Son's marriage with myself Col Glascock was deeply in debt notwithstanding he owned a handsome farm with about 7,000 acres of land, and also several negroes.

At the time of our marriage *three years ago*, my husband was in business for himself, and owned a Drug Store the sales of which amounted to nearly *Seven Thousand* Dollars a year (a *very* prosperous business for so small a town as McMinnville). Instead of selling for *cash* as Druggists generally do, he sold almost entirely on credit. When we had been married about fifteen months, his *Father* induced him to sell out in order to lend *him* the money to pay a portion of *his* debts promising to return the money in a short time as he would sell his land and buy back very soon. I tried hard to keep my husband from selling out, for I knew that he would not be able to induce the gentleman to sell to him again, and furthermore I did not believe that his Father would ever return the borrowed money. He only received a thousand dollars in actual cash for his Drugs— The remainder of the payment was in notes for *nine* and *twelve* months. His last stock of Drugs had not been paid for, but his Father promised to have the money ready whenever the payment became due.

His Father appropriated the Thousand Dollars besides about *Four Thousand Dollars* in notes of hand from customers who were owing him. It is needless to weary you by a detailed account of his Father's extravagance and ingratitude. Suffice it to say that *not one dollar* was ever returned and when the Drug debts became due my husband was obliged to give the notes which he had received for the remainder of the money due him for his Drug Store. Have you perceived that he never received one dollar from the sale of his business. A little over a year ago, my husband at the urgent request of the citizens of this place was induced to assume the proprietorship of this Hotel. Still trusting to his Father's promises to pay the money, he consented to take the Hotel and was obliged to buy the furniture belonging to the House. About nine months after he took the Hotel, his Father went off, leaving all his property in the hands of two lawyers whom he directed to sell *everything* to pay his debts. His wife, daughter and youngest son[7] were thus left—without a home, without a servant and with no means of procuring either. My husband immediately wrote to his mother to come and make their home with him, for as long as he had a crust of bread in world, or a roof to cover his head, they should be cheerfully shared with them. From August of last year until February of this year they lived with us, when my husband was obliged to sell the furniture in order to pay the former proprietor, from whom he had purchased. We are now boarding, and he is now worth nothing. Had he lost every thing through his own extravagance, I would not murmur, but when he started out to make his own living, he asked no assistance from his Father (though the latter was *then* well able to afford it) but by diligent attention to business while a clerk and through the kindness of a few friends he was enabled to set-up in business for himself. No man was ever more popular than he was. Every one loved and respected him, and well did he deserve their good will, for he was kind and considerate to all, a consistent church member, and a strictly moral and upright man. This character as well as his energy and devotion to business gained him the custom of this and the neighboring counties, and of course he could not fail to succeed. But a *mistaken sense* of filial duty induced him to sacrifice everything to an idle and extravagant Father, and *now*, in the flower of his manhood—at the age of *Twenty Five years*, he is with scarcely a dollar in the world. He cannot bear to be idle and is using every endeavor to get into some kind of business, but so far he has been entirely unsuccessful.

There is no opening *here* for business, not even a vacant clerkship. I am teaching Music in The *Female* College[8] at this place, and have been in that position for several years. He was bitterly opposed to my teaching, but was over ruled by my determination, and the urgent request of this community. I have wearied you I know with this recital, but I could not help it for I wished to prove to you in how much need he stands of a situation. What I have written to you, you will please keep private, for during all his trials and difficulties he has never made any complaint of his Father's conduct, or spoken of him with the least degree of disrespect and I would not have him think that *I* would do so. From his mother I learned the particulars of his unkind treatment, from one who of all others should have been the first to lend him a helping hand.

Hoping you will excuse me for appropriating so much of your valuable time I will close with the earnest wish that if you cannot secure the appointment for him of which I have spoken, that you will use your influence to obtain some other one for him. Trusting that you will give me an early reply, I remain

Yours respectfully   Mrs Lucy A. Glascock

Direct to McMinnville Tennessee

ALS, DLC-JP.

1. Lucy A. (Faxon) Glascock (b. c1838), New York native, was the wife of James Glascock (b. c1835), a Virginian who kept the Warren House in McMinnville. 1860 Census, Tenn., Warren, 211; *Population Schedule of the United States Census of 1850 (Seventh Census) for Warren County, Tennessee* (McMinnville, 1958), 131; *Mitchell's Tenn. State Gazetteer* (1860–61), 119.

2. Lucy A. (Mrs. Charles) Faxon (c1804–1874). 1860 Census, Tenn., Montgomery, 116; *Goodspeed's Montgomery*, 1030–31.

3. Charles O. Faxon, editor of the Clarksville *Jeffersonian*; Henry W. (1826–1864); Leonard G. (b. 1827), who had moved to Illinois (see *Johnson Papers*, III, 444–45n); James G. (1831–fl1886); George B. (1838–fl1886); and John W. (1840–fl1886). *Ibid.*

4. On March 20 Faxon had recommended Robert B. Hickman and C. B. Wilcox. John Faxon, who wrote on the same day claiming to be a unionist and asking the senator's influence for a clerkship, had been assistant supervisor of state banks and cashier of the Bank of Tennessee at Rogersville, as well as local editor for the *Jeffersonian*. Nonetheless, he ultimately went South, serving in Co. A, 14th Inf., CSA, made up of men from Clarksville and Montgomery County. John W. Faxon to Johnson, March 20, 1861, Johnson Papers, LC; *Tennesseans in the Civil War*, I, 203; II, 151.

5. Robertson Topp and H. Coffin, respectively president and superintendent of the Memphis and Ohio Railroad, which linked with the Louisville and Nashville at Clarksville to become the Memphis branch of the L & N. *Report to the General Assembly on the Condition of Railroads in Tennessee* (Nashville, 1859), 445; Thomas D. Clark, *The Beginnings of the L & N* (Louisville, 1933), 57.

6. Census returns appear to substantiate the story of George Glascock's vicissitudes as detailed here by his daughter-in-law. In 1850 Glascock (b. c1803), a native of Virginia, possessed property valued at $10,000; in 1860 his real estate was worth $36,000, but his personal wealth was estimated at only $3,550. In 1850 he owned seven slaves; in 1860, only two. *1850 Census, Warren County*, 131; 1860 Census, Tenn., Warren, 13; 1850 Census, Slave Schedule, Tenn., Warren, 546; 1860 Census, Slave Schedule, Tenn., Warren, 2.

7. Mary Jane Glascock (b. c1820), a Virginian, daughter Fanny (b. c1840), a music teacher, and son Thomas (b. c1845), a student, both born in Tennessee. 1860 Census, Tenn., Warren, 13.

8. Cumberland Female Seminary, established in 1850 by the Middle Tennessee Synod of the Cumberland Presbyterian Church, became Cumberland Female College four years later and continued to function until 1900. Womack, *McMinnville at a Milestone*, 231–32.

From Thomas A. R. Nelson

Jonesboro' Tenn. 5th April 1861—

Hon. A. Johnson,
Dear Sir.

Your despatches did not reach me until to day because I spoke at Greeneville and Jonesboro' on Monday—and went to Newport on Tuesday from whence I have just returned.

I have only been in town two days in all since my return home and am scarcely able to say who should be Post Master here. The sentiment seems to be that if Williams[1] had applied openly and publicly in the first instance, he could have got the majority, but many of the citizens, who would otherwise have supported him, are unwilling to do so because they do not like the idea of Crouch[2] appointing his successor.

By looking at the two Petitions on file you can form a pretty correct opinion as to which of the applicants has the majority and I think the office should be given to whichever seems to be the choice of the people. Dawes'[3] friends say he has a decided majority and that many of Williams friends who would have signed the Petition in the first instance, were unwilling to do so in consequences of Crouch's recommendation.

Yours respectfully,   Thos. A. R. Nelson.

ALS, DLC-JP.

1. John E. Williams.
2. For William H. Crouch, see *Johnson Papers*, I, 418n.
3. William Dawes received the appointment, serving from April 9, 1861, until April 22, 1865. See Letter from William Dawes, March 13, 1861; Dawes to Johnson, February 14, 1861, Johnson Papers, LC.

From Charles A. Rice

Knoxville, Friday, April 5, 1861.

Private
Hon. A. Johnson
Greeneville, Tenne.
Dear Sir.

The prompting of this letter may be attributed to the fact of my being an applicant for the appointment of P.M. at this point, taken in connection with the prevailing opinion, that your wishes and influence have been consulted, and may still be controling with the present Powers at Washington, in the distribution of the Federal offices in E. Tenn.

I would have addressed you at an early day, but for the fact, that I had a number of friends in the upper counties, including Col. Nelson, who were interested for me, and who, I believed, would ask your attention to my claims; besides, our Representative, Mr Maynard, was in the city, holding my petition, ready to present it at the proper time, and to represent to the Department my qualifications & eligibility for the position. My petition was gotton up in December— Hence, I felt, without assuming that my capacity & fitness for the discharge of the duties of the office, were superior to those of other applicants, that I had some prior claims, growing out of my *early* move in the matter—when public opinion was so violently arrayed against Mr. Lincoln, rendering it almost *criminal* for a man to tolerate the *idea* of Mr. Lincoln's administering the Government, to say nothing of *holding an office* under his administration. *The friends of the Union*—embracing many of my old *political* friends, & many, also, of both wings of the old Democratic party, & some of *your* personal & political friends—I presume you saw the names on my petition—commended my independent & open course, & signed my paper very cheerfully. There were understood to be other applicants, but they were not known,—would not avow it openly.— But, really, I have said much more on this subject than I intended— please excuse me for inflicting the task upon you, of reading such a lengthy story, which will not be likely to possess any interest, *at this late period*, especially.

The leading object of my letter, however, is to set myself right with you, in regard to the views I entertain, as to present party movements. I am for breaking down old party lines. It is certainly no time *now*, to cavil about "political parties." I am for the UNION PARTY—for the CONSTITUTION & GOVERNMENT OF THE U.S. Hence I can affiliate with all those who go for the Union, the Constitution & the enforcement of the laws, *first principle*—are unwilling to sacrafice their Country for sake of *party*, or *self aggradizement*. Having said this much I need hardly say, that I do not sympathise with the "Knoxville Whig," in its "wholesale attack" upon you, in its issue of this week—now just out.[1] My connection heretofore with that paper,[2] and the press at Knoxville, would very naturally lead you to suppose that my sentiments & sympathies were truly echoed by the "thunder" of the Whig: but, if you were familiar with the history of my political *status*, you would be prepared to know, that I did not look upon the "Whig" as being always a "chart and compass"[3] for me. Although my personal relations are friendly enough with the editor—could not well be otherwise, as our wives are related[4]—yet we do not agree in *every thing*. His prejudices are too strong, his feelings too bitter.

I heard early in the week, that he intended an attack upon you in his paper of to-morrow; so I made it convenient to call *at his residence* to enquire the nature of his assault, and to ascertain his *programme of the war* to be waged against you & other Union men in the state. After hearing his statement, I, modestly of course, questioned the propriety of his policy—assuming that, I was opposed to any renewals of *old party slang*—I was for, forgetting the past, and looking at the *present* and *future*—that you had, by your noble defence of the Union & the Constitution, entitled yourself to the respect & confidence of every loyal Union man in the country—that your preference for your old political friends, for office, was nothing but what was natural—just what a Bell-Everett man would do—bestow favors upon his own *party* associates & friends. Still, I failed to convince him that he was in error—that his policy was calculated to arouse old party prejudices, and renew party spirit, which I thought ill-timed & unnecessary.— I have mentioned these matters to you, merely to give you a fair view of the relations, personal & political, that exists between the "Whig" (& its editor) & myself so that you may not be prejudiced against me, on account of the *singular*, not to say *unnatural* ebullitions that paper occasionally puts forth.

Not that, I suppose you will feel *alarmed* at any *guns* that may be fired from the battery of the "Whig," but I have felt that I was but doing myself an act of justice, under the existing circumstances, to thus, *confidentially*, say what I have. If you shall, in your final verdict, see proper to use your influence for my appointment, I shall know it, by hearing the announcement of the fact of my election, and shall esteem it as a *personal* favor to myself, as well as a compliment to those through whose kindness & confidence, I have been recommended to the P.O. Department[.]

> I have the honor to be,
> With much respect, yrs. &c.
> Chas. A. Rice

ALS, DLC-JP.

1. Brownlow had questioned Johnson's fidelity to the Union cause because of his rumored support of secessionist William D. McNish for Nashville postmaster. Knoxville *Whig*, March 30, 1861.

2. Rice had become part owner of the *Whig* in 1855 and sole owner in 1858. According to John Bell Brownlow, the Parson had sold the paper, continuing, however, as its editor, in order "to be rid of the labor of publishing." Early in 1859 Brownlow repurchased the *Whig*. Ben Harris McClary, ed., "The Sale of Brownlow's Knoxville *Whig*," ETHS *Publications*, No. 35 (1963), 97–98.

3. Found in a hymn of the period, "Jesus Savior Pilot Me," by Edward Hopper.

4. Brothers Thomas W. and James Gaines of Virginia were great-grandfathers of Eliza O'Brien Brownlow and Amanda Gaines Rice. Mrs. Hal T. Spoden (Sullivan County Historian) to Andrew Johnson Project, January 16, 1974; Calvin E. Sutherd, *A Compilation of Gaines Family Data* (Fort Lauderdale, Fla., 1972), 227ff, 287ff.

From Samuel Evans

April 6, 1861, Blountville; ALS, DLC-JP.

Asks Johnson to address Sullivan County on the political issues of the day, for "there is more of the Secession element in Sullivan than in a majority of the County's in E. Tennessee." Defeated in February on the question of disunion, "They are endeavoring to revive the old party

lines between Whig & Democrat, and branding those who disagree
with them and stand by the Union as *Black Republicans*." [See Letter
from Sullivan County Citizens, May 6, 1861.]

From Richard M. Edwards

Cleveland Tenn April 8th 1861

Hon A. Johnson
    Your efforts in the U. S. Senate during the past session of Con-
gress have given entire satisfaction to the whole Union party of this
part of the state. They look to you as the leader of the Union cause,
and all with one accord have said you should be retained in your
position. But within the last two days reports are circulated here
greatly to your prejudice. It is said that yourself and Etheridge have
agreed together in reference to the policy of transferring Tennessee
to the Southern cottonocracy and that your programme is to have
Etheridge run for Gov & yourself to be returned to the Senate, &
there to throw your united influence in favor of the project of turning
Tennessee over to the Southern concern. I am free to say that I dis-
believe the whole story.
    Yet I think it proper to give you a chance to deny the imputation.
    Several Union men have requested me to apprise you of the report
and request a denial or confirmation of the statement.
    We want to *know* upon whom we may rely in the coming contest;
knowing as we do that the "big shock" is yet to come—that the cause
of the Union will loose many and that the most intensely bitter and
vindictive contest ever known in the state will shortly be on us. To
the Union Democracy (of whom we have a heavy majority here)
your late speeches are perfectly satisfactory; and if you still occupy
the same position which you expressed in the Senate they will still
be for you.
    Another part of the story in reference to the combination is that
the Breckinridge disunionists are to be placed in and retained in
office entirely to the exclusion of Union men so as that they may aid
the disunion movement by their influence and position[.][1]
    Your response it is hoped will clearly refute all such charges—as
your past history affords no just grounds for their promulgation or
belief[.]

Very truly   Your friend & obt servt
R. M. Edwards

P.S.   I dislike post scripts but I must add an item: Brabson has
reported here that you have all the appointments in Tennessee in
your pocket and hence you are held responsible for the appointment

of the officers. At this place, T. W. Johnson the old P. M.[2] is retained who is a red hot disunionist & his son another disunionist who now lives in Georgia is mail agent on the E. T. & G. R. R. through the influence of S. A. Smith a *rank disunionist*.[3] If your influence is to be given to the disunion office seekers to the exclusion of your Union friends you will loose very nearly all you have gained[.]

Have you had anything to do with the Appointments? If so you have been imposed on by Smith & Rowles[4] *who always have been your enemies*.

Your friend   R. M. Edwards

ALS, DLC-JP.

1. Although he appeared to be Lincoln's patronage agent for Tennessee, Johnson tended to favor his old allies among the Breckinridge Democrats, many of whom later sided with the Confederacy. Bell Unionists, dissatisfied with evidences of partisanship in the dispensation of Federal patronage, by April were convinced that, a "political combination" between the Lincoln administration and Johnson having been effected, the senator would give Democrats the Federal appointments in Tennessee. J. Milton Henry, "The Revolution in Tennessee, February, 1861, to June, 1861," *Tenn. Hist. Quar.*, XVIII (1959), 111–12; Robert W. Winston, *Andrew Johnson: Plebeian and Patriot* (New York, 1928), 187; Knoxville *Whig*, March 30, 1861.

2. Thomas W. Johnson (b. *c*1812), a Cleveland hotel keeper, had been appointed postmaster in 1856. Wooten, *Bradley County*, 178; 1860 Census, Tenn., Bradley, 7.

3. For Samuel A. Smith, former congressman from the third district, see *Johnson Papers*, III, 447n.

4. George W. Rowles was a prominent Cleveland attorney. *Ibid.*, I, 413n.

From Amos Kendall

Washington April 9th 1861

Hon Andrew Johnson

Dear Sir,   Dr. F. B. Culver[1] who married my second daughter now deceased, is desirous of procuring the office of Paymaster in the army, and I am informed you are inclined to aid him. He has for some years resided in this City where he came from the State of Arkansas, of which, I suppose, he remains a citizen. I shall be much obliged by any aid you can render him.

Allow me to thank you most cordially for your efforts to stem the tide of secession and save our invaluable Union. I only regret that old age makes it impossible for me to stand by you in the very front of the fight, yet, I am ready to devote what of mental and physical powers I have to the great cause whenever I can see where to strike.

With highest respect   Amos Kendall

Present.

ALS, DLC-JP.

1. Frederick B. Culver, a Louisville, Kentucky, physician who married Kendall's daughter Adela (d. 1851), was now living in Washington, D. C., at 355 11th West. Stickney, *Amos Kendall*, 540; *Boyd's Washington and Georgetown Directory* (1860), 60.

To Ward H. Lamon,[1] *Washington, D. C.*

Washington City April 16h 1861

Col W. H. Lamon,
Dear Sir,

It is with pleasure, I recommend to your favorable consideration Dr W. J. C. Duhamel[2] of this City, the present practicing Physician of the United States Jail, for Continuance as such. Dr Duhamel, has dischar[g]ed all the duties, as I am advised, as practicing physician, with promptness, efficiency and Skill, giving general Satisfaction, to the patients and the appointing power.

While he is a good citizen and a talented man he is also for the Union, and has exerted his influence for its preservation— If you can find it consistent, to continue him in his present position, you will Confer a favor on me that will be highly appreciated[.]

Very respectfully &c   Andrew Johnson

ALS, CSmH-Ward Hill Lamon Col., #378.

1. Ward H. Lamon (1828–1893), Virginia-born attorney, was one of Lincoln's law partners (1852–59) and a staunch friend. He had accompanied the President-elect as a bodyguard in February, 1861, personally surveyed the Charleston situation for Lincoln in March, and was appointed marshal of the District of Columbia in April (1861–65). Returning to the practice of law after the war, he traveled extensively and collaborated in writing a controversial biography of Lincoln (1872). *DAB*, X, 562–63.

2. William J. C. Duhamel (1827–1883), a native of Maryland who possessed $8,000 in real estate and $1,000 in personal property, resided at 496 North I Street, Washington, D. C. A graduate of the University of Maryland (1849), he was for ten years the physician for the United States prisons in the District of Columbia and a surgeon in the Army of the Potomac. His postwar letters to the President reveal that, having been a friend since 1857, he was endeavoring to keep Johnson informed of a possible plot to implicate the latter in Lincoln's assassination. He is said to have been a member of the White House staff during the administrations of both Buchanan and Johnson. 1860 Census, Washington, D. C., 4th Ward, 14; *Appleton's Cyclopaedia*, II, 251; *Boyd's Washington and Georgetown Directory* (1860), 67, 225; Columbia Historical Society *Records*, XLVIII–XLIX (1946–47), App. 343; Duhamel to Johnson, August 10, 1867, Johnson Papers, LC.

To Abraham Lincoln, Washington, D. C.

April 16, 1861, Washington, D. C.; LS, DLC-Lincoln Papers.

Endorsing Charles H. Foster of North Carolina for a Federal appointment, Johnson adds that he hopes "the President will find it consistent with the public interest and sound policy to distribute as near as may be a fair proportion of the patronage of the government, among the border States."

From Alexander J. D. Thurston

Nashville 20th April 1861

Hon Andrew Johnson,
Washington City
My dear & Kind Sir

We are all a blaze of Excitement and Everything in Confusion— Tennessee will go out of the Union in a very few days, the Citizens are arming and drilling to resist the North— A number of Volunteers will leave in a very few days for the Southern Confederacy— Our Legislature meets next Thursday, by Proclamation of Gov Harris—

You my dear Sir have been posted here as sending traitorous dispatches to some one in the State—[1]

Are you coming home soon. the State needs your services and advice and I beg of you to hasten home immediately—

I know you are a true southern man, not willing to submit to one single thing that infrings the smallest right of your State, and for that very reason hasten home, and meet the fanatics who would brand you with the name of traitor— Senator Johnson I revere you too much as a man to tamely hear these Epithets, unrebuked and passed unheeded—

No one yet knows the purport of your dispatch, but it is said Govr Letcher[2] stopped it, on account of its treasonable nature—

I understand it is in the hands of Gov Harris, what disposal he will make of it I am unable to learn— Please hasten home and God bless and protect you[.]

Very Respectfully   Your Sincere friend
A. J. D. Thurston

ALS, DLC-JP.

1. The Nashville *Patriot* of this same date, quoting a Virginia paper, reported: "An infamous and traitorous telegraph from Andrew Johnson of Tennessee stopped."

2. John Letcher (1813–1884) of Virginia, Jacksonian Democrat, served as congressman (1851–59) and wartime governor (1860–64). Though originally opposed to secession, he nevertheless vigorously supported the Confederate cause when he felt Lincoln's troop requisition gave his state no alternative. Resuming his Lexington law practice after the war, he later served in the Virginia house of delegates. *DAB*, XI, 192.

Speech at Knoxville[1]

April 27, 1861

He came out manfully on the side of his country—in favor of the enforcement of the Laws, and the preservation of the Union, at whatever cost. He held up the movers and originators of Secession to merited scorn and contempt. He traced their treason back to the days of South Carolina Nullification—quoted Gen. Jackson upon them—argued the question of Secession—and in a word, delivered arguments, at once unanswerable, and convincing, on the part of the people. His speech was received with great applause, and highly commended by men of talents, who have never heretofore agreed with the Governor in sentiment. Whilst he avoided personalities, he dealt out a full measure of justice to the disappointed politicians, designing demagogues, and actual traitors, seeking to break up the Government, and to destroy the country. Meanwhile, the speech was well calculated to allay, if not totally to obliterate every vestige of party asperity which may have formed a lodgement in the hearts of any of our people. In a spirit of fraternal feeling, he referred to the past political conflicts, that had engendered heart-burnings, and acrimonious feelings during which Democrats had said things hateful to the feelings of Whigs, and Whigs had alike wounded the feelings of Democrats; but now that our beloved country was imperiled, he counselled the exercise of a forgiving spirit—the blotting out of all past differences. Turning to Mr. Nelson,[2] who had arrived after he commenced speaking, on the down train, he passed a just and handsome compliment upon him, and stated that while they battled against each other for years, in a courteous and honorable warfare, they were now shoulder to shoulder, in battling for our common country.[3]

Knoxville *Whig*, May 4, 1861.

1. Johnson was met at the depot by Knoxville Unionists and taken to the Franklin House, where an "immense crowd" had gathered for a Union meeting. He was introduced "from a stand erected on Gay Street, in front of Morrow's Bank, and spoke for more than two hours, with great effect." Although this report contains much editorial comment, it is included as an example of the tenor of Johnson's speaking on the hustings. Knoxville *Whig*, May 4, 1861.

2. Thomas A. R. Nelson.

3. Johnson had half finished when a demonstration nearly interrupted the meeting. "The Brass Band that come up with the Monroe Volunteers, struck up at just such a distance as to interrupt the speaker and his crowd; and in the highly excited state of the public mind, the interruption was calculated to bring on a collision." According to editor Brownlow, when other bands and military companies carrying secessionist flags arrived, it was with difficulty that an "effusion of blood" was avoided. *Ibid.*; see also Temple, *East Tennessee*, 19.

To Knox County Representatives[1] [Nashville]

Knoxville, April 28,1861.

To Messrs. J. S. Boyd, John Williams and R. H. Armstrong:

By firmness and deliberation the state may be saved. With reasonable time for a canvass, East Tennessee will give twenty thousand majority against secession.[2]

Andrew Johnson,
T. A. R. Nelson,
Horace Maynard,
C. F. Trigg,
O. P. Temple.

Oliver P. Temple, *East Tennessee and the Civil War* (Cincinnati, 1899), 191; Knoxville *Whig*, May 4, 1861.

1. James S. Boyd, John Williams, and Robert H. Armstrong. Boyd (1802–1884), a Virginia native, was an Opposition party state senator (1859–61) representing Knox and Roane counties. A merchant in Carmi, Illinois (1833–55), he moved to Campbell's Station, Knox County, and became a farmer. After the war, he served as county trustee (1870–72). Armstrong (1825–1896), son of Drury P. Armstrong and an American party member, served in the house (1855–61). For Williams, see *Johnson Papers*, II, 317–18n; Robison, *Preliminary Directory, Knox*, 6, 17.

2. On June 8, 1861, East Tennessee voted against secession, 32,923–14,780. Campbell, *Tenn. Attitudes*, 291–92.

From Robert Johnson

Nashville Tennessee April 29th 1861

Dear Father

Since writing you on Saturday, I have no additional news to write you— The Legislature is now in Session, *Secret*, and doing nothing—[1] I have no doubt but what an ordinance of Secession will be enacted in a few days, which may be left to a vote of the people, but doubtful— The only thing that will induce them to do so, will be, that they are afraid of rebellion and Civil war within the limits of the State which would be the case, and in all probability the people will rebel in any event—

The excitement is cooling down here and I believe a reaction will take place if the people have time to reflect and reason the matter over with themselves— The Union members held a meeting at my room last night, they are few, but determined to stand to the last— We will vote against all of their propositions[2] & as soon as an ordinance of Secession is passed, will leave, protesting against all the proceedings of the Legislature, including its secret sessions &c[.]

I find a pretty strong Union feeling existing here, but it is silenced by the mob and dare not express their sentiments—but the time will come when the usurpers and despots will be hurled from power and place, by an outraged people— I am for East Tennessee holding on, and never enter the Southern Confederacy— I never will, so help me God, be bound down by Jeff Davis &Co— Dr Jennings[3] & R. J. Meigs Esq called to see me yesterday— they are perfectly furious — Meigs is preparing to go to California—[4] I have had a great many Union men to call on me, but they are all alarmed and afraid to say anything on the street— Herman Cox still stands firm[.]

I will be at home sometime during the present week and I will give you in detail the exact state of things going on here—[5]

Etheridge made a speech at Trenton last Monday, which is said to be the most bitter speech ever heard fall from the lips of man— he was not permitted to speak at Paris—[6]

Yours &c   R J

I will write to morrow[.]

ALS, DLC-JP.

1. On April 18 Governor Harris called the legislature into a second extra session which convened a week later. His opening message requested a declaration of independence and a union with the Confederacy. Because of "grave and solemn matters" to be considered, and "with a view to the public safety," both houses elected to hold secret sessions, the legislators recalling that the Declaration of Independence and the Constitution had been framed behind "closed doors" and that the U. S. Senate frequently resorted to executive session beyond public view. On May 3 Robert Johnson moved to rescind secret sessions, but the motion was laid over indefinitely. Three days later the Assembly passed an ordinance providing for a referendum on a declaration of independence and a bill to raise a provisional army. *Tenn. Acts*, 1861, Ch. I; 2nd Extra Sess., Ch. III; *Tenn. House Journal*, 1861, 2nd Extra Sess., 12–13, 48, 63, 105; White, *Messages*, V, 278–89.

2. In addition to voting against the convention bill, the sixteen determined unionist representatives, virtually all from East Tennessee, voted against proposals to raise a provisional force (H. R. No. 1), to appoint commissioners to form a military league with the Confederacy (Senate Res. No. 18), and to nullify all Tennessee debts to citizens of nonslaveholding states. Although most of these unionists tardily returned after the legislature's May 9–June 17 recess, Robert Johnson and James Britton continued to absent themselves. Daniel Trewhitt of Hamilton County failed to report to this session at all. *Tenn. House Journal*, 1861, 2nd Extra Sess., 32, 57, 43, 60.

3. Thomas R. Jennings, former state senator and professor of anatomy at the University of Nashville. See *Johnson Papers*, I, 57n; *Nashville Bus. Dir.* (1860–61), 200.

4. Meigs shortly resigned his office as state librarian. Isham G. Harris to Senate and House, June 18, 1861, in White, *Messages*, V, 310.

5. Johnson was now in Greeneville.

6. Unionist Emerson Etheridge spoke at Trenton on April 19, but was prevented from doing so at Paris four days later by an eruption of disorder in which a number of persons were wounded and one killed. Memphis *Avalanche*, April 20, 1861; Gideon J. Pillow to L. P. Walker, April 24, 1861, *OR*, Ser. 1, LII, Pt. II, 69.

From Sullivan County Citizens[1]

Blountville, Tenn., May 6, 1861.

Messrs. Nelson and Johnson: ——

Hon. Sirs:

The citizens of our county, learning by your handbill, that you intend speaking in our town on to-morrow, the 7th inst., called a large meeting to-day in their Court House, and with absolute unanimity passed a resolution requesting you not to speak in our county. We were appointed a committee to make known this request to you, which request we most respectfully urge you to consider in view of the excited state of the public mind. Believe us, sirs, we intend no disrespect.

L. F. Johnson, Chrm.[2]

Knoxville *Whig*, May 18, 1861.

1. Johnson and Nelson were scheduled to appear in Blountville. According to Brownlow, *"their own friends,"* alarmed by the recent burning of a unionist's house and fearing for their personal safety, prepared this letter sent to intercept them as they arrived by train at Bluff City. David Sullins, a Methodist minister and one of the signers, recalled many years later that, when it was discovered that Johnson and Nelson, accompanied by the latter's son David and son-in-law Samuel Cunningham, were traveling by private conveyance, he rode out to warn them about the mood of the crowd, which was equipped with shotguns and "a good deal of whiskey." Pausing at the outskirts of town while the wishes of the assemblage were ascertained, and determining that only four persons favored their speaking, they proceeded to Kingsport. Knoxville *Whig*, May 18, 1861; David Sullins, *Recollections of an Old Man: Seventy Years in Dixie, 1827–1897* (Bristol, 1910), 192–97.

2. The letter was signed by forty-two others, including William Gammon, secretary.

[To Amos A. Lawrence,[1] Boston, Mass.]

Knoxville Tenn May 15th, 1861.

Amos A. Lawrence Esqr
(Near) Boston Mass.

Dr Sir:

I received your kind favor on yesterday & hasten to reply.

Thank you for the high regard you Seem to have for my patriotism & my devotion to my country.

What assurances can I have from you & your people of *material aid*, in the way of money, men & arms, if I can succeed in arousing any people to resistance to this damnable treason in the South? This is very important. We have a formidable union element in East Tennessee which can be judiciously managed if we can obtain the aid alluded to. Harris, Governor of this State, will not let us have arms nor money—therefore, we *must appeal* to you.

Let me hear from you forthwith.

Very Respy Yr. Obt. Svt.
Andrew Johnson

L [forgery], DLC-JP2.

1. This is the first installment of a "correspondence" between Johnson and Amos A. Lawrence, New England businessman and philanthropist. The Lawrence letters are authentic, even though not all were received by the senator; all three of the "Johnson" letters [May 15, 23, June 6] were forgeries written by Knoxville Postmaster Charles W. Charlton in a shrewd scheme to elicit financial assistance for the Harris regime. Charlton, engaged in monitoring the mail of Brownlow and other unionists, had intercepted a Lawrence letter, now lost, offering sympathy and "*material aid*" to East Tennessee. According to Charlton's apologia in 1870, a local "committee"—members not identified— decided that Lawrence's letter was "a *vital* one, for it looked to the *sudden arming* of an *enraged* population, and, as a result, a terrible civil revolution in our own midst." With this excuse the committee, "guided by a profound conviction of duty," decided to reply "in order to get further information concerning so momentous a movement." Protesting that what he did was done by the committee's "dictation and their approval," he concluded, "If we did wrong it was one of the errors of an exciting period, when passion swayed the judgment, and when indiscretion got the better of prudence." At no point did he allude to what Brownlow in 1861 denounced as an effort "to steal money upon the credit of Johnson's name and political position, from a Northern Capitalist." Knoxville *Whig*, August 10, 1861, June 22, 1870.

Speech at Elizabethton[1]

May 15, 1861

He commenced at the beginning of this Southern exasperated state of feeling and traced it on up to the present day. He showed most conclusively that the whole affair was conceived in sin and wickedness, and nurtured and brought forth in iniquity. He told the people that the first secession movement that there is any account given of took place in the Garden of Eden, where the serpent beguiled our fore-parents and made them eat of the forbidden fruit, after which they seceded and retired from all the enjoyments which had been placed before them in Paradise. He said that Judas, after he had betrayed our Saviour for the thirty pieces of silver, also seceded, and immediately put an end to his existence. He showed most plainly that no State, under the National Constitution, had any authority whatever to secede from the General Government, which had been erected and sanctioned by all the States.[2]

Louisville *Journal*, May 23, 1861.

1. Upon arrival Johnson and T. A. R. Nelson were escorted to the public square and presented with "Union badges" in a ceremony "conducted by a coterie of the ladies . . . whose fair hands had constructed them in a most tasteful and elegant manner." Although Johnson, preceded by Nelson's two-hour oration, spoke for something over three hours, only these few sentences were reported.

2. Nathaniel G. Taylor then spoke briefly. See *Johnson Papers*, II, 229n.

From Amos A. Lawrence[1]

(Near)   Boston. May 18. 61.

Dear Sir   If yr note to me were printed in our newspapers it would be good for Ten Thousand dollars in three days time. But of course I must only use it as a private letter.

In order that you shall be sure of something at once I write below this a draft[2] wh. some of yr Union bankers or merchants may be willing to take at the usual prem. for Eastn. exchange. Probably Gardner & Co, Evans & Co, Douglass & Co[3] of Nashville will know it.

The Govt. will soon exhibit a power wh. will astonish even you. The Nullifiers have been playing into Scott's hand for three weeks & now they have lost the game.

Yrs with regd   Amos A Lawrence

Boston. May 18th, 1861. At sight without grace pay to Andrew Johnson on order One Thousand dollars for value recieved & charge to my account.[4]

Amos A Lawrence

Messrs Mason & Lawrence & Co[5] Boston.

Let. Bk. Copy, MHi-Amos A. Lawrence Papers; also Copy, DLC-JP2.

1. This and other "Letters written by Seces[s]ion[ists] Charlton, Haynes and others—the Lawrence Correspondence—" were "Captured with the effects of Isham G. Harris," probably when Nashville fell to the Federals in 1862, and thus found their way into the Johnson Papers. Undated endorsement, Johnson Papers, Ser. 2, LC.

2. Scrawled across the top of the letter is the notation: "If you cannot use this draft, return & tell me what to send."

3. All three firms were wholesale dry-goods establishments located on the public square.

4. Across the face of the draft is written, "Accepted Mason Lawrence & Co."

5. Robert M. Mason and Amos Lawrence had formed a partnership as Boston commission merchants in 1843; eventually Mason ceased activity, but Lawrence continued to use the name. The firm became the selling agency for many textile enterprises, especially the Pacific Mills at Lawrence, for many years the largest of their kind in the United States. *DAB*, XI, 47.

From Amos A. Lawrence

Boston. May. 22. 61.

Dear Sir

A meeting of gentlemen has just been held at my office[1] to consider the subject of maintain'g the Union men in E. Tenn. & a comee. of three consistg. of Mr Edw. Everett,[2] Judge Parker[3] & Judge Hoar[4] was chosen to urge the necessity of support upon the Nat. Govt. They are now writing a letter to the Prest. This will all be done in a manner not to come before the public.

I have a letter from Mr A. T. Stewart[5] of N. Y. who will bring it before the "Union Defence Comee"[6] of the State. This too will be done so as not to create difficulty for you at home.

You must have some more money & I hope to send you a mod. sum.

Yours respy & truly
Amos A. Lawrence

Hon. And. Johnson. Knoxville.

Let. Bk. Copy, MHi-Amos A. Lawrence Papers. [Intercepted in Knoxville post office; see Letter from Amos A. Lawrence, May 15, 1861.]

1. An attached memorandum, signed by fourteen prominent men, recorded "that a crisis exists in East Tennessee" and recommended that "citizens of Massachusetts" contribute to the Union cause. A second page lists twenty-one contributors and the amounts, totaling $1,760, pledged "to sustain Andrew Johnson & the Union men of Tenn." Amos A. Lawrence Papers, Massachusetts Historical Society.

2. Edward Everett (1794–1865) of Massachusetts, perhaps most widely known for the extended dedicatory oration which preceded Lincoln's pithy Gettysburg Address, had a long and varied career. Unitarian minister, Harvard professor, and editor of the *North American Review*, he had served as congressman (1825–35), governor (1836–40), minister to Great Britain (1841–45), president of Harvard (1846–49), secretary of state (1852–53), senator (1853) and vice-presidential candidate on the Constitutional Union ticket in 1860. In 1864 Everett chaired a committee which raised more than $100,000 "for the relief of the loyal and suffering East Tennesseans." *DAB*, VI, 223–26; *BDAC*, 870; Everett, *Account of the Fund for the Relief of East Tennessee* (Boston, 1864).

3. Joel Parker (1795–1875), New Hampshire-born jurist, had been a state legislator (1824–26) and chief justice of the state supreme court (1838–47) before his appointment as Royall Professor of Law at Harvard (1847–68). Parker was the author of numerous books on legal and political subjects, including *Personal Liberty Laws (Statutes of Massachusetts) and Slavery in the Territories* (Boston, 1861), and *The Right of Secession* (Cambridge, 1861). *DAB*, XIV, 230–31; *NCAB*, XII, 113.

4. Ebenezer R. Hoar (1816–1895), brother of Congressman George F. Hoar, was Massachusetts state supreme court judge (1859–69), U. S. attorney general (1869–70), and congressman (1873–75). *BDAC*, 1060.

5. Alexander T. Stewart (1803–1876), Irish-born merchant, had come to New York about 1820. From a small inheritance he imported Irish lace

and established what became a successful wholesale and dry-goods business, opening in 1862 the world's largest retail store, which counted among its customers some of the country's wealthiest and most fashionable people. Increasing his wealth and influence with lucrative army and navy contracts, he also acquired a controlling interest in numerous New England textile mills. Throughout his lifetime a supporter of many causes, he contributed generously during the war to the sanitary commission. *DAB*, XVIII, 3–5.

6. Composed of prominent New Yorkers and chaired by John A. Dix, this committee had been organized soon after April 20, when a large public meeting was held in Union Square to raise funds, supplies, equipment, and troops during the national emergency created by the fall of Sumter. Stewart was a member of the committee, which ultimately disbursed over $1,000,000 appropriated by the city government; it also served as an executive arm of the Federal government during the mobilization effort. DeAlva S. Alexander, *A Political History of New York* (4 vols., New York, 1906–23), III, 7–8; *American Annual Cyclopaedia* (1861), 533–34.

[*To Amos A. Lawrence, Boston, Mass.*]

Knoxville Tenn May 23, 1861

Amos A. Lawrence Esqr
(Near) Boston, Mass.
Dr Sir:

Yr letter came promptly to hand, containing draft for $1000.— For the *present* it would not do to attempt to have it cashed, as I would be *suspected*. All my movements are narrowly watched by *certain men*— However, I will still retain it, &, if I can use it, safely, hereafter, I will do so.

If I could command $5000—or $10,000—Say $10,000—[1] I have no doubt I could hold this State onto the *Federal Union*. Such enthusiasm you have never witnessed, as is exhibited throughout the State in behalf of our cause. Besides our election comes off on the 8th of June, & much is to be done in the meantime.

Let me, therefore, suggest that you send me $10,000—in Northern or Southern Currency in *large bills, not* by express, but in a letter *through the mails*.[2] Thus I can get the money, use it, & *run no risk.* DO IT PROMPTLY! ! I am making speeches daily to *immense crowds.*

Yur Obt. Svt. Andrew Johnson.

Can you give us no assurance that we can get men & guns before the 8th of June? Keep me advised.   A. J.

L [forgery], DLC-JP2.

1. On the following day Charlton, transmitting to his friend Governor Harris Lawrence's communication of May 18, observed: "another letter from Amos A. Lawrence to Andrew Johnson. I hope I may so mannage this matter as to Secure, *at least*, $10,000 for the use of the State! *Time will develop!*" Harris, much less inclined to mince words, noted on the envelope, "Charlton hopes to steal $10000 from Lawrence." Charlton to Harris, May 24, 1861, Johnson Papers, Ser. 2, LC.

2. Aware that he risked personal exposure if he attempted to forge Johnson's signature on a draft to be honored in Tennessee, Charlton now resorted
to a request for cash, with the significant reminder that it be sent *"through
the mails."*

From John W. Ford

Chattanooga May 25. 1861.

(*Private*)

Hon Andrew Johnson
Dear Sir:

Hood of the "Gazette" who went to Washington for the purpose
of trying to get the Post-office here has returned, and says that he will
be appointed about the first April and that you have recommended
him. I do not believe this for two reasons: First: I know you have
not ben in the habit of recommending men for office who have always
belonged to the opposition party of Tennessee, under all its *aliases*—
2d—I do not believe that you would recommend any man for the
office of Post-Master here, with the view of ousting the present
worthy Democratic incumbent, who has always ben your friend—[1]

After the disruption of the Charleson Convention Hood published
an Editorial which I clipped from his paper, and Commented upon
in the Reflector of the 8th May[2]—and which I herewith enclose to
you— You will see that he therein denounced you "as the embodiment of political depravity"—"for years advocating doctrines worse
than Sewards"— I have no doubt that while at Washington, he was
playing the *todie* around you—but you could not fail to know his
motive— He is a great liar and will stoop to any low device to accomplish his ends.— I have as an old friend felt it to be my duty to
write you this much in reference to him—

I have also clipped an Editorial article from the Reflector of the
15th May, in which I defend "My Political position,"—[3] I do this
for the reason, that I have not the least doubt but what the hungry
office hunters from Chattanooga, have represented me to be a Secessionist.— I occupy the same grounds now that I occupied in that
article.— if that article makes me a Secessionist then I am one, not
otherwise.—

I am as ever, *truly*
Your *friend*   John W. Ford

ALS, DLC-JP.
   1. Harvey T. Phillips.
   2. This issue of Ford's *Hamilton Reflector* is not extant.
   3. This editorial has not survived.

From Jeptha Fowlkes

Nashville Ten. May 29. 1861.

Private
Hon. A. Johnson
My dear Sir:

I shall go to Richmond Va. in 2 or 3 days—passing by Greenville Te. It is very important that I see you— I have much valuable information for you; without which you can't correctly shape your own course. The State, will certainly go out, by a large vote—on 8th. great personal hostility exists toward you in West & Middle Tennessee— So much so, that, I do not believe you could Safely travel over; even the R.R. lines passing through these two sections without indignity, if not violence! I want to see you, Nelson & Brownlow![1] You have resisted the action of the State to the largest extent in yr. power & unsuccessfully! The die is cast & irrevocably! Resistance to *the will* of state, as expressed at Ballot-box cannot avail; & it will bring to you Consequences to be avoided; & I will if possible stop & interchange with you such views, as I have on the subject. I beg you will until I can see you, avoid all controversies, & all Collisions of whatsoever character! I mean the full import of my suggestions— one, of two lines of policy, are left, in my judgment! A separation is now irresistable! After the vote is cast,—& state, is out, opposition & resistence to the Southern movement, will not be tolerated! our people are a unit. 40.000 troops can be concentrated upon Miss: within a few hours! 1.500.000 men are really drilling in the South! with the bitterest feeling of hostility to the North.— I repeat a separation & two or more govemts are, now, inevitable! Ground your arms until I can see you. Can't you meet me at Knoxville? It may be pregnant with consequences, that I see you in person & soon. Within 3 days I shall be at Knoxville. Meet me with Nelson if practicable.

Yr. fnd.   J. Fowlkes

ALS, DLC-JP.

1. According to Postmaster Charlton, Fowlkes acted "very improperly" during his visit to Knoxville in early June, seeking an interview with Brownlow, Temple, and others, and being "closeted with them *that day* & *night*." The doctor "left *next morning*, without seeing a single *Southern Rights man*! He acknowledged that he had shown Brownlow a Copy of the Boston letter" —a disclosure "Exceedingly unfortunate, for Johnson will know all about it so soon as he (B) can communicate with him." Late in the summer Brownlow publicly applauded his "personal friend" Dr. Fowlkes, who although a secessionist, was "liberal, generous, and kind," having "come here to East Tennessee upon a mission of mercy." Charles W. Charlton to Isham Harris, June 6, 1861, Johnson Papers, LC; Knoxville *Whig*, August 24, 1861.

From Amos A. Lawrence[1]

(near) Boston, May 29. 61.

Dear Sir

I have already written you that some gentlemen here have requested a com[mitt]ee consisting of Mr Everett, Judge Thomas[2] & Judge Hoar (both of the Supreme Court—) to address a letter to the Govt. at Washn. in behalf of yr people. Also that Mr Stewart of N Y a member of the Union Defence Comee has brought the subject before that Comee. Whether your friends have derived any encouragement from either of these sources, I am not informed.

An appeal from the Union men of Tenn. publishd in our newspapers wd call out "material aid" if that were wanted. In fact I have something wh. has been placed in my hands already, but am at a loss to know how to send it to you, or to yr friends. I sent something but have not learned whether it was recd.

You will soon see & feel the majesty of the Govt. The people are united to a man North of the Potomac. Money is abundant at 6% & the Govt. can have any am't. Provisions are cheap, some kinds (fish for instance) lower than ever before. And every man is ready to march. The women even wear uniform & go thro. the drill, & practice target shooting.[3] We "Union" men denounce our Mr Bell as a traitor, & the Breckinridgers denounce Breckinridge.[4]

Resp'y & truly Yrs
Amos A Lawrence

Hon. Andrew Johnson, Tenn.

ALS, DLC-JP; Let. Bk. Copy, MHi-Amos A. Lawrence Papers.

1. Although Johnson makes no reference to this letter in his June 25 communication to Lawrence, this copy, at least, did not fall into Charlton's hands; probably it was waiting for the senator when he returned to Washington on June 21, inasmuch as his usual endorsement, "Amos A. Lawrence Attended to," appears on the envelope. See Letter to Amos A. Lawrence, June 6, 1861, note 1.

2. Benjamin F. Thomas (1813–1878), a Massachusetts lawyer and compiler of *Thomas' Town Officer: A Digest of the Laws of Massachusetts . . .* (rev. ed., Worcester, 1856), was state legislator (1842), state supreme court judge (1853–59), and congressman (1861–63). There is no explanation for Lawrence's mention of Thomas, instead of Judge Joel Parker, as a committee member. A letter from Secretary of War Cameron to the committee in June and Lawrence's letter of May 23 clearly indicate that Everett, Parker, and Hoar constituted the committee. *BDAC*, 1702–3; *NCAB*, V, 220; Cameron to Everett, Parker, and Hoar, "Committee of the Citizens of Boston," June 13, 1861, Edward Everett Papers, Massachusetts Historical Society.

3. Although it would be difficult to document this sweeping statement concerning feminine military activities north of the Potomac, the New York *Herald* of April 29 reported that a women's drill team had been organized in that city. Mary E. Massey, *Bonnet Brigades* (New York, 1966), 39.

4. Both the Constitutional Unionists, a sizeable group in New England, and the Breckinridge Democrats, a significantly smaller number, were becoming disillusioned as Bell and Breckinridge appeared to be moving toward secession. Despite his protestations of loyalty, Bell was charged with disunionism: "When he undertakes to say that in a certain anticipated contingency Tennessee must take up arms against the Union, he openly advises treason." Boston *Advertiser*, May 9, 1861.

[*To Amos A. Lawrence, Boston, Mass.*]

Knoxville Tenn June 6. 1861

Amos A Lawrence Esqr
(near) Boston, Mass
My dear Sir:

I receied your two letters to day.[1] Thank you, most sincerely, for your proffered aid. We need it—need it badly. As yet I have not been able to use your draft—am afraid to do so. Send me, if you can, 5 or $10,000 in New England Currency in *large bills, by mail*, via, *Cincinnatti*. Be sure to do it *promptly*. *Do not delay*. I Can now purchase a lot of arms if I had the means.

How do you propose to introduce aid or arms into E. Tennessee? By what *route*, & by what method? Answer Soon.[2]

Respectfully Yr Obt Svt.
Andrew Johnson.

L [forgery], Copy enclosed in Charles W. Charlton to Isham G. Harris, June 6, 1861; DLC-JP2.

1. Probably the Lawrence letters of May 22 and 29. Although neither is found in the cache of Charlton letters captured with Harris' effects in Nashville, they are the only possible Lawrence letters still to be acknowledged at this date, inasmuch as Charlton's forgery of May 23 had already dealt with Lawrence's message of May 18. That the May 29 communication reached Johnson late in June (see Letter from Amos A. Lawrence, May 29, 1861, note 1) may perhaps be explained by Lawrence's having dispatched two identical letters, one addressed to the senator in Washington and the other to Knoxville, indicating his uncertainty about Johnson's whereabouts.

From André Froment

June 8, 1861, New York, N. Y.; ALS, DLC-JP.

A representative of the New York City Common Council desires to send Johnson an engraved copy of resolutions saluting him as "most 'faithful, among the faithless' . . . the uncompromising friend of the Union" who "by his patriotic course . . . has endeared himself to every Union-loving citizen thrughout the land"; invites him to "accept the hospitalities" of the city with the assurance that "the use of the Governors Room [would] be tendered to him for the purpose of receiving the calls of his friends and countrymen."

From Knox County (Ky.) Citizens

June 10, 1861, Barbourville, Ky.; ALS, DLC-JP.

George M. Adams, Sr., and thirteen others, believing it unsafe for Johnson to travel to Washington through Virginia, suggest that he go via Cumberland Gap and stop in Barbourville; given three days' notice, "our people would flock from all parts of the Country to See, & hear from one of the Champions of Constitutional liberty."

From Amos A. Lawrence[1]

Boston. June 14. 61.

Dear Sir

Please to indicate the way by wh. you can recieve a good supply of arms. Probably via Cincinnati will be most convenient.

Enclose yr letter to some friend in Washn. who will deliver it at once to Mr Cameron,[2] & address this letter to Mr Edw. Everett with the request to have it opened by Mr Cameron. If you choose, you can address the letter to Mr Cameron himself. What you want will be forwarded at once. I have just the assurance in writing from the right quarter & through Mr Everett that you will have all the arms you require.

The money in my hands of wh. I advised you will pay freight.

This is sent to Edw. N. Maxwell[3] of Louisville to be forwarded. Probably Larz Anderson[4] of Cincinnati will be glad to do anything in that quarter.

Respecty. & truly Yrs
Amos A Lawrence.

Hon. And. Johnson, Tenn.

Let. Bk. Copy, MHi-Amos A. Lawrence Papers.

1. This is the second of the Lawrence letters (see Letter from Amos A. Lawrence, May 29, 1861) which did not fall into the hands of the Charlton "committee"; nor, for that matter, does it appear to have reached Johnson.

2. Simon Cameron, secretary of war.

3. Edward N. Maxwell, publisher of the 1859–60 Louisville, Kentucky, directory, was a printer and proprietor of Maxwell & Co., booksellers and stationers at 451 Main Street. Martin F. Schmidt, "The Early Printers of Louisville, 1800–1860," *Filson Quarterly*, XL (1960), 328.

4. Larz Anderson (1803–1878), elder brother of Sumter's defender Maj. Robert Anderson, was a Harvard graduate and Cincinnati attorney whose five sons served in the Union army. Alfred Tischendorf and E. Taylor Parks, eds., *The Diary and Journal of Richard Clough Anderson, Jr., 1814–1826* (Durham, N. C., 1964), xxvi; Charles T. Greve, *Centennial History of Cincinnati* (2 vols., Chicago, 1904), I, 837; *Williams' Cincinnati Directory* (1861), 41.

From John T. Jones[1]

Harrison Tenn June 15th 1861.

Hon. Andrew Johnson
Dear Sir

My only apology for adressing you at the present time is the deep interest I feel, and the strong desire I entertain for the honor and Loyalty of East Tenn. and knowing you to be a faithful champion of the laws and the Constitution and true to our Federal Government I have thus made free to write my present sentiments and what I believe to be the sentiments of much the largest portion of our citizens— for your inspection—

And First we feel that East Tennesseeans should take a bold and independant stand against the corrupt proceedings of our state Legislature and the dictations of Gov Harris. That we disregard in *toto* the result of the mock election of June the 8th.[2]—and mantain at all hazards our integrity to the Federal Union its Constitution and laws. That we seperate from the disloyal and rebellious divisions of the state and establish our selves as a new & loyal State in the Federal union—Can we not do it? Shall we not do it? I do hope our convention at Greenville[3] will take some descisive steps in the matter. Cut us loosse from middle and west Tennessee though I doubt not if they had not been intimidated they would have stood by the Union.

East Tenn has not and I yet believe can not be intimidated and emasculated with our 19 or 20 thousand majority for the Union or against Secession— let us organize a State—a new State will it do? Is it not right?— We anticipate some definite action on the part of our convention—Some concentration of the union elements of East Tennessee in such a manner as will secure at least a degree of safety—

Our people will not tamely submit to the oppressive and degrading exactions that will no doubt be attemped to be imposed by the Rebel leaders in Tenn— We will fight—If not by and under the authority of State or Federal Government—then by *Guerilla bands*— on our "*own hook*"[.][4] I have all ready a company of one hundred and fifty ready to die, rather than submit to the reign of corruption now being exercised, and will I doubt not only in a more agravated manner continue to be exercised over us—

In the name of Heaven urge upon the Convention the necessity of Loyal and energetic action— Let us never submit to the debased leaders of the Rebellion[.]

Yrs Truly   J. T. Jones

ALS, TKL.

1. John T. Jones (b. *c*1821) was a Virginia-born physician with $2,000 personal property. 1860 Census, Tenn., Hamilton, 7th Dist., 153.

2. At Harris' bidding, the legislature had passed on May 6 "An act to submit to a vote of the people a Declaration of Independence" which stipulated that Tennesseans were to go to the polls June 8 to choose between "separation" and "no separation" from the Union. Without waiting for the popular vote, the governor continued his headlong rush to align Tennessee with the Confederacy: military appointments were made and confirmed, a defensive position planned and implemented, and volunteer companies received into military service. Two-thirds of the state appeared predominantly Confederate, but East Tennessee, demonstrating a strong Union sentiment, saw its political leaders—men like Johnson, Nelson, Brownlow, Thomas Arnold, and Oliver P. Temple—speaking out forcefully in a series of rallies and in the well-publicized Knoxville convention of May 30–31. Although the balloting showed a majority of about 55,000 for "separation," loss of both the official returns and the recorded vote of several counties lends credence to the view that chicanery was not absent in the hard-fought referendum. Out of thousands of ballots cast, Shelby and Lauderdale counties returned only five and seven votes respectively for "no separation," while Franklin, Humphreys, and Lincoln reported not a single "union" ballot. Middle and West Tennessee favored "separation" at a ratio of 7–1 and 4–1, while East Tennessee took the opposite stand by more than 2–1. Temple, *East Tennessee*, 179–223, 340–43; White, *Messages*, V, 289–306.

3. When the Knoxville convention reassembled in Greeneville on June 17, a new set of conditions prevailed. What had been termed "opposition" before June 8 could now be labeled "treason"; evidence of disagreement with majority opinion, whether overt or covert, could endanger one's safety and that of family and friends. Nevertheless, according to Oliver P. Temple, a major participant, the delegates were in a defiant mood. How should such strongly felt opposition be exhibited? Temple was gratified that, as the four-day meeting progressed, emotions cooled and a carefully worded, yet contemptuous, set of resolutions won approval. Condemning as "Unconstitutional and illegal" the action of the General Assembly "looking to a separation of Tennessee from the Government of the United States," and deploring the prospect of civil war, the delegates sought the legislature's consent to the creation of a separate state composed of the counties of "East Tennessee, and such other counties in Middle Tennessee as desire to co-operate with them." On June 29 the legislature unanimously rejected the memorial because the men assembled at Greeneville had not been "selected with the view to the formation of East Tennessee into a new State," nor had the elections of February 9 and June 8 constituted referendums upon the question of separate statehood. Temple, *East Tennessee*, 343–65; White, *Messages*, V, 311–15.

4. A colloquial expression, common in the mid-nineteenth century—found in *Uncle Tom's Cabin* (1852) and in *Tom Brown at Oxford* (1861)—even as in the twentieth, to describe one who takes action independently, without anyone else's authorization. *OED*, V, 374.

Speech at Lexington, Kentucky[1]

June 18, 1861

He openly charged that the Secessionists of the State were aiming to subvert the liberty of the people & establish Kingly Govt. styled Govr. Harris King Harris & said the secessionists called him King.

He denounced the late Legislature as subsidized & corrupted by the Govr. & held secret sessions the better to enable them to carry out their nefarious designs— That the vote on secession was control'd by armed bands of soldiers & that the reign of terror was in force—[2] that E. Tennessee would resist the State & fight for the Union, if they could procure arms— Arms was all he wanted & Tennessee would triumphantly reject the Southern Dictator & support the stars & stripes.

He said if Despotism were approaching at all as he believed it was, that it was approaching from the South & not from the North. That the South had made the North our ennemies, by its unjust conduct— That if Lincoln were to blame at all, it was not because he had done too much to sustain the Union, but because he had not done enough[.]

He denounced & condemned every act of the seceding States & Confederate Govt. & every prominent man connected with them, as traitors ambitious, unprincipled & conspired to subvert liberty and establish despotism. He knew the men well & named a long list—

Jeff Davis he said was infanitely worse than Cataline—[3] He was Cataline without Catalines good traits. Cataline had some good traits Davis had not one. He was equally bitter agst Govr. Harris & associates of the *secret Legislature* of Tennessee & the leading secessionists of the state.

It is understood that his object is to obtain arms & pass them thro Ky. to E. Tennessee— He appealed to Ky to stand firm & join Tennessee to plant the stars & stripes on the intermediate mountains, the highest peak, & fight & gloriously die if necessary, together (Ky & Tennessee) for the Union.[4]

* * * * * * *

He declared that sooner than submit to the Southern Confederacy & call Davis or Harris Master, he would yield to the Autocrat of Russia—that then he would be *subject to one he would be proud to call master.*

* * * * * * *

He said he was no fugitive—tho he had heard that the Govr. of Tennessee had issued a warrant for him as a traitor.[5] Whether true or not he did not know—nor did he care or trouble himself about it. He denied the letter to A. Lawrence[6]—but eulogised the act of Lawrence in giving money to preserve the Union. That if the Govr had such a letter it was robbed from the mail & he was a robber— If there were no such letter, there was forgery to injure an innocent man. Robbery or forgery was inevitable[.] Such were the evils consequent upon the doctrine of Secession.[7]

ALS, Nicholas D. Coleman, June 19, 1861, to "Dear Sir," DLC-JP.

1. Unreported in the press but preserved in the letter of an unfriendly auditor, this three-hour speech was widely applauded and frequently mentioned during the following weeks; together with others delivered "along the Mountain route from E. Tennessee to this place," it was a source of encouragement to Kentucky unionists at a crucial time in the state's deliberations over secession. A future Missouri governor, Thomas T. Crittenden, visiting in Lexington at the time, later wrote nostalgically, "I don't think it has ever been exceeded in patriotism, pathos and force in the United States," adding that it gave the Union men "more unity and backbone than had been displayed before." The barebones version offered here was written by Nicholas D. Coleman, who felt it his duty not only to report Johnson's "most vindictive hatred and hostility towards the South and all men who are for the South" but also to reveal that "he contemplates the blackest treason against the sovereignty of Tennessee." Coleman (1800–1874), a native Kentucky lawyer and Jacksonian congressman (1829–31) who migrated to Mississippi in 1837, served as Vicksburg postmaster (1837–50) and prospered as attorney, commission merchant, and railroad promoter before moving to New Orleans (c1855). A member of the state senate in 1861, he opposed disunion until Louisiana joined the Confederacy. Although it cannot be ascertained precisely when Johnson acquired this document, he did not forget the author; in September, 1865, when Coleman came to Washington seeking a pardon, the President had him placed under the strictest surveillance and refused his request. Coleman to "Dear Sir," June 19, 1861, Johnson Papers, LC; "Selections from the Autobiography of Governor T. T. Crittenden, Part I," *Missouri Historical Review*, XXVI (1931), 10; *BDAC*, 721; James T. McIntosh, ed., *The Papers of Jefferson Davis* (2 vols., Baton Rouge, 1971–   ), II, 159n; Lafayette C. Baker, *History of the United States Secret Service* (Philadelphia, 1867), 586–88.

2. Given the temper of the times, it is difficult to assess with accuracy these allegations. The same line of argument was followed by the Greeneville Convention, whose meeting, held nine days after the June 8 election, coincided with Johnson's speech; in its "Declaration of Grievances" the convention maintained that, "with but few exceptions," the canvass was free only in East Tennessee; elsewhere, particularly in "the larger parts of Middle and West Tennessee," speeches and discussions advocating the Union cause were forbidden, unionist papers not allowed to circulate, and Union ballots made public in an election ostensibly conducted by secret vote. Moreover, the unanimity of the secession return in many large counties where but a few weeks previously Union sentiment was strong "proves beyond doubt, that Union men were overawed by the tyranny of the military power and the still greater tyranny of a corrupt and subsidized press." A modern historian, attesting to the pressure exerted in Middle and West Tennessee, notes the determination of the Nashville disunionists that there should be no opportunity "to vote secretly for Union" and points out that in numerous localities "Military companies added to the hysteria of the occasions." *Proc. E. Tenn. Conv.* (Greeneville), 20; Hamer, *Tennessee*, II, 548–49.

3. Lucius Sergius Catilina (c108–62 B.C.), a Roman aristocrat who had been both praetor and governor of Africa, planned two conspiracies. The first, in 65 B.C., was rumored to be a plot to murder the consuls and seize control of the government; the second, which followed his failure to be elected consul in 63, an armed insurrection. *Encyclopaedia Britannica* (1971 ed.), V, 83.

4. At this point Coleman remarked, "In his speech he cautiously felt his way & finding his audience to suit he poured out all his bitterness the amount of which against the South really astounded Me. The audience was largely Union & gotten up by active efforts—messengers musick & a flourish. Those of us who are southern attended to know from his own words, the true objects of his mission[.]"

5. The Knoxville *Whig*, May 25, 1861, claimed that Johnson, Nelson,

Baxter, Temple, Maynard, Trigg, Brownlow, and George W. Bridges, if captured, were to be taken "in irons" to Montgomery, where they would be tried for treason or held as hostages.

6. The attack on Johnson for trafficking with the abolitionist Amos A. Lawrence had appeared in the Richmond *Enquirer* on June 11. The senator, innocent of any correspondence with the Bostonian, could sincerely and indignantly deny complicity. See Letter from Amos A. Lawrence, June 22, 1861, note 2.

7. Eschewing further "coverage," the writer here turned his full attention to an assessment of the speech and speaker: "Much more of such stuff, constituted his address— It was a tirade of vindictive abuse—a tissue of misrepresentations from beginning to end— What I considered most outragious was his resolve to raise up armed opposition to the stand of Tennessee. The people by a large majority have voted to unite the States destinies with the Confederate States—and now one of the citizens of Tennessee is raising armed resistance to that solemn decision. It is understood that Johnston, goes this morning to Cincinnati to speak to night & make arrangements for arms. As Lincoln has furnished arms to the *secret Black Republicans of Kentucky*, which were brought, in the dead hour of the night, into the state & distributed to selected individuals, no doubt Johnston, will obtain as many as he wants for the Black Republicans of E. Tennessee—& endeavor to pass them through Kentucky, from Cincinnati." Earlier he had declared, "The whole speech was characterized by the most disgusting misrepresentations of facts & results of action; partial to the North & prejudicial agst the South—full of suppressions of truth & ingenious suggestions of falsehood thereby coloring & perverting the true state of affairs as they transpired & as they now exist."

From John R. McClanahan[1]

Memphis, June 19th 1861

Andrew Johnson Esqr
Late U.S. Senator &c.
Greenville, Tenn
Sir:

The patriotic Sense of all this portion of Tennessee being fully develloped, and that of the whole State becoming rapidly right, it has become dangerous to the persons of Traitors to remain longer within her borders. I therefore take the liberty of warning you, in the language of your friend Lincoln at Washington "to disperse in twenty days;"[2] and I suggest further, That your personal safety might require you to leave much sooner.

Our own self respect as *gentleman and freeman*, as well as a proper regard for the purity of our Commonwealth and the respectability of our State Soverignty imperatively require that you should leave Tennessee at once and forever. You can probably find a Congenial home and associations among your Northern allies.

Yours   Jno. R. McClanahan
of the Memphis Appeal

ALS, DLC-JP.

1. John R. McClanahan (c1798–1865), a native of South Carolina, was editor and copublisher of the Memphis *Appeal*, listing $5,000 real and $16,000 personal property in the most recent census. Robert Talley, *One Hundred Years of the* Commercial Appeal, *1840–1940* (Memphis, 1940), 19, 46; 1860 Census, Tenn., Shelby, 140.

2. In his proclamation calling for 75,000 volunteers, Lincoln had admonished those comprising and supporting the Confederate States of America "to disperse and retire peacefully . . . within twenty days" from April 15, 1861. John G. Nicolay and John Hay, eds., *Abraham Lincoln: Complete Works* . . . (2 vols., New York, 1920 [1894]), II, 34.

Impromptu Speech at Cincinnati[1]

June 19, 1861

Fellow-Citizens: I must confess, I was all unprepared for the manifestation of good feeling which has greeted me so unexpectedly on this occasion. I feel myself all unworthy of such a reception. ("Yes you are!") My connection with the earnest endeavors of the patriots of the land to preserve the Union of the States has been but the promptings of duty.

Each and every loyal citizen owes the same allegiance and is bound, in honor, to perform the same duty. I feel that I have endeavored to perform all that is required of me in the present crisis, and have an approving conscience. Whatever the remainder may do, one portion of my own State will stand firm by the Stars and Stripes, which you have displayed here to day. The flag which was borne by Washington—by the patriots of 1812—by Scott in the war with Mexico, must be defended in every extremity and at all hazards. I trust to God that it will yet waive in triumph over a united people.

All we ask in my portion of Tennessee is not to be invaded, but if invaded, as has been threatened, all we want is to be placed in a condition to defend ourselves and the Stars and Stripes, under which we are ready to shed our blood.

I did not intend to make a speech, but simply to return you my heartfelt thanks for this magnificent though unexpected reception. Again, gentlemen, I thank you from the bottom of my heart.

Cincinnati *Enquirer*, June 20, 1861.

1. With an alleged threat of assassination hanging over his head, Johnson was persuaded to leave Tennessee on June 12 for Washington, boldly departing by buggy in daylight on a public road via Cumberland Gap. In Kentucky the journey became a veritable triumphal procession. Arriving in Covington on June 19, he was attended by the Kanton Union Guards as a *corps d'honneur*; a band playing "Hail Columbia" conducted him from the train to a waiting carriage which, under escort of several military organizations, carried him by ferry across the Ohio to the Burnet House, where a crowd of

several thousand clamored for a speech; Johnson obliged with these impromptu remarks. Temple, *East Tennessee*, 344; Cincinnati *Enquirer*, June 20, 1861; George Fort Milton, *The Age of Hate: Andrew Johnson and the Radicals* (New York, 1930), 107.

Speech at Cincinnati[1]

June 19, 1861

Fellow-Citizens— In reply to the cordial welcome which has just been tendered to me, through your chosen organ—in reply to what has been said by the gentleman[2] chosen by you to bid me welcome to Cincinnati—I have not language adequate to express my feelings of gratitude. I cannot find language to thank you for the tender of good fellowship which has been made to me on the present occasion. I came here without any expectation that such a reception was in store for me. I had no expectation of being received and welcomed in the language, I may say the eloquent and forcible language of your chosen organ. I am deserving of no such tender, so far as I am concerned.

I might conclude what little I am going to say by merely responding to, and endorsing every single sentence which has been uttered on this occasion in welcoming me in your midst. [Applause.]

For myself I feel that while I am a citizen of a Southern State— a citizen of the South and of the State of Tennessee, I feel at the same time that I am also a citizen of the United States. [Applause.] Most cordially do I respond to what has been said in reference to the maintenance of the Constitution of the United States, in all its bearings, in all its principles therein contained. The Constitution of the United States lays down the basis upon which the Union of all the States of this Confederacy can and may be maintained and preserved, if it be literally and faithfully carried out. [Applause.] So far as I am concerned, feeling that I am a citizen of the Union—that I am a citizen of the United States, I am willing to abide by that Constitution. I am willing to live under a Government that is built upon and perpetuated upon the principles laid down by the Constitution, which was formed by Washington and his compeers, after coming from the heat and strife of bloody revolution. [Applause.]

I repeat, again, that I have not language adequate to express my gratitude for and appreciation of the kindness which has been manifested in regard to my humble self. I cannot sufficiently thank you for the manifestation of your appreciation of the course I have pursued, in regard to the crisis which is now upon this country. I have no words to utter, or rather I have words which will not give utterance to the feelings that I entertain on this occasion. [Applause.] I feel, to-day, a confidence, in my own bosom, that the cordiality and the sympathy and the response that comes up here from the people of Ohio is heartfelt and sincere. I feel that, in reference to the great question now before the people, those whom I see before me, are honest and sincere. [Applause.] I repeat again, and for the third time, that I have no language in which I can express my gratitude to you, and at the same time, in which I can express my devotion to the principles of the Constitution and the flag and emblem of our glorious Union of States. [Applause.]

I know that there has been much said about the North, much said about the South. I am proud, here to-day, to hear the sentiments and the language which have been uttered in reference to the North and the South, and the relations that exist between these two sections. [Applause.] I am glad to hear it said in such a place as this that the pending difficulties—I might say the existing war—which are now upon this country do not grow out of any animosity to the local institution of any section. [Applause.] I am glad to be assured that it grows out of a determination to maintain the glorious principles upon which the Government itself rests—the principles contained in the Constitution—and at the same time to rebuke and to bring back as far as may be practicable, within the pale of the Constitution, those individuals, or States even, who have taken it upon themselves to exercise a principle and doctrine at war with all government, with all association—political, moral and religious. [Applause.] I mean the doctrine of Secession, which is neither more nor less than a heresy—a fundamental error—a political absurdity, coming in conflict with all organized government, with everything that tends to preserve law and order in the United States, or wherever else the odious and abominable doctrine may be attempted to be exercised. I look upon the doctrine of Secession as coming in conflict with all organism, moral and social. I repeat, without regard to the peculiar institutions of the respective States composing this Confederacy, without regard to any Government that may be found in the future or exists in the present, this odious doctrine of Secession should be crushed out, destroyed and totally annihilated. No Government can stand, no religious, or moral, or social organization can stand where this doctrine is tolerated. [Applause.] It is disintegration—universal dissolvement—making war upon everything that has a tendency to promote and ameliorate the condition of the mass of mankind. [Applause.] Therefore I repeat, that this odious and abominable doctrine—you must pardon me for using a strong expression—I do not say it in a profane sense—but this doctrine I conceive to be *hell born and hell bound*, and one which will carry everything in its train, unless it is arrested and crushed out from our midst. [Great Applause.]

In response to what has been said to me here to-day, I confess
when I lay my hand upon my bosom, I feel gratified at hearing the
sentiments that have been uttered—that we are all willing to stand
up for the constitutional rights guaranteed to every State—every
community, that we are all determined to stand up for the preroga-
tives secured to us in the Constitution as citizens of States composing
one grand Confederacy, whether we belong to the North or to the
South, to the East or to the West. I say that I am gratified to hear
such sentiments uttered here to-day. I regard them as the most conclusive evidence that there is no disposition on the part of any citizens
of the loyal States to make war upon any peculiar institution of the
South, [Applause] whether it be slavery or anything else—leaving
that institution, under the Constitution, to be controlled by time,
circumstances and the great laws which lie at the foundation of all
things which political legislation can control. [Applause.]

While I am before you, my countrymen, I am in hopes it will not
be considered out of place for me to make a single remark or two,
in reference to myself as connected with the present crisis. My position in the Congress of the United States during its last session, is,
I suppose, familiar to most, if not all of you. You know the doctrine
I laid down then, and I can safely say that the opinions I entertain
now on the great questions of the day are just as they were then. I
have not changed them. I have seen no reason to change them. I believe that a Government without the power to enforce its laws, made
in conformity with the Constitution, is no Government at all. [Ap-
plause.] We have arrived at that point or that period in our national
history, at which it has become necessary for this Government to say
to the civilized, as well as to the pagan world, whether it is in reality
a Government, or whether it is but a pretext for a Government. If it
has power to preserve its existence and to maintain the principles of
the Constitution and the laws, that time has now arrived. If it is a
Government, that authority should be asserted. I say, then, let the
civilized world see that we have a Government. Let us dispel the
delusion under which we have been laboring since the inauguration
of the Government in 1789—let us show that it is not an ephemeral
institution; that we have not imagined we had a Government, and
when the test came, that the Government frittered away between our
fingers and quickly faded in the distance. [Applause.] The time has
come when the Government reared by our fathers should assert itself,
and give conclusive proof to the civilized world that it is a reality and
a perpetuity. [Applause.]

Let us show to other nations that this doctrine of secession is a
heresy—that States coming into the Confederacy, that individuals
living in the Confederacy, under the Constitution have no right nor

authority, upon their own volition, to set the laws and the Constitution aside, and to bid defiance to the authority of the Government under which they live. [Applause.]

I substantially cited the best authority that could be produced upon this subject, and took this position during the last session of Congress. I stand here to-day before you and advocate the same principles I then contended for. As early as 1833, (let me here say that I am glad to find that the Committee which have waited upon me on this occasion, and have presented their sentiments to me through their organ—I am glad to find that they represent all the parties among which we have been divided.) As early as 1833, I say, I formed my opinions in reference to this doctrine of secession in the nullification of the laws of the United States. I held these doctrines up to the year 1850, and I maintain them still. [Applause.]

I entertained these opinions, as I remarked before, down to the latest setting of Congress, and I then reiterated them. I entertain and express them here to-day. [Applause.]

In this connection, I may be permitted to remark that, during our last struggle for the Presidency, all parties contended for the preservation of the Union. Without going further back, what was that struggle? Senator Douglas of the State of Illinois was a candidate. His friends presented him as the best Union man. I shall speak upon this subject in reference to my position. Mr. Breckinridge's friends presented him to the people as the Union candidate. I was one of Mr. Breckinridge's friends. The Bell men presented the claims of the Hon. John Bell of Tennessee for the Presidency, upon the ground that he was the best Union candidate. The Republican party, so far as I understand them, have always been in favor of the Union. Then here was the contest: between four candidates presented to the consideration of the people of the United States. And the great struggle between them and their advocates was who was entitled to pre-eminence as a man in favor of the preservation of the Union of these States. Now where do we find ourselves? In times gone by you know we had our discussions and our quarrels. It was bank and anti-bank questions, tariff and anti-tariff, internal improvement and anti-internal improvement, or the distribution of the money derived from the sale of public lands, among the several States. Such measures as these we presented to the people, and the aim in the solution of all was how best to preserve the Union of these States. One party favored the measures as calculated to promote the welfare of our common country; another opposed them, to bring about the same result. Then what was the former contest. Bringing it down to the present times, there has been no disagreement between Republicans, Bell men, Douglas men and Breckinridge men, as regards the preservation of the union of States. Now, however, these measures are all laid aside—all these party questions are left out of consideration, and the great question comes up whether the Constitution, as adopted by the old articles of confederation and afterwards re-affirmed in the adoption of the Constitution of the United States—I say now, when the great question arises, involving the preservation and existence of the Government of the United States, I am proud to meet this vast concourse of people, and hear them say that they are willing to lay aside all party measures—all party considerations, and come up to join in one fraternal hug to sustain the bright stars and broad stripes of our glorious Union—all willing to unite, I repeat, in one fraternal hug—all willing to co-operate for the consummation of a sublime purpose, without regard to former party differences—that we are all determined to stand fast by the Union of these States. [Applause.] So far as I am concerned I am willing to say in this connection that I am proud—I am gratified to stand here among you as one of the humble upholders and supporters of the stars and stripes that have been borne by Washington through a seven years' revolution—a bold and manly struggle for our independence—and separation from the mother country. That is my flag—that flag that was borne by Washington in triumph. Under it I want to live and under no other. It is that flag that has been borne in triumph by the Revolutionary fathers over every battle field, when our brave men after days of toil and danger laid down and slept on the cold ground with no covering but the inclement sky, and arose in the morning and renewed their march over the frozen ground, as the blood trickled from their feet—all to protect that banner, and bear it aloft triumphantly.

I repeat that I am proud to be in your midst—am amongst this vast number to uphold the flag that was borne by Washington—the emblem of the Union of States. [Applause.] I have intimated that I should make some allusion to myself. I have indicated to you what were my opinions and my views from 1833 down to the moment I stand before you. With the facts in relation to the contest which took place recently in the State of Tennessee, you are all familiar. No longer ago than last February there was an extra session of the Legislature called. There was then a law passed authorizing a Convention to be called. The people of that State voted it down by a majority of sixty-four thousand.[3]

In a very short time afterward another session of the Legislature was called. This legislature went into secret session in a very short time. While the Southern Confederacy, or its agents, had access to it, and were put in possession of the doings and proceedings of this secret session,[4] the great mass of the people of my own State were not permitted even to put their ears to the keyhole, or to look through a crevice in the doors, to ascertain what was being done. A league with the Southern Confederacy has been formed, and the State has been handed over to that Southern Confederacy, with Jeff. Davis at its head. We, the people of Tennessee, have been handed over to this Confederacy, I say, like sheep in the shambles,[5] bound hand and foot, to be disposed of as Jefferson Davis and his cohorts may think proper.

This Ordinance was passed by the Convention with a proviso that it should be submitted to the people. The Governor was authorized to raise 55,000 men. Money was appropriated to enable him to carry out this diabolical and nefarious scheme, depriving the people of their rights, disposing of them as stock in the market—handing them over completely, body and soul, to the Southern Confederacy.

Now you may talk about slaves and Slavery, but in most instances when a slave changes his master even he has the privilege of choosing whom he desires for his next master,[6] but in this instance the sovereign people of a free State have not been allowed the power or privilege of choosing the master they desired to serve. They have been given a master without their consent or advice. No trouble was taken to ascertain what their desires were—they were at once handed over to this Southern Confederacy.[7]

* * * * * * *

But while this contest has been going on, a portion of our fellow citizens have been standing up for the Constitution and the Union, and because they have dared to stand upon the great embattlement of Constitutional liberties, exercising the freedom and the liberty of speech, a portion of our people have declared that we were traitors; they have said that our fate was to be the fate of traitors, and that hemp was growing and that the day of our execution was approaching—that the time would come when those who dare stand by the Constitution and the principles therein embraced, that the expiation of these deeds would be upon the gallows. We have met all these things. We have met them in open day. We have met them face to face—toe to toe—at least in one portion of the State. We have told them that the Constitution of the United States defines treason, and that definition is, that treason against the United States shall consist only in levying war against the General Government of the United States. We have told them that the time would come when the principles of the Constitution and the law defining treason would be maintained. We have told them that the time would come when the judiciary of the Government would be sustained in a manner that it could define what was treason under the Constitution and the law made in conformity with it, and that when defined, they would ascertain who were the traitors, and who it was that would stretch the hemp they had prepared for us. [Applause.]

I know that in reference to myself and others rewards have been offered, and it has been said that warrants have been issued for our arrest.[8] Let me say to you here to-day that I am no fugitive, especially no fugitive from justice. [Laughter.] If I were a fugitive, I would be a fugitive from tyranny—a fugitive from the reign of terror. But, thank God, the county in which I live, and that division of the State from which I hail, will record a vote of 25,000 against the secession ordinance.[9] The county in which I live gave a majority of 2,007 against this odious, diabolical, nefarious, hell-born and hell-bound doctrine.[10]

Cincinnati *Gazette*, June 20, 1861; also printed in Cincinnati *Enquirer*, June 20, 1861, and Frank Moore, ed., *The Rebellion Record* (11 vols. and supp., New York, 1861–68), II, 148–51.

1. Upon Johnson's arrival at the Burnet House it was announced that he would deliver an address at 3:00 p.m. Appearing on the eastern balcony at the appointed hour, he spoke to "a very large number of persons." Cincinnati *Enquirer*, June 20, 1861 (Brackets in the original, taken from the *Gazette*).

2. William S. Groesbeck (1815–1897), a native of New York and member of one of the earliest Cincinnati families, was a prominent lawyer, member of the Ohio constitutional convention (1851), commissioner to codify the state laws (1852), Democratic congressman (1856–58), representative to the Washington Peace Conference (1861), and state senator (1861–64). A noted orator, he often officially welcomed dignitaries to the city or presided over special celebrations or observances; on this occasion he received Johnson with a "brief address" which was "loudly cheered." Groesbeck subsequently served as counsel to Johnson during the latter's impeachment and trial. *Ibid.*; Greve, *History of Cincinnati*, II, 210–16; *BDAC*, 979.

3. Authorities differ as to the actual vote, but the secretary of state recorded 57,798 "for convention" and 69,675 "no convention"—a difference of 11,877. White, *Messages*, V, 272.

4. Henry Hilliard of Alabama, dispatched by the Confederate government as commissioner to Tennessee, met with the second special session of the legislature, called April 25 and held in secret. On April 30 he addressed a joint session and the next day the Assembly adopted a resolution authorizing the governor to enter into a military league with the Confederacy. The commissioners then appointed by Harris drew up an agreement with Hilliard, which took effect May 7. *Ibid.*, 288–93.

5. A slaughterhouse.

6. A singularly unrealistic statement!

7. Here the *Gazette* reports that Johnson discussed the Tennessee secession ordinance, the loyalty of East Tennessee to the Union, and Governor Harris' refusal to furnish arms to the section.

8. See Speech at Lexington, Kentucky, June 18, 1861, note 5.

9. In the forthcoming August state election, Greene County rejected the permanent Confederate Constitution (which Johnson calls "the secession ordinance"), 2,369–827, the East Tennessee vote being 27,738–15,494. Summary sheet from original returns, Tennessee State Library and Archives; White, *Messages*, V, 332.

10. The *Gazette* reported that the speaker, continuing for another fifteen minutes, made "humorous allusions to the 'bravery' of the Secession soldiery" and appealed for the preservation of the Union.

From Amos A. Lawrence[1]

(near) Boston. June 20, 61.

Dear Sir

The Telegraph announces yr arrival in Lexington on yr way to Washn.

Presuming that you have not recd my last letters, I write to say that Mr Everett has recieved a handsome letter from the Secy. of war,[2] expressing deep interest in yr success, & offering an abundant supply of arms as soon as he shall be advised by what route they can be transported. Of course you will advise with him at once. If you will send my draft to L. B. Bacon[3] 59 Murray St New York, he will remit you a N. Y. check for the amount, & for $750 in addition.

Having arrived at Washn. you will probably be convinced that the Rebellion will be crushed. But if you have any doubts they will be solved when you come farther North. We can send 100,000 well drilled men from this State by Oct 1st, armed & equipped, & when there are no more men, then "Masstts will go herself."[4] There is little done but to drill, & work on the land. Money is abundant & food cheap.

Resp'y & truly Yrs
Amos A Lawrence

Hon Andrew Johnson, USS. Washn.

Let. Bk. Copy, MHi-Amos A. Lawrence Papers.
1. There is no evidence that either Johnson or Charlton received this letter. Apparently Lawrence, more than a week after the Richmond *Enquirer*'s June 11 revelation of the fabricated correspondence, was still unaware of the duplicity which had been practiced on him.
2. Simon Cameron; his letter to Edward Everett has not been located.
3. According to *Trow's New York City Directory* (1861), 45, Lora B. Bacon was an "agent."
4. The source of this patriotic effusion has not been found.

From William F. Lockwood[1]

Omaha City N. T. June 20th 1861

D Sir

I am now at this place holding a Term of the Supreme Court of the Territory. I had hoped to meet Mr Milligan here, but was disapointed sorely. Is he likely to accept the appointment[?][2] if not there is a citizen of this Territory—Mr Taylor[3] whom we should be pleased to have receive it.

I received my appointment as one of the Judges for this Territory on the 27th of April.

I regret much to learn of the treatment you received on your way home in Virginia in June.[4] I hope very much when the loyal people of that State, will vindicate you against such insults.

Your friends here and I can assure you that all of the people stand in that relation, feel a deep interest in yourself & the result of the contest in Tennessee as connected with your notions. We hope it will be all right with you, but greatly fear the contrary. But one thing is certain, your efforts in behalf of our glorious union will be remembered with gratitude by the friends of the Union throughout the Country & if there ever shall be restoration of the union you will be one of those whom the nation will revere as one of its noblest and ablest defenders.

We do not know whether you will be able, whether you will be allowed to attend the approaching session of Congress. I hope you will be as your presence there will be of great importance to the Country at this time.

I address this letter to you, at Washington, as I suppose it would not in any event reach you in Tenn.

If it should please you to answer this address me at *Dakota City Neb. Ty.*

Your Friend   Wm. F. Lockwood

Hon. Andrew Johnson
Washington D. C

ALS, DLC-JP2.

1. William F. Lockwood, a native of Connecticut, had moved to Nebraska Territory where he served as associate justice of the district court. *U. S. Official Register* (1863), 270; Lanman, *Biographical Annals*, 262.

2. Appointed by Lincoln associate justice of Nebraska Territory on March 27, 1861, Sam Milligan never served. According to his memoirs, he "resigned the commission," feeling that he was in no position to leave his family and property in Greeneville. Subsequently he came under suspicion of the Confederate authorities and fled to the Union lines in April, 1864, seeking refuge ultimately in Nashville, where he was successively "Supernumerary Clerk" in Governor Johnson's office, commissioner of banks, and state supreme court judge. Sam Milligan, Memoir (Microfilm in Tennessee State Library and Archives), 96–98, 104–5, 108, 110–12; *U. S. Official Register* (1861), 194; see also Basler, *Lincoln Papers*, IV, 295n.

3. Possibly William H. Taylor, Otoe County Republican who served in the Sixth Territorial Assembly (1859) and as a nonvoting delegate to a convention (1859) to discuss the southern border and the subject of annexation to Kansas of the territory south of the Platte River. David H. Price, "Sectionalism in Nebraska," *Nebraska History*, LIII (1972), 458; Nebraska State Historical Society *Collections*, XVI (1911), 120; *Publications*, XVIII (1917), 377.

4. On his way to Tennessee in April Johnson had witnessed several mobs gathered at Virginia railroad stations chanting, "Hang the traitor!" On one occasion he is said to have drawn a revolver on assailants—one of whom

pushed his way close enough to reach out and pull his nose. The train sped
through Bristol without its customary stop, reportedly on orders from Jefferson Davis, who probably did not desire an incident that might make Andrew
Johnson a martyr and jeopardize the growing southern sentiment in the border
states. Knoxville *Tri-Weekly Whig*, May 4, 1861; James M. Morgan, *Recollections of a Rebel Reefer* (Boston, 1917), 36–37; Milton, *Age of Hate*, 105–
6, 698; Lately Thomas, *The First President Johnson* (New York, 1968),
191–92.

From Anthony Ten Eyck

Detroit, Mich. June 21, 1861

Hon. Andrew Johnson
Washington
My dear Sir,
    Presuming upon our friendly acquaintance & intercourse, at the
St Charles,[1] during the winter I was acting as Clerk of Mr. Stuarts
Pub. Land Com,[2] of which you was a member, I take the liberty of
presenting to you a matter of much personal interest to me, & asking
your kind generous assistance, so far as you feel you can consistantly
render it—
    My name is before the Sect' of State (with testimonials in its sup-
port from Judges, Clergymen, Editors of leading state papers, our
Post Master,[3] V. Presdt Hamlin, the U. S. Senators from this state,[4]
& other respectable & influential citizens, of different politics) for
the apptment as *Consul General at Frankfort on the Main*, made
vacant by the death of a Mr. Hosmer,[5] of this State, who had lately
been appointed—
    It was thought the Administration would be glad of an oppor-
tunity of acknowledging their appreciation of the patriotic motives
of their fellow citizens, in rallying to the support of the constitutional
govt, of their common country without regard to previous political
ties & associations, by granting this appointment to one who had
not been of their political organization, but who was labouring zealously for the maintainance of the Constitution & the Union— It was
this view of the matter that induced the application— My wife's
health had been failing all winter & spring, & our physician advised
a change of climate & travel abroad, as the most likely to produce
favourable results— I wanted some such appoinment to enable me
to go, as I had not the pecuniary means, otherwise, to do so— Here
you have my case.
    I have the capacity & the Experience, (having been Commissioner
at Sandwich Island)[6] & the testimonials as Secty' files will show I
have the character & integrity, to warrant me in claiming peculiar
fitness for the place—

What is necessary now in the case, particularly, is to induce the Presdt, or Sect'y, or Assistant Sect'y, to call up the case for action & determination.

This can only be done, by some generous friend of influence, & of democratic antecedents— Your position with the admn, & before the Country, is such, that I have no doubt a word from you, verbally, or in writing, would induce prompt & favorable decision in the case — I submit whether you feel that you can take any action in the matter. Trusting you may find it consistent with your views & feelings so to do, & at an early day.   I remain,

Yours Very respectly & truly

Anthony Ten Eyck

ALS, DLC-JP2.

1. During much of his service as senator, Johnson stayed at the St. Charles Hotel, located at the northeast corner of Pennsylvania Avenue and Third Street. Bryan, *National Capital*, II, 445n; *Johnson Papers*, III, 204n.

2. Ten Eyck was clerk for the Senate public lands committee (1857–59), a Detroit post office clerk (1859), and assistant postmaster (1861). *Ibid.*, 439n; *Johnston's Detroit Directory* (1861), 27; *U. S. Official Register* (1859), *439.

3. William A. Howard (1813–1880), Detroit lawyer and Republican congressman (1855–59, 1860–61), was appointed postmaster by Lincoln in 1861 and removed by Johnson in 1866. After the war he remained active in politics and served as governor of Dakota Territory (1877–80). *BDAC*, 1083; *DAB*, IX, 282–83; Michigan Historical Commission, *Michigan Biographies* (2 vols., Lansing, 1924), II, 419–20.

4. Zachariah Chandler and Kinsley S. Bingham.

5. Rufus Hosmer, politician, sometime lawyer, and editor of the Detroit *Advertiser* (1849–54, 1855–61), had been appointed March 11, 1861, but never served, dying in Lansing on April 20. William Stocking, "Wielded a Strong Pen," *Michigan History*, XXV (1941), 29–33 (originally printed in the Detroit *Free Press*, February 20, 1898); *Senate Ex. Journal*, XI (1858–61), 296, 304.

6. Ten Eyck, who had served as commissioner of Hawaii (1845–49), evidently was unsuccessful in his application, inasmuch as William W. Murphy, a native New Yorker currently residing in Michigan, received the Frankfurt appointment September 30, 1861. However, Ten Eyck did receive a commission as additional army paymaster. *Johnson Papers*, III, 439n; *U. S. Official Register* (1861), 7; *Senate Ex. Journal*, XI (1858–61), 504, 538.

To Meda Blanchard,[1] Washington, D. C.

Washington, June [21?], 1861.

Mrs. Meda Blanchard:

Dear Madam: Learning that you have just finished a successful course of culture of your musical gifts, under the most eminent masters of Italy, and that you are about to commence what we are sure will be a most brilliant professional career, we take this mode of making known to you that we would esteem it a great kindness and rare privilege if you would favor the residents and strangers now in Washington by giving your opening concert[2] in this your native city.

We remain, dear madam, your friends and servants,

William H. Seward,
Montgomery Blair,
Caleb B. Smith,
Edward Bates,
Salmon P. Chase,
Gideon Welles,
Andrew Johnson,[3]

Washington *Evening Star*, July 2, 1861.

1. Meda Blanchard, a beautiful singer recently returned from two years of study in Italy, called at the White House several days before her July 6 concert to thank Mrs. Lincoln for her patronage. While there she was invited to sing for a group of guests, only to have the President himself descend from his office and, after Madam Blanchard had finished her selections, request her to sing the "Marseillaise." It might be noted that, although at least one volume has been written attesting to Lincoln's love of music, described by the author as "something passionate," Johnson's perhaps perfunctory—or even gently coerced—signature among Madam Blanchard's petitioners is one of the few instances we have of the Tennessean's concern with the muse. Kenneth A. Bernard, *Lincoln and the Music of the Civil War* (Caldwell, Idaho, 1966), 36.

2. The concert, with Signor Lotti, tenor "from New York," Prof. Amasa McCoy, Shakespearean reader, and Mr. Harry Schermon, pianist and accompanist, as assisting artists, was held in the hall of Willard's Hotel with the President and Mrs. Lincoln, Secretary Seward, members of the diplomatic corps, and the "elite" of Washington in attendance. Madam Blanchard may not have been at her best—"sang well, though with a voice fatigued apparently by over practice, and affected by the oppressive atmosphere"—but her audience was appreciative, responding with "repeated bursts of rapturous applause." *Ibid.*, 37–38; Washington *Evening Star*, July 8, 1861.

3. The names of thirty-five more legislators and prominent Washington citizens, including N. P. Willis, Thurlow Weed, N. P. Banks, and A. E. Burnside, followed.

From Edward B. Boutwell[1]

Washington June 22nd 1861.

Dear Sir:

I have been unjustly punished by Isaac Toucey,[2] late Secretary of the Navy, because I am a Southern man and a Catholic. My punishment has been continued and my promotion stopped, notwithstanding I am a Union man, because Mr. Welles,[3] coming from Connecticut, adopts all the prejudices of Mr. Toucey against Southern men. You know and can appreciate the difficulties a Southern man has to contend against, who remains faithful to the Constitution of his Country, and therefore, you must agree with me that a Southern Union Navy officer ought not to be set a side to advance Northern men. This Secretary Welles is doing in my case.

I am respectfully Your Ob Servt
E B Boutwell
Com U S Navy

Hon Andrew Johnson
U S Senate

ALS, DLC-JP.

1. Edward B. Boutwell (c1800–fl1866), a Virginian, entered the navy as a midshipman (1819) and rose to the rank of commander (1850), serving as captain of the *U.S.S. John Adams* in the Pacific Squadron during the mid-1850's. Although the evidence is inconclusive, his complaints of ill-treatment at the hands of Toucey and Welles probably stem from allegations by American missionary interests that Boutwell treated the natives with undue harshness during the *Adams'* visit to the Fiji Islands in 1855. Suspended from duty (1858) for five years, he tendered his resignation in July, 1861. The department refused to accept it and he was dismissed by presidential order on August 12, 1861. Edward B. Boutwell, ZB-File, Naval Records Col., RG45, National Archives.

2. Isaac Toucey (1792–1869), a Connecticut lawyer, served as Democratic congressman (1835–39), governor (1846–47), attorney general in Polk's Cabinet (1848–49), U.S. senator (1852–57), and secretary of the navy under Buchanan (1857–61). *DAB*, XVIII, 600–601; *BDAC*, 1722.

3. Gideon Welles (1802–1878), Connecticut native, inherited wealth and added to his income as part owner and editor of the Hartford *Times* (1826–36). A Democratic member of the state lower house (1827–35), he was later chief of the bureau of provisions and clothing for the U.S. navy (1846–49). After leaving the Democratic party in consequence of the Kansas-Nebraska Bill, he helped establish the Republican Hartford *Evening Press* in 1856. As secretary of the navy in the Lincoln and Johnson administrations, Welles served with efficiency amid constant controversy. *DAB*, XIX, 629–32; see also John Niven, *Gideon Welles: Lincoln's Secretary of the Navy* (New York, 1973).

From Amos A. Lawrence[1]

(near) Boston, June 22. 61

Dear Sir

I learn that my letter to you (with the $1000=draft) is in the newspapers.[2] Please to inform me whether the draft has been negotiated by you. If not, I presume it was stolen by the traitors & therefore will not be paid by Mason & Lawrence if presentd.

Yr Obt Svt Amos A Lawrence

Hon. Andr. Johnson
Washn

ALS, DLC-JP.

1. Beyond all question, this note reached Johnson.

2. Under the heading, "Andrew Johnson's Treason Discovered," the Richmond *Enquirer* of June 11 had exposed this "perfidy and corruption on the part of one who has held so high an office in the government of our country," adding that the "infamous wretch . . . ought to be arrested at once." The circumstances under which the *Enquirer* achieved this "scoop"—so disastrous for the Charlton "committee's" plans—are obscure. Jeptha Fowlkes, a Memphis doctor and, at this stage of the sectional quarrel, a would-be peacemaker among Tennesseans, passed through Knoxville in early June, having in his possession a copy of the May 18 Lawrence letter which he had evidently obtained from Governor Harris in Nashville. After consorting with his erstwhile Whig friends "Brownlow Temple & others," and, according to Charlton, "without seeing a single *Southern Rights man!*," he went on to Richmond, whether or not via Greeneville to visit Johnson, as originally proposed, is not known. Given the nature of the Lawrence letter and the skulduggery implied, it is surprising that Brownlow, who was privy to the letter in early June, did not expose it then in his paper. Subsequently, on June 22, he assured his readers: "We knew it two weeks ago—we saw copies of them [the letter and accompanying draft] before the late election—and Gov. Johnson was furnished with them." In light of Fowlkes' apparent desire to bring Tennesseans together in this time of crisis, one wonders about his motivation in permitting publication of so controversial a communication. True, he was not a close associate of Charlton and those Knoxville Democrats who hoped through deception to fleece well-to-do New Englanders. Perhaps he fell in with those in Richmond who were less interested in northern money for the Confederate cause than in castigating Johnson and destroying, if possible, his effectiveness as a rallying point for moderate Tennessee, nay southern, sentiment in those tense weeks of the "phony war" before Bull Run. Certainly the tone of the editorial comment accompanying the Lawrence letter was one of virulent personal attack upon the integrity and patriotism of the Tennessee senator. Charlton to Harris, June 6, 1861, Johnson Papers, LC; Knoxville *Whig*, June 22, 1861; Letter from Jeptha Fowlkes, May 29, 1861. For full text of the *Enquirer* article see To the *Union and American*, June 30, 1861.

From Lexington (Ky.) Citizens

June 22, 1861, Lexington, Ky.; ALS, DLC-JP.

Sanders D. Bruce, chairman of arrangements, invites Johnson to join in "a grand Picnic Celebration" on July 4—"an occasion for the renewal of *National patriotic feelings*, as opposed to the lamentable and mischievous *sectional predjudices* which have been so industriously propogated of late years, with too much success, by designing politicians—"

Response to Washington Serenade[1]

June 22, 1861

Mr. Johnson said that Mr. Lincoln had done no more than his duty, and that if he had done less, he would have deserved the halter himself. He said he stood by the President in all his acts, and called upon all good citizens everywhere to do the same. Let millions of money be expended, let our most precious blood be poured out; but above and before all things, let the Union and Constitution be preserved. The speaker showed clearly that the war was not brought about by the North, but on the fulfillment of every citizen's greatest privilege—the election of our Chief Magistrate—which was done honestly and fairly, there arose in the South a few dishonest politicians, who were bound to break up the Union and the Government. Then was practically inaugurated the principle of Secession. South Carolina must first make friends with the hydra-headed monster, and thrust its acquaintance upon the other Southern States by its brutal assault on Fort Sumter, thus causing blood to flow and the cannons to reverberate over the South, until every Southerner should be filled with the spirit of war. He showed that the doctrine of Secession would utterly abandon the idea of ever constructing another Republic, because its tendency was to destroy and not to inaugurate any system of equality among men, and destroy that principle which enables men to govern themselves. Hence, to acknowledge the doctrine of Secession would be to invite despotism and anarchy. And shall we permit it? [Cries of "No, never!"] the hue of march has already begun on Washington, the capital of our nation, founded by the father of our country, George Washington; and, my friends, let me tell you that anarchy and destruction are treading closer upon your heels than you are aware, if you allow this principle or its advocates to gain a foothold upon the soil of American freedom. This man Beauregard,[2] or No-regard (cries of blackguard), as some call him, fired upon our gallant Anderson when he was informed that he and his men were upon the point of starvation, and would evacuate the fort in three days, unless supplied with provisions. Pryor was there, and desired that the cannon's roar should be heard by Virginia, as that State was then wavering on the point of secession, and he desired to make her decide in favor of "protection of the rights of the South."[3] Hence, the war upon a little band of the most gallant, though starving men in the service. He referred to the historical records of the past to prove the spirit of anarchy among bad men, and proved the present Southern movement to eclipse them all. What principles have we lost by the continuance of this Union? [Cries of "none."] Then stand by it! ["We will," "we will."] Compromise! Where can compromise be found but in the Constitution of the United States? I look upon it as one of the best compromises that ever could be made. ["Good!" "good!"] Hence I look upon it as our God bidden duty to stand by it; by the Government which was framed by Washington; which was sustained by Jackson; which was fought for by our good old patriot Scott. ["Bravo!" and "Huzza for Gen. Scott," and the cheers heartily given.] He then paid a very high compliment to Gen. Scott. He believed South Carolina and the whole South would be as quiet as a lamb if the old man Jackson had been at the head of the nation last Fall; and could Clay and Webster respond to their cries for compromise, it would be as it often has been, in the language of Andrew Jackson: "The Federal Union—it must and shall be preserved." They may burn our fields; destroy our property; nay, our best blood may and will be sacrificed, but East Tennessee cannot be converted into a land of slaves! They may confiscate my little property I own in Tennessee. My life may be required to lay upon the altar of my country, *but let my country be saved*! She is right, and right and justice must prevail, while the stars and stripes continue to float over us.

New York *Tribune*, June 25, 1861, quoting the Philadelphia *Press*, n.d.

1. On June 22 Johnson, having arrived the previous day, was serenaded at his hotel, the St. Charles, by the 25th Pa. Rgt. band, with a large crowd in attendance. Washington *National Intelligencer*, June 24, 1861.

2. Pierre G. T. Beauregard (1818–1893) of Louisiana, a West Point graduate (1838), served on Gen. Winfield Scott's staff during the Mexican War and as chief engineer at New Orleans (1858–61). Superintendent of West Point when his native state seceded, he was removed because of his outspoken secessionist views. Resigning from the United States army on February 20, 1861, he was immediately commissioned a brigadier general by the Confederate government and assigned to Charleston where, acting under orders from Jefferson Davis, he demanded the surrender of Ft. Sumter. In June he was given command of one of the two Confederate armies in northern Virginia. *DAB*, II, 111; see also T. Harry Williams, *P. G. T. Beauregard: Napoleon in Gray* (Baton Rouge, 1955).

3. Roger Pryor of Virginia, ex-congressman who believed an attack on Sumter would bring Virginia into the Confederacy, assured a Charleston audience on April 10, 1861, that if South Carolina would strike a blow and "blood is shed, old Virginia will make common cause with her sisters of the South." Quoted in Samuel W. Crawford, *The History of the Fall of Fort Sumter: The Genesis of the Civil War* (New York, 1898), 305; Charleston *Courier*, April 11, 1861.

From John Campbell[1]

419 Chestnut St Phila
24th June 61

Dear Sir

I wrote to you some time ago in Tennessee— I sent the letter under cover to Col Forney clerk of the H R in order that he might forward it to you inasmuch as I did not know your residence[.] I am glad that so far you have escaped assassination and personal injury and hope that you will live to see this treasonable heresy utterly crushed and that I will live to assist in elevating you to be chief Magistrate of the whole U S'— It is impossible for me to see clearly all the details of the policy to be pursued to speedily put down the rebellion and to restore to a distracted Country and to a misinformed people, peace and harmony—but I think that I see some of those details — The hints that I give to you may or may not be useful to you at all events they are intended for your good. Living in the North as I do, I have a better opportunity of knowing its public opinion than you—to the best of my ability I will post you— The present war has been accepted as a dire necessity not from any desire to wage war for its own sake but to defend the Government Union and Constitution from paracidal and sacriligious attacks— No portion of our people has shown so much alacrity in rushing to defend our flag as the Democracy[.] 75 per cent of the soldiers belong to our party— Do not you for a moment believe that the Democratic party is extinct— It will be again the National party purified by a terrible ordeal— The Republican Press the Cabinet at Washington and other Republican officials are anxious to make people believe that partyism is ignored for the time being— I wish that it were so— I say to you that in the dispensation of places in the Custom House Post office Navy yard Mint Arsenal &c so far as Phila is concerned even day laborers unless they are black Republicans cannot get a days work.[2] I think that it is as well that you should know this— I am opposed to this odious and vindictive distinction being made— If this present administration desires to shorten the war they ought to adopt such a course of policy as will knit together all our people— I send to you 2 documents one an address of the Republican Ex Committee (here called the peoples party) the other the resolutions passed at a more partisan nominating Convention[.][3] you can judge from them how far the Republican party desires to Conciliate the people— There is another evil to be complained of—to wit the appointment of unfit persons to responsible Commands in the Army— You will talk to Gen. Scott upon this matter— again there are bad and corrupt men who have been making money out of the necessities of the times—by furnishing rotten clothing and diseased food to the Troops[.] Our Governor Curtin[4] is bitterly denounced for being one of the principle men in these base transactions— I state these matters to you so that you may understand something of the state of parties here yet for all this my duty is to aid public opinion to support the Government to crush the rebellion—

The Events that have occurred since January last have caused you to become a noted and marked man[.] God has conferred upon [you] great Courage and a keen perception of right from wrong[.] the noble stand that you have taken for the Unity of the Republic has told well upon the hearts of the American people[.] The Vantage ground gained you must not lose— your Cincinnatti speech has been published in our Phila papers—[5] remember that what I write to you is out of pure friendship— I never saw you but once— Col. Wm C Patterson,[6] a Tennessean by birth brother to General Patterson first directed my attention to you— since then having watched your Course I find that you are up to the standard of patriotism that I admire—

You can if any portion of this letter is necessary use it— I do not know what you may do after the adjournment of Congress—but I would say to you if you can you ought to pay Phila a visit— I am using every exertion to get you recognized as our National Leader— I mentioned your name incidentally to Henry M Phillips[7] who was a member of last Congress but one— he is no friend of yours[.] There is no Democratic newspaper here— There is to be a penny paper named Union[8] started here on the first of July— I cannot guess what its tone will be— It is said that it is to be devoted to the *Dollar Interest*[.] I will post you after it shall have appeared— I intended to have gone on to Washington to see you but as I can do you no service by going—I believe it is as well to remain here. If you require any information that you think that I can give let me know — Do not feel any delicacy in requesting me to serve you in any way that I am able— I shall comply with your request with alacrity and do not imagine that I am useless— *There is no one man single handed* in Phila can be of more use to you than I.

There is one item I wish to direct your attention to— You no doubt have read Mr Holts letter—[9] it was carefully prepared and well written[.] you will be called upon to speak in the forthcoming session of Congress[.][10] Let your speech be well and carefully matured—full of patriotism and avoiding clap trap[.][11] let it be worthy of a statesman— You must have it stereotyped[12] for Circulation— I have acquaintances and Connecions all over the Country— If your speech is enveloped and franked I will see that it will be mailed to every person whom I know[.] I may have forgotten some things— I dotted [*sic*] down such ideas as came uppermost in my mind— If in the multiplicity of business you consider my Correspondence either unimportant or intrusive I shall cease it[.]

One of your truest friends
John Campbell

ALS, DLC-JP.

1. John Campbell (b. *c*1810), publisher, author, and Philadelphia bookseller, had been secretary of the Social Reform Society (1844), an organizer of the Social Improvement Society, and from 1845 to 1852 the most active exponent of the rights of labor in Philadelphia. Contributing to *Young America* and Greeley's New York *Tribune*, he served as the latter's reporter in the

Philadelphia labor movement for several years. Author of *Negro-Mania; Being an Examination of the Falsely Assumed Equality of the Various Races* (1851) and *A Theory of Equality; or, The Way to Make Every Man Act Honestly* (1848), he had early applauded Johnson's Union stand. 1860 Census, Pa., Philadelphia, 7th Ward, 295; Commons, *History of Labour*, I, 516; Campbell to Johnson, January 17, March 1, 1861, Johnson Papers, LC.

2. Philadelphia, like many other northern cities, was suffering from the general business depression caused by a sudden loss of southern markets and the defalcations of indebted southern merchants. By December, 1860, over twenty thousand laborers were unemployed in Philadelphia alone. Stampp, *And the War Came*, 123–25; Nicholas B. Wainwright, ed., *A Philadelphia Perspective: The Diary of Sydney George Fisher . . . 1845–1871* (Philadelphia, 1967), 389.

3. Confronted by the southern challenge to national unity, many Philadelphians hoped to revive the "People's Party," a coalition of Republicans and Americans in the late 1850's, and to nominate for a recently vacated congressional seat a candidate unfettered by existing party designations, one dedicated solely to preservation of the Union. This effort failed when a convention, claiming to be of the People's party, rejected "concensus" resolutions and selected a partisan Republican as its candidate. Dusinberre, *Civil War Issues in Philadelphia*, 77–78; Philadelphia *Bulletin*, June 22, 24, 25, 1861.

4. Andrew G. Curtin (1815–1894), prominent Whig-Republican lawyer and later Democratic congressman (1881–87), served as governor (1861–67) and strongly supported the Lincoln war effort. Yet Pennsylvania was ill prepared for war, and its governor was described by a contemporary as lacking "the requisite ability" and "moral influence" to deal with the situation. Alluding to conditions at Camp Curtin, near Harrisburg, the critic described a "shocking scene of filth, discomfort and disorder," and noted that the men in the field had insufficient food, no comforts, and were fast becoming demoralized. *DAB*, IV, 606–7; *BDAC*, 766; Wainwright, *Fisher's Diary*, 389–90.

5. Speech at Cincinnati, June 19, which was published in the Philadelphia *Inquirer* June 24, 1861.

6. William C. Patterson (1813–1883), financier and president of the Pennsylvania Railroad (1849–52), was born in Claiborne County, Tennessee, but educated in Philadelphia. A Mexican War veteran, he served for three months on the staff of his brother, Gen. Robert Patterson. When the Bank of Philadelphia was near collapse, William successfully conducted its affairs, keeping the loss much smaller than anticipated; also for a time he helped manage the consolidation of city and county governments in Philadelphia. *NCAB*, XIII, 334.

7. Henry M. Phillips (1811–1884), attorney and Democrat, served in Congress (1857–59) and held a variety of civic posts (1867–82). *BDAC*, 1454.

8. There is no evidence that the proposed "Union"—evidently intended as the organ of business Democrats—ever materialized.

9. Joseph Holt, Kentuckian and former member of Buchanan's Cabinet, opposed Governor Beriah Magoffin's neutrality proclamation and took a strong stand on his state's remaining in the Union. On May 31 he wrote a lengthy address—printed in pamphlet form—against any concessions to the Confederacy. Moore, *Rebellion Record*, I, Doc., 283–92.

10. See Speech in Support of Presidential War Program, July 27, 1861.

11. An effort "to convince or gain applause . . . by the use of cheap, empty, or meretricious means." *Webster's Third International*.

12. A method developed in the late eighteenth century for printing by transfer from a metal plate cast from a mold of the original type. *OED*, X, 925.

From William P. Fessenden[1]

June 24 [1861]

My dear Sir—

I Saw Secretary Chase this morning, and he asked me where you could be found—Saying that he wished you to dine with him & two or three friends to day at 5. P M.[2]

He requested me, if I met you, or could find where you were, to bring you along— I have called at [your] lodgings,[3] but did not find you[.]

His house is at the Corner of 6th St. & E.

Yours very truly   W. P. Fessenden

June 24—[1861]   Monday—

ALS, DLC-JP2.

1. Fessenden of Maine, chairman of the Senate finance committee, had been in Washington since early June conferring with Treasury Secretary Chase. Francis Fessenden, *Life and Public Services of William Pitt Fessenden* (2 vols., Boston, 1907), I, 186.

2. Although Chase was wont to conduct business over the dinner table, there is no specific evidence that Johnson on this occasion dined with Fessenden and the secretary, both of whom were known to be sympathetic with the plight of border unionists. David Donald, ed., *Inside Lincoln's Cabinet: The War Diaries of Salmon P. Chase* (New York, 1954), *passim*; Potter, *Lincoln and His Party*, 115–16.

3. The St. Charles Hotel.

From Joseph M. Kennedy

June 24, 1861, Washington, D. C.; ALS, DLC-JP.

Census office employee, recalling that "I was engaged with you and my Father [J. C. G. Kennedy], sending Union documents to the Southern States," asks support for a lieutenancy in the U. S. cavalry.

From John J. Roane[1]

Washington June 24th/61.

(Private)

My Dear Sir

Fearing I might not find you at home I have hastily dropped a few lines stating the purpose of my call in addition to paying my personal respects; I feel assured that you will forgive this trespass, for I have known you long & ever esteemed you as a friend & acquaintance, flattering myself that I, & my history are not entirely unknown to you & therefore not unworthy of a share of your regards— before you left Washington after the adjournment of congress I sought you more than once, but had not the pleasure of seeing you except when you seemed much engaged on the street & sickness finally prevented the prosecution of my wish until your departure. you have now my dear Sir returned, to our city in good health, I hope, & certainly with a reputation enhanced by loyalty & evidences given of both moral & personal intrepidity & I seek you again & with a hope that I may not be considered a bore or that I ask too much when I crave your aid in obtaining relief from impending distress— I am extremely poor, & actually want bread. I cannot beg it, but beg *employment* which can give it, & I am aware what the leverage & weight of character can justly effect & to obtain them in uplifting the prejudices of want is desirable. I have therefore approached you with a hope that a spirit of Christian commiseration may prompt an interest in my behalf. a good word from you to any head of Department would secure me a place where by labor I could earn a living— Do I ask too much? I hope not,— I flatter myself that I have some little claims on my country & if I may be pardoned I will state them.— I left Princeton College in 1812 & returned to Va & served out the war, served some years in the Ho of Delegats & in Congress, have been a clerk in the Patent Office for sixteen years & finally special agent of the treasury a place given me by Mr Guthrie at the instance of Mr Pierce which I was constrained to resign owing to a severe affliction of my head which confined me in the Infirmary in Balt some months— I am a Union man & altho for Bell & Everett at first, yet believing Mr Lincoln fairly & constitutionally elected I resolved to await his course & the acts of his administration—heard his inaugural was satisfied & up to this date commend his administration. I am enrolled with the soldiers of 1812 for the defence of our capitol— I have two sons in Philadelphia who voted the Lincoln ticket— My distinguished relative Judge Spencer Roane[2] denounced secession as arrant treason & can but look upon it as such & nothing mortifies so much as that my native state should suffer herself to be dragged into the villainous pool of disloyalty & swept on by the Phrenzied movement of more southern states— I have thus my dear sir stated my claims for *employment*, tho in a disjointed way. My former friends in Virginia now denounce me & seem to have lost evey kind feeling for me owing to my antagonistic views & my sons who have heretofore aided me have become now unable to do so any longer owing to the galling pressure of the times & want of employment in their respective trades— I will do myself the honor of waiting on you as early as I can,— with my sincere good wishes for your welfare

I am yours most truly
J J Roane

ALS, DLC-JP2.

1. John J. Roane (1794–1869), native Virginian, was a member of the Virginia house of delegates (1820–23), a Democrat in Congress (1831–33), patent office clerk (1836–51), and treasury department special agent from time to time after 1855. *BDAC*, 1524–25.

2. Spencer Roane (1762–1822), prominent Virginia jurist, was elected to the house of delegates (1783–84) and the state senate (1788–89). Appointed to the Virginia general court in 1789, he was later elevated to the state supreme court of appeals (1794–1822). Though a proponent of state rights, Roane seems to have been equally committed to the inviolability of the Union, seeing in state rights a device to protect an appropriate balance within the national framework. Judge Roane's declaration: "it is *treason* to secede," was made at a meeting of the Virginia electoral college in 1808; subsequently in 1814 when the Union appeared to be threatened by the Hartford convention, he denounced its tactics and supported possible presidential use of troops to suppress insurrection. John Roane, congressman (1809–15, 1827–37) and father of John J., was Spencer's first cousin. *DAB*, XV, 642–43; Edwin J. Smith, "Spencer Roane," *The John P. Branch Historical Papers*, II (1905), 18; Margaret E. Horsnell, Spencer Roane: Judicial Advocate of Jeffersonian Principles (Ph. D. dissertation, University of Minnesota, 1967), 174; [Lyon G. Tyler], "Roane Family," *William and Mary Quarterly*, Ser. 1, XVIII (1910), 199; Milwaukee *Sentinel*, November 14, 1860.

From George A. Woodbridge

June 24, 1861, La Crosse, Wis.; ALS, DLC-JP.

A northern schoolteacher, having resided in Nashville for some years and knowing Johnson to be sympathetic to "union men of all sections, & especially with those who have been compelled to leave the state which has the honor of being so ably represented by your self," recounts the circumstances of his exile and solicits a consulship or similar post abroad.

From O. S. Baker

June 25, 1861, New York, N. Y.; ALS, DLC-JP.

Admiring friends in New York City, pleased that Johnson has arrived safely in Washington, desire to send assistance "to those you have left behind . . . Either in Men, Money or Arms."

From Mark W. Delahay

June 25, 1861, Nebraska City, N. T.; Autograph Circular Signed, DLC-JP.

Surveyor general for Kansas and Nebraska reports that unionists from Texas, Arkansas, and Missouri have removed to Kansas for safety. Inasmuch as more than thirty million acres in that state alone, and an even larger quantity in Nebraska, lie unsurveyed, asks Congress to appropriate additional funds for public surveys so that bounty land will be ready for soldiers in the present war.

From Amos A. Lawrence

(near) Boston. June 25. 61.

Dear Sir

Enclosed are two letters[1] wh. induced me to take pains to obtain some action from Govt. in favor of yr people, & to collect a little money ($1750), wh. wd serve to pay expenses of transporting arms.

Were it necessary, I wd send you Secy. Camerons letter to Mr Everett offering all the arms you require, & requests informatn. as to the point where shd be deliverd. Probably you have seen him (Mr C.) ere this. If not please do so, or send a confidentl. person.

I am somewhat mortified by the deception practiced, & particularly so because it has caused inconvenience & risk to yr. self.

Resp'y & truly Yrs
Amos A Lawrence

Hon. Andrew Johnson.
U S Sen.   Washn.

ALS, DLC-JP2; Let. Bk. Copy, MHi-Amos A. Lawrence Papers.

1. Probably copies of Charlton's "Johnson" missives of May 15 and 23, although the envelope endorsement is merely the terse comment "Containg [sic] letters forged to Mr Lawrence of Boston."

From Pitser Miller

Louisville, June 25 1861

Hon Andrew Johnson
Washington City

D. Sir.   I thought of writing to you several times previous to our Election[1] but did not do so until a short time ago, which I am certain from the time did not reach you at Greeneville[.] I was in Lexington the 22nd, where I learned you had been and had made a long speech[.] Some said you had said you had been shot at near

Cumberland Gap & that you was going to Washington to get arms to supply the East Tennesseans with but on closer enquiry I could find no person that had heard you say it but several said they heard all you said and nothing of the kind was uttered. I was glad to hear it[.] I too have fought & abused & argued against Secession & voted against Representation but a majority of my state have gone for it — I want no Civil War so I cease forever the agitation hoping a kind providence will do something to reconcile and restore order[.][2]

I wrote a long Letter to Mr. Seward about 10 days ago which contained my views fully[.] the Aim of it the War if prosecuted against us would destroy both parties or rather destroy the Goverment & the Confederacy[.] And I ask you as an old friend an old Supporter & Admirer to use your influence to stop this war[.] If Mr Lincoln had when he came into office withdrawn [from] Pickens & Sumpter & the officers from the 7 Seceding States the agitation [of] Davis Yancy &c could not have kept the Conservative Element 15 Months out of the Union & the best thing for all hands now would be to with draw the preparations for War & let peace Reign and the arts & sciences flourish & happiness prevail[.] It is not my place to brag but the north Can not Subjugate the South, I have done nothing but that to be a good Citizen all my life[.] I have a large Interest at Home[.] my property is there[.] I cant dispose of it yet[.] I am made to support the war[.]

I would come on to Washington at the meeting of Congress if I thought I was safe & would not be inconvenienced in getting home in any way[.] would be glad to hear from you[.]

Very Respectfully yr. obt St.
Pitser Miller

ALS, DLC-JP.

1. The June 8, 1861, Tennessee referendum on secession.
2. Although a wealthy slaveholder, Miller remained loyal to the Union, spending the war years in Bolivar, from which place he wrote Johnson in 1862 asking for a writ of election in order to send congressmen from his district and in 1863 complaining about foraging activity of Union troops. Miller to Johnson, November 29, 1862, March 7, 1863, Johnson Papers, LC.

To Amos A. Lawrence, Boston, Mass.[1]

Washington D. C. June 25th, 1861.

(Private.)

Amos A. Lawrence Esq.

Dear Sir

Your letter of the 22nd. ins't has been received. The draft referred to by you has never been received by me. From the publication referred to in the Richmond Enquirer, I take it for granted that the draft was intercepted at that point, and I am in possession of some facts which induce me to believe that it was remitted to Gov. Harris, present Governor of Tennessee.[2]

It, having been abstracted from the mails, of course should not be paid.

The letter referred to in the Enquirer dated "near Boston May 18th, 1861," seems to have been written or predicated upon one received from me. It reads for instance as follows: "If your note to me were printed in our newspapers, it would be good for ten thousand dollars in three days time, but of course I must only use it as a private letter."

If I ever wrote any letter to you on the subject of money to be expended in sustaining the Union in Tennessee or elsewhere, I do not now remember it.

In making this statement, I do not intend to disclaim any letter written by me upon this or any other subject, for I would have been more than gratified to have received means from you or any other person to be expended or used in a proper manner for the purpose of saving the Union and thereby preserve the integrity of the Government, for I feel that money could not be expended in a more holy or just cause.

I have made this statement believing that some person may have written a letter to you and forged my name, for the purpose of using it in such manner as would operate to the injury of the Union party in Tennessee.

I hope that you have preserved the original letter and that you will enclose it to me, so that, if a fraud, I can detect and expose the rascal who perpetrated the act.

I will add in conclusion that some means could be very judiciously used in the Eastern portion of the state in maintaining their position in adhering to the Union. We have some fear of invasion and are determined to resist to the last extremity. We hold the other two divisions of the state as being in rebellion, and shall ask the cooperation of the Federal Government in the enforcement of the law and a compliance with the constitution of the United States.

Most of the presses have been subsidized, those remaining must be sustained and others established. In fine any material aid to be used in sustaining the Union and the constitution, and in crushing out the abominable heresy of secession will be gratefully received, and faithfully applied to that purpose, and accounted for.[3]

I have the honor to be Your Obt. Sert.

Andrew Johnson.

L, MHi-Amos A. Lawrence Papers; in hand of William A. Browning.

1. There can be no question about the authenticity of this letter, although it is not in Johnson's hand. Apparently a worsening of his bad arm, or the general pressure of affairs upon his return to Washington in mid-June, or both, led to his employing an amanuensis for most of his correspondence, including this letter in the hand of William A. Browning, a former land office clerk. Washington *Evening Star*, April 5, 1861.

2. Johnson's comments on the forged May 18 letter cannot but appear somewhat ingenuous, if not downright evasive, if we are to believe Brownlow that the senator had been "furnished" with copies of the letter and draft early in June, either by Dr. Fowlkes or by Brownlow himself.

3. Having discovered, through exposure of the Charlton fraud, that Lawrence and his associates had planned to send financial assistance to East Tennessee, Johnson in his first bona fide letter to the New Englander, goes out of his way to emphasize that "any material aid" would be used most productively in behalf of the Union cause. In thus continuing to focus Lawrence's philanthropic and patriotic attention on East Tennessee, Johnson unwittingly prepared the way for the machinations of the wily Carlyle Murray "of Adair Co. Ky." See Letters from Amos A. Lawrence, August 9, 1861, and Carlyle Murray, July 12, 1861.

From John Bell Brownlow[1]

Knoxville Tenn
Wednesday 26th June 1861

Gov. Johnson

I have time to write you but a few lines as the Train for Nashville leaves in half an hour. A very worthy citizen of this place of Northern birth[2] leaves this morning to settle in Chicago or Boston. This letter will be mailed at Chicago or Boston by the gentleman referred to. For fear that the secessionists here will telegraph to Nashville and have him *searched*, I will have this conveyed upon the person of his wife, whom I suppose they are not despicable enough to examine. I enclose you the proceedings entire of our Convention.[3] It was a glorious affair. An entire success. The proceedings of the convention are already bringing forth good fruit. It is unnecessary to comment. You know all. I would also call your attention to the comments thereon in the paper. Your son Robert came down on yesterday with the expectation of going to the meeting of the Legislature, but upon consultation with friends concluded not to go. He stayed last night with Col. John Williams.[4] Col. Williams will not go to Nashville. I told your son that I would write to you and he bade me say that your family are all well[.]

Very Truly   John Bell Brownlow

P. S.

A report was circulated here day before yesterday that you were coming through Kentucky within a few days march of Knoxville with several thousand troops— The secessionists were actually credulous enough to believe it. In consequence of it, on yesterday and to day four or five companies numbering about 375 or 400 men were sent from this place to guard Cumberland and Wheeler's Gaps.[5] If you were coming with an army you would have a *small* force to beat back. I want you to caution Carter[6] as to the manner of his return. Though the force sent from here would be insignificant to meet a force of any magnitude, yet it is sufficient to capture Carter.

J B. B.

It would be well for Carter to keep on the lookout. The secessionist in E Tenn are greatly frightened. There is no telling when we can get another letter to you.

ALS, DLC-JP.

1. At this time John Bell Brownlow (1839–1922), eldest son of the Parson, was assisting his father in publishing the Knoxville *Whig*. Accompanying the latter north in 1862, he participated in various Union rallies and eventually became a lieutenant colonel of the 9th Tenn. Cav., USA. Returning to Knoxville, he edited the *Whig* (1865–69) and served as his father's personal secretary when Brownlow entered the Senate. The son remained in Washington for a number of years holding various government posts prior to establishing the Knoxville real estate firm of J. B. and W. G. Brownlow. Knoxville *Journal*, October 27, 1922; *Tennesseans in the Civil War*, I, 342.

2. Probably Milford C. Butler (c1824–c1876), native of Massachusetts, a language professor at East Tennessee University (1858–61) and a loyalist whose mail was pilfered by Confederates who also threatened his life. When he and his wife went north after his June 15 resignation, they left behind property worth $3,000. He became principal of Poland Academy in Poland, Ohio, returning later to Knoxville to serve as principal of the Classical Preparatory School of the University (1869–70); from 1870 until his death he was principal of the Knoxville Female Academy. 1860 Census, Tenn., Knox, 12th Dist., 27; Moses White, *Early History of The University of Tennessee* (Knoxville, 1879), 71, 72; Laura E. Luttrell, "One Hundred Years of a Female Academy," ETHS *Publications*, No. 17 (1945), 80; Stanley J. Folmsbee, *East Tennessee University, 1840–1879*, The University of Tennessee *Record*, LXII (1959), 44; Butler to Oliver P. Temple, January 19, 1865, Temple Papers.

3. The Greeneville Union Convention, June 17–20, 1861.

4. For John Williams, see *Johnson Papers*, II, 317–18n.

5. In late June and July there were rumors of Johnson's being seen in the Cumberland Gap area—an apparent case of mistaken identity embarrassing to the Confederate force sent to capture him. An undated clipping from an unidentified newspaper of the period reports there were 1,500 Confederates in Kentucky and 400 in Tennessee at Cumberland Gap, "waiting to capture Andy Johnson" before advancing to Somerset. Wheeler's Gap is in Campbell County, near Jacksboro. Knoxville *Whig*, July 27, 1861; clipping in Johnson Papers, LC.

6. James P. T. Carter (1822–1869), brother of Samuel P. and William B. Carter and a native Tennessean engaged in iron manufacturing before 1860, had accompanied Johnson north after the state seceded; he later became a colonel of the 2nd Tenn. Inf., USA. Appointed by Johnson secretary of Arizona Territory (1866–67), he later served as acting governor (1867–69). John S. Goff, "Colonel James P. T. Carter of Carter County," *Tenn. Hist. Quar.*, XXVI (1967), 372–82.

From Edward Cooper[1]

Cincinnati June 26, 1861

Hon & Dear Sir,

Pardon the infliction I make in asking you to confer with Mr Etheridge to whom I have enclosed a few letters, in favor of an appointment to a chaplaincy in the U. S. Army. I am anxious to return to Tennessee & in connection with the Governments agency for restoring order and obedience to law. My knowledge of the Topography of the Country—the people—and the base appliances of the corrupt press of Memphis, will greatly add to my professional usefulness in Serving the army and winning back the best portion of the Old School Presbyterian influence to patriotism.

An interview with Mr Etheridge will, I trust, Satisfy you that your favorable influence for me will not be misapplied. I do not multiply papers, for I am confident that you and Mr Etheridge ought to have the influence to bring the appointment,—for no men have done more under the most difficult and dangerous circumstances than you to Sustain the administration in saving the best government that ever existed.

Be pleased also to inform when Mr Carter[2] will be here. I have a package of pistol caps for Mr Brownlow, which I wish to Send by him, in order to avoid the danger of interception by express.

With Great Respts Yours Truly
Edward Cooper

Hon A Johnson   Washington

ALS, DLC-JP2.

1. Edward Cooper (b. c1818), New York native and Old School Presbyterian minister and teacher, possessed $4,240 in real estate and $1,200 in personal property. Apparently associated with the Female Institute in Brownsville, founded in 1850 by the West Tennessee Baptist Convention, he seems to have maintained a boardinghouse for teachers. 1860 Census, Tenn., Haywood, Brownsville, 49; Cooper to Johnson, March 17, 1861, Johnson Papers, LC; *Goodspeed's Haywood*, 828.

2. Probably James P. T. Carter.

From R[obert] G. Huffaker

June 26, 1861, Somerset, Ky.; ALS, DLC-JP.

Native Kentuckian and former wholesale grocer applies for some situation with the Federal government, perhaps buying horses and mules. "Oweing to my union Sentiments I have been compelled to give up my Business and leave the town of Nashville, leaving the Rebels in my Debt $20,000, being all I possess."

From Henry Watterson[1]

Chronicle Office[2] June 26th [1861]

My Dear Gov;

Forney has presented my name to the Secretary-of-War for a third-class ($1,600) vacancy, which has recently occured. Gen'l Cameron replied that he would make the appointment, if it was agreable to you. When I assured you last winter that I would not hold office,[3] I was honestly desirous of making my living by my profession, as a journalist; and I have not been disappointed in my expectations. But affairs have changed, father and mother are with me, and a position of the kind has become necessary to me, upon their account. With the same repugnance to official service, which I then entertained, these circumstances force me to abandon my preference for a season at least. The object of this note is simply therefore to ask your good word with the war-office without desiring to vex you with my own, private affairs, when your mind must be so full of public business. I hardly need add Governor, that I sincerely regret this necessity, nor how very much gratified I shall feel, if you will assist me in relieving it; which will require only a word of approval, with which I shall be doubly grateful, if you can mention the weakness of my sight, which some-what retards an over-use of my eyes.[4]

Very truly yours
Henry Watterson[5]

ALS, DLC-JP.

1. Watterson, former clerk in the land office, and at this time reporter for the Washington *States*, which was in its closing days, would shortly embrace the Confederate cause. *Johnson Papers*, III, 477n; Joseph F. Wall, *Henry Watterson: Reconstructed Rebel* (New York, 1956), 32–35.

2. The Washington *Chronicle*, a daily, was started in 1861 by John W. Forney. Watterson was an occasional correspondent for Forney's Philadelphia *Press*. *Ibid.*, 26–27.

3. See Letter from Henry Watterson, March 20, 1860, *Johnson Papers*, III, 476–77.

4. A severe case of scarlet fever during childhood impaired Watterson's sight, which was further damaged by an accident blinding his right eye. Wall, *Henry Watterson*, 9.

5. He did not receive the position and shortly afterwards left Washington for Tennessee. *Ibid.*, 33.

From Samuel K. N. Patton[1]

Campbells Rest Tenn   June 27th 1861

Hon A Johnson
D Sir

East Tennessee is anxiously looking and listning for the sound of
old Abes Horn—& would rejoice at the sight of his troops or the
sound of the horsemans Bugle— We would like to see some 10 or
15 thousand men in Tenn[.] their number would soon be doubled
if it was necessary— We would want the Best kind of Armes (Minnie Rifles) probably would suit us best. With such a force Secession
would be soon stoped— East Tennessee can stope the waar herself
if well armed and drilled, an army would form a neucleus around
which the union men could gather and drill[.]

We have an abundant harvest and can feed them cheap and well[.]
dont wait too long[.] the Secession party are catching the young and
thoughtless[.] they are going into the army[.] they could be Secured to the Lincoln troops, as they are called, if the U S flag was
unfurled to the Breeze and a call made for volunteers under it, By
the by, cant you get some place for me, under old Abe[.] I am not
so hide bound but I would take any profitable office, one in which I
could serve my country with credit to myself and profitt to my
country[.]

If the troops come here I would like to be Commissary or Colonel
of a Regiment of East Tennesseeans if nothing higher[.] Try what
you can do for me— I have heretofore applied for an Indian agency[.]
the papers were Sent to the president[.] you might hunt them up if
you want any evidence as to how I stand at home.

Yours   S K N Patton

P S

I wont be verry particular as to the office[.] I only want one which
will be honerable and proffetable—

S K N Patton

ALS, DLC-JP.

1. For Patton, currently a Washington County member of the legislature,
see *Johnson Papers*, III, 465n.

To Michael Goldman,[1] Rutledge

Washington City, June 27th, 1861.

Michael Goldman Esq.

My dear Sir:

I have to day succeeded in obtaining from the P. O. Department Warrant No. 6.716 on the U. S. Treasurer for $444.^{60}/$_{100}$, payable to your order. The Treasurer makes the warrant payable at the sub-Treasury, Philadelphia, Penn. I herewith enclose the receipt which is to be signed and returned as soon as possible to the U. S. Treasurer.

I have been assured that on to morrow there will be a draft issued for the amount due you from the Census Bureau.

You will please let me know what disposition I shall make of them. I have not been able to receive a letter or newspaper since I left Tenn on the 12th of the month.

There are steps now being taken to open a daily stage line from London Kentucky to Russellville, Tenn, with a view of opening up more immediate & reliable mail facilities with Eastern Tennessee. There will be a special agent sent out in a few days for the purpose of making all necessary arrangements. Perhaps you might find it to your interest to see the agent while there, and put in a bid. The Government is making vigorous and determined efforts to preserve its integrity and crush out the odious doctrine of secession. Write soon and send your letter by way of *Cumberland Gap.*

Your friend   Andrew Johnson

Everything goes on smoothly.

L, DLC-JP; enclosed in Goldman to Johnson, November 9, 1863.

1. Michael Goldman (b. *c*1813), Pennsylvania-born Rutledge census taker and mail contractor, had $1,000 in real and $1,500 in personal property. During the fiscal year 1860–61, he claimed $1,818.50 for his postal services. 1860 Census, Tenn., Grainger, Rutledge, 157; *U. S. Official Register* (1861), 530*.

From Salmon P. Chase

TREASURY DEPARTMENT
June 29, 1861

My Dear Sir,

After the Cabinet meeting today I got hold of our "great and good friend" the President, who expressed the strongest wish to gratify you and endorsed "Approved A. Lincoln" on the order I drew. I then took it to Gen. Thomas[1] who promised to have it properly directed &

signed & to send it to me or to you. I also saw Cameron who promised the guns—two rifles & two Smooth bore.[2] So there need be no more delay[.]

Very truly   S P Chase[3]

Hon. A. Johnson

ALS, DLC-JP.

1. Lorenzo Thomas (1804–1875), adjutant general of the army (1861–69), was a West Point graduate (1823), a veteran of the Seminole and Mexican wars, and Winfield Scott's chief of staff (1853–61). When President Johnson dismissed Secretary of War Stanton in February, 1868, he appointed Thomas secretary *ad interim* and requested him to take possession of the department; Stanton, in turn, had Thomas arrested under the Tenure of Office Act. Although acquitted, he retired from the army in 1869. *DAB*, XVIII, 441–42.
2. At this time the United States army possessed two types of cannon—the twelve-pounder "Napoleon," a smoothbore gun-howitzer used extensively in the war, and the cast-iron ten-pounder, a rifled cannon invented by Robert P. Parrott. Francis A. Lord, *Civil War Collector's Encyclopedia* (Harrisburg, Pa., 1963), 24–29.
3. Endorsed by Johnson: "From Secretry Chase in reference to the raising of troopes in Tenn & Ky—"

From William R. Fleming[1]

Lexington Ky, June 30. 1861

Hon Andrew Johnson
My Dear Sir
I have intended writing you several days ago but concluded I would wait and see the result of the action of a certain defeated Candidate for Congress in the 9th district of our State, Col. John S. Williams of Cerro Gordo notoriety—[2] He is trying to raise a company of soldiers in Ky for what purpose no one knows except what he says himself[.] I understand he has said he would intercept if possible the arms intended for East Tenn. and I think it quite probable he would make the attempt at Paris—Bourbon County where Secession has more advocates than at any point along the route— This route was suggested by you when I had the pleasure of seeing you here[.] You will perhaps remember me as the person who called upon you at the Hotel & drove you to see the monument of Mr Clay in the afternoon. I gave you also on the eve of taking leave of you on the night of your speech my name & desired to serve you in any way I could. I still desire to do so—if I can & refer you to Hon J. J. Crittenden, Geo. W. Dunlap,[3] Members of Congress from this State— as to my position standing &c &c[.] I suggest that in case you should desire to send arms to East Tenn that to avoid all danger, I would suggest they be stopped at Maysville 65 miles east of Cincinnati

thence to Flemingsburg (my native Town) Mt. Sterling Richmond —thence through Whitley County to avoid the Cumberland gap, as it is said here that men are to be stationed there to get hold of them, how true it is I am not prepared to say— you can better judge than I the correctness of the rumor— I go in a few days to Maysville & Flemingsburg where I shall remain for some two weeks, and if I can serve you or your cause, I will be glad to do it[.] Write to me direct Flemingsburg Ky where I shall be glad to hear of your success in any thing—

The sacrifice you made in stopping with us was not so great I hope as you feared it would be[.] The speech you made for us will not be forgotten by us, & as I told you that it satisfied the wavering & made for the gallant Crittenden many votes[.] We intend taking the position defined by you, & we do not doubt of ultimate & complete success of a cause so just & good. I hope & trust that you may be able to accomplish great good during the coming Session of Congress although things look gloomy enough in almost every direction[.] I send you enclosed some few extracts which I have cut from newspapers in order that you may see the estimation in Ky place[d] upon your services—reputation &c[.]

I presume you will hardly return to Tenn before the adjournment of the approaching Congress— I shall be happy when not conflicting with your duties to have you drop me a line occasionally giving me a short a/c [account] of your doing's &c &c[.] If Mr Carter[4] is still with you please remember me kindly to him— Wishing you good health happiness &c

I remain dear Sir Your obliged friend &c
Wm. R. Fleming

ALS, DLC-JP.

1. William R. Fleming (b. c1815), a native of Kentucky, as a young man moved to Philadelphia, where he was a "merchant" at 153 Market Street. Returning to Kentucky about 1859, he married and, according to the census, was worth $20,000. 1860 Census, Ky., Scott, 37; *McElroy's Philadelphia Directory* (1850), 134; (1856), 204; G. Glenn Clift, comp., *Kentucky Marriages, 1797–1865* (Baltimore, 1966), 193.

2. John S. Williams (1818–1898), lawyer and politician, served as a Whig, and later a Democrat, in the Kentucky house (1851–54, 1873–76) and as a Democrat in the U. S. Senate (1879–85). A Mexican War veteran who distinguished himself at Cerro Gordo, he was appointed brigadier general, CSA, and commanded in East Tennessee, opposing Burnside's advance to Knoxville. After the war he was a railroad promoter and farmer. *BDAC*, 1822; Boatner, *Civil War Dictionary*, 927; Collins, *Kentucky*, II, 130.

3. George W. Dunlap (1813–1880), commissioner of the Kentucky circuit court (1843–74), member of the state house of representatives (1853), and recently elected Unionist congressman (1861–63), returned to the practice of law in Lancaster after the war. *BDAC*, 836.

4. James P. T. Carter, who had accompanied Johnson on his flight from Tennessee.

From Alexander R. McKee[1]

Somerset Ky 30th June/ 1861.

Hon Andrew Johnson
Dear Sir

We are exceedingly apprehensive that an effort will be made by a detachment of Virginia Rebels to take the guns about to be, or being, forwarded to the Loyal men of East Tennessee— Our Trator Govenor[2] was seen in Company with a few of his Traitorous gang a few days ago, at the Rail Road Depot Lexington—whispering something—*Treason no doubt*, to his satelites who were on the eve of departure on the Eastern train— We believe their mission was to inform Jeff Davis or some of his crew, that East Ten—was about to be furnished with arms, by way of Kentucky—and if possible to have them taken after the waggons pass Cumberland Gap— Kentuckians will protect them to the borders' and if assailed any-where near there will protect them farther or die in the attempt[.]

We do not know, what plan you have devised or how you propose gitting the guns to the Loyal men of your state, and are at a loss to act in concert— an agent should be sent to Knox Co.—Laurel Co. &c. with full instructions— If you find it necessary to Telegraph me on the subject, do so in the alphabet enclosed[.][3] send your Telegraph to Lexington with directions to enclose by mail to me at Somerset, and also at Mt Vernon Kentucky[.]

Verry hurriedly & truly your fried
Alexr. McKee

Hon Green Adams[4] will hand or enclose you this note, and will inform you who I am[.]

Mc

ALS, DLC-JP.

1. Alexander R. McKee (b. *c*1815) was a coal merchant with $22,000 in real and $3,500 in personal estate. 1860 Census, Ky., Pulaski, 88.

2. Beriah Magoffin, though a believer in the right of secession, deplored piecemeal secession. Refusing Lincoln's call for troops, he also turned down a similar request from Davis, although secretly permitting Confederate recruiters within the state. After the legislature refused to call a convention, the governor had proclaimed the state's neutrality on May 20. *DAB*, XII, 200.

3. The code was as follows:

a b c d e f g h i j k l m n o p q r s t u v w x y z
6 1 x ▽ z △ 9 c v 7 4 3· Χ = ‖ 5 □ $ 8 ∼ 10 17 22 30 75 100

4. Green Adams (1812–1884), elected to Congress as a Whig (1847–49) and as an American (1859–61), also held several appointive positions, including judge of the Kentucky circuit court (1851–56), sixth auditor of the treasury (1861–64), and chief clerk of the House of Representatives (1875–81). *BDAC*, 459.

From James L. Slaughter[1]

London Laurel County Kentucky
June 30th, 1861

Honl Andrew Johnson.

I am the man that you stoped with when you was Comeing from Barbersville in Companey with Adams and Joplin—[2] I have some newes to Tell you[.] Mr. Newby[3] at the foot of the Cumberland Mountain on the other Side in Ten brought the news that thair was Three hundred and fifty of the Rebles Station at the Gap—and Two hundred at Big Creek[.] the news came to me this evening by the mail Carrier[.] thair had been moore of the Rebbls came to the Gap[.] the number now is One *Thousand*— the Rebbles has planted their Cannon on the Kentucky *Soil* and they are wateing for you—to come with your *armes*[.]

I have One request to ask of you[.] I want you to Send me One of Sharpes best Rifles[4] with all that belongs— Send the Box by Express —in care of John Carty of Lexington[.][5] pay all charges to Lexington— when you Shipe the Box drop me a line[.] we all want to here from you[.] I will pay you for the gun at any Time[.] all well[.]

You[r]s &Co James L. Slaughter
Send the gun quick[.] we may nead it—   J. L. S

ALS, DLC-JP.

1. James L. Slaughter (b. *c*1824), a Kentucky-born merchant, possessed $4,400 in real and $19,370 in personal property. 1860 Census, Ky., Laurel, London, 135.

2. Green Adams and possibly James Joplin (1807–1900), a Virginia native residing in Hardin County, Kentucky. Julia H. S. Ardery, comp., *Kentucky Records* (2 vols., Baltimore, 1965–72), I, 229.

3. Possibly James Newby (b. *c*1830), a wagonmaker. 1860 Census, Tenn., Claiborne, 9th Div., 165.

4. Invented by Christian Sharps of Philadelphia in 1848, this rifle was the first really satisfactory breech-loading gun. *Encyclopaedia Britannica* (1971 ed.), XX, 671.

5. John Carty (1806–1867) was a well-known grocer and commission merchant. Collins, *Kentucky*, II, 195; *Williams' Lexington Directory* (1859–60), 43.

Knoxville, June 13. 1861

Hon. I.G. Harris,
   Nashville.

   Dr Sir:

      You now perceive how
difficult it will be to detect Brownlow in his
answer to the enclosed letter. In his last issue
he says his letters are intercepted at Nashville, & that
you folks are boasting of opening Johnson's letters.

                                    Yours &c
                                    C. W. Charlton

   P. Since writing the above I have seen the Johnson
letter in the Virginia papers! So this ends the correspondence
between Amos & Andy. Sorry for it, for I wanted to
pursue it, and was just on the ~~was~~ eve of getting for the
State about $10,000 of Lawrence's money!

503   C.

Charles W. Charlton to Governor Isham G. Harris, June 13, 1861:
The "*Amos & Andy*" correspondence.
Courtesy Library of Congress.

Amos A. Lawrence, portrait by Eastman Johnson.
Courtesy Harvard University Portrait Collection.

To Nashville Union and American[1]

June 30, 1861

ANDREW JOHNSON AND THE CHARGE MADE AGAINST HIM
BY THE RICHMOND ENQUIRER.

From the Richmond Enquirer.

We have just seen a letter from Amos A. Lawrence, of Boston, well known to the country as one of her men of capital and a leading Black Republican, in the full confidence of President Lincoln and his Government at Washington. It is addressed to Andrew Johnson, of Tennessee, and encloses a draft for one thousand dollars, *as part of the pay* intended for his services in betraying those confiding portions of the people of Tennessee who have stood by him in support of the maintenance of the Federal Union. We give this letter to the public. It was intercepted in its passage to Johnson, and is now in possession of a reliable gentleman of this city, well known to the country. There is no doubt of the genuineness of the letter.

Let the people of Tennessee ponder over this letter, and ask themselves if so base a traitor should longer exist in her midst. Note the remark of Lawrence, that, if the information given by this infamous wretch was printed in the Northern newspapers, "*it would be good for ten thousand dollars in there* [three] *days time.*" This thousand, however, is given him in order that "*he* (Johnson) *may be sure of some thing at once.*" Never, perhaps, have we been brought to witness such perfidy and corruption on the part of one who has held so high an office in the Government of our country. So blasting a crime cannot be resisted with too dire a vengeance by the people of Tennessee. He ought to be arrested at once.

[Lawrence to Johnson, May 18, 1861, is printed here.]

No one I am sure, could have been more surprised than I at the appearance of the above article.— As I had *never* written to Amos A. Lawrence, Esq., upon the subject of East Tennessee affairs, with the view of obtaining either money or other material aid, I saw at a glance that forgery, fraud, and robbery of the mails formed the basis of this mendacious article, and I therefore wrote to Mr. Lawrence,[2] (*the first and only letter ever written by me to Mr. L. upon any subject whatever,*) requesting him to forward to me the original letter or letters upon which his draft had been predicated.

I have just received his reply thereto, in which he expresses his regret at the deception practiced, and encloses two letters, purporting to have been written by me, as follows:

[Johnson to Lawrence, May 15, June 6, 1861.]

I pronounce both of the above letters deliberate, wilful, and unmitigated forgeries, perpetrated, no doubt, with the view not only of injuring me, but of damaging the Union party of Tennessee by connecting my name with Northern men and Northern means in a manner supposed to be obnoxious to the noble patriots of my own State.

The letter of the 15th ultimo, it seems, is the private letter to which Mr. Lawrence refers in his letter as published in the *Enquirer*, and upon which the draft was drawn. This is the first forgery.

The letter of the 6th instant clearly shows that the draft, which could not be made available, so palpable was the fraud, was to be retained and used in the work of injuring me, just as circumstances might favor; while the call for "$5,000 or $10,000 in New England currency, in *large bills*," if favorably responded to, would have served individual purposes, and, I doubt not, would have been unhesitatingly used therefor. To make this fraud and bold attempt at robbery still more conclusive, I will state the fact that, on the 15th May, the date of the first letter, I was present at and addressed a large Union meeting in Elizabethtown, and one hundred and eighteen miles from Knoxville, where the above letters were written and mailed; and on the 6th June, the date of the second letter, I was filling one of a series of appointments at Montgomery, about forty miles west of Knoxville. This town of Knoxville, let it be remembered, is about seventy-five miles distant from Greenville, by postoffice address. I shall add further, that there is not, either in the body of the letters or the signatures thereto, the slightest similiarity to my handwriting or signature.

It would have been impossible for such a fraudulent and mail-robbing transaction to have been carried on in the postoffice at Knoxville without the knowledge or consent of the postmaster,[3] and he and his confederates must be held responsible for it by an enlightened public judgment. Time may develop all the facts connected with this and other transactions of a similar character perpetrated at this same post office.

I have not made this statement of facts for the purpose of exonerating myself of treachery, treason, and corruption, based upon the publication of the Richmond *Enquirer*, for I feel that I stand beyond the reach of their shafts of calumny and defamation; but my object is to expose the dishonorable and wicked means resorted to by "secession" to carry out its nefarious and corrupt designs in attempting to overthrow and break up the best Government the world ever saw.

ANDREW JOHNSON.

Washington, June 30, 1861.

Nashville *Union and American*, July 9, 1861.

1. In an effort to counter the adverse publicity consequent upon the publication of the spurious Lawrence correspondence in the Richmond *Enquirer*, June 11, 1861, and subsequently reprinted in Tennessee, Johnson inserted this

disclaimer in the *Union and American*, a onetime supporter now become a Confederate organ. The editors remained unconvinced, observing: "We consider it proper to give him the benefit of his wholesale denial. But we feel sure that, when this matter is probed to the bottom, he will be found to have had some understanding with LAWRENCE, whose guilt is confessed in sending aid to him. He certainly had an understanding with the Washington Administration relative to military assistance, as he frequently threatened, in his speeches, that such aid would be furnished. LAWRENCE was clearly a secret agent of the Administration in the matter." Nashville *Union and American*, July 9, 1861.

2. Letter to Amos A. Lawrence, June 25, 1861.

3. Johnson was quite right, in view of Postmaster Charlton's preoccupation with the interception of unionist mail—not only Johnson's, but also that of T. A. R. Nelson, Brownlow, and a Massachusetts professor of ancient languages at East Tennessee University, Milford C. Butler. When the forgery was revealed, Charlton wrote Harris that Brownlow "says his letters are intercepted at Nashville & that you folks are boasting of opening *Johnsons* letters. . . . Since writing the above I have seen the Johnson letter in the Virginia papers! So this ends the correspondence between *Amos* & *Andy*. Sorry for it, for I wanted to pursue it, and was just on the eve of getting for the State about $10,000 of Lawrence's money!" Charlton to Harris, June 13, 1861, Johnson Papers, LC; Folmsbee, *East Tennessee University*, 44–45.

From Roderick R. Butler

Rep Hall Nashville July 1st /61

Hon A. Johnson

Dear Sir this body will adjourn this day after having created offices sufficient for all[1] I suppose and sufficient increase the storm of indignation that is still in Eastern Tennessee[.] the Legislature refused the petition of East Tennessee asking for a division of the State[2] and refered the question to the next General assembly[.] my own opinion is that when the Kingston Convention[3] asembles that a State Government will be organised[.] I send you the report of the committee to whom the question was refered[.][4] I find that East Tennessee has many frinds in Middle & West Tennessee who say that whenever a blow is struck at East Tennessee they are with her and I dont belive an effort will be made to coerse her[.] they will be afraid of the policy of [illegible] and if East Tennessee will make a bold strike she will have but little difficulty in sustaining herself[.] Wm H Polk is a canidate for Govnor[.][5] his announcement produced a flutering in King Harris ranks[.] perhaps we can make an arrangement with him by giving him the heavy majority of East Tennessee to favor our moove[.] I will lay the suggestion before our frinds in Knoxville tomorrow[.] Robert has not been here[.] we thought it best[.] this body have been very concilitory indeed but it was not because they desired so to do but as we all beleve the Greeneville Convention made them open their eyes. I have conversed with many

Gentlemen of both sides and but one opinion prevails as to the Critenden amendments[.][6] all agree that if they were passed Tennessee would take imediate steps to go back into the Federal union and I trust the Republican Party will have the good judgment to pass them imediately[.] I have heard several members of this body say who voted for separation that if they were passed they would take grounds for going back[.] it will have a powerfull effect and no mistake[.] I have an arrangement so I can communicate with you and will advise you of our moove[.] I had in my possession two pension certifi[c]ates one belonging to David D. Sturt[7] the other George Brown[8] Invalid pensioners and I lost both of them and I have hunted every where for them[.] they both reside in Johnson County[.] will you be so kind as to procure duplicates as they are reflecting upon me[.] it is true at the presant they will do them no good but they are after me every day for them[.] please Govenor attend to it as it will relieve me much[.] the law requires an affidavit but I presume the department will issue them upon my statement endorsed by yourself[.]

I am truly   R R Butler

ALS, DLC-JP2.

1. Probably a reference to the many military positions authorized by the Act of May 6, filled by the governor and confirmed by the legislature on June 29. See *Tenn. Senate Journal*, 1861, 2nd Extra Sess., 169–72; *Tenn. House Journal*, 1861, 2nd Extra Sess., 188–91, 194.

2. The Greeneville convention's memorial requesting separate statehood was presented on June 20; nine days later it was rejected by the General Assembly, which adopted a joint house-senate report. *Ibid.*, 192–93; *Tenn. Senate Journal*, 1861, 2nd Extra Sess., 176–77; *OR*, Ser. 1, LII, Pt. I, 178–79; Nashville *Republican Banner*, June 30, 1861.

3. One of the Greeneville resolutions had provided for the assembling of an East Tennessee constitutional convention at Kingston, subject to the call of the president, Thomas A. R. Nelson, who scheduled a meeting for August 31. However, Nelson's arrest by the Confederate authorities and his acquiescence in Tennessee's secession precluded the Kingston meeting. Knoxville *Whig*, August 3, 1861; *OR*, Ser. 1, LII, Pt. I, 176–77.

4. Probably the joint house-senate report on the Greeneville convention resolutions, found in *Tenn. House Journal*, 1861, 2nd Extra Sess., 192–93.

5. Polk, brother of the President, was defeated by incumbent Governor Harris, 74,973–43,342. *Tenn. Official Manual*, 170; *Johnson Papers*, II, 299n.

6. Crittenden's compromise amendments, debated throughout the winter of 1861, had failed in the Senate early in March but continued to receive considerable press and public support. Nevins, *Emergence of Lincoln*, II, 390–91, 402.

7. David D. Stuart (b. c1791), a Johnson County farmer with $6,000 in real and $1,000 personal property. No pension record has been found. 1860 Census, Tenn., Johnson, 6th Dist., 85.

8. George Brown (c1784–1874), North Carolina native and Carter County farmer, claiming "an injury" as a result of lifting logs while building a blockhouse at Ft. Armstrong in Alabama during his three-month enlistment in the War of 1812, was awarded an annual invalid pension of $93, beginning July 3, 1852. *Ibid.*, Carter, 31; *House Ex. Doc.* No. 119, 35 Cong., 1 Sess., 51; George Brown, "Old War" Invalid Pensions, RG15, National Archives.

From Leslie Combs[1]

Lexington July 1/61

Private

Dr Sir.

1st My Son in law—Capt Bruce,[2] will this day, commence organizing the *Home* guard into Battallions Regts—Brigades & Divisions—with Commanders *Duly elected*—not appointed by our Govenor—

2nd Northern & central Kentucky are pretty well Supplied with arms, but we need, *speedily*, 5000 Stand for South-Eastern Kentucky on the line of Tennessee—all loyal counties & ready to help East Tennessee in her trouble—

3rd The Gov. & his co-conspirators have not yet consented to submit to the popular voice—but are operating to get up a row before our August election— They have Several plans— One is to stop guns from *crossing Ky*—to E. Tennessee—

4th Looking to this, I have notified our friends in Ky Central R. R. & all along the Wilderness road to Cumberland Gap to be on the alert, *as if* the Guns were to be conveyed by these roads— I think the Gov &Co will thus be thrown out—

5th I have *only* mentioned to my Son in law the *true* route is to land at Louisville—Rail road to Lebanon—.then Taylor, Casey & Wayne Counties & to your line— You must have Waggons at Lebanon & mounted unarmed men to meet them as Soon as possible & be ready to protect them.

6th

Your men can leave Tennessee in Squads or Companies as may be best & march back an army—fully organised &c &c—

I hope to be in Washington the first of next week & will see you— I shall stop at Willards—

Yours truly   Leslie Combs

Hon A. Johnson U. S. Senate
Washington D. C.
P. S. Address Col Sanders D. Bruce Lexington Ky.

ALS, DLC-JP.

1. Leslie Combs (1793–1881), War of 1812 veteran, general of the Kentucky militia, and lawyer-businessman widely known as "the friend of Henry Clay," had served in the Kentucky house (1827–29, 1833, 1845–47, 1857–59). An active Unionist, he was elected clerk of the Kentucky court of appeals (1860–66). *DAB*, IV, 328; "Life of General Leslie Combs," *American Whig Review*, XV (1852), 53–62, 142–55.

2. Sanders D. Bruce (1825–1902), born in Lexington and educated at Transylvania College, went into the mercantile business. A staunch Union

man, he was appointed inspector general of the Kentucky Home Guard and elected colonel of the 20th Ky. Vols. Resigning his commission in 1864, he removed to New York City, where in August, 1865, he began the sporting journal *Turf, Field, and Farm* and wrote several books on horses. *NCAB*, VI, 321–22; *Who Was Who in America* (5 vols., Chicago, 1943–73), I, 155.

From John Dainty[1]

Philada July 1 1861

Dr Sir

I have had you[r] portrait engraved of which I send proof.[2] Will you please have your friends examine it for correction and suggest any alterations which would improve the likeness and send them by return mail[.]

Respy yours   John Dainty
728 Sansone St

To Hon Andrew Johnson

ALS, DLC-JP.

1. John Dainty (b. *c*1807) was listed in the census as a shoe dealer and appeared in Philadelphia directories variously as a shoe manufacturer, merchant, copperplate printer, and publisher. 1860 Census, Pa., Philadelphia, 24th Ward, 9th precinct, 53; *McElroy's Philadelphia Directory* (1860), 209; (1862), 145; (1863), 183; (1864), 160.

2. This likeness, engraved by Adam B. Walter of Philadelphia, was published by Dainty along with an excerpt from Johnson's Speech at Cincinnati, June 19, 1861. Print No. USZ61–181, LC. See frontispiece.

From Mathew J. J. Cagle[1]

Springfield Ill
July 2d 61

To the Honerable <u>Andruw Johnson</u> of <u>Tenn</u>

Dear Sir

I for the first time Avale my Self of the oppertunity of wrighting you A few lines to Infom you whoo I am And my Condition and the Condition of things in my Section of Contry in Tennessee I[n] which I Shall Ask Some Advise And I hope you Excuse me if you will not give it[.] I am now in Springfield *Ill* wher I Shall Remane Some 4. or, 5 days[.] I am from Dickson County *Tenn*[.] I was Acting as Justice of the peace for the 9th District[.] I was a Striker for Douglass, for which Information I Refer you to *W. R. Hurly*[.] I Being

A Douglas man and then Contending for Slaves under twelve years old and over fifty to be Taxed as other property[2] Created a prejudice Against me[.] And when this Revolution taken place I was questioned how I stood And Whether I wold take the Oath to the Southern Confederacy or not[.] I Answered them I was A Union man And wold not take the Oath And Continued to Argue for the Stars And Stripes And Advised my friends Not to Vounteer[.] they (the Secessionist) there upon Sent A Company of Armed men to take me And deal with me if I Still refused to take Oath[.] then my friends Advised me to leave And I Started But on Reflection I was not Satisfyed to leave So I went Back And tried to feel around Some But was watched[.] tho I Can Start A. *Capt* Company in my County And from what I Can learn others Can do the Same in other places And as Soon as I Can Read [*sic*] and Drill Some I Am Redy for to Searve the Stars And Stripes *And will do it*[.] But I lack Some infomation which I hope you will Give me[.]

I want to know how my men will Be payed And how I am to get the lawful authority to Rase and muster in to Searvis these men And when the Union men of *Tenn* will get assistance And in what maner And whoo will take Charg of the Union men in Our State And wher I am to look to for Arms[.]

I am her with out means[.] Answer Soon And give me Some Advise[.]

Yours with mutch Respect &C

M. J. J. Cagle

ALS, DLC-JP.

1. Mathew J. J. Cagle (b. *c*1829), Illinois native and Unionist, was a Dickson County farmer who represented that county in the state legislature (1867–69) and served on a state committee to encourage the settlement of immigrants in Tennessee. 1860 Census, Tenn., Dickson, 82; Robison, *Preliminary Directory, Dickson*, 17.

2. Article II, Sec. 28 of the Tennessee Constitution of 1835 provided for the taxation of "slaves between the ages of twelve and fifty years." *Tenn. Official Manual*, 86.

From A. D. Ferren

July 2, 1861, Jackson, Mich.; ALS, DLC-JP2.

Offers Johnson an opportunity to offset his reported "heavy pecuniary loss" consequent upon his Union stance by delivering patriotic lectures in several Michigan cities. If he is averse to speaking with an admission fee—"fearing that it might excite prejudice against you"—perhaps he would "lecture for the benefit of the widows and orphans of those who may fall in battle for the Union," or some other cause deemed proper.

From Henry T. Johns[1]

Cheshire Berkshire Co. Mass.
July 2. 1861

Hon. A. Johnson
Honored Sir

I am pastor of the M. E. Church in this place; am 33 yrs of age, 9 of which have been spent in the ministry and 6 of those years in the South.

I desire to be connected with Tennessee's struggle for herself in the Union. I have not rugged strength enough for a private, military skill for an officer, but I have strength and ability for the work of praying & preaching. I have no doubt that U. S. Regiments will be formed in Tennessee and to one of those Regiments I desire to be connected as Chaplain[.]

While I sympathize with the North in her efforts to preserve our nationality, I can but more deeply sympathize with the efforts of those states, whose Union men walk in constant peril of their lives[.]

I want to be among your Union men. Chaplains are elected by the field & company officers of the respective regiments, but that would follow your recommendation as a matter of course[.]

Obtain me this post and I will come and share your destinies.

My friends think I have enough of the Ad-Captandum[2] to make an effective chaplain[.]

For character and adaptation, I have recommendations from Hon. H. L. Dawes, Gov. Briggs, Col. Briggs, Rev G. Haven Chaplain of Mass. 8th &c &c &c[.][3]

Please take this among your other various duties and thus add one more bond to my gratitude.

Situated as Tennessee now is, I cannot expect she will pay her Chaplains as Mass. does ($118 pr. month). If the coming session of Congress should graft this feature into the Army,[4] then I should receive pay for my services, if not labor and honor must stand for pay.

God bless you, sir, and preserve you, that when your death hour comes, it may be amid the quiet of home, beneath the avenged flag of our Union[.]

Yours *fraternally*
Henry T. Johns.

ALS, DLC-JP.

1. Henry T. Johns (1828–1906), Pennsylvania native, served with the 49th and 61st Mass. Vols. as first lieutenant, was cited for gallantry during the Appomattox campaign, and subsequently was employed by the land

office. Henry L. / Martha J. Johns, WC–623, 146, Pension File, RG15, National Archives; *OR*, Ser. 1, XLVI, Pt. I, 1094.

2. See Speech on Secession, December 18–19, 1860, note 16.

3. Henry L. Dawes (1816–1903), Massachusetts lawyer, state legislator, congressman (1857–75), and senator (1875–93), is chiefly remembered as the author of the Dawes Act of 1887, which granted U. S. citizenship and 160–acre homesteads to Indian heads of families who met certain conditions. George N. Briggs (1796–1861), Massachusetts governor (1843–51) and one of the founders of the Republican party in that state, was a staunch supporter of Abraham Lincoln. His son, Henry S. Briggs (1824–1887), a Massachusetts lawyer, commanded a battalion in the Army of the Potomac during the peninsular campaign and later became a brigadier general. Gilbert Haven (1821–1880), later a Methodist Episcopal bishop, served for three months in 1861 as chaplain of the 8th Mass. Vols., then traveled abroad in 1862. Following his return, he was appointed pastor to a Boston congregation (1863–66), then served as editor of the Methodist journal *Zion's Herald* until his election as bishop in 1872. He published numerous religious works. *DAB*, V, 149–50; *BDAC*, 788; *NCAB*, I, 114–15; XIII, 261–62; Boatner, *Civil War Dictionary*, 86; William Gravely, *Gilbert Haven, Methodist Abolitionist: A Study in Race, Religion, and Reform, 1850–1880* (Nashville, 1973).

4. In early May the war department had issued a general order relating to the formation of volunteer units, including the appointment of regimental chaplains. On July 22 Congress approved the general order, providing for chaplains' pay and allowances comparable to those for captains of cavalry ($70 per month, with rations and forage). It is presumed that chaplains serving with the Tennessee regiments in Kentucky were covered by this legislation. *U. S. Statutes*, XII, 270, 595; *Revised Regulations of the Army of the United States, 1861* (Philadelphia, 1862), 351; *OR*, Ser. 3, I, 154; Roy J. Honeywell, *Chaplains of the United States Army* (Washington, D. C., 1958), 104–5.

From James D. Martin[1]

Somersette Ky July 2nd/61

Hon. A Johnson
Dear Sir

You will I have no doubt be surprised, at receiveing a Letter from me at this time. I hope however you will excuse me for what might seem an intrusion, but for and under the circumstances which I write my object is two fold which you will Learn as you read. And first haveing Learned that you were in Washington for the purpose of making arrangements by which our friends in E. *Ten.* might be protected in *their rights*, by furnishing arms &c &c I have thought it right to app[r]ise you of the fact, that there is at this time stationed at Cumberland Gap six hundred Jeff Davis soldiers and that they are being daily reinforced. They have also a considerable force at every gap on the Ky line to prevent the shipment of arms into East Tennessee. Since I Left Greeneville I have been constantly Labouring in the Union cause, making speeche &c &c, & here Let me remark that if it should become necessary for your safety either as it regards your person or the transmission of arms to Tennessee, that there can be 5.000 brave Kentuckians raised *in the mountains* that would be proud to accompany you either as a body guard or an escort for the safe delivery of arms in Tennessee at any point you may designate.

And secondly as you are well aware all business has been suspended in Greeneville makeing it absolutely necessary for me to remove to some other Locality in order that I might be able to make a support for my family but to my discomfiture I have found Kentucky no better for my business, notwithstanding they are all for the *stars* & *stripes* here yet there is no money[.] there is nothing that I can do for a Support. If I would I might have availed my self of an appointment in the Southern Army but a sense of duty to my country would not permit me to accept an appointment at their hands however Lu[c]rative it might be notwithstanding all of my nearest relations are extremely southeron.

This is therefore to ask your aid in my behalf to obtain an appointment in some of the departments in Washington city that would be at Lea[s]t sufficient for a support for myself & family until our Loved country can be restored, & peace & plenty reign where all is now one wide spread & universal ruin. An early answer will be anxiously Looked for.

Most Respectfully   James D. Martin
Formerly of Greeneville E. Tennessee

P. S.
I have just Learned that Capt Garrard[2] of Clay county Ky has raised 5000 volunteers for the U. S. service[.]

Our P. M. here is a Secessionist.[3] I will have to send this to an other office to be mailed[.]

ALS, DLC-JP.
    1. Probably James D. Martin (b. *c*1830), a Virginia-born Greeneville dentist. 1860 Census, Tenn., Greene, 83.
    2. Theophilus T. Garrard (1812–1902), Kentucky state representative (1843–44), senator (1857–61), and captain in the Mexican War, was promoted to colonel of the 7th Ky. Vols., USA, and later to brigadier general. In 1860 he had $7,000 in real and $13,000 in personal estate. Boatner, *Civil War Dictionary*, 326; 1860 Census, Ky., Clay, 12; Speed, *Union Cause*, 75–76; *Appleton's Cyclopaedia*, II, 608.
    3. Probably F. J. White, who was appointed in 1855 and served until 1861. *U. S. Official Register* (1855), *263; (1859), *127; (1861), *257.

From John E. Patterson[1]

Oberlin O July 2d 61

Hon Andrew Johnson

Sir your position since your Boyhood has ever had an upward tendency & for which I am glad and feel proud of *you*. I have not seen you since your days of boyhood but for all the time since then to the present I have had much pleasure in reading you mooving on upward & ever in the right course & on the right side. I know you have forgotten me long since & why—you have—it is plain & but reasonable—that it would be so. as your way has been upward & you well—merit your present attainments—while my position is but an Humble *one*, and my way through Life up to the prest has been Ruff & hedged up—on every side, but like you Sir—I have ever lived in love with moral and upright Character & am still so inclined to fill that space to the utmost of my ability[.] it is my true sentiment though it is much like self praise—to speak thus of myself— yet I am glad to know—that it is none the less *true* & like you *Sir* I have ever tried to reach after all and every Honorable persuit—as is my *Motto* through life—but to the substance that leads me to drop this line to your Honour. 1st we was will [well] acquainted & play mates & neighbours in your days of Boyhood[.] Many play of marbles & other amusements of youthful enjoyment we had in the yard of your mothers home—as we my mother—to yours was near neighbours—even for a time on the same lot & when she lived on the orchard place on the land of Mr Suggs[2] south of his residence toward the Creek—all of which is now fresh to my mind & I fondly look back at those days—of our Boyhood—& often review your march *upward* & *upward* with pleasure & when I have read through the News papers that Andrew Johnson is a self made *man* I in my mind can confirm the fact as no man of this day—knew more of you & yourse of early life than does myself & my Brother Henry[3] & we often fondly speak of you as he to was a playmate of the same days & now I go on to tell you—who we *are* and of our origin[.] We are the Sons of Chancy Patterson or Chancy Harris as Stephen Harris her last Husband gave the Name of Harris—but Harris was not the farther of us— Our mother has been dead some twenty one years— twelve years after her decease—we Henry and myself & our families left Raleigh mooved to the State of Ohio where we now live in much *Cumfort* & have raised a family here— Henry & *me* lear[ne]d the trade of Bricklayer & plasterer under Old Mr Henry S. Gorman & John. S. Gorman[4] his son all of Raleigh & I supposed you may remember them[.] they both of them has died long since[.] There is many little things that I could tell you of—that might cause you to recolect us—but I will not truble you with them now—as I feel that you is a business man in matters of great moment—in these times of Excitement & will hardly condesend to Notice a line from so Humble and Remote Person & the more do I suppose so—as I am a man of Colour & you a Member of *Congress*—but I hope you will pardon me at least—if I have intruded & pass me off unnoticed if you choose— but *Sir*—you may say that I have gone far out of my way—in this matter— Yet I can assure you that while I write this I am fondly delighted even to think of you and of bygone days of Boyhood— I cannot even hope or expect you to Condecend to drop me an answer yet there is no man that would be more glad of the Honour to Receive a letter from you— perhaps you will at least send me a scrap of some of the debates in the Approaching Congress[.] if so I will feel much obliged[.] the Honourable Mr Blake[5] from our District sends me such ocationaly— I will not say more[.] Brother Henry join me in this and offer you our Highest Regard and do assure you that the Name & acts of Andrew Johnson stands highest in order in this state & you are well known here by character as a great man— and a self made man &c[.]

Yourse &   John. E. Patterson

P S Remember the poor & the needy while it is well [with] you[.] you number but one—but you are of much *weight* & influence[.]

ALS, DLC-JP.

1. John E. Patterson (b. c1804), a mulatto, is listed in the census as a mason with $4,000 in real estate and $100 in personal property. 1860 Census, Ohio, Lorain, 83.

2. Not identified.

3. Henry J. Patterson (b. c1809) was a master mason with $1,500 in real estate and $200 in personal property. His daughter Mary Jane (1840–1894), born in Raleigh and brought to Ohio by her parents, was probably the first black woman to receive an A. B. degree (Oberlin College, 1862) and the first black principal (1871–84) in the Washington, D. C., schools. *Ibid.*, 71; Robert S. Fletcher, *A History of Oberlin College* (2 vols., Oberlin, 1943), II, 534–35; Sylvia G. L. Dannet, *Profiles of Negro Womanhood* (2 vols., Chicago, 1964–66), I, 301.

4. Irish-born Henry S. Gorman died in Raleigh in 1840, having been preceded in death by his son John S. (1836), then residing in Tuscaloosa, Alabama. Carrie L. Broughton, comp., *Marriage and Death Notices from Raleigh Register and North Carolina Gazette, 1826–1845* ([Baltimore, 1946]), 343, 359.

5. Harrison G. O. Blake (1818–1876), Vermont-born Republican congressman (1859–63), moved to Ohio where he engaged in mercantile pursuits, studied both medicine and law, and served in the state house of representatives (1846–47) and senate (1848–49). *BDAC*, 562.

From Amos A. Lawrence

(near) Boston. July 3d, 61.

Dear Sir   The newspapers assert that arms are going forward to yr people. There must be some risk of their being intercepted. If you wish to have the assistance of some responsible men in Kentucky who will do what they undertake, call on the writer of the enclosed letter Judge Bullock of Louisville;[1] or on the person to whom the letter is addressed, also a Kentuckian but living in Massachusetts (& a brother in law of Mr Wigfall)[2] an energetic & loyal man. He is my neighbour & I know him well.

Mr Bland Ballard[3] of Louisville brother of the P. Mastr. there is a good man, & ready to do anything.

Mr Speed[4] mentioned in the letter is a lawyer, & reliable for all he undertakes.

Probably Caleb Logan,[5] Chanseller of Ky is an unconditional Union man, & if so very reliable.

I hope that the forged letters may have done something toward this movement of the arms. If so they will not have been written for nothing.

Resp'y & truly Yrs
Amos A Lawrence

Hon. Andrew Johnson, U S Sen.

Let. Bk. Copy, MHi–Amos A. Lawrence Papers.

1. Edward I. Bullock (1808–1883), Virginia-born lawyer, was a Democrat who served as attorney for Fulton County, Kentucky, and circuit judge of the first district. The letter referred to does not appear in the Johnson Papers. William E. Connelley and E. Merton Coulter, *History of Kentucky*, Charles Kerr, ed. (5 vols., Chicago and New York, 1922), V, 35.

2. Simon (or Simeon) S. Bucklin (*fl*1893), the husband of Mary Frances Cross (sister of Wigfall's wife), was a Boston wholesale dealer in leather goods in 1861. After the war he moved to Providence where he was president of a life insurance company (1867–74) and a machine manufacturing concern (1876–77). John T. Trezevant, *The Trezevant Family in the United States* (Columbia, S. C., 1914), 60; Adams, Sampson & Co., *Boston Directory* (1861), 484; Sampson, Davenport & Co., *Providence Directory* (1867), 38; *ibid.* (1874), 59; *ibid.* (1876), 64; *New-England Historical and Genealogical Register*, XLVII (1893), 225.

3. Bland Ballard (1819–1879), a prominent Louisville attorney opposed to slavery, was appointed U. S. district judge (1861–79) by Lincoln. Andrew J. (1815–1885), also a lawyer, and clerk in his younger brother's court, was not the Louisville postmaster; the previous incumbent, F. S. J. Ronald, had been replaced by John J. Speed in March, 1861. Thomas M. Green, *Historic Families of Kentucky* (Baltimore, 1959 [1888]), 78–79; Margaret M. Bridwell, "Notes on One of the Early Ballard Families of Kentucky," *Filson Quarterly*, XIII (1939), 11.

4. Probably James Speed (1812–1887), a lawyer practising in Louisville almost continuously from 1833 until his death. Elected to the legislature in 1847, he was defeated as a delegate to the Kentucky constitutional convention of 1849 because of his emancipationist views: hostile to slavery, he had written a series of letters to the Louisville *Courier* attacking the institution. Adviser to Lincoln on affairs in Kentucky, he was appointed attorney general in late 1864, resigning in July, 1866, in opposition to Johnson's policies. *DAB*, XVII, 440–41.

5. Caleb W. Logan (1819–1864), a Louisville attorney, served in the state legislature (1850) and as judge of Louisville chancery court (1855–62). Green, *Historic Families*, 148–50.

From William R. Hurley

Washing[ton] D C July 4th 1861

Hon A Johnson
Dear Sir

I received two letters from Brownlow yesterday, & also two Copies of the "Whig" Containing the full proceedings of the Greenville Convention. Brownlow mentioned in his letter of 26th ult. that he had also sent three Copies to you. If you have not received them and will leet me know it I will send you one. The convention has stated the grievances first rate. I am anxious to hear how it is received at Nashville. Brownlow says that Col Cummings[1] or that four Companies of his Regiment had gone to Cumberland Gap, and about the same number would go to Wheelers Gap, to prevent arms from going. I saw the President and he said— *"See Andrew Johnson & whatever he Can not do: I Can not."* I saw Col Meigs[2] & he Telegraphed to a man in the Quarter-masters Department, the fact contained in Brownlows letter. Our union friends in Tenssee are [in need of] aid from the Federal Government. I have many letters from the south some from Citizens of Georgia & some from Alabama (sent by han[d] to Kentucky & there mailed) asking aid. I have urged this matter for two months, but without avail except in fair promises to relieve them as soon as possible. I know you *feel* anxious, and that you have vast influence with the government. I hope you will succeed.

Verry Respectfully Yours &C
W R Hurley

P. S. I saw Ex-Gov Bebb[3] to day who told me that his appointment to Tangiers would not support his family (being only a salary of $3000) and that he could not accept it. It *would* support me & wife which is all the family I have. It was given as a Tennessee appointment, and the Governor says he would use his influence to get it for me. Now I am sure that you Can get it for me if you choose to do so, and beg of you to give me your influence. I feel confident that I could fill it as well as Gov Bebb. I have never before asked any office and if you believe I Could fill it, I have no hesitancy in asking your aid, as you are well aware that I have supported you for every office you ever asked for.— You now have a chance to reciprocate the favor, & I hope you will recommend me to the President. A few lines, simply endorsing me would be sufficient. I want a foreign mission—or some better position—than I now hold[.][4]

WRH

ALS, DLC-JP2.

1. David H. Cummings (c1818–fl1894), Virginia-born Knoxville editor who had served in the Mexican War, was colonel of the 19th Tenn. Inf., CSA (June 11, 1861–May 10, 1862). In 1860 he was farming in Anderson County where he owned $40,000 worth of real estate. 1860 Census, Tenn., Anderson, 158; *Tennesseans in the Civil War*, I, 214–15; *Knoxville Blue Book* (Knoxville, 1894), 258; see also *Johnson Papers*, I, 491n.

2. Probably Montgomery C. Meigs, who became quartermaster general May 15, 1861.

3. William Bebb (1802–1873), former Whig governor of Ohio (1846–48), was a schoolteacher in his early years before studying law and opening an office in Hamilton. In 1852 on a visit to Wales, his father's homeland, he persuaded a number of Welshmen to settle in East Tennessee on a tract of land which he purchased and where he lived until the war, when he relocated in Illinois. In July, 1861, he was appointed consul to Tangiers but failed to serve. *NCAB*, III, 140; Ohio Historical Society, *The Governors of Ohio* (Columbus, 1954), 57–60; *Senate Ex. Journal*, XII (1861–62), 488, 537.

4. Currently clerk in the sixth auditor's office, Hurley did not receive a diplomatic appointment; in February, 1862, he was seeking the Nashville postmastership which went to John Lellyett. See Hurley to Johnson, February 24, 1862, Johnson Papers, LC.

From Ezra R. Andrews[1]

BENTON & ANDREWS,
STATIONERS AND PRINTERS,

Rochester, N. Y. July 6 1861

Hon. Andrew Johnson
Dear Sir;—

The noble stand taken and maintained by Wm. G. Brownlow, of Knoxville, Tenn., in sustaining the flag of our Union there, and the pecuniary losses to which he has subjected himself,[2] has created the desire with many here to contribute to sustaining him by subscribing for his Paper. Many will gladly make the small contribution, without the pleasure of reading it, but there are others who are unwilling to do so unless they can have the assurance that the paper can be received. Upon inquiry at our Newspaper offices I find that no exchanges are now received from Tennessee; we are therefore at loss to know through what channel to communicate with Mr. Brownlow, to ensure his receiving a draft, and whether we can secure the papers. If you will have the kindness to give me such information on the subject as will lead to the accomplishment of our wishes, you will lay upon us a lasting obligation.

Also, as chairman of the Lecture Committee of the Rochester Atheneum and Mechanics Association,[3] I extend to you an invitation to deliver one or more lectures in our Course for the winter of 1861–2. The citizens of this place desire very much to make the personal acquaintance of one to whom they now look with feelings akin to reverence—one whom they consider the Saviour of his section of our country from the pollution's of treason, and of the human race from the effects of the most damning rebellion which has blotted the page of history since the "secession of Satan."

The rostrum of our Association has been graced by such celebraties as Chapin, Beecher, Parker, King, Hopkins, Willats [Willett], Pierpont, in Religion; Wilson, Cass, Doolittle, in Statesmanship; Prentice, Raymond, Greeley, in Politics, Agassiz, Silliman, Mitchell, and shall I say, Maury, in Science; Curtis, Taylor, Holmes, Emerson, in Literature, and hosts of others in all the walks of life. Our regular course it is expected will commence on Thursday evening, November 14th, and be continued each Thursday evening until some time in February. If it should not be convenient to arrange for that evening (Thursday of any week) and the evening following, in case you should favor us with two, please name the time, and we will accommodate ourselves to your convenience. I doubt not if you will allow us to announce to the Chairmen of Committees of other Associations, that you will lecture next winter, you will receive sufficient invitations to make the visit in this section both lucrative and agreeable[.][4]

Any further information with reference to our Association can be obtained from Hon. Alfred Ely,[5] M. C. from that district.

Yours truly   Ezra R. Andrews[6]

Cor. Sec. Roch. Ath. & Mech Assoc.

ALS, DLC-JP.

1. Ezra R. Andrews, printer, was a director of the Rochester Atheneum and Mechanics' Association. *Rochester* Daily Union *Annual City Directory* (1859), 17, 53.

2. Because of the blockade, southern boycotting, and the loss of advertising, Parson Brownlow's Knoxville *Whig* was in financial trouble. As a result, he suspended the tri-weekly edition on August 3, and substantially reduced the format of the weekly. Knoxville *Whig*, June 29, August 3, 1861.

3. Founded in 1849, the Association flourished in the 1850's as a center of adult intellectual life, maintained an extensive reading room containing a library of 8,000 volumes, and sustained an annual series of lectures. John H. French, *Gazetteer of the State of New York* (Port Washington, N. Y., 1969 [1860]), 403; Blake McKelvey, *Rochester: The Flower City, 1855–1890* (Cambridge, Mass., 1949), 42, 198–99, 292.

4. Johnson subsequently received a number of invitations to lecture in up-state New York. See Johnson Papers, LC, *passim*.

5. Alfred Ely (1815–1892), Rochester lawyer and Republican congressman (1859–63), was captured by the Confederates while observing the first battle of Bull Run and incarcerated in a Richmond prison for nearly six months. *BDAC*, 860.

6. Believing that Johnson had accepted the invitation through Ely, Andrews wrote the following month suggesting that a formal date be set. Apparently Johnson replied that he could not make "a positive engagement," prompting Andrews to ask again in December whether there was "any probability that you will be able to leave your public duties long enough to make a tour through this State between this time and the first of April?" Andrews to Johnson, August 15, December 9, 1861, Johnson Papers, LC.

From James Culbertson[1]

Carter County Kentucky July the 6th 1861

Gov A- Johnson
Dear sir—

It is delighfull apleasing to me to heare of your fortunate Escape from your vile se[c]eding Enomies[.] nothing that has trancepierdo in all the history of the secession movements are more gratifying to the union party her in Kentucky— I am her fighting for the cause day after day[.] I addressed some three hundred pursons—on yesterday at olive hill[2] some several Reblies present—but I understand from friends that pretty mutch convin[c]ed them of their Eror but let that be as it may— I am to address a p[o]rtion of the people of the West ende of this County on next saturday[.] We will keep the union men warm her so mutch so that I think all will be rite in this parte of the state— I only landed her from Virginia on the second of this month an exile form my country for my country cause[.] I was born and rared in east but moved to wist last Nov a yeare ago. I fought for my country untill my life could only pay the bill If I could have been bought— I rite to you in as mutch as you have just escaped alike deficulty and know how men feel under such circumstances[.] I think it is vital importance to the united states troops and to boath states Tennessee and Virginia that a Sufficint army who would be concentrated and [on] the line betwene Virginia and Tennessee so as to cut all communication off betwene the East and West so as to opperate in consorte With Each other—East or Wist—and holde possession of the Railrode so as to leave no chance for supp[l]ies to the east & the union men in that portion of Virginia should be supplied With arms, to defende themselves and With some supporte from the Goverment Would soon be able to defende themselves against the secession party in the counties of the southern parte of the state [and the] army could be held in check[.] I am Will acquainted

With that portion of boath States and Will do all I can to release my friends and save the union[.] (all my blood connection) are prety mutch in East Tennessee, and Westen Virginia. Esqr John Kilgore[3] of your own county of Green that di[e]d some ten or fiften years ago Was my own uncle my mothrs Brother[.] No doubt you knew him Well— If you can so arange it I Will be one in the fight if the govrment can give som office that Will allow me to ride on horse back as i am to olde to Walk— This move will cut off al supplies that are now pascing through the pound gap[4] that leads direct from the south east corner of Kentucky to abingdon by Way of Russell county[.] a few hundred men could keep all that portion Lee Scott and Wise and those other counties with the union men already their [sic] in purfect submishion to the laws of the goverment— their are some sevral thousand cattle in the upper county of Kentucky that Will fall into the enomys hand If some thing are not speedyly don by the govrment to prevent it. all that portion of the State from Cumberling Gap to the Levisa forke[5] are open and supplies continually pasing through to the south and cannot be prevented only by an army of sufficint force[.] Cattle will soon be for market and should be prevented immediately[.] my family are in the county [which] adjoins the State of Virginia and binds [sic] on the Pound gap and a good tun pike Road passes through this gap to Wise court house thene through Russell thence to abingdon about sixty miles in all—. It seems To me that this kinda of an arangement would affect the Rebles more than any other and would advance the union more than any perhapps in the policy of Goverment— should this line of policy be addopted you should bare in mind that it will take a strong forse to holde that possition being placed betwine the too extreams— It might be well for the Goverment to sende an agent for the purpos of securing all the cattle in the uper Kentucky[.] any thing to prevent the Stock from falling in the hand of the enemy— be assured of this one thing that is I will do all I can for the union and the cause— If a course of policy like this should be pursued ther should be a large supply of Exter guns for the union men of the country. I could be of advantage to the army—gide the scouting parties as I am vary well acquainted with the country. I have some military Expearance.

In conclution let me give you some of my troubles[.] I lefte Virginia fo good about the tenth of may took shelter in Letcher in this sate leaving my family behinde[.] I got a friend to go bring my family to me but when the disunions found that I had made my escape they theatened to make discant [descent] upon me so that in order to make the thing sertain and my escape shure I was compled [to] leave home at night for feare being picked up before I could make my final escape to this parte of the state wheare I finde stronge union men at all most every pointe— sence I commenced this letter I learne form a friend that I affected some ten or fifteen changes at my las speaking soundly converted to the union— We are her whear paper are deare as you may see from this sheete[.] please look over this badly addressed letter and the numerous Mistakes as I am somwat deranged on the subject.

please let me heare from you as soon as poible[.] direct your letter Olivehill Carter County Ky.

Yours truly   James Culbertson

ALS, DLC-JP.

1. James Culbertson (1802–1884) of Scott County, Virginia, was referred to as "Captain." Olga J. Edwards and Izora W. Frizzell, *The "Connection" in East Tennessee* (Washington College, Tenn., 1969), 219.

2. Olive Hill is a small village fifteen miles west of Grayson, the seat of Carter County, Kentucky.

3. John M. Kilgore, head of a large household in 1830 and a justice of the peace, was the son of North Carolinian Charles Kilgore, a Revolutionary War soldier, whose daughter Mary was the wife of James Culbertson (1764–1823). 1830 Census, Tenn., Greene, 227; Edwards and Frizzell, *East Tenn. "Connection,"* 190–91.

4. Pound Gap, near Pound, Virginia, and Jenkins, Kentucky, is in Wise County, Virginia.

5. Levisa Fork, near the Kentucky-West Virginia line on the edge of the Cumberland Plateau, flows north from the Virginia line to the Big Sandy.

From Librarian of Congress[1]

Library of Congress.
July 6. 1861.

Hon. Andrew Johnson,
Sir:

There is charged to your account in the Library—

Wheeler's History of N. Carolina
Haywood's History of Tennessee
Sabines American Loyalists
Holmes' Annals, 2d. vol.
Moultries Revn. & S. Carolina, 2 vols.
Remembrancer, 10th, v. pt. 2
Hazlitt's Shak[e]speare, 2d. v.
AEsops' Fables,

If you have no further use for the above books will you be pleased to have them returned that your account may be adjusted?[2]

Very respectfully Your obt. Servant
Rob Kearon[3]
for the Librarian

ALS, DLC-JP.

1. John G. Stephenson, *U. S. Official Register* (1861), 215.

2. Johnson did not return these volumes until the next year, the first six titles on March 5, and the last two on January 31, 1862. Borrowers' Ledger, Library of Congress, Nov. 1859–May 1861, LC.

3. Rob Kearon was a messenger in the Library of Congress. *U. S. Official Register* (1859), 195.

To Simon Cameron, Washington, D. C.

Washington City July 6th 1861—

Hon S. Cameron
Dear Sir

I have just learned that there is some 30 boxes of minie Rufles at the Arsenel—and that they can be sent instead of the musket— These are the kind of gun above all others, needed by our people— they are accostomed to the use of rifles.[1] These 30 boxes would make one rifle Company for evry Regimet— We must have the rifles if possible— Get an order at once and they can be packed and sent with the Muskets— Prompt action is indepensibly necessary— Mr Carter[2] who will hand you this note will take the order and have it attended to—[3]

Your frind   And. Johnson

P. S. I will see [illegible]—

ALS, DNA-RG156, Let. Recd., War Dept., 1825–1861.

1. The rifle, with its spirally grooved bore, was a more accurate weapon than the old smoothbore musket.

2. Probably James P. T. Carter.

3. In his reply Cameron referred Johnson to "Bull" Nelson, "who has the requisite authority to act in the premises." Cameron to Johnson, July 8, 1861, Johnson Papers, LC; Secretary of War Military Book 45, July–Aug. 1861, RG107, National Archives.

From James H. Embry[1]

Maysville Ky July 7th 1861

Hon. Andrew Johnson
Dr Sir—

I promised you during your stay in Richmond to write you from this place as to the best route to carry your guns to East Tennessee—

I suggested then as the safest route Maysville, Flemingsburg Sharpsburg Mt. Sterling Winchester Richmond thence through Laurel & Whitley Counties to the Tennessee line— I Still think it the best— I have conversed with prominent Union men in the several Towns named in the last four days[.] they assure me that there is no difficulty to be apprehended in shipping the guns by the route suggested—

I saw Mr Prentice[2] on the 29th of June in Louisville & he expressed the opinion that Col John S. Williams the late Secession Candidate in this District was secretly raising a force to intercept & take your guns on their way through Ky— I have feared the same thing— I learn however that he is in Nashville or was on Thursday last— It may be that he will urge Middle Tennessee to send a force at once to East Tennessee to capture them when they cross the line— I do not think he could successfully raise a force here to effect such a purpose—

I saw Gen. Combs on Sunday last in Lexington & he said that the best route for the guns was through Louisville, Lebanon & Wheelers Gap— It would be the speediest, but I doubt whether it is the safest—

He said he would be in Washington on the 4th & see you—

I understand there is a Secession force at Cumberland Gap & at Wheelers Gap for the purpose of intercepting the guns. I cannot vouch for the truth of the rumor—

I return home to day week & would like to hear from you— I expect to see my Father[3] on Friday next & he will be directly from Nashville— If I obtain any information from him that would be of service to you I will Communicate it—

Yours very truly   James H. Embry

ALS, DLC-JP2.

1. Probably James H. Embry (b. *c*1828), a Nashville lawyer in 1850, who a decade later had moved back to his native Kentucky. Subsequently a judge, he was recommended in August, 1867, as governor of Wyoming Territory but did not receive the appointment. His sister Marie L. Embry (b. *c*1827) was the wife of Joseph S. Fowler. Porch, *1850 Census, Davidson,* 173; 1860 Census, Ky., Madison, 418; Applicants, Vol. E, May 1867–August 1868, p. 61, Johnson Papers, Series 6A, LC; Embry to Johnson, March 11, 1862, Johnson Papers, LC; *DAB,* VI, 564.

2. George D. Prentice (1802–1870), Connecticut native, first editor of the *New England Review* (1828–30), a Hartford weekly, and author of a *Biography of Henry Clay* (1831), had been invited by Kentucky politicians to edit the Louisville *Journal,* an anti-Jacksonian newspaper which he converted into a prominent Whig voice. A unionist who upheld Lincoln's administration, he was influential in preventing the secession of Kentucky. *DAB,* XV, 186–87; John J. Piatt, ed., *The Poems of George D. Prentice* (Cincinnati, 1887), vii–xlv.

3. Bowling Embry (*c*1803–*fl*1878), Kentucky-born farmer with $18,000 real property in 1850, later served as Nashville's postmaster (April, 1867–March, 1869). Porch, *1850 Census, Davidson,* 173; Wooldridge, *History of Nashville,* 130; Embry to Martha J. Patterson, February 19, 1878, Johnson Papers, LC.

From John G. Eve[1]

Hon Andrew Johnson

You will not perhaps recollect having been introduced to me at the Burnett House Cincinnati by Capt. Nelson[2] but that for the present is not material. I write to make some suggestions to you. Cumberland Gap is now blockaded or invested by about 700 Tennesseans & Virginian's[.] They are located on the summit on the right of the road as you come north. This is the latest information— We learn further that they got there without treading on the "*Sacred*" soil of Kentucky—[3] How they did this I cannot very well imagine. The troops are variously armed with shotguns Rifles &.c— They are under the command of Col Powell.[4] Some eight miles below at the Baptist Gap[5] 200 Confederate troops are stationed— Some 27 miles still lower down at the Big Creek Gap there are some 500 troops stationed[.] Wheelers Gap still lower down *five* miles is not as yet, so far as we have learned, guarded. The direct road from Williamsburg Whitley Co, Ky passes through Wheelers Gap.

These passes are guarded, as they say, to prevent the ingress of Andy Johnson's arms into East Tennessee. Our people from Lexington Ky to each of these Gaps are anxious to assist in taking arms through to East Tennessee and to assist them if necessary. I would suggest however that it takes more than mere bravery in a battle and that our people are almost wholly undisciplined—and if those arms are sent through that a regular force ought to be sent with them. It is true this would violate the neutrality of Ky according to Magoffins proclamation[6] but what does that amount to. Why need our people longer advocate that doctrine? Can they hope to have any influence, by such a course, in bringing back the seceded states, which have said there is no hope of reconciliation except in their recognition as an independent Confederacy? Besides have not the people of Ky spoken in thunder tones their devotion to the Union as it was and as it is—[7] The people in this section look on that proclamation as all Bosh— They are anxious that a Federal force shall be sent here to rout the Confederate troops and drive them from our border. This may not be wisdom on our part but so it is. I speak here more particularly of the Mountain people.

A Regiment has been raised in the counties of Knox, Whitley Laurel & Clay whose services are now or will be tendered to the general government[.] But I have got off my subject[.] How would it do to place the arms at about two points in Whitly and Knox where they could be guarded well and have it communicated to the Union men of Claiborne & Campbell Co's [Tennessee] (that is I mean the first supply of arms) and let them organize in squads & companies privately & come over & get their arms & accoutrements[.] There are several passes for horsemen between the Baptist Gap and Big Creek Gap through which they might thus come. Having thus armed the Union men in those counties it would be more easy to attack and (their retreat being cut off) take the troops stationed at either one of those Gaps and thus pass the remainder of the arms through to East Tennessee.

Droves of Horses and mules are continually passing through here via Cumberland Gap to the South— Cattle are occasionally passing.[8]

We have traitors in our midst who keep up communication with Va & Tenn[.]

We dare not write letters to Tennessee for fear of their being intercepted.

We learn that men passing through the Gap are questioned very closely as to what their business is. I do not know that any one has as yet been stopped. I have just learned that they are expecting to have 3000 troops there in a few days[.] If this war continues and I think it will for some time it will be difficult to get troops through Western Virginia and you know how it is in this state that there is a space between the Gap and Lexington Ky of about 125 miles where there is no Rail Road and most of the way is a dirt road.

Now is it not almost a military necessity for the Government to build a Rail Road from Lexington Ky to Morristown in East Tennessee if this war is at all likely to continue?[9] I presume you will attend immediately to your project of a daily mail line to East Tennessee[.] if so have the routes so changed that one will run from Lexington Ky to this point a distance of 98 miles and the other from this point to Russelville Tenn about 70 miles— You will remember there is more difference than that in the roads— The routes now are from Lexington Ky to London & from London to Russelville. I make the above *suggestions* for your consideration— If they are not good of course you will not adopt them. I should be much pleased to hear from you if you have spare time from your duties[.]

Very Respectfully &c
John G. Eve

ALS, DLC-JP2.

1. John G. Eve (b. c1836), a lawyer who became colonel of the 49th Ky. Inf., USA, was involved with the initial distribution of the "Lincoln guns" to home guard units in Knox and Whitley (Ky.) counties. *OR*, Ser. 1, XXXIX, Pt. II, 146, 296, 330; 1860 Census, Ky., Knox, 28; Eve to Green Adams, July 2, 1861, Johnson Papers, LC.

2. William ("Bull") Nelson (1824–1862), Kentucky native and An-

napolis graduate (1846–7–8), entered the navy as a midshipman in 1840, serving in the Mexican War, and was subsequently promoted to lieutenant. A strong unionist, he was sent by Lincoln to Kentucky early in 1861 to arm the loyalists and organize army regiments, not only to save the state from possible secession but also to prepare for an invasion of East Tennessee. In September he became brigadier general of volunteers; later he joined Buell's Army of the Ohio, serving with distinction at Shiloh and Corinth and participating in several Kentucky campaigns. Peremptory by nature and a strict disciplinarian, Nelson strongly reprimanded General Jefferson C. Davis in September, 1862, for alleged negligence—an act which cost him his life on September 29 when Davis shot and mortally wounded him at the Galt House in Louisville. *DAB*, XIII, 426; A. M. Ellis, "Major General William Nelson," Kentucky State Historical Society *Register*, IV (May, 1906), 56–64; U. S. Naval Academy Alumni Association, *Register of Alumni, Graduates and Former Cadets and Midshipmen* (Annapolis, 1967), 4.

3. Although the idea that Kentucky's soil was "sacred" is found in the April 17 resolutions of the state's Union party central committee and had been endorsed by the leading unionists of the state, the phrase is more generally associated with Governor Magoffin's neutrality proclamation of May 20. However, the latter borrows only the intent, not the actual wording—"sacred" does not appear in his statement. Speed, *Union Cause*, 47–49, 57–60; Moore, *Rebellion Record*, I, Doc., 74; Coulter, *Civil War in Kentucky*, 38–45, 55–56.

4. Probably Col. Samuel Powel, 29th Tenn. Inf. Rgt., CSA. *Johnson Papers*, I, 512n; *Tennesseans in the Civil War*, I, 235–37; *Battles and Leaders*, III, 16.

5. Baptist Gap, in Cumberland Mountain, Claiborne County, is southwest of Cumberland Gap.

6. Magoffin's neutrality proclamation of May 20, 1861. Moore, *Rebellion Record*, I, Doc., 264–65.

7. Various resolutions of mass meetings throughout early-to-mid-1861 indicate that many Kentuckians deplored the action of the South, supported Crittenden's resolutions, and hoped to stay in the Union. *Cong. Globe*, 37 Cong., 2 Sess., App. 80–82; Coulter, *Civil War in Kentucky*, 38–43.

8. One observer complained that "fat cattle, mules by droves, and loads of bacon are daily passing through Cumberland Gap to the rebels." Given arms, the Kentucky unionists would "soon put a stop to the business." *Frank Leslie's Illustrated Newspaper*, July 6, 1861.

9. During the 1850's several companies had been chartered to construct a line between East Tennessee and central Kentucky, but none had built more than a few miles of track. Nor, despite a general recognition of the military necessity for such a road, would any significant progress be made during the war. Riley O. Biggs, The Development of Railroad Transportation in East Tennessee during Reconstruction (M. A. thesis, University of Tennessee, 1934), 55–63, 118–22; Coulter, *Civil War in Kentucky*, 252–53.

From George Worsham[1]

Phila, Pa. July. 8th 1861—

Dr Sir:

I can truly say without flattery that your course has commanded the admiration and awakened the sympathies of all good men and all true lovers of the Union every where irrespective of party. All true patriots ignore party creeds and past feuds and recriminations, and rally on one common platform—the broad platform of the Constitution and the Union.

Thousands upon thousands of the Democratic party voted the Republican ticket in the North, and elected Mr. Lincoln, not for the purpose of breaking up the Democratic party, but to break down the political power of a proud, haughty, insolent oligarchy, who had been ruling the nation for more than half a century under the pretext of protecting one peculiar species of property to the exclusion of all other interests. We became tired of having the task imposed upon us, quadrennially, of saving the Union by voting in accordance to the dictation of a haughty, overbearing minority. The true Democracy of the North, enlightened by a free press and free schools, has learned to know its power, both moral and physical, and has the courage to assert its rights, and to maintain them, in spite of the dictations of haughty, overbearing minorities. The North is not Abolitionized— Not one in twenty would interfere with the institutions of the South. Full nine tenths of the Republican party are willing to leave the extension of slavery to the natural laws of climate, soil, productions and the increase of population, satisfied that neither freedom nor slavery can be imposed upon an unwilling people in a Republican government. It is useless, however, to disguise the fact, that the Abolitionists did not take up a Presidential Candidate as usual, but threw their vote and influence in favor of the Republican party, and now claim the triumph of the Republican party, an Abolition victory.

Mr. Lincoln would have been elected without the aid of the Abolition element in the demoralized state of the Democratic party. Look at the overwhelming majorities in the Northern States so lately Democratic.[2] The Abolitionists were always disunionists, like their Southern antitypes, and disorganizers of the political parties. They were the patrons and supporters of Abolition "Sewing circles," "Abolition fairs"[3] "and Abolition lectures," which were got up for the support of the "Abolition cause," and the under ground railroad. To this disorganizing minority of the past and the present, Wm. B. Thomas,[4] Collector of the Port of Philadelphia, and B. Rush Plumly,[5] Appraisor at large, both belong. The latter has been a strolling Abolition lecturer of the true Garrison and Wendell Phillips school. It is idle to conceal the fact, or deny it—

It is known that the Collector of the Port, through his subordinates exerts or wields a tremendous power over the party in Pennsylvania. Thus far the Abolition element has dictated all the Appointments at the Customs, and revived the most intense party feeling and animosity, at a time when Patriots bury the recollections of the past in temporary oblivion[.] "To the victors belong the spoils," but the Abolitionists are not the victors. It is useless to deny that the Abolition element in the Republican party headed by Mr. Thomas and his satellites, did not pack the convention in the Second Congressional district in Penna. which nominated Mr. Chas. O'Neal,[6] and resulted in the election of Mr. Biddle,[7] in a district in which the Republicans had an overwhelming majority, thus evincing that the Abolition element is in the minority, though it assumes to control, even at the expense of intensefying party feeling and party rancour. It is to be hoped that the Senate will refuse to confirm all such nominations as disorganizing and dividing the people of Pennsylvania, now a unit, on the present momentous crisis.

I belong to the toiling millions who get their bread by the sweat of their brow. I make no pretensions to learning. I am a Democrat and like thousands more who voted for and elected Mr. Lincoln, the very man for the times, I too voted for him; but if the Abolition, and not the Democratic element, through him and the Senate is to rule and control the party, the North will soon become divided and demoralized. We can spare the Abolitionists for they won't fight, unless it is for the Spoils of office.

I have been a voter forty years. I am no stranger to the history of parties in this State, or to the history of parties in the United States — I never held an Office nor desired one. I am for my country; the *whole* country, uncontroled by Northern Abolitionists or Southern Oligarchs. But if such nominations as I have named be confirmed by the Senate (for it is such appointments which give the real *bent* of a party, not the foreign ministers) than I hazzard nothing in the prediction, that when we have put down the rule of Southern Oligarchs and monarchists, we will have the task imposed upon us of putting down northern Abolitionists also, before the Country can be restored to its quiet, Democratic equilebrium. While we are fighting to put down the one, let us try to nip the other in the bud, before it grows to such gigantic dimensions as the present. Many of the leading Abolitionists ignore the truth of the insperation of the Bible, and recognize only the God of Reason.[8] What can be expected from them.

Respectfully &C—   George Worsham
Phila Pa.

Hon. Andrew Johnson—

ALS, DLC-JP.

1. This unusually literate and articulate representative of "the toiling millions" appears to have eluded the scrutiny of posterity.

2. In Worsham's own Pennsylvania, as well as in Indiana and Illinois, three states which had returned Democratic electors in the 1856 presidential campaign, the Republicans outpolled the combined vote of the two Democratic candidates. If we include the six states—Connecticut, Iowa, New York, Ohio, Rhode Island, and Wisconsin—which had been in the Democratic fold in

1852, we find a similar Republican success story in 1860. In these nine states the popular vote was 1,386,035 for Lincoln as against 1,061,145 combined vote for both Democrats. Arthur M. Schlesinger, Jr., ed., *History of American Presidential Elections, 1789–1968* (4 vols., New York, 1971), II, 1152.

3. The role of women in the American Anti-Slavery Society was primarily that of fund raising through "Fairs" at which a variety of manufactured and homemade items—made in "Fair Circles"—were sold. These fairs, which developed rapidly, represented a means not only of raising money but also of propagating antislavery doctrine. Otelia Cromwell, *Lucretia Mott* (Cambridge, Mass., 1958), 154, 156, 178.

4. William B. Thomas (b. 1811), wealthy Philadelphia flour manufacturer and outspoken abolitionist, was an organizer of Philadelphia's Republican party, known locally as the "People's" party. Defeated for mayor in 1856, he was instrumental in swinging Pennsylvania's support behind Lincoln's nomination, for which he was rewarded with the collectorship. Although Thomas vocally advocated recognition of southern independence in February, 1861, he also organized, financed, and commanded an elite home front militia regiment popularly called the "Custom's Guards." Stephen N. Winslow, *Biographies of Successful Philadelphia Merchants* (Philadelphia, 1864), 75, 79; Dusinberre, *Civil War Issues in Philadelphia*, 33, 189.

5. B. Rush Plumly (1816–1887), an ardent abolitionist and treasurer of the Consolidated Coal Company of Philadelphia, served as a major in the Union army and in March, 1864, was appointed chairman of the board of education for the Department of the Gulf, supervising schools for newly emancipated blacks, a post he retained until June, 1865. Sherwin, *Prophet of Liberty*, 520; Wendell P. and Francis J. Garrison, *William Lloyd Garrison: The Story of His Life* (4 vols., London, 1889), IV, 124n; *Cohen's Philadelphia Directory* (1860), 732; Howard A. White, *The Freedmen's Bureau in Louisiana* (Baton Rouge, 1970), 167–69.

6. Charles O'Neill (1821–1893), a Philadelphia attorney who served in the state lower house (1850–52, 1860) and senate (1853), was later elected as a Republican to Congress (1863–71, 1873–93). When he lost the mayor's race to Charles Biddle in 1859, a contemporary referred to him as a "man of no mark or reputation." *BDAC*, 1408–9; Wainwright, *Fisher's Diary*, 395.

7. Charles J. Biddle (1819–1873), a lawyer and brevet major in the Mexican War, was elected Democratic mayor (1859–61) and congressman (1861–63), later becoming editor in chief of the Philadelphia *Age. BDAC*, 551.

8. The charge of godless deism was a perennial nineteenth-century allegation leveled against those with differing views. Moreover, the Garrisonian wing of abolitionism, arraigning the lethargy of many orthodox Christians and their churches, seemed to afford some basis for the charge. Even John Humphrey Noyes in the 1840's complained about the Anti-Slavery Society's falling into "the hands of Unitarians, Universalists, and other free-thinkers," and asserted that it had embraced a "positive hostility to the more orthodox churches." Walter M. Merrill, *Against Wind and Tide: A Biography of William Lloyd Garrison* (Cambridge, Mass., 1963), 182, 186.

From C. B. Ryan[1]

Travisville Tenn July 9th 1861

Hon Andrew Johnson
Sir

Our whole county was thrown in to intense excitement yesterday by the arival among us of some 300 Volunteers from East. Tenn for the purpose they say of making all the Union men leave or swearing them to support the Jeff Davis Confederacy but they have not attempted to do either the one or the other yet and just so soon as they do attempt it we are determined to defend ourselves the best we can[.] we can whip double the number that is here but we donot intend to make the first attact[.] we have no arms except our Country rifles and shot guns which we intend useing if they should make any attempt to drive out the union men of Fentress County. if we can get help we are determined not to submit to them, and if we can not get it a great many of us will have to leave for Kentucky until the government can send us aid[.] I See in the papers that you are making arrangements for arms and men for the defence of East Tenn. Fentress County is determined to stand with East Tenn in any event. I can refer you to the Hon. Horace Maynard as to responsibility of myself[.] if you can take time to drop me a line please do so and direct your letters to me at Albany Ky[.]

I Remain your Obedient Servant
C. B. Ryan

ALS, DLC-JP.
1. C. B. Ryan (b. c1830), a Kentucky-born merchant, was postmaster in 1863. 1860 Census, Tenn., Fentress, 93; *U. S. Official Register* (1863), 634.

From Michael Goldman

Rutledge Tenn
July 10th 1861

Andrew Johnson
His Hon—

Dear Sir I Recd your letter dated June 27th, & am much obliged to you for your kindness. those warrants I desire sent or paid to, the firm of Henry, Smith & Townsand[1] No 17 & 19 Warren St. New York City, & placed to the credit of Easley & Williams[2] Rutledge, *Tenn.* please feel yourself authorized, to assign, my name as transfered to said firm, & oblige me Michael Goldman— I do trust in god that the united states will persavere—and over rule those Radigals of the South— The daily stage line from London to Russellville, I doubt never can be performed by horse power. the distance is 96 miles and four or five mountains to cross— it cant be done— but I should like the contract, was in the hands of good union men. I am told the company who own it are rabit Secessionists— its not worth my while to bid for said rout. it would take much capital which I have not got—though I would like to get acquainted with

the agent, if I knew his name, and knowed when he would be out—
please write me all the particulars— Union sentiments stand here
as you left them, only they made up a company, in this County, say
Beanstation—and I suppose, there are some three or four hundred
volenteers—stationed at Cumberland Gap, to kill you when you
come back. they say there are more to be sent there. Mr Edmonds[3]
at Rogersvill Contractor, from Rogersville to Knoxville [for] horse-
mail on our road, *ceased* carrying the mail the day after the Election,
and commenced again on the first day of July for the South[.] if I
were the government—I never would pay him any more—or any
others that had forfeite their contracts— I am still carrying the mail
for the united States, and will continue to do So untill instructed to
the Contrary—or that they take my contract by force. if the P. O. D.
would Send orders to me I would try and collect from all offices that
they might wish—and render to them a strict account— I was at
Dandridge on yesterday[.] those rampant Secessionists keep growl-
ing—A G. Wadkins [Watkins], John Hooper, Crozier, & Company
are to have a grand demonstration above Bean Station on the 16th of
this month—[4] so says there advertisement— *Ben. Branner*[5] has a
Company of Cavelry at Cumberland gap[.] I am in haste— my
friend & neighbor—Tho Lathim[6] is going to Thorn Hill and I will
have this mailed there so it will be sure to go on that rout. please
write me soon[.] I will be so anxious to hear[.]

Your friend   M. Goldman

I wish I could talk [to] you fifteen minutes[.]

ALS, DLC-JP.

1. Josiah J. Henry, Thomas U. Smith, and John J. Townsend were dry
goods merchants. *Trow's New York City Directory* (1861), 389, 804, 858.

2. Probably Joseph Williams (b. *c*1830) who, though designated as a
farmer in the 1860 census, possessed $17,225 in personal property and
$24,000 in real estate; Warham Easley, Jr. (b. *c*1818), was a merchant with
$18,000 in real estate and personal property valued at $24,700. 1860 Census,
Tenn., Grainger, 157.

3. W. F. Edmonds (b. *c*1832), listed as a physician in the 1860 census,
had been a bidder (1859) for post routes in upper East Tennessee. *Ibid.*,
Hawkins, 13; *House Ex. Doc.* No. 86, 36 Cong., 1 Sess., 317, 318–19.

4. No information concerning this meeting has been found.

5. Benjamin M. Branner (b. *c*1830) was lt. col., 4th Tenn. Cav. Batta-
lion, CSA, resigning in June, 1862, after his unit became part of the 2nd
Cav. Rgt. In 1860 he had $20,000 in real and $30,000 in personal property.
After the war he was a principal stockholder and director of the East Tennessee and Virginia Railroad. 1860 Census, Tenn., Jefferson, 188; *Goodspeed's Knox*, 846; *Tennesseans in the Civil War*, I, 25, 52; John B. Lindsley,
Military Annals of Tennessee: Confederate (Nashville, 1886), 626; *Annual
Report of the East Tennessee and Virginia Railroad . . . 1868–69* (Knoxville,
1870), 7.

6. Thomas Lathim (b. *c*1822), a clerk, had $700 in real and $13,200 in
personal property. 1860 Census, Tenn., Grainger, 163.

From J. K. Ingalls

July 10, 1861, New York, N. Y.; ALS, DLC-JP.

Land Reformer writing on New York Kansas Relief Committee letter-head expresses apprehension about land bounties for veterans. Although the advocates of homestead legislation favor just recompense, "they would deeply regret the entailment of a dangerous monopoly of the public domain." Assignable land warrants, of doubtful benefit to the soldier, would in practice "furnish convenient 'scrip' and legal sanction to a monopoly as dangerous to our liberties and to the interests of the people, as it is insidious and unscrupulous in the means it adopts to promote its ends."

From George M. Adams[1]

[July 11, 1861?]

Memo for Gov Johnson
We want bacon beeves &C stopped from sending through Cumberland Gap & other points above & below the Gap & some person given the authority[.]

The regiments raised in the mountains of Ky— Let us know if they will be permitted to remain in Ky & East Ten and how long they will have to remain in service[.]

If it is necessary to Commission persons here to take in Volunteers —appoint T T Garrard of Manchaster Clay Co Ky—G. P Brown of London Ky—J. W Redgell of Barbourville Ky—Robt Boyd[2] of Williamsburg Whitley Co Ky & if necessary send blanks to fill up for who we think are the right men[.]
See Greene Adams when you get to Washington[.]

G. M Adams

learn who Capt Nelson & learn who he is[3]

ALS, DLC-JP; enclosed in Letter from William Nelson, July 11, 1861.

1. George M. Adams (c1809–1875), brother of Congressman Green Adams, was a Barbourville merchant, who served as captain and commissary of subsistence for volunteers (1861–62). Ruth R. Seibel (Coeditor, *Adams Addenda*, St. Louis) to Andrew Johnson Project, February 20, 1975.

2. Theophilus T. Garrard of Manchaster; G. P. Brown (b. c1813), Tennessee-born merchant and farmer of London, Kentucky, had been a member of the legislature (1850); Joel W. Ridgell (b. c1816), Kentucky-born lawyer, became a colonel in the Federal army, resigning in January,

1863; Robert Boyd was a mail contractor and later a member of the state senate (1867–75). Collins, *Kentucky*, II, 141, 458; Connelley and Coulter, *Kentucky*, II, 115, 1120; 1860 Census, Ky., Laurel, 132; Knox, Barbourville, 28; *House Ex. Doc.* No. 86, 36 Cong., 1 Sess., 310–12, 315.

3. Undoubtedly inspired by a Louisville *Courier* (June 21) column headed "Andrew Johnson, who he is and what he is after," and noting that the "traitor" had passed through enroute to Washington for arms. Knoxville *Register*, June 27, 1861.

From William Nelson

Cincinanti O. July 11th 1861

Dear Sir

Dont fail to get the 300 Sharp rifles at the Navy Yard and the two Howitzers— Press the matter. If necessary go and see Chase[1] about it. He is the steam Engine of the Administration and a friend of mine—

See the Adjutant General and make him and the Cheif of the ordnance[2] [give] the order for the additional 3000 stand of arms and accoutrements for the Kentuckians to be mustered in. Responses for letters written by me when in Washington are already coming to hand. Our affair, that is the transportation to Cumberland Gap is perfectly easy— no interruption will occur. I have everything arranged to insure their safe transportation by two routes to insure things going straight[.]

I have not seen anything of Carter.[3] I called for him at your Quarters at *one* o'clock, as we agreed, but I did not find him and I was compeled to go ahead. In my letters from Barbourville I learn that they the Secessionists of Tennessee are on the lookout for Carter and I fear that he will find some serious difficulty in getting through—

One matter is money! I required from the Quarter Master General[4] that $20,000 be placed to my credit in New York for me to draw against. But this is but a drop in the bucket, and my future promptitude of action will in a great measure depend upon my pecuniary supplies being kept up—

Jim Clay[5]—Roger Hanson,[6] Cal. Morgan,[7] the two young Breckinridges,[8] Stevenson[9] formerly in Congress and many others have gone towards Virginia by way of *Cumberland Gap* so it is said. But Jim Clay, and some others returned this morning saying that their horses had *foundered*. I suppose the Hill people have *foundered for him*[.][10]

Dont fail on the Sharpes rifles! See that equipments are sent for the Cavalry Regiment authorized—or that I am authorized to purchase them. They were not ordered when I left— Excuse me, I am hurried having written at least 20 letters today:

So the following is what I wishe attended to viz

1"—The Sharps rifles— the Secretary of War to write to the Secy Navy a letter for them and they will be given to you— If there is any hesitation see the Presidnt and *Chase*

2"—Get the Adjutant Gen'l to order the 3000 additional muskets and accoutrements.

3.—Money! Money!! Money!!!

4.—The arms and equipments for the mounted Regiment authorized, or authorized me to purchase————

5. I must buy sufficient provision to last us thro' the gap, but my horses are ample for this purpose[.]

Yours very truly   W. Nelson

Hon A. Johnson Senate

ALS, DLC-JP.

1. Treasury Secretary Salmon P. Chase, with whom Nelson, because of friendship, was corresponding. See Nelson to Chase, July 16, 1861, Johnson Papers, LC; Donald, *Chase Diary*, 13.

2. Lorenzo Thomas was adjutant general, and James W. Ripley, acting chief of ordnance.

3. Probably James P. T. Carter. See Letters from James P. T. Carter, July 15, and from William Nelson, July 16, 1861.

4. Montgomery C. Meigs. See *Johnson Papers*, III, 179*n*.

5. James B. Clay (1817–1864), Lexington lawyer and son of Henry Clay, was chargé d'affaires to Portugal (1849–50), congressman (1857–59), and delegate to the Washington Peace Conference. Attempting to "go South," he was captured by home guards and held at Camp Dick Robinson, near Bryantsville, until tried by a civil court which failed to indict him. Refugeeing to the South, in the summer of 1863 he ran the blockade to Canada where he died of tuberculosis. *BDAC*, 704; Connelley and Coulter, *Kentucky*, III, 6; Zachary F. Smith and Mary Rogers Clay, *The Clay Family*, Filson Club *Publications*, No. 14 (Louisville, 1899), 180.

6. Roger W. Hanson (1823–1863), a Mexican War veteran and state legislator (1853, 1855) who was defeated for Congress by James B. Clay, became a colonel of the 2nd Ky. Cav., CSA, in September, 1861. Captured at the fall of Donelson, exchanged, and promoted to brigadier in December, 1862, he was mortally wounded at the battle of Murfreesboro. *DAB*, VIII, 232–33; *Confed. Mil. Hist.*, IX, 239–41.

7. Calvin C. Morgan (1827–1882), two years younger than John Hunt Morgan, was a captain, aide-de-camp, and agent for his brother and was captured with him in 1863. The two Morgans had served together in the Mexican War and were business partners in a wool-processing business. Cecil F. Holland, *Morgan and His Raiders: A Biography of the Confederate General* (New York, 1942), 24, 26, 254; "Henrietta H. Morgan, Mother of Heroes," *Confederate Veteran*, II (1894), 331.

8. Robert J. (1834–1915) and William C. P. (1837–1904), sons of the Reverend Robert J. Breckinridge, were both lawyers. Robert raised a regiment but resigned in 1862 to serve briefly in the Confederate Congress. Returning to the army as a colonel of cavalry, he was taken prisoner in February, 1865, resumed his law practice after the war, and served as judge of the eighth

Washington City, Aug. 6th. 1861.

To

His Excellency, Mr Lincoln,
President,
Sir,

We have received entirely reliable information from East Tennessee up to Saturday the 27th. ult. On Friday, the 26th. of July, three Commissioners from the Confederate States, called upon the Central Union Committee at Knoxville, Tenn. and endeavoured to prevail upon them to abandon the Government of the United States. This the Committee at once declined to do.

We deem it our duty to inform the President that up to July 27th. eighty thousand (80.000) Southern troops had passed into Virginia over the East Tennessee and Virginia Rail Road.

Our object in making this communication, is not to be importunate, but to keep our Government informed of the true condition of our people, and of the intentions of our enemies.

Very Respy. &c.

Andrew Johnson

Wm. B. Carter

Letter from Andrew Johnson and William B. Carter to Abraham Lincoln,
August 6, 1861.
Courtesy Library of Congress.

Check for compensation, July 15, 1861. *Courtesy National Archives.*

Receipt for compensation and mileage, August 6, 1861.
Courtesy National Archives.

district court of common pleas (1876). William, who married a grand-daughter of Henry Clay, became a Confederate colonel; later he was editor of the Lexington *Observer and Reporter* (1866–68) and congressman (1885–95). *BDAC*, 592; Connelley and Coulter, *Kentucky*, III, 18; [A. C. Terhune], "Robert J. Breckinridge," *Confederate Veteran*, XXIII (1915), 271.

9. John W. Stevenson (1812–1886), a Virginian, served as a Democrat in the Kentucky legislature (1845–49), and in Congress (1857–61); after the war he became lieutenant governor and governor (1867–71), U. S. senator (1871–77), and president of the American Bar Association (1884–85). Although sympathetic to the Confederacy, he refrained from active participation and during Johnson's presidency supported his policies. *DAB*, XVII, 633–34; *BDAC*, 1655.

10. Nelson's ironic reference suggests that the return of Clay and his companions was prompted by mountaineer hostility rather than by lamed horses.

From Peter H. Grisham[1]

Camp Joe Holt— Clark Co.
Indiana— July 12. 1861.
Opposite Louisville Ky.

Hon. Andrew Johnson: —

Dear Sir:— I lately came out from East Tennessee and joined the Company of Union Volunteers making up at Liberty Kentucky by Capt. Mitchell[2] under Genl. Rosseau.[3] You may not remember me, I used to Clerk for Valentine Sevier and George Jones[4] in Greeneville— I came out to Kentucky directly from our East Tennessee Convention at Greeneville; at which I was a delegate from Washington Co.— I stopped in Morgan Co. E. Ten one week where I own some land. They are nearly all Union fighting men there. Montgomery is their town, where you spoke recently[5] & where you made quite a mark—for the people almost worship you. It is nearly 2 weeks since I left E. Tenn. and I heard there were certainly 500 secessionists in Campbell Co. at the Gaps and 400 was at Clinton with 2 Cannon. I have heard since in Ky. that 600 more joined them last week & the Ky. papers state that many are going that way from different towns & cities in Ky. in order to seize Union arms going to E. Tenn. &c.— Genl. Rosseau told me to day that this regiment will be likely to go there when the men are properly drilled—which I am told will take a month & that will be too late I fear—for the Union men, if not already fighting in E. Tenn., I think will be certainly this week. The men who went with you through Cumb. Gap were at the Greeneville Convention & the delegates from Union, Campbell, Anderson & other Counties particularly Morgan Co. asserted that their Union men would shoot them down man by man if they undertook to take the gaps of Cumbd.—

I hope there will be concert of action by Kentucky & Tennessee in opening the gaps & arming our E. Ten. Union men. I am well acquainted with & saw at Convention your sons Robt. & Charles. Please excuse haste &c.

Yr. Fr. &c. P. H. Grisham.

Write Care Capt. Mitchell

ALS, DLC-JP.

1. Peter H. Grisham (b. *c*1827), a clerk and schoolteacher in Jonesboro in the 1850's, after the war became a government clerk, first in the pension office and then in the third auditor's office of the treasury. 1850 Census, Tenn., Washington, 235; Ross Smith, *Reminiscences of an Old Timer* ([Jonesboro], 1930), 5, 59; Grisham to O. P. Temple, April 20, 1880, Oliver P. Temple Papers.

2. Probably Edward J. Mitchell (*c*1836–*fl*1887), of Indiana, captain of Co. F, 2nd Ky. Cav., USA, who enrolled at Camp Jo Holt, Jeffersonville, in July, 1861, and resigned in September, 1862. One month earlier Gen. William Nelson had observed that the captain, then under arrest for being absent without leave, had never worked well with his lieutenants; his resignation should be accepted for the good of the company. Edward J. Mitchell, Compiled Service Record, Civil War, 2nd Ky. Cav., and File 12181–1884, Volunteer Service Branch, RG94, National Archives.

3. Lovell H. Rousseau (1818–1869), Kentucky native, moved to Indiana in 1840 and was elected to the legislature (1844–45, 1847–49). After service in the Mexican War he became a leading Louisville attorney. Elected to the state senate in 1860, he resigned the following year to raise troops for the United States, establishing Camp Jo Holt across the river from Louisville. Commissioned brigadier general of volunteers in October, 1861, he served first in the Army of the Ohio and, after his promotion to major general, with the Army of the Cumberland. Resigning in November, 1865, to sit as a Republican congressman (1865–67), he strongly opposed Radical Reconstruction policies and was reprimanded by the House for his violence toward Josiah B. Grinnell of Iowa, who had insulted him. He reentered the regular army in 1867 and was sent to Alaska to receive that territory from the Russians. Summoned from there to appear at Johnson's impeachment trial, he arrived too late to testify. *DAB*, XVI, 194–95; *BDAC*, 1545.

4. For Sevier and Jones, see *Johnson Papers*, I, 4–5n, 275n.

5. During their two-week swing around upper East Tennessee, Johnson and Nelson had been in Montgomery on June 6. Alexander, *T. A. R. Nelson*, 79.

From George W. Keith[1]

Monticello Ky. 12th July 1861

Hon Andrew Johnson Sen. Tennessee
Dear Sir

Knowing your position & the labors imposed on you it is with reluctance I now for the first time attempt to trouble you[.]

The emmergency of our Condition in Morgan Scott & Fentress Counties with very precarious condition of East Tennessee generally impels me to call on you for some exertion on your part for our protection[.]

There are about 400 Secession Troop in Morgan & Fentress

Counties[.] the first Squad of 210 passed through Montgomery peacably by the Flag that waved over you & Col. Trigg[2] but on Tuesday last (the 9th) a second Squad passed through after having beaten & abused one of our peacable & unoffending Citizens of Morgan to wit James Jones[3] on account of his Union sentiments came on through Montgomery with their secession Flag halted opposite our Flag & one of their ensigns[4] snatch it down while from three to four of the men stood with fixed [bayonets?] upon each man & child with their muskets in a ready position (our women were excited looking on as he started of with our flag when my wife sprang at him & the first motion took it from him[.] he then waved his Southern flag over her & told her & all there that soon they should all bow to it—) I was not there but came home shortly afterwards[.]

Our folks would have followed them but for the fact that we had information that upwards of 200 hundred more would pass the next Wednesday the 10th[.] we determined if they insulted us to whip them[.] I was asked to go to Scott County & send men to Montgomery by 11 Oclock which I rode all night to do & sent over 100 & came on to Kentucky Wayne County to meet B. T. Staples[5] & other who started on the 26th June to Cincinnatti to procure assistance if possible[.] the Reb foes of Morgan & Scott Counties found out that mission North and have instructed the stationed rebels & those in Ky. to inter-cept all the passes & capture them a victory they shall be diprived of if possible[.]

My greatest object is inform the proper authority they are rushing all the forces they can into the Western portion of East Tenn. & all along the line of Kentucky to prevent or deprive us of all possible assistance in the way of arms or men & coerse us into submission before the August election[.][6]
All of which I have been and am contending against with scarcely any amunition or other hopeful means of success and at the same time to prevent the capture of Staples Hall & Duncan[7] & for the restoration of our Government—knowing that they have sworn I shall not live but I hope I will yet be able to see them disappointed[.]

I think if Hon. Maynard was instructed he would give us the news by express if no other way. I would have no hope of geting any thing through the mail from your or Sect. *Cameron*[.]

In haste your Obt. Servant

G. W. Keith

To Hon Andrew Johnson Sen.
Washington City D. C.

ALS, DLC-JP.
1. George W. Keith (b. c1814), a Morgan County merchant, farmer, and schoolteacher, was court clerk (1848–56), county surveyor (1858–60),

state senator (1865–69), and clerk and master of chancery court (1870–82). In late September, 1861, he enlisted at Camp Dick Robinson in the 2nd Tenn. Inf., USA, and served as regimental quartermaster until mustered out in October, 1864. Robison, Biog. data; Ethel Freytag and Glena K. Ott, *A History of Morgan County, Tennessee* (Wartburg, Tenn., 1971), 128, 311–12, 363, 364.

2. Connally F. Trigg (1810–1880), a native of Abingdon, Virginia, moved to Knoxville where he became a law partner (1855–59) of Oliver P. Temple. Overwhelmingly elected as a Union candidate to represent Knox and Roane counties in the February 9 "convention or no convention" election, he was later characterized by Temple as an "ardent, bold, uncompromising Union man, with the courage to proclaim his opinions in terms sometimes startling." In July, 1862, Lincoln appointed him U. S. judge for the district of Tennessee. Trigg had been traveling and speaking along with Johnson, Nelson, and Baxter. Temple, *Notable Men*, 208–11; Caldwell, *Bench and Bar*, 305–6; *Senate Ex. Journal*, XII (1861–62), 416, 436.

3. Either James Jones (b. c1794), a native Virginian, or James Jones (b. c1830), born in Tennessee, both farmers. 1860 Census, Tenn., Morgan, 2nd Dist., 21, 22.

4. During the first decades after the Revolution, an ensign was the lowest commissioned infantry officer in the U. S. army, as well as in the Tennessee militia. Although the rank disappeared from the regular army after the War of 1812, it continued to be in use in the state forces. *OED*, III, 202; Heitman, *Register*, II, 568; *The Militia Law of . . . Tennessee* (Nashville, 1840), Sec. 67.

5. Benjamin T. Staples (1817–1863), a Morgan County farmer with an estate of $8,000, a Bell supporter in 1860 and a strong unionist, canvassed his county against secession and served as a delegate to the Knoxville Convention of 1861. Arrested by Confederates in December, 1861, and imprisoned in Knoxville, he was released and fled to Kentucky; returning later to Nashville, he was appointed adjutant of a regiment of Tennessee cavalry. In March, 1863, along with other officers, he was taken prisoner by the Confederate guerrilla Champ Ferguson. As Staples was being taken to Knoxville, he was murdered by a guard. 1860 Census, Tenn., Morgan, 66; Temple, *Notable Men*, 54, 191–94.

6. In the impending Kentucky legislative election, the Southern Rights party made little effort to put a ticket in the field; the result was a decisive victory for the Unionists. Coulter, *Civil War in Kentucky*, 97–98.

7. Probably John Hall (b. c1820), a Morgan County farmer who later became court clerk (1875–76), and James S. Duncan (c1819–1863), a Morgan County farmer with $15,000 realty, who was killed in March, 1863. 1860 Census, Tenn., Morgan, 38, 61; Freytag and Ott, *Morgan County*, 363; James S. Duncan, Compiled Service Record, RG94, National Archives.

From Carlyle Murray[1]

Boston July 12th 1861.

Hon Andrew Johnson
United States Senate

Sir   Permit one who admires you as a man—& loves you for your patriotism to trespass on your valuable time for a moment. I am a Kentuckian born near the Tennessee line, and like yourself an unconditional Union man. Disabled by wounds received in Mexico,[2] that will prevent my taking the field in person—I am yet anxious to do all I can for my bleeding Country in this her hour of sorest need. All honor to you, & your co-patriots in East Tennessee. The Government should aid them at once. They have my active sympathy, & I desire to show it—, by giving them my little mite & my prayers. God will doubtless receive the last— will you my dear Sir please tell me what I shall do with the first? Will you please write me to whome, how, & where I shall send a few contributions to aid the Union cause and gallant men of your State.

Oblige me Sir   And believe me your obt. friend & St
Carlyle Murray.

ALS, DLC-JP2.

1. This is the first of a series of letters from the Kentuckian Parker H. French, alias Carlyle Murray, alias Christopher Monroe, alias Charles Maxcy (or Maxy). A charismatic adventurer "affable in nature," fluent of tongue and pen, and a shrewd judge of character, French first came to public notice in 1850 as the leader of a California-bound wagon train—an enterprise in which he mulcted both suppliers and participants. Abandoning his companions at El Paso, he fled to Mexico where he was imprisoned for some eighteen months after attempting to rob a packtrain loaded with silver. In California he practiced law, was elected to the legislature from San Luis Obispo (1854), and coedited the Sacramento *State Tribune* (1855). Caught up in William Walker's Central American schemes, he was designated Nicaraguan minister to the United States and, after presenting his credentials in 1856, came briefly under indictment for violation of American neutrality laws; thereafter he resided in New York, where his occupation was listed as "chemist." Soon after Murray's "association" with Johnson and Lawrence, this "unconditional Union man"—now exposed as a swindler and Confederate sympathizer—was apprehended by Federal authorities and incarcerated at Ft. Warren. Following his release in February, 1862, he seems to have settled in St. Louis as a commission merchant and "speculator." Ironically, despite his multifarious activities, much information about this colorful character, including birth and death dates, remains yet to be established. Edward McGowan, *The Strange Eventful History of Parker H. French, with Introduction, Notes and Comments by Kenneth M. Johnson* (Los Angeles, 1958); Rex W. Strickland, *Six Who Came to El Paso: Pioneers of the 1840's*, Texas Western College Southwestern *Studies*, I, No. 3 (El Paso, 1963), 19–25; *Trow's New York City Directory* (1860), 305; *OR*, Ser. 2, II, 1275; *Edwards' St. Louis Directory* (1867), 352; *Gould's St. Louis Directory* (1873), 296.

2. Although he led Johnson and others to believe he was wounded in the Mexican War, French actually lost his right arm in 1850 during a gunfight at Corralitos, Mexico. Strickland, *Six Who Came to El Paso*, 24–25; see also Amos A. Lawrence to John M. Forbes, August 10, 1861, Amos A. Lawrence Letter Book, New England Emigrant Aid Company Records, Kansas State Historical Society.

Speech to Missourians in the District of Columbia[1]

July 12, 1861

Fellow Citizens—and I must address of course that portion of my fellow citizens from Missouri, who have so kindly tendered their approbation and respect, but whilst speaking to them, I address you with equal sincerity, and tender my thanks for the kindness you have manifested on this occasion. I can only repeat here what but a few moments since I said to those gentlemen, who I fear from partiality more than from a correct appreciation of my course have been induced to make the manifestation they have on this occasion,—but let that be as it may, I say such a manifestation coming from that section of our country which they represent—The State of Mo., which is so closely identified, with Tennessee in sympathy, in interest, in feeling, and in everything that should characterize them in the future as in the past, renders me on the present occasion incompetent to return my gratitude in that language and in that form which my heart would dictate or judgment approve. But while I may not be capable of reducing it to sentences and frases handsomely rounded and made to fall pleasant upon the ear, I trust and hope that they will not the less convey the sincere feelings of my heart, and my devotion to the country. (Applause.) [2] As the Address just made has very clearly indicated the perilous condition of the country with which they have been partial and kind enough to associate my own name, and with it the State which I have the honor in part to represent in the Councils of the Nation, I must be indulged while I submit a few remarks with reference to the position that she occupies, and I trust in God will ever occupy in all time to come. ("Amen," and applause.) In Tennessee as in most of the States that have attempted to break up the Government, and to withdraw from the Confederacy there has been a reign of terror gotten up. In some portions of the State the people notwithstand[ing] the fact that by their Bill of Rights, and by the Constitution they have the privilege of speech guarantied to them, and also the right to keep and to bear arms, have had these fundamental and sacred privileges denied them. Even you who reside in the District of Col.[3] cannot appreciate these things as we do who reside in Tennessee, and the other States still further South. You have never been denied these high privileges. You have never been waited upon by mobs and informed that you must not appear before the people and discuss questions involving their highest and their dearest interests. You have never been driven back at the front of the bayonet, as it were, at the violence and threats of the mob. You have not experienced these things, hence, here in your midst, and elsewhere further North, and even further West, it is not a very difficult matter to be a Union man. (Applause.) But when we go a little further South, and Southwest there is some responsibility both as regards life & property, as well as reputation, and all those rights which are sacred & dear to man. When you have to defend a position which, and a party who is trodden with treason and threatened with confiscation of property—denied the privilege of speech,—in fact everything that pertains to freemen, why then it is a very different position to occupy from what it is here.

When I go to my own State how does the case stand there? Why we find three thousand officers scattered throughout the State for the purpose of organizing companies and battalions to assist the Confederate cause as it is styled. And in a very short time a large army is well disciplined and equipped, and portions stationed in different sections of the State to brow-beat and to deter any and all who might dare to defend the cause of these States. This has been the course pursued there. Rewards have been offered, and high premiums held out, for the heads of all prominent Union men.[4] Such persons have been compelled to ride from point to point with one hand upon a knife, and another upon a pistol or a gun to protect themselves from the wily and insidious assaults of assassins. These are some of the perils which the people there have had to undergo; but thank God in one portion of the State we did meet them, and there were some men engaged in it who had the courage, moral & physical to meet this terrible exigency. They were met face to face, and met in their own way—and pardon me for saying so here tonight, for I make the statement in no spirit of egotism—that in every county in the Eastern portion of the State in which T. R. Nelson, and myself addressed the people they rolled up a large majority in favor of this glorious Union.[5] (Loud & prolonged applause.) My friends, I did not refer to this for the purpose of attaching any importance either to Mr Nelson, or myself, but to show of what inestimable value is the privilege of speech, which if it could have been exercised in all portions of the State, I have no doubt Tennessee would today have been standing in this galaxy of States one of the brightest jewels that now adorns this mighty and glorious Diadem. And this too by a majority ranging from 25 to 50,000. I trust in God that the time will yet come, when the beautiful banner of our country which was borne by Washington in the Revolution, by Jackson & Scott in the war of 1812, and in the war with Mexico, will again be unfurled from every Court-House, from every Cross-Roads, and from every public place throughout the width and breadth of the State. ("Amen" and applause.) I believe that time will come and that shortly. (Applause.) And, notwithstanding that today when it is understood that I came here to discharge my public duty and that I would make an effort to take back relief and assistance to a gallant, generous, frugal, and independent, but an oppressed people, why even the very passes of the mountains have been blockaded. They have been shut up to prevent any ingress, as it was said, of arms and the munitions of war that might be sent or carried to the relief of that people. How does the matter stand there: Why even the arms that have been manufactured by the Government and placed in the State by the proper authorities for the protection of the people have been seized by a little petty tyrant named Harris who has assumed—or it has been assumed by some for him in some of the newspapers—the title and position of Governor:—and the Union loving people denied the use of them. This is our condition. Had the people there 10,000 stand of arms, they would tomorrow occupy the most important position in this whole programme of war that is going on. They would control the only remaining stream that now supplies and keeps alive the Southern Confederacy.[6] But they are powerless. With railroads running in from the West, and then on the East, if any time they attempted to strike a blow their people would be overrun by the Myrmidons to be furnished by this Southern Confederacy. And let me ask you here tonight, if, while these gallant men are struggling against such odds for the maintenance of their rights, the preservation of their freedom and their position in this glorious Union, and for the ascendency of the Stars & Stripes which was borne by the Father's of your Country, you will—even at this distance—be willing to stand by, and see them struggle in vain. ("No." "No"., and loud applause.) I know that hearts are patriotic here as elsewhere, and there is no patriotic heart—there is no one who loves liberty—loves his brethren who will be willing to stand by, and see a brave, struggling & suffering people, trod beneath the iron heel of a base usurper. (Thats so, and applause.)

I am aware that much has been said about despotism and tyranny, and all that; and that there has been a charge of a disposition on the part of the Free States, of the Non-slaveholding States, to wage a war of extermination and to destroy some institutions which are peculiar to the South. Pardon me for saying here tonight, (for I do it in mere justice to those places where I have been within the Free States) that wherever I have been this doctrine and this sentiment have been disclaimed. (Applause.) I have heard in every audience I have addressed in the Free States, "It is no war upon Southern institutions," (Applause) it is no war upon Mo; it is no war upon Tennessee. Instead of its being a war upon your institutions, it is an prompt and effective relief. But when we turn round and look at the South we find that it is a war made by them upon the Constitution and the Union of the States. They are determined, if they possibly can effect it, to destroy this Gov. and establish one for themselves, disconnected, and different far from the present glorious form of Government under which we live. And just here I must be permitted to remark that my own honest convictions are that the character & genius of the Government they propose to establish—if they succeed in overturning this present one—which I don't think there is any possibility of—(Thats so) will be absolutely or partake to a very great extent of Monarchy itself.

[(]A Voice. Full Monarchy.[)] We have reached that period in the history of our country when a large portion of the people—especially a large proportion of those who assume to be leaders—seem to have lost confidence in the integrity and capability of the people for self-government, and are now endeavoring to subvert the present form of Gov. in the hope that after we have had wars, blood shall be shed, lives sacrificed, the substance of the people exhausted, and themselves wearied, fatigued, and worn out, that then the masses of the people will be glad to accept of any sort of Government for the sake of peace and repose. This is that at which they are aiming.

But let me refer to a few facts in connection with this subject. Was there not conclusive evidence adduced in the Senate during last May,[7] that no compromise was desired. We remember the resolution that was passed in the Senate when the proposition was made that the time had arrived when it was necessary to legislate for the protection of slave property.[8] When these propositions were made by Mr A. G. Brown, that they all voted against, and defeated them, thus showing that further legislation was not necessary. We find that instead of the election of the present incumbent to the White House being a cause for the dissolution of the Gov. it was made a mere pretext, and taken as a favorable occasion for breaking up the Gov.

I must be permitted to enlarge upon this point, and I trust you will bear with me, for the time has arrived when we should talk about facts and apply them to the present condition of the country. You know as well as I do that on the 4th of March last, if all the Senators had remained in their places, that they were within six of a majority.[9] If these men from the South entertained such serious apprehensions that inroads would be made upon the institutions of their section, let me ask you if they did not have it in their power being within a majority of six to arrest and prevent evey successful inovation that might attempted to be made, by the Administration. Why not then have remained then and if inroads were attempted, within the Senate, within the pale of the Constitution, according to law, and the forms of Government resist all the encroachments—and thereby give evidence that we were its faithful vigils by staying at our posts and defending the Constitution in accordance with the Constitution and Laws. (Applause.) This is not all. In this connection we know that if these fears were apprehended what is it that Mr Lincoln could have done. They were alarmed! The Government was to be upturned. What could he have done with a majority against him?

("Nothing") It is as my friend says he could have done nothing. He could not even have formed his Cabinet if the Senate as originally constituted had opposed him. He could not have appointed a Foreign Minister, or made a treaty inimical to the South, for such action could not have been valid unless approved by a two third vote. He could not even have drawn his salary without the consent of the Senate. I merely enumerate these things to show that this apprehend[ed] danger is a mere pretext for breaking up the Government. There was no cause whatever for it.

You know it has been alleged that first slavery was to be abolished in the District of Columbia, and next it was to be prohibited in all the Territories; but the third, last, and most important move was to follow these two moves. That these were laid down as entering wedges. And upon this point I wish to be understood. When these things were done,—which in themselves were not much cared for, only as they were as the outposts—then slavery was to be interfered with in the States. There is where the dread was, that when they went on excluding slavery from the Territories, and the Free States became so numerous as to reduce the remaining slave States to one fourth, that then under the Constitution—having done two other things—they would come forward with an amendment to the Constitution, confering power upon Congress to interfere with it in the States. Understand me if you please—for I want your attention upon this point—and when the facts are submitted, and they are connected it strips this nefarious move of the South of every vestige, pretext; it leaves it without the slightest foundation beneath the shining sun. Now how does the matter stand, and how did it stand at the adjournment of the last Congress? There were 34 States in the Confederacy. Seven went out.

Now I wish your attention to one point, and I will nail it in on the one side, and clinch it on the other.[10] (Laughter) Now, what was done at this precise period of our history when the Slave States were reduced below one fourth. We find that there were three Territorial bills passed by a two thirds majority, in neither of which was anything said in regard to the prohibition of slavery. What more was done? Why in the sixth section of the bill conferring power on the Territorial Legislature they go on and instead of conferring power issue a negative,—or in other words impose a negative power that they shall have no power to legislate so as to impair the value of private property, or to tax one description of property higher than another; and all shall be taxed according to value.[11]

Now mark you, that these three Territorial bills embraced and covered every square inch of Territory owned by the United States.

After the passage of this slavery prohibition then a negative was put upon the Leg. that they should have no power to legislate or impair the value of private property in any sense of the word whatever. Then what becomes of the Territorial question? Now, how much of it is left? Is there any more left of the Territories. There they are all embraced. There is the negative on your Terr. Leg. settling all that thing about Squatter, Popular, or any other kind of Sovereignty by which we think proper to call it. Now how does the "big" or remaining end of the question stand—for this is what I call putting the nail through upon that point. At this very period when the Constitution was to be so amended as to confer power upon Congress to interfere with slavery in the States an amendment is brought forward by Mr Corwin, a representative from a Free State which says that the Constitution shall never be so amended as to authorize Congress to interfere at any time with the subject of slavery in any sense whatever.[12] Then there are the Territories on the one hand, and here is an amendment passed by two thirds of Congress, putting the negative directly upon Congress, and making such a proviso a part of the Constitution[.] My friends are you not aware of the fact that there are some portions of your Constitution which cannot be amended—even under the 5th section which provides for amendments to the Constitution.[13] Now putting this together, "being past by two thirds," and that too when we were but one fourth—putting your Territorial bills together, putting the amendment to the Constitution together, how much of the slavery question is left? I call this clinching the nail upon that subject. Then where does it bring us? It brings us to the conclusion that all this attempt at secession, and all this civil war, and this blood which is now being spilt and shed has been unnecessary and unjustifiable. We see that it is a war that has been made without cause, or the least foundation, and therefore should be instantly put down. And then on the other hand we see that while we have been fearing apprehended aggressions upon the South here is a war against the Gov. and as I have before said without any just cause, for this battle could have been fought in the Union, without the sacrifice of life, in accordance with Constitution and law. But they seem to have preferred making war upon the Gov., upon the Constitution, and tearing down the Flag of their country, and running up seven stars in its stead.[14] How does it stand on the other side? My friends, I have heard it asked in Tennessee & Ky, and doubtless you have heard the same question propounded in Mo, "With whom do you intend to take sides in this issue?—the North or the South? Those who talk thus seem to regard this trouble as a war between the North and the South. But my friends, it is no such thing. I told the people in my own State, and in other places, and I tell the Nation here, tonight, that so far as I am personally

concerned and the Union men of Tennessee are concerned, my own
and their stand is by the Government. (Loud & prolonged applause.)
It is by the Stars & Stripes; it is by the Union of the States. It is not
with the South, or the North, but it is with the Gov. standing by the
Flag of the Country, and institutions founded and reared by our
Forefathers. This is where we stand. (Applause.)

Fellow citizens, we have reached that crisis in our Gov.,—or perhaps it would be more correct to say that this Gov. like all others
has three trying ordeals through which it must pass. First a nation
has a severe struggle in achieving its Independence[.] Such was our
case. We commenced as a handful in the Revolution and we know
that Washington and his peers waded through a seven years war;
and that they slept upon the cold, damp, ground with no covering
but the inclement sky; but notwithstanding this, rose in the mornings and renewed the march, and traversed the frozen ground, the
blood gushing from their heels. These privations were submitted to
achieve our Independence from a British despotism. This was the
first struggle, the first ordeal. The next was in 1812. After having
started and become an independent people it became necessary in
assuming our position among the Nations of the Earth to have a
struggle with external, and with Foreign foes. It was in 1812 when
our soil was again contaminated by such a foe; and the same year
when our seamen were imprisoned and incarcerated in floating
dungeons upon the high seas. It was at this time, while engaged in
contending against Foreign foes that the second trouble came upon
us. But under the lead of Jackson & of Scott, and a long list of
patriots, whose names I might mention, but hardly think it necessary, we passed through the second ordeal, and proclaimed to the
world that notwithstanding we had just emerged into a state of Independence, we were powerful enough to maintain our character as an
independent and separate power among the Nations of the Earth.
(Applause.) The second ordeal having been safely and creditably
passed, we now come to the Third. And these are ordeals through
which our Nation must pass. And what an important ordeal is it.
Now the Gov. is struggling with itself as it were for existence. Striv-
ing with an internal foe—against traitorous arms, that have been
lifted, and traitorous hearts that have determined to strike the Gov.
down. (Applause.) This is the ordeal. The contest has come, and
now the question is, is there sufficient patriotism, sufficient power,
sufficient energy, in the Gov. to uphold its existence, and strike
down this band of traitors and conspirators who are trying to destroy the liberties of the people. ("There is," and loud applause.)
My own honest conviction is that if this Gov. has been a delusion; if
we have been laboring under a dream, imagining that we possessed

a Gov. when in fact we have had none, the time has now arrived in our history when this delusion should be dispelled. Now is the time when this idea should be converted into a great fact or vanish into thin air. If we in reality have a Gov. that has the inherent power to enable it to preserve itself then this fact should be clearly demonstrated. (Applause.) And when it becomes necessary to assert that power, it doesn't make any difference who the enemy is. If this war is against traitors, against men who have lost confidence in the capability of man for self-government, it is not the less just on that account, nor worthy of less vigor. If S. C. and the other seceding States will attempt to dissolve their allegiance to this Gov. and make war upon their own countrymen, they at once render themselves as much of an enemy as any foreign power, and should be dealt with as we would any other foe, only with more severity as they are traitors. (Loud applause.) Civil war is more to be deprecated than any other kind of warfare, and those who have been the immediate cause, should be treated with unusual vigor & severity. ("Thats so," and applause.)

Then, we know how the facts are. We know who commenced this war and whos are in wrong.[15]

*　*　*　*　*　*　*

I would to God that peace might be restored to our land, and the evils of war thus averted, but as I have before remarked, I believe the time has come when the plethora[16] has become too great in the body politic. The dimensions of the tumor have become so great, its properties so inflammable, that nothing will now do but the effectual application of the Surgeon's knife. (Enthusiastic applause.) And even addressing it to this extreme, if it become necessary to amputate a limb, or to take out a tumor with the Surgeon's knife, I say let the work be thoroughly done. (Loud applause.) I proceed upon the idea that the system has reached that point or condition when nothing else will answer. ("Thats so.") War is to be abhored and deprecated; but when it becomes necessary in the maintenance of a great principle, every patriots services, and if need be his life should be given cheerfully. In this exigency I hope none will talk of treaties. What better treaty, what better compromise can you make than the Constitution of the U. S. which was framed by Washington, Jefferson, Madison, Monroe, and other patriots. Some have spoken of subjugation. An attempt was being made to subjugate the South. My friends is it any subjugation to be forced to comply with the provisions of a Constitution, formed by such men as Washington & the others I have mentioned and under which we have lived so long and happily. This Constitution subjugates none, but it protects all in the enjoyment of their rights. (That's it.) Let me ask this concourse of people before me, how many of you have lost any of your privileges by this Constitution. (None.) Do you feel as if you were in subjugation by living under the Constitution of your Fathers, and the law made in conformity to it. If any of you have lost your rights under this Constitution, let me ask you if our Southern brethren are getting their rights under the present state of things in that section. (Laughter.) Go there and examine the rate of taxation; and other outrageous wrongs, and then let me know your opinion.

Then, fellow citizens, as we have entered into this struggle, let us feel as if we were acting upon principle, and not engaged in a conflict of one section against the other section. We are contending for the Constitution which protects each and all in the full enjoyment of their rights as sacred by the patriots of the Revolution. This being so let us feel it. Let me ask you is there a patriot before me, who loves his country, loves the Stars & Stripes, who is wedded to this Union, who, when he turns his eyes Southward, and beholds the grave of Washington, is willing to see the 7 star flag unfurled over it. ('No' Never.") Again gaze upon that marble slab contributed by the State of Tennessee with a view to its having a place in that unfinished shaft in your vicinity[17] and read the inscription, "The Federal Union it must & shall be preserved." Where is the patriot who will not cheerfully go to protect his tomb from desecration by those who are seeking to reverse this beautiful motto.

Draft report, DLC-JP5E.

1. Missourians resident in Washington had procured "the services of Dodsworth's fine band accompanying the New York Seventy-first regiment," and assembled at the St. Charles Hotel to endorse Johnson's patriotic course. The delegation assured the senator that Tennesseans "will hereafter teach their children the name of Andrew Johnson when asked for an example of loyalty and courage" and that "on the scroll of American history . . . the characters of fidelity and courage . . . will be appended, in conspicuous lines, to the honored name of Andrew Johnson." Johnson's response was taken down by a Francis W. Crane, who submitted it to the senator for his correction. That this document is to be found in the Johnson Papers without evidence of any published version suggests that Crane, contrary to his original expectation, did not retrieve his notes in order to "have it publised [sic] in every Union Paper" in Missouri. Washington National Intelligencer, July 12, 15, 1861; Washington Evening Star, July 13, 1861; Crane to Johnson, July 17, 1861, Johnson Papers, LC.

2. Here someone—Crane? Johnson?—deleted as repetitious the following: "In presenting myself before you in compliance with the request that has been made and in answer to what has in part been said in regard to my own State, I must be permitted to offer a few remarks while I am before you. (That's what we want.)"

3. A reference to the limitations upon full citizenship, such as the right to vote, experienced by Washington residents.

4. See Speech at Lexington, Kentucky, June 18, 1861, note 5.

5. In the June 8 referendum East Tennessee had voted against separation, 32,923–14,780. White, Messages, V, 304; Campbell, Tenn. Attitudes, 292.

6. The Tennessee River.

7. Either Johnson misspoke or the reporter made a mistake; the Senate action occurred in May, 1860.

8. See Speech on the Seceding States, February 5–6, 1861, note 45.

9. This assertion reflects Johnson's presumption of party-line voting by all senators.

10. In carpentry the nail, driven through the board, is clinched by bending it flat on the opposite side.

11. Colorado achieved territorial status February 28, 1861; Nevada and Dakota followed on March 2; just as Johnson asserts, the sixth section in each territorial act did "issue a negative." *U. S. Statutes*, XII, 172–77, 209–14, 239–44.

12. The joint resolution offered by Thomas Corwin of Ohio, passed March 2, 1861, and sent to the states, read as follows: "*Article Thirteen.* No amendment shall be made to the Constitution which will authorize or give to Congress the power to abolish or interfere, within any State, with the domestic institutions thereof, including that of persons held to labor or service by the laws of said State." *Ibid.*, 251.

13. Article V provided that the first and fourth clauses of Art. I, Sec. 9, could not be amended until 1808. The first clause concerned the slave trade; the fourth allowed taxation only in proportion to population, a restriction not amended until 1913 (16th Amendment). The article also prohibited any amendment which would deprive a state, without its consent, of equal suffrage in the Senate.

14. The first Confederate flag, the "stars and bars," adopted on March 4, 1861, consisted of three wide stripes, two red flanking a white, and a circle of seven stars on a blue field, representing South Carolina, Alabama, Mississippi, Georgia, Florida, Texas, and Arkansas. The more familiar battle flag—thirteen stars on a blue St. Andrew's cross over a red background—was designed by Beauregard after the battle of Bull Run to avoid confusion on the battlefield between the "stars and bars" and "stars and stripes." Two more Confederate flags followed, utilizing the thirteen stars in a blue St. Andrew's cross in the upper corner. Boatner, *Civil War Dictionary*, 284.

15. Pages 22–26 of the manuscript are missing.

16. A bodily condition characterized by an excess of blood.

17. In accordance with a suggestion from the Washington Monument commissioners, the Tennessee General Assembly passed a resolution in December, 1849, authorizing the state's contribution to the proposed structure. The governor's 1851 annual message reported that a slab of marble from Hawkins County had been selected, inscribed, and sent to Washington. Described as "four feet long, two feet thick, and eighteen inches deep, of a dark chocolate color, highly finished," the slab was inscribed with the state name and Jackson's famous toast on Jefferson's birthday, 1830: "Tennessee—The Federal Union. It must be preserved." Although the cornerstone was laid in 1848, the monument was not completed until 1884. White, *Messages*, IV, 384, 400–401; WPA, *Washington, City and Capitol* (Washington, D. C., 1937), 319–22.

Remarks on Senators-elect from Virginia[1]

July 13, 1861.

Mr. JOHNSON, of Tennessee. It is with no ordinary pleasure that I rise to present the certificates of the Senators elect from the Commonwealth of Virginia, for the purpose of having them read at the desk; and I move that they be permitted to come forward, be quali-

fied, and take their seats. I look upon this as a favorable omen. The
return of the Old Dominion to this body, I think, is indicative of
future good, and the future restoration of the Union of these States.

[Following the reading of the credentials as certified by Governor
Francis H. Pierpont, James Bayard of Delaware objects on the ground
that the Pierpont government is not the duly elected body of Virginia
and moves that the credentials be referred to the committee on the
judiciary.]

Mr. JOHNSON, of Tennessee. I hope the motion of the Senator
from Delaware will not prevail. These certificates from the Commonwealth of Virginia afford *prima facie* evidence that the election
has taken place regularly, and that these gentlemen have been regularly certified here as the Senators from that Commonwealth. Is
there any proof before this body, presented in any way, that the
election has not taken place regularly, according to the Constitution
of the United States and of the State of Virginia? The certificates
themselves furnish *prima facie* evidence that these gentlemen are
the Senators elect from the Commonwealth of Virginia. The other
great fact is equally clear, without regard to what the Senate did
yesterday, that these vacancies did exist on the 9th of the month,
when this election took place. That fact is known to this body; it is
known to the country. The late Senators from Virginia were not
here.[2] The vacancies did in fact exist when this election took place.

These are facts within the cognizance of this body. They are
known to every member here. Here are the certificates of election of
these gentlemen, and there is not a single scintilla of proof from any
quarter that they are not the Senators, and have not been properly
and regularly elected. There is no one else claiming the seats, no
one making a contest for them. There is not a particle of evidence
from any quarter that these gentlemen are not the Senators elect
according to the forms of law and the Constitution.

How was it in the case from Indiana? There was a contest about
the election of the Senators from that State a few years ago, and
papers were presented protesting against their election before they
were sworn in. They, however, came forward with their certificates,
and were qualified, and the matter was investigated afterwards.[3] It
strikes my mind that it is clear and conclusive, upon the proof now
before the Senate, that the gentlemen, whose credentials have been
presented, are the Senators elect from Virginia; and there can be no
objection to their being qualified and taking their seats. Then, if
their seats be contested, or any proof presented that the election did
not regularly take place, the subject can be referred to the Committee on the Judiciary, or the Senate can take such course as it thinks
proper. Why should there be a reference of these credentials, when

there is no intimation, no evidence in the world, except that these gentlemen are Senators from the State? It is known that the old State government is in rebellion, making war upon the Government of the United States. As it appears to my mind, there can be no reason, at this stage of the proceeding, why this reference should be made; and I hope that the Senators will be permitted to go forward and be qualified, and take their seats according to the custom of the Senate.

[Willard Saulsbury of Delaware asks how, if those "seats were vacant yesterday, the Senate . . . could have expelled those gentlemen?" Inasmuch as Mason and Hunter had been considered members upon their expulsion July 11, the election of the senators-designate, having occurred prior to the vacancy, is therefore void. Lyman Trumbull, observing that "scarcely a Senator here . . . was not elected in advance, before the office became vacant," favors accepting the credentials and administering the oath on the ground that the old regime is in rebellion. A side exchange between Bayard and John P. Hale of New Hampshire reveals that the former regards recognition of the new senators as constituting recognition of the rebellion, which Hale denies.]

Mr. JOHNSON, of Tennessee. I will answer the question of the Senator from Delaware [Mr. Saulsbury] by asking another question. Because the Senate, on the 11th of this month, voted for a resolution expelling certain Senators,[4] he assumes the fact to be that no vacancy existed prior to that time. I want to ask the Senator the simple question, if the vacancy did not exist prior to that time?

[Saulsbury, repeating his argument that by expelling the southerners on July 11 the Senate had recognized them as being in full membership up to that date, maintains that the resolution declaring the seats vacant since the beginning of the session on July 8 should have been adopted.]

Mr. JOHNSON, of Tennessee. It seems that the Senator and myself agree in the substance of what we have stated to the Senate. I understand him to admit the existence of the fact of a vacancy in the Senate of the United States from Virginia prior to the 11th of July, when the Senate passed the resolution to which he refers. If that fact exists, as it does, a mere reconsideration of the resolution now would not affect it one way or the other; for the passage of the resolution on the 11th did not do away with the fact.

Mr. SAULSBURY. Will my friend allow me a moment? I said that the Senate, being the judges of the election and qualification of their own members, had the right to treat the seats of the former Senators from Virginia as vacant from the time they withdrew; and if they had so treated it there would have been a vacancy.

Mr. JOHNSON, of Tennessee. Then the right of the Senate to treat it as a vacancy must grow out of the existence of the vacancy itself, which proves conclusively that the vacancy existed, and substantially commits the gentleman himself to the existence of a vacancy. But the question is not whether the Senate proceeds on the idea of a vacancy or not. A Senator, in tendering his resignation, frequently tenders it to the Legislature. It is not necessary to tender it to the Senate. It is for the Legislature of the State to determine that fact; and the Legislature of the Commonwealth of Virginia now proceed upon the existence of the fact. On the 9th day of July they assumed that vacancies existed in the Senate of the United States, occasioned by the withdrawal and abdication of R. M. T. Hunter and James M. Mason from the Senate of the United States. Is there a Senator upon this floor, of any party, who does not admit the existence of that fact? It is for the Legislature to determine. They have assumed what is true, that vacancies existed; and assuming that to be so, they have taken the regular steps, and have filled those vacancies. They have not been, as has been indicated here, elected for regular terms; but the Legislature have proceeded to fill vacancies which existed at the time of the election. That is the fact. If that fact did not exist, the reconsideration of the resolution adopted by this body would not bring it into existence; and the mere fact of the Senate passing a resolution, does not do away with the existence of the fact which the Legislature of the State of Virginia assumed to exist. There can be no question about that.

The case is clear in another point of view. According to the custom and usage of the Senate, here is *prima facie* evidence that an election has taken place, which entitles the members elect to appear and be qualified and take their seats; and then, in the event that any contest arises, it is competent for the Senate to refer it to the Committee on the Judiciary, or to any other committee, in its discretion, to ascertain all that may be necessary of the circumstances appertaining to the election.

I think, sir, there can be no question as to the existence of the fact of vacancies, and surely there can be none as to the power of the Legislature to fill the vacancies. That has been done. It is competent, under the Constitution, for each House constituting the Congress of the United States to judge of the elections, returns, and qualifications of its members. That is a clear, general power; and, according to the uniform construction of this constitutional provision, it is our duty, upon the presentation of these certificates, no contest being made, to permit the Senators to be qualified and take their seats as members of this body.

The Senator from Illinois has referred to some cases that have heretofore occured.[5] Let me refer to some others. It is not long since Oregon was admitted as a State. Do we not remember that before her admission two gentleman[6] presented themselves here, were in the lobbies, were inside of the Senate, contending for seats as Senators of a State that was not then in the Union? If we were to construe the Constitution very strictly, or wanted to make an *ad captandum* argument, we might say that an election of Senators which took place prior to the admission of a State into the Union was not valid under the Constitution of the United States; but under the Constitution, the Senate having the general power to judge of the elections, returns, and qualifications of its members, they were permitted to take seats, notwithstanding they were elected prior to the admission of the State into the Union.[7] How was it with the State of California? Her Senators were here for weeks anxiously waiting, impatiently waiting, for the Congress of the United States to admit California as a State. The election took place; they were here before the State was even in the Union; yet, dealing with the case under the general power of the Constitution, this body recognized, and admitted to seats here, Senators who had been elected prior to the admission of California into the Union.[8]

Upon these precedents I might safely rely if the cases were parallel; but they are not parallel. Is there the slightest resemblance between the cases? I am not questioning the power in the one case, while I am contending for it in the other. I am merely contending that these precedents are much stronger than the case now before the Senate.

It seems to me that there is not much in what the Senator from Delaware [Mr. Saulsbury] said as to the action of the Senate. The great fact exists. The action of the Senate one way or the other does not do away with the fact. There were vacancies here from the State of Virginia. The Commonwealth of Virginia, the loyal portion of it acting under the Constitution and the law, have proceeded to fill those vacancies, and have done it; and the gentlemen so elected not only have the right to take their seats, but it is the constitutional duty of this body, upon the presentation of this paper, regular in every particular, to admit them. This ought to be allowed simply as a matter of right; and I think the Senate and the other branch of Congress, in cases of this kind, should be inclined, even where there is doubt, to put the most liberal construction; and to give their action the largest margin it is possible to give. Will the United States stand by and see a loyal portion of a State, maintaining all the authorities, prevented from having a fair and equal participation in the Government, and to that extent favor and tolerate and sanction open rebellion and encourage insurrection in another portion of the same State? If there is a State government in existence as a part of this Confederacy, and that State government has sent Senators here with certificates made out in the usual and regular form, it is the duty of the Government to come up to the relief of the State of Virginia, the loyal portion of it, and take it by the hand, and sustain it against rebels and traitors who are trying to overthrow it and to overturn the Government. It is our duty, I repeat again, our constitutional duty, to sanction and sustain, as far as it is possible, the State government in making the great move that she has made, which I conscientiously believe will result in the overthrow of treachery and treason to the people of the United States. We should give them all the aid we can; we should stand by the loyal men; we should give them encouragement; we should develop the Union sentiment, so that it may, if possible, arrest and crush out a set of usurpers who have sprung up in the land, and are trying to override and tread beneath their feet the great majority of the people.

I say it is the duty of the Senate and the duty of the House of Representatives to stand by these loyal men, to stand by Virginia as long as she is loyal to the Constitution, to stand by the Union sentiment, to stand by that sentiment in the State which is trying to sustain and will in the end sustain the supremacy of the Constitution and the laws. To refer the case to the committee without a single fact being presented, without one single reason being given, when there is no real objection made to these Senators taking their seats, strikes me as very singular. The form of the credentials is regular; they come from an organized Legislature loyal to the Government; the vacancies exist, and yet it is said these credentials must be referred. The session is nearly at a close; it will come to a close in a few days; and yet these gentlemen are to be kept out of their seats by the proposed reference of the case. Is any reason given for it? Is there any fact to be investigated? What is it for but delay? What is it for but to impede and to embarrass the Union sentiment that is rising and growing throughout the land? Whether it is intended for that or not, that is the effect it is calculated to have.

I trust and hope that the Senate will without hesitancy permit the Senators to be qualified and take their seats with their compeers in this body to battle with us for the preservation and for the existence of the Government, and against those who are making war upon it, and in the end help us to crush out a set of traitors who are attempting to overthrow the Government and all that is sacred and dear to man.[9]

Cong. Globe, 37 Cong., 1 Sess., 103–4, 105, 106.

1. Two days earlier the Senate had voted to expel James Mason and R. M. T. Hunter of Virginia, along with other senators from seceded states. Johnson, without prior introduction, gained the floor to present the credentials of Waitman T. Willey and John S. Carlisle, elected by the "restored government of Virginia," a regime established by thirty-four trans-Allegheny counties in Wheeling on June 11. Francis H. Pierpont, a Wheeling attorney and coal dealer, had been elected governor, two senators and three congress-

men chosen, and a unionist legislature organized. Edward C. Smith, *The Borderland in the Civil War* (New York, 1927), 185–220; Nevins, *War for the Union*, I, 142–43. For Hunter and Mason, see *Johnson Papers*, II, 104n, III, 29n.

2. Mason and Hunter had not returned to the Senate after Virginia seceded and were formally expelled July 11. *Cong. Globe*, 37 Cong., 1 Sess., 64.

3. In 1855 Indiana Democrats, quarreling among themselves, refused to select a senator, leaving one seat vacant for two years. Two years later, with both seats up for election, the factions managed to caucus and support the reelection of Jesse Bright and the election of Graham Fitch. When the Republicans refused to go into joint session, the Democrats, holding a majority in both houses, held the election, which was contested. Although their credentials were debated for a year, both Bright and Fitch took their seats and participated fully in the work of the Senate. Emma L. Thornbrough, *Indiana in the Civil War Era, 1850–1880* (Indianapolis, 1965), 78.

4. On July 10, Clark of New Hampshire introduced a resolution calling for the expulsion of Mason and Hunter of Virginia, Thomas L. Clingman and Thomas Bragg of North Carolina, James Chesnut, Jr., of South Carolina, A. O. P. Nicholson of Tennessee, William K. Sebastian and Charles B. Mitchell of Arkansas, and John Hemphill and Louis T. Wigfall of Texas. The following day, after considerable discussion, the resolution was passed. *Cong. Globe*, 37 Cong., 1 Sess., 40, 64.

5. Trumbull had reminded his colleagues that the "Senator from Delaware was elected before the vacancy which he filled existed," and that the "Senators from Minnesota were admitted long before the State of Minnesota was a member of the Union." *Ibid.*, 104.

6. Joseph Lane and Delazon Smith. *Ibid.*, 35 Cong., 2 Sess., 1019.

7. The senators' credentials were presented and the oath administered on February 14, 1859, the same day that Oregon was officially admitted. *Ibid.*, 1012, 1019.

8. Californians had adopted a constitution on November 13, 1849, at the same time electing members to the legislature. Convening in joint session, the legislature chose William M. Gwin and John C. Frémont as the state's first senators. On September 10, 1850, one day after California officially became a state, the new senators were seated. Walton Bean, *California: An Interpretative History* (New York, 1968), 133–34; *BDAC*, 149.

9. The motion to refer to the judiciary committee the petition for admission of the new Virginia senators was voted down, 35–5; Carlisle and Willey at once took the oath of office and were seated. *Cong. Globe*, 37 Cong., 1 Sess., 109.

From John B. Haskin[1]

Washington Sunday,
July 14th, 1861.

My Dear Sir

There will be a caucus of Senators, in relation to the Secretaryship, tomorrow morning at 11 O'Clock— You will place Col: F.[2] under obligations of lasting gratitude, to you, by being present, and assisting him—

Yours truly   John B. Haskin

Hon: A Johnson—

ALS, DLC-JP.

1. John B. Haskin (1821–1895), New York lawyer, was a Democratic congressman (1857–61). *BDAC*, 1021.

2. John W. Forney, a candidate for secretary of the Senate, was elected the following day. *Cong. Globe*, 37 Cong., 1 Sess., 119; see also *Johnson Papers*, II, 32*n*.

From Samuel S. Bush[1]

Louisville Ky
July 15 1861

Hon Andrew Johnson
Dear Sir

Dr Hale[2] is here from Fentress Co. E Tenn— He says 400 Middle Ten Troops came into that Co on last Monday evening— He represents that they are without arms or Ammunition— Not a pound of powder in the Co. The people, he says are determined to Expel them and he came here to try to get arms— He wants Rifles of some sort. —the Enfield—Halls or the Minnie Rifle.[3] That his people know nothing of any gun but the rifle— He requests me to write you to know within what time he can be furnished with a 1000 Rifles— If they cant possibly get rifles they want the next best gun they can get.—Such an One as will be suited to a Guerilla warfare— I would be very much pleased if you would write immediately— Twenty Cos in the S. E. part of Ky are preparing to assist E Tenn[.]

Allow me to suggest that the Communication between Ky & E Tenn is greatly interrupted by the Seccession post masters in the South E quarter of the State— I have been in that quarter of the State recently and have seen a number of E Tennesseans who tell me that they have not recieved a line from Ky, owing to this interruption. They should be removed at once[.]

Write, if you please, at once. The Guns can be sent to James Speed or the Surveyor of the port in this City and will be forwarded by them to Clinton Co Ky and deposited some-where near the line from whence they can be easily obtained by the Fentress Co people. You will probably remember me— I was 5 years ago a Citizen of Sumner Co Tenn. Met you once at Col Guild when John K Howard was present[.][4] I was the person who brought Howard the information of his fathers having been Killed in the East by a Collission of the Cars[.][5]

Yours Respectfully   S. S. Bush[6]

ALS, DLC-JP.

1. Samuel S. Bush (b. *c*1825) was a Sumner County farmer with $600 in real estate and $250 in personal property. 1860 Census, Tenn., Sumner, Gallatin, 16th Dist., 113.

2. Jonathan D. Hale (b. *c*1817), who had just written Johnson from Cincinnati, was a Fentress County physician with $8,125 in personal and $2,500 in real property in 1860. Two days before this letter he was reported to be raising a "Lincoln company" in Fentress; in 1863 Gen. George H. Thomas called Hale his "chief of scouts." 1860 Census, Tenn., Fentress, 76; *OR*, Ser. 1, XXIII, Pt. II, 586; Albert R. Hogue, *Mark Twain's Obedstown & Knobs of Tennessee: A History of Jamestown and Fentress County, Tennessee* (Jamestown, 1950), 38, 57; Hale to Johnson, July 14, 1861, Johnson Papers, LC.

3. The Enfield musket, a British gun popular in the South, was also used by northern regiments, particularly during the early part of the conflict, since the government had purchased 428,000 stand when hostilities began. Patented in 1811 by J. H. Hall, the Hall rifle, a breechloader used early in the war, was a modification of the Minié rifle, initially developed in France and manufactured in the United States during the 1850's. Lord, *Civil War Collectors' Encyclopedia*, 240, 247; William B. Edwards, *Civil War Guns* (Harrisburg, Pa., 1962), 67, 242–55; Jack Coggins, *Arms and Equipment of the Civil War* (Garden City, N. Y., 1962), 31–32.

4. Josephus C. Guild (1802–1883), born in Virginia and reared in Houston and Sumner counties, was a lawyer and chancellor (1859) for Sumner, Montgomery, and Robertson; he later moved to Nashville and served as a judge (1870–77). Compiler of *Old Times in Tennessee* (1878), he enjoyed the title of "colonel" as a legacy from the Seminole campaign (1836). John K. Howard, onetime political friend of Johnson, was a lieutenant colonel in the 7th Tenn. Inf., CSA; wounded at Gaines' Mill, he died in Richmond July 9, 1862. Caldwell, *Bench and Bar*, 297–99; Acklen, *Tenn. Records*, I, 288; *Tennesseans in the Civil War*, I, 189; see *Johnson Papers*, II, 263*n*.

5. Jacob Howard, former Greeneville merchant, had been killed in a New Jersey train wreck on the Camden and Amboy Railroad, August 29, 1855. "In Memoriam, Jacob Howard," Sam Milligan Memoir; *Johnson Papers*, I, 215*n*.

6. An attached letter from Joseph Holt supports Bush's statements and expresses the hope that his letter "will receive from the government immediate attention." Holt to Johnson, July 15, 1861, Johnson Papers, LC.

From James P. T. Carter

Barbersville Ky July 15/61

Hon' A Johnson
Dear Sir

I arrived at this place, this morning at 3 o clock by private conveyance from London. Quite a number of East Tennesseeans have been on the look out for me, to capture me thinking they would get valuable information as to the plans of the Government in suplying the Union men of E Tenn with arms. I shall leave here to night with a guide to make a passage at some point th[r]ough the mountain moast direct to Knoxville. From the moast reliable information I can gather the number of troops at Cumberland Gapp dose not exceed three hundred & Fifty all told, which have three small pieces of cannon planted on the west sumit that over looks the gapp[.] They also have Wheelers & Babtist Gapps garded with about two hundr[ed] men each.

I have made an arraingement to send a man by Cumberland Gapp
& meet me at Knoxville by which means I hope I shall be able to give
perfectly reliable information as to the entire strenght of the *traitors*
in East Tenn. in order to do this I shall have to employ some safe
person to bring all communications to this place to be mailed as all
mail communication is cut off by this rout with Tenn.

I remained one day in Cincinatti. Saw Leut Nelson.[1] I think his
plan a very bad one for getting through with our arms. his idea is
to shipp the arms in small lots to Nicholasville thence to Barbersvill
& make a depot at the latter place. I objected to it moust strenuously
for just so soon as he makes the attempt in that way a portion of the
armes will be captured & the Briges on the Lexington Road will be
burned, (so say the sperinntendent of the Road)[.][2]

My sugistion to him was this. That he make his arrraingements
to have a sufficent number of waggens in Cincinatti to haul the guns
& amunition over to Covington a mediately after the 2 o'clock t[r]ain
leave for Lexington[.] Let the R Road agent take possession of the
telegrphy office & put all on a special train & leave Covvington at 8
or 9 o clock P M.

After I saw Liut Nelson I meet with G W Fulton the superintendent & laid the above plan before him, which he endorses, and informed me that he has the intire control of the Telegraphy[.] The
agent is anxious to do every thing in his power to fasilatee the transportation, & requested me to say to you that it would be best for you
not to leave Washington untill after the arms have been shipped as
your departure will be too generally known & the enemy will be on
the allert. I think his surgestion a good one[.] conscider it for your
self.

I cannot give you as much information as I would like as I have
rather a bad chance to get posted my self as I cant get out[.] I am
stopping at Mr Adams,[3] & have been so private so far that none of
his family but his wife knows that I am here[.]

From all that I can geather I very much feer that the traitors are
plainig the same desperate game hear that they plaid in Tennessee.

Yours Respectfully
Jas P. T Carter

ALS, DLC-JP.

1. "Bull" Nelson, under orders of July 1 from the war department, was
engaged in planning an expedition for the relief of Kentucky and Tennessee
by distributing arms and raising three regiments. See Letters from William
Nelson, July 11, 16, 1861; Lorenzo Thomas to Nelson, July 1, George D.
Ruggles to Nelson, August 13, 1861, copies in Johnson Papers, LC.

2. George W. Fulton was superintendent of the Kentucky Central Railroad. Several months earlier, when he had become superintendent of the

Covington and Lexington, he was described as "a gentleman whose invariable courtesy of deportment is the index of integrity and character." *OR*, Ser. 1, XVI, Pt. II, 488; Louisville *Journal*, February 21, 1861.

3. See Letter from George M. Adams, July 23, 1861.

From Johnston H. Jordan[1]

Cincinnati O. July 15/61—

Andrew Johnson— U S S.
Washington D C.

Dear Sir: Among the many delays and other things which surprise me, connected with this "War" nothing astonishes me *so much* as the neglect or delay, on the part of the Government, in sending *arms and assistance* into East Tennessee!

I saw the necessity of it, and urged it upon the Powers at Washington, *more than* a *month ago*[2]: —and I supposed, certainly, that as soon as *you got to Washington*, if not before—*it would be done*.

It does seem to me that there is *no time to be lost*, if this is going to be done, with any hope of its being of any service! For several days past Gov. Harris has been moving troops towards Knoxville,[3] for the purpose, of course, of *subduing* and *crushing out* the Union men.

To day a gentleman—a Union man—from *East Tennessee*, arrived in this city, for the express purpose of urging our people, and Gov. Dennison,[4] to *send them arms and ammunition*—but *especially the latter*:—that Secession troops were already overrunning the country (a Company of them being stationed *on his farm*, when he left!.)—and that if the Union men in East Tennessee do not *soon* get assistance of this sort, at least, *it will be too late!*— they will be overrun—crushed out—driven off—or killed!

If arms & ammunition are *sent here—to Cincinnati*, there need be no difficulty in getting them to Knoxville, or into the hands of Union men in East Tennessee. I would myself agree and undertake to put 5000 or 10 000 stand[5] safely there *inside of ten days*.

Let the arms be sent here— let us have three days notice—and we will *put them into the proper hands*, in a very few days.

They can be shipped per Railroad to *Danville Ky*—then carried *in the farmers wagons*, by Kentuckians, from there to Knoxville— *or to the Union men*.

I should like no better job—if I had the *arms* and the *authority*— than to do just this thing!

Cannot something of the sort be done—and that *immediately*?

Is the Administration paying any attention to *Kentucky*?[6] There is *mischief* brewing there—and that *very shortly*! It would be well to keep an eye on Magoffin and his Secession colleagues—and *especially* would it be well to get possession of that *Louisville Railroad*, as far as the Tennessee line. *In a short time it will be too late*! O! the want of *fore thought*!

Truly Yours,
J. H. Jordan, M. D.

ALS, DLC-JP.

1. Johnston H. Jordan seems to have pursued careers as a doctor in both Cincinnati and Indianapolis and as a newspaper publisher and editor in the latter city. The author of *Anatomy, Physiology, and the Laws of Health* (1857), he was associated with the *Western Universalist* during the mid-1850's and with the Indianapolis *Gazette* just before, during, and after the war, selling out in 1868 because it was not profitable. A staunch Republican who, as here, urged upon Lincoln vigorous prosecution of the war, by the election of 1864 he was a critic of the administration, identified with the Chase supporters. Berry R. Sulgrove, *History of Indianapolis and Marion County, Indiana* (Philadelphia, 1884), 244; Donnal V. Smith, "Chase and the Election of 1860," *Ohio Archaeological and Historical Quarterly*, XXXIX (1930), 785; Winfred A. Harbison, "Indiana Republicans and the Re-election of President Lincoln," *Indiana Magazine of History*, XXXIV (1938), 41; Jordan to Lincoln, April 4, 5, July 4, October 9, 1861, Lincoln Papers, LC.

2. Earlier in the month Jordan had written Lincoln urging him to set as priority "No. 1" aid to East Tennessee unionists who were "in danger of being *overrun* by the Secessionists!" Jordan to Lincoln, July 4, 1861, *ibid.*

3. On July 11, 1861, following expressions of concern from secessionist East Tennesseans, Confederate War Secretary Leroy P. Walker directed Governor Harris to dispatch two regiments to upper East Tennessee; a week later such arrangements were completed, and another regiment had arrived in Knoxville. On July 26 Felix Zollicoffer was appointed to command the district of East Tennessee with headquarters in Knoxville. Actually, these were not the first secessionist forces to be active in East Tennessee. Before the June election Confederate troops were reported in Knoxville, where companies of volunteers were being raised. Alabama and Mississippi troops also had moved through the town on their way to the Virginia front. *OR*, Ser. 1, IV, 364–67, 374–75; Ser. 2, I, 827–28; James C. Stamper, Felix Zollicoffer: Tennessee Editor, Politician and Soldier (M.A. thesis, University of Tennessee, 1967), 68; Rothrock, *French-Broad Holston Country*, 129–30.

4. William Dennison (1815–1882), former Whig lawyer and now Republican governor of Ohio (1860–62), dispatched state troops to aid the loyal citizens of western Virginia and advocated that similar measures be used in Kentucky; in time he assumed virtually complete control over railways, telegraph lines, and express companies in Ohio. Appointed postmaster general by Lincoln in 1864, he remained until 1866, when he resigned because of his opposition to Johnson's policies. *DAB*, V, 241–42; Ohio Historical Society, *Governors of Ohio*, 76–79.

5. A complete set of arms for one soldier. *Webster's Third International.*

6. From the beginning of hostilities Lincoln realized the strategic importance of Kentucky and treated his native state with the utmost consideration, giving assurances that, as long as Kentucky did not commit an overt act against the United States, he did not plan to move troops through the state. As a result of this lenient policy, Kentuckians continued a busy and profitable trade with both North and South. Not until August 16 was commercial intercourse with the Confederacy prohibited, and even then the Federal government allowed a liberal permit system which made possible some trade with

the South. The end result was to keep Kentucky in the Union, despite the Confederate-sympathizing Governor Magoffin. Nevins, *War for the Union*, I, 133–34; Coulter, *Civil War in Kentucky*, 53–54.

From Theodore Smith

July 15, 1861, Ellicottville, N. Y.; ALS, DLC-JP.

New York banker, eager because of family health to relocate in a warmer climate, wants to know "what part of [Tennessee] you consider most healthy and agreeable, as a residence—and whether the com[in]g fall & winter, such part of the state would probably be a safe & agreeable place to reside." Assures Johnson that he shares in the "wide spread gratitude and admiration that Every where among loyal men, prevails for your unflinching devotion and patriotic Exertions for the Union."

From Washington, D. C., Citizens

July 15, 1861, Washington, D. C.; ALS, DLC-JP.

Charles Gumber and seventeen other "citizens, Soldiers Mechanics & Tradesman" beseech Johnson to urge upon Congress a general relief bill which will "make us comfortable and Safe while in discharge of our duties to our Country," inasmuch as "We are daily Subject . . . to have our Families thrown out upon the Streets our Little Household Furniture distrained for Rent due" and are "Subject to be warranted at any and all times for Small debts for food & Fuel[.]"

From William O. Bourne

New York, July 16, 1861.

Hon Andrew Johnson,
Dear Sir,

I take the liberty of enclosing to you one hundred copies of "THE IRON PLATFORM," for June,[1] which I hope you will find not only worthy of your attention, but worthy of your approval, and that you will place them in the hands of your friends.

I have an unalterable faith in the loyalty and patriotism of the people of the South, and although there is a great apparent defection at the present time, I attribute it to the persistent frauds and wicked schemes of the traitors and terrorists who have madly hoped to accomplish by violence, usurpation, and imposture, what they could not achieve by the legitimate instrumentalities of truth and constitutional rights. With this conviction I aim to appeal to the reason, patriotism, and fraternal feelings of the masses, being thoroughly convinced that if we can reach them by some strong and well individualised *movement of the people*; independent of any of the old partisan caucuses and machinery, we shall be able to facilitate a popular reaction which will expedite with great force the triumph of those military agencies which the government has unhappily been compelled to organise and call for in order to preserve our popular institutions from overthrow.

It is, perhaps, unfortunate for a man to be *independent* in his mode of presenting truth to the public, yet I cannot avoid the conviction that in the wreck of old platforms, and party organizations, a noble and enduring Iron Platform can be constructed which will reëstablish the grand ideas of popular liberty and Union on a basis which will forever defy the imposture of secession, and the diabolism of rebellion and bloodshed.

I wish that some means could be adopted by yourself and friends to circulate my tract liberally among the people of Tennessee and Virginia. I believe that the masses of the people can be reached by proper means, and while ALL the men and money are called for and appropriated necessary to crush the Rebellion, yet it would be a grand moment to circulate liberally just such documents as I propose.

It was my expectation to have the privilege of a personal interview with you in Washington, that I might be able to explain such matters as you might be disposed to inquire into. In the hope that you will visit New York,[2] and favor me with an interview, I am

Your Obt Svt
Wm Oland Bourne

ALS, DLC-JP.

1. *The Iron Platform*, "devoted to the Union and free labor," was published in New York City from May, 1856, to September, 1864. The June, 1861, issue contained an "elegant extract" from the Memphis *Avalanche* calling for the "scalps of Johnson and Etheridge," for, just as farmers hang "a dead crow as a warning to others . . . the skin upon Emerson and Andy's ugly craniums must hang high up in the Capitol at Montgomery." New York Public Library, American History Division, to Andrew Johnson Project, November 8, 1972.

2. The same day Bourne, on behalf of the "Working-Men's Committee," dispatched an invitation for Johnson to visit New York to speak. Bourne to Johnson, July 16, 1861, Johnson Papers, LC.

From William Nelson

Cincinnati O. 16 July 1861

Dear Sir

Enclosed herewith is a letter a copy of one sent to Mr Chase by me,[1] and a parellel one—being sent by me to the Adjutant General of the Army (General Thomas)[.] Please *pitch in* and see that my demands are complied with. See that the Quarter Master General (Meigs)[2] and the Commissary General (Joe Taylor)[3] are instructed to meet my demands in their departments. I have asked far less than the regulations allow, but still sufficient.

On one consideration and with the acquiescence of all parties in the Hill country, I shall assume the Command of the Expedition and go ahead so soon as my arrangements will permit.

Our freind Carter[4] is a magpie, a chuckle head,[5] a chatter-box. When he left here for Tennessee I gave him a hundred dollars and bade him with many a prayerful insistance that he would keep mum, until he got into Tennessee[.] I charged him solemly, seriously and with much imposing both to keep his mouth shut, not to open his lips to any, even his own father if he should unexpectedly turn up concerning the business in hand. Well sir he had scarcely got to Lexington, four hours from here only, when he picks up a man named Stevenson[6] with whom he had a sort of an acquaintance, being introduced to him when going through with you. To this man Stevenson, our friend Carter tells of the whole matter in hand. What we are doing, the number of muskets, of artilley, of Cavalry Equipments, of regiments to be raised and when raised, and where going. The men who are expected to go; *who has* the business in hand, and to crown all, the *time that we are to* move.

The whole matter has been sent to Magoffin, telegraphed to Tennesse, and is as well known as if it had been published in the newspapers[.]

This of course complicates matters. Strong guards are now necessary to guard the stores in ther transit through Kentucky to prevent their destruction by secessionists who are on the lookout for any thing passing. Mr. Carter has done the expedition more mischeif than 5000 Secessionists could have done— Such a tee total absence of discretion and common sense is astonishing and when coupled with the fact of having been so solemnly charged to preserve the strictest silence, it is provoking[.]

I am urging on matters with the fiercest energy, and will telegraph you the moment we are ready to move. You will then leave Washington City incog: and come along without being noticed by papers and join us. Dont even take leave of any but your most intimate friends for I again insist that secrecy is necessary to success[.]

Go to the War Department and see my Estimates in the Quarter Masters and Commissary Departments, and insist on their being filled, and paid for as the payments fall due[.]

See General Riply[7] in the ordnance office and let him hurry up his muskets, accoutrements, his artillery with its harness and fittings of all sorts and his cavalry arms. The Cavalry will furnish their own horses, saddles &c. &c—

Make things go with a rush.

Yours truly   W. Nelson

Hon. A. Johnson of Tennessee

ALS, DLC-JP.

1. Nelson wrote Chase describing in detail plans for an East Tennessee expedition, listing military appointments, routes to be used, and military supplies needed, as well as the security precautions that had been worked out for the success of the undertaking. Attached to his letter was a copy of the form which he was using in his appointment of officers to the expedition. Nelson to Salmon P. Chase, July 16, 1861, copy in Johnson Papers, LC; Nelson to Adjutant General, July 16, 1861, *OR*, Ser. 1, IV, 252–53.

2. Montgomery C. Meigs.

3. Joseph P. Taylor (1796–1864), younger brother of the President, was a professional soldier who entered the regular army in 1813 and served in the subsistence department for most of his military career, becoming commissary general of subsistence on September 29, 1861. Boatner, *Civil War Dictionary*, 827; New York *Times*, July 3, 1864; Holman Hamilton, *Zachary Taylor* (2 vols., Indianapolis, 1941–51), I, 262n.

4. James P. T. Carter, who had accompanied Johnson in his flight from Tennessee in June, 1861. Temple, *East Tennessee*, 344, 368.

5. A blockhead, numbskull, dolt. *Webster's Third International*; *OED*, II, 400.

6. Possibly Congressman John W. Stevenson who, along with Governor Magoffin, was accused of southern sympathies. Magoffin's early refusal to supply Union troops and his subsequent "neutrality" policy had the effect of favoring the South. Coulter, *Civil War in Kentucky*, 48–56, 319.

7. James W. Ripley (1794–1870), Connecticut native and West Point graduate (1814), served in the War of 1812, under Jackson in the invasion of Florida, and in the Mexican War, rising to the rank of lieutenant colonel. At the outbreak of the Civil War he was on a special mission in the Orient. Returning home on April 23, 1861, he was appointed army chief of ordnance with the rank of colonel and the following August was promoted to brigadier general. Retired on September 15, 1863, he continued to serve as inspector of armaments until 1869. *DAB*, XV, 625.

From William Nelson

Cincinnati. O July 17th 1861

Dear Sir

Enclosed is a duplicate of a letter addressed by me to General Meigs Quarter Master Genl: requiring that besides expenses already incurred $100,000 should be placed at my credit with the assistant Treasurer in New York City.

This money is absolutely necessary. I must have it to check against. I must be able to buy cattle on the hoof to feed our men, to buy flour as we want it, to pay for all the thousand little wants which are absolutely necessary. The officers of the army whose opinion I have asked insisted that I should ask, considering the size and distance of the undertaking, 250,000$ but I think that you and I are smart enough to get a long on less— I have sent a Copy of all these papers to Chase secretary of the treasury[.] he is a friend of mine. Pitch in, fiercely! have this money arranged before you sleep. I want all the blanks that are necessary from the office of Adjutant General, Quarte Master General, and Commissary General[.] also, I want a quantity of Hardees tactics and army regulations[1] for distribution among the green officers.

I will have the finest Brigade of Kentuckians you Ever saw. You will work hard in Tennessee to Equal them—

I hear continually of Carter— He has gone on his way rejoicing, and blabbing! I am so provoked that I half wish that they would catch and hang him[.]

I want Dr J. J. Mathews[2] of Louisville a newly appointed a Brigade Surgeon to be ordered to report to me for duty in the Tennessee Expedition[.]

Now read over my wants and Enforce them—

1st I want the 100,000$, we must have it

2d Blanks of all the Departments

3. Army Regulations & books of tactics

4. Dr Mathews

See that the Q. M. General & that Commissary general[3] meet promptly all my demands of them. If money is the sinew of war we must have our share of it[.]

Yours truly,   W. Nelson

Hon A. Johnson Senate

ALS, DLC-JP.

1. William J. Hardee (1815–1873), West Point graduate and instructor who became a Confederate general, was the author of a manual, *Rifle and Light Infantry Tactics* (1855), adopted as an army textbook. Only a few days before Nelson wrote, a disturbance, quelled by armed guards acting for customs surveyor Cotton, had erupted at the Louisville L & N depot, "in consequence of a secession trunk filled with Hardee's Tactics." *DAB*, VIII, 239–40; see also Nathaniel C. Hughes, *General William J. Hardee: Old Reliable* (Baton Rouge, 1965); New York *Tribune*, July 17, 1861.

2. John J. Mathews became surgeon with the 5th (Rousseau's) Rgt. and later with the 32nd, before resigning in February, 1862. On July 16 Nelson formally requested his appointment for the expedition. Connelley and Coulter, *Kentucky*, II, 1120, 1131; Nelson to Salmon P. Chase, July 16, 1861, copy in Johnson Papers, LC; Nelson to Adjutant General, July 16, 1861, *OR*, Ser. 1, IV, 253.

3. Montgomery C. Meigs and Joseph Taylor.

From William Nelson

Cincinnati O 18th July 1861

Dear Sir

I wrote to you this morning Enclosing you certain papers, and a requisition on the Quarter Master General for one hundred thousand dollars[.]

I write again to urge you to insist upon my requisition being complied with:[1]

This money is absolutely necessary to pay the daily incidental Expenses of moving so large a body of men, and such a tremendous train as that we will move with. It is to buy cattle to feed the men, forage for Horses, shoeing horses, and mules, repairs, in sho[r]t you can imagine the thousand Expenses necessery to such a movement. There are contingent expenses, as well as subsistance, and must be met with in cash and I must be able to check on some fund. See Meigs! see Col. Joe Taylor! See Cameron!! see Chase!!! see the President!!!! See everybody-but hav it done! Never quit the grit.[2]

Your truly   W. Nelson

Hon A. Johnson
Washington City

ALS, DLC-JP.

1. Johnson evidently interceded on Nelson's behalf, for two weeks later the Kentuckian telegraphed, probably in reply to an inquiry, "Treasury notes can be used." Nelson to Johnson, [July] 30, 1861, Johnson Papers, LC.

2. This particular expression does not appear in the usual sources of nineteenth-century colloquial speech. No mean phrasemaker, Nelson himself may have coined the rhyming admonition to stick to the struggle.

From John Orf[1]

New york, July. 20, 1861

My Dear Sir!

In consideration of affair's, patriler [particularly] of your owen State, I can not help to call your attention to my sugestion made to you in my former letter[2] to wich I undoubtably expected to receive a answer up to this time all tho in vaine. if my proposition therein made to not meet your approvell, or if you have not the convidence in my ability (on account of being a stranger to you that I know not.) how ever you may depent up on my sugestion as well as my proposition to you was made in good faith. and if you should consend to appley with the same, you will [find] that the Military opperations you so may under take in your State will be of nothing less, then a contineal Success in every instance.

because I am satisfied, that I have assertained the weeke side of the Rebell forcess, and I should take the attvanteche at evy instance of it. You may think if I possess sufishent [ability?] to comand a military Corps, Why did I not offer my service allready to the proper Authority.

Allow me then to explane: this.

nameley: I have used up every Cent. of means for the Organisation of a German Working men's Newespaper. wich was intended to be commenced last Prest Campaign; had I been successfull to bring out said Paper at that Time, Then; I would have ben by means, to enable me; to organise a Regt. wich would have ben, long a goe in Actual Service, but in the contruary I would not, for being not only in tirely out of means, but also sick for som 5 Months and as I have seen the way Brigade Generals & Collonals' have [been] appointed, most of them have not the slitest Idea about military tactics—I have determent to take no minor position wathever, being however very angst to become ingached in the present Ware. I have taken the liberty to offer my Service, as I thought to the proper men, particlar when I lernet, that you could obtain the appointment as a Genrl. in reverance of Organising a Legion of som 12, 15, or 20,000. Men in the free States[.] I thought would be a practible sujestion becouse, Who would be able to obtain a said Number in a very short time. The[y] in conction with forces of your own State would be sufishend, to quelle, sussesions in a very shorte time and so protect the Loyal Citizens of your State from further misshive [mischief].

but owing to the Circumstance that I am not able to express my selve by Writing I desired to have a persenal interfiew where I am satisfied I would be abel to satisfey you as well as the Prest. That I possess sufishend Quallifation for all I should ask to become intrusted with, becouse I never make it a practic, to protent to do a thing wich I may et not be able to do. in hope that I may receive a answer as earley as possible

I remain very respectfully
your most Obt. Hub. Servand   John: Orf
Editor of the Am: Patriot & Working Union

Hon: Andrew Johnson
U. St. Senator
Washington D. C.

ALS, DLC-JP.

1. Although John Orf appears to have been a quondam journalist, he was at this time a Dayton, Ohio, painter. Despite a frenetic campaign—characterized by appeals not only to Johnson and the President but also to the

secretaries of war and treasury—to raise a regiment called "Zach Taylor's Sharpshooters," a search of the available military records discloses no evidence that he was successful. *Williams' Dayton Directory* (1860–61), 141; John Orf to Johnson, August 5, December 10, 1861, Johnson Papers, LC; Orf to Salmon P. Chase, December 9, 1861, RG94, Letters Received, Volunteer Service Branch, National Archives; Orf to Edwin M. Stanton, April 24, 1862, RG107, Letters Received, National Archives; Sara D. Jackson (National Historical Publications Commission) to Andrew Johnson Project, November 14, 1974.

2. His former letter is not extant.

3. No paper of this title has been found.

Bill Appropriating Arms To Loyal Citizens[1]

July 20, 1861

Mr. JOHNSON, of Tennessee. I rise for the purpose of asking the unanimous consent of the Senate to introduce a bill of which no previous notice has been given.

A BILL

Making an appropriation to pay the expenses of transporting and delivering arms and munitions of war to the loyal citizens of the States of which the inhabitants now are or hereafter may be in rebellion against the government of the United States, and to provide for the expense of organizing them into companies, battalions, regiments, or otherwise, for their own protection against domestic violence, insurrection, invasion, or rebellion.

Be it enacted by the Senate and House of Representatives of the United States of America in Congress assembled, That the sum of two million dollars be, and the same is hereby, appropriated, out of any money in the treasury not otherwise appropriated, to be expended, under the direction of the President of the United States, in supplying and defraying the expenses of transporting and delivering such arms and munitions of war as in his judgment may be expedient and proper to place in the hands of any of the loyal citizens residing in any of the States of which the inhabitants are in rebellion against the government of the United States, or in which rebellion is or may be threatened, and likewise for defraying such expenses as may be properly incurred in organizing and sustaining, while so organized, any of said citizens into companies, battalions, regiments, or otherwise, for their own protection against domestic violence, insurrection, invasion, or rebellion.[2]

Mr. JOHNSON, of Tennessee. My intention is, to make a motion to refer the bill to the Committee on Military Affairs and the Militia. I will simply state, in this connection, that the object of the bill is, substantially, to call upon the Government to protect the loyal citizens of the rebellious States in their constitutional rights. The loyal citizens of those States feel that this Government is bound to protect them in the enjoyment of a republican form of government. They feel that this Government is bound to protect them against rebellion, against invasion, against insurrection, and against domestic violence. The object is simply to call upon the Government to protect them in the enjoyment of their constitutional rights, or to place them in such condition that they will be enabled to enforce them. I move that the bill be referred to the Committee on Military Affairs and the Militia, and be printed.

The motion was agreed to.[3]

Cong. Globe, 37 Cong., 1 Sess., 216; DNA-RG46, 37 Cong., 1 Sess., (37A-B1).

1. The antecedents of this measure, so vital to Johnson's constituents and so potentially far-reaching in its effect, are at best obscure. Apparently the Tennessee senator, acting independently, prepared and introduced the bill. That it moved so rapidly to final passage is probably evidence of the widespread, exaggerated misconception of the number of loyal southern and border citizens eager to spring to arms in support of the Union.

2. This text, which did not appear in the Congressional Globe, is found among manuscript bills in Senate archives. The Globe at this point provided only a brief paragraph statement of the proposed measure.

3. Three days later the bill, S. 38, was recommended for passage by the military affairs committee. With minor adjustments in phraseology, it passed the Senate the same day and the House on July 27, to be signed into law by the President on July 31. Cong. Globe, 37 Cong., 1 Sess., 226, 298, 365.

From Brotherhood of the Union

July 22, 1861, New York, N. Y.; L, DLC-JP.

Transmitting resolutions of thanks to a southerner for his Union stand during "our existing difficulties," which "originated in the unholy aspirations of dangerous men," Circle 1674 (John Commerford, Ira B. Davis, and J. K. Ingalls, committee) congratulates Johnson on "his patriotism in surmounting the apprehension of individual ruin, or the fears of threatened assassination" and pledges Brotherhood support "to sustain the government" to the end that "the deluded will throw down their arms and unite with us in resuming the proud position which is our common inheritance."

From George C. Rhodes[1]

Nashville Tennessee
July 22 1861

Hon. Andrew Johnson
Sir.

There is a business going on to a very great extent here that ought to be stopped, and I know no one, who would be so apt to attend thoroughly and promptly to it as yourself.

The U. S. Government have furnished a considerable quantity of arms to Union men, or ostensible Union men in Kentucky. A camp has been formed at a point fifty miles from here on the railroad[2] commanded by a Confederate General Withers[3] composed exclusively of Kentuckians, and whole companies of the men are armed with the identical weapons sent there (into Ky) by the U. S. Government and hundreds of the men are those who took the oath of allegiance. They say in explanation that they swore to support and defend the Constitution, the President has violated it and is trying to subvert it, hence obedience to their oath is best carried out by joining the Confederates.

Supplying arms to Kentucky, or any people when many are disloyal is a mistake, for they ultimately fall into the hands of traitors.

Union men are quiet and honest rebels are busy, thieving and lying, and in nine cases out of ten circumvent the Union men.

I hope for the sake of the Union men here this business will be stopped.

Geo. C. Rhodes

ALS, DLC-JP.

1. Not identified.

2. Camp Boone, located near the Memphis branch of the L&N Railroad and close to the Kentucky border of Tennessee near Clarksville, was a Confederate recruiting station. *Battles and Leaders*, I, 337; Coulter, *Civil War in Kentucky*, 104–5.

3. William T. Withers (1825–1889), a native of Harrison County, Kentucky, and a veteran of the Mexican War, had been a law partner of Judge William L. Sharkey of Mississippi. An opponent of secession, he offered his services to the Confederacy when hostilities began, raising troops in Kentucky before returning to Mississippi, where he commanded an artillery regiment. *NCAB*, VI, 516; *OR*, Ser. 1, IV, 367, 378.

From George M. Adams

Barbourville Knox Co Ky
July 23 1861

Dear Governor

Your friend Carter[1] reached my house on the morning of the 15 instant just before day and remained till that evening about dark without any of the traitors in our midst suspecting he was here— he then left here with a guide who knew how to pilot him through the mountains down through Whitley County and they crossed into Tennessee some distance above big Creek Gap— we also sent a son of David Cottrells[2] with him & he has just returned and they reached Knoxville on the 18th safely— on the 18th young Mr Cottrell Come out toward home some 15 miles & on the morning of the 19th some twenty Cavalry passed him in great haste, swearing they intended taking you at all hazards. (Supposing that Carter was yourself) the Cavalry were from Cumb. Gap & had gotten wind that you had gone through the mountains— I have not heard any thing further from Carter but suppose they did not get him[.]

Mr Cottrell says there are 8 or 900 rebels at Cumberland Gap, and a few at the other gaps below Cumb. Gap & Jacksborough— and I will enclose you to night Brownlows Whig of the 20th so you can see they are blockcading some distance below or sending a good many traitors—

Mr Cottrell says in the neighbourhood of Knoxville Hatten had a regiment but they had orders to start to Virginia in a few days—[3] there were also 500 Rebels at Knoxville without arms— and while he was there he saw a regiment of 1000 arrive & it was reported there would & generally believed there would be another regiment there in two hours. They were from Alabama[.]

As it will not be long before arms will leave Cin for our friends in East Tennessee I must urge upon you the necessity of having them well protected— we are all right here and determined to carry arms to your Citizens at all hazards—but the length of time it will take to haul them through Ky to the Gap the rebels will be able to give them word & they can & I believe verily will send several thousand men up to Morristown directly & in two days they Can reach the Cumb. Gap—, and I must talk plain to you for myself & nine tenths of the people in these Mountains look upon Neutrality as little better than treason in its practical effects & as the arms are not to leave till after the election in Ky[4] is it not best at once to send several regiments all the way along with the arms— I verily believe it will Crush out secession in Ky. it will show the secessionists this goverment is and will protect the Union men in E Tennessee & every where else that they are loyal— and it is said by young Mr Cottrell that the friends about Knoxville were of the opinion if arms Come on to the Gap for E Tennessee & there was not a strong force with them they would send any number of rebels up there and crush them out & you are aware if you are acquainted with the young man who is a son of David Cottrell that he is inteligent & knows what he is talking about[.]

Yours sincerely   G M. Adams

Andy Johnson
Washington City

ALS, DLC-JP2.

1. See Letter from James P. T. Carter, July 15, 1861.

2. David C. Cotrell [Cottrell?] (b. c1800), a Claiborne County farmer with $13,525 in real and $15,000 in personal property, had a thirty-year-old son, David, who lived with his father. 1860 Census, Tenn., Claiborne, 9th Subdiv., 190.

3. Robert Hatton, former congressman, was colonel of the 7th Tenn. Inf. Rgt., CSA. Ordered on to Virginia and promoted to brigadier general, he was killed at Seven Pines in May, 1862. *Tennesseans in the Civil War*, I, 188–89; see also *Johnson Papers*, II, 474n.

4. In the August 5 general election three-fourths of the legislature chosen
was unionist. The guns were never forwarded to East Tennessee but were
used for regiments mustered in Kentucky. Speed, *Union Cause*, 119, 133, 163,
181; Coulter, *Civil War in Kentucky*, 97–98, 102.

From Henry S. Townsend

July 24, 1861, New York, N. Y.; ALS, DLC-JP.

Notifies Johnson that the $663.55 forwarded by him has been received
and placed to the credit of Easley and Williams, Rutledge, Tennessee,
merchants.

From William Nelson

Cincinnati Ohio
25th July 1861

Dear Sir

The defeat at Meannassus[1] shook Kentucky like an earthquake, but
like an earthquake it passed away, and the Union people righted
themselves straight up, stiff and strong.

It has intensified feeling on both sides. I happened fortunately to
be in Lexington when the news arrived: The Union Club met in the
Hall in which you made your speech and *I* made my *first stump
speech*.[2] It was necessary for me to do so. The leaders were so
alarmed that I had to pitch in and remind them that we were not
yet whipped not by a damned sight— We had failed to carry Man-
nassus, it is true, but that was all, and all that remaned was gather
up our broken forces and try it again, and again, and again, till we
did it; for do it we would. We have the leisure, the men and the
money and above all the determination. We got up such an Enthusiasm as quite to drown the howl of the secessionists who were cele-
brating the ruin of their Country in the street.

Please find out why the arms have not come: The invoices have been
in my hands a week, but not a gun has come. We want them now—
for if Kentucky wavers, your residence in Tennessee will [be] at an
End— The knowledge that those guns are here will have an em-
mense moral effect.

Next— The Quarter Master General and the Adjutant General
as well as Commissary general have all failed to send me the *blank*
necessary to carry on the business.[3] Without the blanks of the Adjutant General I am unable to muster in any men. They were promised me on the 8th July and I have not received them yet[.]

Carter is in East Tennessee. He was escorted by a foot patrol in
charge of a mountain man around the Cumberland Gap[.]

My letters tell me that there are 570 armed secessinist at the Gap and that they are fortifying themselves.

Governor Magoffin proposes to issue a proclamation denouncing my carrying arms thro the state with a guard.[4] He proposes *to see them* through safely if I dare muster a guard to go with them—I did so,   ⌐ when I heard the proposal[.]

You must not lose any more battles about Washington— It does the Union Cause no good to say the least[.]

General McClellan should insist on having good and experienced officers to command his columns and Brigades. It is high time to drop politics and fight for the constitution and the Union—and to select men who know a little of military science to do it— Unless this is done I fear another disaster—

Dont forget to see that I am supplied with money, and to attend to the request contained here in[.]

Very truly Yours   W. Nelson

Hon. Andy Johnson
Seneate   Washington Cy

ALS, DLC-JP.

1. The first major battle of the Civil War, fought at Bull Run, or Manassas Junction, Virginia, July 21, 1861, resulted in a complete rout of the Federal army. When the news reached Lexington, southern sympathizers so exuberantly displayed Confederate flags and banners that the mayor mobilized the home guard to prepare for an emergency which did not materialize. Nevins, *War for the Union*, I, 214–20; Speed, *Union Cause*, 111–12; Daniel Stevenson, "General Nelson, Kentucky, and Lincoln Guns," *Magazine of American History*, X (1883), 134.

2. Nelson was in Lexington four days earlier but there is no report of this speech. *Ibid.*, 133.

3. A week earlier Nelson had telegraphed, "The muster Rolls & other blanks from the adjt Genls Office have not arrived. see what detained them[.]" Nelson to Johnson, July 17, 1861, Johnson Papers, LC.

4. This statement reflects Nelson's prior impression of Magoffin's proclamation issued August 3 to the effect that "certain arms belonging to the State" which had been "lately seized . . . and taken away from their place of deposit in Mayfield" [Maysville, where the "Lincoln guns" were to be redistributed in eastern Kentucky] were to be turned in to county court judges. Moore, *Rebellion Record*, II, Doc., 474–75; Speed, *Union Cause*, 104.

Remarks on War Aims Resolution[1]

July 25, 1861

Mr. JOHNSON, of Tennessee. I move that the resolution which I introduced yesterday be now taken up, and considered by the Senate.

The motion was agreed to; and the Senate resumed the consideration of the following resolution:

Resolved, That the present deplorable civil war has been forced upon the country by the disunionists of the southern States now in revolt against the constitutional Government and in arms around the capital; that in this national emergency Congress, banishing all feeling of mere passion or resentment, will recollect only its duty to the whole country; that this war is not prosecuted[2] upon our part in any spirit of oppression, nor for any purpose of conquest or subjugation, nor for the purpose of overthrowing or interfering with the rights or established institutions of those States, but to defend and maintain the supremacy of the Constitution and all laws made in pursuance thereof, and to preserve the Union, with all the dignity, equality, and rights of the several States unimpaired; that as soon as these objects are accomplished the war ought to cease.

[Trusten Polk of Missouri moves an amendment striking all words after "southern" and through "capital," inserting in lieu thereof "and the northern States," so the resolution would read: "That the present deplorable civil war has been forced upon the country by the disunionists of the southern and the northern States." Admitting that there are no northern states in revolt, he nonetheless insists that there are "disunionists in the North as well as in the South." When Polk's amendment receives only four votes, Trumbull proposes to strike out "and in arms around the capital" and "subjugation."]

Mr. JOHNSON, of Tennessee. Mr. President, I hope those words will not be stricken out. I think the resolution sets forth what is literally true. Are not these revolted States in arms around the capital? No longer ago than last Sunday the capital was within the sound of the roar of their cannon. Does not that seem as if they were around the capital? The resolution simply states a fact, and that the intention is to preserve the Constitution, to enforce the laws, and to preserve the Government. They are now in arms around the capital, and the roar of musketry and artillery is almost within our hearing, or has but scarcely ceased. It was heard no longer ago than last Sunday.[3]

The intention of the resolution was to state what is literally true. If the Constitution is supreme and is sustained, and the laws made in pursuance thereof are enforced, everybody must comply, and rebels will be made to know their places and to take their true position in the country. If you assert the supremacy of the Constitution and the laws made in pursuance thereof, of course all those in rebellion against them must submit, and they are subjugated. Of course, the resolution contemplates the enforcement of the laws and a submission of the rebels to the laws and the Constitution. The resolution simply states that we are not waging a war for the subjugation of States. If the Constitution is maintained and the laws carried out, the States take their places and all rebel citizens must submit. That is the whole of it.[4]

Cong. Globe, 37 Cong., 1 Sess., 257–58.

1. During a routine business session on the previous day Johnson had presented a resolution on the objects of the war; upon the elaborately courteous suggestion of Sumner, it had been ordered printed for subsequent consideration. *Cong. Globe,* 37 Cong., 1 Sess., 243; see also printed War Aims Resolution, Johnson Papers, LC.

2. Agreeable to the proposal of Jacob Collamer of Vermont, Johnson had changed "waged" to "prosecuted" when the resolution was first introduced. *Cong. Globe,* 37 Cong., 1 Sess., 243.

3. A reference to the Federal defeat on Sunday, July 21, at Bull Run, some twenty-five miles from Washington.

4. Proposing that the phrase "and in arms around the capital" be changed to "in arms against the Government," Collamer then discoursed on the meaning of the word "subjugation." The extended exchange thus initiated became heated when Breckinridge disputed the facts in the resolution, asserting that "the present condition of affairs is due principally to the absolute refusal of the majority in this Chamber to agree to any proposition of adjustment" and further that "the rupture which took place in the harbor of Charleston" did not justify presidential actions which "have made one blaze of war from the Atlantic to the western borders." Rebuttal from John Sherman and James Doolittle, along with remarks from Ira Harris of New York in support of the resolution as Johnson had presented it, followed. After a bare quorum had been assembled with difficulty, the original resolution was adopted, 30–5. *Ibid.,* 258–65.

From Amos A. Lawrence

(near) Boston July 26. 61

Dear Sir

The enclosed letter is from a reliable person in Louisville.[1] I send it to you in the hope the Govt. will be ready to render assistance promptly when it is required.

The $1800 wh. I collected for you was for the transportation of the arms, or for yr own personal expenses in the present emergency. As it did not seem to be required for either, I returned it to those who had given it: not thinking that I had any right to appropriate it otherwise.[2]

The recent defeat will not discourage enlistments here except in proportion as it diminishes confidence in the policy of the Govt., wh. seems to have been adverse to the plan of Gen. Scott.[3]

Resp'y & truly Yrs
Amos A Lawrence

Hon. And. Johnson.
Washn.

ALS, DLC-JP.

1. This unidentified correspondent, perhaps one of the Louisville contacts mentioned in his letters of June 14 and July 3, noted the effect of Bull Run upon Kentucky and described the belligerence of secessionists who milled about the streets shouting for Jeff Davis. Observing that the southern and

western portions of the state were strongly disunionist, he defended the adherence of "loyal sons" to the neutrality policy—"remember there is a large
Confederate force in Tennesee close to our border, our Governor a secessionist, and the State Guard rotten to the core"—and argued that Kentucky's
neutrality protected "the whole southern border of Illinois, Indiana & Ohio
for a distance of some seven hundred miles." Anon. to Dr—, July 22, 1861,
Johnson Papers, LC.

2. Impressed by Johnson's suggestions, made on June 25 and reiterated on
July 31, that the loyal press of East Tennessee was in dire need of financial
support, Lawrence, having already returned the money collected for the transportation of arms, not only forwarded Johnson his own $200 subscription but
also wrote on August 2 "To the gentlemen who subscribed before & to others
who take an interest," inviting them to send the senator "by mail whatever
they are willing to give"—for "there can be no doubt about the urgency of
their [East Tennesseans'] case." Draft, Amos A. Lawrence Papers, Massachusetts Historical Society.

3. General-in-Chief Winfield Scott's "Anaconda Plan," proposed in May,
had envisioned a slow strangling of the Confederacy by land and water operations; however, northern public opinion, scorning Scott as superannuated, demanded a swifter attack. Boatner, *Civil War Dictionary*, 13; Elliott, *Winfield
Scott*, 722–24.

From Benjamin F. Smith

Sullivan County
Milan Missouri July 26th 1861

Hon. Andrew Johnson.
Respected Sir.

Will you favor me with Some documents—eulogies on Douglas[1]
Speeches &C—for the absense of J B Clark,[2] the Member of this
district I request you to oblige. Will you be kind enough to furnish
something reliable concerning the Manasses Junction—or what you
think probable will result there and at Richmond and if the Government anticipates A conflict with a foreign enemy ere Richmond is
taken. Will there be a movement to East Tenn. this fall— Our State
(*Mo.*) is Cursed with a desperate Guerilla warfare—inaugurated
by Govr C. F. Jackson.[3] Our district (composed of four Counties)
has a regiment ready to be received in to service during the war[.]
We expect an attack from our desperate Neighbors that are lurking
in the brush by day & night organizing undoubtedly to Commence
A savage desperation. We are yet without arms to contend on a
field with any number.— We are in a critical situation here. Our
county must now undergo a sorrowful revolution. One party or the
other will have to vamose[4] these precincts[.] We have undertook
a dangerous revolution for pledging ourselves to sustain our delegates in the State Convention in changing our State Constitution so
as to depose the state officers and the immediate ordering of an election to fill the said vacancies from Gov.—down[.]

The Convention is now in session[.][5] we expect their action will be decisive and determined[.] And—Jackson (the Governor) will make a desperate attempt at arms to replace himself but we'll fight him and all his minions sure on the bloody field if they don't abide the ballot box though the latter they most probably will not recognize, but continue the accursed war they have already inaugurated[.] I am sorry to inform you that my father (George Smith) Brothers Uncles and Cousins Morelocks[6] & all my old friends from Greene Co Ten now here are my political foes to the last extremity. Once we all went to gether in the old 11th district Greene Co Tenn)[.] We divided on Douglas & Breckenridge, I voting for the former[.] Now we have forever Squared up our friendly associations on this great issue which is Life or death to our Country[.] I am insane or they are blind to Justice right and truth. The subject is one of frightful contemplation— the result will be ruinous to some of us, but my confidence in the Government remains unshaken[.]

"The Stars & Stripes forever"

Allow me to subscribe myself
Your friend and humble servt,
Benjamin F. Smith

Address—Milan,—Mo—
Sullivan

ALS, DLC-JP2.

1. Stephen A. Douglas had been eulogized on July 9 by six of his former colleagues, including Lyman Trumbull of Illinois and Jacob Collamer of Vermont. *Cong. Globe*, 37 Cong., 1 Sess., 27–31.

2. John B. Clark (1802–1885), a Fayette lawyer, was clerk of Howard County, Missouri (1824–34), state representative (1850–51), and Democratic congressman (1857–61). Expelled from the House on July 13, he served in both Confederate Congresses, as senator in the first and representative in the second. *BDAC*, 698–99.

3. Claiborne F. Jackson (1806–1862), chosen governor in 1860, was a proslavery man, a member of the "Central Clique" which had turned against Thomas Hart Benton. Although he had favored compromise prior to Sumter, Jackson sought to take the state out of the Union after Lincoln's call for troops. Thwarted in this effort, he and many members of his legislature withdrew to Neosho, where they enacted a secession ordinance in the fall of 1861. *DAB*, IX, 538; Richard S. Brownlee, *Gray Ghosts of the Confederacy: Guerrilla Warfare in the West, 1861–1865* (Baton Rouge, 1958), 11–18.

4. Vamoose, slang for "depart quickly" and derived from the Spanish *vámonos* ("let's go"), first appeared in print during the 1840's in George W. Kendall, *Narrative of the Texan Santa Fe Expedition* (2 vols., New York, 1844). Its use in Missouri, undoubtedly dating from the time of the Santa Fe trade, was given wider currency by returning Mexican War soldiers. Mathews, *Americanisms*, II, 1807.

5. The State convention, which had met in March "to consider the relations of Missouri to the Union" and voted that there was no cause for seceding, reconvened on July 20, after Governor Jackson embraced the Confederacy. Declaring the offices of governor and lieutenant governor vacant, the convention proceeded to fill these places with unionists and to set up a pro-

visional government, choosing Hamilton Gamble as governor. Brownlee, *Ghosts of Confederacy*, 11–12, 19–20; John McElroy, *The Struggle for Missouri* (Washington, D. C., 1909), 48–50, 136–37.

6. Smith's brothers were Michael J., twenty-five, a teacher, and Martin V., twenty-one, a farmer, both Tennessee-born and living in 1860 with their father, George. His uncle and cousins were probably David Morelock (b. c1813) and his family of nine. In addition there was Tennessee-born Susan Morelock (b. c1810), a farmer according to the 1860 census, with sons Jacob M., twenty-six, born in Tennessee, and Edward, fifteen, born in Missouri, and George R. Morelock, twenty-six, a Tennessee-born farmer. David and George R. lived in Milan, the Smith family in Lindley. 1860 Census, Mo., Sullivan, 656, 757, 841.

From George M. Adams

Barbourville Knox Co Ky
July 27 1861

Dear Governor

William G Hilton[1] who lives 7 miles South of Greenville (your town) has just called to see me who is just from your place— he says the rebels have 750 men well armed stationed there—and there are certainly at Brush Creek Washington County [10?] miles from Cumb. Gap 3000 troops armed with Minnie rifles and that this information may be relied upon as he was in their Camps & knows it—and there are 600 at Carters depot and some Companies in Monroe County— On last Saturday he heard your Son Robt address 500 Citizens in the second district[2] & he has raised a light horse Company— James P McDowell is your candidate for the Legislature[.]

And there is now here from Sneedsville C L Barton[3] one of the delegates that was at the Greenville Convention—also John D Mitchell[4] from the same place & J W Jarvis a brother of L M Jarvis[5] who is said you would know and two other men & they report a reign of Terror by sending secessionist armed among them and you may know there is some truth in the matter when such men have to leave in the night & travel all the way here through Lee Co Va & Harlan Co Ky through the mountains on *foot*— they are very anxious about arms & assistance in the way of Gov troops to assist them— Old Davy Cottrell & one of his sons are also with us for fear they will be hung or outraged if they remain— R L Stanford[6] from Sullivan Co Tenn was here yesterday morning, but as he said he was on his way to Washington to see you I will not give you his report of the troops in East Ten, although it was much larger than I have learned from other sources— I enquired particularly of Hildreth[7] if your wife & family were well & he says they are and they have gone and are now living at Col Danl Stovers & that Judge Pattersons family are going there in a few days[.][8]

I am Satisfied that from evey thing I can learn that is reliable the traitors intend to prevent voting in E Tennessee at both the August elections[9] & more particularly that they will break up the vote for the Convention and I am further fully satisfied they will Concentrate a large force to prevent Johnsons arms as they call them from going to our loyal brethren in E Tennessee—so you must prepare for it— Hildreth will leave here the day after to morrow & return to your town if he is not taken up. I think he is smart enough to get back[.]

Your freind sincerely

G M Adams

Honl Andy Johnson
Washington City

ALS, DLC-JP2.

1. Not identified.

2. Robert's speech seems not to have been recorded for posterity.

3. Charles L. Barton was a delegate from Hancock County to the Greeneville Convention, June 17–20, 1861. *Proc. E. Tenn. Conv.* (Greeneville), 14.

4. John D. Mitchell (b. *c*1838) was a Tennessee-born Sneedville merchant. 1860 Census, Tenn., Hancock, Sneedville, 1.

5. Probably Lewis M. and Joel W. Jarvis. The former (b. *c*1831), a Virginian who came to Sneedville in 1841, was a dry-goods merchant, circuit court clerk (1860), and subsequently (1863) captain of Co. E, 8th Tenn. Cav., USA. After the war he became a lawyer and state legislator (1865–68). Joel Jarvis (*c*1827–1862) served as a private in Co. B, 1st Tenn. Cav., USA, for one month before dying of measles. 1860 Census, Tenn., Hancock, Sneedville, 1; *Goodspeed's East Tennessee*, 872, 1221; *Tennesseans in the Civil War*, II, 532; Lewis M. Jarvis, Joel W. Jarvis, Compiled Service Records, RG94, National Archives.

6. Dr. Robert L. Stanford (*c*1815–1869), a native of North Carolina, was a prominent Sullivan County unionist, serving as a delegate to both the Knoxville and Greeneville conventions. In 1860 he declared $15,000 worth of personal property and $28,000 in real estate. When Tennessee seceded, he fled to Kentucky, was appointed a surgeon of volunteers with the rank of major, and with General Burnside's command returned to Tennessee in September, 1863. A personal and political friend of Johnson, he served as president of the Johnson Club in Memphis after the war. Becoming state treasurer, he removed state funds to Memphis (1868), depositing them in a bank which failed. Although some of the money was recovered, Stanford committed suicide. 1860 Census, Tenn., Sullivan, 28; Temple, *Notable Men*, 51; *Proc. E. Tenn. Conv.*, 6, 15; Thomas W. Humes, *The Loyal Mountaineers of Tennessee* (Knoxville, 1888), 159–63; Verton M. Queener, "A Decade of East Tennessee Republicanism," ETHS *Publications*, No. 14 (1942), 64–65.

7. Not identified.

8. David T. Patterson and Daniel Stover were Johnson's sons-in-law, the latter living at Carter's Depot in Carter County. Daniel Stover (1826–1864), a farmer and prominent unionist, had represented his county at the East Tennessee Union conventions at Knoxville and Greeneville. In February, 1862, he enlisted as a Union soldier and during the spring of 1863 recruited the 4th Tenn. Inf., composed of exiles from Carter, Cocke, Grainger, Greene, and Johnson counties. His regiment reported to Camp Spear at Nashville on August 31, 1863, but Stover, becoming seriously ill, never commanded in the field and died the following year. *Tennesseans in the Civil War*, I, 383; Frank

Merritt, *Early History of Carter County, 1760–1861* (Knoxville, 1950), 166, 167; *Tenn. Adj. Gen. Report* (1866), 99; Temple, *Notable Men*, 51.

9. In the August state elections the Confederate faction won a decisive victory, Governor Isham Harris defeating the Union candidate, William H. Polk, by a margin of 30,000 votes and the legislature emerging with an overwhelmingly Confederate majority. East Tennessee's response reflected that section's union sympathies, with 27,115 votes for Polk and 14,887 for Harris; on the vote to ratify the Confederate Constitution, 27,738 were opposed and 15, 494 favorable. White, *Messages*, V, 332.

From J. Pringle Jones[1]

Reading, Pennsylvania
July 27, 1861

Hon: Andrew Johnson.

Although I have not the honour or the pleasure to be personally known to you, I feel that, in times like these, men, whose hearts beat together for their whole country, may offer to each other their thoughts and suggestions for the common good, without any previous acquaintance or the formality of an introduction. I greatly mistake your manly nature, if I need offer an apology for the liberty I am now taking.

It seems to me that in territory, circumstanced as is the North-Western part of Virginia, as Missouri, and, as, I hope, your own glorious Eastern Tennessee soon will be, in all of which the friends of the Union are in the ascendancy, and in the two former of which they have the legal and law making machinery of society in their hands, something of a legal kind might be done which would tend greatly to the repose of society *by bringing the enemies of the Union under the pressure of liens upon their estates.* We know how that idea was worked out in England by the seventh Henry and with what good effects.[2]

It might be necessary, nay, it would certainly be so, to purify the judiciary before the proposed legislation is invoked, a thing which they wisely propose to do in Missouri.[3] It would be better to say, perhaps, that the judiciary must be brought into harmony with that legislation before the full benefit of it can be obtained.

The legislation that I would propose would be simply this: to require every [well known and leading][4] secessionist, who by speech, by writing, or by arms had vindicated the treason, at any time within the year preceding his arrest, to enter into bond with two freehold sureties, for his keeping the peace and being of good behaviour, in a sum equal to half the value of his property, and for the period of ten years or more. This bond I would have entered of record and make a lien upon the real estate of all parties to it, & would make any after vindication of the treason by speech, writing or by arms, of the principal, a cause of forfeiture. Every magistrate should have power to issue the warrant and to require the bond, and to take it, and it should be his duty to file it of record in the proper office. The forfeiture of the bond I would have declared, upon the complaint of any citizen, duly established to the satisfaction of the circuit judge, *without the intervention of a jury*, in open court, after due notice to the principal and his sureties.

These are the outlines of a system, very much to be amplified in details, by which in a very short time all the principal secessionists of a region would become bound *by their property*, which is after all a stronger bond, than oaths of allegiance or the sense of honour and duty or the vague and uncertain terrors of the penal law, in restraining men. Men will run the risk of their lives here and of their souls hereafter, much more readily than of their houses and lands. Besides, in binding up one traitorous malefactor two others will have to be bound along with him.

Take NorthWestern Virginia, for example, and suppose a Law, like the one proposed, to be enacted at Wheeling—and applied in Berkeley County.[5] How soon would the whole batch of traitors, that has been afflicting that County, find itself encumbered in the meshes of such a law—inextricably, and how tame and submissive they would straightway become. I do not approve of terrorism—especially of that awful kind which proceeds from the unregulated and irregulable (if there be such a word) passions of a mob—and I would avoid, what will otherwise become inevitable, by some such legislation as is here suggested.

If I were to write any more, you would begin to suspect that I was some fossil correspondent of the Richmond Inquirer, revived— which, upon my honour, I assure you I am not. If you doubt it, your clerk, Mr Forney, I think, will vouch for me. And so, with the respt which a true heart must always feel for a brave, devoted and loyal senator of the United States,

I remain your very obedient servant   J. Pringle Jones,
Reading, Penna. 27 July, 1861.

ALS, DLC-JP.

1. J. Pringle Jones was president judge of the Berks County courts. *Boyd's Directory of Reading* (1860), 215.

2. Henry VII's Statute of Fines, the revival of a law dating from the reign of Edward I, was intended as a means of securing clear titles to land after the upheavals of the civil wars, thereby reducing the current "host of vexatious law-suits." From the feudal practice of "a money payment . . . by a tenant to his lord on a particular occasion (as a transfer of a tenant right)," the statute was later used as a method of alienating entailed land, the use which this correspondent has in mind. Gladys Temperley, *Henry VII* (Westport, Conn., 1971 [1914]), 260; Francis Bacon, *History of the Reign of King Henry VII*,

ed. J. Rawson Lumby (London, 1889), 260; *Webster's Third International*.

3. Prompt military intervention by Federal officers in Missouri prevented a Confederate seizure of the state in July and forced Governor Jackson to evacuate the capital, leaving a vacuum in civil government. The convention elected in January to deal with Missouri's relations with the Federal government reconvened on July 22 to reorganize the state government. Among the recommendations submitted to the convention three days later was a proposal calling for the appointment of four additional supreme court justices, making seven in all, to hold office until November, when the legislature was to be elected. Arthur R. Kirkpatrick, "Missouri in the Early Months of the Civil War," *Missouri Historical Review*, LV (1960–61), 247; Moore, *Rebellion Record*, II, Diary, 41.

4. Brackets are in the original.

5. As the northwestern Virginia counties drew apart from seceding Virginia, Berkeley and Jefferson, a virtual enclave of Maryland and Confederate Virginia, were areas of disaffection with the emerging unionist movement symbolized by the Second Wheeling Convention of May, 1861. They became part of the new state of West Virginia only when annexed by the first legislature. Charles H. Ambler, *West Virginia: The Mountain State* (New York, 1946), 329–35, 405; Ambler, *A History of West Virginia* (New York, 1963), 326, 349.

Speech in Support of Presidential War Program[1]

July 27, 1861.

Mr. JOHNSON, of Tennessee. Mr. President, when I came from my home to the seat of Government, in compliance with the proclamation of the President of the United States calling us together in extra session, it was not my intention to engage in any of the discussions that might transpire in this body; but since the session began, in consequence of the course that things have taken, I feel unwilling to allow the Senate to adjourn without saying a few words in response to many things that have been submitted to the Senate since its session commenced. What little I shall say to-day will be said without much method or order. I shall present the suggestions that occur to my mind, and shall endeavor to speak of the condition of the country as it is.

On returning here, we find ourselves, as we were when we adjourned last spring, in the midst of a civil war. That war is now progressing, without much hope or prospect of a speedy termination. It seems to me, Mr. President, that our Government has reached one of three periods through which all Governments must pass. A nation, or a people, have first to pass through a fierce ordeal in obtaining their independence or separation from the Government to which they were attached. In some instances this is a severe ordeal. We passed through this ordeal in the Revolution; we were seven years in effecting the separation, and in taking our position amongst the nations of the earth as a separate and distinct Power. Then, after having succeeded in establishing its independence, and taken its position among the nations of the earth, a nation must show its ability to maintain that position, that separate and distinct independence against other Powers, against foreign foes. In 1812 this ordeal commenced, and terminated in 1815. Our Government has passed through this ordeal.

There is still another ordeal through which a nation must pass. After having passed through these two, it has to contend against internal foes; against enemies at home; against those who have no confidence in its integrity, or in the institutions that may be established under its organic law. We are now in the midst of this third ordeal, and the struggle through which this Government is passing now is to determine whether it is capable of maintaining its existence against internal foes and domestic traitors to the Constitution. The problem now being solved before the nations of the earth, and before the people of the United States, is whether we can succeed in maintaining ourselves against the internal foes of the Government; whether we can succeed in putting down traitors and treason, and in establishing the great fact that we have a Government with sufficient strength to maintain its existence against whatever combination may be presented in opposition to it.

This brings me to a proposition laid down by the Executive in his recent message to the Congress of the United States. In that message the President said:

> This is essentially a people's contest. On the side of the Union, it is a struggle for maintaining in the world, that form and substance of Government, whose leading object is to elevate the condition of men; to lift artificial weights from all shoulders; to clear the paths of laudable pursuit for all; to afford all an unfettered start, and a fair chance in the race of life. Yielding to partial and temporary departures, from necessity, this is the leading object of the Government, for whose existence we contend.[2]

I think the question is pretty clearly stated in that paragraph. It is now a contest for the existence of the Government against internal foes and traitors. It is a contest whether a people are capable of governing themselves or not. We have reached that crisis in our country's history, and the time has arrived when, if the Government has the power, if the people are capable of self-government, and can establish this great truth, that it should be done; and this is the ordeal through which we must pass in the establishment of this great truth, or this great problem of man's capability of self-government. I trust and hope that we shall succeed in the experiment; I feel confident we shall; but the time has arrived when the energies of the nation must be put forth, when there must be union and concert on the part of all those who agree in man's capability of self-government, without regard to their former divisions or party prejudices, in order to demonstrate that great proposition.

Since this discussion commenced, it has been urged and argued, by Senators on one side, that there was a disposition to change the nature and character of the Government; and that, if we proceeded as we were going, it would result in establishing a dictatorship.[3] It has been said that the whole framework, nature, genius, and character of the Government would be entirely changed; and great apprehensions have been thrown out that it would result in a consolidation of the Government or a dictatorship. Sir, I agree that there is an effort, a very great effort, being made to change the nature and character of our institutions, and the whole framework of the Government. We find, in the speech delivered by the distinguished Senator from Kentucky, [Mr. Breckinridge,] the other day, the following paragraph, alluding to what will be the effect of the passage of this joint resolution approving the action of the President:

Here in Washington, in Kentucky, in Missouri, everywhere where the authority of the President extends, in his discretion he will feel himself warranted by the action of Congress upon this resolution to subordinate the civil to the military power; to imprison citizens without warrant of law; to suspend the writ of *habeas corpus*; to establish martial law; to make seizures and searches without warrant; to suppress the press; to do all those acts which rest in the will and in the authority of a military commander. In my judgment, sir, if we pass it, we are upon the eve of putting, so far as we can, in the hands of the President of the United States, the power of a dictator.[4]

Then, in reply to the Senator from Oregon, [Mr. Baker,] he seems to have great apprehension in reference to his allusion to a dictator.[5] The Senator goes on to say:

The pregnant question, Mr. President, for us to decide is, whether the Constitution is to be respected in this struggle; whether we are to be called upon to follow the flag over the ruins of the Constitution? Without questioning the motives of any, I believe that the whole tendency of the present proceedings is to establish a Government without limitation of powers, and to change radically our frame and character of Government.

Sir, I most fully concur with the Senator that there is a great effort being made to change the nature and character of our Government. I think that effort is being demonstrated and manifested most clearly every day; but we differ as to the parties making this great effort. I think the question is fairly and properly stated by the President, that it is a struggle whether the people shall rule; whether the people shall have a Government based upon their intelligence, upon their integrity, upon their purity of character, sufficient to govern themselves. I think this is the true issue; and there is an effort being made, and that effort has been long contemplated, to overthrow and upturn the institutions of this Government that we call free, which is based upon man's capability of self-government.

The Senator alludes furthermore in his speech to a conversation he had with some very intelligent gentleman who formerly represented our country abroad.[6] It appears from that conversation that foreigners were accustomed to say to Americans, "I thought your Government existed by consent; now how is it to exist?" and the reply was, "we intend to change it; we intend to adapt it to our condition; these old colonial geographical divisions and States will ultimately be rubbed out, and we shall have a Government strong and powerful enough." The Senator seemed to have great apprehensions based on those conversations. He furthermore read a paragraph from a paper[7] indicating that State lines were to be rubbed out. In addition to all this he goes on to enumerate that the writ of *habeas corpus* has been violated, and he says that since the Government commenced, there has not been a case equal to the one which has recently transpired in Maryland.[8] I shall take up some of his points in their order, and speak of them as I think they deserve to be spoken of. In his speech, he says:

> The civil authorities of the country are paralyzed, and a practical martial law is being established all over the land. The like never happened in this country before, and would not be tolerated in any country in Europe which pretends to the elements of civilization and regulated liberty. George Washington carried the thirteen colonies through the war of the Revolution without martial law. The President of the United States cannot conduct the Government three months without resorting to it.

The Senator puts great stress on the point, and speaks of it in very emphatic language, that General Washington carried the country through the seven years of the Revolution without resorting to martial law during all that period of time. Now, how does the matter stand? When we come to examine the history of the country, it would seem that the Senator had not hunted up all the cases. We can find some, and one in particular, not very different from the case which has recently occurred, and of which he was speaking. In 1777, the second year of the war of the Revolution, members of the Society of Friends in Philadelphia were arrested on suspicion of being disaffected to the cause of American freedom. A publication[9] now before me says:

> [Johnson reads an abbreviated account of the arrest and confinement of twenty Pennsylvania Quakers on suspicion of "being disaffected or dangerous to the United States." Faced with the impossibility of obtaining a hearing before the supreme executive council of Pennsylvania, the prisoners sought writs of habeas corpus to require their being brought before the court. In response the state legislature, at the instance of the council, enacted an *ex post facto* law suspending the habeas corpus act.]

Thus, Mr. President, we find that the writ of *habeas corpus* was suspended by the authorities of Pennsylvania, during the Revolution, in the case of persons who were considered dangerous and inimical to the country. A writ was taken out and served upon the officers, and they refused to surrender the prisoners, or even to give them a hearing. If the Senator from Kentucky had desired an extreme case, and wished to make a display of his legal and historical information, it would have been very easy for him to have cited this case—much more aggravated, much more extravagant, much more striking, than the one in regard to which he was speaking. Let it be remembered, also, that this case, although it seems to be an extravagant and striking one, occurred during the war of the Revolution, under General Washington, before we had a President. We find that at that time the writ of *habeas corpus* was suspended, and twenty individuals were denied even the privilege of a hearing, because they were considered inimical and dangerous to the liberties of the country. In the midst of the Revolution, when the writ of *habeas corpus* was as well understood as it is now, when they were familiar with its operation in Great Britain, when they knew and understood all the rights and privileges it granted to the citizen, we find that the Legislature of Pennsylvania passed a law repealing the power to issue the writ of *habeas corpus*, and went back and relieved the officers who refused to obey the writs, and indemnified them from the operation of any wrong they might have done.[10] This occurred in the Revolution, during the very period referred to by the Senator from Kentucky. If he wanted a strong and striking case, one that would bear comment, why did he not go back to this case, that occurred during the period to which he referred in our revolutionary struggle for independence? But no; all these cases seem to have been forgotten, and the mind was fixed down upon a case of recent occurrence. There is a great similarity in the cases; but the one to which I have alluded is much more extravagant than the one referred to by the Senator. It was in Philadelphia, where Congress was sitting; it was in Pennsylvania where these persons, who were considered inimical to the freedom of the country, were found. Congress was appealed to, but Congress executed the order; and the Legislature of Pennsylvania, after it was executed, though it was in violation of the right to the writ of *habeas corpus*, passed a law indemnifying the persons that had violated it, and made it retrospective in its operation. Hence we see that the Senator's case does not amount to much. We find a much more extravagant case when we were struggling for our independence as a people, when this course was sustained by the authorities of the country. What is our case now? We are not struggling for the establishment of our nationality, but we are now struggling for the existence of the Government. Suppose the writ of *habeas corpus* has been suspended: the question arises whether it was not a justifiable suspension at the time; and ought we not now to indorse simply what we would have done if we had been here ourselves at the time the power was exercised?

The impression is sought to be made on the public mind that this is the first and only case where the power has been exercised. I have shown that there is one tenfold more striking, that occurred during our struggle for independence. Is this the first time that persons in the United States have been placed under martial law? In 1815, when New Orleans was about to be sacked, when a foreign foe was upon the soil of Louisiana, New Orleans was put under martial law, and Judge Hall was made a prisoner because he attempted to interpose.[11] Is there a man here, or in the country, who condemns General Jackson for the exercise of the power of proclaiming martial law in 1815? Could that city have been saved without placing it under martial law, and making Judge Hall submit to it? I know that General Jackson submitted to be arrested, tried, and fined $1,000; but what did Congress do in that case? It did just what we are called on to do in this case. By the restoration of his fine—an act passed by an overwhelming majority in the two Houses of Congress—the nation said "we approve what you did."[12] Suppose, Mr. President, (which may have been the case,) that the existence of the Government depended upon the protection and successful defense of New Orleans; and suppose, too, it was in violation of the strict letter of the Constitution for General Jackson to place New Orleans under martial law, but without placing it under martial law the Government would have been overthrown: is there any reasonable, any intelligent man in or out of Congress who would not indorse and acknowledge the exercise of a power which was indispensable to the existence and maintenance of the Government? The Constitution was likely to be overthrown, and the law was about to be violated, and the Government trampled under foot; and when it became necessary to prevent this, even by exercising a power that comes in conflict with the Constitution in time of peace, it should and ought to be exercised. If General Jackson had lost the city of New Orleans, and thereby the Government had been overthrown, by refusing to place Judge Hall and the city of New Orleans under martial law, he ought to have lost his head. But he acted as a soldier; he acted as a patriot; he acted as a statesman; as one devoted to the institutions and the preservation and the existence of his Government; and by so acting the Government was saved and preserved.

Then, sir, the power which has been exercised in this instance is no new thing. In great emergencies, when the life of a nation is in peril, when its very existence is flickering, to question too nicely, to scan too critically, its acts in the very midst of that flickering, in the very midst of that crisis, when the Government is likely to be overthrown, is to make war upon it, and to try to paralyze its energies. If war is to be made upon those who seem to violate the laws of the United States in their efforts to preserve the Government, wait until the country passes out of its peril; wait until the country is relieved from its difficulty; wait until the crisis passes by, and then come forward, dispassionately, and ascertain to what extent the law has been violated, if indeed it has been violated at all.

A great ado has been made in reference to the Executive proclamation calling out the militia of the States to the extent of seventy-five thousand men. That call was made under the authority of the act of 1795, and is perfectly in accordance with the law. It has been decided by the Supreme Court of the United States that that act is constitutional, and that the President alone is the judge of the question whether the exigency has arisen. This decision was made in the celebrated case of Martin *vs.* Mott.[13] The opinion of the court was delivered by Judge Story. Let me read from the opinion of the court:

[Joseph Story defended the right of Congress to take action during threat of danger and to invest the President with the authority to decide when it is necessary to call out the military forces. Although these powers are limited, they can be "exercised upon sudden emergencies, upon great occasions of state, and under circumstances which may be vital to the existence of the Union"—when the public interest can be served only by "prompt and unhesitating obedience" to presidential orders.]

We see, then, that the power is clear as to calling out the militia; we see that we have precedents for the suspension of the writ of *habeas corpus*. It must also be evident that this is an unpropitious time to be making war upon the Government, while it is in its greatest peril, and thereby paralyze, weaken, and destroy public confidence in the Government, when there is a power actively contending in the field to overthrow and upturn our institutions and destroy the Government itself.

The next objection made is, that the President had no power to make additions to the Navy and Army.[14] I say, in these two instances, he is justified by the great law of necessity. At the time, I believe it was necessary to the existence of the Government; and it being necessary, he had a right to exercise all those powers that, in his judgment, the crisis demanded for the maintenance of the existence of the Government itself. The simple question—if you condemn the President for acting in the absence of law—is, do you condemn the propriety of his course; do you condemn the increase of the Army; do you condemn the increase of the Navy? If you oppose the measure simply upon the ground that the Executive called them forth anticipating law, what will you do now? The question presents itself at this time, is it not necessary to increase the Army and the Navy? If you condemn the exercise of the power of the Executive in the absence of law, what will you do now, as the law-making power, when it is manifest that the Army and Navy should be increased? You make war upon the Executive for anticipating the action of Congress. What do gentlemen do now, when called upon to support the Government? Do they do it? They say the President anticipated the action of Congress. Does not the Government need an increase of the Army and the Navy? Where do gentlemen stand now? Are they for it? Do they sustain the Government? Are they giving it a helping hand? No; they go back and find fault with the exercise of a power that they say was without law; but now, when they have the power to make the law, and when the necessity is apparent, they stand back and refuse. Where does that place those who take that course? It places them against the Government, and against placing the means in the hands of the Government to defend and perpetuate its existence. The object is apparent, Mr. President. We had enemies of the Government here last winter; in my opinion, we have enemies of the Government here now.

I said that I agreed with the Senator from Kentucky that there was a design—a deliberate determination—to change the nature and character of our Government. Yes, sir, it has been the design for a long time. All the talk about slavery and compromise has been but a pretext. We had a long disquisition, and a very feeling one, from the Senator from Kentucky. He became pathetic in the hopelessness of compromises. Did not the Senator from California [Mr. Latham] the other day show unmistakably that it was not compromise they wanted?[15] I will add, that compromise was the thing they most feared; and their great effort was to get out of Congress before any compromise could be made. At first, their cry was peaceable secession and reconstruction. They talked not of compromise; and, I repeat, their greatest dread and fear was, that something would be agreed upon; that their last and only pretext would be swept from under them, and that they would stand before the country naked and exposed.

The Senator from California pointed out to you a number of them who stood here and did not vote for certain propositions, and those propositions were lost. What was the action before the committee of thirteen? Why did not that committee agree?[16] Some of the most ultra men from the North were members of that committee, and they proposed to amend the Constitution so as to provide that Congress in the future never should interfere with the subject of slavery. The committee failed to agree, and some of its members at once telegraphed to their States that they must go out of the Union at once.[17] But after all that transpired in the early part of the session, what was done? We know what the argument has been; in times gone by I met it; I have heard it again and again. It has been said that one great object was, first to abolish slavery in the District of Columbia and the slave trade between the States, as a kind of initiative measure; next, to exclude it from the Territories; and when the free States were three fourths of all the States, so as to have power to change the Constitution, they would amend the Constitution so as to give Congress power to legislate upon the subject of slavery in the States, and expel it from the States in which it is now. Has not that been the argument? Now, how does the matter stand? At the last session of Congress seven States withdrew, it may be said that eight withdrew;[18] reducing the remaining slave States down to one fourth of the whole number of States. Now we have reached the point at which the charge has been made, that whenever the free States constituted a majority in the Congress of the United States, sufficient to amend the Constitution, they would so amend it as to legislate upon the institution of slavery within the States, and that the institution of slavery would be overthrown. This has been the argument; it has been repeated again and again; and hence the great struggle about the Territories. The argument was, we wanted to prevent the creation of free States; we did not want to be reduced down to that point where, under the sixth article of the Constitution, three fourths could amend the Constitution so as to exclude slavery from the States. This has been the great point; this has been the rampart; this has been the very point to which it has been urged that the free States wanted to pass. Now, how does the fact stand? Let us "render unto Caesar the things that are Caesar's."[19] We reached, at the last session, just the point where we were in the power of the free States; and then what was done? Instead of an amendment to the Constitution of the United States conferring power upon Congress to legislate upon the subject of slavery, what was done? This joint resolution was passed by a two-thirds majority in each House:

Resolved by the Senate and House of Representatives of the United States of America in Congress assembled, That the following article be proposed to the Legislatures of the several States, as an amendment to the Constitution of the United States, which, when ratified by three fourths of said Legislatures, shall be valid, to all intents and purposes, as part of the said Constitution, viz:
ART. 13. No amendment shall be made to the Constitution which

will authorize or give to Congress the power to abolish, or interfere, within any State, with the domestic institutions thereof, including that of persons held to service or labor by the laws of said State.[20]

Is not that very conclusive? Here is an amendment to the Constitution of the United States to make the Constitution unamendable upon that subject, as it is upon some other subjects; that Congress, in the future, should have no power to legislate on the subject of slavery within the States. Talk about "compromise," and about the settlement of this question; how can you settle it more substantially? How can you get a guarantee that is more binding than an amendment to the Constitution, which is unamendable, that Congress in the future shall not even legislate on the subject? This places the institution of slavery in the States entirely beyond the control of Congress. Why have not the Legislatures that talk about "reconstruction" and "compromise" and "guarantees," taken up this amendment to the Constitution and adopted it? Some States have adopted it. How many southern States have done so?[21] Take my own State, for instance. Instead of accepting guarantees protecting them in all future time against the legislation of Congress on the subject of slavery, they undertake to pass ordinances violating the Constitution of the country, and taking the State out of the Union and into the southern confederacy.[22] It is evident to me that with many the talk about compromise and the settlement of this question is mere pretext, especially with those who understand the question.

What more was done at the last session of Congress, when the North had the power? Let us tell the truth. Three territorial bills were brought forward and passed. You remember in 1847, when the agitation arose in reference to the Wilmot proviso. You remember in 1850 the contest about slavery prohibition in the Territories. You remember in 1854 the excitement in reference to the Kansas Nebraska bill, and the power conferred on the Legislature by it. Now we have a constitutional amendment, proposed at a time when the Republicans have the power; and at the same time they come forward with three territorial bills, and in neither of those bills can be found any prohibition, so far as slavery is concerned, in the Territories. Colorado, Nevada, and Dakota, are organized without any prohibition of slavery. But what do you find in these bills? Mark, Mr. President, that there is no slavery prohibition; mark too, the language of the sixth section, conferring power upon the Territorial Legislature:

SEC. 6. *And be it further enacted*, That the legislative power of the Territory shall extend to all rightful subjects of legislation consistent with the Constitution of the United States and the provisions of this act; but no law shall be passed interfering with the primary disposal of the soil; no tax shall be imposed upon the property of the United States;

nor shall the lands or other property of non-residents be taxed higher than the lands or other property of residents; nor shall any law be passed impairing the rights of private property; nor shall any discrimination be made in taxing different kinds of property; but all property subject to taxation shall be in proportion to the value of the property taxed.[23]

Can there be anything more clear and conclusive? First, there is no prohibition; next, the Legislature shall have no power to legislate so as to impair the rights of private property, and shall not tax one description of property higher than another. Now, Mr. President, right here I ask any reasonable, intelligent man throughout the Union, to take the amendment to the Constitution, take the three territorial bills, put them all together, and how much of the slavery question is left? Is there any of it left? Yet we hear talk about compromise; and it is said the Union must be broken up because you cannot get compromise. Does not this settle the whole question? There is no slavery prohibition by Congress, and the Territorial Legislatures are expressly forbidden from legislating so as to impair the rights of property. I know there are some who are sincere in this talk about compromise; but there are others who are merely making it a pretext, who come here claiming something in the hope that it will be refused, and that then, upon that refusal, their States may be carried out of the Union. I should like to know how much more secure we can be in regard to this question of slavery. These three territorial bills cover every square inch of territory we have got; and here is an amendment to the Constitution embracing the whole question, so far as the States and the public lands of the United States are concerned.

I am as much for compromise as any one can be; and there is no one who would desire more than myself to see peace and prosperity restored to the land; but when we look at the condition of the country, we find that rebellion is rife; that treason has reared it[s] head. A distinguished Senator from Georgia once said, "when traitors become numerous enough, treason becomes respectable."[24] Traitors are getting to be so numerous now that I suppose treason has almost got to be respectable; but God being willing, whether traitors be many or few, as I have hitherto waged war against traitors and treason, and in behalf of the Government which was constructed by our fathers, I intend to continue it to the end. [Applause in the galleries.]

The PRESIDENT *pro tempore.* Order!

Mr. JOHNSON, of Tennessee. Mr. President, we are in the midst of a civil war; blood has been shed; life has been sacrificed. Who commenced it? Of that we will speak hereafter. I am speaking now of the talk about compromise. Traitors and rebels are standing with arms in their hands, and it is said that we must go forward and compromise with them. They are in the wrong; they are making war upon the Government; they are trying to upturn and destroy our free institutions. I say to them that the compromise I have to make under the existing circumstances is, "ground your arms; obey the laws; acknowledge the supremacy of the Constitution—when you do that, I will talk to you about compromises." All the compromise that I have to make is the compromise of the Constitution of the United States. It is one of the best compromises that can be made. We lived under it from 1789 down to the 20th of December, 1860, when South Carolina undertook to go out of the Union. We prospered; we advanced in wealth, in commerce, in agriculture, in trade, in manufactures, in all the arts and sciences, and in religion, more than any people upon the face of God's earth had ever done before in the same time. What better compromise do you want? You lived under it until you got to be a great and prosperous people. It was made by our fathers, and cemented by their blood. When you talk to me about compromise, I hold up to you the Constitution under which you derived all your greatness, and which was made by the fathers of your country. It will protect you in all your rights.

But it is said that we had better divide the country and make a treaty and restore peace. If, under the Constitution which was framed by Washington and Madison and the patriots of the Revolution, we cannot live as brothers, as we have in times gone by, I ask can we live quietly under a treaty, separated as enemies? The same causes will exist; our geographical and physical position will remain just the same. Suppose you make a treaty of peace and division: if the same causes of irritation, if the same causes of division continue to exist, and we cannot live as brothers in fraternity under the Constitution made by our fathers, and as friends in the same Government, how can we live in peace as aliens and enemies under a treaty? It cannot be done; it is impracticable.

But, Mr. President, I concur fully with the dislike expressed by the distinguished Senator from Kentucky to a change in the form of our Government. He seemed to be apprehensive of a dictatorship. He feared there might be a change in the nature and character of our institutions. I could, if I chose, refer to many proofs to establish the fact that there has been a design to change the nature of our Government. I could refer to Mr. Rhett; I could refer to Mr. Inglis;[25] I could refer to various others to prove this. The Montgomery Daily Advertiser, one of the organs of the so-called southern confederacy, says:

Has it been a precipitate revolution? It has not. With coolness and deliberation the subject has been thought of for forty years; for ten years it has been the all-absorbing theme in political circles. From Maine to Mexico all the different phases and forms of the question have been presented to the people, until nothing else was thought of, nothing else spoken of, and nothing else taught in many of the political schools.[26]

This, in connection with other things, shows that this movement has been long contemplated, and that the idea has been to separate from and break up this Government, to change its nature and character; and now, after they have attempted the separation, if they can succeed, their intention is to subjugate and overthrow and make the other States submit to their form of government.

To carry out the idea of the Senator from Kentucky, I want to show that there is most conclusive proof of a design to change our government.

I quote from the Georgia Chronicle:

Our own republican Government has failed midway in its trial, and with it have nearly vanished the hopes of those philanthropists who, believing in man's capacity for self-government, believed, therefore, in spite of so many failures, in the practicability of a republic.[27]

"If this Government has gone down," asks the editor, "what shall be its substitute?" And he answers by saying that, as to the present generation, "it seems their only resort must be to a constitutional monarchy." Hence you see the Senator and myself begin to agree in the proposition that the nature and character of the Government are to be changed.

William Howard Russell, the celebrated correspondent of the London Times, spent some time in South Carolina, and he writes:[28]

[Russell claimed to have heard on all sides expressions favorable to monarchy—"if we could only get one of the royal race of England to rule over us, we should be content!"—and even to returning to "the British connection."]

This idea was not confined to localities. It was extensively prevalent, though policy prompted its occasional repudiation. At a meeting of the people of Bibb county, Georgia, the subject was discussed, and a constitutional monarchy was not recommended for the southern States, "as recommended by some of the advocates of immediate disunion."[29] Here is evidence that the public mind had been sought to be influenced in that direction; but the people were not prepared for it. Mr. Toombs, of Georgia, during the delivery of a speech by Mr. A. H. Stephens, before the Legislature of that State, did not hesitate to prefer the form of the British Government to our own.[30]

Not long since—some time in the month of May—I read in the Richmond Whig, published at the place where their government is now operating, the center from which they are directing their armies which are making war upon this Government, an article[31] in which it is stated that rather than submit to the Administration now in power in the city of Washington, they would prefer passing under the constitutional reign of the amiable Queen of Great Britain. I agree, therefore, with the Senator from Kentucky, that there is a desire to change this Government. We see it emanating from every point in the South. Mr. Toombs was not willing to wait for the movement of the people. Mr. Stephens, in his speech to the Legislature of Georgia, preferred the calling of a convention; but Mr. Toombs was unwilling to wait. Mr. Stephens was unwilling to see any violent action in advance of the action of the people; but Mr. Toombs replied: "I will not wait; I will take the sword in my own hand, disregarding the will of the people, even in the shape of a convention;"[32] and history will record that he kept his word. He and others had become tired and dissatisfied with a government of the people; they have lost confidence in man's capacity for self-government; and furthermore, they would be willing to form an alliance with Great Britain; or, if Great Britain were slow in forming the alliance, with France; and they know they can succeed there, on account of the hate and malignity which exist between the two nations.[33] They would be willing to pass under the reign of the amiable and constitutional Queen of Great Britain! Sir, I love woman, and woman's reign in the right place; but when we talk about the amiable and accomplished Queen of Great Britain, I must say that all our women are ladies, all are queens, all are equal to Queen Victoria, and many of them greatly her superiors. They desire no such thing; nor do we. Hence we see whither this movement is tending. It is a change of Government; and in that the Senator and myself most fully concur.

The Senator from Kentucky was wonderfully alarmed at the idea of a "dictator," and replied with as much point as possible to the Senator from Oregon, who made the suggestion. But, sir, what do we find in the Richmond Examiner, which is published at the seat of government of the so-called confederate States?

In the late debates of the congress of this confederacy, Mr. Wright, of Georgia, showed a true appreciation of the crisis when he advocated the grant of power to the president that would enable him to make immediate defense of Richmond, and to bring the whole force of the confederacy to bear on the affairs of Virginia. It is here that the fate of the confederacy is to be decided; and the time is too short to permit red tape to interfere with public safety. No power in executive hands can be too great, no discretion too absolute, at such moments as these. We need a dictator. Let lawyers talk when the world has time to hear them. Now let the sword do its work. Usurpations of power by the chief, for the preservation of the people from robbers and murderers, will be reckoned as genius and patriotism by all sensible men in the world now, and by every historian that will judge the deed hereafter.[34]

The articles of their leading papers, the Whig and the Examiner, and the speeches of their leading men, all show unmistakably that their great object is to change the character of the Government. Hence we come back to the proposition that it is a contest whether the people shall govern or not. I have here an article that appeared in the Memphis Bulletin, of my own State, from which it appears that under this reign of secession, this reign of terror, this disintegrating element that is destructive of all good, and the accomplisher of nothing that is right, they have got things beyond their control:

In times like these, there must be one ruling power to which all others must yield. "In a multitude of counselors," saith the Book of Books, "there is safety;" but nowhere are we told, in history or revelation, that there is aught of safety in a multitude of rulers. Any "rule of action," sometimes called the "lah," is better than a multitude of conflicting, irreconcilable statutes, Any one head is better than forty, each of which may conceive itself the nonpareil, *par excellence*, supreme "*caput*" of all civil and military affairs.
Let Governor Harris be king, if need be, and Baugh a despot.[35]

"Let Governor Harris be king, and Baugh a despot," says the Bulletin. Who is Baugh? The mayor of Memphis.[36] The mob reign of terror gotten up under this doctrine of secession is so great that we find that they are appealing to the one-man power. They are even willing to make the mayor of the city a despot, and Isham G. Harris, a little petty Governor of Tennessee, a king. He is to be made king over the State that contains the bones of the immortal, the illustrious Jackson. Isham G. Harris a king! Or Jeff. Davis a dictator, and Isham G. Harris one of his satraps. He a king over the free and patriotic people of Tennessee! Isham G. Harris to be my king. Yes, sir, my king! I know the man. I know his elements. I know the ingredients that constitute the compound called Isham G. Harris. King Harris to be my master, and the master of the people that I have the proud and conscious satisfaction of representing on this floor! Mr. President, he should not be my slave. [Applause in the galleries.]

The PRESIDENT *pro tempore*. Order! A repetition of the offense will compel the Chair to order the galleries to be cleared forthwith. The order of the Senate must and shall be preserved. No demonstrations of applause or of disapprobation will be allowed. The Chair hopes not to be compelled to resort to the extremity of clearing the galleries of the audience.

Mr. JOHNSON, of Tennessee. I was proceeding with this line of argument to show that in the general proposition that there was a fixed determination to change the character and nature of the Government, the Senator from Kentucky and myself agree; and so far I think I have succeeded very well. And now, when we are looking at the elements of which this southern confederacy is composed, it may be well enough to examine the principles of the elements out of which a government is to be made that they prefer to this. We have shown, so far as the slavery question is concerned, that that whole question is settled; and it is now shown to the American people and the world that the people of the southern States have now got no right which they said they had lost before they went out of this Union; but, on the contrary, many of their rights have been diminished, and oppression and tyranny have been inaugurated in their stead. Let me ask you, sir, to-day, and let me ask the nation, what right has any State in this so-called confederacy lost under the Constitution of the United States? Let me ask each individual citizen in the United States, what right has he lost by the continuance of this Government based on the Constitution of the United States? Is there a man North or South, East or West, who can put his finger on one single privilege, or one single right, of which he has been deprived by the Constitution or Union of these States? Can he do it? Can he touch it? Can he see it? Can he feel it? No, sir; there is no one right that he has lost. How many rights and privileges, and how much protection have they lost by going out of the Union, and violating the Constitution of the United States?

Pursuing this line of argument in regard to the formation of their government, let us take South Carolina, for instance, and see what her notions of government are. She is the leading spirit, and will constitute one of the master elements in the formation of this confederate government when it is formed. What qualifications has South Carolina affixed upon even members of the Legislature? Let us see what are her notions of government—a State that will contribute to the permanent formation of the government that is to exist hereafter. In the constitution of South Carolina it is provided that—

No person shall be eligible to a seat in the House of Representatives, unless he is a free white man, of the age of twenty-one years, and hath been a citizen and resident of this State three years previous to his election. If a resident in the election district, he shall not be eligible to a seat in the House of Representatives, unless he be legally seized and possessed, in his own right, of a settled freehold estate of five hundred acres of land and ten negroes.[37]

This is the notion that South Carolina has of the necessary qualifications of a member of the lower branch of the State Legislature. Now, I desire to ask the distinguished Senator from Kentucky—who seems to be so tenacious about compromises, about rights, and about the settlement of this question, and who can discover that the Constitution has been violated so often and so flagrantly, yet never can see that it has been violated anywhere else—if he desires to seek under this South Carolina government for his lost rights? I do not intend to be personal? I wish he were in his seat, for he knows that

I have the greatest kindness for him. I am free to say, in connection with what I am about to observe, that I am a little selfish in this; because if I lived in South Carolina, with these disabilities or qualifications affixed upon a member, I would not be eligible to a seat in the lower branch of the Legislature. That would be a poor place for me to go and get my rights; would it not? I doubt whether the Senator from Kentucky is eligible to-day to a seat in the lower branch of the Legislature of South Carolina. I do not refer to him in any other than the most respectful terms, but I doubt whether he would be qualified to take a seat in the lower branch of her Legislature. I should not be, and I believe I am just as good as any who do take seats there.

In looking further into the constitution of South Carolina, in order to ascertain what are her principles of government, what do we find? We find it provided that, in the apportionment of these representatives, the whole number of white inhabitants is to be divided by sixty-two, and every sixty-second part is to have one member.[38] Then all the taxes are to be divided by sixty-two, and every sixty-second part of the taxes is to have one member also. Hence we see that slaves, constituting the basis of property, would get the largest amount of representation; and we see that property goes in an equal representation to all the numbers, while those numbers constitute a part of the property-holders. That is the basis of their representation.

Sir, that is not the place for me to go to get my rights, nor do a large proportion of my people think it is the place for them to go to get their rights. Notwithstanding they have been borne down; notwithstanding there has been an army of fifty-five thousand men created by the Legislature; notwithstanding $5,000,000 of money has been appropriated to be expended against the Union;[39] and notwithstanding the arms manufactured by the Government, and distributed among the States for the protection of the people, have been denied to them by this little petty tyrant of a king,[40] and are now turned upon the Government for its overthrow and destruction, those people, when left to themselves to carry out their own government and the honest dictates of their own consciences, will be found to be opposed to this revolution.

Mr. President, while the congress of the confederate States was engaged in the formation of their constitution, I find a protest from South Carolina against a decision of that congress in relation to the slave trade, in the Charleston Mercury, of February 13. It is written by L. W. Spratt to "Hon. John Perkins, delegate from Louisiana."[41] It begins in this way:

From the abstract of the constitution for the provisional government, published in the papers this morning, it appears that the slave trade, except with the slave States of North America, shall be prohibited. The congress, therefore, not content with the laws of the late United States against it, which, it is to be presumed, were readopted, have unalterably fixed the subject, by a provision of the constitution.

He goes on and protests. We all know that that constitution is made for the day, just for the time being, a mere tub thrown out to the whale,[42] to amuse and entertain the public mind for a time. We know this to be so. But in making his argument what does he say? Mr. Spratt, a commissioner who went to Florida, a member of the South Carolina convention that took the State out of the Union, says in this protest:

[Denying that the struggle is merely between two sections "that for some unaccountable reason . . . have become opposed to each other," Spratt asserts that "the real contest is between two forms of society." The South is establishing "a *slave* republic," but the "contest between democracy and slavery is not yet over. . . . both forms of society exist within the limits of the southern States; both are distinctly developed within the limits of Virginia; and there . . . the war already rages."]

Hence we see the propriety of Mr. Mason's letter,[43] in which he declared that all those who would not vote for secession must leave the State, and thereby you get clear of the excess of population to the slaves. They must emigrate.

Like an excess of alkali or acid in chemical experiments, they are unfixed in the social compound. Without legitimate connection with the slave, they are in competition with him.

The protest continues:

[Even South Carolina, so apparently dominated by slaveholders and so completely accepting of the institution, may soon face an invasion of "abundant pauper labor" which will permit democracy to "gain a foothold, and . . . here also the contest for existence may be waged" between slavery and democracy. After further warnings of the danger inherent in the growth of a nonslaveholding population in the new southern Confederacy, Spratt reiterates that "Slavery cannot share a government with democracy."]

In this connection, let me read the following paragraph from De Bow's Review:

All government begins with usurpation, and is continued by force. Nature puts the ruling elements uppermost, and the masses below and subject to those elements. Less than this is not government. The right to govern resides in a very small minority; the duty to obey is inherent in the great mass of mankind.[44]

We find by an examination of all these articles, that the whole idea is to establish a republic based upon slavery exclusively, in which the great mass of the people are not to participate. We find an argument made here against the admission of non-slaveholding States into their confederacy. If they refuse to admit a non-slaveholding State into the confederacy, for the very same reason they will exclude an individual who is not a slaveholder, in a slaveholding State, from participating in the exercise of the powers of the Government. Take the whole argument through, and that is the plain meaning of it. Mr. Spratt says, that sooner or later it will be done; and if the present revolution will not accomplish it, it must be brought about even if another revolution has to take place. We see, therefore, that it is most clearly contemplated to change the character and nature of the Government so far as they are concerned. They have lost confidence in the integrity, in the capability, in the virtue and intelligence of the great mass of the people to govern. Sir, in the section of the country where I live, notwithstanding we reside in a slave State, we believe that freemen are capable of self-government. We care not in what shape their property exists; whether it is in the shape of slaves or otherwise. We hold that it is upon the intelligent free white people of the country that all Governments should rest, and by them all Governments should be controlled.

I think, therefore, sir, that the President and the Senator from Kentucky have stated the question aright. This is a struggle between two forms of government. It is a struggle for the existence of the Government we have. The issue is now fairly made up. All those that favor free government must stand with the Constitution, and in favor of the Union of the States as it is. That Union being once restored, the Constitution again becoming supreme and paramount, when peace, law, and order, shall be restored, when the Government shall be restored to its pristine position, then, if necessary, we can come forward under proper and favorable circumstances to amend, change, alter, and modify the Constitution, as pointed out by the fifth article of the instrument, and thereby perpetuate the Government. This can be done, and this should be done.

We have heard a great deal said in reference to the violation of the Constitution. The Senator from Kentucky seems exceedingly sensitive about violations of the Constitution. Sir, it seems to me, admitting that his apprehensions are well founded, that a violation of the Constitution for the preservation of the Government, is more tolerable than one for its destruction. In all these complaints, in all these arraignments of the present Government for violation of law and disregard of the Constitution, have you heard, as was forcibly and eloquently said by the Senator from Illinois, [Mr. Browning,][45] before me, one word said against violations of the Constitution and the trampling under foot of law by the States, or the party, now making war upon the Government of the United States? Not one word, sir.

The Senator enumerates what he calls violations of the Constitution—the suspension of the writ of *habeas corpus*, the proclaiming of martial law, the increase of the Army and Navy, and the existing war; and then he asks, "Why all this?" The answer must be apparent to all.

But first, let me supply a chronological table of events[46] on the other side.

[The table lists the dates on which southern states seized Federal forts and other property between Fort Moultrie and Castle Pinckney on December 27, and Fort Barrancas and the Pensacola Navy Yard on January 11; included also is the *Star of the West* incident, January 9.]

These forts cost $5,947,000, are pierced for one thousand and ninety-nine guns, and are adapted for a war garrison of five thousand four hundred and thirty men.[47]

We find, as was shown here the other day, and as has been shown on former occasions, that the State of South Carolina seceded, or attempted to secede, and withdrew from this confederacy of States without cause. In seceding, her first step was a violation of the Constitution. She seceded on the 20th of last December, making the first innovation and violation of the law and the Constitution of the country. On the 27th day of December what did she do? She seized Fort Moultrie and Castle Pinckney, and caused your little band of sixty or seventy men under the command of Major Anderson to retire to a little pen in the ocean—Fort Sumter.[48] She commenced erecting batteries, arraying cannon, preparing for war; in effect, proclaiming herself at once our enemy. Seceding from the Union, taking Fort Sumter [*sic*] and Castle Pinckney, driving your men in fact into Fort Sumter, I say were practical acts of war. You need not talk to me about technicalities, and the distinction that you have got no war until Congress declares it. Congress could legalize it, or could make war, it is true; but that was practical war. Who began it? Then, sir, if South Carolina secedes, withdraws from the Union, becomes our common enemy, is it not the duty, the constitutional duty of the Government and of the President of the United States to make war, or to resist the attacks and assaults made by an enemy? Is she not as much our enemy as Great Britain was in the revolutionary struggle? Is she not to-day as much our enemy as Great Britain was during the war of 1812?

In this connection, I desire to read some remarks made by the Senator from Missouri [Mr. Polk] in his speech the other day, in regard to this general idea of who made the war. He said, speaking of the war:

[Polk charged that the President, ignoring the will of a Congress which refused to move toward war, was solely responsible for the present conflict.]

The Senator from Kentucky [Mr. Powell] spoke pretty much in the same language. Speaking of the refusal of Kentucky to respond to the first call of the President for seventy-five thousand men, he said:

[Powell defended Kentucky's neutrality as true unionism, which avoids shedding "a brother's blood, whether he be from the North or the South," in order that "compromise and conciliation" may be invoked.]

I desired in this connection to place before the Senate the remarks of both the Senators from Kentucky and the Senator from Missouri, and to answer them at the same time. The Senator from Missouri says the war was brought on since the 4th of March by the President of the United States of his own motion. The Senator from Kentucky [Mr. Powell] pronounces it an unjust, an unrighteous, and an unholy war. Sir, I think it is an unjust, an unrighteous, and an unholy war.

But, sir, I commenced enumerating the facts in regard to the question of who commenced the war. How do they stand? I have just stated that South Carolina seceded—withdrew from the Confederacy; and in the very act of withdrawing, she makes practical war upon the Government, and becomes its enemy. The Star of the West, on the 7th [9th] of January, laden simply with provisions to supply those starving men in Fort Sumter, attempted to enter the harbor, and was fired upon, and had to tack about, and leave the men in the forts to perish or do the best they could. We also find, that on the 11th of April General Beauregard had an interview with Major Anderson, and made a proposition to him to surrender.[49] Major Anderson stated, in substance, that he could do no such thing; that he could not strike the colors of his country, and refused to surrender; but he said, at the same time, that by the 15th of the month his provisions would give out, and if not reinforced and supplied, starvation must take place. It seems that at this time, Mr. Pryor,[50] from Virginia, was in Charleston. The convention of Virginia was sitting, and it was important that the cannon's roar should be heard in the land. Virginia was to be taken out of the Union, although a majority of the delegates in the convention were elected against secession, and in favor of the Union.[51] We find that after being in possession of the fact that by the 15th of the month, the garrison would be starved out and compelled to surrender, on the morning of the 12th they commenced the bombardment, fired upon your fort and upon your men. They knew that in three days they would be compelled to surrender; but they wanted war. It was indispensable to produce an excitement in order to hurry Virginia out of the Union, and they commenced the war. The firing was kept up until such time as the fort was involved in smoke and flames, and Major Anderson

and his men were compelled to lie on the floor with their wet hand-
kerchiefs to their faces to save them from suffocation and death.
Even in the midst of all this, they refused to cease their firing, but
kept it up until he was compelled to surrender.

Who then commenced the war? Who struck the first blow? Who
violated the Constitution in the first place? Who trampled the law
under foot, and violated the law morally and legally? Was it not
South Carolina, in seceding? And yet you talk about the President
having brought on the war by his own motion, when these facts are
incontrovertible. No one dare attempt to assail them. But after Fort
Sumter was attacked and surrendered, what do we find stated in
Montgomery when the news reached there? Here is the telegraphic
announcement of the reception of the news there:

Montgomery, Friday, *April* 12, 1861.
An immense crowd serenaded President Davis and Secretary Walker,
at the Exchange Hotel to-night.

Mr. Davis refused to address the audience,[52] but his Secretary of
War did. The Secretary of War, Mr. Walker,[53] said:

No man could tell where the war this day commenced would end,
but he would prophesy that the flag which now flaunts the breeze here
would float over the dome of the old Capitol, at Washington, before
the 1st of May. Let them try southern chivalry and test the extent of
southern resources, and it might float eventually over Faneuil Hall
itself.[54]

What is the announcement? We have attacked Fort Sumter, and
it has surrendered, and no one can tell where this war will end. By
the 1st of May our flag will waive in triumph from the dome of the
old Capitol at Washington, and ere long perhaps from Fanueil Hall
in Boston. Then, was this war commenced by the President on his
own motion? You say the President of the United States did wrong in
ordering out seventy-five thousand men, and in increasing the Army
and Navy under the exigency. Do we not know, in connection with
these facts, that so soon as Fort Sumter surrendered they took up the
line of march for Washington? Do not some of us that were here
know that we did not even go to bed very confidently and securely,
for fear the city would be taken before the rising sun?[55] Has it not
been published in the southern newspapers that Ben McCullock[56]
was in readiness, with five thousand picked men, in the State of
Virginia, to make a descent and attack the city, and take it?

What furthermore do we find? We find that the congress of
this same pseudo-republic, this same southern confederacy that
has sprung up in the South, as early as the 6th of March passed a
law preparing for this invasion—preparing for this war which they
commenced. Here it is:

That in order to provide speedily forces to repel invasion, maintain the rightful possession of the confederate States of America in every portion of territory belonging to each State, and to secure the public tranquillity and independence against threatened assault, the President be, and he is hereby, authorized to employ the militia, military, and naval forces of the confederate States of America, and ask for and accept the services of any number of volunteers, not exceeding one hundred thousand.[57]

Senators talk about the enormous call of the President of the United States for seventy-five thousand men, when your forts were surrendered, and when the President of the so-called southern confederacy was authorized to call out the entire militia, naval, and military force, and then to receive in the service of the confederate States one hundred thousand men; and yet there is alarm here at the President calling out seventy-five thousand men to defend the capital and the public property. Are we for the Government, or are we against it? That is the question. Taking all the facts into consideration, do we not see that an invasion was intended? It was even announced by Mr. Iverson upon this floor that ere long their Congress would be sitting here and this Government would be overthrown.[58] When the facts are all put together we see the scheme, and it is nothing more nor less than executing a programme deliberately made out; and yet Senators hesitate, falter, and complain, and say the President has suspended the writ of *habeas corpus*, increased the Army and Navy, and they ask, where was the necessity for all this? With your forts taken, your men fired upon, your ships attacked at sea, and one hundred thousand men called into the field by this so-called southern confederacy, and with the additional authority to call out the entire military and naval force of those States, Senators talk about seventy-five thousand men being called out by the President of the United States, and the increase he has made of the Army and Navy. Mr. President, it all goes to show, in my opinion, that our sympathies are with the one government and against the other. Admitting that there was a little stretch of power; admitting that the margin was pretty wide when the power was exercised, the query now comes, when you have got the power, when you are sitting here in a legislative attitude, are you willing to sustain the Government and give it the means to sustain itself? It is not worth while to talk about what has been done before. The question on any measure should be, is it necessary now? If it is, it should not be withheld from the Government.

Senators talk about violating the Constitution and the laws. A great deal has been said about searches and seizures, and the right of protection of persons, and of papers. I reckon it is equally as important to protect a Government from seizure as it is an individual.

I reckon the moral and the law of the case would be just as strong in seizing upon that which belonged to the Federal Government as it would upon that belonging to an individual. What belongs to us in the aggregate is protected and maintained by the same law and [sic] moral and legal, as that that belongs to an individual. These rebellious States, after commencing this war, after violating the Constitution, seized our forts, our arsenals, our dock-yards, our custom-houses, our public buildings, our ships, and last, though not least, plundered the independent treasury at New Orleans of $1,-000,000.[59] And yet Senators talk about violations of the law and the Constitution. They say the Constitution is disregarded, and the Government is about to be overthrown. Does not this talk about violations of the Constitution and law come with a beautiful grace from that side of the House? I repeat again, sir, is there not to be more toleration to violations of the Constitution for its protection and vindication than there is to violations of it, in order to overthrow and destroy the Government? We have seen instances, and other instances might occur, where it might be indispensibly [sic] necessary for the Government to exercise a power, and to assume a position that was not clearly legal and constitutional, in order to resist the entire overthrow and upturning of the Government and all our institutions.

But the President issued his proclamation. When did he issue it, and for what? He issued his proclamation calling out seventy-five thousand men after the congress of the so-called southern confederacy had passed a law to call out the entire militia, and to receive into their service one hundred thousand men. The President issued his proclamation after they had taken Fort Moultrie and Castle Pinckney; after they had fired upon and reduced Fort Sumter. Fort Sumter was taken on the 12th,[60] and on the 15th he issued his proclamation. Taking all these circumstances together, it showed that they intended to advance, and that their object was to extend their power, to subjugate the other States, and to overthrow the Constitution and the laws and the Government.

Senators talk about violations of the Constitution. Have you heard any intimation of complaint from those Senators about this southern confederacy—this band of traitors to their country and their country's institutions? I repeat, substantially, the language of the Senator from Illinois, [Mr. Browning:]

Have you heard any complaint or alarm about violations of constitutional law on that side? Oh, no! But we must stand still; the Government must not move while they are moving with a hundred thousand men; while they have the power to call forth the entire militia and the army and the navy. While they are reducing our forts, and robbing us of our property, we must stand still; the Constitution and the laws must not be violated; and an arraignment is made to weaken and paralyze the Government in its greatest peril and trial.[61]

On the 15th of April, the proclamation was issued calling out seventy-five thousand men, after the confederate States had authorized one hundred thousand men to be received by their president—this man Davis, who stood up here and made a retiring speech—a man educated and nurtured by the Government;[62] who sucked its pap; who received all his military instruction at the hands of this Government; a man who got all his distinction, civil and military, in the service of this government, beneath the stars and stripes, and then, without cause—without being deprived of a single right or privilege—the sword he unsheathed in vindication of that flag in a foreign land, given to him by the hand of his cherishing mother, he stands this day prepared to plunge into her bosom! Such men as these have their apologists here in Congress to excuse and extenuate their acts, either directly or indirectly. You never hear from them of law or Constitution being violated down there. Oh, no; that is not mentioned.

On the 15th the President issued his proclamation calling seventy-five thousand men into the service of the United States, and on the 17th this same Jefferson Davis, being President of the southern confederacy, issued a proclamation proposing or opening the door to the issuance of letters of marque and reprisal,[63] and that, too, in violation of the pseudo-hermaphrodite government that has been gotten up down there. In retalliation for the proclamation issued by the President of the United States, he, in violation of the constitution of this pseudo-confederacy, issued his proclamation proposing to issue letters of marque and reprisal. In other words, he proposed to do what? To open an office and say, we will give out licences to rob the citizens of the United States of all their property wherever it can be picked up upon the high seas. This he proposed to do not only in violation of the constitution of the confederate States, but in violation of the law of nations; for no people—I care not by what name you call it—has a right to issue letters of marque and reprisal until its independence is first acknowledged as a separate and distinct power.[64] Has that been done? I think, therefore, Senators can find some little violation of constitution and law down there among themselves. Sir, they have violated the law and the Constitution every step they progressed in going there, and now they violate it in trying to come this way. There was a general license offered, a premium offered, to every freebooter, to every man who wanted to plunder and play the pirate on the high seas, to come and take a commission, and plunder in the name of the southern confederacy; to take, at that time, the property of Tennessee or the property of Kentucky, your beef, your pork, your flour, and every other product making its way to a foreign market. Mr. Davis authorized letters of marque and reprisal to pick them up and appropriate them. After that, their congress saw that he had gone ahead of their constitution and the laws of nations, and they passed a law modifying the issuance of letters of marque and reprisal, that they should prey upon the property of the citizens of the United States, excepting certain States—excepting Kentucky and Tennessee—holding that out as a bait, as an inducement to get them in.[65]

I do not think, therefore, when we approach the subject fairly and squarely, that there was any very great wrong in the President of the United States, on the 19th, issuing his proclamation blockading their ports, saying you shall not have the opportunity, so far as I can prevent it, of plundering and appropriating other people's property on the high seas. I think he did precisely what was right. He would have been derelict to his duty, and to the high behest of the American people, if he had sat here and failed to exert every power within his reach and scope to protect the property of citizens of the United States on the high seas.

Senators seem to think it is no violation of the Constitution to make war on your Government; and when its enemies are stationed in sight of the capital, there is no alarm, no dread, no scare, no fright. Some of us would not feel so very comfortable if they were to get this city. I believe there are others who would not be very much disturbed. I do not think I could sleep right sound if they were in possession of this city; not that I believe I am more timid than most men, but I do not believe there would be much quarter for me; and, by way of self-protection, and enjoying what few rights I have remaining, I expect it would be better, if they were in possession of this city for me to be located in some other point, not too inconvenient or too remote. I believe there are others who would feel very comfortable here.

Then, Mr. President, in tracing this subject along, I cannot see what great wrong has been committed by the Government in taking the course it has taken. I repeat again, this Government is now passing through its third ordeal; and the time has arrived when it should put forth its entire power, and say to rebels and traitors wherever they are, that the supremacy of the Constitution, and laws made in pursuance thereof, shall be sustained; that those citizens who have been borne down and tyrannized over, and who have had laws of treason passed against them in their own States and threatened with confiscation of property, shall be protected. I say it is the paramount duty of this Government to assert its power and maintain its integrity. I say it is the duty of this Government to protect those States, or the loyal citizens of those States in the enjoyment of a republican form of government; for we have seen one continued system of usurpation carried on, from one end of these southern States to the other, disregarding the popular judgment; disregarding the popular will; setting at defiance the judgment of the people; disregarding their rights; paying no attention to their State constitutions in any sense whatever. We are bound, under the Constitution, to protect those States and their citizens. We are bound to guaranty to them a republican form of government; it is our duty to do it. If we have got no Government, let the delusion be dispelled; let the dream pass away; and let the people of the United States, and the nations of the earth, know at once that we have no Government. If we have a Government, based on the intelligence and virtue of the American people, let that great fact be now established, and once established, this Government will be on a more enduring and permanent basis than it ever was before. I still have confidence in the integrity, the virtue, the intelligence, and the patriotism of the great mass of the people; and so believing, I intend to stand by the Government of my fathers to the last extremity.

In the last presidential contest I am free to say that I took some part. I advocated the pretensions and claims of one of the distinguished sons of Kentucky,[66] as a Democrat. I am a Democrat to-day; I expect to die one. My Democracy rests upon the great principle I have stated; and in the support of measures, I have always tried to be guided by a conscientious conviction of right; and I have laid down for myself, as a rule of action, in all doubtful questions, to pursue principle; and in the pursuit of a great principle I can never reach a wrong conclusion. I intend, in this case, to pursue principle. I am a Democrat, believing the principles of this Government are Democratic. It is based upon the Democratic theory. I believe Democracy can stand, notwithstanding all the taunts and jeers that are thrown at it throughout the southern confederacy. The principles which I call Democracy—I care not by what name they are sustained, whether by Republicans, by Whigs, or not—are the great principles that lie at the foundation of this Government, and they will be maintained. We have seen that so far the experiment has succeeded well; and now we should make an effort, in this last ordeal through which we are passing, to crush out the fatal doctrine of secession and those who are coöperating with it in the shape of rebels and traitors.

I advocated the professions of a distinguished son of Kentucky at the late election, for the reason that I believed he was a better Union man than any other candidate in the field.[67] Others advocated the claims of Mr. Bell, believing him to be a better Union man;

others those of Mr. Douglas. In the South we know that there was no Republican ticket. I was a Union man then; I was a Union man in 1833; I am a Union man now. And what has transpired since the election in November last that has produced sufficient cause to break up this Government? The Senator from California[68] enumerated the facts up to the 25th day of May, 1860, when there was a vote taken in this body declaring that further legislation was not necessary for the protection of slave property in the Territories. Now, from the 6th of November[69] up to the 20th of December, tell me what transpired of sufficient cause to break up this Government? Was there any innovation, was there any additional step taken in reference to the rights of the States or the institution of slavery? If the candidate whose claims I advocated had been elected President—I speak of him as a candidate, of course not meaning to be personal—I do not believe this Government would have been broken up. If Stephen A. Douglas had been elected, I do not believe this Government would have been broken up. Why? Because those who advocated the pretensions of Mr. Lincoln would have done as all parties have done heretofore: they would have yielded to the high behest of the American people.

Then, is the mere defeat of one man, and the election of another, according to the forms of law and the Constitution, sufficient cause to break up this Government? No; it is not sufficient cause. Do we not know, too, that if all the seceding Senators had stood here as faithful sentinels, representing the interests of their States, they had it in their power to check any advance that might be made by the incoming Administration. I showed these facts, and enumerated them at the last session. They were shown here the other day. On the 4th of March, when President Lincoln was inaugurated, we had a majority of six upon this floor in opposition to his Administration. Where, then, is there even a pretext for breaking up the Government upon the idea that he would have encroached upon our rights? Does not the nation know that even Mr. Lincoln could not have made his cabinet without the consent of the majority of the Senate? Do we not know that he could not even have sent a minister abroad without the majority of the Senate confirming the nomination? Do we not know that if any minister whom he sent abroad should make a treaty inimical to the institutions of the South, that treaty could not have been ratified without a majority of two thirds of the Senate?

With all these facts staring them in the face, where is the pretense for breaking up this Government? Is it not clear that there has been a fixed purpose, a settled design to break up the Government and change the nature and character and whole genius of the Government itself? Does it not prove conclusively, as there was no cause, that they simply selected it as an occasion that was favorable to excite the prejudices of the South, and thereby enable them to break up this Government and establish a southern confederacy?

Then when we get at it, what is the real cause? If Mr. Davis had been elected President of the United States, it would have been a very nice thing, he would have respected the judgment of the people, and no doubt his confidence in their capacity for self government would have been increased; but it so happened that he was not elected. They thought proper to elect somebody else, according to law and the Constitution. Then, as all parties had done heretofore, it was the duty of the whole people to acquiesce; if he made a good President, sustain him; if he became a bad one, condemn him; if he violated the law and the Constitution, impeach him. We had our remedy under the Constitution and in the Union.

What is the real cause? Disappointed ambition; an unhallowed ambition. Certain men could not wait any longer, and they seized this occasion to do what they had been wanting to do for a long time —break up the Government. If they could not rule a large country, they thought they might rule a small one. Hence one of the prime movers in the Senate ceased to be a Senator, and passed out to be president of the southern confederacy. Another, that was bold enough on this floor to proclaim himself a rebel, retired as a Senator, and became secretary of state.[70] All perfectly disinterested, no ambition about it! Another, Mr. Benjamin, of Louisiana—one that understands something about the idea of dividing garments; who belongs to that tribe that parted the garments of our Saviour, and for his vesture cast lots—went out of this body and was made attorney general, to show his patriotism and disinterestedness—nothing else! Mr. Slidell, disinterested altogether, is to go as minister to France. I might enumerate many such instances. This is all patriotism, pure disinterestedness! Do we not see where it all ends? Disappointed, impatient, unhallowed ambition. There has been no cause for breaking up this Government; there have been no rights denied, no privileges trampled upon under the Constitution and Union, that might not have been remedied more effectually in the Union than outside of it. What rights are to be attained outside of the Union? The seceders have violated the Constitution, trampled it under foot; and what is their condition now? Upon the abstract idea that they had a right to secede, they have gone out; and what is the consequence? Oppression, taxation, blood, and civil war. They reasoned upon the principle of a madman, who happened to discover somehow that man had dominion over the beasts of the forest; and because he had, he said he had a right to shear a wolf. A friend remonstrated with him, and asked him if he had considered the danger and the difficulty of the attempt to shear a wolf; and after the shearing was over, what would it be worth? "Oh no," said he, in the midst of his frenzy and madness, "I have a right to shear a wolf, and therefore I will shear a wolf."[71] Yes, they have sheared the wolf, and what has come? They have gone out of the Union; and, I repeat again, they have got taxes, usurpations, blood, and civil war.

I said just now that I had advocated the election to the Presidency of the distinguished Senator from Kentucky, on the ground that he was a good Union man. I wish we could now hear his eloquent voice in favor of the old Government of our fathers, and in vindication of the stars and stripes, that have been borne in triumph everywhere until a very recent date. I hold in my hand a document which was our text book in the campaign. It is headed "Breckinridge and Lane Campaign Document No. 16. Who are the disunionists? Breckinridge and Lane the true Union candidates." It contains an extract which I will read from the Senator's address on the removal of the Senate from the old to the new Chamber. I would to God he was as good a Union man to-day as I think he was then:

Such is our country; ay, and more—far more than my mind could conceive or my tongue could utter. Is there an American who regrets the past? Is there one who will deride his country's laws, pervert her Constitution, or alienate her people? If there be such a man, let his memory descend to posterity laden with the execrations of all mankind. * * * * * Let us devoutly trust that another Senate, in another age, shall bear to a new and larger Chamber this Constitution vigorous and inviolate, and that the last generation of posterity shall witness the deliberations of the Representatives of American States still united, prosperous, and free.[72]

Now this was the text—an extract from a speech of the Senator, after the nomination was made:

When that convention selected me as one of its candidates, looking at my humble antecedents and the place of my habitation, it gave to the country, so far as I was concerned, a personal and geographical guarantee that its interest was in the Union.[73]

In addition to that, in Tennessee we headed our electoral ticket as if to give unmistakable evidence of our devotion to the Union, and the reason why we sustained him, "National Democratic ticket. 'Instead of dissolving the Union, we intend to lengthen it and to strengthen it.'—*Breckinridge*."[74] Where are his eloquent tones now? They are heard arraigning the Administration for what he conceives to be premature action in advance of the law, or a slight departure from the Constitution. Which is the most tolerable, premature action, action in advance of law, a slight departure from the Constitution, (putting it on his own ground,) or an entire overthrow of the

Government? Are there no advances, are there no inroads, being made today upon the Constitution and the existence of the Government itself? Let us look at the question plainly and fairly. Here is an invading army almost within cannon shot of the capital, headed by Jeff. Davis and Beauregard.[75] Suppose they advance on the city tonight; subjugate it; depose the existing authorities; expel the present Government: what kind of government have you then? Is there any Constitution in it? Is there any law in it? He can stand here almost in sight of the enemy, see the citadel of freedom, the Constitution, trampled upon, and there is no apprehension; but he can look with an eagle eye, and, with an analytic process almost unsurpassed, discriminate against and attack those who are trying to manage your Government for its safety and preservation. He has no word of condemnation for the invading army that threatens to overthrow the capital, that threatens to trample the Constitution and the law under foot. I repeat, suppose Davis, at the head of his advancing columns, should depose your Government and expel your authority: what kind of government will you have got? Will there be any Constitution left? How eloquent my friend was upon constitutions. He told us the Constitution was the measure of power, and that we should understand and feel constitutional restraints; and yet when your Government is perhaps within a few hours of being overthrown, and the law and Constitution trampled under foot, there are no apprehensions on his part; no words of rebuke for those who are endeavoring to accomplish such results.

The Old Dominion has got the brunt of the war upon her hands. I sympathize with her most deeply, and especially with the loyal portion of her citizens, who have been brow-beaten and domineered over. Now the war is transferred to Virginia, and her plains are made to run with blood; and when this is secured, what do we hear in the far South? Howell Cobb, another of these disinterested patriots, said not long since, in a speech in Georgia:

> The people of the gulf States need have no apprehensions; they might go on with their planting and their other business as usual; the war would not come to their section; its theater would be along the borders of the Ohio river and in Virginia.[76]

She ought to congratulate herself upon that position, for she has got the war. Now they want to advance. Their plans and designs are to get across into Maryland, and carry on a war of subjugation. There is wonderful alarm among certain gentlemen here at the term "subjugate." They are alarmed at the idea of making citizens who have violated the law simply conform to it by enforcing their obedience. If a majority of the citizens in a State have violated the Constitution, have trampled it under foot, and violated the law, is it subjugation to assert the supremacy of the Constitution and the law? Is it any more than a simple enforcement of the law? It would be one of the best subjugations that could take place if some of them were subjugated, and brought back to their constitutional position that they occupied before. I would to God that Tennessee stood to-day where she did three months ago.

Mr. President, it is provided in the Constitution of the United States that

no State shall, without the consent of Congress, lay any duty of tonnage, keep troops or ships of war in time of peace, enter into any agreement or compact with another State, or with a foreign Power, or engage in war unless actually invaded, or in such imminent danger as will not admit of delay.[77]

The State authorities of Tennessee, before her people had even voted upon an ordinance to separate her from the Union, formed a league by which they transferred fifty-five thousand men, the whole army, over to the confederate States for the purpose of prosecuting their war. Is it not strange that such a palpable violation of the Constitution should not be referred to and condemned by any one? Here is a member of the Union, without even having the vote taken upon an ordinance of separation or secession, forming a league, by its commissioners or ministers, and handing over fifty-five thousand men to make war upon the Government of the United States, though they were themselves then within the Union. No one seems to find fault with that. The fact is, that, in the whole progress of secession, the Constitution and the law have been violated at every step from its incipiency to the present point. How have the people of my State been treated? I know that this may not interest the Senate to any very great extent; but I must briefly refer to it. The people of a portion of that State, having devotion and attachment to the Constitution and the Government as framed by the sires of the Revolution, still adhering to it, gave a majority of more than twenty thousand votes in favor of the Union at the election.[78] After that, this portion of the State, East Tennessee, called a convention, and the convention published an address, in which they sum up some of the grievances which we have been bearing in that portion of the country. They say:

The Memphis Appeal, a prominent disunion paper, published a false account of our proceedings, under the head "the traitors in council," and styled us, who represented every county but two in East Tennessee, "*the little* batch of disaffected traitors who hover around the noxious atmosphere of ANDREW JOHNSON's home." Our meeting was telegraphed to the New Orleans Delta, and it was falsely said that we had passed a resolution recommending submission if seventy thousand votes were not cast against secession. The dispatch added that "the southern rights men are determined to hold possession of the State, though they should be in a minority."[79]

They had fifty-five thousand men and $5,000,000 to sustain
them, the State authorities with them, and made the declaration that
they intended to hold the State though they should be in a minority.
This shows the advance of tyranny and usurpation. By way of showing the Senate some of the wrongs which that people have borne and
submitted to, who are loyal to the Government—who have been deprived of the arms furnished by the Government for their protection
—withheld by this little man Harris, the Governor of the State—I
will read a few paragraphs from the address: [80]

[The four paragraphs of the Greeneville convention address painted
a chilling picture of the plight of unionists in East Tennessee and inveighed against "the pretended majority" which reveals "an utter contempt and disregard of law; a determination to force every Union man in
the State to swear to the support of a constitution he abhors; to yield his
money and property to aid a cause he detests; and to become the object
of scorn and derision, as well as the victim of intolerable and relentless
oppression."]

These are some of the wrongs that we are enduring in that section
of Tennessee; not near all of them, but a few which I have presented
that the country may know what we are submitting to. Since I left
my home, having only one way to leave the State through two or
three passes coming out through Cumberland Gap, I have been advised that they had even sent their armies to blockade these passes
in the mountains, as they say, to prevent JOHNSON from returning
with arms and munitions to place in the hands of the people to vindicate their rights, repel invasion, and put down domestic insurrection
and rebellion. Yes, sir, there they stand in arms environing a population of three hundred and twenty-five thousand loyal, brave, patriotic, and unsubdued people;[81] but yet powerless, and not in a
condition to vindicate their rights. Hence I come to the Government,
and I do not ask it as a suppliant, but I demand it as a constitutional
right, that you give us protection, give us arms and munitions; and
if they cannot be got there in any other way, to take them there with
an invading army, and deliver the people from the oppression to
which they are now subjected. We claim to be the State. The other
divisions may have seceded and gone off; and if this Government will
stand by and permit those portions of the State to go off, and not
enforce the laws and protect the loyal citizens there, we cannot help
it; but we still claim to be the State, and if two thirds have fallen off,
or have been sunk by an earthquake, it does not change our relation to this Government. If the Government will let them go, and not
give us protection the fault is not ours; but if you will give us protection we intend to stand as a State, as a part of this Confederacy,
holding to the flag that was borne by Washington through a seven
years' struggle for independence and separation from the mother

country. We demand it according to law; we demand it upon the guarantees of the Constitution. You are bound to guaranty to us a republican form of Government, and we ask it as a constitutional right. We do not ask you to interfere as a party, as your feelings or prejudices may be one way or another in reference to the parties of the country; but we ask you to interfere as a Government according to the Constitution. Of course we want your sympathy, and your regard, and your respect; but we ask your interference on constitutional grounds.

The amendments to the Constitution, which constitute the bill of rights, declare that "a well regulated militia being necessary to the security of a free State, the right of the people to keep and bear arms shall not be infringed."[82] Our people are denied this right secured to them in their own constitution and the Constitution of the United States; yet we hear no complaints here of violations of the Constitution in this respect. We ask the Government to interpose to secure us this constitutional right. We want the passes in our mountains opened, we want deliverance and protection for a downtrodden and oppressed people who are struggling for their independence without arms. If we had had ten thousand stand of arms and ammunition when the contest commenced, we should have asked no further assistance. We have not got them. We are a rural people; we have villages and small towns—no large cities. Our population is homogenous, industrious, frugal, brave, independent; but harmless and powerless, and rode over by usurpers. You may be too late in coming to our relief; or you may not come at all, though I do not doubt that you will come; they may trample us under foot; they may convert our plains into graveyards, and the caves of our mountains into sepulchers; but they will never take us out of this Union, or make us a land of slaves—no, never. We intend to stand as firm as adamant,[83] and as unyielding as our own majestic mountains that surround us. Yes, we will profit by their example, resting immovably upon their basis. We will stand as long as we can; and if we are overpowered, and liberty shall be driven from the land, we intend before she departs, to take the flag of our country, with a stalwart arm, and a patriotic heart, and an honest tread, and place it upon the summit of the loftiest and most majestic mountain. We intend to plant it there, and leave it, to indicate to the inquirer who may come in after times, the spot where the Goddess of Liberty lingered and wept for the last time, before she took her flight from a people once prosperous, free, and happy.

We ask the Government to come to our aid. We love the Constitution as made by our fathers[.] We have confidence in the integrity and capacity of the people to govern themselves. We have lived entertaining these opinions; we intend to die entertaining them. The battle has commenced. The President has placed it upon the true ground. It is an issue on the one hand for the people's Government, and its overthrow on the other. We have commenced the battle of freedom. It is freedom's cause.[84] We are resisting usurpation and oppression. We will triumph; we must triumph. Right is with us. A great and fundamental principle of right, that lies at the foundation of all things, is with us. We may meet with impediments, and may meet with disasters, and here and there a defeat; but ultimately freedom's cause must triumph, for—

> Freedom's battle once begun,
> Bequeathed from bleeding sire to son,
> Though baffled oft, is ever won.[85]

Yes, we must triumph. Though sometimes I cannot see my way clear in matters of this kind, as in matters of religion, when my facts give out, when my reason fails me, I draw largely upon my faith. My faith is strong, based on the eternal principles of right, that a thing so monstrously wrong as this rebellion is, cannot triumph. Can we submit to it? Can bleeding justice submit to it? Is the Senate, are the American people, prepared to give up the graves of Washington and Jackson, to be encircled and governed and controlled by a combination of traitors and rebels? I say let the battle go on—it is freedom's cause—until the stars and stripes (God bless them) shall again be unfurled upon every cross road, and from every house top throughout the Confederacy, North and South. Let the Union be reinstated; let the law be enforced; let the Constitution be supreme.

If the Congress of the United States were to give up the tombs of Washington and Jackson, we should have rising up in our midst another Peter the Hermit, in a much more righteous cause—for ours is true, while his was a delusion—who would appeal to the American people and point to the tombs of Washington and Jackson, in the possession of those who are worse than the infidel and the Turk who held the Holy Sepulcher.[86] I believe the American people would start of their own accord, when appealed to, to redeem the graves of Washington and Jackson and Jefferson, and all the other patriots who are lying within the limits of the southern confederacy. I do not believe they would stop the march, until again the flag of this Union would be placed over the graves of those distinguished men. There will be an uprising. Do not talk about Republicans now; do not talk about Democrats now; do not talk about Whigs or Americans now; talk about your country and the Constitution and the Union. Save that; preserve the integrity of the Government; once more place it erect among the nations of the earth; and then if we want to divide about questions that may arise in our midst, we have a Government to divide in.

I know it has been said that the object of this war is to make war on southern institutions. I have been in free States and I have been in slave States, and I thank God that, so far as I have been, there has been one universal disclaimer of any such purpose. It is a war upon no section; it is a war upon no peculiar institution; but it is a war for the integrity of the Government, for the Constitution, and the supremacy of the laws. That is what the nation understands by it.

I have already detained the Senate much longer than I intended when I rose, and I shall conclude in a few words more. Although the Government has met with a little reverse within a short distance of this city, no one should be discouraged and no heart should be dismayed.[87] It ought only to prove the necessity of bringing forth and exerting still more vigorously the power of the Government in maintenance of the Constitution and the laws. Let the energies of the Government be redoubled, and let it go on with this war—not a war upon sections, not a war upon peculiar institutions anywhere; but let the Constitution and the Union be its frontispiece, and the supremacy and enforcement of the laws its watchword. Then it can, it will, go on triumphantly. We must succeed. This Government must not, cannot fail. Though your flag may have trailed in the dust; though a retrograde movement may have been made; though the banner of our country may have been sullied, let it still be borne onward; and if, for the prosecution of this war in behalf of the Government and the Constitution, it is necessary to cleanse and purify that banner, I say let it be baptized in fire from the sun and bathed in a nation's blood! The nation must be redeemed; it must be triumphant. The Constitution—which is based upon principles immutable, and upon which rest the rights of man and the hopes and expectations of those who love freedom throughout the civilized world—must be maintained.

The people whom I represent appeal to the Government and to the nation to give us that constitutional protection that we need. I am proud to say that I have met with every manifestation of that kind in the Senate, with only a few dissenting voices. I am proud to say, too, that I believe old Kentucky, God bless her! will ultimately rise and shake off the stupor which has been resting upon her; and instead of denying us the privilege of passing through her borders,[88] and taking arms and munitions of war to enable a downtrodden people to defend themselves, will not only give us that privilege, but will join us and help us in the work. The people of Kentucky love the Union; they love the Constitution; they have no fault to find with it; but in that State they have a duplicate to the Governor of ours.[89] When we look all around, we see how the Governors of the different States have been involved in this conspiracy—the most stupendous and gigantic conspiracy that was ever formed, and as corrupt and as foul as that attempted by Catiline in the days of Rome. We know it to be so. Have we not known men to sit at their desks in this Chamber, using the Government's stationery to write treasonable letters;[90] and while receiving their pay and sworn to support the Constitution and sustain the law, engaging in midnight conclaves to devise ways and means by which the Government and the Constitution should be overthrown? The charge was made and published in the papers.[91] Many things we know that we cannot put our finger upon; but we know from the concert of action, the regular steps that were taken in this work of breaking up the Government, or trying to break it up, that there was system, concert of action. It is a scheme more corrupt than the assassination planned and conducted by Cataline in reference to the Roman Senate. The time has arrived when we should show to the nations of the earth that we are a nation capable of preserving our existence, and give them evidence that we will do it.[92]

Cong. Globe, 37 Cong., 1 Sess., 288–97; *Speech of Hon. Andrew Johnson of Tennessee, on the War for the Union . . . July 27, 1861* (Washington, D. C., 1861).

1. On July 27 Solomon Foot of Vermont, the president *pro tempore*, called up joint resolution S. 1, to "approve and confirm certain acts of the President of the United States for suppressing insurrection and rebellion," and recognized Johnson. *Cong. Globe*, 37 Cong., 1 Sess., 288.

2. Lincoln's Special Session Message, July 4, 1861. Richardson, *Messages*, VI, 30.

3. During the current debate John C. Breckinridge, Trusten Polk, and Lazarus W. Powell had all condemned the President's high-handed action in precipitating the country into a war, as well as his exercise of unconstitutional authority in prosecuting the effort to coerce states back into the Union. All claimed to see great danger in Lincoln's course. *Cong. Globe*, 37 Cong., 1 Sess., 47–49, 64–71, 137–41; for Polk and Powell, see *Johnson Papers*, III, 205–6n, 354n.

4. Breckinridge's speech of July 16 opposing the resolution to approve presidential action. *Cong. Globe*, 37 Cong., 1 Sess., 140.

5. Edward D. Baker was quoted by Breckinridge as having said that he favored dictatorial powers for the President because, for the purposes of waging war, "nothing was so good as a dictator." Baker interrupted the Kentuckian, protesting that he had been "misrepresented"; that he had actually said, "in order to save the Union [he] would take some risk of despotism"— would "risk a little to save all." *Ibid.*, 140–41.

6. Breckinridge gave no clue as to the identity of this former diplomat, referring to him only as "a very excellent and distinguished man." *Ibid.*, 140.

7. The Kentucky senator designated the unnamed source as "a leading, able, influential paper in one of the northern States." *Ibid.*

8. Following his arrest and imprisonment on May 25, 1861, John Merryman of Maryland, an ardent secessionist, obtained from Chief Justice Taney

a writ of habeas corpus directing that he be brought before the Federal court in Baltimore. The commander at Ft. McHenry refused to comply, on the ground that the President had suspended the writ. In *Ex parte* Merryman Taney asserted that, under the Constitution, only Congress had the power to suspend habeas corpus. Lincoln, advised by Attorney General Edward Bates that Taney was in error, disregarded the chief justice's opinion and allowed the military to proceed with its case. *Ex Parte* Merryman, Federal Cases No. 9487 (1861); Pfeffer, *This Honorable Court*, 159; McPherson, *Great Rebellion*, 154–61.

9. Thomas Gilpin, *Exiles in Virginia: With Observations on the Conduct of the Society of Friends during the Revolutionary War Comprising the Official Papers of the Government Relating to That Period 1777–1778* (Philadelphia, 1848), 37–42.

10. On January 5, 1778, the supreme executive council of Pennsylvania notified Congress that the prisoners were detained by the United States and "that a considerable expence hath been paid by this State removeing [sic] them to Winchester." After Congress had decreed their release, on March 19 the council ordered that they be returned to Shippensburg and "that the whole expence of arresting & confining the Prisoners sent to Virginia, the expences of their journey, & all other incidental charges, be paid by the said Prisoners." *Minutes of the Supreme Executive Council of Pennsylvania* (16 vols., Harrisburg, 1838–53), XI, 395, 460–61.

11. In March, 1815, Judge Dominick Hall of the U. S. district court sought to interfere with Andrew Jackson's enforcement of martial law in New Orleans by issuing a writ of habeas corpus for Louis Louaillier, a member of the Louisiana legislature whom Jackson had arrested. Seized by Jackson and locked in the barracks with Louaillier, Hall was released several days later and banished from the city. Following the announcement of peace, the judge returned to New Orleans, issued a summons against Jackson charging him with refusal to recognize habeas corpus in the case of Louaillier, and fined him $1,000. Marquis James, *The Life of Andrew Jackson* (New York, 1938), 260–64.

12. Johnson was among the "overwhelming majority" in the House of Representatives who approved the bill, signed by President Tyler on February 16, 1844, to indemnify Jackson for the fine and the accrued interest ($2,-732.90). *Ibid.*, 760; *Cong. Globe*, 28 Cong., 1 Sess., 120, 288; see also *Johnson Papers*, I, 119–20.

13. Martin v. Mott, 12 Wheaton 19 (1827), 29–30.

14. In a speech on July 10, Polk of Missouri had accused the President of issuing a proclamation "calling for an increase of the Army and the Navy to the amount of about eighty-three thousand men" without a law upon which to base such an order. The Constitution, Polk pointed out, invests Congress with the exclusive power to "raise and support armies." On the next day and in a similar vein, Powell of Kentucky, citing the statute of 1795 as the only authority by which the President could summon the militia, argued that if the call of April 15 was not for the purpose of protecting the capital but for "making war on the sovereign States of this Union," then it was unwarranted under the Constitution. *Cong. Globe*, 37 Cong., 1 Sess., 48, 67.

15. Milton S. Latham, speaking on July 20 in favor of joint resolution S. 1, reviewed the circumstances surrounding the outbreak of hostilities and averred that secession was a "deliberate, willful design" of some southern politicians who had blocked all efforts at compromise. *Ibid.*, App. 19–22.

16. In the Senate Committee of Thirteen Crittenden's proposal to extend the Missouri Compromise line was defeated, 6–6. Davis and Toombs presented the extreme southern demands, which included protection of slave property in the territories—a position patently unacceptable to the Republican members. Seward, at this time considered an ultra on the question of slavery, proposed nonetheless a constitutional guarantee of slave property in the states where

it existed and suggested that states modify their personal liberty laws; the guarantee did not, however, include the territories. Northern Democrats Bigler and Rice submitted plans looking toward the extension of the Missouri Compromise line, with guarantees for slavery where it existed and more efficient state laws for the recovery of fugitive slaves. Aside from Seward's efforts, the committee Republicans—Collamer, Doolittle, Grimes, and Wade—made no proposals and, along with Toombs and Davis, voted down Crittenden's compromise. On December 28 the committee reported that it had been unable to reach agreement. *Senate Report* No. 288, 36 Cong., 2 Sess.; Nevins, *Emergence of Lincoln*, II, 390–97; Nichols, *Disruption of Democracy*, 414–16; William E. Baringer, *A House Dividing: Lincoln as President Elect* (Springfield, Ill., 1945), 206–7.

17. Toombs had wired his Georgia constituents as early as December 23, advising them that both the Senate Committee of Thirteen and the House Committee of Thirty-three were controlled by "your enemies," the Republicans, and suggesting that secession was their only recourse. Hunter and Mason joined in a telegraphic dispatch on January 26, summarizing the hopelessness of the situation for the South and asserting that only "prompt and decided action, by the people of Virginia in Convention" could avert "impending civil war" and reconstruct "a Union already dissolved." McPherson, *Great Rebellion*, 37–41; Phillips, *Toombs, Stephens, Cobb Correspondence*, 525.

18. South Carolina, Mississippi, Florida, Alabama, Georgia, Louisiana, and Texas had seceded by early February; Virginia's secession convention was meeting when Congress adjourned, and the state left the Union on April 17. Morris, *Encyclopedia of American History*, 228, 230; Nichols, *Disruption of Democracy*, 498.

19. Mark 12:17.

20. Introduced by Thomas Corwin of Ohio, this resolution had been approved March 2, 1861. *Cong. Globe*, 36 Cong., 2 Sess., 1236; App. 350; *U. S. Statutes*, XII, 251.

21. No southern state had adopted the proposed amendment; Ohio, Maryland, and Illinois had ratified it, but the New England states rejected it, while others took no action. Herman V. Ames, *The Proposed Amendments to the Constitution of the United States*, American Historical Association, *Annual Report, 1896*, II, 196.

22. On May 6 the Tennessee legislature voted to submit the question of secession to the people. The ensuing June 8 election merely endorsed, 104,-913–47,238, the actions of the Assembly, which had already aligned Tennessee with the Confederacy. Campbell, *Tenn. Attitudes*, 198–206.

23. *U. S. Statutes*, XII, 174, 211, 241.

24. Attributed to Robert Toombs. James Z. Rabun to Andrew Johnson Project, February 18, 1975.

25. A leading southern fire-eater, Robert Barnwell Rhett, Jr., editor of the Charleston *Mercury* after 1857, worked to create dissension within the Democratic party and defeated efforts in the legislature to postpone a secession convention. John A. Inglis (b. c1814), a Maryland native who represented Chesterfield County, South Carolina, in the convention, served as chairman of the committee which drafted the secession ordinance. A chancellor, he owned thirteen slaves and in 1860 declared his real property at $17,000 and personal estate at $45,550. For Rhett, see *DAB*, XV, 527; *Johnson Papers*, I, 314n; for Inglis, see Ralph Wooster, "Membership of the South Carolina Secession Convention," *South Carolina Historical and Genealogical Magazine*, LV (1954), 193; Kibler, *Benjamin F. Perry*, 346.

26. Johnson was using a clipping from an unidentified newspaper which quoted this passage from the *Advertiser*. See Johnson Papers, Series 20, LC.

27. Augusta *Chronicle and Sentinel*, January 26, 1861.

28. Letter dated April 30, in London *Times*, May 28, 1861; New York *Tribune*, June 11, 1861.

29. At a meeting on December 15 to consider Federal relations, Bibb County cooperationists considered the "doctrine of immediate secession to be ill-advised, rash, and dangerous," but carefully avoided denunciation of its proponents. Their resolutions included support for a convention, concern for a "provisional" government, and praise for the republican system. Macon *Telegraph*, December 19, 1860.

30. When Stephens, in a speech delivered on November 14, 1860, asked somewhat rhetorically, what government could compare with that of the United States, even "with all its defects," Toombs had replied from the floor, "England." Candler, *Confederate Records*, I, 189; Moore, *Rebellion Record*, I, Doc., 221.

31. Richmond *Whig*, May 17, 1861.

32. Stephens quoted Toombs as having said on the preceding day, "I ask you to give me the sword, for if you do not give it to me, as God lives, I will take it myself." Quoting from the Atlanta *Locomotive*, the New York *Times* of November 20 paraphrased the passage: "His defence was now his strong arm, and if Georgia said he shouldn't take up his sword, he intended to do it anyhow." The printed version intended for wide circulation reads, "we now stand without a shield . . . and we demand at your hands the sword for our defence, and if you will not give it to us, we will take it—take it by the divine right of self-defence, which governments neither give nor can take away." New York *Times*, November 20, 22, 1860; *Speech of Hon. Robert Toombs, delivered in Milledgeville on Tuesday Evening, November 13, 1860, before the Legislature of Georgia* (Milledgeville, 1860), 6–7; Moore, *Rebellion Record*, Supp. I, 367.

33. Johnson was referring to the strained relations between the two countries caused by Napoleon III's annexation of Savoy and Nice. Adolphus W. Ward and George P. Gooch, eds., *The Cambridge History of British Foreign Policy, 1783–1919* (3 vols., Cambridge, 1922–23), II, 441–51.

34. Richmond *Examiner*, May 8, 1861.

35. Memphis *Bulletin* not extant.

36. R. D. Baugh (b. c1815), a Memphis merchant and cotton broker, had been mayor since 1857. Keating, *Memphis*, II, 28; *Twyman's Memphis Directory* (1849), 10; 1860 Census, Tenn., Shelby, Memphis, 2nd Ward, 17; *Goodspeed's Shelby*, 885.

37. Art. I, Sec. 6. Johnson does not cite the whole section—a candidate for the house may also be eligible by owning real estate, debt-free, in the amount of £150.

38. *Ibid.*, Sec. 3 of amendments ratified December 17, 1808.

39. An act "to Raise, Organize and Equip a Provisional Force, and for other purposes," passed by the Tennessee Assembly on May 6, empowered the governor to raise a volunteer army of 55,000, and authorized him to "dispose of five million dollars of the bonds of the State of Tennessee" for this purpose. *Tenn. Acts*, 1861, 2nd Extra Sess., Ch. III; White, *Messages*, V, 311.

40. A reference to Governor Isham Harris.

41. Leonidas W. Spratt (1818–1903), a first cousin of James K. Polk and a native South Carolinian, graduated from South Carolina College (1840) and practiced law in Florida before returning in 1850 to Charleston, where he continued his law practice and became editor of the *Southern Standard* (1853), for which he wrote a series of articles, later published as *The Foreign Slave Trade: The Source of Political Power—of Material Progress, of Social Integrity, and of Social Emancipation to the South* (Charleston, 1858). At the Southern Commercial Convention of 1858 at Montgomery, Spratt had advocated reopening the slave trade. A member of the South Carolina house of representatives (1858–60), he became a delegate to the secession convention, later representing that body as a commissioner to the Florida secession convention. During the war he was a Confederate colonel, subsequently resuming the practice of law in Charleston and later returning to Florida. John Perkins,

Jr. (1819–1885), a lawyer, cotton planter, and congressman (1853–55), was chairman of the Louisiana secession convention and served in the Confederate Senate (1862–65). In this letter Spratt expresses the fear that the clause prohibiting the foreign slave trade will become part of the permanent Constitution, because "the same men who have prepared the provisional will prepare the permanent constitution." May and Faunt, *South Carolina Secedes*, 213; Nevins, *Emergence of Lincoln*, I, 16; Avery O. Craven, *Growth of Southern Nationalism, 1848–1861* (Baton Rouge, 1953), 369; *BDAC*, 1446; Charleston *Mercury*, February 13, 1861.

42. An old expression originating from the attempts of sailors to prevent whales from causing damage to small vessels; the practice is explained in Jonathan Swift's *A Tale of a Tub* (Oxford, 1920 [1710]), 40.

43. James M. Mason's May 16 letter to the editor of the Winchester *Virginian* appeared in the New York *Tribune* of May 23 and the Washington *National Intelligencer*, May 25, 1861.

44. "What Is a Constitution?" *DeBow's Review*, XXX (1861), 306.

45. Orville H. Browning (1806–1881), a native Kentuckian, moved to Illinois in 1831 and practiced law in Quincy. A member of the state senate (1836–43) and a founder of the Republican party, he was appointed to the Senate (1861–63) to fill the vacancy caused by the death of Stephen A. Douglas; subsequently he became Johnson's secretary of the interior (1866–69). Browning had spoken two days earlier. *BDAC*, 613; Maurice G. Baxter, *Orville H. Browning: Lincoln's Friend and Critic* (Bloomington, Ind., 1957); *Cong. Globe*, 37 Cong., 1 Sess., 263–65.

46. Johnson's dates are substantially those found in McPherson's *Great Rebellion*, 27–28, with the exception of the seizure of Ft. Barrancas and the Pensacola Navy Yard, which he dates January 12 instead of 11.

47. Although the source of these figures has not been found, they conform generally to data reported in the *National Intelligencer*, January 21, 1861.

48. Anticipating an attack on Moultrie, Anderson had moved his "little band" to Sumter on December 26; the following day South Carolina troops occupied both Moultrie and Castle Pinckney. E. B. and Barbara Long, *The Civil War Day by Day: An Almanac, 1861–1865* (New York, 1971), 15–16; Nevins, *Emergence of Lincoln*, II, 368.

49. Beauregard's representatives—James Chesnut, Stephen D. Lee, and Alexander R. Chisholm—demanded the evacuation of the fort, which Anderson refused, indicating, however, that he would be starved out in a few days. After consulting with Secretary of War Leroy P. Walker, Beauregard inquired precisely when the Union force would be obliged to withdraw. When Anderson replied that he would not leave before the fifteenth, the Confederates, fearing reinforcements and supplies were on the way, notified him that this was unacceptable and opened fire on the morning of April 12. According to a student of the Sumter crisis, a formal surrender was never demanded, but reports to that effect were circulated in the North for propaganda purposes. Long, *Civil War Almanac*, 55–56; Stampp, *And the War Came*, 282; McPherson, *Great Rebellion*, 113–14.

50. Congressman Roger A. Pryor. See *Johnson Papers*, III, 420n.

51. Assembling on February 13, Virginia's convention met until the firing on Sumter, when the moderates capitulated to the ultras and a secession ordinance was adopted on April 17. Of the 152 delegates, 62 were identified as unionists, 43 as moderates, and 46 secessionists; 1 was unclassified. Wooster, *Secession Conventions*, 142–43, 148–49.

52. According to report, Davis was ill and could not speak. New York *Tribune*, April 15, 1861.

53. Leroy P. Walker (1817–1884), native Alabamian and lawyer, was a state legislator (1847–50), delegate to the Nashville Convention of 1850, and circuit court judge (1850–53). Following Alabama's secession, he was appointed to the Confederate cabinet in February, 1861; resigning in Sep-

tember, he became a brigadier, held commands at Mobile and Montgomery, and served as judge of a military court (1862–65) before resuming his law practice after the war. *DAB*, XIX, 351; see also William C. Harris, *Leroy Pope Walker: Confederate Secretary of War* (Tuscaloosa, 1962).

54. New York *Tribune*, April 15, 1861.

55. In the weeks following Sumter, Confederate troops poured into Virginia, occupying the Shenandoah Valley, Harper's Ferry, and Manassas, and blocking the approaches into Virginia from Washington. Rumors circulated that an attack on the capital was imminent. Unprepared to defend itself at the time of Sumter, the city by the end of April had been sufficiently fortified to withstand an attack. Nevins, *War for the Union*, I, 77–79, 112–13.

56. Ben McCulloch (1811–1862), a soldier, adventurer, and Texas lawman, was in command of Lone Star troops in February, 1861. Commissioned a Confederate brigadier, he commanded in Arkansas and Missouri before being killed at Elkhorn Tavern in the spring of 1862. A year earlier newspaper stories in the South reported rumors that McCulloch was organizing troops for a descent on Washington. *DAB*, XII, 5–6; New York *Tribune*, March 29, 1861; Richmond *Enquirer*, April 4, 1861; New York *Times*, April 11, 12, 1861.

57. *Journal of the Congress of the Confederate States of America, 1861–1865* (7 vols., Washington, D. C., 1904–5), I, 110; McPherson, *Great Rebellion*, 117.

58. On December 11, 1860, when Alfred Iverson of Georgia spoke against Lazarus W. Powell's resolution recommending establishment of the Committee of Thirteen, he declared: "if Maryland secedes from the Union and joins us, as she ought to do, in my humble conception, and a southern confederacy be formed of all the slave States, I see no reason why Washington city should not be continued the capital of the southern confederacy." *Cong. Globe*, 36 Cong., 2 Sess., 51.

59. This figure, reported to Congress early in the year, was the occasion for a House resolution introduced by John A. McClernand on February 4, calling on the President "to communicate . . . the facts . . . and what, if any, steps he has taken or contemplates to recover possession of said treasure and property." According to a contemporary source, the seizure of the New Orleans mint cost the United States $576,926. *Cong. Globe*, 36 Cong., 2 Sess., 730; *American Annual Cyclopaedia* (1861), 319.

60. Although the attack began at 4:30 a.m. Friday, April 12, the fort capitulated about 2:30 p.m. the following day, with the official surrender and evacuation on Sunday, April 14. Long, *Civil War Almanac*, 56–59; McPherson, *Great Rebellion*, 113–14.

61. A paraphrase either of Browning's remarks of July 18, or of his July 25 speech. *Cong. Globe*, 37 Cong., 1 Sess., 188, 263.

62. Educated at West Point (1828), Jefferson Davis had served in the Mexican War and as secretary of war (1853–57), congressman (1845–46), and senator (1847–51, 1857–61). *BDAC*, 784.

63. Under date of April 17, Davis invited "all those who may desire, by service in private armed vessels on the high seas, to aid this Government in resisting so wanton and wicked an aggression, to make application for commissions or Letters of Marque and Reprisal." Moore, *Rebellion Record*, I, Doc., 71.

64. Given the lack of clarity in "the law of nations" on this matter, Johnson's categorical statement is not warranted. In May, 1861, England had recognized the belligerency of the Confederate States in order that southern ships on the high seas might have the status of lawful belligerents. The U. S., however, chose to regard the war as a domestic insurrection, thus claiming that Confederate privateers were, in effect, pirates. Hersch Lauterpacht, *Recognition in International Law* (Cambridge, 1946), 21, 298, 303.

65. On May 6, 1861, the Confederate Congress, recognizing the existence

of a state of war between the Confederacy and the United States, authorized the President to issue commissions or letters of marque and reprisal for seizure of vessels and cargoes belonging to United States citizens, excepting those of slave states and territories, including Kentucky and Tennessee, which had refused to cooperate in those "acts of hostility and wanton aggression . . . plainly intended to overawe, oppress, and finally subjugate the people of the Confederate States." James D. Richardson, comp., *A Compilation of the Messages and Papers of the Confederacy* (2 vols., Nashville, 1905).

66. Johnson had supported John C. Breckinridge's candidacy in 1860.

67. Throughout the 1860 campaign Johnson vigorously denied accusations that Breckinridge held disunionist views. Although believing in the right of secession, the Kentuckian favored compromise as a means of saving the Union and supported the Crittenden Compromise. After Sumter he took the position that the Union no longer existed and that the time had come for Kentucky to make a decision; when the state abandoned her neutrality and ordered Confederates out of her boundaries, he fled to escape arrest. On December 2 the state senate declared him a traitor and formally expelled him. *Johnson Papers*, III, xxvii; *DAB*, III, 9–10; Lucille Stillwell, *John Cabell Breckinridge* (Caldwell, Idaho, 1936), 78–81, 98–105.

68. Milton S. Latham's speech of July 20, 1861. *Cong Globe*, 37 Cong., 1 Sess., App. 19–22.

69. The date of Lincoln's election.

70. Robert Toombs of Georgia.

71. On several occasions Johnson had used this fable, borrowed from Edmund Burke, illustrating the folly of a futile adherence to principle—in this case, urging a costly war for the maintenance of "rights." See *Johnson Papers*, III, 662–63, 664n; IV, 234.

72. Vice President Breckinridge's ceremonial address was delivered on January 4, 1859. *Cong. Globe*, 35 Cong., 2 Sess., 203–4.

73. A passage from the Kentuckian's speech accepting the nomination of the Baltimore convention. Nashville *Union and American*, June 30, 1860.

74. "Instead of breaking up the Union, we intend to strengthen and to lengthen it," appears in the Nashville *Union and American*, July 7, 1860. Earlier, in his acceptance remarks, Breckinridge had more fully articulated the same sentiment: "Instead of looking to the breaking up of the Confederacy, I observe that one of the resolutions seems to contemplate the extending of it—lengthening its cords, and extending its boundaries." *Ibid.*, June 30, 1860.

75. Although Washington remained uneasy about a Confederate strike after Bull Run (July 21), Davis and his generals, Joseph E. Johnston and Beauregard, had decided not to advance on the capital. Nevins, *War for the Union*, I, 217, 220; Alfred Roman, *The Military Operations of General Beauregard in the War Between the States 1861 to 1865* (2 vols., New York, 1884), I, 110–11, 114.

76. This statement, attributed to Cobb, was given to the Louisville *Journal* by "one of the most respectable citizens of Fayette county [Ky.]," who had recently returned from New Orleans and reported that Cobb, traveling on the same train, had included these sentiments in several speeches at various points along the route. Cobb, in a letter to the Atlanta *Confederacy*, denied the report. Louisville *Journal*, April 27, May 10, 1861.

77. Art. I, Sec. 10.

78. In the June 8 referendum East Tennessee had voted against separation, 32,923–14,780. White, *Messages*, V, 304; Campbell, *Tenn. Attitudes*, 292.

79. This statement is part of the Declaration of Grievances, which served as a preamble to the resolutions of the Greeneville Convention of June 17, 1861. The New Orleans *Delta* reported: "A resolution passed by the [Knoxville] Convention declares, in substance, that if seventy thousand votes are cast against secession, it (the Convettion [*sic*]) recommends resistance to the

act of secession; if less, submission." New Orlean *Delta*, June 1, 1861; *Proc. E. Tenn. Conv.* (Greeneville), 20.

80. *Ibid.*, 23; New York *Tribune*, July 4, 1861.

81. A sweeping statement which exaggerates not only the total population of East Tennessee but also the unanimity of opinion in that section.

82. U. S. Constitution, Second Amendment.

83. Adamant: "A stone believed to be of unpenetrable hardness." *Webster's Third International.*

84. Joseph Hopkinson, "Hail Columbia," st. 1.

85. Byron's *The Giaour*, ll. 123–25.

86. Peter the Hermit (c1050–1115), a French monk also known as Peter of Amiens, was one of the initiators of the First Crusade (1095), which was virtually annihilated in 1096. Joined by additional crusaders the following year, Peter and his band, after many hardships, stormed and captured Jerusalem in July, 1099. Johnson's reference to Peter's cause as a "delusion" may reflect a secular bias against a crusade to recover a religious site. *Encyclopaedia Britannica* (1971 ed.), XVII, 743.

87. Johnson's effort to minimize the disorderly rout of Federal troops at Bull Run is rather transparent.

88. Consonant with the policy of neutrality adopted by the legislature in May, Kentucky denied to both sides the right to transmit arms and munitions through that state. Coulter, *Civil War in Kentucky*, 52–56.

89. Johnson attributes Kentucky's quasi-secessionist stance to Governor Beriah Magoffin, who had been the architect of her neutrality and who continued to allow Confederate recruiting. The historian of Civil War Kentucky, however, has assessed Magoffin as a moderate, sympathetic to the South, but a strong constitutionalist. Although Unionists desired his impeachment, he was allowed to resign in 1862, after approving a moderate conservative in his place. *Ibid.*, 143–44; Lowell H. Harrison, "Governor Magoffin and the Secession Crisis," Kentucky State Historical Society *Register*, LXXII (1974), 91–110; see also *Johnson Papers*, III, 416n.

90. Referring to Toombs, Floyd, and other southerners, a New York *Tribune* article, entitled "Treason at Washington," observed: "They use the franking privileges of the Government, its mails, its official seals, to hatch and promote treason. And in due time, they and their co-traitors in the House of Representatives, after doing all the harm they can by remaining in Washington, will draw their pay from the Federal coffers, pack up their stationary, go home, and take up arms against the Constitution and the Union." New York *Tribune*, January 22, 1861.

91. In all probability the *Tribune* article cited above is the source of these remarks. Southern congressmen and senators had met the night of December 13 to draft a manifesto; in early January southern caucuses had assembled, ostensibly to plan consolidation of a separate South. The *National Intelligencer* reported such "secret sessions," as did the New York *Times*. Washington *National Intelligencer*, January 11, and New York *Times*, January 7, 1861, quoted in McPherson, *Great Rebellion*, 37, 391–92.

92. At this juncture John P. Hale of New Hampshire interrupted to propose that further consideration of the subject be postponed until Monday, July 29, and that the Senate proceed to executive business. After a brief exchange between Collamer and Sumner on Hale's proposals, both resolutions were adopted. Johnson did not subsequently resume his remarks. *Cong. Globe*, 37 Cong., 1 Sess., 297.

From Alfred M. Coffin[1]

OFFICE OF A. M. COFFIN
COMMISSION MERCHANTS,

No. 54 Front Street,
New York July 29 1861

My Dear Sir

Tax us. We will pay it. If evey dollar and Every life of this generation be required we'll give all that we may transmit to poterity our Country United and free—
We will:

Put brave men to Command[.] take good Care of the Soldiers. Place Chaplins in the Hopitals. Look well to the Contracters that they do not rob the Soldiers— There are some most Consumate rascals in the midst of the Contracters[.]

Your friend   A M Coffin

ALS, DLC-JP.

1. Alfred M. Coffin, a New York merchant living at 36 W. 39th St., two weeks earlier had voiced his "love for the man who sacrifices so much for the Union as Andrew Johnson" and had invited the senator to a public dinner given by "your friends of both parties." Much earlier Coffin had been among those who hastened to applaud Johnson's December Union stand. *Trow's New York City Directory* (1861), 166; Coffin to Johnson, December 22, 1860, July 17, 1861, Johnson Papers, LC.

From Francis Lieber

July 29, 1861, New York, N. Y.; ALS, DLC-JP.

German-born historian and political theorist teaching at Columbia College wants copy of Johnson's remarks on the suspension of habeas corpus [Speech in Support of Presidential War Program, July 27]. "May God prosper you and all who struggle, by word or sword, to save the *integrity* of our *Country*."

From Michael L. Patterson

Greensburg Indiana July 29th 1861.

Hon Andrew Johnson
Sir

I hope you will not think me out of place by writing these lines to you. I left Greeneville East Tennessee on the 23d Inst. and have come to this place, and while stopping here I thought I would say a few words to you, concerning the condition of things in and about greeneville. Reuben Arnold[1] has been appointed Col, H. G. Robinson[2] appointed Major by Gov. Harris to get up a Regment at Greeneville and they are doing all that they can and when I left there they said that they had the number of manes [names] for one Company in Greene Co. Col. now Capt. Sam Powel had made up a company in Hawkins Co.[3] and brought them to Greeneville and camped just above the Depot on Saturday before I left. Arnold mustered his men some 23 in number—Stating that all of his men would not be in until Tuesday the day I started. I understand through Dr. S. P. Crawford[4] (who is now a Rebel) that Gov. Harris told him that he Harris had had Several letters written to him, that the Union men was burning, shooting and Killing the Rebels in E Tenn, and calling on him to send and station troops in our civil East Tenn country, and Harris Did send about two thousand to B[r]ush-Creek W. [Washington] Co. there was about 600 men at Cumberland Gap, about 300 at wheelers Gap, 200 Guarding the Loudun bridge—&c. &c. the Rebels are saying that the union men shall stop their Drilling, &c[.]

when I reached Nashville I learned that those troops at Bush Creek had been sent to Va. we are in a terrible state of Excitement. the union men are geting verry impatient waiting for arms. Some are for submitting to the vote of the state while others are standing firm and loyal to the Constition & laws. Jas P McDowel is the nominee for the County, & Jas Britton Jr.[5] for Floater— I think McDowel is a submissionist. and you Know the firmness of Mr. Britton— Now at the request of Gen Sam Milligan & your Son Robert, and my own desire, I would ask you to give me a letter immediately giving us all the satisfaction to [sic] you can, when the probability of troops and arms will reach East T and the moovement & doing about Washington. We are all in suspense, and are [waiting] verry anxiously to know what is going on and what doing &c— I will start back Home in the course of 5 days, and I want to hear from you before I go. It would not be safe for me to carry your letter from here to Tenn, and what ever you may pen I shall not attemp to carry it, only from memory[.] your letter will be distroyed before I leave hear—also, Gen Milligan & Robert both stated to me, to say to you when I got where I could write to you, that in their Judgments & opinions you had better not attempt to come Home until these deficulties were settled, and I concur with them. there is a terrable state of feeling now raging among the Rebels—and if they had any chance they would do some mischief to you and it would be impossible for the union men to give much aid unless they were armed— Robert also suggested to me to say to you that a change in the Post master at

Greeneville would be a good thing. I dont think Elbert[6] will do[.]
all persons are dissatisfied with him only the *Rebels*, and he stands
to day reguarded by the union men that he has Sworn to Suport the
Constn. of U. S. and has not Come up to his oath, he is charging
every person 5¢ postage[7] and has been for Some weeks[.] He Done
it before he had any commission from the Confederate Department
and at the proper time and place I would be glad to have him removed—and Some good Union man in his place. all our Union mail
matter stops either on the line or in the post office's and we Know
not where but so it is we get none any more. All the news that we
get is Rebel news. and as you Know they can & do out *lie* the Devil
himself. for my part, I am going home, and try to wind up my buisness as well as I can and then I am going where I can live under the
Stars & Strips[8] provided they Can not be raised again in E Tenn, for
to live under the Rebel flag—I will not, to take an oath to support
the Southern Confederacy constition, I will not— the Constition of
the United States must be preserved, and the laws complied with—
& obeyed—and if this is not done in the south, then I will go north
of Masons & Dickson line—and pitch my camp—

Gov. If you have time to write please write immediately—so I can
get your letter before I leave here, then if you can write in time Back
your letter to Greensburg Decator Co. Indiana.

Gov. my office is not worth any thing to me now—[9] the Courts
are about suspended, and I would Say to you, that if there is vacancies in any clerk's office at Washington, and you can get a Situation
for me I would be under many obligations to you— I am thrown out
of buisness or nearly So, and I must do something with my pen—to
live— I shall expect aword from you[.]

                              Yours Respectfully—   M. L. Patterson

ALS, DLC-JP.

1. Reuben Arnold became a lieutenant colonel of the 29th Tenn. Inf.
CSA, when it was organized in September, 1861. *Tennesseans in the Civil
War*, I, 235; see also *Johnson Papers*, I, 534n.
2. H. G. Robertson was formerly editor of the Greeneville *Democrat. Ibid.*,
III, 197n.
3. Samuel Powel raised Company K, composed of men from Hawkins
County, during July and August. This unit and others assembled at Henderson's Mills in Greene County were organized into the 29th Tenn. Inf.,
CSA. Powel, who became a colonel, was reelected in May, 1862, resigning in
November of that year. *Tennesseans in the Civil War*, I, 235–36; see also
Johnson Papers, I, 512n.
4. Dr. Sean P. Crawford. *Ibid.*, III, 304n.
5. James Britton, Jr., was a Greeneville lawyer. *Ibid.*, I, 497n.
6. Elbert Biggs had been postmaster since 1856. *Ibid.*, II, 391n.
7. Confederate postal regulations in effect since June 1 required all postmasters to reject U. S. postage and collect five cents for all letters moving 500
miles or less within the Confederacy and ten cents on those transported more
than 500 miles. Knoxville *Whig*, May 25, 1861.

8. Patterson returned home and the following January made his way North through rebel lines; failing to obtain a civilian post, he served as colonel of the 4th Tenn. Inf., USA. After the death of Johnson's son-in-law, Daniel Stover, Patterson commanded the regiment. See Michael L. Patterson to Johnson, January 31, 1862, Johnson Papers, LC; *Tenn. Adj. Gen. Report* (1866), 98–99.

9. Patterson was clerk of the circuit court at Greeneville. See *Johnson Papers*, III, 388n.

From Daniel S. Heffron[1]

Utica, N. Y. July 31, 1861.

Hon. A. Johnson:

Dr. Sir:

I write to you in behalf of the "Utica Mechanics Association", a Literary Association of this City, that provides an annual course of Lectures before its members and our citizens generally. We wish to know if we can secure your services, Hon. Senator, for a Lecture either on Nov. 20th or 27th or some Wednesday evening in December or January, 1862.

Choose your own subject, & either write your lecture, or give us a talk, as you would talk to your own loved citizens of Tennessee. We want to hear the man that the people would delight to honor.

Other cities on the line of the Central Rail Road would like your presence also for an evening lecture of an hour more or less.

If you will promise to come, and desire it, I will secure you appointments for the week: say Monday evening in Buffalo, Tuesday in Rochester, Wednesday evening in Utica, Thursday in Syracuse, going back 2 hours ride only, Friday in Albany and Saturday in Newburgh—New York.

As to compensation, please make it as reasonable as engagements will permit. We usually pay about $50 per night,[2] while in Buffalo, Rochester, Albany & New-York they afford to pay more. But state your own terms.[3]

Yours truly,   D. S. Heffron
Chairman of Lect. Com.

P. S. I refer you to Hon. Roscoe Conkling,[4] of our District, in Congress.

ALS, DLC-JP.

1. Daniel S. Heffron (b. c1818) was superintendent of common schools and chairman of the board of the Utica Mechanics' Association. 1860 Census, N. Y., Oneida, Utica, 3rd Ward, 22; *Utica City Directory* (1860–61), 20, 98.

2. Remuneration for lectures in the years between 1840 and 1860 ranged from a few dollars to around sixty-five dollars. Starr King, the prominent Unitarian divine, when questioned about his fees, remarked that he lectured

for "Fame—Fifty and My Expenses." Waldo W. Braden, "The Lecture Movement: 1840–1860," *Quarterly Journal of Speech*, XXXIV (1948), 209–10;
Carl Bode, *The American Lyceum* (New York, 1956), 201.

3. Johnson did not go, nor was he able to accept other such invitations.
See Letter to Benjamin A. G. Fuller, August 27, 1861.

4. Roscoe Conkling (1829–1888), lawyer and politician, had been briefly
mayor of Utica (1858) before serving as a Republican in the House (1859–
63, 1865–67) and the Senate (1867–81). A Radical Republican, he advocated a stern Reconstruction policy. *DAB*, IV, 346–47; *BDAC*, 728; David
M. Jordan, *Roscoe Conkling of New York* (Ithaca, 1971), 16–20.

From John T. S. Nicholson

July 31, 1861, Clarksville, Tenn.; ALS, DLC-JP.

Foreman on the Clarksville *Jeffersonian* and "the only Union man in
this city" is willing "to do anything to save my country" but particularly
wants a clerkship in Washington. "It is not safe for me to be here any
longer, I fear, and if this note is seen . . . I will be dealt with in a manner, which would end my days." Urges great caution in use of the mails:
"We can get no letters by mail now, and the post-office department of
the Rebel Government have authorized the Postmaster to examine all
letters going East or West, or North." If Johnson's reply should "fall
in the hands of the Rebels . . . I am done for."

From William H. Seward

[cJuly 31, 1861?], Washington, D. C.; LS, DLC-JP.

Cryptic note from secretary of state requesting Johnson to "have the
goodness to come and see me at your earliest convenience—if possible,
this evening at my house."

To Amos A. Lawrence, Boston, Mass.

Washington City, July 31st 1861.

(Private)
Amos A. Lawrence Esq
Dear Sir,

I have to acknowledge the receipt of your letter of the 26th inst,
enclosing a communication from a gentleman (whose name you do
not give) in Louisville in regard to East Tennessee affairs.[1]

Referring to your generous and patriotic offers of aid for the
Union cause in my State as expressed in the correspondence resulting from the attempted fraud upon you by the forgery of my name,
I will state that I have succeeded in providing, through the Government, means for the defense of East Tennessee,[2] but there still re-

mains a cause in which your liberality can be properly and most advantagously exercised.

The Union papers of that section of the State—East Tennessee— are now reduced to two or three. Foremost among them is the Knoxville Whig, edited by the Rev. Wm. G. Brownlow.

Brownlow is a patriot, ardently devoted to the Union cause and the influence of his paper is very great.

His press must be sustained, but his circumstances will not admit of his bearing the entire burden.

His paper has been suppressed by secession Post Masters, his subscription lists fail him, he is sustaining pecuniary losses with every issue of his paper, everything is done by secessionists to intimidate him;[3] but, conscious of the right, he stands forth the fearless advocate of the Government of our fathers.

I have said thus much, Sir, in behalf of that paper, entirely without the knowledge of the distinguished editor, and without any idea of appealing for pecuniary aid for him personally.

His paper boldly advocates the cause of our people, and it ought to be sustained.

Rather let us establish more such papers than that these should go down for the want of aid.

Every cent that may be placed in my hands or in the hands of others for that purpose shall be faithfully applied and accounted for.

I should not even have written this letter had I not been taxed individually to the utmost of my ability.

Please favor me with a prompt reply.

Very Respectfully, Your Obt. Sert.
Andrew Johnson.

Copy, DNA–RG59, Misc. Lets. and Newspapers Relating to the Civil War, 1861–1865, Box 1, Parker H. French; also in "Documents," *Tennessee Historical Magazine*, Ser. 2, II (1932), 293.

1. See Letter from Amos A. Lawrence, July 26, 1861; the "gentleman in Louisville" has not been identified.

2. A reference to the weapons under the control of Gen. William Nelson, to be distributed in Kentucky and Tennessee. See Letters from James P. T. Carter, July 15, Nelson, July 16, and George M. Adams, July 23, 1861.

3. Brownlow's financial woes became apparent in July when, in a column headed "We Must Have Money!," he urged subscribers and advertisers to pay up their accounts. Later in the month, though noting that his subscriber list was still large, the editor pleaded for advanced subscription payments because of reduced advertising—a penalty inflicted by the blockade—and announced a reduction in the size of the paper. As for complaints that subscribers were not receiving their papers, the Parson charged "foul play . . . at the hands of unprincipled men, handling them as route agents, and Post-Masters." Knoxville *Whig*, July 5, 27, September 3, 1861.

To Carlyle Murray, Boston, Mass.

Washington D. C. July 31st. 1861

(Private:)
Carlyle Murray Esq
Dear Sir,

Your letter of the 12th ins't, expressing a desire to aid in the Union cause in East Tennessee, has been received.

I thank you, Sir, for your generous offer of assistance to that people, and, in reply to your request that I should advise you as to how you can best serve them, I have to state that I have succeeded in providing, through the Government, means for the defense of East Tennessee, but there still remains a cause in which your liberality can be properly and advantageously exercised.

The Union press of that section of the state is now reduced to two or three. Foremost among them is the Knoxville Whig edited by the Rev Wm. G. Brownlow.

Brownlow is a patriot, ardently devoted to the cause of the Union, and the influence of his paper is very great. His press must be sustained, but his circumstances will not admit of his bearing the entire burden.

He is sustaining losses with every issue of his paper, it has been suppressed by secession Post Masters, his subscription lists fail him, every thing is done to intimidate him; but, conscious of the right, he stands forth the fearless advocate of the Government of our fathers.

I have said this much, Sir, in behalf of that paper, entirely without the knowledge of the distinguished editor, and without any idea of appealing for pecuniary aid for him personally.

His paper boldly advocates the cause of our people, it is doing noble service and ought to be sustained.

Every cent that may be placed in my hands or in the hands of others for that purpose shall be faithfully applied and accounted for.

I should not even have written this letter (except simply an acknowledgement of your kind favor of the 12th ins't) had I not been taxed individually to the utmost of my ability.

Please favor me with a prompt reply, if you determine to do so.

Very Respectfully Your Obt. Sert.
Andrew Johnson

L, DNA-RG59, Misc. Lets. and Newspapers Relating to the Civil War, 1861–1865, Box 1, Parker H. French.

From John G. Buxman

August 1, 1861, New York, N. Y.; ALS, DLC-JP.

A northerner, engaged for the past six years in manufacturing and mining in White and Van Buren counties, has been obliged to flee Middle Tennessee to avoid being forced to use on behalf of the state Confederate government his "considerable knowledge . . . regarding the manufacture of Saltpetre (more than any other man in the State). . . . Our disunionists stated that I would in this capacity be of more service to their cause, than a Legion of soldiers." Seeks government position.

From Middleton Goldsmith[1]

Washington Aug 1st 1861.

To Senator Johnson.

Sir.

I thought that perhaps it might be well to remind you of the substance of some remarks of mine in reference to the Medical Corps of the volunteers to [be] raised and organized in Kentucky and Tennessee[.]

The suggestion was to this effect

1st That the applicants for medical appointments should be examined by a board of surgeons to be stationed at Louisville.

2d That those appointed by the War department after this examination, should be ordered to Louisville to receive instruction in the details of Camp and Hospital practice. I need not remind you of the fact those who would probably be appointed from your State and ours however well they might be qualified for the discharge of the ordinary duties of their profession, have no acquaintance with the details of camp and Hospital service so far as such service differs from the Common practice of medicine and surgery. I refer more particularly to the method of keeping the necessary records accounts —Making returns and all the matters relative to the hygiene of Camps and Hospitals as well as those modifications of the general rules of practice which experience has shown must obtain in field and Hospital practice[.]

My impression is that a short course in instruction say for two weeks would be sufficient for the purpose. A somewhat extended observation of the medical service among volunteers has forced the above convictions upon me. If upon Consideration of the subject, it seems to you of importance enough to give it your attention I hope when you have a fit occasion you will bring the matter to the notice of the proper department.

For myself I have only to say only this that I am the Surgeon in attendance upon the Louisville Marine Hospital[2] in which the service is almost identical in diseases and practice with that of Military Hospitals, and that I would cheerfully render the service of teaching so far as that instution under my care affords the opportunity and continue the instruction at Camp Joe Holt just opposite Louisville if the department should think well of the project and would give me the opportunity[.]

Senator Foote[3] of Vt. could inform if you desired it whether my professional status is such as to give weight to my opinions and assure proficiency in such duties. I would gladly if thought best to appoint some other instructor give him all the aid I can—by giving him the use of my wards for the purpose—

Let me add that I desire no compensation for the service which I propose.

Very respectfully   M. Goldsmith
Professor of Surgery in the Kentucky School of Medicine—
Professor of Clinical surgery in the Louisville Marine Hospital

P. S. I leave for Louisville in the morning, so find it impossible to get an audience from the Secretary of War.

ALS, DLC-JP2.

1. Middleton Goldsmith (1818–1887), Maryland-born physician, studied medicine and served as a ship's surgeon before becoming interested in medical research. With his father, also a surgeon, he specialized in the removal of gallstones without operating. A founder of the New York Pathological Society for medical research, he taught at Castleton (Vt.) Medical School (1844–56) and served as dean of the medical faculty of the Kentucky School of Medicine in Louisville. Enlisting in the Union army as brigade surgeon, he was assigned to Buell's corps and later served as medical director of the army hospital at Jeffersonville, Indiana. He continued his interest in medical research, working briefly in Louisville before returning to Vermont in 1866. *NCAB*, XXIII, 344.

2. The Louisville Hospital Company, incorporated in 1817, first opened on Chestnut Street in 1823. Affiliated in 1827 with the local medical school, the Louisville Hospital became known as the Marine Hospital because of the frequent admission of transient rivermen. There was also a U. S. Marine Hospital in Louisville, built in the 1840's and located on High Street. *Tanner's Louisville Directory* (1859–60), 320; Emmet F. Horine, "A History of the Louisville Medical Institute," *Filson Quarterly*, VII (1933), 142; Evelyn C. Adams, "Dr. Richard Ferguson (1769–1853)," XXXVI (1962), 178; Eugene H. Conner and Samuel W. Thomas, "John Croghan (1790–1849)," XL (1966), 227n.

3. For Solomon Foot, see *Johnson Papers*, III, 167n.

From Buffalo Young Men's Christian Union Society

August 2, 1861, Buffalo, N. Y.; ALS, DLC-JP.

William C. Bryant, lecture chairman and attorney, learning of Johnson's proposed appearance in Rochester, observes that Buffalo would also be honored by a visit from "the statesman and orator whose patriotic labors and sacrifices have established for him so lasting a claim to the gratitude and affection of his country."

From Samuel P. Carter[1]

Barbourville, Ky. Aug. 2d, 1861.

Hon Andrew Johnson
U. S. Senator,
Dr Sir

My brother James will give you all the Tenn. news & explain to you the reason why I have not proceeded at once to E. T. At the request of Mr. Adams[2] I have commenced drilling Ky Volunteers assembled at this place— Many E. Tennesseeans are [due her]e in a few days—& it shall be my special business to look out for them. If I had authority to muster them into service here & could place arms in their hands, at once, they might be organized & be made in a very short time efficient. I would suggest the propriety of urging the Govt. to send some regulars—the more the better, to accompany the expedition & the vital importance of having Genl. Anderson or some other regular army officer to take charge of the military movement— Some 200 additional rebel troops were passed yesterday, on thier way to Cumberland Gap—making the force there from 800 to 1000. The people here are very impatient for action—& are anxious to be mustered into the U. S. Service— Much enthusiasm— & determination to have the Gap prevails—

I am respectfully, Yr. Obt. Servt   S. P. Carter

ALS, DLC-JP.

1. Samuel Powhatan Carter (1819–1891) of Elizabethton, the only American officer to serve both as a rear admiral and a major general, was a graduate of the naval academy (1846), an instructor (1850–53), and assistant to the executive officer at the academy (1857–60). Stationed in Brazil when the war commenced, he declared his unionism, and his services were sought by Johnson and other East Tennesseans. Early in July he was detailed by the navy to the war department for special duty in East Tennessee to raise and drill volunteers, and his efforts produced the first Union troops in the state. In May, 1862, he became a brigadier general, but his naval promotions continued, and at the time of his retirement he was a rear admiral. DAB, III, 543–44; Boatner, Civil War Dictionary, 130.

2. Congressman Greene Adams.

From Amos A. Lawrence

(near) Boston. Aug. 2. 61

Dear Sir
    Yours of the 31st is recd.
    Enclosed please find a check for $100 payab. to yr order, wh. please to send to Mr Brownlow.
    As soon as I have any liesure I will attempt to collect some money for him among my friends: tho. this is not so easy to do as it was a few weeks ago. The loss by rebel repudiation of debts falls heavily on us.[1]

Resp'y & truly Yrs
Amos A Lawrence

Hon. Andrew Johnson
U S Sen.

ALS, DLC-JP.
    1. On May 21 Jefferson Davis had signed a bill prohibiting payments to northern creditors. Although at least half this debt—which some contemporary estimates placed as high as $300,000,000—was owed to New Yorkers, other seaboard merchants, such as Lawrence, were hard hit by the policy. Moore, *Rebellion Record*, I, Doc., 265; Foner, *Business & Slavery*, 218, 302; Fite, *Social and Industrial Conditions in the North*, 107–8.

From A. J. Mershon[1]

Rogersville Madison Coty Ky
August 2nd 1860 [1861]

Mr. Andw. Johnson
    Sir I hope that the cause will be a sufficient excuse for a stranger writing to you with out a formidable introduction.
    I have Just returned from Cumberland Gap. there was a report here that there was Confederate troops there but the *Traitors* denied it. and the friends here requested me to go and examine and learn the truth of the matter which I did and found about 1800 rebel troops stationed there[.] they are located on the Virginia road[.] there tents are situated on both sides of the Virginia road commencing right in the Gap and extending a long around the mountain barely leaving room for a waggon to pass between the Tents. They have six pieces of Cannon all of which are located in Ky 4 situated on the right & 2 on the left of the road below those building in the Gap. all of them with their mouths Pointing down into Ky. They say their only object is to capture you on your return home— They

have all the Gaps Guarded or stoped up by roling Stones & falling trees in them. David Cockerel[2] is now in Ky with many others from E Tennessee numbering some 50 or 60 in all who have had to flee their Country to save their lives many of them leaving their families behind them to the mercy of the traiterous retches and their crops half harvested, &c &c[.]

Those men have awaken a sympathy in the mountains of Ky and they are turning out in great numbers and there are many in this county around here who seem anxious to go. If the govern will endow me with the Power to get up a Company I would gladly assist in repelling those traitors at least from Ky & E Tennessee. I served in the Mexi War in the 16th U. S. Infantry, Col Tibbat[ts] & Capt T. T. Garrard's[3] Company E.   for reference see our Congressman Honl. G. W. Dunlap who Knows me[.] please get me the authority to raise a Company. I can furnish the Department with satisfactory recommendations as to my military Qualifications. please attend to this for me at the earliest convenience and forward to Richmond Ky and oblige one who is willing and even anxious to relieve an oppressed people.

Respectfully Your obt servt
A. J. Mershon

My respects to Hol G. W. Dunlap.

ALS, DLC-JP.

1. A. J. Mershon succeeded George W. Ballew as representative from Madison County in the Kentucky state legislature (1865–67). Collins, *Kentucky*, II, 494.

2. David C. Cottrell.

3. Col. John W. Tibbatts and Capt. T. T. Garrard. William H. Powell, comp., *List of Officers of the Army of the United States from 1779 to 1900* (Detroit, 1967 [1900]), 630, 325; Smith, *War with Mexico*, II, 417.

From John W. Thomson

August 2, 1861, Hillsboro, Ohio; ALS, DLC-JP.

Unionist refugee from Giles County, "completely overrun by secessionists," inquires whether "anything can be accomplished by union men returning to East Tennessee and aiding their brethren there in holding on to the union."

From Samuel P. Carter

barboursville Ky. Aug. 3d 1861

Hon. Andrew Johnson,
U. S. Senator,
Dear Sir,

Capt. Cooper,[1] of Campbell Co., I think, arrived this afternoon forced to fly from his home. He reports that about 150 Tennesseans will be at Boston, in this state, to night, & that in a day or two—about as many more will be in Ky. for arms. I regret not a little that there are, as yet, no arms to give them, or even authority to muster them into the U. S. Service. I shall do what I can to provide for them. Capt. Cooper, I understand, commands the company which is at Boston tonight. He remained at home until the election. He reports that the rebels, as far as he could hear, had lost ground at the polls —In three precincts, no vote had been given with, perhaps, a single exception, for the so-called, confederate Constitution—[2] He represents that a reign of terror prevails in E. Tenn, & bad at [as] things now are, they will be much worse in a few days. O that the means for resistance were here. I would again urge the necessity of the Governments sending troops to accompany the expedition—10,000 would not be too many—independent of those that can be raised in Ky. And *let there be sent a competent army officer* as a leader[3]— together with efficient regular officers to conduct the operation[.] Success is most important, to the general Govt. as well as to E. Tenn. & Ky. It will not do to risque a defeat—unless you would have E. Tenn. lost. Such will not be the case if the Govt. will send competent officers & plenty of men— an incompetent, inexperienced leader will only result in disaster. I should think that troops might be sent from Ohio & Indiana. The mere appearance of these would encourage Kentuckians & induce many more to tender their services to the Govt. than are now likely to do so— I need not say that whatever is to be done, should be done quickly.[4]

You can tell James[5] that, I heard through a couple of Tenns. who came in on foot to day—the rebels are on the look out for him & breathe the direst threats against him. The men said it would not do for him to return to Tenn. at present.

I have been engaged in drilling Ky. volunteers, today—& shall continue to employ myself in that way until I can get Tennesseans together, when I hope to devote myself to their improvement.

Do not forget the additional troops—& above all things the *mili-*

tary Commander, for I do not think the volunteers, on this side [of] the mountain, at all events, will have confidence in any other.

In haste— Yours Respectfully

S. P. Carter[6]

There should, of course, be a good Engineer officer, as well as some of artillery.

ALS, DLC-JP.

1. Joseph A. Cooper (1823–1910), Kentucky-born farmer of Cove Creek, Tennessee, had served in the infantry in the Mexican War. A Whig opposed to secession, he was an influential delegate to the Knoxville convention before enlisting as captain, 1st Tenn. Inf., at Whitesburg, Kentucky, in August, 1861. Named a brigadier general in July, 1864, he failed in a bid for the U. S. Senate (1868), became collector of internal revenue, Knoxville district (1869–79), and subsequently moved to Stafford County, Kansas, where he farmed for the rest of his life. *DAB*, IV, 407; Temple, *Notable Men*, 101–8.

2. Whatever the situation in specific precincts, a comparison of the total East Tennessee vote on the Confederate Constitution (August 1) with the June 8 poll on separation from the Union does not reveal a significant disparity of sentiment, the earlier response showing 32,923–14,780 against separation, and the latter 27,738–15,494 opposed to the Constitution. These figures suggest that "the rebels" had not "lost ground at the polls." Campbell, *Tenn. Attitudes*, 292; White, *Messages*, V, 332.

3. This statement should probably be read as a reflection on Bull Nelson, and perhaps interpreted as a puff for the writer's brother, James P. T. Carter.

4. A reference to the murder of Duncan in *Macbeth*, Act. I, sc. 7.

5. James P. T. Carter.

6. The following day Carter wrote Johnson that he would leave on August 5 for Williamsburg to rendezvous with Captain Cooper's company of Tennesseans "now there." Carter to Johnson, August 4, 1861, Johnson Papers, LC.

From Samuel J. Pooley

Liberty Corner Somerset County

New Jersey Aug the 3d 1861

To/Hon Andrew Johnson

Washington

My dear sir,

How great the contrast, between Critenden & Breckinridge.[1] The former brings experience & wisdom [to] gether & places their leaves around his honored head,[2] to the Union of his & our Fathers while the latter leans to & favors its opponents & destroyer. Now how can Mr. B win that place back in my esteem, which he formerly held. Indeed it is hardly a question with me, who is the worse, Davis or Breckinridge. If Mr B had not been a stump Candidate for the Presidency Douglas would have been elected & Davis & his Co-Traitors would have been baffled in their purpose to destroy the Union. But the Union is not destroyed & God will not let it be destroyed[.] it will live, live long after its enemies shall have descended into their dishonored graves, & if the Expression is not out of place, I hope that the Devil will get them[.]

Yours Very Respectfully
Samuel James Pooley

ALS, DLC-JP.

1. The former vice president was by now clearly on his way to the Confederate fold. In antiwar remarks in the Senate on July 16 and August 1, he had indicated his southernism and his intention to resign should Kentucky sustain the Federal government's course against the seceding states. Returning to Kentucky, he was speaking to followers at Mays Lick when he was warned to flee; he ultimately made his way to Confederate lines. The state legislature requested his resignation on October 2 and the Senate expelled him December 2. *Cong. Globe,* 37 Cong., 1 Sess., 137–43, 376–80; 2 Sess., 9–10; Stillwell, *Breckinridge,* 99–104.

2. In the Pythian games of the ancient Greeks, leaves of laurel were used to crown victors; hence, a crown of honor. *Webster's Third International.*

From William S. Doak[1]

London Ky. Augt 5th— 61.

Hon. A. Johnson.
Dear Sir.

The arms for East Ten. are not making much progress in this way, & affairs, there, are becoming desperate, many men have been forced to flee into Ky. some of them from Green County. By reports from these men & a letter from S. S. Doak[2] of Camp Creek. dated 17th July, I learn that East Ten. was being filled with Southern troops, & the union men were getting afraid to speak or write their sentiments.

20.000 Sou. troops are reported in E. Ten. but I think many of them have gone on into Virginia. There are about 1000 at Cumberland Gap, & a few more companies scattered along at different points of the mountain down to Big Creek Gap. I suppose they could concentrate 10. or 12.000 men at Cum. Gap in a few days.

Our people (of Ky.) are beating up recruits for the U. S. service, a great many are anxious for the fight, but one thing is in the way, we don't know who is to be the commander[.] We have no one here that we can trust. We have plenty of men true & brave enough, but they have no experience. Lieut. Nelson, now at Cin. I suppose wants to be the Gen. for this expedition but Kentuckians don't want him & our people will not fight under him.[3] The man we want is Gen. Robert Anderson, & I write now cheifly for the purpose of asking your assistance, in securing the appointment to him. Give us Anderson & our people will fight & fight hard & with the full faith that they never will be whipped. Gen. Scott himself could not secure more devoted soldiers, in the mountains of Ky. than Robert Anderson.[4]

In the present stage of the game I don't think those arms ought to pass into East Ten. with less than 20.000. men.

Why can't the Government be still awhile in Virginia; defend the fortifications along the Potomac; let McClellan & Anderson secure the East Ten. & Virginia Railroad, & Fremont take a trip down the Mississippi, seize their contraband cotton & open a southern port & let the British have a little to stop their grumbling.

But whatever may be done, give us Gen. Robert Anderson, & Deo volente East Ten shall be free again.

Yours truly   W. S. Doak
London Ky.

Hon. A. Johnson.

ALS, DLC-JP.

1. William S. Doak (1829–1882), son of President Samuel W. Doak of Tusculum College, was born at Tusculum and graduated from the college in 1815. Licensed by the Cincinnati Presbytery two years later, he served as a minister and a practicing physician in Kentucky and Tennessee before becoming professor of philosophy and political science and president of Tusculum (1865–82); at his death he was also state superintendent of public instruction (1881–82). Tusculum College, *Alumni Catalogue 1794–1929* (Cincinnati, 1929), 14; Harry E. Mitchell, *The Mitchell-Doak Group* (n.p., 1966), 212.

2. Samuel Snapp Doak (1832–1873), William's nephew and a Greene County native, graduated from Tusculum (1852), taught there and at Hiwassee College, reorganized and reopened Tusculum in the fall of 1865, and served both as vice president and professor of mathematics (1866–73). *Ibid.*, 215; Tusculum College, *Alumni Catalogue*, 37; Donald Mitchell, Spencertown, N. Y., to Andrew Johnson Project, February 6, 1974.

3. Nelson, who had a quick temper and dictatorial manner, became increasingly unpopular among some Tennesseans. So disliked was the "Bull" that "the day he gets placed among Tennessee troops in battle," wrote one East Tennessean from Camp Calvert in November, "will be a dark day for him." Cincinnati *Commercial*, November 16, 1861; *Battles and Leaders*, I, 375.

4. Anderson, the "hero" of Ft. Sumter, was a solid, amiable man whose reputation was currently high among moderate unionists of the border states. That he should be compared with the octogenarian Scott affords a clue to the writer's concept of vigorous leadership. W. A. Swanberg, *First Blood: The Story of Fort Sumter* (New York, 1957), 34, 37.

From John Orf

Newyork August 5, 1861.

Hon Andw. Johnson!
My Dear Sir!

Your letter of date July 22. has been recieved, accept my thanks for the Hon: of answering it. it must have been de laite at our Post

Office, but no account of it[.] I reley axspected no answer, and ther-
for (paticular on account of the onsuccessfull Result of our Couse
at Bull's Rune—July 21.—) I send a letter to Prest Lincoln—dated
this day a week.[1] I allso send a other letter to him with the same
Maile of yours requesting him to accept my proposed Plane and in-
diufituly [individual?] Service for the Time of War; and request me
to come to Washington at onced for anable me to make a full explanation in regard do it, as ther is no time to be lost, to be ready at
the proper time; said Plaine in detail is about the following! namly:
—as I prvsely [previously] have sujjested to yu—To Authorise me
to Organise a Corp's under the Name "*Union Defence Leg[ion]*"
wich I propose to organise by establishing Recruting Offices at New
york Philadelphia, Boston Pittsburg and eather Cincinnati or Dayton, Oh wich in cours of two Mth. will be organised, trilled; and
ready for Service. in that time I am fully convinced that said "*Legion*" according to the mode I persoe will reach the Number of from
20 to 25,000 or more if required, consisting of Infantre so trilled
that they my be used to do Eavery Service—in the Battell field. Rifle
men well trilled in Scirmisse and Bayonett, also in the Field Manov-
ering and Artillery trilled in every kind of Artillery operation[.]
Sabeures [sappers] to erect with the assistance of the Legion fortifications ware ever it my be desirable.
Now Sir sence you have Hon: me with a Kindly answer and as we
both advocate one and the same princable in political affairs, I have
no hesitation to entrust you with the Plan of how to opperate namley:
I [pro]pose to the Prest, as the only true and Effective mesure, to
goe and acoopey [occupy] Tennessee and North Carline erect forti-
fication at the Northern Line of this two states as well as thir Southern Line ware ever a Rail Road croses the Line, betwen Memppis
Ten. and the Atlantic Ocean. of course the Union men of this two
States (Who as I see my [by?] a act of Congress shall be funished
with Arms and Amution) I could join in with said Legion, and if I
should be entrusted with the Commend of said Legion. (to wich I
know in advance would be found competent during the Organisation
of said Legion) you my feel assured That sessesionism will [be]
found no wares by the first of May next. Now Sir I find in your letter
the favorable offer, that you would Serve me in any application. I
then mereley ask you, to consolt with the Presitent, in reference of
my Plaine of Opperation as in reference Who [how?] the military
especily the Field and Subaltern Officer should be trilled to make
our next Engagement with the Rebbeles more honorable &cc, and
besuech the Prest to request me to come to Washington for a personal Explanation. That would be about all I have a wright to ask
from you. of course I have not the means at present, having used

up every Cent in the Organisation of my Paper, and being Sick for som 5 or 6 Month's. however if I receive a letter from the Prest. to come, I have friends a know [enough] who will furnish me with the amount to pay my travelling Exspence[.]

Main vile I remaine very Respectfully

your most Obt. Humbl Service

John: Orf

N. B.

Allow me jet to Remark, that my desire is non ambition, but only a Patriotic feeling to maintain the only Asyle [asylum] to every one for freedom Seeking Indiufidual and bewared [sic] for destruction, and If our present Prest. Sec of Ware and Comander in Chief, are endowed with a simler feeling of our Patriotic Father Washington The [sic] will ondoubtly treed [treat] me as he hase donne to fourners, Who just arrived her, and I reside mor then 21 year in this Contry, and posess equale as much Military tallent as any one.

J. O.

ALS, DLC-JP.

    1. Not found.

From Edmund W. Crittenden[1]

Pittsburgh August 6, 1861

Hon. Andrew Johnson
Washington, D. C.

Dear Sir,—I have just read an abstract of your recent speech in the Senate[2] and— approving as I do most heartily the sentiments therein expressed, will feel exceedingly obliged by your sending me half a dozen or more copies of it for distribution among my friends when it is printed as I presume it will be at an early day. And if the assurance of the hearty sympathy as well as the highest admiration of your patriotic course in the present crisis in our National affairs, will encourage you to persevere in the Herculean work that is before you, then be assured that the writer cherishes these sentiments with his whole soul. But sympathy and admiration do little good without corresponding action. I would fain render you any assistance that I can personally. I am a Kentuckian, settled here temporarily on account of my business connections & duties. I have spent much of my time traveling through Ky. since these troubles commenced. My business partner in Louisville[3] has recently returned from the Eastern part of the state where he has spent some six weeks organizing *Union lodges*[4]—an association with which I presume you are familiar. He writes me that all the hardy mountaineers want, is arms & ammunition and they will turn out 10,000 or 20 000 strong and *"see Johnson through."* This is their usual expression[.] In our county of about 1300 voters—some of whom, of course are secessionists, there were 400 volunteers enrolled for this service in two days. This is in accordance with my own observation when I passed through a portion of the same region in April last. In view of what I *suppose* you will need on your return to Tennessee, I will venture to recommend to you to provide for the prompt delivery of at least 20000 stand of arms at such point as you may direct before you leave Washington. Then as you return, stop at Louisville, Covington, Frankfort, Lexington and as many other places as you can and *make your appeal directly to the* PEOPLE to volunteer for the restoration of constitutional law & order in Tennessee. Gen. Rousseau told me he would go with his brigade that he is now raising if so ordered— for he is subject to Government orders—and you will find strong & warm friends in all the above-named places. And allow me to add, with all due respect to the *great men* of Ky. that the *people* are far ahead of the *politicians* in their loyalty and readiness to *act* in the premises. In fact it has been the potential voice of the *people* that has kept Ky. in the Union in spite of her leading politicians. The whole mountain region of Ky. Virginia East Tennessee, N. Carolina and North Alabama, I am satisfied are as true to the Union today as any Northern state. Should you be chiefly instrumental in developing these Union elements, and by restoring your own state lead the other states by her example to take the same course, following successively the examples of W. Virginia & Missouri, yours will be a most enviable position. The *people* will not overlook such services; *history* will record the story in glowing pages; but what will be still better you will have the consciousness of having devoted yourself to your country's service in the time of her greatest trial and won a victory for which all the honours a nation can heap upon you will be light compared with what you will feel in your own bosom—the approving smile of Heaven. GOD SPEED THE WORK!

If you should think it better to pursue a more *private* course in Ky. than the one suggested, send your card to *N. B. Gantt*—firm of Crittenden & Gantt, 3rd street near Main, in Louisville and he will put you in communication with the Union Lodges there and elsewhere thoughout the state.

As to the transportation of arms, I think they can safely be shipped at Covington and reach *Nicholasville* by Railroad. This takes them two thirds across the state, and although I would advise having strong guards and every precaution taken, I think the Union men now so far outnumber the Secessionists that they will hold the latter at bay and prevent any successful attempt at seizure. As to violation of *neutrality*, this game is played out by the Secessionists themselves, they having in numerous instances violated it. And now that the elections are all over, I am for fighting them the way & after the examples they have set.

If you pass through here and can stop over a train or two the people would be glad to give you a friendly greeting. If you can consistently gratify them in this you may do good to the cause and I shall be most happy to be the medium of communication, if you will write or telegraph me when you are coming.

Very Respectfully   E. W. Crittenden

ALS, Johnson-Bartlett Col.

1. Edmund W. Crittenden, coal dealer and resident of Louisville, Kentucky, resided at 7th between Walnut and Chestnut streets. *Tanner's Louisville Directory* (1859–60), 58.

2. Probably the Speech in Support of Presidential War Program, July 27.

3. N. Beall Gantt (b. *c*1830), a coal dealer and partner of Crittenden, resided at 7th between Grayson and Walnut streets. In 1860 he had $10,000 worth of personal property. *Ibid.*, 88; 1860 Census, Ky., Jefferson, Louisville, 6th Ward, 96.

4. Although the Union League ultimately became a militant organization formed by hard-core Republicans to bolster the Union party and discredit the Democratic, the first clubs were started in the border states during the secession crisis. Accustomed to a Masonic-type ritual, members developed signs and passwords, and were sworn to secrecy. The first such group was formed in Missouri in January, 1861, and spread to Kentucky, where one was organized in Louisville in May. Within six weeks it was said that in that city alone there were six thousand members of the secret society bound by oath to fidelity to the Union. Clement M. Silvestro, *Rally Round the Flag: The Union Leagues in the Civil War* ([Ann Arbor, 1966]), 4; *Battles and Leaders*, I, 375.

To Abraham Lincoln, Washington, D. C.

Washington City, Aug. 6th. 1861.

To His Excellency, Mr. Lincoln,
President,
Sir,

We have received entirely reliable information from East Tennessee up to Saturday the 27th. ult. on Friday, the 26th. of July, three Commissioners from the Confederate States,[1] called upon the Central Union Committi at Knoxville, Tenn. and endeavoured to prevail upon them to abandon the Government of the United States. This the Committee at once declined to do.

The commissioners then informed the Union Committee that the Government of the Confederate States would allow the loyal citizens of East Tennessee until Friday the 16th. inst for consideration, and that if they did not determine, by that day, to yield willing obedience to the new Government, they would be compelled to obey, and be *forced* to serve in the Southern army. Your Excellency will at once see that the condition of the people of East Tennessee is such as to require the most prompt and energetic action on the part of our Government—

In the midst of the general gloom which hangs over our people, we are happy in being able to give your Excellency every assurance that their loyalty is not diminished, but increased, as their dangers become more threatening— Although they are encompassed with enemies, our brave men are daily organizing, and are only waiting for you to place arms in their hands with which they may strike in defence of themselves & their Country—

We deem it our duty to inform the President that up to July 27th. eighty thousand (80.000) Southern troops had passed into Virginia over the East Tennessee and Virginia Rail Road—

Our object in making this communication, is not to be importunate, but to keep our Government informed of the true condition of our people, and of the intentions of our enemies.

Very Respy. &c.

Andrew Johnson

Wm. B. Carter[2]

LS, DLC-Lincoln Papers. In Carter's hand.

1. On July 20 Gen. Leonidas Polk wrote Col. Robertson Topp, Judge J. Caruthers, Dr. Jeptha Fowlkes, and Col. D. M. Leatherman ordering them to East Tennessee for the purpose of pursuading the people there to abandon their opposition and unite in support of the Confederacy. Knoxville *Whig*, August 24, 1861.

2. William Blount Carter (1820–1902), an East Tennessee unionist, son of Alfred M., brother of James P. T. and Samuel P., and nephew of Congressman William B. Carter (*Johnson Papers*, I, 218*n*), was a Presbyterian minister whose ill health forced his resignation from his Rogersville church. By 1861 he was a special agent of the post office department, receiving a yearly salary of $1,600, and was also farming and managing his father's Carter County estate. After the secession of Tennessee, he went north, traveling about Kentucky and Ohio giving Union speeches. Subsequently, in September, 1861, he submitted to Lincoln an elaborate bridge-burning scheme which called for the simultaneous destruction of all the major railroad bridges in East Tennessee. Although adopted, the plan was never fully implemented by the military and was only a partial success. Near the close of the war he became the leader of the conservative or opposition forces then clamoring for an armistice with view to a peace settlement. Octavia Z. Bond, *The Family Chronicle and Friendship Book* (Nashville, 1928), 535; Temple, *Notable Men*, 88–93; *U. S. Official Register* (1861), 448*; *OR*, Ser. 1, IV, 284, 317, 320, 359–60, 364–65.

To Simon Cameron, Washington, D. C.

August 7, 1861, Washington, D. C.; L, DNA-RG107, Appl., 1820–1861, Tenn. #4, Wm. P. Chambliss.

Johnson and Emerson Etheridge recommend that Capt. William P. Chambliss of Giles County, a former member of the legislature, be promoted to major, inasmuch as "Tennessee has received no appointments under the increase of the Army." [Appointed captain in April, 1861, Chambliss was not breveted major until May, 1862.]

From Samuel P. Carter

Barboursville Ky Aug 7th 1861.

Hon. Andrew Johnson
U. S Senator
Dear Sir,

I am extremely sorry to inform you that Hon. T. A. R. Nelson was taken by the rebels at Chadwells gap—about 12. miles East of Cumberland gap—on Sunday night—by a guard of Virginians it is said—[1] They arrived at Cumberland gap—early monday morning & Nelson—his son David—Willis, & others of the party, were seen by young Willis[2] of Hawkins Co. soon after their arrival. Young Willis has just arrived here— he talked with Nelson & knows him— They left the gap monday afternoon under a guard of 300 men— ostensibly for Knoxville—designing afterwards to carry him to Richmond Va. Nelson said he thought the rebels would hang him unless he should be rescued by E. Tennesseans. I do not believe the scoundrels will dare to carry their threats into execution, or if they do I hope every prominent Secessionist in E. Tenn. will be sacrificed— The people here are greatly excited & are most anxious to make a move— they are restrained with the greatest difficulty. There are between 200 & 300 E. Tennesseans here & at Williamsburg. I start to the latter place in an hour. Maynard left this yesterday afternoon for Washington.

Mr. Willis says he heard at Tazwell that the Union majority in E. Tenn. was 35000.[3] In many places they did not allow the secessionists to vote, while at others they showed no disposition to do so.— Do hurry in aid.

I must act without authority & muster the E. Tennesseans into service— If I only had arms for them we would not defer action at some point in the mountains. Now is the time to strike— It is most galling to be kept in idleness—

In haste, yours truly
S. P. Carter

ALS, DLC-JP2.

1. In August, 1861, defying Confederate sentiment in the state at large, the voters of the first district elected Nelson to the Federal Congress. Informed that a warrant for his arrest had been issued to take effect if his election bid was successful, he set out from Rogersville, traveling at night via Jonesville, Virginia, in an effort to reach Kentucky and thence to Washington. On the night of August 4, after crossing the Clinch River at Kyle's Ford, his party was captured while passing over Wallen Ridge into the Powell River valley of Virginia. Alexander, *T. A. R. Nelson*, 87–89.

2. Possibly Iredell [Indell?] Willis (b. *c*1841) or I. [T.?] W. D. Willis (b. *c*1835), a farmer. 1860 Census, Tenn., Hawkins, 2nd Dist., 112, 114.

3. On August 1 Tennesseans held a gubernatorial election and at the same time voted on the Confederate Constitution. Although the result demonstrated a preponderant Confederate sympathy statewide, returns in East Tennessee, as expected, ran counter to the trend, with East Tennesseans opposing ratification, 27,115–14,887. White, *Messages*, V, 332.

To Henry S. Lane[1] and Others, Indianapolis, Ind.

Washington D C. August 7. 1861.

Gentlemen:

We have received your letter of 5th., instant, inviting us to visit Indiana, at such time as may suit our convenience, and, while there, to regard ourselves as the guests of the State.[2] At any time we would have felt ourselves highly honored by such a manifestation of regard, but especially do we feel so, at this unhappy period in our country's history. Educated, as we have been, to consider ourselves *Citizens of the United States*, and, under the Constitution, "entitled to all privileges and immunities of Citizens in the several States," we cannot but appreciate in its fullest extent, this manifestation of your approval and regard— At a time when, in some parts of the country, loyalty to the Constitution is punished as a crime, it is encouraging to the friends of public liberty to find that, elsewhere—as in Indiana—none are regarded, as enemies, other than traitors in arms and those who give them "aid and comfort." We do not despair of the Republic: We look confidently to the period when the Constitution will be maintained and its authority obeyed on every rood of soil o'er which the ensign of our nationality has ever floated— The energies of our people may be strained; their resources may be taxed, and their patriotism and capacity for self-government again severely tried; but History will yet attest their power, to meet every emergency which the enemies of the Government may create.

Our immediate engagements, here, and our relations to our personal and political friends at home are such, that we cannot *now* name a day when we can visit your state, but we hope to be able to do so soon, and will hereafter advise you when.

We recognize among the names before us many which have been

long and eminently connected with the public service—and to each of you we offer, individually, assurances of our high personal regard.

We have the honor to be Your Obt. Servts.
Andrew Johnson.
Em: Etheridge

To Hon H. S. Lane,[3]

L, In-Indiana Div., John Brayton MS Col. In Etheridge's hand.

1. Henry S. Lane (1811–1881), Kentucky native, began law practice in Indiana in 1834, served in the state senate (1837) and house (1838–39), and as a Whig congressman (1840–43). After service in the Mexican War, he turned to banking and was permanent chairman of the 1856 Republican convention. Inaugurated Indiana governor January 14, 1861, he resigned four or five days later to become senator (1861–67). *BDAC*, 1189.

2. Assured that he would be accorded a "reception worthy of your position and distinguished services," Johnson had been invited to remain as "the guest of the State" so long as it remained hazardous for him to return home. Indianapolis Citizens to Johnson, August 5, 1861, John Brayton Collection, Indiana State Library, Indianapolis.

3. Other addressees were William M. Dunn, Albert G. Porter, James A. Cravens, John Law, John P. C. Shanks, George W. Julian, William Mitchell, Albert S. White, Schuyler Colfax, Richard W. Thompson, J. P. Usher, John D. Defrees, and George W. Ewing.

From Montgomery Blair

Post Office Department
8th August 1861

Dear Govr

I am very much inclined to think that your man Carter will not be of any use to you in the business you desire to set him upon.[1] His letter to the President,[2] which was read to us last night I saw staggered you a good deal as well as myself, and his talk this morning indicates weak nerves as well as a weak head: If you think it best, however, I will send him his commission,[3] as I fully recognise it to be your prerogative to lead in Tennessee matters.

Very truly Yours,   M Blair
Postmaster General

To The Honble Andrew Johnson
of U. S. Senate.

ALS, DLC-JP.

1. Given the tone of Johnson's and William B. Carter's recent letters to Lincoln, it can be assumed that the senator contemplated using Carter to facilitate the transport of arms to the beleaguered East Tennesseans, now under extreme pressure from the Confederates.

2. Although Carter's letter has not been found, in all likelihood he detailed the plan for the notorious bridge-burning incident of November 8–9.

It is interesting to note that Johnson was taken aback by this bold and, as it turned out, foolhardy proposal.

3. Probably a reference to Carter's pending appointment, apparently upon Johnson's recommendation, as special postal agent, a position which might serve as a cover for whatever role the senator hoped to have Carter play in getting military equipment into East Tennessee.

From Amos A. Lawrence

(near) Boston. Aug. 9. 61

Dear Sir

Enclosed please find a check for Two hundred dollars for Mr Brownlow, handed to me by friends.

Mr Murray[1] of Adair Coy. Ky is here, & I shall tomorrow put him in the way of collecting more.

Did you recieve one hundred dollars from me a few days ago?[2]

Yr Obt Srvt Amos A Lawrence

Hon. Andrew Johnson
U S Sen.

ALS, DLC-JP.

1. See Letter from Carlyle Murray, July 12, 1861.
2. Lawrence had enclosed this sum in a communication of August 2. See also Letter to Amos A. Lawrence, August 14, 1861.

From Carlyle Murray

Boston Aug 9th 1861

(Private)
Hon Andrew Johnson
Dear Sir.

When I wrote to you on the 12th ultimo, I was peculiarly anxious & exercised about the condition & prospects of East Tennessee. I am not a man of wealth, but I was solicitious to give *her* my mite, and for this purpose wrote to Mr Etheridge as well as yourself. Mr E answered my letter in a few days. About the same time I met a friend who was going to penetrate East Tenn after visiting Washington & Cairo. To him I gave $100. with instructions to use his own discretion; & either hand it to the Hon Mr Etheridge in Washington, or take it with him to your State & hand it over to some responsible Patriot, for the benefit of the cause you both so nobly represent— as he might think most judicious. I have not heard from him since his departure, but I am certain it will be faithfully applied.[1] It was all I was able to give at the time, as my health is delicate—never having wholly recovered from the wounds received in Mexico.

But I love this dear old Union, & our country Starry Banner, under which groups so many holy memories, & countless hopes, not only for ourselves, but for the teeming million yet unborn destined to occupy this broad Continent; So that on the reception of your letter, I felt it a duty to do something, either directly or indirectly, toward sustaining the Paper of the fearless Mr Brownlow; whose patriotism & indomitable pluck is the admiration of all good men, & whose many excilent qualities of both head & heart, illustrates him as peculiarly fitted to uphold our Countrys cause in the meridian round about him. And especially so, as I personally know something of the influence of the "Whig"—of the facts you mention—and of the great necessity of supporing him in his heroic struggles.

Actuated by an earnest desire to be of service to him, and thus to the Cause—thinking the case urgent, & not being able to spair the means myself just at this juncture; and lastly, on the hurry of the moment not noticing your letter was marked "Private"; I took counsel of the best motives of our nature—and of anxiety for our imperrilled Union, and lade your letter before Mr Abbot[2] & Amos Lawrence of this city. They promptly & cordially agreed with me, that the Rev Mr Brownlow & the "Whig" should be sustained and kept going under all circumstances; and that evry armed Patriot we could help raise up in your State, was equal to two Northern Soldiers sent there—not only because they are already on the ground, but because their hardy habits—local knowledge & experience makes them so.

Thinking with me too, that the aid might be needed at once, they have this morning, throug Mr Amos Lawrence, sent you a check for Two hundred ($200) dollars to cover any immediate want of Mr Brownlow; and have in connection with myself, arrainged a plan to secure through our friends here, a much larger sum; which I shall probably remit to you in a few days. That is, if you remain in Washington, or where the mails or Express can reach you in safety. In connection with this, let me entreat you Sir, to be constantly on your guard; for the Arch Trators have set a price on your head;[3] & the sluthe Hounds are on your track if you venture within their scent. Remember you are dear to us all, and your Country needs your life, and not your death, in this vexed hour of trial. I shall tremble for your safety should you return to Tennessee.

You may depend on our discretion & secrecy in this subject matter. For I desire the whole affair should be kept quiet & out of the Paper. Its publication could do no earthly good, and might do injury both to you in Tenn and myself in Kentucky.

If I have done wrong in showing your letter, I hope you will forgive me for the sake of the motive that made me offend.

If I can be of service to you or the cause, command me at once. I shall be here a month or so, & then return to Ky.

Please inform me what amount will probably carry the "Whig" through[4] (with its own meager resources) until Congress meets? And also of your own movements as to time & place; so that I may communicate with you—drect me how; for should Kentucky declair as she should, & I hope she will, I shall try to play a part, feeble as I am, near our State lines.

Hopeing I shall hear from you immediately, I will subscribe myself your humble & obt Servt.

Carlyle Murray.
No 6 Newton Place Boston, Mass.

ALS, DLC-JP.

1. Although the thought is ungenerous, it cannot but strike the reader that this resourceful man, according to his explanation, so designed his giving that it was virtually impossible for Johnson to discover whether the $100 had actually been contributed. It may be noted that Johnson's August 14 response reports the arrival of the $200 from Lawrence but is notably silent on any sum from Murray.

2. Abbott Lawrence (1828–1893), Amos Lawrence's cousin and the youngest son of Abbott Lawrence (1792–1855), was a member of A & A Lawrence & Co., commission house, and of James W. Paige & Co., another large merchantile firm, until he retired from business to become a lawyer (1863). Samuel A. Green, "Memoirs of Abbott Lawrence," Massachusetts Historical Society *Proceedings*, XLII (1908), 41–47.

3. There is no specific evidence for this assertion. However, Johnson had been threatened by "infuriated mobs" while touring East Tennessee during May and June, and Col. Thomas C. Hindman, with a regiment in Knoxville, had proposed to arrest him. Moreover, as Johnson left East Tennessee in mid-June, James Lafferty, a militia officer, confronting the senator at Bean Station, called upon the assembled crowd to arrest him as a traitor, but no move was actually made to do so. The New York *Tribune* of June 23 reported that Johnson had suffered a "narrow escape from assassination in Virginia." Temple, *Notable Men*, 401–3; Temple, *East Tennessee*, 197–98; Washington *National Intelligencer*, May 24, 1861.

4. This inquiry is part of the trap Murray was preparing for Amos Lawrence and the other well-to-do New Englanders whom he planned to bilk. Although Brownlow, hurt both by the blockade and by loss of advertisers, was in financial need, ultimately it was not lack of money, but rather orders from the Confederate government which caused the editor to suspend publication of the *Whig* in October. Coulter, *William G. Brownlow*, 158–59, 179; William G. Brownlow, *Sketches of the Rise, Progress, and Decline of Secession* (Philadelphia, 1862), 100, 249; Knoxville *Whig*, July 6, 1861ff.

From C[icero?] Baakee

August 12, 1861, New York, N. Y.; ALS, DLC-JP.

In response to a letter from Johnson, has "called together about one hundred of our most prominent Citizens" and believes that New York businessmen will be able to collect $50,000 for East Tennessee relief within a month. Johnson, as the "representative of the unionists of E.

Tenn.," seems to be the logical person to "appropriate" the funds "to
the best advantage for the glory of the cause." Hopes the senator will
address the citizens' meeting called to launch "this noble undertaking."

To Amos A. Lawrence, Boston, Mass.

Washington City, Augt. 14th, 1861.

Amos A. Lawrence Esq.
Dear Sir,

Your letter of the 2nd. ins't, enclosing draft for $100", and that
of the 9th. ins't, with draft for $200" enclosed, have been received.

The amount, in connection with some other funds intended for
the same purpose, has been forwarded to the Rev. Wm. G. Brownlow by a special agent,[1] who will properly use and account for the
same.

Very Respectfully, Your Obt. Sert.
Andrew Johnson.

L, MHi-Amos A. Lawrence Papers.

1. That Johnson had delivered to William B. Carter $325 designated for
Brownlow is attested by a "Memorandum of William B. Carter" dated August
13, 1861, found in the Johnson Papers, LC.

To Carlyle Murray,[1] Boston, Mass.

Washington Augt. 14th 1861.

Carlyle Murray Esq,
Dear Sir,

I have received and read with interest your letter of the 9th ins't.

The amount therein referred to as coming through Amos A.
Lawrence Esq has been received and, in connection with other funds
has been conveyed to Mr. Brownlow. I see from the papers this
morning that the publication of the "Knoxville Whig" has been
ordered to be stopped,[2] and I fear it cannot be resumed until the
supremacy of the constitution and the law is asserted and maintained
in Tennessee or the Eastern portion thereof.

The Government is taking the necessary steps to that end, and I
hope it will be accomplished at no distant day.

Hundreds, not to say thousands, of East Tennesseans are now
making their way into Kentucky, seeking protection and *supplies*
to sustain them against the usurpation and tyranny now imposed by
the Confederate States. Many of them have been compelled to leave
their families to the *tender mercy* of secessionists, but they intend to

return with arms in their hands to drive their oppressors beyond the boundaries of the State.

I hope and trust that you, sir, familiar with the character of our people, may have it in your power to contribute much personally and pecuniarily to relieve them from their oppressed condition. You know their love for the Union and the Government of our fathers. They never will, if they have the means of resistance placed in their hands, submit to be slaves. They may be conquered; their fields may be converted into graveyards and they may no longer realize the blessings of free government; but they will never consent to become the subjects of a Southern monarchy. Death, extirpation and the extinction of their name and race would be regarded by them as far more preferable than life without freedom and the proud distinction of being a citizens of this glorious Union. My heart, my hopes and my destiny are with them and with them I intend to live or perish.

I shall pursue no doubtful course. In matters of this kind, I am controlled and actuated as in matters of religion. When I cannot see my way clear as to the future; when my facts or data all give way, and my reason fails me, I draw upon my faith, and, relying upon a great principle of right, lying at the foundation of all things, I cannot believe that this hell-born doctrine of secession will triumph, and that its corrupt and traitorous followers can succeed.

I shall be either at this point, Cincinnati, or Lexington, Ky, just at such times as I can most conveniently aid the cause of the Union in my section of the State of Tennessee: I may therefore be addressed at either of those places with perfect safety, for the Post Masters at those points will be instructed to forward to me whatever mail may be sent to their offices when I am in another city. I may visit Phila., New York, and Boston. If so I will be much gratified to see you and have a personal interview.

Accept assurance of esteem, & believe me

Your Obt. Sert.
Andrew Johnson

L, DNA-RG59, Misc. Lets. and Newspapers Relating to the Civil War, 1861–1865, Box 1, Parker H. French; also in "Documents," *Tennessee Historical Magazine*, Ser. 2, II (1932), 294.

1. Apparently Johnson also sent, under Emerson Etheridge's frank, a copy of his letter to Lawrence of the same date. David R. Barbee, "Two Andrew Johnson Letters," *Tennessee Historical Magazine*, Ser. 2, II (1932), 294.

2. Although a Washington newspaper reported that the *Whig* had been suppressed by order of General Zollicoffer, it continued to appear until October 26. However, the Parson was continually harassed by Confederate soldiers stationed in Knoxville, and rumors constantly circulated concerning his imminent arrest. Evidently the Confederate authorities were trying to avoid the Federal precedent of suppressing the Louisville *Courier* and the New York

Day Book. Washington *Evening Star*, August 14, 1861; *OR*, Ser. 1, VII, 804; Coulter, *William G. Brownlow*, 178–79; Knoxville *Whig*, October 26, 1861.

From Alvan C. Gillem[1]

Fort Taylor Florida.
August 16, 1861.

Sir.

I Under no other than the existing state of affairs should I have taken the liberty of addressing you but these are no ordinary times, and all lovers of our Country seem to be more firmly bound to each other, to put down rebellion & punish traitors.

I desire to express to you the sincere pleasure I experienced from a perusal of your noble effort in the Senate in behalf of the loyal citizens in the rebelious states & more particularly of those of Tennessee. I am a native of that state & *know* that there are thousands of patriotic citizens there who would hail with joy any effort that might be made to deliver them from the present reign of terror. I had hoped that this effort would have been made, before the people, had been called upon to go through the *forms* of an election on the so called declaration of Independence.[2]

I am certain that at this day a majority of the people of Tennessee are true to the Union. Can it be possible that in the short interval from February to May 104.500[3] intelligent American citizens could have changed their minds on so important an issue as the dismemberment of a nation? without the introduction of any new element of discontent, unless we except the conflict at Sumpter as such, & who were responsible for that conflict, a major & a few half starved officers & men of my regiment,[4] or Davis & Beauregard? That attact was made, as it was openly boasted of here & elsewhere to *force* the border slave states from the Union, or to use the common term of the day to *Coerce* them into submission to the so called southern Confederacy.

Entertaining the views I do you may easily believe that I read with pleasure your appeal in favor of assistance to the Union men of Tennessee,[5] & though but a Captain, I am ready at any time to go to the assistance of the loyal citizens of my native State.— Believing the doctrine of state allegiance to be distructive to all government, I acknowledge now, & after all the benefits of care & education bestowed on me by the nation I should consider it the basest ingratitude to fail in my duty at this hour of trial.

There can be but one nation on this continent. This is the first opportunity which has ever occured of testing the strength of our government & unless this rebellion is put down in such a manner as to *awe* the evil disposed—we are a ruined people.

Hoping you will excuse this intrusion,

I am very Respectfully
Alvan C. Gillem
Capt 19th Infty.

Since writing the above I have been informed that Brigadier General Geo. Stoneman[6] has applied to the war Dept for my services with his command[.] I am very anxious to go with him into active service and any assistance you may render me will be thankfully received[.][7] I have been ten years in the army and hope in the promotions now being made that the few remaining Tennesseans will not be forgotten. I should like to be attached to the cavalry now being raised.

Very respectfully your obt Servt.
Alvan. C. Gillem

Hon. Andrew Johnson U. S. Senator
Washington City D. C.

ALS, DLC-JP.

1. Alvan C. Gillem (1830–1875), native Tennessean and West Point graduate (1851), served against the Seminoles and on the western frontier before casting his lot with the Union and being assigned to Ft. Taylor, Florida. Although he did not get the transfer to Stoneman's command, nor yet to the cavalry, for which he asks in the postscript, he was sent to the western army in Kentucky, fought at Shiloh and Corinth, and began to advance in rank and responsibility. A friend, even protégé, of Johnson, Gillem was commissioned colonel, 10th Tenn. Vol. Inf., provost marshal of Nashville (August-December, 1862), adjutant general of Tennessee (1863–65), and brigadier (August, 1863) and major general, U. S. Vols. (November, 1865). Active in state politics during Reconstruction, he served as one of three vice presidents at the constitutional convention (January, 1865), briefly as a member of the legislature (April-May, 1865), and as commander of the district of East Tennessee (1865–66). Under congressional Reconstruction he commanded the 4th military district (Mississippi, Alabama) in a way offensive to the radicals and, shortly after Johnson left the White House, was transferred to the Texas frontier, later commanding troops in the Modoc Indian war (1873). *DAB*, VII, 287; Robison, *Preliminary Directory*, *Jackson*, 19–20.

2. An allusion to the June 8 election on the adoption of a secession ordinance. White, *Messages*, V, 289–91.

3. The differences in popular response may be partially explained by the wording of the questions. In February the two-part ballot offered a choice of "Convention" or "No convention," and a second choice among union or disunion candidates in the event that "Convention" won. "No convention" prevailed, 69,675–57,798; more decisive was the candidate vote, in which Union men triumphed 91,803–24,749 over disunionists. By June, the choice was between "separation" or "no separation," with the vote ranging from 102,173 to 108,511 for separation—depending on the prejudice of the contemporary source—to 47,238 opposed to separation. At no time was there an indication that 104,500 "changed their minds," though Gillem's claim approximates a widely accepted figure for the total "separation" vote. *Ibid.*, 272n, 302–3n.

4. Prior to Sumter Maj. Robert Anderson had just taken command of companies from Gillem's former regiment, the 1st Artillery, which had been stationed in Charleston harbor since 1857. *Battles and Leaders*, I, 50–51.

5. An allusion to Johnson's Speech in Support of Presidential War Program, July 27, 1861.

6. George Stoneman (1822–1894), a New York West Pointer (1846), served in Gen. Stephen Kearny's "Mormon Battalion" and in the Southwest until 1855. In command at Ft. Brown, Texas, at the beginning of the war, he fled east, saw action in the Potomac and West Virginia theatres, and was for a time chief of the cavalry bureau before joining the western army in the winter of 1863–64. Captured at Clinton, Georgia, during the Atlanta campaign, he was exchanged and returned to duty in October, 1864, when he conducted a successful raid into southwest Virginia and central North Carolina in conjunction with Sherman's march to the sea. Thereafter he held commands in Petersburg and Richmond (1865–69) and in Arizona until retirement in 1871. Beginning in 1879 he served as a railway commissioner in California and later as Democratic governor of his adopted state (1883–87). *DAB*, XVIII, 92.

7. Later in the year, having heard that Samuel P. Carter, a navy captain, was ineligible for appointment as brigadier general, Gillem again sought Johnson's assistance, this time for command of the Tennessee brigade in the planned invasion of East Tennessee. Unsuccessful in this request, he was not promoted to brigadier until August, 1863. Gillem to Johnson, November 29, 1861, Johnson Papers, LC.

From Benjamin T. Staples

Jamestown Russell Co. Ky.
August 16th, 1861.

Hon Andrew Johnson
Dear Sir.—

I arrived at this point to day in Company with about 240 men from Morgan, Roan, Scott, Fentress, and Overton Counties. We have just decided to proceed to Camp Robinson, near Lancaster.— We are out of money—and travelling on the hospitality of our Union friends of Ky. We left our homes by different routs, and are together by chance.—

The state of things in East Tennessee is indiscribable.— Many of our people are prisoners in the rebel Camps.— Squads of Cavalry are Continually Scouring over the Country taking what they like— pasturing their horses in Corn fields—taking prisoners all they can. The line between Tennessee and Kentucky is the main line of their Operation.[1] The East Tennesseeans are trying to get to Kentucky by thousands, for the purpose of Arming and Organizing—and then going back to releive those we have left behind us.— We expect now, to reach Camp Robinson in three or four days, and hope to meet many of our friends there—and if possible hope you will be there soon to aid us, by your Council.— If you know where Maynard is,

Communicate the above to him, that he may assist if possible in giving us aid.—

G W Bridges[2] was taken prisoner on the 7th. of August.— he came to Monticillo and ventured back to see about his family, who was coming by Jamestown, and was taken three miles inside the Kentucky line.— Myself and G. W. Keith came with him to Monticello and considered him out of reach of the enemy— We have not been back home since.—

To conclude.—I cannot write all.— we need help and must have it or we are lost.—

> Your Friend B. J. Staples
> of Morgan Co. E. Tenn.

ALS (and Copy), DLC-JP; Louisville *Journal*, August 28, 1861; Knoxville *Register*, September 19, 1861; Memphis *Appeal*, August 30, 1861.

1. In an obvious effort to arouse sympathy and inflame the reader against the Confederates, the newspaper version of this letter elaborates on the preceding lean account of conditions in East Tennessee as follows: "You may rest assured that the state of things in East Tennessee is indescribable. Many of our people, upon bare suspicion, are arrested and taken prisoners, insulted, abused, and carried into rebel camps, there to be disposed of as the rebel mob thinks proper. Squads of cavalry and infantry are continually scouring over the country, offering our people, male and female, every indignity that these ruffian bands are capable of; destroying our crops and substance without regard to the condition or circumstances of the persons; pasturing their horses in our cornfields, wasting our hay-stacks, taking provisions of every description without regard to quantity, not even asking the price or tendering an equivalent therefor in any shape whatever.

"The violators of law, of order, and the Constitution are upon us in the name of secession. I may say to you, in fact, that the destroyer is upon us. We still have hope, and look to the Government of our fathers for protection and support against usurpation and our ruthless invaders. May God and the Government come to our aid and rescue us from the hands and destruction of the vandals now upon us! The heart and the feelings of the people of Tennessee are still for the Union, and will so continue as long as there is one gleam of hope left to an oppressed and down-trodden people. Let us have arms and the munitions of war and we will drive these invaders of human rights beyond the borders of our State, or the last man will perish in the attempt." Louisville *Journal*, August 28, 1861.

2. For George W. Bridges, see *Johnson Papers*, III, 295n.

From Benjamin A. G. Fuller[1]

> Augusta. (Me) Aug 17/61

Hon. Andrew Johnson,
Dear Sir,

Before you receive this letter, you will probably have learned from the newspapers that the Democratic State Convention of Maine, was controlled by the Anti-War party, which voted down a resolution offered by the minority setting forth "that we are opposed to the present War—except so far as necessary to suppress rebellion, and maintain the Constitution and laws of the United States."

This majority would vote only for the first clause—without the exception. Upon this nearly one half withdrew, held their convention, made their nomination & passed loyal & patriotic resolutions.

How large a portion of the Democracy of Maine is represented by this majority I cannot say, but the Douglas vote was over 40,000 to about 6.000 for Breckenridge, and the supporters of the latter, having called their own Convention, at another time & place it was not anticipated that they would come into ours, & hence no efforts were made to meet the contingency, & thus by a quiet movement, they came in in full force, to surprise & control the loyal side.[2]

I have stated these facts, that you may be able to understand the condition of things, and appreciate the saddened feelings with which the minority left the Convention, and the importance of the effort they are making to counteract at the polls the evil tendencies of the doings of our State Convention, as put forth by the majority.

If a large party is to arise at the North, opposed to sustaining the Government in all constitutional means to suppress the rebellion, the dreadful consequences are too apparent, and who can say that every Northern State would not become the theatre of these terrifying heart rending scenes which now afflict Missouri, Virginia, & your own State to some extent?

The difficulty with many honest, but misguided men is that they do not distinguish between supporting the government & supporting the Administration, and all its political theories between the suppression of rebellion, and making war upon the South.

Feeling the momentous importance of keeping the Northern sentiment loyal and conservative, the State Committee of the Convention which nominated Col Jameson[3] have deemed it of such consequence as to justify an application to yourself and Mr. Holt to aid us by your personal efforts in our midst in effecting this great object. And I therefore write to invite you, in their behalf, to visit Maine, and address the people upon the great issues now before us, at such time before election as may be convenient to you, in company with Mr Holt, if he can join you.[4]

If it be possible for you to comply, please to inform me at what time & upon how many occasions, you could address us[.]

Allow me to add that we do not expect you to give both your time, labors & substance but all expenses will be most cheerfully provided[.][5]

Very respectfully Your obt Servt
Benj. A. G. Fuller, Ch. St. Com.

(Maine Election) Sept. 9.

ALS, DLC-JP.

1. Benjamin A. G. Fuller (1818–1885), prominent Democratic lawyer and editor of the Augusta *Age*, was the uncle of Melville W. Fuller, chief justice of the U. S. (1888–1910). Louis C. Hatch, ed., *Maine: A History* (5 vols., Portland, 1919), III, 639; Willard L. King, *Melville Weston Fuller: Chief Justice of the United States, 1888–1910* (New York, 1950), 30; *NCAB*, I, 31.

2. The Maine Democratic party had divided into a Douglas faction, later called "War Democrats," and a Breckinridge faction, known as "Anti-War," or "Peace Democrats." In the summer of 1861, under the guise of called separate conventions, the Breckinridge men surprised and outmaneuvered the Douglasites at their Augusta convention by appearing with bona fide credentials in majority strength; the Douglas wing withdrew because of a platform argument and nominated a separate candidate for governor. Fuller's account is in essence confirmed by the recollections of former Senator (1847–53) James W. Bradbury, chairman of the convention committee on resolutions. Joseph Williamson, "The First Democratic State Convention in Maine during the Rebellion," Maine Historical Society *Collections*, Ser. 3, II (1902), 279–84.

3. Though ill, Charles D. Jameson (1827–1862), a successful lumber shipper and manufacturer, accepted the War Democrats' nomination for governor, a patriotic gesture rendered futile by factionalism in the party. In the ensuing election the Republican incumbent, Israel Washburn, received 58,689 votes, Jameson, 21,935, and Anti-War Democratic ex-Governor John W. Dano, 19,801. Commissioned a colonel in 2nd Maine Inf. and brigadier general, U. S. Vols., Jameson became ill after the battle of Fair Oaks and died of "camp fever." Boatner, *Civil War Dictionary*, 434; Hatch, *Maine*, II, 442.

4. Joseph Holt, Buchanan's postmaster general and briefly secretary of war, was at this time working for the Union cause in his native state of Kentucky. Holt toured New York and Massachusetts on behalf of the Union, but Johnson declined all invitations to speak in the North in order to be nearer East Tennessee and to foster aid for Tennessee unionists in Kentucky. *DAB*, IX, 181–82; Letters to Benjamin A. G. Fuller, August 27, 1861, and to Edmund B. Miller, August 28, 1861; see also *Johnson Papers*, III, 430n.

5. Two days later Judge Bradbury wrote in the same vein: "Abolition fanaticcism has enabled the Brakenridge element to Stir up an anti war spirit, which may go so far as to cripple the government in the defense of its authority and the suppression of rebellion." He further observed, "The anti war movement is disunion by consent. The 'not an inch' abolition policy is disunion by refusing to distinguish between the rebel traitors from choice, and the timid union men, who need something to strengthen them in their embarrassments." James W. Bradbury to Johnson, August 19, 1861, Johnson Papers, LC.

From Carlyle Murray

Boston Aug 19th 1861

Hon Andrew Johnson
U S Senate Washington D. C
Sir.

Both myself and Mr Amos A Lawrence, wrote to you some days since in refference to some pecuniary aid we designed for that staunch patriot, the Rev Mr Brownlow.

We heartily agree with you as to his exalted worth, and the necessity of sustaining him and his Paper in East Tennessee.

His value, and this necessity, not only commends itself to the judgement of our New England Friends, but also to their feelings—hence we had made arrangements to enable you to sustain him.

But in the last few days we have seen a notice going the rounds of the Journals, to the effect, that Mr Zollicoffer[1] at the head of a band of Rebbels, had made a descent on Knoxvill—suppressed the "Whig", and arrested Mr Brownlow.[2] To besure we have also seen, what amounts to a semi-contradiction; but the high-handed lawless tyranny of the act, is so much in keeping with the general conduct of the Secessionist, that we have but little hopes of its proveing a canard.

But it may be only a rumor. You are probably acquainted with the true facts of the case, which I beg you will impart to me at your earliest convenience. If our fears are well founded, then we have met with a serious misfortune. If the "Whig" is not suspended, we will aid it throug you as soon as you inform us of the fact. If Mr Brownlow needs personal aid on account of his heavy losses—or if he desires, and you think it advisable, to start another paper in some new locality, I have no doubt we can raise amonge a few of us the necessary amount.

In doing thus, we desire to act with secrecy and delicacy, so as to avoid jarring his sensativeness or his independence. For it would be truly a duty and not a favor—for us to help him.

I beg you will inform me as to the true state of the case; and give such suggestions in the premmises as you may think judicious. Trusting I may soon hear from you, and that I may in some manner be useful, I will

> Subscribe myself, Your humble and obedient Servt
> Carlyle Murray.
> No 6 Newton Place.

ALS, DLC-JP.

1. Felix K. Zollicoffer (1812–1862), newspaper editor, Whig politician, and Confederate general, was born in Maury County. Graduating from Jackson College, Columbia, he engaged in newspaper work with several papers, including the Columbia *Observer*, *Southern Agriculturist*, Huntsville (Ala.) *Mercury*, and the Nashville *Republican Banner*. Named state printer (1842), he was adjutant general and state comptroller (1845–49); he also served in the state senate (1849–51), and in Congress (1853–59). He attended the Washington Peace Convention (1861), was commissioned brigadier general in charge of East Tennessee operations, and died at the battle of Mill Springs, Kentucky, early in 1862. *DAB*, XX, 659–60; *BDAC*, 1863; Stamper, Zollicoffer, *passim*.

2. Actually, Zollicoffer, ordered to "Preserve peace, protect the railroad, and repel invasion," exhibited considerable leniency toward East Tennessee unionists at this time, making no attempt to silence Brownlow until October. *OR*, Ser. 1, IV, 374; Coulter, *Brownlow*, 165–67; Stamper, Zollicoffer, 70.

To André Froment,[1] New York, N. Y.

Washington City, Aug. 20, 1861

André Froment, esq., Chairman Special Committee, New-York City.
My Dear Sir:

I have the honor to acknowledge the receipt of your letters of 24th June and 8th ult.[2]

I hope you will pardon the delay in acknowledging the kindness so unexpectedly bestowed in the invitation from the Common Council of New-York to accept the hospitalities of that city. It has arisen solely from the great pressure of public business, and the uncertainty of my future movements, in consequence of the alarming state of affairs in that section of the country to which I belong.

It has been my desire to accept this invitation. It comes from New-York City; it comes from a people whom I have ever regarded as generous, warm-hearted, and loyal.

I therefore regret to say that I am at last compelled to decline the honor of a public reception, as tendered by your Committee.

The circumstances at present surrounding me are such as to render it impossible for me to make any positive arrangement, or designate any time at which I could visit your city.

I return my sincere thanks to you, and, through you, to those whom you represent, for this manifestation of regard, and approval of the course I have pursued in connection with the present state of affairs.

Upon my advent into public life, I took my stand in favor of free government based upon an enlightened public judgment. From 1833 down to the present time I have uniformly advocated the Union of the States, the Supremacy of the Constitution, and the enforcement of the laws made in pursuance thereof.

To their maintenance the best efforts of my life have been devoted, and for their continuance and preservation, if necessary, life itself will be sacrificed.

All true patriots and lovers of our race should be willing to come forward and perish in this last struggle for the perpetuation of a Government based upon the virtue, integrity, and capacity of man for self-government. These were the principles that carried us through the Revolution, and upon which Washington, Jefferson, and a long list of patriotic worthies, established our present unparalleled form of Government.

Accept assurances of esteem,
And believe me, yours truly
Andrew Johnson

New York *Tribune*, August 22, 1861.

1. André Froment, alderman of the fifteenth district, was a clerk-agent residing at 66 E. 31st Street. *Trow's New York City Directory* (1861), 307.

2. On behalf of the Common Council Froment actually had written three times in June. See Letter from Froment to Johnson, June 8, 1861; Froment to Johnson, June 10, 24, July 8, 1861, Johnson Papers, LC.

From Rachel T. Strickland[1]

Philadelphia Aug. 21st 1861.

Hon. Andrew Johnson,

Sir Altho personally unknown to you, I have ventured to ask you to loan me fifteen or twenty dollars in a case of great emergency — I together with my Son Frank was obliged to leave Nashville Tennessee without bringing any thing with us and are now without any means as my Son to whom I look for Support is out of employment owing to these disastrous times— I know you will not refuse to assist the widow of the late Architect of the Capitol of Tennessee who now is entirely without the means of living— be pleased to direct to 929 Race Street near 10th at your earliest convenience & oblige

Your grateful friend.   R. M. S.

Mrs. William Strickland Philadelphia

ALS, DLC-JP.

1. Rachel T. Strickland (1789–1866), a native of New Jersey but long-time resident of Philadelphia, married William Strickland, architect and engineer, in 1812. Of their six children who lived to maturity, the two boys, Francis M. (*c*1818–1895) and Jesse H. (*c*1826–1899), served briefly in the 8th Tenn. Cav., USA. Agnes A. Gilchrist, *William Strickland: Architect and Engineer, 1788–1854* (New York, 1969), 137–38; *Tennesseans in the Civil War*, I, 339–40; II, 589.

From George D. Blakey[1]

Russellville Ky Augt 22nd 61

Gov Johnson

Dear Sir   Hoping and believing that you have not forgotten me tho our acquaintance is but limited & my position but humble & believing that you feel some sympathy for me in this my xposed position 50 miles north of Nashville & 50 of Clarksville I take the liberty on my arrival safe at home to drop you a line[.] I had hoped that after our late election in which treason was so signally rebuked that Traitors would not have been so rampant. But Sir they are nothing daunted & are as sanguine of taking Ky off as if they had carried the State by an over whelming majority. I understand that it had been agreed upon in my absence that I should be shot at the Depot on my return but no demonstration was made & I have been permitted to live now 20 hours after my arrival. They perhaps have concluded that it might be safe to be more sly about it. You may remember that the head & font of my offending[2] is that I voted for Lincoln & that I now assert Loyalty to the Union as one of the essentials of Christianity. During my stay of 3 weeks in Washington you were the only man of rank who sought counsel of me as regards Ky hence I came away as I went only a wiser & more subdued man. I think the days of law & order in Ky have gone by & that this neutrality of ours was only a trick of the enemy to enable them the more readily to Capture the State[.] And when the President conseted to respect the wolf in sheeps clothing when he failed to enforce law & order in Ky as well as Tenn he lost sight of that illustrious example set by Son of Man when he said to the first great Secessionist on a High mountain "get behind me Satan[.]" If Fort Sumpter had been re-enforced in Novr & rebels shot as they came within reach of her guns she had not fallen[.]

If the President had xercised this right view, before called in question of sending troops in Ky & Tenn for protection of the Loyal Citizens the reign of Terror had not been inaugurated. But enough of this[.] It now only remains to do the best we can & sell our lives at the best possible price. If the President should at any time determine to do any thing for Ky or Tenn I do hope he will select Genral officrs at least from among men with clean records. If it should be known that Genrl Buckner[3] is to command I presume he could raise a strong army of Traitors as I find he is quite a favorite with them[.] He was on the Cars with me yesterdy on his way to the Southern Confederacy & I had a good opportunity of taking observations[.] I tell you he will not do to command Loyal men[.] In this my opinion has undergone no change[.] The Rebels here are more active than ever[.] They certainly contemplate some action at an early day. They are in an encampment drilling in this county. Camp Boone near Clarksville is being reenforced daily from this State[.] I know not that before you get this I may have fallen at their hands or in their hands[.] But I intend to stand my ground Trust in God & keep my powder dry.[4]

My Kind regards to Mr. & Mrs. Underwood[.][5]

Very Respectfully yours &c
Geor. D. Blakey

ALS, DLC-JP.

1. George D. Blakey (1809–1886), physician and native of Logan County, Kentucky, who later moved to Bowling Green, was Cassius M. Clay's choice for lieutenant governor when Clay ran for governor of Kentucky in 1851 on the antislavery ticket. Like Clay, Blakey liberated his slaves and joined the

Republican party. In 1866 he was appointed commissioner to make awards to "legal owners of slaves enlisted into the Union Army." Cassius M. Clay, *The Life of Cassius Marcellus Clay* ([Berea, Ky.], 1968 [1886]), 166; James R. Bentley, ed., "The Civil War Memoirs of Captain Thomas Speed," *Filson Quarterly*, XLIV (1970), 271n.

2. "The very head and front of my offending." Shakespeare, *Othello*, Act I, sc. 2.

3. Simon Bolivar Buckner (1823–1914), Kentucky native and West Point graduate (1844), taught at the Academy, served in the Mexican War, and resigned from the army in 1855. Appointed a major general in the Kentucky militia, he worked for the state's neutrality, although offered commissions by both North and South. In September, 1861, following the Federal invasion from Cairo, he joined the ranks of the Confederacy. Captured at Ft. Donelson, he was exchanged in August, 1862, served under Bragg in the Chattanooga campaign, and in 1864 was given command of the Department of Louisiana. After Appomattox he worked in New Orleans both on a newspaper and in the insurance business. Returning to Kentucky, he became editor of the Louisville *Courier* (1868), Democratic governor (1887–91), and vice-presidential candidate on the conservative National Democratic ticket in 1896. *DAB*, III, 234–36; Boatner, *Civil War Dictionary*, 95–96; see also Arndt M. Stickles, *Simon Bolivar Buckner: Borderland Knight* (Chapel Hill, 1940).

4. Attributed in Hayes, *Ballads of Ireland*, I, to Oliver Cromwell as he was about to cross a river to attack. Stevenson, *Quotations*, 1650.

5. Probably Warner L. Underwood (1808–1872), a Bowling Green attorney, who served in the state lower house (1848) and senate (1849–53), in Congress (1855–59), and as U. S. consul to Glasgow (1862–64). He had talked about Kentucky's neutrality with Lincoln during April. Collins, *Kentucky*, I, 88; *BDAC*, 1740.

From Charles A. Eames[1]

Lewisville Kentuckey
Augt 22/61

Hon Andrew Johnson
Washington D C

Dear Sir I am just from East Tenn & haveing this moment met a Gentleman from Washington that said he saw you & talked with you & thinking it a good chance for you to hear from your family I write. Your family were well when I Left home on Tuesday Last[.] Your Son Roberet will have to keep close[.] Now I hurd divers Men say at Knoxvill since the procklamation of Mr Zolicoffer[2] that if he did not hush up & give way to cecession they would arrest him & hang him. Nelson is Released on parole of honor & Mr Bridges I cant say what will become of him[.] they caught him as he Returned after his wife & children[.][3] we are to be a persecuted people[.] they have about 10 thousand men at cumberland Gapp now well armed & have ordered 10 thous more from Corinth Miss to come in there to put East Tenn down[.][4] what shall we do[?] if the Governmt dont stop them they will press us in to servis without a Doubt & it Does Look to Bad that 30 thousand good Union Men of East Tenn have to go to this unreasonable war against their will & consent for I know that is wahat they are up to[.] now Davis says in 40 d[a]ys all of us must Leave the State & take the Oath[5] & at the same time they will not Let them Leave[.] they Stop all at the Ky Line & that Shews to me plainly that Harris is determined to force us to his call[.] what will be come of us all[?] it does seem that the Governnt ought to save us from such distruction Both of Lives & property as they will make of us when they come to force us out for we shall Resist a Draft[.] we have no gunns nor powder at all[.] if we had them or could geat them it would be Different with us[.] we geat No news at all therefore we dont know what to expect or what to do[.] may the time soon come when you may be able to help us by sending Arms to us & a good Man to head us[.] I find many Rabid cecesion Men here & the southern part of Ky is nearly all cecession & if this State dont watch it will be caught knapping in this case[.]

I am from Washington Co E T[.]   C. A. Eames[6]

ALS, DLC-JP2.

1. Charles A. Eames (b. c1827), a Washington County boot maker, possessed personal property worth $10,000 and real estate valued at $12,000. 1860 Census, Tenn., Washington, 3rd Dist., 51.

2. On August 7 Zollicoffer issued a proclamation designed to be conciliatory, appealing to unionists to abide by the decision of the ballot box in the state election. He assured East Tennesseans that Confederate troops were there to preserve peace and would protect those who pursued their "lawful avocations" without giving aid to the enemy; however, he also warned that "Treason to the State cannot, will not be tolerated." On August 18 he promulgated another order which was as much a caution to Confederates to observe the "most scrupulous regard for . . . personal and property rights" as it was an admonition to unionists. Not until November did Zollicoffer make an effort to apprehend Johnson's sons and son-in-law. Knoxville *Whig*, August 10, 24, 1861; *OR*, Ser. 2, I, 847; IV, 388.

3. George W. Bridges of Athens, having been elected to the 37th Congress, was arrested en route to Washington. He escaped in time to serve the last week of the term before joining the Union army. See *Johnson Papers*, III, 295*n*.

4. On August 13 Gen. Leonidas Polk, commanding in West Tennessee, was ordered to send the 14th and 15th Miss. Inf. regiments to Russellville, Jefferson County, East Tennessee; at the same time an Alabama regiment was similarly dispatched. *OR*, Ser. 1, IV, 387.

5. Jefferson Davis' August 14 proclamation ordered all males over fourteen who were not citizens of the Confederate states but were "adhering to the Government of the United States," and who did not declare their intention of becoming citizens, to leave within forty days or be treated as "alien enemies." Richardson, *Messages and Papers of the Confederacy*, I, 131.

6. A marginal note reads: "I Shall Return to Tenn this week & will say to some member of your family that I hurd from you & that at this time you was in usual hea[l]th[.]"

From James Culbertson

August 23, 1861, Catlettsburg, Ky.; ALS, DLC-JP2.

Virginia refugee once again shares his views on appropriate Union military strategy. Having only a small pocketknife to defend himself, he urges Johnson "to see the president" and "till him to sinde me a fire shooter that will do about 7 inches in length and one of coult Revolvrs or sharps Rifle[.]" Offers to return them at the end of the war, "If needed."

From Carlyle Murray

Boston Aug 23d 1861.

Hon Andrew Johnson
U. S Senate Washington City D. C.
Dear Sir

Your letter of the 14th. inst is before me;—a letter that does honor both to your head and your heart.

I am as little versed in compliment, as I am in flattery; but I must say, that the exalted sentiments and unflinching patriotism expressed in your communication, makes me more hopeful and determined for the future, and draws me nearer unto you as a man and a Christian. I thank you for them.

God knows that I would willingly give my life—my all, to serve our unhappy country, and to crush the audacious traitors, who would violate the chastity of our Queenly Capitol by their incestious embrace—wretches who would pollute her as a wanton, and then proclaim her dishonor as a triumph.

It is this feeling—this desire (without alloy) to serve her in any capacity however humble and private, that induces me again to address you. My Friend Mr Amos A Lawrence, handed me this morning, the enclosed clipping from one of our Dailys[1] (which you see denies the suppression of the Knoxvill Whig) and suggested I should enclose it to your attention.

Do please find out the truth of the matter if possible, and let me know. The reason why I am thus urgent, is because we know the value of the Whig, and are convinced that its continuance is of the utmost importance; and would consider ourselves culpable to have it go under for the want of means.

I have a hope that my own native State—Noble Old Kentucky, will throw off the criminal nutrality that now binds her like the shirt of Nessus,[2] and be ready to sustain the heroic mountaineers of East

Tennessee. I presume you will be occupied in Lexington, in organise-ing and arming your repatriated constituents, so that they may re-turn, and defend "the ashes of their Fathers and the Temples of their God?"[3] If so—does the Government furnish you *all* you require? Are there not some equipments—some essentials needed which she does not furnish, and which we may help you in procureing? If there are, there are many here that would be glad to aid the cause;—and I am personally at your command, without any other aim, than to serve my Country without stint and without price.

If hostilities should break out in my Section of the State, I shall re-turn to Kentucky at once—otherwise I shall remain here some-time. I think it would be profitable to the cause, and gratifying to you individually, if you could visit Boston before going West, as you have many, very many friends in New England; and especially in this City. They would give you a truly generous welcom; and your humble servant would take pleasure in being counted among them.

My Dear Senator, your faith in the future sounds both sublime and prophetic, and reflects on my own feelings with a healthy luster. The ways of Providence are inscrutiable;[4] and this rebellion, is work-ing out some great problem in the Divine economy of Nations. Some body has said, that Revolution like the Plow, only fertilizes the soil only by rending its bosom—or, like the devouring flame that con-sumes the litter and the stubble of decaying nature, from the black-ened waste of which springs the germs of a new and richer harvest. God grant it may be so in our case, and that this civil tempest, may leave our political atmosphere in a purer and a healthier State.

I can but reiterate my offer of time, and means to serve our holy cause— command, and direct me if you see occasion; for in default of others, my Country is Father, Mother, Wife & children to me.

I am my Dear Sir,

Your Sincer Friend and humble Servt,
Carlyle Murray.
No 6 Newton Place.

ALS, DLC-JP.

1. The Boston *Advertiser*, citing the Washington *Republican*, quoted from a "private" letter of Brownlow which stated that, while "notice [has] not been served on me yet," he had been "driven to the wall with more subscribers on my list than the eight secession papers of East Tennessee all put together;" he would "starve, or beg my bread of Union men," before he would "surrender to this vile heresy of secession." Boston *Advertiser*, August 23, 1861.

2. According to Greek mythology, the blood of the centaur Nessus, slain by Hercules, when placed on the latter's robe by his jealous wife, so burned him that he immolated himself in order to put an end to his excruciating agony. Jerome I. Rodale, *The Phrase Finder* (3 vols. in 1, Emmaus, Pa., 1953), 666.

3. Paraphrase of Macaulay, "Horatius," st. 27, *Lays of Ancient Rome.*
OED, I, 486.
    4. Paraphrase of Abraham Cowley, *The Essays and Other Prose Writings*,
ed. Alfred B. Gough (Oxford, 1915 [1668]), 75.

From George Ryan[1]

                              Xenia Green County Ohio August 24th 1861
Messrs Andrew Johnson and Emerson Etheridge
Dear Sirs   I was drove from Tennessee about the first of June
1861[.] I lived in nine miles of Murfresborough Rutherforde County[.] I was in Town the Seconde monday in February and the de-
moracey and Some few of the oposition ware down on you and the
thinge gru worse and wose. I was for the unnion all the time and
Said that Johnston and Eathridge had made the best Speeches of
any members in Congress[.] you may depend It mad the disunionist
hot and I Still avocated that you had done right[.] at last I receved
A letter from one of my relations from ohio[.] this was enoughf[.]
you may depend the devils ware after me thick and fast[.] they give
me two days to leave and after conculings [counsellings] of my
friends I conclude to leave and I am heare in Xenia ohio[.] I had to
leave my lands and all of my property Just So—and now Genlemen
I want to see you both Just to Know what is the best course to pursue[.] I think If I could See Either or both of you we coulde make
Some araingements to go back with an armey to Tennessee and
drive them devills from the State[.] If you receve this letter I hope
that you will answer it Imediatley and If you come this way when
you return home I hope and trust that you will Stop hear and make
a Speech to the people of Xenia and If you will do So pleas tellegraph
to me when you will come to this place[.] I am a Strainger to you
both but It dont take Tenn people longe to be come acquainted[.]
I woulde rather See you than any men on this Earth[.] Last April
was a warme time In Murfressborough[.] If my Self or Andrew
Johnson Maynard Nelson or Browlow had of been In Murfressborough they woulde of hunge us as Shure as any thinge but thnks
to the lorde we ware not Theire[.] what do you think that Such men
as me had better to do[?] I left one Hundred and about thirty achers
of land and about one thousand dollars in note and acunts and nearley
all of my pursonal property is theire—but my object in wrightinge
this letter So is to let you Know that the olde Democratick party and
Some of the oposition party in Tennessee think no more of you than
the ranke's abolitionst in ohio[.] J M Avent[2] and olde Samuel
Rucker[3] E. A. Kibble[4] Steph White[5] and Benjamin Lillard[6] ware

verry Sever on you— I do wish from my harte that I coulde See you[.] I want to go back to Tennessee to help to whip out disunionism but I am in bad health at this time[.] I do hope that you will come to Xenia as Soon as possible— If I had one Hundred thousand dollars I woulde be in Tennessee in Shorte notice and my worde for It I make cecessinist feel awfull[.] I hope that you wrighte to me Soon or tellegraph to me in Xenia for you both have lots of friendes in this place and they woulde all be glad to See you[.] I Saw in the papers tha Brownlow had chaning [changed] his Vews on political topics but I dont blieve a worde of It.— pleas Send me your last [s]peech that you mad this call Cession[.] I me[a]n Mr Johnson Speech[.][7] you may depend Gentlemen I woulde like to See A Tennessee friend[.] It woulde be A greate treate to me but purhaps I have tired you patie[n]ce wrighting so much but pleas excuse me[.] It is like talkinge to you[.]

I remain yours respectefully

George Ryan

Messers Johnson & Etheridge M. C.

ALS, DLC-JP.

1. Probably "G. Rion" (b. c1816), native Tennessean and Rutherford County farmer who possessed $16,000 in real and $300 in personal property. The oldest of his six children, a son Marion, aged twenty in 1860, evidently remained in Tennessee. 1860 Census, Tenn., Rutherford, 8th Dist., 99; Ryan to Johnson, Emerson Etheridge, and Horace Maynard, February 2, 1862, Johnson Papers, LC.

2. James M. Avent (1816–1895), a former Virginian, was a prominent and wealthy Murfreesboro attorney. A "Democrat of the old 'Jacksonian school,' " he was senior partner in the well-known law firm of Avent, Smith, & Avent. *Goodspeed's Rutherford*, 1022; Deane Porch, comp., *Tombstone Inscriptions of Evergreen Cemetery* (Murfreesboro, 1968), 141.

3. Samuel R. Rucker (1794–1862), a native of Virginia and state representative (1827–29), was a Murfreesboro lawyer and landholder possessing $27,500 in real and $37,000 in personal property. 1860 Census, Tenn., Rutherford, Valley, 162; Robison, *Preliminary Directory, Rutherford*, 49.

4. Edwin A. Keeble (1807–1868), a Virginia-born lawyer and landowner of Rutherford County, with $66,650 in real and $54,360 in personal property, was mayor of Murfreesboro (1838–55), Democratic presidential elector in 1856, speaker of the Tennessee house (1861–63), and elected "without opposition" to the Confederate Congress in 1863. *Ibid.*, 33; 1860 Census, Tenn., Rutherford, Murfreesboro, 19.

5. Stephen B. White (b. c1815), a native Tennessean, was a farmer holding $51,000 in real and $38,000 in personal property. *Ibid.*, 2d Dist., 14.

6. Benjamin Lillard (b. c1787), a Virginia-born farmer, owned $57,500 in real and $34,550 in personal property. *Ibid.*, Bushnell Creek Dist., 136.

7. Speech in Support of Presidential War Program, July 27, 1861.

From John Lellyett

BURNET HOUSE,
JOHNSON, SAUNDERS & CO.
Proprietors.

Cincinnati, Aug 26, 1861

Hon. Andrew Johnson
Washington, D. C.

Dear Sir,—I have not troubled you with any of my favors for a long time, and now it is not from any promptings of a selfish character that I address you.

Last winter, I twice perhaps, or at least once, wrote you, urging you to come to Tennessee, and address the people. I saw our friends in taking the anti-coercion by-path, would fall into the broad road to disunion. I so told them, and so intimated to you. Alas! I was right! When I saw you and Etheridge in March, at Washington, I asked that you or he, or both, should make a few speeches through our part of the State at the earliest possible day. I said something was necessary to give the people the right tone—the Union men. I wanted Etheridge to take the race for Governor, that he might canvass the State, imparting a *tone* of *decision* to the contest, that by his election we might achieve no barren victory. My ideas were right about these things. I knew our friends stood upon hollow grounds.— grounds undermined and filled beneath, with the explosives of hell by their own hands. The match was in the hands of their enemies, I was right.

I only mention these things that I may obtain for a moment your ear, and due consideration to what I now suggest.

Since the Middle of July I have spent nearly all my time in Kentucky. I now tremble for the fate of that State. The hell-hounds of Nashville predict, that in Sixty days she will be in the Southern Confederacy. They are moving heaven and earth to accomplish their object. The elections are all now over, and the field is free. Our more judicious friends are alarmed— Prentice[1] and Harney,[2] and the Speeds,[3] and all that coterie of patriots about Louisville, dream dreadful dreams. But the body of the Union Men of Kentucky see not the danger—and there all the danger lies. They have not the *animus* to meet the danger which is coming up against them. Their hearts—the great deep of their hearts,—needs to be stirred by just such words of counsel and exhortation as *you* can lay before them. Prentice thinks so too. Let me therefore, appeal to you, as you regard the position of Kentucky—aye, as you regard the future of your country—as you regard the success of this great struggle for the preservation of constitutional liberty—come to Kentucky. You, and Etheridge, and Maynard, and Joseph Holt could save Kentucky from great danger. The loyal men of Kentucky must be aroused to the fighting point. Nothing less will save her.

I suppose I have said enough. Pray take the matter under consideration; and whatsoever you determine to do, do quickly. No time to be lost.

A horrible condition of tyranny prevails at Nashville. May they place upon every man's leg there a block and chain! They had no manhood to resist the usurpation. Now let it stamp them in the dust, until

> "The land's despair
> Shall cry to heaven, and bondage grow
> Too vile for even the vile to bear."[4]

I suppose I may be considered at length an exile. I withstood and defied the scoundrels until they ceased to menace me; but yet having left, I am continually warned not to return. Well, the place is too infernally disagreeable, even if it were not dangerous. I shall bide my time.

Yours Respectfully   John Lellyett

ALS, DLC-JP.

1. George Prentice.

2. John H. Harney (1806–1867), former college professor and president of Louisville College (1839–43), began in 1844 publication of the Louisville *Democrat*, which he edited until his death. Elected to the Kentucky legislature (1861–62), he served as chairman of the committee on Federal relations which drafted the resolution demanding that Confederate and Tennessee troops be withdrawn from Kentucky soil. However, during the war his criticism of the "arbitrary arrest and deportation of citizens" led to his arrest and a brief investigation by the military. Following the war he urged moderate treatment of former rebels. *Appleton's Cyclopaedia*, III, 85.

3. James and Joshua F. Speed. The latter (1814–1882), a Louisville businessman and close friend of Lincoln, had served one term in the Kentucky legislature (1848). His friendship with Lincoln had begun when he operated a store in Springfield, Illinois; continuing to maintain this close association, he often visited Lincoln in Washington after the latter became President. *Ibid.*, V, 626.

4. Lellyett had incorporated this bit of poesy in "Letters to Georgia's Great Commoner" which appeared over the signature "J. L. Nashville" in the Nashville *Patriot*, January 16, 1861. Its ultimate source has not been located.

From William Lellyett

Louisville, Aug. 26. [1861]

Hon. Andrew Johnson:

Dear Sir,

Believing that you have considerable influence with the President
of the United States, and are devoted in earnest to the maintenance
of the Government, I take the liberty to make some suggestions in
relation to Kentucky, which you may lay before Mr. Lincoln or the
proper Department, if you think them worth notice. I am now a
resident of Kentucky, and an Inspector appointed by Mr. Gallagher[1]
under the supervision of Mr. Chas. B. Cotton Surveyor of this port;[2]
and I have a good opportunity to observe the matters whereof I
speak.

Our ambiguous position of quasi neutrality is an exceedingly
troublesome one. The rebels, assisted by Kentucky Secessionists,
are making this State a feeding trough for treason, in spite of the
Surveyor's vigilance. Disloyal men in Louisville are in the habit of
loading wagons with the most dangerous contraband goods—even
fire arms and swords, and material for the manufacture of Cannon,
percussion caps and swords. When these wagons get a little way
from the city, which they manage to do in spite of the most careful
watching, they are taken under escort by bands of armed traitors;
and nothing but a strong military force could stop them without
danger of bloody collision. This should be avoided, if possible. Last
Saturday, a company of eighty-five Home Guard were called out to
assist the Inspectors, and proceeded down the railroad to a point on
the Lebanon Junction, and brought back the contents of six wagons
—consisting of Seventy-eight bars of black tin, for tempering metal
to be used in making cannon, a quantity of thin sheet copper, for the
manufacture of percussion caps, one or two barrels of opium,[3] forty-
five boxes of tin plate some sheet iron, and some thin sheet brass, to
be used in making sword hilts. The loyal Guard met with no resistance; but some traitor exposed their lives to emminent peril by
removing a rail from the track, and throwing off the cars. Several
were badly bruised, and one inspector had his arm broken.[4]

If the military could be used in this way, it would soon put a stop
to the wagon business. But prominent men of Louisville, of the milk-
and-water sort, discourage the Home Guard from rendering the
assistance in which they display an admirable alacrity, if left to
themselves. Now, sir, I think it is high time the Government [sh]ould

place an able General of the regular army at the head of our loyal military, so that we will not be dependent on the meek and timid counsels of milksop civilians. We only want a military head. There are brave men innumerable, ready to serve under him.

Again, I hear but little of our U. S. District Attorney and Marshall.[5] Both ought to be always present in Louisville, as their principal duties are here at present. The Surveyor is annoyed by threats of suits when he makes surveys. His countenance should be strengthened by the presence of these officers. We want *nerve*. The Secessionists, though in the minority, are strengthened by Tennessee; and it seems to me that five or ten thousand men should be kept in readiness at New Albany, to assist loyal Kentuckians in any case of emergency. The removal of Reausseau's Brigade from Jeffersonville —or Camp Jo Holt,[6] dampens the feeling of Union men, and encourages the rebels. It is time Kentucky were looked after in earnest. Give us a head—a head with *teeth* in it, that will bite.

Very respectfully   W. Lellyett

ALS, DLC-JP2.

1. William D. Gallagher (1808–1894), Pennsylvania-born poet, journalist, and government official, was reared in Ohio, published his first poem when he was sixteen, and became a newspaper man in Cincinnati in 1828, in due time editing the *Mirror* and later the *Gazette*. He continued to write poetry and music, his popular ballad "The Spotted Fawn" appearing in 1845. After two years in Washington (1850–52) as private secretary to Thomas Corwin, he moved to Louisville, where he purchased a half interest in the *Courier*. Following this unsuccessful venture, he acquired a farm near Louisville, where he edited a number of farm publications. As a delegate to the Republican National Convention in 1860, he supported Lincoln and later became private secretary to Treasury Secretary Salmon P. Chase. Lincoln later appointed him special collector of customs for the upper Mississippi Valley and in 1863 surveyor of customs at Louisville. *DAB*, VII, 102–3; *NCAB*, IX, 250–51; see also W. H. Venable, "William Davis Gallagher," *Ohio Archaeological and Historical Quarterly*, I (1887), 358–75; II (1888), 309–26.

2. Charles B. Cotton (b. *c*1827), a Louisville lawyer, was surveyor of the port in 1861. 1860 Census, Ky., Jefferson, Louisville, 4th Ward, 46; *U. S. Official Register* (1861), 69; (1863), 91.

3. A medicinal item in the midst of war materiel.

4. The "Special Correspondent" of the New York *Tribune*, writing from Louisville on August 25, the day after the seizure and derailment, gave a nearly identical description of the incident, agreeing in all the details and adding that the "Seventy-eight pigs of black tin would make the mouths of Nashville rebels water," while the copper, no doubt, was eagerly awaited by the "piratical portion of the Professors in the University of Nashville," who "have made a cap factory of their laboratory." New York *Tribune*, August 30, 1861.

5. James Harlan (1800–1863), Frankfort lawyer and Whig, had served in the House (1835–39), as Kentucky secretary of state (1840–45), and in 1845 had been elected to the lower house of the Kentucky legislature. A staunch unionist, Harlan had, in March, 1861, opposed secessionist legislation, and in May, together with John J. Crittenden, James Speed, and others, had formulated plans for distributing the "Lincoln Guns" to Kentucky unionists. For his services Lincoln rewarded him with the appointment of district

attorney of Kentucky, a position he held until his death. Alexander H. Sneed (b. 1830), the marshal, a lawyer with $9,000 in personal estate, had represented Boyle County in the legislature (1859–61). *DAB*, VIII, 267; Collins, *Kentucky*, II, 85; Louisville *Journal*, May 6, 1861; 1860 Census, Ky., Boyle, Danville, 4.

6. New Albany and Jeffersonville, Indiana, across the Ohio River from Louisville, were adjacent to Camp Jo Holt, where Gen. Lovell Rousseau's command was located during the summer of 1861; however, if rumor became fact, they were about to be transferred to Missouri. When warned that disorder might arise if he were to parade his three thousand men through Louisville in a farewell gesture, Rousseau is said to have responded that he would march even if the streets "should be made to run with blood." David G. Farrelly, "John M. Harlan and the Union Cause, 1861," *Filson Quarterly*, XXXVII (1963), 10–11.

To Benjamin A. G. Fuller, Augusta, Me.

Washington City Augt. 27th 1861.

Benj. A. G. Fuller Esq
Sir:

Your letter of the 17th ins't,[1] tendering an invitation to visit Maine and address the Union men of that State, has been received.

I tender you my sincere thanks for the complimentary manner in which you have been pleased to refer to my course, and for the interest you manifest in an acceptance, on my part, of your kind invitation. I assure you it would gratify me to comply with your request, and tender whatever aid I could furnish to the cause of the Union in your own State; but, Sir, I must go among my own people. They have been driven from their homes, outraged, and oppressed. A reign of terror, instituted by this abominable heresy of secession, has compelled them to desert their wives, their children, and all that man holds dear on earth.

They are in Kentucky in large numbers and have formed a noble band to fight gloriously for the defense of our common country. Their sacrifices have been great, but God grant that in the end they may triumph.

I am advised that my presence among them is desirable, and I shall go as speedily as circumstances will admit to render whatever assistance lies in my power.[2]

Accept assurances of esteem
& believe me Yours Truly,
Andrew Johnson

L, MH.

1. It is quite probable that a telegram received the previous day from Senator William P. Fessenden—"Will you come to Maine where you can do great good and address the union democrats"—prompted this response to the

earlier invitation. Fessenden to Johnson, August 26, 1861, Johnson Papers, LC.

2. Three days later the Tennessee senator reached Cincinnati on his way to Kentucky.

To Edmund B. Miller, Chicago, Ill.

August 28, 1861, Washington, D. C.; L, ICHi.

Declines invitation to speak at Chicago Young Men's Literary Association in order to be nearer East Tennessee to aid his people, "the loyal, brave and hardy mountaneers [who] have been driven from their homes . . . to seek an asylum in the adjoining State of Kentucky"; hopes that "returning with the Stars and Stripes at their head, they may drive their oppressors from the land they have so ruthlessly invaded."

Speech at Cincinnati[1]

August 31, 1861

It was my intention to have gone through this city quietly and unobserved, although I am free to say that the approbation which you, my fellow-citizens, have bestowed upon my conduct, is appreciated, and will ever be held in affectionate remembrance by me.

A few weeks since, when it was my privilege to pass through Cincinnati,[2] you were pleased to bestow upon me a demonstration of your approbation far beyond my merits or my worth.

My efforts still continue unabated in trying to carry out those measures which are necessary to sustain the Government in its emergency; and I hope that nothing will ever transpire which will tend to abate these efforts.

I have to-night read with great pain and regret the reported recantation, by a distinguished citizen of Tennessee, of the views hitherto expressed by him.[3] I regret this step on the part of that distinguished citizen for two reasons. I regret it on account of our cause, but I regret it more on his own account. If it were my case, I do not hesitate to say that rather than make such a recantation, I would be screwed down in my iron coffin and buried in the earth the feet foremost.[4] But I trust that it is not so, and of what I know of that distinguished citizen, I do not believe the report to be true.

A few weeks since when I passed through your city, the crisis was thickening, and since then it has continued to grow thicker and blacker, and if the result of the contest has chilled, (I mean the battle fought at Manassas,) and dispirited you, how much more heavily must it have fallen upon the lovers of the Union in the Southern

States, and how much greater must have been its tendency to discourage the Union men there. But I tell you that if the sullen, smothered, Union feeling of the South has receded, it is like the smothered fires of Vesuvius, which only fall to gather more lava and more heat, that when the time comes they may burst forth with the more destructive fury.— (Cheers.) When the time comes in which the smothered sentiments of Southern Union men shall burst forth, they will visit destruction upon those who have exiled them from their homes and devastated their property.— Manassas should but stimulate you to make such a demonstration as will teach traitors, both North and South, (for I tell you that you have them here) that there is a power in this government sufficient to preserve it from destruction, and that you are determined that the Union shall be preserved. (Cheers.)

We have heard much said about the rights of this section and of that section, about the right of this sort of property and to that sort of property, but I tell you that the true cause of this strife lays deeper than any such current. Ever since men began to be organized into civilized communities, there have been those who contended that all power originated in usurpation, and that the few were born to rule the many. This is the principle which underlies the contest now going on. (Cries of that's so.)

And if this rebellion should succeed in destroying the Government, as I pray God it may not, then there would be established upon its ruins either an aristocracy or a monarchy. The question submitted to you is not "Shall we stop at Manassas?" but the issue is, you must either conquer them or they will conquer you. If they take Washington, do you think they will stop? No. They will take Baltimore; and if they take Baltimore, they will want Philadelphia; and having Philadelphia, they will march to New York, until, as their Secretary of War said in Montgomery, they will dictate the terms of their compromise within the walls of Faneuiel [sic] Hall.[5] I speak plainly; it is their intention to give you a military dictatorship. The same bayonets which destroy this Government will dictate the next. Instead of a Constitution, they will give you swords and bayonets. We need not mince or hesitate in this matter. To speak in common parlance, you must either whip them or they will whip you. They are, many of them, insolent, proud braggarts, like spoiled children; and badly spoiled, at that. You must whip it out of them, or they will whip you.— [Loud applause.]

Much has been said about compromises.— What! compromise with rebels, with arms in their hands? Compromise with traitors who would subvert your Constitution? Do you want any better compromise than the Constitution made by Washington and the patriots of the Revolution,—a Constitution beneath which they lived, and which they sealed with their blood?

If they don't want to change the Government, why subvert it? If they do not wish to form another, why destroy this? I ask this simple question! If we cannot live on terms of peace and friendship under a Constitution, can we hope so to live under a mere treaty? If the day should ever come, and I pray God that it never may, when you shall make any other compromise than that of unqualified submission to the Constitution and Laws! What then? Do treaties change the geographical, commercial, or social relations of nations? Your treaty of peace would be one of continual war. You can not have peace without the Constitution. You must meet the question fairly now. You must fight it out. [Cries of that's the talk.] (Renewed cheers.)

Suppose a treaty should be made with the rebels, would any of the disturbing elements which brought about the present difficulty be got rid of? Not one. Such a treaty would be one of war. It could not be otherwise. We could not escape a fight under it, and if the fight must come, it had better come now. [Great applause.]

It is said that Beelzebub was once an angel in heaven, but he rebelled, and tried to overthrow the government of Jehovah and the result was he was kicked out of heaven by the angels.

Whenever virtue compromises with vice; vice makes an inroad upon virtue. If virtue compromises with vice to-day; to-morrow there must be another compromise, and the next day another, until virtue is clean gone and vice rules instead. If truth compromises with falsehood, falsehood will encroach upon truth, until falsehood becomes truth, and truth falsehood. Compromise between right and wrong to-day, and you must compromise again to-morrow, and again the next day, and so on until right is gone and wrong supplies its place. The time for compromise is gone by; now is the time to put down crime and punish vice—the time to stand on those great principles of truth which underlie the Constitution. Now is the time to act.

I saw the other day a very good figure by which a noble son of Kentucky, the Hon. Joseph Holt, had well illustrated the present difficulty by the story of the child which was brought to Solomon, being claimed by two women. When the Judge offered to divide the child, the pretended mother said, "yes, I am content to take half," but the true mother said "no, rather than hurt the child, give it to her."[6] So with us, let us not submit to have our Union divided, though the false mother may be willing to take the half, but instead of giving it to them we will take it all. [Long and loud applause.]

I intend to fight in defense of this government as long as life shall last. It is wrong to destroy the best government ever devised for the use of man. I would rather see this continent swept back into a howling wilderness than to see a monarchy planted on the ruins of this republic. I would rather see this race swept out of being than that the sun should set forever in darkness upon man's hope for self government. The fall of this Government would be to the world an argument that man's capability of self government was at an end, which lies at the foundation of our noble structure. Now is the time to establish the truth of what we hold to be true. What if our flag has been trailed in the dust and sullied, let it be placed in stalwart hands; baptize it in the sun's fire, and, bathing it in a nation's blood, establish its reputation on a firmer basis than ever before. Never surrender. When Paul Jones, the naval officer, was in an engagement in which his ship was riddled and likely to be sunk to the bottom of the ocean, his lieutenant, becoming scared, struck his colors; the enemy, seeing the colors struck, and being hard by, called out through a trumpet, "Do you surrender?" Without replying, but seeing that the colors were down, Paul Jones pulled out his pistol and killed the lieutenant, then, again hoisting his flag, answered, "No, I am just getting ready to fight."[7] Let that be the feeling in the North—we are just getting ready to fight.

I do not wish to refer to my State in any feeling of egotism. But where can I look, save to that environed spot, Eastern Tennessee? It is my home. It was there I selected her who is the mother of my children. It was there that their infant minds were taught by their loving grandparents[8] to love virtue, to be good and true. The people there are a brave people—I love them. They took me by the hand and encouraged me step by step until I gained my present position. What though I am driven from the State and my family cannot follow me? What though thousands are leaving the State in obedience to the proclamation of Davis?[9] What have I done? What has my son done? What have these my friends done? What is the head and front of their offending, but love for our country? My intention is to perish in the effort or restore to Tennessee her former rights unimpaired.

I will stand by these loyal people. They never deceived, they never betrayed me. They never were false to their pledges, and I never will be false to mine.

How long has it been since we praised in strains of poetry and eloquence the glories of Warsaw?[10] Now, tell me, is not the tyranny of Davis worse than any tyranny exerted by Russia over Poland? I am not given to bragging, but my former acts must be a sure indication of my future course. I intend to be with that people, and stand by them through the rain and the heat, with toil and with the sword, until, if needs be, I have poured out the last drop of my blood a willing libation upon the altar of my country's liberty.[11]

Cincinnati *Commercial*, September 2, 1861; New York *Tribune*, September 4, 1861.

1. Arriving from Washington the preceding evening with Gen. William T. Sherman's family, Johnson had taken lodging in the Burnet House, where he was enthusiastically welcomed and serenaded by Menter's Band. This speech was the first of many which he would make in Ohio and Kentucky during the next three months in an effort to build Union morale and end Kentucky's neutrality. Cincinnati *Enquirer*, September 1, 1861.

2. See Impromptu Speech at Cincinnati and Speech at Cincinnati, both June 19, 1861.

3. We can speculate that Johnson had just received a copy of Brownlow's *Whig* of August 24 in which, following his capture and temporary imprisonment in Richmond, Congressman Thomas A. R. Nelson had, upon his release and return to East Tennessee, published an address to the people of that section advising them to abstain from further opposition to Confederate authority. Alexander, *T. A. R. Nelson*, 91–93.

4. An extensive search into burial customs has failed to cast much light on this rather obscure reference. Although the speaker may possibly have been impressed by the current interest in the metallic casket, which had been gaining in popularity during the course of the previous decade, it seems more plausible to assume that an "iron coffin" would afford the maximum security for one who had steadfastly held to his principles, refusing to recant. In similar vein, it may be hypothecated that perpendicular interment—a practice scarcely common but not unknown among certain Indian tribes—implies greater defiance than does the ordinary recumbent burial. John Brickell, *The Natural History of North Carolina* (Murfreesboro, N. C., 1968 [1737]), 386.

5. On the evening of April 12, with Sumter under seige, Leroy P. Walker had regaled the cheering crowd gathered at the Exchange Hotel in Montgomery with this boast; that "the flag which now flaunts the breeze here would float over the dome of the old Capitol" before May 1 and "might float eventually over Faneuil Hall itself." New York *Tribune*, April 15, 1861.

6. 1 Kings 3 : 16–27.

7. Traditional accounts of the encounter between the *Bonhomme Richard* and the English *Serapis* (1779) have held that John Paul Jones shot "Lieutenant Grub" (Midshipman Beaumont Groube) for striking the colors near the battle's end and that he uttered his famous "I have not yet begun to fight" just before victory was won. According to a modern biographer, Jones did not fire on his own officer but instead hurled a pistol at the chief gunner, who panicked when he found that the ensign and staff had been shot away; moreover, the captain made his pithy exclamation early in the action. Samuel Eliot Morison, *John Paul Jones: A Sailor's Biography* (Boston, 1959), 230–36.

8. Mary McDonough Johnson Daughtry (1783–1856) and Sarah McCardle Whitesides (c1794–1854). See *Johnson Papers*, I, 634; III, 293n.

9. A week earlier Brownlow's *Whig* had commented: "Many are leaving East Tennessee . . . under the impression that, [wit]hin forty days they will be forced to leave the State and have their effects confiscated." Knoxville *Whig*, August 24, 1861.

10. The Polish cause was traditionally dear to Americans, who remembered with gratitude the Revolutionary War service of Generals Thaddeus Kosciuszko and Casimir Pulaski. When news of the 1830 Warsaw uprising reached the United States, an "outburst of enthusiasm for the fighting Poles" found expression in oratory, poetry, historical writing, and newspaper editorials. Jerzy Jan Lerski, *A Polish Chapter in Jacksonian America: The*

United States and the Polish Exiles of 1831 (Madison, Wis., 1958), 14, 17–27; Joseph A. Wytreval, *America's Polish Heritage: A Social History of the Poles in America* (Detroit, 1961), 132–34.

11. Possibly a paraphrase of Thomas Moore, *Lallah Rookh: Paradise and the Peri*, st. 11: "O! if there be, on this earthly sphere, / A boon, an offering Heaven holds dear, / 'Tis the last libation Liberty draws / From the heart that bleeds and breaks in her cause!" Stevenson, *Quotations*, 1107. When Johnson finished, the Reverend William B. Carter was called for; his brief remarks were followed by those of the Reverend Granville Moody, who "gave a few sledge-hammer arguments against the rebels." Cincinnati *Commercial*, September 2, 1861.

Appendix

Andrew Johnson in the U. S. Senate[1]
1860–61

36 CONGRESS, 2 SESSION
December, 1860–March, 1861

Journal	Globe	Date	Subject
	23	Dec. 10, 1860	Named member of committees on public lands, to audit and control contingent expenses, and the District of Columbia.
	23	Dec. 10	Moves that bill (H. R. 24) securing homesteads for actual settlers on public domain be referred to committee on public lands; agreed to.
41	82–83	Dec. 13	* Joint Resolution for Amendments on Presidential, Senatorial, and Judicial Selection (S. 48); read and passed to second reading.
41	83	Dec. 13	* Resolution Proposing "Unamendable" Amendments Affecting Slavery; ordered printed.
49–50	117	Dec. 18	Moves consideration of his joint resolution (S. 48); agreed to.
	117–19, 134–41	Dec. 18–19	* Speech on Secession.
59	181	Dec. 21	Votes for bill (S. 377) authorizing extension of Baltimore and Ohio Railroad into District of Columbia; passed.
60	182	Dec. 21	Moves that his joint resolution (S. 48) and all other resolutions relative to subject be referred to select committee; agreed to.
73	248	Jan. 5, 1861	Presents pension petition of Ellen Morris, widow of Revolutionary War officer Lewis R. Morris; referred to committee on pensions.
87	305	Jan. 10	Votes for resolution calling for information *re* appointment of acting secretary of war [Joseph Holt]; adopted.
	309	Jan. 10	* Reply to Jefferson Davis.
107	409	Jan. 16	Votes against motion to postpone Crittenden's resolutions in order to take up bill (H. R. 23) for admission of Kansas; motion not agreed to; votes against Clark of New Hampshire's amendment designed as substitute for Crittenden's resolutions; agreed to.

1. The data in this Appendix are drawn from the *Journal of the Senate* and the *Congressional Globe*. Asterisks indicate items printed in Volumes III, IV, or V.

Journal	Globe	Date	Subject
128	489	Jan. 21	Votes for bill (H. R. 23) admitting Kansas; passed.
139	536	Jan. 24	Named member of committee on public buildings and grounds.
169	639	Jan. 30	Votes against Pacific railroad bill (H. R. 701), providing for transportation of mails, troops, munitions, and military stores; passed.
174	685–86	Feb. 1	Moves to postpone discussion of Virginia peace mission until following Monday to consider Indian appropriation bill (H. R. 865); agreed to.
184	728	Feb. 4	Moves to postpone until next day question of printing President's message accompanying resolutions of Virginia legislature; agreed to.
	744–50, 766–72	Feb. 5, 6	* Speech on the Seceding States.
	783, 788, 791	Feb. 7	Denies Louis T. Wigfall's allegation that he was "in close conclave" with William H. Seward and Henry Wilson before delivering his Speech on Secession; unsuccessfully opposes order clearing galleries after applause provoked by Wigfall's reply; seeks withdrawal of motion to postpone consideration of Wigfall's remarks on his speech; motion carried.
202	813	Feb. 8	Opposes extending patent rights on McCormick reaper; votes for resolution (H. R. 71) providing additional time for testimony on McCormick patent; adopted.
233	918	Feb. 15	Submits committee report *re* compensation of Mrs. Elizabeth A. R. Linn, pursuant to Senate resolution of March 20, 1860; intends to amend first appropriation bill to do so.
275	1065	Feb. 20	Votes against bill (H. R. 338) paying treasury notes and fixing duties on imports; passed.
289	1130	Feb. 23	Votes for appropriation bill (H. R. 299) paying expenses incurred in suppressing Indian hostilities in California; passed.
290	1132	Feb. 23	Votes for joint resolution (H. R. 70) to quit title to Iowa lands; passed.
294	1138	Feb. 23	Amends civil appropriation bill (H. R. 895) to pay Mrs. E. A. R. Linn $2,672; accepted.
302	1164	Feb. 25	Votes for postal bill (H. R. 950) *re* discontinuing service to states withdrawn from Union; passed.
310	1184	Feb. 25	Votes against civil appropriation bill (H. R. 895); passed.

Journal	Globe	Date	Subject
	1185	Feb. 25	Seeks to get consideration of Crittenden resolutions; no action.
	1247	Feb. 27	Favors continuing debate on army bill (H. R. 299) and postponing consideration of Crittenden resolutions until evening; debate on H. R. 299 continued.
	1281	Feb. 28	Opposes paying workmen's compensation from Senate contingent fund; suggests appropriation from treasury.
	1350–51 1354–56	Mar. 2	* Speech in Reply to Senator Lane.
	1386	Mar. 2[3]	Opposes all amendments to joint resolution (H. R. 80) amending Constitution to prevent congressional interference with slavery.
383	1403	Mar. 2[4]	Votes for joint resolution (H. R. 80) to amend Constitution; passed.
387	1405	Mar. 2[4]	Votes for joint resolution (S. 54) proposing amendments [Crittenden] to Constitution; failed.
395–96	1413	Mar. 2[4]	Reports on Senate employees; printed.

36 CONGRESS, SPECIAL SESSION
March, 1861

Journal	Globe	Date	Subject
412–13	1446	Mar. 8	Named member of committees on commerce, public lands, and to audit and control contingent expenses.
	1456	Mar. 14	Seeks to remove name of Albert G. Brown of Mississippi from resolution declaring certain Senate seats vacant.
427	1498	Mar. 23	Moves that Senate go into executive session to consider nominations sent by President; agreed to.
	1524–25	Mar. 28	* Remarks on Contingent Expenses.

37 CONGRESS, 1 SESSION
July–August, 1861

Journal	Globe	Date	Subject
20–21	17	July 6	Named member of committees on commerce, public lands, territories, and to audit and control contingent expenses.
27	54	July 10	Votes for bill (S. 1) authorizing use of volunteers to aid in enforcing the laws and protecting public property; passed.

Journal	Globe	Date	Subject
30	64	July 11	Opposes resolution that Senators Mason, Hunter, Clingman, Bragg, Chesnut, Nicholson, Sebastian, Mitchel, Hemphill, and Wigfall be "expelled"; supports amendment that these names be "stricken from the roll, and their seats declared vacant"; original resolution adopted.
	80	July 12	Suggests that resolution relating to replacement of Senate messengers be referred to committee to audit and control contingent expenses; agreed to.
	81	July 12	Questions Wilson of Massachusetts concerning pay of army chaplains.
	103–6	July 13	* Remarks on Senators-elect from Virgina.
	127	July 15	Demands "yeas" and "nays" on question of increasing standing army and opposes permanent increase of army; no action taken.
68–69	216	July 20	Asks unanimous consent to introduce a bill (S. 38) to arm loyal citizens of states in rebellion; agreed to.
	216	July 20	* Bill Appropriating Arms to Loyal Citizens.
69	217	July 20	Moves to postpone until following Monday consideration of joint resolution (S. 1) approving certain acts of President for suppressing rebellion; agreed to.
72	220	July 22	Moves, "on account of indisposition," that consideration of resolution (S. 1) be postponed until following Wednesday; agreed to.
74–76	226	July 23	Moves amendment of bill (S. 38) to arm loyal citizens, specifying appropriation of $2,000,-000, and further amends bill to include states threatened by rebellion; both agreed to; amended bill (S. 38) passed.
80	235	July 24	Named member of conference committee on resolution (S. 5) to pay widow of Stephen A. Douglas amount due late senator.
84	243	July 24	Votes for bill (H. R. 76) paying police organized by U. S. to protect Baltimore; passed.
84–85	243	July 24	Presents resolution on war aims.
91	258–60	July 25	* Remarks on War Aims Resolution.
92	265	July 25	Votes for war aims resolution; passed.
96	275	July 26	Votes for joint resolution (S. 10) declaring determination of Congress to maintain supremacy of government and integrity of Union.

Journal	Globe	Date	Subject
96	276	July 26	Moves that consideration of joint resolution (S. 1) to approve certain acts of President in suppressing rebellion be postponed until next day; agreed to.
	288–97	July 27	* Speech in Support of Presidential War Program.
107	332	July 29	Named member of select committee to investigate abandonment and destruction of naval yards and government properties at Pensacola, Norfolk, and Harper's Ferry (Globe, July 30). [No evidence that Johnson served.]
117	336	July 30	Votes against tariff bill (H. R. 54) providing increased revenue from imports; passed.
126	364	July 31	Votes against conference committee report on bill (S. 36) constructing armored ships and floating batteries; rejected.
133	372	Aug. 1	Votes for conference committee report on bill (S. 3) providing for better organization of military establishment; concurred in.
167	400	Aug. 2	Votes for tariff bill (H. R. 54) in order to sustain credit of government and protect against "an invasion"; passed.
184	442	Aug. 5	Votes for bill (S. 69) increasing pay of military personnel; passed.
189	451	Aug. 6	Votes for resolution giving year's salary to former Senate Secretary Asbury Dickens in recognition of faithful service; adopted.
194	454	Aug. 6	Reports, from committee to audit and control contingent expenses, resolution making allowance to D. R. McNair, former Senate sergeant-at-arms, and moves passage; refused and carried over.

37 CONGRESS, 2 SESSION
December, 1861–March, 1862

Journal	Globe	Date	Subject
32	32	Dec. 9	Votes for resolution creating joint committee on conduct of war; adopted.
42–43	71	Dec. 12	Moves to refer to select committee that portion of presidential message relating to construction of Kentucky-Tennessee-North Carolina railroad; agreed to.
52	110	Dec. 17	Named member of joint committee on conduct of war.
67	159	Dec. 23	Named chairman of select committee on "a railroad to connect

Journal	Globe	Date	Subject
			the loyal portions of Tennessee and North Carolina with Kentucky."
87	206	Jan. 7, 1862	Votes against bill (S. 101) increasing number of West Point cadets; rejected.
97–98	263–64	Jan. 10	Votes for resolutions expelling Waldo P. Johnson and Trusten Polk of Missouri; adopted.
106	291	Jan. 13	Votes to allow Frederick P. Stanton, contesting Kansas senatorial seat of James H. Lane, to take a seat on the floor and to address Senate; carried.
108	309	Jan. 14	Votes for resolution directing secretary of war to inform Senate concerning war contracts and bounties; passed.
151	520	Jan. 28	Votes for bill (S. 169) authorizing President "in certain cases" to take possession of railroad and telegraph lines; passed.
157	555	Jan. 30	Reports, from select committee, bill (S. 179) for construction of military railroad connecting Kentucky, Tennessee, and North Carolina; passed to second reading.
	584–89	Jan. 31	* Speech on Expulsion of Senator Bright.
169	608	Feb. 3	Moves consideration of bill (S. 179) to construct Kentucky and Tennessee military railroads; fails.
176	655	Feb. 5	Votes for resolution expelling Bright of Indiana; adopted.
	707	Feb. 7	Introduces letter from Flag Officer A. H. Foote describing capture of Fort Henry.
193–94	738	Feb. 11	* Resolution on Washington's Birthday Celebration.
208	814	Feb. 14	Presents petition of Jesse Ellis, invalid pensioner; referred to committee on pensions.
215	845–46	Feb. 17	Introduces resolution (S. 51) expressing appreciation to army and navy for "the recent series of brilliant victories"; adopted.
247	993–94	Feb. 27	Votes for resolution allowing Benjamin Stark of Oregon to take senatorial oath; adopted.
270	1083	Mar. 5	Votes to amend army officers' pay bill (S. 175) so as to pay chaplains $100 a month; passed. [Last vote in Senate; confirmed as military governor of Tennessee—March 4.]
291	1165	Mar. 11	Replaced as member of committee on conduct of war.

Index

Primary identification of a person is indicated by an italic *n* following the page reference. Identifications found in *Johnson Papers*, Volumes I, II, and III, are indicated by a Roman numeral and page number in parentheses immediately following the name.

Abercrombie, Anderson, 346
Ableman v. Booth, 215, 256n
Abolitionists: blamed for anti-war spirit, 684n; and the church, 59–60, 553n; denounced John Brown's raid, 135; as disunionists, xxxi, 32, 33, 84, 122, 136, 191, 242–45, 259n, 454, 551; Johnson called, 129, 449; repudiated in North, 83–84
Adams, George M., 485, 556n, 582; from, 556–57, 594–95, 602–4
Adams, Green, 525n, 526, 556, 659
Adams, John, 38, 140
Adams, John Quincy: and Treaty of Ghent, 346, 347n
Adams Express Company: delivers southern mail, 281, 282n, 381, 427
Adams-Onís Treaty: and Florida's offshore islands, 409n
Agassiz, Louis, 542
Alabama: act for statehood, cited, 228, 258n; CSA rgt. in East Tenn., 595; flag, 364n; Johnson burned in effigy in, 288; secession of, 92, 153, 184, 185n, 250, 267, 269n; Union sentiment in, 173, 371, 540, 668
Alexander, James H., 335, 336n
Alexander, Reuben F.: from, 88
American Anti-Slavery Society: "fairs" promoted by, 553n
American Revolution: writ of habeas corpus suspended in, 606–7, 609, 610
Anderson, Isaac: from, 306
Anderson, Joseph (III, 362n), 418
Anderson, Larz, 485n
Anderson, Richard K.: from, 93
Anderson, Robert, 112, 113n, 282, 436, 646n, 659, 681n; evacuates Fort Moultrie, 251, 260n; at Fort Sumter, 506, 625–27, 646n; from, 307; preferred for East Tenn. expedition, 664–65; removal of recommended, 382, 383n
Anderson, Samuel R. (II, 325n), 313, 350n, 388; Bank of Tenn. president, 343; from, 432; Nashville postmaster, 344
Anderson County: unionists, 559

Andrews, Ezra R., 542n; from, 541–42
Anthony, Henry B., 110, 433, 434n
Appointments, Presidential: confirmed, 397n, 500, 502n, 534n, 539n, 541n; requests for, (civil) 421, 472, 654, 657, (diplomatic) 501, 513, 540, (military) 519, 521, 534, 544, 671; see also Patronage; Tenn. appointments
Appropriations, 708, 709; for arms for loyal citizens, xxii, 557, 593n, 710; in S. C. for new government, 165n
Arkansas: as border state, 165n; land office appointment in, 352; secession of, 187, 302, 304, 305n, 366, 367n, 401, 402n, 422–23, 425–26, 452–53, 453n; unionists, 187, 402n, 453n, 514
Arms and munitions: bill for appropriations for, 592–93; cannon, 523n; Confederate, 660; for East Tenn. rgts. in Ky., 549, 596n; individual sidearms, 526, 546n, 557, 558, 581n, 602, 691; Johnson's requests for, 491, 638–39, 646, 670; for Ky., 531, 557, 558; threatened capture of, 526, 535–36, 539; transferred to southern arsenals, 209, 409n; transportation of, 531, 535–36, 546–47, 548, 557, 582, 599, 665, 668–69, 673; for Va. loyalists, 543–44, 691; see also East Tennessee: arms for; "Lincoln guns"
Armstrong, Joseph R., 271n; from, 271
Armstrong, Robert H., 474n
Army, U. S.: cannon in use in, 523n; chaplains for, 519, 534, 535n; pay increase bills for, 710, 711; scouts, 544; wartime increase in, defended, 612–13
Arnold, Charles, 393n; from, 391–93
Arnold, John Q., 188, 190n
Arnold, Reuben (I, 534n), 188, 288, 289n, 452, 651, 652n
Arnold, Thomas D. (I, 33n), 418n; unionist leader, 487n

Tennessee, anti-Johnson (*cont.*)
452, 456–57, 468–69, 472, 482, 486, 487n, 663n, 680n; as a border state, 165n, 166, 377; as a Confederate state, 475n, 487n, 497, 615, 631, 637–38, 648n; convention election (Feb. 9) in, xxiii, 124n, 171, 185, 188–91, 195, 263–76 *passim*, 280, 282, 285–90n, 298–300, 310, 312, 323, 328, 335, 341, 349, 350n, 351, 356, 362, 383–84, 430, 496, 498n, 680n; Democratic defeat (1860) in, 355, 364n; district system for elections, 200, 202n; disunionist officeholders in, 203, 285, 287, 289, 295, 309, 324, 412, 417, 427, 456, 470, 536, 580; drought in, 384n; early history, 245–48; election (June 8) in, 474n, 486, 487, 489n, 514, 565, 572n, 637, 644n, 648, 680n; election (Aug. 8) in, 429–30, 530n, 603, 604n, 662, 663n, 672n; Johnson on secession of, 163–64, 356, 488, 489n, 497, 615, 620; Johnson urged to visit, 183–84, 271, 331, 401, 423, 472; and Miss. River navigation, 25–26; partisan politics in, 414n, 419–20, 438, 467–70n, 473; provisional army raised in, 475n, 497; reaction to Lincoln in, 62, 67n, 275, 297, 301, 325, 368, 401, 406, 450, 467; refugees from, 519, 532, 657, 661, 693; rgt. chaplains for, 534; secession of, 474, 475n, 486, 487n, 515, 644n, 679, 680n; state bonds for East Tenn. & Va. RR, 147; ultra men in, prepare for war, 158; Union party in, 516, 527; unionism suppressed in, 475n, 489n, 564–66, 638; unionist sentiment in, 38, 79–80, 81n, 102, 111–12, 114, 118–31 *passim*, 148, 156–58, 165–70 *passim*, 172n, 180n, 183–84, 188–90, 195, 202, 208, 248, 252, 266–82 *passim*, 287–88, 295, 298, 311, 328–30, 333–35, 343, 415–17, 424, 430, 431n, 452, 460, 467–69, 483, 488, 489n, 533, 559, 570, 663, 679, 680n; Va.'s secession and, 323; Washington Peace Conference delegates selected, 191, 192n; *see also* East Tennessee; Middle Tennessee; West Tennessee; individual counties and towns

Tenn. appointments: customs collectors, 296, 412–13; district attorneys, 125, 390–91, 394, 403, 431, 433, 456; marshals, 298, 308, 337, 348–49, 351–52, 383, 385, 396–97, 404–5, 417n, 427–

Tenn. appointments (*cont.*)
28, 431, 433, 437; pension agent, 451–52; postmasters, 51–52, 118–19, 186, 203, 277, 285, 287, 289–90, 292–93, 294–95, 307, 312, 324, 337, 339–40, 344–45, 365, 367, 382, 385–87, 394, 397–99, 402, 403n, 404–6, 412, 413n, 415, 424, 427–29, 431, 432, 433, 435, 437–38, 450, 455, 456, 459–60, 466–68, 470, 481, 651–52; route agents, 312–13, 334, 335, 338–39, 344–45, 396, 413–14, 417–18, 429, 433, 462, 464, 470, 474n; special postal agent, 674n; *see also* Patronage

Tenn. Constitution of 1835: and tax on slaves, 533n

Tenn. Historical Society, 278

Tenn. legislature: act passed to raise provisional force, 475n, 622, 645n; adopts declaration of independence, 475n, 486, 487n; addressed by CSA commissioner, 496, 498n; attempts to remove Johnson from Senate, xxx, 101, 107, 117, 123n, 147, 156, 157n, 158, 167, 168n, 169, 172, 330, 412n; convention bill in, 157–58, 163, 169, 171, 178, 266, 383–84; conventional interest bill in, 158, 160n; convict-lease bill in, 344n; extra sessions called, (1st) 287n, (2nd) 472, 474, 475n, 486, 488, 496, 498n; Harris' messages to, (Jan. 7), 168, 264n, 287n, 325n, (Apr. 18) 475n; Johnson's advice to, 162–64; Johnson's influence on, 329; Robert Johnson on, 112, 157–58, 159n, 172, 173n, 178, 474–75; military appointments authorized by, 530n; militia bill in, 158, 159n, 172, 173n, 178, 251–52, 260n, 264n; rejects East Tenn. petition for separate statehood, 272n, 529, 530n (*see also* Greeneville Union Convention); resolution on Washington Monument (1849), 573n; secession ordinance passed in, 474, 475n, 497; and southern convention call, 114, 115n; supports slavery amendment, 184–85; Union sentiment in, 475; and Washington Peace Conference, 268; *see also* House of Representatives, Tenn.; Senate, Tenn.

Tenn. press: denounces Johnson, 101, 112, 160

Territories: Confederate emissaries to, 458; restrictions on acquisition of, 88; slavery in, 39–41, 50–51n, 56–57, 80, 94, 122, 131–34, 136–37, 140, 145n, 161,

The Papers of Andrew Johnson

Monticello, the type chosen for this series, is a Linotype design based on the first successful American face, which was cut by Archibald Binny at Philadelphia in 1796. The clean legibility of Monticello, especially in the smaller sizes, suits it admirably for a series in which documentation is extensive.

Volume 4 of *The Papers of Andrew Johnson* was composed and printed letterpress by Heritage Printers, Inc., Charlotte, North Carolina, and bound by The Delmar Company, also of Charlotte. The text paper is Library Text, manufactured to the specifications of the National Historical Publications and Records Commission by the S. D. Warren Company, Boston, Massachusetts; illustrations were printed by offset lithography on Warren's Lustro Offset Enamel Dull Cream. Columbia Mills, Inc., Minetto, New York, manufactured the binding cloth. The book was designed by Hugh Bailey and Helen Orton.

THE UNIVERSITY OF TENNESSEE PRESS